SALMON P.
CHASE

 LINCOLN'S VITAL RIVAL

WALTER STAHR

SIMON & SCHUSTER

New York London Toronto Sydney New Delhi

Simon & Schuster
1230 Avenue of the Americas
New York, NY 10020

Copyright © 2021 by Walter Stahr

First Simon & Schuster hardcover edition November 2021

SIMON & SCHUSTER and colophon
are registered trademarks of Simon & Schuster, Inc.

For information about special discounts for bulk purchases,
please contact Simon & Schuster Special Sales at 1-866-506-1949
or business@simonandschuster.com.

The Simon & Schuster Speakers Bureau can bring authors to
your live event. For more information or to book an event,
contact the Simon & Schuster Speakers Bureau at 1-866-248-3049
or visit our website at www.simonspeakers.com.

Interior design by Kyle Kabel

Manufactured in the United States of America

1   3   5   7   9   10   8   6   4   2

Library of Congress Cataloging-in-Publication Data

ISBN 978-1-5011-9923-3
ISBN 978-1-5011-9925-7 (ebook)

In memory of John Roland Stahr
October 29, 1932, to October 14, 2020

Contents

Introduction

Zion Church, the largest black church in Charleston, South Carolina, was packed for a political meeting on the afternoon of May 12, 1865. Most of the five thousand people present had started their lives enslaved and gained their freedom only a few weeks earlier, when the Union army finally arrived in town. The main topic for this meeting, as the last rebel die-hards fought the last battles of the Civil War, was reconstruction—the process of forming new state governments in the South, and whether blacks as well as whites would participate in this process. The afternoon's first speaker, a white Union general, said that blacks had earned the right to vote through their service during the war. The remarks of the second speaker, a black army major, were interrupted by the arrival of the chief justice of the United States.[1]

The black crowd stood and cheered, and the military band played "Hail to the Chief," as Chief Justice Salmon Portland Chase walked down the aisle and up to the platform. "More than anyone else, he looked the great man," one of his friends recalled: six feet tall, solid, strong, clean shaven, nearing sixty. The crowd cheered Chase not because of his work on the Supreme Court (he had been chief justice only for a few months) or because of his work as Treasury secretary during the Civil War (although some called him "Old Greenbacks" for his role in creating the new green paper currency). No: the black Charleston crowd cheered because Chase was known as a lawyer who had defended fugitive slaves and a leader who, in his various government roles, had always argued against slavery and in favor of black rights.[2]

1

Chase did not disappoint his audience. He said that their future was at last largely in their own hands. "Let the soldier fight well, let the preacher preach well, let the carpenter shove his plane with all his might, and the planter put in and gather in as much corn or cotton as he can. . . . Act thus, and I have no fears for your future." He told them that he had been speaking for black voting rights for twenty years, since a similar speech in Cincinnati, Ohio, but he cautioned that mere speeches did not have much effect, for in spite of his efforts, blacks still could not vote in Ohio. Chase had been pressing the new president, Andrew Johnson, to insist on black voting in the reconstruction process, and he believed that the president might well follow this course. If there was a delay, however, Chase advised the blacks of Charleston that they should "go to work and show that the United States government was mistaken in making the delay. If you show that, the mistake will be corrected." When he finished, the crowd cheered Chase nine times.[3]

Who was Chase, chief justice at this critical, fluid moment in American history? How did his views change from his youth, when he wrote that "little cause exists for that sickly sympathy which many at the North feel or affect to feel with the fancied suffering of the slave," to his mature years, when he became a leading antislavery agitator? Why did the Republican Party, the party which Chase had done more than any other man to create, choose Abraham Lincoln rather than Chase as its presidential candidate in 1860? Why did Lincoln select his rival Chase for the vital task of managing the federal finances during the Civil War and then, near the end of the war, make him chief justice of the United States? And why was the chief justice touring the South in the last days of the Civil War and giving what many would view as a controversial, political speech?[4]

Born in rural New Hampshire in 1808, Chase spent some of his youth in southern Ohio before returning east to attend Dartmouth College. After graduation, he lived four years in the nation's capital, Washington, DC, teaching school and reading law. He moved to Cincinnati to start his legal career, where he married the first of three wives, all of whom died young. He was elected to the city council as a member of the Whig Party in 1840, but a year later, disgusted by the subservience of the two main political parties, the Whigs and the Democrats, to the slave states and the slave masters, Chase left the Whigs and joined the tiny Liberty Party.

Chase's course, in the 1840s and early 1850s, was very different from that of Lincoln, another midwestern lawyer active in politics. While Chase was busy building and leading antislavery parties, Lincoln remained a loyal Whig, perhaps holding antislavery opinions but rarely expressing them in speeches. In the 1844 presidential election, Lincoln gave speeches for his Kentucky hero, the senator and slaveholder Henry Clay. Chase worked this year for the Liberty Party, publishing a "Liberty Man's Creed," in which he declared that the party was simply carrying out the dreams of George Washington and Thomas Jefferson, to end slavery through peaceful political processes.

A year later, Chase received a silver pitcher from the free blacks of Cincinnati to thank him for his legal work representing those accused of being fugitive slaves. In a speech that would often be quoted against him, Chase urged the state to amend its constitution so that blacks would have the right to vote. "True democracy makes no enquiry about the color of the skin, or the place of nativity, or any other similar circumstance," he said. Lincoln, in the course of his long legal career, never represented a fugitive slave; he once served as lawyer for a master in an attempt to keep a black woman and her children in slavery in the free state of Illinois. Chase represented alleged fugitives so often that he was known as the "attorney general for runaway negroes."[5]

In 1848, near the end of his single term in Congress, Lincoln campaigned for the Whig presidential candidate, Zachary Taylor, another southern slaveowner. Chase was the key leader that year in forming the Free Soil Party, a combination of the Liberty Party with antislavery elements of the Whig and Democratic Parties. After the Free Soil national convention, of which he was the presiding officer, Chase campaigned relentlessly for the Free Soil Party, helping it secure almost 15 percent of the votes in the northern states. Early in the next year, an even split between the two major parties in the Ohio legislature allowed the Free Soil Party, through a coalition with the Democrats, to send Chase to Washington as one of the state's two federal senators.

The major speeches of Chase's six years in the US Senate were speeches against slavery, notably against the Fugitive Slave Act of 1850 and the Kansas-Nebraska Act of 1854, which he denounced for opening the immense northern part of the Louisiana Territory to slavery, and thereby violating the Missouri Compromise. Chase helped start the fire and fan the flames of northern outrage against the Nebraska bill, and from this conflagration would emerge a new political party, the Republican Party, committed to Chase's brand of political antislavery. It was only at this stage, in the midst of the furor against the Nebraska bill, that Lincoln started to give speeches against the extension of slavery, although he remained a Whig until early 1856.

Meanwhile, in 1855, the Republicans of Ohio nominated and then elected Chase as the first Republican governor of a major state. He served two terms, each of two years, working to protect black rights and to strengthen education. "No safer or more remunerative investment of revenue is made by the state than in the instruction of her youth," he declared. In 1858 some national Republican leaders favored Stephen Douglas, the Democrat, over Abraham Lincoln, the Republican, in the Illinois senate race, hoping that Douglas would divide the Democratic Party. Chase was one of the few out-of-state leaders who supported Lincoln, speaking in Chicago and elsewhere in that memorable campaign. But even though Chase and Lincoln were now in the same party, they did not yet agree on black rights. Chase would never have said (as Lincoln did in the course of this campaign) that he was not "in favor of bringing about in any way the social and political equality of the white and black races" and that he was not "in favor of making voters or jurors of negroes, nor of qualifying them to hold office, nor to intermarry with white people."[6]

Chase was a leading candidate for the 1860 Republican nomination, but it was Lincoln who received the nomination at the Chicago convention, in part because he was seen as less radical on the slavery issue than Chase or his former Senate colleague, William Henry Seward. Chase was understandably disappointed, but he overcame his chagrin and campaigned widely and effectively for Lincoln, speaking in the East, in New Hampshire and New York, and in the West, in Ohio, Indiana, and Michigan, and even in the slave state of Kentucky. The next year, as some of the Southern states seceded, and as civil war approached, Lincoln offered Chase the second most prestigious position in his Cabinet, as secretary of the Treasury. Chase accepted, starting work in March 1861.

Chase managed, in his three years at the head of the Treasury, to raise the hundreds of millions of dollars necessary to enable the Union to win the Civil War, in part through direct appeals to the public to invest in government bonds. He also used the wartime crisis to create a national bank system and a single national currency. Before the war, American currency was a confusing mix of foreign and domestic coins and more than ten thousand different types of banknotes—difficult to value and easy to counterfeit. After the war, currency consisted of coins minted by the federal government and notes printed and backed by the federal government. Before the war, there were no national banks, only a host of almost two thousand state banks, ranging from the large and stable to the small or spurious. After the war, under legislation devised and pushed through Congress by Chase, there was a strong system of national banks.[7]

Chase did not forget the slaves or former slaves during the Civil War. No other member of the Lincoln Cabinet was in such close touch with the army officers, government officials, and private volunteers working to help the blacks who fled from slavery to freedom. Chase pressed Lincoln to emancipate the slaves, he favored enlisting black volunteers into the army, and he urged Lincoln to insist that Southern blacks have the right to vote. He was Lincoln's one serious rival within the Republican Party for the 1864 presidential nomination, something that now seems odd and outrageous but seemed less so at the time, when presidents generally served a single term and were often succeeded by their senior Cabinet officers. Chase pulled out of the race in February but continued his Treasury work until June, and then campaigned for Lincoln's reelection in the fall. When Chief Justice Roger Taney, whose most famous opinion was that blacks could never be citizens, died in October, Lincoln considered many men before naming Chase, whose views on civil rights were almost the complete opposite of Taney's, as the nation's next chief justice.

Chase remained deeply concerned about blacks and black rights while on the Supreme Court. Within weeks of becoming chief justice, he organized the admission of the first black member of the bar of the court. On the eve of Lincoln's second inauguration, in March 1865, the nation's foremost black leader, Frederick Douglass, called for tea at the home of his friend Chase, whom he had known since "early antislavery days." A few weeks later, just before Lincoln's assassination, Chase wrote the president two long letters, urging him to speak out for black voting rights. Chase was not satisfied with Lincoln's approach, giving voting rights only to a few intelligent blacks or former soldiers; Chase wrote the president that he was now "convinced that universal suffrage is demanded by sound policy and impartial justice alike."[8]

On the morning that Lincoln died of his bullet wounds, April 15, it was Chase who administered the oath of office to the new president, Andrew Johnson. Both in person and by letter, while he was on the southern tour that took him to Charleston, Chase pressed Johnson to adopt the approach he called "universal suffrage and universal amnesty," linking suffrage for blacks with amnesty for former rebels. After encouraging Chase for a while, Johnson rejected that approach and allowed whites to control the first phase of reconstruction. But by the time Chase died in 1873 at the age of sixty-five, black men had the right to vote throughout the United States, and there was a black member of the Senate and several black members of the House of Representatives. Much work remained, but Chase could take considerable pride in what he and his colleagues had accomplished in ending slavery and securing black rights.[9]

Millions of Americans see Chase's name every day—the Chase National Bank was named for him by friends not long after his death—but they know little about his life and work. If Americans know anything about Chase and slavery, they do not know how his views evolved over time; how he gradually became one of slavery's most vocal and successful opponents. If Americans know anything about Chase's relations with Lincoln, they know that he was Lincoln's rival but not that Lincoln could never have become president without the vital work that Chase had done in the two preceding decades—forming and building antislavery political parties—nor the way in which the sixteenth president respected and relied upon Chase. The purpose of this book is to tell Chase's story, from birth to death, for a new generation of Americans.

CHAPTER I

"He Called Me Yankee"

⁑ 1808–26 ⁑

S almon Portland Chase never liked his name. In his early twenties, Chase wrote to a college classmate that he was thinking of changing his "awkward, *fishy* name" to something more impressive, like Spencer Payne Cheyce. Five years later, he had another idea: Samuel Paca Chase, taking the names of one of the early justices of the Supreme Court, Samuel Chase, whom Chase believed was a distant relation, and William Paca, another signatory of the Declaration of Independence, apparently simply because his last name started with *P*. During the Civil War, when an admirer wrote that he was thinking of naming his son Salmon Portland, Chase replied that he "had the misfortune to be born about a year after my uncle Salmon Chase died at Portland; and to have a sort of monument to his memory made of me by giving me the name of Salmon Portland." His uncle "was an excellent man and Portland a very respectable city; but somehow I never liked the name derived from them." Chase urged the father to think of "the feelings of your boy, fifteen years hence or twenty," and to find a better name.[1]

Cornish, New Hampshire, where Chase was born on January 13, 1808, was a town of about sixteen hundred people, on the edge of the Connecticut River, among green hills and fertile farmland. Chase's great-grandfather Samuel and his family were the first to settle in Cornish, just before the American Revolution. Samuel's family was large, and his children had large families, so that according to one local history, Chase was for many years the most common surname in the town. By 1808, a number of these men had left Cornish and distinguished themselves elsewhere. One of Chase's uncles, Dudley, was the Speaker of the House in Vermont; he would go on to serve as federal senator. Another uncle, Philander, was the first Episcopal minister in New Orleans; he would go on to become the first Episcopal bishop of Ohio and then Illinois, as well as the founder of Kenyon College. Yet another uncle, Baruch, was a leading lawyer in Hopkinton, New Hampshire. All of these Chase men were graduates of Dartmouth College, located in Hanover, New Hampshire, about twenty miles north of Cornish, also on the Connecticut River. Chase's father, Ithamer, did *not* attend college; some sources say that he stayed home to run the farm while his brothers went to school. "An upright Christian man," as his son recalled him, Ithamer served as a member of the state legislature and as justice of the peace.[2]

The parents of Chase's mother, Jannette Ralston Chase, moved from Scotland to New England just before the American Revolution. Chase's grandfather Alexander Ralston, according to a local history, owned not only the Ralston Tavern in the center of Keene, New Hampshire, about fifty miles south of Cornish, but also "several farms and much other real estate"—so much so that, in some years, Ralston "was the largest taxpayer in the town." Chase's parents married in Keene in 1792, settled in Cornish, and soon had a large family: Salmon was the seventh of eleven children. He started attending school in Cornish, but in late 1815 or early 1816 the family moved to Keene, where his father started a glass factory with two partners. This proved precisely the wrong time for the farmer to enter the glass business, because the end of the War of 1812 brought imports of cheaper, better British glass. Moreover, the worldwide bitter cold weather of 1816—the result of the eruption of Mount Tambora in what is now Indonesia—depressed the New England economy. There was deep snow on the ground in New England through June, so that crops froze and failed throughout the region.[3]

Perhaps because of these stresses, perhaps because of genetic factors, Ithamer Chase suffered a stroke in the summer of 1817. A few days later, the father of the nine-year-old boy was dead at age fifty-four. Salmon Chase wrote later that "they called it the numb palsy. No remedies availed. He lingered some days, and then we were called into his room. Father was dying. How still the room was, except the heavy breathing and the ominous rattle. He could not speak to us, and we stood mute and sobbing. Soon all was over. We had no father. . . . The light was gone out from our home."[4]

Ithamer Chase left behind not only ten children—one had died as an infant—but also substantial debts. The family moved to less expensive quarters, and several of the older children moved out; the second son, Dudley, went to sea and died of disease in the Caribbean. Salmon Chase, who had studied up to this point at home and in local schools, spent several months, perhaps a whole school year, at a school in Windsor, Vermont. The school was run by Josiah Dunham, a former newspaper editor for the Federalist Party, the party of John Adams and Alexander Hamilton and the opponents of Thomas Jefferson and James Madison. Chase remembered finding and reading the back issues of Dunham's paper, "fiercely Federal in sentiment" and harshly critical of President James Madison. In the first two decades of the nineteenth century New England was the stronghold of the waning Federalist Party, and although Chase never *called* himself a Federalist, he imbibed some Federalist ideas—especially about banks and commerce—that never left him.[5]

In early 1820, when he was twelve, Chase learned that he would be leaving New England for Ohio, to live and study there with his uncle Bishop Philander Chase. Young Chase was thrilled, not because he was especially religious, but because Ohio was the heart of the West. As people flooded into Ohio from the East, the population soared: from 230,000 in 1810, to 580,000 in 1820, to almost 940,000 in 1830. Land was cheap—under the Land Act of 1820, one could purchase eighty acres from the federal government for only $100—and thousands were moving to Ohio, buying up land, clearing forests, plowing fields, forming farms, building new communities. Chase was born in New England, and would spend many years in Washington, but the West would be his real home.[6]

On the first leg of his first trip to Ohio, Chase was with his oldest brother, Alexander, and Henry Schoolcraft, later a famous scholar of Native Americans, who were on their way to join an official expedition exploring the Great Lakes. When they reached Buffalo, the three travelers had to wait for Lake Erie to melt before they could continue. Their vessel, the *Walk-in-the-Water*, the first steamboat on the Great Lakes and one of the first steamboats in the world, used both a steam engine and sails to travel from Buffalo to Detroit in less than three days, stopping along the way at Erie, Cleveland, and Sandusky. "The accommodations of the boat were all that could be wished," Schoolcraft wrote in his account of the expedition, "and nothing occurred to interrupt the delight which a passage at this season affords." Thus did Chase experience for the first time the transportation revolution, one in which he would play a minor supporting role as lawyer and legislator. Over the course of his lifetime, better roads, along with steamboats and railroads, would shorten journeys from months and weeks into days and hours.[7]

Young Chase disembarked from the *Walk-in-the-Water* in Cleveland, while his brother and Schoolcraft continued on to Detroit. Cleveland at this time was just a village of five hundred people, among them a friend of the bishop's who had agreed to host the boy. Chase recalled that he "spent several days—perhaps a couple of weeks—at his house on the west bank of the Cuyahoga [River], amusing myself by going down to the ferry and playing ferryman, taking passengers to and from the Cleveland or eastern side, and sometimes paddling down toward the lake till the waves rolling in rocked my canoe." Eventually Chase set out to cover the last hundred miles of his journey, south and west to Worthington, Ohio, traveling in the company of two priests, heading to an Episcopal convention. Chase remembered that "great forests stretched across the state" and that the road was so poor they sometimes lost their way in the woods.[8]

With its schools and small-scale factories, its village green and churches, including the Episcopal church of which Chase's uncle was the rector, Worthington was a bit of New England, transplanted to rural central Ohio. Worthington had tried and failed to become the state capital, losing out to nearby Columbus, where the legislature had started to meet a few years before Chase arrived in Worthington.[9]

Born in 1775, Philander Chase had already lived a remarkable life by the time his nephew Salmon came to live with him. As a student at Dartmouth, after reading an Episcopal prayer book, Philander left the Congregational Church, which was so pervasive and powerful in New England, to join the far weaker Episcopal Church. He was ordained an Episcopal priest in 1799 and converted his family, among others; Salmon recalled worshipping as a boy at Trinity Episcopal Church in Cornish. After appointments in New York, Philander Chase was assigned in 1805 to the new territory of Louisiana, where he organized the first Episcopal church in New Orleans. After five years there and five years as the rector of a parish in Hartford, Connecticut, he went to Ohio, organizing the handful of Episcopal congregations there into a diocese, of which he was ordained the first bishop in 1819. The Episcopal Church in Ohio was

*Bishop Philander Chase, the uncle with whom Chase lived as a boy in Ohio,
and whom he later recalled as "tyrannical."*

small and struggling, so, to make ends meet, Bishop Chase ran a farm near
Worthington and served as the president of the Worthington Academy,
also known as Worthington Seminary. The bishop's family consisted of his
second wife, Sophia, their two children, and a son by his first marriage,
Philander Jr., a minister who did much of the teaching at the seminary.[10]

Bishop Philander Chase was an intelligent, diligent, difficult, dispu-
tatious man. The Episcopal church in Worthington was founded and, for
many years, headed by Deacon James Kilbourn, who also served the community in various other capacities, including as land agent and member
of Congress. In 1820, the year in which Salmon arrived in Worthington,
Bishop Chase filed canon law charges against Kilbourn. We do not know
the details, only that the bishop charged the deacon with improper and
immoral conduct. Rather than face trial—in a church court that would
no doubt be dominated by friends of the bishop—Kilbourn resigned his
ministry.[11]

A few years later, after founding and presiding over Kenyon College, Philander Chase resigned after a bitter dispute with the trustees. Salmon Chase was not especially surprised, writing to a cousin that the bishop was "never qualified for the government of young men." Chase explained that "for founding a college, for encountering and overcoming obstacles where everything depends upon energy and impulse, he is admirably qualified—but in duties which demand mildness, patience, and forbearance he will always be wanting." Later still, when Chase recalled his years with the bishop, he was even more pointed: his uncle was "quite tyrannical."[12]

If the uncle was difficult, the nephew was not easy, either. Chase would later remember how one of his older schoolmates in Worthington called him a Yankee, "which with them was a reproachful epithet." Chase replied, "Tom, if you call me Yankee again, I'll kick you." The boy insisted that Chase was indeed a Yankee, and Chase immediately kicked him. Tom ran off to the bishop, who summoned his nephew, and asked why he had kicked his classmate. "Because he called me Yankee," Chase replied. "Well," said Philander, "are you not a Yankee? I am, and I regard it as a credit and not a reproach." All right, said Chase, but he would not have the boys insult him with the term. Chase "knew by the look of the old gentleman that my case was won; and, sure enough, I was let off with a very slight reprimand."[13]

Chase did not enjoy his two years in Worthington: "There were some pleasant rambles, some pleasant incidents, some pleasant associates, but the disagreeable largely predominated. I used to count the days and wish that I could get home or go somewhere else and get a living by work." He spent more time working on the farm than he spent at school: milking and tending cows, chopping wood and building fires, sowing and tending and harvesting crops. He did well in his first school year, meriting a prominent place in the graduation ceremony and delivering a short speech in Greek in which he compared the apostles John and Paul. For much of Chase's second school year, however, the school was for some unclear reason not in session. Chase recalled that "my scholarship, such as it was, grew rusty."[14]

In the summer of 1822 the trustees of Cincinnati College offered Bishop Chase a position as its president, at a salary of $1,800 a year plus moving expenses. His duties, they assured him, would be light. The bishop explained to Philander Jr. that he was inclined to take the post for the sake of his wife. "To have removed her from New York to the woods and thus buried her alive has always stung my conscience with a kind of remorse," he admitted. In Cincinnati, "she will find those who resemble the elegant society to which she has been accustomed. Here her pure mind will not be so frequently disturbed by the viperlike hissing of envy or the toadlike croaking of malice and atheism." After moving his family to Cincinnati in the fall (over what he termed "indescribably bad roads"), the bishop reported that he had placed Salmon in the freshman class at the college. "I know he is too young: but what could we do? Except for his disposition of becoming too well acquainted with the city, which I will repress or break his pate, he would do well enough." Indeed, that very evening, the bishop lamented, young Salmon was out in the city, absent without leave.[15]

Cincinnati, which would be Chase's home for the next year, and to which he would return and live most of his life, was an amazing place in the early part of the nineteenth century. The population was surging: from 2,500 in 1810, to about 10,000 in 1820, to almost 25,000 by 1830. Steamboats were central to this growth, moving people and goods up and down the Ohio River, while the engine and steamboat factories provided work for hundreds of Cincinnatians. Other factories made furniture, cloth, clothing, glassware, and other goods. Cincinnati was the hub of a large, rich agricultural area, in both Ohio and Kentucky, and the center of the American pork trade. Frances Trollope, the British writer who lived in Cincinnati in the latter part of the 1820s, described how a walk was spoiled when "the brook we had to cross [was] red with the stream from a nearby pig slaughter-house, while our noses . . . were greeted by odors that I will not describe, and which I heartily hope my readers cannot imagine."[16]

Cincinnati was the first place where Chase lived among African Americans. His part of New England was almost entirely white, with only eight hundred blacks in New Hampshire and nine hundred in Vermont, according to the 1820 census. In contrast, Ohio was home to almost five thousand blacks, of whom about a thousand lived in and around Cincinnati. Most of these African Americans were former slaves, living in shacks, speaking poor English, working as laborers. As a legal matter, some of the city's blacks were *still* slaves, for they were fugitives subject to recapture by agents for their masters, and all free blacks feared being kidnapped and claimed as fugitives. As a practical matter, however, such captures were not that common in Cincinnati at this time, and the black community there was making modest progress in the years following Chase's arrival. Foreign visitors almost invariably contrasted the free state of Ohio with the slave state of Kentucky, just across the Ohio River. Alexis de Tocqueville, the French traveler and author, whom Chase would meet a few years later in Cincinnati, wrote that on the Ohio side of the river, "everything is activity, industry," while on the Kentucky side, "you think yourself on the other side of the world; the enterprising spirit is gone."[17]

By December 1822, the bishop could write to his son that "Salmon has done wonders." The boy was spending almost all his time with his tutor, and he would soon take "an examination which will entitle him to a place among the Sophomores." Chase probably did not have to work too hard to gain a place in the sophomore class at the age of fifteen, for he recalled later that it "was not a study-loving set of boys who resorted to Cincinnati College at that time." If Bishop Chase had remained there for two or three more years, Salmon Chase would be known as a graduate of Cincinnati College, now the University of Cincinnati, rather than of Dartmouth.[18]

In the summer of 1823, however, Bishop Chase, frustrated that he did not have enough priests to serve the "fainting, famishing, dying" congregations of Ohio, and exasperated at the failure of the eastern bishops to respond to his letters, decided that he would set out for England, to raise funds there for a new Episcopal college in Ohio. At first, the plan was for Salmon to remain in Cincinnati under the care of a minister, but then it was decided that the boy would accompany Uncle Philander and his family as far as upstate New York. The Chase family set out by wagon in early August, with the bishop holding the reins, and Salmon probably walking ahead. It took them more than a month to make their way to Kingston, New York, where the bishop planned to place his wife and children with her family while he was abroad. Here Salmon and Philander Chase parted ways, with the bishop heading south to New York City to board his boat for England, and the boy taking the steamboat north to Albany, New York, then walking east over the hills of Vermont to New Hampshire. He would never forget, he wrote later, "the sensations with which I saw the Monadnock Mountain lift up his crest towards the sky after so long an absence. He stood there like a sublime friend to welcome me home while yet afar off. I was greatly fatigued when I arrived thus near to my home and was still some ten miles off, and it was near night. I had a dollar or two left, and I hired a man to take me with his wagon the remaining distance and before bedtime had received again the welcoming embraces of my mother and my sisters."[19]

Chase must have written letters to his family during the three years that he spent in Ohio, but none have survived. The first letters that we have from Salmon Chase date from late 1823 and early 1824, after his return from Ohio, while he was studying to prepare for college and also teaching school to help pay his college expenses. Chase did not much like teaching, writing a few years later about the difficulties of trying to instruct "forty noisy dirty ragged young idiots." In another letter, he said he would "sooner undertake to teach the wild Indians than again undertake to instruct the *savages* of our enlightened land." Yet like many other educated but impecunious young men at this time, Chase had no choice; teaching school was the best way for him to earn money.[20]

Chase's tone in these early letters was light. In one, he wrote about a girl in town who was "one of the best, not to say the very best young lady that you ever saw, the very vision of perfection, language would fail to express her numerous excellences. So I must leave your own imagination to supply all deficiencies." In another, he wrote that among ladies of the town, "there's one always sails with all her streamers flying and under a full press of sails, another but scarce moves along, while a very, very few keep the mean path . . . never attempting to lift themselves to the stars and never sinking into the mud and filth of this nether world." In July 1824 he wrote that, although he probably could enter Dartmouth in the junior class and thus complete college in two years, he thought it would be better to have an additional year of college. His mother must have informed him that there was no money, for the next month, he took and passed the examination to become a junior. "My examination was by no means a severe one," he wrote his sister, "and consequently I bore it very well."[21]

Dartmouth College, when Chase arrived on the Hanover campus in the fall of 1824, had only a few faculty members and about 150 students. Chase was only sixteen, but he was not the youngest student on campus; there were boys of fourteen as well as men in their twenties. Some of the students were well prepared, having attended prestigious private schools, and others, like Chase, less well prepared, having studied here and there. The curriculum included Latin, Greek, literature, history, geography, theology, and mathematics. In theory, the students rose each day at five, attended daily chapel services, and prepared their lessons. Most of them, like Chase, lived in small groups, renting rooms and arranging for meals from local families.[22]

Dartmouth College had just survived an attempt by the New Hampshire Legislature to repeal the college's charter and turn the school into a public university. From the perspective of the Chase family, and others close to the college, the legislature might as well have closed the school's doors: a public university would be nothing like their small, serious school. In early 1819 the Supreme Court, in a strong opinion by Chief Justice John Marshall, decided that the state legislature had violated the federal constitutional prohibition against "impairing the obligation of contracts" when it passed laws that abrogated the original charter of the college. Every Dartmouth student knows today that this was the case in which, near the end of his oral argument to the court, Daniel Webster declared that Dartmouth was "a small college" and "yet there are those who love it." Webster's famous words did not appear in print, however, until much later, so it is unlikely that Chase knew about them. What he *would* have known, from family and friends, was that their beloved college had escaped only because of a great lawyer and a great chief justice.[23]

Dartmouth College, where Chase was a student from 1824 through 1826,
and to which he returned often in later life.

Chase's letters from Dartmouth provide a wonderful window into the college and his character. A few weeks after he arrived, answering a question about the local women, he wrote, "I have not seen a single fair face since I have been here near enough to distinguish form and features." As to his studies, Chase admitted, "I love not conic sections so well as I ought," but he believed that "I shall bend my mind to them sufficiently to get them and get them well too." The junior class was "far from being contemptible either as to numbers or talents, and one would need considerable exertion to keep a middling rank." Their first examinations were approaching, and some of his classmates were studying "as if their lives depended upon their appointments," by which he meant their grades. Chase hints here at what he would later admit: that he did not work too hard at Dartmouth.[24]

The presidential election of 1824 was approaching, a confused five-way contest that would ultimately be resolved in the House of Representatives. John Quincy Adams, son of the young nation's second chief executive, John Adams, prevailed over General Andrew Jackson through what Jacksonians denounced as a "corrupt bargain" between Henry Clay and Adams, making Adams president and Clay the secretary of state. Chase probably favored Adams, the candidate from New England, but he did not write about the election, at least not in the letters that remain. In March 1825 he reported that the college had placed lighted candles in all the windows, "a grand illumination . . . in honor of the president's inauguration." In the summer of that same year, writing to his sister, Chase said that their cousin Joseph Denison now had his college degree and that he longed to have his own. Then Chase turned around and mocked college by quoting the Scottish poet Robert Burns: "A set of dull conceited hashes, confuse their brains in college classes; they gang in stirks [go in as young cattle] and come out asses."[25]

Friendships, above all, are what come through in Chase's college letters. In one letter, he noted that his friend "old Bison" had "fallen in love for the ninety-ninth time," this time to a woman from Hartford. "But as he is a sworn squire of dames, I suppose that his present will last no longer than his former flames." Chase added that their friend George Punchard, later a leading minister, "has grown fat and hearty as a buck." Some of the friendships that Chase formed at Dartmouth would last the rest of his life: Charles Cleveland, a member of the class of 1827, became a noted classics scholar, one of Chase's constant correspondents, and (through Chase's influence as Treasury secretary) the American consul in Wales. Chase had at least two female friends: he wrote letters during and just after his college years to Adeline and Lauretta Hitchcock, two sisters from Keene, where Chase was spending some of his college vacations.[26]

In the spring of 1826, Chase's senior year, there was an intense religious revival in Hanover. Before this, his Christianity had been the calm, rational religion of an educated Episcopal bishop. In his first letter about the revival, Chase wrote that he was "not taught to believe much in the efficacy of such things," by which he probably meant that his uncle did not believe in revivals. Now, however, like so many other Americans in the early nineteenth century, Chase was swept up in an exciting and emotional Christianity, in a religion that threatened damnation and promised salvation. Writing to a college classmate who was away from school, Chase reported that "compared to last fall, the college seems very sober this spring, I assure you. In the chapel this evening, you might have heard a pin drop, so attentive and silent were the students." In another letter, he noted the leading role of women of Hanover in the revival, saying that "the revival commenced among the young ladies, all of whom without exception have become seriously disposed."[27]

Chase wrote several letters about the revival, including one to the Hitchcock sisters in which he explained that he had completely changed his view about *The History of the Decline and Fall of the Roman Empire* by Edward Gibbon. He had been reading and enjoying the six-volume work before the revival but now denounced it as "poisonous"— probably because the author attributed the decline of Rome to the rise of Christianity. Gibbon, he claimed, "would I fear have made me an infidel had it not been that, during the revival which has commenced here, it has pleased God of his infinite mercy to bring me as I would humbly hope to the foot of the cross." Another Dartmouth student, writing at this same time, described the revival as "powerful, astonishing, glorious," and listed Chase as one of the student leaders who had knelt to "lift their supplications, humble, fervent, and earnest." Another Dartmouth student, less enthused, recalled years later that "all wholesome discipline was abandoned" and that "in the end, all the functions of college life were suspended for one week by a decree of the faculty."[28]

Writing to Denison in June, Chase exhorted his cousin to lead a more religious life. "How important it is that we grow in grace day by day and that we do not suffer ourselves to be led back into the world by any of the numerous temptations which daily beset us." He urged Denison to use his influence to convert people. "Let your friends and acquaintances see that you are anxious for their eternal welfare and exhort them in the spirit of Christian love to flee from the wrath to come." Chase reported that there was a revival in a nearby town, and "glorious days seem to be near the Church of Christ. Christians are losing many old prejudices which formerly were wont to divide them from each other." He hoped that soon all Christians would "be of one heart and one mind" striving to "do most to build up the kingdom of the Redeemer." Chase would remain religious throughout his life, but he was never quite *as* religious as he was during this first flush of enthusiasm.[29]

Chase graduated from Dartmouth in August 1826, eighth out of his class of thirty-seven. His class rank was just high enough to entitle him to membership in the Phi Beta Kappa Society. After graduation, Chase spent some time in Hopkinton, New Hampshire, staying with his sister, Abigail Colby, and talking with the local Episcopal priest, a distant relative, about his future. Chase recalled later, "I had not relinquished the idea of being a minister; but greatly doubted whether I had any right to assume so sacred an office." The eighteen-year-old was more inclined to become a lawyer, following the advice of his brother Alexander, eleven years his senior, who wrote him that "if you feel an ambition to be extensively useful to your species by being advanced to rule over them, and be known and distinguished as a man both at home and abroad," then he should "become an honest and conscientious and moral lawyer."[30]

In November, armed with not much more than a couple of letters of introduction, Chase set out from New Hampshire, hoping to find a teaching position somewhere near Philadelphia or Baltimore. Chase did not want to teach for the rest of his life—he still viewed teaching as tedious—but he was realistic enough to know that teaching was how he would earn his living while he prepared for another profession. Finding nothing much in the middle states, Chase went on to Washington, DC, where he knew that he could at least call upon his uncle Dudley Chase, about to start his second term in the Senate.[31]

Salmon Chase was already an unusual young man when he left New England and arrived in the nation's capital. More than six feet tall, with thick brown hair and large, expressive brown eyes, he made a favorable first impression. In an era when few attended and fewer graduated from college, Chase was an honors graduate of one of the nation's best colleges. He was a serious, sober, eloquent young man, eager to see the world and to make his mark upon it. First, however, Chase would have to find some kind of work in Washington.

CHAPTER 2

"Metropolis of the Nation"

১৯২ 1826–30 ৯৬

A few days after arriving in Washington in December 1826, Chase wrote a long letter to the Hitchcock sisters in New Hampshire. "You will be somewhat surprised," he started, "to learn that I have taken up my residence in the metropolis of the nation." He described Washington in almost breathless terms. The Capitol, where Chase would spend so much of his life, first as senator and then as chief justice, was a "most magnificent building," and he especially admired its four immense historical paintings—scenes from the American Revolution—in the Rotunda. Chase had not only visited the White House; he had met the president at a public reception. Although Jackson's supporters mocked John Quincy Adams as "King John," Chase had "never met a man whose appearance was in my estimation more unkingly." The sixth president was "diminutive," with "blue eyes and a short nose," and "exceedingly plain in his dress and his manners."[1]

As to himself, Chase told the sisters that he hoped to start his own school in January. Writing the next day to a college classmate, Chase was even more positive, saying that school would open on the second Monday of January. An Episcopal priest whom Chase did not name (probably William Hawley, rector of St. John's Episcopal Church) had promised "to use all his influence in my favor, and his influence is by no means small." His uncle, Bishop Chase, now back from England, had written to his friend Henry Clay, the secretary of state, about his nephew, who believed

21

that Clay would "befriend me as far as his multiplicity of associations will permit." In an advertisement for his Select Classical School in a local paper in late December, Chase listed Secretary Clay, Senator Chase, and Reverend Hawley as references. By the middle of January 1827, Chase could write to his college classmate Thomas Sparhawk that he had twenty pupils in his school already, including the children of Clay and Attorney General William Wirt.[2]

Years later, recalling these first few weeks in Washington, Chase would paint a darker picture, writing that, after his advertisement yielded only one potential student, he went to his uncle Dudley, begging him for a position as a federal clerk. Senator Chase refused, saying that he "once obtained an office for a nephew of mine, and he was ruined by it." At the time, Chase was deeply disappointed, but, looking back, he was pleased, for if he had obtained a clerkship, "it is almost certain I would have remained a clerk." The only way Chase obtained pupils was when another schoolteacher, who felt that he had too many students, divided them with Chase, keeping the girls and giving Chase the boys. So it was the seren-dipitous kindness of a stranger, at least as much as his own credentials, that gave Chase the pupils he needed in order to remain in Washington.[3]

Chase did not have many friends in the capital during his first few months there. Writing to his friend Hamilton Smith in May 1827, Chase explained that there were distinct tiers of Washington society: a first tier, composed of members of the Cabinet and their families; a second level, "the lawyers physicians divines and gentlemen generally"; a third tier, "the mechanics and artisans"; and below them, "the laborers and slaves." These "classes are almost as distinct from each other as the castes of the Hindus," he observed, and "few have a very extensive acquaintance beyond the class to which they belong." So far, Chase knew only a few members of the first tier of Washington society, men whose sons were among his pupils.[4]

Religion would always be a central part of Chase's life, and so, on Sundays, he went to church, often attending churches of different denomi-nations. He recalled later that he became a member of St. John's Episcopal Church, on the north side of Lafayette Square, and "for a long while was a teacher in the Sunday school." He formed a friendship with Reverend Henry Van Dyke Johns, the rector of Trinity Episcopal Church, and one Sunday afternoon, they rode to Rock Creek Church, the oldest Episcopal congregation in the district, so that Johns could hold services there.

Chase wrote in his diary that the building was "dilapidated" and the congregation "very small," but "even that rude place might be a fitting temple for the most high, if humble hearts and contrite spirits were met to worship there." Chase often attended services at the New York Avenue Presbyterian Church, describing the pastor, John Nicholson Campbell, as "one of the most popular preachers at Washington." One Sunday, when bad weather caused other churches to cancel services, Chase went to Ebenezer Methodist, near the Washington Navy Yard. The enthusiastic preacher described in detail the tortures of hell and the pleasures of paradise. The congregation participated fully: "some shouted aloud in anticipation of heaven," while others "shrieked in dread of hell" and "sobs and groans resounded through the house." Chase did not mention it in his diary, but this was an interracial congregation, of which there were many before the Civil War.[5]

Chase was in many ways like John Quincy Adams: sober, serious, self-critical. In his diary, at the age of twenty-five, Adams wrote that he was "not satisfied with the manner in which I employ my time. It is calculated to keep me forever fixed in that state of useless and disgraceful insignificancy which has been my lot for some years past." Chase wrote in his diary in almost identical terms at about the same age. "The night has seldom found me much advanced beyond the station I occupied in the morning, and the end of the year has at length come round and finds me almost in the very spot I was in at its commencement. I have learned little and forgotten much and ready to conclude of the future from the past I almost despair of ever making any figure in the world." The two men came from such similar Puritan backgrounds that they echoed each other.[6]

Chase and Adams had another similarity: they lacked the common touch. In late 1827, at a banquet in Baltimore, celebrating the anniversary of a victory over the British in the War of 1812, Adams offered a curious toast, thoroughly confusing his listeners. The toast, Chase wrote to a friend, was "another proof if any were wanting of the saying great men are not always wise. The president made an effort at easy dignity and failed most completely." In another letter, after meeting Adams at a reception, Chase described him as "cold and reserved" and "peculiarly unfortunate in his demeanor." One of Chase's clerks would later recall that he never heard Chase "make a joke or tell a story. He never indulged in light or trifling conversation. He did not possess in the slightest degree the charming quality of humor."[7]

It was not until November 1827, almost a year after he arrived in Washington, that Chase mentioned for the first time that he was studying law with William Wirt, whom he described as "one who wins the affections and prepossesses the judgment almost instantaneously." Originally from Maryland, the son of immigrants, Wirt had lived as a young lawyer in Virginia, where he became a protégé of Thomas Jefferson. In 1807 President Jefferson asked Wirt to serve as the lead prosecutor in the treason trial of Aaron Burr—the former vice president who was accused of attempting an armed rebellion in the Southwest. President Madison made Wirt the district attorney for the Eastern District of Virginia in 1816, and, the following year, President Monroe appointed him attorney general. John Quincy Adams, when he became president in 1825, retained many of Monroe's appointees, including Wirt, who would serve until 1829, the longest tenure of any attorney general. But being attorney general was not a full-time job in the early nineteenth century, so Wirt tutored law students such as Chase. He also had an active private law practice, which often kept him away from Washington for weeks.[8]

William Wirt, attorney general for Presidents James Monroe and John Quincy Adams, and Chase's friend and legal mentor in Washington.

Chase spent more time with the Wirt family than with Wirt himself. The lady of the house, Elizabeth Gamble Wirt, was from a leading Richmond family and was then working on the book for which she would become famous: *Flora's Dictionary*, listing more than two hundred flowers and explaining their meaning in the language of love. Chase described Mrs. Wirt as "a very interesting and agreeable woman, though somewhat inclined like most of her sex to remember the faults of the absent." There were ten children, including two boys in Chase's school, and two girls, Elizabeth and Catherine, about the same age as Chase. Elizabeth was a "modest girl," Chase wrote, "with a richly cultivated mind and a most amiable disposition. Her sisters, four in number, do not equal her as to sweetness of temper but all are uncommonly intelligent." A few weeks later, Chase wrote to another friend that "there are two unmarried daughters who are old enough to go into society, both possessing highly cultivated minds, fine taste, and elegant manners." At least at first, it seems that Chase did not have a strong favorite among the two sisters; he liked them both and indeed penned a poem to praise them both. He shared the poem with several friends and was annoyed when it made its way into the papers.[9]

In the spring of 1828 Chase wrote a friend that he had spent three of the past seven evenings with the Wirt family, listening to the sisters play music and enjoying their educated conversation. In another letter, he described them as "highly amiable and lovely girls, as artless and frank as if they had been born and educated in the western forests, yet uniting to this lovely simplicity elegance of manners, refinement of taste, strength of mind, and a cultivated intellect. They share largely in that vivacity and openness which distinguishes Southern manners, while they exhibit not a little less that elegance and cultivation of mind which mark more frequently the character of the Northern lady." Contradicting his earlier description of Washington society as divided into rigid castes, Chase described the Wirt circle as including men of "all professions, the lawyer, the physician, the minister of peace, and the man of war; and of all ranks, the judge, the advocate, the poor student." Chase was distressed to hear in June that the two Wirt sisters had (in his words) "mortgaged their fair hands to two young officers in the army." Chase's information was not quite correct: Liz Wirt had received a proposal from Edward Hazzard, one of the army engineers working on the first stages of the Baltimore & Ohio Railroad, but she had not accepted. As she explained in a letter to her father, "you are my *beau ideal,* and I don't think I can have anything to say to any *beau* who does not bear at least some faint resemblance to you."[10]

Elizabeth Gamble Wirt, author and wife of William Wirt. It appears that there are no surviving portraits of the Wirt sisters, so this portrait of their mother, made in about 1810, is our best approximation of the Wirt sisters when Chase knew them.

In July William Wirt invited Chase to join him, his two daughters, and their teenage brother William on a trip to New England, where they would place the boy in a boarding school. Wirt promised Chase that the two of them would work on Chase's legal preparation along the way, but the young man declined the invitation, writing to a friend that he would "keep close to my books while he is gone and astonish him by my acquisitions when he returns." Perhaps Chase did not join the Wirt vacation because he did not want to spend weeks in close contact with the sisters when he could not hope to marry either of them. The problem was not only Hazzard and the other army officer; the key problem was his own poverty. When a friend teased him about his "Dulcinea"—the beautiful product of the imagination of Don Quixote in the novel by Cervantes—Chase wrote that he had "no such attachment" but that *if* he allowed himself "to think of these things, I know no one to whom I would sooner offer heart and hand. But I hold it the merest folly in a young man, not possessed of an independent fortune, who is pursuing the study of law or medicine, to clog his free steps by incumbrances like these." In another letter, Chase explained that he would "deem a young man guilty of gross infatuation who could permit himself to fix his affections, even were he sure they would be reciprocated, upon one educated as they have been in the bosom of affluence, accustomed to every indulgence, unused to the smallest degree of self-denial, and consequently utterly unfitted for the duties of a poor man's wife, unless he had more certain and assured prospects of professional success than I can anticipate."[11]

While the two older Wirt sisters were away in New England, Chase offered to teach their younger sisters Latin. Mrs. Wirt was not happy, writing to her husband that Chase had "overrated their capacity and his love of *truth* and *blunt sincerity* induced him to let them understand as much, which has so discouraged them, that they are quite heartsick about it." She added that Chase "has not the wit to discover that he is in fact a *hard task Master*—and not the gentle and encouraging friend that they had a right to expect." A few weeks later, she was pleased to report that the girls were now taking dancing lessons, and that this had provided an excuse to terminate their Latin lessons with Chase. Not long after Wirt returned to Washington, Latin again caused tension: Wirt wrote Chase a long, harsh letter claiming that his sons (after months under Chase's instruction) now pronounced Latin improperly. We do not have Chase's response, but it seems that he both defended himself and explained his own poor Latin training. Wirt sent back an apologetic letter, and the case was closed.[12]

Wirt guided Chase in his legal studies, but, perhaps more important, the two talked about literature, politics, and history—and especially Thomas Jefferson. For Wirt, Jefferson was not a remote ancient figure but a friend, mentor, and client, one who had died only a few months before Wirt first met Chase. After the deaths of John Adams and Thomas Jefferson, on July 4, 1826, the citizens of Washington asked Wirt to deliver a funeral oration, soon printed as a pamphlet. Adams and Jefferson, Wirt declared, were "apostles of human liberty," sent to lift Man "to the station for which God had formed him, and to put to flight those idiot superstitions with which tyrants had contrived to enthrall his reason and his liberty." Wirt also shared with Chase lesser details, such as that "Mr. Jefferson was only sixteen when he began to keep regular files of newspapers" thus making himself "master of all that was passing in his own age." Chase would keep just such newspaper scrapbooks later in his life. As a boy, Chase probably heard harsh words about Jefferson, for Jefferson and his successor, Madison, were not popular in New England. But after his time with Wirt, Chase revered Jefferson.[13]

Chase learned about the ways of Washington by attending debates in Congress, by reading the papers, by talking about politics with friends. The main issue on the agenda of Congress in early 1828 was the tariff; Northerners wanted a high tariff to protect their industries from imports; Southerners wanted a low tariff because they imported many goods and thus *paid* the tariff. After Congress enacted a new, higher tariff in May, there were protests in Southern states, especially South Carolina, where people compared the "tyrannical" new tariff with the British tax laws that led to the American Revolution, and some even suggested that the state should secede from the Union.[14]

By this point, Chase had abandoned all thoughts of becoming a minister; he wanted to be a lawyer and a political leader, like his role models William Wirt and Daniel Webster. He had not abandoned, however, his Puritan religious intensity. Urging his friend Sparhawk to study harder, Chase wrote, "I regard this world not as a place of leisure—not as a place for selfish exertion, but as a vast theater upon which each man has a part allotted to him to perform and duties to discharge which connect him closely with his fellowman. I confess I desire to be distinguished, but I desire more to be useful, and were the choice of exalted honor and undying fame or extensive and humble usefulness offered to me, I do not think I should hesitate a moment in my choice of the latter." Chase continued: "I do not regard myself as at liberty to make any disposition of my time that may suit my inclination but esteem it as a sacred trust committed to me by my God every moment of which ought to be devoted to a diligent preparation to discharge any duties which He may call upon me to perform."[15]

The Wirts, like most leading families in Washington, owned slaves. There were more than six thousand slaves in the District of Columbia at this time, in a total population of about forty thousand. Living and working in this society, it is not surprising that Chase sometimes sounded like a Southerner when talking about slaves. "The truth is," he wrote his friend Smith, "that little cause exists for that sickly sympathy which many at the North feel or affect to feel with the fancied suffering of the slave. The master has a far more just claim upon our commiseration, for it is a truth that the people of the South live in continual apprehension of an insurrection among their slaves." In another letter to Smith, Chase mocked a scheme to colonize former slaves on the Pacific coast. The distance and difficulties were too great, and besides, he wrote, "the climate is not congenial to the negroes," so that they would "*long* remain in a weak and helpless condition." Agreeing with those who favored African colonization, Chase wrote that "Africa is their home; they are more willing to go there; and are sure if industrious, when they arrive, of a competence." And yet Chase also recounted to Smith a conversation with a slave boy about colonization, in which the boy said he did not want to leave "all he holds dear. He feels in all its force that *amor patria* which makes the Greenlander prefer the rough and bleak land which God hath given him to the fairest portion of the earth. America is as much the home of the negro whose fathers' fathers have lived here and died as it is of the American white man, whose foot not many centuries ago had never pressed the soil which he now so proudly claims as his own peculiar inheritance." It is hard to imagine a young Southerner acknowledging in this way that blacks have as much right to America as whites. Perhaps the best way to describe Chase's views on slavery at this point is that they were not well formed; he had not thought much about slavery, he did not write much about it in his letters, and he was not yet writing essays and briefs on slavery and related issues.[16]

Later in his life, when Chase wrote about these early Washington years, he did not recall that he had laughed at the "fancied suffering of the slave." What he remembered instead was that, at the request of some leading Quakers, he drafted a petition to Congress seeking the abolition of slavery within the District of Columbia. "The existence among us of a distinct class of people, who, by their condition as slaves, are deprived of almost every incentive to virtue and industry, and shut out from many of the sources of light and knowledge, has an evident tendency to corrupt the morals of the people and to damp the spirit of enterprise, by accustoming the rising generation to look with contempt upon the honest laborer, and to depend for support too much upon the labor of others." There is no way of knowing whether Chase *agreed* with these arguments or simply devised them as a lawyer for his clients, but it is perhaps indicative that he did not sign the petition.[17]

The year in which Chase got to know the Wirts, 1828, was also the year of the bitter election between John Quincy Adams and Andrew Jackson. Chase was strongly in favor of the incumbent and opposed to Jackson. He wrote that he feared that "the Jackson men will gain the day. It has been truly said that they have the huzza boys with them and unfortunately they are a majority in this land of equal rights and unequal sense." Chase added that he hoped that recent reports about "the private and public character of Gen. Jackson will awaken the people to a sense of their danger." Adams supporters called Jackson a murderer, for the way in which he had summarily executed military prisoners, and a bigamist, for the way in which he had married his wife while she was still legally married to another man. In another letter, Chase wrote that "among all the political men in the United States, the most morally pure, the most politically upright and consistent are the president and his Cabinet." Chase believed that Jackson would not have many votes north of the Potomac River, except perhaps in New York.[18]

Chase was right in thinking that Jackson would not win many votes in New England, but he received some votes even there, and he carried almost every state *outside* of New England. As the results trickled into Washington in early November 1828, Chase predicted disaster. "If I do not mistake the signs of the times," he wrote to Thomas Sparhawk, "you and I will live to see this Union dissolved, and I do not know that New England has much reason to deprecate such an event." The "signs of the times" that Chase thought were "fearful omens" included "the proceedings at the South during the last summer" (the protests against the 1828 tariff), "the measures adopted as preparatory by the South Carolina delegation in Congress last winter" (their preparations for secession because of the tariff), and "the recent election of an ignoramus, a rash, violent military chief to the highest civil office."[19]

Writing his cousin Joseph Denison a few days later, Chase said that the election of "a man whose every act proclaims his unfitness to rule a free people, conclusively evinces that the day is past when New England's voice was heard with deference. We are henceforth a proscribed people—cut off from the race of honor and doomed to be hewers of wood and drawers of water for the people of the South and West." Perhaps, Chase mused, New England would be better off as an independent nation. "Having immense internal resources, strong in mutual attachments, united by the ties of similar religious and civil institutions, and more than all mighty through the virtue and intelligence of the people, what has New England to dread or rather what has she not to hope from a *dissolution of the Union?*" Chase was fortunate that these were private letters, not public statements, for they would surely have been quoted back against him later, when he and others opposed Southern secession.[20]

On January 1, 1829, Chase was among those at the annual White House reception, the last that would be held under President Adams. Chase noted in his diary, the first diary entry that survives, that "the lady who leaned upon my arm was one of the most brilliant in the room, and I shone a little by reflected light. She was elegantly attired in a Scottish dress of the most tasteful description." The young lady, whom Chase did not name, was Elizabeth Wirt, who wrote to her father that she wished he could have seen her in her Scottish costume. "Everybody said they had never seen me wear anything half so becoming, and even Mr. Chase observed that it was the prettiest dress in the room. I held his arm all the time." Hazzard had by this time written to the Wirts to say that he would no longer court Elizabeth because she seemed not to care for him. Elizabeth was not sorry to part with him, writing to her father that he "has more feeling than sense. I should get tired of him as a companion, for he has few resources of conversation."[21]

A few days later, Chase marked his twenty-first birthday. Quoting Macbeth's grim speech, Chase wrote in his diary that "tomorrow and tomorrow and tomorrow creeps in this petty pace from day to day." Unlike Macbeth, however, Chase did not despair. "Even now there is time if I will but resolve and resolutely act to do much. Knowledge may yet be gained and golden reputation. I may yet enjoy the consciousness of having lived not in vain. Future scenes of triumph may yet be mine." Many would later call Chase ambitious, and comments like this show that he was: he hoped to work hard, to do well, and to make his mark on the world.[22]

Chase learned from his law books but learned more important lessons by watching lawyers at work. On February 14, for example, Chase watched in awe as Daniel Webster argued an interstate property dispute in the United States Supreme Court. "He states his case with great clearness and draws inference with exceeding sagacity. His language is rich and copious; his manner dignified and impressive; his voice deep and sonorous; his sentiments high and often sublime." In its ruling a few days later, the Supreme Court agreed with Webster, declaring that "fundamental maxims of a free government seem to require that the rights of personal liberty and private property should be held sacred." Years later, when he was chief justice, Chase would quote this language in one of his own opinions, on the constitutionality of the notes issued by the federal government during the Civil War.[23]

Daniel Webster, the famed lawyer, orator, and senator. Chase heard Webster speak both in court and in the Congress, and recalled his kindness following Webster's death.

The first few months of 1829 were hard for Chase, for he knew that the new president would not keep Wirt as attorney general, and that the Wirt family would leave Washington soon after the inauguration. On inauguration day, March 4, Chase noted in his diary that Wirt and the other members of the Adams Cabinet were invited but did *not* attend, for they did not wish "to hear themselves abused by insinuation." After delivering his inaugural address, which, according to Chase, nobody in the audience could hear, Jackson mounted his horse and rode to the President's House, followed by the crowd. "The people rushed into the building,"

Chase wrote. "They swarmed in every room. They pried into every corner. Those who entered first into the building were obliged to find their way out through the windows, for to return through the doors was almost an impossibility." Jackson had to spend the night in a hotel "so that the ravages of the mob might be repaired, and the building prepared once more for his habitation." On April 8 Chase recorded that "the loveliest part of Mr. Wirt's family left Washington for Richmond," where the sisters would visit relatives before moving to Baltimore. A week later, Chase wrote that the "remainder of Mr. Wirt's family left Washington today." At the end of the month, he wrote Sparhawk that "this administration was appropriately denominated some weeks since as 'the millennium of minnows.' It is so truly. From all quarters have applicants for office been flocking, of all kinds and conditions."[24]

Sparhawk had apparently teased him about Liz Wirt, because Chase responded that he wished he could "cherish the anticipations to which you obviously allude." But he could not. "If I were a little more advanced in the world, even one short year, it might be. But ignorant as I am of my future destinies, uncertain even as to the place where my lot may be cast, I feel it would be unjust to her to attempt to win her affections." And yet, he added, "so strangely inconsistent is man with himself, I always forget all this when in her presence, and half of my thoughts are employed upon this very subject, and though conviction constantly extinguishes the taper of Hope, yet it is constantly relumed in my brain."[25]

Wirt was not the only man to lose his post when Jackson took over from Adams, for Jackson was the first president to make a clean sweep of the executive branch, removing essentially all his predecessors' appointees. There were no civil service protections at the time, so Jackson removed not merely Cabinet members but also minor clerks. Chase was appalled by the new chief executive's course. "He speaks of the subordinate officers of the Government as his slaves. 'My clerks must do this, my clerks must do that.' If anyone has happened to incur his displeasure, 'Let him be removed.' If a head of a Department remonstrates, 'You, Sir, hold your office at my will.'" In another letter, Chase fumed that "good men are displaced to make room for others of more questionable character. Experience is sent to beg, and inexperience is elevated to power and place and trust. Learning gives way to ignorance, and it is curious to remark that the head of the nation is the most ignorant man in the Cabinet, and from him downward, influence is in direct proportion to narrowness of soul."[26]

Probably through his friend Reverend John Nicholson Campbell, Chase was invited to give an oration on July 4, 1829, at the Presbyterian church. The event was rained out, so Chase did not give the speech, but he printed a version in a newspaper, and it shows better than any other source we have his political and constitutional views at this time. Chase started with an attack on what he called "extreme democracy": the increasing tendency of voters not merely to elect men to represent them, but to instruct their representatives in detail on how they should vote on the issues. Chase was equally opposed to the way in which the electoral college had changed since the first presidential elections. Those elected to the college were now committed to vote for a particular candidate, such as Adams or Jackson; they were no longer free, when they gathered in their state-by-state meetings, to discuss the candidates and to vote their consciences. After quoting Alexander Hamilton, who praised the way in which the members of the electoral college would gather and *deliberate*, Chase denounced the new system as a perversion of the Constitution.[27]

More generally, Chase was troubled by the emergence of strong political parties. "Young as I am," he wrote, "I have witnessed the partial career of one who, by the magic influence of party names, controlled a state more absolutely than if a scepter were in his hand. . . . He was the high priest of a party, and the excommunications of the Vatican, in the plenitude of papal dominion, were not more dreaded than his." Chase did not mention his name, but he was writing about Martin Van Buren, known already as the Little Magician, whose faction of the Democratic Party dominated New York politics and who now had national power as Jackson's secretary of state.[28]

Chase feared that at some point, Congress, "regardless of everything but sectional and individual interest," might enact "partial and oppressive legislation" so severe that it would divide the Union. Again, although he did not mention the tariff, Chase surely had the strong Southern opposition to the 1828 tariff in mind. In an eerie preview of what the Southern states would say in 1861 as they seceded, Chase sketched what one state might say to the others as it seceded from the Union. "We have implored your *forbearance*, and you have multiplied your *exactions*; we have remonstrated with you as brethren, and you have spurned us as *slaves*. Henceforth we are separate and forever. If you attempt to force us into submission, we are prepared to resist. If your armies are sent hither, we are ready to meet them. And upon the graves of our fathers every man of us will perish before we return to a connection which we *abhor*."[29]

Chase discussed westward expansion and education, and especially the need to extend education to remote western regions. "No people can be *truly* free," he wrote, "unless they are exempt from the debasing influence of ignorance and vice. Upon the knowledge and integrity of the people rests the whole fabric of self-government." Chase knew, from his time in Ohio, and from the newspapers, that people were moving west. "The day is not very distant when on the shores of the mighty Ohio, and on the shores of the mightier Mississippi, and far beyond where, as yet, the foot of the pioneer hunter has alone trodden, there will be congregated a mass of human beings, far outnumbering the whole of our Atlantic population." Chase viewed this expansion with mixed emotions, because people were moving west more rapidly than civilizing institutions, such as schools and churches. Chase called upon westerners to strengthen their civic institutions, and he called upon *all* Americans to work for individual and national self-improvement. In this way, he concluded, "our beloved country" would become "more great, more glorious, more virtuous, and more free," and its anniversary would be celebrated "to the thousandth and ten thousandth generation."[30]

At about this same time, summer of 1829, Chase received another invitation: to deliver a master's oration at the Dartmouth commencement. All graduates of the college were entitled at this time to receive a master's degree three years after the bachelor's degree, without any further course work, but the faculty would select one or two each year to represent the group with a master's oration. Chase accepted the honor and fixed as his topic "The Relative Importance of the Western States in the American Union." He left Washington at the end of July and spent several happy days in Baltimore with the Wirt family. "In the evening, I walked with Elizabeth and the younger girls" to see the imposing column for the city's nearly complete monument to Washington. Chase, however, "thought little of the Monument . . . or of anything but the noble creature at my side." When they returned to the Wirt house that evening, "the younger members of the family surrounded me. Rosa and Ellen had chairs before me . . . young Agnes, a lovely girl of fourteen, threw herself carelessly on the floor. To be in the midst of such a circle and to be conscious that I shared in the affections of that circle was an exquisite delight."[31]

After a pleasant trip up the Chesapeake Bay, Chase took a carriage through New Jersey, complaining in his diary that "the Jersey roads are certainly the worst in the nation." By the time he reached Boston, he was quite ill, but he continued by stage to Hopkinton, New Hampshire, where his mother was then living. "Here I remained sick nearly a fortnight and, of course, did not deliver my master's oration." On the way home from New England, he was able to pass another few days with the Wirt family in Baltimore, spending an hour with Elizabeth alone. Chase returned to Washington in early September feeling much like "a dog that is dragged back to a chain from which he has been temporarily freed."[32]

As he struggled through dense legal texts to prepare for the bar exam, Chase dreamed of a simpler and fairer legal system. He wrote to Sparhawk that he would "desire to see all the dark and circuitous bypaths which conduct to the sanctuary of justice converted into a broad and beaten highway. I would be glad to see the sun of jurisprudence shining with unclouded effulgence upon all, the rich and the poor, the learned and the ignorant, not hidden by clouds or obscured by a disastrous eclipse as it now is." Chase was also, as he studied for the bar, considering where he would live and work as a young lawyer. He was inclined to Baltimore, where he could spend time with the Wirt family and other friends, but there was a problem: under the local rules, he could not practice in the civil courts until after he had lived in Maryland for three years. So Chase was also looking at other possibilities, including Louisiana, Ohio, and New York.[33]

Chase confessed later that he barely passed the bar. "I had not been a diligent student and knew very little law. I had read a good many pages but had not read very thoroughly." He was examined in open court by the venerable William Cranch, who had already served for decades as the chief judge of the United States Circuit Court of the District of Columbia. Chase wrote that Cranch "knew me and knew my circumstances. I had been in the habit of going up and playing chess with him, and he always beat me." When the judge indicated that he thought Chase should study for another year, the young man pleaded that he had already made his arrangements to go west and practice there. Cranch relented and instructed the clerk to swear Chase in as a member of the bar.[34]

Chase passed the bar in December, but did not leave Washington until February 1830, in part to allow time for the smooth transfer of his school to his college classmate Hamilton Smith. In late December

Chase went to see the first few miles of the Baltimore & Ohio Railroad, the first major rail line in the United States. He marveled at how the smooth rails and iron wheels reduced friction "almost to nothing" and raved about the railroad's "incalculable importance" because it "makes Cincinnati and Baltimore neighboring cities and renders every kind of communication between them as easy as it is now between Baltimore and New York. It will open to the West a market for their produce and facilitate the introduction of the manufactures of the East." Chase was right in his predictions, although it would take longer than he hoped for the railroad to cross the Allegheny Mountains; the line would not reach the Ohio River until 1853.[35]

On the first day of the new year, "while all the world" went to the president's mansion to "pay their respects to General Jackson," Chase visited with other friends. A few days later, however, Chase and a friend went to another White House reception, where Chase met Jackson. Chase shook hands with the president, but he was not much impressed. "General Jackson is not a man of the mind. In his manners, he is graceful and agreeable, and much excels his predecessor in the art of winning golden opinions from all sorts of men." Chase was even more hostile toward Martin Van Buren, describing him as "cold, selfish, intriguing, base, and faithless," and praying that Van Buren would "never reach the gold round to which he so ardently aspires"—meaning the presidency. Chase hoped that the next president would be Henry Clay but for some reason did not use his time in Washington to get to know Clay better. Chase noted in his diary that he attended a reception at Clay's house only after declining several earlier invitations, and that he stayed there for only a half hour, "glad to escape the scene of ceremonious frivolity."[36]

In January 1830 Chase received a letter in which Liz Wirt revealed how far she was from the stereotype of the shallow Southern woman. She started by complimenting a recent article in a local weekly paper, the *American Spectator and Washington City Chronicle*, which she assumed was from Chase's pen. She wished that she had his pen at her command, for she would like to call upon "the Ladies" to "unite immediately in putting down the use of all strong drink at their parties—to exclude from their invitations all who are not satisfied with the lemonade and wine that is offered to them but call for brandy." (Chase agreed; he did not drink much himself, and he was soon active in the temperance movement.) She would also "object to ladies waltzing with gentlemen but allow them to do so with each other—as there is an almost irresistible association in the music and grace and movement of the waltz." Instead of all this, Liz Wirt suggested "that the young people form a literary association, to meet periodically at each other's houses and to spend *one hour* in reading some literary work . . . after which, they should pass the remainder of the evening in conversation and music, to the exclusion of dancing."[37]

Chase took Liz Wirt's letter and (with minor edits) published it in the newspaper as "An Address of a Lady to Her Peers." In a draft letter to Elizabeth, he wrote that she would "see with what promptitude I have obeyed your commands." Then he continued with a personal plea: "You must long since have discovered that my affection for one member of your family far transcends the limits of ordinary friendship, and, therefore, I may speak of it to you without reserve." His strong feelings for her, and his doubts about "my future prospects in life," had combined to prevent him from speaking; they had "produced a constraint which perhaps has been construed into coldness and a silence which may have been construed as neglect." Chase had hoped, during his most recent visit to Baltimore, to speak with Liz alone, in order to "put an end" to this "alternation between life and death," but there was "no favorable opportunity." Now he asked her to "solve the doubt for me. May I hope? Or may I not?" Chase added in a postscript that he was not sure where he would start his legal career: perhaps in Cincinnati, perhaps in western New York.[38]

This was Chase's draft, now in the Chase Papers at the Historical Society of Pennsylvania. The final version of the letter is not among the Wirt Papers at the Maryland Historical Society, but it seems that it was not as ardent as the draft. Liz Wirt responded that she had not yet seen the issue of the newspaper with the address to the ladies. She did not answer Chase's question about marriage (assuming that the question survived in the final letter), but she suggested that she cared for Chase. "You do me but justice in believing that I cannot be indifferent to anything that relates to your happiness and prosperity—far from it—I take a most sincere and lively interest in all that concerns you." She was "not competent to advise or to decide between the North or the West," but she feared that if Chase went to Cincinnati, "we should lose you forever." Upstate New York did not seem that far to Liz Wirt; she and her father and sister had spent time there during their New England tour. But Cincinnati, she wrote, was so far that it was like the "country from whose bourn no traveler returns."[39]

If Chase replied to Elizabeth's letter, his response has not survived. In a way, he answered her by moving to Cincinnati, the place where she believed he would be lost to her. Chase believed that he would have more opportunity in Cincinnati, a rapidly expending city, than in a more settled place such as Baltimore or upstate New York. He explained in a letter to his friend Charles Cleveland, "I would rather be *first* in Cincinnati than first in Baltimore, twenty years hence. And as I have been first at school and college (except at Dartmouth, where I was an idle goose), I shall strive to be first wherever I may be."[40]

Chase's interest in Elizabeth Wirt did not prevent him seeing other young women in the weeks before he left Washington. He visited the home of Samuel Ingham, secretary of the Treasury, and spent time there with Mary Maxcy, daughter of a senior Treasury official, writing in his diary that "her face is not one which a sculptor would choose for a model; yet it is beautiful in feature and still more beautiful in expression." Chase was "very nearly falling in love with this lady," and indeed he wrote some poetry for her, but she had one critical flaw: "She is disinclined to religion and its duties; I value them more than any earthly possession."[41]

On another page of his diary, Chase described a visit to northern Virginia with his friend Thomas Swann, another of Wirt's law students, and a future mayor of Baltimore. While there, they met two "agreeable, intelligent young ladies who had read much" and "made subtle distinctions with a skill worthy of old Aristotle." Chase wrote that "I don't like argumentative ladies. They have no right to encroach upon our privileges." He was not entirely serious here; he did like learned women, such as the Wirt sisters, but he also had a sense of male privilege.[42]

Chase also used his last weeks in Washington to attend debates in Congress and arguments in the Supreme Court. Chase was in the Senate chamber for what one scholar has called "the greatest debate in the history of the Senate," between Daniel Webster and Robert Hayne of South Carolina, in which Webster declared for "Liberty and Union, now and forever, one and inseparable!" Chase was also in the basement of the Capitol, in the courtroom of the Supreme Court, to hear Webster argue a case against Wirt. Chase thought Wirt had the better of the argument because of his careful preparation. "No part of the cause had been unseen," he enthused to his friend Cleveland. "No corner or nook which was not to him a familiar haunt." It was, Chase concluded, well worth one's time "to listen to the utterance of such men."[43]

Just before leaving for the West, Chase went to Baltimore to see the Wirt family one more time. "It was not as it was wont to be," Chase wrote in his diary. When he called at the Wirt house, "some of the family were sick, others did not appear, and they who did seemed changed. Perhaps it was but the picturing of my fancy, but I fear not." The next morning, "coming out of church, I met one of the young ladies. I had not seen her the preceding day and perhaps my own manner was somewhat affected by the reception I had met. She accused me of coldness. I defended myself as well as I could and went home with her. I called again the next day and bade them farewell." After moving to Cincinnati, it seems, Chase did not write to Elizabeth, and she did not write to him. When he learned in 1831 that she had married Louis Goldsborough, a young naval officer, Chase wrote to a friend that "had circumstances been different, I would have shivered a lance for the prize. But who can control his destiny?"[44]

CHAPTER 3

"*First* in Cincinnati"

⟫ 1830—35 ⟪

When Chase departed from Washington in early March 1830, he planned to make a tour "of the whole West and Southwest," especially Louisiana, and then "fix myself where circumstances might seem most favorable." When he reached Cincinnati, however, after ten difficult days on the road, Chase learned that his proposed business in Louisiana was "in such a state as to render that journey inexpedient at least for the present." So Cincinnati would be "the future scene of my professional labors, and here if anywhere must I build up my reputation." He was encouraged by what he saw of the local legal profession, for the "lawyers here are far from being a very talented or highly educated body of men." There were exceptions, but Chase was sure that with hard work, he would succeed.[1]

Cincinnati had changed dramatically in the seven years since Chase had seen the city. The population had doubled from twelve thousand to more than twenty-four thousand, although the *Cincinnati American*, when it published the census figures in the summer of 1830, estimated that the true number was about twenty-eight thousand. Chase wrote to an eastern friend that the city's population was composed "almost wholly of young people. A grey head is a rare sight, though there is a goodly number of grandfathers and grandmothers among us, for marriage is not put off here so long as it is now in New England." In a newspaper essay, intended for an eastern audience, Chase described the steamboats on the Ohio River as "stately structures" well suited for "the river they rush along and the

41

mighty territory whose productions they carry to a distant market." Not far from the busy riverfront were the factories, "the steam mill, and the cotton factories, and the sawmill factories, and others that we have not room to enumerate." These workplaces, Chase wrote, were "the principal source of the wealth and prosperity of our city," for "it is labor that gives value to everything."[2]

At first, Chase did not much share in the prosperity of Cincinnati. Because the county court was not in session when he arrived, he could not be admitted to the bar until June, so he worked as a clerk in the office of a more senior lawyer. Even after becoming a bar member, Chase did not open his own law office until September. He wrote to his brother that month that he wished he could describe "a long list of suits in court, and crowding clients, and other agreeable things of that nature"—but he could not. "You must remember that I have had an office only from the beginning of the month, and that here—where the members of the bar are so numerous, and business generally has formed a channel for itself—it is idle for a young man to expect much business at the start." A few months later, he confessed to a friend that he had "little professional business— very little." And a few months thereafter, seeking yet another loan from a friend, Chase wrote that the "law is but a barren field. It yields little reward to the arduous tillage. Or possibly I should say that the harvest is slow of growth and only ripened by a succession of summers."[3]

Chase did not waste time, however. He worked his way through legal books, such as a three-volume treatise on the law of evidence, and more general books, such as a history of the United States. He spearheaded the formation in late 1830 of the Cincinnati Lyceum, a group of about a hundred men that met once a week for public lectures. Starting in New England, lyceums were forming at this time in many American cities and towns, for reasons that Chase set out in an essay in the *Cincinnati American*: "Knowledge, like light, spreads itself far and wide. A beacon's radiance reaches far but the illumination of a single powerful intellect reaches farther." A lyceum would rely not upon one powerful intellect but on many speakers and would benefit not only those who attended the lectures but also all those with whom they shared the knowledge they gained. Although the members of the Cincinnati Lyceum were men, ladies were welcome to attend the lectures, and many did, for there is a letter to the editor complaining that their bonnets made it hard for people to see the speaker. During the first winter of the lyceum, Chase gave several lectures himself, including one in December on the life of the English lawyer and reformer Henry Brougham, and one in March about the effects of mechanization on society. Chase revised these two lectures and published them as essays in the *North American Review,* the leading intellectual periodical of the nation.[4]

Chase opened the Brougham essay with five paragraphs in praise of biography. "History seldom condescends to the teaching of individuals," he wrote, "and when she does, instructs rather in the arts of war than in the works of peace," with a focus on wars and battles. Biography "teaches by better examples than these," and "she deems it no unworthy task to tell with what self-sacrificing spirit philanthropists have labored on through difficulty, and discouragement, and opposition, to give some effect to some grand scheme of benevolence, in many instances dying without one glimpse of the glorious triumph which was destined to crown their exertions." Biography "helps us to a better understanding of the way in which the great machine of society works. Thoughts and feelings are the prime forces that act upon it, the thoughts and feelings of individual men." Because sometimes one person, whether through chance or force of character, is in a position to control "the destinies of whole nations," in order to understand history we must understand "individual character and conduct."[5]

Chase praised especially Brougham's efforts to improve education, to spread knowledge, and to end slavery. He quoted from a recent speech in which Brougham insisted that there was "a law above all the enactments of human codes," a law "written by the finger of God on the heart of man," and this law rejected the idea that "man can hold property in man." There was a link, Chase wrote, between Brougham's work for education and his work against slavery. "His great principle seems to be, let an enslaved nation be enlightened, and there is no power on earth that can detain it from freedom; let a free people be enlightened, and there is no power on earth that can reduce it to bondage." These were notable comments from a man who would devote his life to antislavery, and they suggest Chase was changing his mind about slavery. Aside from this one essay, however, there is nothing to show that he did anything for slaves or antislavery during his first five years in Cincinnati.[6]

Chase liked his second essay, about the effects of machinery on society, even better than his first. He commenced by setting out the arguments of those who feared that the increased use of machines, such as those being invented and improved to process cotton, would increase poverty and widen the gap between rich and poor. Drawing on the Scottish economist Adam Smith, and on his own experiences in the United States, Chase disagreed, seeing the Industrial Revolution as a source of not only wealth but also widely shared wealth. He admitted that new machines would sometimes end old jobs, but he saw this as a temporary phenomenon to be cured by new jobs in new industries. Chase looked forward to railways "stretching over mountains and plains, linking together and making near neighbors of distant territories." He was especially excited about the intellectual and social effects of the printing press and related systems: "Knowledge is widely diffused through all classes of society and is yet to be diffused far more widely. An unprecedented demand for useful information is everywhere made. Through the instrumentality of the press, and the modern engines of swift conveyance, sympathies are established between individuals, who entertain similar sentiments, though residing in opposite hemispheres." Again, Chase would himself participate in this process: through newspaper articles, pamphlets, speeches, and letters, working to establish sympathies for antislavery.[7]

Indeed, Chase was already involved in the process of diffusing knowledge through one particular paper, the *Cincinnati American*. Because he had so little legal work, Chase wrote to an eastern friend in early 1831, he was "living on ink" by writing articles for the newspaper, in which he had a "pecuniary interest." Among the Chase Papers at the Library of Congress, in Washington, DC, is a scrapbook with dozens of articles clipped from the *Cincinnati American* from this period. Some articles were surely written by Chase, for they are signed S.P.C., and other unsigned articles were probably his work, for they are in his style and in his scrapbook. In June 1831 the publishers announced that the *Cincinnati American* would be edited for a while by an editor pro tempore. Although the paper did not name the temporary editor, in all likelihood, it was Chase.[8]

Several of his contributions to the *Cincinnati American* are interesting in light of his later life. In an article about the Supreme Court, the future chief justice declared that of all "the admirable institutions of our country, none affords more signal proofs of the wonderful wisdom, virtue, and foresight of the framers of the Constitution than the Supreme Court. None has more effectually answered to its designed end; none has been more cautiously restrained within its assigned limits; and none has more eminently contributed to the welfare, tranquility, and happiness of the whole country." Among the justices, Chase praised especially John Marshall and Joseph Story. The nation was blessed, he wrote, to have Marshall as its chief justice, a man whose decisions "by their wisdom, their justice, and their explicitness, commend themselves equally to the understanding, the conscience, and the heart of all her citizens." Chase was writing at a time when many Jacksonians believed that the Marshall Court had not kept within its "assigned limits"; that by invalidating state statutes under the federal Constitution, the court was improperly interfering with state governments. Congress had considered bills to make the Senate the ultimate arbiter of constitutional questions, or to require that the court have a supermajority to invalidate a state law, or to prevent the court from reviewing the decisions of state supreme courts. In early 1831 more than fifty Jacksonian members of the House voted to repeal the main provision used by the court to review state court decisions. The bill did not pass, but in praising the Supreme Court, Chase was taking a controversial position: he was defending an institution under attack.[9]

The future Treasury secretary also wrote five articles about banks and currency. American currency at this time was a confusing mixture of coins, mostly imported, and banknotes, issued by banks chartered by the state legislatures. In theory, banknotes were redeemable at the head office of each bank for specie—that is, for gold or silver coins. In the first article in this series, Chase noted some of the problems of this system: the value of banknotes varied with the distance and strength of banks, so that a $5 note from one bank might be worth far less than a $5 note from another; as such, it was difficult for people to know how to value banknotes, especially those from small or distant banks. Furthermore, banks often failed, and the many different banknotes were also easily forged. Chase also decried the way in which governments sometimes "debased" their currency by adding other metals to supposed gold and silver coins. "Suppose the government to make a law requiring all citizens to receive debased coinage at its nominal amount—that which is called a dollar being in fact so debased as to be worth only [part] of a dollar, what it be but to take from the pocket of every creditor in the community one dollar out of every ten, and make a payment of it to his debtor? . . . He who had bought could satisfy the law by paying nine-tenths of the purchase money, and he who wished to buy would be obliged to pay a nominal price one-tenth higher, than before the debasement of the currency." In Chase's view, this would be "intolerable."[10]

In his 1831 essays, Chase praised the Second Bank of the United States, the sole national bank at the time. Chase wrote that it played an "indispensable" role for the federal government: holding all the government's deposits, paying all the government's bills, and helping the government market its debt. The bank was also critical in limiting the state banks; the bank did not have a formal regulatory role, but its purchases of state banknotes, and demands upon these banks to redeem these notes for specie, served as a brake on unsafe banks. Noting that President Jackson opposed the Second Bank of the United States and questioned its constitutionality, Chase predicted rightly that the president would veto legislation to extend the bank's charter.[11]

The *Cincinnati American* and Chase opposed Jackson on other issues as well. When Jackson vetoed the bill to provide federal funds for a new road between Maysville, Kentucky, and the Ohio River, claiming that the federal government could not support local construction projects, the *American*, in an article signed *C*, mocked the president's reasons as "political humbug." Like most men in the West, Chase supported roads and canals, and saw no constitutional reason why the federal government could not support them as well. In a private letter attacking the Maysville road veto, Chase denounced Jackson as a dictator like Napoleon I. Indeed, Chase thought that the late French emperor was better than Jackson, for Napoleon "had a soul capable of magnificent designs," whereas Jackson was "weak, credulous, vindictive, and narrow-minded." Jackson strongly supported Indian removal—forcing the eastern natives to leave their lands and to move west of the Mississippi. When Congress passed and Jackson signed the Indian Removal Act in 1830, Chase wrote that he hoped that the Indians were not "deprived of one jot or tittle of their just rights." If he were an Indian, Chase continued, "I would stand out to the bitter end—and appeal to God and Nature and Humanity for defense against the most enormous oppression that blots the record of Time."[12]

It seems that Chase's work for the *Cincinnati American* ended in the summer of 1831, perhaps because the publisher hired a permanent editor, or perhaps because Chase was leaving for a trip east. Why he left Cincinnati for two full months is puzzling, because after his return, he complained that his absence had prevented him from obtaining clients for the winter court session. Chase's first stop was White Sulphur Springs, Virginia, where he spent a few days with William Wirt and his family. White Sulphur Springs was at this time the leading resort in the South—the place to which elite Southerners and a handful of Northerners repaired for weeks of relaxing and socializing. Henry Clay, William Wirt, and Senator John Tyler of Virginia, a future president, all visited the Springs, as did many other leaders whose names are no longer known. Unfortunately, we do not have a letter or diary entry from Chase describing his own impressions of the Springs.[13]

Armed with letters of introduction from Wirt, including one to Daniel Webster calling Chase "one of the finest intellectual specimens of your own intellectual country," the twenty-three-year-old went to Boston. He recalled later that he received a "kind reception" there and "felt myself quite a character." Chase also spent time in New Hampshire, where his aging mother was living with Chase's older sister Abigail Chase Colby and her husband, Dr. Isaac Colby Jr. As it turned out, this would be the last time that Chase would see his mother alive; Jannette Chase would die the next spring, unable to fulfill her dream of moving west with the Colby family. Chase also visited New York City, Baltimore, and Washington before returning to Cincinnati in early November.[14]

Chase was somewhere in the eastern states, perhaps in Baltimore, when the Anti-Masonic Party gathered there in September 1831 for its national convention, generally viewed as the first national nominating convention in American history. Many early American leaders were members of the Masonic order, a secretive fraternal organization. In the fall of 1826 an upstate New York Mason, William Morgan, announced plans to publish a book exposing the secrets of the Masons. Morgan was arrested on trumped-up charges, then seized from jail by a group of men and never seen alive again. When Masons impeded the investigation and prosecution of those involved in Morgan's abduction and presumed murder, outrage against the order turned first into a movement and then into a political party in upstate New York and New England.[15]

Anti-Masons achieved considerable success in local and state elections in several states; for example, William Henry Seward, who would serve with Chase in the Lincoln Cabinet, was elected to the New York State Senate in 1830 as an Anti-Mason. A year later, he and other Anti-Masons were hoping to broaden their party and become the main anti-Jackson party in the next presidential election. But there were other anti-Jacksonians, the National Republicans, the heirs of the Adams party, many of whom wanted to see Henry Clay nominated and elected president. Before the Anti-Masons nominated Chase's mentor Wirt for president, Chase would have agreed with the National Republicans and not the Anti-Masons. His father had been a Mason, and Chase recalled later that he "always supposed the order did a great deal of good in their way." After the Wirt nomination, however, Chase had more mixed emotions.[16]

Wirt himself had mixed emotions, explaining in a long letter to Chase that he had not sought the nomination. "I am perfectly aware, with you, that I have none of the captivating arts and manners of professional seekers of popularity. I do not desire them. I shall not change my manners; they are a part of my nature." He would be happy if the people would "take me as I am," but if not, "they will only leave me where I have always preferred to be, enjoying the independence of private life." Fortunately for the shy Wirt, presidential candidates were not yet expected to campaign, so he did not have to travel the country giving speeches and shaking hands.[17]

In December the National Republican Party met in Baltimore and nominated Henry Clay for president. Chase was disappointed; he had hoped the National Republicans would follow the lead of the Anti-Masons and unite all the anti-Jackson forces behind a single coalition candidate: William Wirt. He wrote a friend that "if when Mr. Wirt was nominated, there had been a frank surrender of prejudices, and a ready and general consolidation upon him, I have no doubt that Jackson could have been defeated." Rather unrealistically, Chase suggested that Clay should have stepped aside for Wirt and that the "only effect" of the Clay nomination was "to strengthen Jackson and make the assurance of his reelection doubly sure."[18]

At about this same time, late 1831, Alexis de Tocqueville and his friend and traveling companion Gustave de Beaumont arrived in Cincinnati in the course of their long tour of the United States. Tocqueville was not yet the most famous foreign observer of American life. In fact, he was not famous at all; just a young French traveler asking question after question. Chase was one of the half dozen people whom Tocqueville interviewed in Cincinnati; it seems that they were introduced by Chase's friend Timothy Walker. Chase told Tocqueville that he believed that "we have taken democracy here about as far as it can go." The system of "universal suffrage" (essentially all white males were entitled to vote in

Ohio) had in Chase's view produced "some quite poor choices, especially in the cities." The most recent members of Congress from Cincinnati, he contended, "were absolutely unworthy of the choice." Chase was especially troubled by the way in which the Ohio legislature selected judges for seven-year terms; he would have preferred a state parallel to the federal system, with judges appointed by the president, confirmed by the Senate, and then serving until resignation or death. "In America, judges are supposed to maintain a balance among all parties, and their special role is to counter the enthusiasms and errors of democracy. If they are merely an emanation of democracy and dependent on it for their future, they cannot enjoy the necessary independence."[19]

Alexis de Tocqueville. The intrepid, inquisitive French traveler interviewed Chase in Cincinnati in late 1831.

After Tocqueville and Beaumont left Cincinnati, Chase wrote to a friend that he feared the French travelers did not understand how and why Cincinnati had grown so rapidly. The French travelers appreciated the site of Cincinnati, Chase believed, but not the "moral and intellectual advantages of the place—its churches and free schools; its exemption from the curse of slavery and the certainty felt by the parent that his child, however poor, would here be instructed in the elements of knowledge and the principles of duty." When Chase argued that "these contributed more to the prosperity of Cincinnati than all physical circumstances, they seemed at a loss how to understand me." The letters of Tocqueville and Beaumont, however, show that they understood quite well. Beaumont contrasted the free state of Ohio with the slave state of Kentucky: "the two states enjoy absolutely identical material advantages," but "Ohio enjoys a prosperity to which Kentucky does not even come close." Tocqueville wrote home from Cincinnati that "everything that is good and bad about American society stands out here with such relief that it is like reading a book with large letters intended to teach children how to read."[20]

In the spring of 1832 Chase formed a legal partnership with two other young lawyers from the East: Timothy Walker and Edward King, son of Rufus King, federal senator and founding father. Isaac Jewett, who worked for Chase, Walker, and King as a law clerk, wrote home to Boston that Chase had "literary merit" and "great promise," but Jewett considered Walker as the one destined to become the "lion of the West." Chase himself also saw Walker as a rival, writing that he was "at present" working with Walker, but "it cannot always be so." It seems the law firm did not have much legal work, because Chase and Walker worked on the side this year to start the *Western Quarterly Review*, a new periodical modeled on the leading Southern literary journal, the *Southern Review*. They drafted a prospectus, sent copies to newspapers and potential authors, and offered to pay authors $3 per printed page, a high rate that one newspaper editor mocked, saying the review would never sell enough copies to pay this much. Among the potential authors whom Chase contacted were William Wirt and Daniel Webster. All of them liked the idea of a new journal, but none of them agreed to write, so the project soon folded.[21]

In June 1832 Chase's brother-in-law Dr. Isaac Colby, sister Abigail Chase Colby, and younger sister, Helen Chase, arrived in Cincinnati and rented a house. Chase, who had been living in rented rooms, now moved in with the Colbys, where, in his words, he was "far more comfortably situated." Another family that would prove important in Chase's life arrived in the fall: that of Reverend Lyman Beecher, a leading Presbyterian minister and a founder of the American Temperance Society. Several of

Beecher's thirteen children would become even more famous, including the author Harriet Beecher Stowe. Within a few weeks of the Beechers' arrival in Cincinnati, Chase was attending Beecher's church and praising his sermons in the pages of his diary. It seems almost certain that Chase met the younger Beechers, including Harriet, twenty-one at the time. In a brief biography of Chase, she would later write that his "fine person, his vigorous energetic appearance, and the record of talent and scholarship that he brought with him" secured him "the patronage of the best families" in Cincinnati.[22]

Chase followed national politics closely, and the threats of South Carolina to secede in response to the high tariffs of 1832 appalled him. In an article for the *Illinois Monthly Magazine*, signed only with the initial *C,* Chase urged the South to wait and see how the tariffs would work in practice. Only if Southerners "become thoroughly convinced that their fathers and our fathers erred in their efforts to establish and consolidate the Union; that those were vain efforts to change the principles of repulsion, which the very nature of things has planted between the North and the South, into principles of attraction and cohesion; when they are fully satisfied by the clearest reasons and most certain facts, that the great experiment has resulted in nothing but ruin to the South, and unnatural prosperity to other sections"—only then, Chase wrote, should they consider cutting "the cord which binds them to their brethren." Chase went further, asking how the national government should respond if South Carolina purported to withdraw from the Union. Should the national government "yield everything without a struggle, and withdraw its custom-house, its courts, and its officers from her territory? We think otherwise. A state is no more at liberty to recede from a contract than an individual. If an individual refuses to comply with the terms of his contract, he must be compelled by force." If South Carolina used force, then the other states would have to "subdue force by force. South Carolina cannot be permitted to withdraw in peace." Chase did not explain why his views on secession had changed, from his private letters a few years earlier, in which he mused about the possibility that New England would withdraw after the election of Jackson, to this public condemnation of the possible secession of South Carolina. But Chase now accepted the argument of Webster: that secession would lead to civil war. Or, as Jackson would put it a few months later in response to South Carolina's threats of secession and civil war, "disunion by armed force is treason."[23]

As the election of 1832 approached, Chase wrote a friend that although he personally preferred Wirt, the main task was to defeat Jackson, and, for that reason, he would "vote for Mr. Clay and use all my little influence to advance his cause." The president had recently vetoed the bill to extend the charter of the Bank of the United States, and Chase believed that opposition to the veto would help Clay's chances; that Clay would prevail over Jackson in both Ohio and Indiana. "Everything is at stake," Chase insisted. "Jackson is plainly endeavoring to set himself above the law and the Constitution. If he should be reelected, all is lost." In that scenario, Chase continued, the only solution would be impeachment, "and who shall impeach? A venal Congress?"[24]

In spite of the efforts of Chase and others, Jackson won the fall election in a landslide, carrying sixteen out of the twenty-two states, and even winning in some New England states. Why, Chase asked in the aftermath, "why could not Mr. Clay and his friends see, a year ago, that the salvation of the country was put in jeopardy by his continuance in the field?" Even if all the votes for Clay, Wirt, and other opposition candidates were combined, however, Jackson would have won.[25]

The 1832 election more or less coincided with the arrival of cholera in Cincinnati. Chase's friend Jewett, in an October letter home, reported that the disease was killing twenty to thirty people per day, in all parts of the city and all classes of society—often killing people within a few hours of their first symptoms. "The theater is closed. The magistrate's offices are no longer open. Several hotels have ceased to entertain gourmands. The markets are ill-supplied." More than five thousand people had fled the city, and legal business was at a standstill. A few weeks later, Chase wrote in similar terms, saying that more than five hundred people had already died. Chase himself was sick in November, although he insisted to his correspondent that it was only a "bilious fever" and that he was on the mend. In December, however, Chase was again sick, and, for a few days, he was near death. He wrote in his diary in January 1833 that he thanked God for his recovery; that on his deathbed, he had reviewed his life. "And I resolved, if I should recover, to try to do more for God than I had before done—to live a more godly life."[26]

Chase started in late 1832 a major research and writing project: to gather, organize, and annotate all the statutes of Ohio. Up until then, the statutes were scattered in chronological volumes, many of which were rare; for instance, there was only one remaining copy of the territorial laws for 1792. There was no easy way to find statutes by subject or to determine whether a statute had been revised or repealed. Chase hoped to help other lawyers find statutes more easily, but he also wanted to make a profit; he entered into a contract with a publisher. Chase's three volumes, published over three years, presented the statutes in date order but added indices and notes, so that it became possible to find all statutes about voting procedures, for example, and to learn that one act had been revised by another. Chase decided to include, in the first volume, what he called a preliminary sketch of the history of Ohio. In a letter to his friend Cleveland, he wrote that he was finding the task almost impossible because there were almost no reliable histories from which to work. "I know I shall fall far short of my conception of what such a thing should be."[27]

Chase's forty-page historical essay is interesting both for what it says and what it does not say. Unlike his private letter, in which he sided with the Indians against Jackson, in this public history Chase was much more hostile to the natives, referring once to "murderous invasions of the savages." He summarized and praised the Northwest Ordinance of 1787, especially the provision banning slavery in the Northwest Territory, which ensured that Ohio was a free state. In describing the 1802 state constitution, Chase noted that the powers of the governor (which he would himself exercise in the late 1850s) were "very limited." Chase approved of the way in which the Ohio constitution denied the governor a veto over legislation, calling the veto an "anomaly in republican government." In his private remarks to Tocqueville, Chase had criticized excessive democracy; now, in this public history, he praised "universal suffrage" in Ohio, saying that the "unlimited extension of the elective franchise, so far from producing any evil, has ever constituted a safe and sufficient check upon injurious legislation." Chase overlooked how the state constitution denied the right to vote to blacks, although blacks voted at this time in several states, and he did not mention that women could not vote in Ohio, although they had enjoyed this right in New Jersey until 1807.[28]

Chase summarized in his history many of the statutes passed by the first few state legislatures, but he did not mention the Ohio Black Laws, which he would later oppose and help to repeal in 1849. Under the first of these so-called Black Laws, passed in 1804, no "black or mulatto person" could move to Ohio without a court certificate proving that he or she was free, and nobody in Ohio could hire a black or mulatto person who did not have such a certificate. Under an 1807 law, no "negro or mulatto person" could move into Ohio without filing, within two months of arrival, a bond signed by two men promising to pay up to $500 "for the good behavior of such negro or mulatto." It seems that the immigration provisions of these two laws were rarely enforced, for the state's black population grew rapidly. Another section of the 1807 statute, however, was generally enforced: a provision that prohibited blacks from testifying in civil or criminal cases involving whites. This meant that if a white person committed a crime against a black, he could not be prosecuted if the only witnesses were the victim or other blacks. Finally, although Ohio already had a system of public schools, one that Chase praised in his history, blacks were generally excluded from attending them. Chase noted the exclusion without comment or criticism. In short, if he had tackled this project ten or twenty years later, when his views on slavery had changed, Chase would have written quite a different history of Ohio.[29]

When the first volume was published in 1833, Chase sent copies to friends and leaders, including James Kent, former chancellor of New York, and a leading scholar of American law. In his cover letter to Kent, Chase explained that he hoped, with his preface, not only to sketch the history of the state but also "to inculcate national ideas and national sentiments." Kent responded with praise for Chase's "great work," saying that it "does credit to your enterprise, industry, and accuracy." Justice Joseph Story thanked Chase in similar terms and "wished with all my heart that other states would follow your example." Unfortunately, from Chase's perspective, the book did not sell well. The state agreed to purchase only 150 copies, fewer than he had expected, and a fire burned several hundred copies of the second volume. In total, Chase received about $1,000 for all his work on three volumes, or about $30,000 in today's money.[30]

In late 1832, at about the same time that he started work on his statute publication project, Chase started doing legal work for the Second Bank of the United States as the junior partner of Daniel Caswell. Although Jackson had vetoed the bill to extend the bank's charter, the federal charter still had more than three years to run, and, after that, the bank would continue for a while under a Pennsylvania charter. At first, Chase shared the bank's legal work with Caswell, whom he described to a friend as "one of our ablest lawyers," but in early 1834 Caswell decided to move to Indiana and sold his share of the business to Chase.[31]

Our main sources of information about Chase's work for the Bank of United States are about twenty letters he wrote to Timothy Kirby, agent of the bank in Cincinnati, and to Herman Cope, third assistant cashier of the bank, based in Philadelphia. Many of these were opinion letters, for which Chase researched and answered a legal question raised by bank officials. For example, in one missive, Chase advised Cope about improvements made by a tenant on a factory site owned by the bank; in Chase's view, the bank could retain the improvements or dictate terms for their removal. In another letter, he explained why he did not think that the Ohio courts would grant an injunction (sought by some bank officials) against a tenant cutting down trees on a farm. Other letters summarize the status of the dozens of cases that Chase was handling for the bank in the courts of Ohio.[32]

Chase's other clients at this time included Lafayette Bank of Cincinnati, authorized by the state legislature in early 1834 and organized later in the year, with Chase serving both as lawyer and one of the first directors. Again, our information about Chase's work for Lafayette Bank is limited, consisting mainly of diary entries noting that he attended meetings of its directors. There are a few more revealing items, however. In February 1836 Chase spoke with a couple of investors about "the investment of a hundred thousand dollars surplus capital belonging to the Lafayette Bank." One of those with whom he spoke was Josiah Lawrence, president of Lafayette Bank, who "declined on the ground that, being president of the bank, it might be said he had improperly used its funds." There is also a letter, almost illegible, from Lawrence to Chase, discussing tensions between the directors of the bank, all based in Ohio, and the shareholders, many of them in New York. What is clear, even from these limited sources, is that Chase's role with Lafayette Bank was quite different from his role with the Bank of the United States. He was not just an outside lawyer for the Lafayette Bank but rather part of the management team.[33]

Chase was busy not only with his statutes project and with his work for bank clients, but also with civic and religious work. He was the founder and for ten years the president of the Young Men's Bible Society of Cincinnati, an affiliate of the American Bible Society, the purpose of which was to print and distribute the Bible as widely and cheaply as possible. The annual reports of the national society show that the Cincinnati affiliate, under Chase, was especially successful. "In addition to the supply of their own city," the Cincinnati group provided Bibles to "steamboats, to German immigrants, and to the destitute generally in Hamilton County," the county of which Cincinnati was the principal city. Chase was also active in the American Sunday School Union, noting in his diary that Sunday school instruction was necessary for "diffusing religious knowledge and creating a taste for general information." In his first government position, he served as a school inspector for the city of Cincinnati, the start of a lifelong interest in public education. He was a leader of the Young Men's Temperance Society of Cincinnati, lamenting in a speech to that group that there were more than two hundred "tippling shops" in the city. Addressing the Agricultural Society of Hamilton County, Chase sounded very much like Thomas Jefferson, praising the many small independent farms and urging farmers not to neglect their general education, since farmers were the majority of America's voters. When a Young Men's Colonization Society for Hamilton County was formed, its leaders invited Chase to speak about whether "the voluntary colonization of the blacks to the coast of Africa is a powerful work of extending civilization and Christianity to that great, but as yet, barbarous continent." The colonization speech, if Chase gave one, does not survive.[34]

When the Whig Party was formed, in 1834 and 1835, to oppose Andrew Jackson and promote internal improvements, young men like Chase were its leaders in Cincinnati. They achieved their first success in the fall election of 1834, replacing a Jacksonian with a Whig as Hamilton County's representative in Congress. A few weeks later, while in Columbus on bank business, Chase joined with many members of the legislature in a public letter supporting Justice John McLean as the Whig candidate for president. Justice McLean already had a long record of public service, including as the innovative postmaster general in the administrations of James Monroe and John Quincy Adams. In February 1835 Chase continued his McLean campaign, writing to Samuel Vinton, an Ohio Whig in Congress, to urge that the Whigs in Washington nominate McLean. Chase explained that he and others in Cincinnati favored McLean over the other Ohio candidate, General William Henry Harrison, because McLean's election would put an end to "military rule." Neither Chase, nor McLean, nor others, seemed to view his position on the Supreme Court as precluding him from becoming a presidential candidate, and Chase himself, thirty years later, felt free to seek the presidency while serving as chief justice. In the end, the efforts of Chase and others for McLean came to naught, for the justice firmly withdrew his name from consideration in late summer 1835.[35]

Chase's diary entries for his first few years in Cincinnati mention various young women, none of them apparently serious romances. Chase later recalled that, when he first met his first wife, Catherine Jane Garniss, in the fall of 1831, her "appearance did not please me" and that he thought her "an affected and shallow girl." Nor did Chase like her father, John Garniss, noting in his diary that he "heard as usual not a little slander" during one conversation with him. Chase did not spend much time with Catherine until early 1833, when the severe illness of Chase's brother-in-law Dr. Colby forced Chase to move out of the Colby home and into a boardinghouse, where, by chance, the Garniss family also lived. Now Chase started to call upon Catherine Garniss from time to time. On the first of May 1833, for example, the two of them went together to hear speeches by the students at a local school for young women. "We came home under a broiling sun and agreed upon a ride in the evening and by moonlight." Chase closed his diary entry for the day with a hint of humor as well as New England austerity: "Must think more and eat less, tomorrow."[36]

Chase's diary is far from complete for these years, so we do not know when and how he proposed. Nor do we have any diary or letters from Catherine that would give *her* side of the story. One of Catherine's friends recalled much later that she first described him as "uncouth" with an "unmanageable mouth" but that she hoped to "polish him up a little." Evidently she succeeded in these efforts, for on March 4, 1834, in the parlor of the Garniss home, Reverend Lyman Beecher married Salmon Chase and Catherine Garniss. Chase was twenty-six, and his wife was twenty-two.[37]

At first, the couple lived in a boardinghouse along with Chase's sister Helen, but, after a while, they moved in with Catherine's parents. Chase was happy. In the summer of 1835 he wrote to his closest friend, Charles Cleveland, head of a young ladies' school near Philadelphia, that he wished Charles could know his wife. "I think her a paragon of perfection. She

seems to me not so pretty indeed as when we were first married but tenfold more lovely and tenfold dearer." Chase had hoped "to visit the East
this summer, but my wife's health is delicate, and I cannot leave her."[38]

Charles Dexter Cleveland, Chase's lifelong friend, who grieved
with Chase after the death of each of his three wives.

Catherine Chase's health was "delicate" because she was expecting a
child, a daughter Catherine Amelia, born on November 16, 1835. For a
few days, Chase's wife was unwell, and he thought about postponing a
business trip to Philadelphia, but she urged him to go, telling him that it
would improve his reputation. Chase left Cincinnati on about November
21 and received, while he was away, a few reports about his wife's health.
On his return trip, on Sunday, December 6, he received three letters at
Wheeling, at the time in western Virginia, now in the state of West
Virginia. The first letter reported that his wife's health was improving;
the second reported a "sudden and alarming" change for the worse; and
the third, dated December 2, said that his wife had died. Chase hastened
home, praying that the letter was wrong, but when he reached the Garniss
house, the "black crape on the door announced that death was within."[39]

For weeks, Chase was overcome with grief. He visited Catherine's grave every day of December. On Christmas morning he awoke with only one thought: "my wife—my dear wife—gone—never to return." The next day, he went to his office and spent an hour or two "in fruitless attempts to prepare an argument" in a banking case in the United States Supreme Court. On Sunday, December 27, he wrote Charles Cleveland that "what grieves me most is that I was not, while my dear wife lived, so faithful with her on the subject of religion as I should have been, and I have now no certain assurance that she died in the faith." He wished that he had not "contented myself with a few conversations on the subject of religion, with a few recommendations of religious books, with faint prayers," so that "she might have been before her death enrolled among the professed followers of the Lamb." Two days later, he noted that "the nurse came downstairs with my dear little motherless child," and that he was thankful for the nurse and for his daughter's good health. On the last day of the year, Chase recorded all the changes 1835 had brought: the birth of his child, the death of his wife, the publication of the third and final volume of his book. His wife had joked that she would keep the book "for her oldest son. Alas she never saw the final volume."[40]

CHAPTER 4

"Some Great Scheme"

⁓ 1836–41 ⸲

n the latter part of the 1830s and the first years of the 1840s, Chase
went from a rank-and-file Whig, with no strong views on slavery; to a
prominent local Whig, with definite antislavery views; to a Liberty Party
leader who denounced the Whig Party as subservient to the slaveholders.
Chase's legal work also changed during these years, as he started to represent
fugitive slaves and abolitionists in court cases. He continued to handle commercial cases for banks and other clients, but the cases for which he became
known were those in which he worked without pay for black defendants.
The story of this transition tells us much not only about Salmon P. Chase
but also about the emergence of antislavery politics in America.

First, however, a word about words. Although Chase was often called
an abolitionist, and although he had many friends among the abolitionists, he said consistently that he was *not* an abolitionist, but merely an
antislavery man. For Chase, an "abolitionist" was someone like William
Lloyd Garrison, the Boston editor who demanded the immediate libera-
tion of all America's slaves, and who famously declared, in the first issue
of his paper *The Liberator*, that on the subject of slavery he did not "wish
to think, or speak, or write, with moderation." Because he viewed the
Constitution as sanctioning and supporting slavery, Garrison denounced
the document as a "covenant with death and an agreement with hell."
Garrison generally did not vote and did not endorse political candidates
in his paper, viewing it as pointless. For Garrison, abolition was a moral

crusade, not a mere political position. Chase agreed with Garrison that slavery was evil but disagreed about almost everything else, beginning with the Constitution, which he regarded as the great charter of freedom. As Chase read it, the Constitution at most tolerated slavery as an exception, in the slave states, but established freedom as the general national rule. Chase believed that the federal government could not emancipate slaves in the slave states—that was an issue for the states—but the federal government should not impose or assist slavery, either. So, for example, Congress should end slavery in the District of Columbia and repeal the Fugitive Slave Act of 1793—the federal law that allowed masters to capture slaves who escaped from a slave state to a free state. The best way to achieve change, he believed, was through politics, by building a broad antislavery political party. He hoped and expected that, once an antislavery party took control of the national government, the states would change their own laws and that slavery would end, though he was vague about how this would occur. But the first task was to wrest control of the federal government from the Southern slave owners.[1]

These were not yet Chase's views in 1836, when he was simply a standard Whig. Indeed, although this was a presidential year, the young man paid little attention to politics; he struggled to do his legal work through his grief. In January he spent three days in court as one of the prosecutors—states and counties often hired private lawyers to serve as temporary prosecutors—in a high-profile murder trial. Chase's hour-plus closing speech was "listened to with great attention by a crowded audience." One of the defense lawyers, a senior member of the local bar, was, in Chase's view, "very verbose" and "very repetitionary," speaking more than five hours. Even in the midst of a murder trial, Chase missed his wife. "How much do I regret that I cannot tell her of my speech and impart to her all my feelings?" he wrote in his diary. Near the end of the defense speech, Chase left the courthouse and went to his wife's grave site, where he prayed for "strength and patience."[2]

Three months later, in April, Chase wrote Charles Cleveland that "the calamity, which has fallen upon me, was so severe, so overwhelming, so unexpected, that I have hardly yet recovered from it sufficiently to perform any duty, which the exigency of the immediate occasion does not imperiously require." He prayed that the death of his wife would "lead me to look less to earth as a permanent abode and more to that world of bliss and glory whither I humbly hope my dear wife has gone before me. Still, however, I cannot but feel the difference between the world with her and the world without her." Chase described his late wife as almost a saint. "She was universally beloved by her acquaintances, for she never permitted herself to indulge a wish which would involve the slightest inconvenience to another."[3]

In the summer of 1836 Chase was wrenched from his private grief, and from his quiet legal practice, by riots in Cincinnati. The principal target of the rioters' wrath was James Birney, who had owned slaves in Kentucky and Alabama, then freed them and converted to the cause of abolition. Birney moved to Cincinnati in 1835 and started a weekly antislavery newspaper, the *Philanthropist*. Chase probably met Birney through his brother-in-law Isaac Colby, an abolitionist friend of Birney's. Most whites in Cincinnati opposed Birney, claiming that his presence and his paper hurt the city's connections with the South. In late July, after a mass meeting attended by many of the city's leaders, including some of Chase's clients, a formal letter was presented to Birney, demanding that he cease publication. Birney refused.[4]

On the night of July 30 an anti-abolition mob attacked the office of Birney's printer, destroying the press, then attacked other offices and houses, including Colby's office. Chase recalled that his sister Abigail Colby, terrified, fled from her home to his. After attacking abolitionists, the mob attacked blacks and black residences, dispersing after midnight only when the mayor, who had been a silent spectator during the destruction, told them that "we have done enough for one night." On the next night, a riotous mob gathered outside a hotel where they believed that Birney was hiding. Chase recalled that he "stood in the doorway and told them, calmly but resolutely, that no one could pass." Although the news accounts of this second night do not name Chase, they confirm his recollection that a mob gathered and then dispersed at the hotel.[5]

Chase and a few friends published a call for an August 2 meeting of all those in the city who opposed mob violence. But when he and his colleagues arrived at the appointed time and place they found a meeting already in progress under the firm control of the anti-abolitionists. Chase and his friends did not try to wrest control of the meeting, which passed modest resolutions condemning violence. In a long public letter to the *Cincinnati Gazette,* however, Chase responded to the claim that he had said that he would pay $10,000 to support an abolitionist press. What he actually said, Chase wrote, was that he would pay almost any amount rather "than see an abolitionist press put down by a mob." He explained that "much as I have deprecated the course of the abolitionists, I regard all the consequences of their publications as evils comparatively light when compared with the evils produced by the prevalence of mob spirit."[6]

Both the printer of the *Philanthropist* and the leaders of the Ohio Anti-Slavery Society hired Chase to represent them, in separate civil cases, against some prominent members of the anti-abolition mobs. Chase explained in a letter to his friend Cleveland that the defendants were so angry at the abolitionists that they would probably regard even the lawyers like Chase "as personal enemies." He was prepared to lose some of his legal business, however, because "a man must perform his duty and leave consequences to Him, who requires the duty." The cases would take some time in the courts, but eventually Chase would win verdicts for his clients in both cases against the rioters.[7]

On March 10, 1837, James Birney arrived at Chase's office with an urgent, difficult legal problem. The Birney family housekeeper, Matilda Lawrence, had been arrested as a fugitive slave. Matilda was about twenty years old, "of striking beauty and engaging manners," according to one account, the slave and probably the daughter of her master, Larkin Lawrence. Indeed, during a trip to New York City, Lawrence had passed Matilda off as his daughter, and she begged him for her freedom, a request he refused. As they headed back to Missouri, the steamboat tied up at the wharf in Cincinnati, and Matilda simply walked into the city. Soon thereafter, she started working for the Birney family.[8]

Lawrence sent an agent, John Riley, to Cincinnati to find and return Matilda, and she was now in the county jail. Birney shared with Chase the paperwork for the case to date: Riley's affidavit, the magistrate's order authorizing her arrest, and the order committing her to prison. In the affidavit, Riley stated that he was the agent of Larkin Lawrence, that Matilda was Lawrence's slave, and that she escaped in February 1836 and was hiding in Cincinnati. The magistrate simply repeated and relied upon Riley's claims, although he added one detail, referring to Matilda as a "colored girl." On this thin basis, she now faced life as a slave.[9]

Chase agreed at once to take the case. Using the ancient English procedure for challenging illegal detentions, Chase applied for and obtained a writ of habeas corpus, a court order directing the sheriff to bring Matilda to court, and for both sides to appear in court, the next morning. Chase and Birney (formerly a lawyer in Alabama) then worked into the night to prepare

Chase's argument. The next morning, Chase and his junior partner were in the courtroom of Judge David Kirkpatrick Este, the presiding judge of Hamilton County. Matilda sat in the prisoner's dock. Riley was represented by three lawyers, including a former Jacksonian member of Congress, Robert Lytle, and the county prosecutor Nathaniel Read. All three of Riley's lawyers had been leaders in the anti-abolition movement a few months earlier. Three strong men also accompanied Riley, to take Matilda away if, as expected, the judge ruled in their favor. William Henry Harrison, clerk of this court and future president of the United States, was probably in the courtroom as well.[10]

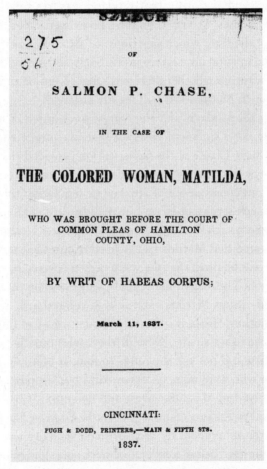

SPEECH

2 7 5
5 6

OF

SALMON P. CHASE,

IN THE CASE OF

THE COLORED WOMAN, MATILDA,

WHO WAS BROUGHT BEFORE THE COURT OF
COMMON PLEAS OF HAMILTON
COUNTY, OHIO,

BY WRIT OF HABEAS CORPUS;

March 11, 1837.

CINCINNATI:
PUGH & DODD, PRINTERS,—MAIN & FIFTH STS.
1837.

Chase's argument in the Matilda *case, in pamphlet form, was an early and influential argument that the Constitution did not authorize fugitive slave legislation.*

At the outset of his argument, Chase noted the intense community interest on both sides of the case. "I feel the responsibility which rests upon me as an advocate; I perceive the responsibility which rests upon the court; not to the community alone, not alone to the humble individual who sues for protection here, but to conscience and to God." If the court ruled erroneously that Matilda was a slave, it would "consign to human bondage a human being, rightfully free;" if the court erred in the other direction, it would only "deprive a master of the services of a single individual, legally a slave."[11]

Chase then argued that slavery was "admitted, on all hands, to be contrary to natural right." Chase cited not only *Somerset v. Stewart,* the famous English case declaring that England was free soil, but also two recent Southern cases. Slavery "can have no existence beyond the territorial limits of the state which sanctions it." Matilda was now in Ohio, "by whose fundamental law slavery is positively and forever interdicted." The question was thus whether there was some exception to these general rules under which Matilda was still legally a slave.[12]

Reviewing the affidavit and the magistrate's orders, Chase insisted that they were not a sufficient basis for Matilda's arrest and detention. The Fugitive Slave Clause of the Constitution provided that "no person held to service or labor in one state, under the laws thereof, escaping into another, shall, in consequence of any law or regulation thereof, be discharged from such service or labor, but shall be delivered up on claim of the party to whom such service or labor may be due." Nothing in Riley's affidavit suggested that Matilda had escaped from a slave state into a free state, so there was no proof that she was a person covered by this clause of the Constitution. The magistrate's orders were based on the affidavit and equally invalid, unless Matilda's status as a "colored girl" was sufficient to justify detention. "If so, if color be sufficient cause of imprisonment, let us know the exact shade. Who in the courthouse is guilty? Who innocent?" Chase did not ask the judge to look at Matilda, and those in the courtroom who were more or less as dark, but his point was made.[13]

Those involved in Matilda's arrest and detention, Chase continued, had failed to follow the procedure set out in the Fugitive Slave Act, which allowed a master or his agent to "seize or arrest such fugitive from labor" and take the fugitive before a federal or state court judge or magistrate to prove his status. This was not what Lawrence or his agent had done; they had relied upon state officers to arrest and detain Matilda, acting,

Chase said, without any basis in state or federal law. Moreover, he continued, there were questions about the constitutionality of the Fugitive Slave Act itself.[14]

At this, according to the report of the case, Robert Lytle jumped up and demanded to know "whether they would, at this late day, permit any discussion as to the constitutionality of the act of Congress, and urged that such discussion was irrelevant to the case before the court." Judge Este responded that he was "disposed to hear counsel with patience," that he was not inclined to "prescribe to counsel what course of argument should be pursued." Chase resumed, with some heat, "The constitutionality of the act of Congress is not relevant to this case! What then are we discussing? Is it not the validity of the magistrate's commitment?" The magistrate had no power to commit Matilda to prison "unless derived from the act of Congress, and the act of Congress can confer no power at all, if unconstitutional."[15]

The Constitution, Chase said, both creates the national government, giving it certain limited powers, and forms a compact among the states, binding them in certain respects. The Fugitive Slave Clause was a compact among the states, not a grant of power to the federal government, for it did not mention the federal government and did not grant Congress any powers. Chase noted that the Fugitive Slave Clause was not part of Article I, the principal source of the powers of Congress, but rather was in Article IV, along with the Full Faith and Credit Clause, another compact between the states, but one with a sentence giving Congress implementing authority. The Fugitive Slave Clause had no such language granting power to Congress. Chase asked the court to consider whether those who drafted and ratified the Constitution would have wanted to create a system in which "any person can be dragged, by any other person who chooses to set up a claim against him as a fugitive servant, to undergo trial for his personal liberty"—a trial in which mere local magistrates would decide whether a person was free or slave, without the possibility of any effective appeal.[16]

Chase also argued that the Fugitive Slave Act was contrary to the Fourth and Fifth Amendments, which protected against "unreasonable searches and seizures" and promised that "no man shall be deprived of life, liberty, or property without due process of law." In practice, there was not much process under the Fugitive Slave Act; the master or his agent seized the supposed slave, presented a flimsy affidavit to the magistrate, and then transported the person into a slave state. "Can we wonder that, upon pretense of seizing fugitives from labor, under the provisions of this act, unprincipled persons have kidnapped free persons and transported them out of this state, and sold them into slavery? Is not this inhuman and infamous practice the natural and inevitable consequence of this act? And can such an act consist with that security from unreasonable seizure, which the Constitution solemnly guarantees to the people? I think not."[17]

Chase then turned to the Northwest Ordinance, which "lies at the foundation of all our institutions" in Ohio, and which prohibited slavery in the Northwest Territory and the states formed from it. The ordinance provided that its terms should be treated as "a compact between the original states and the people and states in the territory, and forever remain unalterable, unless by common consent." The prohibition on slavery in Ohio, therefore, was "impressed on the soil itself" and could not be varied by state or federal law. Chase did not explain as well as he should have why this mattered; he should have argued that by bringing Matilda to Ohio, her master had freed her.[18]

We do not have the arguments of Riley's lawyers because Chase and Birney, when they printed a pamphlet about the case, omitted them. Judge Este ruled that Matilda was a fugitive slave. Riley and his men took Matilda from the courtroom to a boat bound for the South, and we do not know her history after that. Chase was right about the Constitution: the Fugitive Slave Clause was a compact rather than a grant of power to Congress, and the Fugitive Slave Act violated other provisions in the Constitution, such as the right to trial by jury. As a tactical matter, however, Chase's decision to spend his time on the Constitution, rather than on the facts, was a mistake. It was not likely that a local judge in Cincinnati would find that the Fugitive Slave Act of 1793 was contrary to the Constitution, but he might well rule that there was inadequate proof that a particular person was a fugitive slave.[19]

Chase was also the key lawyer in the second phase of the *Matilda* case, the state's criminal prosecution of Birney for violating state law by harboring a fugitive slave. Chase and Birney lost in the lower court, but they appealed to the state supreme court, where Chase's arguments were better than his original *Matilda* argument. He focused on the question of whether Matilda was a fugitive slave under the Constitution or the Ohio statute. "Was she held in service in one state, and did she escape into another state? Plainly not. At the time she left the individual who claimed to be her master, she was within the territorial limits of Ohio [on a boat tied to the Ohio shore] by the consent of that individual. If she had ever been a slave, she ceased to be such at the moment that she was brought by Lawrence within these limits." When Matilda walked off the boat and into the town, it "was in no just sense of that term an escape" but instead the "first exercise of that freedom which the Constitution of Ohio would confer upon her."[20]

This line of argument proved far more practical, for Chase and others, than attacks upon the constitutionality of the fugitive slave laws. The state supreme court found there was no proof that Birney knew Matilda was a fugitive slave at the time that he hired her. The court thus reversed Birney's conviction without reaching Chase's constitutional arguments, saying they were "of a character too important in their bearing upon the whole country to be adjudicated upon without necessity."[21]

Chase did not give up on his constitutional argument. In an 1838 essay in the *Cincinnati Gazette*, under a classical pen name, Marcellus, he commented on the failure of the Ohio legislature to provide for trial by jury for those accused of being fugitive slaves. Insisting again that he was "not an abolitionist," Chase extended and improved upon the arguments that he had made in the *Matilda* case about why the Fugitive Slave Act was contrary to the Constitution. He noted that other states, including New York and Massachusetts, had passed laws to provide jury trials for those in Matilda's situation, and he urged Ohio to follow their example. The Fugitive Slave Act, because it was unconstitutional, was "no obstacle to legislation on the same subject by a state legislature; much less does it excuse a state legislature from its first and highest duty to the people—that of securing to every member of the community the complete enjoyment of his natural and social rights."[22]

Chase's argument in the *Matilda* case was (in the words of two leading historians) the "first major abolitionist challenge to fugitive recaptures." His *Matilda* pamphlet was the first step on the road that led to his becoming known as "attorney general for the fugitive slaves." After the *Matilda* case, he started to receive letters from the South asking for his help in finding good homes in Cincinnati for freed slaves, and letters from the North asking for advice on questions about alleged fugitive slaves. His *Matilda* argument was also an important first step toward his political antislavery position: that the federal government had no role in slavery, even with respect to fugitive slaves, and that slavery was merely a "local institution" of the slave states. But the *Matilda* argument was not, as some have suggested, the Rubicon in Chase's life, after which he was completely committed to antislavery. It was a single case, albeit an important one, in the midst of a busy legal career. Chase was still a Whig in politics, not the antislavery agitator he would become.[23]

As a director of the Lafayette Bank, Chase had an inside view of the most serious financial crisis of the first half of the century: the Panic of 1837. Like other Whigs, Chase deplored President Jackson's decision in 1833 to withdraw federal funds from the Bank of the United States and place them in various "pet banks" favored by Democrats. Chase also disapproved of Jackson's specie circular, an 1836 order requiring settlers to pay for federal lands in specie (gold or silver) rather than with bank bills, as had been customary. Historians and economists are still debating whether and to what extent these policies caused the financial crisis. But there is no debate over a few key facts. On May 10, 1837, all the banks in New York City suspended specie payments—that is, they announced they would no longer pay in specie to those presenting their banknotes for redemption. Such suspensions were not uncommon in the nineteenth century and often not that dire: the banks were still open for business, and their depositors were not wiped out; they simply could not withdraw specie from their bank accounts for the time of the suspension. The suspension of specie payments in New York in 1837, however, was soon followed in Cincinnati and elsewhere, leading to a nationwide economic depression. Railroads suspended construction; factories closed their doors; workers lost their jobs.[24]

In the midst of this downturn, in the fall of 1837, Chase went east, stopping first in Richmond, Virginia, where he visited the widow of his mentor William Wirt, who had died a few years before. Upon reaching Baltimore a few days later, Chase wrote a warm letter to Mrs. Wirt, saying that he was sending her the finest cheese that Baltimore had to offer and urging her to visit him in Cincinnati, "the beautiful city by the beautiful river." From Baltimore, Chase went to Philadelphia, New York, Boston, and New England.[25]

Each party in the 1838 Ohio election blamed the other for the deep economic downturn. Democrats demanded, among other things, that Ohio follow the example of Massachusetts and enact bank regulations. After the Democrats prevailed, the legislature passed a banking law imposing capital requirements, creating a board of three bank commissioners, and requiring that the commissioners visit every bank in the state at least once every year. The bank commissioners were authorized to inspect the books and records of the banks and to "make such other inquiries as may be necessary to ascertain the actual condition of the said institutions and their ability to fulfill all the engagements made by them."[26]

This language, which sounds pretty standard in the twenty-first century, was radical in the 1830s, when only a few states had rudimentary bank regulations. One Whig paper claimed that the only reason the Democrats formed the bank board was "to create three fat offices, to be filled by some of their cormorant partisans, that thus the party may have three stout electioneers constantly perambulating the state at the *expense of the people!*" In May 1839, when the bank commissioners arrived in Cincinnati, the *Cincinnati Advertiser,* a Democratic paper, reported that Lafayette Bank had tried and failed to obtain a court injunction to prevent them from carrying out their inspection. "On the policy, propriety, or *necessity* of the application for such an injunction, we make no comment; our readers can draw their own conclusions and act accordingly." The *Advertiser* was suggesting that the Lafayette Bank had something to hide; that customers should withdraw their funds.[27]

The *Cincinnati Gazette,* a Whig paper, immediately defended the Lafayette Bank, most of whose directors were Whigs. The *Gazette* reported that the judges could not rule on the requested injunction because they were shareholders in another bank that would be affected by whatever they decided. After another attack in the *Advertiser*, the editor of the *Gazette* spoke with "the best source of information—Mr. Chase, the counsellor alleged to have prepared the motion. His information corresponds with that received from the judge. Notice of the motion was given; the bill and exhibits were prepared. These were handed to the judges, for perusal out of court, a common practice, adopted to save taking up time in reading them to the court. Mr. Hatch, one of the commissioners, conversed with the judges and expressed his wish that the case should be acted upon. But the court declined to act, as I have stated. No motion was made in court, no opinion was expressed or intimated by the judges. Such are stated by Mr. Chase, the counsel, to be the facts." It seems that Chase's argument was that the bank commissioners were seeking customer records that were not covered by even the broad language of the new statute.[28]

By the end of 1838, the Chase household consisted of himself, his little daughter Catherine, his sister Helen, then in her early twenties, and two nieces, Eliza Whipple and Jenny Skinner, not yet twenty. Late this year or early in the next year, Chase met through his nieces the young woman who would become his second wife: Eliza or Lizzie Smith, daughter of a local merchant. Helen later recalled Lizzie Smith as "the loveliest, most fascinating, graceful person I ever knew." We do not know much more about her: only one of her letters survives, and (unlike with his first wife) Chase did not write about this courtship.[29]

A few days before the date set for the wedding, September 26, 1839, Chase received an angry letter from John Garniss, the father of his first wife. Garniss was annoyed that Chase had not told him about his plans to marry again, and, above all, Garniss did not want his granddaughter to participate in the wedding ceremony. "I beg in the name of my dear child that her child may not be an actor in this pageant." Chase wrote later that his daughter Catherine, not quite four at the time, "was ardently attached" to Eliza, "whose gentle and winning endearments had gained her heart even before I was married to her." So it seems likely that little Catherine *was* among those who attended this double wedding, for Chase's sister Helen married on the same day to a young Episcopal minister. Chase was thirty-one years old; his bride, only seventeen. Eliza Chase moved into the house with her new husband, her new stepdaughter, and (it seems) her friends the two Chase nieces.[30]

Only a few months later, however, on February 6, 1840, little Catherine died of scarlet fever. "I have lost my only child, my sweet little Kate," Chase wrote to his friend Cleveland. Since his daughter had reached the age of four and survived the most serious childhood diseases, measles and whooping cough, Chase had expected that she would live to adulthood, to become his "own counsellor and friend." Now she was gone, and Chase could only hope that "this bereavement may be sanctified to me and mine—that our hearts may be fixed on heavenly things—and that our spirits may be purified from the defilements of the world." With his wife in 1835, his sister in 1838, his daughter in 1840, and others to follow—death was a constant part of Chase's life.[31]

His grief was softened by the arrival of a new daughter, formally named Catharine Jane Chase, but known informally as Kate, born in August

1840. Chase wrote to Cleveland that he was thankful that both his wife and child were healthy. Eliza was "an invaluable treasure and support, combining in a wonderful degree the warm affections and simple confidence of youth, with the mature judgment of far riper years." Moreover, he continued, "we are one in the most important respect—one in a common dependence on the Savior and in a common hope of the eternal life." Many of Chase's diary entries from this period are religious. At the end of one month, for example, he noted, "This is the last weekday of a month by no means adequately improved. How little have I done for the Savior or for souls! With only two or three have I conversed on religious subjects at all." He was trying to memorize the longest psalm in the Bible, the 119th Psalm, and meant "to continue to do so until I can repeat it with facility from beginning to end." He was also teaching Sunday school, noting that he should "pay more attention" to the speeches he prepared for these classes to "try to make them more interesting and instructive."[32]

Chase's diary also shows how much time he spent on bank work in late 1840 and early 1841. Most days, he spent about an hour at the offices of Lafayette Bank, in the elegant new building on Third Street that it shared with the Franklin Bank. Chase served not only on the board of directors but also on the executive committee and the exchange committee—the latter of which was charged with deciding whether to accept, and at what rate, the banknotes of other banks. The multiplicity of banks, the paucity of information about their finances, and the prevalence of counterfeit banknotes all made such decisions a difficult part of every banker's daily life. Chase also continued to do some legal work for the Bank of the United States, now in the process of winding down its operations. In early 1841, however, he parted ways with the bank because of a fee dispute. "I feel quite confident," Chase wrote to Kirby, "that I can make as much money if not more if left at liberty to act for clients who will not now employ me because I represent the bank, than with the arrangement proposed." A financial summary shows that Chase owed the bank more than $2,000 in late 1839, in the depths of the financial crisis, but that he had almost canceled this debt through his legal work for the bank by early 1841, often earning several hundred dollars in a single month of work.[33]

In March 1840 the Whigs in the First Ward of Cincinnati nominated Chase as one of their candidates for city council. Each ward, at this

time, elected three members to the council, which totaled twenty-one
members. Chase and other Whigs prevailed in the April election, with
each of the First Ward Whig candidates receiving about four hundred
votes, and the three Democrats, about two hundred votes apiece. The
Cincinnati City Council met once a week, and Chase was almost always
at the meetings. For Chase, still quite committed to temperance, this
was the main issue facing the council. There were hundreds of taverns
and coffeehouses selling alcohol, and the city council was licensing yet
more, in part because the license fees provided a significant source of
city income.[34]

William Henry Harrison, neighbor and friend of Chase in Cincinnati.

By this time, Chase had overcome his aversion to military candidates
for political office and supported General William Henry Harrison, the
Whig candidate for president. Chase knew Harrison personally. He lived
on a farm in North Bend, about ten miles outside of Cincinnati; he served
for a while as clerk of one of the city courts; and he attended and addressed

a meeting of Chase's chapter of the Young Men's Bible Society. In May 1840 one of Chase's college classmates, Albert Hoit, came to Cincinnati in order to paint Harrison's portrait and asked Chase to introduce him to Harrison. Taking his wife and niece along, Chase went with Hoit to North Bend to call upon the general. Harrison was most affable, insisting that they all stay for dinner, even stoking up the fire himself. Harrison agreed to sit for a portrait by Hoit and, when the painting was done, Chase deemed it "a fine likeness." A few weeks later, Chase and Harrison met by chance on the street in Cincinnati, and Harrison asked whether Chase knew Gamaliel Bailey, who had taken over as the editor of the *Philanthropist* after James Birney moved to New York. When Chase replied that he knew Bailey well, Harrison asked Chase to see Bailey about an article in the *Philanthropist* charging Harrison with talking out of both sides of his mouth about slavery. Chase discussed the matter with Bailey, but without much effect; before long, Bailey was urging his readers to vote for neither of the two major party candidates, which he saw as subservient to the South, but to support instead the candidate of the new Liberty Party, Chase's friend and former client Birney.[35]

Gamaliel Bailey, editor first of the Philanthropist *in Cincinnati and then the* National Era *in Washington, DC.*

The 1840 campaign was among the most intense in American history, with Whigs using as their symbols the log cabin and the cider jug, because a Democratic editor had unwisely said that Harrison would be content to retire to his log cabin where he could drink hard cider. Whigs claimed that the Democratic candidate, incumbent president Martin Van Buren, lived in luxury at the presidential mansion, unlike the modest Harrison, who had once lived in a log cabin. Democrats could have turned around this argument, pointing out that Harrison's father was a wealthy Virginia planter and that the general's current home was no log cabin, but for some reason did not.[36]

Chase was more worried than excited by the contest between Harrison and Van Buren. In a letter to his friend Cleveland, he wrote that he was "disgusted with party strife and am greatly chagrined on seeing the means to which both parties resort to gain their ends." He believed that Van Buren and the Democrats were corrupt, and that Harrison was "animated by a sincere and elevated patriotism." But Chase was concerned about "the results of this excited contest upon the religious and moral character of the country" and lamented that the Whig songs and slogans, celebrating Harrison and his supposed love of hard cider, were "calculated to promote intemperance." Moreover (and here he sounded like Bailey), "the complete subservience which both parties have manifested to the South upon the great, and, in my judgment, vital question of slavery" made him almost "inclined to withdraw from the contest in despair." Chase was not yet "willing to take part in the third party movement," regarding it as "premature," but he hoped that "before a next presidential election, antislavery feeling will be too widely diffused to permit a repetition of the scenes of 1840."[37]

In the end, William Henry Harrison carried nineteen states and 234 electoral votes; Martin Van Buren, only seven states and 60 electoral votes. Harrison and Van Buren each received more than a million votes, while Birney polled only 6,225 votes. In many states, there was not a single vote for Birney, because the Liberty Party was not organized enough to print and distribute ballots. (In the nineteenth century, ballots were printed by the political parties.) In Ohio, most of Birney's votes came from the Western Reserve, the northeastern counties of the state, originally claimed by Connecticut and settled largely by immigrants from New England. In the southern counties, including Chase's own Hamilton County, Birney received only a handful of votes.[38]

Chase was always a serious reader. In late 1840 and early 1841 he was reading a history of the French Revolution, an account of travels in East Asia, and the French original of *Democracy in America* by Alexis de Tocqueville. His diary for this winter shows that he also read three books that were important in changing his mind about slavery.[39]

William Ellery Channing, a leading Unitarian minister and reformer, started his long essay on *Emancipation* with an account of the British West Indies, five years after the British Parliament abolished slavery there. Channing contrasted the peace and prosperity of the British islands with the brutality of slavery in Spanish Cuba, still importing thousands of slaves from Africa each year. As for the United States, Channing argued that the free states should not interfere with slavery in the slave states but should "free ourselves from all obligation to use the powers of the national or state governments in any manner whatever for the support of slavery." He urged an amendment to the Constitution repealing the Fugitive Slave Clause but commented perceptively that the provision was "undergoing a silent repeal." As antislavery sentiment increased in the North, "the difficulty of sending back the fugitives increases."[40]

William Jay, lawyer and son of the first chief justice, John Jay, was the author of *A View of the Action of the Federal Government, in Behalf of Slavery.* Jay detailed not only some familiar ways in which the federal government supported slavery—by the slave trade in the District of Columbia—but also some that were less familiar, such as diplomatic efforts with Britain to secure extradition of fugitive slaves from Canada. In a prescient passage, Jay predicted that Southerners would persist in their efforts to extend slavery, and to create one or more new slaves states, by annexing the Mexican province of Texas to the United States: "It would be folly to suppose that the project of annexation is abandoned by either the South or by Texas; nor does it need the gift of prophesy to foresee that the first favorable opportunity of making war upon Mexico will be readily embraced by the federal government." Within a few years, Texas would join the Union as a slave state, and war with Mexico would follow.[41]

Theodore Weld, editor of the *Emancipator*, an abolitionist paper in New York, argued in *The Power of Congress over the District of Columbia*

that Congress had the authority to abolish slavery in the district. This
might seem so obvious that it would not require a fifty-page pamphlet;
after all, the Constitution gives to Congress the "power to exercise exclu-
sive legislation, in all cases whatsoever, in said District." But Southern
legislators insisted that Congress had no authority to end slavery there
because the District of Columbia was composed of land ceded by Virginia
and Maryland, and also that abolition without compensation would be
an impermissible taking of private property for public purposes. Weld
noted that nothing prohibited Congress from compensating the masters, but he would prefer abolition without compensation, because, in
his view, abolition would not involve taking private property; it would
be protecting the most basic property right, ensuring that "every man's
right to his own body shall be protected." Weld also quoted dozens of
founders, including George Washington, Jefferson, Madison, and Jay, to
prove that the founding generation expected and supported a gradual end
for slavery in the United States, including in the district.[42]

With these authors fresh in mind, Chase spoke about slavery in January
1841 at the Cincinnati courthouse. We do not have Chase's full speech,
only a brief report in the *Cincinnati Gazette* saying that he "addressed
the meeting at considerable length on the power and duty of Congress
to prohibit, without further delay, slavery and the slave trade in the
District of Columbia; and on the unconstitutionality of the various rules
and practices by which Congress had abridged the right of petition on
this subject." (The "rules and practices" in question included the "gag
rule," by which Congress precluded consideration of petitions calling for
limiting or abolishing slavery, a rule against which John Quincy Adams,
now a member of the House, was fighting.) The editors of the *Cincinnati Republican* refused to report on the meeting, explaining that "the
Constitution was adopted in an *honest* spirit of compromise and that our
Southern brethren are entitled to a peaceful enjoyment of all the rights
and privileges secured to them by that sacred instrument."[43]

Chase drafted a letter to the paper's editors, asking them if they
could point to "any compromise of the Constitution which the meeting
attacked" or "any right or privilege secured by [the Constitution] to the
South which the meeting assailed?" He argued that the "Constitution
contains no provision which sanctions slaveholding or slave trading in the
District of Columbia. On the contrary, the Constitution expressly declares
that no person shall be deprived of life, liberty, or property without

Cincinnati as it appeared in the early 1840s,
when Chase was a young lawyer there.

due process of law." This prohibition applied to all persons, of whatever color, and yet "every person who is brought into the District and held as a slave, and every child born there and held as a slave, is deprived of liberty without any process of law at all." Chase added that, in his view, the Constitution did *not* prohibit slavery in the slave states, because the Due Process Clause was a limit only on the federal government, not upon the states. In this, he echoed a unanimous 1833 decision of the Supreme Court, holding that the federal Bill of Rights did not restrict the actions of state governments.[44]

At the time of this January 1841 speech, Chase still considered himself a loyal Whig. Between the election in November and the inauguration in March, he wrote several letters about appointments in the new Whig administration, including a February letter to president-elect Harrison. After suggesting three men for patronage positions, Chase turned "with extreme reluctance" to address a policy point. He had heard that Harrison, in his inaugural address, would argue that Congress should not abolish slavery in the District of Columbia. Knowing that he could not persuade Harrison to advocate freeing the slaves there, Chase urged a more plausible course: silence. "I would most respectfully suggest whether every allusion to the topic of slavery had not better be avoided," he wrote. "It is not a subject on which Congress will be at all likely to act during your presidency, while it is a subject which cannot be touched without grievously offending one side or the other and producing a schism which may be attended with fatal consequences." Chase closed with the prayer "that the latter part of your illustrious career may correspond with its commencement and its course thus far, and that the confiding acclaims which greet your accession to the presidency may be changed into grateful benedictions when you retire from it."[45]

On March 4, 1841, the day on which Harrison was inaugurated in Washington, Chase was on the Ohio River. Eliza Chase was bound for New Orleans with her baby, Kate, and her sister Frances. Chase joined them as far as a few hours south of Louisville, Kentucky, for the day was "very pleasant," as was the company. "Nothing marred our enjoyment," he wrote in his diary, "but a cold which the baby had taken the first night on board." After telling the captain and doctor to take "especial care of my wife and little one," Chase disembarked from the southbound steamship and boarded one heading north. When the boat stopped in Louisville, he purchased a fictional account by the British writer Harriet Martineau of the black revolution in Haiti, which he read all the way back to Cincinnati, for the book "interested me greatly."[46]

Chase was also reading about temperance in early 1841, including Dr. Ralph Barnes Grindrod's five-hundred-page *Bacchus: An Essay on the Nature, Causes, Effects, and Cure of Intemperance,* which presented the emerging medical evidence about how alcohol entered the bloodstream and the brain, concluding that alcohol was a *"positive and effectual poison."* In the most controversial section of the book, Grindrod argued that, because devout Jews avoided alcohol during Passover, the "wine" shared at the Last Supper was probably more like grape juice. Chase told his diary that he was "fully persuaded that no alcoholic wine was used at Institution of Lord's Supper and that the use of such ought to be discontinued everywhere." After opposing particular licenses at earlier meetings, Chase declared at the March 15 council meeting that he would "vote for no more licenses to sell intoxicating drinks whether to taverns or other houses." Such positions would earn him praise in the *Philanthropist* and the votes of temperance men, but would lose him votes among the increasing immigrant population, mainly German, in the council elections set for Monday, April 5. This election would turn, one paper predicted, "wholly on the license question, without any reference to the two great political parties of the day."[47]

The returns were still being counted when, on Thursday, April 8, dreadful news reached Cincinnati: the president, after a short illness, had died five days earlier in Washington. Chase was in court, arguing a case, when the first report of Harrison's death arrived. At a special city council meeting that afternoon, Chase proposed and the council adopted a resolution lamenting the death of Harrison, "whose simplicity of manner, benevolence of heart, and undeviating integrity of conduct justly and greatly endeared him to all." Later, Chase attended a meeting to arrange with the various churches that they should all toll their bells in mourning. The next day was Good Friday, so Chase went to Episcopal church for services that were (in his words) "indescribably solemn." In the afternoon, he attended a meeting to plan the local services for the late president. Someone suggested that Judge Jacob Burnet, an early settler like Harrison, should give the eulogy. "I can't do it," said the judge. "He and I were the last of a band of thirty who were associated here forty-five years ago. He is gone, and I am left alone." There was, Chase noted, hardly a dry eye in the room.[48]

A few days later, the Cincinnati papers—still full of stories about Harrison's death and speculation about the new president, John Tyler—reported the results of the city council elections. Most but not quite all of the temperance candidates were defeated. In the First Ward, the three winning candidates each had about 560 votes, while Chase and the other temperance candidates each had only about 350 votes. Those in favor of more taverns had prevailed, the *Philanthropist* lamented, because the "principal portion of the clergy threw cold-water on the cold-water enterprise," and the press, "with one or two exceptions, did the same thing." Chase did not even mention the election in his diary, focusing instead on the death of Harrison and his current court cases.[49]

In one of these cases, Chase represented yet another fugitive slave, Mary Towns. The case was assigned to Judge Nathaniel Read, one of the lawyers who had represented the slave catcher in the *Matilda* case, now promoted to the state bench. Chase argued that the Fugitive Slave Act was contrary to the Constitution because it did not provide for trial by jury, but he also presented an affidavit from Towns in which she said she came to Cincinnati ten years earlier under a "written license" from one "who had full authority to give such a license," and that she "never did escape from Kentucky." Why the judge accepted the affidavit is mysterious, because under state law, blacks were not allowed to testify. But Read did accept the Towns affidavit and essentially accepted Chase's argument, finding that the master's affidavit was "vague" and "did not state that she escaped into this state." Judge Read declared that Mary Towns was free—an unusual verdict in fugitive slave litigation.[50]

Chase rejoiced over the *Towns* case in a letter to his friend Cleveland, writing that the judge ruled that the fugitive slave exception in the Ohio constitution "must be construed strictly" and that "every person *not precisely within its terms* must be regarded as free." It was not enough for a master to allege that a slave escaped from his residence in a slave state, for the slave might later have received or purchased freedom before coming to Ohio. "She must have escaped *from the state*, under the laws of which she was held to service, *into this state*." Only four years earlier, when he made similar arguments for Matilda, "they were then treated with ridicule or disregard." Now they were "recognized as law." In this same letter, Chase reported that he had given a speech to a recent gathering of those "opposed to the political encroachments of slavery at a village about ten miles from the city." Chase closed his letter by saying that he intended to leave Cincinnati soon "with my wife and child, neither of whom are very well, and make my way slowly through Virginia to Washington." From there he would go to Philadelphia, where he hoped to see his friend around the middle of July.[51]

Chase did not keep a diary for the second half of 1841, or perhaps a volume of the diary is simply lost, so it is hard to trace his movements. We know that he was in Cincinnati, with thousands of others, when the late president's body arrived there on July 5, 1841. "There was neither bustle nor parade of any kind," a paper reported, "but the countenance of everyone, as he followed the hearse, bore an impress of deep sorrow." Chase was also present two days later when the casket was walked slowly through the streets of Cincinnati to the waterfront and placed on a boat to carry it to North Bend, to be buried there. He was still in Cincinnati at the end of July, because he defended a man accused of interfering with an officer who was attempting to arrest a "runaway negro." But by late August, it seems, Chase was back east, seeing friends and doing business.[52]

Chase was thus probably out of town when the local Whigs gathered on August 21 to select their candidates for state senator and state representatives. The leading Whig paper of Cincinnati, the *Daily Gazette*, included Chase in a list of six plausible party nominees for state senator. A few days later, it reported that the convention had nominated Oliver Spencer, a lawyer about Chase's age, for state senate, without any explanation of why Spencer was chosen over Chase and the others. The *Philanthropist* claimed that the Whigs passed over Chase, in spite of his "knowledge, integrity, and usefulness," simply because he was "thoroughly antislavery in his opinions and practices." According to the *Philanthropist*, "the Whig convention at Carthage was as much an anti-abolition as antidemocratic convention," and Chase, after coming in a strong second at a similar convention a year earlier, this year "received only six votes out of 102." Forty years later, a friend elaborated (or perhaps exaggerated), saying that the Whigs rejected Chase because he was an abolitionist. This defeat (the friend claimed) showed Chase "that there was no place in the Whig Party for him and his principles." Modern biographers have accepted this, writing that Chase's defeats in April and August were the reason that he shifted to the Liberty Party.[53]

Nothing in Chase's papers, however, suggests that he sought the Whig nomination. On the contrary, there are two long letters to Chase from his Cincinnati friend and law partner Flamen Ball, one in late August and one in early September, neither of which mentions the Whig county convention. In the second letter, Ball described for Chase the terrible antiblack riots in Cincinnati in early September, in which several blacks were killed; Ball could easily have continued to describe how local Whigs had abandoned Chase because of his antislavery views. Moreover, there was ample room in the Northern Whig party for antislavery Whigs. For example, Ohio congressman Joshua Reed Giddings was both an opponent of slavery and a staunch Whig during the 1840s. William Henry Seward, governor of New York from 1839 through 1842, was another leading antislavery Whig. So Chase could have opposed slavery and defended fugitive slaves in court cases, and not only remained a Whig but also probably achieved success as a Whig. Why did he leave one of the two dominant political parties and join the apparently pointless Liberty Party?[54]

The best answer to this question, and it is only a partial answer, is from Chase's own writings from this period. He became convinced that the Whig Party, like the Democratic Party, could not oppose slavery *as a*

party because it was subservient to the South. He was also deeply troubled
by the role of Whig leaders in the antiblack riots in Cincinnati, both in
1836 and again in 1841. William Harrison's death, which made John Tyler
the tenth president, was another reason that Chase changed parties. Now
there was no local friend in the White House, but a total stranger. Now,
instead of Harrison, who had pledged to secure a federal charter for a new
national bank, there was Tyler, who vetoed bills to create a new national
bank. Now, instead of a president who Chase expected would be neutral
on slavery, the new president was yet another Southern slave owner.[55]

In a revealing letter, Chase wrote his friend Charles Cleveland in October 1841 that after the recent riots, Cincinnati had "a most unenviable
distinction for lawless violence." What especially angered him was the
role of city leaders who condoned or only feebly condemned the violence.
Chase insisted that he was not an abolitionist, but he had decided to
join the antislavery movement. He now viewed slavery "as an influence
perverting our government from its true scope and end, as an institution
strictly local, but now escaped from its proper limits and threatening to
overshadow and nullify whatever is most valuable in our political system."
Antislavery, Chase wrote, "aims at a complete deliverance of the government of the nation from all connection with and all responsibility for
slavery." Political antislavery, at least Chase's version of antislavery, would
concede that the Southern states were free to maintain slavery within their
borders if they wished, but antislavery would "examine fully the merits
and demerits of the system of slavery itself." Once slavery was "agitated
as a political question, great light must be thrown upon it." Chase was
well aware that political antislavery would be "unpopular" at first, but
he had faith that it would "gain friends constantly."[56]

Chase's conversion to the antislavery cause was a gradual one and, like
many conversions, not easily explained. Part of the process was intellectual: reading William Jay and others persuaded him that the antislavery
interpretation of the Constitution was correct. Part of the process was
personal: getting to know Isaac Colby and other abolitionists persuaded
Chase that they were not raving lunatics but serious, sober, righteous
men. Chase was also getting to know, after the *Matilda* case, individual
black people, both his clients and community leaders. Surely this helped
to change his views on black slavery. And part of the process was spiritual:
Chase came to see slavery as contrary to the central commandments of
Christianity, to love God and love our neighbor.[57]

Whatever the conversion process, it is clear that by December 1841, Chase was committed to the antislavery cause. He placed a small advertisement in the *Philanthropist* urging all the "friends of liberty" in Ohio to attend an end-of-the year state convention in Columbus. When the two hundred delegates gathered, they adopted an address, drafted by Chase, which provides the best early statement of his antislavery views. He started by emphasizing that he and his colleagues had not separated "from the parties with which we have heretofore acted without reluctance and a struggle. Many of us have, until quite lately, indulged the idea that this separation was not absolutely necessary." They had hoped that one or both of the main political parties would begin to oppose slavery and seek to deliver "the people of this country from the manifold evils they suffer in consequence of the ascendency of slaveholding influence, in all the departments of our national government." But such hopes had been "repeatedly disappointed" and were now "finally relinquished."[58]

Chase quoted Thomas Jefferson, who declared in the Declaration of Independence that "all men are created equal," and he quoted from Madison, whose notes of the 1787 Constitutional Convention, kept private while those who participated in the convention were alive, were first published in 1840. In a key passage, Madison stated that the Philadelphia delegates "thought it wrong to admit in the Constitution the idea that there could be property in man." All the Liberty Party wanted, Chase wrote, was to follow through on the vision of these fathers of the nation. "Their creed is our creed," he declared. "Their faith is our faith." The Constitution they drafted and ratified "designates all the inhabitants of the states as persons and nowhere recognizes the idea that men can be the subjects of property." The Constitution "found slavery and left it a state institution," dependent upon the slave laws of the slave states; the Constitution gave slavery "no national character, no national existence." Chase's reading of the Constitution was thus quite different from that of not only the Southern slave owners but also the Northern abolitionists, both of whom agreed that the Constitution sanctioned and protected slavery.[59]

Chase insisted that the Liberty Party was not seeking to interfere with slavery in the slave states. This was a crucial concept, not only in the Liberty Party but also later in the Free Soil and Republican Parties.

The Liberty Party "would not interfere with the restoration of fugitives from service, on claim of the party to whom their services may be due," but would insist that this constitutional clause applied only "to cases of escape from the state under the laws of which the service may be claimed to be due into another state." As we shall see, Chase's position on the fugitive slave problem would change over time; he would soon argue that there was no constitutional basis for a federal fugitive slave law. What the Liberty Party wanted, Chase wrote in all capitals, was "the absolute and unqualified divorce of the government from slavery." He did not spell out in this address what such a "divorce" would mean in practice, but, at a minimum, he had in mind abolishing slavery in the District of Columbia and preventing its spread to other federal territories.[60]

Chase closed by placing himself and his colleagues under the "banner of constitutional liberty." In a hint of what would become the 1848 slogan of the Free Soil Party, he wrote in 1841 that the Liberty Party would inscribe on its banner "Liberty, Equal Rights, Protection to Free Labor, General Education, Public Economy." The party would rally under this flag "with firm resolution never to abandon the contest, never to relax our exertions, until our great object shall be happily accomplished. Last year, the Liberty Party counted her voters by the thousands; this year, she counted them by tens of thousands; next year, she hopes to count them by hundreds of thousands." A decade earlier, in his essay on Henry Brougham, Chase had imagined a reformer, completely committed to a cause, working "through difficulty, and discouragement, and opposition to give effect to some great scheme of benevolence." At the time, Chase himself had no such cause to which he was committed. But in 1841 he found his great cause, his life's work: political antislavery. Now he would face years of difficulty, discouragement, and opposition.[61]

CHAPTER 5

"To Limit and Localize...Slavery"

ༀ 1841–48 ༀ

As soon as he joined the Liberty Party, Chase set out to change it. He saw three related tasks. First, Chase wanted to distinguish the Liberty Party, a political party, from abolitionism, a moral movement. Second, he hoped to broaden the party, to persuade antislavery Whigs and Democrats to join, and to extend the party into border slave states such as Kentucky. Third, Chase tried to reverse a decision made in early 1841: that James Birney should be the party's presidential candidate again in 1844. He wanted someone more popular than Birney, someone more political, someone who could attract more than just abolitionists.[1]

One of the first letters Chase wrote after joining the party was to Joshua Leavitt, an eastern preacher, editor, and party leader. We do not have Chase's letter, only Leavitt's icy response, informing him that Birney had been duly named at a national convention called by the national committee, of which Leavitt was a member. As for the word *abolitionist*, Leavitt wrote that he was proud to be an abolitionist and that he expected "to be one, and to continue my efforts of all sorts, until slavery is actually abolished." In Leavitt's view, the term was "so far fixed to us that we have no alternative but to go on and make it respectable."[2]

Chase also started to correspond with Joshua Giddings, the antislavery Whig member of Congress from the Western Reserve. Trying to persuade

James Birney, the Liberty Party presidential candidate in 1840,
whom Chase wanted to replace with an alternative for 1844.

Giddings to leave the Whigs for the Liberty Party, Chase argued that because of the confusion in the Whig Party following Harrison's death, the Whigs could no longer expect to prevail in state elections. "If we must be in a minority, why not be in a minority of our own—rather than in a minority of men who despise us or affect to do so?" he asked. Chase believed the Liberty Party might "secure the balance of power in the legislatures of the free states" and then "accomplish immense good for the country." Chase referred here to a key role of state legislatures at this time—selecting federal senators. An even division in a state legislature between the two major parties might give an antislavery party the "balance of power" and thus allow it to select a senator. This is how Chase himself, in a few years' time, would go to Washington as a federal senator.[3]

Treating Giddings as if he were a member of the Liberty Party rather than the rival Whigs, Chase wrote to him in January 1842 that many were unhappy with the nomination of Birney, and raised two possible alternatives: John Quincy Adams and William Henry Seward. Chase did not need to detail for Giddings their antislavery qualifications: how Adams had argued against the "gag rule" that prevented Congress from considering antislavery petitions; how Seward had refused a request from the governor of Virginia for three men who had helped a slave escape, saying that there was no law of New York that recognized that one man could be the property of another. Leavitt might fear "disturbing the present nomination," but Chase feared that it would be impossible to persuade many people to vote for "one so little known as Mr. Birney is and who has seen so little of public service."[4]

Writing Birney directly, Chase expressed similar concerns. The party's vice presidential candidate, Thomas Morris of Ohio, was honorably prepared to step aside "if any man more likely to strengthen the cause could be selected," and Chase was sure that Birney had "similar sentiments." Chase raised with Birney the same two names: Adams and Seward. Birney replied that he did not see how "any abolitionist conversant with our cause could have thought, at this stage of it, of going out of our ranks for candidates for any office. Out of our ranks all public men are of the Whig or Democratic party. How can they be abolitionists?" When Birney shared Chase's letter with Leavitt, he wrote back to Birney that he was astonished that a "raw recruit" like Chase would write in such terms. In Leavitt's opinion, Chase seemed to think "that there is very little practical wisdom among those who raised the Liberty Standard while he was worshipping the Log Cabin, and that therefore all that has been done needs undoing that it may be done right." Leavitt's irritation is understandable: he was more than a decade older than Chase and had devoted years to the abolitionist cause. Perhaps more remarkable is that, over time, Leavitt came to work with and listen to the brash young western lawyer.[5]

Chase was not easily discouraged. He wrote to Lewis Tappan, the New York merchant, publisher, and abolitionist, including a copy of the Ohio liberty address, and raised the possibility of Seward as a presidential candidate. Tappan approved of Chase's speech and agreed with him on the need to broaden the antislavery party, replying to Chase, "If we could get half a dozen first-rate men into Congress—men of mind, courage, and eloquence—we could do more good than to elect an antislavery governor of a great state." He promised to speak with Seward and then shared the New York governor's response with Chase: Seward did not see how he could accept a Liberty nomination without seeming to oppose the "generous and

*Lewis Tappan, New York financier and philanthropist, with whom
Chase worked in the early Liberty Party.*

patriotic [Whig] party" of which he was a member. A few months later, Chase wrote Tappan again to ask a slightly different question: whether Seward could be persuaded to "become the candidate for the presidency of a party based on the principles set forth in the Ohio liberty address?" Chase believed that "with Seward as our champion, and constitutional liberty and free labor as our watchwords, we could carry several states in 1844, and a majority at the next subsequent election." But, he continued, "if the Liberty Party perseveres in its present courses as adopted in some states, with Mr. Birney as a candidate, it will, I fear, become extinct." Chase was already thinking about the possibility of a new party, broader than the Liberty Party, with someone like Seward as its candidate.[6]

Chase also pursued Adams, asking the former president through Giddings for his views on slavery in the District of Columbia (probably hoping to publish the response in the *Philanthropist*). Adams received this letter, for it is among his papers at the Massachusetts Historical Society, but it seems that he did not reply. So Chase wrote again to Tappan, sending along a proposed joint letter to Adams. "We are among those who earnestly hope that you will permit yourself to be named as the candidate of the friends of Free Labor, Liberty, and the Constitution for the highest national office." Since the only copy of this letter is the draft, in the Chase Papers, it seems that Tappan did not sign and send the letter on to Adams.[7]

Through these and other letters, Chase formed alliances and friendships that would in many cases last for decades. For example, he started a correspondence in early 1842 with Cassius Marcellus Clay, a cousin of Henry Clay's and the leading antislavery Whig in Kentucky. Chase urged the former Whig congressman to start an antislavery party in his state,

Cassius Marcellus Clay, leader of the Kentucky antislavery movement and friend of Chase.

but Clay responded that it was impossible: he would be denounced as an abolitionist and lose all his political sway. Nevertheless, Clay would become Chase's principal point of contact in Kentucky and vice versa; for example, in one letter, Clay asked Chase to find him a white nurse "capable of controlling five children."[8]

Thaddeus Stevens, antislavery lawyer from Pennsylvania, leader of the radical Republicans, and one of the House managers in the impeachment of Andrew Johnson.

Chase also wrote for the first time in 1842 to Thaddeus Stevens, then an obscure lawyer in Gettysburg, Pennsylvania. Chase complained to him about the way in which some eastern leaders were confusing abolitionism with antislavery: "Abolition seeks to abolish slavery everywhere. The means which it employs correspond with the object to be effected—they are of a moral nature—argument, persuasion, remonstrance, and the like. The Liberty Party seeks to abolish slavery wherever it exists within the reach of the constitutional action of Congress . . . and to deliver the government from the control of the Slave Power." Chase and Stevens would work closely together during the Civil War, when Stevens, by then a congressman, chaired the House Ways and Means Committee. At about the same time, Chase wrote his first letter to Gerrit Smith, an upstate New York philanthropist and abolitionist, "for the purpose acquainting you with the views and purposes of the Liberty men in this quarter." Chase and Smith would often disagree, but they were in constant correspondence until near the end of Chase's life, with about fifty letters from Chase to Smith in various archives. It was also in this period that Chase started to write to Charles Sumner, a Harvard Law School lecturer and Boston lawyer. Sumner was more of an intellectual than a politician: fluent in five modern languages, a deep reader and frequent traveler. The correspondence would turn into a close friendship, with Chase and Sumner each destined to play a major role in the Civil War and Reconstruction.[9]

Charles Sumner, the Massachusetts antislavery leader with whom Chase started to correspond in the early 1840s, and who would remain his friend until Chase's death in 1873.

Chase's political work was not limited to writing letters. Among the Chase Papers at the Historical Society of Pennsylvania is a handwritten 1842 list of the men in Hamilton County who had pledged to vote for Leicester King, the Liberty Party candidate for governor that year. It seems likely that Chase secured some of these names through face-to-face meetings. He also spoke at Liberty rallies in the spring and summer. In Ohio's October election, King received about five thousand votes, more than five times as many as Birney's total two years earlier.[10]

Chase's personal life in these years was difficult. In May 1842 he and his wife, Eliza, welcomed a daughter, Lizzie, but they mourned and buried the little girl in August. A second daughter, also called Lizzie, was born the next year. Even more difficult for Chase, he learned in September 1842 that Eliza had tuberculosis in both lungs. "The treatment in this case seems to me to be very simple," the Chase family doctor wrote: "plain nutritious diet; daily exercise in the open air; sponging the chest every morning with tepid water; gradually allowing it to become cooler." But the physician's confident tone could not hide the terrible truth. Tuberculosis, also known as consumption, was the leading cause of death among American adults. The disease seemed to strike the young more often than the old, and women more frequently than men, so much so that women lived shorter lives than men. Eliza would have known that the disease was not romantic or poetic, that it was dreadful and relentless, for two of her sisters had just died of consumption. Both she and Chase would have known at once that she would probably die herself within a few years.[11]

There was also a significant change in Chase's professional life at the end of 1842: he resigned or was removed as a director of Lafayette Bank. He did not explain his departure at the time, at least not in any surviving letter, and offered a questionable one later. "As a director of the Lafayette Bank," Chase wrote in 1853, "I was an earnest and constant advocate of resumption [of specie payments], and I had the satisfaction of seeing that institution among the first to resume. My ideas on this subject, however, were not popular among the stockholders or the directors of other banks, and finally I and the other directors who insisted that the bank should be conducted on specie principles were turned out of office, and I lost its business." This explanation is odd because it would have been suicidal for Lafayette Bank to resume specie payments while other banks in Cincinnati were not making such payments; the only way to resume was in unison, which is what happened. Moreover, Chase did not lose the legal business of Lafayette Bank; he continued to represent it in court even after he ceased to serve as a director. What seems more likely is that, after Chase left the Whig Party and started to have Democratic ideas about banks, he was no longer welcome on Lafayette's Whiggish board.[12]

Chase and his friend Gamaliel Bailey (still editing the *Philanthropist*) turned their attention in early 1843 to William Jay as a possible presidential candidate, hoping to capitalize not only on Jay's own "irreproachable character" but also that of his late father. Tappan reported back to Chase that Jay was not interested, saying that he did not think an abolition candidate could obtain a single electoral vote. A few weeks later, Chase wrote to Jay directly, asking if he knew of an antislavery Episcopal minister who might take charge of Chase's home church, St. Paul's, in Cincinnati. Jay wrote back that he rejoiced to get such a question; it made him feel that he was not alone in the Episcopal church, and that there were a few others who did not forget "their relationship to the poor slave and their obligation to do justice and love mercy." And Jay sounded a bit more encouraging about the Liberty Party, writing that the party was doing "more than I formerly anticipated from its efforts."[13]

Chase and Bailey arrived in Buffalo in August 1843 for a national Liberty convention without what they wanted most: an alternative to Birney as the party's presidential candidate. But they achieved success on other fronts, as when the convention adopted a platform that sounded very much like Chase: more political than moral. When he returned to Cincinnati, Chase wrote to Tappan about Birney that "the thing is as it is, and we must make the best of it." They would not be able to get as many votes for Birney as they would have obtained for Jay, and not nearly as many as Adams would have won, but they "must give him what votes we can" and make a better nomination next time. Half in jest, Chase added that he hoped in 1849 to be able to greet Tappan as secretary of the Treasury.[14]

In the summer of 1843, in a packed courtroom in Cincinnati, Chase tried what would prove to be one of his most important cases, *Jones v. Van Zandt*. His client was John Van Zandt, described by the *Philanthropist* as an "honest, hard-working, benevolent farmer." The year before, while heading north from Cincinnati in his wagon in the predawn darkness, Van Zandt met nine black people walking on the road in the same direction. He offered them a ride, and one of them, Andrew, took the reins. An hour or two later, two white men stopped Van Zandt, claiming that the blacks were fugitive slaves fleeing from Kentucky. Andrew leapt from the wagon and escaped, but the others were taken back to Kentucky. Their owner there, Wharton Jones, sued Van Zandt in federal circuit court, seeking both the $500 penalty provided by the 1793 Fugitive Slave Act for a person who harbored or concealed a fugitive slave, and damages for the loss of the slaves' services, especially Andrew.[15]

The federal circuit courts in the early nineteenth century were staffed by justices of the Supreme Court and district judges, and Chase was probably pleased to learn that the *Van Zandt* case would be tried by his friend Justice John McLean, sitting as a circuit court judge. After the lawyers for Jones presented their case, Chase asked McLean to "overrule the evidence"—in other words, to direct a verdict for his client. Both sides argued this motion at length, with Chase questioning again the constitutionality of the 1793 act, arguing that Van Zandt had no notice that the black people were fugitive slaves and contending that his client had not harbored or concealed the alleged fugitives; after all, they were not hiding in a house but instead riding with him along the open road.

Justice John McLean, friend and neighbor of Chase in Cincinnati,
and perennial presidential candidate.

McLean denied Chase's motion, but Chase renewed his points in his closing. Bailey wrote in his paper that Chase's three-hour closing speech, "whether viewed as a legal argument or a specimen of oratory, has seldom been equaled."[16]

Chase's task in the *Van Zandt* case was made more difficult by the Supreme Court's recent decision in *Prigg v. Pennsylvania*. Justice Joseph Story declared in the principal *Prigg* opinion that the Fugitive Slave Act was "clearly constitutional in all its leading provisions," except for the part of the act that authorized state magistrates to enforce it. "As to the authority so conferred on state magistrates," Story wrote, "state magistrates may, if they choose, exercise the authority unless prohibited by state legislation." Some states would soon follow the suggestion in Story's final phrase and pass personal liberty laws, prohibiting state officers from helping in the capture and rendition of fugitives. But the phrase was of no use to Chase in the *Van Zandt* case because Ohio law at this time *required* state officers to assist in arresting fugitives. In a separate opinion in the *Prigg* case, McLean agreed with Story about the constitutionality of the 1793 act but dissented on a procedural point. Chase used one bit of McLean's opinion—in which he said that everyone in a free state was presumptively free—to argue that Van Zandt was entitled to believe that the blacks whom he met, even after midnight, were free men and women. In general, however, Chase disliked and disagreed with *Prigg v. Pennsylvania,* denouncing it in a private letter as "a decision worthy of the judiciary of Pandemonium"—John Milton's name for the capital of hell in his epic poem *Paradise Lost.*[17]

After the closing arguments, Judge McLean instructed the jury, and they returned a verdict against Van Zandt for $1,200 in damages. Chase moved for a new trial on various grounds, and McLean granted his motion. McLean and his colleague on the Ohio federal circuit, District Judge Humphrey Leavitt, also asked the Supreme Court to consider and decide more than a dozen questions raised in the *Van Zandt* case. The questions included whether the circumstances of the case (blacks walking north after midnight) were sufficient to put the defendant on notice that these people were fugitive slaves, and whether the 1793 act was consistent with the Northwest Ordinance and the Constitution. Federal law, at this time, allowed circuit judges, when they disagreed, to raise questions for the Supreme Court, more or less forcing the higher court to take up the case and consider the issues.[18]

Once Chase knew that the *Van Zandt* case was heading to the Supreme Court, he sought other lawyers to help him, writing to Thaddeus Stevens in Pennsylvania and William Seward in New York. It seems that Stevens did not respond—at least, there is no response in the Chase Papers—but Seward agreed readily. For the next few years, however, there was not much for Chase and Seward to do because the case was far down on the court's docket. Chase used the case, however, as an excuse for frequent letters to and from McLean, who kept him apprised not only on the status of the case but also on national politics.[19]

In March 1844 Chase attended what he described as a "great anti-Texas meeting" in Cincinnati. For many people, the main reason to oppose making Texas part of the United States, through annexation, was that there were already about thirty thousand slaves in Texas. If Texas became part of the United States, it would soon become one or more slave states, extending slavery and increasing the power of slave states. Annexation might also lead to war with Mexico, which still viewed Texas as a rebellious province, not an independent nation. The leaders of this Cincinnati meeting were Whigs, but Chase drafted the resolutions, which William Birney, son of the presidential candidate, described to his father as a "signal triumph" for the local Liberty Party. The attendees decided to pose written questions to the presidential candidates about Texas, and Chase also drafted these letters, claiming that the people of Cincinnati were "irreconcilably opposed to any enlargement of the domain of slavery." A week later, he went to another local mass meeting, this one composed largely of Democrats who supported bringing Texas into the Union as a slave state. At one point, Chase leaped to his feet to oppose the "slavery doctrines" embedded in the resolutions. Bailey reported in the *Philanthropist* that Chase's remarks were greeted with applause but were then followed by a rabid speech "in favor of slave owners and slave breeders."[20]

Writing to James Birney at this time, Chase agreed with him in opposing the annexation of Texas but disagreed with him about the history of Florida and Louisiana. In a recent public letter, Birney had conceded that the treaties for acquiring those territories had secured the rights of slaveholders to their slave property. Chase responded that the Louisiana Purchase Treaty of 1803 and the Florida Purchase Treaty of 1819 had promised the residents of these new territories *freedom*, without regard to color. These guarantees meant that both territories, and all states created from them, were free, and that Congress had no right, in the Missouri Compromise of 1820, to consign part of the Louisiana Territory to slavery. (The compromise admitted Missouri as a slave state, Maine as a free state, and excluded slavery from any states formed in the Louisiana Territory north of the southern border of Missouri.) Chase was making a novel and important argument: instead of assuring slaveowners (as he had in the past and would in the future) that the antislavery party would not challenge slavery in the existing slave states, Chase was now saying that slavery was illegal in Florida, Louisiana, Arkansas, and Missouri. He soon renewed this argument in speeches at Liberty rallies, saying that, under the Constitution, slavery "was to be confined to the original states" and that it was not allowed in the Florida or the Louisiana Territory.[21]

When the Whigs gathered in Baltimore in early May 1844, they nominated their great hero, Henry Clay, for president. At the Democratic convention, later the same month, the delegates deadlocked for days and eventually nominated a dark horse, James Polk, a former representative from and governor of Tennessee. The Democrats also adopted an aggressive platform, calling not only for the annexation of Texas but also for the acquisition of all of the Oregon Country, at the time owned jointly with Great Britain. Chase probably agreed with his friend Bailey, who wrote in the *Philanthropist* that Polk was a "man of small talents" who secured the nomination only because he was "in favor of the immediate annexation of Texas" and because he had strong support from the slave states. A friend wrote to Chase that many Democrats, after their convention, "seem to have become enlightened and speak out indignantly against the domination of a slaveholding oligarchy." In an effort to unite the party, Polk promised that, if elected, he would serve only a single term. But many Northern Democrats were not mollified, especially former president Martin Van Buren and other Barnburners, so called because they would supposedly rather burn down the barn than yield.[22]

Chase planned to continue speaking at Liberty rallies during the summer, but in late June he received an alarming letter from his wife. She was in Cumberland, Maryland, on her way east to see relatives, and reported that she was coughing "incessantly" and unable to sleep at night "on account of my cough." Leaving his daughters with his sister Alice, and writing to his clients that he would be away for a few weeks, Chase hastened to Maryland, then continued with his wife to New York City. Eliza's health improved, and she and Chase spent some time in New England. There is no Chase diary for this period, nor are there many letters, so it is not clear whether Chase and his wife were back in Cincinnati when their daughter Lizzie died there in late July 1844 at just eighteen months.[23]

A week later, a Liberty convention nominated Chase to represent Hamilton County as the member of Congress for its district. It was an honor for a man not yet forty; a recognition that Chase was the leading Liberty man in the county and, indeed, in all of Ohio. Chase declined, though, writing that "considerations of a private nature, which I am not at liberty to disregard, constrain me—and so long as they exist, will constrain me—to decline becoming myself a candidate for any political station." Chase did not explain further, but he probably did not want to leave his grieving wife for a campaign. Yet Chase did speak at a few Liberty rallies in the fall of 1844 and published in the *Philanthropist,* bylined S.C., one of his strongest antislavery statements, the "Liberty Man's Creed."[24]

He opened by quoting Jefferson: "I believe all men are created equal; that they are endowed by their Creator with certain inalienable rights, among which are life, liberty, and the pursuit of happiness." He alluded to the *Somerset* principle: "I believe that slavery is so odious that nothing can uphold it except positive law, and that all such law violates inalienable rights, and ought to be immediately abrogated." Then, in very short form, he made his argument about the views of the founding generation on slavery: "I believe that the settled policy of the American government, at the time of the adoption of the Constitution, was to limit and localize, not to extend and nationalize slavery." Turning to the Constitution, he declared: "I believe that the Constitution of the United States confers on Congress no power to establish or uphold slavery anywhere; but, on the contrary, expressly prohibits the general government from depriving any person of liberty except by due process of law." This implied that "slavery in the District of Columbia and the Territory of Florida, and in all the states created out of any territory of the United States, is anti-constitutional."[25]

After regretting the control that the slaveholders had over the federal government because each slave was counted as three-fifths of a person for purposes of allocating seats in Congress, Chase argued that "the offices of government ought to be filled by non-slaveholders" and that the "policy of this government should be directed to the establishment of liberty, the procuring and extension of markets for free labor, and the discontinuance of all forms of oppression." If Chase really meant that *all* federal offices, including the minor local offices in the Southern states, should be filled by antislavery men, this was radical indeed. Southern fear of such appointments was a major factor in secession after Abraham Lincoln's election in 1860.[26]

Chase's 1844 creed continued: "I believe that whenever Liberty men shall obtain the control of Congress, all laws for the maintenance of slavery in the District and in Florida, and for the special encouragement of slave labor, will be repealed; and that the coastwise and interstate slave trade will be prohibited." Chase rarely raised the possibility of prohibiting the interstate slave trade, but such a prohibition would have dealt a death blow to slavery, for masters in the Upper South, who generally had more slaves than they could use on their farms, depended upon selling slaves to the Lower South, where masters needed new slaves.[27]

"I believe that if Liberty men will do their duty," Chase continued, "being constant in season and out of season, and always faithful to their nominations, the antislavery strength of the country will be concentrated at the ballot box in less than four years, that a Liberty president and Congress will be elected in 1848, and that the census of 1850 will not include a single slave." Chase was exaggerating for effect here, suggesting what *could* be achieved, rather than making a practical political prediction. He concluded: "I believe that the work has to be done, and that it might as well be done in four years as in forty. I believe that I will do my share of it."[28]

Voting in the 1844 presidential election started in early November and continued through early December. When the votes were finally counted, Polk had prevailed over Clay in one of the closest contests in American history; a shift of a few thousand votes would have made Clay the next president. The Liberty candidate, Birney, received 62,054 votes, many times more than he had received four years earlier, but fewer than Chase and others had hoped. Some Whigs claimed that Birney had cost Henry Clay the election, because if one added up the votes for Clay and Birney in New York, they exceeded those for Polk in that state, and if Clay had carried New York, along with his other states, he would have prevailed. This was not the way in which Chase and Bailey thought, however. They saw no real difference, on slavery, between the two major parties; the only way forward, in their view, was through the Liberty Party or another antislavery party.[29]

In a letter to his friend Charles Cleveland in February 1845, Chase lamented the indifference to the plight of the slaves. The slaves "seem to be cut off from the sympathies of mankind," he observed. "The brazen wall of oppression separates them from the kindly flow of the compassion of human hearts. Our pulpits resound with the evils of Catholicism, the dangers of unbelief, the wants of the heathen. But alas, who cares, or caring, dares to speak, of the multitudes perishing in our very midst?" Chase also commented on the legislation making its way through Congress for the annexation of Texas. "You must know that I never had much objection" to annexing Texas, except on two points: "the assumption of her debt" and the "continuation of slavery being provided against." As to the first point, Congress had resolved that it would not pay Texas's debts; as to the second, "we must provide against it at the ballot box!" For a man who, less than a year earlier, had denounced the Texas annexation at public meetings, these were rather remarkable statements. Perhaps Chase realized that annexation was inevitable and wanted to focus his energies elsewhere.[30]

In early 1845 Chase was involved in a fugitive slave case with an unusual and important aftermath. Samuel Watson, born a slave in Virginia, was sent by his master to Arkansas, where he worked for several years before a new master sent an agent to bring him back to Virginia. On their eastward journey, when the steamboat stopped in Cincinnati, Watson walked off the boat and into the city. He returned to the riverside that evening, where the agent found him "leaning quietly against a post." Fearing that Watson would leave again, the agent arranged for local officials to arrest him. Chase somehow learned of the arrest and obtained a writ of habeas corpus, setting up a hearing before Judge Nathaniel Read.[31]

At this hearing, in a packed courtroom, Chase and his two colleagues made arguments similar to those Chase had made before: that a boat tied to the Ohio shore was legally within Ohio; that the moment a master brought a slave into the free state of Ohio, the person was free; and that by walking off the boat, Watson was not escaping from slavery but merely exercising his freedom. Chase also argued that when the United States acquired the Louisiana Territory from France in 1803, "slavery ceased to be a legal relation in that territory, and all the laws authorizing slaveholding in it, or in any of the states created out of it, are unconstitutional and void." Congress had no power, under the Constitution, Chase said, to create or maintain slavery; only the original slave states had such authority. Slavery was also inconsistent with the terms of the treaty with France, in which the United States promised liberty to all the inhabitants of the territory. Chase was now testing in court the argument he had devised during the campaign, based on the Louisiana Purchase Treaty.[32]

A decade later, the *New-York Tribune* published an account of Chase's work in the *Watson* case, saying that his speech for Watson "was such a one as no mere platform speaker, however gifted," could make, for Chase "had a living, agitated, trembling subject in the man Watson." Chase's "softest whisper could be heard, so anxious was the hush in that hall, but when he closed his glorious appeal, the delighted audience vociferated their applause."[33]

Two lawyers opposed Chase: one the son and the other the nephew of Justice John McLean. Both McLeans disputed Chase's points, and then Judge Read announced his decision: Watson was a slave. As the agent and his hired hands came forward to seize the man, he turned to Chase and his colleagues.

"Have you done everything?" Watson asked. "Can nothing further be done for me?"

Chase answered Watson that they had done all they could, to which the black man responded, "God Almighty bless you, then. I'll never forget you!"[34]

After the hearing, when Read published his decision, there was much in the opinion with which Chase agreed. "I regret deeply that slavery exists," the judge declared, calling the practice "the only blot upon the white pennant of universal liberty, which we have flung upon the free air, for the admiration and imitation of the world." Read also agreed with Chase that, as a general rule, when a master brought a slave to Ohio, the slave became free. But Read created an exception to this rule for slaves in transit along the Ohio River, saying that otherwise Ohio would be denying the people of Virginia and Kentucky "the right to navigate the Ohio with a slave." Chase would have noticed that Read did not cite any cases in support of his "right of transit" and resolved to challenge this supposed right in another case. Read also rejected Chase's novel argument about the Louisiana Territory, saying that slaves were not included among the "inhabitants" promised freedom by the treaty.[35]

Some free black leaders in Cincinnati decided to honor Chase for his work on the *Watson* case and other similar fugitive slave cases. They paid a silversmith to create an elegant silver pitcher and presented it to Chase at a ceremony in one of the city's black churches. Andrew Gordon, a barber whom a historian has called "one of the state's premier black orators," presented the pitcher to Chase, telling him the black community would never forget his labors for "our downtrodden and oppressed people."[36]

The silver pitcher presented to Salmon Chase by the black community of Cincinnati in 1845 to thank him for his work on their behalf. One of Chase's most prized possessions, the pitcher was passed down through the family until 2013, when it was donated to the Cincinnati Museum Center.

Chase started his speech on a general, philosophical level, contrasting aristocracy and democracy. In a monarchy or aristocracy, he said, "the rights or rather the privileges of a class may be created by law and secured by law." But in a democracy, "which recognizes no class or privileges, every man must be protected in his just rights, or no man can be, by law. The moment the law excludes a portion of the community from its equal regard, it divides the community into higher and lower classes, and introduces all the evils of the aristocratic principle." Because of this, Americans believed that "all legal distinctions between individuals of the same community, founded in any such circumstance as color, origin, or the like, are hostile to the genius of our institutions, and incompatible with the true theory of American liberty."[37]

Applying these general principles to the question of suffrage, Chase denounced the provision in the Ohio constitution denying blacks the right to vote, declaring that "true democracy makes no enquiry about the color of the skin, or the place of nativity, or any other similar circumstance or condition." By mentioning "place of nativity" Chase was taking a stand not just on racial rights but also on the rights of immigrants—an issue that would be debated furiously in American politics. Chase insisted that the 1831 state statute denying black children the right to attend Ohio's public schools was contrary to the state constitution, which promised public education for "every grade, without any distinction or preference whatever." Likewise, he condemned the Ohio law that prohibited blacks from testifying in court, saying that "almost all humane and benevolent people" opposed this form of exclusion.[38]

Turning to the slave states, Chase elaborated on his Watson argument. "I claim that nowhere, unless within the limits of the original states, can a single person be enslaved, except in violation of the Constitution and the Law." Slavery in Louisiana, Arkansas, and Missouri, the three states formed so far out of the Louisiana Territory, was contrary to the Constitution, including the Fifth Amendment, which prohibited the federal government from depriving anyone of life, liberty, or property without due process. Sounding like a preacher—and he was, after all, in church—Chase declared that slavery was contrary to the Bible: "Slavery did not descend from Heaven, as some Divines profanely teach; it came up from beneath, it did not come down from above. Let us hope, however, that it will go down, and that right speedily, to the place of its origin, and know no resurrection."[39]

Chase congratulated his black audience on the progress they had made in Cincinnati. "Debarred from the public schools, you have established schools of your own; thrust by prejudice into obscure corners of the edifices in which white men offer prayer, you have erected churches of your own." Chase had recently attended the commencement of "the Colored High School," and "every intelligent countenance and every generous aspiration of that youthful band of happy scholars added fresh strength to my desire for the advancement of the race to which they belonged." He exhorted the black community to "go forward as you have begun. Be assured that upon yourselves lies the chief responsibility of the work of your social and civil redemption." For himself, Chase pledged that he would persist in the cause until "every vestige of oppression shall be erased from the statute book" and until the sun in its daily passage across "our broad and glorious land" would see not "the footprint of a single slave."[40]

Chase arranged for his Watson argument, Gordon's speech, and Chase's response to be printed in a pamphlet. This would ensure that his words would reach not only his immediate black audience but also a larger white readership, at a time when almost no whites would agree with Chase about black rights. Chase's pamphlet would be quoted against him in future political campaigns, under headlines such as "Chase in Favor of Nigger Suffrage" and "Chase in Favor of Nigger Children Attending the Same Public Schools with the Whites." Chase treasured the silver pitcher for the rest of his life, writing to Gerrit Smith that he would "rather possess the smallest evidence of the regard from the oppressed and injured" than an expensive gift from the Russian tsar. After the 1860 presidential election, some editors confused Lincoln and Chase, and claimed that it was the president-elect who had spoken to a group of grateful blacks in Cincinnati. When the editor of the *New York Times* wrote Lincoln to ask if he had given the silver pitcher speech, he answered that he had not; and, indeed, that he "was never in a meeting of negroes in my life." The silver pitcher thus might serve as a symbol of the differences between Chase and Lincoln in their prewar relations with blacks. Chase was known as the friend of blacks and he met with them often; Lincoln had not attended any meeting with blacks before becoming president.[41]

Chase's main project in the spring of 1845 was to arrange a Southern and Western Convention of the Friends of Constitutional Liberty, to be held in Cincinnati in June. As its name suggested, Chase and Bailey sought to attract men from slave states as well as free states, and they hoped to bring national leaders such as Seward. Although more than two thousand people attended, there were very few from slave states, and no leading antislavery Whigs. "I want to see and know Ohio, and I greatly want to see and know you," Seward wrote privately to Chase, but he claimed that after six years of public service, he needed to focus on his private law practice. In a public letter, however, Seward denounced slavery, as did William Jay and Horace Greeley, the eccentric but influential founder and editor of the *New-York Tribune*. All these letters were read aloud at the convention and printed in the reports of its work.[42]

When Chase called the convention to order, on the morning of June 11, the immense hall was filled with delegates and observers. In the afternoon session, Chase delivered the address he had drafted, an essay of about ten thousand words, soon printed as a pamphlet. Chase started with a detailed history, quoting from and interpreting the Declaration of Independence, the Northwest Ordinance and the Constitution. He quoted Washington, Jefferson, and others to show that the revolutionary generation hoped and expected that the Southern states would before long abolish slavery. Chase then described how, contrary to these early expectations, the Slave Power now dominated the federal government. Most of the presidents, starting with Washington, had been from the slave states; most of the justices of the Supreme Court were from the slave states; and the Three-Fifths Clause ensured that the slave states had more than their fair share of members of the House. Even at the lower levels of the federal government, most of the federal employees in Washington were from the slave states: more than one hundred each from Maryland and Virginia but only six from Ohio. The result was that, at every turn, the interests of the slave states, and especially slave owners, prevailed over those of the free states and freedom.[43]

The immediate reaction to Chase's address was mixed. One delegate, Quintus Atkins, complained about a passage in which Chase criticized both the Whig and Democratic Parties, saying that the Democrats were not true to their professed democratic principles. For Atkins, this looked like "awful squinting towards the Democratic Party." Chase responded in a long letter, saying that he tried to reflect not only his own views but also those of the Liberty Party, and that he was not urging a union of the Liberty and Democratic Parties, but rather damning the Democrats for their failures. Seward generally approved of Chase's address but told him he wished he had omitted the comments about the Whigs and the Democrats, because they would prevent the speech from being printed in Whig or Democratic newspapers. William Jay applauded the address more fully, writing to Chase that it was "noble and dignified." In the longer run, Chase's address would become an important source of ideas in the antislavery movement, the Republican Party, and postwar policy.[44]

The health of Chase's wife, Eliza, continued to decline in early 1845. He wrote his friend Cleveland that: "Her disease seems to make slow but certain progress, and the hope of a favorable event has become exceedingly faint." In late July Chase departed for the East, accompanied by Eliza, his sisters Alice and Helen, and his daughter, Kate, now almost five years old. Chase hoped to consult some doctors there about Eliza's condition and also to visit some antislavery leaders, such as Gerrit Smith and William Seward in upstate New York. All of this proved impossible. Writing to Smith from Buffalo, Chase explained that the "health of my dear wife, to benefit which was the primary object of my journey, has become so very precarious that we are under the necessity of retracing our steps." They traveled slowly, not reaching Cincinnati until the middle of August.[45]

There, at the end of September 1845, Eliza Ann Smith Chase, not yet twenty-four years old, died of tuberculosis. Writing to his friend Cleveland on the day of the funeral, Chase said that he had "laid all that was mortal of my precious wife in the tomb, and I feel as if my heart was broken. I write weeping." His one consolation was that, during her last months, they had "spoken of her probable departure, and she seemed always to have her hope in Christ; and during the few days before her death, I repeatedly spoke to her of the Savior, and she expressed her trust in Him as the sufficient foundation of her hope." Four weeks later, Chase wrote to Cleveland again that he could not yet believe that his wife was gone. "Like the weeping Rachel, my heart refused to be comforted." Yet somehow Chase carried on through his grief, both with his legal work and with his antislavery crusade.[46]

About two hundred Liberty Party men gathered in Columbus in late December 1845 for their state convention, with Chase presiding as well as drafting the resolutions. The first resolution declared that the Liberty men were not "indifferent in regard to questions of currency, trade, and territorial extension" but regarded all these issues as less important than the paramount question of "slavery and freedom." Another resolution praised "the independent Democracy of New Hampshire" and its "able and intrepid" leader, John Parker Hale. (The "Democracy" in the nineteenth century was another term for the Democratic Party.) A former member of Congress, exiled from the Democratic Party because of his antislavery views, Hale was leading a strong third party in New Hampshire, styling itself the Independent Democracy. At the convention, Chase's name was among the four suggested for the Liberty candidate for Ohio governor. After he declined, the convention nominated his friend Samuel Lewis, a former superintendent of state schools.[47]

Chase wrote to Hale a few weeks later, introducing himself and saying that he had "long thought it of great importance to base the action of the Liberty Party upon Democratic principles." He believed that "the Liberty Party can accomplish little as such"—in other words, in its current form. "But taking the name of Democrats, which justly belongs to us, and contending for Liberty for all as the consequence of Democratic principles, we can compel the whole body of the existing Democracy except such parts as are incurably servile to come upon our ground." Chase longed "to see the Liberty Party completely merged in a True Democracy, organized not in one state only but in every state where there are freemen enough to organize it." This was the first time, but far from the last, that Chase would write about combining the antislavery party and the Democratic Party. Other people talked about merging the Liberty Party with the Northern Whig Party, for there were far more antislavery Whigs than antislavery Democrats. But Chase, partly because he generally agreed with the Democrats on economic issues, and partly because he viewed himself as a Jeffersonian Democrat, always favored merging with the Democrats and opposed merging with the Whigs. Others were less convinced, including Hale, who wrote back that he did not "know not what to say in answer to your suggestions."[48]

In May 1846 news arrived in Cincinnati and elsewhere that Mexican forces had attacked American troops along the Rio Grande River. Many Whigs believed that President Polk had provoked the attack by sending an army into a region that Mexico viewed (with considerable justification) as Mexican territory. "Our government has been utterly wrong in this whole matter," declared Horace Greeley in the *New-York Tribune*. "No true honor, no national benefit, can possibly accrue from an unjust war." Polk, in his war message to Congress, insisted that "Mexico has passed the boundary of the United States, has invaded the territory of the United States, has shed American blood upon American soil." Polk did not ask Congress to declare war against Mexico; instead, he asked its members to declare that a state of war *already existed* and to appropriate funds to

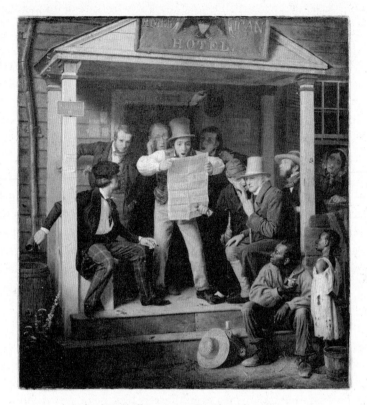

Richard Woodville's painting War News from Mexico *captures the eagerness with which Americans read the papers in the nineteenth century and the way in which news was shared.*

carry on the war. Congress soon passed Polk's war resolution, with some Whigs joining so that they would not be seen as denying financial support for troops in the field.[49]

Most Liberty men deplored the Mexican War, but Chase's views were more mixed. When his friend Cassius Marcellus Clay wrote from Kentucky that he would be leading a company of volunteers to fight in Mexico, Chase did not attempt to dissuade him. Indeed, Chase defended Clay in a letter to Gerrit Smith, writing that Clay hoped "to contribute to [the war's] speediest termination, by aiding in striking such blows as would compel the Mexicans to ask for peace." Clay also believed, wrote Chase, that by leading troops, he could "so effectively silence the clamor of his adversaries that he would, on his return to Kentucky, be enabled to wield a far more potent influence than ever in behalf of Liberty." Smith was not persuaded, however, writing back that Clay was "guilty of going forth to murder his innocent fellow men."[50]

In June 1846, during a speech Chase gave at a Liberty rally near Cincinnati, opponents threw "rotten eggs and other missiles" at him. Chase paused, and a hostile voice from the crowd shouted, "Why don't you go where the slaves are?" Chase responded, "I *am* where they are. What slavery can be worse than that where free discussion, the only safeguard of liberty, is suppressed by violence?" That same month, the New Hampshire Legislature elected John Hale to a six-year term as one of the state's two federal senators. (Federal senators were selected by state legislatures, not elected by the people, until the Seventeenth Amendment was adopted in 1913.) Abolitionist and antislavery newspapers rejoiced in Hale's election, for he would be the first true antislavery man in the Senate. Hale's election was the result of a coalition between the Whigs and the Hale Democrats—just the sort of balance of power coalition that Chase had predicted a few years earlier and that would elect him in a few years' time.[51]

Although the war was far from over, Polk asked Congress in August 1846 for an appropriation to acquire territory from Mexico in the peace negotiation. During the House debate on this request, David Wilmot, a Pennsylvania Democrat, proposed an amendment: "that, as an express and fundamental condition of the acquisition of any territory from the Republic of Mexico . . . neither slavery nor involuntary servitude shall ever exist in any part of said territory, except for crime, whereof the party shall first be duly convicted." This was the Wilmot Proviso, based on the Northwest Ordinance, never enacted into law yet still a milestone in American history. The House adopted Wilmot's proposal, and the appropriation, on sectional votes, with almost all Northern members voting in favor, and almost all Southern members voting against. Disregarding party lines in this way was unusual, up to this point in American history. The appropriation then moved to the Senate, where it died at the end of the congressional session. Although the proviso did not become law, Chase felt encouraged to see so many Northern Democrats voting in its favor, writing to Giddings that "Wilmot's Proviso will exert a tremendous influence."[52]

Chase and Giddings were writing each other at this time about a possible meeting to discuss Whig-Liberty cooperation. Chase told Giddings frankly that he disagreed with the Whigs on many issues. "I do not believe in a high tariff, a Bank of the United States, or any system of corporate banking." (This was a surprising statement from a man who had, a decade earlier, strongly supported the Bank of the United States and served as a director of Lafayette Bank.) Giddings responded that, however much they might disagree about banks and tariffs, Whigs and Liberty men would probably agree on questions such as repealing Ohio's odious Black Laws. Chase replied that what he had in mind—and hoped Giddings had in mind—was "a union among antislavery men upon an antislavery platform without reference to former party connections." Chase also shared with Giddings a copy of his Liberty Man's Creed, saying that it had been "widely circulated and everywhere endorsed by the Liberty Press."[53]

In the course of this correspondence, Chase congratulated Giddings on being nominated for Congress. Giddings might have congratulated Chase for the same reason, for the local Liberty Party nominated Chase for Congress in early September, and this time he did *not* decline. When Giddings read part of Chase's letter at a Whig political rally, however, suggesting that Chase favored the Whigs, a reader wrote the *Cleveland American* to criticize Chase for abandoning his principles. Chase responded in a letter to the editor, and in a letter to Giddings, that he was committed to the principles of the Liberty Party. Chase carefully did not say that he was committed to the party itself, for he was not; he was seeking a way to build a broader antislavery party.[54]

In Ohio, most men who voted for the Liberty Party were former Whigs. Worried that Whig defections would allow the Democrats to prevail, the Whig candidate for governor, William Bebb, started to call for repeal of some of the state's Black Laws. "The law by which negro children are prevented from enjoying the benefit of our common schools," Bebb said in a speech, "should be repealed. The law that compels negroes to give security for their good behavior should be repealed. The law that prevents them from giving testimony in our courts should be repealed." Some Democrats immediately attacked Bebb, calling him an abolitionist and arguing that the state should retain the Black Laws, especially those that (at least on paper) limited black immigration to Ohio. "What can hinder the people of the state from complete inundation by the useless, toil-worn slaves of the masters of Virginia?" asked one paper. "Repeal the laws, and what shall keep the poorhouses from being glutted, and the county treasuries from impoverishment?" On the Black Laws, Chase agreed with Bebb and other antislavery Whigs, even while he agreed with Democrats on issues such as banking laws.[55]

Like many nineteenth-century elections in Ohio, the gubernatorial election of 1846 was close. Bebb prevailed with 118,857 votes, while the Democrat David Tod had 116,849, and the Liberty man Samuel Lewis, 10,799. In Hamilton County, as expected, Chase ran a distant third for the House seat. But Chase was encouraged by the serious discussion of repealing the Black Laws and by Lewis's strong showing.[56]

In November 1846, at the age of thirty-eight, Chase took a pause from politics and legal work to marry for the third time. His bride, Sarah Bella Ludlow, was the twenty-six-year-old granddaughter of one of the founders of Cincinnati, Israel Ludlow. Chase probably met Belle, as he called her, through her father, an abolitionist colleague of James Birney. Both of Belle's parents had died before she married, so the wedding was held at the home of her aunt Sarah Ludlow McLean and her husband, Justice John McLean. The minister was Charles McIlvaine, the Episcopal bishop of Ohio. After the wedding, Chase and Belle went away for a couple of weeks, leading to the first letter we have from Chase's daughter, Kate, age six. "How soon will you be back?" she demanded to know.[57]

After years of delay, Chase and Seward learned in late 1846 that the Supreme Court would consider and decide the *Jones v. Van Zandt* case that winter. Justice McLean (now Chase's relative through their marriages into the Ludlow family) informed Chase that the court would not hear oral argument but would consider written briefs. The court's rules allowed for more than one brief from parties represented by more than one lawyer, and so Chase and Seward each drafted and submitted to the court, in February 1847, a detailed written argument. Chase's *Van Zandt* brief ran to more than one hundred printed pages.[58]

Like any good lawyer, he focused closely on the words of the statute, the 1793 Fugitive Slave Act, and on the wording of the plaintiff's complaint. For example: Chase contended that Van Zandt did not "harbor" or "conceal" the slave who escaped because he was sitting in the driver's seat, visible to all, driving the wagon. Nor did Van Zandt harbor any of the other slaves, because they were traveling along the road, not hiding in a house or other enclosed space. Chase also insisted that the phrase "after notice" in the statute required notice from the owner to the person accused, so that even if the alleged fugitives told Van Zandt they were fugitives, that was not enough, for that was not notice from their owner.[59]

Chase renewed and extended his arguments about why the 1793 act was unconstitutional. The Constitution did not refer, at any point, to slaves; the so-called Fugitive Slave Clause applied only to *persons* held to service in one state who escaped into another state. If alleged fugitive slaves were *persons*, they were protected by the Fifth Amendment, which declared that "no *person* shall be deprived of life, liberty, or property without due process of law." The process in federal fugitive slave cases, Chase argued, was "no process of law at all"; it was as if a man found his missing horse in his neighbor's barn, but instead of going to court to prove title to the horse, he seized the animal and then showed an affidavit to "his own hired magistrate." Fugitive slaves were also protected by the Fourth Amendment, which provides that "the right of the people to be secure in their persons, houses, papers, and effects, against unreasonable searches and seizures, shall not be violated." How, Chase asked rhetorically, "can the people be subjected to seizures more unreasonable than under this act of Congress?" There was also the Sixth Amendment, which promised the right to a jury trial—a right, under the act, not granted to alleged slaves. The proper construction of the Fugitive Slave Clause was that it was a mere compact among the states, akin to other compacts among the states, and not a grant of power to Congress, and thus Congress had no authority to legislate on the matter at all.[60]

Chase concluded by expressing the hope that the court would construe the Constitution to bring it into line with "that other Constitution, which, rising, in sublime majesty, over all human enactments—antedating them all, surviving them all—finds its seat in the bosom of God." He noted that on questions "which partake largely of a moral and political nature, the judgment, even of this court, cannot be regarded as altogether final. The decision to be made here must, necessarily, be rejudged at the tribunal of public opinion." He alluded to the way in which William Lloyd Garrison attacked the Constitution, and he prayed the court would "rescue the Constitution from the undeserved opprobrium of lending its sanction to the idea that there may be property in men."[61]

The Supreme Court took less than a month to decide the *Van Zandt* case against Chase and his client. The decision was unanimous. On the notice point, the court ruled that notice from the owner was not required; it was sufficient if the defendant knew or should have known from all the circumstances that those whom he had helped were fugitive slaves. On the harbor or conceal point, the justices decided that any action making it harder for a master to recapture his fugitive slave was "harboring and concealing" under the act. And, without addressing Chase's arguments in any detail, the court said that the Fugitive Slave Act was constitutional, saying that the courts had long agreed on the "validity as well as the expediency of the act."[62]

Chase was disappointed but not much surprised by the Supreme Court's decision. In a letter to his friend Lewis Tappan, he commented that "truth is truth" and "it will prevail at last." Indeed, some of the points in Chase's brief—widely circulated in pamphlet form—would "prevail at last" after the Civil War in the Fourteenth Amendment, the first section of which would require the *states* as well as the federal government to respect the rights of all citizens. Chase was pleased that the *New-York Tribune* had printed part of Seward's *Van Zandt* argument and that the case had brought him closer to the former New York governor, whom he regarded "as one of the very first public men of the country." Chase wished that "the liberal-minded of all parties could be prevailed upon to take him up for the presidency," but he predicted this would prove impossible in the present party situation. "In the presidential chair or out of it, however, William H. Seward will possess an honor and estimation with the lovers of truth, humanity, and freedom which is better than the presidency."[63]

In a letter to John Hale, Chase commented that it was "strange that the proslavery construction of the Constitution, so utterly indefensible, upon history or by reason, should be so tamely acquiesced in by the courts." Chase agreed with Hale that they "should be open, bold, indignant, and emphatic in our denunciation" of this view of the Constitution. "If the courts will not overthrow it," he predicted, "the people will, even if it be necessary to overthrow the courts also."[64]

John Van Zandt did not live long after the Supreme Court's decision. Chase saw the farmer once in Cincinnati in April 1847 and related in a letter that "consumption is doing her deadly work upon him surely though slowly." When Chase asked Van Zandt whether he regretted helping the fugitives, "the old man's eye lighted up" as he insisted that he did not regret *anything* he had done to help them. A few weeks later, after Van Zandt died, Chase reported to Sydney Howard Gay, editor of the *National Anti-Slavery Standard*, that Van Zandt died confident that he had "done no wrong," and that "in succoring the needy and delivering the oppressed he was just following in the footsteps of Him who 'went about doing good.'"[65]

This spring of 1847 was a season of death for Chase. His older brother Alexander, who had been living with Chase and his wife in Cincinnati, died in late March, apparently of a stroke. When his friend and physician Noah Worcester died of consumption, Chase wrote in his diary that he was "learned, without pretension; cheerful, without levity; earnest, without fanaticism; he was a good physician, a good citizen, a good friend. I wish his Christian character had been more open to observation." Then two weeks later, Edmund Smith, younger brother of Chase's late wife Eliza, also died of consumption. "He was conscious almost to the last moment, and perfectly resigned," Chase wrote in his diary, adding, "I trust he has found acceptance with God." The fall, however, brought new life: a daughter, Janet, known as Nettie, who would be one of Salmon Chase's only two children to survive him.[66]

Chase continued in 1847 both to work within the Liberty Party and to explore alternatives. He wrote Hale and Tappan to raise the idea of recruiting antislavery men from all the parties to form a Liberty League—a group committed "to vote for no man who is not reliably known to be opposed to the extension of slavery and in favor of expelling it from all the ground which it now unconstitutionally holds, and of discouraging and discountenancing it by example and recommendation." What Chase had in mind, at least at first, was *not* a new political party, for he wrote that "to build up a new party is by no means as easy as to compel old parties to do a particular work." Looking at the two major parties, Chase predicted that the Whig nominee for president in 1848 would be General Zachary Taylor, a Southern slaveholder who was winning glory in the ongoing Mexican War. The proper Democratic response, Chase thought, would be to nominate someone like the Barnburner leader Silas Wright of New York, to embrace the Wilmot Proviso, and thus to "rally the antislavery sentiment against the hero sentiment." In a July 1847 letter to Preston King, another leading New York Democrat, Chase went further, suggesting that if the Democrats would nominate Wright, on a Wilmot platform, he would support them. "For myself," Chase wrote, "I sympathize strongly with the Democratic Party in almost everything except its submission to slaveholding leadership and dictation."[67]

By this time, American troops under General Winfield Scott were marching from Veracruz toward Mexico City, which they would capture in September 1847. Democrats looked forward to the peace negotiations, hoping that the United States would obtain as part of the treaty at least California and New Mexico, perhaps much more. Many Whigs wanted "No More Territory," saying that the United States did not need additional land. One Whig paper argued that the only sure way to prevent the extension of slavery was not to acquire territory into which slavery could extend, while another predicted presciently that if the United States acquired a large part of Mexico, "the mighty question involved in the Wilmot Proviso will be let loose with its disastrous consequences, and the Union will be violently rent asunder." Chase agreed with the Democrats on this point. The "cry of no territory," he wrote to Hale, was "the merest delusion and the most palpable deception." The Whig slogans, "no territory" and "withdraw our troops," were "humbug" in Chase's view because "we must have territory and we cannot withdraw our troops. Let us have an honorable peace and free territory."[68]

Some Whigs, notably Senator Thomas Corwin of Ohio, a presidential candidate, blamed the Liberty Party for the Mexican War, arguing that if the Liberty men had just voted for Clay in 1844, he would be president, and there would be no war. "They prate a good deal about the sufferings of the poor slave," said Corwin in a speech, "and yet by their ill-advised, impolitic, and reckless course have made his condition infinitely worse, and in all probability entailed upon the country perpetual slavery." Chase was with Corwin on the platform for some reason, and Corwin asked Chase whether he regretted having voted for Birney. When Chase shook his head no, Corwin said that he felt sorry for Chase, adding, "I do not question your sincerity, but I pity your ignorance." Chase, sending clippings about Corwin to his friend Sumner, wrote that he had hoped the senator would come around to an independent antislavery stance. "He is where he was, however," he conceded, "and there I must leave him, until he comes to a better mind."[69]

Another Whig, Abraham Lincoln, at the time a freshman member of Congress, questioned Polk's claim that he called for war because Mexico had "shed American blood upon American soil." Unlike Chase, whose main concern about the Mexican War was the extension of slavery, Lincoln said nothing in this speech about slavery; his concern was just to attack Polk. Lincoln posed a series of questions and demanded that Polk answer them "fully, fairly, and candidly." If he did not, Lincoln would be "fully convinced, of what I more than suspect already, that he is deeply conscious of being in the wrong; that he feels the blood of this war, like the blood of Abel, is crying to Heaven against him . . . that originally having some strong motive . . . to involve the two countries in a war, and trusting to escape scrutiny by fixing the public gaze upon the exceeding brightness of military glory—that attractive rainbow that rises in showers of blood—that serpent's eye that charms to destroy—he plunged into it, and has swept *on* and *on*, till, disappointed in his calculation of the ease with which Mexico might be subdued, he now finds himself he knows not where." Not surprisingly Polk ignored Lincoln and his questions.[70]

Within the Liberty Party, in late 1847, eastern leaders wanted to nominate candidates before the end of the year, but Chase and Bailey wanted to delay nominations until the spring. Bailey was now in Washington, where he was the publisher and editor of the *National Era*, a weekly antislavery paper. In a letter printed in Bailey's paper, Chase said that by delaying their nominations, the Liberty men could show antislavery men in other parties that "nothing is to be expected from the old parties." Then the Liberty men could invite all those opposed to slavery to "come with us, and aid in the selection of true antislavery candidates and give them your support." Chase wrote to John Hale that he hoped events would "prepare the way for the organization not of a Liberty Party, exactly, but of an Independent Party, occupying Liberty and Liberal ground, making Slavery or Freedom the paramount issue." Here was the template for the new party that Chase, Bailey, and others would form the next year: the Free Soil Party.[71]

The Liberty Party had called for a national convention in Buffalo in late October. As the date approached, there was discussion about not only whether this should be a nominating convention but also whether Chase should be nominated for vice president. Chase discouraged this idea. As he wrote to an antislavery lawyer in New York, "I am comparatively young, and unknown, and my services to the cause have been slight in comparison with many others." Bailey agreed. "Were we united, were there no prospect of disgraceful distractions, were there grounds for anticipating a marked increase of the Liberty vote and a steady growth of the party for many years to come," Bailey wrote to Chase, "I should say by all means accept the nomination." Given their doubts on all these points, however, Bailey advised Chase to wait.[72]

Chase traveled to Buffalo to delay nominations, but when the convention voted in favor of immediate nominations, Chase announced that Ohio would "cheerfully submit" to the majority's approach. The convention nominated Hale for president, and someone suggested Chase for vice president, but he "peremptorily declined," after which Leicester King, a judge and former Ohio state senator, received the nomination. Gerrit Smith tried to persuade the convention to adopt a resolution declaring that slavery anywhere in the United States, even the original slave states, was contrary to the Constitution. Chase led the effort to defeat this proposal, viewing it as a serious misreading of the Constitution, placing vague language about "freedom" over specific limits on the federal government's powers.[73]

Chase was not too troubled by these late 1847 nominations, because he believed that both Hale and King would make way if a broader antislavery coalition formed in 1848. And he was quite encouraged by another convention that more or less coincided with the one in Buffalo: a gathering of Barnburner Democrats in Herkimer, New York. The Barnburners were livid that the mainline Democrats had refused, at their state convention in Syracuse, New York, even to consider antislavery resolutions. Chase wrote to Sumner to rejoice that the Barnburners had "repudiated the Syracuse Servilism. They resolved that the Wilmot Proviso—the stone which the builders rejected—should be made the head of the corner." Chase suggested the possibility of a "great convention of all antislavery men" in Pittsburgh in May or June 1848. If the Liberty men could unite with both the Barnburner Democrats from New York and Conscience Whigs such as Sumner from Massachusetts, they could perhaps gain hundreds of thousands of votes, perhaps carry several states, perhaps force the election into the House of Representatives—perhaps even *win* the presidential election in the House.[74]

On his way back from Buffalo to Cincinnati, Chase stopped for two weeks in Columbus to try another fugitive slave case. Chase's client was Francis Parish, a lawyer in Sandusky, Ohio, charged with harboring two Kentucky slaves, Jane Garrison and her five-year-old son, and with obstructing their arrest. The evidence for the slaveowner was principally from his agent, a Colonel Mitchell, who testified that when he approached Parish's house and asked whether Jane Garrison and the boy were there, Parish said that they were, and that first Jane and then the boy came out of the house. When Mitchell announced that he was there to arrest the blacks and take them back to Kentucky, Parish asked on what authority. Mitchell answered that he had a power of attorney, and Parish said that was not enough; he would need a court order. At this point, according to

Mitchell, Parish pushed Jane and her son back into the house and closed the door.[75]

The evidence in defense of Parish came from several respected figures, including two judges. They testified that Mitchell had told a very different story at a prior trial, right after the events in question, when Mitchell had agreed to Parish's version of events, and admitted that Parish had not "directed or pushed the servants into his home." After a full day of deliberation, the jury found against Parish, imposing two fines of $500 each. Chase moved for a new trial, and Justice McLean granted his motion.[76]

There is an interesting contrast here between Chase and Lincoln, for at almost this same time, in October 1847, Lincoln was involved in a fugitive slavery case in Illinois, representing the master rather than the slave. Lincoln's client, Robert Matson, brought a woman and her children from Kentucky to Illinois, holding and working them as slaves in southern Illinois. Matson claimed that he was a Kentucky citizen and that the slaves were only in the state "temporarily"—even though this temporary residence had lasted for two years. The Illinois court made short work of this argument, ruling that the alleged slaves were free. Some of Lincoln's biographers do not even mention the *Matson* case, others downplay it, and a few condemn Lincoln's choice to take on the case. A lawyer does not have to represent every client who walks through his door. Lincoln deserves blame for agreeing to represent Matson in this case, just as Chase deserves credit for working to free his many black clients.[77]

When Chase reached Cincinnati in December 1847, he found the Ohio River flooding the city. In a letter to the *National Era*, over his pen name Marcellus, Chase reported that "the water has entered many of the buildings near the river, and serious apprehensions are entertained that the stores and dwellings on Front and Columbia Streets will be invaded." The other main issue in town was the price of pork, which was worth only half as much as in the prior year. "This great reduction in the price of our staple indicates, of course, a corresponding reduction in the income of the state during the next year, and many already begin to predict hard times." Turning to politics, Chase wrote that there was "unusual interest" in the imminent Democratic state convention. Rank-and-file Democrats, Chase claimed, were committed to the Wilmot Proviso, but this "Herkimer [antislavery] spirit is much dreaded by many, perhaps most, of the Democratic leaders." Quoting but not naming his friend Edwin Stanton, an Ohio lawyer who would later join Chase in the Lincoln Cabinet, Chase wrote that if the Columbus convention followed the lead of Syracuse and took no stand on slavery, "there must be another Herkimer"—that is, an antislavery revolt against the mainstream Democrats. In a postscript, Chase advised that the Ohio River was still rising and that some churches were providing shelter "for families driven from their homes."[78]

Chase worked steadily in the first few months of 1848 to build a broad antislavery coalition. He went from Cincinnati to Columbus in January, hoping to work with antislavery Democrats such as Edwin Stanton to persuade their state convention to adopt strong antislavery resolutions. In this he was disappointed, for Stanton did not even show up in Columbus, and the resolutions of the convention were weak. Chase was writing at this time both to leading Whigs, including Charles Sumner and Joshua Giddings, and to leading Democrats such as Ohio's Jacob Brinkerhoff and Benjamin Tappan (Lewis Tappan's older brother). He was also courting editors, including Edward Hamlin of the *Cleveland True Democrat*, which declared in early March that there were enough antislavery men to "control the next presidential election. For this purpose, they must unite. They must set aside their party bickerings and party prejudices and come together for the salvation of the Constitution and the cause of liberty."[79]

In March and April Chase circulated in Ohio a printed letter, calling for the "friends of Freedom, Free Territory, and Free Labor, without distinction of party, to meet in Mass Convention, at Columbus, on Saturday, the seventeenth day of June, the anniversary of Bunker Hill." Explaining why a convention was necessary, Chase noted that the United States was about to acquire an immense territory from Mexico. The Slave Power, he warned, would demand that this region become first slave territories and then slave states, and would further demand "that the trade in living men and women shall be permitted in them by the national authority; that free labor and free laborers shall be virtually excluded from them by being subjected to degrading competition with slave-labor and slave-laborers." More than two thousand men, from all Ohio parties, signed Chase's call, which started to appear in the newspapers in mid-May. Some, however, refused, with Brinkerhoff writing to Chase that the movement was bound to fail, while others were horrified. Lewis Tappan chastised Chase for deserting the Liberty Party.[80]

At the Democratic National Convention in Baltimore in late May, the party nominated Senator Lewis Cass of Michigan for president, adopted a platform that condemned abolitionists, and insisted that each state should decide for itself on slavery. Barnburners were outraged when the convention, faced with two delegations from New York, opted to seat half the delegates from each side, thereby denying seats to half the anti-slavery New Yorkers. They were equally appalled by the platform, which in no way criticized or questioned slavery, and by the choice of Cass, whom they derided as a "dough-face"—an insulting term for a spineless, Southern-sympathizing Northern politician. Immediately afterward, Barnburners started making plans to hold their own convention in upstate New York.[81]

At the Whig National Convention in Philadelphia in early June, the party nominated Zachary Taylor, an army hero with no known political positions, for president. Their choice for vice president was Millard Fillmore, an upstate New Yorker notably soft on slavery. The Whigs attempted to sidestep the slavery issue by adopting no platform whatsoever. Antislavery Whigs, both in Philadelphia and elsewhere, were incensed. Within a few days, a half dozen Whig papers in Ohio had announced that they would not support Taylor. Ohio's *Ashtabula Sentinel* declared that Western Reserve Whigs would refuse to back "a man whose hands are red with the blood of innocents and who is in favor of extending the curse of slavery upon territory now free."[82]

On June 20 and 21, 1848, Chase and about a thousand others gathered in Columbus for what they called the "State Independent Free Territory Convention." As Chase hoped, this state convention endorsed the idea of a national coalition convention to take place in Buffalo on the ninth of August and deferred nominating state or national candidates until then. In addition, the Columbus convention adopted a strong set of antislavery resolutions, drafted by Chase, insisting that there should be no more slave states and no more slave territory. Even the state's leading Whig paper expressed mild praise for Chase's work at the convention, saying that he was "distinguished for his energy and ambition" and now "stands at the head of the free territory interests in Ohio."[83]

The very next day, the Barnburners gathered in Utica, New York, and nominated former president Martin Van Buren as their candidate for president. Chase was disappointed that the Barnburners had nominated Van Buren rather than waiting for the Buffalo convention, writing to Hale that he "would have greatly preferred a general convention and united action and a different nominee." Among other things, Chase reminded Hale of the way in which Van Buren had pledged in his 1837 inaugural address to oppose any attempt by Congress to abolish slavery in the District of Columbia. But Chase was prepared to forgive the man he had once called "cold, selfish, intriguing, base, and faithless"—even to support him—if Van Buren would now commit himself to antislavery.[84]

By July, Chase was in favor of Van Buren, writing to the former president's son that "the best possible nomination for the presidency has been made at Utica, provided the name of John McLean can be associated with it." Chase's support for McLean was odd: the justice might have been antislavery in his private letters, but in his judicial opinions, McLean almost always ruled against slaves and those attempting to assist them. For example, he had joined in the unanimous opinion in the *Van Zandt* case. In a couple of letters to McLean, Chase tried to see whether he would accept a nomination, but the justice was evasive. At the end of the month, Henry Stanton, an antislavery leader in New York, known to history as the husband of the suffragist Elizabeth Cady Stanton, wrote to Chase that he was "satisfied that Mr. Van Buren must be the man for the presidential candidate. There is no avoiding it. Nor am I satisfied that it would be well to do so if we could. He is strong in states and regions where the antislavery aspects of the question have not taken very strong hold. Besides, the main prop of the Slave Power has been the Northern Democracy; and he is the man to shiver that in pieces and forever." Chase agreed.[85]

When Chase reached Buffalo in early August 1848, he found the city thronged; perhaps ten thousand or even twenty thousand people were present. There were delegates from every free state and three slave states: Delaware, Maryland, and Virginia. There were Liberty men like himself, Henry Stanton, and Joshua Leavitt. There were antislavery Democrats, including Preston King, Samuel Tilden, David Dudley Field (leading New York lawyer and law reformer), and Benjamin Butler (not the future general but the New York lawyer of the same name). And there were antislavery Whigs such as Joshua Giddings, Charles Francis Adams (son of the late John Quincy Adams), and Richard Henry Dana Jr. (the Boston lawyer and author of *Two Years Before the Mast*). A number of black leaders were present, too, including Frederick Douglass, already famous for his first autobiography and now editing an abolitionist newspaper in nearby Rochester. Whether Chase met Douglass at this time or had met him somewhat earlier, we do not know. Douglass would later recall that he knew Chase from "early antislavery days" and that Chase welcomed him "to his home and to his table when to do so was a strange thing."[86]

The Buffalo Free Soil Convention was really two parallel conventions: a public outdoor convention of thousands and a private "conference committee," in the Universalist Church, of about a hundred men. This smaller group, chaired by Chase, included the major leaders, and nominally reported to the larger gathering. Chase, the principal author of the resolutions of the Buffalo convention, simply copied from his Columbus resolutions in many places. "No more slave states and no more slave territory," the Buffalo platform declared. To reassure Southern states, however, the platform also confirmed that slavery was a matter of state law: "We therefore propose no interference by Congress with slavery in any state where it exists." For Chase, this was a retreat from his earlier argument that slavery was not allowed in any state formed from the Louisiana Territory, but he knew that such a compromise was necessary to secure moderate votes. The Buffalo platform also addressed issues *other* than slavery, advocating cheap postage; retrenchment of federal expenses; river and harbor improvements; and tariffs sufficient to allow for the "earliest practical payment of the national debt." [87]

Building on the land reform ideas of the radical reformer George Henry Evans, the Free Soil platform called for the federal government to grant "reasonable portions of the public lands" to "actual settlers." The phrase *free soil* thus had two meanings: Chase and others wanted to see free states formed from the western territories, and, as a means to this end (and to the broader, fairer distribution of land), they wanted to see land granted to those who actually settled the territories. "We inscribe on our banner," Chase and the platform declared, "Free Soil, Free Speech, Free Labor, and Free Men," and under this banner "we will fight on and fight ever, until a triumphant victory shall reward our exertions." A few months later, Chase recalled in a letter that, at one point, he had deleted those words, thinking them "too magniloquent," but ultimately had restored them. In hindsight, "really, it now seems to me one of the best resolutions in the set." Indeed, Chase's call for free soil and free men would become central not only to the Free Soil Party but also to its successor the Republican Party, and in American history.[88]

After the platform was drafted and agreed upon, it was read to the crowds outside, who cheered it sentence by sentence. The conference committee then returned to the church, with Chase again in the chair, to nominate candidates. Benjamin Butler, Van Buren's friend and former law partner, read aloud a letter from the former president opposing the extension of slavery into the territories and expressing support for the convention. Stanton followed by saying that Hale would "submit to the action of this convention." The delegates voted, with Van Buren receiving 244 votes and Hale, 183 votes. Chase then recognized the venerable abolitionist Joshua Leavitt. According to a young lawyer from Indiana, George Julian, later a leading Republican member of Congress, Leavitt was "full of emotion and seemed at first to lack the power of utterance, while the stillness of death prevailed in the convention." Leavitt explained why even he, who had worked so long for the Liberty Party, was now leaving it to support Free Soil and Van Buren. At this, Julian recalled, "the mingled political enthusiasm and religious fervor of the convention broke over all bounds and utterly defied description." The delegates agreed to make the nomination of Van Buren unanimous and, after a short break, named Charles Francis Adams candidate for vice president. There had been some talk about Chase as the vice presidential nominee, but he discouraged the idea, thinking that the new party needed a stronger name than his own.[89]

At about nine thirty in the evening, Chase, as president of the conference committee, mounted the outside platform and announced the nominations. The name of Van Buren, he declared, was "always illustrious but rendered doubly so by the conduct of his friends at this convention." The name of Adams was "honored" both because of Charles Francis as well as his famous father and grandfather. The crowd greeted the nominations with "indescribable" enthusiasm. "The tent was filled to its utmost capacity," reported the *Buffalo Daily Republic*. "All were cheering, swinging their hats and handkerchiefs." There was a marching band, there were banners, there were a few further speeches, and then the national Free Soil Convention adjourned.[90]

Chase was rightfully proud of his work in Buffalo. He and his friends had managed the delicate task of merging three political factions—the Liberty Party and the antislavery Whigs and Democrats—into a single new national party, the Free Soil Party. Chase had earned and received praise for his work, with one paper commenting that "there was no man at the Buffalo convention more deservedly influential and more generally respected than Mr. Chase." The convention was the end of a long and often lonely process for him, creating a broader national antislavery party. Now another difficult undertaking was about to begin: transforming the enthusiasm of the convention into actual votes for the Free Soil ticket.[91]

CHAPTER 6

"Ambitious as Julius Caesar"

⁓ 1848–49 ⁓

After the intense week of the Buffalo convention, Chase spent a few days with his brother Edward in nearby Lockport before traveling by train to Cleveland. Upon his arrival, he addressed a crowd and announced through the *True Democrat* that he would speak almost daily for the next two weeks in northwestern Ohio. This kind of county-to-county campaign was necessary because the population of the state was so scattered. Aside from Cincinnati, with about a hundred thousand residents, and Cleveland and Columbus, with about sixteen thousand each, the people of Ohio lived in or near small, rural towns. Face-to-face politics was even more necessary because there were only ten Free Soil papers in the state, with small circulations. To spread the Free Soil gospel, Chase had no choice but to go directly to the people.[1]

Writing home to his wife on August 19, Chase reported that he had already given speeches in Painesville, Jefferson, and Orwell. His "delightful traveling companions" were John Vaughan (former editor of the *Cleveland True American*) and James Briggs (editor of the *True Democrat*). The countryside was "beautiful" and the people "remarkably intelligent." A few days later, Chase wrote to Van Buren that, although the people of the Western Reserve were enthusiastic for Free Soil, some were troubled by the stance Van Buren had taken while president about slavery in the District of Columbia. This letter "crossed in the mail" with Van Buren's lengthy letter accepting the nomination, addressed to Chase and published in the papers in late August. On the question of slavery in the district, Van Buren waffled, both defending his prior position and saying that if he was elected, and if Congress passed a bill to end slavery in the district, he would not veto the bill. It was hardly the strong statement for which Chase had hoped.[2]

Chase wrote to Belle on August 24 that he was up early and thinking of her, "towards whom my heart always yearns. . . . I love to think of your goodness, your sweetness, your good sense and untiring devotion." Chase had already given ten speeches, in seven places, of about two hours each, yet he assured his wife that his health was fine. He spoke that day in Cleveland to what the *True Democrat* called a "listening, intelligent, reasoning crowd composed of men of principle, independence, and high determination." The next day, describing for his wife how the three men had traveled by two-horse buggy from Cleveland to Chardon, Chase wrote that "Mr. Briggs is a careless driver. Often, as we came along, he would get talking so earnestly that he would let the horses go as they pleased, and in some cases we came near capsizing."[3]

Chase spoke in Painesville on August 26 to an audience of about two thousand people including (he noted in a letter to his wife) "near one hundred ladies." According to the *True Democrat,* Chase contrasted the situation in the early days of the republic, when all accepted that "slavery was a local institution" and that the "states alone where it existed had the right to regulate and control it," with the present, when the slave masters claimed that slavery was "a fact, not an institution—a relation existing of right, standing on the same footing as the relation of parent and child—and that being such a relation, it can be carried out of the limits of the local law and retain its binding force." From Cleveland, where he was spending Sunday, Chase wrote Belle that "we intend to go to Medina tomorrow, the next day to Elyria and Oberlin, the next day to Norwalk and the next to Sandusky and the next to Detroit." After these speeches, Chase intended to return to Lockport and Buffalo, to be there in time for the state fair in early September. He closed by asking Belle to kiss their daughters, Kate and Nettie.[4]

After his exhausting travels in August and early September, Chase was back in Cincinnati by the middle of the month, and although he wrote some political letters over the next few weeks, it seems that he gave no further political speeches. Perhaps he was silent because of articles such as one that appeared in late August in the *Cleveland Herald,* a

Whig paper, asserting that Chase was "an aspirant for the office of United States senator." The *Herald* claimed that he hoped to secure the seat by "electing enough pledged Van Buren members to hold the balance of power on joint ballot in the legislature." A few weeks later, the *Herald* printed a letter predicting that "every member of the next legislature from the Reserve, except senators who hold over, will be a Van Buren man. Holding the balance of power, as they will, I trust that the place William Allen has heretofore occupied in the US Senate will be filled with a Free Soil man, such a man as Giddings, Chase, [Benjamin] Tappan, or [Columbus] Delano." The *Herald* commented that "this explains the zeal of Chase and Tappan!"[5]

The editors overstated when they suggested that Chase was campaigning for himself rather than for the Free Soil cause. But the *Herald* was right on certain points. The second term of one of the state's two senators, William Allen, would end in March 1849. The new legislature elected in October 1848 would select his successor in late 1848 or early 1849. None of the parties named their candidates for senator—that was not the custom at the time—and the Free Soil Party did not nominate candidates for the statewide offices. But in some places, there were three-way contests for the legislature, with Whig, Democratic, and Free Soil candidates all seeking a single seat. It was thus possible that neither of the major parties, the Whigs or the Democrats, would have a majority in the legislature, that the Free Soil faction would hold the balance of power, and that the legislature would choose a Free Soil senator.[6]

In late September Chase was upset to learn that a Free Soil convention in Franklin County had nominated him for governor. Such a nomination violated an unwritten understanding between the Free Soil Party and the Whig candidate for governor, Seabury Ford: the Free Soil Party would not interfere in the race for governor, and Ford would not interfere in the presidential race. Chase wrote at once to the *Ohio Standard*, a new Columbus paper edited by his friend Edward Hamlin, and the *True Democrat*, through his friend John Vaughan, to state that he did *not* want to be a candidate for governor. Chase's private view was that Ford would be elected, but he noted that some former Democrats among the Free Soilers would vote for the Democrat, John Weller. Chase's letter appeared in the papers, but some men voted for him nevertheless.[7]

———

For several days after the October 10 state election, it was not clear who would be the next governor: Whigs claimed that Ford would win, while Democrats insisted that it would be Weller. It was not until October 27 that the *Ohio State Journal* printed official results showing that Ford had prevailed by about three hundred votes out of almost three hundred thousand cast. The legislative results were even less clear, in part because of a dispute about Hamilton County. During the prior winter, the Whig legislature had passed a law dividing the county into two districts: an urban district and a rural district. The Whigs hoped in this way to secure the two rural seats rather than see all five seats go to the Democrats, based on their strength in Cincinnati. Democrats denounced this law as unconstitutional and claimed the two disputed seats for Alexander Pierce and George Pugh. Whigs insisted that the law was perfectly proper and that the disputed seats belonged rightfully to George Runyan and Oliver Spencer.[8]

The legislative situation was also unclear because the party labels, such as Free Soil, did not capture the complex views of individual legislators. Most Free Soil members, for example, coming from the Whig party, remained close with their Whig friends and would favor an antislavery Whig or a Whiggish Free Soiler for senator. Other Free Soil members leaned toward the Democrats. In a letter to his wife, Chase even made up a word to describe these members: "Democratish Free Soilers." Some Whig members could not forget or forgive the way in which Joshua Giddings had left their party to join the Free Soil Party, and so they would not vote for him for Senate, even though they might agree with him on all the issues. In short, any tally of the numbers of members of the legislature in the three parties was both provisional (because of the election disputes) and imprecise (because of the personal preferences of legislators).[9]

Overlooking these complexities, some papers were speculating in late October that the Democrats and Free Soil legislators in Ohio would collaborate to elect their state's next United States senator. Chase's friend Gamaliel Bailey, in the *National Era*, wrote that if the Free Soil members indeed held the balance of power in the Ohio legislature, "their responsibility will be a heavy one." The Free Soil members would want to send to Washington a new federal senator "thoroughly versed in the principles, policy, and aims of the Free Soil movement" and one who had "by his acts proved his fidelity to its interests." Salmon Chase was just such a man. "Many years ago, when no distinction was to be won by connection with the antislavery cause, but when its adherents suffered political and social ostracism, he openly identified himself with it and has ever since been known as a wise, steadfast, and powerful upholder of its interests. No man was more influential in the organization of the present Free Soil movement."[10]

These preliminary discussions in Ohio about the choice of the state's next federal senator took place in the final weeks of the national presidential contest. Many Whigs feared that if antislavery Whigs deserted their party to vote for Free Soil, the Democrats and their candidate, Lewis Cass, would prevail. In a long open letter to Ohio Whigs, Horace Greeley, editor of the *New-York Tribune*, urged them to remain true to the Whig Party. Greeley said that there was simply no chance this year of electing a Free Soil president; even if Van Buren could carry a few states and thereby force the election into the House of Representatives, the ultimate victor would be Cass, because Democrats controlled more state delegations in the House. So the next president would be either Taylor or Cass, and even though Taylor was a Southern slave owner, and Cass a Northerner who did not own slaves, Greeley insisted that the general would prevent the spread of slavery, while Cass and the Democrats would allow and even encourage the practice. Greeley was not the only antislavery Whig who urged Northern Whigs to stick with Taylor rather than defect to Van Buren: Lincoln, Seward, and many other prominent Whigs campaigned for him. Likewise, many antislavery Democrats, such as Thomas Hart Benton in Missouri, campaigned for Cass. Perhaps sensing that there was little point, Chase did not return to the campaign trail in the final weeks of the presidential election.[11]

For the first time in American history, voters in the various states went to the polls on the same day to elect a president: November 7, 1848. Within a few days, the papers were reporting that Taylor had prevailed over Cass in a close contest. Nationwide, the Taylor-Fillmore ticket received about 47 percent of the votes, Cass about 42 percent, and Van Buren a respectable 10 percent. Van Buren did well in New York, New England, and western states such as Wisconsin. But in Ohio, as Greeley had feared, Taylor and Van Buren more or less split the antislavery vote, so that Cass carried the state. Although Van Buren did well in the Western Reserve, he received only about a tenth of the overall state vote. Chase was disappointed, writing to Sumner that "here in Ohio, we did not do near so well as we expected—not near so well as we should have done had the vote been taken immediately after the Buffalo convention."[12]

As the new state legislature gathered in Columbus in December, Chase wrote in hopeful terms to a Free Soil friend. Chase believed that the election returns would show traditional Democrats that they "must give up their alliance with the slaveholders" or else give up "their ascendancy in the free states." Chase thus expected that "sooner or later, the old Democracy must join us." He also predicted that many "true-hearted and honest Whigs" would be disappointed by Taylor on slavery issues and soon join the Free Democrats—the term he often used for the Free Soil Party. Chase noted that some people were talking about making him senator, and he would not pretend that he was "indifferent to such a mark of confidence as an election to that office would be." But he insisted that the first task was to strengthen the Free Soil Party. If "the final triumph of our cause can best be promoted by my services in the Senate, and the legislature are willing to elect me, I will try to do my duty to the Free Democracy and our noble state." But if "the majority of our friends shall think the best interests of the cause require another man and he can be elected, I shall rejoice in his election and do all I can to aid his efforts in the Senate by mine among the People." Chase added that it would be better from a personal perspective to stick to his legal career. "In a pecuniary point of view, my law office is the best office I can hold."[13]

Early on December 4, the date set for the start of the state legislative session, the Democratic members of the House, including Pierce and Pugh from Hamilton County, gathered in the House chamber and declared themselves to be the House of Representatives. A few hours later, the Whig members gathered on the other side of the chamber and declared that *they* were the lawful House. Day after day, for several weeks, the chaos continued, with two rival groups holding separate meetings, and some Free Soil members suggesting possible compromises. The state Senate, with eighteen Whigs and eighteen Democrats, was also divided, and took more than a week, and dozens of ballots, to select its speaker. The *Ohio State Journal* reported on December 19 that "men go to the statehouse with their pockets swollen with concealed weapons, and bullies armed to the teeth stand by to enforce the claims of their friends to seats in the legislature. The sales of pistols, revolvers, and other articles of private warfare in this city during the past three weeks have been enormous." In an era when violence among legislators was common in Washington, violence in the divided Ohio statehouse seemed quite possible.[14]

By this time, Chase was in Columbus, in part to prepare for legal arguments in cases before the state supreme court, in part to work with the Free Soil legislators. He explained to his wife on December 20 that the "grand matter in controversy is whether Messrs. Pugh and Pierce or Messrs. Spencer and Runyan are entitled to seats." If Pugh and Pierce received House seats, the Democrats expected, with the help of a few Free Soil members, to elect a speaker and thus control the House; if Spencer and Runyan obtained the seats, the Whigs expected, again with the help of a few Free Soil members, to control the House. "It is impossible to predict how matters will turn out," Chase wrote, but his "impression" was that the Democrats and Free Soilers would together control the House. In this scenario, "it is quite possible that I may be ultimately elected to the Senate." There were obstacles, however: "My location is unacceptable to some of the Free Soilers, all of whom are from the Reserve; and my political position is unacceptable to many of the Democrats, who naturally enough prefer a man acting fully with themselves." But since neither group could elect a senator without help from the other, and since "I am perhaps more acceptable to *both* though not to each, than any other individual, I may be elected."[15]

Thus did Chase outline and predict what would happen over the next few weeks: two of his Free Soil friends would vote to award the two contested seats to the Democrats; then the Democrats would join with the Free Soilers to select Chase as the federal senator. Chase did not predict, however, all the twists and turns of the tale, including how he would draft, and Democrats and Free Soilers would pass, a bill to repeal some of the state's ancient and odious Black Laws.

One of the new Free Soil legislators with whom Chase worked closely this winter would become a lifelong friend: Dr. Norton Townshend. Born in England in 1815, Townshend was in Cincinnati, studying medicine, at the time of the *Matilda* trial. As he watched Chase at work in that case, Townshend recalled thinking that "there is a man I can and will vote for whenever I have an opportunity." After further medical studies in Europe, Townshend returned to Ohio, where he worked as a doctor and joined the Liberty Party. He attended the Buffalo convention and decided to run as a Free Soil candidate for the Ohio House. He won election in October and, by December, was in the midst of the negotiations about how to organize the legislature.[16]

In Chase's December 20 letter to Belle, he described how he had drafted a statement about the impasse for Townshend and how Townshend had prepared a set of compromise resolutions. The doctor presented these documents the next day, and the Democrats, in Chase's words, accepted the "proposition of peace and conciliation" so that "the responsibility of organizing or refusing to organize is thrown upon the Whigs." Chase now realized that it would not be possible for all the Free Soil members to agree on the question of who was entitled to the Hamilton County seats; some members would side with the Whigs, while others (Townshend and John Morse, a member of the House from Lake County) would side with the Democrats. Chase himself believed that the Democrats Pugh and Pierce should get the disputed Hamilton seats, but "many of our friends here hold a different view," and "the most that can be hoped for is toleration of each other's differences."[17]

The legislators at last accepted Townshend's approach on December 23 and agreed on a temporary organization of the House. "The honor belongs to the Free Soilers," Chase wrote a friend with pride. Many members departed immediately for home to spend Christmas with their families, but Chase remained in Columbus, explaining to Belle that he had been so busy with politics that he had not had time to prepare for his supreme court arguments. He was annoyed by the "constant allusions to my position as a candidate for the office of senator and am almost tempted to withdraw altogether from it. I think it a mere possibility that I may be elected." The Free Soil men from the Western Reserve favored Giddings; if the Whigs agreed with them, Giddings would be elected. Democrats favored a traditional Democrat, and perhaps some Whigs would join them to defeat Chase. "My only chance is that the Free Soilers being unable to carry Giddings, and the Democrats, unable to carry a candidate of their own, they may unite upon me."[18]

In spite of the winter weather, more than a hundred Free Soil delegates, including Chase, gathered in Columbus on December 28 and 29 for their annual state convention. Once again he drafted the resolutions, which addressed many issues other than slavery, often in Democratic terms. For instance, Chase called for a ten-hour limit on the workday, taxes on corporations, repeal of the state's Black Laws, and a convention to revise the antiquated 1803 state constitution. He confided to his wife that many Whigs opposed his draft, so that it was hard to get it through the committee and accepted by the convention. "We had some very strong men in the committee, exceedingly Whiggish in their views, and at times I thought the result very doubtful," he penned. "By patience and perseverance, however, we carried everything through at last quite to our minds." Chase was especially excited that "we have assurances from leading Democrats that they will now go for the absolute repeal of the Black Laws." By tilting the platform toward the Democrats, Chase was killing two birds: strengthening his support for the senate seat and working to pass important reform legislation.[19]

Chase stayed in Columbus in early January 1849, working on cases in the courts, including one in which he represented Lyman Beecher and the biblical scholar Calvin Stowe (father and husband, respectively, of Harriet Beecher Stowe) against those who claimed that because they were "New School" Presbyterians, they could not teach at Lane Seminary. Chase's argument, accepted by the state supreme court, was that the plaintiff, the founding donor of the seminary, did not have standing to control the trustees in their choices. This was just one of a dozen cases over a three-year period that Chase argued in the state supreme court, on banking, property, and procedure issues.[20]

Chase was also busy with politics, noting in his diary on January 5 that he had a "long walk and conversation with Lucian Swift," a state senator from Akron who was sometimes viewed as a Democrat, sometimes as a Free Soiler. Swift "intimated his desire of my election as senator," and the two men also talked about the question of which newspaper editor would receive the coveted state printing contract.[21]

Two days later, even though it was a Sunday—a day Chase normally reserved for church and religious reading—he spent hours "preparing bill for separate schools for colored children, embracing a clause for the repeal of all the black laws." Although some black children were already attending integrated public schools in Cleveland and private black schools in Cincinnati, about three-quarters of black children in Ohio were not attending school of any sort. In terms of the proportion of black children getting an education, Ohio was behind New York and the New England states, but ahead of New Jersey, Indiana, and Illinois. The first five sections of Chase's bill would change Ohio law to require (not merely permit) the formation of separate colored school districts in places where colored children did not already attend public schools with white children. These colored school districts would be governed by trustees elected by the colored men in the district—a first small step toward black suffrage in Ohio—and supported by the school taxes collected from the colored population of the district. Buried in the sixth section of Chase's bill was the repeal of the state's Black Laws, listing several by name and date, but also repealing "all parts of other acts, so far as they enforce any special disabilities or confer any special privileges on account of color." Chase also worked this day on what he termed a "bill to prevent kidnapping," the all-too-common practice of kidnapping free blacks on the basis of false claims that they were fugitive slaves.[22]

After the conclusion of his court cases, on about January 12, 1849, Chase headed home to Cincinnati, leaving behind the school bill to be introduced by Morse, and the kidnapping bill to be introduced by Albert Riddle, a Whig Free Soiler from the Western Reserve. Chase stayed in constant touch with Columbus, however, writing long daily letters to friends there. On January 16, for example, he wrote to Edward Hamlin, contrasting his situation in Cincinnati, sitting by his fire with his wife, with Hamlin's in Columbus, "scribbling some editorial for the paper, perhaps a defense of Townshend and Morse." Chase wished that Hamlin could have more comfortable surroundings and "a long, long list of faithful paying sub- scribers, constituting a congregation that the Pope—and every editor, you know, is an infallible Pope—might be proud to preach to." Chase wrote Hamlin again the next day, asking him what had happened to the bill for colored schools and repeal of the Black Laws, and asking for letters directly from Morse and Townshend, noting, "I am very anxious to hear from them." On January 19 Chase wrote Morse to say that he agreed that the choice of senator should not turn on personal considerations. "Let that man be elected, if his election be possible, whose success will most certainly and most efficiently promote the triumph of our cause in our state and nation." Chase could not resist adding, however, that since Giddings already represented the Western Reserve and the former Whigs in Congress, it would make sense to elect "a Free Soiler from the southern part of the state, acceptable to the old Liberty men and Democratic Free Soilers."[23]

Chase wrote Hamlin again on January 20, saying that he was glad to hear that the prospects were good for passing the bill to repeal the Black Laws. "The repeal of those laws is an object dearer to me than any political elevation whatever; and is worth more to us as a party than the election of any man to any office in the gift of the legislature." Chase asked about the status of the anti-kidnapping bill. "With a little improvement," he observed, "it might be made a complete safeguard, not only against the use of our officers and the use of our jails for the recapture of fugitive slaves, but also against the kidnapping by force or fraud of free persons." After hearing from Riddle that he did not have much hope that the legislature would take up the kidnapping bill, Chase wrote to encourage him. Chase viewed Riddle as a friend (indeed, he described him as such in a letter to his wife) but Riddle was not in favor of sending Chase to the Senate, writing to Giddings that Chase was "a noble man, but as ambitious as Julius Caesar." Like many others from the Western Reserve, Riddle favored Giddings. The *Cleveland True Democrat*, for example, praised both men but added that Chase was "a young man" who could afford to "work and wait."[24]

Chase decided to write to Giddings directly, to avoid misunderstanding, and to stress that he was more interested in the cause than in personal promotion. We do not have the letter to Giddings, only a summary that Chase sent to Townshend. "I gave him full credit for all that his most partial friends claim; admitted that if we were both out of Congress, he ought to be preferred over me; but stated that I could not help believing, since he was already in Congress, and looking to other aspects of the case, that my election this winter would be a greater gain to the Free Soil cause than even his own." Chase wrote in similar terms to Hamlin, saying that because Giddings was already in Congress, it would make more sense to send Chase. "I may be wrong in this," Chase added, "misled perhaps by the ambition so freely ascribed to me. If so, let Giddings be chosen. I shall not complain."[25]

Writing to Stanley Matthews, another ally in Columbus, Chase pressed him to work for the Morse bill. In the course of a long letter (he seemed to write only long letters this winter), Chase related how "an old negress, grimy, black, fat, squat, and odorous" came to his office and asked him to prepare a legal document, or what she called a "scription." She had purchased her own freedom, she explained, and now she wanted to purchase the freedom of her son, for $350. "She had been advised to have him go to Canada, but she wanted him with her in her old age, and if he should go to Canada and come back, he would always be afraid of everyone he saw." Chase drafted the document for the woman and contributed a few dollars toward her son's freedom; she left grateful for his help. "That old woman," Chase wrote, "may be in heaven, when many of the earth's proud ones may lack a drop of water to cool their burning tongues."[26]

Chase's encounter with this black woman illustrates his attitudes toward blacks at this time. He might mock her, but he also helped with her legal problem, just as he was helping to repeal the hated Black Laws. The woman went to Chase's office because he was known as a friend of colored people. Chase knew poor blacks, like this woman and Matilda. He knew black community leaders such as Andrew Gordon, who had presented him with the silver pitcher. He knew black students, such as those at the black high school where he attended commencement. And he knew national leaders, including Frederick Douglass and John Mercer Langston, Oberlin graduate and future member of Congress. Chase could not understand all the problems black Americans faced, especially those in slavery. But he knew far more about these problems, and sympathized far more with blacks, than any other mainstream political leader at the time, with the possible exception of his friend Seward.[27]

In the state legislature, in late January, Morse and Townshend voted with the Democrats in order to grant the two disputed Hamilton County seats to the Democrats, Alexander Pierce and George Pugh. Whig papers were outraged; the *New-York Tribune,* for example, criticized Morse and Townshend for disregarding both state law and the wishes of their Whig constituents. Free Soil papers were more interested in the progress the legislature was making to repeal the Black Laws. Morse's bill passed the House on January 30 by a vote of fifty-two to ten, with most Whigs not bothering to vote. Hamlin predicted to Chase that the "bill will pass the Senate without much difficulty." In the pages of his paper, Hamlin not only rejoiced at the passage of the bill but also defended Morse and Townshend against the charge of "making a corrupt bargain with the Democrats, by which Mr. Chase was to be elected to the US Senate. No man would suspect a thing of this kind or make the charge but one who would have made a similar bargain had he had an opportunity." Hamlin was right on this: the Whigs were working just as hard as Democrats to arrange a deal with the Free Soil members about the Senate seat and the state offices at stake.[28]

Chase returned to Columbus on February 2, in part to press for repeal of the Black Laws, but also to work toward the Senate seat. The Senate amended the Morse bill so that it would not repeal the law against blacks serving on juries, nor the law denying them access to poor relief. Then, after a short debate, the Senate passed the amended bill on February 5 by a vote of twenty-three to eleven. Five of the senators who voted against the bill were Democrats, six were Whigs. A few days later, the House accepted the Senate version of the bill, and thus it became law. The *Huron Reflector* called the bill "a noble victory for the cause of liberty, humanity, and justice." The *Ohio State Journal* approved of the repeal but did not think it mattered much, saying that the Black Laws, "with the exception of the 'testimony clause,' were to all intents a dead letter." In Fairfield County, not far from Columbus, an angry meeting denounced the repeal as an instance of "Free Soilism, abolitionism, demagogism, and negroism." The *Daily Standard* lamented the Senate amendment, saying the bill would have been better in the form passed by the House, but it still viewed the bill as "a great victory—a victory for humanity over oppression." Chase agreed: this was a triumph both for him personally and for Ohio's blacks. After more than forty years, the hated laws limiting black immigration and black testimony were gone.[29]

Chase's prospects for the Senate seat, he wrote to his wife on February 7, were "by no means flattering." A few days later, the *Zanesville Courier* reported that although there was a bargain between the Free Soilers and the Democrats to make Chase senator, "the signs are now that he will be fooled." David Disney, a former Democratic member of the legislature, recently elected to Congress, was in Columbus, "and he has great influence over the Locos." ("Locofoco" and "Loco" were the derisive nicknames for the Democrats.) Disney wanted the Senate seat for himself, but even if he could not get it, he would "defeat Chase." On February 11 Chase told his wife that there was no progress on the Senate question: "The caucus of the Democracy on Friday evening determined nothing. There was a good deal of bickering and some anger among them, but nothing was concluded." Chase claimed that he was not sure that he even wanted the Senate seat. "How much better is a quiet spirit, satisfied with the allotments of a limited sphere, devout towards God, and loving towards men, than the restless anxiety of ambition."[30]

Two days later Chase wrote Belle again, informing her that the Whig caucus had decided to push Justice McLean as senator. Chase was almost amused, for it was "quite certain that the judge cannot command the Free Soil vote." On the Democratic side, he learned that the caucus had decided to cast "one or two complimentary ballots" for William Allen and then give their votes to Chase. If the Democrats "adhere to this understanding—and there is very little doubt but they will—I shall be elected." But the *Ohio State Journal* reported on February 15 that Chase would not get the seat because some Democrats from Hamilton County (there were six, including Pugh and Pierce) refused to vote for him. "They cannot be brought to vote for Chase—they would fear to do so and return to their constituents." The *Journal* did not explain why these men would not vote for Chase, but it seems likely that they were traditional Democrats who hated the idea of a Free Soil senator.[31]

Chase was discouraged, writing his wife on this day that there was "more delay, and more disappointment, foreshadowing, I fear, the final disappointment of my hopes!" Every hour was being used, he explained, to persuade Democrats to vote against him, "and I have no strength to spare, as none of the Whig Free Soilers are for me." Chase was right in his vote count; if all the Whigs and Whiggish Free Soilers voted against him, he would need all the Democrats and independent Free Soilers in order to get a majority. He could not afford a single Democratic defection. By February 20, he was more hopeful, for the legislature had decided to vote in two days, and it was "generally supposed that I shall be elected senator." Even the *Ohio State Journal* conceded that Chase would probably be elected, reporting that the "refractory Locofocos have been, after much tribulation, gathered into the fold again," and that an agreement was in place by which Chase would be elected senator and two Democrats sent to the state supreme court.[32]

On the morning of February 22, all 106 members of the Ohio legislature gathered in joint session to select a federal senator and various state judges. Under the rules, it was not enough to secure a plurality of votes; one had to have a majority—in other words, at least fifty-four votes. On the first ballot, Thomas Ewing (who had somehow supplanted McLean as the Whig candidate) received forty-one votes; William Allen, twenty-seven; Salmon Chase, fourteen; Joshua Giddings, nine; and various other candidates, one or two. This was the complimentary vote for Allen that Chase had predicted. On the second ballot, all but one of the Democrats shifted from Allen to Chase, and he also gained some of the scattered votes, so that he had fifty-two votes—almost but not quite enough. On the third ballot, Chase amassed fifty-five votes, a majority, but this ballot was set aside because a clerk had counted one member's vote twice. The fourth ballot confirmed that Chase had prevailed with fifty-four votes. The papers reported that he received all the Democratic votes plus those of five Free Soilers, including Morse, Townshend, and Swift. The legislators proceeded at once to select two judges for the state supreme court, both Democrats, and a circuit judge, a Free Soiler. That evening, according to the *Ohio State Journal*, Chase "gave a supper to his Locofoco friends" at the American House Hotel, then "took the seven o'clock stage for home."[33]

Whig papers denounced Chase for his ambition and for making an improper bargain. The *Ohio State Journal* claimed that "every act of his was subsidiary to his own ambition. He talked of the interests of Free Soil; he meant his own. He harangued on the benefits of electing a Free Soil senator; he intended that none but himself should be that senator." The *Pittsburgh Gazette* described Chase as a "Locofoco Freesoiler" who could "be counted on as an opponent of General Taylor's administration." In the *New-York Tribune,* Greeley offered a more measured critique, calling Chase "a man of decided ability, of good personal character, an early and ardent abolitionist, formerly a Whig, but now sympathizing on most leading questions with the opposite party." Chase would probably be a better senator than his predecessor, Allen, for he favored both land reform and shrinking the federal government, "especially of our national expenditures for army and navy, as well as a most devoted champion of Free Soil and Free Men." But the *Tribune* viewed Chase's election as "a fraud upon the public will of the state" achieved only by disregarding a "plain and important provision of law": that is, the law dividing Hamilton County into two electoral districts.[34]

Democratic papers were generally pleased with the selection. The *Cincinnati Enquirer* commented that it would have preferred a traditional Democrat such as Allen, but since that was not possible, Chase was the next best choice. It praised him as "a gentleman of fine talents and upright character, from whom a liberal, nay, a Democratic, course may be expected on all questions of general politics." The *Enquirer* claimed that Whigs were outraged not because of the bargain that promoted Chase but by their own failure to strike a bargain to promote a Whig such as Giddings. The *Cleveland Plain Dealer* described Chase as a "sound constitutional lawyer" who was opposed to "all kinds of legislative monopolies, such as banks and tariffs." Chase would vote with the Democrats on all issues other than slavery and would "plant his battery where it will tell with most effect on the slaveholding bulk of Taylor Whiggery."[35]

Free Soil papers, of course, celebrated Chase's victory. The *National Era* declared that he was "a man of signal ability, great dignity of character, and purity of private life. He has won an enviable reputation at the bar and distinguished himself by his efforts in the cause of Free Soil." And, just as predictably, Southern papers were appalled. The *Memphis Eagle* opined that Chase was "a mad fanatic, an unscrupulous abolitionist, a man of very ordinary abilities, and altogether incompetent to the honors conferred upon him." Chase was a "special advocate for the runaway slaves. For this latter effort, he was presented with a silver vase by the darkies and gave a public levee to his colored brethren. Such a man will disgrace the Senate."[36]

Many historians, echoing the Whigs, have criticized Chase for improper ambition or improper tactics in the election of 1849. John Niven, his most recent biographer, claimed that "all of Chase's activities in church, education, and community affairs were aimed at his own advancement politically" and that his "driving ambition to achieve his goal at any cost more than countered his many good and strong qualities." Doris Kearns Goodwin, in her great book on Lincoln and his rivals, quoted from Whig papers to argue that the "suspicions and mistrust engendered by the unusual circumstances of the Senate election would never be wholly erased." The common criticism of Chase's ambition is curious: historians do not criticize Lincoln or John F. Kennedy for their ambition. And the questions about Chase's tactics in the first weeks of 1849 also beg scrutiny. There has never been any suggestion that Chase or his supporters bribed Democrats to vote for Chase for Senate. What they did was to work out a legislative compromise, in which Free Soil men obtained some benefits—repeal of the Black Laws and Chase's election—and Democrats also achieved some of their goals—control of the legislature, election of judges. To put the point another way, what the Democrats and their allies (Morse and Townshend) did was the same kind of deal that the Whigs and their allies (Riddle) tried and failed to make because Giddings had alienated some of Whigs. To his credit, Giddings himself did not complain, writing to Charles Sumner that he viewed the election of Chase as a "great victory."[37]

CHAPTER 7

"Freedom Is National"

☙ 1849–50 ❧

t is one of the curious coincidences of Chase's life that, when he arrived in Washington in early March 1849, to serve his single six-year term in the United States Senate, Abraham Lincoln was still in town, having just completed his single two-year term in the House of Representatives. The House was not in session after Monday, March 5, the date of Zachary Taylor's inauguration and the day on which Chase, delayed on the road, finally arrived in the capital. The custom at this time was for the Senate, but not the House, to meet for a short session after a new president's inauguration, to consider the chief executive's nominations for his Cabinet and other positions in the government. Former congressman Lincoln remained in the capital for a few weeks, however, to argue a case in the Supreme Court and to press for patronage positions for Whig friends as well as for himself; he hoped to become the head of the federal land office.[1]

Although they had some mutual friends—notably Joshua Giddings, who stayed at the same boardinghouse as Lincoln—nothing suggests that Lincoln and Chase met at this time. Giddings was not in town; Chase had tried to persuade him to stay for a few days after the end of the House session, so that they could talk face-to-face, but Giddings left before Chase arrived. If Lincoln and Chase had met, however, and talked about politics, they would not have found much on which they agreed.[2]

For Chase, of course, the most important issue facing the nation was slavery; he wanted to see Congress abolish slavery in the District of Columbia, prevent slavery's expansion into new territories, repeal the Fugitive Slave Act, and perhaps even limit the interstate slave trade. Lincoln, during his two years as a member of Congress, said almost nothing about slavery. This was not because there were no House debates about aspects of slavery while Lincoln was a member; there were. In April 1848, for example, Giddings gave a strong House speech against slavery and the slave trade in the District of Columbia. Speaking to the slave states, on behalf of the free states, Giddings said: "You shall not bring us to share with you in the guilt and the turpitude of this traffic in human flesh now carried on here under our protection." What the free states wanted, he continued, in words very like those of Chase, was the "separation of this government from all interference with slavery." Lincoln may have agreed with Giddings in quiet conversations, but he would not speak out against slavery like Giddings or Chase.[3]

When Lincoln did write or speak about the politics of slavery, it was often to denounce the abolitionists rather than the slave masters. Lincoln wrote to a friend in 1845 that "if the Whig abolitionists of New York had voted with us last fall, Mr. Clay would now be president, Whig principles in the ascendant, and Texas not annexed." In a campaign speech in 1848 in Massachusetts, Lincoln attacked the Free Soil Party, saying that it had no principles other than its purported opposition to the extension of slavery, and that a better way to oppose extension was to vote for the Whigs, because a vote for the Free Soil Party was effectively a vote for the Democrats. Later in the same campaign, in a speech back home in Illinois, a paper reported that Lincoln criticized "with the most scathing language the 'consistency' of the abolitionists" because they both "professed great horror at the extension of slavery" while they "aided in the election of Mr. Polk, for which, with its disastrous consequences, they were responsible."[4]

Near the end of his term, in early 1849, Lincoln presented to the House what he called a bill to "abolish slavery in the District of Columbia, by the consent of the free white people of said district, and with compensation to owners." Lincoln's proposal provided that no new slaves could be brought into the district, other than slaves of members of Congress while serving in Congress; that children born to slaves in the district after the effective date of the act would be free from birth, although required to serve their masters as apprentices until they reached adulthood; and that masters could, if they wanted, free their slaves and receive fair compensation from the federal government. Lincoln's bill would only take effect if ratified by the white voters of the district. Moreover, Lincoln's plan would require the district authorities to "provide active and efficient means to arrest, and deliver up to their owners, all fugitive slaves escaping into said district." Lincoln abandoned his proposal soon after presenting it, explaining years later that he realized the bill could not pass. Chase would have viewed Lincoln's proposal as far too timid; under Lincoln's language, a child who was enslaved in the district on the effective date of the act would remain enslaved there for the rest of his or her life, as long as his master did not decide to free the slave. Chase would have especially disapproved of Lincoln's requirement that federal authorities help slaveowners recover their fugitive slaves; this was just the kind of federal involvement in slavery which Chase wanted to end.[5]

On March 6, the morning after his arrival in Washington, Chase went first to the home of his closest friends in the capital, Gamaliel and Margaret Bailey, and then called upon the other senator from Ohio, the Whig Thomas Corwin. Although Chase and Corwin were from different parties, Corwin now offered, as was the custom, to present his new colleague's credentials. They went to the Capitol with Senator John Hale of New Hampshire, with whom Chase had worked over the years, and now met in person at last. Hale happily introduced Chase to other senators, including Andrew Butler of South Carolina, Henry Foote of Mississippi, and Sam Houston of Texas. The slave state senators, Chase wrote to his wife, were "civil enough, but I dare say wished in their hearts that I was anywhere other than in that chamber." Chase also saw Seward this morning, another colleague whom he was meeting in person for the first time. Corwin formally presented Chase to the Senate, and Chase took the oath of office. Among the sixty senators at this time were many of the greatest ever: Henry Clay, John Calhoun, Daniel Webster, Thomas Hart Benton, Stephen Douglas, and Jefferson Davis. Salmon Chase was now one of them.[6]

Within a few days, Chase had been to the White House and met the new president. Chase wrote to his wife that Zachary Taylor "was very kind and sociable with me, and when I left asked me to come again." Chase used his weeks in Washington to form or renew friendships, including with Elizabeth Wirt Goldsborough, now living in Baltimore while her husband, Louis Goldsborough, was at sea on a naval assignment. Elizabeth and Chase had not written to one another after he moved to Cincinnati, but he now visited her in Baltimore, and she followed up their conversation by sending him a pamphlet by her husband, refuting the arguments of a pacifist who claimed that "all war is forbidden by Christianity."[7]

Chase hoped that the Democrats in the Senate would view him as one of their number. An early indication that this would not be the case came when the Democrats announced committee assignments: Chase was not placed on any Senate committee whatsoever. Later in his six-year term, he would receive a few minor committee assignments, but he was never a member of the Democratic caucus.[8]

The main business of this short Senate session was to consider nominations. Although the Senate was controlled by Democrats, and all Taylor's nominees were Whigs, the nominations were generally approved immediately, for Democrats as well as Whigs believed that a president was entitled to appoint his supporters. There was only one exception during this session: the Senate rejected the nomination of Edward McGaughey, a Whig member of Congress, to become a territorial governor, because of what the *New York Herald* called his "unpatriotic, un-American" opposition to the Mexican War. Chase was among those who voted to confirm McGaughey. The Senate also spent several days debating whether Democrat James Shields, originally from Ireland and now a resident of Illinois, was entitled to his Senate seat. Shields claimed that his election to various local offices showed that he had been a citizen for more than the required nine years, but his opponents countered that the only proof of his citizenship was a more recent court order. The Senate decided against Shields, with Chase again in the minority, writing to his wife that Shields would have been treated differently if he was part of "the cottonocracy of Massachusetts or the slaveocracy of Virginia."[9]

When Chase returned to Cincinnati in late April, the city was in the early stages of a cholera epidemic. Most of the deaths were among the poor and the immigrants, but nobody was safe: Chase's friend Judge Charles Brough died in May. Chase's few diary entries for this spring were somber. He was reading a biography of William Wilberforce, the British abolitionist and Christian leader. "How his example shames and humbles me," he wrote in his diary. The next day, Chase regretted that he devoted "too little time" to morning prayer and that he had not "been bold for Christ as I should have been." Then he chided himself for being "too cold" in family prayers. "When shall I feel the glow and flame I would fain realize?"[10]

The compensation of senators, at this time, was modest indeed: only $8 for each day they attended a Senate session. So, to make ends meet, Chase had to keep working as a private lawyer. In the summer of 1849 he commenced one of his most interesting cases, representing Henry O'Reilly in his telegraph disputes with inventor Samuel F. B. Morse and his colleague Amos Kendall. O'Reilly was born in Ireland in 1806, moved to America at the age of ten, and established himself as an editor and entrepreneur in Rochester, New York. Starting in 1846, the ebullient O'Reilly entered into a series of contracts with Kendall to build telegraph lines using Morse's patented technology. For a while, O'Reilly worked well with Kendall, but by the time Chase joined O'Reilly's legal team, the man had become a bitter competitor of Kendall and Morse. O'Reilly sought to build his own telegraph line from Louisville to New Orleans, claiming that he was not using or infringing upon Morse's patents. O'Reilly called his company the People's Line and cast himself as the free-market competitor of the monopolist Morse. Kendall and Morse sued O'Reilly in several courts, including Kentucky, where Morse obtained an injunction, keeping O'Reilly from erecting his New Orleans line through that state.[11]

Chase's first task for O'Reilly was to argue, in a federal circuit court in Frankfort, Kentucky, that this injunction should be lifted. His luggage had been lost in transit, and, as he wrote Belle, he was in "a very pretty fix—with one shirt answering both for night and day and promising to make a very rowdyish appearance tomorrow, which will be its third in succession." Chase also had only "one pair of pantaloons, with a rent on one side, just below the angle of the pocket hole, which has been rather ashamed of itself for some time but is now kept in countenance by the breaking of a button-hole in front, which allows a yawning gap in a very awkward place." Chase had resolved to try his hand at sewing to repair the damage.[12]

During breaks in the legal argument, Chase met with O'Reilly and others to learn about the technical side of the telegraph. The case went on day after day, and Chase was impatient to be home, for his wife was expecting a baby. At last, on June 13 the judges ruled in O'Reilly's favor, lifting the injunction so that he could resume construction in Kentucky. This decision was reported in papers as far away as New Orleans and New

York, and the *Louisville Courier* said that Chase had impressed the people of Frankfort as a lawyer and a gentleman. "Whatever political differences may exist—however much some of our fellow-citizens may differ with him on some topics—no such differences prevented gentlemen of all parties in Frankfort from freely expressing their sentiments respecting him."[13]

Almost as soon as he was back in Cincinnati, Chase started to receive telegrams from O'Reilly demanding that he come to Louisville, where Morse's lawyers were seeking another injunction. Chase responded that he could not leave Cincinnati, for his wife was due to deliver any day, and other family members had symptoms "of the prevailing epidemic." O'Reilly kept up the pressure, however, and Chase relented, working for a week in Louisville in late June. He arrived back in Cincinnati at daybreak on July 1 to find large fires burning—"a preposterous remedy for cholera," he wrote in his diary, "giving an aspect of gloom to everything hardly to be surpassed." Chase was just in time for the birth, on the evening of the next day, of his daughter Josephine, or Josie. Chase's family now consisted of Belle and their three daughters, Kate, Nettie, and Josie.[14]

In a long letter on July 4, Chase reported to an eastern friend that the cholera was "absolutely fearful" in Cincinnati. "Near nine hundred died last week, and the number of deaths this week will probably exceed a thousand. Its ravages are greatest among the poor emigrants, who are crowded together in miserable quarters, and who cannot be persuaded, I am told, to observe the least caution." (By this time, about half the population of Cincinnati was foreign born, mainly from Germany and Ireland.) "When there is enough and to spare for all God's creatures," Chase continued, "how sad that the millions perish for lack of such knowledge, and lack of the ordinary comforts of life, while the few are surrounded with all the appliances of luxury! I am thankful that my own condition is one of ease and comfort; and yet I feel as if it were almost criminal to enjoy it while so many suffer such sad extremes of wretchedness and destitution." In a similar letter, to his sister-in-law, he wrote that the daily deaths meant that "everyone must or should feel that his own turn may be next."[15]

Chase left Cincinnati in mid-July for Cleveland, where he was slated to speak at a Free Soil convention timed to coincide with the anniversary of the Northwest Ordinance. When he reached there, however, he felt quite ill, though he assured Belle that he had no symptoms of cholera. After a week in bed in Cleveland, Chase went home and resumed legal and political work. He was trying to bridge the divide between the Free Soil and Democratic Parties. Writing to a Boston abolitionist, Chase said that he was "still a Liberty man, because I am a Democrat. I am still resolute in the determination not to rest satisfied until every legitimate and constitutional power of the government shall be put in action against slavery, because slavery is inconsistent with the great democratic ideal of equal rights among men." Writing to an Ohio Democrat, Chase stressed that he agreed fully with the Democrats "on the subjects of trade, currency, and special privileges. . . . But I cannot, while boldly asserting these principles in reference to those subjects, shrink from their just application to slavery."[16]

Chase spent August and part of September in New England, partly to speak with political friends, mainly to work on the O'Reilly case. He visited several cities to interview and take the testimony of witnesses, including Joseph Henry, a leading expert on electromagnetism. He spent a quiet Sunday with his oldest sister, Hannah Whipple, and her family in Concord, New Hampshire, and gave a political speech in Boston. After visits to Philadelphia and Washington, Chase went back to Ohio by way of Pittsburgh, where he gave another political speech (lost to history because, as the local reporter noted, "the lights were dim and uncertain" so he could "take no notes").[17]

When Chase reached Washington in early December 1849 to attend the winter session of Congress, he found a letter waiting from his friend John Dix, an antislavery Democrat from New York. Dix wrote Chase that Congress would have its "hands full this winter, with California asking for freedom, and eight states prepared to secede if they are not permitted to extend the evil of slavery." California, in the midst of its gold rush, with a population of perhaps a hundred thousand people, had adopted a new state constitution that would prohibit slavery. Now it was awaiting approval from Congress. Some Southerners were threatening to secede if California was admitted to the Union on this basis, for it would give the free states a majority in the Senate. New Mexico posed another point of contention: many Northerners wanted to organize it as a free territory; Southerners opposed this and wanted to award half of New Mexico to Texas. Indeed, some Texans claimed that if they did not get all the territory to which they were entitled—on the basis of ancient and dubious claims—they would go to war against New Mexico. Dix was inclined to dismiss such threats, writing Chase that "the wolf may be at the door," but "we may be permitted to doubt until we see him." There was "no public evil so great as that of carrying slavery into territory which is free." Chase agreed.[18]

Not much happened in the Senate for the first few weeks of December, because the House could not agree on who should be its speaker, and the Senate did not want to start work until the House was organized. Chase spent some of his time in the House, listening to the debates, writing letters to friends. He was in the hall when Robert Toombs of Georgia declared that if "by your legislation, you seek to drive us from the territories of California and New Mexico, purchased by the common blood and treasure of the whole people, and to abolish slavery in the district, thereby attempting to fix a national degradation upon half the states of this Confederacy, *I am for disunion.*" Contrary to the House rules, Southern members applauded Toombs. Chase viewed all this as just "theater," writing to his friend Hamlin that "the whole scene was dramatic and entertaining. One or two were frightened by the stage thunder, but most understood the manufacture, and disregarded it."[19]

Although most members of Congress left their wives and children at home, Chase brought Belle to Washington this winter, along with their three children and Belle's younger sister, Kate. Chase did not explain why in his letters, but surely part of his thinking was that he did not want to be apart from his wife for the next seven or eight months. It turned out, however, they were unable to stay together after Belle suffered in mid-December what Chase described as the "most threatening symptoms of rapid consumption."[20]

As he explained to his friend Hamlin, neither he nor his wife had "confidence in the efficacy of ordinary treatment," but both had some hope "in the water cure, especially in the hands of a judicious physician." After the death of his first wife, Chase distrusted traditional doctors, who relied on strong drugs and purges, and turned instead to homeopathic doctors, who relied more on the body's natural processes. The water cure, also known as hydropathy, was a homeopathic approach, involving fresh air, ample exercise, loose clothing, and bathing in cool or even cold water. Water cure doctors tried to help their patients, many of whom were women, take charge of their own health. Dr. George Dexter advertised that, at his facility in Morristown, New Jersey, he could cure "gout, rheumatism, bronchitis, consumption, dyspepsia, constipation, diarrhea, paralysis," and other diseases. Chase went with Belle and the children to Dexter's clinic on December 22. Josie and Nettie would stay there with Belle, with help from a nurse, and nine-year-old Kate would attend a boarding school in New York City under the charge of Mrs. Henrietta Haines.[21]

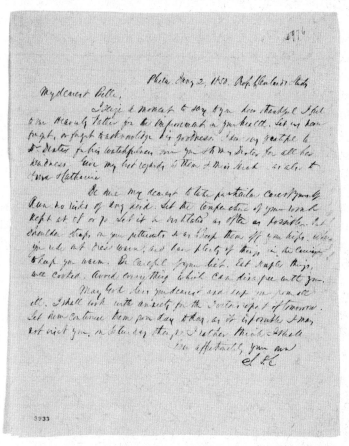

A relatively legible sample of Chase's handwriting: a letter to his wife, Belle, from January 1850, thanking "our Heavenly Father" for her health.

On January 2, 1850, on his way back to Washington, Chase wrote to Hamlin that he had been watching his wife through the holidays, "never leaving her except when obliged to do so for her own sake, administering to her comfort in every way possible to me. For the first three days after our arrival . . . she mended daily. Then came a sudden change for the worse which filled me with dismay. Then she rallied again, and I hung between hope and despair. But now today, God be praised, she seems better than at any time since we left Washington." Once back in the capital, Chase received frequent letters from Dr. Dexter, and rare letters from Belle, reporting her progress. Chase wrote to his wife every day, sometimes more than once a day. He assured her of his love, he relayed news from Washington, he urged her to take care of her health, he reminded her of their common Christian faith. "May God our Father," he closed one letter, "watch over you and bless you. Kiss our little darlings for me."[22]

Chase hoped to work in Washington during the weeks and to see his wife in New Jersey on some weekends, but he was hindered by the schedule—for the Senate generally met six days a week—and by the weather, such as a snowstorm that delayed him for twenty-four hours. Chase found it difficult to concentrate on his work in Washington; he was so worried about his wife, fearing that she would weaken and die, like his second wife Eliza, and like so many others. A grim reminder of mortality arrived in the form of a telegram reporting that his sister Hannah had died in New Hampshire. Chase wrote to his friend Sumner that "a sweeter, kinder, more affectionate heart never yearned towards a brother." Chase had seen Hannah only a few months earlier and had not imagined "that it was our last meeting on this earth. But God has so willed it." Death, he wrote, had "pursued me incessantly ever since I was twenty-five." Indeed: two of his wives, three of his children, and four of his siblings had died, and his third wife was now in danger of death. "My path has been—how terribly true it is—through the region of his shadow. Sometimes I feel as if I could give up—as if I *must* give up. And then after all I rise and press on."[23]

Chase made his first short Senate speech on January 10. The issue was whether the upper chamber should print resolutions from the Vermont legislature opposing the extension of slavery. He hoped the Senate would do so, as well as print all similar popular petitions and resolutions, because he hoped that information and discussion would lead to "an amicable solution." Chase warned the South, however, that the North would not be swayed by threats of disunion, and he disagreed with those who claimed the South had somehow been slighted. "Have any states of the South . . . lacked their full proportion of all the honors of this Confederacy? Have they not had their full proportion, *at least*, of all the power of this Confederacy? Do they not at this moment, in this hall, and in the other hall, exercise all the power, to say the least of it, which to them legitimately belongs?" Chase echoed here the Slave Power argument he had been making since 1841: that slave owners had *more* than their fair share of political power. Even if Congress admitted California as a free state, and New Mexico as a free territory, the South would have no just cause to complain, Chase argued, for Congress would merely be extending the principles of the Northwest Ordinance. He hoped the current crisis could be resolved "in the spirit of the fathers" so that "this Union will be made what the fathers of the republic designed it should be made, an example of freedom to the nations of the earth."[24]

Chase's speech elicited an angry response from Andrew Butler of South Carolina, who accused him of pretending to seek compromise while really making "odious and arrogant distinctions between different sections of this Confederacy." To prove his point, Butler had the clerk read into the record a letter that Chase had sent to Ohio Democrat John Breslin, which had somehow made its way into the newspapers. "No Democrat," Chase had written, at least none with "any real faith in the great cardinal doctrines of democracy, that all men are created equal by nature . . . can doubt that slaveholding is greatly inconsistent with democratic principles." Senator Butler, who owned more than sixty slaves, and who considered himself a far better Democrat than Chase, accused the freshman senator from Ohio of seeking the "unconditional submission of one section"—the South—in his vision of free democracy.[25]

Two weeks later, on January 24, Butler gave a long speech in favor of a stronger fugitive slave law, during which he reviewed how the free states had (in his view) improperly failed to honor their constitutional obligation to help masters recover fugitives. Butler claimed that one of the Ohio senators had supported a resolution saying that federal officers could swear to support the Constitution but use a "mental reservation" to exclude the Fugitive Slave Clause as "null and void." Chase asked Butler whom he meant. "I allude to the senator himself," Butler replied. When Chase denied that he had endorsed such a resolution, Butler responded that the papers attributed the resolution to him. "If the senator relies upon no better authority than the newspapers," Chase said with a smile, "he will find himself often misinformed."[26]

When Butler finally concluded, Chase rose to defend himself. Referring to the Breslin letter, Chase explained that although he had intended it as a private letter, he was not ashamed of what he had written. "My opinions . . . all men may know, and these opinions I am ready to defend. They are not sectional opinions, unless the opinions of Washington, Jefferson, and Madison were sectional also, for every position which I maintain is fortified by their authority." As to the supposed resolution, Chase insisted again that he had not voted for any "mental reservation" language. "I hold no doctrine of mental reservation. Every man, in my judgment, should say precisely what he means."[27]

In late January Henry Clay sketched for the Senate his ideas for compromise—the outline of what we know as the Compromise of 1850. The Kentucky senator's proposed compromise consisted of eight elements, including admitting California as a free state and strengthening the Fugitive Slave Act of 1793. Chase was not impressed, writing to Edward Hamlin that Clay was offering "sentiment for the North" and "substance for the South." On February 5 the Senate was crammed to capacity to hear Clay's main speech in support of his proposal. "Never, on any former occasion," he began, "have I risen under such feelings of deep solicitude. I have witnessed many periods of great anxiety, of peril, even of danger to the country; but I have never before arisen to address any assembly

Henry Clay presents his compromise proposals to the United States Senate in early 1850. Chase is among those portrayed, a few seats behind Clay, with his hand to his chin.

so oppressed, so appalled, so anxious." Again, Chase was not impressed, writing his wife that, although Clay "made a powerful effort," the speech was a confused mix of "beauties and blemishes" because he tried "to plead at the same time the cause of slavery and freedom."[28]

Chase realized that the only way to defeat Clay's compromise was through political pressure, and he wrote at least six times this winter to Lewis Tappan, the well-connected New York leader, encouraging him and others to speak out against the extension of slavery. Chase even drafted six petitions for Tappan to circulate, leaving blank the names of the cities from which they would be submitted. "My hope is in the overruling Providence of God," Chase wrote Tappan. "I put no trust in politicians."[29]

Congress would devote the winter and spring to considering Clay's proposals, with senator after senator making major speeches. When it was announced that, in spite of his grave illness, John Calhoun would speak on March 4, Elizabeth Goldsborough asked Chase to find her a place on the Senate floor. Chase found her request puzzling, for the South Carolina senator's speech was already printed. But perhaps Elizabeth knew best, for she was there to see Calhoun, more dead than alive, hobble into the Senate chamber, take his seat, then sit wrapped in a black cloak as his protégé, Senator James Mason of Virginia, standing at his desk directly behind Calhoun, read out what everyone believed would be the great senator's final Senate speech.

"I have believed from the first," Calhoun's speech started, "that the agitation of slavery would, if not prevented by some timely and effective measure, end in disunion." Antislavery agitation, Calhoun claimed, had strained and snapped many of the "common cords" that bound the states together, including the national churches and national political parties. "If the agitation goes on, the same force, acting with increased intensity . . . will finally snap every cord, when nothing will be left to hold the states together except force." How to save the Union? The only way was to adopt measures that would prove to the Southern states that "they can remain in the union consistently with their honor and safety." However dramatic the scene, Chase was not persuaded by Calhoun's points; he reported to a friend the next day that Calhoun's speech had "produced next to no effect."[30]

Three days later, on March 7, Daniel Webster rose to give his principal speech, again eagerly awaited. "I wish to speak today," he started, "not as a Massachusetts man, nor as a Northern man, but as an American. I

speak today for the preservation of the Union. 'Hear me for my cause.'"
Much to the surprise of those who had thought him to be an opponent of
slavery, Webster supported every one of Clay's resolutions, including the
proposal to strengthen the fugitive slave law. Chase wrote to Sumner that
Webster's speech was an "absolute and unconditional surrender." Sumner
agreed, urging Chase to speak soon, to answer both Calhoun and Webster.
Chase now had what Sumner called a "great opportunity."[31]

But on March 11, long before Chase could get the floor, William Henry
Seward gave a stirring antislavery speech. In the most famous section of
the speech, he declared that "there is a higher law than the Constitution,
which regulates our authority over the [western] domain and devotes it
to the same noble purposes" as those of the Constitution. Seward's words,
printed promptly, elicited both praise and condemnation. A Vermont
paper said that Seward had expressed "clearly, boldly, and eloquently
the prevailing sentiment of the free states." Southern papers denounced
Seward and his speech, saying that a man who answered only to his ideas
about "higher law" could never be trusted.[32]

Chase was frustrated, writing to Sumner on March 15 that "we are
in the midst of sad times, but I hope in God. He, I think, has not yet
abandoned us to the madness or meanness of the politicians." He assured
his friend that he meant to "speak fully," but could not say when, since "a
junior senator, especially of my stamp, has hardly a fair chance." Sumner
sent Chase several letters full of ideas and arguments, and, finally, Chase
reached an agreement with another senator so that Chase would have
the floor on the afternoon of March 26. His letters to his wife grew very
short as he turned all his attention to writing and editing his speech.[33]

The most dramatic event in the Senate on March 26, 1850, however, was
not the first part of Chase's speech: it was an episode in the ongoing feud,
which seemed likely to lead to a duel, between the massive Thomas Hart
Benton of Missouri and the diminutive but combative Henry Foote of
Mississippi. Benton, who had not said much so far during the debates,
rose to insist that the admission of California could not be postponed any
longer. Foote, who viewed Benton as a traitor to the South, responded
with personal ridicule. Benton reminded Foote that, under Senate rules,
"personalities and attacks upon motives are forbidden." Foote responded
that if Benton "feels in the least aggrieved at anything which has fallen

from me, he shall, on demanding it, have full redress accorded him, according to the laws of honor. I do not denounce him as a coward"— although it seemed he was doing just that—"but if he wishes to patch up his reputation for courage, now greatly on the wane, he will certainly have an opportunity of doing so." Benton had to be restrained by friends as he lunged for Foote, shouting "Can I take a cudgel to him here?"[34]

Only after this drama, and some routine matters, did Chase rise to speak. He gave his version of the history of slavery in the colonies and the states, starting with the founding of Jamestown—the first permanent English settlement in America, where the first enslaved Africans were brought ashore, in 1619. He quoted from Washington, Jefferson, and Madison to show that they hoped to see an end to slavery. He emphasized Jefferson's role in drafting the Northwest Ordinance and excluding slavery from the Northwest Territory. He detailed how slaveholders had come to dominate the national government: to control the presidency, the Congress, and the courts. Then Chase paused and said that he did not want to be misunderstood.[35]

"I take no sectional position. The supporters of slavery are the sectionalists, if sectionalists there be. Freedom is national; slavery only is local and sectional. I do not complain at all that the offices of this country have been filled by Southern gentlemen. Let them have the offices, if only they will administer the government in accordance with its original principles. But I do complain that it has not been so administered; that its powers have been perverted to the support of an institution which those principles condemn." The phrase "freedom is national" would become the rallying cry of the Republican Party, but it is usually attributed to Sumner, perhaps because his 1852 speech was reported far more widely than this 1850 address by Chase.[36]

Christopher Wren, architect of St. Paul's Cathedral in London in the late seventeenth century, is buried in the cathedral, with an epitaph that translates as: "If you seek his monument, look around you." Chase closed the first day of his speech with a similar tribute to Jefferson, saying that if a foreign visitor should ask to see Jefferson's monument, Chase would not take him to see the grave and obelisk at Monticello, the late president's Virginia plantation, but to the Northwest, to see the results of the Northwest Ordinance. "Behold on every side his monument," Chase would say to the visitor. "These thronged cities, these flourishing villages, these million happy homes of freemen, these churches, these schools . . . these institutions of education, religion and humanity, these great states . . . these, these are the monuments of Jefferson."[37]

On the next day, March 27, the battle between senators Benton and Foote resumed. After some angry words, including another hint by Foote that they should fight a duel, Vice President Millard Fillmore called a halt, because it was the agreed time for Chase to speak. Once again he was speaking to a Senate distracted by the prospect of a duel, not paying attention to a junior antislavery senator.[38]

Chase opened by saying that, in light of the history he had outlined the day before, there was no basis for the assertion by Calhoun and others that a balance between slavery and freedom was somehow an essential element of the Constitution. Turning to Clay's compromise, Chase favored the immediate admission of California as a free state. He argued that it was premature to attempt to resolve the boundary between Texas and New Mexico. He agreed with Clay that the slave trade should be abolished in Washington, but contended that (for the same reasons) slavery itself should be abolished in the district. Just as Congress had prohibited the Atlantic slave trade, Congress should prohibit the interstate slave trade. "Is it less cruel, less deserving of punishment, to tear fathers, mothers, children from their homes and each other, in Maryland and Virginia, and transport them to the markets of Louisiana or Mississippi?" Congress could not enact the proposed new fugitive slave law, Chase said, because the Fugitive Slave Clause was merely a compact among the states. He devoted several paragraphs to this constitutional argument and only a few sentences to a critique of the pending bill, although Chase did argue that the bill would allow "seizures without process, trial without a jury, and consignment to slavery beyond the limits of the state without opportunity of defense." Chase knew more about fugitive slave litigation than any other senator, and he should have used his courtroom experience to describe in more detail the injustice of the fugitive slave process.[39]

Chase opposed both Clay's proposal to allow slavery in the western territories and Webster's claim that slavery was effectively excluded from the West because of the arid climate and harsh terrain. "Neither soil, nor climate, nor physical formation, nor degrees of latitude will exclude slavery from any country," he asserted. As to Webster's argument that it was pointless to "reenact the will of God," Chase disagreed again, saying that all "just legislation must be a reenactment of the Divine will." He dismissed Southern threats of disunion, saying that the South had made such threats before, and, furthermore, that the South could not achieve its goals, such as extending slavery or preventing slaves from escaping, by leaving the Union. Then he closed with a paean to the Union and the Northwest Ordinance, saying that the people of the Northwest would insist that the principles of the ordinance should be extended to the whole West.[40]

"I have finished my speech," Chase wrote to his wife that evening, "and oh how far short I fell of what I hoped to do!" He planned to revise the speech and give it to the printers in two days, but in the end, it took him more than a week. One reason was the death of John Calhoun on March 31 and the long official funeral service on April 2. "Thus has terminated an uneasy, restless, earnest life," Chase wrote to his wife about Calhoun, "a life which if devoted to a noble cause would have been illustrious beyond that of any of our modern statesmen; but devoted, as it was, to the propagandism of slavery." Then he stopped himself in midsentence, adding: "Let Him judge who looks upon the heart." Chase was disappointed that his oration did not attract more attention, but this was, to some extent, his own fault, for the speech was long on facts and short on passion, and he waited too long to release it in printed form. The speech first appeared in print in the April 4 edition of the *National Intelligencer*; it did not appear in the *National Era* until April 11; and it did not appear at all in many newspapers, since by the time it was in print, it was old news. Another problem, not Chase's fault, was that he was neither a Whig nor a Democrat, so Whig and Democratic newspaper editors did not devote space to his speech. The *New-York Tribune*, the most important Whig paper, sided with Chase on slavery, but it ran only a very brief summary of his speech, buried in the daily congressional report.[41]

Some of Chase's frustration spilled out in his letters, such as one to Tappan, in which he wrote that "this unfortunate speech of mine has not had a fair chance in the world." He conceded in a letter to Stanley Matthews that "I am not a rousing speaker at best" but complained that the news was dominated by the quarrel between Benton and Foote. When Sumner wrote Chase that it was good to know that Seward was "with us," Chase replied that Sumner was wrong about Seward. "He holds many of our antislavery opinions, and will never, I believe, abandon them." But Seward, he said, intended to support Taylor, who was inclined to attempt nothing more than the admission of California. "He is too much of a politician for me." A few days later, Chase wrote to Hamlin that Seward was really just a "Whig partisan."[42]

Over the objections of Chase and others, the Senate in April formed a committee of thirteen members, headed by Clay, soon known as the Compromise Committee or the Omnibus Committee, because it would place all the proposals into one bill, like passengers in an omnibus. As this committee was working, Chase wrote to raise with Frederick Douglass a larger question: What would happen to former slaves after slavery ended? Echoing current scientific experts, Chase wrote that "the black and white races, adapted to different latitudes and countries by the influences of climate and other circumstances, operating through many generations, would never have been brought together in one community, except under the constraint of forces, such as that of slavery." Thus, although he was strongly opposed to "any discrimination in legislation against our colored population," Chase believed that the two races would probably have to separate when slavery ended. He posed another question to Douglass: What did he think about the possibility that black Americans would move to the West Indies or South America "not under the constraints of any colonization scheme, but of choice and free will?" Douglass wrote back that in his view, climate and geography were not relevant. "*We are here*, and here we are likely to be," he stated.[43]

Chase expressed similar views when John Mercer Langston and his brother Charles Langston, black leaders in Ohio, raised similar questions in a letter to him. Chase responded that he believed it likely that the white and black races would eventually separate, but there should be "no *violence*, no *compulsory emigration*, no *legalized injustice* of any description." The Declaration of Independence, in Chase's view, meant that blacks "have the same natural rights as other men," and, in a democracy, "there is no reliable security for the rights of any unless the rights of all are also secured."[44]

When the Omnibus Committee reported to the Senate on May 8, Chase was dismayed. He wrote to a friend that the report "yields everything to the South, not even retaining for the North the poor concession . . . of a declaration that slavery does not now exist and probably will not be introduced into the territories acquired from Mexico." Chase noted that Southern extremists were also not satisfied with the report "because it does not secure them against the future assaults of the antislavery men." The Southern men were right, he continued, "for if this legislative compromise should be enacted, it would add but fuel to the flame of antislavery zeal." Two days later, Chase wrote another friend that he thought the Southern opposition to the Clay compromise was "the

*John Mercer Langston, a graduate of Oberlin College, friend of Chase,
leader of the Ohio black community, and, later, member of Congress.*

action of adroit men, accustomed to play boldly, who hope to win by it a
portion of California." Chase hoped, however, that Southern opposition
would continue "long enough to kill the Omnibus Monster."[45]

Chase's wife and younger daughters spent a few weeks in Washington
in late April and early May. As the weather grew warm, however, Chase
wanted his wife in a cooler climate and under the care of a good physician. Chase was concerned about not only his wife but also little Josie,
who seemed to be sick more often than she was well. On Saturday, May
18, Chase, Belle, her sister, and the two children took the train to New
York City. They spent Sunday there, for Chase was averse to travel on
the Sabbath, and then the women and girls continued to Northampton,
Massachusetts, where Belle would be under the care of another water cure
practitioner. Chase left New York by Monday's overnight train to be back
in the Senate on Tuesday morning.[46]

Perhaps because Zachary Taylor opposed the Clay compromise, Chase started to warm to the president. "I do not think him a statesman," Chase wrote to his wife after a visit with Taylor, "but that is not his fault. He did not make himself president; the people are responsible for that. I believe him honest, and that is much in these days." Chase remained hopeful that the omnibus bill would be defeated, writing that "in the hands of any other man than Clay, it would fail beyond peradventure." In late June, during a short visit to see his wife in Massachusetts, Chase wrote to Sumner that "those of us who are opposed to the omnibus bill believe that it will be defeated by a majority of four votes at least. But those who favor it seem equally sanguine that it will pass by the same majority. Who is right will not be seen for several weeks, I fear, as the discussion moves on slowly."[47]

Chase was reading a book by Dr. Samuel Sheldon Fitch, probably his *Six Lectures on the Uses of the Lungs; and Causes, Prevention, and Cure of Pulmonary Consumption, Asthma, and Diseases of the Heart*, first published in 1847. Naturally, Dr. Fitch could not know what we understand about tuberculosis today, and effective antibiotic treatments for the disease were a century in the future, but he proposed some commonsense suggestions for consumption patients, such as exercise in the open air. Chase was impressed and wanted Belle to see Fitch. So in early July he went to New York, where they consulted Fitch together. The doctor suggested a facility near Morristown, New Jersey. Chase placed Belle there and then headed back to the capital, arriving late on July 9 or early on July 10.[48]

Chase thus may or may not have been in Washington when President Zachary Taylor, after a short illness, died in the late evening of July 9. Millard Fillmore took the oath and became president the next day. Chase wrote Belle that Washington was "full of rumors about Mr. Fillmore, the new Cabinet, and the effects of the change of administration upon the slavery question." After attending the funeral services in the White House East Room, Chase wrote her that "nobody *knows* what Mr. Fillmore will do, but the general opinion is that he will be controlled by the Clay and Webster influence." Indeed, this would prove the case: Fillmore named Webster as his secretary of state and threw his support behind Clay's compromise, leaning on legislators with promises of patronage.[49]

The national tragedy of Taylor's death was followed for Chase with personal tragedy; he received a telegram from Morristown on Sunday, July

28, saying that his year-old daughter Josie was dead. He wrote to his wife with "tearful eyes" and a "sad, sad heart" to lament and to console. "Surely I do not weep for her. She is happier now than either of us could be were all the blessings we covet ours; and she is spared a life of sickness and suffering which might have and very probably would have been hers had she lived." He longed to be with Belle but could not leave Washington. "The great questions which we have been discussing all winter approach their decision. A single vote may be of vast consequence." He would stay in Washington for a few days, and then "I shall come to you."[50]

On Wednesday, July 31, in a sweltering Senate chamber, Chase was part of a curious coalition that defeated the omnibus bill. In a series of votes, the opponents of Clay's compromise removed section after section from the bill, until the only provision left was the one that would admit Utah as a territory. The opponents of compromise rejoiced, with Seward "dancing about like a little top," and Chase shaking hands with Pierre Soulé, the pro-slavery senator from Louisiana. After this defeat, Henry Clay, old and tired, essentially gave up; he spent almost all of August on vacation. The relentless Stephen Douglas, Democrat from Illinois, did not give up, and on Thursday and Friday, at his suggestion, the Senate considered the bill to admit California.[51]

Chase finally left Washington on Saturday, August 3. Belle needed a change of scene, so he used this short trip to move his family to the mineral spring resort at Schooley's Mountain, New Jersey. One advantage of this change was that there was a new train service, twice a day, the terminus of which was only fifteen miles away from the resort. Even though it was summer, young Kate was not with her stepmother, aunt, and sister, but still at school in New York. Chase wrote his daughter on her tenth birthday in August to urge her to write more often and to tell the truth. "More than anything else," Chase wrote, he wanted her to become "a sincere, devoted Christian," one who was "true, gentle, forbearing towards your companions, loving all around you." It seems, from other letters, that Chase kept Kate at school, rather than with her stepmother, because he feared that Kate would be too much for Belle. "You are apt to presume a little on your strength," he wrote his wife, "and have had some severe warnings against *presuming too much*."[52]

Chase was back in Washington on Friday, August 9, in time to vote against what he derided as the "Texas Surrender Bill." The proposed legislation fixed the border between Texas and New Mexico, giving Texas some but not all of the territory it had claimed, and in return promised Texas compensation and implicitly allowed slavery in the New Mexico Territory. Chase thought it outrageous to give Texas half of New Mexico and to pay her "ten millions of dollars in consideration of her withdrawing her unfounded pretension to the other half." Chase blamed the new Fillmore administration, claiming that it had pressured New England Whigs into supporting the bill. A few days later, he was pleased to see the Senate vote to admit California as a state. Douglas was trying to push the pieces of the compromise through the Senate one by one, as separate bills, and so far, he was succeeding.[53]

When Chase heard that Charles Sumner's brother had died, he wrote to console his friend, saying that "often and often has the blow fallen upon me." The health of his wife was "so precarious that I have no respite from intense solicitude. You may well suppose that under the circumstances public life is irksome to me. Gladly would I retire and leave its duties and distinctions . . . to others. But I seem to myself to have no choice. So few are the faithful to Freedom [that] it would be criminal in me to think of retiring." Chase was writing not to complain but to urge Sumner not to discourage those seeking to make him a federal senator. "You must not decline, nor even show any repugnance to acceptance. It is a time of trial for the friends of freedom," and "our side needs encouragement." Sumner did not decline.[54]

As for Chase, he remained in Washington day after day as the Senate worked its way through bill after bill. It was not until August 19 that the chamber started to debate a specific fugitive slave bill. To solve what Southerners saw as the problem of hostile state statutes and officials, the bill proposed a system in which only *federal* officials would be involved. Federal district judges would appoint at least one federal commissioner for each county. Masters or their agents could seize a supposed fugitive slave and bring him before one of these commissioners, who would then decide whether the person was indeed a fugitive slave—on the basis of affidavits, without in-court testimony, cross-examination, or jury trial. Any person who aided or sheltered a fugitive slave, or impeded a slave catcher, or attempted to rescue a fugitive slave would face six months in jail and a $1,000 fine. And any person who failed to assist a slave catcher would also face federal criminal penalties.[55]

Chase, of course, opposed the bill. But, knowing that it would pass, he also worked for amendments. William Dayton of New Jersey offered on August 19 what should have been a commonsense amendment: that those accused of being fugitive slaves and threatened with a lifetime in slavery should have the right to trial by jury. With many senators absent, including John Hale and William Seward, Chase was the strongest voice in favor of this amendment.

"If the most ordinary controversy involving a contested claim to twenty dollars must be decided by a jury," he argued, "surely a controversy which involves the right of a man to his liberty should have a similar trial." Chase warned the Southerners that their bill would create more problems than it would solve. "You may rely upon it that so long as you send your agents into the free states to seize and carry off this class of persons, without any trial, upon no other authority than the claimant, so long you will encounter difficulties and serious difficulties." When Chase finished, there were shouts of "Question! Question!" for many senators were eager to vote and move on. After some further debate, in which Chase crossed swords with Jefferson Davis and Andrew Butler, the question was called on Dayton's amendment. The New Jersey senator and Chase were outvoted twenty-seven to eleven. It is possible that if all sixty senators had been present, Chase might have prevailed on this amendment or on some slight variation. But Douglas was not only counting votes; he was also betting on absences, a good bet in Washington in August.[56]

Chase offered his own amendment on August 23, so the fugitive slave bill would apply in the states but not in the territories. "The object of this amendment," he explained, "is to conform the provisions of the bill to the provisions of the Constitution." Since the Fugitive Slave Clause applied by its terms only to a "person held to service or labor in one state . . . escaping into another" state, Congress could not extend the fugitive slave system to the territories. Not only Southerners but also Northerners opposed Chase's proposal, with Dayton arguing that "in carrying out the Constitution in good faith, according to its spirit, it is right we should give the slave states a remedy for the recovery of fugitive slaves in the territories as well as the states." When the time came for a vote, Chase was alone, with forty-one votes against him.[57]

Later that day, he was in the minority again, when the Senate approved the fugitive slave bill, twenty-seven to twelve. Many Northern senators were absent—either out of town or merely out of the chamber—fearing that whichever way they voted on this controversial bill, they would anger some of their constituents. Even if all of the Northern senators had been present, however, the bill would have passed, with a combination of almost all the Southern votes, Whig and Democratic, and the votes of Northern Democrats sympathetic to the South.[58]

One by one, because of Douglas's diligence, and Fillmore's patronage pressure on reluctant members, and the absence of opponents, the compromise bills passed the Senate and the House and were signed into law by Fillmore. On the evening of September 7 the people of Washington celebrated, marching through the streets with a brass band to salute the senators who had favored the compromise. "The joy of everyone seemed unbounded," reported one paper, because "the factious spirit of Northern and Southern ultraism was crushed, and the danger that they had brought upon the Union had subsided and passed away." Chase, though, did not celebrate. He wrote to Sumner that "clouds and darkness are upon us" and that "the slaveholders have succeeded beyond their wildest hopes twelve months ago."[59]

Chase did not give up, however. On September 18, the day on which Fillmore signed the new Fugitive Slave Act, Chase sought leave to introduce a bill to prohibit slavery in the western territories. Clay, back in Washington, urged the Senate not to consider the bill: "There is, I believe, peace prevailing now throughout all our borders. I believe it will increase and will be permanent and durable. I trust the Senate will at once, and without hesitation, put its face against any further disturbance of this country." Chase disagreed "entirely from the idea of the senator from Kentucky, that these questions are settled." Congress, he said, had merely avoided the matter of slavery in the territories. Then Thomas Pratt of Maryland raised his own bill, to address the problem of slaves escaping from the District of Columbia. When Clay agreed that the Senate should address Pratt's legislation, saying that it would form part of the set of compromise measures, Chase pointed out that Clay had never mentioned this issue as part of his compromise, adding, "I know of no reason why the security of slavery in the district should be preferred to the security of freedom in the territories." But Chase was again outvoted, and the Senate considered Pratt's bill.[60]

In the final weeks of the session, the Senate turned to other issues. Chase and Benton worked together to secure funds for the first federal buildings in Cincinnati and Saint Louis, to serve as combined courthouses and customshouses. Benton noted that they merely sought facilities for the two great cities of the West that were "readily granted to the small towns of the Atlantic coast." More often, however, Chase found himself opposing appropriations. He wrote a friend that he had "no idea of the profligacy and recklessness in expenditure which characterizes the present conduct of our government." The annual appropriation, he feared, would reach $60 million. "It seems useless to resist the current," he conceded. "There are hardly half a dozen of us who have any disposition to do so."[61]

Finally, at noon on September 30, 1850, the ten-month session of Congress, one of the longest of the nineteenth century, was over. From Chase's perspective, it had been a terrible time. His sister and daughter had both died. His wife had contracted a deadly disease. Congress had passed a set of bills, including the Fugitive Slave Act, which he viewed as utterly wrong. Even measures he had supported, such as ending the slave trade in the District of Columbia, came with a stiff price, for Congress had rejected the idea of freeing the slaves there. Most members of Congress seemed determined to have no further discussion of the issues that had been resolved in what was soon termed and praised as the Compromise of 1850. People wanted agitators like Chase to cease bringing up the slavery question. He was understandably discouraged.[62]

CHAPTER 8

"The Question Is Not Settled"

1850−53

On his way home to Cincinnati, on the eve of the October 1850 state
election, Chase stopped in Sandusky, Ohio, to give a speech in which
he denounced Whigs and Democrats alike for their role in passing
the Fugitive Slave Act. The Democratic candidate for governor, Reuben
Wood, prevailed relatively easily, by a margin of twelve thousand votes,
and Chase's friend Norton Townshend won a seat as a Free Soil member
of Congress. In the new Ohio legislature, as in 1848, there would be
a close division between the two major parties, so that the Free Soil
Party would hold the balance of power. Excited, Chase wrote Joshua
Giddings about the possibility that the legislature might select him
as the state's next US senator. Chase was not, however, in favor of an
agreement between the Free Soil and Whig members of the legislature,
even if such an agreement was necessary to elect an antislavery senator.
"Our platform is a democratic platform," he wrote to John Morse, "our
principles are democratic principles, our name is the Free Democracy."
Chase was almost alone in calling the Free Soil Party the Free Democracy
at this time. But he had convinced himself that the day was not distant
when the Free Democrats and the other Democrats of Ohio would unite
in an antislavery coalition.[1]

Chase did not have much time with his wife this winter, for Belle had
decided that she did not want to spend the rest of her life in water cures

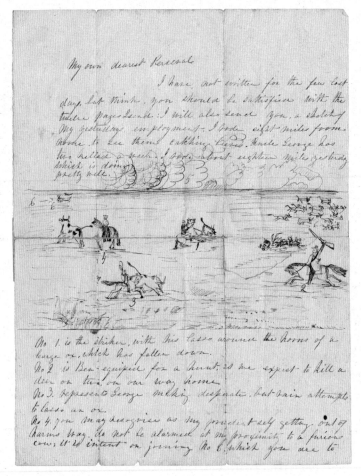

Belle Chase, writing to her husband from Texas in December 1850,
sketched a cattle roundup for him. Belle depicted herself in the upper left
of the sketch, "getting out of harm's way."

or other medical facilities. Instead, she wanted to spend the winter in southern Texas, to see if warm weather would help with her tuberculosis. "I do not at all relish the idea of such wide separation," Chase wrote to Kate in late October, but he was prepared to endure it for the sake of his wife's health. A party of five started by steamboat in November for New Orleans: Belle, her younger brother Benjamin Chambers Ludlow, their older sister, Charlotte Ludlow Jones, her husband, Charles Jones, and three-year-old Nettie Chase. From New Orleans, Belle, Ben, and

Nettie continued by boat to Matagorda, Texas, where they stayed with relatives George and Charlotte Kenner on their cattle ranch. Chase wrote to his wife often, urging her to "omit no care for the restoration of your health. Take all the exercise in the open air you possibly can." Only one of Belle's letters to her husband from Texas has survived: a lovely one, in which she sketched herself on horseback, watching as the men rounded up great herds of cattle. Belle addressed her husband as "my own dearest Perceval," an allusion to one of the legendary knights of King Arthur's Round Table, and she signed herself "ever devotedly your own." In a Christmas letter to Kate, at school in New York, Belle reported that the weather was "warm and soft as summer, and flowers are blooming all around." A month later, she served as scribe for little Nettie, telling Kate that she would like to show her the sights of Texas, including a "real live calf" that she had received as a pet from her uncle George.[2]

Chase returned to Washington in early December for the second session of the Thirty-First Congress, expected to be a short and quiet session. He spent Christmas in New York City, from where he wrote to Belle that she would "hardly know Kate if you were to meet her in a strange place." The girl's manners were "ladylike, without awkward diffidence and yet modest," and she was "much better looking." Kate was by this time writing frequent letters to her father, and he would write back, often criticizing her penmanship or composition. In January, for example, he wrote that she needed to include more detailed descriptions in her letters. "You, I think, are like me. You set down only naked facts without any embellishment whatever." In another letter, he praised her progress, saying that her letter would "do credit to a young lady." But she should "not be content with doing so well. You must try to improve more and more until you write a really elegant hand and express your ideas with ease and fluency." We do not have Kate's letters from this period, only those of her father, which were almost illegible. Chase was aware of the problem, writing to his daughter that she should not "imitate my illegible writing, but follow my precept rather than my practice."[3]

Chase's niece Hannah, daughter of his late sister Hannah Chase Whipple, spent this winter with Chase in Washington. Together they attended Saturday-night parties at the home of Gamaliel and Margaret Bailey, with a group that Chase described to his wife as "the Free Soilers and Liberals in Congress." One key member of this weekly gathering was Sara Jane Clarke, who lived with the Baileys, served as governess for their children, and wrote articles and books under the pen name Grace Greenwood. Chase described her to Kate as "the author of those stories of her pets which you liked so much." Others who attended regularly were Horace Mann, educator, reformer, and member of Congress from Massachusetts; his wife, Mary Peabody Mann; Congressmen George Julian of Indiana and Kinsley Bingham of Michigan; and Apollonia Jagiello, known in the press as the "heroine of Hungary" for her military role in the failed Hungarian Revolution of 1848. Chase did not write much to his wife about these parties, but it is clear from the letters that Bingham and Julian wrote to *their* wives that everyone enjoyed themselves. "We had a glorious time at Dr. Bailey's last Saturday night," Julian wrote, "the most *rollicking* time I have known in Washington." Julian noted that Chase and his niece were among those who stayed, after most of the other guests had departed, and played blindman's bluff, spinning the blindfolded person around three times and then challenging him or her to blow out a candle. On another evening, Greenwood performed a satire on Shakespeare, and the "audience was convulsed with laughter."[4]

Salmon Chase, circa 1850, in what appears to be the first portrait of him.

Knowing that this Congress would not pass antislavery legislation and hoping to make progress on other issues, such as river and harbor legislation, Chase did not raise slavery during this short congressional session. But others did, notably Henry Clay. The aged senator rose on February 16, 1851, to denounce how a Boston mob, of both whites and blacks, had rushed into the federal courthouse to seize and free an alleged fugitive slave. "The question raised" by the Boston rescue, Clay intoned, was "whether the government of white men is to be yielded to a government by blacks." The Senate spent a day discussing whether to seek a report on the Boston riot from President Fillmore and then another two days on whether to refer the report to a committee.[5]

Chase spoke on February 22, saying that he was sorry that the Senate was once again debating slavery. Chase may not have been *that* sorry to see the Senate debating slavery—which he viewed as the most important issue facing the nation—but for political purposes, he wanted to appear reluctant to raise the issue. He explained that although he had opposed almost all the compromise measures, he was prepared in this session to leave them "to the judgment of the people and to postpone further discussion until that judgment should be passed upon them." He reminded his colleagues that he had warned them that the 1850 Fugitive Slave Act would cause controversy. People naturally sympathized with fugitives, and "you cannot legislate it from the breast. Add to this sympathy the conviction very generally felt that this law is unconstitutional [and] the public sentiment of hostility to slavery itself, and it becomes very obvious that the law cannot be executed to any practical extent." Some senators were calling for Fillmore to send federal troops to Boston. "For what end?" Chase asked. "You cannot prevent occurrences like this by all the military force in the world."[6]

In March, after a long stalemate, the Ohio legislature selected Benjamin Wade to join Chase in the Senate. An outspoken opponent of slavery, Wade would in time become a friend and ally of Chase, but at first Chase distrusted him as a Whig. In April, after an even longer impasse, the Massachusetts legislature selected Charles Sumner for the Senate. Chase rejoiced, writing his friend that he hoped that the two of them could room together in Washington in the coming winter.[7]

By this time, Chase was back in Ohio, working on legal cases. After hearing the famous Swedish soprano Jenny Lind at one of her concerts in Cincinnati, and meeting the "Swedish Nightingale" in person as part of a group of officials, Chase wrote to his wife that Lind spoke well—better than he expected—but was "prodigiously ugly." Cassius M. Clay and his wife were in town to hear Lind, too, and Chase was favorably impressed by Mary Jane Clay, writing to Belle that she had "a splendid blue eye and noble forehead." What he admired most, he was quick to add, was "her devotion to her husband." Chase was growing impatient for his own wife to return from Texas, but she did not reach Cincinnati until May, after an absence of about six months.[8]

Chase traveled to Toledo, Ohio, in late May 1851 to deliver a major speech. The proponents of the Compromise of 1850, he noted, claimed to have "settled" the slavery question. "Every man who has an eye to see or an ear to hear knows that the question is not settled. It is more unsettled than ever. The fugitive slave bill has thrown into the cauldron new elements and applied to it fiercer flames. It degrades the state sovereignties; it makes every man's personal freedom insecure; it sends its marshals and deputy marshals among us, to seize any man who may be claimed as a fugitive from service; it clothes its irresponsible commissioners with powers to enforce that claim without affording any adequate defense to its victim."[9]

Chase then turned to his ideas about how best to end American slavery: "In the view of the Constitution, slavery is a mere state concern. It depends wholly on state laws for its existence and continuation. . . . All power to authorize or sustain slavery is carefully withheld from the national government." This meant that the federal government should ensure that there was no slavery outside the limits of the slave states—no slavery in the District of Columbia, for example—and that there should be "no legislation by Congress for the extradition of fugitives from service." But, Chase continued, "within state limits, slavery must be left to the disposition of state legislation." He expected, perhaps naively, that if the federal government excluded slavery from the territories and repealed the fugitive slave laws, the slave state governments would soon pass laws to emancipate their slaves. Chase contrasted this approach, which he called the Jeffersonian, Democratic approach toward ending slavery, with another: the Whig approach. This would involve "emancipation by the general government, coupled with compensation of the masters, and perhaps expatriation and colonization of the slaves," which, in Chase's view, would entail "the creation of an enormous national debt" and the "perpetuation of oppressive tariff and credit systems."[10]

Next, Chase addressed the argument that the South would secede if Congress took the steps he suggested. "This is an old cry and a very stale cry," he contended. The threat of disunion was merely a negotiation tactic: a way for Southerners to scare Northerners so that they could get their way. Chase analogized the states to planets, held in their places by gravity, and said he had "no fear that South Carolina will permanently disappear from the American Constellation." He closed with an inspiring vision of the country's future, in which "the hope of Jefferson" was realized in an expansive Union, with "all free, every right defended, all labor justly rewarded, and not a man enslaved!"[11]

Throughout the night and into the morning, Chase worked with a reporter to turn his notes into a printed version of the speech. "This work was harder than speaking," he wrote to Belle, "but I think by this means a pretty fair report has been secured." Chase also used his time in Toledo to visit with his younger sister Helen, now the wife of the local Episcopal priest, Henry Walbridge, and the mother of a "charming family" of five children.[12]

In late June Chase gave another, similar speech in Ravenna, near Cleveland, at a Free Soil meeting. Giddings, Morse, Townshend, and Samuel Lewis were among the Free Soil leaders present. In a letter to Sumner, Chase called the event "glorious." Belle and Nettie were with him in Cleveland, and from there the family traveled to Lockport, New York, where they visited with Chase's younger brother Edward and older sister Janette. While away, Chase wrote in early July to decline an invitation to attend a convention of Democrats in Fulton County, Ohio, urging the delegates to oppose the fugitive slave law. And later that month, he wrote to a friend that "Mrs. Chase's health is somewhat improved, though the nature of her disease—an affliction of the lungs—does not admit of relief from painful apprehension so long as any unfavorable symptoms remain."[13]

In August 1851 the Ohio Democrats gathered in Columbus and nominated Reuben Wood for a second term as governor. Some members of the state party wanted this convention to endorse the Compromise of 1850, as other Democrats were doing in other states, but the Ohio party declined to do so, instead affirming prior resolutions urging the federal government to "use all power clearly given by the terms of the National Compact, to prevent the increase, to mitigate, and finally to eradicate the evil" of slavery. The state convention also criticized how the Fillmore administration was employing patronage to punish those who refused to implement the Fugitive Slave Act. Some county conventions were using stronger language, including the Fulton convention to which Chase had written, whose delegates declared that they "opposed the fugitive slave law and recommend its immediate repeal," and that they detested how the administration was "turning out of office men merely for not approving of the infamous fugitive slave law."[14]

Although Chase would have preferred a more explicit antislavery platform, he decided that this state Democratic platform was good enough, and he wrote Joshua Giddings that he was inclined to support the Democrats rather than the Free Soil Party in the impending election. "Undoubtedly there is no Old Line Democracy in the country occupying so advanced a position as the Democracy of Ohio. It seems to me that it would be almost criminal to withdraw from them the influence which has brought them into this position and may keep them there." Chase knew Giddings would disagree, but he hoped to keep close with both his Democratic and Free Soil friends. Perhaps Chase was already thinking ahead, hoping that another coalition of Democrats and Free Soilers would elect him to a second senate term. In any case, a few weeks later, Chase wrote the *Toledo Republican* a long public letter explaining why he would accept the Columbus platform and support the Democrats' candidates. Chase quoted from county resolutions, from Democratic newspapers, and from Governor Wood's inaugural address to claim that Ohio Democrats opposed the fugitive slave law and opposed the extension of slavery.[15]

Not surprisingly, Chase's friends in Free Soil Party were horrified that he would abandon them for the Democrats. One county convention declared that Chase's Toledo letter "filled us with shame and mortification. Henceforth he must rank among mere partisan politicians." The *Cleveland True Democrat*, edited by his friend John Vaughan, commented that Chase had hurt himself more than his enemies ever could. The *Anti-Slavery Bugle,* the weekly paper of the Ohio Anti-Slavery Society, said that if Chase could accept Wood in Ohio, he would probably accept whichever candidate the Democrats selected for the 1852 presidential election. This was "but another step in the descent Mr. Chase commenced at Buffalo," when he left the Liberty Party and backed Martin Van Buren. The only Free Soil editor who supported Chase was Gamaliel Bailey, who printed the Toledo letter in full and stressed that Chase was in no way committed to supporting the Democrats in 1852. Meanwhile, Whig papers chuckled at Chase's defection, with Akron's *Summit County Beacon* accusing Chase and Norton Townshend of exploiting Free Soil to gain high office and then deserting the party, in essence telling their friends, "We have no further use for you."[16]

Perhaps troubled by this reaction, Chase did not give speeches for Wood. Indeed, in late September he attended a rally of the "friends of freedom" in Cleveland, where speakers included his friends Samuel Lewis, the Free Soil candidate for governor, and Cassius M. Clay of Kentucky. Chase had not planned to speak, but the crowd called for him, and, according to one paper's report, he assured them that although he "somewhat differed— temporarily he trusted—from those with whom he had long acted," he would never abandon "the cause to which the best years of his life had been devoted." When the election results were tallied, Wood won a second term with more than 145,000 votes, while Lewis received only about 16,000. The *Cleveland True Democrat* complained that the vote for Lewis would have been "larger by some thousands had Mr. Chase stood by his party."[17]

As Chase prepared to leave Cincinnati for Washington in November 1851, he rented a furnished house in Clifton, a village about four miles north of Cincinnati, near the homes of his friends Justice McLean and Bishop McIlvaine. His hope was to provide Belle and Nettie with "a pleasant home in the country" for the months that he was away. Arriving in the capital on the first day of December, in time for the start of the first session of Congress, Chase resumed his frequent letters to his "beloved, afflicted, precious wife." Late one Sunday night he wrote that he hoped and prayed for the restoration of her health: "It may please God to grant my earnest prayer for it. If not, I desire above all things your cheerful loving submission to the Divine Will here and your eternal happiness." As for himself, he admitted that he suffered from "sinful thoughts and inclinations" and that his love of God was "so feeble and cold, that I dare not be confident. Pray for me, my dearest. Let us pray for each other."[18]

In another letter, Chase told his wife that he had just finished reading part of *Uncle Tom's Cabin*, written by his friend Harriet Beecher Stowe and first published by his friend Gamaliel Bailey in the *National Era*. Although Stowe had recently moved to Maine, her novel was based on what she had seen and heard in her two decades in Cincinnati. Chase would have recognized the book's central scene, in which the young slave Eliza escapes from Kentucky to Ohio, across the frozen Ohio River, clutching

Eliza, an enslaved character in Harriet Beecher Stowe's novel Uncle Tom's Cabin, *crosses the Ohio River. Chase, who had represented fugitive slaves like Eliza, wrote in his diary that he could not read Beecher's novel without tears.*

her child to her chest—for Chase had represented women just like Eliza. He would also have recognized one of the minor characters, John Van Tromp, a kindly farmer who shelters Eliza, whom Stowe had patterned after his client John Van Zandt. Although Chase did not often write about whippings and beatings, he would have known that Stowe did not exaggerate when she described the brutality of slavery. Like thousands of others—the novel sold more copies than any other book published in the nineteenth century—he found Stowe's story intensely emotional, writing in his diary, "I cannot read it without tears."[19]

Belle, in her letters to her husband, gave him a positive picture of her health, writing that she was feeling better. But then, in the middle of December, Chase received an alarming letter from her physician Joseph Potter. Belle could not speak above a whisper, Potter wrote, and her feet were swollen due to lung failure. Chase left Washington almost at once. When he reached Cincinnati, he learned that Belle was not even able to go up and down the stairs and that her legs had swollen substantially. Potter told Chase that he had never seen a consumptive patient live for more than a few weeks after such swelling.[20]

Chase and his wife shared a somber Christmas. He wrote his friend Hamlin on New Year's Day that "the physician gives no hope of recovery."

A few days later, he wrote another friend that "I feel like a criminal while absent from my post" in Washington, but "under existing circumstances, my first duty is to her." Although Chase did not mention it, he was thinking about the death of his first wife; how he had been away on business during the last few days of Catherine's life. He would not make that mistake again. Chase was at Belle's side when she died in Clifton on the afternoon of January 13, 1852. She was thirty-one years old.[21]

Papers around the nation noted the death of Sarah Bella Ludlow Chase, generally without comment. One exception was the *Cleveland True Democrat*. Overlooking his recent differences with Chase, Vaughan wrote about how Sarah had "wrestled with disease: never repining, never complaining, and genial in spirit to the last." She had gone to heaven, Vaughan wrote, "and happy will it be for us, if living we should be so beloved, or dying so blessed." Chase was not keeping a diary at this time, and there are no surviving letters from him for a month after his wife's death, but it seems that he remained in Cincinnati for a while, for he is not mentioned in the daily reports of congressional debates until early February. When he went back to Washington, Chase left Nettie behind with relatives in the Cincinnati area.[22]

Even after he returned to the Senate, Chase was slowed and saddened. He wrote to his daughter Kate that they must think of Belle in heaven "whither a purer and gentler spirit has seldom gone." In a letter to Hamlin, on black-bordered paper, Chase predicted that James Buchanan of Pennsylvania, a Southern sympathizer, would get the Democratic nomination for president and that the national Democrats would endorse the Compromise of 1850. A few weeks later, in a similar letter, he anticipated that the Democrats would choose either Buchanan or Lewis Cass of Michigan, the latter of whom he found equally objectionable.[23]

When the Democrats held their national convention in Baltimore in early June, Chase attended for a day or two "as a deeply interested spectator," writing to a friend that all was "confusion." It was indeed a chaotic convention, out of which a dark horse, former senator Franklin Pierce of New Hampshire, emerged at last as the party's presidential nominee. The platform praised the Compromise, especially the Fugitive Slave Act, saying that because the law was "designed to carry out an express provision of the Constitution," it could not be "repealed, or so changed as to destroy or impair its efficiency." Northern antislavery Democrats might achieve some success at a state convention (as in Columbus in 1851), but Southerners and their dough-faced allies could easily outvote them at a national convention (as in Baltimore in 1852). A few days after the convention, Sumner wrote to Charles Francis Adams that Chase viewed the platform and the nomination as "the greatest triumph slavery has ever had." Soon Chase said the same thing in a public letter: he would not support Pierce or the platform; instead, he would support the Free Democrats, the term he preferred for the Free Soil Party—and one that many now accepted.[24]

In late July Chase took a brief break from Congress to travel to Hanover, New Hampshire, to attend his Dartmouth reunion. Chase explained to Kate that he had graduated from the college in 1826, and "since then we have never met. Twenty-six years have rolled away . . . making many and great changes and now my class or so many as can are to meet at the college. I want to be there and shake hands with those who come." In 1826 the journey from Washington to Hanover would have taken at least a week by stagecoach. Now, in 1852, Chase could travel by rail, completing the trip in about a day. On his way back to Washington, he chanced to meet Pierce in Concord, New Hampshire. "He is a very prepossessing man," Chase wrote to Hamlin, "and I am not surprised that he is popular." They did not talk long, but Chase did tell Pierce that the Baltimore resolutions "would prevent me from supporting him."[25]

As the national convention of the Free Democrats, or Free Soilers, set for August in Pittsburgh, approached, there were many who wanted Chase as the nominee. He may have secretly hoped that the convention would nominate him, but he discouraged friends from pressing his name. "Hale is a good enough Democrat," Chase wrote to Hamlin, "far better certainly than Cass or Buchanan or Pierce." Chase added that he wanted "to be out of the scrape for many reasons" including hostile sentiment in Cincinnati and Cleveland. Indeed: there must have been many among the Ohio Free Democrats still smarting at the way that Chase had abandoned them the prior year. Chase did not attend the convention, remaining in Washington, where Congress was still in session, but his friend Townshend went, armed with a letter from Chase declining the nomination, to read aloud if necessary. On the very eve of the convention, Chase heard from a Boston editor that he had a letter from Hale, declining the nomination. Chase telegraphed the editor not to publish it, and he wrote to Hale, insisting that he reconsider. "The spontaneous impulses of the antislavery men everywhere designate you as the nominee," Chase told Hale. "You cannot disregard them without the most serious injury to yourself and the cause." The convention nominated Hale, and he accepted eventually.[26]

As was often the case, Congress procrastinated in the early weeks of the 1852 session, so that there were long hours during the frantic final weeks. Drinking was common in Congress in the nineteenth century and more common near the end of a session. One evening in late August, sitting at his Senate desk, Chase described for his daughter Kate the debate on an important amendment: "A tipsy senator gets up and opposes it. Wine makes him merry, and he makes senators merry. . . . It is sad and wrong; but almost unavoidable when so many men get together under circumstances of so much excitement."[27]

When the first session finally ended, Chase went to Ohio to campaign for Hale for president and Giddings for Congress. He wrote Sumner that "our friends in Ohio are in good spirits, and the vote for Hale . . . will be respectable—not so great as it would have been had there been no conspiracy against me, but still as large, I hope, as that of 1848." This was a curious comment, suggesting that Chase had been hoping for the nomination even as he insisted that he was not interested. Chase spoke to large and enthusiastic crowds in Cleveland, Oberlin, and other towns in the Western Reserve, the region where Free Soil would receive its strongest support. John Mercer Langston, the young black leader, introduced both Chase and Hale when they spoke in the crowded church at Oberlin College, Langston's alma mater, the nation's first mixed-race, mixed-gender college.[28]

In the Ohio election in October, Giddings and Edward Wade (brother of Benjamin) won seats for the Free Soil Party in the House of Representatives. A month later, in the national election, Pierce won a convincing victory, carrying twenty-seven of the thirty-one states, while his Whig opponent, General Winfield Scott, captured only four. Democrats would also control both houses of the next Congress. Hale received 155,210 votes nationwide, fewer than Van Buren in 1848, but the main reason was that the Barnburners and other Democrats had reconciled in New York. Outside of New York, Hale was able to get more or less as many votes as Van Buren received four years earlier. In Ohio, for example, he received 31,782 votes, compared to 35,347 for Van Buren. The dramatic defeat of the Whigs suggested that the party might soon dissolve, paving the way for a new and broader antislavery party. This would indeed happen, but not quite yet—not until 1854, when the Nebraska debate, in which Chase would play such a central part, shattered the old party patterns.[29]

The two greatest Whigs, Henry Clay and Daniel Webster, both died in 1852. Amidst the praise for Webster after his death, Wendell Phillips, the Boston abolitionist, denounced him for his support of the 1850 Compromise. This prompted Chase to write to Phillips that Webster was "my father's friend" and also "showed some personal kindness to me" as a young man. "While, therefore, I acquiesce in the justice of your judgment of his great apostasy . . . I wish for some melting charity mingled with the flashes of just indignation." Chase added that he hoped that Phillips (who, like Garrison, eschewed political parties) could join the political antislavery men. "Will the time never come when the opponents of slavery will see eye to eye—and work shoulder to shoulder?"[30]

Chase was busy at this time with a Supreme Court argument as well as Senate sessions. Over the course of three days in late December, he argued for Henry O'Reilly in his patent case against Samuel F. B. Morse in the highest court in the land. The justices accepted Chase's central argument, expressed in language still cited in contemporary patent cases, that one of Morse's patent claims was too broad; the scientist could not patent the general concept of communicating by electric impulses, only his specific method for telegraphic communication. Chase arranged for his argument to be printed as a pamphlet, and some papers printed parts, with the *Cleveland True Democrat* commenting that it was "worthy of his high standing as an advocate and a scholar."[31]

Not much happened in Congress in the short session from December 1852 and through March 1853. Near the end of the session, however, Chase managed to get an amendment added to the army appropriation bill, providing funds for a survey of the possible routes for a railroad to the Pacific. The *New York Evening Post* complimented the senator from Ohio on his "tact and discernment" in getting this amendment adopted and hoped it would be the "means of not only materially expediting the construction of the Pacific railroad, but of commencing it in a safe and judicious way." Chase immediately thanked John Bigelow, a senior *Post* editor, writing that "so many *cold* words are directed towards me, that a *warm* regard is really refreshing." A few weeks later, when the *Evening Post* moved to a newer and taller building, Chase wrote again, gently teasing Bigelow. "Few certainly would aspire to a higher post than that you occupy." Before this time, Chase had cultivated Ohio editors; now he began reaching out to New York editors, at just the time that their papers, using the telegraph and the rails, and ever-larger printing presses, were coming to dominate the national news industry.[32]

On March 4, 1853, Chase attended the inauguration of Franklin Pierce as the nation's fourteenth president. He approved of some parts of the inaugural address, such as when Pierce pledged "rigid economy in all departments" of the federal government, and disagreed with others, such as the claim that the Compromise of 1850 was "strictly constitutional and to be unhesitatingly carried into effect." In a short special session after the inauguration, the Senate confirmed Pierce's key appointments, including Jefferson Davis as secretary of war.[33]

Successful political parties in the nineteenth century supported their party newspapers through government printing contracts. For example, when the Ohio Democrats, with Chase's help, gained control of the state legislature in the winter of 1848–49, they gave Samuel Medary, editor of the leading Democratic paper, the *Ohio Statesman,* the state senate printing contract. Sometimes the printing spoils were shared between the two major parties, and William Henry Seward proposed such an arrangement in April 1853: to pay the *National Intelligencer*, a Washington Whig paper, to publish some of the recent Senate debates, even though they had already been published in the *Daily Globe.* Chase opposed Seward's motion—indeed, opposed the whole system—arguing that it should be left to private enterprise. To show how absurd the Seward suggestion was, Chase moved that the *National Era* should receive the printing work, as the representative of the Independent Democratic Party.[34]

Chase's motion provoked an angry response from John Weller, the unsuccessful Democratic candidate for Ohio governor in 1848, now a Democratic senator from California. Chase and Weller never liked each other, with Chase once describing Weller in his diary as a "miserable dough-face." Weller now declared that Chase did not represent the "great Democracy of Ohio," but only "a clique for the purpose of destroying the peace and tranquility of the Union." Chase had been elected by a "dishonorable bargain" between Democrats and abolitionists, and there was no way that he could be reelected. In two years, Weller predicted, to laughter from the galleries, Chase would be back in private life, where he could pursue his pointless philanthropic schemes.[35]

Weller's speech elicited a long response from Chase. He defended the
way in which he had been elected, saying that it was natural for the Old
Line Democrats and the Independent Democrats to collaborate, since they
agreed on so many issues, and that neither party had compromised its principles. Chase explained why he preferred to call himself an Independent
Democrat but added that "gentlemen may call me an abolitionist if they
choose, and I will promise not to be at all angry. The name would simply
identify me in sentiment and opinion with some of the greatest and best
men who ever lived, both of our own and other lands." Regarding his
own political future, Chase conceded that it was "very possible that I may
not be reelected. I shall have as little to regret in that event as any man."
As to the cause of freedom, however, he insisted that "no future event is
more certain, in my judgment, than that the principles of this minority
will become the principles of a majority of the American people."[36]

The *New York Herald*, in its summary of the news the next day, called
the Chase-Weller confrontation a "decidedly spicy affair." For the *Baltimore
Sun*, Chase's successful opposition to Seward's motion showed how dangerous it was to elect antislavery senators; a few more such senators could
prevent all "healthy action" in the Senate. An editorial in the *National
Era* made just the opposite point, urging readers in Ohio to elect a legislature that would reelect Senator Chase. Not only was he necessary as
a "friend of freedom" in Washington, according to the *Era*, but he had
also represented Ohio's other interests well in the Senate.[37]

When the short Senate session ended, Chase went back to Ohio by way of
New York City, where he saw political friends and his daughter Kate, and
Lockport, where he saw his brother Edward. When he returned to Ohio,
Chase started to give campaign speeches, often with Joshua Giddings or
Samuel Lewis, the Free Democratic candidate for governor.[38]

Chase took a break from the campaign in June, however, to go to Saint
Louis to help two widows: Mary Gillespie Chase, wife of his impecunious
brother William, and Jane Chase Auld, daughter of Chase's brother Alexander. Both women were struggling on the edge of poverty. Hearing that
Chase was coming to town, Frank Blair, a local lawyer and state legislator,
later a member of Congress and a Union general, wrote to ask him to give
a speech about the Pacific railway. Frank's older brother Montgomery,
also a lawyer, had helped Chase with at least one Missouri legal question

and would later serve with him in the Lincoln Cabinet. Their father was Francis Preston Blair, a newspaper editor and informal adviser to several presidents. In short, the Blair family played an important role in American politics and in Chase's life, eventually becoming his most outspoken enemies.[39]

When Chase arrived in Saint Louis, the mayor of the city and various other leaders seconded Blair's suggestion that he give a speech about railroads. (One of them, Edward Bates, a prominent Whig, would also serve with Chase in the Lincoln Cabinet.) Chase declined, but he did write a public letter pledging his support of what he called "the great work of modern times": the construction of a railroad to the Pacific along the "most direct and practicable route." Chase was pleased by his reception in Saint Louis, bragging about it to both Bigelow and Sumner. "If this note is a little more unintelligible than common in consequence of undecipherable chirography," he started his letter to Bigelow, "place it to the account of the wheezy, huffy, shaking but otherwise very comfortable steamer *Prairie State*, bound from Saint Louis to La Salle [Illinois], whereupon I am at this present writing a passenger." Chase noted that the request for him to speak in Saint Louis was one of the first invitations an antislavery leader had received to deliver an address in a slave state, and that it had been followed by others, including one from Virginia. These invitations seemed to suggest a "modified and may I not add mollified sentiment south of Mason & Dixon's line." Chase forwarded a clipping from a Saint Louis newspaper, with the letter inviting him to speak and his response, in hopes that Bigelow would reprint it in the *New York Evening Post*. Although the *Post* did not reprint the letters, it printed a positive letter from a local correspondent about Chase's time in Saint Louis. "All parties, without distinction, joined in giving him a hearty welcome, and he was received with the distinguished consideration he deserves."[40]

Chase took another break from the campaign in July to go to Philadelphia and Washington. On his way, he stopped for a few days at the home of the railroad entrepreneur Thomas Ellicott, in Chester County, Pennsylvania, and described the house and family to his daughter Kate. "Miss Lizzie," an unmarried daughter of thirty-one, "is the best-looking of them all and is really a very superior woman, with a great deal of sense and a good deal of heart. You need not however be alarmed for me, for a gentleman in New York is said to be her accepted lover, and I look only for *friends* among ladies as I do also among gentlemen." Kate, who was now thirteen, was worried at the prospect that her father would marry for a fourth time; she had come to value her own central role in Chase's life and to oppose any woman in whom he had romantic interests. In spite of Kate's resistance, Chase would continue to have female friends—including Elizabeth Ellicott, who would soon marry another Chase friend, James Shepherd Pike, Washington correspondent for the *New-York Tribune*.[41]

During election season, nineteenth-century newspapers were in the habit of printing the names of their preferred political candidates daily, usually as the first item in the news columns. Free Soil papers in Ohio in 1853, for example, urged voters to support Samuel Lewis for governor and other men for lesser state offices. Whig and Democratic papers printed their own different slates. None of these 1853 Ohio slates named Chase or any other candidate for the federal Senate, although everyone understood that the Ohio legislature elected in October 1853 would decide whether Chase or some other man would serve in the Senate after the end of his first term in March 1855. Occasionally papers would comment about this Senate aspect of the election. The *Portage Sentinel*, a Democratic paper in Ravenna, claimed in June 1853 that Chase, Lewis, and Giddings were on the campaign trail early because they wanted "the balance of power in the next legislature, in hopes thereby to secure the reelection of Salmon P. Chase to the United States Senate." But such comments were rare, not just in Ohio in this year but elsewhere in this era. Senate races were implicit, not explicit, in antebellum America.[42]

Chase, however, was well aware of the stakes in the 1853 state election, and he spoke more often and in more places (at least twenty different Ohio counties) this year than in any prior election. We do not know much about what he said in these speeches, but there are some hints in the newspapers. Chase spoke in Toledo on June 20, for example, to what he described in his diary as a small crowd on a hot evening. A local paper commented that he "stood where he did two years ago, a Democrat of the Jeffersonian school." Chase contended that the federal government should get out of the business of supporting slavery but leave the question of abolition to the states. "It was never the intention of the framers that this should be a great consolidated government, and if Jefferson could see the present centralization of power at Washington, the immense revenue and patronage under the control of the administration, he would be astonished." In a speech in Syracuse, New York, on August 31, Chase attacked the Supreme Court's *Van Zandt* decision in favor of the fugitive slave law by noting that five of the nine justices were from slave states. A reporter hearing this speech called it "able, statesmanlike, convincing" and predicted that Chase would serve in a yet higher office. Another paper commented that Chase held his audience's attention through "clear thought, lucid arrangement, appropriate language, and candid and courteous manner."[43]

In addition to giving speeches, Chase wrote three long letters in late 1853 as part of his quiet campaign for a second Senate term. The first was to Edward Hamlin, detailing his work in the Senate for Ohio and for the West. This letter described, for example, how Chase and Thomas Hart Benton had secured funding for the first federal buildings in Cincinnati and Saint Louis, even when all seemed lost because the parallel House bill did not include such funding. Hamlin or another editor revised and extended this letter into four articles in the *Cleveland True Democrat*, soon reprinted in several other papers. The second and third articles in this series tracked Chase's letter closely, while the first and fourth were largely drafted by the editors. The series started by saying that, after a careful review of Chase's legislative record, the editors were "highly impressed with his industry, his talents, his independence, his judicious management, and in many cases his meritorious success." The final article described Chase as a true Jeffersonian Democrat, committed to preventing federal interference in state affairs and reducing federal expenditures. "The great danger to our institutions is that the national government will go on assuming the exercise of power not granted in the Constitution, until, by reason of the vast patronage and increasing revenue, in the hands of a wicked administration, it will corrupt the politicians gradually, absorb the powers of the states, and become irresistible—and in the end a tyranny."[44]

Chase also started but never finished a long autobiographical letter, perhaps intended as the first pages of a book with his speeches. He did not hide some of his failures. For example, in describing his bar exam in Washington, he admitted that he "had not been a diligent student" and "in fact, knew very little law." Judge William Cranch, however, "knew me and my circumstances. I had been in the habit of going up and playing chess with him, and he always beat me. Besides, he was one of the most benevolent men alive." Chase also described some of the key turning points in his life, such as the anti-abolition riots in Cincinnati in 1836. Noting that his late sister was the wife of one of the abolitionists, Isaac

Colby, Chase said that he came to realize that the abolitionists were some
of the city's most "pure, upright, and worthy citizens."[45]

In the third and longest letter, printed as a pamphlet, Chase contrasted the national Democratic Party, dominated in his view by the Slave
Power, with the Ohio Democrats, committed, in his view, to freedom.
He described and denounced "that great Slave Interest, wielding a capital, invested in human beings, of not less than fifteen hundred millions
of dollars, and controlling directly the political action of near half the
states, and exerting a potential influence over that of all the rest." The
Slave Power was a "great concentrated money and political power, in obedience to which politicians 'turn around and turn around' with as much
facility as Jim Crow ever performed his fantastic feats at the command of
his master." ("Jim Crow," at this time, was a song-and-dance routine in
which a white actor in blackface would mock the language and manners
of black slaves.) Many men, Chase continued, elected to "represent the
interests of farmers, mechanics, laborers, and traders of the free states,"
changed course when they reached Washington. These men voted with
and for the Slave Power, "relying upon party drill and the favor of an
administration, itself indebted to this Power for its existence, to keep
the voters in the traces back home." Chase let his pen run away from him
here, forgetting that many of the Ohio legislators who would decide upon
the next senator were traditional Democrats: they had voted for Franklin
Pierce, and they sought patronage from his administration.[46]

The 1853 Ohio state election was unusual because, although none
of the parties mentioned temperance in their platforms, much of the
campaign revolved around whether or not Ohio should adopt a Maine
law, patterned on the liquor prohibition law passed there two years earlier. *The Freeman's Manual*, for example, contrasted Samuel Lewis, who
openly favored a Maine law, with the Whig and Democratic candidates,
who took no stance on the question, and were, in the editor's view, de
facto opponents of temperance. The *Cleveland True Democrat*, knowing
that women were keener on prohibition than men, urged the women
of Cleveland to pressure their husbands to "do their duty" and vote for
temperance candidates. In some places, there were "fusion slates" that
combined antislavery and temperance candidates. Although Chase was
personally in favor of temperance, he disagreed with making temperance
one of Lewis's key issues, explaining in a letter to Gerrit Smith that there
was no "Rum Power" as dangerous as the Slave Power.[47]

As he toured the state, Chase was hopeful. He wrote Giddings that he believed Lewis would receive at least sixty thousand votes and that the Whig Party was weakening so rapidly that this election would probably be "our last triangular battle." He wrote Sumner that "prospects in Ohio are good" and "we hope to cast such a vote as will, if not elect our candidate, at least put an end to triangular contests." In the end, Lewis received 50,346 votes, fewer than Chase hoped, but far more than any antislavery candidate to this point in state history. William Medill, the Democrat, won the governorship with 147,663 votes, while Nelson Barrere, the Whig, tallied only 85,820. The Whigs suffered disastrous defeats in the legislative races, so that Old Line Democrats would dominate the legislature; they would have no need of Independent Democratic support but could elect one of their own as the next senator. Chase claimed to Hamlin that he was glad not to have a second term in the Senate, saying, "I want to be out of public station and in the ranks." He wrote in similar terms to Townshend: "The legislature is more completely Old Line than I thought possible, which ensures me my walking papers, which I shall receive with great philosophy."[48]

Whatever the legislature did about the Senate seat, Chase's six-year term was far from over. He returned to Washington in December 1853 for what he expected would be a quiet session of Congress. After Hale's retirement, there were only three strong antislavery senators: Sumner, Seward, and Chase. Sumner wrote that "this Congress is the worst—or rather promises to be the worst—since the Constitution was adopted." President Pierce, in his annual message, praised the Compromise of 1850, saying that it had brought "a sense of repose and security to the public mind" and promising that this repose would "suffer no shock during my official term, if I have power to avert it." Neither Chase nor Sumner nor Pierce sensed that 1854 would prove one of the most important years in American history, a year in which Chase would play a central role.[49]

CHAPTER 9

"The Nebraska Iniquity"

·❧ 1854 ❧·

On January 4, 1854, the Senate Committee on Territories, through its chairman Stephen Douglas, reported a bill to organize the Nebraska Territory, roughly the region we know as Kansas, Nebraska, South Dakota, North Dakota, Colorado, Wyoming, and Montana. The key section of the bill provided that when a state or states were organized from this territory, they "would be received into the Union, with or without slavery, as their constitutions may prescribe at the time of their admission." In the report, Senator Douglas argued that by allowing the people of the territory to decide for themselves about slavery, rather than attempting to resolve the contentious question in Congress, he was merely implementing the principles of the Compromise of 1850. Douglas did not mention, but it was widely known, that one of his primary goals in organizing the territory was to prepare for a railroad from Chicago to San Francisco.[1]

Chase was immediately concerned by the Douglas bill, writing to the head of the federal Land Office for an estimate of the size of the territory. A few administration papers, such as the *Washington Union*, applauded Douglas's approach, while Horace Greeley's *New-York Tribune* and a few other antislavery papers attacked the bill as a violation of the Missouri Compromise, which had promised that this region would be free from slavery forever. In general, however, the papers carried little about the Nebraska bill in the first weeks of January. A single sentence in the *New*

York Times on January 19 alerted readers that "the Independent Democrats in Congress will issue an address to the country, setting forth the objections to Douglas's Nebraska bill, and appealing for help to defeat it." Chase was probably the person who tipped the reporter that he was working on an address critical of the Douglas bill.[2]

Before Chase could publish his address, however, Douglas introduced a new version of his bill. The revised legislation proposed a Kansas Territory, roughly Kansas and eastern Colorado, and a Nebraska Territory—everything to the north—and declared that, in order to allow the people of both territories to decide about slavery for themselves, the slavery prohibition of the Missouri Compromise would be "inoperative." The next day, January 24, Douglas sought to start Senate debate on this bill. Several senators, including Chase, asked for time to read and consider the bill. Douglas agreed, setting January 30 as the date to open discussion. What Chase knew, and Douglas did not, was that his manifesto against the Nebraska bill had already appeared in print that morning in the *New York Times* and would appear again that afternoon in the *National Era*. Soon this address, titled the "Appeal of the Independent Democrats in Congress to the People of the United States," would be in almost every paper and in thousands of pamphlet copies. Chase would later describe the appeal as the "most valuable of my works," and historians have called it "a brilliant piece of antislavery propaganda."[3]

Chase and his colleagues in the appeal (Sumner, Giddings, Smith, and two others) denounced the Douglas bill "as a gross violation of a sacred pledge; as a criminal betrayal of precious rights; as part and parcel of an atrocious plot to exclude from a vast unoccupied region immigrants from the Old World and free laborers from our own states, and convert it into a dreary region of despotism, inhabited by masters and slaves." They refuted the argument that the Compromise of 1850 had somehow repealed the Missouri Compromise of 1820. It was not antislavery agitators who threatened the Union, they argued, it was Douglas and the Southern Democrats. "Demagogues may tell you that the Union can be maintained only by submitting to the demands of slavery. We tell you that the Union can only be maintained by the full recognition of the just claims of freedom and man. The Union was formed to establish justice and secure the blessings of liberty. When it fails to accomplish these ends, it will be worthless, and when it becomes worthless, it cannot long endure." They called upon the people to rise in opposition to the Nebraska bill.

"Let all protest, earnestly and emphatically, by correspondence, through the press, by memorials, by resolutions of public meetings and legislative bodies, and in whatever other mode may seem expedient, against this enormous crime." In a postscript, which appeared in the *National Era* but not the *New York Times*, Chase attacked the new version of the bill and asked whether the people would "permit their dearest interests to be thus made the mere hazards of a presidential game." Chase and his five colleagues closed with a personal declaration. "For ourselves, we shall resist it by speech and by vote and with all the abilities which God has given us. Even if overcome in the impending struggle, we shall not submit. We shall go home to our constituents, erect anew the standard of freedom, and call on the people to come to the rescue of the country from the domination of slavery. We will not despair; for the cause of human freedom is the cause of God."[4]

Writing to his friend Hamlin on the day the appeal first appeared in the papers, Chase reported rumors that Douglas had talked with President Pierce about Nebraska and that the "administration, with a good deal of trepidation, has resolved to risk its future on the bill as it now stands." It seems that Chase had not yet seen that day's issue of the *New York Herald,* with a detailed report of how Douglas and several slave state senators had persuaded Pierce, at a Sunday-afternoon meeting, to support a strong version of the Nebraska bill. One of the key senators was David Atchison, "Bourbon Dave," from Platte County, Missouri, just across the Missouri River from Kansas. Atchison and others in his part of the state were determined, by means fair or foul, to prevent Kansas from becoming a free territory or free state. Chase was already counting votes for and against the Nebraska bill, telling Hamlin that Thomas Hart Benton, the other senator from Missouri, and Sam Houston, representing Texas, were both opposed to the Douglas bill. "The signs all point to storms ahead." Writing to his friend John Jay, son of William Jay and grandson of the first chief justice, Chase warned that Douglas intended to drive the bill through the Senate as fast as he could. "Wake up the people," Chase wrote Jay, "for if we don't do it, our American Experiment will fail."[5]

The people were waking up. The *Chicago Tribune* reported that opposition to this "cruel and iniquitous bill" was gaining strength every day from "almost every quarter." The *New York Evening Post*, which had not previously paid much attention to the Nebraska bill, now printed and praised the appeal, saying that Chase had exposed Douglas's "pettifogging." In

Cleveland, a call for a public anti-Nebraska meeting was "signed by the most respectable and influential men of all parties," and the meeting itself was unanimous: Congress should not repeal the Missouri Compromise; Congress should not extend slavery into the Nebraska Territory. Two nights later, at a similar gathering in New York City, a huge map was displayed so that people could see the territory at stake: "more than ten times larger than the state of New York." Again the attendees were from all political parties—"substantial men," in the words of the *New York Evening Post*—determined that the South not break the bargain of the Missouri Compromise.[6]

In a Senate speech on January 30, Douglas denounced Chase and his appeal. Although the Illinois senator stood only five feet four inches tall, he was large-headed and barrel-chested, and so known as the "Little Giant." On this day, Douglas was "violent, abusive, and vulgar," one paper said; another said he "lost his temper before he began." When Chase asked Douglas to yield for a minute, he refused angrily. A senator "who has come to me with a smile on his face" and then "sent forth to the country a document of this kind, filled with misrepresentations and imputations upon my motives, has no right to expect any courtesy at my hands," he roared. Noting that one version of the appeal was dated Sunday, January 22, Douglas accused Chase and his colleagues of desecrating the Sabbath. This was rather rich coming from Douglas, who rarely attended church, whereas Chase almost always attended. When Douglas finished ranting, Chase rose to respond, "manly and self-possessed," according to the *New-York Tribune*.[7]

On February 3 Chase opened his main speech against the Nebraska bill by painting a picture of how the peace at the outset of the congressional session had been shattered. "All at once, there was a change, rattling thunder was heard from the skies, the winds were filled with storms." Who brought on these storms? Not Chase and other so-called agitators, but Douglas and others who deprecated agitation. Why did they do this? "Because Slavery again wants room; because Slavery again wants territory; because Slavery wants more states." What did they now demand? "That a sacred compact should be rescinded; that a compact which had endured during a whole generation of men . . . was now to be set aside and repealed." Before 1854, Chase had not much liked the Missouri Compromise, because it introduced slavery into the southern part of the Louisiana Territory, but now he wedded himself to it and thereby gained the support of the millions who revered the Missouri Compromise almost as if it were part of the Constitution: a time-honored bargain between slavery and antislavery forces.[8]

Chase's key point was that Douglas was wrong in claiming that the 1850 Compromise had somehow repealed the Missouri Compromise. "Did any man, from the North or South, during the long debate on the acts of 1850 ever allege that they would supersede or repeal the Missouri Compromise? No one." More recently, Douglas had reported a bill in 1853 to organize the Nebraska Territory, but had not claimed that the Missouri Compromise had been repealed. Even David Atchison, Chase noted, had stated during the 1853 debate that while he opposed the Missouri Compromise and wished that it could somehow be repealed, it was clear that the "Missouri Compromise cannot be repealed."[9]

The *New-York Tribune* printed a detailed report of Chase's speech, with the editors commenting that "we cannot recall a speech of greater logical ability and compactness." The *New York Times* reported that the "galleries and lobbies were densely crowded," and the whole audience "listened to Mr. Chase's arguments with the most profound attention." The reason, according to the reporter, was that "upon this bill the senator from Ohio expresses sentiments which are held by hundreds of thousands who acknowledge no sympathy with his general political positions." At last, the *Tribune,* the *Times*, and other leading Northern papers were giving Chase the coverage they had denied him during the 1850 debate.[10]

Chase was gratified by the warm reception to his speech. "The ladies even invaded the floor," he wrote to his friend Townshend, and "paid the most profound attention. Even my modesty could not refuse the conviction that I had what people call a success." He pressed Townshend to have the Ohio legislature pass a resolution to oppose the Nebraska bill. "You can hardly be aware how much the silence of our legislature at this juncture cripples and weakens me." Several other state legislatures passed resolutions along the lines that Chase wanted, but not Ohio, where traditional Democrats controlled Columbus.[11]

Douglas was keen to whisk the Nebraska bill through the Senate as soon as possible. Chase wanted to delay, to allow time for Northern senators and representatives to hear from their constituents. "The bill must be kept in the Senate as long as possible," wrote his friend James Shepherd Pike from Washington. "Meanwhile hell must be raised in the North. The ear of Congress is open. It must be deafened with condemnation."

Both to illustrate his points and to prolong the process, Chase offered a series of amendments. For example, he proposed that the bill should state that "the people of the territory, through their appropriate representatives, may, if they see fit, prohibit the existence of slavery therein." When Douglas objected, Chase claimed this showed that the senator did not really believe in "popular sovereignty"; that that was just a phrase to pave the way for slavery.[12]

On March 2, in the course of a debate on one of the Chase amendments, a senator attacked Chase for one of the popular petitions he had submitted, apparently without reading it first. The petition called those who voted for the Nebraska bill traitors. Chase responded that the American people, when they discussed public questions and submitted petitions to Congress, were "not accustomed to measure their language with the precision and the exactness required by the rules of this chamber." Another senator now challenged Chase: Did he approve of the language in this petition? No, Chase responded, he did not. Nor did he consider those who would vote for the Nebraska bill to be traitors. Chase said that he was not in the habit of "indulging in aspersions on Southern gentlemen," for he had received his "professional education from a slaveholder—one of the purest and noblest of men—a man so endowed with gifts of intellect, so graced by the accomplishments of culture, and so refined and elevated . . . that he stood among his compeers, as an American and Christian gentleman, easily first. I refer to William Wirt, to name whom is to praise." Southerners were not persuaded by Chase's tribute to Wirt or his other arguments; all of his amendments were defeated.[13]

The Senate debate on the Nebraska bill ended with an all-night session, starting at noon on Friday, March 3, and finally ending at about five o'clock on Saturday morning. Douglas started speaking just before midnight and continued for three hours, spending much of his time attacking and insulting Chase and Sumner. Violating the Senate traditions of addressing the presiding officer and referring to colleagues in the third person, Douglas told Chase and Sumner that "you degrade your own states" by "arousing passions and prejudices," so that "I am now to be found in effigy, hanging by the neck, in all the towns where you have the influence to produce such a result." Chase said he hoped the people of Ohio would treat the senator from Illinois "with entire courtesy." But Douglas insisted that Chase had insulted him personally, and quoted from the address, in which Chase warned against "an atrocious plot" and "servile demagogues." Douglas especially resented the suggestion that he was pressing the Nebraska bill to further his presidential hopes. "I must be permitted to tell the senator from Ohio," Douglas said, "that I did not obtain my seat in this body either by a corrupt bargain or a dishonorable coalition."[14]

This sentence provoked a minute of complete chaos, with Chase, Douglas, and others all speaking at once, and the presiding officer vainly calling for order. When the Senate finally settled down somewhat, Chase quoted to Douglas the sentence about presidential ambition from the address and explained that he did not intend to impute any improper motive. "I do not think it is an unworthy ambition to desire to be president of the United States." Douglas disagreed with Chase, but, after some further personal remarks, he returned at last to the substance of the bill. One Washington correspondent commented that the printed version of the Douglas speech would "convey but a faint idea of its violence and vulgarity" and that his "sneering tone and vulgar grimaces must be heard and seen rather than described." The Senate finally passed the bill by a vote of thirty-seven to fourteen, with almost all the Southerners, of both parties, joined by more than a dozen Northern Democrats.[15]

As Chase and Sumner had hoped, and as they had urged in their appeal, the free states responded to the Nebraska bill with righteous indignation. Almost every day, from February through May 1854, there was another anti-Nebraska meeting in another city. Petitions flooded into Congress, including one signed by thousands of New England clergymen, denouncing the Nebraska bill as a great moral evil. Chase was particularly pleased to see many traditional Democrats opposing the bill. According to one count, among the Democratic papers in Ohio, only thirteen supported the bill, while forty-one were opposed. And Chase was happy to see the increasingly important German American community opposing the Nebraska bill. One of the main speakers at a Cincinnati meeting in early March was Charles Reemelin, a German American leader who would become a key Chase ally. This was a nonpartisan gathering, but Reemelin said that he "could never forget that he was a Democrat" and that, in his view, everyone present was in some sense a Democrat because they were "all believers in the inalienable rights of liberty." Chase wrote Hamlin that if Reemelin and other prominent Germans would "side with the Independent Democracy, we may hope for great things." Writing to an abolitionist editor in New York, Chase said it seemed "the purpose of Divine Providence to renovate our body politic by an infusion of the vigorous German element."[16]

Some people were already talking about turning the anti-Nebraska outrage into a new political party. An anti-Nebraska meeting in Ripon, Wisconsin, even suggested a name for the new party: Republican. An editor in Middlebury, Vermont, unaware of the Ripon meeting, wrote that there was only one appropriate response to the way in which Southern Whigs had joined the Democrats to vote for the Nebraska bill: "the formation of a great Republican Party of the North." Proponents of the new name liked its classical ring (*res publica* means "public affairs" in Latin) and its American history (Jefferson called his political friends the Republicans). Chase was skeptical at first about the idea of a new Republican Party, hoping to maintain and strengthen the Independent Democratic Party. "No faith must be put in a mere anti-Nebraska movement," he wrote to Norton Townshend in early March. "We must adhere to a Democratic organization such as will bring in German strength." To a leading Ohio Democrat, Chase wrote, "Slavery and Democracy are irreconcilable antagonists," and so the "Independent Democracy should maintain inflexibly their own organization."[17]

Opponents of the Nebraska bill planned a "great state protest rally" in Columbus on March 22, and Chase decided at the last minute that he would travel there to attend. It was a cold, wet day, but a large crowd gathered in the Town Street Methodist Church to hear from Chase and other speakers, and to adopt anti-Nebraska resolutions. Chase denounced the Nebraska bill and then challenged the crowd: "What will you do? Will you stand by those who defend the right against might?" One reporter heard him hint at a new party: "If then you do not make a party that will contain good men at all hazard, they must shrink back and be led by the South."[18]

Back in Washington in April, Chase expected the anti-Nebraska forces to defeat the bill in the House. "There is reason to hope," he wrote to Theodore Parker, a Boston minister and abolitionist, "that the Nebraska iniquity sleeps the sleep that knows no waking, and that the speeches now being delivered concerning it in the House may be classed as obituary notices." Chase wrote to a Connecticut leader that "the Nebraska bill is so damaged that it is not likely that it will ever be taken up by the House. A Nebraska bill may indeed pass the House; but it will hardly be the bill which went from the Senate." President Pierce, however, was pressuring members of the House, offering patronage positions in return for votes. Chase wrote Hamlin in mid-May that "the Nebraska scheme is on its legs again" and that he was "uncertain" whether it would pass the House.[19]

The House passed the Nebraska bill on May 22 by a vote of 113 to 100. Pierce, Douglas, and their allies were able to persuade forty-four Northern Democrats and thirteen Southern Whigs to join them. Alexander Stephens, a Southern Whig leader in the House, later vice president of the Confederacy, wrote a friend, "I took the reins in my hand, applied whip and spur, and brought the wagon out." Douglas also claimed credit for the House vote, writing a few years later, "I passed the Nebraska bill myself." Dismissing the speeches for and against the measure as "nothing," he insisted that what really mattered was "the marshaling and directing of men," and Douglas named Chase as *the* man who played this role against him.[20]

The House version of the Nebraska bill differed slightly from the Senate's, so the upper chamber had yet another late-night debate to decide whether to accept it. Chase started his speech by alluding to Jefferson. "Men have inalienable rights; it is to protect these rights that governments are instituted among men; it is because the prohibition of slavery [in the Missouri Compromise] fulfills the greatest object of government that I revere and defend it." Then he stated more clearly that he would support a new antislavery political party: "I shall rejoice, sir, if the friends of freedom, disregarding the differences which have hitherto been suffered to divide them, shall be found willing to unite for the maintenance and defense of liberty."[21]

Douglas, in response, denounced the emerging anti-Nebraska party: "No sane man can close his eyes to the fact that this great Northern party, which is being organized on sectional issues, contemplates servile insurrection, civil war, and disunion!" he railed. When the Senate passed the bill at about one in the morning, its supporters fired cannons to celebrate what the *Washington Sentinel* called "the triumph of nationalism over sectionalism." Chase wrote that he and some "brother senators" were walking down the "western steps of the Capitol towards our temporary homes" as the cannon fire "echoed and reechoed over the silent city." He told his friend Sumner that "they celebrate a present victory, but the echoes they awake will never rest until slavery itself has died."[22]

Aside from defeating the Nebraska bill, Chase's main priority for this session of Congress was passing homestead legislation, to fulfill the pledge of free soil from the 1848 Free Soil platform. As the Senate debated a homestead bill in July, Chase proposed an amendment so that homesteads would be available not only for American citizens but also for all immigrants who had declared their intention of becoming citizens. Chase explained that "the immigrants whose cause I plead are as intelligent, as worthy, as useful, and as respectable as any other portion of our population." The proper response to immigrants, Chase continued, was "generous confidence" and "honorable treatment" in order "to convince them of the expedience and necessity of divesting themselves, as speedily as possible, of their foreign character, and of putting on, with the rights and privileges, the sentiments also of American citizens. Thus I would seek to Americanize them with generosity and justice."[23]

Chase gave this short speech at a time of increasing immigration and increasing hostility against immigrants. As recently as 1844 and 1845, only about 100,000 immigrants entered the United States each year. By 1853, immigration had increased to 368,000, and in 1854 more than 427,000 immigrants would arrive, mainly from Germany and Ireland. Some were fleeing harsh conditions at home; others were seeking better lives in America. Most immigrants were Catholic, at a time when Protestants viewed Catholics with suspicion or outright hatred. Many recent immigrants were inclined to drink, while American reformers favored temperance or even prohibition. So it is not surprising that those opposed to immigration, opposed to drinking, opposed to the Catholic Church—especially what they saw as Catholic interference in American politics—would form secret fraternal orders and then a parallel political party. The Know-Nothing Party received its name because members of the secret orders, when questioned, were supposed to respond: "I know nothing." According to a platform published in June 1854, attributed to the Know-Nothings—also called the Americans—the new party was committed to repealing "all naturalization laws," to supporting "none but Native Americans for office," and to passing "more stringent and effective emigration laws."[24]

Viewed against the background of increasing anti-immigrant sentiment and the growing Know-Nothing political party, Chase's July 1854 speech was either foolish or brave. He should have realized that there was little chance of reconciling the different versions of the homestead bill so late in the congressional session, and that even if the two houses could agree, President Pierce would probably veto the bill. In other words, there was no point in Chase's amendment to the Senate homestead bill to extend its benefits to immigrants, no point in making a pro-immigrant speech that could be used against him by nativist political leaders. But Chase was not a particularly prudent politician. He would almost always speak out rather than keep quiet. And Chase genuinely believed that immigrants contributed to American prosperity and deserved a fair chance in America.[25]

After the session of Congress ended in August 1854, Chase went to New Hampshire to spend time with family and friends, including his daughter Kate, who was turning fourteen. Chase worried about her, writing to her that she was "now just at that age when girls are apt to feel that they ought to be allowed to think and act for themselves." He was not pleased with the reports he received from Miss Haines about Kate's schoolwork. "To rank eighth in your class ought not to satisfy you and does not satisfy me," he reproached her. The time had come "for you to put on your thinking cap and use your brains and qualify yourself for a part in society." While they were in New Hampshire, Chase and Kate met Maria Eastman, originally from Concord, now the head of a boarding school for girls near Philadelphia, and decided that Kate would attend Mrs. Eastman's school starting in September.[26]

Even in the midst of a vacation, Chase could not resist a chance to attack the Nebraska bill. On a pleasant day in late August, he addressed a crowd of two thousand in Wolfeboro, New Hampshire, not far from the shores of Lake Winnipesaukee. Parts of his speech were light. The crowd laughed when Chase said that he seldom met a man who actually favored the Kansas-Nebraska Act—other than postmasters who owed their positions to the Pierce administration. But much of the oration was dark, for Chase argued that the Nebraska bill was another step in the long process through which the Slave Power was extending slavery. Some had accepted the Fugitive Slave Act of 1850 because they believed it would be the South's last demand. They were wrong. Some men believed that the Kansas-Nebraska Act of 1854 would be the last Southern demand. They, too, were wrong. Chase described "the exulting triumph with which the slaveholders told him, after the bill had passed, that the day was not far distant when there would be slaves in Ohio." For many years, Chase said, the voters of New Hampshire had effectively supported the South by voting for Old Line Democrats. "You, my friends of New Hampshire, have

long been counted as the truest vassals of the Slave Power." The Granite
State must now throw off this yoke and vote for antislavery candidates,
first in the state's 1855 congressional election, then in the 1856 presidential election. The audience responded with "tremendous applause."[27]

When Chase returned to Ohio in early September, his first stop was
Hillsboro, where his daughter Nettie, who was about to turn seven, was
living with the family of Catharine Collins, a cousin of her late mother,
Belle. Chase found his daughter "very well and very happy," with "a great
deal to tell me." A week later, Chase wrote Kate again, describing the
presents that he had sent to Nettie and the Collins family, including a
"panopticon" for Nettie—probably a small circular depiction of a scene.
"They were all much delighted." Chase urged Kate to apply herself to
her schoolwork; "be sure you understand everything as you go along."[28]

Ohio was in the midst of an exciting political campaign, in essence
a referendum on the Nebraska bill. In most of the state's congressional
districts, there were only two nominees: one in favor of the Nebraska
bill—typically an administration Democrat—and one opposed, called
the anti-Nebraska or Fusion or Republican or People's Party candidate.
In only a few districts did Whigs nominate their own candidates; the
party was essentially dead in Ohio, having merged into the fusion movement. Chase supported the anti-Nebraska candidates and hoped "the
voice of Ohio will be emphatically pronounced against the Nebraska
iniquity," but insisted that he would campaign "in my own character as
an independent Democrat, not as a Fusionist, or Republican, or Whig,
for I am neither." A Toledo paper reported that in a speech there Chase
"dissected the Nebraska movement from beginning to end, with a most
caustic severity, yet in a tone and language of great moderation." The
editor commented that the speech was not "raving abolitionism" but
rather a "strong, calm, patriotic, intellectual effort worthy of a senator
from the great state of Ohio." In the town of Findlay, a paper reported,
Chase "held the house spellbound" for three hours, explaining "how all
the fountains of legislation at Washington were poisoned, how the Slave
Power strangled all that rebelled against it, how presidents, speakers,
committees were but the tools and cat's paws of its imperious will."[29]

The results of the Ohio election in October 1854 were remarkable. In every one of the state's twenty-one congressional districts, the

anti-Nebraska candidate prevailed. Never in recent history had one side—
it was premature to call the anti-Nebraska coalition a single party—won
such a stunning statewide sweep. Some of those first elected to Congress in
this wave would become important in Chase's life and in American history,
including John Sherman, later a leading Republican senator, and John
Bingham, a longtime Republican member of Congress, known today as
the principal author of the Fourteenth Amendment to the Constitution.[30]

As the Ohio election returns were printed in the papers, Chase was
in Illinois, giving anti-Nebraska speeches there, ahead of that state's
November congressional elections. (In the nineteenth century, each state
set its own congressional election date, with the result that these elections
were scattered throughout the year.) Chase's first and most important Illinois speech was in Chicago, on the evening of October 12, where he was
greeted with "rapturous applause." Chase devoted most of his address to
reviewing the Nebraska bill and denouncing the way in which it repealed
the Missouri Compromise. The *Chicago Tribune* commented that "we
have not listened to a speech in Chicago more dignified, argumentative,
and forcible than this one by Mr. Chase. Compared with the sophistical
bullying speech delivered by Senator Douglas, at the same place, a few
weeks ago, the contrast was most favorable to Mr. Chase."[31]

Speaking every day except Sunday, Chase went on to Aurora, Belvidere, Galena, Granville, Hennepin, Jacksonville, Joliet, and the state
capital of Springfield, the home of Abraham Lincoln. Chase also traveled
north to Platteville, Wisconsin, to give a speech in the hometown of his
friend Ben Eastman, a member of Congress from that state. The *Belvidere
Standard* praised Chase for his "calm and logical" speech, saying that it
had not heard "a better or stronger advocate of Jeffersonian Democracy."
The *Galena Jeffersonian* said that Chase "comes up fully to the expectations of those who, like us, have never heard him before. Deliberate and
methodical, logical in the arrangement of his arguments, with a fine
person and agreeable voice, he makes an impression the hearer carries
away with him to become the basis of action hereafter. Above all, his
sincerity and singleness of purpose—the absence of all fustian and bom-
bast—recommend him to a warm place in the estimation of all who are
able to discriminate between sense and sound, action and argument." The
Free West, an antislavery paper in Chicago, claimed that "opponents as
well as friends admitted that his efforts were of the highest intellectual
order" and called Chase "the best living representation of the principle

of freedom to which the territory of the Great West was sanctified by the policy of our fathers."[32]

Not all of the press coverage was favorable. The *Illinois State Register,* the Democratic paper of Springfield, said that although there was ample notice of Chase's speech there, "the attendance was very slim—not more than two hundred and fifty persons being present at any one time, and at the close of the speech the number was considerably less." The *Register* dismissed Chase's views as "well known": he "attacks the national administration, the institution of slavery, the fugitive slave law, the Compromise of 1850, [and] the Kansas-Nebraska Act." The speech, it added, "excited no interest or sensation." The *Illinois State Journal*, the Whig paper in Springfield, was in its way even more unkind. Two days after Chase's speech, a small item said that "we neglected yesterday to state that on Wednesday afternoon, Mr. Chase, Democratic senator from Ohio, delivered a speech in the courthouse, and in the evening was followed by Mr. Giddings." This was the entire report. Edited by two close friends of Lincoln's, the *Journal* was still a Whig paper, like Lincoln himself, and the paper was not about to give space to a speech by a *Democratic* senator.[33]

As Chase campaigned in the fall of 1854, people talked with him about what he would do after his Senate term ended in early 1855. Chase wrote to his friend Townshend that some friends, including Ben Eastman, "actually seem to think my name likely to be presented as a candidate for the presidency in 1856. Such an event ought not to be counted among the impossibilities after what has come to pass; but it is among the unlikelihoods, which are next of kin to the impossibilities." What seemed far more likely to Chase was that "I may be a candidate of the People's Movement for governor next year." He was "not anxious for this," he claimed, but was inclined to accept the nomination "if the popular wish shall seem to tend in that direction" because it "would be pleasant to have a popular endorsement of my course." When Hamlin wrote to warn Chase that there was talk about nominating Jacob Brinkerhoff (formerly a Free Soiler and now a Know-Nothing) for governor, Chase responded that "an endorsement of my senatorial course by the people of the state would gratify me, but as my activities in the Senate have the approval of my own conscience, I can do very well without any other endorsement. If the good people desire our friend Brinkerhoff or any other worthy and well-qualified man rather than myself, I shall be the last to object to it."[34]

The anti-Nebraska candidates in Illinois and Wisconsin did not do as well in November as Chase had hoped and predicted: Democrats retained five of the nine congressional seats from Illinois and one of the three seats from Wisconsin. More important, and more worrisome, were the election results in Massachusetts and New York. In the Bay State, the Know-Nothings elected an obscure merchant as governor and voted in all twelve members of Congress, while in New York's confused four-way race for governor, the Know-Nothing candidate came in a close third, with more than 120,000 votes. And the first territorial election in Kansas, in late November, was a scandal, as thousands of "border ruffians" crossed from Missouri into Kansas to vote for slavery. David Atchison, urging his Missouri friends to vote in Kansas, warned that "your peace, your quiet, and your property depend upon your action." More ominously, in a private letter to Jefferson Davis, Atchison wrote that "our people are determined to go in [to Kansas] and take their *niggers* with them." They would, if necessary, "shoot, burn, and hang" the abolitionists there.[35]

Chase wrote Hamlin in late November that he felt increasing "uneasiness" about the Know-Nothings but still thought it "best not to say anything against them. Wait until it becomes necessary, and it may never become necessary. What is objectionable may cure itself. Meantime, antislavery men should be constantly warned of the importance of keeping the antislavery idea paramount." In a long letter to Dr. John Paul, who was both antislavery and anti-immigrant, Chase noted that, in the recent Ohio campaign, some of the anti-Nebraska candidates for Congress "were reputed to be Know-Nothings. I did not hesitate to support them; nor did thousands upon thousands of patriotic foreigners, especially of German immigration." Chase agreed with Paul's mistrust of Catholics to an extent, writing that "in the action of certain Catholic priests and of certain conspicuous foreigners, there has been something justly censurable." He did not elaborate on this point and went on to insist that he would not "proscribe men on account of their birth," nor would he "make religious faith a political test."[36]

As Chase prepared to give a lecture on slavery in Boston in early December, his college classmate George Punchard, now editor of a Boston paper, published a short profile of Chase. He recalled him as "an agreeable companion, a lover of fun, of the strictest integrity, and [with] a high sense of honor, which preserved him from everything vicious, while some were tempted to their ruin." Punchard regretted that Chase would not serve a second term in the Senate and hinted at higher office. "Mr. Chase stands six feet and two inches, perfectly erect and finely proportioned . . . the most noble-looking man in the Senate. He is fit, 'every inch of him,' to be a president."[37]

On the evening of December 7, in spite of bad weather, the Tremont Temple in Boston, home of a racially integrated Baptist congregation, was filled. Chase started his two-hour address on a grand scale: "Descending from age to age, the great controversy of right with wrong, of liberty with slavery, of democracy with despotism, reaches at length our time and devolves upon us." He proposed to contrast views on slavery in the early United States with those of the present, looking at slavery from religious, judicial, and political perspectives. In the early years, he said, many ministers denounced slavery, such as the preacher and theologian Jonathan Edwards, who said in 1791 that in fifty years it would "be as disgraceful for a man to hold a negro slave as to be guilty of common robbery or theft." Over time, however, with Southern pressure, most Northern ministers ceased to speak out against slavery. Religious societies also "yielded to the pro-slavery current," said Chase. "The American Bible Society refused a proffered donation in aid of the supply of Bibles to slaves."[38]

Turning to the courts and court cases, Chase reminded his listeners of the 1772 *Somerset* case, which he characterized as standing for the "great principle that slavery can only be supported by positive law and that where there is no such positive law, there can be no slavery." Under the influence of the *Somerset* case and "of the liberal principles of the Revolution, and the religious teachings of the time," early American state courts "were originally much disposed to favor the claims of freedom." Chase cited in particular a decision by George Wythe, chancellor of Virginia and mentor to Thomas Jefferson, who declared in 1806 that freedom was "the birthright of every human being." Therefore, "when one person claims to hold another in slavery, the burden of proof lies on the claimant." Now, Chase lamented, the state and federal courts were biased against those alleged to be slaves and in favor of those who claimed to be their masters. He described the still-obscure case of a "poor fellow named Scott, originally a slave in Missouri," taken by his master first to Illinois, free by virtue of the Northwest Ordinance, and then to the Minnesota Territory, free by virtue of the Missouri Compromise. When his master took Dred Scott, along with his wife and child, back to Missouri, Scott filed suit, seeking their freedom. After an initial victory in the county court, Scott suffered defeats in the state supreme court and the federal circuit court. Scott's lawyers had recently noticed an appeal to the United States Supreme Court.[39]

"Thirty years ago," Chase said, "I do not doubt that the decision of that high tribunal would have been in his favor. Today my fears for the issue are greater than my hopes." Chase did not mention that he had offered, a few weeks earlier, to serve as counsel for Scott "if necessary," but nothing came of it. Other lawyers, including Chase's future Cabinet colleague Montgomery Blair, represented Scott, in a case the Supreme Court would not decide until 1857, in one of its most momentous and infamous decisions.[40]

In his comments on the political history of American slavery, Chase described and praised Jefferson's 1784 Plan for Government of the Western Territory, noting that it would have covered not only the Northwest Territory but *all* federal territory, including any land acquired in the future. Jefferson's plan provided that after 1800 "there shall be neither slavery nor involuntary servitude in any of said states, otherwise than in the punishment of crimes, whereof the party shall have been duly convicted to have been personally guilty." Chase also highlighted another plan by Jefferson, his 1783 draft Virginia constitution, which would have prohibited the slave trade immediately in that state and prohibited slavery itself after the year 1800. It was, Chase said, "sad to think how near we came to the realization of his generous hope and yet failed." Chase contrasted Jefferson's views with a recent editorial in the *Richmond Examiner* that insisted it was "all a hallucination to suppose that we are ever going to get rid of African Slavery, or that it will ever be desirable to do so. It is a thing that we cannot do without, that is righteous, profitable, and permanent, and that belongs to Southern society as inherently, intricately, and durably as the white race itself." Chase commented that "this theory of slavery denies the very existence of human rights. It derides the great doctrine of the Declaration of Independence as the vain figment of a dreaming philosophy. Man as man, according to this theory, has no rights. Man has rights in and over his fellow man, derived from superior force or superior craft, none in or to himself, against superior force or craft. The weak, the ignorant, the poor, the simple must be guided and made useful, and the shortest and best method of doing this is to enslave them."[41]

Although Chase's Boston speech was mainly a lament about how the nation had departed from its early antislavery principles, he concluded on a hopeful note: "Already upon the mountains, I can almost see the feet of the apostle of deliverance. Already I seem to catch the low murmurs of the song of triumph soon to swell up to Heaven from enfranchised millions. God speed the day when it shall fill the arches of Heaven from all our land and mingle its music with the rejoicings of the angels over a great nation not ashamed to love mercy and not afraid to do justice."[42]

CHAPTER 10

"Our Victory Is Glorious"

1855

During the first weeks of 1855, the last few weeks of his Senate term, Chase took special interest in a judicial reform bill, part of which would relieve the Supreme Court justices from riding circuits and serving as circuit court judges. He approved of this change but suggested an amendment so that, as justices retired or died, their number would be reduced from nine to six. Chase noted that six or seven justices had sufficed until 1837, when Congress increased the number to nine to allow them to handle nine circuits. If the justices did not ride circuits, Chase argued, there was no need for nine justices; a court composed of a chief justice and five associates would suffice. Although Chase did not name names, everyone knew that the oldest member of the court was Roger Taney, born into a slave-owning family in Maryland, and the next oldest was Peter Daniel of Virginia. Chase insisted that his amendment did not reflect disrespect for the court. The judiciary was "a great arm of power," he said, "but its action is quiet and unobtrusive and, for the most part, soothing and healing. So long as its functions are performed in a manner which commands itself to the conscience and reason of the people, the confidence, the attachment, of the people will not be withdrawn."[1]

Chase's unsuccessful attempt to reduce the number of justices was but one example of his efforts while in the Senate to reduce the size and cost of the federal government. Chase opposed the federal subsidy for the Collins Company Atlantic steamship line, saying there would be "steam lines whether the patronage of the government be extended to them or not." He took issue with a bill to authorize the construction of three separate rail lines to the Pacific—each to be paid for with generous land grants, and each on a route selected by certain federal officials—arguing that Congress should not "abdicate the whole power . . . over this great and interesting subject to three executive officers of the government."[2]

Although Chase hoped to avoid debates about slavery this winter, he found himself in the midst of them almost in spite of himself. For example: an Alabama senator opposed Chase's routine request for a few days to consider a bill, criticizing him for his "fanaticism" on slavery. Chase responded that he was not a fanatic; that his views were "shared by thousands and hundreds of thousands of people in the free States. They are not decaying or dying out. They spread and grow stronger day by day." Then a senator from Delaware criticized Chase for this short speech, saying that "agitation" by Chase and others on the slavery issue would lead to the "destruction of the Union." Chase answered that the Constitution and the Union "have survived much misinterpretation and perversion. Both will still survive when the former shall be interpreted in the sense of its framers and in the spirit of liberty, and the latter made efficient to secure the great ends of its establishment, freedom, justice, and happiness for all."[3]

A week later, Chase was part of another such debate, this time on a bill to allow federal officers and anyone else "acting under color of federal law" to transfer lawsuits against them from state court to federal court. Although the bill did not mention the Fugitive Slave Act, its main purpose was to allow those involved in attempts to capture or kidnap alleged fugitive slaves to remove, or transfer, their cases from hostile state courts to friendly federal courts. Chase denounced the bill as an "overthrow of state rights. It is a bill to establish a great central, consolidated federal government. It is a step—let me say a stride, rather—towards despotism." This bill, Chase said, was like the Fugitive Slave Act itself; not authorized by the Constitution. Charles Sumner agreed with Chase, calling the bill "an intrusive and offensive encroachment on state rights," which would be rejected "if the attachment to state rights, so often avowed by senators, were not utterly lost in a stronger attachment to slavery." After a debate that lasted until midnight, the Senate approved the bill, but it died in the House and thus did not become law.[4]

As Chase's term ended, the *New York Evening Post* lamented his departure from the Senate. "We shall miss his eloquence in the debates of that body, the courtesy and dignity which graced the part he bore in them, and his conscientious abstinence from appeals to the prejudices of the day." The *Post* noted his steadfast stance against slavery, but especially praised his work on other issues. "We could always rely on his vote in favor of liberal commercial legislation; we always counted on his opposition to a corrupt or extravagant expenditure or appropriation; and we could always depend on his cooperation to restrain action of the federal government within its proper sphere." In other words, the *Post* approved of the way in which Chase adhered to Jefferson's ideas about limiting the federal government.[5]

On his way home from Washington to Cincinnati, Chase went by way of New York City, seeing John Bigelow and other editors, and by way of Rochester, New York, where he gave a speech to the Ladies' Anti-Slavery Society. Chase urged that Congress repeal the federal law authorizing the coastal slave trade. "Every cargo of slaves which is shipped from Baltimore to the rice fields of the extreme South, go under the American flag and by virtue of that law. Let that trade cease—a trade worse even than the African slave trade." He also called for Congress to repeal the Fugitive Slave Act, saying it made Northerners serve as slave catchers for Southern masters. At this, a voice from the crowd asked, "Would not the South, then, dissolve the Union?" Chase responded that "if there is but one way to preserve the Union, and that is to make you and me slaves, why, then, let the Union perish rather than our freedom!" But he immediately added that he "did not believe there was any danger of a dissolution of the Union." While in Rochester, Chase probably met with Frederick Douglass, who lived and edited his paper there and was closely connected with one of the leaders of the Rochester Ladies' Anti-Slavery Society.[6]

Almost as soon as Chase returned to Cincinnati, in March 1855, he was involved in a complicated fugitive slave case, representing Rosetta Armstead, a sixteen-year-old slave sent by her master, an Episcopal priest in Kentucky named Henry Dennison, to serve his daughter in Virginia. The agent to whom Dennison entrusted Rosetta's transit made the mistake of taking the girl by train from Cincinnati to Columbus, where antislavery lawyers secured a state court order granting her freedom. Dennison then arranged for Rosetta to be arrested by a federal marshal, Hiram Robinson, and transported to Cincinnati. "It was the plan of Dennison and the captor of Rosetta," Chase recalled, "to take her at once to [John] Pendery, the [federal fugitive slave] commissioner, have an

*Frederick Douglass, the most prominent black leader
of the Civil War era, friend and sometimes critic of Chase.*

immediate examination, and carry her off at once into Kentucky." Chase
and his colleagues prevented this by obtaining a habeas corpus order
from another state judge, James Parker, confirming the Columbus order
freeing Rosetta. When Dennison and Robinson arranged for Rosetta to
be arrested again, Chase sought an order declaring them in contempt of
court, and Parker ordered Robinson's arrest. The federal marshal's lawyers
then applied to John McLean, as circuit judge, for an order releasing Robinson. McLean freed Robinson, reasoning that the state courts could not
interfere in the federal fugitive slave process. Chase achieved his principal
goal, however, Rosetta's freedom, when Pendery accepted his argument
that her master had effectively freed her when his agent brought her to
the free state of Ohio.[7]

Many of Chase's letters from early 1855 were about how to secure the Republican gubernatorial nomination in the face of the increasing strength of the Know-Nothings. Responding to rumors that the organization had decided that it would support only its own members as candidates, Chase told his friend Oran Follett, editor of the *Ohio State Journal*, that he would never join their order; that he would not "advance myself at the sacrifice of principles." But neither would he condemn the Know-Nothings. "I have not approved the censure by some antislavery friends upon the K.N. organization." Indeed, some antislavery papers, including the *Ohio Columbian*, edited by Chase's friend Edward Hamlin, had been very harsh in their criticism of the Know-Nothings. Chase believed that the Northern Know-Nothings were becoming more of an antislavery party and less of an anti-immigrant party, so that his friends should "wait and see, and not precipitate by censure in advance, a course which prudence and conciliation may prevent."[8]

Writing to Hamlin, Chase said that he was gratified that several Ohio papers had endorsed him for governor, and that all but one of the Ohio members of Congress supported him. Chase was concerned that the Know-Nothings would nominate their own candidate for governor and the other offices; he wanted, if possible, to keep the antislavery and moderate Know-Nothings together in one party. What Chase feared was what the Democrats hoped for at this point: that there would be competing Free Soil and Know-Nothing tickets, dividing the vote that had been united the prior year, paving the way for Democratic victory. Chase counseled Hamlin to moderate his criticism of the Know-Nothings. "My idea is to fight nobody who does not fight us. We have enemies enough in the slaveholders and their aiders."[9]

In a more personal letter to his friend Norton Townshend, Chase said he regretted that he had "accomplished so little since I have been here [in Washington] compared with what I might have done had I only resolutely applied myself." As to the future, he did not know what was best. "If the People's Movement goes on, and I shall happen to be nominated for Governor upon a platform which I can occupy with a good conscience and a bold heart, I shall remain in Ohio, provided my active services are needed for the canvass." He was also thinking "of making a trip to Kansas," to rally the antislavery settlers struggling there against pro-slavery forces from Missouri. "Sometimes," Chase wrote, "I think it would be better to reject both ideas and stay at home, practice law, and make money. Then again, it occurs to me that it would be a good plan to go abroad, see the old world, and spend money." More or less quoting the poet Robert Burns, Chase asked Townshend for his advice. "Your counsel, dear tittie [sister], don't tarry."[10]

In late March, in a letter from Cincinnati to his friend James Shepherd Pike, now a Washington correspondent for the *New-York Tribune*, Chase reported that "there is a good deal of confusion here about fusion." The Know-Nothings were "rather inclined to dictate terms to the outsiders, and there may be a split among the anti-administration forces." The Free Soilers were "willing to cooperate with the Know-Nothings upon a fair common ticket in which both sides shall be fairly respected as to men, and on a platform of no more slave states and no slave territory. But they insist that the ticket shall be nominated by a people's convention fairly constituted." In other words, if the Know-Nothings held their convention first, and tried to impose their nominees on the Free Soilers, the Free Soilers might nominate their own men, leading to a split. Chase admitted that he really did not know what would happen.[11]

Events soon strengthened Chase's hand. Thousands of pro-slavery men from Missouri crossed into Kansas in March 1855, not in order to settle but simply to vote in the territorial election. In theory, only residents of Kansas could vote in this election, but the armed Missouri interlopers ignored this technicality. The *New-York Tribune* reported that an "army of slaveholders and their jackals" from Missouri had "taken possession of the polls at the point of the bowie knife, voted till they were tired, and elected whomsoever they chose as delegates to the territorial legislature." The *National Era* added that not only did the Missouri ruffians prevent the Free Soil residents from voting; in many cases they forced them "under threats of violence, to vote for pro-slavery candidates." In early April, the municipal elections in Cincinnati were marred by Know-Nothing violence against German Americans; a few men were killed and many more injured. The *Cincinnati Enquirer* asked indignantly whether the city was "to be left to the mercy of an infuriated mob, governed by the worst passions, and regardless both of life and property?" The violence in Kansas increased the resolve of antislavery men in Ohio to elect a strong antislavery man as their governor, and the violence in Cincinnati made the Know-Nothings look like a lawless mob. The *Toledo Blade*, endorsing Chase, explained that "we find no man in Ohio who so unequivocally represents the great idea and the great truths which must triumph or be struck down in the coming contest." Nominating Chase, and electing him by a great margin, would "strike terror into the camp of the traitors at Washington, and stay the brutal aggressions and encroachments of the slave drivers in Missouri."[12]

Chase went to New York City in May 1855 to work on legal cases, then to Philadelphia to see Kate at boarding school, and then to Washington, DC, to visit friends there. While he was in the East, a dispute about him broke out among the papers. The first shot was fired by the *New York Times*, claiming that even if Chase was nominated, he could not be elected governor of Ohio because he was not acceptable to Whigs: "As a propagandist of antislavery doctrine, he probably has few superiors; but he seems to be devoid of the most essential qualities of the effective legislator or statesman. He can scarcely expect the united support of the Whigs of Ohio, when known to be so uncompromisingly hostile to every Whig measure and all Whig policy." The *New York Evening Post* defended Chase, contrasting him with William H. Seward, whom the *Post* said was far too eager to vote for questionable spending. The *New-York Tribune* joined the fray, saying that although the editors differed with him on some issues, he had done well in the Senate. "His career in that body was marked by great ability and by unflinching firmness on the Nebraska question. It was likewise distinguished by the high merit of habitual resistance to all schemes of public plunder." Chase was now the "most suitable man for the state of Ohio to elect as her next governor." Writing to his daughter, Chase commented with a touch of humor that it was "very uncertain whether I shall be governor or even a candidate; but some of the papers begin to abuse me a little, which is a good sign."[13]

The Know-Nothings were the main reason it was uncertain whether Chase would be a candidate. As he explained to Edward Pierce, a young protégé of Sumner, he was "aware of the plan to supersede me by Mr. Brinkerhoff. It is the Know-Nothing game. They tell me their only objection to me is that I am not a member of the Order, while Mr. B. is, and I have no doubt that the nomination would be given to me without hesitation if I should only join." But Chase refused to join the Know-Nothings, saying: "I can tell no lies, wear no double face, proscribe no worthy foreigner or religionist—not to be fifty times a governor." Chase's supporters were increasingly confident, and some were resolved to walk out of the Republican state convention if he was not nominated. "If the Know-Nothings suppose they can inveigle Mr. Chase's friends into a convention where he is to be sacrificed because he is not a member of the Order," the *Ohio Columbian* declared, "they will find themselves grievously disappointed." Chase was aware of their plans to walk out of the convention and did nothing to discourage them.[14]

In late May and early June, he exchanged a half dozen letters with Lewis Campbell, a member of Congress and Know-Nothing leader, although he claimed to Chase that he had nothing to do with what he termed "the organization called the Know-Nothings." Chase wrote Campbell that, in his view, a state ticket headed by a Know-Nothing would be defeated. Such a ticket would lose "the whole German vote" and "the Free Soil vote, even if no separate ticket be nominated, is alienated." Campbell responded that he thought Chase was foolish to refuse fusion with the Know-Nothings, for that was the only way to keep the "rotten Ohio Democracy" from carrying the state. The congressman told Chase that he did not care who was nominated, although at this very time, Campbell was writing friends to urge that they nominate Brinkerhoff rather than a "milk and water Yankee who plays the game of fast and loose on all the great questions of the day." Chase answered Campbell that he would not unite with the Know-Nothings, he would not adopt their doctrines, but he would *cooperate* with them on an antislavery platform, as he had cooperated with some Know-Nothings the prior year.[15]

Three conventions in June improved Chase's chances to secure the nomination in July. On June 5 the Know-Nothings of Ohio gathered in Cleveland and adopted nativist resolutions, including one suggesting that immigrants should have to wait twenty-one years before they could vote, but also adopting antislavery resolutions—including one denouncing plans to extend slavery into Kansas. Most important, from Chase's perspective, this convention did not name candidates for statewide offices, so there would be a clean slate for the Columbus convention in July. When the national Know-Nothing Party, meeting in Philadelphia, resolved on June 13 to endorse the Compromise of 1850 "as a final and conclusive settlement," many of the Northern delegates walked out. This group, led by Thomas Ford, a lawyer from Mansfield, Ohio, gathered at a nearby hotel and pledged themselves to restore the Missouri Compromise. Meanwhile, a group calling itself the Know-Somethings of Ohio, a more moderate version of the Know-Nothing Party, met in Cleveland on this same day.

James Ashley, a young friend of Chase's and later a leading member of Congress, attended the convention and reported to Chase that when his name was mentioned as a possible candidate for governor, it "brought down the house."[16]

Chase himself was more and more confident that he would receive the nomination for governor at the Republican state convention. In a public letter in mid-June, he wrote that "all minor differences of opinion must be disregarded for the sake of agreement and harmony on the common platform of *no slavery outside of the slave states*. Upon this platform all must be welcome, of whatever birth, and of whatever creed." In a private letter to James Pike, Chase said that after the recent "explosion in Philadelphia," it seemed likely "that I shall receive the nomination of the thirteenth of July convention, and that everything will go harmoniously." In a letter to Kate, Chase wrote that "the prospect now is that I shall be nominated for governor. If I am and accept, I shall not be able to spend much time in New Hampshire this summer."[17]

Still, up to the very day of the Republican convention, newspapers disagreed about whether Chase would be nominated. The *Cincinnati Gazette* predicted a deadlock between Chase and Brinkerhoff and that some third man would get the nomination. The *Ohio Statesman*, the state's leading Democratic paper, reported that many county conventions were opposed to Chase and that "the returns for the last twenty-four hours look decidedly against Mr. Chase." The *Cincinnati Enquirer*, another important Democratic paper, believed that Chase would be nominated. The Know-Nothings would be forced, according to the *Enquirer*, to change their war cry from "Down with the foreigners and Catholics" to "War to the knife on the South and up with the niggers." The *Ohio Columbian* insisted that the people favored Chase for governor—that the only opposition was from a handful of Know-Nothing politicians—and then quoted county resolutions strongly endorsing him.[18]

According to the *Ohio State Journal*, "Hundreds of the best and ablest men" gathered in Columbus on July 13 for the Republican state convention. When the time came to nominate a governor, Chase received 225 votes, more than twice as many as his nearest rival. "The result on being announced was received with loud cheers," the paper reported. Equally important, from Chase's perspective, his friends controlled the platform committee, and the platform was exclusively an antislavery document, without any hint of nativist language. True, the convention nominated

Know-Nothings for other offices, such as Thomas Ford for lieutenant governor and Brinkerhoff for chief judge, but this did not especially bother Chase. Indeed, he was happy to see Ford rewarded for his strong antislavery stance in Philadelphia.[19]

Candidates did not generally make acceptance speeches at antebellum political conventions, but Chase decided to speak to this convention. He started with false modesty, claiming, "Ohio has many citizens better fitted for the position in which you would place me." He insisted, however, that there was no person in the state more strongly committed to the principles of the party—namely, that the "spread of slavery, under all circumstances, and at all times, must be inflexibly resisted" and that "Kansas must be saved from slavery by the voters of the free states." Alluding to the abolitionists, Chase insisted that he was not one of them, for he would not interfere with slavery in the slave states. Alluding to the Know-Nothings, Chase said that he was ready to campaign "side by side with all men who are willing to unite with me for the defense of freedom." He concluded with the hope that "the time might soon arrive when the sun in his course over this continent would find with his beams no slave."[20]

As transportation improved, and expectations changed, more candidates engaged in itinerant political campaigns, traveling from place to place to shake hands and make speeches. Chase was at the forefront of this trend in 1855. He realized that many people in Ohio distrusted him, including Whigs who viewed him as a Democrat and conservatives who viewed him as an abolitionist. So starting in early August and continuing to the eve of the October election, Chase went to every corner of the state, speaking in fifty-seven places spread among forty-nine counties. To some extent, he could travel by rail, but many places weren't served by railroads, so Chase had to travel by carriage, in open wagons, on horseback, in canal boats, and even by canoe. We know when and where he spoke, for some papers printed his schedule, but we do not know much about what he said, for the papers did not often report his speeches.[21]

One exception is the speech that he gave at Circleville, a county seat of about three thousand people, on August 4. Chase supposedly lacked a sense of humor, but the newspaper report of this speech is filled with humorous sentences that were surely funnier in person than in print. When he spoke of Thomas Jefferson, for example—and Chase almost always spoke about Jefferson—he said sarcastically that it was "possible that posterity might pronounce Mr. Jefferson as great a man as Franklin Pierce or Stephen A. Douglas." The South's policy of admitting states in pairs, one slave and one free, was like insisting that "whenever American liberty should be in a pregnant condition and about to bring forth new states, that it should have twins, [and] one of them should be a black baby and the other a white baby." Opening the Nebraska Territory to slavery, while claiming (as Douglas did) that slave owners were not likely to take slaves there, was as if "a neighbor should let down the bars of your cornfield, and say in extenuation that he knew his hogs loved corn, but he did not think they would go in."[22]

In his speech in Cincinnati on August 21, printed soon as a pamphlet, Chase started by recalling how he had arrived in the city more than thirty years ago "as a mere boy." Few people had lived in Cincinnati as long as Chase, and "to none of you, I am sure, is the prosperity of this beautiful city or the advancement in all respects of her noble institutions more dear." Chase challenged those who called him a disunionist to find a single sentence in any of his speeches in which he expressed anything less than love of the Union. "No man, fellow citizens, cherishes a warmer or more earnest devotion to the Union of these States than the man who now stands before you. Founded on the principles of the Declaration of Independence, cemented by the Constitution, and protected by the patriotism of the people, it seems to me fit to endure forever." The real disunionists, Chase said, were the secessionists in the South. He quoted a resolution, adopted recently at a meeting in South Carolina, hailing the "Disunionists of 1776" and suggesting the state should follow their example. Northern Democrats, Chase noted, did not denounce these Southern disunionists; they worked with and, indeed, for them in Washington. "Do you not know that from the disunionists are selected chiefs of committee in the Senate and the House of Representatives, foreign ministers and heads of departments? Why, the disunionists of [Carolina] are the rulers of our national rulers."[23]

Responding to those who called him an abolitionist, Chase said that he would "not undertake to define abolitionism" but would instead describe "frankly" his position on slavery. It was, he said, simply the position of "Washington, Jefferson, and Franklin": namely, that the Constitution "conferred on Congress no power to institute or maintain slavery by national legislation" nor "any power to interfere by national legislation with slavery in the states." (Chase was simplifying the complex position of Washington and Jefferson on slavery; after all, Washington signed into law the Fugitive Slave Act of 1793.) He claimed that neither he nor any other Republican leader wanted to interfere with slavery in the slave states. "Ohio Freedom will not interfere with Kentucky Slavery, but Kentucky Slavery must not interfere with Ohio Freedom." (Kentucky leaders would view many of the measures Chase supported, such as repealing the Fugitive Slave Act, as interfering with slavery.) Chase repeated that his approach was the same as that of the founders, for "all these illustrious men hated slavery" and "all of them longed for the coming time when the whole land should be delivered by the constitutional action of the national and state governments from this, its greatest curse."[24]

Chase then recounted the history of the Nebraska bill: how Douglas and Pierce had used every means "to seduce or intimidate senators and representatives to disregard the wishes of their constituents and vote for the repeal" of the prohibition against slavery in the Nebraska Territory. "At length, over violated rules and outraged rights, the Slave Power and its allies forced their way to nefarious victory," he said. Recalling the midnight when the bill finally passed the Senate, Chase described how "with great sorrow," he and his friends walked down the steps of the Capitol amidst the booming cannons. "But *thank God* the smoking thunder of that night awoke the people!" In the ensuing election, the Northern people ousted most of those who had voted for the Nebraska bill, especially in Ohio, which sent "twenty-one representatives to execute, in the legislature of the nation, the will of the people of Ohio."[25]

Recent events in Kansas and Missouri, Chase said, proved that Ohio was right to oppose the Kansas-Nebraska bill. In the territorial election, "ruffian bands of Missourians, armed with bowie knives and revolvers . . . marched into the territory, seized upon the polls, and fraudulently deposited their Missouri ballots as Kansas ballots." The Kansas legislature was now dominated by Missouri men, and "its enactments for the establishment of slavery rival in atrocity the worst edicts of Nero or Caligula." (Indeed, under the new Kansas slave code, merely speaking against slavery was a crime and encouraging slaves to rebel was a crime punishable by death.) Chase recounted the recent case of a minister from Ohio, a "mild and forbearing" man, who was "charged only with avowing himself in favor of making Kansas a free state." This minister was "seized by a mob of ruffians . . . dragged to the river's bank, where his face was painted black, and marked with the letter *R,* and then, upon two pine logs lashed together . . . pushed out into the turbid waters of the Missouri, to live or die as the event might determine." (The minister survived the ordeal.) In another case, a quarterly conference of Methodist ministers was attacked by a mob. One minister was seized while preaching, and the others escaped "amidst threats of tar, feathers, and hemp from the mob, amply provided with these things."[26]

Chase mocked the argument that the Pierce administration was not responsible for the dreadful violence in Kansas. "Not responsible! Is not the president charged with the duties of executing the laws of the United States? Is not Franklin Pierce president? When has he attempted to enforce those laws in Kansas?" Pierce was quite ready, Chase noted, to use federal troops to ensure that a single fugitive slave was taken from Boston to slavery in the South. But the president had done nothing to protect the settlers of Kansas from the violence of the Missouri ruffians. Moreover, Pierce had rewarded some of the Missouri leaders by giving them federal positions. "If these facts do not establish the complicity of the administration in the Kansas outrages," said Chase, "it is impossible to establish any proposition upon evidence."[27]

Political opponents did not generally debate one another in the nineteenth century, but on August 30 Chase and John Bingham for the Republicans, and William Medill and George McCook for the Democrats, chanced to meet at Carrollton, Ohio, each side having scheduled speeches there for that day. They agreed to engage in an impromptu debate, with each of the four having one hour to speak. Medill started and, according to a Republican paper, essentially accused Chase of being a Know-Nothing. Chase was next and spoke "with a coolness and firmness of tone that seemed to delight the heart and win the approval of almost every listener." When it was McCook's turn, he wanted to ask Chase questions and to have the time that Chase spent answering deducted from Bingham's time. Chase declined, since this was not the agreed-upon format, and the flustered McCook then gave a disjointed speech. After Bingham spoke, McCook rose again to pose his questions, and this time Chase answered. "The scene closed by a unanimous cheer for Chase," the Republican paper crowed.[28]

Historians have often dismissed Chase as a public speaker. One wrote that his "oratorical skills were limited" and another that "his emotional content was nil." But those who heard him in the mid-nineteenth century had a different view. After Chase spoke in Platteville in 1854, a correspondent wrote that "verily such a speech was never heard here before." Chase's "clear, frank, and manly" speech in Dayton in 1855 caused "several old-line Whigs" to declare that he would now have "their hearty support." The *New York Evening Post* reported in 1856 that if Republicans nominated Chase for president, his friends would "insist upon him taking the stump, where, they assert, he appears to greater advantage than any statesman now in public life." In an article published in 1871, an Ohio editor recalled hearing Chase speak in small rooms, to audiences of only twenty people, and at mass meetings, to crowds of thousands. "His speeches, whether in the schoolhouse or in the Senate, whether before large or small audiences, were always characterized by the same unbending regard for truth and justice, by the same calmness and self-possession, by the same strength and clear statement of his case, the same considerate regard for the opinions of others." This editor attributed Chase's continued political power to the close connection he formed with the people, through years of stump speaking.[29]

There were three candidates in 1855 for Ohio governor: Salmon Chase for the Republicans; the incumbent governor, William Medill, for the Democrats; and Allen Trimble, an aged former governor, for the faction of Know-Nothings who were not prepared to accept Chase as their candidate. The papers supporting Trimble argued that Chase was too soft on immigrants. Recalling his proposal to extend the homestead law to reach immigrants, the Trimble men claimed that "soon the sons of American families will look in vain for fields which have been taken from them" by immigrants. The Trimble papers also attacked Chase as an abolitionist or, in the words of one paper, "a genuine dyed-in-the-wool-abolition-ist-disunionist."[30]

Democratic papers echoed the Trimble papers in attacking Chase as an abolitionist. Using Chase's silver pitcher speech against him, headlines claimed that he was "In Favor of Negro Voting" and "In Favor of Nigger Children Attending the Same Public Schools with the Whites." Chase was "In favor of negro suffrage! In favor of negro jurors! In favor of negro office holders! In favor of conferring upon negroes the political privileges of white citizens!" Some Democrats said that Chase was effectively a Know-Nothing, like the others on the "Fusion Know-Nothing ticket."

One paper charged Chase with "duplicity" on the question of how soon immigrants should get voting rights, quoting a letter in which he had endorsed a shorter period and remarks he had supposedly made urging a longer period, even "ten, twelve, or fifteen years." Although Chase himself said not a word about temperance, the *Cincinnati Enquirer* argued against him by reminding readers that he was in favor of a Maine law to limit liquor sales.[31]

Like Chase, Republican papers maintained that Kansas was the central issue in the Ohio campaign. They claimed that Medill, during the congressional debate of the prior year, had left his post in Columbus to go to Washington to press Democratic members to vote for the Kansas-Nebraska bill. Medill and Wilson Shannon, the new governor of the Kansas Territory, were close friends, so that a vote for Medill was effectively a vote for Shannon, who wanted to establish slavery in Kansas. "If you want to sustain the Missouri ruffians who have invaded Kansas," one paper warned, "vote the Democratic ticket. If you want to encourage the men who run ministers of religion out of Kansas and make it the penitentiary or death to speak in favor of freedom, vote the Democratic ticket. If you want Kansas made a slave state, vote the Democratic ticket. If you want the battle for freedom given up, and all the remaining territory of the Union given over to slavery, vote the Democratic ticket." In other words, vote for Salmon P. Chase.[32]

Chase often advised Kate to observe more closely and write more fully. "You must keep your eyes open, my dear child," he wrote her. "They were given you expressly to see with; and your mind was given you expressly to observe with." Chase's own letters to his oldest daughter were often short and general, but on Sunday, September 30, he wrote a detailed description of his campaign travels, one of the best letters he ever wrote her. He had given a speech on Thursday in Van Wert, near the Indiana border, and was committed ("without my consent") to speak that same evening in Delphos, fifteen miles to the east. There was a new railroad track between the two places, "but no train going, so a party of my political friends volunteered to take me down on a handcar," a small railway car powered by its passengers. It was "rather dangerous," Chase noted, "for who could tell but we might meet a train or perhaps another handcar, or but that a switch might be out of place." As they approached Delphos, they saw a light and wondered whether it was a locomotive coming in the opposite direction. A voice called out, telling them to "Come on!" and then shouted at them to "Stop! Stop!" They braked just short of a gap in the tracks, where a drawbridge over a canal was open.[33]

The next day, Chase had to travel fifteen miles from Delphos to Kalida. The only transport available was an open wagon, in which Chase and a colleague took their seats, "having a buffalo robe spread over the backseat which we occupied, to make it softer." They started off "through the woods, across mud holes, over corduroy bridges, jumping and jolting to the town of Kalida." After his speech, Chase departed in the same wagon for Charloe, hoping to make it there by nightfall. Along the way, he and his driver had to cross the Auglaize River at a ford, which they reached at twilight. "The water was rushing over the dam in great volume and roaring loudly," he recounted, "and just below sweeping furiously along, as if it would carry all before it. I confess I felt somewhat alarmed, but in we went. In a moment, the water was sweeping over the sides of the wagon." They emerged from the water, but made slow progress on the rutted road, blocked at places by fallen trees. At last, they asked for shelter at a cabin and were placed "in the loft, among the oats, corn, old clothes, etc." Chase slept soundly and the next morning covered the last few miles to Charloe in a canoe, paddled by two men from the cabin. "The morning was glorious," he told Kate. "The sun's radiance was flashed back from the glassy surface of the swift river. The willows lined the bank, and here and there an enormous sycamore stretched its arms far over the stream, turning down till their extremities touched the water."[34]

Over the next week, the last week before the election, Chase spoke in Antwerp, Napoleon, Toledo, Wauseon, and other towns. He continued speaking right up through the day before the election, when he was in Tiffin, roughly 160 miles north of Cincinnati. Indeed, it is not clear whether he was able to get home to vote there on Tuesday, October 9. At first, it seemed that Chase had lost the election. Wednesday's headline in the *Ohio Statesman* hailed the "glorious Democratic gain" and claimed Medill the victor. By Thursday, however, as more ballots from more counties were counted, it was clear that Chase had won. His strength was in the Western Reserve, where he received two-thirds of the vote. Statewide, the final counts were Chase, 146,770 votes; Medill, 131,019 votes; and Trimble, 24,276 votes. Republicans would also control both houses of the new state legislature.[35]

These Ohio votes were still being counted when Chase gave a speech so conciliatory that it probably disappointed his supporters: "We have not come together to rejoice over the victory of a party but the triumph of a great principle. Our contest has not been with enemies but with fellow citizens and neighbors. The weapons of our warfare have been arguments, not bayonets; our conquest is a conquest of reason, and not a conquest of force." In his private letters, Chase was more exultant. He wrote to Charles Sumner that "our victory is glorious and complete. Even the nomination of Trimble, designed to work me harm, has done good in separating me from the proscriptive Know-Nothings." Writing to James Grimes, the new Republican governor of Iowa, Chase said that "never was such an effort made to kill off a man as was made to kill off me." He had faced "detraction," "vituperation," and "proscription," and yet had emerged "stronger today in Ohio than ever."[36]

Some of the congratulatory letters Chase received urged him to run for president the next year. And Chase himself was seriously thinking about this possibility. In a letter to Kinsley Bingham, the new Republican governor of Michigan, Chase wrote that, in order for Republicans to win the presidential election in 1856, they would "need the liberal Americans [Know-Nothings], and we shall also need the antislavery adopted citizens. Neither of these great classes can be spared without imminent danger of defeat." In addition, they would "need and must have a large accession from the Democratic element." He believed that "the elements required for a presidential election have been harmonized in my election in Ohio" and could be united again next year. Moreover, his "uniform opposition to extravagant appropriations in Congress" would help him win votes in the general election. "That it would be gratifying to me to be selected as the exponent of the anti-Nebraska sentiment of the country, it would be mere folly to deny."[37]

Chase's victory in Ohio was a bright spot in an otherwise dark election season for Republicans. In some states, they suffered defeat at the hands of the Democrats, while in others they fell to the Know-Nothings. A leading Democratic paper in New York commented in late October 1855 that "nobody believes that this Republican movement can prove the basis of a permanent party." It was not just Democrats who doubted Republican chances. The Boston minister Theodore Parker, friend and correspondent of Chase, predicted in a letter to William Herndon, Abraham Lincoln's law partner, that there would be two Northern candidates in the coming election, "one Republican, one Know-Nothing," and that the Know-Nothing nominee would "get the most votes." Indeed, although there were rudimentary Republican organizations in some states, no National Republican Party existed at this point; no national committee to organize a national convention, much less a national campaign.[38]

Chase started working, right after his own election in Ohio, to solve this problem. He went to Toledo in early November for a quiet meeting with some political friends, including Edward Hamlin and James Ashley. Chase and his colleagues agreed upon the idea of a preliminary national convention, to be held in Pittsburgh on February 22, 1856, in order to set the date and time for a second, nominating convention, probably in June. They started sending letters, a few of which have survived, such as one from Chase to John Hale: "We think here that the Republican organization should be got in working order and to do that it would be wise to hold an informal gathering of such as can attend say at Pittsburgh on 22 February to organize a Republican National Committee and counsel together." A similar letter, from Chase's lieutenant Alfred Stone, was addressed to Cassius M. Clay, and printed in the *New-York Tribune.* "Does the proposition to hold this [Pittsburgh] meeting strike you favorably?" Stone asked Clay. "Might we expect a representation at this meeting from Kentucky and other Southern states?" Clay's response, also in the *Tribune,* supported the proposed Pittsburgh meeting and Chase's concept of a broad Republican Party. "Let Whig and Democrat, Know-Nothing and Anti-Know-Nothing, Catholic and Protestant, native born and adopted, and all shades of opinion, be urged by the great necessity of immediate action."[39]

One person who did not agree with Chase about a broad movement was his old friend Gamaliel Bailey, who wrote to Chase that his position toward the "detestable organization," the Know-Nothings, was "not so satisfactory as that of Seward. You temporize with it—he opposes it boldly and outright." Bailey warned Chase that he would not "go with you into any association with Republicans *and* Know-Nothings, with members of two parties, with men trying to serve two masters."[40]

Chase and Bailey probably discussed their disagreement face-to-face in late December, for Chase was in Washington, and he generally stayed with the Baileys when he was there. On December 29 Chase and Bailey both attended a dinner at the Maryland home of Francis Preston Blair, the senior Jacksonian statesman, to discuss the Republican Party. The other guests were Charles Sumner; Preston King, former member of Congress and future senator from New York; and Massachusetts representative Nathaniel Banks, who was seeking to become Speaker of the House and was sometimes named as a possible presidential candidate. Blair had also invited William Henry Seward, but he declined, claiming that he had a rule against "taking part, personally, in plans or schemes for political action."[41]

None of the six participants described the conversation at the Blair dinner in any detail, but it seems that they agreed to support Banks in his campaign in the House for Speaker, to hold a preliminary February Pittsburgh convention, and then to hold a national nominating convention, perhaps in Cincinnati in June. After talking with King, Seward complained that the proposed Pittsburgh convention "was to be on the Ohio plan, half Republican and half Know-Nothing." In other words, Seward was unhappy that Chase had persuaded the other leaders to accept his "Ohio plan" and to include moderate Know-Nothings as well as ardent Republicans under the broad Republican tent.[42]

CHAPTER 11

"Avowed and Determined"

1856–57

After spending the first days of the new year in Washington to argue a case in the Supreme Court, Chase headed to Columbus, where, as one paper noted, his "inaugural address will be looked for with great interest." The statehouse was still under construction, so the inauguration could not be held there; instead, it was at the nearby theater serving as temporary quarters of the Ohio House. One paper reported that "the large hall of the Odeon was densely packed" on the afternoon of Chase's inauguration "with the most eminent citizens of the state and the fairest ladies in the land." Another said that "the ladies were there by hundreds, taking full possession of the seats of the members" and that Chase "read his inaugural in a clear, distinct, and effective manner, commanding undivided attention throughout."[1]

In a section of the address that is especially interesting in light of his later work, Chase commented on currency, which at this time consisted of coins, some foreign and some minted by the federal government, and banknotes, issued by more than a thousand state banks—some sound and some spurious. "A sound and sufficient currency," Chase declared, "is indispensable to the welfare of every civilized community. The best practicable currency, in my judgment, would be a currency of coin, admitting the use of large notes only for the convenience of commerce. Such a currency, however, is only attainable through the legislation of Congress." Chase

suggested that the state legislature might want to allow for additional
banks in Ohio, but "the utmost care should be used to secure the prompt
and certain convertibility of every note issued, into gold or silver coin,
upon demand of the holder, to protect the community." In Chase's view,
there was no problem with a "mixed currency of coin and notes exchange-
able for coin at the will of the holder without loss," but he declared that
"all mere paper money systems, pregnant with fraud and fruitful of ruin,
justly incur universal reprobation."[2]

The section of Chase's message most widely reprinted denounced
the Douglas version of democracy and lamented the chaos in Kansas.
He argued that there could not be true democratic government when
one part of the population (black) was enslaved by another part of the
population (white). True democracy requires, as a foundation, respect
for "inalienable rights." In Kansas, the false version of democracy had
led to "invasion, usurpation, violence, bloodshed—almost to civil war."
The correct approach was to apply in Kansas and in other territories the
approach adopted for Ohio and the rest of the Northwest Territory by the
Ordinance of 1787— namely, the prohibition of slavery.[3]

Most Ohio papers printed Chase's address, with Republican papers
praising and Democratic papers attacking his ideas. The *Ohio State Journal*
said that it was "conceded on all hands to be the best state paper ever to
have emanated from our state executive." The *M'Arthur Democrat* claimed
that Chase "recommends that negroes shall have the benefit of school
along with white children, or that you shall be taxed to provide schools
for them." This was a rather creative reading of a single sentence in which
Chase said that "universal education is our cheapest defense, and surest
safeguard, and most enduring wealth." Outside of Ohio, the *New-York
Tribune* devoted several columns to excerpts from the address, with Horace
Greeley commenting that it was "marked by Mr. Chase's characteristic
clearness and vigor of statement." In the *National Era*, Gamaliel Bailey
praised the address as "a state paper of the first order."[4]

When Chase moved to Columbus in early 1856 to become governor, he
and his daughters lived together in one household for the first time in
many years. Nettie was eight, and Kate was fifteen. At first, the family boarded with the P. T. Snowden family, near the statehouse. Chase
enrolled the girls in a local school, arranged for private French lessons, and

worked on his own French, reading a French daily devotional and novels by Victor Hugo. Nettie recalled that her father "was particularly fond of studying the Bible in different languages," including French, German, and Greek, and regretted "that he knew nothing of Hebrew to help him to a fuller understanding of the greatest of books." Chase's other reading in this period included Edmund Spenser's sixteenth-century epic poem *The Faerie Queene*, and *The History of the Decline and Fall of the Roman Empire* by Gibbon, the very book that Chase had denounced as "poisonous" while an ardent college student.[5]

*Kate Chase as she looked in the early 1850s,
before she charmed men in Columbus and Washington.*

Even as a teenager, Kate attracted admirers, as evidenced by a cryptic letter from her father in the summer of 1856 while he was away in Cincinnati. "*Go nowhere and with nobody and do nothing* of the least consequence without consulting freely with your aunt Charlotte," he admonished. "You are at a time of life when all your acts will be observed." This letter may be related to a few entries in Chase's diary about "trouble" with Kate, who was reportedly walking out in public with a married man. When Chase explained his concerns, Kate seemed "really penitent."[6]

Those who met Kate Chase in these years did not forget her. A young local newspaper reporter, William Dean Howells, later a leading American author, recalled that after dinner at the Chase home, the group played charades, and Howells was almost overcome with nerves. "Nothing but the raillery glancing through the deep lashes of her brown eyes which were very beautiful could have brought me to the self-sacrifice involved." Carl Schurz, born in Prussia, now a rising political leader in Wisconsin, and later a member of the Senate and the Cabinet, recalled that at their first meeting, Kate "saluted me very kindly, and then let herself down upon her chair with the graceful lightness of a bird that, folding its wings, perches upon the branch of a tree. She was then about eighteen years old, tall and slender, and exceedingly well formed." Chase and Schurz were talking politics, and Kate "took a lively and remarkably intelligent part" in their conversation. Isabella Trotter, a British visitor, wrote home that Kate's figure was "tall and slight, but at the same time beautifully rounded, her neck long and graceful, with a sweet, pretty brunette face. I seldom have seen such lovely eyes and dark eyelashes; she has rich dark hair in great profusion, but her style and dress were of the utmost simplicity and grace." Trotter was also impressed by Chase, "a first-rate man in talent and character," and noted that "with good reason [he] worships his daughter."[7]

Only after winning a second two-year term as governor in 1857 would Chase purchase a house in Columbus, on the corner of Sixth and State Streets. It was a substantial Gothic stone house with a large yard surrounded by an iron fence. Chase sent Kate to Cincinnati to purchase furniture for it and then sent letter after letter of advice and instruction. "Let me again remind you not to buy anything in Cincinnati," he wrote her, "which you can as well buy in Columbus." He added that he feared "I am trusting a good deal to the judgment of a girl of seventeen; but I am confident I may safely trust yours." When Trotter visited the Chase house a few months later, it reminded her of "an English rectory standing in a little garden." She approved of what Kate had done with the interior, especially the drawing room, "such a *bijou* of a room," with pale white walls, a marble table in the center, and a marble Greek bust. "The simplicity and beauty of the room could not be surpassed."[8]

The Chase house in Columbus, at the corner of East State and Sixth Streets.
Chase and his family lived here for two years, until he moved to Washington in
early 1861 to join the Lincoln administration.

Nettie did not attract as much attention as her half sister, Kate. Howells and Schurz did not mention Nettie at all in their memoirs, while
Trotter, in her 1859 book about her American travels, mentioned Chase's
second daughter but did not describe her. In a letter to Kate, Chase
praised Nettie as "artless, guileless, truthful, affectionate, and winning,"
adding that it was "by loving others that she makes them love her." In a
diary entry in early 1857, he noted that, in a family political discussion,
Nettie had defended a legislator expelled for a fistfight on the House
floor, "but abandoned him on learning that he was proslavery." It seems
safe to assume that both Nettie and Kate shared their father's antislavery
opinions. By the end of her time in Columbus, Nettie was enrolled in the
"art section" of the school, developing the talents she would use later in
life as an illustrator of children's books.[9]

Chase had no wife, but there were women in his life. Elizabeth Ellicott
Pike, wife of his friend James Pike, wrote not long after Chase's inauguration to ask the "great and illustrious governor" to write to "this the
truest of thy friends." In another letter, she wrote that "at intervals the
desire to see you comes upon me so strongly that I wish to disembody
my spirit and send it to you upon a sheet of lightning or a whirlwind."
Chase responded that although he did not deserve her warm words, it was

*Salmon Chase and his two daughters, Nettie on the left and Kate on the right,
in a photo made at Mathew Brady's Washington studio in about 1857.*

"very pleasant to feel that one is liked by a noble woman and noble man."
He added: "I put you first because all my experience of life has taught
me that the grammarians have committed a sad mistake in declaring
the masculine the worthier pronoun. Ask Mr. Pike if I am not right."[10]

Chase also kept in touch with Elizabeth Wirt Goldsborough, with
whom he had been so in love in his youth and who now lived in Annapolis, where her husband was the superintendent of the Naval Academy.
Thanking Chase for one of his letters, she wrote that her mother believed
that only one other person, her late husband William Wirt, could write
such a "beautiful letter." Warning that she would always "speak plainly
and frankly," Elizabeth said that although she opposed the extension of
slavery, "there ought to be a doctrine of noninterference with the rights
and privileges of the Southern states, where slavery exists as a matter of
hereditary property." She urged Chase to stress this point more and not

to let his name "be associated and confounded with the host of unscrupulous and fanatic abolitionists." In the summer of 1857 Chase and his daughters visited the Goldsborough family, after which Elizabeth wrote to thank him and to say she hoped they could see each other more often.[11]

Susan Walker, the unmarried sister of Chase's former law partner Timothy Walker, was another of Chase's frequent correspondents. In late 1852, less than a year after the death of his third wife, Chase noted in his diary that he had called upon Susan Walker in Washington, which was "indiscreet and wrong." We do not have the letters between the two of them, only notes in Chase's diary of letters sent and received. In early 1857, however, Margaret Bailey wrote Chase that she had asked Susan Walker why she and Chase never married. "Because we know each other too well," was the reply. Margaret wrote that she "never did believe you would marry Miss Walker," although she could not quite explain why. "We women often get ideas through our instincts which we don't trouble ourselves to test by our reason, and we should be none the wiser if we did." She predicted that Chase would someday "settle down with a middle-aged lady" and "live out comfortably your three-score years and ten."[12]

Last but not least, there was Charlotte "Lottie" Eastman, widow of Chase's friend Ben Eastman, who died young in early 1856. Chase described her to a friend as "a sweet and lovely woman, unaffected and unpretending, good-looking enough, though no longer young, to be pleasant to the eyes, and intelligent enough, though not learned, to be an agreeable talker." Chase started to correspond with the widow soon after her husband's death and would see her from time to time, either in Washington or at her home in Beverly, Massachusetts; she may have visited Columbus in 1859. It was not until after the Civil War, however, that the friendship between Chase and Eastman would grow into something more intense.[13]

Chase had hardly settled into his routine as governor when he learned of the Margaret Garner fugitive slave case, famous at the time and even more famous today as the background of Toni Morrison's novel *Beloved* and the opera *Margaret Garner*. Eight members of the Garner slave family crossed the frozen Ohio River on the night of January 27, 1856, from Covington, Kentucky, to Cincinnati. The next day, as federal marshals approached the house where the Garners were hiding, Margaret Garner, terrified that her child would be returned to slavery, used a knife to slit the throat of her

Thomas Noble's painting The Modern Medea *shows Margaret Garner explaining to her captors why she killed her daughter rather than see the girl enslaved again. Chase attempted to secure freedom for Garner and her family.*

three-year-old daughter, nearly cutting off the girl's head. She slashed at her other children, injuring them, but was restrained and then captured by the marshals, along with the others. The papers quoted Margaret as saying that "she had killed one, and would like to kill the three others, rather than see them again reduced to slavery." The seven surviving Garners were jailed, and a legal battle commenced between federal authorities, who wanted to see them declared fugitive slaves and returned to their Kentucky masters, and Ohio state authorities, who wanted to hold them to face state criminal charges and thereby keep them out of slavery, even if one or more of them was convicted.[14]

On the day after the arrest, Cincinnati judge John Burgoyne, who had already issued a writ demanding custody of the Garners, arrived in Columbus to confer with the governor. Chase recalled that Burgoyne asked whether "the executive of the state would sustain the process of the state in the midst of a community in which, by most persons, any decision against the claims of masters would be regarded as little better than treason." He responded that "the process of the state courts would be enforced in every part of the state" and "authorized him to say to the sheriff that, in the performance of his duty, he would be sustained by the whole power at the command of the executive."[15]

For the next few weeks, as lawyers argued the *Garner* case in several Cincinnati courts, Chase followed "with great interest" in the papers. He would have agreed with the *New-York Tribune* when it declared that Garner proved that slaves hated slavery. "Like the rest of us, they yearn for freedom, and having achieved freedom, though but for a few days, they welcome the grave as the alternative to bondage." Then, on February 28, the federal district judge in Cincinnati, Humphrey Leavitt, ruled unexpectedly that the Garners should be returned to Kentucky. Federal marshals, accompanied by a large crowd, immediately took the Garners from the Cincinnati courtroom to a Covington jail. Chase was later criticized for failing to defend the Garners, but there was no way for officials in Cincinnati to confer with the governor in Columbus before obeying Leavitt's order and handing over the family. Chase learned about the order only by reading about it in the newspapers *after* the Garners were already in Kentucky.[16]

The Hamilton County prosecutor wrote Chase to suggest that he ask the governor of Kentucky to arrest the Garner adults as fugitives from Ohio's justice system and return them for trial on the pending state charges against them. Chase was reluctant—he recalled that "the indicted prisoners could hardly be considered as having fled from justice in Ohio"—but he agreed when a friend volunteered to go to Kentucky to attempt to purchase the freedom of the three surviving Garner children. Two men, one bearing Chase's official letter to the Kentucky governor, and the other seeking to purchase the children, went to Kentucky and obtained an order from the governor to deliver up the adults. The masters of the Garner slaves, however, were not taking chances; they had already put the family on a steamboat heading south. Chase learned this by reading in the papers that, in the predawn darkness on March 8, the steamboat carrying the Garners collided with another boat on the Ohio River. Several passengers drowned, including one of the Garner children. The *Louisville Courier* reported that Margaret Garner "exhibited no feeling other than joy at the loss of her child." The surviving Garners were placed on another boat for New Orleans, and in early 1864 Chase would write that "nothing has been heard of the Garner family since." Chase hoped that they were among the many slaves who had found their way to freedom by that point in the Civil War, but he did not know. Some members of the family did live to see freedom, but not Margaret, who was later reported to have died of typhoid fever in Mississippi, still enslaved.[17]

The day-to-day work of the governor of Ohio was far less dramatic than the *Garner* case. Like most governors at this time, Chase did not have veto authority, much less the line-item veto. He followed the work of the state legislature, and sometimes supported or opposed a particular bill, but legislation was not a major part of his work. The key offices in the state, such as the treasurer and the attorney general, were elected, not appointed by the governor. To the extent that Chase did have the power to appoint, he sometimes tapped friends, but, other times, he chose political opponents such as Edward Mansfield, the first commissioner of statistics in Ohio, responsible for an annual statistical report. When asked, Chase said that he appointed Mansfield simply because he was best qualified for the post. The governor had the power to pardon, and Chase's files contain many letters about pardon applications, often letters from Chase seeking further information.[18]

Chase also handled requests from other states for the extradition of prisoners, and one sees in these letters the meticulous lawyer at work. For example, when Chase received a request from Pennsylvania to extradite a man charged with seduction, fornication, and bastardy, he responded that the female accuser was over twenty years of age, so that the defendant could not be charged with seduction, and that the other crimes were not punishable by imprisonment in the penitentiary, so that extradition was not available under Ohio law. Occasionally, even a ministerial task could be pleasant. As Chase hoped, the legislature elected Benjamin Wade for a second Senate term in March 1856, and Chase had to sign the formal papers confirming the selection. "Five years ago," Wade wrote to Chase, "no prophet" could have predicted that the "abolitionist" Wade would become a federal senator or that "the abolitionist and agitator S. P. Chase would be the governor of Ohio to sign his credentials." Chase probably smiled as he signed the papers.[19]

Although he did not ignore his work as governor, Chase devoted much of the first few weeks of 1856 to organizing the National Republican Party and especially to persuading people to attend the proposed Pittsburgh convention. His principal aide in this work, James Ashley, reported to Chase in January that he had received forty-one replies to his circular letter urging a Pittsburgh gathering and that all but a few were favorable. Chase and his friends then printed their convention call in the papers. Horace Greeley, in the *New-York Tribune*, urged that every state send a few sound delegates to the Pittsburgh convention.[20]

The Know-Nothing Party, officially renamed the American Party in 1855, planned to hold its own national nominating convention in Philadelphia on the same auspicious day that the Republicans were meeting in Pittsburgh: Washington's birthday, February 22. Chase hoped that, as in the prior year, the American Party would divide over slavery, so that the liberal Americans would join the Republicans. Chase's main agent in this effort was Thomas Spooner, a Know-Nothing who was now more committed to antislavery than to nativism. The prior fall, Spooner had drafted resolutions for the Ohio American Party, declaring that "proscription on account of birth or creed is unwarranted by American principles." Chase urged his friend Charles Cleveland to reprint these resolutions, and he encouraged Spooner and other friends to attend the Philadelphia convention and advocate for an antislavery platform.[21]

As Chase hoped, there was a respectable gathering in Pittsburgh on February 22, with more than a hundred Republican leaders from more than twenty states. The Ohio delegation included many Chase supporters, such as Ashley, Giddings, Reemelin, Stone, and state treasurer William Gibson. Other friends and correspondents of his were present, including Kinsley Bingham, governor of Michigan; George Julian, former and future member of Congress from Indiana; and Joseph Medill, formerly an Ohio editor and now one of the senior editors of the *Chicago Tribune,* the most influential Republican paper in the West. Horace Greeley and Edwin Morgan, future governor, were among those present from New York. There were a few men from slave states as well, including Kentucky, Maryland, Missouri, and South Carolina. Francis Blair attended and served as chairman, causing comment about the seeming contradiction of having a slave owner preside over an antislavery convention. Chase himself was *not* among those in Pittsburgh, both because he was busy in Columbus as governor and because of the custom that candidates did not attend conventions in the nineteenth century.[22]

The key issues facing the Pittsburgh convention were the time and place for the national nominating convention. The delegates opted for a relatively late date, June 17, so that the Republican convention would be after the Democratic convention, set for April. Chase's friends pushed for Cincinnati, arguing among other points that there were "superior reporters in that city, and the proceedings would be fully reported in the

English and German newspapers." But friends of other candidates did not want to give Chase the advantage of a hometown convention, and so Philadelphia was selected instead.[23]

The delegates were hammering out these issues when a telegram arrived from Spooner, who had followed Chase's suggestion and was attending the American Party convention in Philadelphia: "American Party no longer united. Raise Republican banner. No further extension of slavery. Americans are with you." Spooner's message, however, was only partly correct. Yes, a handful of American Party leaders from Northern states had walked out and would support Republicans in the fall. But the remaining delegates in Philadelphia had nominated former president Millard Fillmore and adopted a platform stressing national unity. The American Party would pose serious problems for both Democrats and Republicans in 1856.[24]

Chase was pleased with the Pittsburgh convention—especially by reports remarking on his strength in the party. "Had the Pittsburgh convention been a nominating convention," one friend wrote, "you would have had the nomination for the presidency by two to one." Similarly, Ashley assured Chase that "a large majority of the delegates at Pittsburgh were of our way of thinking, and had there been a nomination, you would have gotten a large majority." Chase's friend John Bigelow, who reported on the convention for the *New York Evening Post*, wrote Chase that there had not really been much discussion about candidates in Pittsburgh. "For my own part, of course," Bigelow added, "I would prefer to have a personal friend nominated for the presidency rather than a stranger, but I am prepared to support with all my might any man who is nominated fair and square in opposition to the nationalization of slavery." Chase probably read this as indicating that Bigelow would support him, when, in fact, he was already quietly working for a rival, the California explorer John Frémont.[25]

The main candidates for the 1856 Republican nomination were Chase, Seward, McLean, and Frémont. Chase and Seward were both strong antislavery men who had served in the Senate. Some former Whigs would favor Seward because he used to be one of them, while other men, who had partnered with Chase in the Liberty or Free Soil Parties, would line up behind him for similar reasons, seeing the Ohio governor as the true antislavery candidate. None of the papers viewed Chase's history as a

Democrat as a disabling factor, for he was always a Democrat of a curious kind, more ardent about slavery than any other issue, and not a member of the Democratic caucus in the Senate. Seward had the advantage of his friend and adviser Thurlow Weed, editor of the *Albany Evening Journal*, and veteran of countless conventions and campaigns. Although Seward was interested in the nomination, Weed believed it was not in Seward's interest to be nominated this year, when the new party would probably meet defeat. Weed already had his eye on 1860. John McLean was not known for his antislavery views—indeed, his judicial opinions generally supported slavery—but he was favored by conservatives and some editors hoping to see the Republican Party carry conservative states. Horace Greeley wrote to a friend that "if McLean is the man for Pennsylvania and New Jersey, then I am the man for McLean."[26]

John Frémont was famous because of his explorations of the West, recounted in books edited by his extraordinary wife, Jessie Frémont, daughter of Senator Thomas Hart Benton. Finding himself in California in 1846 in the midst of a revolt against Mexican rule, Frémont sided with the rebels, helping California achieve its brief period as the independent Bear Flag Republic. When the United States seized California, Frémont was appointed military governor, but he ignored orders from the War Department, resulting in a court martial and dismissal from the army. Although President Polk commuted the sentence and reinstated Frémont, the colonel resigned and returned to California as a private citizen. In late 1849 the territorial legislature named him as one of the state's first federal senators, but statehood was delayed for months by the debate over the Compromise, so that Frémont did not take his seat in the Senate until September 10, 1850, the day after California became the thirty-first state. During the last weeks of the debate over the Compromise, the new senator did not make any speeches about slavery. Indeed, during his brief stint in the upper chamber, Frémont made almost no remarks whatsoever, other than to support a bill to change the rules for gold mining in California. When Mississippi's Henry Foote accused Frémont of pushing this bill for personal reasons, the two senators got into a fight in the Capitol Rotunda, during which Foote struck and hit Frémont above the eye, drawing blood. One paper reported that before Frémont could "return the compliment," other members separated them.[27]

Frémont departed from Washington as soon as the congressional session ended in late September and went to California, where he tried and failed to win a second Senate term. He had done nothing to distinguish himself in the Senate; nor did he side with the anti-Nebraska forces in 1854 and 1855. Why, then, was Frémont a leading candidate for the 1856 Republican nomination? It was precisely *because* Frémont had such a thin record that leaders such as Francis Blair and newspapermen like Bigelow favored him. They believed that Frémont would appeal to former Know-Nothings, to former Democrats, and to lukewarm former Whigs. Blair apparently revealed to Chase and the others who attended the December 1855 dinner that Frémont was "his man" for the nomination the next year.[28]

In late March 1856 a letter from former senator Thomas Hart Benton appeared in the papers, saying that he had no interest in a presidential nomination and criticizing both parties for their "slavery agitation," which, in his view, "would end disastrously for the Union." In the letter's key line, Benton wrote that "a new man, unconnected with the agitation, is what the country wants." Benton did not name his "new man," but it seemed that he had his son-in-law Frémont in mind. Chase disagreed, writing to Bigelow that "this policy of 'new men' is almost always fatal and would now be certainly so. It would ensure defeat without an accompanying benefit. The overthrow which it would bring would leave the opponents of the administration demoralized, disorganized, and without power." Chase insisted that he was not reacting to the implicit "personal disparagement of myself" as an "agitator." What he feared, he wrote, was that if the Republicans nominated someone without a strong antislavery record, Gerrit Smith and others would nominate an abolition candidate, and "thousands upon thousands of earnest antislavery men would rally under the abolition banner," with the result that the Republicans would "carry no Northern state."[29]

Gamaliel Bailey agreed with Chase, writing to him in April that "the Republican movement is about to slip from the control of men of principle into the hands of place hunters and politicians." Bailey would prefer Chase or Seward as the party's candidate. "I have confidence in you both and would rather suffer defeat with either of you on our principles fairly and squarely stated, than secure success with untried men without principle." As to Frémont, Bailey wrote, "you know him. He is an amiable, honorable gentleman, with a gift for exploration and adventure, but without knowledge of politics or political men, or the value and aims of our movement." Without giving up his own hopes, Chase signaled to Seward that he preferred him over Frémont, writing Seward to praise a speech and to predict that his "place hereafter" would be "higher and more conspicuous still."[30]

While Republicans were debating whom to nominate for president, the struggle continued between proponents and opponents of slavery in Kansas. At a Columbus rally in March to raise funds for those heading from the free states to Kansas, Chase gave a short speech. He noted a recent proposal in Mississippi to impose a tax on slaveowners to raise funds "to aid in sending armed men with their slaves into that [Kansas] territory." This showed that "now not only Missouri, but the whole South, [is] making preparations to send armed forces there, to prevent the settlers of Kansas from exercising that right of 'popular sovereignty' said to have been guaranteed them by the Kansas bill." Among the best-selling books of the spring was an account of the conflict and violence in Kansas.[31]

Sumner wrote to Chase in May, saying that he would speak soon in the Senate about Kansas and promising "the most thorough and complete speech in my life." In the course of his five-hour address, spread over two days, which he titled "The Crime Against Kansas," Sumner attacked the Pierce administration for supporting the pro-slavery settlers, and denounced some of his fellow senators, such as Andrew Butler of South Carolina, whom he said was pledged to his mistress, the "harlot Slavery." Like abolitionists who accused Southern masters of raping their slaves, Sumner was (almost) accusing Butler not just of preferring slavery as a system but also of preferring slaves as sexual partners. Two days later, after the Senate had finished its work for the day, and Sumner was sitting at his desk in the Senate chamber writing letters, Preston Brooks, a member of Congress from South Carolina and Butler's cousin, approached Sumner.

Brooks told Sumner that he had insulted his state and his relative, then suddenly attacked Sumner with a thick gutta-percha cane, with blow after blow, on the head, the neck, the arms, while Sumner was trapped by his desk, bolted to the floor. When Senator John Crittenden of Kentucky tried to intervene, shouting "Don't kill him!" at Brooks, Laurence Keitt, another South Carolina member of Congress, raised his own cane, shouting back at Crittenden, "Leave them alone, God damn you!" Brooks kept striking Sumner even as the cane broke into pieces, and Sumner wrenched the desk from the floor. When Brooks finally stopped

SOUTHERN CHIVALRY — ARGUMENT_{versus} CLUB'S.

Preston Brooks, of South Carolina, assaults and nearly kills
Charles Sumner on the floor of the United States Senate, June 1856. This print
represents the northern view; for Southerners, Brooks was a hero.

and stalked off, the bleeding Sumner was carried from the chamber by
his colleagues, nearly dead.[32]

As soon as he read about the attack on Sumner, Chase dashed off a
letter to his fallen friend. "How I wish I could have been near when the
dastardly ruffian struck you down! One arm at least would have been
prompt in your succor and defense." Chase approved of Sumner's Kansas
speech, "your noble defense of freedom," or at least the summary that had
appeared so far in the *New-York Tribune*. "God bless you," Chase closed,
"and God grant that Northern endurance may at length be at an end."[33]

The papers were still reporting on this savage attack on the Senate
floor when news arrived that Missouri ruffians had attacked the antislavery
town of Lawrence, Kansas. The *New-York Tribune* denounced the "border
ruffians" and claimed that Lawrence was "in ruins," with "several persons slaughtered." The *Ohio State Journal* quoted from an eyewitness who
claimed that there were "several dead bodies in the streets" and that, after
fleeing for his life, he could see the smoke from the burning town from
fifteen miles away. The *Cincinnati Gazette* commented that "in Kansas, in
Washington, everywhere [Southerners] exhibit the same intolerance, the
same hatred of freedom, of courage and manhood . . . everywhere they
seek to trample the weak under foot."[34]

The attacks on Sumner and on Lawrence should have helped Chase and hurt Frémont in the race for the Republican presidential nomination. After all, Chase was a close friend of Sumner's and a strong supporter of free Kansas. There were no primaries to bind the Republican delegates heading to Philadelphia; they could vote for Chase if he was their choice, in light of recent events. But the editors who had decided upon Frémont were not swayed. Starting on May 18 and continuing for several weeks, the *New York Evening Post* printed a series of articles by Bigelow about the adventures and triumphs of Frémont. Even more important, on June 6 the *New-York Tribune* endorsed Frémont for the Republican nomination. Greeley explained that if the opponents of slavery were strong enough to elect any of their candidates, he would prefer Seward or Chase, because of their "early, earnest, faithful, protracted, unswerving service to the cause." But the *Tribune*'s editor believed that the Republicans were *not* yet strong enough to elect such a candidate; they would need someone who could appeal more broadly, someone like Frémont or McLean. Greeley tried his best to paint Frémont as an antislavery advocate, claiming that he was "one of the men who by prompt and determined action at the critical moment made California a Free State."[35]

In spite of these articles, Chase still had some hope in early June of obtaining the Republican nomination. In a letter to his New York friend and lawyer Hiram Barney, he urged him to "go to work yourself in right earnest. There are many who agree with you in New York. Get them to move and to show themselves in Philadelphia. The politicians are not omnipotent—the people will go for something, if we only exercise faith and add to faith virtue." In a letter to Hamlin, Chase wrote in similar terms: "It seems to me that if the wishes of the people could prevail, I would be nominated." But he also realized that the convention would probably choose Frémont, so he authorized two friends to withdraw his name, if necessary, to preserve party unity. On the eve of the convention, Chase's friend James Pike, in his report to the *Tribune* from Philadelphia, said simply, "Frémont's nomination is inevitable." And indeed, after Thurlow Weed withdrew Seward's name, and a friend read Chase's letter aloud, withdrawing his name, the convention had no difficulty nominating Frémont. The platform echoed Chase in many places, such as when it argued that "our Republican fathers" wanted to keep slavery out of the federal territories. Indeed, the platform went beyond Chase in some respects, such as where it declared that Congress should "prohibit

in the territories those twin relics of barbarism: polygamy and slavery."
This was a slap at the polygamous Mormons in the Utah Territory and
also a hint that slaveholders slept with both their white wives and their
black slaves.[36]

"Some of my friends were a little disappointed by the result of the
Philadelphia convention," Chase wrote to a cousin. "They thought it not
quite just to set aside the framers and builders of the cause for a new
architect." But he had "personal confidence" in the nominees and said he
would "labor earnestly for their election." Chase's friends were, in fact, more
than a little disappointed. Barney lamented in a letter to Chase that even
Bailey had "worked among antislavery men for McLean" at the convention
and that "the *Tribune* and *Evening Post* and a hundred other papers" were
strong for Frémont. "You have had nobody really and actually at work for
you." Elizabeth Pike wrote to Chase that she simply "hated" the Frémont
nomination. "It seemed to me that if ever the Republican Party could hope
to have a man of their own, one who had represented their faith and fought
their battles, it was now, when they could point to the bleeding wounds
of Kansas and say: behold! But they were afraid to risk it."[37]

The election of 1856 was another triangular contest. Democrats nominated
James Buchanan of Pennsylvania on a platform that endorsed the Compromise of 1850, including the Fugitive Slave Act, and opposed "agitation
of the slavery question under whatever shape or color the attempt may be
made." Buchanan lived in southern Pennsylvania, only a few miles from
the slave state of Maryland; he was a Northern man with many Southern
friends. Both the American Party and the fading Whig Party nominated
Millard Fillmore; they argued that the only way to preserve the Union
was to vote for the former president. It was "madness or folly," the Americans said, for Republicans to "believe that our Southern brethren would
submit to be governed" by a Republican president; they "must see that
if this sectional party succeeds, it leads inevitably to the destruction of
this beautiful fabric reared by our forefathers." Democrats agreed with
the Americans on this point: the Republicans were a mere sectional party,
and Republican success would end the Union.[38]

Starting in July and August, and especially in September, Chase
campaigned around Ohio for Republicans. Speaking to a crowd of five
thousand gathered on a high bluff about a mile outside of Zanesville,

he spoke mainly about "the wrongs the Free State men have endured in Kansas from Border Ruffian legislation and Presidential injustice." The *Ohio State Journal* described the speech as "strong in argument, felicitous in illustration, and manly in its style." He was one of several speakers in Sandusky, in early September, to a crowd estimated at between thirty thousand and forty thousand. While there, news arrived that Hannibal Hamlin, the Republican candidate for governor in Maine, had won his race. This cheered Chase and other Republicans, who viewed it as indicating that Republicans would prevail throughout the North. When Chase spoke in Cadiz, Ohio, the local Democratic paper mocked him, saying that he gave "the same speech he delivered here last fall, but not delivered half so well." Charles Dana, an editor of the *New-York Tribune*, seeing that Chase was out on the campaign trail while Seward was sulking at home, wrote to his colleague Pike that Chase was "about ten times as much of a man" as Seward.[39]

Because John Frémont would not get any votes in the Southern states, the only way for him to win in the electoral college was to carry almost all the Northern states, especially the most populous ones: New York (with thirty-five electoral votes), Pennsylvania (twenty-seven), Ohio (twenty-three), Indiana (thirteen), and Massachusetts (thirteen). Three of these states, Pennsylvania, Ohio, and Indiana, voted twice, once in October to select state officers and members of Congress, and once in November, on the same day as other states, to elect the president and vice president. Chase predicted that Republicans would win in Ohio in October, and they did, though not by the massive margins that he had predicted. But the party lost in Indiana and Pennsylvania, which essentially ended Frémont's chances. Chase did not give any further speeches.[40]

James Buchanan carried nineteen states in the 1856 presidential election: all but one of the slave states and five of the free states: California, Illinois, Indiana, New Jersey, and Pennsylvania. Frémont carried eleven states, including Ohio and New York. Fillmore, the American Party nominee, carried only Maryland, but he received more than 20 percent of the national popular vote. There was a sectional pattern to the election results, not only between but also within states. In Ohio, Indiana, and Illinois, Republicans generally carried the northern counties, and Democrats and Americans, the southern counties. In Illinois, for example, Republicans received more than 80 percent of the votes in the northern tier, but only 2 percent of the votes in the southernmost county, Alexander County.[41]

The 1856 results provided the road map for Republican victory in 1860. The new party would need to carry a few more free states, including Pennsylvania, to win the White House. To do this, it would need to do a better job of attracting moderates in states such as Illinois, Indiana, and Pennsylvania, including the "liberal Americans" who Chase believed truly belonged in the Republican Party. He was hopeful, as evidenced by a letter he wrote to Charles Sumner, who was still convalescing from the vicious attack by Preston Brooks: "We have lost the battle, but we are stronger than anything except victory could make us. Let us profit by our mistakes and make victory sure, by higher faith and better works, next time."[42]

Chase spent the last days of 1856 and first of 1857 working on two documents: his annual message and his speech for the dedication of the new statehouse. The message was a thirty-page printed document filled with financial details but also with interesting ideas. For example, after noting the increasing importance of railroads, Chase urged the legislature to create a state railroad regulation commission, something that would become common in the late nineteenth century but barely existed at this time. He also urged the legislature to review and reform the laws denying rights to married women, asserting, "Instances not unfrequently occur of gross oppression though the absolute control given to the husband over personal estate and particularly over household goods." Chase lamented the plight of Ohio settlers in Kansas, reporting that "they are practically disenfranchised by odious test oaths; that many of their number have been killed; many robbed; and all subjected to grievous indignities and injuries."[43]

After almost two decades of work, and with some work still remaining, the Ohio statehouse was ready to dedicate and open on January 6, 1857. Thousands of people, including hundreds of ladies in hoopskirts, pressed in when the gates opened at seven in the evening. The *Ohio State Journal* reported that "the fretting, the scolding, the complaining of the daughters of fashion were of no avail; tighter and tighter, closer and closer, the living, breathing mass was packed together." As governor, Chase made the principal speech of the evening, giving a brief history of the statehouse and naming some of the illustrious men who had served as legislators. He closed with a benediction of the building: "May the counsels of truth and justice and public virtue preside in its halls; may discord and faction be put far from them; and may the free and united people who reared it, and whose temple it is, watch over and cherish within its walls the form and spirit of their republican institutions." After the speaking, there was dancing, and the last guests did not leave until the sun rose the next morning.[44]

A few weeks later, Chase was in Cleveland to lecture on the Italian astronomer Galileo. Describing Galileo's trial by the Catholic Church for the heresy of asserting that the sun was the center of the solar system, Chase related how, after the guilty verdict was pronounced, Galileo kneeled and "called God to witness that he utterly renounced, abjured, and detested the opinions he had formerly taught." No one, Chase continued, was deceived by this extorted renunciation. "Even his enemies must have felt that, whatever might be wrung from his lips, his mind remained unchanged." The triumph of the judges, in having secured these statements from Galileo, was temporary, for they "could torment, they might even destroy the teacher; but the truth he proclaimed was beyond their reach." On the surface, Chase was talking about science and history, but surely some thought about the parallels between Galileo's insistence that the earth rotated around the sun, and Chase's assertion that the Constitution was a charter of freedom.[45]

Other lectures and letters were more political. In lieu of a promised lecture, which he had to cancel because of pressing work in Columbus, Chase sent a letter to the state teachers association. It was a paean to public education. Noting that he had been a teacher himself and thus knew something of the "responsibilities, trials, and aspirations" of teachers, he declared that "no safer or more remunerative investment of revenue is made by the state than in the instruction of her youth. Stinginess here is not economy. It is waste, and the worst description of waste: the waste of mind." The schoolhouse was more important than the courthouse or even the statehouse, for it was in the schoolhouse that future judges, legislators, and even presidents were formed. "To make the schoolhouse efficient, teachers must be not only qualified but honored. The responsibility of their trust, the magnitude of their work, and the dignity of their calling must be acknowledged, and not coldly acknowledged only, but thoroughly appreciated."[46]

Chase spoke several times at events to celebrate the completion of the rail line from Baltimore to Saint Louis by way of Ohio. The most important speech was in Baltimore, where he was introduced by his friend Thomas Swann, formerly a law student with Chase under William Wirt, and now the mayor of Baltimore. Maryland was a border state, with more than eighty thousand slaves and a government dominated by slave owners. Chase extolled how the railroad would bring the people of the different states closer together, while admitting that they would continue to disagree on some points. "We will maintain our respective positions with candor, courtesy, firmness, and resolution; and we will refer whatever questions may be between us to the great American tribunal of popular discussion and popular judgment." He insisted that there was "no evil for which disunion is the proper cure."[47]

In early March 1857 the Supreme Court finally decided the *Dred Scott* case. As Chase feared and expected, the court ruled against Scott, finding that as "a negro, whose ancestors were imported and sold as slaves," Scott was not a citizen and thus was not entitled to sue in the federal courts. This should have been sufficient; if Scott had no right to sue, then the Supreme Court had no right to consider other issues in the case. But Chief Justice Roger Taney's opinion proceeded to consider Scott's argument that his time in the Minnesota Territory had made him free and ruled that because slaves were a form of property, Congress had no authority under the Constitution to prohibit slavery in any federal territory.[48]

Like other Republicans, Chase disagreed strongly with the *Dred Scott* decision. The legislatures of several states, including Ohio, passed resolutions condemning the ruling. More usefully, Ohio enacted three new laws to strengthen the position of alleged fugitive slaves. The most important of these made it a crime to bring into Ohio any person "with the intent to hold or control" that person as a slave. This meant that not only would a master with a slave, stopping in Ohio on his way up or down the Ohio River, possibly lose the slave; the master himself would face criminal sanctions. A second law prohibited the use of state jails for holding alleged fugitive slaves. A third law prohibited "slaveholding and kidnapping in the state of Ohio." Although there was an exception for actions taken under the federal Fugitive Slave Act, any actions that were *not* authorized by the federal statute, such as seizing an alleged fugitive without process, were prohibited. Chase noted in his diary that he was in the statehouse on the day that these bills were passed and reported to a friend that "I aided them as far as I could properly do so."[49]

Nativist members of the legislature lobbied at this time for a state constitutional amendment to impose a one-year waiting period before a newly naturalized citizen could vote in state elections. This posed a difficult issue for Chase, for he did not want to offend either the immigrants or the nativists who had supported his election. In a long letter to Frederick Hassaurek, a German American leader in Cincinnati, Chase said that he believed the proponents of the amendment were merely concerned about "indiscriminate, hasty, and sometimes fraudulent naturalization just upon the eve of an election." Chase also sent Hassaurek a proposed resolution, which he had edited some, suggesting changes in the federal immigration laws. Hassaurek responded that he and other German leaders would oppose the state constitutional amendment but could support the resolution. In part because of quiet pressure from Chase, the proposed amendment did not pass the legislature.[50]

Some of Chase's political friends urged him not to run for a second term as governor, warning that if he lost in Ohio, he would hurt his chances for the presidential nomination in 1860. Others, however, insisted that he had to run for a second term. Chase was ambivalent, writing to his friend Edward Pierce that he wished he could avoid another campaign "without seeming to shrink from some danger and without giving just occasion of dissatisfaction to our friends." By May 1857, Republican papers in Ohio were rejoicing that Chase would seek reelection. The *Ohio State Journal* claimed that there were "thousands of men who opposed his election two years ago" who would now "give him a cordial and substantial support." Another Republican paper said simply that Chase was "the man" to carry the party this year.[51]

In the summer of 1857 Chase was involved in another fugitive slave case, again involving conflict between the state and federal governments. The case started with an unsuccessful attempt to arrest a fugitive slave at a farm near Urbana, Ohio. A few days later, federal deputy marshals returned to arrest the owner of the farm where the fugitive had been living and working. After getting into an argument with the farmer's friends, the marshals arrested four men for interference with federal officials. As they attempted to take their four prisoners to Cincinnati, however, the marshals were stopped by a large crowd, including state officials, bearing a state judge's writ of habeas corpus for the men's release. Shots were fired, and the state officials arrested the federal marshals for attempted murder. Judge Humphrey Leavitt soon issued his own federal writ of habeas corpus, directing that the prisoners be brought to Cincinnati, where he would decide whether they should be released. Chase asked the Ohio attorney general, Christopher Wolcott, to argue in Cincinnati on behalf of the state. For the *Cincinnati Enquirer,* this meant that Chase "sanctioned, justified, adopted, and countenanced the infamous conduct of the sheriff and people of the Underground Railroad counties in their violent and outrageous conduct." This was "the equivalent of a declaration of war on the part of Chase and his abolition crew against the United States courts."[52]

On the very day that this article appeared, June 10, 1857, Chase learned of an even more serious crisis. After giving a speech at a college commencement, the governor returned by train to Columbus. Francis Wright, the state auditor, met Chase at the station to report that more than $500,000 was missing from the state treasury—leaving it nearly empty. The treasurer, William Gibson, claimed that this deficit was entirely the fault of his Democratic predecessor and brother-in-law, John Breslin. At the very least, however, Gibson, who had taken office almost a year and a half earlier, had failed to report the deficit. Chase had no way of knowing whether Gibson was telling the truth—that the deficit was entirely Breslin's fault—or whether Gibson had also taken money from the treasury.[53]

Chase demanded that both Wolcott and Gibson come to Columbus. Wolcott arrived Thursday and Gibson late Friday. Gibson was a friend of the governor's. "I loved him," Chase would soon tell Wright, "and still cherish my affection for him in spite of the great wrong he has done me and all of us." But Chase had decided that the man could not be trusted. On Saturday morning, June 13, Chase met with Gibson and demanded his resignation. The treasurer refused. At a second meeting, in the afternoon, Chase said that if Gibson did not resign, he would have him indicted and arrested, creating a vacancy that would enable Chase to appoint his successor. At this, Gibson relented and resigned. Chase named Alfred P. Stone as the new treasurer and waited at the treasurer's office until Stone had signed the mandatory personal bond, for $250,000, and obtained the required signatures of six sureties to back it up. Chase did not go home until eleven thirty that night.[54]

A partisan newspaper war over these events started at once and lasted for months. On June 14 the *Cincinnati Enquirer* accused Gibson, whom it called "one of Chase's lieutenants," of robbing the people of Ohio, while

Republican papers defended Chase and Gibson, insisting that Gibson's only crime was failing to report Breslin's crimes. The *Enquirer* countered that "a corrupt and willful concealment is quite as censurable as the original defalcation." Republican papers, including out-of-state papers such as the *Chicago Tribune*, alleged that Breslin had used state funds for Democratic political purposes. Indeed, it would eventually emerge that Breslin *had* used the state treasury to support Democratic banks and newspapers.[55]

Chase's main focus, in late June, was finding funds to pay the state's bills, both in Ohio and in New York, where interest payments were due on the first of July. On June 18 Francis Wright reported to the governor that after a "hasty examination" of the state's finances, it seemed that a loan of $200,000 would be necessary. Chase immediately wrote to John Andrews, president of the State Bank of Ohio, seeking a loan in that amount. Andrews explained that, because of the bank's structure, the loan could not be approved in Columbus; he would need approval from the bank's branches around the state. It was not until June 27 that Andrews informed Chase that the branches had approved the loan. The governor was also in close touch with Wright, whom he had sent to New York City to deal with issues there, including questions there about whether some of the assets the state believed it owned free and clear were subject to liens and thus not available. Chase was "much relieved" by a telegram from Wright, also on June 27, reporting that these issues were resolved. The state did not default.[56]

After speaking with Chase, Wolcott filed a civil suit on behalf of the state against Gibson, Breslin, and their sureties, seeking to recover for the state the amounts missing from its treasury. Breslin fled to Canada. According to a report by Thomas Sparrow, the Democrat appointed by Chase to investigate, Breslin's flight "was accompanied by declarations that he resorted to it in order to avoid inquiry. He said to one of the witnesses that he would not be taken; his person they should never have under any circumstances." After a grand jury indicted Breslin and Gibson, Breslin's friends floated a settlement proposal. If Breslin's sureties would pay the state $250,000, would Chase and Wolcott agree to drop the criminal charges against Breslin and the civil case against Breslin and the sureties? Chase refused.[57]

Meanwhile, in the Urbana fugitive slave case, Judge Humphrey Leavitt had ruled that the state could not interfere with the federal fugitive slave process and therefore ordered that the prisoners be released. Chase would probably have let the matter rest if the federal officials had not also arrested several of the Greene County officials involved, including the sheriff and the prosecutor. Chase had been planning a trip east and decided to stop in Washington, to speak with President James Buchanan and see if some compromise was possible.[58]

In Washington, Chase and his military aide, Henry Carrington, met quietly with Buchanan and his secretary of state, Lewis Cass. Chase suggested that the president should direct the federal district attorney in Cincinnati to drop the federal cases against state officials, and that Chase would in turn drop the state cases against the federal marshals. It seems that Buchanan was polite but made no promises. Chase also asked Cass to make a formal request to the British government for the extradition of Breslin from Canada, which was still British territory. The secretary of state was not enthused, explaining to Chase that although there was an extradition treaty with Great Britain, this case did not come within the terms of the treaty. Chase did not give up, writing several letters to Cass, without results. In the end, after several years in Canada, Breslin managed to get the state charges against him dropped, and returned to the United States. Gibson, although tried and convicted, secured an order for a second trial, which was never held, because of the Civil War. He, too, eventually got the charges against him dismissed.[59]

On August 12, 1857, the Republicans of Ohio gathered in convention in Columbus. After the usual preliminaries, one of the delegates rose to nominate Chase for a second term as governor, saying that it was pointless to go through the process of ballots and moving that he be nominated by acclamation. "The question was then put, and every delegate in the convention responded aye," the *Ohio State Journal* reported. The convention was starting to consider the candidates for lieutenant governor when Chase arrived in the hall to "the loudest cheers that were ever heard in that building." He gave a short speech, saying that anyone who wanted to know his political principles could read them in prior speeches and statements. "I am ashamed of none of them. I have stood where I expect to stand until the great end for which we labor is achieved. . . . I stand, as I have ever stood, the avowed and determined advocate of the cause of liberty and human rights, wherever, and by whomsoever, assailed." The platform, adopted later in the day, was everything that Chase wanted.

One resolution condemned the *Dred Scott* decision, and another protested against "the arrest and vexatious prosecution, under writs of federal commissioners, of our judges, sheriffs, justices of the peace, and citizens."[60]

That evening, after the convention was over, some two thousand to three thousand people gathered informally on the steps of the statehouse. The main speaker was Robert Warden, a former Democrat, now Republican, and later one of Chase's first biographers. The crowd called for the governor, who appeared amid loud huzzahs and spoke for a few minutes in his usual strong style. After several more speeches, the meeting ended around eleven thirty, but a "large number, headed by the band, marched to the residence of Governor Chase and gave him a serenade." Chase thanked them and then "invited his friends into his house, where they were regaled with hot coffee and eatables."[61]

As in 1855, there were three candidates for governor in 1857: Chase for the Republicans; Henry Payne, a Cleveland lawyer and financier, for the Democrats; and the improbably named Philadelph Van Trump for the American Party. Democrats renewed their attacks on Chase as the friend of the slaves and the blacks, with several papers printing what they called the "Congo Creed," quoting especially from Chase's 1844 Liberty Man's Creed, in which he had advocated that blacks should vote and attend public schools with whites. Even a dozen years later, very few Ohioans agreed with him on these issues, so Republican editors tried to change the subject, to charge the "Congo Democracy" with being servants of the slave masters. Democrats also linked Chase with Gibson, charged Chase for failing to discover the deficit, and claimed that Gibson had used the Treasury for personal purposes. The *Cincinnati Enquirer* said that Chase would have been a more effective governor "if he had not been consumed by a vain and ambitious desire to be president of the United States." Because of this, the paper alleged, Chase neglected his work in Columbus and "goes flitting over the state like an itinerant lecturer," speaking about "bleeding Kansas" and the *Dred Scott* decision, issues that had nothing to do with Ohio.[62]

Chase's main speech of the campaign was in Cincinnati on the evening of August 20. He was introduced by his friend Alphonso Taft, Cincinnati lawyer and soon to be the father of the future president and chief justice William Howard Taft. In the first part of his speech, Chase claimed that "Breslin took every dollar of the money. There was not one dollar of the people's money taken by any officer of the Republican administration.

There was not one dollar of it in the Treasury when the Republican Party assumed the government." Chase admitted that "Gibson concealed the fact. He did grossly wrong. It cannot be denounced too strongly. It cannot be palliated." The governor noted that Breslin had been indicted and then fled to Canada and that Buchanan and his secretary of state had so far refused to seek extradition. If the Buchanan administration would just devote to this extradition effort some of the energy that it devoted to "catching runaway niggers," he said pointedly, Breslin would soon face justice. Chase also blamed the current administration for the violence in Kansas. On the topic of slavery and the Slave Power, Chase declared: "I want to see slavery overthrown and intend to help overturn its power; I want to see the power of two hundred fifty thousand slaveholders over thirty million of the people cease."[63]

"Tell us something about state rights!" someone in the crowd called out.

"I am bringing you to that question," Chase said, because "these aggressions of slavery encroach upon state rights." He then reminded the audience of some recent incidents in which slave owners had used federal marshals to capture (in the governor's view, to kidnap) blacks in Ohio whom they claimed as their slaves. "I believe with Jefferson that the cardinal principle of our Union is the preservation of the reserved rights of the states and . . . if we wish to maintain our liberties, we must have our [state] laws obeyed." Chase's remarks were greeted with "hearty applause."[64]

As he had during the 1855 gubernatorial campaign, Chase spent several weeks in 1857 traveling around the state and giving speeches. The *Ohio State Journal* reported on September 14 that he had spoken every day, except Sundays, for the past two weeks, sometimes having to travel all night between events, "yet never in one instance failed to keep his appointments at the time and place specified." The paper quoted Chase as saying that he "has never spoken so much and at such remote points in so short a space of time, and yet he never felt less fatigue." When it was all over, the governor wrote to Sumner that he "spoke forty-six times in forty-two counties, traveling, by night and day, sometimes in railway cars and sometimes over the roughest roads, in carriages, over thirty-seven hundred miles."[65]

Knowing that he would be away on the campaign trail for weeks, Chase parked his two daughters with the Collins family in Hillsboro. In a long September letter to Nettie, about to turn ten, Chase described his travels, telling her that one of his speeches was in Gallipolis, named after its French or Gallic settlers. "The people seemed well pleased" by his speech there and "said I would get a great many more votes there than I did when I was elected governor two years ago." Upon leaving Gallipolis, he went on, one of their horses "became so lame he could not travel, and we were therefore obliged to walk back to town, the driver leading the lame horse." With new horses, they traveled through the night over a "very rough road," reaching their destination, Ironton, about nine the next morning. He spoke there in the afternoon and was glad that "the next day was Sunday, when I could rest and go to church instead of speaking."[66]

Chase continued traveling until the day before the election, speaking in Zanesville on that day, over the din created by what he described in his diary as "Congos" beating drums and shouting insults. On Election Day, October 13, he returned by train to Columbus, where he voted himself. Then he waited as results arrived by telegraph from around the state, first in the form of predictions by local editors about their counties. On the morning of Thursday, October 15, the *Ohio Statesman*, the leading Democratic paper, claimed on the basis of some official results and some estimates that Payne would probably prevail over Chase. As of that evening, the *Ohio State Journal* speculated that "the Republican state ticket is elected" but admitted that "we are not by any means sanguine." The governor himself, in a letter this day, conceded that "there is a likelihood that I am defeated," blaming a coalition of Democrats and Know-Nothings, "made effective by the wretched misconduct of our own treasurer, Gibson."[67]

It was not until Saturday evening, October 17, that the *Ohio State Journal* claimed victory for Chase, estimating that his margin over Payne would be about one thousand votes. Sure enough, in the final, official count, Chase edged out Payne, 160,568 votes to 159,095, with Van Trump collecting 10,272 votes. The *New York Evening Post* rejoiced, saying that Chase was "superior by a head and shoulders to any governor that Ohio had before him." The *Cincinnati Enquirer,* however, disagreed and complained that Chase won only because of illegal black voting in the Western Reserve, where election judges would allow some blacks to vote in spite of the provision in the state constitution limiting the vote to white males. The *Ohio Statesman* echoed this complaint, saying that the new legislature ought to make it a crime punishable by ten years in the penitentiary for an election judge to permit a black man to vote. It seems unlikely that Chase really owed his election to black votes, but some African Americans *did* vote in Ohio, thanks to a state supreme court decision allowing men who were more than half white to vote, and election judges willing to see white features in the faces of partly or perhaps wholly black men. Democrats viewed this as a problem—indeed, a crime—while Chase considered it a step in the right direction.[68]

Chase's October victory in Ohio looked even more impressive in November, when Republicans suffered defeats in other key states. In New York, Democrats prevailed by about twenty thousand votes. In Pennsylvania, the second most populous state, Democrats prevailed by forty thousand votes. Republicans prevailed in Massachusetts only because they nominated for governor a candidate, Nathaniel Banks, who straddled the line between Republican and Know-Nothing. These results helped Chase in the informal conversations (of which he was well aware) about who should be the Republican presidential candidate. Chase was also aware, however, that 1860 was still a long way off. He cautioned his young friend Edward Pierce in Boston not to get too excited too soon.[69]

Chase spent December 1857 in Columbus working on his annual message and watching national events. As Congress gathered in Washington, the main issue was once again Kansas—particularly the Lecompton Constitution, drafted by a proslavery convention held in Lecompton, Kansas. Rather than put the whole draft constitution to a vote, as was customary, the Lecompton delegates offered Kansas residents only two choices: the constitution with the provision protecting slavery forever, and the constitution without this one provision but with other controversial provisions, such as one prohibiting free blacks from entering Kansas. President Buchanan, in his annual message, endorsed both the Lecompton Constitution and the ratification process. Senator Douglas immediately denounced the ratification process because it did not give residents of the Kansas Territory the right to accept or reject the whole proposed state constitution.[70]

This division in the Democratic Party, between the Buchanan and Douglas factions, led to a division in the Republican Party, with some eastern Republicans—notably Greeley—supporting Douglas and effectively abandoning Illinois Republicans. In an editorial on December 21, for example, the *New-York Tribune* declared that Douglas was "right" about Kansas and predicted that Douglas would "save his party in Illinois from defeat next year, which otherwise was morally certain." Abraham Lincoln wrote to his friend and senator, Lyman Trumbull, asking what the *Tribune* meant "by its constant eulogizing, and admiring, and magnifying of Douglas? Does it, in this, speak the sentiments of Republicans in Washington? Have they concluded that the Republican cause, generally, can best be promoted by sacrificing us here in Illinois?" Sumner and Chase, although they did not yet know Lincoln, agreed with him. Sumner wrote to Chase that "our experience of Douglas, I think, would prevent any strong confidence in his labors for the good cause. His essential baseness has been too often manifest." Chase regretted that "some of our friends and papers should seem to play into the hands of Douglas. What we have seen, heard, and felt of him will make it impossible for us to trust him." He was worried not only about Illinois but also about "an obvious disposition among many to place our cause on the lowest possible ground—to connect it with the least possible advocacy of principle; and to seek success by means which will make success worse than useless." In other words, Chase feared that Greeley and others were repeating the errors of 1856. "The party for which I labor," he declared, "must be a manly, honorable, honest, freedom-loving party, which has principles and dares assert them, and representatives of its principles and dares assert them."[71]

CHAPTER 12

"Your Noble Lincoln"

✦ 1858–59 ✦

hase's January 1858 message to the legislature focused on finances and financial policy. He described what we call the Panic of 1857, starting with the failure in August 1857 of the Ohio Life Insurance and Trust Company, continuing with the suspension in October 1857 of specie payments by the banks of New York City, and leading to recession and even depression by the next year. Chase's explanation of the panic was simple, perhaps simplistic: he blamed "the spirit of speculation; eager desires for great and sudden gains; the spirit of ostentation and luxury." He cited figures to show how the number of banks had increased in recent years and that many banks had inadequate reserves. He called again for national currency reform. "A leading object in all regulations of currency should be to secure the interests of the masses of the people," he declared, which, in his view, could not happen "while the laborer is paid in paper, subject to continual fluctuation, and exposed to all the hazards of financial disorder."[1]

Turning to his own state's finances, Chase showed (with detailed tables and estimates) that the state would need to reduce spending or increase taxes. He recommended a slight increase in state real estate taxes to close the gap between spending and revenues in the next fiscal year.[2]

In the last section of his message, Chase attacked the pro-slavery Lecompton Constitution and President Buchanan—whom he called the agent of the slave masters—for trying to force the people of Kansas to accept slavery. The governor also denounced the *Dred Scott* decision, saying that the Supreme Court had "promulgated the revolting doctrine that the Constitution of the United States establishes and guarantees slavery in all the national territory, and consequently that there is no foot of all our widely extended domain, outside of states whose constitutions prohibit slavery, where the free laborer can find a home exempt from the intrusion of that very peculiar institution." These developments, Chase said, raised fundamental questions: "Shall the government of this country be administered by the people, for the people, or by a privileged class, for a privileged class? Is the constitution, in fact, what it is now claimed to be, the bond and guaranty of slavery; or what the fathers of the republic believed it to be, the shield and safeguard of liberty? Does it establish slavery everywhere, outside of free states, or liberty everywhere, outside of slave states?"[3]

This portion of Chase's message was widely reprinted. The *Toledo Blade* said the message showed "how much better off we should be as a nation if Governor Chase stood in the shoes of James Buchanan." Lincoln almost certainly read Chase's message and may have had the phrase "by the people, for the people" in mind when he proclaimed in his Gettysburg Address in 1863 that the purpose of the Civil War was to defend "government of the people, by the people, for the people."[4]

Ladies and gentlemen crowded the statehouse on January 11 for Chase's second inauguration. Summarizing the key principles of the Northwest Ordinance and the Ohio Constitution, the governor said they included the "absolute freedom of every individual, guaranteed and secured by impartial law" and "just protection to all forms of worship and all religious organizations." There was "nothing narrow, nothing illiberal" in these principles; they "welcomed the immigrant together with the home born to the fullest participation in the inestimable blessing of popular institutions." Without naming the Know-Nothings, Chase was again stating for all to hear that he would oppose their efforts against Catholics or immigrants.[5]

Many of the letters that Chase received in the first half of 1858 concerned the 1860 Republican nomination for president. James Ashley, after a visit with Greeley in New York, reported that the editor was "warmly against Seward and at present favorable to you." Greeley cautioned that there was "no telling but a new man may be born before 1860, as Frémont was in

1856." But if "the convention was held *now*," Ashley wrote, "Greeley would go for you." Giddings wrote from Washington that almost all the members of the Ohio congressional delegation supported Chase. Representative John Bingham confirmed his strong support in a letter to Chase. A Boston editor, after speaking with Republicans in New Hampshire, assured Chase that his native state would "at the proper time" support him. Theodore Parker, the Boston minister, wrote Chase that the nation would need in 1860 "a man for the presidency who has never yielded to the South; we don't want a fanatic, a dreamer, an enthusiast; we don't want a coward, or a trimmer." Calvin Stowe, husband of Harriet Beecher Stowe, wrote Chase that *"now is the time, and you are the man*. Depend upon it, I am right. Instead of struggling under a mountain, as you have . . . for fifteen years past, you will ride triumphantly on the topmost wave."[6]

One of Chase's main rivals for the nomination, William Henry Seward, made a mistake in early 1858 that seemed likely to help Chase. Speaking in favor of an army appropriation bill that was opposed by most members of the Republican Party, Seward blurted angrily, "I know nothing, I care nothing—I never did, I never shall—for party." John Jay wrote to Chase that Seward's attack on his own party had "seriously damaged his chances." Chase disagreed with Seward about the army, writing to Bigelow that West Point and the Naval Academy "tend to enlargement both of army and navy, which cannot be too jealously watched. Our true reliance in times of emergency should be upon volunteers." Another rival, Nathaniel Banks, was, at least according to Chase's correspondents, not sufficiently committed to Republican principles.[7]

Reading such letters from friends, as well as the newspapers, Chase was understandably encouraged. He wrote to Jay that he was gratified by the "many indications of a disposition to urge my name by the friends of our principles." It would indeed be "an honor to be the representative of our cause in so great a contest" and perhaps to help to settle the question of the expansion of slavery "peacefully, honorably, and advantageously for all." Sometimes, Chase confessed, "my imagination is fired with such ideas and hopes as these. But I know too well the uncertainties of the future, and I am too little satisfied with my own fitness for such a work to be greatly engaged in such thoughts." He was sufficiently engaged, however, to write a long letter to his friend Hiram Barney, who was on his way to Washington, apparently as an unofficial agent for Chase, listing the senators and representatives Chase thought would support his candidacy. "Write me in detail all you learn respecting each individual," he instructed Barney.[8]

Although Chase had no formal role in the legislative process, he tried to stay in Columbus while the legislature was in session, so that he often had to decline out-of-state speech invitations. Knowing that his responses to such invitations would be published, however, Chase used them to strengthen his support. Writing to decline an invitation to speak in Richmond, Virginia, Chase praised the state as the parent of Ohio, because it was only after Virginia yielded its territorial claims that Ohio could be formed. The slave state of Virginia might seem an odd place to seek Republican support, but Chase knew that it would have delegates at the 1860 Republican National Convention, and hoped that some of them would favor him.[9]

Chase tried this year to attend as many college commencements as possible. He explained to a friend that "our educational institutions, next to our religion, are the mainstays of our civil life, [so] it seems to me a special duty in my present position to give all the attention to them I can consistently with other valid claims upon me." Chase attended at least four college graduations this year: in Athens, at Ohio University; in Hudson, at Western Reserve College; in Marietta, at Marietta College; and in Oberlin, at Oberlin College. Chase would speak at these events, but only briefly, for the main speakers were generally the students themselves.[10]

Governor Chase had an even closer relationship with Wilberforce College, in Xenia, Ohio, the first private black college in the United States, for he was among its initial trustees—a group that one paper called "many of the most learned and distinguished men in the state of all denominations and parties." Four of these initial trustees were black, and one of them, Bishop Daniel Alexander Payne of the African Methodist Episcopal Church, especially impressed Chase. A few years later, forwarding an article about Payne and his work as president of Wilberforce to a British friend, Chase described him as "black as the ink I write with and very capable and intelligent." Chase would later leave $10,000 in his will to Wilberforce College, one of the largest gifts the school received in the nineteenth century.[11]

Chase was in frequent contact in the spring and summer of 1858 with Republican leaders in Illinois, Kansas, Massachusetts, and elsewhere. He

Daniel Alexander Payne, who served with Chase on the initial board of trustees of Wilberforce College and later served as the college's president. Chase supported Payne's work, leaving the college $10,000 in his will.

noticed (but apparently did not comment upon) the unusual decision of the Illinois Republican Party to nominate Abraham Lincoln for the Senate seat held by Stephen Douglas. Antebellum political parties did not nominate candidates for the Senate; they waited until after they had won control of a state legislature to discuss whom they should select as their senator. Chase also noticed Lincoln's speech on the occasion of his nomination, in which he declared that "a house divided against itself cannot stand. I believe this government cannot permanently endure half *slave* and half *free*." Either the opponents of slavery would "place it where the public mind shall rest in the belief that it is in the course of ultimate extinction," he continued, or the advocates of slavery would "push it forward till it shall become alike lawful in all the states, *old* as well as *new*, *North* as well as *South*." Southerners, claiming that Lincoln was an abolitionist, would often cite his reference to the "ultimate extinction" of slavery. Chase had of course been saying similar things for years, although he also made clear that Republicans would not interfere with slavery in the Southern states. Chase heartily approved of what he called, in one of his first letters to Lincoln, "that noble speech of yours at Springfield."[12]

Chase intended to take part in this year's campaign, both in Illinois and in Ohio, but first he went to the East. Traveling by rail, along more or less the route that had taken him eight weeks to cover in 1823, Chase and his daughter Kate reached Boston in only two days. On arrival, Chase received a polite note from Governor Nathaniel Banks suggesting that Chase join him at the statehouse early the next morning, so that they could travel together by carriage to Cambridge for the Harvard University commencement. The two governors were among the distinguished men on the platform for the commencement, at which one of the honorary degrees went to Banks. Another was bestowed upon Judge Edward Bates of Missouri, who was also being mentioned as a possible Republican nominee. On Sunday, July 25, Chase attended services at Theodore Parker's Unitarian church in Boston. Parker's congregation included many of the most famous men and women of Boston: William Lloyd Garrison, Louisa May Alcott, author of *Little Women,* and the poet and author Julia Ward Howe.[13]

From Boston, Chase went to Hanover, where he had what he termed a "delightful visit" at the time of the Dartmouth commencement. In the absence of the head of the alumni association, Chase was called upon to preside over the alumni dinner, telling those gathered that their beloved alma mater, now almost ninety years old, had three thousand living children. "Wherever any of us go, even to the ends of the earth, our thoughts fondly wander back to old Dartmouth." The guests included John Wentworth, a former and future member of Congress from Chicago, and William Evarts, a Republican lawyer in New York City and a future secretary of state. Chase and Kate then visited family and friends in Concord and stayed a day or two in Exeter, New Hampshire, with Amos Tuck, business leader and former member of Congress, and one of Chase's political friends and correspondents.[14]

After a few days in Essex County, Massachusetts, where he called upon the poet and abolitionist John Greenleaf Whittier, and spent a Sunday with R. P. Waters, leader of the movement to encourage migration to Kansas, Chase went back to Boston. There was a dinner to honor him, hosted by the governor and attended by forty Republican leaders, at which Chase spoke briefly about his New England heritage. According to the *Boston Courier,* he "made a very fine impression upon the company, most of whom had been strangers to him before this time." That night, an eager crowd went to the Revere House hotel, where Chase was staying, and demanded with shouts and cheers that he give them a speech.[15]

Speaking from the hotel's high balcony, Chase started by saying that his ancestors were "among those who shared the earliest trials of this commonwealth," and that he was proud to share in "the faith of the fathers of New England." He recalled that "some years ago, many years ago, more years ago than I should like to tell if there were any ladies present"—the crowd laughed—"I was riding along the banks of the Ohio with that illustrious citizen of Massachusetts whose remains now repose upon the shore of Marshfield [Daniel Webster], and he said to me, contrasting the appearance of one shore with the other, the great progress of Ohio with the slow progress of Kentucky, 'My young friend, do you know what has made all this difference? It is the Ordinance.'" The Northwest Ordinance, Chase continued, prohibiting slavery, protecting religious freedom, encouraging education, was a gift from Massachusetts, for Nathan Dane, a delegate to the Confederation Congress, was one of its principal authors. The duty of the present generation was to adhere to "those principles which came to us in the *Mayflower*, which were reiterated in the Ordinance, and which are now scattering their manifold blessings over the great West." To do this, they should "disregard hereafter those petty differences which we have suffered to divide us; not to inquire whether a man was yesterday or day before a Whig, American, or Democrat."[16]

Chase saw many people in Boston, but two he especially hoped to see, James and Elizabeth Pike, were not there; they had left town a few days before Chase arrived, so that James could work in Maine for Republican candidates. Chase wrote to Elizabeth that he was "*so* disappointed" because he had "much to talk about both to you and to him which I cannot well write." James had apparently hinted that the Pikes might come to Ohio in the fall. "Do, do, do come," Chase urged Elizabeth, and "come straight to one house in Columbus where your welcome shall be as cordial as you could wish."[17]

After visiting Providence and Newport, Rhode Island, Chase went to New York City, where he attended a reception to honor Cyrus Field, the American entrepreneur who had just completed the first transatlantic telegraph. A New York reporter for the *Cleveland Herald* wrote that the "large and elegant parlors were filled to overflowing with lawyers, judges,

merchants, etc. Your governor was voted the best-looking man present."
Many New Yorkers, the correspondent added, "would like to hail Mr.
Chase as the next president of the United States." The celebration of this
first Field telegraph proved short lived, for the line soon failed, and it
would take eight years before a second, permanent line was in place.[18]

The Ohio political campaign of 1858 was unusual in that, unlike most
races between 1830 and 1860, it was not triangular: there were no Whig
or Know-Nothing or American candidates, only Republicans on one
side and Democrats on the other. Chase was happy that his approach
to Know-Nothings, which he described as conciliation without "aban-
donment of principle," had brought all the factions into the fold of the
Republican Party.[19]

While Chase had been in the East, the Republicans of Ohio's Seventh
Congressional District bypassed their incumbent Republican member of
Congress and nominated instead Thomas Corwin. Seeing this as a rebuke
to Chase, Democratic papers rejoiced, for Corwin was a moderate Whig,
not an ardent Republican. To prove that there was no tension between
them, Chase joined Corwin on the platform in late August at a rally in
Columbus. In the course of his speech, Corwin said that the Whigs had
accused him of selling out their party to Chase.

"By the way," he said, turning to Chase, "I have not received the
consideration; fork over."

The governor, laughing, "heartily gave his hand to Corwin." The
banter and laughter continued during Chase's speech, when he alluded
to Corwin's dark complexion and nickname, Black Tom. Chase said that
although he was "rather averse to compromises" he would make a compromise with Corwin: if he would work with Chase in opposing the extension
of slavery, Chase would "not find fault—with his color." The next day,
Chase clipped the report of the rally from the *Ohio State Journal* and sent
it to John Bigelow, who ensured that a similar report soon appeared in
the *New York Evening Post*.[20]

A few days later, on September 10, Chase was the guest of honor in
Put-in-Bay, Ohio, on the anniversary of the naval battle there during the
War of 1812. The *Ohio State Journal* reported that the "scene was truly
grand," with six large lake steamers moored in the small bay, along with
a Treasury revenue cutter, whose men climbed into the rigging to cheer

the governor. As he landed, militia companies fired their cannons, and then a procession formed and "marched to the lively music of several bands to a beautiful grove on the island, where a stand had been erected to accommodate the officers and speakers of the day." Chase gave a "short but happily conceived address" in which he "drew a vivid parallel between the Northwest of 1812 and 1858." In a letter to Kate, Chase wrote that "no description can do justice to the scene," as they departed after the event: "the boom of cannon, the bray of trumpets, the shrill of fifes, the clatter of drums," and the great steamboats themselves, like living creatures upon which "hundreds of Lilliputians were riding."[21]

Chase traveled around Ohio in September, mixing nonpolitical events, such as county fairs, with political conversations and campaign rallies. He was the principal speaker one evening in Cincinnati at what Republican papers called "the largest political gathering ever held in this city." Thousands of men marched with flaming torches; there were fireworks and militia companies and illuminated signs. Chase started by saying that he came not as governor or as a candidate but as a "simple citizen." Last year "I met my political antagonists—I call them not enemies, for I will not recognize any of my fellow citizens of Ohio as my enemies—and we defeated them." This year, Chase continued, he "rejoiced to see the people united—the whole people—because, regarding this great multitude, I cannot think there is anybody in the city who is *not* here tonight." The crowd laughed and cheered.[22]

The heart of Chase's speech, widely reprinted, was a commentary on popular sovereignty. "The Democracy preach to you 'popular sovereignty.' I believe in 'popular sovereignty.' It is a good thing and a right thing. It signifies that the people ought to rule—and they do rule, when they have a chance. But human rights underlie popular sovereignty. Every man feels that he ought to be a freeman; that he is entitled to 'life, liberty, and the pursuit of happiness.'" Liberty, Chase continued, was "inalienable. It cannot justly be taken from one man and given to another. It is for this reason that I condemn the institution of slavery. It ought not to exist anywhere." Chase added quickly, however, that Democrats were wrong to claim that Republicans intended to interfere with "vested rights." Chase wanted any slaveowners in the audience—and surely there were some, with Kentucky a short ferry ride away—to "note that we preach no such doctrine. We mean to leave slavery in the states where our fathers left it. We will leave it to the disposal of the people where it exists."[23]

On Election Day, October 12, Republicans prevailed in Ohio, electing
fifteen out of their twenty-one congressional candidates, including Chase's
friends Ashley, Bingham, and Corwin. The party also did well in Indiana, Iowa, and Pennsylvania, the other states that voted on this date, so
that the *Illinois State Journal* could proclaim a "clean Republican sweep!"
The election season was not over yet, however, with campaigns still in
progress in the seven states that would vote on November 2, including
Illinois, Massachusetts, and New York. Chase was following these races
closely, especially in Illinois. The debates there between Lincoln and
Douglas were reported not just in the local papers but also nationwide,
and Chase clipped a few of the news reports and pasted them into one of
his scrapbooks.[24]

Chase supported Lincoln, and he would have agreed with much of
what Lincoln said in the course of this campaign, but not everything.
For instance, Chase never would have uttered what Lincoln said in the
September 18 debate in Charleston, Illinois: that he was not "in favor of
bringing about in any way the social and political equality of the white
and black races" and that he was not "in favor of making voters or jurors
of negroes, nor of qualifying them to hold office, nor to intermarry with
white people." Lincoln claimed that "that there is a physical difference
between the white and black races which I believe will forever forbid the
two races living together on terms of social and political equality. And
inasmuch as they cannot so live, while they do remain together, there must
be the position of superior and inferior, and I, as much as any other man,
am in favor of having the superior position assigned to the white race."[25]

Buchanan was so determined to stop Douglas that he encouraged
Buchanan Democrats to run against Douglas Democrats for Illinois legislative seats. Many eastern Republicans favored Douglas over Lincoln
precisely because of this division between Douglas and Buchanan; they
hoped that the split among the Democrats would spread nationwide.
The *New York Times,* for example, praised how Douglas was fighting both
Buchanan Democrats and Lincoln Republicans. Even if Lincoln won,
according to the *Times*, there was "no reason to believe" that Lincoln
would "render to the country any service to be compared with that of his
predecessor," Douglas. Such attitudes made it hard to persuade out-of-state
Republican speakers to come to Illinois, so the *Chicago Tribune* rejoiced

Abraham Lincoln, rival, friend, and colleague of Chase.

when it was able to announce on October 19 that Governor Chase would campaign in Illinois. On the next day and for several days thereafter, the *Tribune* printed his campaign schedule, starting with a great Republican rally in Chicago on October 26.[26]

Chase spoke for about two hours to a packed house in the Chicago Metropolitan Hall, "reviewing the slavery question and the position of the political parties in reference to it, from the beginning of the government to the present time, in a most cogent and convincing argument." The *Tribune* did not provide a more detailed report of Chase's speech, explaining that "the time for effectual assistance from printed speeches is past." Over the next few days, the last week of the campaign, Chase spoke at least seven times: in Rockford, Warren, Geneseo, Mendota, Rock Island, and Princeton, Illinois. The *Davenport Iowa Democrat*, describing Chase's visit to nearby Rock Island, said that he gave "a regular old-fashioned speech," denouncing the repeal of the Missouri Compromise and the "humbug which the Democracy set up in the form of popular sovereignty." The *Mendota Press* noted that bad weather kept people from coming to hear speeches there by Chase and Owen Lovejoy, Republican member of Congress and brother of the abolitionist martyr Elijah Lovejoy, who had died defending his printing press from a pro-slavery mob in 1837. Those who did come heard Chase give what the *Press* called a "dignified but telling speech." Chase himself, writing a friend, said that with the exception of the Chicago effort, his speeches "were as good as I can make."[27]

Some Democratic papers in Ohio attacked Chase for interfering in another state's politics. "This is what naturally might be expected of a presidential aspirant like Mr. Chase," sniffed the *Cleveland Plain Dealer*. "He wants Mr. Douglas out of the way, and he will join the administration forces there to crush him out." The *Cincinnati Gazette* defended Chase, noting that Democrats had not complained about out-of-state support for Douglas. "But for Gov. Chase to make half a dozen speeches, in a canvass so confessedly important in its bearing on the politics of the whole country, is a grave and unpardonable offense. Shame on such hypocritical prudery! Gov. Chase is doing a good work, on the right side."[28]

Overall, however, there was not much press coverage of Chase's speeches in the Illinois campaign, in part because he was speaking late in the process and in part because Illinois Republicans were keen to counter the Democratic argument that Lincoln was in favor of black rights. So even Republican papers did not want to highlight the efforts of Chase and Lovejoy, whom one of the Democratic papers derided as "two of the great nigger equality champions." The leading Republican paper of Springfield, the *Illinois State Journal*, did not even mention that Chase was in the state.[29]

The weather in Illinois on Election Day, November 2, was miserable, as it had been for several weeks. At first, it seemed to Republican editors that they would prevail; more than one newspaper printed a headline along the lines of "Lincoln Elected." In some sense, Republicans did prevail, for Republican legislative candidates received more votes than their Democratic rivals. But because of the way in which the districts were drawn, Democrats would have slight majorities in both houses of the state legislature, so they could elect Douglas for another Senate term. Chase wrote to an Illinois editor that, although he was disappointed that they had not managed to elect "your noble Lincoln," he was pleased that Douglas had only a "minority in the popular vote." Lincoln was grateful to Chase, writing early in the new year to thank him for being "one of the very few distinguished men whose sympathy we in Illinois did receive last year, of all those whose sympathy we thought we had reason to expect. Of course, I would have preferred success; but failing in that, I have no regrets for having rejected all advice to the contrary, and resolutely made the struggle."[30]

After the frenzy of the campaign, the last two months of 1858 were comparatively quiet for Chase. Thanksgiving was observed in some places and not others at this time, but Governor Chase asked the residents of Ohio to set aside Thursday, November 25, "as a day of public thanksgiving and prayer to Almighty God." He urged the people of the state to observe the day "by abstinence from ordinary labors" and "by public and private offerings of praise and gratitude for the multiform and manifold blessings and benefits, national, social, and personal, which God hath been graciously pleased to bestow upon us." It was probably in this year that young William Dean Howells was a guest of the Chase family for Thanksgiving. "The turkey was set before the governor, who carved it," he recalled, "and then it was brought to the guests by a shining black butler, instead of being passed from hand to hand among them, as I had always seen it done." Howells and a colleague from his newspaper "were the only guests; and after dinner, the family did not forbid itself the gaieties befitting its young people's years," including charades.[31]

"The foremost concern of an intelligent and prosperous people," Chase declared in his January 1859 message, "is public instruction. The mind of every community is the motive power of its advancement, and the measure of its education is practically the measure of its production." Chase was justly proud of Ohio's education system, especially when compared with Southern states, where white elites saw little need to educate poor whites, much less slaves. But he recommended improvements, such as establishing state "normal schools," to better train teachers. Chase reviewed in turn the state's programs to help the poor, the insane, the blind, and the deaf. In a section of the message on crime and punishment, he noted that there had been only eighty murders the previous year and suggested that the legislature revise state law so that it did not require the death penalty whenever a defendant was convicted of first-degree murder. "I am persuaded that, in many instances, murder escapes all punishment, or all adequate punishment, through the reluctance of juries to find verdicts which must necessarily be followed by sentence of death." Chase denounced intemperance, saying that alcohol abuse caused illness, poverty, and violence, and suggesting the creation of what we would call an alcoholism treatment center. The governor did not discuss slavery, however, saying that his views on the subject were well known and he need not repeat them.[32]

A few weeks later, Chase received a troubling letter from his oldest and closest friend among national editors, Gamaliel Bailey of the *National Era*. Seward's friends and supporters, Bailey reported from Washington, viewed the 1860 nomination as "now or never" because of their man's advancing age. Bailey advised Chase to stand aside for Seward. "You are in the prime of life and have the promise of continuing so; you have not yet attained your full stature or status—he has—every year adds to your strength." Striving for the 1860 nomination "against the settled feeling of Seward's numerous friends would provoke unpleasant and damaging discord and tend hereafter to weaken your position." Bailey added that he was so sick that his wife and friends were insisting that he retire from the paper and travel to Europe.[33]

Chase responded that, although he appreciated Bailey's friendship, he could not agree in this case with his analysis. There was not much difference in age between Chase, who had just turned fifty-one, and Seward, who was not yet fifty-eight. For Seward's friends to claim that he deserved the nomination because of his age was "babyish." A contest between the two of them for the nomination would be a friendly one, for Chase admired Seward; "no man will ever hear me denying his great abilities and merits." Chase contended that he had no *right* to abandon the race at this time. "A very large body of the people—embracing not a few who would hardly vote for any man other than myself as a Republican nominee—seem to desire that I shall be a candidate in 1860. No effort of mine, and, so far as I know, none of my immediate personal friends, has produced this feeling. It seems to be of spontaneous growth. Under these circumstances," he continued, "those to whose judgments I am bound to defer" insisted that Chase leave his name among those "from whom the selection is to be made." Chase closed by telling his friend Bailey that he prayed for his health.[34]

At almost this same time, late January 1859, an even more influential editor, Horace Greeley, hinted in the *New-York Tribune* that he would favor Seward. Greeley started his editorial with a list of more than a dozen possible Republican nominees, including Seward, Chase, and Bates—but not Lincoln—and insisted that his main goal was to find a candidate who would win in the general election. But then Greeley praised Seward. "Where is the other possible candidate for president whose public utterances are so replete with a wise humanity, a generous philanthropy, a statesmanship entitled to the proud designation of Christian?" Greeley suggested that Chase would be his second choice, calling him one of the "ablest and most deserving Republicans" and praising his stance against wasteful federal spending. But then Greeley questioned whether Chase favored the high protective tariffs that were, for him and other former Whigs, an essential public policy. Thurlow Weed happily reprinted Greeley's editorial in his *Albany Evening Journal*, as did many other papers.[35]

In spite of the tension between Chase and Bailey, Chase worked hard in early 1859 to raise money for his friend's proposed trip to Europe, in the form of investments in the Chicago Block Company. Although structured as a for-profit company, backed by Chicago real estate, this was more of a charity than a company, for the promoters made no effort to confirm that the real estate was worth more than the $5,000 that they sought to raise, and they gave all the money they brought in straight to Bailey for his trip expenses. Chase wrote letter after letter urging Republican leaders to help Bailey by investing in the company. In the midst of all this work, he read in the *Ohio Statesman* that Bailey had "abandoned" him and that the *National Era* would soon support Seward. Bailey must have shared with friends in Washington, who shared with the *Statesman* correspondent, the views that Bailey had expressed in his letters to Chase. Bailey responded with an editorial, saying that although he was a personal friend of Chase, "the *National Era* is not committed to Mr. Chase, Mr. Seward, Judge McLean, Mr. Hale, Mr. Banks, or any other man, as a candidate for the presidency." This was helpful, but it would have been *more* helpful if the *National Era* had simply endorsed Chase.[36]

Some Republicans, especially in Pennsylvania, favored high protective tariffs and disfavored Chase as a "free trader." His friends worried that this might prevent him from receiving the Republican nomination, for Pennsylvania would have more delegates at the national convention than any state other than New York. Chase responded with letters to editors and friends, such as one in which he said that he was in favor of a "moderate revenue, economically used in administration, collected by a tariff of duties, so arranged as to afford the greatest possible incidental benefits to industry." Soon the *New-York Tribune* was echoing his letters, reporting that Chase was fully committed to tariffs and believed they "should be arranged so as to promote as efficiently as possible the development of American industry."[37]

One cold evening in February, Chase was summoned from his library by his daughter Kate, who heard someone groaning just outside the family's front door. Upon opening the door, Chase found his sister Alice on the ground, moaning in pain. Alice, who had been living with Chase for a few months, had walked to a lecture at the Episcopal church and suffered a stroke on her return. Chase carried her into the house and sent for doctors. "All was in vain," he wrote, for Alice died the next day at the age of fifty-three. Ten Chase children had survived childhood; now all of his siblings but two, Edward and Helen, were dead. In a letter to John Jay, Chase wrote that his sister's death "admonished me effectively of the rapidly approaching day when I too must depart. God grant that it may be with the same hope and the same affection which gathered around her liberated spirit."[38]

In late 1858 and early 1859, Chase followed closely what we know as the Oberlin-Wellington Rescue Case. The dispute started in September 1858, when two white men from Kentucky and a federal marshal from Ohio seized a fugitive slave from Kentucky, John Price, on the farm where he had lived on the outskirts of Oberlin. The slave catchers paused to have dinner in a hotel in nearby Wellington, unaware that a large group of men from Oberlin, both black and white, indignant at Price's seizure, were on their way there. The Oberlin men, reinforced by many from Wellington, surrounded the hotel and demanded that Price be released. Charles Langston, a black leader whom Chase knew as an acquaintance if not a friend, played the role of peacemaker for a while, speaking first with the crowd outside, then with the three men holding Price inside. When these negotiations failed, the crowd stormed the hotel, rescued Price, and returned with him to Oberlin. From there, he departed quietly for freedom in Canada.[39]

In December, a federal grand jury in Cleveland, carefully selected by the Democratic clerk of the court to exclude Republicans, indicted thirty-seven men, some white, some black, from Oberlin and Wellington for violating the Fugitive Slave Act. Three Oberlin leaders, including a prominent theology professor, were indicted even though they were not in Wellington on the morning of the rescue; their alleged offense was "aiding and abetting," encouraging the others to resist the Fugitive Slave Act. Two of Chase's friends, Albert Riddle and Rufus Spalding, agreed to serve as defense lawyers for the defendants.[40]

The prosecutors decided to try the defendants one by one and selected as their first target Simeon Bushnell, a young clerk who drove the wagon carrying Price back to Oberlin. The jury, carefully selected to exclude antislavery men, found Bushnell guilty, and the judge sentenced him to sixty days in prison and a substantial fine. When the prosecutors suggested that this same jury would try the second case, that of the black leader Charles Langston, the defense lawyers objected so strenuously that the judge ordered the marshal to take into custody all the defendants he could find and arrest. Soon twenty men, black and white, including the theology professor, were in the Cuyahoga County Jail.[41]

The second trial, of Langston, in April and May 1859, ended with another guilty verdict. When the judge asked the defendant if he had anything to say before he was sentenced. Langston responded with a long speech, reprinted in many papers, in which he denounced the Fugitive Slave Act and, indeed, the whole federal judicial system: "I was tried by a jury who were prejudiced; before a court that was prejudiced; prosecuted by an officer who was prejudiced; and defended, though ably, by counsel that were prejudiced. And therefore it is, your honor, that I urge . . . that I should not be subjected to the pains and penalties of this oppressive law, when I have *not* been tried, either by a jury of my peers or by a jury that was impartial." Somewhat stunned, and perhaps persuaded, the judge sentenced Langston to only twenty days in prison.[42]

At this point, defense lawyers Riddle and Spalding applied to the state supreme court for a writ of habeas corpus, arguing that there was no legal basis for the federal court's conviction and detention of their clients. Chase instructed the state's attorney general, his friend Christopher Wolcott, to have Ohio join the case on the side of the prisoners, and Wolcott's points echoed those that Chase had made in previous cases, including a detailed argument against the constitutionality of the federal fugitive slave laws. The state court set May 25 as the date for oral argument in Columbus. Antislavery leaders announced plans for a grand rally in support of the prisoners, to be held in Cleveland on the twenty-fourth.[43]

Chase was in his Columbus office on the morning of the rally when he received an urgent telegram from Cleveland warning that there might be violence and pleading for him to come there at once. He hastened to the train station and reached Cleveland within a few hours. When the governor arrived at the rally, he found a crowd of about ten thousand listening to fiery speeches. In his own brief speech, Chase urged restraint, saying, according to the news accounts, that "he had not come to counsel any violence." He sided with the prisoners, calling them "some of the most respected citizens of the state" who had "done what they believed to be right"—what almost every man would view as right. And for this, they were charged and confined, which Chase said was simply "wrong." The correct response, however, was to use the ballot box to change the government. "If the government does wrong, turn it out. Dismiss the unworthy servants and put in those who will do your will."[44]

Near the end of his speech, little noticed at the time, Chase issued a direct challenge to the federal government: "If the process for the release of any prisoner should issue from the courts of the state, he was free to say that so long as Ohio was a sovereign state, *that process should be executed.*" In other words, if the state supreme court, in the pending case, ordered the release of the Oberlin prisoners, Chase would implement the order—regardless of whether it was consistent with federal precedents such as the Supreme Court's decision in *Van Zandt.*[45]

The next day, Chase was in the courtroom to show his own support for the defendants. In the morning, the prisoners' private lawyer argued that the Fugitive Slave Act was invalid because it violated the "inviolable right of persons to personal liberty." After the noon break, the two lawyers representing the federal government said that they would not make any oral argument but would rely upon their written points. Wolcott's strong, detailed argument took the rest of the day and the next morning. After considering the matter for a few days, the judges announced their decision on May 30, ruling against the prisoners. Chase was surprised, for the lead opinion against the prisoners was by Judge Joseph Swan, an antislavery friend of his, who wrote that however much he might personally oppose slavery, the Fugitive Slave Act was constitutional, and he would "refuse the experiment of initiating disorder and governmental collision." There was a strong dissent by Jacob Brinkerhoff, who would have released the prisoners because he agreed with Chase and Wolcott that the fugitive slave law was contrary to the Constitution. The *Cleveland Daily Leader,* echoing Chase, commented that the "free people can only take an appeal through the ballot boxes," and "this they will do."[46]

It was only a few days after this controversial decision that the state Republican convention met in Columbus. Although the state constitution did not yet limit a governor to two terms, Chase did not want a third term, and the convention nominated as his successor his friend William Dennison. Outraged by Swan's decision in the *Oberlin* case, the convention refused to nominate the judge for another term on the state supreme court, even though judges customarily received repeated nominations. Another part of the convention's response to the *Oberlin* decision was a plank in the platform, drafted by Chase, that demanded "the repeal of the Fugitive Slave Act of 1850, as subversive of both the rights of the states and the liberties of the people, and as contrary to the plainest duties of humanity and justice." Another plank, also by Chase, claimed "for all citizens, native and naturalized, liberty of conscience, equality of rights, and the fullest exercise of the right of suffrage." This addressed the concern of some German American leaders that Ohio would follow the lead of Massachusetts, which had recently imposed a two-year waiting period before naturalized citizens could vote.[47]

The fugitive slave language in the Ohio platform, easily understood in the Ohio context, was harder for Lincoln to understand and accept in Illinois. After reading about the Ohio platform in the papers, Lincoln wrote at once to Chase to say that the Ohio fugitive slave plank was "already damaging us here in Illinois" and that if such language were introduced at next year's national convention, it would "explode it." The problem, Lincoln wrote, was that many Republicans believed that the Constitution required that a fugitive slave "shall be delivered up," and these men looked "upon the plank as dictated by spirit which declares that a fugitive slave 'shall not be delivered up.'"[48]

Chase answered that, like Lincoln, he wanted to avoid "extremes which may endanger the success of the Republican Party." But Lincoln's own "noble speech" in Springfield showed that avoiding extremes was "not at all inconsistent with the boldest and manliest avowal of our great principles." He went on to explain that, in light of recent events in Ohio, "some kind of statement in favor of the repeal of the Fugitive Slave Act of 1850 was indispensable" in the state Republican platform.

He also set out in brief the reasons why he and others favored repeal: "There are many who believe that [the Fugitive Slave Act] is entirely unconstitutional because Congress has no power of legislation upon the subject, or because it provides no trial by jury; while others think it unconstitutional in part because it vests judicial power in commissioners and for other reasons. These, as well as all others who have any sympathy with our general movement, agree that it is unnecessarily harsh and severe and marked by many repulsive features, while thousands who do not concur in our movement . . . agree that it is next to worthless as a practical measure." Chase sent Lincoln a copy of Wolcott's points, a version of the argument Chase had been making for years, that the Fugitive Slave Clause was merely a compact among the states, not a grant of power to Congress, and so there was no constitutional basis for a federal fugitive slave law.[49]

Lincoln was not persuaded. He admitted to Chase that the Constitution did not state that Congress had authority to implement the Fugitive Slave Clause but said that, in his view, "whatever the Constitution says 'shall be done' and has omitted saying who shall do it, the government established by that Constitution, by implication, is vested with the power of doing." Moreover, he noted, "the Constitution was adopted, in great part, in order to get a government which could execute its own behests, in contradistinction to that under the Articles of Confederation, which depended, in many respects, upon the states, for its execution." (Lincoln was right that under the Articles of Confederation, the predecessor of the Constitution, the national Congress had almost no power.) Lincoln stressed, however, that his purpose was not to debate with Chase the constitutional question but rather to raise the political point that pressing for repeal of the Fugitive Slave Act as part of the national platform would split the Republican Party.[50]

While Chase was busy with politics in Ohio, his ailing friend Gamaliel Bailey boarded a steamship bound for Europe, in hopes of improving his health. "The prayers of thousands follow him abroad," Chase wrote to Sumner, who was also abroad, still recovering from the Brooks assault. Bailey died a few days later at sea, apparently of complications from a severe cold. "What a dreadful blow our dear friend's death was," Chase wrote to Elizabeth Pike. "I loved him so much. He was so true, so genial, so thoughtful, so generous, so entirely manly." Some papers speculated that Chase's friend Donn Piatt, who had been working to raise funds for the Chicago Block Company, would now take over the *National Era* and make that paper a "Chase organ." Elizabeth wrote to warn Chase against Piatt. Her husband, whom she playfully referred to as "the tyrant who holds a legal control over my actions," advised her "to wait until I see you, to communicate my opinions of other people," but she was sure that Chase would burn her letter, so she would write freely. Although Piatt was generous and devoted to Chase, she said, "he has the judgment of a mere child." If Bailey had known the means by which Piatt raised money for the Chicago Block Company, its beneficiary would have been "disgraced and humiliated to the end of his days." She urged Chase not to put Piatt in a position where he could damage Chase's chances to become president. Chase responded with the suggestion that her husband, James Pike, might want to take over the paper. In the end, neither man became the editor, and the *National Era* folded within a few months, unable to help Chase in the presidential year.[51]

Over the summer, Chase made a short trip to the East. His first stop was New Haven, Connecticut, where he attended the Yale University commencement, making a short speech at the alumni dinner. He claimed that as a son of Dartmouth, he was a cousin of all those present, for Harvard, Yale, and Dartmouth were three sisters—the three New England colleges formed before the American Revolution. Chase went next to Plymouth, Massachusetts, where twelve thousand people attended the laying of the cornerstone of the Pilgrim Monument. Chase said that he "came with no prepared speech, with no set phrase, but with a heart brim full of love for New England." He drew a parallel between the Pilgrims, who crossed the Atlantic to create New England, and the New England leaders who crossed the Alleghenies to establish Ohio. The people of Ohio were "gathered from many lands," Chase said, "and we have no narrow, no sectional, no proscriptive spirit." Massachusetts, Virginia, and South Carolina had helped to populate Ohio, as had Germany and Ireland. "From every quarter of the world, we welcome those whose love of liberty and free institutions directed them to our shores, and, in doing so, we build a monument worthy of the descendants of the Pilgrims."[52]

From New England, Chase went to New York City, Washington, and Philadelphia, speaking in each place with political friends. In a letter to Republican senator Simon Cameron, the most powerful politician in

Pennsylvania, and also one of the most corrupt, Chase suggested that they meet in Philadelphia. He hoped for support from the Keystone State, especially after the first ballot, when the Pennsylvania delegates would probably vote for Cameron as the state's favorite son. We know that Chase visited the senator at his home, but not what they discussed, although the *New York Herald* said that they talked about how to prevent Seward from getting the nomination. Chase probably assured Cameron about the tariff, insisting that his position was consistent with those of Pennsylvania Republicans.[53]

Simon Cameron, Lincoln's first secretary of war, friendly with Chase but not capable of managing the rapidly expanding War Department.

Chase was working in the West as well as the East. One of his key correspondents was Joseph Medill, editor of the *Chicago Tribune*. Medill wrote Chase in June to explain that he intended to publish soon an editorial advocating that the Republicans choose a western candidate. In

the view of the editors, Medill wrote, it was too early for the paper to
endorse Chase in particular. "The moment we take sides for you in our
columns, it will be a signal for the Seward organs to make fight against
you." After attending the Republican convention in Minnesota, Medill
reported that Seward's friends were "pretty certain and confident" but
that he was "quietly confident that a delegation can be secured for you."
A few weeks later, Medill wrote to Chase that more and more men were
talking about Edward Bates, the preferred candidate of the powerful Blair
family, and that Seward's chances seemed to be fading.[54]

Another key Chase correspondent was Carl Schurz, the German American leader in Wisconsin. Through a mutual friend, Schurz let Chase know
that he feared that a Seward administration would result in substantial
increases in government spending: "Political immorality, the loose views
of political and private honesty, which have been and are so predomi-
nant in the party organization of this country, are in my opinion no less
dangerous an evil than slavery itself," he said. Writing to Chase directly,
Schurz warned that if the "contest between you and Mr. Seward should
become too animated, if a drop of animosity should be infused into it, the
nomination would fall upon neither of you, and the convention would see
itself obliged to take up some neutral, indifferent availability."[55]

Ohio Democratic papers claimed in August 1859 that Republican leaders
were forcing candidates for the state legislature to promise that, if elected,
they would choose Chase as the state's next federal senator. Republican
papers called this a "fabrication," but there must have been some basis
for the claim, for Chase wrote to Edward Pierce that "there seems to be
a general opinion that if we have the legislature, I shall be elected to the
Senate in the place of Pugh." The governor was doing all he could to
ensure that Republicans would control the next state legislature. Starting
in late August, and continuing through early October, Chase gave dozens
of campaign speeches, in every corner of the state.[56]

In his principal speech, at Sandusky, Ohio, Chase discussed the *Lem-
mon v. New York* case, then pending in the New York state courts. The
issue was whether slave owners could keep slaves in New York if they
were "in transit" between two slave states. Chase predicted that, even if
the former slaves prevailed in the New York courts (as they would the
following year), they would lose in the United States Supreme Court.

The slave masters would establish "that they can take their slaves into New York . . . to any state of the North, and that they can hold them there during all the time that is convenient for them to be passing through." Chase also denounced the revival of the illegal Atlantic slave trade. In a recent case in South Carolina, a jury had refused to convict defendants accused of importing slaves from Africa. An even more recent case involved what Chase described as "the landing of six hundred negroes from a slave ship in Florida," which the local federal marshal claimed he could not prevent because "he had no means furnished him." Why not? Chase asked. Because President Buchanan did not want to offend the Southern masters who were "in favor of the slave trade, lest he finds it hard to secure the nomination at Charleston"—the site of the Democratic convention in April 1860. Chase's hard-hitting speech was widely reprinted.[57]

Both Stephen Douglas and Abraham Lincoln campaigned in Ohio in September 1859: Douglas for Democrats, and Lincoln for Republicans. Starting his speech in Columbus with characteristic humor, Lincoln said that the audience should not expect from him eloquence such as that of Chase. On the morning of Lincoln's speech, the *Ohio Statesman* had accused him of favoring black suffrage, and Lincoln refuted the charge, insisting again that he was not "in favor of making voters or jurors of negroes, nor of qualifying them to hold office, or intermarry with white people." In the main part of his speech, Lincoln denounced Douglas and other Democrats for pretending that blacks were not human and had no rights under the Constitution. Chase was out on the campaign trail himself, but his and Lincoln's paths never crossed. After Lincoln returned to Illinois, he wrote Chase to voice his "great regret at not meeting you personally while in Ohio." The governor wrote back to praise Lincoln's "two admirable speeches" in Ohio and to say that he likewise regretted that they had not been able to meet. "But I trust we shall yet meet—and that I shall have the pleasure of expressing to you personally the sentiments of true regard with which I am, sincerely yours, S. P. Chase."[58]

On Election Day, October 11, Republicans triumphed in Ohio. Dennison received 184,557 votes; his Democratic rival, only 171,226. Republicans would control both houses of the state legislature, so that they could elect Chase as their next federal senator. The *New-York Tribune*, commenting on Chase's work as governor and alluding to his future service as senator or perhaps even president, said that the "people of Ohio were never served more ably, wisely, and uprightly. We rejoice in the faith that his services are not lost to the country and wish that men of similar character and caliber could oftener be chosen to stations of like eminence and responsibility."[59]

A week after this election, the first "rather confused telegraphic reports" arrived in Ohio of an attack by John Brown and a handful of supporters, black and white, on the federal arsenal at Harpers Ferry, Virginia, his failed attempt to start a slave rebellion. Almost immediately, Democratic papers attacked Chase for encouraging the violent abolitionist Brown. The *Cincinnati Enquirer* argued on October 19 that "Brown and his followers are but the advance column of the partisan disciples of Seward and Chase, who . . . stand ready to deluge the land in blood to carry out their fanatical views." The *Illinois State Register* said that when men like Chase "by specious demagoguism, in the name of freedom and liberty, daily labor to weaken the bonds of our glorious governmental fabric . . . is it to be wondered at that ignorant, unprincipled, and reckless camp followers of the party for which these leaders speak, attempt, practically, to illustrate the doctrines which they preach?" In a private letter to the editor of the *Cincinnati Gazette,* Chase described Brown as misguided: "How rash—how mad—how criminal thus to stir up insurrection which if successful would deluge the land with blood and make void the fairest hopes of mankind! And yet how hard to condemn him, when one remembers the provocation: the unselfish desire to free the oppressed."[60]

Chase did not mention in this letter, nor did the papers report, that the connection between Brown and Chase was closer than just their shared hatred of slavery. In late 1856, when Brown had visited Columbus, Chase had donated, or persuaded a friend to donate, $25 to support Brown in his Kansas work. The governor also wrote a short note recommending Brown "to the confidence and regard of all who desire to see Kansas a free State." The abolitionist took this note, along with other recommendations, to the East. A few months later, when Brown wrote Chase for help raising further funds in Columbus, the governor replied that he was "sorry to say that on consideration I do not find there is any probability of obtaining any contributions here beyond the twenty-five dollars I obtained for the captain [Brown] when here early last winter." Chase used the third person because he thought he was writing to Nelson Hawkins, a friend of

Brown's; in fact, Hawkins was Brown's pseudonym. Fortunately for Chase, these letters were not published until long after his death.[61]

On October 23, as papers were still reporting Brown's raid, Chase gave a speech in Cincinnati in which he stressed that the Republican Party was moderate—indeed, conservative. "We wage no war with any section of our common country. We insist only that the few shall not be permitted to control the many—that the government of the people shall be in the hands of the people, and not in the hands of a privileged class; that the slaveholders of the slave states shall not force their slavery either into the free states or the free territories of the republic." He also argued that the Republican Party was not just about slavery; it was the party of reform, the party of good government. "Let us unite," he urged, "to arrest the fearful tendencies of the federal government to corruption and prodigality; to secure to labor its just rewards; to protect and cherish our industry; to elevate the tone and scope of our foreign intercourse; to cultivate a higher and nobler sentiment of nationality; to make our country the glory of all lands and an example of all nations."[62]

Unfortunately for Chase, few papers printed this speech. Medill explained to him that "in the present excited state of the public mind growing out of the Harpers Ferry affair, it is doubtful whether the publication of your speech in our paper would be of much use." The Chicago editor also warned Chase that the friends of various candidates, including Cameron and John Read, another Pennsylvanian, were talking about naming Lincoln as the vice presidential candidate. "This has set Lincoln's friends to talking of him for the first place on the ticket, on the grounds that he is a stronger and more available man than either Cameron or Read—even in Pennsylvania." (An "available man" in the nineteenth century was one likely to be elected.) Chase probably sensed, rightly, that Medill now supported Lincoln rather than him.[63]

At the end of November, Chase received an alarmed letter from the Virginia governor, Henry Wise, reporting that he had heard of plots in Ohio, Pennsylvania, and New York to send armed groups to rescue John Brown before his imminent execution. Wise asked Chase to take steps to prevent any armed incursion from Ohio into Virginia and then—oddly—warned Chase that "necessity may compel us to pursue invaders of our jurisdiction into yours; if so, you may be assured that it will done with no disrespect to the sovereignty of your state." Chase responded on December 1 that there was not much he could do to stop the alleged Ohio plot without further details. He assured Wise that if people committed crimes in Virginia and then escaped into Ohio, he would take appropriate steps to extradite them to face charges. Ohio could not "consent, however, to the invasion of her territory by armed bodies from other states, even for the purpose of pursuing and arresting fugitives from justice." There was no armed attempt to save Brown, and he died on the scaffold the next day. In a sense, Brown failed, for his raid on Harpers Ferry did not lead to a slave rebellion. In another sense, he succeeded, for his raid and the *reaction* to his raid did more than any other single event to lead to the Civil War.[64]

In December the Republican National Committee met in New York City to decide upon the time and place for party's national convention. Chase knew many of the men on this small committee: Cassius M. Clay of Kentucky, Thomas Spooner of Ohio, Carl Schurz of Wisconsin, and Gideon Welles of Connecticut, an editor with whom Chase had corresponded about the possibility of publishing a volume of his speeches and who was a committed Chase supporter at this point. A few days before the meeting, Chase wrote in detail to Spooner, pressing for a western site for the convention, such as Pittsburgh, Wheeling, or Cincinnati. In the end, the committee fixed the opening date of the convention for June 13 (later changed to May 16) and settled upon Chicago as the venue. Lincoln was not yet viewed as a serious candidate for the presidential nomination, so the friends of Chase and Seward readily agreed to Chicago, something they surely would not have done if they had known how this would help Lincoln secure the nomination.[65]

CHAPTER 13

"The Interests of the Cause"

❧ 1860 ❧

C hase started his final annual message as governor with a not-so-subtle allusion to the corrupt Buchanan administration, saying that public positions were "sacred trusts" and that the people had the right to "fidelity, zeal, and unremitting diligence" from their public servants. Most of this address was about finances, but Chase also recommended repeal of a recent law requiring election judges to "reject the votes of persons who appear to have a distinct and visible admixture of African blood." This statute was an attempt by the legislature to reverse a decision of the state supreme court that those who were more than half white could vote under the language of the state constitution allowing white male adults to vote. Chase argued that the statute "gives to judges of elections, under a loose and uncertain rule, a large and dangerous power capable of being perverted to extreme abuse." Chase also pressed the legislature to address the problem of kidnapping of blacks, saying that, in many cases, "the territory of Ohio has been clandestinely entered, and peaceful inhabitants, guilty of no crime but color, have been cruelly kidnapped." The federal fugitive slave law, "believed by a large majority to be unconstitutional," had been implemented in Ohio in a way "which could not fail to excite the deepest feeling." Chase recommended that the legislature reinstate the laws, passed by the Republicans and then repealed by the Democrats, to prohibit slaveholding and kidnapping in Ohio and to make it easier for those seized to file habeas corpus challenges.[1]

Near the end of this January 1860 message, Chase responded to the Southern threats to secede if a Republican was elected president in November. "Ohio has uttered no menace of disunion when the American people have seen fit to entrust the powers of the federal government to citizens of other political views than those of a majority of her citizens. No threats of disunion in a similar contingency by citizens of other states will excite in her any sentiments save those of sorrow and reprobation. They will not move her from her course. She will neither dissolve the Union by herself nor consent to its dissolution by others." Chase insisted that, in the South as well as the North, "the people desire Union and concord, not discord and disunion."[2]

Some out-of-state papers printed parts of Chase's message, including the *Chicago Tribune*, but the *New-York Tribune* printed only a few dull financial paragraphs. Within Ohio, there was a predictable division about the message between Republican and Democratic papers. The *Cleveland Daily Leader* said that no governor of Ohio had done more to earn the gratitude of the people: "well done, good and faithful servant." The *Cincinnati Enquirer*, on the other hand, claimed that an allusion to John Brown showed that Chase was "an admirer of Brown, thinks him a hero, and only regrets that he did not succeed in his horrid mission." In fact, in the sentence partially quoted by the *Enquirer*, Chase condemned incursions into other states and especially "attempts to excite within their borders, servile insurrections," for such insurrections would tend to "involve the country in the calamities of civil, as well as servile, war." When Chase and others referred to "servile war," they had in mind the racial violence of the Haitian Revolution of 1791 to 1804—violence many feared would be reprised in the American South.[3]

In late January former governor Chase and his successor, Dennison, participated in one of the grand political events so beloved in the nineteenth century: a joint gathering of the legislatures of Ohio, Kentucky, and Tennessee. Chase started his short speech by praising the latter state's Andrew Jackson and quoting his famous toast: "Our federal Union, it must and shall be preserved." Chase was sure that not only the three states represented this day but all the states loved the American Union. "The number of people who, either at the South or at the North, really believed that the time for the dissolution of this Union has actually come is too small to excite alarm. And if there be others who suppose that in some future contingency the destruction of the noblest political fabric ever reared by man may become desirable, we may safely trust the logic of events for the demonstration of their error." Because of this strong commitment to the Union, "we will compose whatever differences have arisen or may arise, in the spirit of our fathers." Unlike his final message as governor, this speech was widely reprinted.[4]

Chase's first political goal in 1860 was to persuade the state legislators to select him for the Senate term that would start in March 1861. Republicans had comfortable majorities in both houses of the Ohio legislature, and friends such as Rutherford Hayes, the city solicitor of Cincinnati and future president, assured Chase that almost all Republicans would support him. But a few of the nominally Republican legislators were more Whig than Republican, and they wanted to prevent Chase's election to the Senate by delaying the election until a special session after the presidential election. These men recalled the way in which Free Soilers and Democrats had combined in 1849 to send Chase to the Senate, and they thought it would be poetic justice for a combination of Whigs and Democrats to prevent his election in 1860. As the date of the Republican caucus approached, there was intense speculation in Columbus about whether the dissident members could delay or prevent the election.[5]

When Republican legislators gathered and debated on the appointed night, February 1, Chase received fifty-one votes, with seventeen scattered among rivals, including quasi-Whigs such as Thomas Corwin and Columbus Delano. (Delano, a former Ohio representative, was a distant cousin of Sara Ann Delano, at this time a child in Newburgh, New York, and later the mother of Franklin Delano Roosevelt.) The Republican plan was for the two houses of the state legislature to meet the next afternoon in joint session for the election. First, however, the House and the Senate had to vote separately to hold a joint session, and it seemed that there might be enough votes in the House (all the Democrats and a few apostate Republicans) to defeat the resolution. One Republican member wrote from Columbus late that night that "the Democrats are quite confident that they can secure the cooperation of the requisite number of the so-called Republicans to prevent an election. We shall see."[6]

On the next day, three House Democrats were—for some reason—absent. Other Democrats and some Republicans tried to delay the vote by floating one motion after another—hoping that the missing members would arrive and give them the votes they needed to defeat Chase. George Andrews, nominally a Republican, offered an amendment to express the sense of the Ohio House that no man should become senator "who entertains sentiments of hostility to the enforcement of the Fugitive Slave Act, or who entertains sentiments favoring negro equality with white citizens, either in the elective franchise or in the admission of colored children into our schools." Chase's friend Richard Parsons, Speaker of the House, ruled this amendment out of order and made similar rulings on other dilatory motions. Finally, someone called the previous question, and by a vote of only fifty-one to forty-nine, the House agreed to go into the joint session with the Senate.[7]

The rest of the day was less dramatic. At the outset of the joint session, Chase's friends defeated another halfhearted attempt at delay, and then forced a vote. Chase received seventy-five votes; his Democratic rival, Pugh, fifty-four; and Corwin, five. When the news of Chase's victory arrived in Cincinnati and Cleveland, local Republicans fired cannon salutes. In Columbus, several hundred friends and supporters crowded into Chase's house to celebrate. The *Ohio State Journal* called the party "an occasion of as great enjoyment as can be experienced without the society of ladies."[8]

It was a close call. If Chase had been defeated in his effort to return to the Senate, it would have been national news and would have essentially ended his presidential campaign. His victory was expected, however, so it did not attract much attention from the press. The next stage of Chase's quest for the national presidential nomination would come in late February, as Republicans met in small district conventions in Ohio's twenty-one congressional districts, each of which was entitled to send two delegates to the National Republican Convention. Many of the Chicago delegates selected at these district conventions were firm Chase men, but others were not; those chosen included both Corwin and Delano. Some of these conventions expressed a preference for Chase, but most expressed no preference, wanting to leave the delegates to the national convention free to confer and choose the best candidate. This was consistent with what Chase was writing in letter after letter—that he loved the cause better than himself—and consistent with the way nineteenth-century politics generally worked. Men were chosen as delegates for the national convention in order to exercise their judgment there, not to act as puppets of their county conventions.[9]

In late February two important editorials appeared, and two important speeches were made, on the national stage. The *Chicago Tribune*, whose editor Chase had courted the prior year, now endorsed Lincoln, saying that although he was "not learned, in a bookish sense," he was "master of the great fundamental principles, and of that kind of ability which applies them to crises and events." Somewhat as it had done in 1856, the *New-York Tribune* argued that if the Republicans were strong enough to elect any of their candidates, they should nominate Seward or Chase, each of whom was "a statesman of unquestioned ability, unsullied integrity, broad national views and feelings, and thoroughly Republican principles and aspirations." But in the more likely scenario that the Republicans were not strong enough to sweep the North with Seward or Chase, they should nominate Bates, who would have greater appeal to conservatives and former Whigs.[10]

In his speech in New York City at the Cooper Union on February 27, 1860, Lincoln echoed and amplified on Chase's argument about how those who founded the republic and drafted the Constitution opposed the extension of slavery into the territories. It was the solemn duty of the Republicans, Lincoln declared, to prevent the spread of slavery. "Let us have faith that right makes might, and in that faith, let us to the end dare to do our duty as we understand it." Lincoln's great speech impressed and excited not only those in his audience but also the tens of thousands who read it in the newspapers. Suddenly Lincoln was not just the favorite son of a distant western state; he was a leading national candidate. Lincoln followed up his New York success with a quick speaking tour through New England.[11]

William Seward's main goal in his Senate speech of February 29 was to sound moderate, so he insisted that Republicans would not interfere with slavery in the slave states. Seward closed with a stirring answer to those who predicted that the Union would dissolve if a Republican were elected president. The chief bonds of the Union, "those which render it inseparable and indivisible," were not the railroads and telegraphs linking the states, or the trade between them, but rather the "millions of fibers of millions of contented happy human hearts, binding by their affections, their ambitions, and their best hopes" all Americans to one Union. Seward's speech impressed those who heard it and those who read it, including Chase, who called it "very able" in one letter and even "great" in another, although he added that he "did not like some of his expressions."[12]

William Henry Seward, with whom Chase served first in the Senate and then in the Lincoln Cabinet. "He is too much of a politician for me," Chase wrote of Seward.

Unlike the speeches of Lincoln and Seward, widely reprinted, Chase's long speech on February 23, 1860, was neither printed nor noticed. He addressed the Young Men's Association of Albany, New York, on the topic of "the Mississippi Valley and the American Union." As in other speeches, Chase argued that the Northwest Ordinance had created a region characterized by "freedom not serfdom; freeholds not tenancies; democracy not despotism; education not ignorance . . . progress, not stagnation or retrogression." Chase highlighted the connections between the states of the Mississippi Valley and downplayed the differences between free states and slave states. "With the people of these states, attachment to the Union is . . . a sentiment, deep, loyal, and abiding as that of devoted sons for a venerated mother." The *Albany Evening Journal* reported that "Chase's lecture last night before the young men's association was an eloquent production, to which a large audience listened with deep attention. Its theme, the Mississippi Valley considered in relation to the Federal Union, was handled with the comprehensive grasp of a far-seeing statesman." This was the paper's entire report—two sentences. It was not surprising that the *Journal*, edited by Seward's colleague Weed, would not devote much space to a speech by Chase, but it seems that no other paper noticed the Albany address. Chase bears at least part of the blame, for it seems that he did not provide newspaper editors with excerpts.[13]

More than four hundred Republicans, representing almost every county in Ohio gathered in Columbus on the first of March. The main purpose of this state convention was to select four at-large delegates to attend the Chicago convention. Friends of Chase, however, also suggested a resolution to state that "while the Republicans of Ohio will give their united and earnest support to the nominee of the Chicago convention, they would indicate as their first choice and recommend to said convention the name of Salmon P. Chase of Ohio." The convention approved this by a vote of 375 to 73, after which there were "prolonged cheers for S. P. Chase and the Republican cause," according to the *Ohio State Journal*. Writing to Benjamin Wade, whom some were considering as an alternative Ohio nominee, Chase claimed the resolution was "altogether spontaneous" and hoped that Wade would "take hold with us." Wade did not respond. When the *New-York Tribune* reported that Chase would probably not receive the entire vote of the Ohio delegation because some of the delegates selected at the district conventions would support other candidates, Chase was annoyed, writing a friend that although the Ohio delegation was perhaps not "*perfectly* unanimous," he expected that it would vote together.[14]

The news for Chase from other states in the month of March was mixed. Charles Cleveland wrote from Philadelphia that Chase should not be discouraged by the decision of the Pennsylvania state convention to support Cameron. Cleveland expected that, after voting for Cameron on the first ballot in Chicago, the Pennsylvania delegation would support someone else on the second and subsequent ballots, probably Chase or Seward. Alluding to Cameron's reputation for corruption, and the

Republican commitment to reform, Cleveland said that it "would be too consummate a farce to have Cameron for our standard-bearer." Edward Pierce wrote from Boston that all the delegates from Massachusetts (even Pierce himself) would support Seward. This was a disappointment, for Chase had hoped that the Massachusetts delegation would first support Banks as a favorite son and then divide among other candidates. Amos Tuck, after a business trip to Michigan and Wisconsin, wrote Chase that most Republicans in those states supported Seward. What surprised and troubled Tuck was "the conviction that we must take Seward if we are to name a man representing the principles of the Republican Party, and if we leave him, we must have a modification in the person of Bates or [John] Bell"—another conservative, from Tennessee. Soon Chase heard a similar message from Carl Schurz, the Wisconsin leader, when he visited Columbus. Chase reported to a friend that Schurz "has the opinion that if Seward must be set aside as unavailable at Chicago, Chase must be also." Chase disagreed; he believed that if he was nominated, he would have support from "the conservatives of New York," from "more Americans than anyone but Bates can get," and from "a democratic element of support which no other candidate can command."[15]

But Chase was realistic enough to see that Seward would probably get the Chicago nomination. Chase was keeping a list of those named as Chicago delegates, and, at some point, he "added them up" to estimate that Seward would have at least 162 votes on the first ballot—not enough for nomination but a commanding lead. "Should the nomination fall to him," Chase wrote to James Pike, "I shall not at all repine. If the best interests of our cause and country will be best promoted by it, I shall not only not repine, but shall rejoice. Many, however, think he cannot be nominated; many, that if nominated, he cannot be elected; many, that if elected, his administration will divide the Republicans, reorganize the Democracy, and insure its triumph." In another letter, alluding to Seward's connection with Thurlow Weed, and Weed's reputation for corruption in the state capital of Albany, Chase wrote that "if Albany is to be transplanted to Washington, the party cannot survive." Still, he preferred the nomination of Seward, whom he viewed as a real Republican, to the nomination of Bates or Bell, the elderly conservatives whose names were often mentioned this spring. "I have lost patience with what I hear of hunting of the fossils," Chase wrote to a friend. "It will do for paleontologists but not for Republicans."[16]

For several weeks, starting in March, Chase toyed with the idea of a trip to Washington, to meet with leaders there, many of whom would be important delegates in Chicago. "I wish I could come to Washington without seeming to seek votes," he wrote to Pike. Finally, in late April, Chase and his daughter Kate traveled with Dennison and his wife to the capital. While they were all there, John Gurley, an Ohio member of Congress, gave a dinner to honor Governors Chase and Dennison. Guests included candidates for the nomination—Seward, Chase, and Wade—as well as other leaders, notably Frank Blair, whose family was strongly supporting Bates. A letter from Chase suggests that many of the jokes at dinner were about Seward as the next president. "Seward was evidently quite conscious and hopeful, though a good deal annoyed occasionally."[17]

While Chase was in Washington, the Democratic convention in Charleston, South Carolina, divided into two parts, one Northern and one Southern, each of which adjourned without making a nomination. The Northern convention had balloted more than fifty times, with Douglas receiving a majority, but not the two-thirds majority required by Democratic rules. Writing from Washington to his friend Henry Cooke, editor of the *Ohio State Journal*, Chase said, "I am now satisfied that, since the adjournments of Charleston, it has become certain that our nomination will be given to Seward unless the demands of opposition to his nomination can be concentrated on the choice of Ohio."[18]

In the week before the Chicago convention, a new party, the Constitutional Union Party, held its national convention in Baltimore. More than five hundred delegates, most of them former Whigs or Know-Nothings, crowded the hall and cheered speeches denouncing both the Democrats and the Republicans. The convention nominated John Bell of Tennessee (sixty-three years old) for president and Edward Everett of Massachusetts (sixty-six) for vice president and adopted a platform that merely endorsed "the Constitution of the country, the Union of the states, and the enforcement of the laws."[19]

Republican papers mocked the party, the platform, and the aged candidates, but the Constitutional Union Party posed a real threat to the Republicans. If Bell could obtain as many votes in 1860 as Millard Fillmore had won in 1856, the Republican nominee would not carry enough states to win in the electoral college. In this scenario, the new president would be selected by the House of Representatives, with each state delegation having one vote. The *Baltimore Sun* reported that fourteen state delegations were controlled by the Democrats, fifteen by the Republicans, three delegations were equally divided, and one delegation was controlled by the American Party. Since it would take a majority of delegations (seventeen) to elect a president, neither the Democrats nor the Republicans would be in control; the divided states would hold the balance of power, and the House might select Bell as the compromise candidate. This was the hope of the Constitutional Union Party, and the fear of the Republicans, on the eve of the Chicago convention. To win, Republicans needed to find a candidate who could carry all the states that John Frémont had carried in 1856, and Pennsylvania with its twenty-seven electoral votes, and one or two of the other Northern states that Frémont had not carried, such as Indiana, Illinois, and New Jersey.[20]

Chase remained in Columbus as the delegates gathered in Chicago, since it was considered improper for candidates to attend conventions. Although he had many friends in Chicago, there was no single manager of the Chase campaign—no one like Thurlow Weed for Seward or Judge David Davis for Lincoln. Candidates did not really appoint managers in the nineteenth century; these men appointed themselves on the basis of their long friendships with the candidates. There was nobody like Weed in Chase's life, other than perhaps Gamaliel Bailey, but he was no longer alive, and even if he had lived, he was not a master of practical politics like Weed.[21]

Writing from Chicago on May 13, Edward Pierce advised Chase that neither he nor Seward would be nominated. Seward's problem was that delegates from Pennsylvania, Indiana, and Illinois all insisted that if Seward was nominated, he would not win their states in November. Chase would receive some convention votes from "New Hampshire, Rhode Island, Connecticut, Massachusetts, and your own state," said Pierce, but nowhere near enough for nomination. Chase's problem was similar to that of Seward: with his long radical record, he could not carry the critical conservative states in the fall election. Pierce's letter to Chase was similar to a report by a *New York Herald* correspondent, filed late on the evening of May 15: "The Seward men are not a little frightened at the earnest opposition to him from all quarters except New York. The announcement by Mr. [Andrew] Curtin, the Republican candidate for governor of Pennsylvania, that his own defeat will surely follow Seward's nomination; by Mr. [Henry] Lane, of Indiana, that his state can be carried by any other

Republican candidate than Seward; by the Illinois delegation, that the Republicans of southern Illinois will vote for Bell if Seward is nominated; by the New Jersey delegation, that Seward's nomination will give the state to the Democrats . . . have produced a reaction in the ranks of the various delegations that injures Seward's chances materially." In other words, even before the Chicago convention opened on May 16, delegates were turning away from Seward because they feared that he could not win critical states in the fall. And delegates were not turning to Chase because they believed he would have similar problems.[22]

The voting for the presidential nominee, on Friday, May 18, was in a fixed geographic order, starting with Maine, proceeding through New England and the Atlantic states, before reaching the newer, western states. Each state was entitled to four "at-large" votes and two votes for each congressional district. In the first round of voting, Maine gave ten votes to Seward and six to Lincoln. New Hampshire gave seven votes to Lincoln and one each to Seward and Chase. Massachusetts gave Seward twenty-one and Lincoln four votes. The votes of Rhode Island and Connecticut were scattered among several candidates, with Chase getting one from Rhode Island and two from Connecticut. Already, after New England voted on the first ballot,

The temporary convention hall in Chicago, known as the "Wigram," site of the 1860 Republican National Convention, at which delegates nominated Lincoln.

Seward and Chase were in trouble, receiving fewer votes than expected. In contrast, Lincoln was getting more votes than expected. Like partners in a bridge game, delegates were signaling one another, asking whether Lincoln was the best choice. Unlike a bridge game, the convention was not quiet. At critical moments, the roar for Lincoln was deafening. "Imagine all the hogs ever slaughtered in Cincinnati giving their death squeals together," Murat Halstead wrote for the *Cincinnati Commercial*, along with a "score of big steam whistles." This, too, was a signal to the delegates.[23]

New York, as anticipated, voted unanimously for Seward. Lincoln obtained four votes from Pennsylvania, however, which had been expected to vote entirely for Cameron, and fourteen votes from Virginia, which had been presumed to support Seward. When it was time for Ohio to vote, fourteenth in the order, the delegates responded to these Lincoln signals. Thirty-four Ohio delegates voted for Chase, but eight voted for Lincoln and five for John McLean. (Chase would learn later from the newspapers that Columbus Delano was one of those who supported Lincoln on the first ballot, and Corwin one of those who voted McLean.) When the first round was finished and the results tallied, Seward had 173½ votes; Lincoln, 102 votes; Cameron, 50½ votes; Chase, 49 votes; and Bates, 48 votes. Because some delegations had more members than they had votes, the rules allowed for half votes.[24]

In the second round, Seward received 184½ votes; Lincoln, 181; and Chase, only 42½. In Ohio and other delegations, votes were switching from Chase and other candidates to Lincoln. The most important switch was by Pennsylvania, which awarded almost all its votes on the second ballot to Lincoln, the result of a late-night bargain between managers: Pennsylvania would support Lincoln if he would include Cameron in his Cabinet. On the third ballot, yet more votes shifted to Lincoln, so that he was within a few votes of the required majority. Just before the official result of this ballot was announced, as the clerks were checking their figures, David Cartter of Cleveland, a friend of Chase's and former member of Congress, rose and said that four Ohio votes would shift from Chase to Lincoln. "This announcement," according to the official report of the convention, "giving Mr. Lincoln a majority, was greeted by the audience with the most enthusiastic and thundering applause. The entire crowd rose to its feet, applauding rapturously, the ladies waving their handkerchiefs, the men waving and throwing up their hats by thousands, cheering again and again."[25]

Chase learned the result by telegraph at about three in the afternoon. We do not have (as we do in the cases of Seward and Lincoln) an account of his initial reaction to the nomination of Lincoln. The *Ohio State Journal* reported that the Republicans of Columbus were elated by the selection, firing a cannon salute on the grounds of the statehouse. The *Ohio Statesman* claimed that local Republicans were disappointed by the choice of Lincoln over their favorite, Chase, but this seems to reflect Democratic hopes for division among Republicans rather than Republican reactions. The *Statesman* mocked Lincoln as a mere "third-rate county court lawyer."[26]

Chase had mixed feelings about the Chicago convention. Believing that Lincoln was right on the central issue, slavery, Chase approved the nomination. He was happy with the platform, opposing the expansion of slavery, and attacking the fraud, corruption, and extravagance of the Buchanan administration. Although the platform did not go as far as Chase would have liked—it said nothing about repealing the Fugitive Slave Act, for example—he understood the reasons for reticence. But Chase was angered by the failure of the Ohio delegation, on the first ballot, at least, to give him a unanimous vote, as other delegations did for other candidates. Even in his letter congratulating Lincoln, Chase noted the "generous, unanimous, and constant" support of New York for Seward, and of Illinois for Lincoln, and regretted "the failure of the delegates from Ohio to exercise the same generous spirit." In a letter to a friend in Kansas, Chase wrote that the Ohio delegates were "bound in honor to carry out the expressed wish of the majority of the Republicans of the state, without regard to personal preferences. Had Wade or Corwin received the same expression from the state convention, I would have suffered death sooner than allow my name to be brought into competition with them." Although Chase often claimed that he did not care whether he was nominated, he *did* care, and he was angry at those he viewed as the faithless delegates.[27]

Chase's private anger at the Ohio delegates, however, was far less important than his strong public support for Lincoln, starting just after the convention and continuing right through Election Day in November. Chase was completely committed to the Republican cause. He understood that it was not at all sure that the Republican Party could carry enough states to elect Lincoln. By custom, Lincoln could not campaign for himself; he would have to rely upon Chase and other Republican leaders. If Lincoln was elected president, he could not accomplish much without Republican control of the House (at present, more or less evenly divided between Republicans and Democrats) and more Republicans in the Senate (at present, dominated by Democrats). And in forming his Cabinet, Lincoln would reward those who helped most in the election. Elizabeth Pike alluded to this in the midst of the campaign, when she suggested to Chase that their families should travel to Europe together the next year—"if you are not secretary of state." For all these reasons, Chase threw himself into the Lincoln campaign.[28]

Salmon Chase as he looked while serving in the Lincoln Cabinet.

Chase's first speech for Lincoln was on May 22, at an evening rally on the statehouse steps in Columbus. The huge crowd and the "all-pervading enthusiasm," he said, showed that Lincoln would prevail. Even the slave states, Chase argued, would benefit from a Republican administration: a clean government in Washington and freedom in the western territories. "In the Southern states, there are thousands, kept down by poverty and social distinctions, who long for schools and churches, and for unrestricted opportunities of self-culture and elevation in the social scale. We Republicans propose, by keeping the territories in reserve for them, to furnish them these advantages." Lincoln's life story proved Chase's point: "His grandparents were natives of Virginia, his parents of Kentucky, and they were poor. Young Lincoln left the unfriendly atmosphere of slavery, in his native state, and removed to Indiana, where he could breathe free air and carve out for himself a more favorable destiny." Chase also praised the nomination of Hannibal Hamlin for vice president, saying that he knew Hamlin well from their time in the Senate. Chase closed with "a stirring appeal to Republicans to do their whole duty in the coming campaign. There is now every indication of success, but success is never won without effort, and it is always well to make assurance doubly sure."[29]

In late June the Democrats gathered in Baltimore but divided again into two groups. The Northerners nominated Stephen Douglas, and the Southerners, John C. Breckinridge for president. Chase and other Republicans were encouraged by the division among the Democrats but realized that much hard work was still required to elect Lincoln. Caleb Smith, a former member of Congress from Indiana and a future colleague in the Lincoln Cabinet, wrote to invite Chase to speak in Indianapolis. Although Indiana had voted exclusively for Lincoln at the Chicago convention, Smith told Chase that there were many in the state who hoped to see Chase become president someday. Chase responded that he did not fault the Indiana delegation for supporting Lincoln, saying, "I am sure that they acted as they believed the interests of the cause required, and, if the result shall be the gaining of Indiana and Illinois to the Republican side, thereby not merely advancing the cause but securing the success of the faithful and able Republicans who are candidates in those states, I shall be more than satisfied." Chase was more or less admitting to Smith that, if nominated, he would not have carried Illinois or Indiana in the 1860 presidential election. Chase's past positions on black rights would have made him utterly unacceptable in the southern parts of those two states.[30]

Chase went to Michigan in August, where he gave speeches to large crowds in Detroit, Pontiac, and Ypsilanti. Chase focused mainly on Douglas, because he knew that Douglas was Lincoln's main rival in this region. Although Douglas spoke often about democratic government and popular sovereignty, Chase argued that the way in which the Democrats had treated Kansas proved that they did not really believe in democracy. The governor of Kansas was appointed by the president, not elected by the people of the territory, and the governor could veto legislation unless passed by two-thirds majorities in both houses of the legislature. Similarly, the judges of the territory were appointed by the president and answered to him, not the people of Kansas. Douglas would hand the people of Kansas over, "bound hand and foot," to those who were keen to see Kansas become a slave state. Chase and Douglas were "as wide apart as the poles," for Douglas "follows the false light of despotism, and I follow the light of freedom."[31]

On August 24 Chase addressed a mass meeting in Richmond, Indiana, one of the vital states for Lincoln. Chase started by saying that it was good to see so many young men and especially "the women of the land: our mothers and our sisters and our sweethearts"—the crowd laughed when he said that he was sorry that he did not have a sweetheart himself—and to see women "taking part in our struggle as in the days of the Revolution." Using both humor and reason, he stressed that the Republican Party did not threaten the slave states: "We do not propose to invade any of the rights of the slave states; we do not propose to violate the Constitution in any way. But what is it we say? We say to our slaveholding friends that if slavery is a good thing, we want you to keep that good thing to yourselves; if it is a blessing, we desire you to enjoy the whole of that blessing." The Republicans did not object to slavery in the slave states, Chase said, they objected only to the Slave Power and the way that slavery interfered in the national government and with the free states.[32]

Chase then described, in more detail, what he meant by the Slave Power. He estimated that there were about four hundred thousand masters of about four million slaves in the United States. He noted that in the slave states, almost none of the government offices were held by anyone other than slaveholders. "There never was such an aristocracy before. It has the land; it has the labor; it has . . . the whole political power . . . and nobody can write, preach, or pray unless just as this aristocracy chooses." The Slave Power, Chase noted, also controlled the Supreme Court, since five out of the nine seats were essentially reserved for the South, even though the population of the South was far smaller than that of the North. Chase illustrated with a story about a conversation he had had with David Atchison, the slave-owning senator from Missouri, in which Atchison chided Chase for refusing to compromise. Chase responded with a proposal: "You have had this government for fifty years; now let us have it for the same length of time, and we will be even." The Indiana crowd laughed and cheered.[33]

Reading in the papers that Chase would speak in the East, Elizabeth Pike urged him to make time to see the Pike family. Her husband, she reported, strongly favored Lincoln, but she was less enthused. "I find Lincoln a conservative old Whig," she wrote. "I am ashamed for my want of true patriotism but confess my interest in the coming canvass to be abated by my own disappointments." Chase's first eastern stop was Exeter, New Hampshire, where, on the morning of September 4, he and other Republicans paraded through the town, accompanied by several marching bands and greeted by banners such as "Liberty National, Slavery Sectional." There were two speeches in the morning and another two in the afternoon. Much of Chase's speech was a history lesson; a local paper reported that "he took up each presidential election and reviewed the course of the different administrations." When he mentioned Lewis Cass, the Democratic nominee in 1848, Chase described him as "a very clever man" but one whose "backbone was omitted." John Hale, on the platform with Chase, interrupted to tell him that Cass was a native son of Exeter. The local paper reported that "Chase then apologized in a humorous and happy way."[34]

Three days later, Chase was the principal speaker at a county fair in Middlebury, Vermont. According to a local paper, he gave a fine speech "whose only fault was that it was too short." Among other things, Chase spoke about "the Ohio agricultural society and recommended its adoption by Vermont. He paid a fine tribute to the dignity and worth of agriculture, and to the character of the New England agriculturist, and concluded his address with an impressive appeal in the behalf of liberty and union." The leaders of his place of birth, Cornish, New Hampshire, seeing that Chase was in New England, begged him for a speech there. "I retain the most affectionate remembrance of my native place," Chase responded, and "would rather speak there than in any town in New England." But he was already heading back to the West and could not turn around to speak in New Hampshire.[35]

As soon as he returned to Ohio, Chase was out on the campaign trail for Lincoln and other Republicans. He spoke essentially every day except Sundays from September 13 through the state election day, October 9. Indiana, Iowa, Ohio, and Pennsylvania would all vote for members of Congress on this day, and these elections would influence the November 6 presidential election. As Chase explained to a friend in New York City, declining or at least postponing an invitation to speak there, "we have

a number of doubtful congressional districts, and I feel bound to contribute all in my power to securing a Republican Congress to sustain the
administration of a Republican president." One paper reported that in
one of his speeches, Chase "traced the history of the country in connection
with slavery, from the days of Washington and Jefferson, down to those
of Webster and Clay, saying that to his latest day, he would never forget
the proud form and beaming eye of Henry Clay as he exclaimed on the
floor of the Senate, 'there is no power on earth that shall induce me to vote
for the extension of slavery.'" But Douglas and others had now extended
slavery, claiming that Clay himself would support their version of "popular
sovereignty." Douglas was insulting the memory of Clay, declared Chase;
it was "a sham and a cheat."[36]

Chase had correspondents all over the North but not many in the
South. One of the exceptions was William Mellen, a lawyer with whom
Chase had a brief partnership in Cincinnati and who now managed a coal
company in Kentucky. When Mellen warned Chase that the Republicans
would receive almost no votes in Kentucky, Chase answered that the "great
tide of liberal opinion is slowly if surely making its way into the slave
states." He predicted that, once Lincoln was president, "a great change
will take place in all the South. The planters and slaveholders will find
that the Republican Party proposes no interference with them whatever
within state limits, and a sense of security will lead to greater toleration, and the sentiment of emancipation will find advocates in growing
numbers and of increasing power. I shall not be at all surprised to see
Missouri, Delaware, and Maryland join the free states and ranks in the
first Republican presidential term." The hope that Chase expressed here
was the Lower South's fear: that the border slave states, losing slaves and
gaining immigrants, would soon become free states, changing the balance
of power in Washington and perhaps allowing someday for a constitutional
amendment to end slavery altogether.[37]

The results in Ohio in the October 1860 elections were mixed. In the
statewide contests, Republicans had majorities of about twenty thousand,
so the state seemed safe for Lincoln. But in the congressional races, Democrats gained two seats previously held by Republicans. The Ohio votes
were still being counted when Chase departed for New York to speak in
some of the close congressional districts there. The three parties opposing
Lincoln had formed a joint list of candidates for the electoral college in
New York; they argued that voting for this "Union ticket" was the only

way to save the Union from the secession and civil war that would surely follow the election of Lincoln. Without the thirty-five electoral votes of New York, there was simply no way for Lincoln to win in the electoral college. So Chase's trip there was important not just for the congressional candidates; it was critical for Lincoln as well.[38]

In his first speech in New York, at Fort Plain on September 16, Chase analyzed what would happen if the fusion ticket prevailed in New York, and the House attempted to select the next president. He noted that, under the Constitution, the House could choose only among the three candidates having the highest number of electoral votes, and predicted that this would exclude Douglas from consideration. At most, Bell would probably have only three state delegations in his favor, so he would also not become president in the House. Lincoln and Breckinridge would each have the support of about fifteen delegations, not the required majority of seventeen, so the process would drag on for months—perhaps until Inauguration Day. In that scenario, Chase believed, the question would become whether the Senate, under the rules provided in the Constitution, could select a vice president, for that person would become president in the absence of a president duly elected by the House.[39]

Chase's main point was that nobody should want the uncertainty and instability that would arise from a prolonged congressional debate about who should serve as the next president. His other point was that Bell and Douglas men should realize that neither of their candidates would emerge from this process as president; by voting for the fusion ticket, they were voting for Breckinridge and nationwide slavery. Chase closed, however, by predicting that the voters of New York would not be deceived by the fusion ticket, and that they would vote for Lincoln and liberty.[40]

Chase gave an entirely different speech the next day, in nearby Troy, to fifteen hundred people packed into a theater. "Without any preliminary remarks," the *Troy Times* reported, Chase launched into his argument: "that it was not the agitation for Freedom which prevented the dispatch of important public business by Congress, but the agitation for Slavery." Republicans favored homestead legislation, so that settlers could obtain and improve western land. Democrats, however, in deference to the slave interest, opposed homestead legislation, and President Buchanan had vetoed a homestead bill. Republicans favored limited, economical government, while Democrats, and Buchanan in particular, were profligate spenders. When Buchanan arrived in office, there was a surplus of $17 million in the Treasury. "What did he do with it? Why, he spent it!" exclaimed Chase. To increase federal revenues, Republicans had framed and passed a tariff bill in the House. "Agitation for freedom did not prevent them from carrying it through the House," he explained, but Democratic senators, "too busy agitating for Slavery," had set the tariff bill aside, where it would probably "sleep forever." Third, and most important, Republicans wanted to create free states from the western territories. This was not a new policy, Chase said; it was the policy of Jefferson, who had proposed that all states formed from federal territory should be free states. Democrats, however, had not only blocked the admission of Kansas as a free state but also now opposed the admission of any new free states.[41]

Chase then turned to slavery, attacking the slavery policies of the other parties and defending that of the Republicans. "We don't propose to interfere with slavery in Virginia and South Carolina," he emphasized. "The institution is just as much beyond our power in these states as it is in Russia. True, if Russia succeeds in getting rid of slavery, no man, I think, will grumble; and if Cassius Clay shall succeed in emancipating the slaves of Kentucky, or Frank Blair those of Missouri, no man will regret the progress of civilization." This, Chase said, was how slavery would end in the South: the Southern people would "take up this question and settle it among themselves, just as you settled it here"—an allusion to the gradual end of slavery in New York. Chase again closed by predicting that Lincoln would win: "Lincoln is to be elected president. There is no power on earth capable of preventing it."[42]

After several more speeches in upstate New York, Chase spent Sunday with friends in New York City. Then he was out speaking again at rallies in Brooklyn and Queens and Newark, New Jersey. The *New-York Tribune*, which published column after column of Chase's speeches, commented in late October that he had "been speaking daily in our state for the last fortnight, mainly in the close congressional districts, and has done yeoman service. He speaks very plainly, without parade or ornament; but no man better understands the great principles which underlie the canvass or has a better faculty for making others understand them."[43]

When Chase returned to Ohio, he decided that he would make his final speech of the campaign in Covington, Kentucky, just across the river from Cincinnati. Some friends warned that the locals there would "make trouble," but he decided (as he put it in a letter to John Greenleaf Whittier) that he would speak "at whatever hazard and no matter what the consequences to myself." In the end, although there was some shouting and fighting at the door of the lecture hall, there was none inside, where "the order was almost perfect and the attention very profound." Chase estimated in another letter that only about a hundred people in his Covington audience were in Lincoln's corner, while the others were in favor of Bell or Douglas or even Breckinridge.[44]

Chase started his Covington speech by quoting Andrew Jackson: the Union "must be preserved!" He was sure "that the masses of the American people are entirely sound on the question of the American Union—that among their most cherished sentiments, there is not one more deeply cherished than that implied in the simple yet most emphatic language of the patriot-hero of Tennessee; and that whatever temporary discontents may prevail in this or that section of the country, disunion will never be admitted as a fit remedy for them by the common sense or common patriotism of the country." Chase insisted that the Lincoln administration would not interfere with slavery in the slave states: "I am a Republican, and I intend to vote for Abraham Lincoln; but I would not be a Republican if I believed that the Republican Party meditated hostile aggression upon the constitutional rights of any state or any citizen of any state." Nor would he "vote for Lincoln were I not firmly persuaded that he has a heart large enough and an intellect comprehensive enough to administer the government for the good of the whole people, whether they live in the North or the South, the East or the West."[45]

After Chase finished speaking, he was handed a page with a few questions, which he read aloud and answered. Asked whether Lincoln recognized a state's right to secede from the Union, Chase said that he believed that Lincoln did not recognize such a right, other than the last-resort right of revolution. As heirs of the American Revolution, Republicans accepted that there was a right of revolution; that the people could rise up and throw off a tyrannical government. The right of revolution was, however, outside the legal system; the question of secession was whether there was an implicit legal right for a state to leave the United States. On this, Chase and other Republicans were adamant: no state had the right to secede. The legality of secession would be one of the major issues Chase was to face as chief justice, but long before that, secession would pose practical issues for Lincoln as president and for Chase as a member of his

Cabinet. One of the Covington questioners raised this more immediate issue, asking Chase how Lincoln would respond to Southern secession. "Of course I do not know what he will do," Chase replied, "but I have no doubt *he will do right*."[46]

On Election Day, Chase voted, along with more than four and a half million other men, in what a leading scholar has rightly called "the most consequential presidential contest in all American history." By midnight, the telegraphic reports made it clear that Lincoln would become the next president. In the end, he carried every Northern state other than New Jersey, and even there he received four electoral votes because of the curious way in which the state allocated its electors. The results in some of the states were close: Lincoln received only 50.7 percent of the vote in Illinois and 51.1 percent in neighboring Indiana. The efforts of Chase and others in Kentucky and other border states did not work: Lincoln obtained a mere 1,365 votes in Kentucky and 2,294 votes in Maryland. In most Southern states, he received no votes whatever, because no one dared to print or distribute Republican ballots. Nationwide, Lincoln received only 39.8 percent of the popular vote. None of this mattered, however, in the electoral college, where he would have 180 votes, far more than the required majority of 152 votes.[47]

Chase wrote to his friend John Jay on Election Day that "we take the final step today. Mr. Lincoln will be president, and the Slave Power will be overthrown." The next day, Chase wrote to Lincoln himself: "I congratulate you and thank God. The great object of my wishes and labors for nineteen years is accomplished in the overthrow of the Slave Power." Indeed, in the nineteen years since Chase had joined the tiny Liberty Party, no man had done more than him to prepare the way for this Republican victory. "The lead is yours," Chase wrote to Lincoln, and "the "responsibility is vast. May God strengthen you for your great duties."[48]

CHAPTER 14

"Inauguration First, Adjustment Afterwards"

◁ 1860—61 ▷

Within days of Lincoln's election, Chase started to receive letters urging him to serve in the new president's administration. The *New-York Tribune*'s Charles Dana wrote that the nation faced not only the slavery question but also the "plunder question." Without Chase in the Cabinet, Dana did not "see how we can hope to resist the vast power and unknown genius of the thieves." Dana did not name names, but he was worried about Seward, and even more about Seward's friend Thurlow Weed, viewed as corrupt even by the standards of Albany. James Pike reinforced the point, writing, "The brand of corruption must be extinguished by the superior blaze of honesty, if possible." George Fogg, secretary of the national party committee, wrote that "thousands of our best and wisest men" wanted to see Chase as secretary of state, the foremost position in the Cabinet. Lincoln would need "the best and ablest men" so that "great principles which underlie our movement, reaching back nearly twenty years" would be "impressed upon and into the government."[1]

Chase responded to all these letters in more or less the same way. "I greatly prefer to work in a legislative than in an administrative position," he wrote to Dana. "It is more pleasant on many accounts. Still, I do not say that I would refuse the post you refer to. Indeed, it would be rather superfluous to decline what has not been offered." In a letter to Hiram

Barney, Chase added a few paragraphs about his personal financial situation. During his four years as governor, he had not practiced law; his income, in addition to his salary, came from rental properties and small loans that he had made. Several of those who owed Chase money had not paid their debts, so that he now might have to sell some of his real estate in order to repay his own creditors. Would Barney arrange a loan, secured by Chase's real property, of about $20,000? This would "consolidate my entire indebtedness and relieve me from great anxiety and the necessity of sales."[2]

In this same time period—the first few days after Lincoln's election— the papers reported that the key federal officers in South Carolina had resigned their posts, that the state legislature had called for an early election and convention to consider secession, and that other Southern states were also talking about secession. Like other Republicans, Chase questioned whether the Southern newspaper editors advocating secession represented more than a minority of their readers and doubted that the secessionists would follow through on their threats. So he was not much concerned at first, writing to Illinois senator Lyman Trumbull on November 12 that "no disunion need create alarm except the disunion of the Republican Party."[3]

In late November Chase received a letter from his late wife's sister Ruhamah Ludlow Hunt, wife of a prominent lawyer in New Orleans. Seeing that Chase would probably be a member of the Lincoln Cabinet, she wrote to ask for some reassuring statement from Chase that she might publish in the New Orleans papers. Chase responded that he deplored disunion and that if he were president, he would "expend every expedient of forbearance consistent with safety." In the next sentence, however, he said that "the laws of the Union should be enforced, through the judiciary where practicable, but against rebellion by all necessary means." Chase did not say—perhaps he did not yet realize—that when the slave states seceded, they would insist that the federal laws, notably the federal tariff laws, did not apply within their borders. Enforcing the laws of the Union "by all necessary means" would then lead to armed conflict between the seceded states and the federal government. Chase suggested that the slave states should recognize, after the Republican election victory, that they would not be able to extend slavery and create more slave states. "Disunion, certainly, is not extension. Disunion, rather, is abolition, and abolition through civil and servile war, which God forbid!" Chase did offer one olive branch: to solve the fugitive slave question, he suggested federal compensation for those whose slaves escaped, explaining that Southerners did not really want the return of rebellious slaves, and Northerners could not really return fugitives to slavery. Compensation would make Southern masters whole without offending Northern consciences. Ruhamah Hunt did not publish the letter, explaining to Chase that there was nothing in it that would allay Southern fears.[4]

In his message to Congress in early December, Buchanan blamed Chase and other Northern agitators for the current secession crisis. "The incessant and violent agitation of the slavery question throughout the North for the last quarter of a century has at length produced its malign influence on the slaves and inspired them with vague notions of freedom," he claimed. Southern masters now feared that their slaves, influenced by Republican agitation, would rise up in revolt, and it was this fear that led them toward secession. Buchanan did not believe that states had the right to secede, but, in the next breath, he said that there was nothing the federal government could do to prevent secession. "Poor old imbecile Buchanan, or accursed old traitor Buchanan, I don't know which he is," Chase wrote to his friend Elizabeth Wirt Goldsborough.[5]

Chase had not encouraged his friend Fogg to see Lincoln, but Fogg went in any case, visiting Springfield in early December and then stopping in Columbus to see Chase on his way back east. Fogg then reported by letter to Lincoln that Chase would give the incoming administration "every aid in his power" but would prefer to remain in the Senate rather than take a seat in the Cabinet. Fogg told the president-elect that he had "little doubt that [Chase] will be compelled to see his duty in the acceptance of a position as your constitutional adviser, should you ultimately decide—as I think you will—that no other man can bring to your aid and to the aid of the country the same amount of character, strength, and confidence."[6]

While Buchanan was fretting in Washington and Lincoln forming his Cabinet in Springfield, other leaders proposed compromises. Senator John Crittenden suggested several constitutional amendments, one of which would protect slavery in all territory "now held or hereafter acquired" south of the Missouri Compromise line. Senator Seward also proposed a constitutional amendment providing that no further amendment could "authorize or give to Congress any power to abolish or interfere, within any state, with the domestic institutions thereof, including that of persons held to labor or service by the laws of said state." Seward's friend Weed, in the *Albany Evening Journal,* suggested that Congress should simply legislate to restore the Missouri Compromise line.[7]

Chase was utterly opposed to any such compromise. He drafted, but it seems did not publish, a point by point response to Weed's editorials. He wrote to Fogg that the Northern people wanted Congress to leave the "business of Union saving alone and just attend to the business of legislation." Congress should "admit Kansas, pass the tariff bill . . . pass the homestead bill and enact whatever laws may be necessary to enforce existing laws"—and not waste time on possible compromises. He wrote to Seward that he did not "like the idea of any propositions for adjustment" at this time. "Necessary legislation promptly acted on and tranquil resolution to meet responsibilities when they devolve on us . . . seem to me to comprehend the whole duty of Republicans just now."[8]

During December, press attention turned toward the harbor of Charleston, South Carolina, where about a hundred federal soldiers, under Major Robert Anderson, were holding one federal fort and leaving two other forts more or less unguarded. When Anderson requested more troops, and Buchanan refused, Secretary of State Lewis Cass resigned in protest, and there were reports that General in Chief Winfield Scott would also resign. The secession of South Carolina on December 20 did not make much stir in the North because it was widely expected. What did make a stir was the news that Anderson had quietly moved his troops on the night of December 26 from Fort Moultrie (on a sandy peninsula and thus vulnerable) to Fort Sumter (on an island and thus supposedly "impregnable"). Southerners were outraged and claimed that Anderson's movement was a violation of a pledge by Buchanan not to strengthen the federal position in Charleston Harbor. The *Ohio State Journal* predicted on December 29 that Buchanan, the "imbecile old traitor," would probably surrender Fort Sumter to the rebels. In that case, the paper said, Scott would surely resign his commission.[9]

This was the background for a remarkable December 29 letter from Chase to Scott, condemning Buchanan for meeting with representatives of the rebel state of South Carolina and for even considering the surrender of Fort Sumter. "Rebellion is treason until successful—which God forbid! for successful rebellion must needs be followed, and followed with swift steps, by civil and servile war." Chase reminded Scott that he had the same army rank as George Washington. "Preserve the Union which he established. Sustain Major Anderson. Reinforce him, if necessary. Permit no obedience, by any officer under your command, to any order of the president or secretary, requiring the surrender of posts or stores to rebels or traitors." Chase knew that he was asking Scott to disregard the usual military deference to civilian authority, but in the present crisis, Chase viewed as paramount "the higher and holier duty of maintaining the Union." General Scott did not have to face the choice that Chase feared, for Buchanan did not order the surrender of Fort Sumter. Indeed, early in the new year, pressed by Scott and Northern Cabinet members, Buchanan ordered an unsuccessful attempt to reinforce Anderson at Fort Sumter.[10]

On January 2, 1861, Chase received a letter from Lincoln. "In these troublous times, I would like a conference with you," the president-elect wrote. "Please come visit me at once." The times were indeed troublous. Two days later, the day that Chase arrived in Springfield, the headlines in the local *Illinois State Journal* announced "Startling News! War Commenced!" The telegraphic report claimed that South Carolina forces, from Fort Moultrie, were firing artillery shells upon Major Anderson and the federal troops in Fort Sumter. This account would soon prove false, but other reports, such as that the governors of Georgia and Alabama had seized the federal forts on their coasts—without even waiting for secession votes—would prove correct. Indeed, over the first two weeks of the new year, governors in the Lower South would seize almost all the federal forts, arsenals, and customshouses in their states, shifting both the military balance of power and the political balance of the secession debate. Formal approval of secession, in state-by-state secession conventions, would follow soon thereafter: in Mississippi on January 9, in Florida on January 10, in Alabama on January 11, in Georgia on January 19, and in Louisiana on January 26.[11]

Not long after Chase arrived, Lincoln called upon him at his Springfield hotel. It was the first time that the two men had met, and both were favorably impressed. In a letter to a friend, Chase praised the president-elect's "ability, sincerity, fidelity to political principle, and absolute integrity of character." In another letter, Chase wrote that Lincoln was "a genuine patriot of the old school and loves the country and the cause with the devotion of a son." Lincoln wrote to one of his friends to commend Chase's "ability, firmness, and purity of character." Henry Villard, the

Springfield correspondent this winter for the *New York Herald,* reported that while Chase was in town, Lincoln spent most of his time with his visitor and "improved every opportunity to manifest the high regard he entertained for, and the implicit confidence he placed in the counsels of, the distinguished Ohio statesman." On Sunday morning, for example, Lincoln invited Chase to join him and his wife, Mary, in their pew at the local Presbyterian church, where they heard what another member of the congregation described as "a most excellent sermon."[12]

According to Villard, the main purpose of the meetings between Chase and Lincoln was to confer about the national situation. Villard reported that Chase and Lincoln were not inclined to concession or compromise. This was not "from any feelings of hostility towards the South, but from the conviction that the cotton states are determined to go out of the Union, no matter what peace offerings in the form of Northern concessions may be offered to them." Chase and Lincoln also talked about the possibility that the legislatures of Ohio and Illinois would adopt what Villard called "strong and explicit Union resolutions" and "prepare for the necessity of maintaining the Republican administration and the federal laws . . . by getting their militia systems into working order."[13]

The two men also talked about the Cabinet. Lincoln told Chase that Seward had privately accepted his offer to appoint him secretary of state. The president-elect hoped that Chase would fill the second most prestigious post in the Cabinet, as secretary of the Treasury, both because of his respect for Chase and to create balance between factions: Seward was the leader of the former Whigs, and Chase, of the former Democrats. But Lincoln was not prepared to make Chase an offer quite yet. One complication was Simon Cameron, who had visited Springfield a few days before Chase, and to whom Lincoln had given a letter promising him a senior post, either at the head of the Treasury or the War Department. Lincoln soon received angry letters and visitors telling him that he could not appoint the corrupt Cameron, and Lincoln now regretted making Cameron the written offer. He told Chase that he had just sent Cameron a letter rescinding the prior offer, but that he did not yet know whether Cameron would yield gracefully. (Cameron would not yield but instead insist upon what he viewed as his rightful reward.) The other complication, Lincoln explained to Chase, was Pennsylvania more generally: Would the many protectionists in that state accept Chase, supposedly in favor of free trade, as the head of the department in charge of tariff policy? Lincoln tried to assure Chase that, if he could overcome these obstacles, he would make him secretary of the Treasury.[14]

In a letter to George Opdyke, a friend and future mayor of New York City, Chase wrote that his own "disinclination to enter the Cabinet at all— well known to you—was not, as you may readily conceive, at all abated by this expression of Mr. Lincoln's contingent wish that I should do so; and I frankly said to him that I desired no position and could not easily reconcile myself to the acceptance of a subordinate one, but should gladly give to his administration, as a senator, all the support which a sincere friend—personal as well as political—could give." By the time Chase left Springfield on Monday, January 7, however, he had softened and warmed to Lincoln. They each agreed to consider the matter further. As Chase put it to Illinois congressman Elihu Washburne, nothing "was decided firmly, but the matter was left open for further reflection on both sides."[15]

There is evidence pointing both ways as to whether Chase wanted to be part of the Lincoln administration. Right after his trip to Illinois, Chase urged Opdyke and Barney, former Democrats who were now Republicans, to go to Springfield and "discuss everything frankly and unreservedly" with Lincoln, especially the "proper financial and economic policy of the administration." Chase feared that "unless this be done, those views will have no effective representation in administration councils unless [Gideon] Welles or [Amos] Tuck have a seat, which is not certain." This certainly suggests that Chase was pressing Lincoln (through Opdyke and Barney) to place him in charge of the "financial and economic policy of the administration." Yet, at almost the same time, Chase wrote Francis Blair, another former Democrat, that he was "indisposed to take" the Treasury position but would do so if Blair and other leaders thought he should. In even stronger terms, Chase wrote John Jay to ask whether he would "be willing to take charge of a broken-down department, as a member of a Cabinet with which you could not be sure of six months' agreement, and enslave yourself to the most toilsome drudging almost without respite for four years, exchanging a position from which you could speak freely to the country during half the year and during the other half retire to books [and] travel?" Perhaps Chase both wanted and dreaded the position of Treasury secretary.[16]

When the newspapers confirmed that William Seward would indeed be secretary of state, Chase congratulated him heartily. "The post is yours by right, and you will honor the post." Chase also urged Seward to proceed cautiously in the Senate speech he was about to make. "To me, it seems all important that no compromise now be made . . . but that the people of the slave states and all the states be plainly told that the Republicans have no propositions to make at present." If Seward received this letter before his speech—and the timing suggests that he did not—he ignored it, for his highly anticipated and widely reported speech placed him squarely on the side of compromise. Chase especially deplored Seward's suggestions for "constitutional guarantees to slavery in the states" and (in violation of the Chicago platform and, indeed, every Republican platform) for opening "the whole of Arizona and New Mexico to slavery."[17]

The papers were also reporting that Lincoln was likely to give a place in his Cabinet to Caleb Smith, another politician with a tarnished reputation. Chase wrote Lincoln to advise him that Smith's "reputation has been so seriously affected by his railroad and other transactions that his appointment to a place in your Cabinet would impair the credit and endanger the success of your administration." Chase assured Lincoln that he had nothing against Smith personally; he was a strong speaker for the Republican cause. But Chase reminded Lincoln that the Chicago convention had selected Lincoln rather than Seward in large part because of confidence that Lincoln would give the nation a clean administration—and fears that Seward and Weed would not. It was vital for Lincoln to follow through on the promise of good government. Lincoln did not respond to this letter, and when he finally appointed his Cabinet, on the day after his inauguration, he would include both Cameron and Smith.[18]

In another letter, sent through a friend, Chase explained to Lincoln why Republicans should not discuss compromise before inauguration. The secessionists were trying to "precipitate revolution and, in order to effect their object, misrepresent to the people of the slave states the objects and purposes of the Republicans." The only effective way to refute their claims was "through the inauguration and action of a Republican administration." Once Lincoln was in office, "I am sure the deceived people of the South will soon be brought to a temper of mind in which they will fairly consider fair propositions of adjustment, and I believe that propositions can be made, which, if not acceptable to the politicians, will be acceptable to and accepted by a large majority of the people and of the slaveholders of the slave states." Rather than discuss compromise, Chase believed it would be far more useful for Congress to pass legislation so that the states that had not yet selected House representatives for the next Congress would do so in early March. This would allow Lincoln, after the inauguration, to call Congress into a special session in March or April rather than waiting for the customary December gathering.[19]

Writing to Charles Sumner on January 26, Chase set out what he called his "motto" for the secession winter: "inauguration first, adjustment afterwards." He repeated the phrase in a letter to Lincoln two days later, in which he warned that the Republican Party would lose in the fall elections in Ohio and elsewhere "if the pledge given at Chicago is violated by the passing of an enabling act for the admission of New Mexico as a slave state" or if Republicans voted to approve the Crittenden constitutional amendment. What especially worried Chase were the reports from Washington that Lincoln approved of such compromises. Chase urged Lincoln to advise his friends "that you desire the adoption of no compromise measure before the Republicans become charged with the responsibility of administration through your inauguration. Inauguration first, adjustment afterwards." Chase shared his motto with an editor, and soon it was in all the leading Republican newspapers, often in the prominent place usually reserved for the names of candidates.[20]

As Southern states seceded, most of their representatives in Congress resigned their places, often with elaborate farewell speeches. Most but not all: Andrew Johnson, Democratic senator from Tennessee, refused to resign and denounced secession. Chase noticed his speech, writing Johnson to compare him favorably with Andrew Jackson. Since the departing Southerners were almost all Democrats, Republicans gained control of the Senate and passed in late January the bill to admit Kansas to the Union. The free state of Kansas, of which Chase had dreamed and for which he had worked so hard, was at last a reality. He rejoiced.[21]

As perhaps the most prominent Northern opponent of compromise, Chase would seem a curious choice to send to a national compromise convention, but that is just what happened in February 1861. The legislature of Virginia had issued a call in January for all the states to send delegates to a convention in Washington to make an "earnest effort to adjust the present unhappy controversies." The legislature of Ohio, like several others, hesitated over whether to send delegates but finally resolved to send a delegation, with instructions to seek an adjournment of the convention until April. On the last day of January, Governor Dennison named a delegation of seven men, headed by Chase but composed mainly of conservatives. Chase was not at all enthused. He wrote to Joshua Giddings that there was not another man on the delegation from whom he could "expect any cordial sympathy in resistance to the surrender of our principles." He was inclined "to decline the appointment but fear doing so will make bad worse." Chase wrote another correspondent that "our friends insist on my going, and I have determined to do so, though I would rather go anywhere else." Leaving Columbus almost at once, Chase arrived in Washington in time for the first day of the convention, February 4.[22]

About sixty men gathered that day in Willard's Hall, a lovely little former church that was now part of Willard's Hotel, to start work as delegates to what the papers were calling the Peace Convention. There were delegates from some slave states, including Virginia, but none from the seven states that had already seceded. Indeed, delegates from six of those states were meeting this same day in Montgomery, Alabama, to draft the constitution for what they called a new nation, the Confederate States of America, and to select a new president, Jefferson Davis. Nor were there any delegates at the Washington conference from some of the most ardent Republican states, such as Michigan, Minnesota, and Wisconsin. But by the end of the convention, twenty-two states *were* represented, and many of the delegates were distinguished. They included former president John Tyler, nineteen former governors, fourteen former senators, and fifty former members of the House. Many delegates were or would become friends of Chase's, including Senator William Fessenden of Maine. Most delegates stayed at Willard's Hotel, leading the *Washington Evening Star* to boast that "probably there were never before collected at any one time together under a single roof so many men of note."[23]

On the evening of February 4, Chase's friend James Shepherd Pike organized a meeting of about twenty Republican members of Congress, all opposed to Seward's inclusion in the Cabinet. Fogg attended and reported to Lincoln that Seward "would insist on being master of the administration and would utterly scorn the idea of playing a subordinate part." Seward was supposedly so eager to compromise, Fogg added, that he would give up "every principle to which yourself and the Republican Party stand pledged." Moreover, Seward and Cameron were reportedly talking about forming a new political party—"a Union Party, or something of the kind." It is hard to imagine that Chase was not aware, at least to some extent, of his friends' efforts to exclude Seward from the

Cabinet. Their campaign continued while Chase and the other delegates worked in the Peace Convention. In mid-February, for example, a British diplomat in Washington reported to London that "a not inconsiderable portion of the Republican Party are disposed to urge Mr. Lincoln to discard Mr. Seward altogether, on account of the disposition he has already manifested to abandon the extreme antislavery principles of the party."[24]

The rules of the 1861 Peace Convention, adopted on February 6, were based on those of the 1787 Constitutional Convention. Voting would be by states, and delegates were supposed to keep their discussions confidential. Some men must have violated this rule, for there were daily newspaper reports about the convention, although the stories were often erroneous. On this same day, the convention appointed a committee, headed by James Guthrie of Kentucky, and including one member from each state, to try to devise a compromise proposal. Chase was not included on this committee; the far more malleable Thomas Ewing would represent Ohio. Chase wrote to a friend on February 9 that "there is a greater disposition to compromise than I would like to see." He and the other delegates from Ohio entertained that evening a half dozen delegates from North Carolina and other states divided between unionists and secessionists. "I really sympathize with them," Chase wrote about the Unionists, "but see no reason why we should sacrifice permanently a large power to help them, for the purpose of gaining a little one."[25]

As Chase and other Republicans counted votes in the Washington convention, they worried that a combination of the Southerners and compromising Northerners would outvote them. They decided to seek delegates from the Republican states that were not yet represented. Chase sent a telegram to the governor of Michigan, suggesting that the state should authorize its two Republican senators to represent it in the convention. Somehow the telegram reached the Democratic press in Michigan, where it elicited predictable outrage. In the end, only one Republican state, the new state of Kansas, would heed Chase's call for additional delegates for the Peace Convention.[26]

The Guthrie proposal, when it finally emerged from the committee on February 15, advocated a seven-point amendment to the Constitution. The first and most important article would divide all the remaining federal territory along the Missouri Compromise line, protecting slavery south of the line and forbidding slavery north of the line. A second section, echoing the Whig position of "no more territory" during the Mexican

War, would make it much more difficult for the United States to acquire territory: by requiring the approval of four-fifths of the Senate for any such treaty. A lengthy third section would preclude Congress from interfering with slavery in the slave states, or from abolishing slavery in the District of Columbia, or from prohibiting the interstate slave trade. Section four would allow states (as well as the federal government) to enforce the Fugitive Slave Clause, and section five would prohibit forever the African slave trade. Section six was designed to protect these provisions from any *later* constitutional amendment, and section seven ensured compensation for masters whose slaves escaped due to "violence or intimidation." Chase, of course, opposed the Guthrie proposal.[27]

For the next twelve days, the Washington convention debated the Guthrie proposal, as well as several amendments and alternatives, and various procedural points. There was a brief pause on February 23, the day that Lincoln reached Washington at dawn, having slipped through Baltimore in the dead of night to evade an assassination plot. That evening, as some papers mocked Lincoln for wearing a disguise on his way through Baltimore, and other papers argued that he had rightly feared assassination, the delegates gathered at Willard's to meet the president-elect. For some reason, it fell to Chase to introduce Lincoln to each of the delegates, perhaps because Chase was the most senior Republican member of the Conference. Lincoln was especially warm toward the Southerners, telling one man whom he recalled from their days together in the House that "you cannot be a disunionist, unless your nature has changed since we met in Congress." Over the next few days, Lincoln spent much of his time with Seward; he saw Chase once or twice, but nowhere near as often.[28]

Chase made his main speech in the convention on February 26, in support of an alternative offered by his friend Amos Tuck: a set of resolutions in which the delegates would confirm their belief that Congress could not interfere with slavery in the slave states and suggest that the states should call a constitutional convention to meet after Lincoln's inauguration. Chase warned the Southern delegates that even if the convention adopted the Guthrie proposal, the Northern states would reject it, for the same reason that they had just elected Lincoln. Tuck's proposal simply asked the Southern delegates to "say to your people that we of the free states have no purpose, and never had any purpose, to infringe the rights of the slave states, or of any citizen of the slave states." Chase closed by reminding his colleagues that Lincoln would take his oath of office on

March 4. "That oath will bind him to take care that the laws be faithfully executed throughout the United States. Will secession absolve him from that oath? Will it diminish, by one jot or tittle, its awful obligation?" If the president did his constitutional duty, "and secession or revolution resists, what then? War! Civil war!"[29]

Chase's plea to replace the Guthrie proposal with the Tuck proposal failed. But later that afternoon, the first article of the Guthrie proposal also failed, with eight states in favor and eleven states against. The delegates adjourned for the remainder of the day and talked among themselves; some sources suggest that Lincoln pressed some of the delegates to vote for the Guthrie proposal. In any case, on the next morning, February 27, with some shifts in the votes, and one critical absence, the first article was approved, by a vote of nine states against eight. The other Guthrie articles were also approved, one by one, with Ohio voting in favor, and Chase dissenting each time. When all the articles had been approved, Chase moved for a vote on the whole proposal, hoping that perhaps the different coalitions that had supported the separate articles would not be able to unite to approve the whole package. Acting as chairman, former president Tyler ruled Chase's motion out of order. The Peace Convention soon closed and dispersed, with the *Washington Evening Star* hailing its "glorious" work.[30]

The next step for the convention's proposal was on Capitol Hill, where it faced long odds. Before Congress can propose a constitutional amendment to the states, two-thirds of each house of Congress must approve the amendment. With just a few days left in the congressional session, and with both Northern Republicans and Southern Democrats opposed to the Guthrie proposal, it soon became clear that the convention's proposal had no chance in Congress, much less in the states. Both sides of Congress were working, however, on a different constitutional amendment known as the Seward amendment or the Corwin amendment, because Chase's rival Thomas Corwin was its main proponent in the House. The Corwin amendment was far shorter and simpler than the Guthrie proposal: it stated that "no amendment shall be made to the Constitution which will authorize or give to Congress the power to abolish or interfere, within any state, with the domestic institutions thereof, including that of persons held to labor or service by the laws of said state." Chase opposed the Corwin amendment because he did not want to rule out the possibility that, at some point in the future, Congress and the states would amend the Constitution to prohibit slavery. Moreover, Chase still viewed concessions as premature; his approach was still "inauguration first, adjustment afterwards."[31]

The newspapers in late February and early March were filled with rumors and predictions about Lincoln's Cabinet. Most of the published lists were headed by Seward as secretary of state, Chase as secretary of the Treasury, and Simon Cameron as secretary of war. But there was doubt even as to these names, especially Cameron. The *New York Times* reported on February 25 that "the opposition to Senator Cameron's occupying a place in the Cabinet was formally withdrawn at Philadelphia while Mr. Lincoln was there" and that Cameron would go into "the Treasury or the War Department." The *New York Herald* of February 28 disagreed, reporting that there was still strong resistance to Cameron's having any place whatsoever in the Lincoln Cabinet: "The fight which has been going on today between the friends of Cameron and Chase is most terrific." And according to the *Washington Evening Star* of March 1, a majority of Senate Republicans had demanded that Lincoln give Chase the Treasury Department, and Lincoln had agreed because Chase had promised that "his friends will cordially support the administration even though it be conservative on the great question of the times." Lincoln himself, on or about March 1, compiled a list of Republican senators and their preferences, noting that most of them favored Chase for Treasury. Both Thurlow Weed and Horace Greeley were in Washington, with Weed pushing for Seward and Greeley advocating for Chase. The *New-York Tribune* reported that Weed was "denouncing Chase" and telling people that if he was appointed, "the nation would fail." As late as March 3, the evening before the inauguration, there were rumors that "Chase would be dropped, and John Sherman selected in his stead" to head the Treasury Department.[32]

In the midst of all this Cabinet commotion, Elbridge Spaulding, a Republican congressman from upstate New York, hosted a dinner for Lincoln at the National Hotel. Almost all those named most often in the papers as likely members of Lincoln's Cabinet were present: Seward, Chase, Cameron, Bates, Smith, and Montgomery Blair, who would become postmaster general. Various congressional leaders were also guests, including Charles Francis Adams, John Sherman, and Elihu Washburne. "The affair was very elegant and highly intellectual," the *New York Herald* commented. Adams, however, disagreed, writing in his diary that the dinner was "quite formal and a little dull."[33]

When Charles Dana wrote to congratulate Chase on his new post at the head of the Treasury, Chase responded tartly on March 1: "I am not secretary of the Treasury, nor do I know that I shall be. Rumor has it that Mr. Lincoln will tender me the appointment. If he does, I shall *consider* the question of acceptance." Chase asked Dana to inform the readers of the *New-York Tribune* that the Treasury position was one "which I do not want and which I shall not take except, if at all, with extreme reluctance." As requested, the *Tribune* printed an article along these lines a few days later, saying that Chase would rather be in the Senate. The paper also published, at Chase's request, Tuck's proposal to the Peace Conference, and Chase's explanation of why it failed.[34]

Inauguration Day, Monday, March 4, "opened cloudy and cheerless," according to one correspondent, but at about nine o'clock, "the sun broke forth bright and glorious." Chase surely started the day, as he did almost every day, with private prayer. At about eleven, he went to the familiar Senate chamber, where the first Senate session of the Thirty-Seventh Congress would start at noon. The senators who were also part of the Thirty-Sixth Congress were dead tired, for they had worked through the night, barely passing the Corwin constitutional amendment at about five o'clock. Many House members were present informally, but Congress had not passed the legislation suggested by Chase to move forward election dates, so the lower chamber could not meet formally for at least a few months. At noon, Chase and the other new senators stepped forward in turn to take their oaths of office. Then, at about one, Lincoln and Buchanan entered the Senate arm in arm. A procession was formed, headed by the marshal of the District of Columbia and including the members of the Senate. They all marched out to take their places on the temporary wooden platform erected over the steps on the east side of the Capitol. A cheering crowd of thousands filled the open space in front of them, and over their heads loomed the building's half-finished new dome, still under construction.[35]

In accordance with the custom at the time, Lincoln gave his inaugural address before taking his oath of office. Chase, sitting among the other senators, probably could not hear much of what Lincoln said. But Chase surely heard the applause at some of Lincoln's key lines, such as when he declared that he would "take care, as the Constitution itself expressly enjoins upon me, that the laws of the Union shall be faithfully executed in all the states," and then added a few lines later that he would use "the power confided to me" in order to "hold, occupy, and possess the property and places belonging to the government and to collect the duties and imposts." Chase would *not* have liked a few sentences in which Lincoln blessed the Corwin amendment, saying that he viewed it as already implied in the Constitution and would "have no objection to its being made express and irrevocable." Lincoln closed with an emotional plea: "We are not enemies, but friends. We must not be enemies. The mystic chords of memory, stretching from every battlefield, and patriot grave, to every living heart and hearthstone, all over this broad land, will yet swell the chorus of Union, when again touched, as surely they will be, by the better angels of our nature."[36]

Chase's daughters, Nettie and Kate, probably about 1860.

That night, Chase and his daughter Kate were part of the crowd at the inaugural ball, held in a temporary structure adjoining the city hall. Kate, now twenty, and Nettie, thirteen, had arrived in Washington not long before this; the family was staying at the Rugby House, a small residential hotel near the White House. Nettie was not too impressed by Washington; she would recall "the enormously wide avenues literally flowing with yellow mud" and the "miserable little houses and shops, with here and there a good building standing up in stately contrast." Kate, resplendent in a white satin gown with an overskirt of cherry silk and a crown of woven roses, turned many heads at the ball. Lincoln and his wife, Mary, did not arrive until after eleven, at which point the dancing stopped, and the band played "Hail to the Chief." The guests "danced, talked, flirted, chatted [and] supped most bounteously," in the words of the *New York Times*. Even as late as midnight, according to the *New York Herald*, there were still "rumors of a change in the Cabinet," and "Chase is again said to be uncertain."[37]

The next afternoon, Chase was in his place in the Senate to hear the opening prayer at one o'clock. After a bit of routine business, Lincoln's senior private secretary, John Nicolay, arrived with a message nominating all seven members of the Cabinet, including Chase for Treasury. The clerks cleared the public from the galleries, and the Senate went into executive session, but, according to the *Chicago Tribune,* it was all over in five minutes, with the entire slate confirmed. Chase wrote three years later that he was not in the Senate chamber when his nomination arrived "and knew nothing of it until a few minutes afterwards, when, returning to my place, I was informed that it had been unanimously confirmed." Chase recalled that he "went at once to the president and expressed my disinclination to accept the position. After some conversation, in the course of which he referred to the embarrassment which my declination would occasion him, I said I would give the matter some further consideration and advise him the next day of my conclusion. Some rumor of my hesitation got abroad, and I was immediately pressed by most urgent remonstrances against any declination on my part. I finally yielded to this and surrendered a position every way more desirable to me, to take charge of the finances of the country under circumstances most unpropitious and forbidding."[38]

Chase was probably right to recall meeting with Lincoln, but perhaps not about the "rumor of my hesitation," for there was nothing about such a rumor in the papers. What the papers *did* report was that Chase met both Tuesday and Wednesday with John Dix, who was serving as Treasury secretary for the last few weeks of the Buchanan administration, and that Chase would take over at Treasury on Thursday. Writing to Lincoln late on Wednesday, Chase said that he doubted his "ability to perform adequately the duties about to devolve on me" but would "give my best endeavor to your service and our country's." He expressed similar concerns when he wrote Dennison to resign his Senate seat, saying that Lincoln had called him "to another sphere of duty, more laborious, more arduous, and fuller far of perplexing responsibilities. I sought to avoid it and would now gladly decline it, if I might. I find it, however, impossible to do so without seeming to shrink from cares and labors for the common good which cannot honorably be shunned." On the morning of Thursday, March 7, in a quiet ceremony at the Treasury Department, Chase took another oath and entered another sphere of duty.[39]

CHAPTER 15

"We Have the War upon Us"

✻ 1861 ✻

By modern standards, Chase did not have the right résumé to be Secretary of the Treasury, for he had not headed a major financial institution. Some scholars have even claimed that "Chase had almost no knowledge of business or finance." In fact, he had more financial experience than other nineteenth-century Treasury secretaries, most of whom were lawyers and political leaders, not financiers. Chase had served not merely as an outside lawyer for several banks but also as an internal manager of the Lafayette Bank, and he had helped Ohio extricate itself from its 1857 financial crisis. As the papers speculated on Lincoln's Cabinet and named Chase as the probable Treasury secretary, none argued that he was not qualified. Those who opposed his nomination did so because he was, in their view, an abolitionist.[1]

Even the most experienced financier would have hesitated to take over the Treasury in March 1861, for the federal finances were in terrible shape. In the early 1850s the federal government had received about $60 million to $70 million in revenue each year, almost all of it in the form of import duties. There was no income tax; there was no Internal Revenue Service, so most of the department's four thousand employees worked at customshouses, ranging from the immense customshouse in New York City to tiny offices in places such as Passamaquoddy, Maine. Federal expenditures more or less equaled federal revenues, and in many fiscal years there was a slight surplus. In the late 1850s, however, revenues declined as a result of the recession, while expenditures increased under Buchanan. The Treasury borrowed to cover the deficits, with the result that total federal debt increased from $28 million at the outset of the Buchanan administration to more than $76 million at the start of the Lincoln administration. The Treasury had to pay ever-higher interest rates, and much of the debt was in the form of short-term notes that would come due soon. Secretary Dix reported to Congress in February 1861 that he had only about $500,000 in the Treasury and that he expected bills for almost $10 million to come due in the next few weeks. Lucius Chittenden, a senior official in the department, recalled that when Chase took over the Treasury, "there was not enough money left in its vaults to pay for the daily consumption of stationery; no city dealer would furnish it on credit."[2]

Chase had no ability to increase revenues or decrease expenditures, at least not in the short term. His only option was to borrow, and even here his choices were limited. Unlike a modern Treasury secretary, who can issue Treasury bills for a few days or Treasury bonds payable over thirty years, Chase could issue only two types of debt: twenty-year bonds paying interest at 6 percent or two-year notes paying 7 percent interest. On March 22, Chase advertised to seek bids for $8 million worth of twenty-year bonds. When he and his assistants opened the bids on April 2, they were disappointed that many were at deep discounts; bankers were demanding a high interest rate in light of the weak federal finances and the prospect of civil war. Chase decided to accept only bids at 94 cents on the dollar and above, selling $3.1 million in bonds in this way and raising the remainder by selling two-year notes at par. The *New York Herald*, reflecting the view of the bankers, criticized Chase: "His refusal to accept bids below 94 will probably keep the Treasury in a comparatively depleted state for some time." When John Jay also questioned this approach, Chase responded heatedly that he had "a clear duty to decline bids so far below par, as were most of those received."[3]

By March 1861, seven slave states had seceded and declared themselves an independent nation. These states had seized the federal forts and facilities within their borders, with two notable exceptions: Fort Sumter, in Charleston Harbor, South Carolina, and Fort Pickens, on an offshore island near Pensacola, Florida. Eight slave states were still part of the Union: Arkansas, Delaware, Kentucky, Maryland, Missouri, North Carolina, Tennessee, and Virginia. Each one was debating whether to secede, and many of their leaders said that they *would* secede if the federal government tried to "coerce" the seceded states. This was why Lincoln, in his inaugural address, had stressed that there would be "no invasion, no using of force against or among the people anywhere." But there was a tension, if not a contradiction, between this assurance and Lincoln's promise that he would enforce the laws of the Union throughout the Union and would hold on to the few remaining Southern federal forts.[4]

Fort Sumter had been in the news often in the first few weeks of the year, but none of the reports suggested that the federal troops there faced serious supply shortages. Lincoln was thus surprised, almost incensed, to learn on the day after his inauguration that Major Anderson and his men there were almost out of food and water. It is not clear when Chase learned of the Sumter supply crisis, but it was not later than March 9, when the whole Cabinet heard a grim report from General Winfield Scott. Lincoln and his Cabinet now faced difficult questions. Should they attempt an armed supply mission, knowing that this might lead to conflict in

Winfield Scott, commanding general of the Union armies at the outset of the Civil War.

Charleston and provoke some of the border states to secede? Or should they order Anderson to surrender Fort Sumter, which was, after all, difficult to defend in the midst of a hostile harbor? But if they did order the surrender of the fort—the most visible symbol of the Union in the South—how would the North, especially ardent Republicans, react?[5]

On March 15 Lincoln asked each Cabinet member for a written opinion on whether the government should attempt to send supplies to Fort Sumter. Most advised against any such undertaking, but Chase disagreed. He recognized the possibility that a supply mission could lead to conflict and further secession. He thought the risks acceptable, however, if Lincoln explained in advance that he was merely "maintaining a fort belonging to the United States" and "supporting the officers and men engaged, in the regular course of service, in its defense." Lincoln did not make any immediate decision about Fort Sumter, other than that he would not yet order Major Anderson to surrender and that he would attempt to gather more information about the military and political situations in South Carolina.[6]

On March 18 Lincoln asked Chase for information about the effects of secession on the federal revenues. As the Southern states seceded, they seized the customshouses in their ports; they were still collecting tariffs but not sending any of the revenue to the federal government, instead keeping it for their own purposes. Lincoln asked Chase for details about this missing tariff revenue and for his views on whether it would be practicable for the Treasury, either alone or in cooperation with the navy, to collect the federal tariffs offshore.[7]

Chase responded that the Treasury was not receiving any revenue or, indeed, any information from the seven seceded states. He estimated the annual revenue loss at about $3.5 million. That figure would only increase if, as some papers were predicting, trade patterns shifted, with ships going to Confederate ports in order to avoid higher federal duties and with goods being smuggled up rivers and into the United States. Chase believed an offshore fleet could collect the duties "with a considerable degree of completeness" if ships were posted near each of the principal Confederate ports: Charleston; New Orleans; Mobile, Alabama; Savannah, Georgia; and Galveston, Texas. The Treasury Department had eleven small ships, called revenue cutters, suitable for this service, although some of them would need to have more guns mounted. Chase did not mention, for Lincoln knew as well as anyone, that armed Northern attempts to stop ships and collect federal taxes outside Southern ports would lead to conflicts—and probably, at some point, to civil war.[8]

On March 28 Lincoln and his wife hosted their first formal dinner at the White House, gathering the Cabinet, a few members of Congress, and their spouses or other family members. The seating chart, prepared by John Nicolay, shows about thirty people arranged around the long table, with Chase sitting between Ellen Hamlin, wife of Vice President Hannibal Hamlin, and Lucinda Kellogg, wife of Illinois congressman William Kellogg. William Howard Russell, the famed British war reporter, was especially charmed by Kate Chase, whom he found "attractive, agreeable, and sprightly." Her father impressed him as "one of the most distinguished persons in the whole assemblage: tall, of good presence, with a well-formed head, fine forehead, and a face indicating power and energy." Russell noted "a peculiar droop and motion of the lid of one eye, which seems to have suffered from some injury, that detracts from the agreeable effect of his face." Indeed, Chase had consulted one of the first American ophthalmologists, who advised that there was "an incomplete paralysis of the orbicular or circular muscle that closes the lids" of the right eye, resulting in "chronic inflammation of the eye." The doctor advised that Chase should make "as little use of the eyes as possible, particularly at night." Like many patients, Chase did not follow his doctor's advice, and Russell was probably noticing the effect of some late nights in the first weeks of the administration.[9]

As the dinner guests were leaving, Lincoln asked his Cabinet members to remain. He then briefed them on a letter that he had just received from Scott, advising that the anticipated surrender of Fort Sumter would probably not "have a decisive effect upon the states now wavering between adherence to the Union and secession." The general urged Lincoln to surrender both Fort Sumter and Fort Pickens in order to "give confidence to the eight remaining slave-holding states." After a few seconds of stunned silence, Montgomery Blair said bitterly that Scott was "playing the part of a politician, not the general." The next day, after a further Cabinet briefing on the situation in Charleston, Lincoln again asked the members for written opinions on whether to send supplies to Fort Sumter. Chase now viewed civil war as almost inevitable and hoped that it might start because of "military resistance to the efforts of the administration to sustain troops of the Union stationed, under the authority of the government in a fort of the Union, in the ordinary course of service." Several other Cabinet members agreed with this approach, and Lincoln soon gave orders to prepare a naval expedition to Charleston.[10]

On April 6 Lincoln sent a messenger to Charleston, with instructions to inform the authorities that a naval expedition was heading there to provide supplies—but not troops—to Fort Sumter. When the messenger arrived, word was relayed to Jefferson Davis. The president of the Confederacy decided not to wait for the arrival of the supply ships; he instructed the Confederate general in Charleston to demand the immediate surrender of Fort Sumter. After Anderson refused to capitulate, early on the morning of April 12 the Confederate forces started to rain cannon shells into Fort Sumter. It took some time for news to travel by telegraph from Charleston to Washington, and the first reports were brief, but Chase would have known of the attack on Fort Sumter late on April 12 or early on April 13. By late on the thirteenth, reports had arrived in Washington that Anderson would surrender. As Chase's friend Edwin Stanton, now a leading lawyer in Washington, put it in a letter: "We have the war upon us."[11]

Lincoln and his Cabinet spent most of Sunday, April 14, in consultation. Among other things, they discussed and agreed upon a presidential proclamation calling upon the states for seventy-five thousand ninety-day volunteers to put down the rebellion. Volunteers were needed because the regular army was both small and scattered: only about fifteen thousand men, mainly in distant western forts. Lincoln specified ninety days because that was all that was allowed by the operative law, the Militia Act of 1795. The president's proclamation also called for Congress to meet in special session on July 4, 1861, a date suggested by Chase, to pass the legislation that would be necessary to fund and fight the war. A few days later, Lincoln issued a second proclamation, imposing a blockade upon the ports of the states in secession, and prohibiting any trade with these states. The blockade proclamation raised difficult legal questions, including whether the rebels were entitled to the status of "belligerent" under international law, questions Lincoln and his Cabinet did not quite comprehend yet.[12]

The president's call for volunteers was greeted with cheers in the North and derision in the South. Virginia immediately seceded from the Union and seized both the federal arsenal at Harpers Ferry and the naval yard at Norfolk. Other slave states, including Kentucky and Maryland, hesitated over whether to secede. On the morning of April 19 a Maryland mob attacked Massachusetts troops as they marched from one train station to another in Baltimore. The troops responded with their rifles, and, within minutes, four soldiers and a dozen civilians were dead, and dozens more on both sides were injured. The governor and the mayor, George Brown, sent a joint telegram to Lincoln, pleading with him to send no more "Northern troops" through Baltimore. At an immense rally in the city that afternoon, Brown told the cheering crowd that it was "folly and madness for one part of this great nation" to attempt to "subjugate the other." Brown claimed that even Chase agreed with him that "when independent, peaceful states determined to go out of the Union," the other states should "let them depart in peace." Brown did not explain how he knew Chase's views.[13]

Chase's friend Alphonso Taft, seeing Brown's remarks in the papers, wrote to Chase to ask whether he had really said any such thing. Chase responded that, a month earlier, he had seen only two alternatives: using military force to enforce federal laws in the rebellious states, or "recognizing the organization of actual government by the seven seceded states as an *accomplished revolution*" and "letting that confederacy try its experiment of separation" while "maintaining the authority of the Union and treating secession as treason everywhere *else*." Thinking that the seven states would return "after an unsatisfactory experiment of secession," and knowing that civil war would involve "vast expenditure and oppressive debt," Chase told Taft that he had for a while favored the second alternative. Everything had changed, however, with the attack on Fort Sumter. Now Chase would "insist on the most vigorous measures, not merely for the preservation of the Union and the defense of the government, but for the constitutional reestablishment of both throughout the land."[14]

By late April, Chase was indeed in favor of the "most vigorous measures." The Maryland legislature was about to assemble, and it was widely feared that it would approve a secession ordinance. Chase wrote Lincoln to urge him to arrest the legislators so that they could not assemble and endorse secession. "The passage of that ordinance will be the signal for the entry of disunion forces into Maryland," he warned. "It will give a color of law and regularity to rebellion and thereby triple its strength. The customshouse in Baltimore will be seized, and Fort McHenry attacked—perhaps taken." Lincoln disagreed, writing to General Scott that the legislators had the right to assemble, and "we cannot know in advance that their action will not be lawful and peaceful." Lincoln did instruct Scott to watch closely and act quickly if the legislators attempted "to arm their people against the United States." But when the Maryland legislators gathered, they voted against secession.[15]

For a few days after the Baltimore riot, there was neither railroad nor telegraph service between Washington and the North; the national capital was isolated and almost undefended. Among the first troops to reach Washington, by way of Annapolis rather than Baltimore, was a Rhode Island regiment, accompanied by the state's dashing young governor, William Sprague IV. Mounted on a fine horse, Sprague marched his troops on April 29 from their quarters to the White House, where they passed in review. It was probably at the reception following this review that Chase met for the first time the man who would become Kate's future husband.[16]

John Hay, the second of Lincoln's private secretaries, commented in his diary on this day that Sprague was "a small, insignificant youth, who bought his place" as governor. Sprague was indeed short, about five foot five; and young, thirty; and wealthy, with a reported net worth of almost $10 million (derived from the family's cotton mills in Rhode Island). Sprague used some of this wealth to secure his election in the spring of 1860; one paper estimated that he spent almost $200,000 paying voters as much as $50 each for their support. Sprague was not really a Republican; he was supported by a coalition of conservative Democrats and Republicans, against a straight Republican candidate whom they denounced as an abolitionist. Sprague was also not especially intelligent; Henry Villard said he had "very limited mental capacity," and Sprague himself, in one of his letters, described his mind as "sadly disconnected." Most worrisome of all, from the perspective of a future father-in-law, Sprague drank too much and indulged other passions; it was rumored that the real reason for his recent trip to Europe was that his girl in Rhode Island, Mary Eliza Viall, was pregnant.[17]

Chase did not know all this in the spring of 1861, and he may never have heard about Viall. What he *did* know was that Kate liked Sprague, that she started to spend time with him, and that some papers soon predicted that she would marry him.[18]

Even as they were considering what to do about the Southern forts and the Baltimore riots, Lincoln, Chase, and the other members of the Cabinet devoted the majority of their time in March and April 1861 to selecting and filling federal positions. There were good reasons for this. Chase and other department heads could not do their work without reliable assistants. Most of the important positions required Senate confirmation, and the special session of the Senate would last only a month, until early April. Lincoln was the head of a relatively new political party, enjoying for the first time the right to make federal appointments; he needed to use his patronage power to cement the party together and to reward those who had helped secure his election.[19]

The patronage puzzle had at least four dimensions. Lincoln wanted to spread the rewards among different states, and Cabinet members wanted to secure positions for their own states. Chase illustrated this with a letter to Seward complaining that although Ohio had one-eighth of the national population and an even greater share of the Republican population, it had only received about a dozen of the coveted diplomatic appointments. Lincoln also wanted to be fair to the various factions within the party. A good example of this concern is a letter from Lincoln to Chase, saying that the "great point in favor" of one candidate was that "Thurlow Weed and Horace Greeley join in recommending him. I suppose the like never happened before, and never will again; so that it is now or never. What say you?" Departments were another factor; Chase had more say than others over appointments in the Treasury Department, though not complete control. Finally, there was the question of friends and family, and trying to find suitable positions for those with close personal ties to important Republicans.[20]

The appointment of Chase's younger brother as marshal for the northern district of New York is a good example of the interplay of these dimensions. Edward Chase, a lawyer in the small town of Lockport, New York, had supported the Republicans, but he was far from a leading lawyer or major political power. Salmon Chase, however, believed that his look-alike brother would make a good marshal and secured support from two New York members of Congress and Attorney General Edward Bates. (Although there was no Justice Department yet, the attorney general had more voice than other Cabinet members in appointments of district attorneys and federal marshals.) Seward objected, saying that Chase was merely seeking a personal favor, while Seward was trying to strengthen the party in upstate New York. Chase replied that he would not abandon his brother "or consent that the decision of the attorney general in his favor shall be rescinded." Seward wrote angrily to Lincoln that "when Mr. Chase out of his department demands as a personal favor an appointment in my state humiliating to me, or the attorney general assumes that he can

better determine who should be marshal in the very district in which I
live, the thing becomes a scandal." The issue was solved by a compromise:
Edward Chase would become marshal, and a friend of Seward would be
ambassador to Nicaragua. Chase wrote to John Sherman, recently elevated
from the House to the Senate, to be certain that these two appointments
would be approved in tandem. Edward Chase did not get to enjoy this
prize for long, dying of a sudden stroke the following year.[21]

The single most lucrative position in the federal government was
the collector of customs in New York City. In addition to a salary, the
collector received tens of thousands of dollars each year in fees, and his
subordinates were expected to contribute 2 percent of their salaries to a
political fund controlled by the collector. Seward and his friend Weed
were keen to appoint one of their friends to this powerful position and
were disappointed when Chase managed to get Lincoln to appoint his
friend Hiram Barney. At almost the same time that the president sent the
nomination to the Senate, Barney arranged the private loan that Chase had
requested a few months earlier. The surviving documents are sparse, but it
seems that Barney and his law partner William Allen Butler loaned Chase
$25,000 at an interest rate of 7 percent. By the standards of the time, the
loan was not unusual, but Chase should have found some other way to
raise funds rather than borrow from one of his principal subordinates.[22]

Chase's most important subordinate during the war years was not in
Washington but in New York City, where the assistant treasurer served
as his agent in the nation's financial center. Since 1853, this position had
been filled by John Cisco, a Democrat, and Chase soon decided that he
wanted to keep Cisco rather than replace him with a Republican. Seward,
of course, had hoped to fill this post with one of his friends, but Chase
resisted, writing to Lincoln that "only bad results" would follow a change.
"Mr. Seward ought not to ask you to overrule my deliberate judgment as
to what is best for the department and your administration," he insisted.
Once again Chase prevailed over Seward, and Cisco served the department
ably for the next three years.[23]

When Chase tried to persuade his friend William Mellen to move
from Cincinnati to Washington to serve as an aide in the Treasury, Mellen
declined, saying that he could not afford to live on a government salary in
Washington. He added that he would be happy to accept special assignments for the Treasury in the West. Within weeks of taking office, Chase
gave Mellen his first such assignment: to check on federal property in

Kentucky. Soon there was another assignment and another, and Mellen ended the war as one of Chase's senior assistants in the West.[24]

In early May Chase advertised another loan, seeking bids on $14 million worth of 6 percent twenty-year bonds. In this case, the statute in question allowed the secretary to accept bids only at par; he could not sell at a discount. Chase heard that there would be bids from Boston for $5 million of bonds at par, but then a New York banker came to Washington and told him that he should not expect any bids at par. Chase hurriedly prepared another advertisement under a more flexible statute, seeking to place $9 million worth of twenty-year bonds at a discount. Opening bids ranged from 81 to 93 cents on the dollar; in other words, none of the bids were as high as some of the bids he had rejected a few weeks earlier. Chase accepted bids of 85 percent and above, thereby selling $6.8 million of bonds, and raised the rest by selling two-year notes. In a sense, the notes were cheaper, for they carried a lower interest rate, but they were also more dangerous. James Gallatin, head of a New York bank and son of Chase's predecessor in the Treasury, Albert Gallatin, reminded Chase that the notes might fall due for payment at the very moment when he found it expensive or even impossible to borrow.[25]

One of those who helped Chase through these difficult days was Samuel Hooper, at the time a Boston banker and later a Republican member of Congress. As Chase opened the bids for one of the loans, he found that he was about $1 million short. He recalled that he summoned Hooper, whom he scarcely knew at the time but who happened to be in Washington, and asked him to take another $1 million of the Treasury notes. Hooper "complied without hesitation" even though "most men would have shrunk" from the risks. The two became good friends.[26]

Two of the bankers who were most helpful to Chase in these early weeks were Jay and Henry Cooke, brothers originally from Ohio. Jay was the head of Jay Cooke & Co., a small private bank in Philadelphia, while his younger brother Henry, who had been close to Chase in Columbus as the editor of the *Ohio State Journal*, was now in Washington, serving as his brother's informal agent. Henry Cooke was more of a journalist than a financier, but Jay was one of the great financiers of the century: inventive, eager and ambitious. Chase was so impressed by Jay Cooke that he persuaded Lincoln in early 1861 to appoint him as the assistant treasurer in Philadelphia, a position second only to that of New York in importance to the department. Cooke declined, however, saying that he could not leave his firm and his many private clients, but assuring Chase that he could call upon him "at all times when my services are required."[27]

Chase was busy with military as well as financial matters in mid-1861, partly because Cameron was a weak and overworked head of the War Department, and partly because the friendship between Chase and Cameron made the secretary of war turn to Chase more often than to Seward or other Cabinet members. The United States did not yet have anything like the Joint Chiefs of Staff or the National Security Council, so there were few other places Lincoln or Cameron could turn for help with military issues. One of Chase's first military tasks was to work with army officers to devise orders for organizing the new volunteer forces. The two young officers with whom he worked on this project were Irvin McDowell, part of the Adjutant General's Office in Washington, and William Franklin, charged with supervising construction of the extension of the Treasury Building. Together they drafted a proclamation for Lincoln, issued on May 3, calling for an increase in the regular army of twenty-two thousand men, and an additional forty-two thousand volunteers, this time to serve for three years. The army men wanted the volunteers to serve in mixed, national regiments, but Chase insisted that the regiments be raised on a state-by-state basis. "He would rather have no regiments raised in Ohio," Franklin recalled Chase saying, "than that they should not be known as Ohio regiments." So the War Department orders, issued on May 4, provided that the governors of each state would name the officers of each volunteer regiment, with the result that most regiments were drawn from single states and known by the names of their states.[28]

Chase recalled that he found McDowell, a native of Ohio, "intelligent and disposed to avoid all extravagances," so that Chase supported his promotion to brigadier general "though I presume he would have been appointed" without such support. On May 16 McDowell gave Chase a four-page sketch of how he would fight the rebels in northern Virginia. Two weeks later, probably at Chase's suggestion, Lincoln placed McDowell in charge of what was at first called the Army of Northeastern Virginia, later known as the Army of the Potomac. The newspapers did not mention the Chase-McDowell connection at the time; it was only later in the year, and especially the next year, that papers called McDowell a Chase protégé. McDowell set up his headquarters at Arlington House, the former residence of Robert E. Lee across the Potomac from Washington. Nettie Chase recalled that there was "no brighter or lovelier spot during the May days of 1861 than Arlington Heights," where McDowell and his "cordial and hospitable wife" hosted the Chase family and others.[29]

Irvin McDowell, commander of the Union forces in the First Battle of Bull Run. Chase and his daughters spent much time with McDowell and his family in early 1861.

On May 25 Cameron sent Chase a note saying that he was going to New York City for the weekend and asking Chase to watch over the War Department. It thus may have been Chase rather than Cameron who first reviewed a May 24 letter from General Benjamin Butler, in charge at Fort Monroe, Virginia, raising a new and important question for the Lincoln administration. Three slaves, who had been working for their master, the colonel of the local Virginia militia, on the construction of trenches and gun platforms to attack the fort, had escaped and rowed themselves to the fort. An officer of the militia, acting as agent of their master, had demanded that Butler return the slaves, citing the Fugitive Slave Act. The Union general refused, explaining that since Virginia claimed that it was no longer part of the federal Union, its citizens could not rely upon that federal law. Moreover, Butler said, since the slaves were working for the rebel army, he would treat them as contraband and set them to work for wages. Northern papers reported, with some amusement, that Butler, a clever lawyer, was putting his legal training to work in his new position in the army.[30]

Lincoln and his Cabinet discussed the issue on May 30 and decided to support Butler's stance. Chase drafted for Cameron the official response to Butler, which said in part that the federal government could neither "recognize the rejection by any state of its federal obligations" nor "refuse the performance of the federal obligations resting upon itself." But the government's paramount obligation was "suppressing and dispersing armed combinations formed for the purpose of overthrowing its whole constitutional authority." Butler should therefore "refrain from surrendering to alleged masters any persons who may come within your lines. You will employ such persons in the services to which they may be best adapted, keeping an account of the labor by them performed, of the value of it, and of the expense of their maintenance. The question of their final disposition will be reserved for future determination." The approach devised by Butler, and blessed by Lincoln and Chase, would prove a turning point in the Civil War, for soon there were thousands of fugitive slaves in contraband camps, working for and getting paid by the Union army. At Fort Monroe, Butler would soon promote Chase's friend and protégé Edward Pierce to serve as the supervisor of the contrabands.[31]

Chase recalled later that Lincoln and Cameron "committed to me for a time the principal charge of whatever related to Kentucky and Tennessee." Chase's papers for 1861 confirm this, for they contain dozens of letters about these two border states. When Lovell Rousseau, a Unionist member of the Kentucky legislature, came to Washington in the early summer, Chase took him under his wing, obtaining for him a commission as a colonel and authority to raise two regiments. Rousseau returned to Louisville, from where he reported to Chase that the *Louisville Courier* had already announced his mission. Rousseau would have preferred to work quietly, but he was working nevertheless and soon had his two regiments in a training camp on the banks of the Ohio River. In June Rousseau wrote to Chase, "The secessionists here are like copperhead snakes; they are rabid, fierce, and unrelenting." This was an early, but not quite the first, use of the word *copperhead* to describe the rebels and their Northern sympathizers.[32]

Benjamin Butler, the cross-eyed general from Massachusetts, who coined the term contraband *to describe the former slaves who found freedom with the Union army.*

William "Bull" Nelson, a burly naval officer, was another Chase protégé from Kentucky. The Treasury secretary helped secure him an army commission and the authority to raise nine regiments from Kentucky and Tennessee. Setting himself up at first in Cincinnati, Nelson sent Chase a constant stream of letters requesting arms and ammunition, and outlining plans for an expedition into east Tennessee. In a July letter to Andrew Johnson, still serving as senator from Tennessee even though his state had seceded from the Union, Nelson said that if Johnson could not get the War Department to approve a particular request, he should see Chase, "the steam engine of the administration and a friend of mine."[33]

George Brinton McClellan, a West Point graduate, Mexican War veteran, and resident of Cincinnati for a few months just before the Civil War, was another Chase correspondent in the summer of 1861. Chase helped secure for young McClellan a commission as major general in the regular army (so that he ranked second only to Scott in the hierarchy) and the responsibility for western Virginia. McClellan moved his forces there and won the first land battle of the Civil War: the skirmish at Philippi in early June. Chase wrote to McClellan at least twice that month, but the letters are lost; all we have is McClellan's response, thanking Chase for his concern and detailing his plans. In early July Chase wrote to McClellan again, urging him to cooperate with Nelson and Rousseau and to prepare for a grand movement: to "march down through the mountain region, deliver the whole of it, including the mountain districts of North Carolina, Georgia, and Alabama, from the insurrection, and then reach the Gulf at Mobile and New Orleans, thus cutting the rebellion in two." It was a rather naïve plan: a thousand-mile march through mountainous terrain, with a small force and without lines of supply. McClellan, however, did not laugh at Chase but wrote him that "the movement you suggest meets with my full concurrence" and that he would start "preparing for it as soon as through with western Virginia."[34]

George McClellan, the "Young Napoleon," who arrived in Washington
in mid-1861 to take over the Army of the Potomac.

As critics had predicted, Cameron proved a poor secretary of war. "No one ever suspected Cameron of honesty," the *Cincinnati Commercial* commented in June, "but there were hopes that he had business capacity." Cameron was "very incompetent," the paper continued, and the "greater portion of the really important work of his department is performed by General Scott and Secretary Chase. Cameron attends to the stealing department." The secretary had "swarms of relatives about him, sons, brothers-in-law, and all that sort of thing. One of his sons is said to have made $22,000 on a single horse contract." Nepotism was not unusual at the time, as evidenced by Chase's work to secure a place for his brother Edward, but Cameron crossed some unwritten line. Trying to defend Cameron, Chase wrote to the *Commercial* that Cameron was "administering his department vigorously, patriotically, and honestly." But Chase also complained to Cameron about the slipshod paperwork provided by his department. By the end of the summer, Chase was telling friends that Lincoln needed a new secretary of war, and that Cameron wanted "to resign and go abroad," but Chase was unsure who would be "sufficient for the great work of the War Department."[35]

In late June the historian John Lothrop Motley arrived in Washington seeking a diplomatic appointment—not for the salary, he assured his friend and patron Charles Sumner, but rather because he had "an inclination almost amounting to a frenzy to be enrolled in public service at this great crisis." Motley spent an evening with Chase and was favorably impressed, describing him to his wife as a "tall, well-made, robust man with handsome features, a fine blue eye, and a ready and agreeable smile— altogether *simpatico*." Motley assured Chase that the "English government would never ally itself with the Southern Confederacy or go any further in the course already taken towards its recognition." Chase in turn assured Motley that the "rebellion would be put down and the Union restored." Motley told Sumner that Chase and Cameron understood that "money, men, beef, bread, and gun powder in enormous amounts are necessary for suppressing this insurrection, but they have not the slightest doubt as to the issue."[36]

Chase contrasted for Motley the population of the North, about twenty-two million people, with the white population of the South, only about five and a half million. Even among white Southerners, Chase noted, there were "large numbers who are fierce against the rebels, and still larger numbers among the ignorant masses, who will be soon inquiring: 'What is all this about? Why is all this bloodshed and misery?'" These people would be "made to understand, despite the lies of the ringleaders of the rebellion, that the United States government is their best friend; that not one of their rights has been menaced—that it wishes only to maintain the Constitution and laws under which we have all prospered for three-quarters of a century."[37]

Already, Chase noted, there was progress in the border states. In Maryland, which had looked likely to secede, the people had just voted for Union. In western Virginia, a convention had declared the state's secession from the Union invalid and was working to form a new state government—not merely for western Virginia, where most people supported the Union, but claiming to represent *all* of Virginia. "This course is supported by United States troops and will be recognized by Congress," Chase predicted, "which has had to deal with similar cases before and is the sole judge according to the Constitution as to the claims of its members to their seats." The same thing would happen in eastern Tennessee, where "there are 30,000 or 40,000 fighting men who will fiercely dispute the power of a convention to deprive them of their rights as citizens of the United States and who will maintain the Union with arms in their hands to the death." Chase expected similar developments in other states, and that such "rebellions against rebellion" would weaken the South—as indeed they would.[38]

"And if all these calculations fail," Chase added, "if the insurrection is unreasonably protracted, and we find it much more difficult and expensive in blood and treasure to put down than we anticipated, we shall then draw the sword which we prefer at present to leave in the sheath, and *we shall proclaim the total abolition of slavery on the American continent*. We do not wish this, we deplore it, because of the vast confiscation of property and of the servile insurrections, too horrible to contemplate, which would follow. We wish the Constitution and the Union as it is, with slavery, as a municipal institution, existing until such time as each state in its wisdom thinks fit to mitigate or abolish it." But, he concluded, "if the issue be distinctly presented, death to the American republic or death to slavery, slavery *must die*."[39]

Thus, even in June 1861, before the first major battle of the Civil War, Chase was thinking about the possibility of an emancipation proclamation.

It was not the course he preferred; he hoped and expected to defeat the rebellion through other means. But Chase recognized that it might be necessary to emancipate the slaves in order to defeat the rebellion of their masters.[40]

Chase rose early on July 4, 1861, to join Lincoln, Cameron, and others before eight on a temporary reviewing platform in front of the White House, as more than twenty thousand New York troops marched along Pennsylvania Avenue. Right after the review, Lincoln, Chase, and the other leaders, escorted by a New York regiment, went to a newly erected hundred-foot flagpole on the south side of the Treasury Building for a presentation of an American flag by Edward Sanford, a New York writer and politician. Sanford told Lincoln and the crowd that the patriotic people of New York had sent this flag to Washington "to be here hoisted, and they asked the government to uphold it forever." The president replied that his role was just to raise the flag, which he would do if there was "no fault in the machinery," but after that, "it would be for the people to keep it up." The crowd laughed and cheered.[41]

Thus did Lincoln summarize with a quip his message to the special session of Congress, read by a clerk when the legislators convened that same day at noon. "This is essentially a people's contest," Lincoln declared. It would be for the people of the United States "to demonstrate to the world that those who can fairly carry an election can also suppress a rebellion; that ballots are the rightful and peaceful successors of bullets." Lincoln still included Southerners among the "people" of the United States, for in his view, except in South Carolina, "Union men are the majority in many, if not in every other one, of the so-called seceded states." The goal of the Union government was simply to protect "loyal citizens everywhere" in their rights, and doing this did not involve "any coercion, any conquest, any subjugation, in any just sense of those terms."[42]

Chase, in his own report to Congress, presented this same day, estimated that in order to achieve the "speedy and complete" suppression of the rebellion, the government would need to spend, in the fiscal year that had just started, about $320 million. This estimate, based on estimates from the other departments, would prove far too low; actual expenditures in the fiscal year would exceed $480 million. Chase believed he could raise the required funds through about $240 million of borrowing and

$80 million of taxes. With hindsight, knowing that the war would cost far more and last far longer, it is easy to say that Chase should have relied less on debt and more on taxes. But like almost everyone else, Chase assumed in July 1861 that the war would be over in less than a year.[43]

Echoing Lincoln, and using the model of a recent French loan, Chase said that, because "the contest in which the government is now engaged is a contest for national existence and the sovereignty of the people," it was proper that "the appeal for the means of prosecuting it . . . should be made, in the first instance at least, to the people themselves." Chase proposed what he called a "national loan," by which the government would borrow from the public at least $100 million, in the form of short-term small-denomination notes, with an interest rate of 7.3 percent. He selected this rate because it was about the market rate and would work out as one penny per day on a $50 note. "To secure the widest possible circle of contribution," the Treasury secretary proposed to accept subscriptions for as little as $50, to accept subscriptions at "the offices of such postmasters and other selected persons in such cities and towns of the Union as may be designated," and to allow subscribers to pay "in installments of one-tenth at the time of subscription and one-tenth on the first and fifteenth days of each month thereafter."[44]

On the tax side, Chase noted that the American people had always relied upon tariffs on imports as the principal source of federal revenue. Chase did not propose to depart from this approach but noted that the present tariff schedule would not yield anything like the required revenue. Chase thus proposed to increase tariff rates and to impose tariffs on some goods at present exempt, notably sugar, tea, and coffee. Even with these new duties, Chase estimated that revenue would fall about $20 million short of his goal of $80 million. As to the remainder, he suggested that Congress should consider "taxes on distilled liquors, on banknotes, on carriages," and perhaps other taxes. Chase also urged Congress to focus on closing the Southern ports or collecting federal tariffs offshore near them. He submitted to Congress three detailed draft bills: one to authorize the proposed national loan and provide other borrowing authority; one to increase tariff rates and impose new tariffs; and one to improve tariff collection.[45]

Northern newspapers praised Chase's report. The *New York Times* said he had "proved himself fully adequate to this emergency by proposing a sound, conservative, and statesmanlike policy." The *Times* was especially pleased that Chase proposed to increase taxes and quoted with approval the section of his report in which he said that "in every sound system of finance, adequate provision by taxation for the prompt discharge of all ordinary demands, for the punctual payment of interest upon loans, and for the creation of a gradually increasing fund for the redemption of principal, is indispensable." The *New-York Tribune* predicted that the people would support the national loan. "If it were generally known today that one hundred million more would end this struggle, and end it by Christmas, that sum would be had in a week at par for a 6 percent loan on twenty years' time. If [the war] is to go on indefinitely, we must borrow at ruinous rates and soon find ourselves unable to borrow at all."[46]

Chase did not simply deliver his report and wait for Congress to pass laws. He worked with key members to ensure that the necessary laws were passed in this short session. Indeed, three weeks before the session started, Chase sent a letter to William Fessenden, chairman of the Senate Finance Committee, asking him to come to Washington to confer about financial legislation. On the House side, Chase's key contacts were Thaddeus Stevens of Pennsylvania, head of the Committee on Ways and Means, and Elihu Washburne, head of the Commerce Committee. There were more than two dozen letters between Chase and members of Congress during the single month of this special session; there were also surely many face-to-face meetings.[47]

Congress moved quickly and passed on July 17 an act based on Chase's proposal, authorizing him to borrow up to $250 million over the next year, using a mixture of means: he could issue twenty-year bonds paying interest at 7.0 percent, or three-year notes paying interest at 7.3 percent, or up to $50 million of small-denomination demand notes paying interest at 6.0 percent and repayable upon demand. As Chase had suggested, Congress authorized him to appoint agents in various places to accept subscriptions and to market bonds in Europe. His discretion was not unlimited, however; he was not allowed to accept bids at less than par for the twenty-year bonds, nor to issue demand notes with a denomination of less than $10, nor to accept payment in any form other than gold or silver coins, or specie.[48]

There was not much press comment on the passage of this bill, for the papers were filled with reports about McDowell's march from Arlington toward Manassas, Virginia. If P. G. T. Beauregard, the Confederate general in command, was in any doubt about the intentions of his West Point classmate McDowell, he could simply read the Washington press. The two armies met and fought on Sunday, July 21, in the first major battle of the war, along Bull Run Creek, about thirty miles west of Washington. Many members of Congress and not a few ladies went out in their carriages to see the battle for themselves. Chase and his daughters remained in Washington, where he met with Lincoln and other members of the Cabinet in the late afternoon and evening, as the initially positive reports turned dreadfully negative. One of the hundreds killed was Colonel James Cameron, the sixty-one-year-old brother of the secretary of war, and Chase immediately penned a kind condolence letter to Simon Cameron.[49]

Nettie Chase awoke early on Monday, July 22, to the unfamiliar sound and sight of horse-drawn ambulances passing by the three-story house that Chase had recently rented on the corner of Sixth and E Streets, north of Pennsylvania Avenue and near the Patent Office. "All that sad and rainy day, the utterly disorganized fugitives straggled down the street by twos and threes, in squads, and sometimes the remnants of a company—all

The Chase house, at the corner of Sixth and E Streets
in Washington, during the Civil War.

inquiring for their regiments, no one knowing where to go nor where to halt, but all footsore and weary, with torn and disordered garments." Quarters for the wounded were in short supply, so Chase opened his house "until we had eight or ten men to nurse back into health and strength again." Chase directed his servants to prepare coffee, which his daughters handed to the soldiers as they passed.[50]

On this same grim Monday, in a postscript to a letter to John Cisco, Chase said that he believed that God would in some way "bring good to our country" from the "great disaster of yesterday." Chase did not blame McDowell for the defeat at Manassas, writing a friend that he "did all that could have been done, in his circumstances," but he was pleased when Lincoln summoned McClellan to Washington to take command of all the Union armies, including the army in northern Virginia. Chase explained that he and others wanted to give command "to one having the prestige of victory as well as undoubted military talents." Lincoln also signed into law an act authorizing five hundred thousand three-year volunteers; three days later, he signed another law providing for another half million men. Lincoln, Chase, and others recognized that the war would now last for many months, if not years.[51]

It was in this difficult time, just before and after the Union defeat at Manassas, that Congress devised and passed the first wartime round of trade, tax, and tariff legislation. On the day after the battle, Chase wrote Fessenden, urging him to change the law that had just passed, so that the Treasury could issue demand notes with a face value of less than $10. Chase did not favor such notes, but it might become necessary for the Treasury to turn to them. Using the draft provided by Chase, Congress prohibited trade with the insurrectionary states except insofar as it was allowed by the president. Lincoln soon delegated the authority to issue trade permits to Chase, for whom this would become a major wartime responsibility. On the tariff front, as the Treasury secretary suggested, Congress both raised rates and imposed tariffs on items that previously entered without tariff. Taxes were more difficult because there were so few recent precedents. Chase admitted, in response to a question from Thaddeus Stevens, that it was difficult to estimate how much revenue a proposed tax would raise but stressed the importance of substantial taxes. Congress enacted two new taxes in August. The first was a one-time direct tax of $20 million, allocated among the states (as required by the Constitution) in proportion to their populations, and then allocated within states based upon the value of real estate. The second was an income tax—the first American income tax—set at 3 percent of all income over $800 per year. Neither tax would provide Chase with immediate revenue; the direct tax was not due until late 1862, and the first income tax payment was not due until 1863.[52]

Before leaving Washington in August, Congress also made a few changes to the loan legislation. As Chase suggested, Congress halved the amount of the smallest demand note, to $5, and simplified the signature requirements for Treasury securities. Chase told Fessenden that banks were pressing to suspend "the Subtreasury Act so as to allow the receipt of specie-paying banknotes for loans and, of course, the disbursement of them for expenditures." In other words, banks wanted to use their own banknotes to purchase Treasury securities rather than having to deliver specie, and they wanted to allow the Treasury to use their banknotes to pay its own bills. "I confess that this proposition does not strike me favorably," Chase wrote Fessenden, "but I submit it to the better judgment of the committee." Congress enacted a cryptic compromise, suspending the Subtreasury Act to allow the secretary "to deposit any of the moneys obtained on any of the loans now authorized by law, to the credit of the treasurer of the United States, in such solvent specie-paying banks as he may select." (The treasurer was an official under the secretary in the department.) Congress also passed at this time the first Confiscation Act, building upon General Butler's contraband policy and declaring that any master who "required or permitted" his slaves to work for the rebel military forces would "forfeit his claim" to such slaves.[53]

In July, over Chase's objection, Lincoln appointed John Frémont to command the Western Department, which covered the vast region from Missouri to New Mexico. The most urgent task was to control Missouri, where Union forces faced both Confederate troops and irregular guerrilla bands. In early August Chase sent Frémont a letter urging economy. "This war must necessarily be an expensive war, and there is great danger that, after a month or two, the people, in view of the magnitude of the burdens it is likely to entail, will refuse their support to the measures necessary to its vigorous prosecution. Already the disgust created by fraud or exorbitance in contracts, and by the improvidence of quartermasters and commissaries, is beginning to show itself." Frémont had just reached Missouri when

Chase sent him this warning; within months, his headquarters there would be infamous for waste and corruption.[54]

Chase went to New York in mid-August to meet with bankers from Boston, Philadelphia, and New York City. He hoped to persuade the bankers to lend the government at least $50 million in return for that amount of the recently authorized short-term notes. The bankers were reluctant; at one point, according to one of the bankers, Chase said that their offer of $3 million was "no more than a little drop for the bucket I must fill. I will go back to Washington, set the printing press to work, and so have paper money made, which you will have to take. It will, of course, depreciate—it may cost a thousand dollars to buy a breakfast then—but won't you give me what I ask? I pray you hear my plea." Later accounts suggested that Chase threatened the bankers—and perhaps there was an element of threat—but the banker wrote that "Mr. Chase seemed almost desperate as he took his seat."

At last, after days of discussion, both with Chase and among themselves, the bankers agreed to lend the government $50 million immediately. Some papers claimed that banks committed to loan a total of $150 million, with further tranches in October and December, while others said that the banks merely reserved the "right to take the remainder, if not taken up in other ways." After returning to Washington by overnight train, Chase wrote to thank John Stevens, one of the key New York bankers, for his "most generous and energetic support of the government." Chase asked Stevens to see that the Treasury would receive at least $1 million on each day of the next week. A few days later, he wrote Stevens again, asking whether the first million had been deposited in New York that day, because "payments today exhausted the balance in the Treasury."[55]

One of the Philadelphia bankers involved in this loan was Jay Cooke, who had by this time become a personal friend as well as financial adviser to Chase. One morning in late August, while Cooke was in Washington meeting with Chase at his house, a messenger came to the door, saying that Lincoln and Bates were in a carriage outside, asking for Chase to join them. Cooke recalled that Chase went out and spoke with Lincoln, who said that he and all the Cabinet were heading out to review some of McClellan's troops. Chase tried to excuse himself, saying that he and Cooke were engaged in important work, but the president insisted, so Chase and Cooke joined Lincoln and Bates in the carriage. As they drove along, Cooke remarked that the attorney general reminded him of his father, with dark hair but an almost white beard. Lincoln quipped that this showed "that he uses his jaw more than his brains." According to the papers, the review of McClellan's troops was an all-day affair, with the general and staff "in full uniform, the former mounted on a spirited dark bay horse and looking the thorough soldier." [56]

Chase and Cooke were probably working this day on a lengthy appeal from Chase, addressed "to the citizens of the United States," which appeared in the papers in early September. "Your national government," Chase started, "compelled by a guilty conspiracy, culminating in causeless rebellion, is engaged in war for the security of liberty, for the supremacy of law, and for the maintenance of popular institutions." To raise the necessary resources, Chase explained, he needed funds from the people as well as bankers. He set out the financial advantages for those who purchased the new notes: investors would receive interest at 7.3 percent, higher than most market rates; they could subscribe for as little as $50; they could pay the amount due over time; and "the whole property of the country was pledged for the interest and final reimbursement of this loan." To those who worried that the Civil War would continue for years, Chase responded that "the well-considered judgement of military men of the highest rank and repute warrant confident expectation that the war, prosecuted with energy, courage, and skill, may be brought to a termination before the close of next spring." Chase said that he would "as speedily as practicable" appoint subscription agents "in the several cities and principal towns" and that, in the meantime, people could subscribe by sending funds to the treasurer at Washington or to the assistant treasurers in Boston, New York, Philadelphia, or Saint Louis. [57]

Chase's appeal did not get as much attention as he had hoped, for the press was reporting on a slavery controversy. Without consulting with Washington, Frémont imposed martial law in Missouri and declared that all slaves of rebel masters there were free. At once, Chase started to hear from leaders in Kentucky such as Lincoln's longtime friend Joshua Speed, who wrote to Chase that Frémont's proclamation threatened all the good work that he and other Union men were doing in Kentucky. "I beg you to look at this question in all its bearings—and don't, for God's sake, allow us to be turned over to the enemy." Responding on September 5 to another Kentucky correspondent, former member of Congress Green Adams, Chase wrote that one could construe Frémont's proclamation as "the simple recognition and enforcement of the [Confiscation] act of

Congress." Chase assured Adams that "neither the president, nor any member of his administration, nor, in my belief, General Frémont himself, has any desire to convert this war for the Union . . . into a war upon any state institutions whatever, whether that institution be slavery or another."[58]

Lincoln's first response to Frémont's proclamation was a polite private note asking him to modify his proclamation so that it would not go beyond the Confiscation Act. Most generals would have complied at once, but not Frémont, who replied that he would not change the proclamation without a direct presidential order. So Lincoln wrote Frémont to order him to limit his proclamation and his actions to the terms of the Confiscation Act. As soon as Lincoln's order appeared in the papers, Chase started to receive letters from those who supported Frémont and regretted Lincoln's decision to overrule him. Joseph Medill, editor of the *Chicago Tribune*, wrote to Chase on September 15 that Lincoln's letter had "cast a funeral gloom over our patriotic city." For Medill, "slavery is at the bottom of the whole trouble," and "until the administration sees the contest in its true light, the blood of loyal men will be shed in vain, and the war will come to naught." But the assistant treasurer in Saint Louis, Benjamin Farrar, wrote Chase on September 16 to denounce Frémont as inefficient and incompetent. Farrar was not concerned about the proclamation—indeed, he did not mention it—nor yet about corruption. He was worried by the military situation, with the state "overrun by bands of plundering traitors" and the rebels in control of "the most loyal portion of Missouri for the want of two thousand troops that could have been spared from Rolla [in Missouri] or from idle thousands at Saint Louis."[59]

The national loan was making some progress by September. Jay Cooke, the key agent in Philadelphia, wrote to Chase that more than a hundred people subscribed at his office on September 7—"clergymen, draymen, merchants, girls, boys, and all kinds of men and women." A week later, the *Philadelphia Inquirer* said that more than eight hundred people had subscribed so far in Philadelphia; the paper printed the names of some of the leading subscribers. A Vermont newspaper boasted that the total national subscription had reached $9 million. Writing to August Belmont, a New York financier spending a few months in France, Chase said that if only he had the energy of French emperor Napoleon III (nephew of Napoleon Bonaparte) and his system of subordinates, "the loan would be taken in this country with as much eagerness as in France." Chase had asked Belmont, as he left for Europe, to inquire whether financiers there would lend to the American government. At present, however, the Treasury secretary believed that "if expenditure can be restricted within reasonable limits, the whole sums needed can be supplied in this country." Chase was a Republican, and Belmont was the chairman of the Democratic National Committee, but that did not prevent them from corresponding and collaborating on wartime financial questions.[60]

To raise the necessary funds, Chase was issuing not only interest-bearing notes for the national loan but also interest-free notes payable on demand. The $5 demand note bore an image of Alexander Hamilton, and the $10 note, of Abraham Lincoln. Chase wrote Hamilton's son that he had decided to use his father's image because he wanted "the people [to] renew their recollection of the first secretary of the Treasury." On September 15 the *New York Herald* reported that more than two hundred clerks were at the Treasury Department late the prior night, "engaged in cutting and trimming demand notes, of the denominations of five, ten, and twenty dollars." Each note had to have two signatures, and "three thousand signatures is a large day's work for a man." To accomplish this, "Secretary Chase and his assistants are obliged to work sixteen hours out of every twenty-four."[61]

The *Herald* described the clerks as men, but other papers said that "demand for Treasury notes is so great that additional clerks, including some ladies, have been employed to cut them up." Years later, the treasurer at the time, Francis Spinner, recalled telling Chase that "young men should have muskets instead of shears placed in their hands, and be sent to the front, and their places filled by women, who would do more and better work." Chase "hesitated for some time," according to Spinner, before he "at length consented that I might send him one woman to test the matter." The news reports, however, backed up by the payroll records, show that Spinner's recollection was incorrect: Chase readily agreed to employ women, for they were at work in the department in the fall of 1861, not the spring of 1862, as Spinner recalled. Chase himself, when asked later why he employed women, responded that he was prompted by "motives of humanity." There were many "refugees and others, deprived of the means of livelihood by the war, and I gave them employment to enable them to provide for themselves and families." Chase and Spinner both forgot to mention another point that persuaded them to hire women: their wages were far lower than those of men. Whatever their reasons, the decision by Chase and Spinner to employ women was momentous, for these women were among the first female federal employees, pioneers for thousands who would follow.[62]

Chase's main problem, however, was not printing and cutting the Treasury notes; it was that the military was spending money faster and faster. Writing to one of the New York bankers on September 10, he noted that the "quartermaster's estimate for the current week is four million; the paymaster's, seven and a half." Chase believed that this particular week's demands were "extraordinary, made necessary by the outfit of the army, in view of movements, and of the approach of winter." Part of the problem, as Chase wrote in another letter, was the lack of coordination between state and federal governments. "In every state, men are raised, armed, and equipped, provisioned, and transported, almost without reference to the general government," even though it was the general government—that is the Treasury Department—that would have to pay the bills. The result was that Chase did not "know what is to be provided, or where, or what the aggregate of expenditures during any given time is or is likely to be."[63]

By the end of September, Chase was back in New York City to meet with bankers again and to seek a further loan of $50 million. The bankers agreed to his request, and, in return, Chase agreed that they be allowed to pay for some of the new notes with old Treasury notes rather than specie. The *New York Herald* reported that there was a "slight difference of opinion" between Chase and the bankers about how to interpret the suspension section of the recent legislation. The bankers believed that Congress had suspended the subtreasury law altogether, so that Chase could and should accept their banknotes rather than insisting upon specie. Chase disagreed, both on legal and policy grounds. In a letter to one of the bankers, as he left New York to return to Washington, Chase hinted at his key concern. Taking banknotes as payment, however "harmless or even beneficial it might be if confined to the New York banks," could not realistically be so confined. Politics would force Chase to accept notes from banks in other places; if he limited the policy to New York, there would be cries from Boston and Philadelphia; if he limited the policy to those three cities, there would be cries from smaller cities and towns; and Chase had no way of evaluating the credit of the more than 1,500 different state-chartered banks.[64]

Meanwhile, in Missouri, Frémont had proved himself incompetent, not only militarily but also politically and financially. He feuded with the state's leading Republican, Congressman Frank Blair, even arresting Blair

at one point. Blair responded with public charges against Frémont, including "gross extravagance, waste, mismanagement, and misapplication of
the public moneys." Lincoln sent Cameron to Missouri to investigate, and
as the war secretary left Washington, Chase encouraged him to be bold.
"We must have vigor, capacity, honesty. If Frémont has these qualities,
sustain him. If not, let nothing prevent you from taking the bull by the
horns." Cameron found that almost everyone in Missouri, other than those
benefiting from Frémont's extravagant spending, favored removing him.
But Cameron did not use his authority to dismiss Frémont immediately;
he instead returned to Washington, where Lincoln discussed the issue
with his Cabinet and decided to replace Frémont with Henry Halleck,
a general known as "Old Brains" because he was the author of a leading
text on army tactics.[65]

While Lincoln's orders relieving Frémont from his western command
were on their way to Missouri, Chase assured antislavery friends that the
president was not firing Frémont because of his proclamation or because
he feared Frémont as a political rival. "He who is thinking about the
presidency in 1864," Chase wrote, "cannot properly perform the duties
of 1861." Chase now believed that Frémont's proclamation was a mistake, "its only effect to excite alarm, discontent, and animosity without
effecting a single step of antislavery progress." He questioned whether
any proclamation would make much difference for the slaves; actions,
not proclamations, were what mattered. He was still opposed to "any
interference by the federal government with slavery beyond that made
necessary by insurrection and consequent military necessity." Chase added
that "if any persons of any complexion or condition offer themselves to the
United States in the war, I am for receiving them and employing them
in civil or military services as circumstances may require." Here, for the
first time, Chase hinted that he favored enlisting blacks into the army.
"If it shall turn out that those received were slaves and that their masters
were loyal, I would compensate them fairly for their loss of services, but
under no circumstances should any person once received into the service
of the United States be reduced to slavery."[66]

Chase's friend Sumner, in a Massachusetts speech at about this time,
argued that slavery was the cause of the rebellion, "its inspiration, its
motive power, its end and aim, its be-all and end-all." In order to win
the war, he stressed, the Union would have to make war upon slavery.
Responding to those who questioned whether the federal government

had the power to emancipate slaves, Sumner quoted John Quincy Adams, who said that in time of war, "not only the president of the United States but the commander of the army has power to order the universal emancipation of the slaves." Sumner did not quite demand that Lincoln issue an emancipation proclamation, but he came close, saying that there was "one spot, like the heel of Achilles, where this great rebellion may be wounded to death." Chase did not yet agree with Sumner, but he would come to concur soon enough.[67]

In the fall of 1861 Chase sent Nettie to a boarding school outside Philadelphia, where she would spend one academic year. Writing from there in September to her sister, Kate, Nettie asked whether William Sprague was back in Washington. "I wish (if you don't think me impertinent) that you would marry him. I like him very much." Sprague was not in Washington;

William Sprague, governor of Rhode Island, who accompanied the state's troops to Washington in early 1861, where he met and, in 1863, married Kate Chase.

after serving as a volunteer aide in the battle at Manassas, he returned
to Rhode Island and remained there until early 1862. We do not have
Kate's response—we do not have any of her letters from this period—but
we know that the twenty-one-year-old visited Newport, Rhode Island,
in late August or early September, and it seems that she visited Sprague
in Providence. Chase drafted a letter to Kate saying that he was "sorry
that you went to Providence if, as I suppose, Gov. Sprague is nothing to
you except a friend. If any other relation is desired by him towards you, I
ought to know it. I am not at all anxious for your marriage to anybody."
He added that, at the right time, he would be happy to see her married
to "a really worthy and good man—a gentleman—and a Christian gentleman—who would be to you the affectionate protector you need." It is
not clear whether he sent this letter to his daughter, but he should have,
for Sprague would prove anything but a Christian gentleman.[68]

Chase continued, in the fall of 1861, to correspond with military
officers, especially in the West. Some of these men were already famous,
such as Robert Anderson, the hero of Fort Sumter. Others would become
famous, including future president Rutherford Hayes, serving as a major
in an Ohio regiment, and William Tecumseh Sherman, a West Point graduate and brother of Senator John Sherman. In September, when Sherman
was promoted to general and appointed to lead Union troops in Kentucky,
Chase praised him to William Nelson as "a man of energy, of wisdom,
of courage." In October Chase shared with General Sherman some of the
country's financial difficulties. "For the last six weeks, requisitions have
largely exceeded even the great sum of a million a day—so largely that
the unpaid requisitions for which no present funds are or can be provided exceed twenty millions." Writing to his brother the senator, Chase
added that he was "almost overwhelmed by the cares and anxieties" of his
department; that the "lack of system, organization, and economy in the
war expenditures" were making it difficult to pay the bills. In November,
after Lincoln relieved Sherman from his duties in Kentucky and assigned
him to the staff of General Henry Halleck in Missouri, Chase assured the
senator that this change was made at his brother's request.[69]

There was constant friction in Washington between General Scott,
the aged hero of the Mexican War, and General McClellan, determined
to be the young hero of the Civil War. When Scott informed Lincoln
that he would like to retire, Chase drafted for the president some of the
kind words that he would use at the retirement ceremony. Chase was

gratified by McClellan's promotion, writing to one of the general's aides, in a letter intended for McClellan, "let us thank God and take courage." In a private conversation with McClellan on the day of his promotion, Lincoln expressed concern about the "vast labor" of managing not only the principal eastern army, the Army of the Potomac, but also all the other Union armies. As Lincoln's secretary Hay wrote in his diary, McClellan dismissed the president's worries, claiming, "I can do it all."[70]

By this point, it was clear that the national loan was not going to provide much more for Chase, so he went to New York in November to confer again with the bankers. The discussion this time focused on the 6 percent twenty-year bonds; the bankers agreed to purchase $50 million of these bonds, at a modest discount to par, over the next few weeks. Chase may still have been in New York when news arrived there on November 16 that an American navy ship, the USS *San Jacinto,* had intercepted and fired upon a British commercial vessel, the RMS *Trent.* Crew members then boarded the *Trent* and forcibly seized four Confederate diplomats bound for Europe, including two of Chase's former colleagues in the Senate, James Mason and John Slidell. The Northern press hailed the captain of the *San Jacinto* as a hero, and the financial markets were not at first worried about the possibility of conflict with Great Britain. On November 19 the *New York Herald* printed a positive report about the Northern economy and federal finances. "After eight months of most costly preparations for war on the part of the federal government, with an immense army and navy to be created . . . the federal government and the people of the loyal states find themselves today in a stronger position financially than they were at the commencement of the year." One of the positive details noted by the *Herald* was that the "associated banks of New York, after accommodating the government with a loan of a hundred million dollars, have a larger specie reserve fund on hand than they have been accustomed to hold in the most prosperous times."[71]

Chase spent much of November working on his annual report, a detailed document expected from each department head at the outset of December. In the midst of drafting and revising, Chase sent a short letter to James Pollock, the director of the mint in Philadelphia. "No nation can be strong except in the strength of God," Chase wrote, "or safe except in His defense. The trust of our people in God should be declared on our national coins." Chase directed Pollock to prepare and use a motto "expressing in the fewest and tersest words possible this national recognition." Some research revealed, however, that the wording of the mottoes was set by Congress, so Chase could not change the wording until Congress revised the law. Near the end of his time as secretary, however, the motto he devised, "In God We Trust," first appeared on coins, and it still appears on American coins and currency.[72]

In a prominent November article in the *Atlantic Monthly* magazine, Edward Pierce, based on his work with the contrabands at Virginia's Fortress Monroe, argued that it would make sense to use the former slaves in the army. The *New-York Tribune* reported that Cameron's imminent annual report would take this approach and contend that it was time to place "arms in the hands of the slaves willing to use them for the cause of the Union." Chase agreed with Cameron and Pierce in thinking the time had come to enlist blacks. Even as he supported Cameron on this point, however, the Treasury secretary chided Cameron for his estimates of expenditures, which he characterized as "based upon mere conjecture," and for what he described as "an entire want of system in the management of our military affairs."[73]

Lincoln's annual message to Congress of December 3, 1861, was a serious, sober, dull document—delivered in writing, as was the custom at the time. The president's message discouraged Charles Sumner and others who had been hoping he would soon issue an emancipation proclamation. "In considering the policy to be adopted for suppressing the insurrection," Lincoln stated, "I have been anxious and careful that the inevitable conflict for this purpose shall not degenerate into a violent and remorseless revolutionary struggle. I have, therefore, in every case, thought it proper to keep the integrity of the Union paramount as the primary object of the contest on our part, leaving all questions which are not of vital military importance to the more deliberate action of the legislature." The government "should not be in haste to determine that radical and extreme measures, which may reach the loyal as well as the disloyal, are indispensable." Lincoln suggested that Congress authorize the purchase of some suitable foreign territory for the colonization of former slaves, prompting one of Chase's antislavery friends to write to him deriding Lincoln's "unstatesmanlike scheme of colonization." Chase's friend hoped the "sword" would "make a nation of four millions of black men free" and that they would be "as free as the white man."[74]

Cameron's report, in its first version, was a far more dramatic document than Lincoln's message, for he argued that the Union should make soldiers of the former slaves: "If it shall be found that the men who have been held by the rebels as slaves are capable of bearing arms and performing efficient military service, it is the right and may become the duty of the government to arm and equip them, and employ their services against the rebels, under proper military regulation, discipline, and command." Anyone reading the newspapers in November would have known the secretary of war's views and that he intended to state them in his report. Lincoln should have insisted on reading the report in draft form, and, if he disagreed, he should have asked Cameron to revise it. But he did not. Instead, Lincoln tried to suppress the report, even as it was appearing in the newspapers. Soon a *second* version of Cameron's report, without the language about arming blacks, was in the papers, along with reports of how Lincoln had demanded the revisions. The *Chicago Tribune*, which had praised the first version of Cameron's report, called the failed attempt at suppression a "fiasco" and denounced how Lincoln had "emasculated" Cameron's proposal.[75]

Chase's own report, delayed until December 9, 1861, was a detailed twenty-page printed document with more than a hundred pages of supporting tables and reports. He recounted the success of his recent efforts to raise funds through loans but also advised that the tariff was providing less revenue than he had hoped; instead of $50 million in the fiscal year that would end on June 30, 1862, he now estimated that tariffs would bring in only about $32 million. Chase urged Congress to increase a few tariffs, on coffee and tea, but thought the time not "propitious" for a general revision of the tariff. "It becomes the duty of Congress, therefore, to direct its attention to revenue from other sources," he wrote. By their terms, neither the direct tax nor the income tax was yet in effect, and Chase urged Congress to reconsider and revise them. The direct tax, he advised, should be increased in order to collect at least $20 million from the loyal states, and Congress should raise another $20 million through taxes upon "stills and distilled liquors, on tobacco, on banknotes, on carriages, on legacies, on paper evidences of debt and instruments for conveyance of property, and other like subjects of taxation." Congress would also need to authorize additional loans; Chase estimated that the Treasury would need to borrow at least another $200 million in the current fiscal year.[76]

The heart of Chase's report, however, was his discussion of currency and his plans to create a national currency. Echoing views he first expressed thirty years earlier in the *Cincinnati American*, Chase lamented that the "value of the existing banknote circulation depends on the laws of the thirty-four states and the character of some sixteen hundred private corporations"—the sixteen hundred different state-chartered banks. Strong banks generally did not issue many banknotes—they could obtain funds on more advantageous terms from other banks—while weak banks "almost invariably seek to sustain themselves by obtaining from the people the largest possible credit in this form." The result was that banknotes often "become suddenly worthless in the hands of the people." Chase suggested that Congress create a single, national currency, with "notes bearing a common impression and authenticated by a common authority," issued and redeemed by banks subject to federal regulation. He did not use the phrase "national banks," but this is clearly what he had in mind: a national system of bank regulation, based on the New York system, which he praised as "practicable and useful." Chase envisaged that "solvent existing institutions" would withdraw their notes issued under state authority and issue new federal notes, so that the existing "heterogenous, unequal, and unsafe" currency would soon be replaced with a "uniform, equal, and safe" currency.[77]

Reaction to Chase's report was mixed. The *Cleveland Daily Leader* praised Chase for writing "a report for the people as well as the financiers." The *Chicago Tribune* agreed that the nation needed "a national currency" to end the cost and difficulty of doing business with different banknotes. The *New York Herald* also supported the currency plan, but the bankers of New York were not pleased, because they did not see a clear plan on how Chase would raise funds in the next few weeks and months. "It is no secret that our bankers do not like Mr. Chase's report," the *New York Herald* reported on December 13. The paper predicted that he would finance the next few months of the war with legal tender notes—that is, with notes that Congress would *require* banks and merchants to accept, even if contracts called for payment in specie. In this scenario, the *Herald* believed, the banks would suspend specie redemption—which might severely affect the economy and federal finances.[78]

Perhaps at Lincoln's request, perhaps on his own initiative, Chase drafted for the president in December a message urging Congress to compensate any border state that would emancipate its slaves. Most Southerners seemed to believe, Chase wrote, that the Republican administration intended to interfere with slavery in the slave states. This was a mere "delusion," and, even now, if the "people of the rebellious districts" would only "reject the counsels of their misleaders, reorganize loyal state governments, and again send senators and representatives to Congress, they would at once find themselves at peace, with no institution changed." To show Southern leaders, however, that they could not extend and perpetuate slavery, Chase proposed that Congress offer federal compensation to state governments that compensated masters for emancipating their slaves. He stressed that the decision on whether and how to emancipate slaves would be up to each border state government. "Such a proposition on the part of Congress would be a distinct and emphatic contradiction of all pretense of federal authority to interfere with slavery within state limits, for it would refer the whole subject to the states and people immediately interested." The proposal would also "furnish clear evidence of the paternal sentiments of the people of the non-slaveholding for the people of the slaveholding states." Lincoln waited awhile, but in March 1862 he revised Chase's draft and submitted it to Congress.[79]

After a gap of more than two years, Chase resumed writing a journal in December 1861, on the very day that he submitted his annual report to Congress. For the next two years, Chase kept a detailed journal, with the help of a department clerk, who turned the secretary's illegible scrawl into a clean copy. Less personal than some of his earlier diaries, because he knew that a clerk would be reading every word, Chase's wartime journals provide invaluable insight into his daily work in the Lincoln administration.[80]

On December 10, for example, Chase noted that the Cabinet discussed prisoner exchanges, with Edward Bates arguing that prisoner exchanges would recognize the Confederates as belligerents. "My own view," Chase wrote, "was that we had already acknowledged the rebels as belligerents by the institution of the blockade, but not as national belligerents" and that prisoner exchanges, if organized by generals rather than governments, would be appropriate and beneficial. The next day, Chase recorded a "multitude of callers at the office," including Senator Benjamin Wade and Representative James Ashley, with whom he discussed the legal status of the "insurrectionary states," whether they were still states or mere territories. Chase also spoke with Montgomery Meigs, the quartermaster general, responsible for military provisions, and John Lee, the judge advocate general, responsible for military justice, about the collection and disposition of the cotton that had come under Union control in the Sea Islands of South Carolina. Should the process be handled by the military, which had officers on the ground, or by the Treasury, which customarily handled abandoned property? They also discussed the question of courts in the Sea Islands and other places under federal control within the rebellious states. Chase noted that "Mr. Lee seemed to favor military commissions for the trial of questions not cognizable by courts martial." Chase and Thomas Key, formerly a lawyer in Cincinnati, now a colonel on McClellan's staff, reviewed a bill that Key had drafted to provide for the compensated emancipation of the slaves in the District of Columbia. After Chase approved the draft, Key shared it with Senator Henry Wilson of Massachusetts, who introduced it in the Senate.[81]

Not trusting Simon Cameron and the War Department, Chase was already taking steps to have the Treasury Department control the Sea Islands, including thousands of black men and women left behind as their white rebel masters fled. On the recommendation of Governor William Sprague, Chase appointed the Rhode Island merchant William Reynolds to go to the islands as a Treasury agent. Chase's initial thinking was that Reynolds would gather and send the cotton to New York, where Hiram Barney would arrange for processing and sale. While Reynolds was on his way south, however, Chase sent a telegram to his Boston protégé Edward Pierce, saying that if he wanted to go to the Sea Islands "in connection with the contrabands and cotton," he should travel to Washington at once. Chase told Pierce that although he was sure Reynolds could handle the business side of gathering and shipping cotton, he did not know whether Reynolds would "sympathize with the laborers" or "strive to promote their personal well-being." Pierce, however, was an ardent friend of the former slaves and familiar with their problems from his work at Fort Monroe. Chase had to work to persuade him, but Pierce agreed to go to the islands as a Treasury agent, and by the end of the year was back in Boston, packing his bags. The *Chicago Tribune*, commenting on Chase's choice of Pierce for this role, said that "no better selection could have been made."[82]

Headlines in the *New York Times* on December 16, 1861, blared that there was "Startling News from England" and the "Imminent Prospect of War." The *Times* and other papers had been predicting that the British government would acquiesce in the seizure of the rebels from the *Trent*, so these reports that the British government was preparing for *war* against the United States, came as a shock. John Cisco wrote to Chase that there was a "feverish excitement" in New York, with some bankers "bereft of their senses." According to Cisco, the banks would probably resolve to suspend specie payments the next day.[83]

Although the bankers did not suspend on that day, Chase went again to New York. The *New York Herald* reported on December 20 that the Treasury secretary had "addressed the bankers at some length" on the prior day, telling them that he "had money enough . . . to carry him through the next thirty days, and it would then be time enough to devise new ways and means." The bankers were dismayed, according to the *Herald*, because Chase's speech failed to "shed any light upon the secretary's schemes." There was a motion to adjourn, which carried, and Chase returned to Washington, seemingly empty-handed. The stock market regained some ground over the next few days, but the New York banks continued to lose specie, partly because they were continuing to pay it to the Treasury for bonds, and partly because people were hoarding gold in the midst of the *Trent* crisis.[84]

As Chase returned to Washington, a British messenger arrived there to deliver the official position of the British government. In brief, Britain demanded that United States return the Confederate diplomats to British custody and apologize for the armed assault on the *Trent*. On December 25 and 26, Lincoln and his Cabinet discussed the *Trent* affair in long, tense meetings. Secretary of State Seward urged his colleagues to agree to the demands, arguing that American legal precedents supported Britain's claims about neutral rights. Chase and the others eventually agreed with Seward. In a long journal entry, Chase wrote that he told the Cabinet that he was worried about the economic effects of the uncertainty about possible war with Britain. He did not want to release the rebel captives; doing so would be "gall and wormwood to me." But he was "consoled by the reflection" that surrendering the diplomats to Britain was "simply doing right; simply proving faithful to our own ideas and traditions under strong temptations to violate them." When Seward's pacific response to the British minister appeared in the papers over the weekend of December 28–29, the Northern public was relieved—indeed, pleased.[85]

The *Trent* crisis had been resolved, but the financial crisis had not. The New York bankers decided, over this same weekend, that they would suspend specie payments starting on Monday, December 30. Chase sent a telegram to Cisco, followed by a letter, directing him to suspend government specie payments. "It is certain that the government cannot pay coin unless the banks do," he wrote. As the year ended, Chase was not sure how he would be paying the increasing cost of the war—other than that he would not be paying with gold coins.[86]

CHAPTER 16

"Slavery Must Go"

EARLY 1862

On the first day of the new year, the president received guests at noon at the White House, and then all the Cabinet members opened the doors of their respective homes at about one o'clock. By custom, anyone decently dressed could call on a Cabinet member on this day, and Attorney General Bates noted that the "constant stream of callers" at his house ranged from "senators down to privates." At the Chase home, his widowed friend Susan Walker (who was staying with Chase at the time) assisted Chase and his daughters with the crowd. Almost all the members of the diplomatic corps called upon Chase, and when the British ambassador arrived, Chase welcomed him in Latin, hoping that the peace between the United States and Britain would be perpetual.[1]

Lincoln and the Cabinet met on the evening of January 6 with the members of the Joint Congressional Committee on the Conduct of the War, recently formed to investigate and oversee the war effort. Chase noted in his diary that several senators "were very earnest in urging the vigorous prosecution of the war, and in recommending the appointment of General McDowell as major general, to command the Army of the Potomac." Although Chase was a friend of McDowell's, and supported his promotion, he also defended McClellan, who was ill with typhoid fever, telling the senators that "if his sickness had not prevented, he would by this time have satisfied everybody in the country of his efficiency and capacity." Chase did agree, however, that "no one person" could manage both the Army of the Potomac and the other federal armies, and that McClellan, "in undertaking to discharge both, had undertaken what he could not perform." The meeting closed with Lincoln saying that he would talk with McClellan about dividing his duties.[2]

On January 9 Henry Cooke and Kate interrupted a meeting at Chase's office to tell him that Nettie, on her way back to boarding school, had fallen ill with scarlet fever. Nettie was with Jay Cooke and his wife at their home outside Philadelphia, and Henry and Kate agreed to go there at once by train and report to Chase by telegraph. Remembering all too well the deaths of three wives and four children, Chase wrote to Kate the next day that he was "very, very uneasy" because "a light case may so easily turn into a serious case." He was pleased that a homeopathic doctor was taking care of Nettie because he recalled "how futile was allopathic practice in the case of my own dear child, whose name you bear," who died at four of scarlet fever. A few days later, Chase wrote to Kate again, thanking her for her letters, giving her some news from Washington, and closing, "May God bless and keep you both."[3]

General McClellan was also seriously ill, with some newspapers hinting that he might die. The general met with Lincoln only once during a three-week period, although he was well enough to confer with aides and to issue some routine orders. As McClellan recovered slowly, Chase spoke on Saturday, January 11, with his friend Thomas Key and through him urged McClellan to "honor the office" by calling upon Lincoln rather than forcing the president to wait upon the general. Chase also spoke this day with his friend Edwin Stanton about McClellan and other generals, but it seems they did not discuss—or were not yet aware of—Lincoln's plans to change the leadership of the War Department.[4]

After church on Sunday, Chase went to the White House for a meeting about military plans. Perhaps prompted by Chase, McClellan had called upon Lincoln in the morning, and the president now suggested that they postpone the larger meeting until the next day, so they could include McClellan. Cameron arrived at Chase's house in the afternoon, and they chatted about the possibility that Cameron would resign his position and go to Russia as the American ambassador there, with Stanton taking over at the War Department. Stanton did not have any military experience, but Cameron and Chase agreed that his energy and organization would help the department. Chase then went to see Seward, who also liked the idea of Stanton as the new secretary. While they were talking, Cameron arrived, incensed by a letter from Lincoln saying that he would "gratify" Cameron by nominating him for the Russian post the next day. Cameron interpreted this letter as a rude dismissal, but Chase and Seward calmed him, telling him that Lincoln intended no such thing and urging him to see the president first thing the next day.[5]

Early Monday, after Lincoln spoke with Cameron and assured him by letter of "undiminished confidence" and "affectionate esteem," Cameron gave Lincoln his resignation. At about midday, the president sent to the Senate the nominations of Cameron for Russia and Stanton for war secretary. In the afternoon, four civilians (Lincoln, Seward, Chase, and Blair) and four generals (McClellan, McDowell, Meigs, and William Franklin) met at the White House. At Lincoln's request, McDowell and Franklin summarized the alternative plans they had prepared, one for an advance on Manassas, the other for an advance by water to a point closer to the Confederate capital in Richmond. McClellan sat in sullen silence, even after Meigs urged him to participate. After a side conversation with Lincoln, Chase told the group that the main purpose of the meeting was to hear and consider McClellan's plans. McClellan answered that he "did not recognize" Chase "as in any manner my official superior" and that he would answer only to the president or the secretary of war—although, with Cameron's resignation, there effectively was no secretary of war at this point. After more whispering between Lincoln and Chase, the president asked McClellan to summarize his thinking. To this, the general replied that "no general fit to command will ever submit his plans to the judgment of such an assembly, in which some were incompetent to form a valuable opinion and others incapable of keeping a secret." Seeing that they could not make progress, Lincoln closed the meeting. A few months later, Chase would cite this as the moment when he ceased to trust McClellan.[6]

Some Democratic newspapers hoped that the nomination of Edwin Stanton was a signal that Lincoln would abandon what they called the "abolition-ist" policies of Chase. Some Republicans, notably Senator Fessenden, were worried about Stanton, who was, after all, a Democrat and a friend of McClellan's. To allay Fessenden's concerns, Chase brought Stanton and Fessenden together for a quiet conversation. Afterward, Fessenden wrote to a cousin that he and Stanton agreed "on every point: the duties of the secretary of war, the conduct of the war, the negro question, and every-thing else." In another letter, the senator said that Chase knew Stanton well and "considers him *the* man for the place and times." With the sup-port of Sumner and Fessenden, Stanton's nomination cleared the Senate easily. Chase was pleased, writing a friend that Stanton would "give a new impetus to movements" as well as "needed guaranties of economy." Chase also warned Cameron against entering into questionable contracts in his last few days in the department. "Let a true and faithful friend take the liberty of begging you to be on your guard and yield to nothing which your own upright judgment would not approve."[7]

Edwin Stanton, secretary of war for Lincoln and Andrew Johnson. Johnson's attempt to remove Stanton led to the first impeachment of a president.

Changing the leadership of the War Department, where Stanton started work on January 20, proved far easier than getting McClellan to move. The first Union victories of the year were won by other generals. In the West, in early February, General Ulysses Grant captured first Fort Henry, on the Tennessee River, and then Fort Donelson, on the Cumberland River. In the East, General Frederick Lander cleared the rebels from the upper Potomac River and thus secured the Baltimore & Ohio Railroad. Chase was elated, writing on February 17 that these "crushing blows" should "dispel all doubt of the ability of the Union to deal with the rebellion" and praising his friend Lander as "a man of the noblest temper and equal genius." Stanton published in the newspapers the congratulatory telegram that he sent to Lander, which said that "you have shown how much may be done in the worst weather and worst roads by a spirited officer, at the head of a small force of brave men, unwilling to waste life in camp when enemies of their country are within reach." Stanton's message was meant for McClellan as much as for Lander.[8]

Joy in Washington over these Union victories was cut short on February 20 by the death of Lincoln's favorite son, eleven-year-old William, or Willie, from typhoid fever. Chase and the other Cabinet members attended the simple funeral services in the Green Room of the White House on the afternoon of February 23. The *New York Herald* reported that Lincoln was "bowed down with grief and anxiety" and that his wife was too distraught to be present. McClellan and Stanton sat side by side among the mourners. After the services, Lincoln, Chase, and others entered their carriages and made their way through a rainstorm to Oak Hill Cemetery in Georgetown, where Willie's body would remain in a vault, pending removal and final burial in Springfield.[9]

Two weeks later, there was another Washington funeral, for Chase's friend General Lander, who had died of pneumonia in his military camp in western Virginia. Lander's body was transported to Washington, embalmed, dressed in full uniform, and then placed in a casket in Chase's parlor, through which hundreds passed to pay their last respects. Lincoln was among those present as Chase came down the stairs with the widow to view her late husband's body before the casket was closed. "Her grief seemed almost insupportable," the *Philadelphia Inquirer* reported, "and she retired after a few minutes, leaning heavily upon the arm of Secretary Chase." The funeral procession formed outside Chase's house, with the widow in Chase's carriage, and went to the nearby Epiphany Episcopal Church, packed with mourners. After the funeral services, the procession formed again and accompanied the casket to the train station through a crowd of about twenty thousand people. Here Lander's body was placed on a train, on its way to burial in his place of birth, Salem, Massachusetts.[10]

Frederick Lander, first Union general to die during the Civil War;
Chase provided his home for holding the funeral.

A few days later, Chase wrote Lincoln a long note to disagree with
McClellan's plans for the Army of the Potomac. Fearing that rebels were
numerous and entrenched at Manassas, the general proposed to put his
army on ships and move them by water to Urbanna, Virginia, near the
mouth of the Rappahannock River. Chase believed that it would make far
more sense for McClellan to march south from Alexandria, Virginia, on
the main road toward Richmond, forcing the enemy to fight somewhere
not far from Washington. McClellan's proposed water movement would
be expensive—cost was always a concern for Chase—whereas "here we
have all our force and material of war, and the enemy is far from his base."
Lincoln agreed, telling McClellan that "going down the bay in search of
a field instead of fighting at or near Manassas was only shifting, and not
surmounting, a difficulty." Already there were rumors that Chase was
trying to have McClellan replaced at the head of the Army of the Potomac—perhaps with General McDowell, or perhaps with General Edwin
Sumner, a cousin of Senator Charles Sumner. General George Meade,

one of McClellan's commanders, wrote to his wife in early March that he heard it "whispered that Generals Sumner and McDowell, the one backed by his cousin the Massachusetts senator, the other by his great friend Secretary Chase, have united their forces with the Frémonters to effect McClellan's destruction." In Meade's opinion, if these politicians succeeded in ousting McClellan from his command, it would mean the end of Union chances in the East.[11]

On Sunday, March 9, startling news arrived in Washington: an ironclad rebel warship, known as the CSS *Virginia* in the South and the *Merrimac* in the North, had attacked and destroyed several wooden Union warships in the Hampton Roads, the broad waters where the James and Elizabeth Rivers empty into the Atlantic Ocean. Chase and the other Cabinet members gathered at the White House, where Stanton worried that the ironclad would steam up the Potomac River and "be in Washington before night." By day's end, there was better news: a telegram from Fort Monroe reporting that a Union ironclad, the USS *Monitor*, had arrived and confronted its counterpart, in a three-hour battle, forcing the *Merrimac* to retreat.[12]

On this same Sunday, reports arrived in Washington that the Confederate army was leaving Manassas. McClellan, assuring Lincoln that he would "move forward to push the retreat of the rebels as far as possible," ordered the Army of the Potomac to march from Washington. When the first Union troops reached Manassas, however, they found no rebels to fight. "The supposed impregnability of Manassas turns out to be a ludicrous sham," the *New-York Tribune* reported, for "the fortifications there consist of only three or four slight earthworks, and a fortified camp of no great strength." Rather than pushing after the retreating rebels, McClellan simply occupied Manassas. The Confederates regrouped just south of the Rappahannock River. This scuttled McClellan's plan to transport troops to Urbanna, because the enemy army was now more or less where he had planned to disembark. So the general decided to transport his army by water to Fortress Monroe, at the tip of the peninsula formed by the York and James Rivers, hoping to march from there westward along the peninsula and to reach Richmond in that way.[13]

As McClellan's troops headed south on their transports, Lincoln issued an order relieving McClellan of responsibility for other armies and departments, explaining that this was necessary because McClellan would be in the field on his Richmond campaign. By the same order, Lincoln placed Henry Halleck in charge of the western armies and John Frémont (still popular among Republicans, although Lincoln and Chase had lost faith in him) at the head of a new department in western Virginia and eastern Kentucky. McClellan was not too troubled by these changes at first, writing his wife that he would be glad to be out of Washington. Within a few days of Lincoln's order, the papers were printing an address from McClellan to his army, patterned on those of the first Napoleon. "I have held you back," McClellan declared, "that you might give the deathblow to the rebellion that has distracted our once happy country." In the coming campaign, he would demand of his troops "great, heroic exertions, rapid and long marches [and] desperate combats." McClellan and his men would "share all these together, and when this sad war is over, we will all return to our homes and feel that we can ask no higher honor than the proud consciousness that we belonged to the Army of the Potomac."[14]

When McClellan reached the peninsula, he was angered to learn that Lincoln had held back part of the Army of the Potomac—the corps under McDowell—to defend Washington. Writing to Lincoln from the outskirts of Yorktown, Virginia, on April 5, McClellan said that he would "have to fight all the available force of the rebels not far from here. Do not force me to do so with diminished numbers." Not getting the answer he wanted from the president, McClellan tried Chase, writing to him through Colonel Thomas Key on April 10: "We are now in front of the enemy who are strongly fortified from Yorktown across the peninsula to the Warwick River," Key wrote, urging the government to send "the whole force originally contemplated when this great movement was commenced." Chase responded to Key that although he had not participated in Lincoln's decision about McDowell, he agreed with it, for Chase believed that McDowell's force, now advancing toward Fredericksburg, Virginia, "could give a much more efficient support to McClellan than if sent into the peninsula."[15]

On Saturday, April 19, Lincoln, Chase, and Stanton left Washington on the first of several military trips this spring. They were joined by John Dahlgren, commander of the Washington Navy Yard, and David Dudley Field, the famous New York lawyer. After boarding the Treasury revenue cutter *Miami* at the Navy Yard, they steamed through rough weather down the Potomac River to Aquia Landing. This was the eastern end of a short but important railroad, connecting Aquia with Falmouth, Virginia, on the north side of the Rappahannock River, opposite Fredericksburg. Part of McDowell's army had just captured Fredericksburg without much difficulty, and the president wanted to discuss the situation with the general.[16]

When they reached Aquia, the senior officer there knew almost nothing; a *New York Herald* reporter who had been with McDowell was better informed. Dahlgren sent word for McDowell to come in the morning, and Lincoln and his colleagues spent what Dahlgren described in his diary as a "gay evening in the little cabin" of the *Miami,* with Lincoln telling jokes "in his usual way." Early the next day, General McDowell briefed the president and his colleagues, explaining that he had only about two thousand troops in Fredericksburg, with the balance of his force, "twenty-five or thirty thousand, rather scattered." When Stanton suggested that Lincoln order Frémont and his troops to come to Fredericksburg to form part of McDowell's force, the president demurred, saying that if he tried to put Frémont under McDowell, "there would be an outcry, for McDowell is junior to Frémont."[17]

The *Miami* started back toward Washington and reached the Navy Yard at about two in the afternoon. "During the whole time, the rain had not ceased, and the weather was nasty." Dahlgren hosted the group for lunch, and then they parted for their respective homes. Chase returned to see Dahlgren in the evening, however, saying that, in his view, Lincoln "was at times indecisive between McClellan, who was assumed to represent the Democrats, and Frémont, who stood for the Republicans." Chase urged Dahlgren to join him the next day at the White House, "to urge my idea of concentrating a large force under McDowell and pushing for Richmond." Dahlgren, not wanting to get involved in army politics, declined.[18]

The major battle of April 1862 was not fought in the East, by McClellan or McDowell, but in the West, by Grant and Sherman. Halleck had hoped to combine the armies of Grant and Don Carlos Buell to attack the rebel army at Corinth, Mississippi. Instead, the rebels attacked Grant at nearby Shiloh, Tennessee. Chase learned about the two-day battle not only from the newspapers but also through long letters from William Nelson and Lovell Rousseau—two of the more than forty generals with whom he would correspond over the course of the war.[19] Nelson, whose regiments rushed to reinforce Grant on the first day of the fighting, told Chase that the battle was a "blunder on our part arising from the sheer stupidity of our generals." So unprepared and inattentive were Grant's troops that the rebels surprised one regiment while it was eating breakfast and "took the whole of them prisoners without firing a shot." Nelson condemned Grant and praised Sherman, calling him "the soul of the battle." Rousseau, whose regiments were also in the thick of the fight, agreed with Nelson, writing, "The battle has blown to the winds all our admiration for General Grant. I never confided in his alleged genius, but believed him energetic, and for that admired him. But he is not a safe man and will bring ruin upon the cause if he has the power." Shiloh was not Grant's finest hour, but he owned up to his errors and learned from them, in a way that McClellan never would have.[20]

The key financial question facing Chase and Congress in the first few months of 1862 was how the government would finance the war while specie payments were suspended. Bankers arrived in Washington in January to meet with Chase and members of Congress. Many newspapers now believed that Congress should authorize the Treasury secretary to issue legal tender notes. Other papers, like the *National Republican*, argued that legal tender notes were unnecessary and unconstitutional, because those who had bargained for payment in gold would be deprived of their property without due process of law. As the bankers departed Washington, several papers printed what they called Chase's summary of his agreement with the bankers. According to this summary, legal tender notes would be "unnecessary" if Congress authorized the Treasury to borrow another $250 million and adopted currency and national bank legislation along the lines suggested in Chase's report. Almost immediately, however, Chase started to hear from bankers and from key members of Congress, including his friend Hooper, who told him point-blank that federal notes "must necessarily be made legal tender."[21]

Chase wrote on January 22 to Elbridge Spaulding, a member of the House Ways and Means Committee, explaining that he and John Cisco had revised Spaulding's draft legal tender bill, preserving the substance but changing some details. The committee approved and reported the revised bill the same day. Some papers claimed that Chase favored the bill, but his letter was equivocal. He described himself as "regretting exceedingly that it is found necessary to resort to the measure of making fundable notes of the United States a legal tender, but heartily desiring to cooperate with the committee in all measures to meet existing necessities in the mode most useful and least hurtful to the general interest."[22]

The committee asked for a more formal expression of Chase's views on the legal tender question, and he responded on January 29, admitting that he felt "a great aversion to making anything but coin a legal tender in payment of debts." The suspension of specie payments, however, and the expenditures for the war made it impossible for the government "to procure sufficient coin for disbursements, and it has therefore become inevitably necessary that we should resort to the issue of United States notes." It might have been possible to issue notes, but not legal tender notes, "if the willingness manifested by the people generally, by the railroad companies, and by many of the banking institutions, to receive and pay them as money in all transactions, were absolutely or practically universal." But some banks and some creditors would refuse to accept such federal notes or take them only at a deep discount, so a legal tender clause was needed for fairness. Chase also stressed the importance of imposing more taxes to back up the notes with revenues, and he provided line-by-line comments on the details of the bill.[23]

On February 3 Chase wrote again to Spaulding, saying that although he "came with some reluctance to the conclusion that the legal tender clause is a necessity," he "came to it decidedly, and I support it earnestly." Chase stressed that "immediate action is of great importance. The Treasury is nearly empty." Chase must have sent this by messenger to Capitol Hill, because Spaulding quoted from this letter in the course of that day's debates. Spaulding and Thaddeus Stevens needed Chase's letter because the opposition in the House to the legal tender language came not just from Democrats but also from some leading Republicans. Justin Morrill, Republican from Vermont, declared that he would "as soon provide Chinese wooden guns for the army as paper money alone for the Treasury." Roscoe Conkling, Republican from upstate New York, warned that people would always prefer gold to paper notes issued by a government in the midst of a civil war. The proposed legal tender notes would depreciate from the day they were issued, Conkling said, until they became as worthless as the paper money issued by the Continental Congress during the Revolution.[24]

A few days later, on February 6, Chase sent a fourth letter to a member of the House, this time to his Ohio friend John Bingham. "The legal tender clause, in my judgment, has become a matter not merely of necessity but of vital necessity. If possible, let the bill go through today. A week will be required after its passage before the notes authorized by it can be

engrossed, printed, and brought here from New York." The House passed
the bill on this day, but not by an overwhelming margin, for twenty-three
Republicans joined the Democrats in opposition. Chase was distressed to
learn from William Fessenden that it would probably take the Senate at
least a week to consider and pass the legal tender bill. He urged Fessenden to pass as soon as possible a bill to authorize another $10 million of
demand notes, on the same terms as the prior year's notes. This emergency
bill passed the Senate on February 7, the House on February 10, and was
signed into law on February 12. The Senate passed the legal tender bill
on February 13, but with some changes, so that a conference committee
was necessary—delaying its final passage until February 25.[25]

In its final form, this first legal tender bill authorized the Treasury to
issue $150 million of demand notes and declared that these notes would
"be lawful money and a legal tender in payment of all debts, public and
private," except for amounts owed to the government for import duties,
and amounts owed by the government for interest, both of which would
still be paid in specie. The bill also authorized the Treasury to borrow
another $500 million in the form of bonds, with interest at 6 percent,
payable in specie. The term of these bonds was twenty years, but the
Treasury could redeem them after five years, and they were soon known
as the five-twenties. Congress had been considering simple twenty-year
bonds; it was Chase who insisted on the five-year redemption clause, so
that if conditions changed, the Treasury could redeem the bonds early
and cease paying interest in gold at 6 percent.[26]

The legal tender bill was an important step but far from a complete
solution of Chase's financial problems. He reported to Thaddeus Stevens
on February 25 that the department had more than $25 million in unpaid
requisitions, that it would take time to prepare and print the new legal
tender notes, and that the notes would depreciate unless Congress soon
passed strong tax legislation, to assure people that the government would
have the funds to redeem the notes rather than issuing yet more notes.
As a stopgap, Chase suggested that Congress authorize the government
to use one-year certificates of indebtedness.[27]

Although Chase and others were keen to see Congress pass tax legislation—Fessenden told the Senate in February that "we must tax speedily,
strongly, vigorously"—the process took many months. In late March the
papers reported that the Treasury secretary was drafting his own bill that
would tax fewer items but tax them more heavily. Chase was supposedly

considering taxes as high as 50 percent or even 100 percent on tobacco and whiskey. Chase decided, however, to leave such questions to Congress. The House passed its tax bill on April 8, the Senate passed a very different bill on June 6, and the final bill did not pass until July 1, almost the end of the session. In its final form, the Revenue Act of 1862, running for more than sixty printed pages in the official compilation of federal statutes, imposed a progressive income tax with no tax due from those whose incomes were less than $600 per year, 3 percent due from those earning between $600 and $10,000. The Revenue Act created within the Treasury Department a new internal revenue office to collect income and other internal taxes, including levies on liquor, tobacco, and playing cards, and license fees for professionals, including bankers, lawyers, and even jugglers. It would be up to Chase, in the coming months, to turn this complex statute into additional federal revenue.[28]

Secretary Chase navigated these financial issues in the midst of talk that he would resign in order to return to the Senate, to take the seat occupied by Benjamin Wade when his term ended in early 1863. According to one Ohio politician, Chase was interested in the Senate seat, or a place on the Supreme Court, because he feared that to "reach the presidency, with Seward's opposition and all the contingencies and very great dangers of managing the finances during this very great crisis, is rather a hard road to travel." Chase discouraged such talk, however, writing to an Ohio editor that he had no interest in the Senate seat. Although he had not wanted the Treasury post initially, he would not now "shrink from its responsibilities. I have entire faith in our ability to crush out the rebellion and entire confidence, if I can get my views of finance into law, that we shall save the cost of the war in our secured and improved currency." Chase also did not want to desert Lincoln at this critical juncture, writing to Jay Cooke in May, "I have always found his judgment wonderfully good."[29]

"We must learn to imitate the grand patience of God," Chase wrote to an antislavery friend, but not "shrink from the imitation of his justice and his constant energy also." Chase's own "constant energy" was especially focused in early 1862 on helping the ten thousand former slaves on the Sea Islands of South Carolina and Georgia. His principal agent in this mission was his friend Edward Pierce, but Chase collaborated with many

others, including the reformer Reverend Mansfield French, who met with
Chase in Washington in January before heading to the Sea Islands. Chase
encouraged French and other Christian ministers to provide "the colored
population of the islands now occupied by the United States" with the
"means of religious instruction, ordinary education, and medical care"
and assured them that the "action of this department, within the range
of its legal authority, will be cheerfully and gladly directed in aid of any
voluntary benevolent movement." From the start, Chase envisaged what
we would call a "public-private partnership" in the Sea Islands; he hoped
for close cooperation among military officers, Treasury agents, religious
leaders, and private volunteers.[30]

Not long after arriving in Port Royal, South Carolina, in January, Pierce
sent the first of many long reports to Chase. His initial question concerned
his relationship with Chase's other agent in the Islands, William Reynolds.
Did the Treasury secretary's instruction that Pierce should "report" to
Reynolds upon arrival mean that he was subordinate to Reynolds? Pierce
believed, based on his conversations with Chase, that he was supposed to
"cooperate with, not to serve" Reynolds, and, furthermore, that he was
to work to secure the good will of the former slaves—"this last being
particularly important, as they were no longer slaves subject to the master's lash but freemen under military discipline." Was this right? Pierce
provided Chase with a concrete example of how he saw things differently
from Reynolds: "The impression seems to be pretty strong here that the
cotton should not be ginned here but in New York because it will take
more time and labor to do it here." But Pierce believed that it was "of
the highest importance that the negroes should be kept at work, and at
work which they have been accustomed to do." Accordingly, if they could
gin the cotton in South Carolina, as they had in the past, Pierce believed
they should do so. Pierce noted that Reynolds had asked Hiram Barney to
send clothes for the freedmen but feared that "the want is probably much
greater than the government will feel able to supply," so Pierce would ask
charitable friends in Boston to send clothing.[31]

Two weeks later, in early February, Pierce sent Chase a far longer
report from Port Royal, which Chase soon shared with the newspapers.
Pierce provided details about the contraband camps and the plantations,
where most of the former slaves were still living, for they were "attached
to the places where they have lived." He believed that the former slaves
would, with proper encouragement, work to raise and process cotton and

other crops. In the longer run, "the opportunity is now offered to us to make of them, partially in this generation and fully in the next, a happy, industrious, law-abiding, free, and Christian people, if we have but the courage and patience to accept it." Reynolds had urged Chase to lease the plantations to white landlords who could raise cotton, on the condition that they agree "to employ the negroes and pay them from ten to twelve dollars per month." Without naming Reynolds, Pierce disagreed about leasing, urging Chase to appoint for each plantation a superintendent charged with operating it for the government and paying the former slaves about forty cents per day.[32]

Not long after this report, Pierce arrived in Washington to consult with Chase. They agreed to implement a system of superintendents and also that Pierce should go to New York and Boston to select those who would serve. As Chase explained in a letter of February 19, he wanted Pierce to appoint superintendents and others on the understanding that their compensation would come from private charitable organizations, with only "subsistence, quarters, and transportation" provided by the government. Chase also directed Pierce to "give all suitable support and aid to any persons commissioned or employed by the associations, for the religious instruction, ordinary education, or general employment of the laboring population." By the time he wrote this, Chase probably had in hand a letter from French advising that many of the former slaves "have only the clothing furnished for last year, which is now nearly worn out, and, without an immediate supply, they must not only suffer but be unable to cultivate the plantations." French also warned Chase that "they are wholly without physicians and means to employ any, and yet are suffering more or less from sickness, and, in not a few instances, dying for want of medical aid." Like Chase and Pierce, French believed that antislavery men and women would be eager to help, and French was one of the lead speakers at a meeting at Cooper Union on February 20, which led to the formation of the New York National Freedmen's Relief Association. A similar charitable organization was already at work in Boston.[33]

Over the next two weeks, Chase was in constant touch with Pierce, French, and others about the Sea Islands. Pierce wrote from Boston that the community was "profoundly moved" by the plight of the former slaves. Since "ladies are to go," Pierce hoped that Susan Walker would "accompany them and inspire all with her good sense and patient humanity." Chase responded on February 24 that Walker and two of her friends, "each

admirable in her way," would go with Pierce. Chase cautioned Pierce, "I
have no fund at my disposal from which I can pay the laborers at Port
Royal, and must rely for that purpose upon the proceeds of the sale of
cotton gathered and raised on the abandoned plantations." Therefore,
the "most careful economy must be observed, to avoid all grounds of just
reproach in conducting this experiment." In a letter to Barney the same
day, Chase instructed him to confer with Pierce and purchase the necessary
ploughs, hoes, and other implements, with the cost to be covered by the
sale of the cotton already in Barney's hands. Chase also instructed Barney
to advance Pierce sufficient funds to pay 1,500 laborers for one month at
the rate of forty cents per day. On February 27, however, he wrote Pierce to
say that he believed that "your rate of wages, forty cents a day, is too high."
The government could not "expend more than is absolutely necessary nor
give wages the practical result of which will be to encourage expectations
which cannot be gratified in the long run." The next day, Chase wrote both
Pierce and Barney, saying that he had heard from Governor Sprague that
there were not enough doctors on the islands, and urging them to send
physicians on the ship that would sail south in a few days.[34]

On March 2 Pierce wrote another long letter to Chase from New York.
The following day, more than fifty people, selected carefully to serve as
superintendents, doctors, teachers, and ministers, would accompany him
aboard the steamship *Atlantic* to the Sea Islands. Pierce explained the
selection processes, noting that he had rejected some pacifists because they
refused to take an oath of loyalty to the federal government, and some
women because they were too young—although he changed his mind
about one young woman after Susan Walker vouched for her. Closing his
letter at midnight, Pierce wrote that he had attempted "to do everything
as if you were looking on, or as you would have done it yourself."[35]

When Pierce returned to the Sea Islands, his letters to Chase resumed.
On March 14 he reported that there was agitation among the blacks on
the plantation of Richard Fuller, a Baltimore minister who claimed that
because he was loyal to the Union, the blacks on his plantation were still
his slaves. "It would be a folly and a crime," Pierce wrote, "to put these
negroes on a different basis from all their neighbors with whom they are
intertwined by kin or friendship. Like the others, they are our allies in
this war." Although Fuller had an argument under the Confiscation Act,
Chase believed that the situation in the Sea Islands required the government to treat all the slaves there as free. As it happened, the minister had

come to see Chase the day before Pierce wrote his letter, asking about the status of his slaves. Chase wrote in his diary that he told Fuller that his former slaves were now free. When Fuller persisted, saying that "his right to them was the same as his right to the land," Chase conceded that legal opinions "would differ on that point," but insisted that he would "never consent to the involuntary reduction to slavery of one of the negroes who had been in the service of the government."[36]

On March 20 the *New York Times* published a letter from Port Royal that praised Reynolds and abused Pierce and French, claiming their "mad scheme" for turning the former slaves into free citizens showed their "utter ignorance of the negro character." Chase wrote at once to Reynolds, saying that he hoped the letter in the *Times* was not written by anyone "connected with you," but that if it was, that person "should be promptly dismissed." On March 30 Pierce wrote to Chase that William Nobles and two other Reynolds agents were "the worst kind of men for their places" and were "doing all they can to defeat the movement entrusted to me— to prejudice the negroes against the superintendents and in every way destroy my usefulness." Pierce pleaded with Chase to send on the next steamer "an order discontinuing these three persons from the service of your department, accompanied by an order from the War Department ordering them to leave Port Royal at once." Reynolds complained to Chase at almost the same time that although he had tried to work with Pierce, it had proved impossible, with Pierce improperly "assuming authority over those employed by me and dictating in matters connected with my department." Chase did not respond to these complaints, other than to write Pierce that the War Department would soon take over the Sea Islands, and that Edwin Stanton would offer Pierce a suitable military appointment if he wanted to continue his work there.[37]

The change that Chase had dreamed of for more than twenty years—freedom for the slaves in the District of Columbia—arrived at last in April 1862, when Congress passed a bill based on the draft of his friend Thomas Key. Just as the authors of the Constitution had avoided the words *slave* and *slavery*, Congress avoided these words now. The first section of the bill provided that on the date it was signed "all persons held to service or labor within the District of Columbia by reason of African descent [would be] discharged and freed of and from all claim to such service or labor." A three-member commission would consider requests from loyal masters for compensation, limited to no more than $300 for each person held to service. The bill also provided for colonization, creating a fund of $100,000, to be distributed as the president directed, in amounts not exceeding $100 per person, among "free persons of African descent, including those liberated by this act," who wished to emigrate to the Caribbean or Africa.[38]

After what Chase described as a "long and exciting session," the House passed the Senate emancipation bill on April 11. Various amendments were offered, including one by Representative Charles Train of Massachusetts, who argued that the $300 per person limit, far less than the market value of many slaves, and the lack of any right to appeal from the commission to the courts, violated the constitutional prohibition against taking private property without due process. The House defeated the Train amendment by a narrow vote, but some papers speculated that the president would not sign the bill without the Train amendment or other changes. On April 16, however, without any changes, Lincoln signed the bill into law, setting off rejoicing among the slaves of the district. Chase rejoiced as well, sending Key a telegram to say that "you never performed a more honorable work." A few days later, Chase received a letter from two black leaders informing him that "the colored people of this district propose to give you a vocal and instrumental concert" to show their "appreciation of your early, consistent, and able services as lawyer, orator, and statesman in the cause of human freedom."[39]

Congress also passed at this time several other laws that Chase had long supported. More than a decade after he and others had called for free soil, the Homestead Act of 1862 allowed citizens and immigrants who intended to become citizens to acquire homesteads of 160 acres. Chase predicted that as soon as the "working millions of Europe" learned of the benefits of this new law, "great numbers will seek American homes." Chase welcomed such immigrants: "Every working man who comes betters the condition of the nation as well as his own. He adds in many ways, seen and unseen, to its wealth, its intelligence, and its power." The Land-Grant College Act provided grants of federal lands to the states on the condition that they use the proceeds from the land sales to create and finance colleges. The Pacific Railway Act provided federal financing for private construction of the transcontinental railroad, started during the war and completed in 1869. Chase was excited about the "great work which is to link the East and the West" and recalled the "old days in the Senate when I ventured almost if not quite alone to stand up for the line which has been finally adopted."[40]

McClellan "dallies and waits in eternal preparation" at Yorktown, Chase wrote in his diary on the first of May. "Strange that the president does not give McDowell all the available force in the region and send him on to Richmond." At last, on May 4, McClellan reported to Washington that he had captured Yorktown; it soon emerged that the rebels had retreated so that the federal troops simply walked into the town. Lincoln decided to go south himself, and on the evening of May 5, Lincoln, Chase, and Stanton once again boarded the *Miami*, this time accompanied by General Egbert Viele.[41]

By noontime the next day, as Chase reported to his daughter Nettie, "our staunch little steamer" was being tossed about on the choppy waters of Chesapeake Bay. Lincoln said that he was "too uncomfortable to eat" and "stretched himself at length upon a locker." The others attempted to eat lunch, but the "plates slipped this way and that, the glasses tumbled over and rolled about, and the whole table seemed as topsy-turvy as if some spiritualist were operating upon it." They reached Fort Monroe at about nine that night and met first with General John Wool (the oldest general in the Union army) and Commodore Louis Goldsborough (the husband of Chase's friend Elizabeth Wirt and head of the naval forces in the area). The meeting with Goldsborough was on his flagship, the *Minnesota*, and as their small tug pulled up to the warship, Chase was daunted by the sight of the narrow steps up the steep side. "But etiquette required the president to go first, and he went," he wrote. "Etiquette required the secretary of the Treasury to follow, and I followed. We got up safely, of course, and, when up, it did not seem so very much of a getting upstairs after all." Following a brief conference over the maps, Lincoln, Chase, and Stanton returned to the *Miami* to sleep.[42]

When the presidential party first arrived at Fort Monroe, Stanton had sent a telegram to General McClellan, suggesting that he come to confer with them. McClellan declined, saying he was too busy to leave for even an hour, and he did not find time to see Lincoln during the five days the president was only a few miles away. Instead of worrying about McClellan, Lincoln and his colleagues decided to focus on matters closer at hand. They started May 7 with a morning tour of the USS *Vanderbilt*, a vessel donated to the government by the wealthy financier Cornelius Vanderbilt and fitted with a metal prow to ram and destroy ironclads. Then Lincoln, Chase, and Stanton toured the USS *Monitor,* the first of the Northern ironclads, described in some newspapers as "a big black Yankee cheese box on a raft."[43]

In the afternoon, at Lincoln's suggestion, several Union warships bombarded the rebel guns at Sewell's Point near Norfolk, Virginia. As they observed the attack, Lincoln and his colleagues saw smoke from behind the point, and said to one another that it must be the *Merrimac.* The Union leaders headed back to Fort Monroe and, from that safe vantage point, watched as the two ironclads confronted each other. Without even a single shot being fired, the *Merrimac* turned and retreated. "The rebel monster don't want to fight," wrote Chase, "and *won't* fight if she can help it."[44]

After this, the group toured Hampton, Virginia, burned by the rebels in July 1861 as they retreated. "I never saw such a ruin—bare, blackened, crumbling walls on every hand," Chase remarked. He was especially moved by the ancient Episcopal church, "where generations of Virginians had been baptized, confirmed, married, admitted to the Communion, and dismissed with tears and benedictions to their last repose." Lincoln, Chase, and Stanton also reviewed the troops at Fort Monroe: "regiment after regiment of infantry, all appearing handsomely and some wonderfully well." Chase was happy to "observe everywhere the warm affection felt and expressed for the president."[45]

Receiving reports that the rebels were abandoning Norfolk, the largest town and key port in the region, Lincoln decided to attempt its capture. On May 9, Chase and Wool boarded the *Miami* to scout for a landing place for the general's troops. Back at the Fort, Chase learned that Lincoln had found another possible landing place on the maps and wanted to see it for himself. This time Chase went in the *Miami*, and Lincoln in a smaller boat nearer the shore—so near that at one point Chase feared that the president might be fired upon by rebels upon the shore. They found another promising location, but Wool preferred the one that he and Chase had found, so that was the landing used. It was night when Chase returned to the fort, where "the preparations proceeded with great activity."[46]

Everyone was up early on Saturday, May 10, and Lincoln, Chase, and Stanton went to the landing place to watch as some of the troops climbed the sandy beach and marched off toward Norfolk. Without explaining his reasons, Stanton asked Chase to accompany the troops on their advance, and he agreed, although there was no way of knowing whether they would face skirmishes or even a full-scale battle later in the day. Chase mounted a horse and together with Viele and a small guard trotted south, catching up with the main body of troops after four or five miles. Here there were some rebel guns in action, a key bridge in flames, and, for a few minutes, there was confusion. Viele, a few days later, wrote that he was impressed by the "facility with which Secretary Chase, without any pretension to military knowledge, comprehended at once the whole situation of affairs." Chase gave a few quick orders: dispatching a courier back for Wool, putting Viele in charge of a column of troops, and sending them off to the left, around the burning bridge.[47]

The Union march continued, through heat and dust. As they approached Confederate fortifications a few miles north of Norfolk, where, in Chase's words "we expected the rebels would fight if anywhere," they learned that the works "had just been evacuated." The Union troops, as they entered these empty defenses, "gave cheer after cheer and were immediately formed into line for the further march, now only two miles, to Norfolk." Not long thereafter, Chase and Wool met "a deputation of the city authorities," who, in a small cottage near the side of the road, surrendered the city to the Union forces. The mayor offered Wool and Chase a ride into the city in his carriage—the very carriage used earlier in the day by the Confederate general as his troops scrambled to leave the town and destroy as much as they could at the naval yard.[48]

At Norfolk City Hall, at about six in the evening, Chase and Wool drafted the brief document by which Wool appointed Viele as the military governor of the city and directed him to protect the residents "in all their rights and civil privileges." After issuing this order, Wool and Chase returned to the carriage and rode back to the landing point, reaching there about eight in the evening. Here they briefed a correspondent for the *New York Times*, one of several reporters who filed detailed accounts on the day's events. It was almost midnight when Chase and Wool returned to Fortress Monroe and reported to Lincoln and Stanton. Both men were, in Chase's words, "delighted," and Stanton "fairly hugged General Wool."[49]

There was more happiness in the morning. As Chase came in for breakfast about seven, Goldsborough "astonished and gratified us" with the news that the "rebels had set fire to the *Merrimac* and blown her up."

Without the base at Norfolk, and without time for the ironclad to reach another base, the rebels had decided to destroy the *Merrimac* rather than see it captured. Sitting at the same table as Stanton, Chase penned a hasty letter to General Ambrose Burnside, commanding federal forces on the coast of North Carolina, urging him to attack now that he need not fear rebel reinforcements from Norfolk. Lincoln and the others decided to see for themselves the remains of the *Merrimac*—the site "where the suicide had been performed," in Chase's words—and also whether warships could reach Norfolk. Boarding the USS *Baltimore* to head up the Elizabeth River, Lincoln, Chase, and Stanton reached the wharves of Norfolk, finding the town quiet on Sunday morning. The civilian leaders did not disembark, simply leaving Wool and Goldsborough there, and, turning the ship north, headed for home.[50]

"So has ended a brilliant week's campaign of the president," is how Chase concluded his third letter to Nettie, "for I think it quite certain that if he had not come down, Norfolk would still have been in the possession of the enemy and the *Merrimac* as grim and defiant and as much a terror as ever." Writing to McDowell a few days later, Chase urged him to action. "It has been one of my prime objects and desires that you should advance towards and *to* Richmond," he advised. "McClellan, surrounded by a staff of letter writers, gets possession of public opinion, and even those who know better succumb. Then he lags. If the president, Stanton, and I had not gone to Fortress Monroe, all would have lagged there too."[51]

Not long after he returned to Washington, Chase learned that the tension in the Sea Islands between Pierce on the one hand and Reynolds and his friend Nobles on the other had turned violent: Nobles had attacked Pierce on the streets a week earlier. Pierce wrote Chase that Nobles had emerged from Reynolds's quarters, "accosted me with abusive language, damning me for reporting him to the Treasury Department, then, before I was aware of his purpose, struck me violently on the head and, knocking me down, continued to beat me." Chase wrote at once to General Rufus Saxton, recently appointed by Stanton to fill a role in the Sea Islands akin to the role Pierce had played for Chase, asking Saxton to investigate and, if proper, punish Nobles. Chase also provided Stanton with everything he knew about the incident. Responding to Pierce, Chase apologized for the attack and tried to persuade him to remain and work with Saxton, whom both Chase and Pierce liked. By this point, however, Pierce was eager to return home.[52]

It was on this same day, May 16, that Chase learned from the newspapers that General David Hunter, the new commander of the military department composed of Florida, Georgia, and South Carolina, had recently issued an order imposing martial law and freeing the slaves in those three states. The general did not explain his order other than to say that "slavery and martial law in a free country are altogether incompatible." Hunter's forces controlled only a small fraction of the territory in his department, yet the order purported to free all the slaves in the three states. Because Chase was leaving for New York City, he could not speak with Lincoln about Hunter's order, so he wrote him a short note, urging him not to revoke the decree: "It has been made as a military measure to meet a military exigency, and should, in my judgment, be suffered to stand upon the responsibility of the commanding general who made it."[53]

Chase did not receive Lincoln's response until May 19, when he returned from New York City. "No commanding general shall do such a thing," Lincoln wrote, "upon *my* responsibility, without consulting me." Chase also saw in the papers that Lincoln had issued a proclamation revoking Hunter's order and reserving to himself the questions of whether he had the power to free the slaves of any rebellious state and whether it "shall have become a necessity indispensable to the maintenance of the government to exercise such supposed power." The president also used this proclamation to press the border states again on the question of gradual compensated emancipation, noting that both houses of Congress were supportive and arguing that if the loyal slave states would just take this step, the rebel slave states would return to the Union. One might question Lincoln's political judgment on this point: it seems unlikely that the slave masters of South Carolina or Alabama would have abandoned their rebellion just because Delaware or Maryland started the gradual emancipation of their slaves, but there is no question that the president was convinced that seeing slavery end in the border states would convince at least some people in the Confederacy that there was no point continuing a war for slavery.[54]

Chase was so angered by Lincoln's decision to revoke Hunter's order that he wrote to Hunter, telling him that he had "begun a great and necessary work." On reflection, Chase realized this was a mistake, so he sent a telegram to Barney to intercept and destroy the Hunter letter. Writing to Horace Greeley, Chase said that although he might not have issued the order if he were in Hunter's place, the order had been issued and should have been accepted. Hunter's order was "a mere anticipation, by only a few weeks, perhaps, of what must be done in some way unless we are prepared to surrender the idea" of conquering the rebellious slave states. Surely the order should "have been allowed to stand until the case could have been clearly and fully stated by [Hunter] himself." But Lincoln had made his decision, and the only course for Chase was to "be thankful for skim milk when one can't get cream."[55]

As strongly as Chase approved Hunter's order declaring the slaves in his department free, he disagreed with a subsequent order from the general decreeing that all the able-bodied black men in his department must serve in the army. Chase learned of this from Pierce, who wrote to describe how Union soldiers rounded up frightened blacks and transported them to Hilton Head. "Sometimes whole plantations, learning what was going on, ran off into the woods for refuge. Others, with no means of escape, submitted passively to the decree." Pierce was in favor of allowing blacks to enlist in the army if they wanted to but condemned forcing unwilling men into service. "It should not be done with white men, least of all with blacks, who do not yet understand us." In a second letter, Pierce wrote, "I think there may be some irregularity, almost aberration, in [Hunter's] mind. This is not the first time since his arrival where he has acted without premeditation or examination, and the next day recalled an order just issued. He has evidently been brooding over the arming of negroes for some time, and seems to be carried away by it, and, in his action, ignores all sources of information." Having ceded control of the islands to the War Department, however, Chase could not do much other than pass these letters on to Stanton, urging that he read them carefully.[56]

On Saturday, May 24, Lincoln sent Chase on a third military mission, this time to see General Irvin McDowell at Falmouth. Reports had arrived in Washington in the morning that Confederate general Thomas "Stonewall" Jackson and his army had routed the federal forces under General Nathaniel Banks at Front Royal, Virginia, about seventy miles west of Washington. Jackson and his men were chasing the federals north, toward the Potomac. Lincoln and Stanton sent orders to McDowell to suspend his planned march south toward Richmond and to send troops north to support Banks. Knowing that these orders would disappoint McDowell—who had hoped for the glory of capturing Richmond—the president sent Chase to speak with his friend. Leaving Washington by steamer in the early afternoon and then boarding a military train at Aquia, it was after midnight when Chase reached McDowell's Falmouth headquarters.[57]

From there, the Treasury secretary sent a steady stream of telegrams back to Washington, reporting on developments and seeking instructions. In his first message, Chase informed Stanton that the division of Brigadier General James Shields was already on the march toward Banks. In another message, responding to a question from Lincoln as to why a brigade was being sent to Alexandria, Chase explained that this was part of the movement, intended to expedite the process. Lincoln wrote to Chase that the rebels were "pouring through the gap" they had made yesterday and that it would be a "very valuable and very honorable service for Gen. McDowell to cut them off." To this, Chase replied that McDowell "appreciates, as you do, the importance of the service he is called on to perform. All possible exertion is being made by him and the officers under him to expedite the movement."[58]

Chase left Falmouth on Sunday afternoon and arrived back in Washington around midnight. Heading straight from the dock to the War Department, he found Lincoln, Stanton and Seward. Chase reported on what he had seen in Falmouth, and they described for him the efforts not merely to reinforce Banks but also "to cut off the retreat of Jackson through Front Royal." Although the Treasury secretary was back at his desk on Monday morning, working on financial questions, he kept closely in touch with military matters as well.[59]

By late June, some of McClellan's troops were so close to Richmond that they could hear its church bells. Rather than wait for an attack upon the city's defenses, the new commander of the Army of Northern Virginia, Robert E. Lee, attacked McClellan. In the course of seven days, in which each side saw more than fifteen thousand men killed, wounded, or captured, Lee forced McClellan to retreat to a defensive position on the James River, at Harrison's Landing, Virginia. Although McClellan and others talked about resuming the advance upon Richmond, it would soon emerge that the last of the seven days, July 1, was the end of the Peninsula campaign, the end for now of the Northern hope of winning the war by capturing the Southern capital.[60]

More and more Southern territory was under Northern control in early 1862, and reports and questions from these places frequently reached Chase's desk. For example, General Ormsby Mitchel wrote Chase a long letter from Huntsville, Alabama, describing how he had captured the town and surrounding region, and how he hoped to see Northern cotton purchasers so that cotton trade could resume. Chase responded by telegram that the government had "no objection to the purchase of cotton wherever the military lines extend." A few weeks later, the general wrote again, asking whether he could issue permits to allow supplies into his region. In yet another message, Mitchel asked Chase about cotton owned by a rebel general: Could he sell the cotton and give the proceeds to the general's wife "on a solemn pledge that it shall not be employed to aid the rebellion?" Chase advised Mitchel to use his discretion.[61]

Lincoln started this spring the process of reconstructing the Union by appointing military governors for some Southern states. In March he named Andrew Johnson military governor of Tennessee, now largely in Union hands, and in May he named Edward Stanly for North Carolina, still largely under Confederate control. Chase did not have much to do with Stanly, but there was a steady stream of letters between Chase and Johnson in Nashville, with the secretary generally deferring to the governor, because he was the man on the ground. For example, Chase asked Johnson to name the person that he wanted as the surveyor of the port of Nashville, and Chase allowed Johnson to issue trade permits in Tennessee rather than insisting that this was a Treasury role. At one point, Chase praised Johnson's work as military governor, writing to him that history would record the names of those who saved the Union, and "high up among these future generations will read the name of Andrew Johnson." In short, Chase and Johnson, who would disagree so strongly after the war, got along well during the Civil War.[62]

One of Stanly's first actions in North Carolina was to "close schools for contrabands at New Bern and other points," leading to criticism in some papers. The *New York Herald* defended Stanly, saying he was "the right man in the right place," unlike the "pious blockhead Pierce, who was sent into South Carolina by Secretary Chase to look after the niggers." A few days later. the *Herald* claimed that Chase was losing popularity because he was becoming an abolitionist like Horace Greeley or Wendell

Phillips. Chase "had acquired a high reputation for his management of the finances of the country [but] if he continues in this course, soon not a shred of it will be left." The next day, the *Herald* accused him of bad faith, saying that he came to New York City and sought funds from the "conservative merchants" on the basis that this would be a war for Union. "But no sooner does he accomplish his object than he turns around and goes to work to make the war a war of abolition. If he had declared this purpose at first, how much money would he have received? Not a dollar."[63]

By far the most important Southern territory under Northern control was New Orleans, the cosmopolitan city of more than 150,000 people near the mouth of the Mississippi River. When General Benjamin Butler arrived there in May 1862, he found a few of the local whites loyal and supportive, but most of them were hostile. Some of the strongest Union supporters were free blacks, especially the educated Creole elite of lawyers, doctors, and editors. Chase's first step with respect to New Orleans was to appoint two special agents to go there, one to take control of the customshouse and the other of the mint. For the customshouse, Chase selected a relative, George Denison, son of Chase's late cousin and college correspondent Joseph Denison. The younger Denison, who had lived in the South before fleeing to the North at the outset of the Civil War, was Chase's principal agent in New Orleans for the next few years.[64]

Chase was also in frequent contact with General Butler, both on routine matters and major issues. In late June he wrote a long letter to Butler about slavery, noting that for many months after the start of the war, "I clung to my old ideas of noninterference with slavery within state limits by the national government. It was my hope and belief that the rebellion might be suppressed, and slavery left to the free disposition of the states." Now, however, Chase had become convinced that, in order to win the war, "slavery must go." He believed that the president had the constitutional power, as commander in chief of the armed forces, to declare the slaves in the rebellious states free; Chase's only doubt was about whether it made sense for Lincoln to *use* this power. But when Chase "saw that to abstain from military interference with slavery was simply to contribute the whole moral and physical power of the government to the subjugation of some four millions of loyal people to some three hundred thousand disloyal rebels, that doubt was gone." Chase predicted that Lincoln would soon follow up on the hints in his order reversing Hunter's proclamation and issue his own presidential emancipation proclamation. Charles Sumner wrote to a friend at this time that Chase "agrees with me that the war can be ended only by emancipation. If we do not declare emancipation, we must make up our minds to acknowledge the independence of the rebels." In other words, the *New York Herald* was right, at least in part: Chase now believed that in order to win the war, to maintain the Union, the war had to become a war against slavery as well as against the Southern armies.[65]

CHAPTER 17

"A New Era"

⚜ LATE 1862 ⚜

There was not much celebration of the Fourth of July in Washington. Churches were serving as hospitals for the wounded from McClellan's army, so their bells did not ring out in the customary way. In letters and conversations in this "darkest hour," Chase called McClellan "the cruelest imposition ever forced upon a nation"—a general who had "cost us fifty thousand of our best young lives." He was sure that the reports that McClellan was about to advance were wrong. "Mac will never be ready to take Richmond," Chase told a friend. "All the reinforcements that can be sent him will not place him in a position to move successfully." McClellan's army "ought to have been already embarked and on its way here, or somebody should have been put in command who has resources and energy to retrieve its disasters."[1]

Hearing similar comments from many sources, Lincoln left Washington to see McClellan and his army at Harrison's Landing. Although the president was encouraged by the troops, telling Chase on his return about their "splendid condition and enthusiasm," he was discouraged by their general, who seemed to have no plan to take Richmond. Instead of talking tactics, McClellan wanted to dictate policy. Reacting to reports that Congress was working on confiscation legislation and that Lincoln was considering an emancipation proclamation, McClellan wrote to Lincoln that "neither confiscation of property [nor] forcible abolition of slavery should be contemplated." Lincoln did not respond to McClellan's letter, even though he read it in his presence, further annoying the general.[2]

On July 11, the day that Lincoln returned to Washington, McClellan wrote to Chase, saying that his army was "in good condition" and that, "as soon as it receives all the reinforcements which the government can readily give it," McClellan would advance along the James River toward Richmond. McClellan told Chase that he was distressed about events in Washington, where he saw an administration "without a policy—civil or military—defined and declared." According to McClellan, the president had "very little of mind or heart—thinks poorly and feels feebly," while the secretary of war had "shown that he is no statesman" and was "certainly not a military strategist." Chase did not respond to McClellan's missive.[3]

As soon as Lincoln was back in Washington, he asked Stanton to order General Henry Halleck to come to Washington. Lincoln also signed an order, dated July 11 but not published until July 23, promoting Halleck to command all the federal armies. Chase was concerned about Halleck's promotion, writing to Kate that since Halleck had been placed in charge of the western army, "inaction has been its most marked characteristic." If Halleck would "act vigorously and yet loyally—showing the same respect for civil authority and the law that General Scott always evinced—and yet infusing new life into the torpor here and energy into the military administration of the government, it may be a great benefit." But "my apprehensions exceed my hopes. We have trifled with our opportunities—mismanaged our forces—and kid-gloved the rebellion, until I begin to fear for the issue."[4]

Lincoln also appointed a new general, John Pope, to command the forces in northern Virginia. One of Pope's first actions was to issue a proclamation to his troops: "I have come to you from the West, where we have always seen the backs of our enemies; from an army whose business it has been to seek the adversary and to beat him when he was found; whose policy has been attack and not defense." Chase hosted a dinner for Pope and noted in his diary that the general "expressed himself freely and decidedly in favor of the most vigorous measures in the prosecution of the war." Pope was not sure about whether the former slaves would make good soldiers, but he "advocated their use as laborers, in the defense of fortifications, and in any way in which their services could be made useful without impairing the general tone of the service." Chase liked

Pope, writing a few weeks later that he "seemed to me an earnest, active, intelligent man, and inspired me with the best hopes."[5]

Congress was still in session in the first part of July 1862, working on several measures important to Chase. One was a bill to authorize the Treasury to issue another $150 million of legal tender notes. Unlike the first legal tender bill, this second bill moved through Congress without much controversy, so that there was no need for Chase to send letters prompting and pleading with Congress. Lincoln signed the bill into law on July 11.[6]

The next day, the Senate passed the House version of a far more controversial measure: the Second Confiscation Act. Section 6 of the bill provided for the forfeiture and confiscation of all property of all persons in the rebellious states except those who, within sixty days after a notice by the president, "cease[d] to aid, countenance, or abet such rebellion." In other words, not just those who volunteered for the rebel army but everyone in the rebellious states would lose their property other than those who could prove that they did not, after the notice period, assist or even "countenance" the rebellion. Section 9 provided that "all slaves of persons who shall hereafter be engaged in rebellion against the government of the United States, or who shall in any way give aid or comfort thereto," would be "forever free of their servitude and not again held as slaves." There was no notice provision in this emancipation section; it would take immediate effect if and when Lincoln signed the bill into law. Section 10 partially repealed the Fugitive Slave Act, saying that no slave escaping from one state to another would be delivered up, unless the master could prove that he had not participated in the rebellion, and that the military would not be involved in arresting and returning fugitive slaves. Section 11 allowed the president to "employ as many persons of African descent as he may deem necessary and proper for the suppression of this rebellion, and, for this purpose, he may organize and use them in such manner as he may judge best for the public welfare." This broad language would authorize anything from hiring black laborers to forming regiments of black soldiers.[7]

There was considerable doubt as to whether Lincoln would sign the confiscation bill. Senator Orville Browning of Illinois told the president bluntly that the bill was unwise and unconstitutional: "I said to him that he had reached the culminating point in his administration, and his course upon this bill was to determine whether he was to control the abolitionists and radicals, or whether they were to control him." If Lincoln vetoed the bill, the conservative Browning predicted, he would "raise a storm of enthusiasm in support of the administration in the border states which would be worth to us 100,000 muskets, whereas if he approved it, I feared our friends could no longer sustain themselves there." According to a letter from Henry Cooke, recounting a conversation with Chase, the Treasury secretary was equally adamant that Lincoln should sign the confiscation bill. Lincoln had not consulted Chase, "nor, so far as he knew, a single member of his Cabinet in regard to the matter. [Chase] was certain that [Lincoln] was writing some kind of a message, for he was closeted all day and even dispensed with the usual Cabinet meeting, yesterday being the regular day. Governor Chase thinks it cannot be possible that Lincoln would do such a thing as veto the bill."[8]

Lincoln was indeed drafting a long veto message, but he did not veto the confiscation bill. Instead, he informed a few key members of Congress that he would disapprove the bill unless Congress clarified that "forfeiture should only apply to real estate during the life of the traitor." The *Chicago Tribune* reported that this demand by Lincoln caused "considerable indignation among radical men" and that William Fessenden in particular was "savage on this back-kitchen style of veto." But the members yielded to the president's demand and rushed through a resolution to "clarify" the bill. Lincoln then signed the confiscation bill into law on July 17, the last day of the congressional session.[9]

In a July 20 letter to his friend Richard Parsons, Chase wrote that the "slavery question perplexes the president almost as much as ever, and yet I think that he is about to emerge from the obscurities where he has been groping into somewhat clearer light." Indeed, the next day, Chase recorded in his diary that Lincoln informed his Cabinet members at a special meeting that he had "determined to take some definitive steps in respect to military action and slavery" and presented them with four draft orders. The first would ratify and extend a recent order by General Pope; it would authorize all military commanders in rebellious states to "seize and use" any property "which may be necessary or convenient for their several commands." The second would allow commanders in these states to "employ as laborers" as many "persons of African descent as can be advantageously used for military or naval purposes, giving them reasonable wages for their labor." The third would require military commanders to keep records regarding property and persons, so that, if appropriate, compensation could be paid after the war. The fourth order related to "colonization of negroes in some tropical country." There was a "good deal of discussion" on these points, Chase noted, without any resolution. Stanton then shared a letter from General Hunter in South Carolina, seeking authority to enlist blacks into the army. Stanton, Seward, and Chase all supported the proposal, but Lincoln was "not prepared to decide the question" and seemed "averse to arming negroes." They agreed to resume their discussion the next day.[10]

A print version of Francis Carpenter's famous group portrait of the Lincoln Cabinet. From left to right: Edwin Stanton, Salmon Chase, Abraham Lincoln, Gideon Welles, Caleb Smith (standing), William Seward (seated), Montgomery Blair (standing), and Edward Bates.

On the morning of July 22, Chase talked with Lincoln about George McClellan. He "urged upon the president the importance of an immediate change in the command of the Army of the Potomac, representing the necessity of having a general in that command who would cordially and efficiently cooperate with the movements of Pope and others." Chase also "urged General McClellan's removal upon financial grounds," saying that Chase could not finance the war effort unless Lincoln would appoint aggressive commanders and take steps "in respect to slavery as would inspire the country with confidence that no measure would be left untried which promised a speedy and successful result." Chase added that if "this was not done, it seemed to me impossible to meet necessary expenses. Already there were $10,000,000 of unpaid requisitions, and this amount would constantly increase."[11]

Chase returned to the White House in the afternoon to continue the Cabinet discussion. According to his diary—our only detailed contemporaneous account of this momentous meeting—Lincoln and his Cabinet agreed to drop for the time being the topic of colonization and to issue the three other orders discussed the prior day: seizing property for military purposes, employing black military laborers, and keeping accounts of such property and labor. "The question of arming slaves was then brought up, and I advocated it warmly. The president was unwilling to adopt this measure," but instead proposed a new proclamation.[12]

The first sentence of the draft proclamation, according to both Lincoln's draft and Chase's diary, would give the sixty-day notice under section 6 of the recent Confiscation Act, warning rebels to "cease participating in, aiding, countenancing, or abetting the existing rebellion, or any rebellion against the government of the United States." Second, Lincoln would again press Congress on his plan to reimburse any loyal border state for the costs involved in emancipating its slaves.[13]

Third, as a military measure, under his constitutional power as commander in chief, Lincoln would declare that as of the first day of 1863, "all persons held as slaves within any state or states" still in rebellion would "then, thenceforward, and forever, be free." Under this sweeping sentence, it would not matter if a particular master could prove his loyalty; if a state was still in rebellion on the first day of the next year, the president would declare all slaves in the state free. Lincoln understood that, in regions under rebel control, rebel masters would disregard the supposed freedom of their slaves, but he expected that slaves would flee their masters to seek freedom in regions controlled by federal forces, as they had already done in large numbers. Lincoln was also confident that, over time, the area under federal control would increase, so that the proclaimed freedom would gradually take effect in the whole rebellious region.[14]

After Lincoln read his draft, Chase told him that he would "give to such a measure my cordial support." He would "prefer that no new expression on the subject of compensation should be made" and he "thought that the measure of emancipation could be much better and more quietly accomplished by allowing generals to organize and arm the slaves . . . and by directing the commanders of departments to proclaim emancipation within their districts as soon as practicable." Having said this, however, Chase stressed that he viewed Lincoln's draft as "so much better than inaction on the subject, that I should give it my entire support." Although Chase did not record the reactions of other Cabinet members, Stanton noted that he and Bates supported the measure, while Seward opposed it, making a "long speech against its immediate promulgation."[15]

Stanton wrote: "Chase thinks it a measure of great danger—and would lead to universal emancipation. The measure goes beyond anything I have recommended." Stanton's notes are unclear as to whether he or Chase said the measure "goes beyond anything I have recommended," but another source suggests that this was Chase. Chase's former attorney general, Christopher Wolcott, who was working at this time with his brother-in-law Stanton in the War Department, wrote home a few days later that Lincoln had proposed to his Cabinet a proclamation to free the slaves on January 1, 1863. "All the Cabinet concurred save Seward, who opposed, and Chase, who doubted, saying 'it was a larger step than he [Chase] ever contemplated.'" Chase noted in his diary that Lincoln decided to publish the "first three orders forthwith" and to "leave the other"—the draft emancipation proclamation—for "some further consideration."[16]

Washington was hot and quiet in August 1862. The members of Congress were at home, where many found their constituents unhappy. John Sherman wrote to Chase from Ohio to warn that "if this war is not pressed with energy, we will have civil war among us within ninety days." It would be such a blessing, the senator wrote, "if in this peril we had a strong, firm hand at the head of affairs." Women and children also left Washington, including Chase's daughters, who went to visit the McDowell family in upstate New York. Kate, however, found the farm "very dull" and went alone to the resort at Saratoga. Chase and a few colleagues were still in Washington, working, said the *Baltimore Sun*, "more hours than the most industrious clerks."[17]

The Treasury secretary spent much of the month selecting, state by state and district by district, those who would fill the new internal revenue positions. The law required the appointment of an assessor and a collector for each congressional district, so Chase needed to consult with representatives, senators, editors, and others to find the right men in each region. For each state, he sent at least one long letter to Lincoln—sometimes more than one—setting out the candidates for each position and explaining his reasons for favoring one candidate over another. There were also face-to-face discussions, such as a meeting on August 15 with Lincoln, Welles, and two others to discuss and resolve the appointments for Connecticut.[18]

Chase continued to press Lincoln, both directly and indirectly, on the question of freeing the slaves and enlisting them in the army. At the Cabinet meeting on August 3, he "expressed my conviction for the tenth or twentieth time, that the time for the suppression of the rebellion without interference with slavery had long passed." Chase argued that, in the Southern states, the "blacks were really the only loyal population worth counting" and that in the "Gulf states, at least, their right to freedom ought to be at once recognized." He reminded Lincoln that the president himself had talked about the "importance of making the freed blacks on the Mississippi, below Tennessee, a safeguard to the navigation of the river." So why not, Chase asked, direct General Mitchel to "assure the blacks freedom on condition of loyalty," to "organize the best of them in companies [and] regiments," and to provide for the "cultivation of the plantations by the rest" of the freed blacks. General Butler should "signify to the slaveholders of Louisiana that they must recognize the freedom of their work-people by paying them wages," and General Hunter "should do the same thing in South Carolina." Lincoln, according to Chase's diary, did not comment on these suggestions.[19]

The next day, Chase sent a long letter to William Cullen Bryant, editor of the influential *New York Evening Post:* "We are now engaged in a desperate civil war with (say) nine states, in which the whites are nearly unanimously against us, and the blacks nearly unanimously on our side." The federal forces were fighting in terrain "with which we are very imperfectly acquainted" and in a "noxious" climate, against an enemy familiar with the terrain, accustomed to the climate, and not "destitute of the valor needed for conflicts in the open field." So far, the federal government had made no use "of the only loyal men in the country, adapted to the work and acquainted with the country." These "loyal men," the blacks, "are ready to help us and themselves, and we reject their aid." The time had come, Chase insisted, to free the slaves, at least in the Gulf states, and to enlist blacks into the Union army. "We must, either by proclamation of the president or by the authorized and required action of the commanding generals of the departments, declare free *all* the slaves of those states and invite them to organize for the suppression of rebellion and the establishment of order." Without using Chase's name, Bryant used some of his arguments in editorials calling for emancipation and enlistment.[20]

There was a break in routine on the evening of August 6, when an immense crowd gathered on the grounds of the Capitol for a Union political rally. Several of the speakers worked for Chase in the Treasury Department. Edward Jordan, solicitor of the Treasury, read a series of resolutions, including one urging the president to "prosecute the war on a scale limited only by the resources of the country," and another declaring that the "national capital is eminently the place where treason should be instantly denounced and punished." Lucius Chittenden, register of the Treasury, sounded similar themes, arguing that there were still traitors in Washington, holding federal offices and using their positions "to give information to the enemy." George Boutwell, former governor of Massachusetts, now working for Chase as the first commissioner of Internal Revenue, declared that slavery was the cause of the rebellion and the treason. "When slavery shall cease to exist, there will be no traitors. That is the beginning and end of this war. Slavery in the beginning, freedom in the end; there is no other solution under the high heaven."[21]

After the first few speakers, the crowd clamored for Lincoln, who was sitting next to Chase on the platform. The president leaned over and asked whether he should not "say a few words and get rid of myself?" Without waiting for Chase to answer, Lincoln rose and went to the podium, where he was greeted with "uproarious enthusiasm." When the cheering died down, Lincoln gave an elegant little speech, praising both Stanton and McClellan for their work and taking the blame for any lack of cooperation between the secretary and the general. According to Chase, Lincoln's "frank, genial, generous face and direct simplicity of bearing took all hearts. His speech is in all the prints and evinces his usual originality and sagacity."[22]

About a week later, Lincoln met at the White House with black leaders to discuss colonization in Central America. Lincoln had long favored colonization as a way of reducing the black population of the United States, and he may have believed that he should not emancipate slaves unless he could also remove them to colonies elsewhere. In any case, he used this meeting to press the black leaders to urge their people to agree to colonization, arguing that there were vast differences between the two races, such that they could never live together in peace in the United States. Reading Lincoln's harsh racial rhetoric in the papers, Chase wrote in his diary that the president should have made a "manly protest against prejudice against color, and a wise effort to give the freemen homes in America!" Chase questioned whether Lincoln would ever issue a general emancipation proclamation, along the lines of the draft he had presented at the Cabinet meeting. An immediate "military order, emancipating at least the slaves in South Carolina, Georgia, and the Gulf states," would do "more to terminate the war and ensure an early restoration of solid peace and prosperity than anything else that can be devised."[23]

Reading the papers, and the telegrams at the War Department, Chase worried about John Pope and his army. Halleck had ordered McClellan to transfer his entire army from the peninsula to northern Virginia in order to reinforce Pope, but McClellan had protested and delayed, with the result that Robert E. Lee was able to move around Pope toward Washington. Chase noted in his diary on August 19 that Lincoln was "uneasy about Pope." A few days later, Chase wrote that "we are all anxious about Pope's position." In a letter to Seward, who was at home in upstate New York, Chase wrote on August 27 that "things don't look very bright." Indeed, on the night of the day that Chase wrote to Seward, Stonewall Jackson's rebel troops, after taking all they could carry, burned the Union supply depot at Manassas Junction, only thirty miles west of Washington.[24]

Over the next few days, Pope and his army fought Lee and his army in the Second Battle of Bull Run, a far larger and bloodier battle than the one fought a year earlier. On the morning of August 30 Chase received a message from McDowell, leading part of Pope's army, saying that the "victory is decidedly ours." Pope sent a similar message that morning to Halleck: "We fought a tremendous battle here yesterday, with the combined forces of the enemy, which lasted with continuous fury from daylight until after dark, by which time the enemy was driven from the field, which we now occupy."[25]

By day's end, however, the tables had turned, with Lee attacking and defeating Pope. The next morning, Sunday, August 31, Chase learned that "we had sustained a serious defeat." He added in his diary that "Fitz John Porter was not in the battle, nor were Franklin or Sumner, with whose corps the result would have probably been very different." This was only partly right: General Porter and his troops *were* in the battle, though Pope would later claim that Porter (a McClellan protégé) had disobeyed orders. William Franklin and Edwin Sumner were not available to Pope, however, because, as Chase wrote, "neither Franklin nor Sumner were sent forward by McClellan fast enough to reach him." With the defeat of Pope's army, and the disarray, there was fear that the rebels might capture the capital.[26]

While the armies fought near Manassas, Chase and Stanton fought against McClellan in Washington. On August 30, as Navy Secretary Gideon Welles was about to leave his office for home, Chase arrived with a draft letter to Lincoln, signed by Chase and Stanton, saying they were no longer willing to be "accessory to the waste of national resources, the protraction of the war, the destruction of our armies, and the imperiling of the Union" that resulted from leaving McClellan in any command position. Chase wanted Welles to sign the letter before it was presented to other Cabinet members, but Welles refused, saying that although he generally agreed with the substance, he disagreed with the procedure. "This method of getting signatures without an interchange of views from those who were associates in council," Welles wrote in his diary, "was repugnant to my ideas of duty and right."[27]

Chase and Stanton were not about to give up. On September 1 Chase went again to Welles's office, this time with a more measured letter signed by Chase, Stanton, Bates, and Secretary of the Interior Caleb Smith. Seward was out of town, but Chase hoped to obtain signatures from both Welles and Blair before presenting the letter to Lincoln. Welles again resisted, saying that they should discuss the issues with the president in a Cabinet meeting. Chase responded that he thought the Cabinet members needed to make it clear to Lincoln that he must dismiss McClellan or lose his Cabinet: "Conversations amounted to but little with the president on subjects of this importance. It was like throwing water on a duck's back. A more decisive expression must be made, and that in writing." Welles declined to sign the letter, but assured Chase that he would support him in a Cabinet meeting.

Later in the day, however, Chase heard rumors that McClellan had spoken with Lincoln and Halleck in Washington and would be given command of the Army of the Potomac again. Thomas Key, still serving on McClellan's staff, visited Chase at his home and "told me he supposed such was the fact."[28]

So it proved. The next day, when Lincoln stepped out of the Cabinet meeting for a few minutes, Stanton told his colleagues that the president had asked General McClellan to take command of the defenses of Washington. Chase wrote in his diary that when Lincoln returned to the meeting, Chase told him bluntly that McClellan's "experience as a military commander had been little else than a series of failures—and that his omission to urge troops forward to the battles of Friday and Saturday evinced a spirit which rendered him unworthy of trust, and that I could not but feel that giving the command to him was equivalent to giving Washington to the rebels." Lincoln admitted McClellan's faults but insisted that he "knows this whole ground—his specialty is to defend—is a good engineer, all admit; there is no better organizer." The president said that it "distressed him exceedingly" to disagree with Chase and Stanton on this issue, that he would "gladly resign his place," but that he "could not see who would do this work as well as McClellan." Chase quickly named Generals Joseph Hooker, Edwin Sumner, and Ambrose Burnside as possible replacements; any of them, he insisted, would be better than George McClellan.[29]

Perhaps to take his mind off McClellan, Chase spent part of September 2 drafting an emancipation proclamation for Lincoln's review. He noted in the draft that Lincoln, in his inaugural address, had assured the slave states that he had no intent to interfere with their institutions, including slavery. Chase's draft suggested that Lincoln should say that he had hoped "to terminate, if possible, the rebellion and the war without interference with that institution in any state, and to leave the whole question of its continuance, amelioration, or abolition to state consideration and determination." Lincoln had tried in various ways to urge the people in the Southern states to reconsider their rebellion, but his pleas had fallen on "deaf ears." The war continued, "with increased violence and ferocity," and the rebels were forcing their slaves to provide, in the fields and in the trenches, "indispensable support to the rebellion." The time had come, therefore, to declare that "all persons within the states which most obstinately persist in rebellion—that is to say in the states of South Carolina, Georgia, Florida, Alabama, Mississippi, Louisiana, Texas, and Arkansas—now held to involuntary service or labor and not for crime, are henceforth and of right free; and it is so declared." Chase soon shared this draft with Lincoln.[30]

Northern papers speculated in early September that General Lee would follow up his success in Virginia by crossing the Potomac and invading Maryland. The *Washington Evening Star* even suggested that it would be a *good* thing if Lee's army entered Maryland: "Let them cross unmolested," and "our forces will make short work of them." Soon the papers announced that Lee was indeed in Maryland, and that his army had taken Frederick and Hagerstown. The *National Republican* reported that the rebels were "confident in their ability to maintain their position in Maryland, to devastate southern Pennsylvania, and even to capture Harrisburg and Philadelphia." McClellan and his army marched out of Washington to confront Lee's forces. Writing from Rockville, McClellan told Halleck on September 10 that Lee was near Frederick with not less than 120,000 men; in truth, Lee had only about 40,000 soldiers with him.[31]

In one of Chase's frequent visits to the War Department to get the latest telegraphic news, he learned from Stanton that Lincoln was thinking of going out to see McClellan and his army in the field. Stanton "commented with some severity" on the president's "humiliating submissiveness to this officer." Chase agreed, writing in his diary that Lincoln, "with the most honest intentions in the world, and a naturally clear judgment, and a true, unselfish patriotism, has yielded so much to border state and negrophobic counsels that he now finds it difficult to arrest his own descent towards the most fatal concessions. He has already separated himself from the great body of the party which elected him; distrusts even those who most represent its spirit; and waits. For what?" Two days later, when Chase again visited the telegraph office, he learned that there were two messages from McClellan. One, to Halleck, reported that McClellan had obtained a copy of an order from Lee setting out his tactical plans. In the other, to Lincoln, McClellan bragged that he had "all the plans of the rebels and will catch them in their own trap if my men are equal to the emergency." McClellan was alluding here to the famous "Lost Order": an order from Lee to his generals, directing their movements, that was misplaced by some messenger and located by two Union soldiers.[32]

On Wednesday, September 17, Lee and McClellan and their armies fought an all-day all-out battle along the Antietam Creek near Sharpsburg, Maryland. It was the bloodiest day in American military history, with more than twenty-two thousand men killed, wounded, or missing.

Chase's diary entry for this day gives no sense that, while he was working in Washington, men were fighting and dying less than seventy miles away. He went to the War Department, where he talked with Stanton about promotions, and then across the street to the headquarters of General Halleck. Here Chase found Lincoln and Senator Reverdy Johnson of Maryland hearing from an army captain about how the rebels had captured Harpers Ferry. Back at his own office, Chase noted that an "enormous" number of demands for payment had arrived: more than $4 million in a single day. "Unpaid requisitions still accumulating, now over $40,000,000," he wrote. "Where will this end?"[33]

The first news regarding the Battle of Antietam started to arrive in Washington on Wednesday evening and Thursday morning. The *National Republican* reported rumors that Lee had "been driven from his position with great loss" and that McClellan was "driving the rebels to the Potomac." A brief telegram to Halleck from McClellan on Thursday morning said that the "battle of yesterday continued for fourteen hours and until after dark" and that the federals now held almost all the battlefield. He added that he expected the fighting to "probably be renewed today."[34]

What McClellan did not tell Halleck was that he had no intention of ordering an attack, even though he had thousands of fresh troops, and Lee had none. A *New-York Tribune* reporter, writing a few days later, called this the "fatal Thursday," when McClellan allowed the "clean, leisurely escape of the foe down into the valley, across the difficult ford [of the Potomac], and up the Virginia heights." Indeed, Lee was so sure that McClellan would not attack that he did not even begin his retreat until Thursday evening.[35]

McClellan sent Halleck three messages on Friday, the first saying that General Lee and his army were no longer at Antietam and the second rejoicing that Lee's army was in Virginia. McClellan called this a complete victory, but the papers noted that it was a victory only in the sense that the rebels were no longer in Maryland; it was not the decisive victory McClellan might have achieved if he had destroyed Lee's army on its retreat to the Potomac River.[36]

Chase was worried not just about the finances, and the generals, but also about the Cabinet. Writing to John Sherman on September 20, he expressed frustration that the men who made up the Cabinet were really just "separate heads of department meeting now and then for talk on whatever happens to come uppermost" rather than for "grave consultation on matters concerning the salvation of the country." He added that "no regular and systematic reports of what is done are made, I believe, even to the president—certainly not to the so-called Cabinet." In a letter to Senator Zachariah Chandler on the same day, Chase insisted that he was not "making any personal complaint of the president. I do not. In every matter connected with my department, he allows me to take whatever course I think best, always giving me a cordial support and manifesting in me all the confidence I can possibly claim." But in his view, this was not enough. The tasks of the different departments were so closely connected that it had "always been thought the duty of the president to convene them regularly for consultation and to take their judgments on all important matters, and in general—though this is by no means obligatory—to act in accordance with the well-considered conclusions of the majority. There is, on the contrary, at present time, no Cabinet except in name."[37]

On this same day, Chase received a long letter from the reformer and former member of Congress Robert Dale Owen, urging an immediate emancipation proclamation. The letter was addressed to Lincoln, but as Owen explained in a cover note, he wanted Chase to review the letter and give it to the president only if he approved. "Our enemies, like the Grecian hero," Owen wrote, "have one vulnerable point. You have not touched it yet. What should have been their element of weakness has been suffered to remain an element of strength. They have nearly a million of able-bodied men of fit age for war or for labor. Holding these men in bondage and employing them to till the soil, they are enabled to send to the battlefield almost their entire adult white population, yet preserve their commissariat sufficiently supplied." The time had come for Lincoln to deprive the rebels of their slaves. "Property in man, always morally unjust, has become nationally dangerous. Property that endangers the safety of a nation should not be suffered to remain in the hands of its citizens." Chase agreed heartily with Owen's letter and immediately handed it to Lincoln. "God grant that it may impel him to action," Chase wrote to Owen.[38]

Two days later, on September 22, as if in response to Chase's prayer, Lincoln presented to his Cabinet a draft emancipation proclamation. Lincoln started the meeting by reading a humorous fictional account of an attack on a wax figure of Judas that had been brought to town by a traveling showman. Did the president mean to suggest that his proclamation would meet a similarly hostile reception? In any case, Chase recorded in his diary, Lincoln enjoyed the humor, as did the other members of the Cabinet— except, "of course," the humorless Stanton.[39]

Lincoln then "took a graver tone" and reminded them that "several weeks ago, I read to you an order I had prepared on [slavery], which, on account of objections made by some of you, was not issued. Ever since then, my mind has been much occupied with this subject, and I have thought, all along, that the time for acting on it might probably come. I think the time has come now. I wish it were a better time. I wish that we were in a better condition. The action of the army against the rebels has not been quite what I should have best liked. But they have been driven out of Maryland, and Pennsylvania is no longer in danger of invasion. When the rebel army was at Frederick, I determined, as soon as it should be driven out of Maryland, to issue a proclamation of emancipation, such as I thought most likely to be useful. I said nothing to anyone, but I made the promise to myself and to my Maker. The rebel army is now driven out, and I am going to fulfill that promise."[40]

According to Chase's account, Lincoln continued by saying, "I have got you together to hear what I have written down. I do not wish your advice about the main matter; for that I have determined for myself." But if any of them had comments on the wording of the proclamation, he would "be glad to receive the suggestions." Lincoln added that he knew that "others might, in this matter, as in others, do better than I can; and if I was satisfied that the public confidence was more fully possessed by any one of them than by me, and knew of any constitutional way in which he could be put in my place, he should have it. I would gladly yield it to him." But the president said he didn't know of any person who had more of the "confidence of the people," and, in any event "there is no way in which I can have any other man put where I am. I am here. I must do the best I can and bear the responsibility of taking the course which I feel I ought to take."[41]

Lincoln then read aloud the draft proclamation. The critical sentence provided that on the first of January 1863, "all persons held as slaves within any state, or designated part of a state, the people whereof shall then be in rebellion against the United States, shall be then, thenceforward, and forever free." Lincoln's draft proclamation (unlike the draft Chase had prepared a few weeks earlier) did not free anyone immediately; the president simply promised that he would free the slaves in any states or parts of states that were still in rebellion in January. Lincoln's draft also pressed again for Congress to enact some scheme of colonization and to compensate any border states that emancipated their own slaves.[42]

Seward offered Lincoln a few comments on phrases, and then Chase spoke. "What you have said, Mr. President, fully satisfies me that you have given to every proposition which has been made a kind and candid consideration. And you have now expressed the conclusion to which you have arrived clearly and distinctly. This it was your right and, under your oath of office, your duty to do. The proclamation does not, indeed, mark out exactly the course I would myself prefer. But I am ready to take it just as it is written and to stand by it with all my heart."[43]

Lincoln published the preliminary emancipation proclamation later that day; it was in the major morning papers on September 23. Republican papers praised the proclamation, but Democratic papers denounced it. One declared that "Greeley, Sumner & Co. have triumphed—abolitionism is rampant in the administration, in Congress, wherever their influence could prevail. The proclamation is an outrage on the humanity and good sense of the country, to say nothing of its gross unconstitutionality."[44]

On the evening of September 24, a large crowd and marching band went first to the White House, where Lincoln spoke, and then to Chase's house. When Chase emerged on the front porch to cheers, someone cried for "light, more light!" Apparently there was no light, for Chase started by saying that "all the light you can have this evening will be light reflected from this great act of the president." He was encouraged by their enthusiasm for the emancipation proclamation and predicted that the American people would likewise endorse Lincoln's decision. Nothing, Chase said, had "ever given me more sincere pleasure than to say amen to the last great act of the chief magistrate. In my judgment, it is the dawn of a new era, and although the act is performed under an imperious sense of duty, created by military exigencies which give him power to perform it, it is nevertheless an act, though necessarily baptized in blood, of humanity and justice." The crowd cheered, and Chase started to excuse himself, but the throng insisted that he continue.

If there is another word to be added tonight, it is this: that the time has come when we should bury all jealousies, all divisions, all personal aims, all personal aspirations, in one common resolve to stand by the integrity of the republic. Let him have the most of our approbation, applause, and confidence who does most, whether in the field or at the head of the nation, or in the Cabinet, for the country. Dismissing all the past, let us look only to the future, and henceforth let the day of dissension, defeat, and discord be ended. Let us do nothing except to work for our country wherever Providence may dictate.[45]

In late September James Garfield arrived in Washington from Ohio. Only thirty years old, the future president was already an accomplished scholar, a former state senator, a general in the Union army, and now a candidate for the House of Representatives in the imminent Ohio election. Garfield had been summoned to Washington to talk with Stanton about his next military assignment. Writing home to his wife, Lucretia, after a dinner with Chase on the day he arrived, Garfield described Chase as "by far the strongest man in the administration" and "thoroughly imbued with a moral and religious sense of the duties of the government in relation to the war." A few days later, Garfield and Chase went together to visit General Joseph Hooker, recovering from a wound suffered at Antietam. Although Hooker had a reputation for drinking and womanizing, Chase liked him, noting in his diary that the general was a "frank, manly, brave, and energetic soldier, of somewhat less breadth of intellect than I expected." Hooker complained to Chase that McClellan had "no dash, no boldness, and is the curse of our army." Chase responded that if he were president, "I would have arrested McClellan for his failure to support Pope and ordered him tried. And if he had been convicted of what I believe him to be guilty of, I would have had him shot." A few days later, Chase and Kate persuaded Garfield to stay with them rather than in a hotel. "I have a delightful room and am much better pleased than at Willard's," Garfield wrote to his wife.[46]

In early October Garfield and Kate took the Chase carriage to go into northern Virginia to meet with Generals Carl Schurz, the German American leader from Wisconsin, and Franz Sigel, also a German immigrant. Garfield immediately liked the two men, describing them to a friend as "full of genius, full of the fire of their own revolution, and inspired anew by the spirit of American liberty." The next day, Schurz showed Kate and Garfield the Bull Run battlefield. "We saw hundreds of graves," Garfield wrote, "or rather heaps of earth piled upon the bodies where they lay. Scores of heads,

James Garfield. The future president spent several weeks as Chase's houseguest in late 1862; some have speculated that Garfield, although married, was fond of Kate Chase.

hands, and feet were protruding, and so rapid had been the decomposition of thirty-four days that naked, eyeless skulls grinned at us."[47]

Garfield's wife, at home in Ohio, wrote to her husband that she learned from friends that "you and Miss Kate are taking dinners out, visiting camps, etc." Lucretia asked whether Kate was "a very charming, interesting young lady? I may be jealous if she is, for you have such a fashion of becoming enamored with brilliant young ladies." Garfield tried to calm his wife, writing that Kate did not have a "pretty face, its beauty being marred by a nose slightly inclining to pug." But he added that "she has probably more social influence and makes a better impression than any other Cabinet lady."[48]

Garfield, who would stay with the Chase family for six weeks, was not the only person charmed by Kate this fall. The famous author Harriet

Beecher Stowe visited Washington for a few days and wrote home that "Chase and his pretty daughters spent last evening with us." Admiral Samuel Francis DuPont, who was in Washington for consultations with Lincoln and Welles, wrote to his wife that Kate was "very bright and affable," with "grace of manner and aplomb of mind." DuPont's only complaint was that a young military officer "monopolized her, and I had no chance for extended conversation." The admiral was somewhat surprised to find that he liked Chase as well, writing that he had "great vigor of mind and is more easy and fluent than I judged him in the Senate." DuPont thought he could detect in Chase the "effects of being a young man under the influence and direction of a man like Mr. Wirt."[49]

October 14 was Election Day in Indiana, Iowa, Ohio, and Pennsylvania. As the election approached, Chase's correspondents in Ohio warned him that prospects were poor. John Sherman wrote in late September that the Union Party—a new name for the Republican Party—was "inert," while the "Peace Democrats have taken possession of the party organization" and were "working with wonderful activity and hope of success." Hezekiah Bundy, the Union candidate for Congress from a district in southern Ohio, wrote Chase that although he personally supported the emancipation proclamation, it seemed that the adverse reaction to the proclamation would "defeat me and every other Union candidate for Congress along the border." Bundy and Sherman were right. Only five Republicans were elected to Congress from Ohio, whose next congressional delegation would be dominated by fourteen Democrats. Garfield was one of the few Ohio Republicans to survive, but he was running in the Western Reserve, a safely Republican district. Democrats also did quite well in neighboring Indiana and Pennsylvania.[50]

The *New York Herald* interpreted these October election defeats as a rebuke to radicals and especially to Chase: "The elections are not an expression of the popular will against the war, but against the conduct of the war, not in favor of secession, but against the Radicalism which has ruled rampantly in Congress and has swayed the councils of the Cabinet, led on by one or two of its members." The paper alleged that Chase had hindered McClellan and promoted McDowell, preventing the capture of Richmond and contributing to the disaster at Bull Run. "The consequence of Mr. Chase thus neglecting his proper business and meddling in the policy and management of the war is the financial depression, which has made a paper dollar in a poor man's pocket only worth about six shillings and has seriously impaired the national credit. The result of the elections in Ohio, his own state, is the most emphatic comment on the course of Secretary Chase." The *Herald* was right that the legal tender notes were now worth less than gold dollars, but this had far more to do with concerns about military reverses and federal finances than any neglect by Chase of his financial tasks.[51]

November 4 was Election Day in New York and seven other states. The Democratic candidate for governor of New York was an upstate lawyer and former governor, Horatio Seymour, and the Union candidate was an antislavery friend of Chase's, James Wadsworth. Although nominally a race for the governor of a single state, this was effectively a referendum on the president and his administration. Democratic papers, day after day, attacked Lincoln and Chase, while Union papers argued that a vote for Seymour was effectively a vote for Jefferson Davis. The *New York Evening Post*, for example, quoted Southern papers to show that they were hoping that Seymour and other conservatives would prevail in the Northern elections. "Every vote given to an opposition candidate at the coming election, under these circumstances, does really and unmistakably give aid and comfort to the . . . rebels."[52]

The *New York Herald* claimed that William Seward, whom it now considered a conservative, silently supported Seymour and that Chase was the only Cabinet member who supported his "pet" Wadsworth. "Secretary Chase is the man who kept McDowell in the army to give us two defeats at Bull Run, to interfere with McClellan's plans, and to prevent the capture of Richmond. Secretary Chase is the Mephistopheles of this war . . . who has sacrificed the lives and the health of thousands of our brave soldiers to his intrigues against McClellan and in favor of incompetent generals. Secretary Chase is the person who has so mismanaged the Treasury Department as to reduce the value of the dollar bill in a working man's pocket to about seventy-five cents. In voting for Wadsworth, you vote for Chase."[53]

Chase believed that George McClellan was the most prominent "incompetent general" and continued to press Lincoln to remove him this fall. In the midst of a bitter election campaign, however, the president did not want to remove a prominent Democratic general like McClellan. Chase feared that if Seymour prevailed in New York, the "effect upon government credit and all effort to maintain the territorial integrity of the republic would be most disastrous." He asked Hiram Barney to use the employees of the customshouse to work for Wadsworth—neither unusual nor illegal in the mid-nineteenth century, when all federal employees were political employees. Less than a week before Election Day, Chase predicted that Wadsworth would carry New York "handsomely."[54]

It was Seymour who prevailed in the Empire State, however, receiving about 306,000 votes, while Wadsworth garnered roughly 296,000. Democrats also carried a majority of the congressional seats in New York, as well as in New Jersey and Illinois. Chase claimed that he was not too troubled by these results. He wrote to Sumner to say that he was encouraged by the outcome in Massachusetts, where Republicans held all ten congressional seats. "We can still save a majority in the House," Chase wrote, and "except for the great loss of the moral prestige and influence of Wadsworth as governor of New York, I think the result not really damaging." Talking with another friend about the *Herald*'s attack on him, Chase said that "newspapers did not make me and could not unmake me."[55]

On the day after the New York election, Lincoln relieved McClellan and appointed Ambrose Burnside to lead the Army of the Potomac. Chase was, of course, happy to see McClellan finally removed. He wrote to General Butler that he would have preferred Hooker as McClellan's successor, but Burnside "has some excellent qualities, and I hope too he may prove to possess all that he needs for his trying post." The main purpose of Chase's letter was to reassure Butler that General Nathaniel Banks, who was on his way to New Orleans, was sent not to supersede Butler "but to conduct an expedition to Texas while you are engaged nearer to your present headquarters." On this point, however, Chase was mistaken: when Banks arrived in New Orleans, he revealed that his orders were, in fact, to replace Butler as head of the department. Chase urged Butler to swallow his pride and serve under Banks, but by the time he received Chase's letter, Butler was already on his way to Washington, having handed command to Banks.[56]

The *New York Herald* claimed that Chase neglected finances, but his files show that he devoted much of his time to the Union's financial problems. Chase wrote often to generals and to political leaders, but he wrote even more often to Barney, head of the customshouse in New York; to John Cisco, assistant treasurer in New York; and to Jay Cooke, his financial adviser in Philadelphia. There was a constant stream of reports from and instructions to other officials within the department. Chase also sought advice from outside experts such as Henry Carey, the famous Philadelphia economist, and John Bonner, financial editor for the *New York Herald*. The financial pages of the *Herald* were much kinder to Chase than the editorial pages, with Bonner even comparing Chase with Alexander Hamilton.[57]

In the quarter that ended on September 30, 1862, federal customs duties yielded only $23 million, and the income tax and all other internal taxes less than $1 million. Chase knew that it would take time before the new tax laws started to produce real revenues. On the expense side, the War Department spent $90 million and the Navy Department another $10 million in this quarter, and expenditures of at least this much would probably continue as long as the war dragged on. Chase bridged the gap mainly with legal tender notes; the Treasury Department issued more than $72 million of legal tender notes in this single quarter. Chase knew that he could not rely upon the legal tender notes forever, though: if the government issued too many, they would fuel inflation and lose their value. In late September Chase noted that the Treasury was about $36 million behind in its payments and "almost without resources, except Treasury notes, of which the faculty to issue only fifty-six millions remains, and customs, which supply about $200,000 per day."[58]

As he pondered the finances, and talked with Jay Cooke and others, Chase focused on the long-term five-twenty bonds. Congress had authorized $500 million of these bonds, but as of the end of September, only $16 million had been issued. Bankers were not especially interested in them, so Chase decided to see whether Cooke could persuade the public to purchase five-twenties. He wrote to Cooke on October 23 to say that he hoped that, by "enlarging your sphere and increasing your compensation so that you can pay subagents and defray expenses of very liberal advertising," purchases might reach "a million of dollars per day." Chase proposed to pay Cooke one half of a percent commission on the first $10 million, and one quarter thereafter, on the understanding that Cooke would pay his subagents a commission of at least one-eighth of a percent on the first $10 million and one-tenth thereafter.[59]

Cooke agreed to these terms, and in early November his advertisements started to appear in Pennsylvania papers. The financier emphasized that the interest of 6 percent, payable in gold, was equivalent to 8 percent, given the current premium on gold. "Farmers, merchants, mechanics, capitalists, and all who have any money to invest" should understand that the five-twenties were effectively secured by the entire American economy, so that they were the "best, most available, and most popular investments in the market." Cooke noted that people could purchase bonds for as little as $50 and could pay for them using either legal tender notes or checks drawn on Philadelphia banks. Chase was encouraged by the initial results, asking Cooke to keep copies of the advertisements and other materials. "I regard this as the second great national or popular loan, and I want to preserve a full record of its progress and results," he said. The progress was modest at first: receipts from the five-twenties were only $8.7 million in the last quarter of 1862. But Chase and Cooke had hit upon the *system* that would enable Cooke in time to exceed Chase's goal of $1 million a day for the Treasury.[60]

On the first of December Lincoln delivered his annual message to Congress. "Fellow citizens," he declared, "we cannot escape history. We of this Congress and this administration will be remembered in spite of ourselves. No personal significance, or insignificance, can spare one or another of us. The fiery trial through which we pass, will light us down, in honor or dishonor, to the latest generation." In the section on finances, drafted by Chase, Lincoln noted that while the legal tender notes (known as greenbacks because of the bright-green back side) had worked well so far, they were not a permanent solution. He urged Congress to consider a system of national banks, issuing notes in standard form, backed by Treasury bonds deposited in the Treasury: "These notes, prepared under the supervision of proper officers, being uniform in appearance and security and convertible always into coin, would at once protect labor against the evils of a vicious currency and facilitate commerce by cheap and safe exchanges."[61]

Three days later, in his own annual report, Chase explained his currency plan in more detail. To the extent that there was inflation, he maintained, the problem was not that the federal government had issued too many greenbacks but that private banks had issued too many of their own banknotes. Congress should reduce the amount of private banknotes through a tax on such notes to create room for more federal notes. "The necessities of war have caused the taxation of almost all forms of value," he said. "Can there be a sound reason for exempting" private banknotes? Henry Cooke wrote to his brother that Chase was not planning "violent measures to drive out the existing bank circulation but will effect that object gradually by a tax of 1 or 2 percent thereon, and by the inducements offered the banks to make the change" from state to federal charters.[62]

Chase wanted to create a uniform, national currency issued by national banks under federal supervision. Under his proposal, banks chartered by the states could decide to convert to become national banks, or new national banks could be formed, in each case by purchasing and depositing Treasury bonds with the Treasury and receiving in return Treasury notes. "The form of the notes, the uniformity of devices, the signatures of national officers, and the imprint of the national seal authenticating the declaration borne on each that it is secured by bonds which represent the faith and capital of the whole country could not fail to make every note as good in any part of the world as the best-known and best-esteemed national securities." The national banks would also provide a market for Treasury bonds and depositories for federal funds. For Chase, a key advantage of the system was the way it would cement the Union together. Every national bank with bonds deposited in the Treasury, and "every individual who holds a dollar of the circulation secured by such a deposit; every merchant, every manufacturer, every farmer, every mechanic, interested in transactions dependent for success on the credit of that circulation, will feel as an injury every attempt to rend the national unity, with the permanence and stability of which all their interests are so closely and vitally connected." Perhaps, Chase speculated, if such a system of national banks and national currency had been in place in 1860, the Southern states would not have seceded.[63]

Chase's report included a Hamiltonian sketch of the immense resources that the United States had for paying its debts—even the unprecedented debts that it was incurring to finance the Civil War. The "gold-bearing region" of the United States stretched from the Canadian border all the way south to Mexico and was "rich not only in gold but in silver, copper, iron, lead, and many other valuable minerals." This region was producing, and would continue to produce, millions of dollars a year in minerals. Every acre of fertile American farmland, Chase continued, was "a mine which only waits for the contact of labor to yield its treasures," and "every acre is opened to that fruitful contact by the Homestead Act." Even in the midst of the Civil War, the United States was attracting thousands of immigrants from Europe each year, every one of whom Chase viewed as an addition to national strength. Indeed, he believed that "properly encouraged by legislation and administration," immigration could contribute as much to national revenues as "the metallic products of the gold-bearing region." Chase also made a Jeffersonian plea for more economical federal government, saying the departments needed "to retrench superfluity; to economize expenditures; to adjust accurately measures to objects."[64]

At first, the press was not enthused about Chase's bank proposal. After the *Chicago Tribune* expressed doubts, he wrote a long letter to the editor, explaining that what he hoped to do was gradually reduce the number of state-chartered banks—about fifteen hundred—and replace them with a smaller number of federally chartered banks issuing a single national currency. Congress, too, was not initially inclined to follow Chase's lead. Thaddeus Stevens, for example, introduced a bill to authorize another $200 million of greenbacks and another $1 billion of bonds, and impose a punitive tax on banknotes issued by state-chartered banks. There was not a word in the Stevens bill about national banks. Chase asked John Cisco in New York to ask the "leading financial gentlemen" there to write "members of the financial committees" urging the national bank plan. "I am firmly convinced that the adoption or non-adoption of this plan is the turning point of credit or discredit. If it be adopted, the finances can be placed on a firm and satisfactory footing." If not, Chase feared the "inevitable wreck."[65]

In the fall of 1862 the *New York Herald* claimed that it was widely accepted that the Lincoln administration was a failure; the only interesting question was whether Chase or Seward was more to blame. Among those who blamed Seward was the radical Orestes Brownson, who accused the secretary of state in a long essay of "shrinking from open, decided, vigorous war" and of striving "to preserve slavery, and to prevent the war from operating its ruin." Another radical editor, tied closely with Chase's friend Charles Sumner, was even more pointed, writing that Seward was a "paralyzing influence" and calling upon Lincoln to remove him at once. The *New York Herald*, with the nation's largest circulation, defended Seward and attacked Chase. According to the *Herald*, the Treasury secretary was responsible not only for mismanaging finances and interfering with generals; Chase was behind the radical attacks on Seward. Chase supposedly told Brownson "how Secretary Seward was guilty of this, and responsible for that, and neglectful of this, that, and the other, until poor Brownson's head was completely turned, and he imagined that he had found in Seward the head, font, body, wings, and tail of the evil spirit of this war." The radical faction was the "malign influence which has caused the disasters of the war" and Chase was "the Cabinet member who is responsible for the failure of the administration."[66]

Seward's friends were attacking Chase in the papers, while Chase's friends were attacking Seward, but the two men themselves were not enemies. They worked together well on joint projects, such as a letter from Seward defending Chase and his department against British complaints about policies designed to deter trade with the South by way of British ports. They socialized with each other from time to time. For example, when Seward hosted a dinner for the first ambassador from Haiti to the United States, a man derided by some papers as a "shiny black negro," Chase was among Seward's guests. After another evening at Seward's house, Chase wrote to Kate that Seward "always impresses me very favorably and not at all as the artful man he is reputed to be. He is certainly able; he certainly sometimes does things he ought not to do; but he does talk and act very much like a man desiring above all things to serve his country." When a New York delegation arrived in Washington to accuse Seward of softness toward the South, Chase told them that they were wrong. Seward, said Chase, had never objected "to any *action*, however vigorous, of a military nature." Although Chase grumbled in his letters that the Cabinet did not meet often enough, he almost never complained about Seward.[67]

The tension between the partisans of Chase and of Seward came to a head after Burnside and his army met a terrible defeat on December 13 at Fredericksburg, Virginia. By the end of the day, according to a British observer, the Union dead were so numerous and "so close to each other that you might step from body to body" across the battlefield. When Republican senators gathered behind closed doors a few days later to discuss the disaster, many of them blamed Seward. According to Fessenden's notes, James Grimes, senator from Iowa, argued that "Seward exercised a controlling influence upon the president and improperly interfered in the conduct of the war, and in a manner injurious to the success of our arms." Fessenden declared that a member of the Cabinet informed him "that there was a backstairs and malign influence which controlled the president, and overruled all the decisions of the Cabinet, and he understood Mr. Seward to be meant." Whether Chase actually told Fessenden that Seward was a malign influence, or whether Fessenden was simply ascribing to Chase the views of the radical editors, we do not know, but the senators believed that Fessenden was paraphrasing Chase. Wade suggested that the Republican senators should all go to the White House and demand that Lincoln rid himself of Seward. Browning disagreed, saying that he had not seen any evidence that Seward opposed "vigorous prosecution of the war" and that they should at all costs avoid open conflict with Lincoln.[68]

When the Republican senators resumed this discussion the next day, December 17, Ira Harris of New York offered a resolution, recommending that Lincoln should change his Cabinet. John Sherman objected that the resolution "might be construed as an expression of opinion that all the members of the Cabinet should go out. He presumed this was not desired. No one wished Mr. Chase to leave the Treasury, which he had managed so ably." Sherman added that "he doubted whether changing the Cabinet would remedy the evil. The difficulty was with the president himself. He had neither dignity, order, nor firmness." After further discussion, the senators adopted a revised resolution calling for a "*partial* reconstruction of the Cabinet" and appointed a committee of nine senators to meet with Lincoln. Chase almost surely heard about these discussions from his friends among the senators, including Fessenden, Sherman, and Sumner.[69]

On the evening of December 18, nine Republican senators met for several hours with Lincoln. According to Fessenden's notes, the discussion focused on Seward and on the lack of Cabinet consultation. Chase was not mentioned. Lincoln defended Seward and told the senators that "what the country wanted was military success. Without that, nothing could go right—with that, nothing could go wrong." The next morning, the president called a special Cabinet meeting, without Seward, at which he informed the others that the Republican senators wanted Seward out of the administration and that Seward had given him a resignation letter. Lincoln added that he was not inclined to *accept* Seward's resignation, and he asked the Cabinet to join him that evening for another meeting with the senators. Chase was reluctant, according to Welles, claiming that he "had no knowledge whatever of the movement, or the resignation, until he entered this room." In the end, however, Chase and the others agreed to Lincoln's request.[70]

On the evening of December 19 Lincoln, his Cabinet other than the secretary of state, and the senators gathered in Lincoln's office. Lincoln started with a speech, saying that although the Cabinet had not been involved in some decisions, he thought "most questions of importance had received a reasonable consideration." Seward had been "earnest in the prosecution of the war" and had consulted with Lincoln and sometimes Chase about his dispatches. Lincoln called on the Cabinet members to comment on "whether there had been any want of unity or of sufficient consultation." According to Fessenden's notes, Chase was uncomfortable and said that he would not have "come here had he known that he was to be arraigned before a committee of the Senate." Chase "went on to say that questions of importance had generally been considered by the Cabinet, though perhaps not so fully as might have been desired, and that there had been no want of unity in the Cabinet, but a general acquiescence on public measures." The discussion continued for several hours, with no resolution.[71]

The next morning, December 20, Chase received a message asking him to come to see Lincoln. As he waited in the president's office, first Stanton and then Welles arrived. The Navy secretary wrote in his diary that when Lincoln joined them, Chase told Lincoln that "he had been painfully affected by the meeting last evening" and that "he had prepared his resignation." As Chase slowly handed him the letter, Lincoln took it from him happily. "This," Lincoln told Welles, indicating the resignation letter "with a triumphant smile," would resolve the difficulty. "I see my way clear."[72]

Chase returned to his department and drafted a letter to Lincoln, saying it seemed that Lincoln planned to refuse the resignations of both Chase and Seward. This would be a political mistake, Chase advised. Recent events had convinced Chase that there was "an opinion too deeply seated and too generally received in Congress and the country to be safely disregarded that the concord in judgment and action essential to successful administration does not prevail among [the Cabinet] members." Chase told Lincoln that neither he nor Seward was essential to the administration, so Lincoln should accept both resignations. "Retiring from the post to which you called me, let me assure you that I shall carry with me even a deeper respect and a warmer affection for you than I brought with me to it."[73]

After drafting this letter, Chase set it aside. When Fessenden stopped by that afternoon, Chase explained why he wanted to resign. Chase and Seward represented different wings of the Republican Party, and if Chase remained after Seward resigned, "he might be accused of maneuvering to get Mr. Seward out." Chase added that "Seward's withdrawal would embarrass him so much that he could not get along with the Treasury. He found that very difficult as it was, and if he had to contend with the disaffection of Seward's friends, the load would be more than he could carry." Chase said it would be better to have a "new hand" at the Treasury. "You or Hooper or Sherman can manage well enough."[74]

Fessenden insisted that Chase think again. "The country has confidence in you," he said. "Congress has confidence in you. It is a critical moment. You know that nothing which has been done has reference to you. You knew nothing of our movement [the movement of the senators to oust Seward] and are in no degree responsible for it. You have no right to abandon your friends in this way, and the step will be ruinous to you as well as injurious to the government."[75]

Late in the afternoon, Chase received a letter from Lincoln, addressed to both him and Seward, asking them to withdraw their resignations and resume their work. The next day, Chase received a copy of Seward's response, telling Lincoln that he would "cheerfully" return to his department. On Monday, December 22, Chase wrote to Lincoln himself, in similar terms, saying that he would yield to the president's judgment. So that Lincoln would understand his thinking, however, Chase sent him a copy of his draft letter. The crisis had been resolved, with both Chase and Seward still in the Cabinet—precisely where Lincoln wanted them.[76]

It was no accident, though, that immediately after this controversy over whether the president consulted often enough with his Cabinet members, Lincoln sought their advice about two important issues: the admission of West Virginia as a state and the form of the final emancipation proclamation.

The Constitution required, before a new state could be formed out of the territory of an existing state, the consent of both Congress and the legislature of the existing state. Congress had passed the necessary legislation to create West Virginia, as had the loyal Virginia legislature, now sitting in Alexandria, elected mainly from the western counties. The key question, as Chase said in his letter to Lincoln, was whether this Alexandria legislature was the legitimate state legislature. In Chase's view, the federal government had answered this question already by, for example, granting seats in the Senate to the Virginia senators elected by the Alexandria legislature: "In every case of insurrection involving the persons exercising the powers of state government, when a large body of the people remain faithful, that body, so far as the Union is concerned, must be taken to constitute the state." For Chase, the illegitimate government was the so-called state government in Richmond, in rebellion against the United States. Some of Chase's colleagues worried that admitting West Virginia would lead to divisions of other states and complicate the eventual reconstruction of the Union. Chase was not too troubled by this risk, telling Lincoln that he did not think it likely that there would be any other new states formed out of existing Southern states. Lincoln agreed with Chase and signed the bill admitting West Virginia as a state.[77]

Even more important to Chase was the final emancipation proclamation. Unlike the preliminary document, Lincoln's draft of the final proclamation announced that the Union would enlist black volunteers into the army—a change of which Chase fully approved. His main concern with the draft was that it would exclude from the emancipation process not only the forty-eight counties about to become West Virginia but also seven Virginia counties in and around Norfolk, and eleven Louisiana parishes in and around New Orleans. Chase contended that, under the confiscation acts, slaves of rebellious masters in these areas should already be free, and slaves of other masters were "practically so." He feared that Lincoln's proposed proclamation would effectively reestablish slavery in these counties and parishes. Chase also advised Lincoln to add some language to make it clear that, in granting the slaves freedom, the president was not "encouraging or countenancing . . . any disorderly or licentious conduct." Finally, he suggested that Lincoln should end the proclamation with some "solemn recognition of responsibility before men and before God." Chase gave Lincoln a draft final sentence: "And upon this act, sincerely believed to be an act of justice warranted by the Constitution, and of duty demanded by the circumstances of the country, I invoke the considerate judgment of mankind and the gracious favor of Almighty God."[78]

CHAPTER 18

"My Fixed Faith"

The first day of the new year was a fine one in Washington, bright and clear and warm. At the White House, starting at about eleven, Abraham Lincoln and his wife received diplomats, Cabinet members, and their families. Chase's family this day consisted of his sole surviving sibling, Helen Walbridge; his daughter Kate, now twenty-two; and his daughter Nettie, now fifteen. Helen, seven years his junior, had recovered from a stroke—"the paralysis never wholly left the side which received the shock" was how Chase described her condition—so that when they arrived at the reception, his first task was to find his sister a "pleasant seat" from which she "could witness everything with the least inconvenience from her lameness." William Seward's eighteen-year-old daughter, Fanny, commented in her diary that Kate looked "like a fairy queen" in her lace dress. "Oh, how pretty she is." Like so many others, Fanny did not notice Nettie—or at least not enough to write about her.[1]

At noon, just before the public was admitted to the White House reception, the Cabinet members and families returned to their own homes to hold their own receptions. Noah Brooks, a young journalist, went from house to house that afternoon with a few California friends. At Chase's door, he reported, they were greeted by a servant, a "likely young gentleman of color who had a double row of silver-plated buttons from his throat to his toes." Soon Brooks and his friends were "in the presence of the secretary of the Treasury, a tall, good-looking man, slightly bald and guiltless of whiskers," as well as his "very beautiful" daughter Kate, whom Brooks described as "slight, graceful, and of the wavy, willowy order of figure." Chase was "easy and gentlemanly in his manners, though he has a painful way of holding his head straight, which leads one to fancy that his shirt collar cuts his ears." At day's end, Chase wrote in his diary entry that the reception "tired me a good deal, but the children enjoyed it greatly."[2]

Because Lincoln did not sign the Emancipation Proclamation until after the public part of the White House reception, Chase did not see the final text until early evening. He was no doubt pleased to see that the president had accepted, more or less without change, his eloquent final sentence. He was troubled, however, that Lincoln had rejected his advice about Louisiana and Virginia, excluding parts of those states from emancipation because they were under Union military control. Still, Lincoln's proclamation granted immediate freedom to slaves in other places under Union control, such as coastal South Carolina, and promised freedom to all the slaves in the rebellious states if and when the Union conquered the rebels.[3]

The reformer Mansfield French wrote to Chase from Beaufort, South Carolina, to describe the celebration when news about the final proclamation arrived there. After the reading of the proclamation, thousands of black people responded by singing "My Country, 'Tis of Thee." None of the whites present could recall ever having heard "the song from a colored man or woman before," so to hear it now in this way was the "most wonderful thing," Reverend French exulted. "God was truly manifest in it."[4]

Chase retained a keen interest in the parts of the South under Union control, especially coastal South Carolina and eastern Louisiana. He and his friends were concerned about the impending auction of the abandoned Carolina plantations, required by the direct tax act of the prior year. French warned Chase from Beaufort that the "sharp-sighted speculators are on hand and with larger purses than those of the friends of humanity. If the plantations fall into their hands, *most* of the colored people will suffer greatly." Chase urged Congress to amend the law so that laborers—by which, of course, he meant the *black* laborers—could secure "homes and homesteads on the lands they have cultivated."[5]

In response, Congress passed a law allowing the president to exclude from the land sale process property needed for military or charitable purposes. Lincoln then issued an order, probably drafted by Chase, appointing a commission—Generals David Hunter and Rufus Saxton, and the three land sale commissioners for South Carolina—to determine which lands should be set aside for such purposes. This commission reserved most of the land on the Carolina islands under Union control; only about twenty thousand acres were sold in early March. Several plantations, about two thousand acres in total, were purchased by blacks who pooled their savings so that they would own their own land. Parts of other plantations, retained by the government, were leased to blacks for the season.[6]

Hunter informed Chase in early February that he planned to draft blacks in the area under his control into the army. Chase objected, writing Hunter that the former slaves, if they enlisted freely, would "feel themselves very different persons from what they would regard themselves if *forced into the ranks*, and into service under white officers. Would they not mistake military discipline for a new slavery?" General Hunter disagreed. In early March, citing his need for more troops to hold and increase the area under Union control, he issued an order to enlist "all the able-bodied male negroes between the ages of eighteen and fifty" within the region under his military control who were not "regularly and permanently employed in the quartermaster and commissary departments or as the private servants of officers." Chase was not surprised to learn from Edward Pierce (who visited the Sea Islands in late March and early April) that Hunter's order was causing considerable distress there. "The laborers are hiding in the woods, where they pass the night, and even old men who are not fit for service are doing this. The consequence is that the labor is greatly deranged, and the greater part of it is being performed by women." In other respects, however, Pierce was encouraged by the progress in the Sea Islands. Blacks were working the land, planting corn and cotton, and the "children are learning well in school."[7]

Chase opposed drafting blacks into the army, but he wanted them to volunteer and to serve as soldiers, not mere workers. He used an invitation to speak, which he had to decline, to explain in a public letter that it was "my fixed faith . . . that God does not mean that this American republic shall perish. We are tried as by fire, but our country will live." Not only would the nation survive, but "slavery, the chief source and cause and agent of all our ills, will die." To win the war, "American blacks must be called into this conflict, not as cattle, not even as contrabands, but as men." Citing the recent legal opinion of the Attorney General Bates, in response to a request from Chase, that blacks born in the United States were citizens, and the example of Andrew Jackson, who "did not hesitate" to use black troops against the British in the War of 1812, Chase called for blacks to "receive suitable military organization and do their part. We need their goodwill and must make them our friends by showing ourselves to be their friends. We must have them for guides, for scouts, for all military service in camps or field for which they are qualified." Lincoln and Chase now agreed fully on this issue. Writing to Andrew Johnson in Tennessee, who was reluctant to anger white masters by raising black regiments, Lincoln said that the "bare sight of fifty thousand armed and drilled black soldiers on the banks of the Mississippi would end the rebellion at once."[8]

From Louisiana, Chase received a constant stream of reports from George Denison and others about the work of Nathaniel Banks, the new commanding general. Denison and Chase disliked the new labor system that Banks had imposed, which required rural blacks to remain on particular plantations, working for the white owners. In their view, Banks had effectively reestablished slavery in rural Louisiana. On the other hand, Chase was pleased with the progress that the general was making in turning former slaves into soldiers. Denison wrote to Chase in March that there were "four full regiments" of black soldiers in the department, and "they compare favorably with any troops in the service." Two of these black regiments were in the thick of the hand-to-hand fighting at Port Hudson, Louisiana, in late May 1863. Chase wrote to a friend that the "most remarkable feature of the attack on Port Hudson was the wonderful bravery displayed by the negro regiments." The courage of the black soldiers had "settled forever the question whether negroes will fight. There will no longer be any objections to the policy of arming them which will be worthy the least consideration."[9]

Chase was already considering the terms on which Louisiana would return to the Union. His principal concern about a draft state constitution, prepared by Stanton's aides, was that it limited voting to loyal white citizens; Chase favored extending the vote to all loyal citizens, including blacks. "Is it not a clear obligation of honor and duty to protect these citizens against the possibility of future enslavement?" Chase asked Stanton. "Can any sure guaranty of such protection be given them, except by recognizing their right to participate in the reconstruction of the state, by voting for the members of the proposed constitutional convention?" Chase also noted pointedly that there were more loyal *blacks* than loyal *whites* in Louisiana. "Very many of that portion of them who have been long free are intelligent, hold property, maintain schools and churches, and are in all respects as well qualified to exercise the right of suffrage as their white fellow citizens." Writing on the same question to the Louisiana planter and politician Benjamin Flanders, whom he had recently appointed supervising special agent for Louisiana, Chase used for the first time a phrase he would employ often: "universal suffrage."[10]

Chase's main priority in the first two months of 1863 was getting Congress to pass financial legislation. In early January, in response to a House resolution asking why the government was months late in paying the soldiers, Chase published a letter pointing out the problems in the existing legislation and pressing for new legislation along the lines of his December report. A week later, Congress passed an emergency joint resolution authorizing another $100 million of legal tender notes. Lincoln signed the measure into law, but he also issued a statement (drafted by Chase) explaining that he was worried about the inflation caused by the legal tender notes and urging Congress to create a system of national banks and to impose a tax on state banks when they issued more state banknotes. The *Chicago Tribune* complained that the president's message was "simply a demand that Chase's financial scheme be adopted."[11]

Two related bills were making their way through Congress at this time: a finance bill to authorize further federal borrowing and to tax private banknotes, and a banking and currency bill to set up national banks and a single, national currency. The House made no progress for weeks on the banking bill because many House Republicans joined Democrats to oppose the Treasury secretary's proposed bill. For example, John Gurley, a Republican representative from Cincinnati, noted that even Chase conceded the national bank system would not make an immediate difference in financing the war. "What the country now needs and expects," Gurley declared, "is some sensible, practical plan whereby money will instantly flow into an empty Treasury to meet the demands of a mighty army and navy, and not the adoption of doubtful theories that can confessedly do nothing for the nation till long after it is either saved or lost." After considerable debate, and several changes suggested by Chase, the House passed its version of the finance bill at the end of January. Chase told his friend William Mellen that there were several provisions of this House bill that still troubled him: he had hoped that the lower chamber would impose a uniform annual tax on state banknotes instead of a complicated graduated tax; and he opposed a provision allowing for federal deposits in state banks, which he characterized as the "virtual restoration of the pet bank system."[12]

Chase also wrote Horace Greeley in late January to chide him for a *New-York Tribune* editorial suggesting that Lincoln should change his Cabinet. "Let us get the measures necessary to the success of any Republican administration adopted, and then let the Cabinet be reconstituted if you will." The Treasury secretary himself was quite ready to return to private life. Far more urgent than Cabinet changes, Chase wrote, was "the banking bill," which he called a national version of the successful New York system. "A state free banking system has been tried in New York for three million people with the best results on state credit and individual well-being. What is so good for three million must be good for thirty million or thirty-three million." What the banking bill needed was "vigorous support from the influential press for a few days or perhaps three weeks."[13]

Greeley responded as Chase hoped. Echoing Chase's report, the *New-York Tribune* argued that the bill would "strengthen the union of the states by the closely interwoven ties of common interest in the permanence and credit of the national government." Other newspapers joined their voices to support the bank bill. Chase also lobbied face-to-face and hosted dinners, one night with ten House members and another with six senators.[14]

Chase's key ally in the Senate was John Sherman, to whom he wrote almost daily in late January and early February. In his main speech on the bank bill, on February 10, Sherman stressed that the new, uniform national currency would benefit especially the remote, rural states because their residents would no longer face questions about out-of-state banknotes. Sherman predicted that the new federal banknotes would one day be accepted "all over the world" as the "standard medium of exchange." The bill would strengthen people's connections with the national government and weaken the "doctrine of state rights, which substitutes a local community—for, after all, the most powerful state is but a local community." Thus did Sherman suggest that the opponents of the banking bill were like the secessionists, more concerned about their states than about the United States.[15]

When the Senate voted on February 12, the banking bill barely passed, twenty-three to twenty-one. Several important Republicans voted against the bill, but it also gained two Democratic votes from Oregon, which did not have a state banking system and was thus keen to see a single national currency. The *Chicago Times,* a Democratic paper, complained that the Senate passed the bill without adequate debate and that Chase had been "personally present each day on the floor of the Senate to push it through." The *New York Herald* commented that three or four senators voted in favor of the bill only as a favor to Chase, so that he could "get the bill before the House, it being well understood that it will be killed there without loss of time."[16]

Chase had no intention of letting the bank bill die in the House. He wrote Lincoln about one reluctant Illinois House member, William Kellogg, asking the president to send for Kellogg and "urge him to support the bill on your account and to support it earnestly." As House members gave speeches throughout the evening, for and against the bank bill, Chase was in the chamber. The next day, the day set for the vote, he was on Capitol Hill again, this time with the new secretary of the interior, John Palmer Usher, described by one contemporary as "fair, florid, well nourished, and comfortable." Chase and Usher settled into the Speaker's room and met there with members one by one, probably talking about patronage as well as the merits of the measure. The Senate bank bill passed the House by a vote of seventy-eight to sixty-four. Kellogg was among the members who voted aye, along with most of those who had attended Chase's dinner party. The jubilant Treasury secretary wrote Lincoln that, because the Senate bill passed the House without any amendments, it "needs your approval only to become law." Lincoln signed the National Banking Act into law on February 25.[17]

In its final form, the National Banking Act authorized any group of five or more people to form a new national bank with a minimum capital of $50,000. Existing banks with state charters could also convert to become national banks by meeting the same requirements. National banks were required to deposit part of their capital into the Treasury in the form of United States bonds, and, in return, the national banks would receive national banknotes, which Chase envisaged would become the new national currency. The act created a new position within the Treasury, comptroller of the currency, with broad powers to regulate the national banks. Chase wanted an experienced banker to serve as the first comptroller and was able to persuade Hugh McCulloch, a respected Indiana banker, to take the post. McCulloch would go on to serve as Treasury secretary himself for three different presidents.[18]

Meanwhile, in early March, a conference committee finished work on a compromise version of the finance bill, authorizing Chase to issue one more round of legal tender notes and imposing taxes on notes issued by banks. There were still some aspects of this finance bill that Chase disliked, but he accepted it, and Lincoln signed it into law on March 3, the day that Congress ended its short session.[19]

Chase's critics have often noted that the Banking Act did not do much to finance the Civil War. They miss the point. Chase used the crisis of the war to force through the National Banking Act, just as Franklin Roosevelt used the crisis of the Great Depression to force through the Social Security Act. In the midst of a later financial crisis, Rahm Emanuel, chief of staff for president-elect Barack Obama, observed, "You never want a serious crisis to go to waste," for it is "an opportunity to do things that you did not think you could do before." There had been no chance, in the 1850s, of persuading Congress to create national banks and a single national currency; nor would there have been much chance for such legislation in the contentious decade after the Civil War. Chase deftly guided the measure through Congress in the midst of the crisis.[20]

All through the winter, as Congress worked in Washington, Jay Cooke's advertisements for the five-twenty bonds appeared in a few Pennsylvania newspapers. But Cooke did not start his real push to sell the five-twenty bonds until late March 1863, as if he had been waiting for Congress to finish its work. Henry Cooke reported from Washington to Jay in Philadelphia on March 24 that Chase was "immensely delighted at the way we are rolling in subscriptions." For that one day, the firm received more than $1 million dollars in subscriptions. Chase told Henry that if the Cooke brothers could raise $1.5 million per day from the sale of the five-twenties, he would have "all he wants" and "would look for money from no other source."[21]

Jay Cooke made brilliant use of the newspapers to sell five-twenties. In late March, for example, several papers published an exchange of letters in which Cooke addressed questions from an anonymous rural correspondent (probably just Cooke himself), such as "Why are they called five-twenties?" and "How does Secretary Chase get enough gold to pay this interest?" Cooke's responses were simple and persuasive. "The duties on imports of all articles from abroad must be paid in gold," he explained,

Jay Cooke, the Ohio financier who helped Chase sell
$1.6 billion of bonds for the government.

"and this is the way Secretary Chase gets his gold. It is now being paid into the Treasury at the rate of $200,000 a day, which is twice as much as he needs to pay the interest in gold."[22]

A few days later, an enthusiastic article in the *Philadelphia Ledger* described the scene at Cooke's Philadelphia office. "It would rejoice the heart of every patriot if he could witness in person the daily operations at the agency of the national loan in this city. The people are there to give aid and comfort to the government by investing their savings and their capital in the five-twenty bonds." Cooke and his clerks "sit amidst piles of orders by mail, flights of orders by telegraph, and incessant orders by word of mouth." There was "a letter from a lady in Camden who orders $300, and there is one from St. Paul, Minnesota, for $12,500." There were also investors coming in person. "Near one of the desks is a nursery

One of Jay Cooke's many advertisements for the five-twenty bonds.

maid who wants a bond for $50, and just behind her, placidly waiting his turn, is a portly gentleman, one of the 'solid men' of Philadelphia, at whom you can scarcely look without having visions of plethoric pocketbooks and heavy balances in bank. He wants $25,000." Both articles were reprinted many times.[23]

Cooke also used an obscure provision in the recent finance act, advertising that "the privilege of converting the present issue of legal tender notes" into the five-twenty bonds would cease on July 1, 1863. Almost all Northerners, by this point, held some of the legal tender notes, and Cooke urged them to convert them into the five-twenty bonds before the deadline. When July arrived, however, five-twenty bond sales were going so well that Chase decided, as a matter of discretion, to continue to accept legal tender notes as payment for the bonds. Cooke also developed a network of dozens of subagents, in cities and towns across the North, who served as local collection points and in some cases placed their own advertisements.[24]

The financial results of this frenzy were impressive. In the first quarter of 1863, the Treasury received only $7.2 million from the sale of the five-twenties. In the second quarter, receipts reached $156.6 million. Cooke filled the newspapers with daily and weekly reports on the sales: $5 million in a single successful day, $10 million in a good week, and with more expected the following week. Writing in May to two agents whom he had asked to explore a European loan, Chase explained why that would no longer be necessary: "The investments of the people in the [five-twenties], together with the regular income from customs and internal duties, more than meet our whole expenditure." There was not a "single unsatisfied requisition" in the Treasury, and he was in the process of paying the troops their salaries for the current month. Chase was also encouraged because the "banking system is received with great favor," and the "national currency bids fair to become, more rapidly than was anticipated, the only recognized currency of the country." He expected that with the "resources created by the more vigorous application to production of all our industries, reinforced by large immigration, and by improved machinery," the Union could "carry on the war for two years longer, if necessary," before the debt became too burdensome.[25]

In early June, in light of the immense scale of the five-twenty sales, Chase reduced Cooke's commission rate from one-quarter percent to one-eighth of one percent, with some exceptions. The Treasury secretary explained to Cooke that he had "no disposition to reduce the compensation either of yourself or your agents below what is just and liberal. On the other hand, I have a duty to the country to perform, which forbids me to pay rates which will not be approved by all right-minded men." Chase also returned to Cooke a check for $4,000 arising from his purchase and sale of railway shares for Chase's personal account. He explained that he had envisaged that Cooke would purchase and hold the shares, not sell them before Chase had even paid for them. He did not want, given his role in the markets, to profit from short-term share price movements. Chase continued to rely upon Cooke both for official and personal financial matters, however, and this, in time, prompted questions from Congress. Even by the loose standards of the nineteenth century, the relations between Chase and Cooke were too close.[26]

When William Sprague arrived in Washington in early March 1863 to
take up the Senate seat to which he had been elected, he resumed his
courtship of Kate Chase. By the middle of May, Sprague could write to a
friend that Chase and his daughter had "consented to take me into their
fold"—that is, that he and Kate were engaged. Navy Secretary Gideon
Welles noted in his diary on May 19, after the couple called upon him
at home, that Sprague was young and rich, and Kate had "talent and
ambition sufficient for both."[27]

Serving as a senator was not a full-time job in the nineteenth century,
and Sprague was more interested in his private business back in Rhode
Island than in the public business. So he suggested to Chase that rather
than buying a home in Washington, he and Kate would live with Chase
in the E Street house, assuming "as much of the pecuniary burden as possible." Chase wrote back to his future son-in-law that he wouldn't "feel
easy with any household arrangement where you will not be the head."
More generally, Chase was pleased to see how much Kate and Sprague
loved each other. Some fathers might hope that their daughters would
love them more than they did their husbands, but (Chase said) he was
not one of them. "I want to have Katie honor and love you with an honor
and love far exceeding any due to me," he wrote, "and I shall feel happiest
when she makes your happiness complete." Sprague responded that he
hoped that their marriage would be characterized by "mutual interests,
mutual forbearance, mutual love" and that he would "very gladly concur
in whatever views your greater experience in such matters may decide for
our domestic arrangements." In the end, Sprague purchased the Chase
house from the landlord and also paid for renovations so that it would
serve both branches of the family.[28]

In the midst of all this sweetness and light, there were some worrisome signs. Urging Chase to secure promotion for a Rhode Island friend,
Sprague wrote that his friend had "pledged to me that from this time,
no intoxicating draughts shall pass his lips." Because "I deem nearly all
our defeats occasioned by this practice" and "I know that in my own life
whatever of improprieties I may be charged with, is from this cause,"
Sprague believed this pledge "guarantees sure success." Thus did Kate's
intended admit in a roundabout way that he sometimes drank too much
and engaged in "improprieties."[29]

A week later, Sprague wrote Chase again, this time about a Treasury permit he wanted in order to purchase cotton from the South. "Will permits be given to anyone who furnish proper bonds," he asked, "thus letting in the Jews and Gentiles in the general rush?" Sprague urged the government to "get out as much cotton as we can, paying as little as possible for it. The cotton is of more value to us than the money to the enemy." The new senator did not seem worried about whether it was proper to press the secretary of the Treasury to favor a future family member in this way.[30]

For the most part, in the first six months of 1863, Lincoln and Chase worked well together. They agreed on emancipation, though Chase still hoped that the president would emancipate all the slaves in Louisiana and Virginia. They concurred on enlisting volunteers among the former slaves in the army. Lincoln deferred to Chase on finances and helped him secure passage of the banking bill. They often agreed on the selection of generals, although this was not because Lincoln consulted with his Cabinet. When Ambrose Burnside resigned in January, for example, Lincoln appointed Chase's friend Joseph Hooker to lead the Army of the Potomac, without conferring with Chase or anyone else in the Cabinet.[31]

One way in which Chase and Lincoln worked together was by sharing letters from third parties. In April, for example, Chase forwarded to the president a letter from Murat Halstead, editor of the *Cincinnati Commercial*. Halstead wrote that Ulysses S. Grant, then stalled in his attempt to capture Vicksburg, Mississippi, was a "poor drunken imbecile. He is a poor stick sober, and he is most of the time more than half drunk, and much of the time idiotically drunk. About two weeks ago, he was so miserably drunk for twenty-four hours that his staff kept him shut up in a stateroom on the steamer where he makes his headquarters—because he was hopelessly foolish." In his cover letter to Lincoln, Chase noted that "reports concerning General Grant similar to the statements made by Mr. Halstead are too common to be safely or even prudently disregarded." Although it now seems that Halstead was right in part, and that Grant did drink too much from time to time, it also seems that Grant did not allow his drinking to interfere with his fighting, so that Lincoln was right to ignore Chase's advice and to keep Grant.[32]

A few weeks later, Chase shared with Lincoln a letter from James Garfield, serving as chief of staff in Tennessee for General William Rosecrans.

Ulysses Grant, general during the Civil War, president thereafter.
In 1863 Chase shared with Lincoln a letter from a friend saying that
Grant was "most of the time more than half drunk."

The future president wrote that he had been trying to impress upon Rosecrans that "our true objective point is the rebel army and not any particular position or territory." Nothing but "hard blows that will break their armies and pulverize them can destroy the Confederacy." Lincoln, in an oft-quoted message to Hooker, would use Garfield's exact words, writing that "*Lee's* army, and not *Richmond*, is your true objective point."[33]

One matter on which Chase and Lincoln did not see eye to eye was how to run the Cabinet. "Our administration," Chase wrote his friend Bishop Charles McIlvaine, "under the president's system, if system it be, is departmental." There were some questions "which the president reserves substantially to himself—for example, those relating to slavery." Most other questions were handled by the heads of the separate departments. "The president sustains me kindly and cordially when I ask him but in general does not interfere at all or even care to be informed as to the line of action I adopt," he explained. The department heads were "not expected to exert much, if any, influence on the action of any other departments than their own; of course, they do not expect to be consulted, except very rarely, in relation to any important matter involved in such action. Not being consulted, they are not informed." This was not, Chase wrote, his ideal of an administration, in which measures would be "gravely and fully considered by all and determined on after such consideration by the head." He added, however, that he might be "all wrong."[34]

Chase and Lincoln also sometimes disagreed about government appointments. In February 1863 Senator James Dixon of Connecticut persuaded the Senate to reject the nomination of Mark Howard for internal revenue collector in Hartford. Dixon had no problem with the way in which Howard, acting under a recess appointment, was doing his work as Hartford collector, but the senator was a conservative who disliked Howard's radical politics. Chase urged Lincoln to resubmit Howard's name, so that the Senate could "reconsider its action, calmly and dispassionately." Gideon Welles in this case agreed with Chase, telling Dixon that he was wrong to involve the Senate in his personal quarrel.[35]

Dixon and Chase reached a compromise, but before Chase could discuss it with Lincoln, he received a letter from the president directing him to prepare the papers to appoint a named successor. After meeting again with Dixon, Chase wrote Lincoln that he and the senator wanted to talk with him "as soon as practicable and submit the matter to your further consideration," saying that he wanted to establish that the president and his advisers could select "fit men for responsible places, without admitting the right of senators or representatives to control appointments." He did not question the Senate's right to confirm or reject presidential appointments, but thought Lincoln was going too far in giving a single senator the right to dictate an appointment in his state. Chase added that "unless this principle can be practically established, I feel that I cannot be useful to you or the country in my present position." Lincoln probably did not appreciate this hint of resignation, but Lincoln, Chase, Dixon, and Welles soon resolved the issue and selected a friend of Welles as Howard's successor.[36]

Another disagreement was about Victor Smith, collector of customs for Puget Sound, in the remote Washington Territory. An Ohio lawyer and friend of Chase's, Smith angered many in the territory by moving the customs collection point from Port Townsend to Port Angeles, even using an armed revenue cutter to force the residents of Port Townsend to yield up the customs records. A grand jury charged Smith with various crimes, but after an internal investigation, Chase cleared him and arranged for the criminal charges to be dismissed. One of Smith's key enemies was the surveyor general for the territory, Anson Henry, an Illinois physician and longtime friend of the president, who was in Washington this spring. After meeting with Henry and speaking with Lincoln, Chase instructed his deputy secretary, George Harrington, to investigate and report.[37]

Returning from a two-week business trip in early May, Chase was dismayed to learn from Harrington that Lincoln had asked him to prepare papers to appoint a successor for Smith. Chase also received two letters from Lincoln, one naming the person he wanted as Smith's replacement, and one explaining that by removing Smith, the president did not mean to "decide that the charges against him are true. I only decide that the degree of dissatisfaction with him there is too great for him to be retained." Lincoln added that since Smith was a friend of Chase, he would try to find another place for him.[38]

Chase wrote back to Lincoln heatedly, saying that he could not serve as secretary if the "selection of persons to fill important subordinate places in the department is to be made not only without my concurrence but without my knowledge." He recognized that the ultimate right of appointment belonged to the president. If "after fair consideration of my views in any case your judgment in relation to a proper selection differs from mine, it is my duty to acquiesce, cheerfully, in your determination; unless, indeed, the case be one of such a character, as to justify my withdrawal from my post." Again, Chase suggested that if Lincoln wanted him to resign, he would do so "unhesitatingly." Lincoln resolved the issue by appointing Chase's choice, Lewis Gunn, who had been Smith's assistant.[39]

Chase sometimes disagreed with Lincoln about more serious matters. One of the main Democratic criticisms of the Lincoln administration was that it made "arbitrary arrests"—arresting not only people who were working for the rebels but also those who simply opposed the war or questioned the administration. In March 1863 Lincoln appointed Burnside to head the army's Department of the Ohio, consisting of Ohio and other midwestern states. Not long after arriving at his new headquarters, Burnside issued general order number 38, threatening to arrest all those within the department who were helping the rebellion. "The habit of declaring sympathies for the enemy will no longer be tolerated in this department," the general declared. Lincoln, who had so readily reversed the orders of

Frémont and Hooker, let this order stand. Nor did he intervene when Burnside sent troops to arrest Clement Vallandigham, a former Democratic member of the House, for the "crime" of an antiwar speech. Instead, Lincoln allowed Burnside to try Vallandigham by military commission and sentence him to spend the rest of the war in military prison. After the trial, however, Lincoln started to face Republican as well as Democratic criticism, with leading papers such as the *New-York Tribune* and the *New York Evening Post* insisting that the arrest and trial were unconstitutional.[40]

Lincoln did not respond by pardoning Vallandigham and thus making him a free man. Instead, he commuted the sentence, changing it from prison to exile in the Confederacy. Chase disagreed. "If Vallandigham violated any law," he wrote to a friend, "he should have been arrested, tried, and convicted." He added that he had "never myself been much afraid of words, and when men—Vallandigham among them—have sought to cripple the financial administration by misrepresentation and vilification, I have preferred to reply by augmented efforts in the service of the country rather than by arrest and imprisonment." In another letter, Chase wrote that he believed the "arrest of Vallandigham was a mistake" and that Lincoln had not solved the problem by sending him into exile. Except in extraordinary cases, "the law in my judgment is sufficient and the regular processes of the law are sufficient." In a few years, as chief justice, Chase would help set limits on military trials of civilians during wartime.[41]

Chase's letters from the first half of 1863 yield scant evidence that he was thinking about the next presidential nomination. One, to an Ohio friend, said that he believed "all Republicans and all Democrats who love the country better than slavery should unite; signify their union by boldly assuming the name of Democratic Republicans; and fight political battles on principles of justice, right, liberty, and national integrity for the masses and against the oligarchy." Some might say that the Union Party, composed mainly of Republicans but also including many antislavery Democrats, was just such a party, but it seems that Chase had in mind a political organization with a more Democratic flavor.[42]

Some of the newspapers, however, started to report that Chase was working toward the 1864 Union Party nomination. For example, the *Buffalo Courier* noted that Lincoln had received letters from Washington Territory praising Gunn as "loyal to the government and to Secretary Chase." This, the editors said, was the "kind of loyalty Mr. Chase appreciates as long as he has longings for the presidential succession." Men in various cities had formed Union Leagues, semisecret clubs of those completely committed to the Union cause. In Utica, New York, according to the *New York Herald*, there were two rival Union Leagues, one favoring Seward and one favoring Chase. The *New-York Tribune* mocked the *Herald*'s report, saying that its editors had not "yet heard a friend of Governor Chase name him as a candidate for next president, though his enemies seem to talk of nothing else."[43]

The *Herald* responded with a long article accusing Chase of "laying pipe in every direction for the next presidency." ("Laying pipe," in the nineteenth century, meant "engaging in political intrigue.") According to the *Herald,* "when Mr. Chase wishes to consult visitors from New York, Philadelphia, or Baltimore about his presidential prospects, he takes them into his carriage and drives them about the suburbs of the city, under pretense of showing them the fortifications." The Treasury secretary supposedly told these friends that he was "not responsible in any degree for the military blunders of the administration and is not sanguine of military success." There was some truth in this, for Chase often wrote that he was not much involved in military matters. The *Herald* claimed that Chase was proud that he had "provided for all legitimate demands upon the Treasury—including, we [the editors] presume, his campaign expenses—and that he will never consent to peace upon the basis of separation and the acknowledgment of the Southern confederacy." There was truth in this as well, for Chase was proud of his work providing for wartime expenses—although nothing suggests that he intended to use government funds for campaign purposes. Even if the *Herald* was somewhat premature in seeing Chase as a candidate, events in the second half of the year would show that he was indeed in the presidential race.[44]

Chase gave a short speech in Boston in early May, praising Massachusetts for its contribution to the Union war effort and singling out its native son Joseph Hooker, "who is now striking a formidable blow against the rebellion between the Rappahannock and Richmond." General Hooker and the Army of the Potomac were indeed fighting on the Rappahannock on this day, midway through the weeklong Battle of Chancellorsville. Initial Northern press reports were positive, but it gradually emerged that Hooker had suffered a devastating defeat.[45]

Writing to friends not long after the battle, Chase blamed two factors for the defeat at Chancellorsville: first, the "disreputable retreat of the Eleventh Corps," perhaps due to the "substitution of Gen. [Oliver] Howard for Gen. [Franz] Sigel in the command," and, second, the "temporary, but for a time serious, injury sustained by Hooker from prostration by a ball which struck and shattered a pillar (wooden) on which he was leaning." Chase had learned of Hooker's concussion, not widely reported, from a nephew on Hooker's staff. Chase also wrote Garfield to report rumors that Lee's army was moving north. "If Lee is actually moving, he will find no divided armies before him as formerly under Pope and McClellan and will have no child's play to encounter. It seems to me, indeed, the very thing to be desired, and I am confident Hooker will make him repent of it."[46]

Lee and his army were, in fact, moving north, heading as we know for the Battle of Gettysburg on the first three days of July 1863. As Hooker moved to counter Lee, Chase was in close touch with him and his chief of staff, Dan Butterfield. On the evening of May 20, Chase left Washington by steamer, heading for Hooker's headquarters. When he returned to Washington the next day, the Treasury secretary pressed Lincoln and Stanton to resolve one of Hooker's key problems: he was not in charge of all the federal forces facing Lee and his army. Chase reported back to Hooker that Stanton assured him that "everything in Virginia east of the Shenandoah Valley was practically though not immediately under [Hooker's] command." Chase was still confident that Hooker could defeat Lee, writing to Kate on June 25 that Lee would "get no great distance, in any direction, without feeling Hooker strike him." The next day, Hooker sent a message to Halleck, asking whether it would not make sense to abandon Maryland Heights and Harpers Ferry, so that the federal troops there could join Hooker's main army and help it defeat Lee. Halleck's response was that these positions were more important than strengthening Hooker's army. When Hooker tried to order troops out of Harpers Ferry the next day, he was incensed to learn that Halleck had instructed the officers there to "pay no attention to Hooker's orders." Hooker sent Halleck an angry request to be relieved. After conferring with Lincoln, Halleck sent orders to relieve Hooker and appoint George Meade to lead the Army of the Potomac.[47]

Chase knew nothing about Hooker's resignation and Meade's appointment until the next day, when, at a special Sunday-morning Cabinet meeting, Lincoln reported that Hooker had asked to be relieved and that

Meade was now in charge. The president explained that he saw in Hooker some of McClellan's faults, such as a "greedy call for more troops." Welles wrote in his diary account that Chase "immediately interested himself for the future of Hooker" and suggested that he "should be sent to Fortress Monroe and take charge of a demonstration upon Richmond via the James River." Welles was pleased that the president "did not give much attention to the suggestion." Chase followed up with a letter to Lincoln, pointing out that Hooker might have assumed (from comments like those of Stanton) that he would have at least some control over all the troops confronting Lee. Chase was not pleading with Lincoln to place Hooker back in charge of the Army of the Potomac—he accepted that decision—but rather was laying groundwork for Hooker's next assignment. Meade would command at Gettysburg.[48]

CHAPTER 19

"Bringing to a Second Birth This Same Mighty Nation"

"This is an anxious day," Chase wrote in his diary on July 1, 1863, as the Union and Confederate armies fought at Gettysburg, about eighty miles north of Washington. "Meade's army seems to be drawing right to the rebel positions. Is he not too far to the right? May not Lee turn to his left and so get between him and Washington? These are questions much discussed." Meade's messages to Washington were "neither frequent nor long," but they indicated "prudence, courage, and activity." All the Treasury secretary could do was wait and watch and pray. Two days later, Chase noted that the news was "neither very good nor very bad." It was not until early on the Fourth that messages arrived in Washington saying that Meade had defeated Lee at Gettysburg.[1]

On this same Fourth of July, the besieged rebels at Vicksburg, Mississippi, finally surrendered themselves and the city to Ulysses Grant. The Vicksburg news would not reach Washington for several days, but Chase wrote to Grant on the Fourth to discuss the cotton trade and to praise the general for the "patient energy and skillful courage with which you have conducted the military operations under your direction." Chase hoped that Grant would follow up with the "rapid and complete suppression of the rebellion in the whole region west of the Mississippi and by the complete control of the [Mississippi] River." There was no hint here of the concern that Chase had raised with Lincoln about whether Grant was the right man to command the western armies.[2]

"God be praised for our victories," Chase wrote a few days later to a Union general. With the fall of Vicksburg, with the imminent fall of Port Hudson (the last major rebel stronghold on the Mississippi River), and with the "rebels exhausted and retreating," Chase believed that the end of the war might be near. Writing on July 10 to John Bigelow, now the American minister in Paris, Chase noted that although the "victory over Lee's army was complete," the rebels were retreating "in good order" toward the Potomac. Chase predicted that "unless Lee manages to escape across the Potomac, there must soon be another battle the result of which can hardly be doubtful, though the issue of battles can never be certainly foreseen." On July 15, after Meade allowed Lee to cross the river without a major battle, Chase wrote that Lincoln was "more grieved and indignant than I have ever seen him."[3]

Chase did not have much time to lament Lee's escape, however, for it coincided with the draft riots in New York City. On July 13 an angry crowd interrupted the process of selecting those who would be drafted, destroyed the draft records, and then burned the building for good measure. Soon mobs, many of them Irish American, were roaming the streets and burning buildings, especially those associated with Republicans, and hunting, attacking, and, in many cases, killing blacks. Chase was rightly worried that the mobs would target the federal buildings in southern Manhattan, including the Sub-Treasury Building, with its storeroom filled with gold, and the nearby customs warehouses, one of which held a hundred thousand rifles. Chase sent messages to Hiram Barney and John Cisco, directing them to take all necessary measures to protect federal property. Chase told Cisco that Lincoln and Stanton assured him that "adequate force is on its way to New York." David Dudley Field sent Chase a telegram from New York, describing the situation as "desperate" and asking him to speak again with Lincoln and Stanton. Chase responded with a list of the regiments that were about to arrive in New York City, saying that the Washington authorities believed this was "ample, when added to the force already there." Federal troops finally restored order in New York City, but not before at least a hundred, and perhaps as many as five hundred, people were dead.[4]

Midway through the draft riots, a message from General Nathaniel Banks arrived in Washington: he and his army had captured Port Hudson,

Hiram Barney, Chase's friend, held the most coveted patronage position in the United States: collector of customs for the Port of New York.

the last rebel fort on the Mississippi. The river was "now open," Banks declared. Chase promptly sent a message to congratulate and encourage Banks. But the Mississippi River was not truly open—not in the way that it had been in the past. Chase loosened the department's rules on trading with the enemy in order to allow steamboats to travel from Saint Louis to New Orleans, but he could not permit trade at all the intermediate points or along the tributaries, for much of that region was still under rebel control. Moreover, as George Denison reported to Chase from New Orleans, the line of division between the federals and the rebels was shifting constantly, making it difficult to know whether goods nominally headed for a region under Union control would wind up in Confederate hands.[5]

Predictably, the papers in New Orleans and Saint Louis soon started to attack Chase's trade restrictions. The *Daily True Delta* in New Orleans declared in August that the "Confederate edicts to burn and destroy are no more destructive to commerce than the acts of the federal Congress and the incomprehensible regulations of the Treasury Department, with its swarm of electioneering spies and agents." Chase was indignant, writing to Denison that "no one knows better than yourself how untrue is the allegation that the Treasury Department has sent forth any swarm of electioneering spies and agents. All the appointments of the department have been made with a simple desire to secure the honest execution of the acts of Congress with as little inconvenience and as much benefit as possible to the people, and at the same time to sustain the president in the measures adopted by him for the suppression of the rebellion." Responding to a petition from a group of Saint Louis merchants, Chase explained that it was more important to prevent trade with the rebels, which would strengthen the rebellion, than to open every possible port along the rivers.[6]

Union forces did not make much progress in August 1863. George Meade and his army were quiet in their camp near the Rappahannock River. William Sherman and his army captured Jackson, Mississippi, and turned the state capital into what he called "one mass of charred ruins," but they did not fight any major battles. William Rosecrans and his army in Tennessee seemed (from the perspective of Washington) almost idle. Chase wrote to Garfield that he could not "help thinking how much [Rosecrans] could do with his splendid army and how much the country needs his doing it. This war, apart from its cost in generous blood, is costing immense treasures. The last forty-five days have added ninety million to our public debt, and I begin to be really alarmed."[7]

Even as Chase wrote to Garfield, Rosecrans was moving artillery into position to bombard the rebels in Chattanooga, Tennessee. The general captured this vital point in early September, but ten days later, Confederate general Braxton Bragg and his army attacked part of the federal army at nearby Chickamauga, Georgia. Chase's friend Charles Dana, now serving as an assistant secretary of war, reported to Stanton from Chattanooga that "Chickamauga is as fatal a name in our history as Bull Run. . . . The total of our killed, wounded, and prisoners can hardly be less than 20,000, and may be much more." Chase told his diary that he was worried by this and other messages arriving from Tennessee. As Rosecrans and the remains of his army retreated into Chattanooga, the War Department sent telegrams to Burnside, in Knoxville, Tennessee, and to Grant, in Vicksburg, Mississippi, asking them to send troops to reinforce Rosecrans. Given the distances and other obstacles, however, it was unclear whether these generals could effectively strengthen Rosecrans and his army.[8]

At about eleven o'clock on the night on September 23, Chase received a message from Stanton, asking him to come at once to the War Department. When Chase arrived, Stanton, "silent and stern," handed him copies of three telegrams from Chattanooga. One was from Garfield to Chase, saying that Bragg "no doubt outnumbers us two to one, but we can stand here ten days if help will then arrive." Another was from Dana to Stanton, urging that twenty thousand or twenty-five thousand troops be sent at once to reinforce Rosecrans. A third telegram was from Rosecrans to Lincoln, saying that "all the reinforcements you can send should be hurried up."[9]

Stanton had summoned Lincoln and others to the War Department, and, starting at about midnight, they discussed the Chattanooga crisis. According to Chase's diary, by far the best account of this meeting, the war secretary started by asking General Halleck pointed questions about whether and when reinforcements would reach Rosecrans. Halleck had to admit that he did not really know. Stanton then made a bold proposal: to use the rails to transfer twenty thousand men from the Army of the Potomac, presently in northern Virginia, all the way to Tennessee to reinforce Rosecrans. Stanton recommended placing Hooker in charge of the troops and claimed that he could transfer most of the men within a week. Both Lincoln and Halleck objected, with the president joking that Stanton could not even "get one corps into Washington in the time you fix for reaching Nashville." Lincoln's skepticism was understandable; he had seen how long it took to move troops in the past. Stanton, "greatly annoyed," according to Chase, said that since he was "overruled," he would "give up the point."[10]

Chase now joined the debate and sided with Stanton. He "hoped the proposition would not be abandoned" and "expressed [his] entire confidence in [Stanton's] ability to do what he proposed." To reject Stanton's proposal "was to refuse to adopt the only plan by which the army of Rosecrans would with any certainty be saved." Seward agreed with Chase, and together they turned the tide, persuading Lincoln to allow Stanton to attempt the rail movement. Chase and the others then went home to their beds, while Stanton remained at the War Department, sending messages through the night.[11]

Returning to Washington a few days later after a brief trip to Baltimore, Chase was cheered by the progress that Stanton was making in transporting the troops by rail to Rosecrans. He wrote to Kate that the "great expedition to reinforce Rosecrans is going on admirably." If nothing went amiss, the first troops would "begin to arrive at Chattanooga or within supporting distance within the next two days." A few weeks later, after Hooker and his troops had won fame for the fighting around Chattanooga, Chase wrote Hooker that it was "providential" that he and his troops went to the West. "It seems clear now that, but for Mr. Stanton's determination in insisting upon these reinforcements going promptly and going under you, Rosecrans's army would have experienced the gravest disasters." Chase did not claim any credit for himself, but he could have, for without his and Seward's efforts at the midnight meeting, Lincoln would not have approved Stanton's plan.[12]

Chase was concerned about blacks not just in the South but also in the North. For example, he sided with his friend Colonel William Birney, son of the late presidential candidate, in controversies arising from his efforts to recruit and train black troops in Maryland. While in Baltimore to meet with Johns Hopkins, the financier and philanthropist, along with "twelve or fifteen of the leading financial men" of Baltimore, Chase took time to visit Birney's camp with John Garrett, president of the Baltimore & Ohio Railroad. Chase noted that Garrett's manner suggested that he did not approve of turning former slaves into Union soldiers, writing in his diary, "The sight could hardly be palatable to one so recently, if not still, thoroughly pro-slavery in his sentiments."[13]

Another example: Chase supported efforts to open Washington streetcars to black as well as white patrons. The Cooke brothers formed the first street railroad company in the nation's capital, the Washington & Georgetown Street Railroad Company, and Chase was one of the first stockholders. Indeed, he even toyed with the idea of resigning his government position and taking over as head of the company. In late 1863, after the *Washington Evening Star* reported that the company was thinking about buying separate cars for blacks, Chase wrote an angry letter to Jay Cooke, urging him to reconsider. "If the colored people are to be confined to special cars," Chase wrote, "let them be *better* than the others so as to compensate in some way for [their] exclusion." Better still, however, would be to have no segregation. "Let all cars be free to all," he urged. "Let all decent people ride in any car convenient when they get in." Cooke did not respond to Chase's letter, and the company did not change its policy until Congress, prodded by black protests, prohibited all Washington streetcar companies from discrimination.[14]

Chase's letter to Cooke, with its bold declaration for black rights, shows well why he was the leading radical candidate for the Union Party nomination. But not all radicals favored him. One of their leaders, Benjamin Wade, told John Hay that Chase "was a good man, but his theology is unsound. He thinks there is a fourth person in the Trinity: S.P.C." Wade preferred Lincoln, as did almost all moderate and conservative Republicans. Frank Blair, member of Congress from Missouri, claimed in a September speech in Saint Louis that Chase was now blocking the Mississippi River with his trade regulations as effectively as the Confederates

Frank Blair, Montgomery's younger brother, was a Union general, a member of Congress, and an even more outspoken opponent of Chase than his brother was.

had blocked it with their cannons. "I shall contend for the free navigation of the Mississippi against the embargo of Chase," Blair declared to
the cheering crowd, "as strongly as I have contended against Jefferson
Davis's embargo, and I don't care what position or what power he holds
or wields in this government." Blair claimed that the Treasury secretary
was a "candidate for Lincoln's seat" and was using his trade regulations
to favor New York and Chicago, and to harm Saint Louis, in an effort to
secure political support.[15]

A week later, in a speech in Rockville, Maryland, Frank's brother
Montgomery, still Lincoln's postmaster general, attacked the radicals for
treating the conquered Southern states as mere territory to be ruled by
Congress. Blair insisted that Lincoln would treat the Southern states as
states and admit them back into the Union without too many limits or
questions. Although Blair barely mentioned Chase, many interpreted his
words as another Blair attack on Chase and wondered whether it indicated
that Lincoln, like the Blairs, favored a conservative approach. Thaddeus

*Montgomery Blair, postmaster general, and member of the
Blair family, Chase's political opponents.*

Stevens, a leading radical, wrote Chase that if Lincoln retained Blair after the Rockville speech, "it is time we were consulting about his successor." In other words, believing that Lincoln was turning conservative, Stevens wanted a radical candidate such as Chase for president.[16]

Stevens was not the only person writing to Chase about presidential possibilities. Charlotte Eastman, the Massachusetts widow, chided him for failing to answer her letters, saying that he ignored her because she could not "help you on one step to place and power." Horace Greeley told Chase in late September that if "in 1864 I could *make* a president (not merely a candidate), you would be my first choice." But Greeley cautioned that he might see things differently in a few months, in which case "I shall put the country first and individual preferences nowhere." Joshua Leavitt, who had known Chase since their work in the early Liberty Party, suggested that Chase think about becoming chief justice rather than president. "A four-year presidency is soon over," he pointed out. It would be better to "have the Supreme Court in your hands for the coming twenty years" and thus to "give steadiness to our cause and stability to our institutions amid whatever political changes may take place."[17]

Chase conceded to Eastman that he was ambitious and that he some-times neglected "duties of friendship." He promised to "direct my ambi-tion to public ends and in honorable ways, and forget friends and their claims as little as possible." Chase thanked Greeley for his support and understood his caution. "I hope that I love our country, and the cause of human progress so intimately connected with the fate of our country, too well to allow any personal wishes or aspirations, from which I do not claim to be more free than other men, to interfere with any duty to her or it." Chase told Leavitt that although a judicial position would be "more agreeable to my personal feelings than any political position," he thought he had done and could do more good in political positions. In the midst this terrible war, Chase would try not to ask anything for himself. "I assert no claim—I only recognize obligation. Neither friends nor country owe me anything. I owe to them all that I can do for both."[18]

The Ohio election for governor in October 1863 attracted national attention—indeed, international interest—because of the stark divide between the two sides. The Union Party, consisting of Republicans and those Democrats who supported the war, nominated John Brough, a businessman and former Democrat, for governor. The Democratic Party proposed Clement Vallandigham (now in exile in Canada) for governor, as a way of protesting against Lincoln, emancipation, and arbitrary arrests. Murat Halstead wrote Chase from Cincinnati to warn that Vallandigham might well win because the voters were outraged by the "radical policy of the president" and the "foolish and hopelessly impracticable proclamation." Republicans worried that if Vallandigham won, there would be civil war in Ohio between pro-Union and antiwar factions. The president told Welles that he was more worried about the Ohio election than any other since his own election in 1860; Lincoln would not have believed, a few years ago, that "one genuine American would or could be induced to vote for such a man as Vallandigham," and yet now here he was, "candidate of a large party."[19]

On Friday, October 9, at the end of a meeting about other issues, Chase told Lincoln that he was thinking of going home to Cincinnati in order to vote for the Union ticket. "I wish you would," said Lincoln. Leaving Washington that night, Chase reached Columbus at two in the morning on Sunday, October 11. In spite of the late hour and the lack of notice, there was a crowd to greet him at the train station and to escort him to his hotel, where he gave a brief speech. Chase spent the rest of Sunday quietly, going to church and seeing friends. On Monday morning he gave another short speech, praising the Union soldiers: "I have seen them in camp and on the march—striplings from the fireside; men in mature manhood; gray-headed sires . . . every man a hero, conscious that he fights for himself and all that is dear to him, because he fights for his country." To sustain the Union soldiers in the field, Chase urged men to vote the Union ticket.[20]

After speeches at the rail stops along the way, Chase gave his main speech in a packed Cincinnati hall on the Monday evening before the Tuesday election. The Civil War, he said, was not a war between the North and the South; it was a war between a small Southern aristocracy and all the other people of the United States. "The simple question before us is this: Is this country worth a war? Are the hopes depending upon the perpetuity of American institutions worth enough to justify us in going to war for the nation's life?" Chase did not shy from the controversy about the Emancipation Proclamation. "In my judgment, the proclamation was the right thing in the right place, and without it . . . we could not have made the progress that we have made." Near the end of his speech, Chase said that he believed "God was in all this business, and out of this great trial of ours is to come forth even a more intelligent, prosperous, and glorious nation than we have heretofore been, based on the one principle, which shall be the admiration of the world: free institutions." Chase closed by urging his listeners to do their own part to save the Union, by voting the next day for the Union ticket. Although the *New York Herald* was usually hostile to Chase, it printed and praised this Cincinnati speech. "With the exception of his radical views in regard to slavery," the editors commented, "every portion of this speech is most statesmanlike, and, taken as a whole, it is really masterly. Its perfect simplicity of style and diction reminds us of President Lincoln's happiest efforts."[21]

On the next day, Chase voted at his local polling place in Cincinnati, and reported in the afternoon to Lincoln that signs looked favorable. That evening, at about ten, when the early returns showed that Brough would prevail over Vallandigham, Chase spoke to an eager crowd gathered in front of his hotel. The news of Brough's victory, he said, would encourage the Lincoln administration in Washington and the Union soldiers in the field. Conversely, word of the Democratic defeat would discourage Jefferson Davis in Richmond and the rebel soldiers. "Every man of them intelligent enough to read and allowed to know the truth will realize that it is useless to wage treasonable war against a united people," he said. At about two in the morning, Chase sent a second telegram to Lincoln, estimating (rightly) that the Union majority in the state would be about a hundred thousand votes. Even Cincinnati, customarily a Democratic stronghold, voted for Brough.[22]

The next day, at the request of Oliver Morton, governor of Indiana, Chase traveled west by train to the state capital of Indianapolis. "At every stopping place," one paper reported, "and indeed many times while the train was in motion, the secretary was laughingly greeted with shouts of 'Greenbacks! Greenbacks!'" Speaking in Indianapolis to a large crowd on the capitol grounds, Chase talked about the greenbacks. He noted that the London papers had predicted the federal government would have to borrow there, but he knew the American people would not want him to accept loans from Britain. He had borrowed from American banks until the bankers said they could not lend any more. Then, Chase said, he turned to the American people. There were thousands of "worthy and reliable men whose paper is good as that of any banks," and he decided to "give such people the preference and make greenbacks representing the wishes of the people." Some "bankers predicted a failure," and some people refused to accept the greenbacks. "But we told them they could take it or none, and we made it a legal tender." The greenbacks, and the new national banks, would create a single, permanent national currency.[23]

In the main part of his Indianapolis speech, which was reprinted widely, Chase discussed the purposes of the war in ways that previewed Lincoln's speech a month later at Gettysburg. Although it was "presumptuous to attempt to penetrate the counsels of Providence," Chase believed that "this nation has a great work before it, which it cannot fulfill while it remains a slaveholding country." He named some of the inventors, and inventions, that had changed life in the nineteenth century: the steam engine, the railroad, the telegraph. These inventions emerged, providentially, when they were necessary for advancing civilization. Now it was "no less necessary that there should be a great nation in the world, governing itself and respecting the rights of every human being of whatever shade of complexion he may be, and that nation is being born—this war is giving birth to that nation—and it will be continued until we are prepared for the great duties Providence has assigned to us." George Washington had believed that "God was in the American Revolution, bringing to birth this mighty nation." Chase declared that God was also "in this war, bringing to a second birth this same mighty nation."[24]

Chase was excited by the warm reception he received in Ohio and Indiana. On his return to Washington, he wrote to an Ohio editor to say that he was particularly pleased that the enthusiasm was "entirely spontaneous and popular. The masses seemed to move of themselves. And it was wonderful to me that so many people whom I never supposed to know anything of my work seemed to understand it perfectly." Writing to his daughter Nettie, however, at her boarding school in New York City, Chase cautioned that "you must not be too elated by the praises just now showered upon your father. Nobody can tell how soon the tide may turn."[25]

Others were far less happy about Chase's election efforts. Edward Bates wrote in his diary that "Chase's head is turned by his eagerness in pursuit of the presidency. For a long time back, he has been filling all the offices in his own vast patronage with extreme partisans and contrives also to fill many vacancies properly belonging to other departments." The attorney general especially disliked some of those whom Chase had persuaded Lincoln to appoint as judges. For example, Bates viewed David Cartter, chief judge in the District of Columbia, as one of Chase's appointments and derided him as "an inbred vulgarian and truculent ignoramus."[26]

Lincoln's secretary Hay wrote in his diary that, when he complained to the president about Chase's political schemes, he responded that he "had determined to shut his eyes to all these performances; that Chase made a good secretary and that he would keep him where he is." Lincoln added that if Chase "becomes president, all right, I hope we may never have a worse man." Hay wrote that Lincoln told him that he had seen all along Chase's "plan of strengthening himself. Whenever he sees that an important matter is troubling me, if I am compelled to decide it in a way to give offense to a man of some influence, he always ranges himself in opposition to me and persuades the victim that he (C) would have arranged it very differently." Chase had disagreed, Lincoln noted, and let people *know* that he disagreed, with Lincoln's reversal of the proclamations of Frémont and Hunter and the recall of Butler from New Orleans. "I am entirely indifferent to his success or failure in these schemes," Lincoln told Hay, "so long as he does his duty as the head of the Treasury."[27]

A few weeks later, Chase suggested that Lincoln should appoint his young private secretary, Homer Plantz, as the district attorney for Florida, based in Key West. Hay objected, telling Lincoln that Plantz would go to Florida with only two purposes: "to steal money for himself and votes for Chase." Hay wrote that Lincoln told him that he "prefers to let Chase have his own way in these sneaking tricks than getting in a snarl with him by refusing him what he asks." Lincoln was "much amused by Chase's mad hunt after the presidency" and again said that he hoped "the country will never do worse." In another conversation, Lincoln told Hay that Chase's presidential aspirations were like "a horsefly on the neck of a plow horse—which kept him lively about his work."[28]

Encouraged by his efforts in Ohio, Chase joined the Maryland campaign as well, speaking in late October at an immense election rally in Baltimore. The principal issue in this campaign was emancipation: whether the state should amend its constitution to free its slaves. Henry Winter Davis, a radical member of Congress and a friend of Chase's, headed those who favored immediate emancipation; Montgomery Blair led those who favored delay. James Garfield, who accompanied Chase to Baltimore and joined him on the platform, wrote home that it was amazing to hear local leaders, "many of them lifelong slaveholders," speak out in favor of "immediate and unconditional abolition in Maryland."

Chase was equally surprised at his warm welcome in Baltimore—the home of the secessionists who, less than three years earlier, had nearly assassinated Lincoln on his way to Washington for his inauguration. In early November Maryland elected a legislature composed mainly of those in favor of immediate emancipation, and the state would soon amend its constitution to abolish slavery.[29]

The main event for Chase in November 1863 was the wedding of his daughter Kate to Senator William Sprague. We do not know the details, but it is clear that the courtship between the fiery Kate and the abusive William was not smooth. He wrote to her in September, after she had visited his family in Rhode Island, that he hoped "we may never undergo another such crisis of great discomfort and discouragement" and that they must "be careful of each other's temper." In October he begged her to

William Sprague and Kate Chase at the time of their 1863 wedding.
The Spragues would later quarrel, have affairs, and divorce.

let him "indulge in the luxuries which are soon to be mine." Chase had cautioned his daughter on this score, but it seems, from a much later entry in her diary, that she did allow William to "indulge" in at least some such "luxuries." In early November William wrote to Chase that he had "taken little or no care of myself" and had "neglected both mind and body." He confessed that "infirmities of nature, increased by improper remedies to assuage the disease, has made my life an excited and eccentric one." William was even more explicit about his alcoholism in a letter to Kate, saying that she should not encourage him to smoke, for if he did, he would drink "brandies and whiskies." He claimed that "you won't have tobacco smoke about, or whiskey and brandy, [and] then we will have no war."[30]

There was no hint of any of this, of course, in the newspapers, which reported that the wedding took place in the Chase home at eight thirty on the evening of November 12. Kate wore a white velvet dress and a Tiffany tiara, a gift from her husband worth $6,000. About fifty people, including President Lincoln, who arrived at the last minute, attended the service, read by a bishop "in the chaste, beautiful, and impressive language of the Episcopal form." Then the doors opened for a much larger crowd to attend the reception, with political and military leaders, accompanied by their wives and daughters. The food and wine were lavish and expensive; Chase spent at least $4,000 on the wedding. John Hay found Kate alone near the end of the evening, tired but pleased. "She had lost all her old severity and formal stiffness of manner and seemed to think that she had *arrived*."[31]

Chase remained worried about his daughter. A week after the wedding, he wrote her that not many "lives are so unclouded as yours has been hitherto" and that he feared that she and her husband would face "dark days." (Few couples would see such "dark days" as Kate and William: alcohol, infidelity, and ultimately divorce.) Chase's hopeful letter continued: "I desire nothing so much for you and your beloved husband as that you may be Christians in heart and life. Then, though sickness and misfortune may come, and death must come, you will indeed be safe, and many will be blessed through you." Chase noted that Lincoln and other members of the Cabinet were on their way to dedicate the military cemetery at Gettysburg. Chase would have liked to join them, to pay his own proper respects, but he felt that he could not leave Washington. "My report is hardly begun, and I must finish, if possible, before Congress comes together."[32]

In late November Lincoln shared with Chase a draft of a proclamation that he proposed to issue in early December, to set what the Southern states would have to do in order to rejoin the Union. Relying upon the presidential pardon power, he promised to pardon those who had participated in the rebellion (other than senior officers and civilians) if they would take an oath to support the Constitution and the Emancipation Proclamation. Lincoln declared that if at least 10 percent of those who were qualified to vote under a state's prewar constitution would take the prescribed oath and would form a new state government, the administration would recognize and sustain that government. Although Lincoln did not use the words *white* or *black,* by referring to the prewar constitutions, he effectively excluded blacks from the new state governments. Lincoln added that he would not object to "any provision which may be adopted by such state government in relation to the freed people of such state, which shall recognize and declare their permanent freedom, provide for their education, and which may yet be consistent as a temporary arrangement with their present condition as a laboring, landless, and homeless class." Lincoln probably had in mind something like the restrictive rules that Nathaniel Banks had imposed upon blacks in Louisiana. And Lincoln cautioned that, as president, he could not determine whether Congress would admit representatives elected under these new state constitutions; that would be up to each house of Congress, under its power to admit members.[33]

Chase responded to Lincoln's draft with a long letter of comments. Once again, he urged the president to extend emancipation to cover all of Louisiana and Virginia. He also pressed Lincoln to delete the sentence about special laws for blacks, saying that "special legislation for colored citizens will be as unnecessary as for white citizens. The demand for labor will secure them employment, and freedom will enable them to buy and build with the proceeds of their labor, while the voluntary charities, already so widely awakened, will, with proper support and countenance from the government, secure to them the benefits of education and religion." Knowing that Lincoln was not yet ready to endorse black suffrage, Chase did not raise this issue with him at this time. But he wrote an abolitionist friend that he was "a good deal disappointed by [Lincoln's] determination to limit his plan for reconstition so that colored freemen could take no part in it" and by the suggestion of "qualified involuntary servitude in the form of apprenticeship of the freed people." Lincoln's final proclamation did not make any of the changes Chase suggested.[34]

Chase expressed the same concerns in a letter at this time to his old friend Thomas Swann, former mayor of Baltimore and future governor of Maryland. "Do not attempt any scheme of apprenticeship," Chase wrote. "Such schemes have always failed and would have the very consequences you so justly apprehend, under present circumstances, from gradualism. Make all free; give fair and even liberal wages; provide schools; and let Christian philanthropy and aspiration for a better condition do the rest."[35]

In Lincoln's December message to Congress, he commended the way in which Chase had managed the federal finances. The president said that since March, when Congress had passed the finance and banking laws, "all demands on the Treasury, including the pay of the army and navy, have been promptly met and fully satisfied. No considerable body of troops, it is believed, were ever more amply provided, and more liberally and punctually paid; and it may be added that by no people were the burdens incident to a great war ever more cheerfully borne."[36]

In his own December report, Chase praised especially the "indefatigable efforts" of Jay Cooke and his subagents, who had sold about $400 million worth of the five-twenty bonds over the past year. "The history of the world may be searched in vain for a parallel case of popular financial support to a national government." Chase also boasted that there were more than a hundred new national banks; what he did not mention was that none of the major New York City banks had converted from state to federal charters. Without the participation of these banks, so central to the national financial system, the national bank system would not succeed, so Chase suggested that Congress amend the national banking act. Comptroller McCulloch, in his report, attached to Chase's, was much more detailed about the changes that Congress should make to refine the national banking law and encourage major state banks to convert to federal charters. Chase and McCulloch both stressed that Congress should tax banknotes issued by state banks, to reduce the use of such notes and to encourage conversion to federal charters.[37]

Chase's main point was that Congress needed to raise taxes, so that the country could rely more on current revenue and less on loans. In October and November 1863, he noted, the federal government spent more than $146 million and collected only about $35 million in revenue. Chase had raised the balance, about $111 million, from loans, mainly through the sales of yet more five-twenties. The internal revenue laws—the income tax, internal duties, license fees, and other measures—were producing far less revenue than Chase had expected. He urged Congress to increase taxes on alcohol, tobacco, petroleum, and other products. The secretary cared less about the details than about seeing more revenues flowing into the Treasury.[38]

With the fall 1863 elections over, people started to think more about the next year's presidential election. Chase wrote to his son-in-law that he "feared that Katie may be a little too anxious about my political future. She must not be so. There is nothing so uncertain as the political future of any man." Although Chase himself would prefer to see Lincoln serve a second term, he doubted the "expediency of reelecting anybody, and I think that a man of different qualities from those the president has will be needed for the next four years." (Chase was alluding here to recent history: no president since Andrew Jackson had served a second term, with some dying in office, others defeated in efforts to secure nomination, and others honoring pledges to serve only a single term.) Chase told Sprague that Lincoln's "course towards me has always been so fair and kind; his progress towards entire agreement with me on the great question of slavery has been so constant, though rather slower than I wished for; and his general character is so marked by traits which command respect and affection, that I can never consent to anything which he himself could or should consider as incompatible with perfect honor and good faith."[39]

In this and other letters, Chase said that all he was doing for his own campaign was allowing others to pursue their plans. "I claim no right to anyone's political support," he wrote to Hiram Barney. "But a very large number of citizens, most of them strangers to me personally—some of them friends of the cause to which I have devoted my life and entitled to every consideration on my part—manifest a strong disposition to require my services in another and higher sphere of duty than any I have heretofore filled." Chase explained to Barney that he was inclined to allow these supporters "to take their course."[40]

At almost the same time, however, Chase launched a major political project: agreeing to work on a biography of himself with John Trowbridge, a minor poet and author who was staying with Chase as a houseguest.

Trowbridge recalled later that Chase was a good if somewhat stiff host: "august in the true sense, sometimes austere, and I can understand why some who did not know him under favorable conditions would think him coldhearted. He was surprisingly unreserved in his expressions of opinion regarding public measures and public men, not even sparing the president." Although "not distinguished for wit," Chase's conversation was "always entertaining" and often "embroidered with a playfulness which the background of his stately presence set off." Chase "strongly disapproved" of Lincoln's habit of "telling all sorts of stories, to all sorts of people, on all sorts of occasions." And yet Chase would sometimes share one of Lincoln's stories with his family and friends and join in the laughter.[41]

One of Trowbridge's other friends in Washington was the poet Walt Whitman, working as a volunteer nurse in the hospitals and living, as it happened, just opposite Chase, on the corner of Sixth and E Streets. "In the fine, large mansion," Trowbridge wrote, "sumptuously furnished, cared for by sleek and silent colored servants, and thronged by distinguished guests, dwelt the great statesman; in the old tenement opposite, in a bare and desolate backroom, up three flights of stairs, quite alone, lived the poet." Using a recommendation letter from Ralph Waldo Emerson, Trowbridge tried to persuade Chase to hire Whitman as a clerk. Chase responded that, as much as he respected Emerson, he considered Whitman's poetry collection *Leaves of Grass* a "very bad book, and he did not know how he could possibly bring its author into the government service."[42]

Trowbridge liked to write for children, and Chase did not want to seem to be seeking votes, so the two of them agreed that the book would be a biography "for the use of boys and girls." While Trowbridge was in Washington, there was not much Chase had to do on the project, other than talk with him. Once the writer returned to Boston, however, Chase had to fulfill his pledge to write him letters about his life. Starting in late December, and continuing until March, Chase wrote two dozen long letters totaling more than forty thousand words. He also wrote to other people, such as his sister, Helen, seeking more material for his biographer.[43]

As he approached his fifty-sixth birthday, Chase had suffered the deaths of two parents, three wives, four children, and nine siblings. Drawing on this, he wrote a kind condolence letter in late December to his friend Susan Walker, whose own sister had recently died. "It is one of the afflictions of absorbing public service that no bereavement seems so great as when one is at liberty to think and feel as in a quiet home and in a time of peace."

From time to time, however, even in the midst of the war, "there seems to come to me a sort of breath from some unseen region of emotion and sympathies and all the currents, just hardening into ice, seem to melt and flow freely." He assured his friend that he shared her grief and hoped that God would "bring you nearer and nearer to Him and make you feel that He is more than a father or mother or sister or brother."[44]

On the day that Chase wrote this letter, the newspapers printed a speech by the abolitionist Wendell Phillips, whom Chase considered an ally if not a friend, attacking Chase on several fronts. For example, Phillips said that Chase had failed to live up to his purported antislavery principles when he failed to use state troops to save Margaret Garner. When Phillips had finished, the crowd called for Horace Greeley, who was in the audience. Greeley praised Chase, saying that the "campaigns of a minister of finance are bloodless—his achievements fail to dazzle the vulgar eye or thrill the popular heart—yet none are more essential, or more exacting in their demands of capacity, integrity, and indefatigable industry." Greeley was clear that he was *not* endorsing Chase for president; he was merely pleading with the disparate members of the Union Party not to fight among themselves yet about who should be their candidate, but to work together to fight the rebellion.[45]

Chase told friends that he was not too troubled by Phillips's attack, but it clearly bothered him, prompting him to write several long letters defending his conduct in the Garner case. Among others, Chase wrote to Henry Ward Beecher, one of the Beechers whom he had met thirty years earlier in Cincinnati, and now the most popular preacher in America. Beecher responded to Chase that he did not think Phillips could change the "conviction of the great mass of intelligent men that you have been soundly, consistently, and wisely faithful to the doctrines of liberty, through good report and evil, in office and out of it."[46]

The president's 10 percent proclamation opened the door for new state constitutions in several Southern states—notably Florida, where the small prewar electorate meant that only 1,400 men would have to take the loyalty oath in order to meet Lincoln's 10 percent threshold. Chase was elated, at the end of December, to hear about a Union meeting in Saint Augustine, Florida, that endorsed the idea of a new state constitution, without slavery. Chase had drafted resolutions for such a meeting and handed them to Lyman Stickney, one of the Treasury officers in Florida, as Stickney left Washington a few weeks earlier. As best Chase could tell, the Florida meeting had adopted his resolutions word for word. He hastened to send a copy of the Florida resolutions to a friend in Louisiana, writing, "I hope your convention will be wise enough to adopt the principle of universal suffrage of all men, unconvicted of crime, who can read and write and have a fair knowledge of the constitution of the state and of the United States." Chase was mainly eager to see new state constitutions adopted so that the Southern states could rejoin the Union and Southern blacks could join in the rights of citizenship. But he also realized that if Florida and Louisiana were once again part of the Union, they would have delegates at the 1864 nominating convention—delegates who might favor Chase for president. It was not an accident that, not long after Homer Plantz arrived in Florida, to take up his post in Key West, Chase sent him copies of some of his recent speeches.[47]

CHAPTER 20

"The Salmon Is a Queer Fish"

⚜ EARLY 1864 ⚜

The friends of Chase and those of Lincoln were working in early 1864 to secure the presidential nomination for their respective leaders. A Washington group that Chase described as "composed of prominent senators and representatives and citizens," headed by Senator Samuel Pomeroy of Kansas, and including John Sherman, supported Chase. In New Hampshire, the state convention resolved in early January with "great enthusiasm" to support Lincoln. Other state conventions soon followed this example and endorsed the president. Answering a letter from James Hall, a state legislator in Ohio, Chase said that while he would "of course" want to have a resolution supporting himself from his home state, if the "majority of our friends in Ohio indicate a preference for another, I shall accept their action with that cheerful acquiescence which is due from me to friends who have trusted and honored me beyond any claim or merit of mine." A few weeks later, Chase wrote in similar terms to a friend in Cincinnati: "So far as the presidency is concerned, I must leave that wholly to the people. Those of them who think that the public good will be promoted by adherence to the one-term principle, and by the use of my name, are fully competent, and far more competent than I am, to bring the matter before the public generally, and the people will dispose of the case according to their own judgment. Whatever disposition they make of it, I shall be content. My time is wholly absorbed by my public duties, and I can best serve the public, and my friends too, by the faithful discharge of them."[1]

The Ohio legislature was in session at this time, and the Lincoln men among the legislators wanted to pass a resolution in favor of the president. One of Chase's supporters in Columbus wrote him to report that they were having difficulty to "suppress any expression favorable to Mr. Lincoln." They managed to prevent an early February caucus of legislators from considering the question. "This will be the last of the matter," another Ohio friend assured Chase. A week later, however, an Ohio legislator informed him that the Lincoln men in Columbus claimed that "Chase and his friends are sending out from Washington secret circulars charging incompetency, unsoundness, etc., in Mr. Lincoln." This friend pleaded for a public letter from Chase confirming that nothing "of the sort was done by you, or with your knowledge or consent." Chase did not respond, perhaps because he knew that Sherman was indeed distributing copies of an article favorable to Chase.[2]

In spite of the struggle between their supporters, Chase and Lincoln remained polite and professional with one another. Their good working relationship seemed unlikely to survive, however, an attack on Lincoln by Chase's political friends in late February. The Pomeroy Circular, so called because it was drafted by Pomeroy or one of his colleagues, contended that Lincoln, even if nominated, could not be elected because of the combined forces that would oppose him. The president's "manifest tendency towards compromises and temporary expedients of policy" would "become stronger during a second term than it has been in the first, and the cause of human liberty, and the dignity and honor of the nation [would] suffer." The circular insisted that it was Chase and not Lincoln who possessed the "qualities needed in a president during the next four years." Chase was a "statesman of rare ability and an administrator of the very highest order," and his "private character furnishes the surest obtainable guarantee of economy and purity in the management of public affairs."[3]

Most Union Party leaders were horrified when the circular was published. The *New York Times*, for example, noted that Pomeroy and his friends suggested they would join the "union of influences" against Lincoln. "Are these men mad? Do they seriously think that they are advancing Mr. Chase's interests by this public notification that they intend to rend the party unless the majority of the party will agree to nominate him?" As to Lincoln's tendency to compromise, for the *Times* this was a strength and not a weakness. The president showed great "practical wisdom" by matching his "policy to the progress of public opinion instead of distracting and alienating the loyal mind of the country by seeking to impose upon it measures it was not yet prepared to accept."[4]

As soon as the circular appeared, Chase sent an apologetic letter to Lincoln saying that although he was aware of the Pomeroy Committee, and had met with some of its members, he was not aware of the circular before seeing it in print. Chase offered to resign, for he would not want to "administer the Treasury Department one day without your entire confidence." Chase assured Lincoln that he viewed him with "sincere respect and esteem, and, permit me to add, affection. Differences of opinion as to administrative action have not changed these sentiments; nor have they been changed by assaults upon me by persons who profess themselves the special representatives of your views and policy." (Here Chase was referring to the Blairs.) "You are not responsible for acts not your own," he continued, "nor will you hold me responsible except for what I do or say myself."[5]

The Pomeroy Circular, when it was published in Ohio, outraged the Lincoln supporters there. One of Chase's friends reported from Cleveland that the circular "arrayed at once men against each other who had been party friends always, and finally produced a perfect convulsion in the party." On the evening of February 26, a group of Union legislators gathered in caucus in Columbus and, after a "stormy session," adopted at about midnight a resolution supporting Lincoln. Some of Chase's friends were not invited to this caucus; others attended for a while and left before the vote; and still others remained but did not vote on the resolution. The result was that the papers reported that the Ohio caucus supported Lincoln unanimously. But the eastern reports of this event were delayed, so Chase did not know about the resolution for a few days.[6]

What he did know was that on February 27 Frank Blair attacked him again, this time in the House of Representatives. Blair demanded an investigation, claiming that "a more profligate administration of the Treasury Department never existed under any government" and that "the whole Mississippi Valley is rank and fetid with the fraud and corruptions practiced there by his agents." Chase believed that he had done all that he reasonably could to investigate and punish corruption, and that Blair's attacks were purely political. "The simple fact that I am named in connection with the next choice of president," Chase wrote to Greeley on February 29, "brings upon me the most unscrupulous attacks of the postmaster general and his brother." Chase feared that he could not do his job—he could not raise the money to pay the army and the navy—while facing the "active and vindictive hostility of the Blairs, made all the more embarrassing by their uncontradicted claim to be the special representatives of the policy and views of Mr. Lincoln." Perhaps, Chase continued, "if my name were withdrawn altogether from consideration, then attacks would be discontinued, and I should be left to do my work." This would be "entirely agreeable to me." Or perhaps, Chase mused, he should resign, so that some other man, such as Samuel Hooper, could take over the department. "This would also be entirely agreeable to me."[7]

On the same day that Chase wrote Greeley, Lincoln responded to Chase's letter about the circular. The president had been aware of the Pomeroy Committee but did not pay much attention to it—or to the circular, which he had not even bothered to read. Alluding to Blair's speech, Lincoln agreed with his Treasury secretary that "neither of us can be justly held responsible for what our respective friends may do without our instigation or countenance; and I assure you, as you have assured me, that no assault has been made upon you by my instigation, or with my countenance." Lincoln added that "whether you shall remain at the head of the Treasury Department is a question which I will not allow myself to consider from any standpoint other than my judgment of the public service; and, in that view, I do not perceive occasion for a change." This was Lincoln's lukewarm way of asking Chase to stay on at the Treasury.[8]

On March 2 Greeley wrote Chase that he had changed his mind about what Chase should do. Previously, the editor did not see why Chase could not be both Treasury secretary and presidential candidate. Now, in light of Blair's attacks, Greeley thought it was time for Chase to say that because he did not want to divide the Union Party, he wanted "those who may have deemed [him] worthy of support for the next president to regard [him] as not a candidate." Greeley insisted that Chase should *not* resign. "There is no other man in America who can manage the finances so successfully as you can." James Garfield agreed that Chase should no longer seek the nomination. "The people desire the reelection of Mr. Lincoln," he wrote to Chase. "Any movement in any other direction will not only be a failure but will tend to disturb and embarrass the unity of the friends of the Union."[9]

On March 4 Chase wrote a friend that the Ohio resolution in favor of Lincoln "affords me a suitable occasion for gratifying my wish to remove my name from the discussions which are becoming more partisan than patriotic or safe." The next day, Chase wrote James Hall, reminding him that he had said he would be guided by the preferences of the people of

Ohio. "The recent action of the Union members of our legislature indicates such a preference. It becomes my duty, therefore . . . to ask that no further consideration be given to my name." Chase insisted that "all our efforts and our energies should be devoted to the suppression of the rebellion and to the restoration of order and prosperity on a solid, sure foundation of Union, freedom, and impartial justice, and I earnestly urge all with whom my counsels may have weight to allow nothing to divide them while this great work, in comparison with which persons and even parties are nothing, remains unaccomplished." Chase gave Hall permission to share his letter with the papers.[10]

Chase's letter to Hall, once made public, won him warm praise from the Union Party newspapers. The *New York Evening Post* commented that his "present step, made at a time when the country needs the concentration of all its strength to be used against the common enemy, will endear him still more to the whole nation." The *Chicago Tribune* agreed, saying that Chase's decision reflected his "good sense" and "large heartedness" and would earn him the "profound respect of the people." The *New York Times* declared, "Chase has done himself new honor in refusing to let his name be longer used in connection with the presidential nomination." The *Times* was especially pleased that, by taking his name out of contention, Chase could continue "in the position whose extremely responsible duties he is discharging with masterly ability."[11]

Horace Greeley wrote in the *New-York Tribune* that there was "no man better fitted for president, by natural ability, by study and reflection, by training and experience, by integrity and patriotism, by soundness of principle and greatness of soul, than is Salmon P. Chase." And although Chase was no longer in the running this year, Greeley hoped the "people will yet have an opportunity to support him as a candidate for our chief magistracy." Addressing the argument that Chase was ambitious, Greeley argued that the "man who had his eye on the presidency yet could avow himself an abolitionist so early as 1842—when we did not dream that one so thoroughly antislavery could be chosen governor, much less president—must be gifted with a prescience almost superhuman. He must cherish, moreover, a profound and thorough faith in the ultimate triumph of justice—the 'sober second thought of the people.'"[12]

Democratic and conservative papers, of course, were far less charitable, arguing that the only reason that Chase was giving up was that he had no chance. The *New York Herald* questioned whether Chase really meant to withdraw from the presidential race. "Secretary Chase is shrewd enough to know," wrote the *Herald*, "that the people are more apt to elect a presidential candidate who seems to decline the honor modestly than a man who appears to seek for it ardently." In its colorful way, the paper continued: "The salmon is a queer fish, very shy and very wary. Often it appears to avoid the bait just before gulping it down, and even after it is hooked, it has to be allowed plenty of line and must be played carefully before it can be safely landed." The *Herald* was sure that Chase would yet "leap" at the nomination, perhaps at the Union Party national convention, set for Baltimore in early June.[13]

When Chase withdrew from the presidential race, the *New York Times* insisted that there was no real difference between the "conservative" Lincoln and the "radical" Chase. Both men favored freeing the slaves and fighting until the rebels surrendered. But there *were* differences between the two men, notably on the question of the role of blacks in reconstruction. We have already seen how Chase objected to Lincoln's suggestion, in his 1863 reconstruction proclamation, that the states could pass laws to limit the rights of blacks. Lincoln and Chase also disagreed about granting blacks the right to vote in Louisiana.[14]

Two black leaders from New Orleans, Arnold Bertonneau and Jean Baptiste Roudanez, arrived in Washington in early March to present a petition with about a thousand signatures, seeking black voting rights in Louisiana. The press reported that when Lincoln met with these two leaders, he told them he would favor their petition if it was necessary for military reasons but not as a mere moral request. Lincoln said they should instead raise the issue with the state constitutional convention about to assemble. After meeting with these impressive representatives of the free black community of New Orleans, the president wrote a private letter to the new state governor, Michael Hahn, noting the imminent constitutional convention. "I barely suggest, for your private consideration, whether some of the colored people may not be let in—as, for instance, the very intelligent, and especially those who have fought gallantly in our ranks."[15]

Chase probably met with Bertonneau and Roudanez while they were in Washington. He certainly agreed with them about black voting rights. In a letter to Greeley, Chase wrote that conservatives seemed to believe that "negroes may fight but must not vote—may use bullets but not ballots.

This seems to me the intensity of meanness." In a letter to Benjamin Flanders, in New Orleans, Chase wrote that "nothing, in my judgment, is clearer than that in states where the colored people constitute so large a proportion of the population, as in the states upon the Gulf, they should be allowed to vote if qualified by having borne arms in defense of the country or by sufficient education." In a letter to Nathaniel Banks, as the state constitutional convention started its work, Chase urged him to encourage the delegates to allow blacks to vote: "Let all who are alike qualified have political rights alike. Let the right to vote be determined not by nativity or complexion, but by intelligence, character, and patriotism." In yet another letter, Chase regretted that Lincoln would not "stand by the loyal men who in the slave states have stood most firmly by the Union, and almost worshipped him because of his proclamation. I mean, of course, the loyal blacks." Lincoln seemed to think, Chase wrote, that "to give negroes, however intelligent, the right of suffrage would jeopardize the success of the Union Party at the next election, when he himself will doubtless be the candidate for reelection."[16]

Chase and Lincoln were both correct, in their different ways, on the subject of black voting rights. Chase was right in thinking that voting rights should not turn on skin color. He had declared himself in favor of black voting rights in his silver pitcher speech in 1845, and he would not change his stance. But Lincoln was right in thinking that on the eve of a close presidential contest, at a time when only a few Northern states allowed blacks to vote, it would be imprudent for the president to take a public stand in favor of Southern black voting rights. Whatever Lincoln said about blacks would not have much influence on the white delegates to the state constitutional convention, but a bold public statement now could have a disastrous effect on his national election campaign.[17]

The Louisiana convention was not prepared to go anywhere near as far as Chase wanted on the question of black rights. The new constitution did prohibit slavery, but Chase had assumed that this would be the case, so he did not view this as a great victory. On voting rights, all the new constitution did was to allow the legislature, at some time in the future, to grant black voting rights on the basis of military service, payment of taxes, or intellectual fitness. Chase did not give up. When a committee solicited a letter from him for a Union rally, Chase responded with predictable praise for the army, but added that "we should not forget one class of defenders of the flag—one class of men loyal to the Union—to whom we yet fail to do complete justice. It will be the marvel of future historians that statesmen of this day were willing to risk the success of rebellion rather than entrust to black loyalists bullets and ballots." Many papers printed Chase's letter, and one Vermont paper commended him for "brave words, bravely spoken."[18]

Chase's home life had a new pattern this winter, after his elder daughter's marriage to Sprague. The young couple were sometimes in Washington, sharing the house with Chase, but often in Rhode Island or elsewhere. Nettie, now sixteen, was at boarding school in New York City, so there were times when Chase was alone in the large house. The letters from him to Nettie were an interesting mixture of affection, admiration, and admonition. Responding to a request from her for "just one word," he wrote that "there is only one which comes near expressing my feeling for you, and that is *love*. Take it, darling." A few lines later, however, he chided her for misspelling the word *precocious* and urged her to make more regular use of her dictionary.[19]

In another letter, after describing for Nettie one of the Washington winter balls, Chase wrote that he "did not feel inclined to participate in such scenes" when he thought about "the suffering which exists throughout the land" and the "dangerous condition of our [national] finances." Then he corrected himself, noting that "almost all men and almost all women need a good deal of relaxation and recreation to keep them in condition to accomplish anything." In this respect, "as in many other things, the middle is best—not too much work and not too much amusement." Chase hoped that Nettie would work on her French because, after he finished work at the Treasury, he hoped to travel in Europe and "shall want you for my interpreter and secretary." Chase's own French was good enough that he could read and write—occasionally using that language in light letters to his friend Charlotte Eastman.[20]

Chase did not entertain often—he was nowhere near as sociable as his Cabinet colleague Seward—but he did host events from time to time. One Friday evening, Chase and Kate organized a private concert at their home by Teresa Carreño, a piano prodigy from Venezuela. Only ten years old, Carreño had already impressed audiences in major concert halls. John Hay, one of Chase's guests this evening, wrote in his diary that Carreño had a "child's smile and a man's power over the keys."[21]

In yet another letter to Nettie, Chase wrote that her letters "give great pleasure. You are certainly the genius of the family for this sort of composition." Chase was so busy with work that he could not write a short letter to his daughter without a two-hour interruption. "I wish I were out of official harness," he griped. "It constantly grows more irksome." He had worked hard, and yet his work was the object of criticism and calumny. "I am thankful, however, that no calumny or reviling can destroy any good I have accomplished. So, dear child, do good for the sake of doing it; not for reward or applause. Your Heavenly Father will see and bless you."[22]

Chase's main task in the first half of 1864 was to raise the money needed to pay for the Union war effort. Within the first few days of the year, Jay Cooke and his subagents sold the last of the $500 million of five-twenty bonds authorized by Congress. Chase wrote to a friend that, after the successful sale of the five-twenties, he planned soon to market a new type of bond: paying interest in gold at 5 percent, redeemable in ten years, and payable in forty years. The Treasury secretary did not, however, appoint Cooke as the principal agent to sell these bonds, known as the ten-forties. Perhaps this was because he did not want to answer more questions from Congress about his relations with Cooke; the House had recently demanded information about whether Cooke had received improper benefits from the sale of the five-twenties. (Chase's answer, long delayed, was that Cooke had fully earned his compensation from the Treasury.) In any case, Chase sold the new ten-forty bonds through the assistant treasurers and the new national banks rather than through Cooke. In Cleveland, for example, the First National Bank of Cleveland and the Second National Bank of Cleveland placed daily advertisements in the city's papers, urging readers to subscribe through them for ten-forty bonds. In total, the Treasury raised more than $114 million through sales of ten-forty bonds in the second quarter of 1864.[23]

For Chase, the national banks were the heart of the new national financial system. The national banks would help the government market its securities, as in the case of the ten-forties. The national banknotes (printed by the Treasury but issued through the national banks) would replace the notes issued by state banks and the legal tender notes (issued directly by the government). The national banknotes would soon become, Chase hoped, the single national currency. The national bank scheme, however, faced a major problem in New York City, the nation's financial center. True, by the start of 1864, there were three national banks there, but they were tiny compared with the existing state banks. The combined capital of the three national banks in the city was only $1 million, whereas the capital of the largest state bank there, the Bank of Commerce, headed by Chase's friend John Austin Stevens, was more than $9 million. Bank of Commerce and other leading banks in New York City served as "bankers to the banks," holding millions in deposits from other banks. In general, banks operating under state charters would only deposit with other state banks, and banks operating under national charters with national banks. So, unless Chase and Hugh McCulloch could persuade some of the key New York state banks to convert to federal charters, they would face difficulties persuading other banks to convert, and the "national banking system" might become a small network of small banks.[24]

Chase and McCulloch used both carrots and sticks to solve this problem. Cooke provided one of the sticks, in the form of the Fourth National Bank of New York City, which opened its doors in February 1864 with a capital of $5 million. The *New York Times* predicted that the new Cooke national bank would "undoubtedly be favored with the accounts of many of the out-of-town national banks and a liberal share of the accounts of the Treasury, besides the usual line of local deposits." Bankers with state charters realized that Cooke's bank and other national banks could start to take their profitable deposits from other banks. Chase wanted Congress to give him another stick: a stiff tax or even prohibition on notes issued by state banks. Any increase in the money supply, whether legal tender notes or state banknotes, contributed to inflation, Chase wrote to a friend, but the "national government has been obliged to issue its legal tender notes" while there was no "necessity for the issue of paper money by the state banks."[25]

He continued: "I know of no just claim which the state banks have to make money for the country. I know that it is a necessity for the nation to have it. I think then that the state bank currency should be withdrawn, and that no currency should be allowed except the national. So far as this consists of legal tender notes, their issue and circulation are a direct gain to the country by a saving of interest, and if not issued in excess, the benefit would be unmixed. So far as it consists of notes of national banks, it is recommended by the indispensable necessity of such institutions to make a uniform national currency permanent [and] by the benefits derived from the support afforded by them to the credit of the government bonds."[26]

On the carrot side, Chase and McCulloch worked closely with Hooper and others to devise changes to the 1863 banking law that would encourage conversions from state to federal charters. As Hooper explained in the House, his 1864 banking bill was designed to "render the law so perfect that state banks may be induced to organize under it, in preference to continuing under their state charters." One provision in the bill even addressed the Bank of Commerce specifically. The 1863 act had imposed "double liability" upon the individual shareholders of national banks: if a bank failed, shareholders would not only lose what they had invested but also be liable for an equal additional amount. The charter of the Bank of Commerce provided that its shareholders were liable only for the amount they had invested, so the bank could not convert to a federal charter with double liability. The final version of the 1864 act solved the problem more elegantly: it exempted all state banks meeting certain high capital and reserve hurdles from the double liability provision—in effect exempting the Bank of Commerce and one or two others without naming names.[27]

Congress passed the new national bank act in June 1864, more or less in the form Chase and McCulloch had wanted. In November the directors of the Bank of Commerce would decide to convert from a state to a federal charter. In his December report, Chase's successor could boast about the "rapid and extensive conversion of state institutions of established character, conducted through a long series of years by men of recognized ability, into banks organized under the new system." Congress also passed the steep tax on state banknotes that Chase had sought, hastening the conversion process. Within a few years, there were more than 1,600 national banks and only about 300 state banks. The national bank system was finally and firmly established.[28]

After withdrawing from the presidential race through his public letter to James Hall, Chase said over and over that he was not a candidate. For example, when the *Albany Evening Journal*, edited by Seward's friend Thurlow Weed, claimed that Chase was using department employees for his campaign, the Treasury secretary wrote to Seward that he had "avoided all thought and talk about the presidential nomination and have certainly neither asked, nor sought, nor expected it myself. The patronage of this department is not and never has been used with reference to that nomination." When Chase heard that some of those hoping to represent

Florida at the national convention planned to support Chase, he wrote angrily to Stickney, "I would not take the nomination of the Baltimore convention if it were tendered to me. The delegates have been almost all elected under pledges, express or implied, that they will vote for the renomination of Mr. Lincoln. The nomination of any other man would be justly regarded as a fraud upon the people."[29]

In other letters, however, Chase sounded at least somewhat like a candidate. The *New York Herald* reported that his friends wanted to postpone the Baltimore convention from June to September "because they have been caught napping and want time to intrigue and buy up the trading politicians among the delegates." A few weeks later, Chase wrote to an Ohio friend that it was now clear that the "importunity of Mr. Lincoln's special friends for an early convention, in order to make his nomination sure, was a mistake both for him and for the country." An early convention in Baltimore would not be "regarded as a Union convention but simply as a Blair-Lincoln convention by a great body of citizens whose support is essential to success." It is hard to understand why Chase would want to delay the Baltimore convention unless he had some hope—perhaps one that he would not admit to himself—that he would be the Baltimore nominee.[30]

The best evidence that Chase was at least a quasi-candidate is that he continued, even after his letter to Hall, to write long letters to John Trowbridge for the biography. Many viewed this as a campaign biography, including the publisher, who asked Jay Cooke for $2,000 so that the book could be rushed to editors around the country just before the Baltimore convention. The first part of the Trowbridge book was a somewhat fanciful account of Chase's early life. The author devoted page after page, for example, to describing how Chase used a canoe to ferry people across the Cuyahoga River when he first visited Cleveland. Many of the letters from Chase to Trowbridge were descriptions of his fugitive slave cases, not really material for a children's book. Trowbridge edited these letters slightly and printed them in a long appendix. Chase was not pleased with the final product. "Should there be a second edition," he wrote coldly to Trowbridge, "I think you can make essential improvements in it."[31]

Complaints about and attacks against Chase continued through the spring of 1864. Welles wrote to Chase that the Treasury was so late in paying navy contractors that some of them might stop work. "The embarrassment occasioned by a delay in the payment of such bills is not confined to the contractors but reaches thousands of mechanics who are dependent upon their daily labor for their support." Chase's response to Welles was that, without adequate tax revenue, "there is no available resource except loans, and it is extremely difficult to obtain, in this way, the means required to meet the very large expenditures under the direction of the War and Navy Departments." A few weeks later, Welles groused to his diary that the "pay of the sailors and workmen is withheld until they are almost mutinous and riotous." He continued: "Chase has not the sagacity, knowledge, and ability of a financier. He is a man of expedients and will break down the government."[32]

Frank Blair attacked Chase again in late April, in a House speech in which he said that Chase was using his department for personal purposes. Blair claimed that Chase had given his son-in-law, William Sprague, a trading permit in the South "by which he will probably make the snug little sum of two million dollars," and that Chase had reserved part of the bond issue for Cooke's personal use and profit. Another member of the House, a New York Democrat named James Brooks, charged a few days later that the rooms in the Treasury Building where the women worked were the scenes of "orgies and bacchanals." The papers gleefully reprinted and amplified these charges. The *Cincinnati Enquirer* reported that Spencer Clark, head of the "greenback factory" within the Treasury, "has employed women of easy virtue, and that the most barefaced treachery is practiced in the department with these women. It is even said that this branch of the service has a few rooms fitted up in oriental style of splendor, and that a regular harem is kept under the control of a leading officer, for the benefit of persons high in the confidence of the president. In fine, the charges amount to this: that the greenback factory is a place of easy virtue for the benefit of persons of easy morals."[33]

On the day of Blair's speech, the Washington papers reported that the president had allowed him to resume his army command. Although the paperwork for this change had been in progress for a while, people naturally viewed Blair's triumphant return to the army as indicating that Lincoln approved of his speech. Chase went on this day to Baltimore to attend and speak at the Sanitary Fair—an event organized by women to raise funds for the private care of sick and wounded Union soldiers. The *Philadelphia Inquirer* reported that Chase "beautifully complimented the ladies" for their work, saying that while England had Florence Nightingale, America had thousands of "equally noble, patriotic, and Christian women." Calm on the outside, the secretary was seething on the inside. He wrote a friend that his "first impulse on hearing of Blair's outrageous speech and its apparent—though I am sure not intended—endorsement by Mr. Lincoln was to resign at once." When Chase returned to Washington, however, he learned that the president, in a conversation with some Ohio members of Congress, had "disavowed in the most explicit terms all connection with, or responsibility for, Blair's assault." Chase was not at all happy, but he did not resign.[34]

A small item in the *New-York Tribune* in May 1864 claimed that Chase had disagreed with Lincoln and Stanton about the recent arrest of journalists accused of preparing and publishing a sham Lincoln proclamation. The nation's leading Democratic paper, the *New York World,* responded that if Chase *really* objected to arbitrary arrests, he would resign. According to the *World*, there were only two reasons why he did not: First, "his friends, who are feathering their nests out of the government, still wish to make money, which they could not expect to do after his resignation." Second, "he has an eye on the chief justiceship of the Supreme Court, which may become vacant in the next presidential term." (Chief Justice Taney was eighty-seven years old, so it was likely the seat would become open soon.) Lincoln "could afford to promise [the seat] as the price of Mr. Chase's withdrawal from the presidential arena, and Mr. Chase would rather accept it than run as an unsuccessful candidate for the presidency. We shall, accordingly, see Mr. Chase supporting for reelection a man whom in his heart he despises and derides."[35]

Chase did not despise or deride Lincoln, but there were radicals who did, and some gathered in Cleveland in late May and nominated John Frémont for president. Chase had lost all respect for Frémont, but he liked the key plank of the Cleveland platform, which called for a federal constitutional amendment to abolish slavery and to establish "absolute equality before the law." A constitutional amendment to abolish slavery (without any language about equality) had already passed the Senate and was about to be considered by the House. Lincoln had been silent on the constitutional amendment, but now—prodded by the Cleveland convention—he told friends that he wanted the Baltimore convention to endorse an antislavery amendment. The Baltimore platform demanded the "complete and utter extirpation" of slavery through a constitutional amendment. As expected, the convention nominated Lincoln for president and, in something of a surprise, proposed Andrew Johnson, military governor of Tennessee, for vice president. In his letter accepting the nomination, Lincoln endorsed the amendment, calling it a "fitting and necessary conclusion to the final success of the Union cause." The Baltimore platform and Lincoln's letter were not enough, however, to get the constitutional amendment over the two-thirds hurdle in the House of Representatives. The House rejected the amendment in late June and would not take up the issue again until early 1865.[36]

As the *World* had predicted, once Lincoln was nominated by the Baltimore convention in early June, Chase supported him. This was not because Lincoln had promised to make Chase the chief justice; the two men had not discussed the question, although some of Chase's friends had already raised the issue with the president. Rather, Chase supported Lincoln and Johnson because he thought they were the best candidates and because he believed in the Baltimore platform. "I do not see how any sincere man," he wrote to one friend, "who holds the views expressed in the Baltimore platform can excuse himself from a zealous support of the nominees of the convention." As for Frémont, Chase wrote that he regretted seeing "some very good men taking part in the Frémont movement. I cannot think that it will be persisted in."[37]

Some of the most furious fighting of the Civil War occurred in May and June 1864, as Grant's army clashed with Lee's near Richmond. Grant's losses, in the two months of the Overland campaign, including battles at Spotsylvania and Cold Harbor, exceeded fifty-four thousand men killed, wounded, captured, or missing. This bloody campaign was still in progress when the marching band of an Ohio regiment, accompanied by some soldiers and others, arrived at Chase's house one mid-June evening to serenade him. At first, Chase tried to decline their call for a speech, saying that he would rather "wait for the consummation for which I most devoutly pray, looking to Him alone who can give us the victory, rather than make speeches upon what is transpiring."[38]

Someone in the crowd, sensing Chase's worries, called out to ask if there was bad news. No, he replied. In fact, the most recent telegraphic reports were hopeful. "But how can we feel like talking when every message brings us tidings of some dear relative who has laid down his life upon the altar of his country?" Only the other day, Chase had learned that one of his own relatives had died in the army near Richmond. "His loss was a trying one; it came home to me. But he was no dearer to me than others are to their relatives."[39]

Then, realizing that he could not send the crowd off in this way, Chase continued: "My friends from Ohio, we have reason to be proud of our state, when the gallant Grant and our own gallant Sherman are so nobly leading, and so many of her sons so bravely fighting among the hosts of freedom." He concluded on a more stirring note: "God bless Ohio and her brave men in the field. God bless our country. Let us pray to Him that He will give her deliverance and secure to us the permanent blessings of freedom."[40]

The last week of June 1864 was one of the hardest of the war for Chase. Like others, he was reading the newspapers anxiously for word about Grant in Virginia and Sherman in Georgia. "Can we keep Grant and Sherman so furnished with men and means that they can inflict decisive blows on the rebellion?" Chase asked his diary on Friday, June 24. "My part is to supply, if possible, the means, and where am I to find them?" Congress had been in session for more than six months and still had not passed the tax and loan bills that the Treasury secretary needed. A conference committee was finishing work on the tax bill, but Chase worried that the legislation was too weak and would not produce enough revenue.[41]

Chase wrote at least ten letters the next day. One was to the Boston financier John Forbes, agreeing with him that higher taxes were essential. "The people who really want the war to be prosecuted are willing to pay the cost in taxes; why won't Congress see it and act upon it?" Two letters were to members of Congress about a bill drafted by the Treasury, authorizing the department's agents to deal with captured or abandoned property in the rebellious states. Chase was keen to see this bill pass, in part because it would generate some additional revenue, and in part because it would give the department authority to provide, through leases of abandoned plantations "or otherwise, for the employment and general welfare of all persons within the lines of national military occupation within said insurrectionary states formerly held as slaves, who are or shall become free." He was hoping to use this broad language and his network of agents to help care for the needs of the former slaves in the ever-increasing Southern regions under Northern military control. Although Congress passed this language in the form requested by Chase, his successor did not attempt to use this authority, leaving the former slaves in the military districts under the control of the War Department.[42]

One of the letters Chase wrote this day was to John Stewart, a New York banker, urging him to accept the position of assistant treasurer in New York City. Chase had been searching for a successor for John Cisco, the current assistant treasurer, since late May, when Cisco said he wanted to resign for reasons of health. Cisco's position was perhaps the most important one in the department other than that of the secretary; Chase often sent several telegrams a day to the assistant treasurer, asking him questions and giving him instructions. After consulting with the key senator, Seward's friend Edwin Morgan, Chase had already offered the position to three other men, all of whom had declined. Now he pleaded with Stewart to reconsider. "Let your country, in this exigency, have the benefit of your services."[43]

John Cisco, the assistant treasurer in New York City. The quarrel over Cisco's replacement led Chase to resign from the Treasury in the summer of 1864.

Even in the midst of the Civil War, Chase did not like to work on Sundays; he believed the Sabbath should be a day of rest and prayer. He spent most of Sunday, June 26, however, hard at work. He started drafting a long letter to Thaddeus Stevens, pressing for higher taxes. He wrote to

Cisco, asking him to talk with Stewart and to underscore that both Chase and Morgan wanted him as assistant treasurer. He wrote to William Cullen Bryant, editor of the *New York Evening Post*, complaining about a couple of recent articles in the paper. "For good-tempered, practical criticism, I am always grateful, and even from ill-tempered, I try to draw lessons." But a recent letter to the editor, Chase said, was merely a mixture of "false and distorted statements of facts, and gross imputations of dishonest and dishonorable motives."[44]

On Monday morning Chase heard from William Orton, the expert he had asked for revenue estimates, that the new tax bill would yield far less than what the Treasury secretary believed necessary. Chase asked Orton to draft, as soon as possible, a supplementary tax bill, writing in his diary that he would "insist" that Congress pass the bill before the imminent end of the session. Learning by telegram that Stewart would not accept Cisco's position, Chase met with Morgan and suggested Maunsell Field, who had served well as assistant treasurer in Washington, to take the more critical position in New York. Morgan countered with the names of two friends. According to Chase's diary, he responded that "either gentleman would be entirely acceptable to me personally, but I thought the public interests would on the whole be best consulted by the appointment of Mr. Field." Morgan complained to Chase that many of the clerks in Cisco's office were Democrats, to which Chase replied that if they were, they were Democrats "of the same class with Andrew Johnson"—in other words, loyal to the Union and the Lincoln administration. At about four in the afternoon, before dealing with an emergency extension of higher tariff rates, Chase sent Lincoln a letter suggesting Field's nomination. "His personal character, intelligence, and ability warrant the expectation that he will perform the duties of the office well and acceptably."[45]

Chase started Tuesday, June 28, by reading from his Bible. "How beautiful and excellent is the order and progress which St. Paul enjoins and illustrates in his letter to the Ephesians," Chase wrote in his diary. "If the world could but learn that lesson, how anxieties and perplexities would lighten and pass away." When he arrived at his department, Chase found a letter from the president saying that he could not appoint Field "without much embarrassment." Lincoln urged Chase to select one of the candidates suggested by Morgan and "send me a nomination for him." Chase sent three letters this day to Lincoln. The first, a short note, simply suggested that Chase and Lincoln should meet face-to-face to discuss the situation. Receiving no response, he sent a second letter, stressing that Field was warmly recommended by "many of the most reliable businessmen of New York" and by many "prominent Republicans," including Greeley. Although Chase recognized that it was important to reward political friends, *this office*, he insisted, should not be controlled "by mere party considerations." In the third letter, Chase told Lincoln that he had sent a telegram to Cisco, begging him to postpone by at least three months his resignation. Chase questioned whether Morgan's candidates, who were in their sixties, were up to the task. "They are both estimable gentlemen, and were the times peaceful and the business of the office comparatively small and regular, I should gladly acquiesce in the appointment of either. But my duty to you and to the country does not permit it now."[46]

Chase devoted most of this long day to legislative work, as Congress raced toward the end of its session. He went to Capitol Hill in the morning to talk with Hooper and Elihu Washburne about the trade bill. He sent two letters to Representative Justin Morrill of Vermont on details in the pending tax and tariff bill. He probably heard from James Garfield that his special committee, appointed to look into the alleged misconduct by the women working at the Treasury, would soon report to the House that there was no real evidence of impropriety. Chase went back to the Hill in the evening, hoping to speak with some House members about the financial bills, but found that they were not in session. Late in the evening, he received a welcome telegram from Cisco saying that he could not resist Chase's appeal and would "therefore consent to the temporary withdrawal of my resignation."[47]

The next morning, June 29, Chase received a letter from Lincoln saying that he did not want to meet with Chase about Cisco's successor in New York. "The difficulty does not, in the main part, lie within the range of a conversation between you and me. As the proverb goes, no man knows so well where the shoe pinches as he who wears it. I do not think Mr. Field a very proper man for the place, but I would trust your judgment, and forego this, were the greater difficulty out of the way." The larger issue was that it had been a "great burden to me to retain" Barney as the head of the customshouse in New York "when nearly all our friends in New York were, directly or indirectly, urging his removal." The recent appointment of a Chase friend as the appraiser in New York, another coveted post, had brought Seward, Morgan, and their friends to the "verge of open revolt," said Lincoln. If he were now to yield to Chase and appoint Field, the president feared it would lead to such a revolt. "Strained as I already am at this point, I do not think I can make this appointment in the direction of still greater strain."[48]

Chase wrote back to Lincoln that he had not been "aware of the extent of the embarrassment to which you refer. In recommendations for office, I have sincerely sought to get the best men for the places to be filled without reference to any other classification than supporters and opponents of your administration." Chase sent Lincoln a copy of Cisco's telegram and noted that his agreement to remain for a while solved the "present difficulty." Chase added, however, that he could not "help feeling that my position here is not altogether agreeable to you; and it is certainly too full of embarrassment and difficulty and painful responsibility to allow in me the least desire to retain it. I think it my duty therefore to enclose to you my resignation." Chase would "regard it as a real relief if you think proper to accept it" and would "cheerfully render to my successor any aid he may find useful in entering upon his duties."[49]

After dashing off this short letter to Lincoln, Chase seemingly gave it no further thought and spent almost the entire day on other issues, notably his long letter to Stevens, which he sent in the late afternoon. Chase and Orton estimated for Stevens that, even with the tax bill that Congress had just passed, federal revenues from all sources in the fiscal year about to start would reach only about $318 million. Expenditures would be about $800 million. In order to raise half the budget in the form of current revenues—which Chase believed essential—Congress needed to impose about $82 million of additional taxes. Chase and Orton suggested specific tax changes for this purpose, such as higher taxes on tobacco and alcohol. The Treasury secretary pleaded with Stevens to consider the effects of inadequate tax revenue on both the national credit and the national armed forces. "Who will not prefer to be taxed twice what is proposed in the bill rather than see the army suffer or its operations hindered?" he asked.[50]

Early the next day, June 30, Chase sent Lincoln a copy of this letter to Stevens, and asked Lincoln to underscore the need for higher taxes with a presidential message to Congress. Chase then went to the Capitol to meet Senator William Fessenden. While they were talking, a messenger arrived and spoke with Fessenden alone for a moment. The senator then turned to Chase and asked whether he had resigned, saying that the messenger was asking him to go to the Senate floor to consider the "nomination of your successor." Chase responded that he had submitted a letter of resignation but that he "had not been informed till now of its acceptance." Fessenden "expressed his surprise and disappointment," and the two men parted.[51]

When he returned to the department, Chase found a letter from Lincoln. "Your resignation of the office of secretary of the Treasury, sent me yesterday, is accepted. Of all I have said in commendation of your ability and fidelity, I have nothing to unsay; and yet you and I have reached a point of mutual embarrassment in our official relation which it seems cannot be overcome, or longer sustained, consistently with the public service." This was all that Lincoln told Chase in his letter, although Chase probably also heard some version of what Lincoln told his private secretary, Hay. Chase's message to Lincoln, Hay wrote in his diary, was essentially that "you have been acting very badly. Unless you say you are sorry and ask me to stay and agree that I shall be absolute and you shall have nothing, no matter how you beg for it, I will go." What Lincoln did not mention to Hay—but surely another reason he accepted Chase's resignation after refusing it before—was that Lincoln was now the Union Party nominee for president. Lincoln no longer needed to keep Chase in the Cabinet as a way of keeping him in line politically.[52]

Like Fessenden, Chase's other friends were horrified by his resignation. How, Jay Cooke asked Chase, could he "leave the helm of finance in the midst of this great storm?" Representative Hooper relayed to Chase a conversation with Lincoln, who regretted that relations between the two men had become so strained. The president told Hooper that he had intended, if Taney died or resigned, to make Chase the next chief justice. Hooper believed the president told him this to demonstrate his true respect for Chase. Lincoln recalled for Hooper that Chase had once told Lincoln that he would prefer judicial to administrative office and that he would rather be chief justice than hold any other position. After hearing this from Hooper, Chase mused that if only he and Lincoln could have had a frank conversation, he would not have had to resign.[53]

"So my official life closes," Chase wrote with a flourish in his diary. "I have laid broad foundations. Nothing but wise legislation—and especially bold yet judicious provision of taxes—with fair economy in administration and energetic yet prudent military action . . . seems necessary to ensure complete success." After writing about some of the details of the recent and imminent legislation, he added: "with these advantages and with all the great work of administration already inaugurated and blocked out, and especially with the still greater advantage of not having the inside and outside hostility to encounter, which I have been obliged to meet, my successor, I think, can get on pretty well." Chase exaggerated, but he *had* laid broad financial foundations upon which his successor and, indeed, generations, could build.[54]

CHAPTER 21

"So Help Me God"

❧ LATE 1864 ❧

During the first few days of July, Chase sent several long letters explaining and defending his resignation. He wrote to Greeley that Lincoln had insisted that the New York appointment be made to satisfy Morgan; Chase had wanted the person selected "mainly on the ground of special fitness for the place," especially because Cisco's position was "next in importance financially to my own." However hard Chase tried, one is left with the sense that his resignation was not well considered; that Chase had failed to follow his own maxim that "a resignation is a grave act, never performed by a right-minded man without forethought." On the other hand, one can also understand Chase's frustration that Lincoln had refused even to talk with him about the Cisco situation, insisting on resolving it through letters, not the best way to bridge differences.[1]

Washington was surprised by Chase's resignation, but it was shocked by Lincoln's choice of David Tod, former governor of Ohio, to serve as his successor at the Treasury. One reporter commented that Tod was a "jolly fellow and a good storyteller" but knew "as little of finance as a cow does of arithmetic." Tod declined within hours of receiving Lincoln's offer, enabling Lincoln to name William Fessenden as the next Treasury secretary. The senator from Maine was an ideal choice: well versed in the nation's finances through his work as chairman of the Finance Committee and well liked by all factions of the Union Party. The *Washington Evening Star* reported that the Senate confirmed the Fessenden nomination "unanimously and joyfully."[2]

William Fessenden, Chase's friend and successor as secretary of the Treasury.
Fessenden held the position for less than a year before returning to the Senate,
where he served until his death in 1869.

Fessenden was reluctant to take up the task, however, worried that the workload would harm or even kill him. Chase urged him to accept and promised to help with the transition. Pressed by Chase, Stanton, and others, Fessenden relented and agreed to serve as Treasury secretary.[3]

Chase woke on the morning of the Fourth of July to the "explosions of cannon, ringing of bells, and [the] whiz-whiz snap-snap of [fire]crackers." He believed that the celebration was excessive in light of recent military reverses for the Union. At noon on this day, Lincoln prevented the Wade-Davis Bill from becoming law by refusing to sign it as the congressional session closed. Cosponsored by Benjamin Wade and Henry Winter Davis, the Wade-Davis bill would have established far stricter standards than Lincoln's 10 percent plan for rebel states seeking to rejoin the Union. Chase had favored the bill because it would, in his words, reject the "idea of possible reconstitution with slavery, which neither the president nor his chief advisers have, in my opinion, abandoned." Chase's view that Lincoln had not yet ruled out reconstruction with slavery might seem odd in light of what Lincoln was saying at this time—the president was now on record in favor of a constitutional amendment to end slavery in all the states—but as we shall see, Chase was not wrong about Lincoln's thinking.[4]

True to his word, Chase worked closely with Fessenden on the transition at the Treasury. On July 5, the morning the new secretary started work, his predecessor pulled up in front of Fessenden's house in his carriage, drove with him to the department, introduced him to key employees, and spent time explaining to him "the state of the finances and the general working of the business." The next day, Chase worked another several hours with Fessenden reviewing the mechanics of federal loans. When Fessenden told Chase, in one of their conversations, that Lincoln had agreed that appointments in the department would be made only with Fessenden's "full consent and approval," Chase asked his diary why Lincoln had not agreed to this approach with him. "I can see but one reason: that I am too earnest, too antislavery, and, say, too radical to make him willing to have me connected with the administration; just as my opinion is that he is not earnest enough, not antislavery enough, not radical enough."[5]

As Chase was preparing to leave Washington for New England, he wrote Kate that he did not plan to return as a resident, but simply as her guest from time to time. He hoped to depart on July 11 but could not do so because Confederate General Jubal Early and his army of ten thousand soldiers were just beyond the northern border of Washington. "We are in a sort of siege here," Chase wrote to a friend. "An assault on the fortifications north of my house, some six or seven miles [distant], was expected this morning, but I have heard no guns and presume the rebels thought better of it." Chase may not have heard the guns, but there was serious fighting on both this day and the next at Fort Stevens, a mere five miles north of the White House.[6]

Chase finally left Washington on July 13, noting in his diary that although none of his other Cabinet colleagues had visited since his resignation, Edwin Stanton had called upon him that morning, "warm and cordial as ever." Because of the Early raid, there was no rail service this day between Washington and Baltimore. So instead of taking the normal route north by train, Chase had to head south by boat on the Potomac before turning north in the Chesapeake and then disembarking at the northern end of the bay. He spent a night with Cooke near Philadelphia, a night in New York City, and then went to Newport, Rhode Island, where he heard a "very good sermon" on Sunday morning.[7]

Chase had been hard at work in various capacities—senator, governor, and secretary—for the past fifteen years. Now, for the first time in ages, he took a two-month vacation. From Newport, he traveled to Boston, seeing Pierce, Sumner, and other friends. He attended services at the Unitarian church in Beverly, Massachusetts, then had a "pleasant talk and walk" with Charlotte Eastman on the acre near the sea "which she calls her farm." A few days later, he was in the seaside resort town of Nahant as a guest of Richard Henry Dana, the author and lawyer, playing croquet with Dana's young daughters, "very merry."[8]

While in Nahant, on August 3, Chase received a letter from William Mellen, reporting from Cincinnati that some friends there intended to nominate Chase for Congress. He drafted a response: "unanimous nomination would command acceptance but cannot compete and must not be regarded as a competitor." In other words, Chase did not want to be a candidate like others; he would only accept nomination by acclamation. There was no telegraph office in Nahant, however, so Chase could not send this until the next day. He wrote Mellen a letter along the same lines. Neither message reached Cincinnati before the convention met there on August 6. Chase's friends tried to secure his nomination but were outvoted by the friends of Benjamin Eggleston, whom the *Cincinnati Daily Commercial* ridiculed as "an illiterate, brawling caucus-monger." Chase was annoyed, writing Mellen that he never consented to the use of his name as a congressional candidate. But this proved a minor matter.[9]

Far more important was whether the Union Party should back someone other than Lincoln as its presidential candidate. With the war effort stalled, with his party divided, and with the people "wild for peace," in the words of Thurlow Weed, it seemed sure that Lincoln could not win reelection. "One thing must be self-evident to him," declared the *New York Herald* in early August, "that under no circumstances can he hope to be the next president of the United States." Lincoln more or less agreed. In late August he wrote privately that it was "exceedingly probable" that he would not win a second term. Even more telling was Lincoln's reaction to a letter from Henry Raymond, editor of the *New York Times*, suggesting that Lincoln offer peace "on the sole condition of acknowledging the supremacy of the Constitution"—leaving all other questions to be resolved by a convention. Lincoln did not reject Raymond's idea because it would mean that the rebel states could rejoin the Union as slave states. Instead, he drafted a commission to allow Raymond to meet with Jefferson Davis in Richmond, to see if the South was prepared to make peace on the Raymond terms. It was only after a few days of reflection and discussion that Lincoln decided not to pursue Raymond's open-ended peace proposal. So Chase had not been wrong to think that the president had not yet abandoned the idea of allowing the Southern states back into the Union with their slaves.[10]

Chase, being in New England, had little sense of what Lincoln was thinking in Washington. But since Lincoln was doubting in Washington, it is not surprising that Chase was wavering in New England. In his August 5 letter to Mellen, Chase raised the impractical idea that Lincoln and Frémont should both withdraw from the race in favor of the governor of Ohio, John Brough. A week later, however, in a private letter that soon became public, Chase wrote that he did not "see any reason for believing that the great cause to which we are all bound can be promoted any better or as well by withdrawing support from the nomination made at Baltimore." Chase instructed his allies to "do nothing, or say nothing, that can create the impression that there is any personal difference between Mr. Lincoln and myself, for there is none. All the differences that exist are on public questions and have no private bearing." When a friend urged Chase in late August to write a public letter in favor of Lincoln, Chase's response was that "I could do nothing now." Answering a letter from Michigan saying that people there wanted to replace Lincoln with Chase as the Union Party candidate, he wrote that "no such movement as the one you suggest seems to me expedient, so far as I am concerned. Whether it would be expedient or patriotic in reference to some *other* name, I am not able to judge." In other words, although Chase was not prepared to run against Lincoln, he did not condemn efforts to find a candidate other than Lincoln.[11]

Perhaps one reason that Chase wavered this summer was that, for once in his life, he was not focused on politics. He dined in Boston with Ralph Waldo Emerson and other New England literary leaders. He had a long talk with the poet and abolitionist John Greenleaf Whittier. He tarried a few days with his friend William Curtis Noyes, a New York lawyer, at his summer home in Litchfield, Connecticut. He visited his mother's grave in

Hopkinton, New Hampshire. He walked in the White Mountains, writing in his diary about the "grand prospects." He stayed with the Spragues in their seaside mansion at Narragansett, Rhode Island, with a "houseful" of guests and "very merry" croquet games. He participated in the celebration of the hundredth anniversary of Brown University, marching in the academic procession and giving an impromptu after-dinner speech.[12]

In the last few days of August, while Chase was in New England, the Democratic convention in Chicago nominated General George McClellan for president and adopted a platform declaring that "after four years of failure to restore the Union by the experiment of war," the time had come "for a cessation of hostilities." Instead of attempting to defend the Lincoln record, the Union Party newspapers now had something to attack: the "peace-at-any-price" Democrats. Then, on September 3, the long-awaited news arrived in the North that General Sherman had captured Atlanta. From despair, the mood in the North turned to elation.[13]

As the situation changed, so did Chase's views. He wrote to Samuel Hooper in early September that he planned to return to Ohio and to support Lincoln. "Under existing circumstances," Chase explained, "none of the personal objections that have been made against Mr. Lincoln can outweigh the fact that only through his reelection will there be any chance for the practical development and application of the principles for which the Republican Party have contended." Hooper agreed, urging Chase to campaign hard for Lincoln, believing this would have "powerful influence throughout the country towards securing a successful result to the elections."[14]

Chase's vacation ended on September 12, when he left Providence by the overnight boat for New York City, sleeping only fitfully. After a day in the city, talking with friends, Chase took the overnight train to Washington. He spent some time at the Treasury Department, meeting Fessenden, Harrington, and McCulloch, and he saw Lincoln, who was "cordial," although they did not have "anything like private conversation." Chase was annoyed that the president did not find time for more than "ordinary talk on ordinary topics," but he was now firmly committed to the Lincoln campaign. "Mr. Lincoln's heart is for Freedom and Union," Chase wrote on September 14, "and I am sure that there is little or no hope for the principles and measures to which the best years of my life have been devoted except through his reelection. The sympathies of all enemies of the country are with the Chicago candidates; the sympathies of those who love the country should be with the Baltimore nominees." Chase wrote Hooper that he would leave Washington soon to campaign in Ohio, focusing first on the October election for state officers and members of Congress.[15]

Chase started his campaign, however, before he even left the District of Columbia. On September 17 he spoke at a flag-raising ceremony, saying that the American flag represented "Union, freedom, and territorial integrity." Inspired by these great ideals, Union soldiers marched "side by side to battle wherever throughout the land rebellion and treason are found in arms. The flag, too, proclaims the conviction of the vast majority of these soldiers and of their fellow citizens at home, that the inestimable benefits represented by these ideas can be most surely realized by ratifying at the ballot box in November the nominations made at Baltimore in June." Two days later, responding to an evening serenade, Chase gave a brief speech, praising Lincoln, Johnson, and the Chicago platform. The first element of the platform was the "Union, one and indivisible." The second was that because the "Union has been assaulted by slavery," so "slavery must die the death which it deserves." Alluding to demands for peace, Chase said that "we want peace, but we want it with a Union made sacred by freedom and made permanent by foundations upon freedom and justice." Both speeches were reported widely.[16]

On September 20, while Chase was talking with George Harrington at the Treasury, they were interrupted by the sound of the clerks cheering. News had just arrived that Philip Sheridan, a diminutive but combative Union general, had defeated Jubal Early in the Shenandoah Valley, killing two generals and capturing more than three thousand rebel soldiers. Here was yet more military progress for Chase and others to use in their campaign speeches. Chase left Washington the next day and, after a delay in Pittsburgh due to a missed train connection, reached Cincinnati just in time for his planned speech there.[17]

The Union rally in Cincinnati on the evening of September 24 was immense, enthusiastic, and successful. The *Chicago Tribune* reported that the "streets were festooned with flags, many private residences were illuminated, bonfires blazed, and rockets showered their fiery dust through the deepening twilight." Twenty thousand people crammed Market Square to hear Chase. He started by reminding people that it was Southern rebels, not Northern Republicans, who had started the Civil War: "They were determined either to rule or ruin the republic. We did not choose to submit to their rule." Chase devoted much of his speech to refuting the key plank in the Democratic platform, which he characterized as claiming that "the war has been prosecuted for four years and that it has been a failure."[18]

To be sure, Chase conceded, "some things have moved a little slower than we thought they should," such as McClellan's Peninsula campaign, which, he said bluntly, was "a failure." But Navy flag officer David Farragut had not failed in August 1864 when he lashed himself to the mast, braved the Confederate guns, and captured Mobile, Alabama. Ulysses Grant had not failed in Virginia, where, with "characteristic obstinacy," he was now threatening Petersburg. Phil Sheridan, "another Ohio boy," had not failed; he had "whipped one of their chosen leaders in the Shenandoah Valley." And William Tecumseh Sherman, "yet another Ohio boy," had not failed to capture Atlanta and was even now "getting ready for another advance."[19]

Over the next week, Chase gave speeches in Indiana, including one where there was an "immense meeting" in spite of the "pouring rain." Venturing into hostile territory, Chase spoke in Louisville, Kentucky, where he told his "large and attentive audience" that Lincoln had "administered honestly, ably, and with substantial progress. He is unanimously supported by the Union men throughout the country." Even if Kentucky voted against Lincoln, it would not change the national electoral result. It would be far better for Kentucky to speak "as Henry Clay would, for the Union and freedom forever." In the last week before the state election, Chase spoke in small towns in southern Ohio, including Chillicothe, Jackson, and McArthur. After a Sunday with friends, Chase returned to Cincinnati and voted on Tuesday, October 11. He sent a telegram that day to Lincoln: "all right in Indiana and Ohio large gains in Congressmen." Indeed, the Union Party won dramatic victories in both states and also in Pennsylvania, gaining twenty seats in the House. "The election in November is now a mere formality," the *Chicago Tribune* exulted. "McClellan will not get an electoral vote outside of Kentucky." Chase was pleased but not so confident, warning a friend that "we must not be found napping."[20]

On the morning of October 13 Chase received a telegram from Edwin Stanton in Washington, reporting that Chief Justice Roger Taney had just died there. Chase wrote back that he had rarely known a man "more kind and genial" than Taney, however widely they differed "on political questions." Fessenden and Sumner had told Chase that it was Lincoln's "intention to offer the place to me in the case of a vacancy," and he was inclined to accept, "for I am weary of political life and work." What, Chase asked Stanton, did he think?[21]

Like Chase's other friends, Stanton thought that Lincoln should appoint Chase and that he should accept the appointment. Charles Sumner wrote Chase on October 14 to say that he had already written to Lincoln, urging "anew the considerations to which he yielded last spring, in favor of your nomination as chief justice. Of course you will accept." Horace Greeley wrote to urge Chase not only to accept but also to change his residence to Maryland, so that, like Taney, he could exert personal political influence there. Greeley presciently predicted that there would be a "great anti-Negro reaction the moment the war is over—an uprising of all that is ruffianly under the direction of all that is rascally in the land to revenge upon the poor negroes the humiliation and discomfiture of the slaveholders. This brutality will have to be resisted everywhere," Greeley wrote, but "Maryland is destined to play a leading, unenviable part in this predestined rebound of the rebellion."[22]

Most Union Party newspapers agreed that Chase was the right man to serve as Taney's successor. "The importance of the appointment can hardly be overestimated," the *Chicago Tribune* declared. The new chief justice would "preside over the arena in which the rebels will appear in brazen front, after the subjugation of their armies, to claim redress for the consequences of their crimes, and restitution for their losses instead of punishment for their treason." The Supreme Court would decide questions about "coercion, confiscation, emancipation, reconstruction, and the formation of new state governments in rebellious territory." For this vital position, Chase was by far the best choice. "With a broad foundation of legal ability and political experience, unsurpassed in faithfulness to principle, or in brilliancy of success by any American statesman, he will bring to the construction of the Constitution an enlightened devotion to liberty tenfold more powerful for good than has been Roger B. Taney's worship of slavery potent for evil."[23]

The *New York Herald* disagreed, saying Lincoln could not make a "worse selection" than Chase: "The position requires a lawyer of profound acquirements. Chase is but a dabbler in legal lore. It requires a man of calm judgment and unbiased opinions. Chase is a partisan. It requires a broad and comprehensive faculty of grasping great questions. Chase's miserable failure in the management of the national finances proves him devoid of that quality." The *Herald* predicted that Lincoln would choose Edwin Stanton, William Evarts, or Maryland senator Reverdy Johnson. Other papers speculated that the president would promote Justice Noah Swayne to chief justice. Chase knew that Lincoln's longtime friend and campaign manager, Justice David Davis, favored Swayne for the coveted post, as did Montgomery Blair and his family.[24]

Chase wrote back to Sumner that, although it was unusual to "say what one will do in respect of an appointment not tendered to him" yet, it was "certainly not awry to say to you that I should accept. I feel that I can do more for our cause and our country and for the success of the next administration in that place than in any other." As Chase perhaps intended, Sumner shared this section of his letter with Lincoln. Chase soon learned that the president did not intend to make the appointment immediately. William Fessenden wrote to Chase that the president had told him that since "things were going on well, he thought it best not to make any appointment or say anything about it until the election was over." Fessenden assured Chase that he believed Lincoln would appoint him, probably when Congress convened and the Supreme Court started work in early December.[25]

Chase's main focus in late October and early November was not on the judicial appointment but on the presidential campaign. He spoke twice in Kentucky, first in Covington, just across the river from Cincinnati, and then in Lexington, in the middle of the state. Chase reported to Stanton that his speech in Lexington was "one of my old-fashioned speeches such as you have heard in old times, only instead of arguing that slavery must be abolished outside of state limits, I argued that under the conditions created by the rebellion, it must be abolished throughout the whole country." In a state where almost all the political leaders were slave owners, in a county where about half the population was or had been enslaved, and at a time when local whites were incensed because slaves were freeing themselves by enlisting in the army, it took courage to argue for the abolition of slavery—but that is just what Chase did.[26]

Chase's speech in Kentucky coincided with a speech by Andrew Johnson to a black audience in Tennessee, in which Johnson said that he hoped some Moses would be found to lead them to freedom. The crowd called out that it wanted no Moses other than Johnson. "Well, then," he replied, "if no better shall be found, I will indeed be your Moses and lead you through the Red Sea of war and bondage to a fairer future of liberty and peace." Johnson looked forward to the day when "rebellion and slavery shall, by God's good help, no longer pollute our state. Loyal men, whether white or black, shall alone control her destinies." Chase later called Johnson's Moses speech the "most heroic utterance which had been made up to that time" and said that it "satisfied me completely."[27]

From Lexington, Chase traveled six hundred miles by train to Philadelphia, where he addressed a packed hall on October 27. ("Hydraulic pressure would not have forced another person into the vast room," said the *Philadelphia Inquirer.*) The Democratic plan for restoring the Union, Chase argued, would not work; the "immediate cessation of hostilities" called for by the Chicago platform would just let the Confederacy survive more or less within its current borders. The Union Party wanted to restore a Union that included "all the old states, all the territory that was ours when the rebellion broke out; to tear down that cursed bunting which goes by the name of 'Stars and Bars' [and] restore the old 'Stars and Stripes' flying over all the republic without a rival." The rebellion was doomed to fail, Chase declared, "unless our people are willing that it should succeed." That was the real question in this election, he said, whether the people of the Union would "consent to the success of the rebellion." The crowd roared back its response: "Never!"[28]

After a couple of speeches in the Philadelphia suburbs, Chase took an overnight train to Cleveland, arriving there at about one in the morning but still finding an enthusiastic crowd at the train station. After a quiet Sunday with his friend Richard Parsons, Chase spoke in another packed hall on October 31. He started this speech by recalling how, more than forty years ago, a young boy got off the boat in Cleveland, on his first trip to Ohio. "That boy stands before you tonight." Again, Chase contrasted the Union and Democratic Parties. The Union Party wanted to abolish slavery throughout the Union, while the Democrats wanted a "Union with slavery established in the territories and guaranteed there. They want a Union with the right of owning slaves in all the states." He closed by asking "every man and every woman here"—interesting at a time when women did not vote—to consider the "importance of the great issues before us and of their right decision," and to devote "every energy from now until the day of election in seeing that the last voter is brought out, the last effort is made, for the success of our holy cause."[29]

Chase went from Cleveland to Detroit and then to Adrian, Michigan, where the procession of party supporters before the rally was more than six miles long. In Chicago, on November 4, Chase spoke in yet another packed hall and declared that the end of slavery was near. Even the Southern newspapers, he noted, were now talking about enlisting blacks in the Confederate army and promising them freedom in return. "Freedom is going there," Chase declared, "and it is just as impossible to prevent it as it is impossible to arrest the progress of events. God is moving among the nations of the earth . . . his decrees go forth, and his angels execute them, and one of these decrees is that there shall be liberty throughout this land." The crowd responded with "loud and long continued cheers." From there Chase took the overnight train to Saint Louis, where he spoke to what he described as "a great and attentive and enthusiastic audience." After Sunday in Saint Louis, Chase returned by train to Cincinnati, reaching there a little after midnight on Election Day, Tuesday, November 8. Chase wrote on that day to George Harrington that he arrived just "in time to become a very minute fraction of Ohio's majority for Lincoln." He was somewhat worried that McClellan might have a slight majority in New York and Pennsylvania, but he felt confident that, even in this scenario, Lincoln would prevail in the electoral college.[30]

By the next morning, it was clear that the president would win in almost every state, although in some states, he just barely slipped past McClellan: for instance, Lincoln received only 51.5 percent of the votes in New York and only 51.6 percent in Pennsylvania. But in the end, he won in every state that voted in this election except for Delaware, Kentucky, and New Jersey. In hindsight, perhaps Chase should not have wasted his time in Kentucky, where Lincoln received only about a third of the vote. Some of Chase's friends had urged him to come to New York City and speak at Cooper Union rather than focus on Ohio and Kentucky. But although he was disappointed by the result in Kentucky—Chase had hoped that McClellan would not receive a single electoral vote—he was not discouraged. He believed that even the white masters of Kentucky would soon see that they were better off without slavery, and he was pleased to have played his part in this process.[31]

After the election, Chase was in a somewhat awkward position in Cincinnati. He had planned to go to Washington right after the election and spend the winter there with his two daughters while working with a young protégé, Jacob Schuckers, on a book of Chase's speeches. But Lincoln had not yet nominated the next chief justice, and Chase did not want "even to seem to urge the offer of the place to me. Respect for Mr. Lincoln and confidence in him appear to me best shown by remaining in the West till his decision is known." So Chase stayed with friends in Cincinnati and waited for the president to make his choice.[32]

Chase knew well that he and Lincoln were not personal friends. But Chase disagreed with the newspapers claiming that the two were enemies. In a long letter to Sumner, Chase explained that there was "a difference of temperament and, on some points, of judgment. I may have been too earnest and eager, while I thought him not earnest enough and too slow. On some occasions, indeed, I found it was so. But I never desired anything else than his complete success and never indulged a personal wish incompatible with absolute fidelity to his administration. To assure that success, I labored incessantly in the Treasury Department, with what results the world knows." And, in the fall campaign, he "gave all the aid in my power to his reelection."[33]

The newspapers disputed among themselves in November about who would be the next chief justice. Some predicted confidently that Chase would receive the nomination. The *New York Times*, however, reported that Ohio leaders were pressing Lincoln to nominate Swayne. The *New-York Tribune* said that Stanton would become chief justice, that Butler would take over the War Department, and that Chase would be sent as ambassador to England. Dismissing this report as fiction, Stanton wrote to Chase that "your experience has taught you that the newspaper reports are all lies, invented by knaves for fools to feed on." The secretary of war's sources told him that "Swayne is the most active and Blair the most confident of the candidates," but Stanton was sure that Lincoln would, in the end, nominate Chase, "if it has not already been done."[34]

Chase's friends also differed on whether he would receive the appointment. Sumner and Fessenden, who were perhaps in the best positions to know, having discussed the question with the president, were confident that Lincoln would not change his mind. Fessenden wrote to Chase that he considered "the matter so well settled that no struggle will be made to prevent it." Horace Greeley, on the other hand, wrote Chase to report that there was a struggle, with Evarts and Stanton among the leading candidates, and no clear answer about whom Lincoln would choose. Samuel

Hooper believed that Chase would prevail but admitted to Chase that he would be "better satisfied when the appointment is made."[35]

For himself, Chase wanted the appointment, but, as he wrote to a friend, he did not want to look like "an applicant or candidate for the position" because it was a position "for which there should be no applicants and no candidates." To another supporter, he wrote that all he could tell from the news from Washington was "that the pot boils. If the Blairs' wishes prevail, yours will not. I have made up my mind to take things as they come."[36]

Chase finally left Cincinnati on November 30 for Cleveland, where he gave a speech at a local college and stayed a few days with his friend Richard Parsons. Writing to Sumner on Saturday, December 3, Chase forwarded a *Cincinnati Gazette* editorial advocating him for chief justice. Chase wanted to be sure that Sumner knew that he had no role in the editorial. "I have feared that the president might suppose that I have some agency in the representations which reach him favorable to my appointment. If he has, I hope you will disabuse him of the impression. I would not have the office on the terms of being obliged to seek for it." Chase probably remained in Cleveland on Sunday—he did not like to travel on Sunday—and departed by train on Monday for Philadelphia. He changed trains there on Tuesday, December 6, and headed for Washington.[37]

If, during his brief stop in Philadelphia, Chase saw the New York morning papers, he would have been discouraged. The *New York Herald* reported that Swayne would become chief justice because Lincoln, after learning that Chase had sent a letter opposing his reelection, would disregard his earlier promises to nominate Chase. According to the *New York World,* as of Monday evening, "both the friends and opponents of Mr. Chase claim to be masters of the situation, but the chances are even against Mr. Chase and in favor of Judge Davis for chief justice and Montgomery Blair for associate." When he reached Washington late Tuesday afternoon, however, Chase learned that Lincoln had nominated him and that the Senate had already confirmed him as the nation's next chief justice. "I cannot sleep," he wrote to Lincoln, "before I thank you for this mark of your confidence and especially for the manner in which the nomination was made. I shall never forget either and trust that you will never regret either. Be assured that I prize your confidence and good will more than nomination or office."[38]

Sumner later told one of Chase's first biographers that, as he was leaving Chase's house on this evening, he met with an angry Kate, who shook her finger at him, saying, "you, too, in this business of shelving Papa? But never mind! I will defeat you all!" Often repeated, the story is probably apocryphal. Kate had a temper, but she was not one to shake her finger at her father's best friend in the Senate. Moreover, Kate would have known that her father had been working hard for weeks to secure this appointment and had no intention of being "shelved" on the Supreme Court.[39]

Most newspapers praised the appointment. The *New-York Tribune*, for example, said that the Supreme Court would have vital work in the reconstruction of the Union. "To no hands could it be so safely entrusted as to those of Mr. Chase." Even the Democratic *New York World* predicted that Chase would be a good chief justice, for he was "a studious man of great capacity for sustained labor." The *World* said that Lincoln was not eager to name Chase; he did so only when he realized that "if he sent in any other name than that of Mr. Chase, the Senate would reject it." Charles Dana agreed with this analysis in a letter from Washington to James Pike. Lincoln was "a man who keeps a grudge as faithfully as any Christian," Dana wrote, and he "consented to Mr. Chase's elevation only when the pressure became very general and very urgent." If Lincoln had tried to name Blair, for example, the nomination would have been "smashed to pieces in a moment."[40]

Chase received dozens of congratulatory letters, some from close friends, others from total strangers. Charles Cleveland wrote from Philadelphia to say that he was pleased for his old friend but even more so for the nation: "I know you will feel the responsibilities of this high position." John Jay, grandson and namesake of the first chief justice, wrote from New York: "May you long live to impress upon the Supreme Court of the nation, that regard for the constitutional right and eternal justice, which has marked your political career, and secured for you the admiration and confidence of your country." William Schouler, a friend and editor, wrote from Boston to remind Chase of a conversation in which he had said that the presidency was "an office worthy of the ambition of any man living, but so far as you personally were concerned, you would rather be chief justice of the United States." Alphonso Taft, father of the future chief justice, wrote from Cincinnati that he had feared Lincoln would name another man. "I will forgive Mr. Lincoln much for this. To be chief justice of the United States is more than to be president, in my estimation." An army chaplain sent a simple message: "God bless you."[41]

Not everyone was pleased by Chase's appointment. The *Cincinnati Enquirer* commented that "Chase has heretofore been noted as a political agitator, not as a lawyer or a jurist. In the latter respect, he always held a very inferior rank in this city and, except in political negro cases, always had an inferior position at the bar. As a jurist, he has but little of the experience or the ability of his predecessors, Marshall and Taney. What he lacks in that respect, he makes up in the violence of his political passions." Gideon Welles, who never liked Chase, wrote in his diary that Sumner claimed that Chase would "retire from the field of politics and not be a candidate for the presidency." Welles did not believe it for a moment. "If he lives, Chase will be a candidate, and his restless and ambitious mind is already at work. It is his nature."[42]

Many claimed later that Lincoln made similar remarks at this time about Chase. For example, Lafayette Foster, senator from Connecticut, recalled Lincoln telling him that Chase would make a "very excellent judge if he devotes himself exclusively to the duties of his office and doesn't meddle with politics. But if he keeps on with the notion that he is destined to be president of the United States, and which in my judgment he will never be, he will never acquire that fame and usefulness as chief justice which he would otherwise certainly attain." Foster, who was not that close with Lincoln, said this in an interview in 1878, after Chase had proved Welles right by running for president in 1868. Like so many who summoned up Lincoln's words years later, Foster probably recalled what he thought the president should have said—not what he actually said.[43]

Far more reliable is a report printed in the *Baltimore American* two days after the Chase appointment. A Maryland delegation, visiting Washington the prior day, congratulated Lincoln on his election and on the appointment of Chase. Lincoln responded that he trusted Chase would make a good chief justice. The "country needed assurances in regard to two great questions, and they were assurances that could better be given by the character and well-known opinions of the appointee than by any verbal pledges. In the appointment of Mr. Chase, all holders of government securities in America and Europe felt assured that the financial policy of the government would be sustained by the highest judicial tribunal. In sustaining that policy, Judge Chase would only be sustaining himself, for he was the author of it. His appointment also met the public desire and expectation as regarded the emancipation policy of the government."[44]

Although the Supreme Court had already started its winter term and was hearing cases day by day, Chase could not yet join its work because he did not have his commission. By law, the commission had to be prepared by the attorney general, and there was no attorney general at this time, for Bates had resigned, and his successor, James Speed, had not been confirmed yet by the Senate. Even after Speed was confirmed, the *Philadelphia Inquirer* reported that "owing to a delay in the attorney general's office today, in not preparing his commission, Chief Justice Chase did not take his seat on the bench but will be inaugurated tomorrow at eleven o'clock."[45]

On the morning of December 15, 1864, the courtroom in the Capitol Building—there was no separate building yet for the Supreme Court—was crowded with those who had come to see Chase be sworn in as the chief justice. Many of his friends were in the courtroom, including Sumner, leaning on a column, and Chase's daughters, whom Noah Brooks described as "gorgeously dressed." Chase knew this room well, for it was the former Senate chamber, which the Senate had recently vacated to move to newer and larger quarters. Before entering the courtroom, Chase took the "oath of allegiance" in the court's private conference room. This was the "ironclad oath," imposed by Congress to keep rebels out of the federal government, so Chase swore that he had not borne arms against the United States, that he had not aided or encouraged those in rebellion, and that he had not participated in any "pretended government, authority [or] power within the United States, hostile or inimical thereto." Then, at about eleven, the justices entered the courtroom in their black robes, each going to stand behind his assigned chair, with Chase at the central chair. Raising his right hand, and reading from a printed page, he took the oath of office, swearing to support and defend the Constitution, in what one report called a "firm, audible voice, amid profound silence." Another report explained that Chase read the oath himself rather than having it given to him by another judge, because there was "no judicial officer higher than he to administer it." After taking the oath, Chase added in a firm voice: "so help me God."[46]

CHAPTER 22

"Universal Suffrage"

1864–65

The Supreme Court of the nineteenth century was quite different from the twenty-first-century court. There were, of course, similarities. Then, as now, cases generally did not start in the Supreme Court; its role was to review decisions made by lower federal courts and state supreme courts in cases involving federal questions. Each day's session opened with the justices, in their black robes, entering the courtroom, and with the crier praying for God to "save the United States and this honorable court!" Unlike today's court, however, where the justices decide which cases warrant their review, the Chase court had almost no control over its docket; parties had the right to appeal. And many of the cases on the docket in the Chase era did not involve any federal question; the parties were from different states, so there was "diversity jurisdiction" in the federal courts, but there were no federal issues to resolve, only standard state law questions. The Supreme Court today would not even consider such cases.[1]

For example, during Chase's first weeks, the court heard and decided *Tobey v. Leonards*, a minor family property dispute. An elderly farmer named Jonathan Tobey transferred land in New Bedford, Massachusetts, to his son-in-law, Horatio Leonard, and the young man's father. The question was whether the parties had, at the time of the transaction, reached an oral agreement that the Leonards would transfer the land *back* to Tobey if he repaid what he owed them. The reason the case was in federal court was that the plaintiff, Stephen Tobey, Jonathan's son and heir, was a resident of Rhode Island and chose to sue the Massachusetts defendants in federal court. But because Tobey was seeking an equitable remedy—an order directing the defendants to return the land—the court had to consider the whole record, of more than three hundred pages, to decide whether there had been an oral agreement, as Tobey alleged. "No important principle was decided," notes one historian, and "the decision made no perceptible mark upon the law." So it is not odd that Chase complained of working "from morning to midnight, and no result, except that [one man] owned this parcel of land or other property, instead of [another man], I caring nothing, and nobody caring much more about the matter."[2]

Although the Chase court decided many trivial cases, it also decided a number of important ones. From February 1790, when John Jay presided over the first session of the Supreme Court, through December 1864, when Chase started work, there were only three cases in which the court ruled a federal statute unconstitutional. But during Chase's eight and a half years as chief justice, the court declared that ten laws passed by Congress were unconstitutional.[3] Some of these were high-profile cases, with the press reporting eagerly on the arguments and commenting on the opinions. Unlike today, however, when papers refer to justices as liberal or conservative, or even as Democrats or Republicans, people did not view the justices in this way. Paradoxically, although the justices were more active in politics than they are today, with Chase and others running for president while serving on the court, the justices were not generally viewed as deciding cases for political reasons, and there was no predictable political pattern to the way the justices lined up in their decisions. There was also a great deal more consensus on the court than there is today; dissents were not common.[4]

Chase took his judicial duties seriously. The court's practice when he became chief justice was to meet in Washington for about fourteen weeks each year, from early December through early March. To reduce the backlog of cases, one of the new chief justice's changes was to increase the number of weeks the court was in session; by the year Chase died, 1873, the court was meeting from early October through April. On each weekday of its session, the court would convene at eleven in the morning and hear oral argument until four in the afternoon. Today the court generally hears only one hour of argument in each case, divided between the two sides. In Chase's era, each side generally had at least two and sometimes four hours, so that argument of a single case often spanned two or three days. W. H. Smith, who served as court crier while Chase was chief justice, recalled that "no matter how long, dull, and prosy an attorney might be in presenting his argument, the chief justice never displayed any impatience, but to all outward appearance paid the closest attention." Chase "took copious notes" and asked questions "only to make more clear some statement." Chase was punctual in starting and ending each day's session. Smith could recall only two instances in which Chase failed to close the session at four. Once the chief justice simply failed to notice the time, and Smith had to remind him. In the other, former senator Thomas Ewing, aged and infirm, was arguing what proved to be his last case before the court. At four o'clock, Chase asked Ewing to pause, conferred quietly with the other justices, then asked Ewing if he would like to finish his argument instead of returning another day. "With tears in his eyes," the lawyer thanked Chase and concluded his remarks.[5]

On Saturdays, the justices would gather at eleven in their private conference room to discuss and decide cases. The chief justice "usually called the case," one of Chase's contemporaries recalled. "He stated the pleadings and the facts that they presented, the arguments, and his conclusions in regard to them." In some cases, Chase had more or less decided the case, so that he was presenting a sketch of his opinion to his colleagues. The justices then discussed the case among themselves until reaching a consensus. The chief justice assigned one of the justices to prepare the opinion—unless the chief was in the minority, in which case the senior associate justice would assign the opinion. The justices did not have clerks to help them draft opinions; each justice researched and drafted himself. Unlike today, the justices did not review draft opinions in printed form, commenting and revising the draft so that all who join an opinion agree with it fully. In Chase's time, each opinion was the work of the individual justice to whom it was assigned. After preparing the draft opinion, the justice responsible read it aloud at a Saturday conference and, if it was accepted, read it aloud in court on Monday. This justice then worked with the reporter and the printer to prepare the printed opinion, and there were often some changes between the opinion as it was first read and the final printed document.[6]

Chase's first task as chief justice, and not an easy one, was to form relations with the other justices. Although he had probably met each of his new colleagues at some time or other, he did not really know them when he became the chief justice.[7]

James Wayne was the senior associate justice. Born in Georgia in 1790, he practiced law there, served three terms in the House, and was appointed by President Andrew Jackson in 1834. Wayne owned slaves in Georgia before the war and joined fully in all the prewar court decisions in favor of slavery. When Georgia seceded, however, Wayne did not resign and return to the South, like his Southern colleague Justice John Archibald Campbell; instead, Wayne stayed in Washington and stayed loyal to the Union. He and Chase became firm friends. Following a visit to the Wayne household in early 1865, Chase described the justice to Kate as "kind and courteous, as he always is."[8]

John Catron, another Southerner, was sick at home in December 1864 and would remain there until he died in May 1865, so that he and Chase never worked together.[9]

Samuel Nelson, born in upstate New York in 1792, was a conservative Northern Democrat. He became a state court judge in 1831 and a justice of the Supreme Court in 1845. Nelson joined the court's opinions in favor of slavery and opposed (quietly) the Emancipation Proclamation, but he and Chase would develop a good working relationship.[10]

Robert Grier was a successful Pennsylvania lawyer and state court judge before President James Polk appointed him as a justice in 1846. Although a lifelong Democrat, Grier was fiercely committed to the Union, writing to a friend early in the war that "we must conquer this rebellion or declare our government a failure." By the time Chase joined the court, however, Grier was aging and failing.[11]

Nathan Clifford, born in New Hampshire in 1803, hoped like Chase to attend Dartmouth, but was unable to raise the funds for college, so he read law for five years before he was admitted to the bar. He moved to Maine, entered politics as a Democrat, served two terms in the House and two years as federal attorney general for Polk. Buchanan nominated Clifford in 1857 for a vacant seat on the court, and although Republicans opposed the nomination, calling Clifford a political hack, the Senate confirmed him in early 1858. All the justices at this time were large men, but the court crier recalled that Clifford was the largest, weighing in at more than three hundred pounds.[12]

Noah Swayne was a successful corporate lawyer in Columbus, Ohio, in the 1850s, where he and Chase met from time to time, although they were not really friends. In 1861, however, as soon as Swayne learned of the death of Justice McLean, he wrote to Chase seeking support to become

McLean's successor on the court. There are no letters suggesting that Chase urged Lincoln to name Swayne, but, of course, he would not have to write Lincoln for this purpose; he could simply speak with him at one of their frequent meetings. Other Ohio Republicans pressed Swayne's case, and Lincoln named him to the court in early 1862.[13]

Justice Samuel Miller practiced medicine in Kentucky for a decade before becoming a lawyer. Starting in the late 1840s, Miller freed his slaves, and in 1850 he moved his family to Keokuk, Iowa, becoming a leading lawyer and Republican there. When Congress revised the circuit court boundaries in 1862, creating a circuit of which Iowa was the central state, Iowa Republicans lobbied the president to name Miller to the Supreme Court. Miller was one of the few justices who urged Lincoln to make Chase chief justice. Chase knew about and appreciated Miller's support.[14]

David Davis of Illinois was the justice closest to Abraham Lincoln. From 1848 through 1862, he was the presiding judge of the Eighth Judicial Circuit of Illinois, traveling from town to town and staying in the same hotels with the lawyers who practiced before him, including Lincoln. Davis was Lincoln's campaign manager in 1860 and joined the Supreme Court in 1862. Although Davis had urged Lincoln to appoint Swayne as chief justice, he and Chase soon became friends. In the spring of 1867, for example, Chase wrote Davis that he had an urge to write him a letter "because, well, because I like you; and my esteem for you and confidence in you have been growing all the time we have been together." Davis responded that he liked Chase, too, and "if I were allowed to speak for my brethren, I think I could say you have been growing in their confidence and attachment ever since your accession to the bench. You certainly have in mine."[15]

Stephen Field, born in New York, was the younger brother of Cyrus Field, the telegraph entrepreneur, and David Dudley Field, the lawyer and legal reformer. Stephen went to California during the gold rush, practiced law and entered politics as a Democrat, and was soon a justice of the state supreme court. When Congress in 1863 created a tenth judicial circuit, composed of California and Oregon, and a tenth seat on the Supreme Court, it was obvious that the seat should go to a lawyer from the West, and Field received the nomination. Like Miller, he supported Chase's appointment as chief justice; indeed, he supported Chase even before Taney's death. In the spring of 1864 Chase and Field chanced to meet on

Pennsylvania Avenue, and Field "expressed the warm wish" that Chase might succeed Taney. Writing about this later to Field, Chase said that "if you have forgotten it, I have not, nor shall I ever forget it. It took me by surprise but was very grateful to my feelings." After hearing a report, apparently without basis, that Field had a drinking problem, Chase wrote in his diary that he would talk to Field "like a brother, for he is one of our best men and dear to me."[16]

Justice Stephen Field, Chase's best friend on the Supreme Court.
"I love him like a brother," Chase wrote of Field.

At the end of his first term on the court, Chase wrote to a friend that he "found all the judges kind and their goodwill has, I think, constantly increased, as they have understood me better." One way he secured their goodwill was by taking more than his fair share of the work of writing opinions. Even during his first term, Chase was the author of ten majority opinions, more than all but one of the other justices. This pattern would continue: the chief justice generally wrote more opinions, and more important opinions, than any other justice on the court. Another way Chase stayed on good terms with his colleagues was by not writing dissenting opinions. In one instance, during Chase's first term, Clifford dissented from an opinion by Wayne. Although Chase agreed with Clifford, he did not join the dissent, writing in his diary that "except in very important cases" he thought "dissent inexpedient." In his nine years as chief justice, Chase would write more than two hundred opinions, of which only eleven were dissents.[17]

Since the first day of 1865 was a Sunday, the customary New Year's receptions were held on the second. Chase, however, did not go out, for he was mourning the recent death of his sister, Helen, the last of his siblings. He apologized for his absence from the presidential reception in a letter to Lincoln, assuring him that "no one more earnestly wishes every blessing of the New Year to you and yours. God grant that you may have the satisfaction of seeing it close with Peace and Union once more

John Rock, the first black member of the Supreme Court bar,
whose admission Chase organized in early 1865.

assured to our beloved Land." Lincoln responded kindly, "Allow me to condole with you in the sad bereavement you mention." Writing to his friend Susan Walker, Chase noted that he was now the last survivor of the eleven children born to his parents. "Several members of my family, as you know, have died very suddenly, and I cannot help feeling that I may be called in like manner." Perhaps, he wrote to Walker, "I shall reach the allotted term of three score and ten—now not remote, but it may be also that a year, a month, a week may bring the end of earth." All Chase could do was his duty "to man and to God," to strive to "be what He requires whether for one day or many years."[18]

One of Chase's early accomplishments on the court was to admit John Rock to the bar of the Supreme Court, making him the first black man entitled to argue cases there. Charles Sumner introduced Rock to Chase, describing him as an "estimable colored lawyer" from Boston who was "cordially recommended" by the state governor and others. Chase waited until late January 1865, when he knew his colleagues better, before raising the issue at a Saturday conference. The other justices did not respond at first, and Chase said he would interpret their silence as "indicating willingness to leave the matter to my discretion as chief justice." Then "one after another, nearly all expressed the opinion that the rule must govern." Since the rule on admission did not refer to race, the justices were indicating that they would not oppose Chase's plan. Had Justice David Davis been present, he might have objected, for he wrote to a friend that admitting Rock was simply political theater; the "negro can never be elevated to social and political rights in this country, and all wise statesmen know it." But Davis was sick at home in Illinois this winter. A few days after this conference, in open court, Sumner made a motion to admit Rock to the bar, and Chase approved it without comment. "I purposely avoided the slightest deviation from my usual formula in admitting whites," he wrote in his diary.[19]

Many of Chase's judicial opinions this winter addressed issues with which he was familiar, either from his antislavery work or his time as Treasury secretary. In his first opinion, Chase considered a case involving the *Circassian*, a British steamship captured as it attempted to slip through the Union blockade to New Orleans. The shipowners relied upon General Butler's proclamation, issued when he first entered New Orleans, on May 1, 1862, to argue that New Orleans was under Union control on the date of capture, May 4, so the capture was invalid under international law.

Chase disagreed, finding that Butler was in control of the city but not yet of the port, rendering the capture legitimate. In *Mrs. Alexander's Cotton*, Chase ruled that seventy-two bales of cotton seized in Texas could not be treated as a naval prize; since the cotton was on land, not water, in a rebellious region, it had to be handed over to the Treasury. In a dispute about whether the ship *Kate* was involved in the illegal African slave trade, Chase ruled against the owners. "In considering this evidence," he wrote, it was right to recall that "for more than three hundred years, the western coast of Africa has been scourged by the atrocities of the slave trade; and that this inhuman traffic, although at length proscribed and pursued with severe penalties by nearly all Christian nations, has continued, with almost unabated activity and ferocity."[20]

Although he was busy with the work of the court, Chase also found time this winter to continue his work for slaves and former slaves. On the last day of January, for example, he spent part of the day in the House of Representatives, which was debating whether to approve the

General William Tecumseh Sherman. Chase wrote to him in early 1865 to deplore the way in which the general was treating blacks "almost as pariahs."

Thirteenth Amendment. The proposed constitutional amendment had two sections: the first prohibited slavery or involuntary servitude, and the second authorized Congress to enforce the first section "through appropriate legislation." Chase had to leave town before the final, dramatic vote, when the House approved the amendment, and the galleries erupted in applause. That evening in Baltimore, the chief justice was on the platform as Henry Ward Beecher spoke at a benefit for the Baltimore Association for the Moral and Educational Improvement of the Colored People. After Beecher finished, the crowd called for Chase, and he responded with a few words, saying how happy he was to be in the free state of Maryland when he learned that the House had finally passed the "constitutional amendment abolishing slavery forever."[21]

Chase also found time to write many personal and political letters. After congratulating General Sherman on his capture of Savannah, Chase chided him for the way in which he had excluded black soldiers from his army and treated black residents as "pariahs" who were "almost without rights." Chase believed that "in the political reorganization of the states in insurrection, political, as well as natural, rights must be conceded to a portion at least of the colored population." In several letters, Chase supported Congress in excluding the representatives from Louisiana, because they were elected only by whites. Chase wrote to Wendell Phillips that "universal suffrage, or at least suffrage for all loyal blacks who might be of sufficient education or had been in the national military service, ought to be made an indispensable condition of the readmission of any rebel state to participation in the national government." In a letter to Francis Lieber, the philosopher and legal scholar, Chase explained why, even though he was now a federal judge, he continued to comment on political issues: "Upon matters which cannot possibly present a question for adjudication by the courts, I feel as free to express my opinion as ever." If the rebel states wanted to rejoin the Union, he told Lieber, the government should insist that they accept "universal suffrage."[22]

On March 4, 1865, Chase took part in the familiar ritual of inauguration, this time as one of the central figures: the chief justice. The weather had been wet, and the streets of Washington were a sea of mud. A little before noon, Lincoln, Chase, and others gathered in the Senate chamber to watch as Andrew Johnson took his oath as vice president. Johnson disgraced himself with a long, drunken speech, saying that he was a man of the people and telling the Cabinet members and even the chief justice that they owed their positions to the people. "Everybody was grieved by the sad misconduct of Andy Johnson," Chase wrote to Susan Walker. Sumner was so outraged that he wanted Johnson to resign, but Chase disagreed. "I honor him greatly as one who risked everything for his convictions," he wrote Sumner, hoping that Johnson would "fully retrieve himself." After Johnson finished his speech and stumbled through his oath, the new senators took their oaths, including Fessenden, who had resigned from the Treasury to return to the Senate, replaced at Treasury by Chase's friend and former assistant Hugh McCulloch.[23]

From the Senate chamber, Lincoln, Chase, and the others proceeded out to the platform on the east side of the Capitol Building. One paper reported that as Lincoln, "in his unassuming way, came into full view of the throng, a loud, long, and enthusiastic cheer welcomed him." The audience continued to cheer as the senators and others took their seats and Lincoln approached the small podium. Sitting in the front row just to the

Chief Justice Chase administers the oath of office to Abraham Lincoln, March 4, 1865.

side of Lincoln, Chase was in the perfect position to see and hear this second inaugural address. He would have noticed that, for the first time, the crowd gathered to hear the president's inaugural address included many blacks. He would have reflected, happily, that none of them were slaves.[24]

Lincoln opened his address by recalling how, when he was inaugurated four years earlier, a dreadful civil war seemed imminent. The cause of the war, Lincoln said, was the dispute over slavery. "To strengthen, perpetuate, and extend this interest was the object for which the insurgents would rend the Union, even by war; while the government claimed no right to do more than to restrict the territorial enlargement of it." Neither side had expected that the war would last so long or cause such fundamental change. Both sides "read the same Bible and pray to the same God, and each invokes His aid against the other." It might seem odd for men to "ask a just God's assistance in wringing their bread from the sweat of other men's faces," Lincoln said, but "let us judge not that we be not judged." The president closed with soaring words: "With malice toward none; with charity for all; with firmness in the right, as God gives us to see the right, let us strive on to finish the work we are in; to bind up the nation's wounds; to care for him who shall have borne the battle, and for his widow, and his orphan—to do all which may achieve and cherish a just and lasting peace, among ourselves, and with all nations."[25]

As the cheers died, and the sun emerged, Lincoln approached Chase, laid his hand on the Bible in the chief justice's hand and repeated after Chase the solemn presidential oath. Later in the day, Chase sent this Bible to Mary Todd Lincoln, with a cover note saying that he prayed that the "beautiful sunshine, which, just at the time the oath was taken, dispersed the clouds that had previously darkened the sky, may prove an auspicious omen of the dispersion of the clouds of war, by the clear sunshine of prosperous peace."[26]

Two days after the inauguration, Chase spent an hour in the evening with Lincoln, talking about reconstruction and the blockade. Lincoln was thinking about opening more Southern ports and declaring the rebellion over in parts of Virginia. In a follow-up letter, Chase suggested that "any proclamation declaring the state no longer in insurrection should recite the fact of the continuous loyal state government." Gideon Welles, hearing that Chase was meeting with Lincoln, was immediately suspicious, writing that it seemed like Chase was trying to increase his authority by extending civil rather than military jurisdiction in Virginia.[27]

When the court session ended, not long after the inauguration, most of the justices left Washington for their circuit duties. Each justice was assigned to a circuit composed of several states. The justice and the local district judge constituted the circuit court and were supposed to hold court at least once a year in each district. For some justices, this involved substantial travel. Stephen Field was assigned the new tenth circuit, made up of California, Oregon, and Nevada. Most of the justices were residents of a state in their circuit, but this was not the case with Chase, who took the circuit Taney had handled, consisting at first of Maryland, Delaware, Virginia, West Virginia, and North Carolina. The rebellion, Chase wrote to Walker, would "relieve me from holding any courts" in Virginia or North Carolina, but he was reading up to prepare for circuit court in Maryland.[28]

While Chase was starting his work on the court, Ulysses Grant and his army spent the winter in trenches stretching for miles near Petersburg, Virginia, waiting for weather that would allow them to move and to fight. At last, on March 30, the *Washington Evening Star* reported that Grant's forces were in motion. On the next day, the *Star* said that the Army of the Potomac was advancing south and west, seeking to cut the rail lines out of Petersburg; if this should happen, the "evacuation of Petersburg and Richmond would shortly follow." Chase arrived in Baltimore on Sunday, April 2, planning to spend the whole week holding circuit court there.[29]

The chief justice noted in his diary that no cases were ready for Monday morning, so there was "nothing to be done except call the docket, and we adjourned." Chase was thus probably not in court when news arrived in Baltimore, at about eleven in the morning, that Grant's army had captured Petersburg, the "hitherto impregnable rebel stronghold." About an hour later came even more momentous news: the general had captured Richmond. The celebrations in Baltimore were more muted than in Washington and New York, however, for this was still a city with many Southern sympathizers. The *Baltimore Sun* reported that the local commanding general ordered his soldiers to "maintain peace and order."[30]

Tuesday was another short day in the Baltimore circuit court, and Chase took the train to Washington to be there for the Richmond celebrations that night. Using thousands of candles, government officials illuminated the public buildings, and people illuminated their homes. The *National Republican* reported that the "demonstration of public joy last night exceeded everything of the kind ever witnessed before in Washington." Never before, the paper added, "were so many people abroad in the thoroughfares and public squares as last evening." Even the secession sympathizers seemed to feel as if a cloud had been rolled away from the heavens above them, and they might participate in the happiness of the better time coming for the whole country." Chase's diary entry was more laconic: "it was superb."[31]

Back in Baltimore, at the end of the week, Chase had dinner with several local leaders, including Thomas Swann and Richard Fuller, the Baptist minister. Chase wrote in his diary that he said after dinner that the "nation was bound to secure the right of voting to the loyal blacks of the rebel states," both for reasons of justice and prudence; that giving them the right to vote would "save us from much discord, violence, and disorder." Chase believed that the other guests agreed; at least they did not disagree. Fuller was glad that his own slaves were now free. "I thank God for emancipation," he said. "It has taken a great burden off my mind."[32]

After holding court in Baltimore on Saturday, April 8, Chase returned to Washington by the evening train. He attended Palm Sunday services at the Wesley Chapel, a Methodist church near his house, where "Dr. Nadal preached as usual." Lincoln returned to Washington this same Sunday after two weeks in Virginia, including a visit to the captured Confederate capital. After talking with Lincoln, Sumner wrote to Chase that the president was "full of tenderness to all and several times repeated 'judge not that ye be not judged.' This he said even when Jeff Davis was named as one who should not be pardoned." Sumner, on the other hand, was more sure than ever of the "utter impossibility of any organization which is not founded on the votes of the negroes." On Sunday night, news reached Washington that Lee had surrendered his army to Grant. Under Grant's generous terms, after surrendering their arms, and promising not to fight further, the former rebels could "return to their homes, not to be disturbed by the United States authority so long as they observe their parole and the laws in force where they may reside."[33]

Not much work was done in Washington on Monday; people were too busy celebrating. Chase took the early train to Baltimore, where he had to hold a few more days of circuit court. On Tuesday, April 11, after dealing with "ordinary business at the court," and dining with Baltimore friends, Chase wrote a long letter to Lincoln. After a few words of congratulation, the chief justice said that he was "very anxious about the future"

and especially about the "principles which are to govern reconstruction."
With respect to Virginia, Chase reminded Lincoln that by the "action of
every branch of the government, we are committed to the recognition
and maintenance of the state organization of which Governor Pierpont
is the head." Lincoln, while in Virginia, had authorized the members of
the rebel legislature to assemble in Richmond "for purpose of recalling
Virginia soldiers from rebel armies." Chase did not know the details of
what the president had said on this point—and indeed they are still
disputed among scholars—but in Chase's view, it would be far better to
"stand by the loyal organization already recognized": the government of
Francis Pierpont.[34]

With respect to the other rebel states, Chase urged Lincoln to adopt
a voter registration process that would include all loyal citizens "without
regard to complexion" and to insist that new state constitutions secure
"suffrage to all citizens of proper age and unconvicted of crime." This
approach was "recommended by its simplicity, facility, and, above all,
justice. It will be, hereafter, counted equally a crime and a folly if the
colored loyalists of the rebel states shall be left to the control of restored
rebels, not likely in that case to be either wise or just." In the case of Louisiana, there already was a government, recognized by Lincoln although
not by Congress, but "happily the constitution enables the legislature to
extend the right of suffrage" to blacks. Chase had no doubt that if Lincoln
declared that the extension of suffrage to "colored citizens on equal terms
with white citizens is believed to be necessary to the future tranquility
of the country as well as just in itself, the legislature will act promptly
in the desired direction."[35]

At more or less the same time that Chase was writing this letter to
Lincoln, the president was giving a speech from the White House steps
about reconstruction and Louisiana. After congratulating the armies,
Lincoln reminded the audience of his 10 percent plan. He noted that
when he presented the plan to the Cabinet, they had all approved except
for one member, who wanted Lincoln to extend emancipation to all of
Virginia and Louisiana and who opposed apprenticeship for the former
slaves. Even this member (Chase, although Lincoln did not name him in
the speech) approved other aspects of the plan and approved formation
of a Louisiana government. Lincoln noted that the new Louisiana constitution prohibited slavery and provided for black education. Responding
to Chase and others who hoped to see blacks vote, Lincoln now spoke in

favor of limited black suffrage, saying that he would prefer to see at least the "very intelligent, and those who serve our cause as soldiers" have the right to vote. His main point was that it was better to work with the current Louisiana government than to start afresh in drafting a new state constitution. "Concede that the government of Louisiana is only to what it should be as the egg is to the fowl, we shall sooner have the fowl by hatching the egg than by smashing it."[36]

After reading the president's speech in the Baltimore papers, Chase wrote him a second, longer letter on Wednesday, April 12. Chase told Lincoln that he believed the main reason that Congress had not yet admitted representatives from Louisiana (as Lincoln wanted so keenly) was that "many of our best men in and out of Congress had become thoroughly convinced of the impolicy and injustice of allowing representation in Congress to states which had been in rebellion and were not yet prepared to concede equal political rights to all loyal citizens." Chase wished that Lincoln had been reading the New Orleans newspapers for the past few months, as he had. "If you had read what I have, your feelings of humanity and justice would not let you rest till *all* loyalists are made equal in the right of self-protection by suffrage." At one time, Chase would have been "reasonably contented" by what Lincoln had proposed in his speech—that is, "suffrage for the more intelligent and for those who have been soldiers." Now, however, he was "convinced that universal suffrage is demanded by sound policy and impartial justice alike." Rather than lengthen his letter to explain his reasons, he told Lincoln that he would "return to Washington in a day or two, and perhaps it will not be disagreeable to you to have the whole subject talked over." Chase signed himself "truly and faithfully yours."[37]

Chase spent the next day in court in Baltimore, hearing and deciding a case about illegal oyster dredging, then returned to Washington late. This was another night of celebration, with large crowds walking the streets, admiring the illuminated buildings. Katie and Nettie went out, but Chase was "tired and declined to go." On Friday, April 14, he wrote several letters, expressing in one the fear that Lincoln, in his recent meeting with Governor Pierpont, had raised the possibility of some combined "rebel-loyal organization" for Virginia. Lincoln should, in Chase's view, have insisted that the rebels recognize both the federal government and the Pierpont state government. "How strange that the president should hesitate about a course so direct and so plain, and prefer, or seem to prefer, one so unfriendly to those who abided in their loyalty."[38]

In the late afternoon of the fourteenth, Chase and Nettie took a carriage ride. Chase intended to stop to see Lincoln—to "talk with him about universal suffrage in reorganization"—but "felt reluctant to call lest my talk might annoy him and do more harm than good." Chase returned home a little after dark and retired about ten. At around eleven, a Treasury clerk arrived and demanded to see the former secretary "on important business." The clerk told Chase that he had just come from Ford's Theatre, where the "president had been shot in his box by a man who leaped from the box upon the stage and escaped by the rear." Chase prayed that the clerk "might be mistaken," but soon three others, including his friend William Mellen, arrived to confirm the dreadful news and to add that William Seward "had also been assassinated" in his home. Chase's "first impulse was to rise immediately and go to the president, whom I could not yet believe to have been fatally wounded; but reflecting that I could not possibly be of any service and should probably be in the way of those who could, I resolved to wait for morning." In a little while, a military guard arrived outside the Chase house, "for it was supposed that I was one of the intended victims." All through the night, Chase wrote, he heard the "heavy tramp-tramp" of the boots of the soldiers on the street outside his house. It was "a night of horror."[39]

"Morning came with a heavy rain," Chase wrote to his friend Charlotte Eastman, "as if the skies were weeping, and the heavens had clothed themselves with mourning." Leaving early, he and Mellen walked the ten blocks to Seward's house on Lafayette Square. Passing near Ford's Theatre on their way, they heard that Lincoln had just died, in a house across the street from the theater. They probably also heard that the assassin at Ford's was the famous Shakespearean actor, John Wilkes Booth, and that he had escaped on horseback. At Seward's house, Chase learned that there was a second assassin, later identified as Lewis Powell, who had entered the house, armed with a pistol and a knife, and then attacked six different people, including Seward, slashed about the face and neck, and his son Frederick, assistant secretary of state, whom Powell clubbed on the head with the pistol (after it misfired) as he tried to keep Powell out of his father's room. Chase heard that there was a "slight chance" that Seward would survive, but almost none for Frederick, "his skull having been penetrated to the brain by what seemed to be a blow from the hammer of a pistol." In the end, all those injured at the Seward house would survive.[40]

Chase then went to the Kirkwood House, the hotel where Vice President Johnson lodged, finding him "full of sorrow and anxiety." McCulloch and Speed arrived soon, saying they wanted to discuss the time and place for administering the oath. The four men agreed that Chase would give the oath to Johnson in the parlor of the Kirkwood at ten that morning. Chase and Speed then went to Speed's office to look at the precedents for swearing in a vice president as the new president. While they were walking, Speed said that at the prior day's Cabinet meeting, Lincoln admitted that he "had made a mistake at Richmond in sanctioning the assembly of the Virginia legislature and had perhaps been too fast in his desires for early reconstruction." Everything Speed said about Lincoln, Chase wrote, "deepened my sorrow for the country's great loss."[41]

Returning to the Kirkwood, Chase met Francis and Montgomery Blair, and "with tearful eye," told them that "from this day will cease all anger and bitterness between us." There were about a dozen men in the

Andrew Johnson, who became president on April 15, 1865,
after the assassination of Abraham Lincoln.

Kirkwood parlor as Chase administered the solemn presidential oath to Johnson. "You are president," Chase then told him. "May God support, guide, and bless you in your arduous duties." After the others had come forward to tender their "sad congratulations," the new president asked Chase if he should make some remarks. Chase said that he thought it would be "better to make a brief announcement to the people in the public prints." Johnson asked the chief justice to prepare something, and Chase left for an hour to write. Chase's draft was short and eloquent, suggesting that Johnson lament the "revered and beloved president" and ask for the "cooperation of all patriots and the prayers of all Christians." Johnson did not wait for Chase, however, and the brief comments he released to the papers were less about Lincoln and more about himself.[42]

The next day, April 16, was Easter Sunday. At the Wesley Chapel, Chase heard Dr. Nadal preach mainly about Lincoln, whom he had known and loved. "Abraham Lincoln was more than a ruler; he was the father of his people. And this day, in which the sun of victory is dimmed by his death—in which the churches of the land would be jubilant with the song of victory—gloom is upon us. We cover ourselves with sackcloth, we sit in ashes, and, as a nation, forget our victories, our power, our renown, in the dreadful calamity which has overtaken us." Nadal praised Lincoln's honesty and mercy. He "never uttered a bitter word even against the enemies of his country. He pursued his end in conquering them and bringing them back to their allegiance by every lawful means, but he never seemed to feel that there was any personal quarrel between himself and even the leaders of the rebellion." Chase's sadness was mixed with anger; he wrote a friend that the assassination was another "manifestation of the fiendish malignity of slavery."[43]

On this Sunday afternoon, several radical members of Congress met with the new president. They pressed Johnson to find, capture, and try Jefferson Davis for treason. (Davis and his Cabinet had fled Richmond just before the Union troops arrived; their whereabouts were not yet known.) One of the members of Congress wrote in his journal that Johnson's response was that "robbery is a crime; rape is a crime; murder is a crime; treason is a crime; and crime must be punished. The law provides for it, and the courts are open. Treason must be made infamous, and traitors must be impoverished." Similar remarks by Johnson were soon in the papers.[44]

Chase met several times with Johnson in the two weeks after Lincoln's death. He pressed the new president to include blacks as well as whites in the process of reorganizing the Southern states. He believed that Johnson agreed, writing to a friend that everything he had seen and heard from Johnson "gives me the greatest hopes. His ideas agree very nearly with my own and, of course, I think them right. So in darkness there is light." Charles Sumner, who met with Johnson several times during these weeks as well, was equally convinced that he favored universal suffrage. Johnson, Chase, and Sumner also discussed the Southern trip that Chase had been considering even before Lincoln's death. The new Treasury secretary, Hugh McCulloch, was planning to send Mellen, now a senior Treasury agent, on a seaborne survey of the key Southern ports, starting in Washington and ending in New Orleans. Chase, with Johnson's support, decided to join Mellen. As Sumner explained in a letter, Johnson believed that "all loyal people, without distinction of color, must be treated as citizens and must take part in any proceedings for reorganization." Johnson was reluctant to announce this policy from Washington but was "willing to make it known to the people in the rebel states." Johnson was sending Chase to the South, Sumner wrote, to "touch the necessary strings, as far as he can." Both Johnson and Stanton wrote official letters asking federal military officers in the South to extend to Chase their "courtesy, assistance, and protection."[45]

Just before he left for the South on April 29, Chase met with Johnson and read him a draft address on reconstruction that he had prepared for the president. "The civil war which has desolated our land, may now be regarded as ended," Chase started. "The time for reorganization and restoration has now come." Some white Southerners, by taking part in the rebel governments, had "disqualified themselves from participation in the work of reorganization." Black Southerners, however, had proved their loyalty. "Tens of thousands of them have enlisted and fought bravely under the national flag, and thousands have sealed their loyal devotion with their blood. It would be equally uncivil and unjust to deny to these loyal men the right of participation in the work of reorganization."[46]

The proper way to reorganize the Southern states, Chase's draft continued, was to enroll the loyal citizens in each state as the state's voters and for them to form a new state government, either by drafting a new constitution or amending the old one. "The first step is the enrollment, excluding no citizen because of nativity or complexion, and this can be effected either through the voluntary action of the loyal people or under the supervision of the national authorities." Sounding more like Lincoln than Johnson, Chase wrote that the war "into which the nation has been forced has been waged in no vindictive spirit nor with any purpose of subjugation." Now that this war was almost over, it was time for "all good citizens, putting aside all evil passions and discarding all idle regrets, [to] address themselves cheerfully to the work before them."[47]

Johnson stopped Chase from time to time as he was reading this draft and asked him to reread a sentence. When Chase had finished, Johnson said that he agreed with everything in Chase's draft, but "I don't see how I can issue such a document now. I am new and untried and cannot venture what I please." Chase responded that if Johnson would just issue "some simple declaration that the colored people are free and are citizens and are therefore entitled to vote in reorganization," the new president would have on his side "all the young brain and heart of the country" and also "all those who feel bound to sneeze when the president takes snuff—no small number—and you will be irresistible." In other words, far from being politically impossible, a fair reconstruction policy would be politically powerful. Chase urged Johnson to secure his place in history alongside Lincoln by taking a stand for suffrage as bold as Lincoln's stand for emancipation. By the end of their long conversation, Chase "almost hoped the president's reluctance was conquered and that the new and crowning proclamation would be issued securing equal and universal suffrage in reorganization."[48]

At about eight in the evening of May 1, 1865, Chase and his seventeen-year-old daughter, Nettie, boarded a federal revenue steamer at the Washington Navy Yard. Among those who joined them were Chase's friend Mellen, the Baptist minister Fuller, and Whitelaw Reid, correspondent for the *Cincinnati Gazette*. They stopped the next day at Fort Monroe, the place where General Butler had coined the term *contraband* to describe the slaves fleeing to the Union army. Chase now disliked the term, writing Stanton to suggest that he prohibit its use in official reports. "Words are things," he noted, "and terms implying degradation help to degrade." Changing ships, and continuing on the *Wayanda*, Chase and his party went to North Carolina, where he met several times with General Sherman. Chase and Sherman did not agree at all about universal suffrage. If the government adopted Chase's approach, Sherman warned him, it would "produce new war, and one which from its desultory character will be more bloody and destructive than the last." In Wilmington, Chase met with a black delegation, members of a local Union League, "of which there are three associations at Wilmington numbering two hundred members each." Their goals were simple: "education, improvement, and suffrage."[49]

Laura Towne's school for freed slaves on Saint Helena Island, South Carolina. Towne was one of the early volunteers to teach on the Sea Islands, and Chase saw her school on his Southern tour in 1865.

Early on the morning of May 11, the *Wayanda*, guided by a local pilot, entered the harbor at Charleston, South Carolina, and docked next to the flagship of Admiral John Dahlgren. After reading and debating so much about Charleston as the Civil War started, Chase was eager to see the place for himself, and his party spent several hours touring Fort Sumter and other sites. There was a pleasant lunch aboard the flagship and an evening reception in town, with the guests including Union Generals Rufus Saxton and Quincy Gillmore. Perhaps the high point of the day for Chase, however, was reading a few recent issues of the *New York Herald*. The most widely read paper in the nation was now urging Johnson to insist that the Southern states give blacks the right to vote. In words that Chase could have written himself, the *Herald* argued that blacks had earned the right through their brave military service. Black voting, the *Herald* claimed, was the best way for Johnson to silence Northern abolitionists and "neutralize the fire-eating political elements of the South for all time to come." Pointing out these articles in a letter to President Johnson and arguing again for universal suffrage, Chase told him that the *Herald* "never sustains a cause, which has been unpopular, until it is about to triumph."[50]

Chase spent the next morning in separate talks with black and white leaders of Charleston. Racial relations were tense; just before Chase arrived, there had been chaos at a meeting called to discuss reconstruction, with blacks insisting they could participate in any public gathering, and members of the "white chivalry" refusing to meet or talk with them. "Crowds of whites collected in the streets giving vent to their indignation," wrote the local reporter for the *New York Herald*. In his talks with white leaders, Chase did not hide his own preference for universal suffrage, although he conceded that Johnson might decide differently. The black leaders Chase met with, he reported to Johnson, "attach very great importance to the right of voting—more perhaps than to any other except that of personal liberty."[51]

Charleston, South Carolina, as it looked when Chase visited during his Southern tour.

Chase had been planning to leave Charleston in the afternoon, but Saxton persuaded him to stay until the evening so that he could speak at a late-afternoon meeting at Zion Church. When Chase and Gillmore arrived, they found it packed with five hundred whites and five thousand blacks. In a letter to Johnson, Chase described the audience as "full of the most ardent loyalty" and "quite as intelligent as a similar gathering in the North." Chase was greeted with cheers and introduced by Saxton as a lifelong "friend of freedom."[52]

At the outset of his speech, Chase explained that he had hoped to avoid a civil war: "I did not desire to see even the great good of emancipation effected at such a terrible cost." But once the "war came," Chase argued for emancipation in the Cabinet. "When that honored man—whose death this nation now mourns, in common with all lovers of freedom throughout the world—when that honored man made up his mind to declare that all men in this land shall be free, none gave it a more hearty sanction or a more emphatic amen than myself." Similarly, Chase said, he "never doubted" that it was right to enlist the former slaves in the Union army. "If we make them freemen, and the defense of their freedom is the defense of this nation, whose duty is it to bear arms, if not theirs?"[53]

Chase urged the blacks of Charleston to work hard. He claimed that their situation was not all that different from that which he had faced as a poor young western boy, with "no capital" other than "a free school education, which, thank God, this country gave to all her white children, and is now going to give to all the blacks who will take it. Well, upon such capital, we went to work, and we came to something. You can do the same thing if you will go to work in the same way." Chase warned that "if you spend your time in fretting because this or that white man has a better time than you or more advantages and take short cuts to what you may think success, you will, in the end, be very sadly disappointed." The right path was plain: "Take things patiently and faithfully; the result will be glorious. Let the soldier fight well, let the preacher preach well, let the carpenter shove his plane with all his might, and the planter put in and gather in as much corn or cotton as he can—working for fair wages, and as he gets able to hire others, paying them fair wages, too. Act thus and I have no fears for your future."[54]

As to black suffrage, Chase noted that he had been pressing for black voting rights for twenty years, since his silver pitcher speech in Cincinnati. "But the colored man did not get the franchise because I said it then. Quite possibly, he may not now." Chase said that he did not know what the Johnson administration would do about black Southern suffrage, then confused the question by saying that "there is not a member of the government who would not be pleased to see universal suffrage." If black voting rights were at first denied, however, Chase counseled patience. In that case, blacks should "go to work and show that the United States government was mistaken in making the delay. If you show that, the mistake will be corrected."[55]

Chase closed with a reflection on life and the afterlife. "When a man has been faithful in the honest performance of his duty, he is thought better off if success attend him in this world. But if it so happens, in the Providence of God, that these material results do *not* follow that performance, still he carries in his own mind the consciousness that he has tried to do what is right in the sight of God, rendering to everybody his due, contributing all he can to the general happiness and improvement, diffusing as much enjoyment and contentment as he can in the little circle of which he is the center." Such a man could go through life "happy as a king, though he may never be a king," and after death could go "where there is an end of controversies, because there is but one God and one Father, before whom all his children are equal."[56]

Chase spent the next few days in the Sea Islands, at this point an almost entirely black community, with only a handful of white schoolteachers and military officers. Having worked so hard with Edward Pierce and others to help the blacks of the Sea Islands, Chase was pleased to see the progress of the black community. On Sunday, his friend Mansfield French preached to a "great crowd of colored people" in the space between "several huge, live oaks festooned with moss," and Chase added what he called a "short exhortation to industry, temperance, truthfulness, and self-education." The chief justice was especially "gratified by the extreme anxiety which almost all manifested for education." As Chase's ship approached Savannah early on May 16, he was awakened as the ship tied up to another vessel. An aide rapped on his door and informed him that "Jefferson Davis is here—he's caught." Thus did Chase learn that, after a monthlong manhunt, federal forces had at last captured the head of the rebellion on May 10. Gillmore told Chase that he could see Davis if he wished, but Chase declined, writing to Johnson that he "would not make a show of a fallen enemy." Chase found Savannah very much like Charleston, and people pressed him to give a speech, but he declined, telling Johnson that he had "determined to make no more addresses, fearing I might be taken for a politician or preacher rather than a chief justice."[57]

The main point of Chase's long letters to Johnson was to press him to adopt a system of universal suffrage. Chase admitted that most Southern whites would prefer a system in which only whites voted, although he noted that some whites who had remained loyal to the Union feared retaliation if the Southern blacks did not also have voting rights. Chase insisted, however, that almost all Southern whites would acquiesce in whatever system Johnson devised. He provided Johnson with detailed suggestions about how best to register the voters and conduct elections, suggesting, for example, that it would be better to have county election boards, rather than military officers, compile the new voting lists. Playing to the president's pride, Chase said that he hoped Johnson would "make your administration so beneficent and so illustrious by great acts that the people will be as little willing to shove Andrew Johnson from their mind as to shove Andrew Jackson." It would be "an exceedingly great pleasure for me if I can in any way promote its complete success."[58]

Chase and his party now headed south to Florida, stopping at Fernandina, Jacksonville, Saint Augustine, and Key West. In Fernandina, Chase was pleased to meet Adolphus Mot, the Chase family's former French teacher, just voted town mayor in an election in which both blacks and whites voted. Mot asked the chief justice to administer the oath, and Chase thus had what he described to Kate as "the honor of swearing in the first mayor chosen by universal suffrage south of Mason & Dixon's line." In Key West, Chase wished Kate could have seen the lush tropical plants and trees. "Still more," Chase wrote, "do I wish that you could have visited old Sandy with us—an old negro, seventy-two years old, active, energetic, with his plantation of every tree and flower that grows here."[59]

After Key West, Chase and his party went to Havana, Cuba. Chase often talked about traveling to Europe, but he never managed to find the time, so his few days in Spanish Cuba were the closest that he would get to the Old World. Chase wrote Kate a long, descriptive letter, relating among other details how the American vice consul told Nettie that she would not want to be seen at the paseo, the ritual evening stroll around the center of the city, because she was not properly dressed. Nettie laughed at his concerns, and they continued on their way in the carriage, although even her father had to admit that his daughter was not quite as handsomely attired as the local ladies. But since Nettie's "purpose was to see rather than be seen, she enjoyed this part of the drive very well."[60]

When the Chase party arrived in Mobile, Alabama, on June 2, or perhaps when they reached New Orleans on June 5, he learned that some Northern papers had attacked him for his Charleston speech. The *New York Herald,* which had completely changed its mind about black suffrage, now called Chase a "great negro worshipper" who was "on a stumping tour along the southern coast, entertaining the negroes with his ideas of reconstruction." The *New York World* said that it was utterly inappropriate for the chief justice to be "perambulating a disquieted portion of the country, making harangues on a disturbing question which the authorities have not yet decided." Chase also learned that Johnson had issued two important proclamations on May 29. The first, of which Chase generally approved, was an amnesty proclamation, granting a general pardon for most but not all who had participated in the rebellion. The second, which deeply troubled him, named a military governor for North Carolina and directed him to organize elections, in which only those who were qualified to vote under the old state constitution would be allowed to vote. Johnson had rejected Chase's advice about universal suffrage.[61]

Chase stayed more than a week in New Orleans, meeting again with both blacks and whites. He was "not much impressed" by a group of the city's leading lawyers, all white, but quite inspired by a dozen leading Creoles, including merchants and editors. They were "gentlemen, of refined manners and more than ordinary intelligence, and to all appearance as white as any equal number of confessed whites in the city." Yet because these mixed-race leaders were deemed black, they did not have the vote. In a letter that was widely reprinted, Chase declined to give a speech to the black people of New Orleans, saying that there was no need to repeat what he had said in Charleston. It was "both natural and right," Chase wrote, "that colored Americans, entitled to the rights of citizens, should claim their exercise. They should persist in this claim respectfully but firmly, taking care to bring no discredit upon it by their own action." The experience of the American states demonstrated, he went on, "that public order reposes most securely on the broad base of universal suffrage. It has proved, also, that universal suffrage is the surest guarantee and most powerful stimulus of individual, social, and political progress."[62]

From New Orleans, Chase and his party made their way slowly up the Mississippi River, pausing to see sights along the way. They stopped at

Vicksburg, where they toured the battlefield in a driving rain. In Memphis, Chase was dismayed to learn that President Johnson had issued a proclamation for Mississippi akin to the North Carolina proclamation. (Johnson would soon issue similar proclamations for almost all the Southern states.) As he was approaching Cincinnati, Chase received the word for which he had been eagerly waiting: his daughter Kate had survived childbirth and delivered a healthy baby boy. Chase discouraged her idea of naming the child Salmon. "My only tolerable name is my surname," he wrote to her, "and William is not only a better one, but is the name of one to whom *your first duties* belong"—namely, her husband. The boy would be William.[63]

In late June, Chase spent a few days in Cincinnati and Cleveland, seeing friends and catching up on his correspondence. He wrote to Sumner that Johnson's refusal to "recognize the colored citizens as part of the people" was a "moral, political, and legal mistake." Chase believed that the "vanquished rebels were ready to accept, though, of course, reluctantly, universal suffrage; a large portion of the loyal whites regarded it as essential to their own safety; the whole body of the colored citizens were anxious for it and will never be satisfied or work contentedly without it." Moreover, Chase was sure that the South would be more prosperous with black voting than without it. He estimated the "commercial and financial value of the products of labor for five years with universal suffrage at not less than five hundred millions of dollars more than their probable amount without it." He was "grievously disappointed."[64]

Chase hoped that Congress would correct President Johnson's error. He wrote to his protégé Jacob Schuckers that Congress could "pass a simple law of reorganization providing for the enrollment of all loyal citizens," and that Johnson would not "interfere" with Congress. Even if Congress did not pass such a law, "we must by no means despair. Truth will prevail at last." Nor did Chase despair of Johnson, writing that Republicans should "hold together and support the president just as far as we can. He will, in almost all things—such at least is my confidence—coincide in judgment with the progressive men of the party."[65]

By early July, Chase was at the Sprague farm in Rhode Island with his daughter and grandson, both of whom were "in excellent health." Chase reported from there to James Pike that he had just learned that four defendants, including Lewis Powell, tried and convicted by military commission for their roles in the Lincoln assassination, and the attempted assassination of the Sewards, had died on the scaffold in Washington. "I sincerely hope we have now seen the last of military commissions. However warranted by laws of war or even indispensable, they should be resorted to as sparely as possible." In a letter to Hiram Barney, Chase used for the first time a phrase he would employ often, writing that he would "prefer universal suffrage and universal amnesty to any policy I have seen indicated." When Barney questioned whether the South was ready for universal amnesty, Chase refined his recommendation: "I am not for universal suffrage and universal amnesty except on condition that the first precede the second by sufficient time and trial to ensure safety. Universal suffrage first and universal amnesty afterwards as soon as safe is my idea."[66]

Chase spent a few days in Hanover in late July to attend the Dartmouth commencement. Perhaps thinking there were no reporters present, he talked freely in an after-dinner speech, saying that "no reorganization of the country will be complete and permanent until every man in it, of whatever color, is allowed to vote." Chase disagreed with those who claimed that Southern blacks were not intelligent enough to vote. In his recent travels, he had found many intelligent men among them: "carpenters, merchants, blacksmiths, preachers." Some of them could construct a political ticket, and "others have sufficient intelligence to vote when it is put in their hands." This, he said, was what most white men did: vote for the ticket of their party, without thinking about individual candidates. Chase's remarks soon appeared in the press, and Democratic papers again criticized the chief justice for making political speeches.[67]

After a few days in Boston, Chase went to Newport, Rhode Island, in early August. His vacation there was cut short by a telegram from President Johnson, asking Chase to come to Washington as soon as convenient to discuss the "time, place, and manner of the trial of Jefferson Davis." Johnson saw this as a simple case: Davis was a traitor and must be tried, convicted, and punished. Chase, however, realized that the Davis case was far more complex. Although from time to time he had called the Southern leaders traitors, he knew that they could not be deemed traitors if their states had legally seceded from the Union. A treason trial would have to take place in the district in which Davis committed treason, presumably Virginia, raising the practical question of whether any Virginia jury would convict him. Indeed, the case might not even reach the jury: advisers warned Johnson that Chase would probably rule, as circuit justice, that secession was legitimate, and that Davis thus could not be tried for treason. Because of such concerns, some papers were already suggesting that a military commission try Davis for war crimes, such as the mistreatment of Union prisoners and the assassination of Lincoln. But a military trial would raise other questions, including whether the government could prove that Davis was personally involved in these crimes. And, thinking about how best to bring the Union back together, Chase hoped that Johnson would adopt Lincoln's merciful policy. Universal amnesty meant amnesty even for Jefferson Davis.[68]

Chase did not discuss any of this with Johnson when they met in Washington in August 1865. Instead, as he reported to Charles Sumner, he told the president that he did not think that the Davis trial was "a proper subject of conference between the president and chief justice." Johnson seemed to accept this. In a second conversation, Johnson talked with Chase "very freely about reorganization." Johnson said that in his view the blacks were entitled to their freedom but had no right to suffrage. Furthermore, he found the argument that they were entitled to vote because of their military service "unsound." After all, there were thousands of "young fellows of sixteen and eighteen who have fought bravely," and nobody believed that this entitled these boys to vote. And there were "multitudes of noble women who have risked so much and labored so devotedly. But nobody asks to have them vote." (There *were* people arguing that women should vote, but Johnson disregarded them.) The president then told Chase that "the races must separate" and alluded to his Moses speech, suggesting that what Johnson had in mind was to move blacks out of the South, as Moses had led the Jews out of Egypt.[69]

At this point, the chief justice interrupted the president, telling Johnson that he had "thrown a new light on your offer to be the Moses of the colored people. I supposed it was an offer to lead them out of their condition as slaves, into a new condition of freedom and citizenship." Chase then explained his own view that "blacks were citizens of the United States and of the states in which they live" and, as such, were entitled to "their fair share of influence and control in the work of reorganization." Johnson "listened kindly" and tried to emphasize the points on which he and Chase agreed, such as the "continued existence of the states" and the "natural rights of all men, white or black." But it seemed to Chase that, from Johnson's perspective, the "natural rights" of blacks were rather limited.[70]

Chase remained in Washington for a few weeks, then went to New York and Ohio, where he served as chair of a two-day Christian convention. In early October Chase spent a week on tiny Gibraltar Island, the private retreat of Jay Cooke, in the midst of Lake Erie. Chase, Cooke, and the other guests spent much of their time fishing. Cooke described in his journal how Chase hooked a large muskellunge, "apparently about half the boat's length," but the fish "rebelled stoutly against being brought before the chief justice of our nation. Perhaps he was a Canadian sympathizer with the Southern rebels." Chase's line snapped just as he was about to bring the struggling fish into the boat. Each day started and ended with prayers, and on Sunday they attended services in both the morning and evening at the nearby Episcopal church, of which Cooke was the principal patron.[71]

When Chase returned to the mainland, he found a letter from Johnson saying that the government might have to "prosecute some high crimes and misdemeanors committed against the United States within the district of Virginia," and asking whether Chase was planning to hold a circuit court in Virginia this coming fall or winter. Johnson did not mention Jefferson Davis, but Chase would have known that was whom Johnson had in mind. Chase responded that neither he nor any other justice would hold a circuit court in Virginia this year: "A civil court in a district under martial law can only act by the sanction and under the supervision of military power, and I cannot think that it becomes the justices of the Supreme Court to exercise jurisdiction under such conditions."[72]

December 1865 was a busy time in Washington. President Johnson delivered his first annual message, a balanced document that managed to please most people. Congress started work but—as per prior agreement among Republicans—did not seat the representatives from the Southern states. Instead, Congress formed a Joint Committee on Reconstruction, to examine the situation in the South. This was not because most Republicans agreed with Chase and wanted to see universal suffrage in the South; in fact, very few agreed with him on this issue. But most Republicans were concerned that the new Southern legislatures were adopting black codes, to limit the rights of Southern blacks, by requiring them to sign yearlong work contracts and by denying them various rights, including the right to own guns or travel without permission. Republicans were also deeply troubled by the frequent reports of white violence against blacks and white loyalists in the South. President Johnson, on the other hand, was far more troubled by the exclusion of Southern representatives from the halls of Congress; he blamed the radical Republicans for seizing power.[73]

The Supreme Court would also face reconstruction issues this winter, starting with the case of Augustus Garland, a respected lawyer from Arkansas who wanted to resume work in the federal courts even though he had served in the rebel Congress and thus could not take the required "ironclad oath." The courtroom was crowded on December 15 as Garland's counsel, Matthew Carpenter, later a leading Republican senator, argued that his client had received a full pardon from Johnson and that the time had come for reconciliation. Attorney General James Speed responded that Congress had broad authority to form the federal courts and to write their rules—including rules about who could practice before the federal courts.[74]

Almost buried in the newspapers were reports that several Southern legislatures had ratified the antislavery constitutional amendment. Even South Carolina, having abolished slavery in its new state constitution, and fearing that without ratification it would not be admitted back into the Union, ratified the amendment in November. Within weeks, however, the same South Carolina legislature passed one of the strongest black codes, essentially requiring blacks to work as servants of white masters. On December 18, 1865, Secretary of State Seward, back at work after recovering from the assassination attempt, certified that because three-quarters of the state legislatures had ratified the amendment, it was part of the Constitution. Thus, slavery and involuntary servitude were formally and finally abolished throughout the United States. In a way, Chase had achieved the goal for which he had worked half his life. In another way, however, he had not yet achieved his goals, for Southern blacks faced a new quasi-slavery in the black codes. So it is perhaps not surprising that Chase did not mark Seward's order in his diary. He was already turning his attention to other issues: urging Congress to use its authority under the new amendment to prohibit new forms of slavery; persuading people that Southern blacks deserved the right to vote so that they could defend their interests at the polls; and arguing for universal amnesty as well as universal suffrage so that former rebels would also have the right to vote.[75]

CHAPTER 23

"The Most Dangerous Man"

1866—67

As the Supreme Court heard and decided cases in early 1866, Congress worked on major issues, including a civil rights act, a constitutional amendment, and a bill to strengthen the Freedmen's Bureau (a government agency to help former slaves). Although the freedmen's bill passed both houses with large majorities, President Johnson vetoed it, arguing that the bureau interfered in the Southern states and promoted the black race at the expense of whites. To avoid a complete break with the president, a few moderate Republican senators voted against the motion to override, so the bill did not become law. Johnson celebrated this legislative victory with an angry speech, saying the radical Republicans were as dangerous now as the Southern secessionists had been. A voice in the crowd called out for names, and Johnson answered, naming Sumner and Thaddeus Stevens as among those opposed to the "fundamental principles of the government." One of Johnson's supporters wrote him that he should have included Chase on this list, for he was "the most dangerous man in the country today. He has ability and cunning sufficient to stimulate men in high places to concoct evil, without the manliness or courage to face consequences." Johnson's correspondent warned that Chase wanted to become the next president—a warning that Johnson was hearing from many quarters.[1]

The Supreme Court heard arguments in three major reconstruction cases this winter. The first was the case about test oaths in federal court,

543

the *Garland* case. Another test oath case, *Cummings v. Missouri,* was even more dramatic. The defendant was a young Catholic priest, John Cummings, charged with the crime of celebrating Mass without having taken the required state oath. The new Missouri State Constitution, adopted in early 1865, required that priests, teachers, and others swear that they had not assisted or even sympathized with the rebellion. It was unclear whether Cummings was in any sense a rebel, but the Catholic bishop for the state had advised priests that they could not swear the oath "without a sacrifice of ecclesiastical liberty." The lawyers for Cummings could not argue that the state law violated the First Amendment because, at the time, the amendment restricted only the federal government; states were free to interfere with religious or other First Amendment rights. Cummings thus had to argue that the Missouri law was a bill of attainder (a law aimed at a specific person or persons) and ex post facto law (a law making illegal something that was legal at the time).[2]

The third major case on the court's docket was *Ex parte Milligan*. Army officers had arrested an Indiana lawyer, Lambdin Milligan, and others in 1864 and charged them before a military commission with plotting to make war against the United States. Milligan and two others were convicted and sentenced to death. Justice Davis, however, persuaded Johnson to delay the executions so that defense lawyers could petition the circuit court for a writ of habeas corpus. Then Davis, as circuit justice, agreed to disagree with the district judge on whether the military commission was an appropriate way to try Milligan, a civilian in a state where there was no active rebellion. The disagreement between the two circuit judges sent the case to the Supreme Court, where Milligan was ably represented by James Garfield, David Dudley Field, and Jeremiah Black, the latter of whom had served in the Buchanan administration as attorney general and secretary of state. The court devoted seven days to oral arguments in the *Milligan* case, with the courtroom packed each day.[3]

The court had not yet decided the test oath cases when its term ended in early April, so Chase announced that they would be continued until the next term, set to start in December. He explained to a friend that it was "too important a question to be disposed of under the pressure and in the hurry of the last days of a very laborious term" and that he intended over the next few weeks to "devote to the careful consideration of the elaborate arguments and numerous authorities on both sides all the time I can command." In another end-of-term action, the court ordered that

Milligan and the other prisoners be released but did not explain its decision through a written opinion. The court's April order about Milligan was short and vague, so it did not attract much attention—nothing like the attention that would come in December, when the court finally issued the full *Milligan* opinions.[4]

Not long after the court's session ended, Chase was distressed to read in the papers a letter from Reverdy Johnson, one of the lawyers in the test oath cases, saying that the court had decided to invalidate the test oaths but was withholding its decision. Chase was amazed that one of the justices would violate the confidentiality of the court to reveal how a case would be decided before the decision was announced. He would have been even more astounded to read the diary of Senator Orville Browning, for Justice Robert Grier had not only told his friend Browning how the case would be decided but also how each of the justices would vote. Chase wrote to Justice Samuel Miller, urging him to write a public letter explaining that the test oath cases were not yet decided. The chief justice feared that if he wrote the letter himself, it would "be imputed to mere partisanship." Although Miller shared Chase's outrage at the breach of confidentiality, he did not want to write a public letter, so the issue died.[5]

As soon as the court finished its work in early April 1866, Chase went to New York City to bid farewell to his daughters and his grandson as they left for several months in Europe. After watching them board the steamboat, Chase wrote to Nettie that it was "hard to part with you" and to think that the ship "was about to carry away across the ocean all the most precious ones in the world to me." The letters Chase wrote to his daughters while they were away were strikingly political, reporting on the deadlock between Johnson and Congress and the 1866 election prospects. Chase explained to Kate that "you and Nettie write such excellent letters that I begin to think that there was a great deal of sense in the remark I once made in answer to somebody who wanted to know my opinion of women's rights: that I was for putting everything in the hands of the women and letting them govern. Certainly I don't see but you and Nettie are as well qualified to take part in affairs as I was at your age." Chase chided eighteen-year-old Nettie about her spelling and punctuation, urging her to see if she could not write better letters than Kate, now twenty-five. "Spur up your Pegasus and make him keep step. Don't be in too great a hurry when you write to write well and correctly. . . . Let Pegasus use his wings, but do you use the reins."[6]

Although Chase and William Sprague shared the E Street house in Washington for several months while Kate was in Europe, their letters to her could not have been more different. Chase's letters were bright and cheerful and informative; Sprague's were dark and worrisome. In his first letter to his wife after her departure, Sprague wrote that he had "taken to whiskey since you left" and that he was "depressed past weakness." He warned that "you know I am fond of the ladies and must not blame me for indulging in that fondness." Indeed, he even came right out and said that he "must get some young woman to live with me." In another letter, Kate's husband admitted that his mind was "sadly disconnected." Some newspapers were commenting on the Rhode Island senator's drinking—one article suggested that he should stop using his shirt collar as a funnel—and Sprague complained that Chase "does not understand such weakness as *mine*." One wonders: Did Chase simply not notice Sprague's problems? Or did he decide not to trouble his daughter while she was in Europe?[7]

In March, while the Supreme Court heard arguments in the test oath cases, both houses of Congress passed a civil rights bill. Responding to the Southern black codes and acting on the basis of the new Thirteenth Amendment, Congress provided in this bill that all persons born in the United States were citizens and that all citizens would have certain basic rights, including the right to make and enforce contracts, and the right to "full and equal benefit of all laws and proceedings for the security of person and property." Andrew Johnson vetoed the bill, claiming it would lead to federal interference in the states and even to interracial marriages. First the Senate and then the House voted in April to override him, making the Civil Rights Act of 1866 the first major legislation passed over a presidential veto. Almost all Republicans voted in favor of the motion to override Johnson's veto, while almost all Democrats voted against it. On the evening of this historic House vote, Chase was in New York City, giving a speech about the hundredth anniversary of the Methodist Church in the United States. He praised Congress for passing the civil rights bill, saying that, in doing so, it reflected the "heartfelt sentiments and the fixed resolves of the whole American loyal people" when it "declared that these emancipated slaves shall be equal in civil rights with all other men."

According to one paper's account, this was greeted with warm applause, but when Chase went on to say that the former slaves must be allowed not merely the rights guaranteed in the new bill but also the right to vote, there was only "feeble applause." Chase's stance on black suffrage was not yet accepted by more than a few white Americans.[8]

Even more important than the Civil Rights Act was the Fourteenth Amendment—the most significant constitutional amendment yet. Congress considered a host of alternative amendments this spring, including one drafted by the chief justice. The first section of Chase's draft was like the second section of the amendment finally adopted. He suggested that "whenever in any state, the elective franchise shall be denied to any of its inhabitants, being male citizens of the United States and above the age of twenty-one years, for any cause except insurrection or rebellion against the United States, the basis of representation in such state shall be reduced in the proportion which the number of male citizens so excluded shall bear to the whole number of male citizens over twenty-one years of age." In other words, rather than require states to allow all men to vote, this section would encourage them to do so by reducing their representation in Congress to the extent that they denied adult males the right to vote. Some women objected strongly to this approach, with Elizabeth Cady Stanton, wife of Chase's friend Henry Stanton, warning that "if that word 'male' be inserted, it will take us at least a century to get it out." Chase's proposed second section suggested that "no payment shall ever be made by the United States for, or on account of, any debt contracted or incurred in aid of insurrection or rebellion against the United States; or for or on account of the emancipation of slaves." He also drafted a joint resolution, through which Congress would promise that as soon as a former Confederate state ratified the amendment, Congress would admit its senators and representatives.[9]

As it emerged from the committee on April 28, 1866, the draft constitutional amendment had five sections. The first section, drafted by Chase's friend John Bingham, provided that "No state shall make or enforce any law which shall abridge the privileges or immunities of citizens of the United States, nor shall any state deprive any person of life, liberty, or property without due process of law, nor deny to any person within its jurisdiction the equal protection of the laws." Section two of the committee draft was like Chase's draft about representation, although it excluded "Indians not taxed" from the calculation, a change to which Chase objected in a long letter to Bingham. Chase's principal point was that, by excluding Indians from the calculation, Congress was sanctioning mistreatment of Native Americans. "Let them be regarded as part of the basis of representation, and a motive of much force will be created for their consideration and protection against wrong and fraud and violence." Chase also highlighted the tension between section one of the amendment, which treated Indians as citizens because they were born within the United States, and section two, which excluded tribal Indians from the apportionment calculation. Bingham did not respond to Chase's letter and the final version of section two retained the "Indian exclusion" to which Chase objected.[10]

Section three of the committee's draft provided that, until July 4, 1870, those who had participated in the rebellion could not vote in federal elections unless Congress removed this restriction. As adopted, section three was more limited: it did not limit voting rights, only the right to hold office, and it only excluded those who had taken an oath to support the federal constitution and then participated in the rebellion. Section four was similar to Chase's draft second section, although more artfully worded; it avoided the word *slave* and referred instead to "any claim for compensation for loss of involuntary service or labor." Section five authorized Congress "to enforce by appropriate legislation the provisions of this article." The committee also proposed a bill, like Chase's resolution, stating that each Southern state would regain its congressional representation once it ratified the constitutional amendment.[11]

One might have thought that Chase would applaud the committee's draft, especially the first section, with its broad language about due process and equal protection, principles for which he had fought so long and so hard. But his initial reaction was cool. In a letter to Justice Field, Chase said that the draft amendment "seems all very well provided it can be carried; but I am afraid that it is, as people say, rather too big a contract." He did not object to anything in the committee's proposal, although he questioned the "sweep of the disfranchisement." But Chase feared that the committee was "undertaking too much" and added that "it seems to me that nothing is gained sufficiently important and unattainable by legislation, to warrant our friends in overloading the ship with amendment freight." In a similar letter to Wendell Phillips, Chase worried that the section denying voting rights to former rebels "looks too much like a device for the security of mere party ascendancy. For my part, I care a great deal more about enfranchisement than disfranchisement and wish to see the Constitution free of everything which can be safely left to legislation."[12]

As the constitutional amendment made its way through Congress, however, and went to the states for ratification, Chase grew much more enthusiastic. On the day after Congress approved the amendment, even before Secretary Seward sent the amendment to the states for their consideration, Chase wrote to Governor William Brownlow of Tennessee, urging him to call the state legislators into session so that they could immediately ratify the amendment. Chase wrote to Nettie that the Johnson administration was "straining every nerve to prevent the [Tennessee] legislature from coming together, or, if assembled, from action." He could not understand why the president opposed the amendment, since by ratifying it, the Southern states would regain representation in Congress—which Johnson claimed was his highest priority. But Johnson was more concerned to keep concepts such as "equal protection" out of the Constitution than he was to see Southern representatives back in Congress.[13]

There was another bill in Congress this spring of great interest to Chase: a proposal to increase the compensation of the justices and to reduce over time the number of justices from ten to seven. Indeed, a draft of the bill can be found among Chase's papers. The House version, which passed easily in March, pruned the number of justices to nine, while the Senate version followed Chase's lead and pushed for just seven justices, but did not increase salaries as he'd hoped. After Congress passed the bill, while it was awaiting President Johnson's signature, Chase wrote Sprague to say that he regretted that the bill left the salaries "untouched." In his view, the chief justice's salary should increase from $6,500 to $12,000, and each associate justice's, from $6,000 to at least $10,000. Chase urged his son-in-law to speak with other senators and "see what can be done."[14]

In its final form, the Judiciary Act of 1866 had only two sections: the first reducing the size of the court gradually, as justices died or retired, from ten to seven members, and the second reducing the number of judicial circuits from ten to nine and changing the boundaries of most of them. For example, the fourth circuit—the one Chase handled—no longer included Delaware but gained South Carolina. In an oversight, Congress had not provided any means of allocating the circuits among the justices, raising questions about which justice was responsible for which circuit, and whether the justices could agree among themselves on allocation or had to wait for legislation. This slipshod work by Congress would impede the justices and the circuit courts for the next few months.[15]

Reconstruction was the main issue in the 1866 congressional elections. Republicans said that the Fourteenth Amendment provided the proper approach for reconstruction and urged voters to endorse the amendment by voting for Republican congressional candidates. Chase was now completely committed to the constitutional amendment and wrote that he almost wished that he could "throw off the judicial robes which deny me political freedom and hasten to the side of those who . . . are fearlessly upholding the right." Democrats denounced the "negro-equality constitutional amendment" and urged voters to reject the amendment by voting for Democrats. Johnson, utterly opposed to the amendment, hoped to combine Democrats with conservative Republicans into a new party. His friends called for a National Union Convention in Philadelphia in August, with representatives from all the states, to celebrate peace and support Johnson. Chase disapproved, writing Nettie that the convention would be "just what patronage, with the help of hungry Democrats, can make it. But it will represent no ideas—nothing but platitudes—will not have the sympathy of the masses, and will fail."[16]

Even before the Philadelphia convention, an ill-fated attempted convention in New Orleans showed that there was no peace in the South. A few radical Republicans had called for a state constitutional convention to meet in New Orleans on July 30, hoping to revise the constitution so that blacks could vote. On the appointed day, the city's police officers, most of them former Confederate soldiers, and their white supporters attacked the delegates and their black supporters on the streets and in the convention hall. By the time federal troops finally restored order, thirty-seven blacks and three whites were dead. In the words of General Philip Sheridan, in his telegraphic report from New Orleans, it was "an absolute massacre." Chase and other Republicans blamed Johnson for the bloodshed; in their view, Johnson was encouraging Southern whites in their efforts to intimidate and attack blacks.[17]

Two weeks later, thousands crammed into a temporary convention hall in Philadelphia for the National Union Convention. The high point came at the outset, as the delegates from Massachusetts and South Carolina, the former centers of abolition and secession, entered the hall arm in arm. Many of the Southern delegates were former senior members of the Confederate army, while some of the Northerners were rabid anti-war Democrats such as Clement Vallandigham. There were almost no Republicans. In short, as Chase predicted, the arm-in-arm convention did not persuade many people who were not already inclined to support the president.[18]

Chase read about the events in New Orleans and Philadelphia in the Boston newspapers, for he spent much of the summer of 1866 in New England, and especially with Charlotte Eastman. He noted (briefly and illegibly) in his diary that one night in August, while he and Charlotte were staying at the home of another friend, Chase went to her room and pulled at the door. It "yielded a little," but he did not force it. The next day, she confided that "she wanted me and would have yielded if I had come in." Chase worried that this incident would tarnish their long friendship, but, at least according to his diary, she remained as warm and friendly as before.[19]

A few weeks later, when Schuckers asked Chase about rumors that he would marry Eastman, he responded that he would probably not marry again. "I don't absolutely renounce the idea, and I know no one better calculated to make the happiness of a home than the dear friend I have mentioned, with whom and in whose neighborhood I have passed some delightful days this summer." Chase continued to think about Eastman, writing Nettie a few months later that he liked her "as well as if not better than ever. But for the look of the thing in an old gentleman like me"—he was fifty-nine years old at the time—"and the feelings of Katie, and I daresay yours too, and some other considerations, who knows what I might not have been tempted to."[20]

Perhaps one reason that Chase did not propose to Charlotte Eastman was that she was not an intellectual woman. In praising her to Schuckers, Chase described her as "intelligent enough though not learned." Chase probably compared Eastman with Susan Walker, who at one point in her life served as a computer (a mathematician) for the federal government and who was now running an industrial sewing school for black women. Chase sometimes found Walker too serious—he noted in one letter that she seemed to prefer "martyrdom"—but he admired her commitment to the cause. Another woman with whom Chase may have compared Eastman was Lizzie Pike, who returned to the United States in the summer of 1866 after spending the war years in Europe, where her husband served as an American diplomat. Shortly before she returned, Lizzie wrote to Chase that although it was "very improper in me to say so," she was "just desperate to see you and hear you talk." She missed the "exhilaration" of "strong personalities" and their "intellectual qualities." Chase responded that it would be a "great pleasure to welcome you and Mr. Pike back to your native land."[21]

Not long after the arm-in-arm convention, Andrew Johnson decided to take his message directly to the people. In late August, accompanied by a large entourage, the president left Washington by train, bound for Chicago, where he was to dedicate a memorial to Stephen Douglas. The real purpose of Johnson's "swing around the circle" was to campaign for conservative congressional candidates. At every stop, he gave speeches, often responding to the crowds. In a late-night speech in Cleveland, for example, Johnson demanded to know whether anyone could "place his finger upon one pledge I ever violated."

A voice called out: "New Orleans!"

Then another urged the president to "hang Jeff Davis."

"Why don't *you* hang him?" Johnson retorted.

"Give us an opportunity!" the crowd yelled.

"Haven't you got the court?" Johnson asked. "Haven't you got the attorney general? Who is your chief justice, who has refused to sit on his trial?"

Near the end of this long, almost incoherent display, Johnson said he did not care about his dignity. The *New York Times,* although it still supported Johnson's policies, reproached him for this remark, saying that the American people could never see the dignity of the presidency diminished "without profound sorrow and solicitude."[22]

Chase wrote to Nettie that Johnson, on this campaign tour, was "mortifying his best and sincerest friends and injuring himself, I fear, beyond remedy." Chase especially resented Johnson's argument that Chase was somehow responsible for the delay in the treason trial of Jefferson Davis. Referring to himself in the third person, Chase wrote a long letter to Schuckers, explaining that the chief justice on circuit tried cases when and as they were ready for trial; that he still did not believe it proper for justices of the Supreme Court to hold circuit courts in Virginia and other regions under martial law; and that Congress had created a new problem with the recent law, the circuit allocation problem, which would prevent him and most of the other justices from attending circuit courts this fall and winter. Schuckers shared this letter with the *New-York Tribune*, which copied Chase's twelve points almost word for word in an editorial in late September. Other papers recognized that the *Tribune* was speaking for Chase, but Republican papers agreed with him, blaming Johnson for the delay.[23]

September brought yet another convention, this one mainly of Southerners opposed to Johnson, in Philadelphia. Chase went to Philadelphia, not as a delegate but as an observer. In private conversations with some of the delegates, he urged them to make the constitutional amendment "the platform for the present campaign, expressing my full belief that, though not all we desire or need, still it was a sufficient basis of reconstruction and a bridge over which we can pass to final and decisive victory." The black leader and editor Frederick Douglass, one of the Philadelphia delegates, delivered a fine speech about how the Declaration of Independence declared that all men—not merely all white men but *all* men—are created equal. It seems that Chase did not meet with Douglass on this trip, but he wrote in his diary that the black abolitionist was "doing himself and his race much good by his presence here. I wish he could come to Congress from his district."[24]

Although Chase did not give speeches during the fall campaign, he was active in ways that many viewed as political. In October, for example, Chase went to Baltimore to attend a meeting of the American Freedmen's Union Commission, a new charitable organization of which he had just been elected president. There were several black men and women on the stage, including Chase's friend Bishop Daniel Alexander Payne, whose opening prayer asked God to bless the United States and to "purge its high places of ungodly politicians." In a speech to a similar meeting in Philadelphia in November, Chase praised both the commission's work in educating Southern blacks and the pending constitutional amendment. "I think a more generous and more magnanimous proposition was never submitted to a people who had been in rebellion than the amendments which have been proposed by Congress," he stated. Chase wrote to a friend that "some people seem dreadfully afraid that I shall harm the dignity of the court or damage my own by taking part in meetings for the promotion of the welfare of such low creatures as 'niggers.'" Chase dismissed such fears, however, writing that "when I see an opportunity to do some good for black or white, I hope always to have courage enough to do it, and let dignity take care of itself."[25]

Voters in the five states that went to the polls in early October roundly rejected Johnson and supported the Fourteenth Amendment. Fifty members of the next Congress, from just these five states, would be Republican, with only eleven Democrats. Cheered by these results, Chase was confident that the amendment would soon be ratified, writing Nettie to predict that Missouri, Maryland, and Delaware would soon join Tennessee as former slave states that had formally approved the amendment.[26]

In late October Chase met with President Johnson and pressed him to reconsider his opposition to the amendment. If, Chase argued, "as everybody expected," the November elections confirmed that the people generally favored the amendment, Johnson "might yield his views to the popular decision, without discredit, and not only without discredit but with honor." Johnson, however, cared not only about Northern opinion but especially about Southern opinion, and there were no elections this fall in the Southern states under military reconstruction. The Southern newspapers, however, were almost all opposed to the amendment: "The Southern states cannot without degradation and dishonor ratify an amendment which inflicts the disgrace of disenfranchisement on a large number of their own citizens," insisted the *New Orleans Crescent*. Of course, the Southern opinion that mattered for Johnson and these editors was only Southern *white* opinion.[27]

Voters in twelve states, including New York, elected members of Congress in early November—again mainly Republicans, but with an important exception: Maryland sided with Johnson. Writing to Benjamin Cowen, head of the Ohio Republican Party, Chase blamed the Maryland result on several factors, including fear among "ignorant and debased" whites of "negro elevation and suffrage." Responding to Cowen's suggestion that the people would call on Chase as another Moses in order to "guide them out of the terrible wilderness," Chase thanked him for his support for the 1868 presidential nomination: "I will not deny that I should be greatly gratified by such a proof of public esteem, and especially by the support of Ohio." William Dean Howells, the author, recalled a conversation with Chase at about this time in which he confessed that the chief justiceship was "not the sort of office he had aspired to, and intimated that it was a defeat of his real aspirations." According to Howells, "it was his constant, his intense, his very just desire to be president; no man of his long time was fitter to be president, unless his ambition was a foible that unfitted him."[28]

Chase had two further conversations with Johnson in November, leading to newspaper speculation. Some papers claimed they were discussing an alternative version of the constitutional amendment; others, that they were talking about the Jefferson Davis trial. According to Democratic papers, the only reason that Chase was delaying the Davis trial was that he did not want to lose Republican support for the nomination. Chase wrote Horace Greeley to explain that he had proposed to Johnson that, if he could not accept the constitutional amendment in its current form, perhaps he could support a revised amendment "with a clause ensuring universal suffrage with universal amnesty." The president, however, was adamant, insisting that Congress had to admit Southern members immediately. According to Chase, he "came away with little or no hope, except in the providence of God and in the constancy of our people and their representatives."[29]

Papers were also reporting, in November, that Senator Sprague had sailed for Europe to discuss with his wife whether they should separate or stay together. The couple apparently agreed to reconcile, for in late November they returned to New York, and in December Chase had a "joyous reunion" with Kate in Washington. Nettie, meanwhile, remained in Dresden, Germany, for the winter to study art and languages. Chase wrote to her that he approved of her "determination to improve yourself in French and German and drawing." He cautioned her to "avoid all society not of the purest and highest character" and, indeed, urged her to "have as little intercourse as possible with English-speaking people. The more you force yourself to talk German and French, the better." He worried about her health and admonished her to "keep your feet dry and warm and your rooms well ventilated, without exposing yourself to draft." Chase recalled, even if Nettie could not, how her mother Belle had died young of tuberculosis.[30]

On December 17, 1866, the courtroom was crowded to hear first Justice Davis and then Chief Justice Chase read their opinions in the *Milligan* case. Writing for himself and four other justices, Davis declared that it was unconstitutional to try civilians in military courts when civilian courts were still open. Writing for himself and three other justices, Chase agreed with Davis that it had been improper to use a military commission to try Milligan but disagreed with Davis's broad constitutional condemnation of military courts. Chase focused on a point James Garfield had stressed: that using a military commission to try Milligan was not allowed by the terms of the Habeas Corpus Act of 1863, in which Congress had limited the use of military commissions. The court could not uphold the trial and conviction of Milligan, Chase wrote, "without disregarding the plain direction of Congress."[31]

For the chief justice, the *Milligan* case was only in part about events in Indiana in the recent past; it was also about the scope of federal authority in the South in the violent present. Chase was well aware that, in many parts of the South, the state civilian courts provided no protection for blacks; only the federal military courts would punish whites for crimes against blacks. A case pending in Virginia at the time the court released the *Milligan* opinions in December 1866 provided a perfect example. James Watson, a white doctor, was on his way to church by carriage when his neighbor's carriage, driven by a black servant, passed too close to the doctor's carriage, causing his horses to run wild for a few blocks. Soon thereafter, Watson sought out the black driver and shot him to death. The local authorities released the doctor after asking him only a few questions, leading one Northern paper to comment that Southern whites seemed to view killing a black as nothing unusual or criminal. Watson was then arrested a second time on the orders of General Sheridan, to be tried by military commission. Johnson ordered Sheridan to release Watson, however, on the basis of the recent *Milligan* decision. Southern papers rejoiced at Johnson's decision, with one announcing that "military commissions are dead." Chase's *Milligan* opinion showed that, in his view, military commissions were *not* dead—at least not if Congress decided they were necessary to control the ongoing white-on-black violence in the South.[32]

On January 14, 1867, the Supreme Court at last announced its decisions in the test oath cases. Justice Field, for a five-member majority, held that both the federal test oath (for lawyers practicing in federal courts) and the Missouri test oath (as applied to a Catholic priest) violated the Constitution. Field found that the test oath requirements were punishments that violated both the ex post facto and bill of attainder provisions of the Constitution. "Even people who agree with the outcome of the test oath

The Supreme Court in 1867 in one of its first group photos. From left to right, clerk Daniel Middleton, Justices David Davis, Noah Swayne, Robert Grier, and James Wayne, Chief Justice Chase, and Justices Samuel Nelson, Nathan Clifford, Samuel Miller, and Stephen Field.

case," wrote Field's best biographer, "would have difficulty denying that Field stretched the Constitution to get there."[33]

Justice Miller, writing for himself and three others, including Chase, dissented strongly. With respect to the federal test oath, Miller noted the broad authority of Congress to make rules for the federal courts and argued that all the law required was that lawyers who wanted to practice in federal courts "take the same oath which is exacted of every officer of the government, civil or military." With respect to the state test oath, Miller cited cases showing that the Constitution "makes no provision for protecting the citizens of the respective states in their religious liberties." Even in more extreme cases, the Supreme Court had refused to intervene when states denied their citizens religious liberty, and Miller and Chase did not see any basis in this case for the federal government to interfere with the state government's choices.[34]

Most Republicans were outraged by the *Milligan* and test oath decisions. The *Chicago Tribune* said these decisions showed a "deliberate purpose of the Supreme Court to usurp the legislative powers of the government" and to "defeat the will of the loyal men of this nation in the interests of a rebellion crushed by military power." The paper urged Congress to require the "concurrence of three-fourths, or at least two-thirds of the whole bench, to pronounce authoritatively against the constitutionality of any act of Congress." Lincoln had warned in his first inaugural, referring to the *Dred Scott* decision, that if the "policy of the government upon vital questions affecting the whole people is to be irrevocably fixed by decisions of the Supreme Court . . . the people will have ceased to be their own rulers." The *Tribune* now quoted Lincoln to warn that if Congress did not impose strict limits on the Supreme Court, "the people will cease to be their own rulers . . . and the rebellion will become as victorious as though Grant and Sherman had surrendered to Lee and [Joseph] Johnston."[35]

As violence continued in the South, Congress devised and passed the First Military Reconstruction Bill. The law divided the ten Southern states other than Tennessee into five military districts, each under the command of an army general to be appointed by the president. The principal duties of these commanders and their troops would be to "protect all persons in their person and property" and to "suppress insurrection, disorder, and violence." The bill also set out how the Southern states could rejoin the Union, starting with elections for state constitutional conventions in which both whites and blacks would vote, new state constitutions that allowed for black voting, and ratification of the pending constitutional amendment. Only after completing this process could the representatives of the Southern states return to Congress. Johnson denounced and vetoed the bill, but Congress immediately overrode him. Although Chase would later oppose military reconstruction, he supported this bill when it first passed.[36]

Congress passed three other measures important to Chase in early March 1867. First, it fixed the circuit allocation issue, giving the justices the authority to allocate the circuits among themselves. Second, Congress passed a new federal bankruptcy law, authorizing the appointment of bankruptcy registers—court officials akin to today's bankruptcy judges. The law provided that the district judges would appoint the bankruptcy registers "upon the nomination and recommendation of the chief justice." At the time, some interpreted this as a slap at Johnson, and perhaps it was, but even today, bankruptcy judges are not appointed by the president but by the judges of the circuit court. Chase would devote much of the next few months to finding and appointing men as bankruptcy registers.

Third, Congress passed the Tenure of Office Act, which provided that presidential appointees confirmed by the Senate could not be removed by the president without Senate consent. This had no immediate effect on Chase but would form the basis of the impeachment of Johnson and the impeachment trial over which Chase would preside in the spring of 1868.[37]

Each session of Congress in the nineteenth century ended at noon on the fourth of March of an odd-numbered year. Normally, a new Congress would not gather until December, so the Fortieth Congress would not have gathered until December 1867. Republicans were worried, however, about what Johnson would do if there was a long congressional recess, so the Fortieth Congress convened and started work on the very day that the Thirty-Ninth ended. "The king is dead," Chase quipped in French to Nettie, "long live the king." One of the first tasks of this new Congress was to fix a gap in the reconstruction law and specify how the new military commanders should register voters. Chase had been considering the registration process since his Southern tour, and perhaps this is why Senator Henry Wilson of Massachusetts turned to Chase for help in drafting a voter registration bill. Wilson introduced the bill in early March, and Congress passed it before month's end. Chase's role in drafting this second military reconstruction bill was not known at the time. If it was, he would have received then some of the criticism he has received since, for he should have realized that preparing a controversial political bill was not an appropriate role for the chief justice.[38]

Indeed, on April 4, lawyers for Mississippi filed in the Supreme Court a petition challenging both military reconstruction laws and seeking an injunction to prohibit President Johnson from implementing them. The state argued that military reconstruction would deprive the Southern states of "every attribute of state authority" and deprive their people of their "most sacred rights." After hearing oral argument, the Supreme Court, in a unanimous opinion by Chase, dismissed the state's petition. Chase relied heavily upon the 1803 opinion of his predecessor, Chief Justice John Marshall, in *Marbury v. Madison*. In that case, William Marbury had been nominated and confirmed as justice of the peace, and his commission signed and sealed, but not delivered by Secretary of State James Madison. "Nothing was left to discretion" Chase wrote. "The law required the performance of a single specific act, and that performance, it was held, might be required" by court order. In the current case, in contrast, Congress had given the president broad authority by the two recent reconstruction laws, and the petition asked the court to declare the laws unconstitutional before the president had even implemented them. Quoting Marshall, Chase said that such an order would be "an absurd and excessive extravagance."[39]

A second Southern challenge to military reconstruction followed almost immediately: Georgia filed suit in the Supreme Court, seeking to prohibit Secretary Stanton and General Grant from implementing the reconstruction laws. As the lawyers presented their arguments, the court-room was crowded, according to the *Philadelphia Inquirer*, with "rebels and their sympathizers, who did not look as though they were aware that the late rebellion was over." On May 13 Chase announced that the court had dismissed the Georgia case and promised that the opinion would follow "hereafter." Republican papers and periodicals, which had been so critical after the test oath decisions, now praised the court, with one calling the reconstruction decisions "unqualifiedly beneficial" because they paved the way for the "speedy reorganization of the South under the Reconstruction Act."[40]

Chase had a chance to see some of the South himself in June 1867, for his fourth circuit now included Virginia and the Carolinas, and he was to hold court this month in North Carolina. To get there, Chase went by boat from Washington to Aquia, the former Union supply base in northern Virginia, and by train from there to Fredericksburg and Richmond. He reported to Nettie that the first miles in the train covered "pretty well-known ground," for he had "traversed it when McDowell was encamped there and afterwards when Hooker was in command." In Richmond, Chase reflected on "pleasant days" with the Wirts and other families "long, long ago." He also recalled more recent events, such as the grim conditions for Union prisoners on Belle Isle and in Libby Prison. South of Petersburg, the next day, the train passed through "Lee's lines of defense and then through Grant's lines of attack. There they stretch away, right and left, for miles and miles. They still look formidable."[41]

When Chase arrived in Raleigh, North Carolina, he was greeted at the station by a crowd, mainly black but including some of the town's white leaders. In brief remarks, Chase thanked the people for their warm welcome. "You rejoice, and I rejoice with you, that at length throughout our country, all men are free—all equal before the law—all assured of fair opportunities for improving their condition in life. You mean, I am sure, to use this freedom and these opportunities for the advancement of the best interests of the whole community." The *Raleigh Daily Standard* said that the "colored people turned out in large numbers" to show their respect for the chief justice and because they knew Chase as "one of their earliest, most zealous, and most steadfast friends."[42]

Chase opened court the next day with a brief explanation of why the justices had not participated in Southern circuit courts until this time. Then he and the district judge, sitting together as the federal circuit court, settled down to the work of trying cases, most of which were mundane. In the evenings, Chase met with the leaders of Raleigh, both black and white. He was especially impressed by James Harris, a young black leader who had studied at Oberlin and was now working with blacks in Raleigh. Chase wrote the abolitionist Gerrit Smith that he "could not put $50 or $100 to a better use than sending it to [Harris] to aid in paying his expenses." As for the whites, Chase wrote to David Davis that they generally accepted that slavery was over, and many agreed that the "negro must vote." On Sundays Chase made a point of attending services at both black and white churches. He described the scene for Smith: the chief justice of the United States in a pew at a black church in the South, "seated between a Union officer and an ex-member of Stonewall Jackson's staff."[43]

One case on the Raleigh docket, *Shortridge v. Macon*, presented important national issues. Pennsylvania plaintiffs had sued a North Carolina defendant to recover a prewar debt. The defendant claimed that he did not owe the plaintiffs because the Confederate government had confiscated all debts owed to Northern creditors, forcing him and others to pay the amounts owed into the Confederate Treasury. This was another case about secession: the defendant argued that secession was legitimate, or at least that the Confederacy was the de facto government of the South during the Civil War, entitled to impose duties on its citizens such as his duty to "pay into the Treasury" the amounts he owed his Northern creditors.[44]

In his *Shortridge* decision, widely reprinted, Chase responded that the Constitution did not grant states any right to secede: "War, therefore, levied against the United States by the citizens of the republic under the pretended authority of the . . . so-called Confederate government . . . was treason against the United States." The chief justice also disagreed with those "learned persons" who contended that "when rebellion attains the

proportions and assumes the character of civil war, it is purged of its treasonable character and can only be punished by the defeat of its armies, the
disappointment of its hopes, and the calamities incident to unsuccessful
war." Chase was responding here to a public letter from Gerrit Smith,
making just this argument. "Courts have no policy and can exercise no
political powers," Chase wrote in his opinion. "They can only declare the
law. On what sound principle, then, can we say judicially that the levying
of war ceases to be treason when the war becomes formidable? That war
levied by ten men or ten hundred, is certainly treason, but is no longer
such when levied by ten thousand or ten hundred thousand?"[45]

Everyone understood that Chase's *Shortridge* decision would affect many
other cases. Southerners were concerned about the status of a wide range
of routine actions by state governments during the war years. Was Chase
suggesting that federal courts would not recognize *anything* done by the
rebel state governments? And then there was Jefferson Davis, recently
released on bail but still facing federal treason charges. Horace Greeley,
who had become a strong advocate for Davis and, indeed, was one of
those who signed the bond that allowed Davis out of prison, criticized
the *Shortridge* decision in the *New-York Tribune*. Chase immediately wrote
Greeley to defend his decision, arguing that the definition of treason in
the Constitution was "so plain that it can't be made plainer." What, he
asked rhetorically, "is the business of a court? To fritter away plain words
by arbitrary interpretation? Or, to declare their obvious meaning and leave
to the political departments of the government the duty of applying the
proper mitigations?" In a similar letter to Gerrit Smith, who had also
signed the bond to release Davis, Chase contrasted his role as a judge, to
declare and enforce the law, with his prior role as a governor, when he
exercised the right to pardon. "As governor of Ohio, I pardoned many a
man whom, had I been judge, I should have felt bound to sentence to the
penitentiary. And the president and Congress in the exercise of political
power and discretion can, whenever they think fit, proclaim universal
amnesty." Chase did not quite say that if he were Johnson, he would
pardon Davis, but he came close.[46]

Chase's home was once again empty in the summer of 1867. Kate and
her son had returned to Europe, where Nettie remained after her winter
in Dresden. In early July Chase reported to Nettie on a conversation with

a young friend from Oregon, who was "now bent on securing for me the support of all the Pacific states in the next presidential nomination. And it does look now that if there were no military names before the public, the choice of the people might fall on me." General Grant was by this time the leading candidate for the Republican nomination, although there was also talk about Butler or Sheridan. "Many seem to think that the nomination of a military candidate is a predestined event, which must take place anyhow, and against which it is useless to make opposition." Chase could "easily see that I am not much more likely to be preferred than I was in 1860 or 1864. So I make myself contented—or try to." Chase did not deny his hopes, for he thought he could accomplish "much that would be beneficial to the country," and he was "not insensible to the distinctions of the Chief Magistracy. But if the people don't want my services, I have no right to complain."[47]

Chase was in a curious political position in the summer of 1867. He was often mentioned as a Republican presidential candidate, but he remained on at least polite terms with Johnson, who saw himself as the leading Democratic candidate. Most Republicans believed that Johnson was trying to impede military reconstruction, but Chase disagreed, writing to John Russell Young, an editor of the *New-York Tribune*, "I see no ground for thinking that the president has not intended to carry out the reconstruction acts in good faith." In a similar letter to his friend Theodore Tilton, editor of a weekly magazine called the *Independent*, Chase wrote that Johnson "assures me now that he is in favor of universal suffrage." If the president did, in fact, tell Chase that he supported universal suffrage, he must have meant universal suffrage for *white* men, for no one in Washington was more opposed to *black* suffrage than Johnson.[48]

The *Tribune* had recently printed and criticized a legal opinion by Attorney General Henry Stanbery interpreting and (in the radical view) emasculating the military reconstruction laws. Chase defended Johnson on this score as well, saying that he "certainly was not to blame for calling for the opinion of the attorney general . . . nor can he be blamed for agreeing with the attorney general on points of construction." Chase defended Stanbery, too, saying that he had known him for many years and was "sure of his great legal abilities and equally sure that he is an upright and loyal man." The papers had also recently printed a letter from General Sheridan to Grant, calling the section of Stanbery's opinion that denied the military officers any right to question a former rebel's claim that he was entitled to vote a "broad macadamized road to perjury and fraud." Chase may not have liked seeing Sheridan's letter in the papers, but he agreed on the substance, so he was pleased when Congress overruled this section of Stanbery's opinion through a third reconstruction law, passed over yet another Johnson veto.[49]

When Johnson asked Chase to visit the White House in early August, the chief justice reported to Greeley that the president "received me kindly, as he always does." Johnson was angry at General Sheridan, especially at his letter "published at New Orleans and New York almost before mailed." Johnson also disagreed with other decisions by Sheridan and "intimated very plainly his intention to remove" Sheridan from his position as the general in charge of reconstruction in Louisiana and Texas. Chase advised Johnson against removing Sheridan, saying that it would reinforce the impression that the president was hostile to the peaceful reconstruction in progress. Johnson then told Chase that he was thinking of "putting General Grant temporarily at the head of the War Department, to which, of course, nobody would object, except that it would imply the displacement or resignation of Mr. Stanton." Chase advised the president against this as well, "expressing a quite decided opinion that no change would benefit the country or ought to be made." In a similar letter to his friend Garfield, Chase wrote that although he was generally not inclined to worry, he was quite troubled now. "The President must yield to the People, or the People will take up and put through impeachment."[50]

Chase was right to predict impeachment, although it would take another few months—and more mistakes by Johnson—before the constitutional process for removal from office gained wide support. For now, Johnson listened to Chase about Sheridan but disregarded his advice about Stanton and Grant. On August 5, Johnson demanded the war secretary's resignation. Stanton refused, saying that "public considerations" required him to remain in office. Republican newspapers agreed, with one declaring that "not until Andrew Johnson has ceased to be president, either by impeachment and removal, or by the expiration of his term, will the people consent that Edwin M. Stanton shall leave his post." On August 11, using an exception in the Tenure of Office Act, Johnson suspended Stanton and appointed Grant interim secretary of war. Both Stanton and Grant were unhappy about the abrupt change, which, as Chase predicted, did not help Johnson politically.[51]

The elections of 1867 were not only a contest between Republicans and Democrats; they were a contest between the radical and moderate factions of the Republican Party. In Ohio, for example, radicals pushed a state constitutional amendment to grant blacks the right to vote—a change that many conservatives opposed. In late September the *New York Herald* reported that Chase was on his way to Ohio to shore up the radicals: "And why not, when his interest in the result is greater than that of any other of our aspiring and scheming politicians?" If the voters of Ohio rejected black suffrage—and the paper believed that they probably would—then Chase would have no chance at the Republican nomination. In that scenario, he would be "a horse too badly crippled to be entered for the presidential sweepstakes."[52]

Ohio was not the only state considering important constitutional changes. Kansas was considering two proposals: one to allow blacks to vote and another for women's suffrage. The *New York Evening Post* reported that Chase had told Lucy Stone, a leader of the women's suffrage movement, that he supported the cause. "I think that there will be no end of good that will come from woman's suffrage, on the elected, on elections, on government, and on woman herself. I have said this in public and in private for many years. I am glad that an effort is making in Kansas to accomplish it, and I shall rejoice when the elective franchise shall be as free to women as it is now to men. I think, too, that this will be no distant day." Many papers reprinted Chase's remarks, especially Democratic publications, hoping to show that Chase was so radical, so extreme, that he wanted even women to vote.[53]

Chase was in Ohio for two weeks in late September and early October 1867. His letters suggest that he spent his time innocently enough: visiting with John Sherman and fishing with Jay Cooke. Johnson's papers, however, include a letter reporting that Chase had visited Cleveland, Columbus, and Dayton. "At each point, he had a private conference with the prominent radicals and revenue officers," urging them to "cooperate with the impeachers." On the Sunday before the election, in response to a serenade outside his Columbus hotel, Chase said that, in his current judicial position, he was "not at liberty to take an active part in a political canvass." Then he continued, saying that it would be "mere affectation if, on an occasion like this, if I should refrain from saying that I abide in the faith and cherish the sympathies you have so often heard me avow. I am not, as you know, a man given to change. My vote, therefore, on Tuesday next will be given for the candidates of the great party whose proud distinction is that it demands equal rights and exact justice to all men." So, after saying that he could not campaign, Chase *was* part of the campaign, although with only a single short speech.[54]

The Republican candidate for Ohio governor, Chase's friend Rutherford Hayes, won by a narrow margin, 243,605 to 240,622. The constitutional amendment, however, failed, with only 216,987 votes in favor and 255,340 against. In other words, there were thousands of Ohio voters who wanted a Republican governor but did *not* want blacks to vote. Even before all the ballots were counted, some papers were proclaiming that these Ohio results doomed Chase's presidential chances. The *Nashville Union* declared him "a political mummy, swathed in his judicial robes." The *Cincinnati Enquirer* commented that if the suffrage amendment had passed, Chase would have been the "next nominee for president of the radical negro-worshippers of the United States." As it was, however, the people of Ohio had "settled this question and consigned this dangerous and subtle demagogue to his political grave."[55]

The *Cincinnati Commercial*, edited by Chase's friend Murat Halstead, believed that Chase still had a chance at the Republican nomination. Halstead asserted that Chase was by "temperament and convictions, one of the most truly conservative men in the country," and insisted further that Chase was not among the radicals who favored the impeachment of Johnson. "On the contrary, it was his opinion that no little mischief was done during the late political campaign by the wild threats of summary impeachment that were freely made." As for the question of black suffrage, Halstead conceded that Chase favored this measure, but argued that nine-tenths of Ohio Republicans agreed. Was this a reason, Halstead asked, to deny Chase the Republican presidential nomination, if he was otherwise the best candidate?[56]

Other papers immediately rejected Halstead's characterization of Chase. The *Buffalo Commercial* laughed that it had "seen many instances of sudden conviction, and remarkable agility in changing political front, effected by elections, yet we do not remember any instance" of so sudden a change as that of Chase, from radical to conservative. The *New York World* commented that what the Halstead article really proved was that Chase realized that Republicans wanted a moderate, like Grant, rather than a radical. "If radicalism had any chance of winning in the presidential election, Mr. Chase, as the ablest of the radicals, would find it for his interest to differ as much as possible from General Grant and trust to the outnumbering strength of the radical wing of the party to give him the nomination. Instead of this, he virtually confesses that there is no chance for the election of a stiff radical and surprises the country by softening down his own politics."[57]

Although disappointed by the Ohio results, Chase did not give up hope. He wrote to a friend that, rather than "seek political refuge in the shadow of a past military name," Republicans would do better to adhere to their "principles and organization, and [to] men fairly representing both." Chase admitted that he would be pleased to be the Republican candidate and thus to have the chance to finish the work "to which my life has been dedicated: the establishment of Union on the basis of equal rights for all, secured by just laws sanctioned by universal suffrage, and the establishment of national and individual prosperity on the basis of uniform currency and inviolable faith." But, he insisted, as he had so often in the past, that he would be "satisfied if the results are attained, whoever may be chosen to lead and direct."[58]

While the newspapers debated whether he was alive or dead politically, Chase went to Baltimore to hear and decide the circuit court case of Elizabeth Turner, a ten-year-old black girl. Two days after slavery officially ended in Maryland, Elizabeth's mother had signed an apprenticeship agreement with her former master, Philemon Hambleton, of Talbot County, committing the girl to serve Hambleton for the next ten years. Hambleton agreed to pay the mother once a year for the girl's services, with a final payment to the girl herself on her eighteenth birthday. The agreement provided that Hambleton would teach the girl the "art or calling of a house servant, and that the master shall provide said apprentice with food, clothing, lodging, and other necessaries."[59]

A lawyer for the Freedmen's Bureau, Henry Stockbridge, filed with Chase a petition for a writ of habeas corpus, arguing that Hambleton was keeping Turner in slavery or involuntary servitude, in violation of the Thirteenth Amendment, and denying her civil rights, in violation of the Civil Rights Act of 1866. The local federal judge had denied similar petitions, but Chase granted the petition, directing that Hambleton produce Turner in the federal court in Baltimore on October 15, 1867. Hambleton and Turner were in court on the appointed day, but Hambleton had not hired a lawyer. Chase was dismayed, according to the *Baltimore Sun,* saying that he "desired the whole case should be fully discussed and would prefer that the respondent should be represented by counsel." There were complex issues, he said, including whether the Maryland law about black apprentices violated the federal civil rights law and whether that law was itself authorized by the Thirteenth Amendment. Chase asked Hambleton: Did he wish to keep the girl? The *Baltimore Sun* reported that Hambleton "said he wished to retain the girl, but he did not feel sufficient interest in the case to spend any money on it. He was satisfied to leave the case with the court."[60]

Chase then turned to Stockbridge, who argued that the indenture for Turner did not meet the requirements imposed by the state to protect white apprentices. The system of black apprentices was "an evasion of the constitutional provision abolishing slavery and involuntary servitude," and Turner was far from the only person affected. "The decision in this case would affect the condition of thousands of colored minors whose term of slavery had been protracted from five to ten years." When Stockbridge was done, Chase said again that he hoped to hear argument on the other side, whether from a lawyer hired by Hambleton or from any other lawyer who wanted to argue the issues. He adjourned until nine o'clock the next day.[61]

None of the local lawyers appeared the next morning to argue Hambleton's side of the case, so Chase read out his opinion. He began by noting that the indenture for Turner did not comply with the state law applicable to white apprentices. "The petitioner, under this indenture, is not entitled to any education. A white apprentice must be taught reading, writing, and arithmetic. The petitioner is liable to be assigned and transferred, at the will of the master, to any person in the same county, and a white apprentice is not so liable." Chase then set out five points that seemed to him "sufficient to decide the case." First, the Thirteenth Amendment "interdicts slavery and involuntary servitude, except as a punishment for crime, and establishes freedom as the constitutional right of all persons in the United States." Second, the "alleged apprenticeship in the present case is involuntary servitude, within the meaning of these words in the amendment." Third, the indenture "does not contain important provisions for the security and benefit of the apprentice, which are required by the laws of Maryland in indentures of white apprentices" and therefore violated the Civil Rights Act. Fourth, the Civil Rights Act was constitutional; it was an appropriate exercise of the broad powers granted to Congress by the second section of the Thirteenth Amendment to enforce the prohibition against slavery and involuntary servitude of the first section. Fifth and finally, "colored persons equally with white persons are citizens of the United States."[62]

Newspapers around the country reprinted Chase's circuit court decision in the *Turner* case. The *Independent* said that Chase would receive the thanks not only of Elizabeth Turner, whom "his just judgment has delivered from oppression," but also of the Republican Party, "proud to recognize him as one of its ablest, purest, and bravest leaders." The *New York World*, on the other hand, derided Chase's decision, saying he wanted to ensure that the "vote of a sixteen-year-old Maryland wench is to be of the same avail, in the government of America, as the chief justice's own." For some Democrats, Chase's *Turner* decision was just part of his attempt to secure the Republican nomination.[63]

The last two months of 1867 were quiet ones for Chase. In early November he went to New York for a few days, to greet his daughters upon their return from Europe. Chase was overjoyed to have Kate and Nettie once more "under his roof" in Washington. In early December, when Congress resumed work, the House was considering a resolution to impeach the president for offenses such as suspending Stanton, impeding military reconstruction, and opposing the pending constitutional amendment. Johnson, in his annual message, did nothing to calm Republicans. He pressed for immediate withdrawal of the federal troops from the South so that Southerners (by which he meant white Southerners) could govern themselves. He denounced the idea of black suffrage, saying that it would "Africanize" the South and force white Southerners to "degrade themselves by subjection to the negro race." Johnson issued this incendiary message on the eve of the House impeachment debate.[64]

On December 7, however, the House impeachment resolution failed. Only fifty-seven members, all radical Republicans, voted in favor, while sixty-eight moderate or conservative Republicans joined the unanimous Democrats in voting against impeachment. The key problem was that, as angry as many Republicans were at Johnson, they did not yet believe that he had committed any crimes. And the Constitution was clear: a president could be impeached by the House only for "high crimes and misdemeanors." Chase, who as chief justice would have to preside over a Senate impeachment trial, if there was one, was relieved; he still hoped that Congress and Johnson could work together rather than fighting a constant war.[65]

CHAPTER 24

"Mad with the Presidential Fever"

⟨ 1868 ⟩

The first days of the new year, cold and wet in Washington, found Chase in a reflective mood. Responding to a letter from a Northern preacher working in the South, Chase wrote that he was "particularly touched" to hear that he had the "confidence of the colored people. I have always said that to possess the affection and true respect of the poor and the oppressed is a worthier object of ambition than any official position, even the highest. In that ambition, I am glad to know I am not likely to be disappointed." Alluding to reports that he would be a presidential candidate, Chase said he believed that he had "been credited with more ambition for place than I feel. Not that I possess any uncommon indifference to the gratification derived from distinction, but to me, great place has always been chiefly valuable as great opportunity for useful service." Chase hoped for the "earliest possible restoration of the Southern states to their old relations, upon the basis of universal suffrage and equal rights." In a postscript, he added that he was not in favor of "immediate amnesty to all." He agreed that some former rebel leaders should not yet have the right to vote, but he wanted "no more disenfranchisement after the complete establishment of universal suffrage than is absolutely necessary to secure the new order of things and the new state constitutions against overthrow."[1]

In a letter to his brother-in-law Henry Walbridge, Helen's widower, an Episcopal priest, Chase noted that he was about to celebrate his sixtieth birthday and to "enter upon the last of the seven decades allotted to man. I do not expect to complete it. Whether I do or not, I want to leave absolutely and with entire satisfaction in the hands of God." Chase confessed that his "duties as judge are rather irksome. If I had been appointed younger, and before becoming so deeply concerned in political matters and so largely identified with political measures, I should have liked the position better than any other." Referring obliquely to the possibility that he would become president, Chase added that "should the people see fit to call me to administrative duties, which I do not really expect, I should be better suited." In either case, however, he would strive to "do my whole duty."[2]

In a strong public letter in January, Horace Greeley urged Republicans to nominate Chase, praising his "talents, character, experience, and eminent services." The editor believed that the key issue in the 1868 election would be black suffrage—whether "four millions of American people shall be permanently disenfranchised, and denied any voice in their government, because of their color." Chase's long support of black suffrage meant that if he was nominated, he would not need to say another word about the question, for the choice of Chase would be "a platform in itself—a very broad and firm one." Ulysses Grant's view on this paramount issue, Greeley continued, was a mystery. Did the war hero really support black suffrage in the South? If so, why was there talk among Democrats about nominating him? For Greeley, Chase was the safer, stronger choice.[3]

As soon as he read Greeley's letter, Chase wrote to thank him and to offer some suggestions. He urged Greeley to reconsider his editorial stance on military reconstruction. "The people don't like military domination," Chase wrote. "True, a majority of our friends like it, because they like whatever seems most hard on the rebels. But a large minority dislike it, and they drop out of the ranks one by one and two by two, until the majority of the people is on the other side." Chase also questioned the way in which the *Tribune* was siding with Grant in his current quarrel with Johnson. Stanton was back in the War Department—the Senate having voted to reinstate him—and the president claimed that Grant had helped Stanton return there by violating a promise to Johnson to remain as interim secretary for a while, even after the Senate vote. Grant denied having made any such promise, and the *Tribune* called this a "question of veracity between a soldier whose honor is as unvarnished as the sun and a president who has betrayed every friend and broken every promise." Such praise for Grant, Chase hinted, was not the best way for Greeley to secure *him* the nomination.[4]

Greeley was not the only editor who favored Chase, but rank-and-file Republicans strongly supported Grant. In state after state, as they met to choose delegates for their national convention, to be held in Chicago in May, Republicans endorsed Grant. Writing to a friend in Ohio, Chase said that it seemed that "while many of the best are for me . . . a larger number, also of the best, prefer another." The chief justice would "like to have an expression of support from Ohio" but would not "complain if it is given to another." Ohio Republicans indeed preferred Grant when their state convention met in early March. Papers were now predicting that Grant would be nominated "virtually without opposition."[5]

Democrats and Southerners did not give up in early 1868 on their efforts to persuade the Supreme Court to declare the military reconstruction laws unconstitutional. The key case involved William McCardle, editor of the *Vicksburg Times*, who had been arrested by military officers and convicted by a military commission. McCardle's crime was to criticize in his newspaper the Republican Congress, its military reconstruction laws, and the generals implementing those laws. In one 1867 editorial, for example, McCardle argued that the five generals in charge of military reconstruction were "infamous, cowardly, and abandoned villains" who should have "their precious persons lodged in a penitentiary." When the local federal district judge denied McCardle's petition for habeas corpus, he appealed to the Supreme Court, relying on a section of an 1867 statute allowing for direct appeals in habeas cases.[6]

As the Supreme Court was considering the *McCardle* case, Congress was deliberating ways to prevent the court from ruling against the reconstruction laws. In late January the House debated a bill to prohibit the Supreme Court from invalidating any federal statute without the votes of two-thirds of the justices. Democrats argued that the bill was unconstitutional; Republicans ignored them. The bill passed the House easily.[7]

The lawyers for McCardle, led by Jeremiah Black, asked the court to set the case for early argument, so that "a case of such transcendent importance" could be heard and decided before the end of the court's session in early April. The lawyers for the government, led by Senator Lyman Trumbull, argued that there was no reason for haste, since McCardle was free on bail. Everyone understood that much would change between April and December, when the next session of the Supreme Court would start. Several Southern states would probably ratify the Fourteenth Amendment, as a way of regaining representation in Congress and participating in the presidential election. The most ardent Southern opponents of the amendment were the former Confederates, but they could not vote under the military reconstruction laws, so it seemed likely that even South Carolina would soon ratify the amendment. If the court did not invalidate the reconstruction laws in early 1868, the Constitution itself would probably be changed by late 1868, with enough states having ratified the Fourteenth Amendment to make it part of the Constitution. Timing was also important in light of the congressional attempt to limit judicial authority; if the court did not rule on the reconstruction laws soon, the two-thirds bill might make it impossible for the court to rule against the laws. Chase and his colleagues pleased neither side completely when they announced, in late January, that they would hear the *McCardle* case the first week of March.[8]

The Chase Court faced an almost impossible task: deciding the *McCardle* case under the Constitution, without prompting Congress to pass legislation to limit the court's ability to decide constitutional questions. Even before Chase and his colleagues heard the *McCardle* arguments, however, the chief justice was presented with another difficult task: presiding over the first impeachment trial of an American president.

It was no secret in Washington that Andrew Johnson disliked Secretary of War Stanton—even hated him. But, since it seemed unlikely that the Democrats would choose Johnson as their presidential candidate, he would be president for just twelve more months, and most people believed that he would not attempt anything against Stanton in those months. So Chase and others were shocked to learn on Friday, February 21, that the president had again attempted to remove the secretary from the War Department. Johnson sent Stanton a short letter informing him that he was no longer secretary of war and directing him to surrender his office to the new interim secretary, Lorenzo Thomas. Once again, Stanton refused to resign or to leave, claiming that he was protected by the Tenure of Office

Act. On Friday afternoon and evening, Stanton and Grant placed troops around the War Department to guard against the possibility that Johnson would use troops against Stanton. Clashes between troops answering to different commanders seemed all too possible. It was a nervous weekend in Washington.[9]

The House of Representatives did not waste time. On Monday, February 24, the lower chamber voted overwhelmingly to impeach Johnson. Every Republican who voted favored impeachment, while every Democrat who voted was opposed. The next day, two men whom Chase knew well, Representatives John Bingham and Thaddeus Stevens, appeared in the packed Senate chamber, walked slowly down the aisle, and announced that the House had impeached Johnson. The House did not yet have specific charges—Stevens said that those would be delivered soon—but the issue was now with the Senate. Its members would determine whether Johnson was guilty of high crimes and misdemeanors and should be removed from office. And that meant that the issue was now with Chase, too, for the Constitution provides that in the case of impeachment of the president, the chief justice presides over the Senate trial. If the Senate convicted and removed Johnson, Chase's old political rival from Ohio, Benjamin Wade, would become president, for there was no vice president and the next in line under the federal succession statute was Wade as president pro tem of the Senate.[10]

Republicans George Edmunds and Jacob Howard, two members of the Senate committee to devise impeachment procedures, visited Chase on February 26 in the court's conference room at the Capitol. The senators asked for his ideas about the procedure for the Senate trial and were surprised when the chief justice suggested that *he* might have a vote—at least in the case of ties—just as the vice president votes to resolve ties on legislative issues. The next day, Chase wrote Howard a short letter, suggesting that the Senate, in its legislative capacity, should not take any steps on the impeachment; instead, it should only act on impeachment as a court, with the chief justice presiding. Disregarding Chase's letter, the Senate spent the first few days of March debating and fixing the procedures for the Johnson impeachment trial, while Chase and the other justices were busy hearing arguments in the *McCardle* case.[11]

On March 4, the date when the House planned to present its articles of impeachment to the Senate, Chase diverted some attention to his own role by sending the Senate a formal letter explaining why he believed it important to distinguish between the Senate as a legislature and the Senate as a court for the trial of impeachment. He noted that the Constitution distinguished between impeachments of the president, in which the chief justice would preside, and impeachments of all other federal officials, in which the vice president would preside—just as the vice president usually presides over the Senate. The reason for this distinction, Chase continued, was to avoid a conflict of interest: if a president were convicted and removed, the vice president would take his place. Although there was no vice president in 1868—there was no procedure yet for selecting a new vice president when there was a vacancy in this office—Chase believed the Senate should observe carefully the distinction between its legislative and judicial roles. In particular, he urged that the "rules for the government of the proceedings of such a court should be framed only by the court itself."[12]

This letter from Chase reached the Senate in the morning, while the senators and the crowds in the galleries were waiting for the House managers to arrive and present their articles of impeachment. "As this was considered a sort of judicial protest against the action of the Senate in adopting beforehand the regulations for the government of the court," the *New York Herald* reported, Chase's letter had the "same effect upon the senators that an exploding torpedo would have on a school of porpoises." Senators gathered in groups, reading and discussing the Chase letter, before finally deciding to refer it to a committee. After the reading of the House articles of impeachment, the Senate agreed that the trial would start the next day and appointed a committee to "wait on the chief justice and notify him of a trial of impeachment over which he is to preside." Informal discussion of Chase's letter then continued. "The radicals are extremely indignant," the *Herald* reported, "and say that it is a piece of impertinence on the part of the chief justice. Chase is strongly suspected of being against impeachment, and the radical senators are already expressing regrets that they will be compelled to have him as a presiding officer during the trial. They charge him with being chagrined at the prospect of Ben Wade going into the White House while his own for securing the Republican nomination is considered gone."[13]

Chase spent the next morning listening to oral arguments in the *McCardle* case. Then, at one o'clock, he and a small committee of senators walked to the Senate chamber. The only way for the public to gain entry was through printed tickets, and, among Chase's papers, there are notes to Elizabeth Goldsborough, promising her tickets. She was thus perhaps among those who watched as Chief Justice Chase entered the Senate chamber and announced that he was there "for the purpose of joining with you in forming a court of impeachment for the trial of the president of the United States, and I am now ready to take the oath." After swearing that "in all issues pertaining to the trial of the impeachment of Andrew Johnson, president of the United States, I will do impartial justice according to the Constitution and the laws," Chase administered the same oath to the senators, one by one, in alphabetical order. When the roll call reached Wade, however, Thomas Hendricks, a Democrat from Indiana, objected, arguing that Wade should not participate because of his personal interest. This started a debate that spilled into the next day, with Chase struggling at times to keep the Senate in order.[14]

The 1868 Senate impeachment trial of Andrew Johnson, with Chase presiding.

During this debate, when one of the senators cited one of the impeachment rules, Chase said that in his view these rules did not yet apply because they had not yet been adopted by the impeachment court. After some debate among the senators, they voted; twenty-four senators sustained Chase on this issue and twenty disagreed. The result of this vote was greeted with applause, which Chase promptly checked with his gavel.

The *Cincinnati Enquirer* reported that the radicals were "furious at the applause from the galleries" and that they "hate the chief justice, who calmly and resolutely asserted the rights and dignities of his high position, and who was so triumphantly sustained." After a bit more debate, Hendricks withdrew his motion, and Wade and the last few senators took their oaths. Chase then had the sergeant-at-arms announce that the court of impeachment was now in session. Next, the Senate followed Chase's suggestion and adopted as a court the impeachment rules it had devised previously as a legislature. Then the Senate adjourned the impeachment process for a week, which would turn into two weeks, to allow the president and his lawyers time to prepare his defense.[15]

As Chase was working on the Johnson impeachment in Washington, Democrats were discussing among themselves who they should nominate for president. There were a host of traditional Democratic candidates, including George Pendleton of Ohio and Horatio Seymour of New York. But some New York Democratic leaders wanted a new approach and a new name. As one of them put it in a February letter to Samuel Tilden, chair of the state party committee, naming any of the traditional Democrats "would bring up *old issues* and prejudices and *insure* defeat." Tilden's correspondent hoped that the platform would "cheerfully accord freedom to the negro and equality before the law" and predicted that on such a platform, "success would be sure." Tilden and other Democrats started to think about the possibility that Chase, who combined lifelong Democratic views with a clean Republican wartime record, would be their strongest nominee.[16]

Chase must have been at least somewhat aware of these New York discussions, for in early March he wrote to a friend that he was "satisfied that I am not a suitable candidate for either party." This is the first time that Chase alluded, at least in surviving letters, to the possibility that he would be the Democratic rather than the Republican candidate. Chase listed the many issues that he would have to face as chief justice in the next few weeks: evidentiary questions in the Johnson impeachment, the propriety of military commissions in the *McCardle* case, and perhaps even the constitutionality of the legal tender law. Chase claimed that he wanted to "dismiss every thought which might incline the scale of judgment either way."[17]

A few days later, on March 12, the *National Anti-Slavery Standard* published a letter from an anonymous Washington correspondent, claiming that Chase was siding with Johnson in the impeachment process. "Salmon P. Chase, mad with the presidential fever, and desperate in the consciousness of baffled plans, meanly jealous of Wade, and, perhaps, cherishing the forlorn hope of a Democratic nomination, joins forces with the enemy and stands as the presidential ally." The correspondent described how he and other guests at a recent reception at the Chase home were shocked to hear the president announced as a guest of the chief justice. "His carping letter to the Senate, his refusal, at first, to obey the mandate to appear as its presiding officer, and his decisions the following day are but the first unfolding of a plot to obstruct and defeat as far as possible the conviction of the president." Some of the Republican senators supposedly involved in the plot were Sprague, Fessenden, and Edmund Ross of Kansas. "The most menacing danger of all, however," the correspondent continued, "is the probable decision by a majority of the Supreme Court in the case of McCardle that the reconstruction acts are unconstitutional." The letter urged Republicans to rise up in the North: otherwise the Senate would acquit Johnson, the court would invalidate the military reconstruction laws, and the "South would then indeed be victorious."[18]

Responding to a friend's questions about this widely reprinted letter, Chase dismissed as a "flat absurdity" the idea that he was an ally of Johnson. "Since his proclamation of a provisional government for North Carolina in order to reconstruct on the white basis, I have been a steady opponent of his plans." Chase favored the congressional policy of reconstruction "so far as it contemplated equal rights for all," but he did not "believe in military domination" and did not believe "that anything has been accomplished by military supremacy in the rebel states that could not have been as well if not better accomplished by civil supremacy authorized and regulated by Congress." As to Johnson, Chase, unlike many Republicans, had not "thought it necessary to revile him. I do not quarrel with people about matters on which I differ from them." Chase had called upon the president at the White House from time to time, and Johnson had indeed attended "that reception of mine to which the correspondent referred." In closing, the chief justice said that he was trying to do his duties as best he could, without reference to parties. "I am of no party on the bench. If I believe an act or part of an act of a Republican Congress to be unconstitutional, I must say so. . . . And so of the Democrats. I expect to please neither at all times. But, God helping me, I will do my duty, sorry only that my limited powers do not allow me to do it better."[19]

It seems that the *Standard* was the first newspaper to raise the possibility that the Democrats would nominate Chase. Soon, however, many papers were talking about Chase as the prospective Democratic nominee. The *New York Atlas,* a leading Democratic paper, commented that it was "by no means impossible" that the party would choose Chase, because the Democrats this year were approaching their choice in an "unfettered and dispassionate" way. The *New York Sun,* now edited by Chase's friend Charles Dana, argued that by naming Chase, the Democrats would prove that they were no longer the party of rebels and rebel sympathizers. Dana was sure that Chase would make a good president, saying, "He is a man of marked abilities and acquirements. At the bar, in the Senate, in the governor's chair of Ohio, as secretary of the Treasury, and now as chief justice, he has displayed talents of a high order. But more than this, he has always claimed to be essentially a Democrat." The *New York Herald* disagreed completely, claiming that Chase was not the "exalted statesman, patriot, and philosopher, as painted only a few weeks ago by Greeley, but a selfish, narrow-minded, and small-potato demagogue."[20]

The *Cincinnati Gazette*, now edited by Chase's friend Whitelaw Reid, commented that all the talk about Chase among Democrats showed how desperate they were. Chase not only approved the military reconstruction laws, but also he wanted to see them extended to provide for "negro suffrage." One thing was certain, the *Gazette* declared, and "for this statement we have the highest authority: that if the Democrats run Mr. Chase, they must come to him and stand upon his platform. He will not go to them." The *Gazette* insisted that Chase had not encouraged the Democratic leaders who were talking about him as their presidential candidate.[21]

Chase commented on the *Gazette's* article in a long letter to Murat Halstead, editor of the *Cincinnati Commercial*. Chase denied that he had said anything like "if the Democrats run Mr. Chase, they must come to him and stand upon his platform." This was "not my way of talking about men and parties." He insisted again that he was "no candidate or aspirant for any political position or distinction. I simply want to do my duty faithfully and impartially." Despite his denials in private letters, Chase issued no public statement, such as the categorical refusal William Tecumseh Sherman would make in 1871, when he declared that he "never had been and never will be a candidate for president; that if nominated by either party, I should peremptorily decline, and even if unanimously elected, I should decline to serve."[22]

In early April Chase's friend Theodore Tilton, editor of the *Independent*, visited Washington. The two men had a long conversation, which Chase thought was "off the record," but which Tilton used as the basis for an editorial in the *Independent*, saying the magazine could no longer support him as the Republican candidate. "We have reason to believe," Tilton wrote, that Chase "would not accept the Republican nomination, even if it were tendered. We have equal reason to believe, also, that he would accept the Democratic nomination, if it could be tendered on a platform not inconsistent with his well-known views of negro suffrage. No one who knows the man will expect him ever to change, modify, or compromise his lifelong and ineradicable convictions in favor of liberty, justice, and political equality." Chase believed not only in "equal civil and political rights of all American citizens, without distinction of color," Tilton wrote, but also "without distinction of sex." It seemed that Tilton was trying to deny Chase not only the Republican nomination—no longer really at issue, given Grant's strength—but also the Democratic nomination, by painting him as an unrelenting radical.[23]

With his anger barely restrained, Chase wrote Tilton a long letter saying that he had invited him into his home as a friend; that he had not realized that he was "on trial before an editor"; and that if he had thought he was on trial, he would have "followed a great military example and observed a prudent silence." (Here Chase was hinting at Grant's silence so far on political issues.) Chase explained that, although he agreed with Republicans on "equal rights protected by equal suffrage," he no longer agreed with them on "impeachment, military commissions, military government," and other issues. This is why he had told Tilton that he would not accept the Republican nomination. As for the Democratic party, he had not said anything about accepting the Democratic nomination, only that it was "not in the least degree likely that it should be offered to me."[24]

In none of these letters or conversations did Chase say that he would not accept the Democratic nomination because he was not a Democrat or because he disagreed with the party. On the contrary, although Chase was a founder of the Republican Party, he proudly retained many of his old Democratic ideas. For instance, he agreed with Thomas Jefferson that "all men are created equal," and for Chase, this included black men. He believed that the federal government was a limited government and that it should not infringe upon states' rights. Before the war, he had worried about West Point, the Naval Academy, and a large, permanent military force; now Chase was troubled by the continued presence of the military in the Southern states, wanting the Southern people to govern themselves. Chase favored small, minimal government; in Jefferson's words, a "government rigorously frugal and simple."[25]

Soon Chase was corresponding with Democratic leaders, notably John Van Buren, a distant relative of the late president, and Alexander Long, a former Ohio congressman, about his Democratic views. "Nothing would gratify me more," Chase wrote Long, "than to see the Democracy turn away from past issues and take for its mottoes: suffrage for all, amnesty for all; good money for all; security for all citizens at home and abroad against governmental invasion." By "good money for all," Chase indicated that he sided with "hard money Democrats," who wanted the government to pay its debts in gold, and opposed "soft money Democrats," who preferred using greenbacks to pay the debt. When Long asked the chief justice point-blank whether he would accept a Democratic presidential nomination, Chase responded that if the party adopted a platform along the lines of his prior letter, then he would "not be at liberty to refuse the use of my name." Chase claimed again, however, that he had "no desire for a nomination."[26]

While the papers debated Chase's presidential prospects, and Chase was writing political letters, Congress and the Supreme Court continued their work. Without much fanfare, both houses of Congress passed in March a bill to repeal the 1867 provision allowing direct appeals to the Supreme Court in habeas corpus cases. The repeal language was added as a last-minute amendment by Chase's friend Henry Wilson, who described the amendment only in dry legal terms. The House accepted the Wilson amendment without debate and passed the bill before Democrats realized that it would deny the court the right to hear the pending *McCardle* case. The Senate passed the amended bill on this day, again without debate, sending it to Johnson for his signature or his veto. When Democrats complained a few days later about what they viewed as improper tactics, a Republican responded that nothing required the sponsor of an amendment to "wake up the slumbering."[27]

March 1868 was an unusually busy month for the Supreme Court: in the second half of the month, the court announced opinions in more than two dozen cases. At their Saturday conference on March 14, the first conference after the close of the *McCardle* arguments, the justices did not discuss the case—not surprising, given how many other cases were on their calendar. A week later, with the repeal bill still on Johnson's desk, the justices decided to postpone consideration and resolution of the *McCardle* case. Word of their decision soon leaked out. Gideon Welles wrote in his diary on March 23 that "the judges of the Supreme Court have caved in, fallen through, failed in the *McCardle* case. Only Grier and Field have held out like men, patriots, judges of nerve." Orville Browning wrote in his diary in early April that the justices decided not to resolve the *McCardle* case because "they did not wish to run a race with Congress." Chase used similar language in a letter to Van Buren, saying that the justices other than Field and Grier did not want to "hasten their decision of an appeal for the purpose of getting ahead of Congress." Chase believed that Congress had the "undoubted right to except such cases as that of McCardle from its appellate jurisdiction" and that it would have been "an indecency to run a race in the exercise of that jurisdiction with the legislature."[28]

On March 25 Johnson vetoed the bill to take away the Supreme Court's right to hear the *McCardle* appeal and other similar habeas appeals. The president noted that the bill would not only eliminate the right to appeal in future cases but also preclude consideration of pending cases, and thus "wrest from the citizen a remedy which he enjoyed at the time of his appeal." Republicans, however, had a two-thirds majority in both houses, so they could and did vote to override the veto. The court did not decide the *McCardle* case before its session ended on April 6; nor did it decide two other similar cases seeking an early ruling on the military reconstruction laws. Southern papers were outraged, saying that the court had failed in its duty to stand up to Congress. The real reason white Southerners were concerned was not McCardle himself, who was, after all, out on bail, but fear that they would lose control over Southern blacks. "The white race in ten states," the *Richmond Enquirer* said, "expected to see the whole fabric of negro rule crushed by the weight of judicial authority."[29]

Chase's main focus in April 1868 was the Johnson impeachment trial. The House's articles generally charged that the president had violated the Constitution and the Tenure of Office Act by attempting to remove Stanton from his office without the consent of the Senate. An eleventh "catch-all" article accused Johnson of this and other misconduct, including denying that the current Congress was indeed a constitutional Congress. Johnson responded that the Tenure of Office Act protected Cabinet officers against removal only by the president who appointed them; since Stanton was appointed by Lincoln, he was not protected when Johnson replaced him. Johnson also argued that if the act precluded the president from removing a member of his Cabinet, it was contrary to the Constitution. And he insisted that when he tried to remove Stanton, he was doing so in order to test the constitutionality of the act in the courts.

These were the main legal issues the Senate would have to resolve, but there were also questions about Chase's role as chief justice in a presidential impeachment trial. Would the chief justice make preliminary rulings on evidentiary questions subject to review by the Senate? In the event of a tie on a procedural vote, would he cast the deciding vote? Would he, like a judge at the end of a jury trial, "sum up the case" for the Senate? Chase would have to resolve these issues without much precedent—this was the first time the Senate had tried an impeached president—in a deeply divided partisan environment.[30]

Chase had friends on both sides of the impeachment process. The House managers, effectively the prosecutors, included Benjamin Butler, one of the generals with whom he had corresponded regularly during the Civil War, and John Bingham, whom Chase had known since their days in Ohio politics before the war. The Johnson defense lawyers included William Evarts, who had hosted Chase from time to time at his Vermont vacation home, and Henry Stanbery, whom Chase had also known in prewar Ohio. Among the senators, Chase's friends included Sumner, one of those most eager to convict and remove Johnson, and Fessenden, one of the moderate Republicans believed likely to vote for the president's acquittal.[31]

Early in the trial, while Butler was questioning one of the House witnesses, Stanbery objected that the question was not relevant. Chase overruled him, and the witness was about to answer, when Senator Charles Drake, a Republican from Missouri, objected to Chase's having ruled at all; in Drake's view, evidentiary questions should be decided by the Senate, without any role for Chase. The chief justice responded that, under customary court practices, and in order to move the trial along, he believed that he should "express his opinion in the first instance" on evidentiary questions, subject to appeal and decision by the Senate. Butler disagreed with Chase, in a long speech filled with references to British precedents.

Other House managers joined with their own speeches. Henry Wilson finally moved that the Senate should "retire for consultation." The Senate divided equally on this motion to retire, and Chase then voted in its favor, thereby breaking the tie and showing that he believed he had the right to break such ties. For some reason, perhaps simple exhaustion, no senator objected when Chase voted to break the tie. (Chase's successor Chief Justice John Roberts stated in 2020 that he would *not* break ties in the first impeachment trial of President Donald Trump, since he did not think the "isolated episodes" of Chase's tie-breaking were "sufficient to support a general authority to break ties.") After a three-hour closed-door discussion among the senators about Chase's role, they opened the doors and adopted a revised rule, giving the chief justice the right to rule on "all questions of evidence and incidental questions" unless a member of the Senate asked to have the question considered by the full Senate, in which case the question would be resolved by the Senate. This rule, more or less the approach Chase had in mind, and essentially the approach used now, was adopted by a substantial majority, thirty-one to nineteen.[32]

Two weeks later, when Chase's former Cabinet colleague Gideon Welles was on the witness stand, and Johnson's lawyers asked the navy secretary about Johnson's reasons for removing Stanton, it was Butler's turn to object. Chase ruled the testimony relevant, and another long debate ensued, stretching over two days. Finally, the senators decided that they would exclude the testimony of Welles and other Cabinet members about Johnson's motives. Chase did not explain his ruling about Welles at length in the Senate but did so in letters and conversations. "Under his oath to preserve, protect and defend the Constitution," he wrote to Long, "the president is bound to disregard an act of Congress which, in his honest judgment, attacks and impairs the executive power confided to him by the Constitution, at least so far as may be necessary in order to obtain a judicial determination of the question of its constitutionality." So if Johnson "honestly believed" that the Tenure of Office Act was unconstitutional, he "committed no misdemeanor but performed a duty in disregarding it in order to obtain a judicial decision." The Senate, in Chase's view, should have allowed Johnson "to put in evidence of the sincerity of his belief and of the purpose of his action," and "no evidence on these points could be so valuable as that of the heads of the departments." Chase was probably right on the evidentiary question, but wrong to share his analysis while the impeachment trial was still in progress.[33]

As the defense lawyers presented their last few witnesses, Chase and others hoped that the trial would soon be over. The *New York Herald* predicted on April 20 that the Senate would vote, one way or the other, by the end of the month. But then the Senate decided that it would allow each lawyer on each of the legal teams to give a closing statement and not limit the length of the statements. Over the course of the next two weeks, the Senate listened as four lawyers on each side delivered long closing arguments. Chase was frustrated, writing to his friend James Pike that there was "too much talking by half." James Garfield agreed, writing to one of his friends that Washington was "wading knee deep in words, words, words."[34]

The talking continued into the first few days of May, with some specu-lation in the papers that once the closing arguments were done, Chase would "charge the jury" in a way that would help Johnson. In a letter to John Van Buren, Chase said that he had decided not to attempt any charge or summary. The chief justice was not a member of the court of impeachment, he wrote, but was merely the presiding officer. "Even if the chief justice were, strictly speaking, a member of the court, he would have no right to charge the other members of the court; he could only express his opinion in common with them." His proper role was more limited: he should "rule preliminarily on questions of evidence," and he should, if requested, "express his opinion on any other question."[35]

After mocking and attacking Chase for years, the nation's most popular paper, the *New York Herald*, started in May to praise and promote him as the next president. The *Herald* called Chase the conservative candidate, in contrast to Grant, who was the "slave" of the radical Republicans. The *New-York Tribune*, for once, agreed with the *Herald,* writing that Chase was "one of the ablest—perhaps the very ablest—of our country's states-men; he is a man of lofty Christian character, spotless reputation, and exemplary life; he is in the ripe maturity of his powers and not a shade beyond it; he is a thorough Democrat, according to the true definition of that much-abused term." But the *Tribune*, unlike the *Herald*, did not see much chance that the Democrats, when they gathered for their convention in New York City in early July, would choose Chase.[36]

The papers were also speculating about how various senators would vote in the impeachment trial, with some suggesting that Chase was pressing senators to acquit Johnson. On May 12 the *New York Herald* reported that Senators Fessenden, Trumbull, Grimes, and Sprague all went home to dine with Chase, as did Senators John Henderson of Missouri and Peter Van Winkle of West Virginia. It was perhaps "a trifling circumstance, but the impeachers take it sadly to heart." The *Washington Morning Chronicle* alleged that Chase had "resorted to an extraordinary amount of dinner diplomacy, and long drives with doubtful senators, to defeat impeachment."[37]

At last, on May 16, the time had come for the senators to vote. Addressing the first senator on the alphabetical list, Henry Anthony of Rhode Island, Chase asked, "How say you, Senator Anthony? Is the respondent Andrew Johnson, president of the United States, guilty or not guilty of a high misdemeanor as charged in this article?"—the catch-all eleventh article. Anthony's answer was "Guilty." Chase asked the same question of each senator in turn, with some answering before he finished the question, and others taking a few moments to respond.[38]

The most doubtful vote was that of Edmund Ross of Kansas, upon whom both sides were counting. The Senate chamber was utterly still as Chase posed the question. Standing at his desk, tearing a small scrap of paper, Ross answered, "Not guilty." Some people gasped, and others whispered to their neighbors, with the noise checked by Chase, who then questioned the next senator on the list. When it was over, thirty-five senators had voted guilty; nineteen had voted not guilty. Since there was no two-thirds majority, Chase announced that Johnson was acquitted on this article—by just a single vote. Republicans then adjourned the Senate for ten days, in part to see if they could find one more vote against Johnson on some other article of impeachment, and in part to allow members to attend the Republican National Convention in Chicago.[39]

At the end of this dramatic day, Chase wrote to an old Cincinnati friend, lamenting that impeachment, which should be a judicial process, "has assumed very much the character of a party question." This, in his view, was the real danger to the nation. "What possible harm can result to the country from the continuance of Andrew Johnson nine months longer in the presidential chair, compared with that which must arise if impeachment becomes a mere mode of getting rid of an obnoxious president?" What, Chase continued, "would be thought of a jury or a court which would convict or sentence a man to the penitentiary, because of 'general cussedness,' to use the current phrase, without sufficient proof of specific charges of offenses or crimes?" (Chase was alluding to Fessenden's comment that there would be no problem convicting Johnson if "general cussedness" was sufficient.) Again, even if one agrees with Chase's views, one must question his judgment in sharing these views while the impeachment trial was still in progress.[40]

Some papers at once blamed Chase for the Senate vote. The *New-York Tribune,* on May 18, claimed that he influenced and even "decided the vote" of Senator Peter Van Winkle, one of the Republicans who voted to acquit, while Senator John Henderson, another such Republican, did so only because of the "chief justice's exertions." The *Tribune* also accused Chase of doing "his utmost" to persuade Anthony and Sprague to vote in the same way, "happily in vain." The *Washington Morning Chronicle* was even more bitter and more specific. On the Sunday before the impeachment vote, the paper reported, Chase took a long carriage ride with Henderson, and the next day, he "managed to have at his dinner table four neophytes in treachery: Fessenden, Grimes, Trumbull, and Henderson." Later in the week, Chase "closeted himself for three hours with Senator Anthony, after dining him at his home, and endeavored to overwhelm him with legal assurances that the president ought not to be convicted."[41]

Chase wrote to Greeley to say that the papers were quite wrong about him pressing senators to acquit Johnson. "I have not interchanged a word with Van Winkle on the subject of impeachment that I remember," he wrote, "and my acquaintance with him is very slight." Until the day before, when he happened to meet him on the street, "all my conversation with Anthony would not occupy ten minutes." As for Sprague, who was, after all, his son-in-law, Chase insisted that he was "not influenced by me, nor did I seek to influence him." The chief justice admitted that Henderson, "a near neighbor," had dined with him and Sprague once or twice during the Johnson trial, "but I am sure that I gave him no advice nor sought in any way to control him." Chase also drafted, but it seems did not send, a seven-page letter to the *Chronicle,* refuting its charges point by point. For example: the supposed dinner with several senators did not happen; what happened was that Henderson rode home with Chase and Sprague, and "instead of going to his rooms to a cold dinner," they asked him to "stop with them and take a warm one."[42]

As everyone expected, the Republican convention in Chicago nominated Grant for president. The Republican platform was moderate; instead of insisting on "universal suffrage," it stated that the "question of suffrage in all the loyal states properly belongs to the people of those states." On the day after Grant's nomination, Chase wrote a long letter to James Gordon Bennett, senior editor of the *New York Herald*, to thank him for the "kind things which the *Herald* has lately said of me." Reminding Bennett how, in the spring of 1865, his paper had briefly advocated "equal suffrage as the best basis for restoration in the Southern states," and noting that eight Southern states had now adopted constitutions with universal suffrage, Chase urged Bennett to renew his support for universal suffrage.[43]

"If the Democratic Party were wise," Chase continued, "it would go beyond instead of falling behind the Chicago declarations on the subject of suffrage." Many of the "ablest colored men in the South are sensible of the dangers of having all the colored voters on one side politically and wish for some action of the Democratic Party which will allow them to act with it." Bennett did not respond to Chase's letter, nor did the *Herald* change its stance against black suffrage.[44]

When the Senate impeachment trial resumed on May 26, the first issue was a motion that the court adjourn until late June; some radicals hoped that with more time, they could uncover evidence that Johnson had bribed senators to vote in his favor. There was a tie on this motion, and, once again, Chase broke it, voting nay. Then the senators voted on two of the other articles of impeachment, with the same result; there were only thirty-five votes in favor of convicting and removing Johnson, not the necessary thirty-six. After this, the Republicans gave up and voted to adjourn indefinitely. Chase announced the adjournment and left the Senate chamber, along with the members of the House and the spectators. When the Senate resumed legislative work a few minutes later, Henry Anthony rose to make a "personal explanation," denying that he and Chase ever discussed impeachment. The Rhode Island senator, although a journalist himself, now condemned "that kind of journalism which penetrates into dining rooms and listens at keyholes."[45]

It was utterly unclear, in May and June 1868, whom the Democrats would nominate for president at their convention in early July. Westerners generally favored Pendleton, former member of Congress from Ohio and leader of the party's soft money faction. Easterners, and especially financiers, opposed Pendleton for just this reason: they wanted a hard money candidate. Some liked General Winfield Scott Hancock, with one newspaper speculating that the general would be popular with a "large class of voters—namely, the soldiers who fought for the Union and not for the negro." Others inclined to former New York governor Horatio Seymour, who insisted he was not a candidate. The *New York Herald* argued that only with Chase could the Democrats win the election. Many Democrats, however, could not stand the chief justice. One of Tilden's correspondents wrote that Chase was "out of the question. He would be the weakest man we could have." Another New Yorker wrote to Tilden that Chase could not excite Democrats; he was a leader in Lincoln's Cabinet, and Democrats viewed the election of Lincoln as "about the greatest calamity that ever befell a great nation."[46]

Chase was doing what he could to persuade Democrats that he was their best choice. In a long letter to August Belmont, the Democratic financier with whom he had collaborated during the war, Chase declared that "for more than a quarter of a century, I have been, in my political views and sentiments, a Democrat, and I still think that, upon questions of finance, commerce, and administration generally, the old Democratic principles afford the best guidance." He reminded Belmont that most of those who had voted in 1849 to send him to the Senate were Democrats and recounted some of his efforts to form a single Independent Democratic Party in Ohio. Chase insisted that he "never favored interference by Congress with slavery in the states" but rather supported emancipation "as a war measure." Chase conceded that he had disagreed with Johnson's reconstruction policy because he limited the "right of suffrage to whites," but he also disagreed with Congress in creating "despotic military governments for the states, and in authorizing military commissions for the trials of civilians in time of peace. There should have been as little military government as possible; no military commissions; no classes excluded from suffrage; and no oath, except one of faithful obedience and support to the Constitution and laws." The *New York Herald* soon printed a similar summary of Chase's views, perhaps because Belmont shared Chase's letter with the editors.[47]

Chase was also assuring Republicans, however, that he had not changed his views on equal rights. He predicted to an Ohio Republican that he would not be the Democratic nominee because of the "almost universal commitment of the party to hostility to the colored people." His "whole life has been devoted to what I believed to be genuine democratic ideas," which for Chase included "equality of political rights without regard to race or color." How could the "Democrats nominate me and at the same time maintain their exception, as I think it, to the practical application of democratic ideas? I have as yet seen no way to overcome this difficulty."[48]

When Chase met in Washington in late May with James Harris, black Republican leader from North Carolina, he gave him similar assurances. A Washington correspondent for a New York paper reported that Harris told Chase that he was dismayed that Chase was considering running as a Democrat. Chase responded that he had "always been an antislavery man and always expected to be; that he never had gone down to any man or party." The Democrats had agreed in 1849 to "repeal the black laws and elect a Free Soiler to the United States Senate. He himself was elected on that coalition, and the bill repealing the black laws passed as he himself had drafted it. He had not gone down to them—they had come up to him. If his friends placed him in a similar position now, he was in their hands." Reading the correspondent's version of this conversation in the papers, Chase commented to Schuckers that it "comes as near the truth as such reporting usually does."[49]

Chase spent the first two weeks of June presiding over the circuit court in Richmond. Once again, there was no treason trial for Jefferson Davis. The principal lawyers, Evarts for the government and Charles O'Conor of New York for the defense, had agreed that the case should be postponed again. After some discussion about the date, Chase announced that he would be back in Richmond in November and would "remain until obliged to attend the Supreme Court at Washington." Chase now thought that the government should drop the prosecution of Davis, writing to a friend that he could "see no good to come, at this late day, from trials for treason. I would rather engage in trials of mutual good will and good help." The chief justice even suggested to one of the Davis lawyers an argument they had not considered. The Fourteenth Amendment was about to become part of the Constitution. Did the section excluding former rebel leaders from holding office preclude any other punishment, such as a trial for treason? Although puzzled about why Chase would want to help them, Davis's attorneys decided that they would raise this point in the fall.[50]

While he was in Richmond, Chase visited with local leaders. "They all greet me kindly," he wrote to Schuckers, "but there is a sad state of things growing out of their past hostility to suffrage and the consequent alienation of the colored people and the white disenfranchisement policy

of Congress, the natural fruit of black disenfranchisement by the whites."
He went on to observe that while there was a "great improvement here in
the temper of the men who took part in the rebellion, that of the ladies,
I fear, is as implacable as ever." Nevertheless, Chase's "faith in universal
suffrage and universal amnesty, always strong, is strengthened by all I
see and hear." Chase told Gerrit Smith that he was pleased by the "fast
progress made in the South towards recognition of the fact that universal
suffrage is their surest guarantee of prosperity." Generous treatment for
former white rebels, Chase wrote, "helps them mightily to see the wisdom
of justice to the black citizens."[51]

When Chase returned to Washington, about June 15, he found his
table filled with letters: from Raleigh, North Carolina, assuring him
that local Democrats would support his nomination; from Philadelphia,
reporting on a meeting there of "Chase Democrats"; from John Van Buren,
asking him to comment on the plight of Northern white workers; and
from William Cullen Bryant, editor of the *New York Evening Post*, urging
Chase to use his strength among Democrats to force the convention to
adopt a universal suffrage platform. Chase assured Van Buren that he
was keen to protect white workers; the purpose of his wartime currency
reform had been to create a single, solid currency for workers. But he
replied to Bryant that he probably would not have much influence on
the Democratic platform, because he expected that "anti-progressives"
would control the convention.[52]

Even as Chase was writing to Bryant that he would not have much
say about the platform, many papers were printing what they called
the Chase platform, "drawn up by Judge Chase himself." This platform
declared that "universal suffrage is a recognized Democratic principle, the
application of which is to be left, under the Constitution of the United
States, to the States themselves." The platform also called for universal
amnesty, denounced military government, and urged that "taxes should be
reduced as far as practicable" and "apportioned so as to bear on property
rather than on labor, while all national obligations should be honestly
and exactly fulfilled." A scrawled letter in Chase's files suggests that he
indeed drafted this document but claimed it was meant as a basis for
discussion, not as a statement of his views. He was "mortified" to see how
it was published, fearing this would be "taken as evidence that I seek the
Democratic nomination and also to dictate the platform to be adopted by
the party, neither of which impressions would be at all correct."[53]

For a man who was not seeking the nomination, Chase spent a lot of time writing political letters in the month before the Democratic convention. He also went from Washington to Baltimore to meet with Tilden and Van Buren, who had traveled from New York just to confer with Chase. The *New York Herald* continued to argue that Chase was the best candidate for the Democrats. The *New York World*, however, after initially favoring Chase, now condemned him for his position in favor of black suffrage. "What he has so ardently desired, the Democratic Party has strenuously resisted and indignantly denounced. The Democratic Party may be unable to revoke what has been done, but they certainly are not going to endorse it, as they would virtually do by nominating a man who makes [black suffrage] the cornerstone of his political creed."[54]

The Chase team in New York in July 1868 was better than the team had been in Chicago in May 1860. Those working for him this time included Long, Van Buren, and Hamilton Smith of Indiana, whom Chase had known since their Dartmouth days. Frederick Aiken, a young attorney and journalist, secured office space across from the hall where the convention was to take place. Kate Sprague traveled from Washington to New York, writing her father from there on July 2 that the "popular voice here is all one way, most enthusiastic." She hoped to see the "bright jewel" of the nomination added to her father's "crown of earthly distinction" and added: "*I believe it will be.*"[55]

The delegates to the 1868 Democratic National Convention came from all the states, including Southern states not represented in Congress because they had not yet accepted the Fourteenth Amendment. There had been a few black delegates at the recent Republican convention, including James Harris of North Carolina, but there were none at the Democratic convention. The *New York Herald* noted that many delegates were former Confederate officers, including General Nathan Bedford Forrest from Tennessee, and "unreconstructed antediluvian state rights leaders of the South," including Robert Barnwell Rhett of South Carolina. Whatever Kate might have thought, such men were unlikely to accept her father as their nominee.[56]

Chase remained in Washington, reading and writing letters. He wrote Aiken that he was watching and waiting "very quietly—so quietly that I am almost ashamed of myself, when I think of your anxieties and labors in New York." On the eve of the convention, Chase received a letter from

Alexander Long, saying that it was essential that Chase confirm that he would "abide by the action of the convention and support its nominees." Chase wrote back more or less as Long requested, but then immediately regretted the letter, writing to Van Buren that they should not use the letter if at all possible. "I have never in my life bound myself to the support of unknown candidates upon an unknown platform," he fretted. Chase may have been reacting to a recent public letter from Frank Blair, saying that the next president should "declare the reconstruction acts null and void, compel the army to undo its usurpations in the South, disperse the carpetbag state governments, and allow the white people to organize their own governments." Many of the Democratic delegates, as racist and revolutionary as Blair, applauded this letter.[57]

The Democratic convention opened with a few formalities on Saturday, July 4. On Sunday, while the delegates rested, Hamilton Smith wrote Chase, urging him not to trust Van Buren and other New Yorkers: "They want Seymour or somebody *less honest than you*." Smith advised that, although the midwestern delegates would support George Pendleton for several ballots, some men, including Clement Vallandigham, would support Chase when it became clear (as Smith believed it would) that Pendleton could not be nominated.[58]

On Monday, July 6, the convention selected Seymour as its chairman, but did not hear from the platform committee and did not vote on candidates. On Tuesday, Chase received a telegram from New York sharing part of the Democratic platform, just announced and adopted, and asking for Chase's comments. He responded that he was "not prepared to say till I have seen the whole." In a letter to Kate, he commented that he could "accept well enough the platform so far as" he had received it, but he could not "say that I like it, nor do I suppose anybody will like it." Later in the day, when he read a summary of the platform in the *Washington Evening Star*, Chase must have been dismayed, for the paper reported that the platform "denounces negro suffrage as the basis for restoration" and "specifically denounces the reconstruction acts as unconstitutional." When he read the full text, Chase must have been even more perturbed, for the platform accused Republicans of subjecting the Southern states to "military despotism and negro supremacy," and called the reconstruction acts "unconstitutional, revolutionary, and void."[59]

As Chase's friends planned, his name was not advanced on the initial day of balloting, July 7. Their strategy was to wait until the convention deadlocked and hope that Chase would then be summoned—somewhat in the manner of James Polk's nomination in 1844. On the first ballot, the votes were scattered among ten candidates. Pendleton claimed the most votes, but he did not even have a majority, much less the two-thirds majority required by Democratic rules. On the fourth ballot, North Carolina voted for Seymour, prompting him to declare that he "must not be nominated by this convention. I could not accept its nomination if tendered, which I do not expect." On the sixth and last ballot of the day, Pendleton received 122 ½ votes, far short of the 212 needed for nomination. Chase wrote to Kate that he was glad his name had not yet been put before the delegates. Indeed, he thought it would be "much better not to have my name go before the convention at all unless it goes upon such a demand as will ensure its acceptance by the necessary vote." Chase did not want just nomination; he wanted acclamation.[60]

The next day, July 8, on the twelfth ballot, the California delegation gave a half vote to Chase. There were prolonged cheers, then some hisses, and then further cheers. There was no long speech for Chase, however, and no other delegates joined in voting for him. At the end of this day, on the eighteenth ballot, General Hancock was in the lead, with 144 ½ votes, followed by Hendricks and then Pendleton. The extra editions of the *Evening Star*, which Chase would have seen at the end of the day in Washington, reported the votes ballot by ballot and added that the Chase men hoped the New York delegation would soon support Chase.[61]

On July 9, before the first ballot of the day, the Missouri delegation urged the convention to nominate Frank Blair, while the California delegation argued for Justice Stephen Field. The Ohio delegation then announced that Pendleton wished to withdraw. Midway through the twenty-second ballot, an Ohio delegate announced that Ohio now supported Horatio Seymour. "Let us vote," he urged, "for a man whom the presidency has sought, but who has not sought the presidency." From the chair, Seymour insisted again that he could not be the nominee, but his friends hustled him out of the hall, and, within minutes, he was the unanimous presidential nominee. The delegates, eager to get home, then nominated Frank Blair for vice president and closed their convention. Writing to a friend late in the day, Chase insisted that he was not disappointed, because he had not expected to be nominated. But he regretted that many Democrats wanted to "overthrow the governments organized" under the reconstruction laws and were prepared to "plunge their states into new disorder and strife."[62]

Kate Chase did not accept defeat so calmly. She wrote to her father that he had been "most cruelly deceived and cheated by the man whom you trusted implicitly": John Van Buren. Without quite explaining what she had expected Van Buren to do, or how one man could sway a whole convention, Kate was sure that if Van Buren had only done his duty, her father would have been nominated. Chase did not share his daughter's anger at Van Buren—they continued their warm correspondence—but he entertained the same unrealistic view that he had come quite close to the nomination. He wrote to Jay Cooke that he would have been nominated on the twenty-second ballot if Ohio had not brought forth Seymour. New York planned on that day to support him, Chase claimed, and "Georgia, Wisconsin, Rhode Island, Massachusetts, Maine, and New Jersey were ready to do the same thing. This prospect enraged some of the Ohio delegates, and those opposed to me were in the majority, and so it was agreed that Ohio should go for Seymour." More objective observers, such as the *Cincinnati Enquirer*, disagreed: "Several states had determined not to back Chase under any circumstances," the paper noted.[63]

Although Chase did not receive the nomination, he did not escape criticism for his attempt. Henry Ward Beecher, in a public letter, wrote that Chase was a "splendid man to look upon, but a poor man to lean upon. Ambition lifts some men towards things noble and good, makes them large and generous. Other men's ambition blurs the sharp lines and distinctions between right and wrong." Frederick Douglass was even more scathing, comparing Chase in his paper to an angel who had fallen from heaven into hell. Chase was "an abolitionist of thirty years standing, a Liberty Party man of the olden time, when that party could count only 7,000 votes in the whole country, an antislavery lawyer, trusted most by the trembling fugitive." Now Chase had descended "to the gutter," from where he begged the Democrats to nominate him. Like Beecher, Douglass blamed Chase's ambition for his fall from grace. "Hereafter let us hear no more of Mr. Chase as the negro's candidate or the negro's friend."[64]

It was especially hard for Chase to explain why, after the convention adopted its platform, he did not withdraw from the process. He wrote to Gerrit Smith that although the platform contained some serious flaws, there was also "so much that was good in it" that he "did not feel at liberty—considering how many had identified themselves with my nomination and how grievously a positive refusal would disappoint them—to come out with such a refusal." Besides, Chase added, he believed that if

he was nominated, he could write an acceptance letter that would interpret the platform in a way "acceptable to the masses of the party and not
inconsistent with my own views." It is hard, however, to avoid agreeing
with Beecher and Douglass that Chase's ambition for the nomination in
1868 made him forget his friends and his principles.[65]

The 1868 election was fought not just with speeches and rallies but also
with knives and guns. Some of the Southern violence was organized by the
Ku Klux Klan; although insisting that he had no role in the organization,
Nathan Bedford Forrest also bragged in the papers that there were fifty
thousand Klan members in Tennessee alone. Other violence seemed to
have no connection with the KKK, although the perpetrators were the
same sort of white Southerners. On September 19 several hundred whites
attacked a black Republican election parade in Camilla, Georgia. The
Chicago Tribune reported that "fifty Republican voters, including their
nominee for Congress, were killed or wounded by a Seymour and Blair
mob." The *Buffalo Commercial* added that "negroes were hunted with
dogs, and when they were caught, butchered in cold blood." On October
22 James Hinds, a white member of Congress who favored black rights,
was shot and killed by a close-range shotgun blast while heading to a
Republican rally in Arkansas. The murderer, never tried, was a leading
local Democrat and suspected KKK member.[66]

Chase did not comment on these attacks, even in his private letters.
Instead, he explained over and over why he would support neither Seymour
nor Grant. Chase did not know Seymour well, but he liked him, describing
him as "pure and estimable and honorable." What Chase objected to was
not Seymour but the Democratic platform and Blair's nomination. He
could not understand what had "possessed" the Democratic convention
to "adopt the anti-reconstruction plank and then give it the worst possible interpretation by the nomination of [Blair] with his letter hardly
dry from his pen." As for Grant, Chase believed that he was a "brave and
most deserving soldier" and a "sincere patriot" and "man of good sense."
But Chase was not sure that the general had "any more respect for the
rights of American colored citizens or more real sympathy with them in
their efforts to elevate themselves than very many Democrats who will
vote for Seymour." So, Chase wrote in late September, "I can't get up any
great amount of enthusiasm on either side."[67]

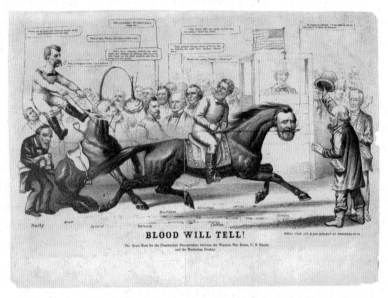

*The 1868 presidential race, with Ulysses Grant leading Horatio Seymour. Chase
is among the spectators; he comments, "We must have another Chase for it."*

There was a flurry of talk in October about the possibility that the
Democrats would drop Seymour and Blair and name Chase and another
as their candidates. Alexander Long wrote to Chase that Seymour might
withdraw and make a "patriotic appeal to the people to seize upon the last
and only hope left of saving themselves and this country from anarchy and
despotism by adopting your platform and yourself." Talk intensified after
the elections in Indiana, Ohio, and Pennsylvania, in which Republicans
carried most of the congressional seats. The *New York World* argued that
if there was any "impediment to success which can yet be removed," it
should be removed at once. The *World* did not name Seymour and Blair,
but it was not hard to determine that they were the impediments whom
the editors hoped to remove—in favor of Chase. Long pressed Chase to
accept the call to become the "candidate of the great conservative masses,
who now turn instinctively to you as their last and only hope for the
preservation of civil liberty and constitutional government."[68]

But Chase was not interested. He wrote to Van Buren that he would
not consent to allow his name to be used as a possible candidate at this late
stage. A week later, he wrote to Thomas Hendricks that the convention's

mistake was not the choice of Seymour; the mistakes were the "sweeping denunciation of the reconstruction laws as unconstitutional, null and void" and the nomination of Blair after his public letter. These mistakes "could not be retrieved by a change of candidates."[69]

On the national Election Day, November 3, Grant and the Republicans defeated Seymour and the Democrats. Grant carried twenty-six states, including all the states in New England and the Northwest. Seymour prevailed in eight states, including New York and two Southern states, Louisiana and Georgia, where white violence kept blacks from voting. Chase did not vote, even though he was not busy with circuit court duties and thus could have gone to Ohio. In an Election Day letter, Chase wrote that his "earnest prayer and confident expectation" was that the nation would now "find peace in the reconciliation of the races and in the recognition and protection of the equal rights of all men."[70]

When Chase opened the circuit court in Richmond a few weeks later, he announced that he would not require all the prospective grand jurors to take the "ironclad oath." He explained that reservations about the oath "expressed by some of the grand jurors known to be among the best qualified for the responsible duties of their position" had led him to the view that the "ends of justice will be hindered and defeated rather than promoted and seconded" by requiring every man to swear the oath. Chase's comments were widely reprinted, as was his circuit court opinion in a case involving Catharine Keppel, a Pennsylvania shareholder in a Virginia railroad company. Keppel sued the company for a dividend paid during the Civil War only to Southern shareholders, leaving shareholders in the North empty-handed. The company answered that the Confederate government had forced it to pay amounts owed Northerners into the Confederate Treasury.[71]

The *Keppel* case, like others, raised the difficult question of the legal effect after the war of the actions of a rebel government during the war. "It is not easy to give a general answer to this question," Chase noted. "On the one hand, it is clear that none of its acts in hostility to the regular government can be recognized as lawful; on the other hand, it is equally clear that transactions between individuals which would be legal and binding under ordinary circumstances cannot be pronounced illegal and of no obligation because done in conformity with laws enacted or directions given by the usurping power." Even though Chase ruled in this case for the Northern side, Southerners were encouraged that he seemed to say that "ordinary transactions" would be recognized and enforced by the federal courts.[72]

The main reason that Chase was in Richmond, of course, was for the Jefferson Davis treason case. Following up on Chase's suggestion, Davis's lawyers moved to dismiss the indictment, arguing that because Davis was now disqualified from holding office by the Fourteenth Amendment, he could not be punished a second time for the same conduct through a treason trial. Richard Henry Dana, an excellent lawyer as well as a famous author, argued for the government that the section of the amendment disqualifying rebel leaders from holding office was not intended as an amnesty and that nobody in Congress or the ratifying legislatures had suggested it would operate as an amnesty. Charles O'Conor responded for Davis that it was "utterly repugnant to the world's ideas of humanity" for the federal government, after dealing with the Southern leaders during the war as "equal and honorable men," to try and hang them after the war as "traitors." Late on Friday evening, after two days of argument, Chase recalled the lawyers and announced that the court was divided, with Chase in favor of dismissing the Davis indictment, and the local district judge, John Underwood, in favor of allowing the prosecution to proceed. This division of opinion on the circuit court would be certified to the Supreme Court, Chase explained, so that the court could review and decide the issue.[73]

Before the Supreme Court could take any action on the Davis case, however, President Johnson issued on Christmas Eve a final amnesty for all those who participated in the rebellion, including Jefferson Davis. A few Republican papers denounced Johnson's order, but Chase, who had been arguing so long for universal amnesty, surely agreed with the president's decision that the time had come to extend amnesty even to Davis.[74]

CHAPTER 25

"Indestructible Union ... Indestructible States"

༄ 1869–70 ༄

A lthough we do not have Chase's diary from early 1869, it seems safe to assume that he watched closely the progress through Congress of the Fifteenth Amendment, to ensure that black Americans would have the right to vote. The House version provided that the "right of citizens of the United States to vote shall not be denied or abridged by the United States or by any state on account of race, color, or previous condition of servitude." The Senate version would have also prohibited restrictions on the basis of "nativity, property, education, or creed." But the Senate approach had no real chance of ratification: New England states wanted to preserve their literacy requirements, and western states, to keep their rules prohibiting Chinese immigrants from voting. Recognizing political realities, the Senate accepted the House version in late February 1869, and the amendment went to the states for ratification.[1]

Chase had been pressing for black suffrage for more than two decades, since his silver pitcher speech, when he said that "true democracy makes no enquiry about the color of the skin." At first, however, Chase was lukewarm about the proposed Fifteenth Amendment. In a letter to an Alabama judge, he wrote that "after the Fourteenth Amendment was adopted, I thought the suffrage should be left to the states after restoration. And I still think so. Centralization and consolidation have gone far enough and too far. And yet inasmuch as the proposed Fifteenth Amendment does not prevent the states from imposing reasonable qualifications, if qualifications should be found necessary, I incline to wish that it may be ratified." Chase added that he would have supported ratification without reservation if "the clause giving Congress power to legislate were left out. I want as little legislation by Congress in respect to the internal concerns of the states as possible."[2]

Within a few months, however, Chase had changed his mind and was pressing a friend in the Ohio legislature, Thomas Yeatman, to lead the effort there to ratify the Fifteenth Amendment. Although Chase would have preferred to "see the principles of the amendment adopted by the states in their constitutions, I have become convinced that the best thing for the South and the whole country is to make sure of their adoption by ratifying the amendment. I feel quite sure that its ratification will be followed very speedily by universal amnesty—by which I mean the removal of all disabilities—and by a great increase of prosperity." Chase was writing "freely as an old friend," but he did not want to see any more of his private letters in public print. "So put this letter in the fire without letting anybody see it," he requested. Yeatman must have ignored Chase's request, for the letter is in the Cincinnati History Library and Archives.[3]

The Supreme Court had several cases on its docket in early 1869 arising out of the 1862 Legal Tender Act. Chase assigned all these cases to himself and managed to resolve three of them without reaching the most controversial question: whether the legal tender requirement was constitutional. In *Lane County v. Oregon*, Chase ruled that the state of Oregon could require each county to pay its share of state taxes in specie. The states existed before the Constitution, Chase noted, and many of its provisions recognized the "necessary existence of the states, and, within their proper spheres, the independent authority of the states." In *Bronson v. Rodes*, Chase ruled that a creditor could enforce an agreement requiring the debtor to pay "in gold or silver coin." Even the Legal Tender Act recognized the distinction between "coined dollars" and "note dollars," so it was not unreasonable to require the debtor to pay in gold as promised. In the third case, *Butler v. Horwitz*, Chase ruled that a lease entered in 1791, requiring annual payments in English golden guineas, was properly interpreted to require payment in gold and not in legal tender notes.[4]

On March 4, 1869, Chase participated for the third time as chief justice in the inauguration of a president, this time of Ulysses S. Grant.

Chase must have reflected, at some point during the day, on the differences among Lincoln, Johnson, and Grant. Chase liked and admired Lincoln while he was alive and still mourned his death; he was deeply disappointed by Johnson, who neither attended Grant's inauguration nor allowed any of his Cabinet members to attend; and Chase was simply unsure at this point about Grant, fearing that a man whose only successes were military might not prove a good president. The inauguration took place on a raised platform on the east side of the now-finished Capitol Building, with an immense, mixed-race audience filling the lawn and using the trees as vantage points. After Grant, Chase, and the others emerged from the building onto the platform, while the cannons were booming and the crowd cheering, Grant whispered a few words to Chase. Then he delivered his brief inaugural address, including a plea for the states to ratify the pending constitutional amendment.[5]

Chase approved Grant's first steps as chief executive. A few days after the inauguration, he wrote to a friend that Grant "means to give us, as far as can be seen, a vigorous, honest, rather nonpolitical administration." (Chase was alluding to the way Grant had appointed not only key political players but also business and military leaders.) A few weeks later, the chief justice was surprised when Grant arrived late in the evening at a dinner hosted by William Evarts to honor General Sherman. Evarts explained to his guests with a smile that he had not invited the president because he knew how much Grant disliked formal dinners, but that he had told Grant that Sherman would "take it as a compliment if his old commander would come in and smoke a cigar." That is just what Grant did: he and the other smokers enjoyed their cigars. Chase was not a smoker, so he did not join this circle, but as he departed, he "had a few moments' pleasant talk with the president and was glad to have it in my power to speak very cordially and with entire sincerity of what has thus far been done."[6]

On April 12 Chase read out two important opinions for the court—opinions that are still cited and discussed. The courtroom was crowded, Chase reported to Nettie, with a "very intelligent and deeply interested audience." First, in a relatively short opinion, for a unanimous court, Chase dismissed the *McCardle* case. Noting that the 1867 provision on which McCardle's appeal was based had been repealed in 1868 while the case was pending before the court, and that the Constitution grants the court appellate jurisdiction only "with such exceptions, and under such regulations, as the Congress shall make," Chase held that the court no longer had jurisdiction. "We are not at liberty to inquire into the motives of the legislature," he explained. "We can only examine into its power under the Constitution, and the power to make exceptions to the appellate jurisdiction of this court is given by express words." In a cryptic final paragraph, Chase noted that the "act of 1868 does not except from that jurisdiction any cases but appeals from circuit courts under the act of 1867. It does not affect the jurisdiction which was previously exercised." In other words, Congress had simply closed one avenue of judicial review; it had not prevented the constitutional questions in the case from reaching the court by some other route.[7]

Second, in a much longer opinion, his most often-quoted opinion, Chase ruled in favor of the state and against the bondholders in *Texas v. White*. The Treasury bonds in question, originally transferred by the federal government to the state of Texas as part of the federal payment to Texas in the Compromise of 1850, were still in the state treasury at the outset of the Civil War. The rebel state government sold the Treasury bonds at a discount during the war, to help finance its war effort. After the war, the reconstruction government of Texas filed suit in the Supreme Court, seeking to recover the bonds from the wartime purchasers or (in some cases) from those to whom the purchasers had since sold the bonds. Since Texas was not yet fully back in the Union—it was one of the last Southern states to regain representation in Congress—the first issue in the case was whether Texas was a "state" entitled to file an original suit in the Supreme Court.[8]

To answer this, Chase reviewed the history of Texas and the United States. When Texas was admitted to the Union in 1845, the state and its people "were invested with all the rights, and became subject to all the responsibilities and duties, of the original states under the Constitution." When Texas attempted to leave the Union in 1861, she drafted a new state constitution, joined the new Confederate government, and contributed thousands of troops to the Confederate army. "Did Texas, in consequence of these acts, cease to be a state?"[9]

It was not necessary, Chase said, to "discuss at length" the question that Americans had been debating for decades: whether a state could legitimately secede from the Union. In the Articles of Confederation, drafted in 1777 and ratified in 1781, the wartime collaboration of the

states was described as a "Union," and "this Union was solemnly declared
to be 'perpetual.'" A few years later, the first words of the Constitution
declared that it was adopted "in order to form a more perfect Union." It
would be difficult, Chase said, "to convey the idea of indissoluble unity
more clearly than by these words. What can be indissoluble if a perpetual
Union, made more perfect, is not?"[10]

The "perpetuity and indissolubility of the Union," Chase continued, "by
no means implies the loss of distinct and individual existence, or the right
of self-government by the states." Both the Articles and the Constitution
recognized and protected the states. "The preservation of the states, and the
maintenance of their governments, are as much within the design and care
of the Constitution as the preservation of the Union and the maintenance
of the national government. The Constitution, in all its provisions, looks
to an indestructible Union, composed of indestructible states."[11]

Chase thus concluded that, however hard Texas might have wanted and
tried to secede from the Union, she had failed. Texas remained, throughout
the Civil War, part of the United States. "The obligations of the state, as
a member of the Union, and of every citizen of the state, as a citizen of
the United States, remained perfect and unimpaired." Some rights of the
state, however, were suspended during the war; nobody would contend,
Chase noted, that Texas was entitled to seats in Congress while she was
waging war against the United States. He thus accepted and embodied
in constitutional law the position that Lincoln had taken during the war:
that the rebellious states remained part of the United States but lost some
of their rights because of their rebellion. This raised the question: Did the
current government of Texas, after the suspension of its rights during the
Civil War, have the right to file suit in the Supreme Court?[12]

To resolve this, the chief justice reviewed the history of Reconstruction,
noting that when the Civil War ended, "there was no government in the
state except that which had been organized for purposes of waging war
against the United States. That government immediately disappeared."
To fill the void, the president had appointed a military governor, who had
organized elections, leading to a new state constitution and a provisional
state government. Congress, starting in 1865, and especially in the 1867
reconstruction laws, had continued the process. It was not necessary, Chase
said, to address whether these laws were in all respects constitutional;
they showed that even Congress recognized the provisional Southern
governments as a form of state government.[13]

Chase devoted special care, in his history of the Civil War and Reconstruction, to the status of the former slaves: "Slaves, in the insurgent states, with certain local exceptions, had been declared free by the proclamation of emancipation; and whatever questions might be made as to the effect of that act, under the Constitution, it was clear from the beginning that its practical operation" would be to free all the slaves. The Thirteenth Amendment had confirmed that the former slaves were now free people. "The new freemen necessarily became a part of the people, and the people still constituted the state; for states, like individuals, retain their identity, though changed to some extent in their constituent elements." It was the people of the Southern states, thus constituted to include the former slaves, who were entitled to the constitutional guarantee of a "republican form of government."[14]

Chase thus concluded that the current Texas government was entitled to file suit as a state. He then addressed whether the bonds belonged to the state, because the wartime transfer by the rebel government was invalid, or whether the bondholders were entitled to the bonds, because the transfer was valid. Building upon his *Keppel* opinion, the chief justice said that some acts of the former rebel state governments would be recognized as valid by the federal courts: "It may be said, perhaps with sufficient accuracy, that acts necessary to peace and good order among citizens—such as, for example, acts sanctioning and protecting marriage and the domestic relations, governing the course of descents, regulating the conveyance and transfer of property, real and personal, and providing remedies for injuries to person and estate, and other similar acts, which would be valid if emanating from a lawful government—must be regarded in general as valid when proceeding from an actual, though unlawful, government; and that acts in furtherance or support of rebellion against the United States, or intended to defeat the just rights of citizens, and other acts of like nature, must, in general, be regarded as invalid and void." In this case, the bonds were transferred by a state war board organized "not for the defense of the state against a foreign invasion, or for its protection against domestic violence . . . but for the purpose, under the name of defense, of levying war against the United States." The transfer agreement was thus a "contract in aid of the rebellion and, therefore, void."[15]

Three of Chase's colleagues—Grier, Miller, and Swayne—dissented from his opinion. In their view, because Texas was not represented in Congress yet, it was not entitled to file suit in the Supreme Court. Some scholars have criticized Chase's opinion, with one complaining that the discussion of secession "hardly seems an adequate treatment of an issue on which reasonable people had differed to the point of civil war." Chase, however, was proud of his *Texas* opinion, writing to Nettie that she and Kate "must pay me the compliment of reading it." He would be pleased to know that his successors on the Supreme Court, in the late-twentieth and early-twenty-first centuries, still cite *Texas v. White* on the rights of the states in the federal system. For example, Justice Sandra Day O'Connor—the first woman ever to sit on the Supreme Court—quoted *Texas v. White* in her 1991 opinion holding that the federal government could not prohibit a state from imposing age limits on state court judges.[16]

Life at the Washington home that Chase and Nettie shared with Kate and William Sprague was disrupted in 1869 by bitterness between Kate and her husband. One cause of the quarrel was a series of Senate speeches in which Sprague insulted almost everyone: senators, lawyers, generals, financiers, and ladies—including his wife. The first speech in the series, on March 15, was the most coherent and calm. Sprague argued that the American financial system was failing and urged Congress to create a commission to study the British system. Four days later, the Rhode Island senator gave another speech, saying that the root of many problems was that there were too many lawyers in Congress. "We have a government of lawyers and judges . . . educated in one line, practiced in one pursuit, educated upon the quarrels and exhibitions of the worst passions of human nature." Senator James Nye of Nevada, a lawyer—although by his own admission not a leading lawyer—responded by asking who had appointed Sprague as judge over the lawyers. Sprague had said that he could not understand some of the legislation of Congress. "Is that a lawyer's fault?" asked Nye, as the galleries laughed. "Perhaps if he had been a little more of a lawyer, he would not have been puzzled so much."[17]

Sprague's third speech, on March 24, was more belligerent, more apocalyptic. "There was less virtue and morality in American society," he insisted, "than in any other civilized society on the face of the earth. The prevailing demoralization was frightful. What mother could send her son out into the world with any confidence that he would be able to resist the temptations that would surround him? What husband could close his door with satisfaction?" People must have wondered: Was Sprague, known for his drinking and womanizing, now accusing his wife of impropriety? The senator said that he had favored the election of Grant "in opposition to the aspirations of one connected with me by family ties" because he believed Grant "had not been contaminated by the politicians and could see through and defeat their machinations." People must have wondered: Was Sprague suggesting that his father-in-law had been contaminated by the politicians? After reciting some of his own background, including how his father was murdered when he was only thirteen, Sprague complained about Nye. "The blow struck by the senator from Nevada the other day dropped deep into my heart and reminded me of the incident I have related." Again, people must have wondered; Did Sprague really mean to compare Senator Nye with a murderer?[18]

The *Chicago Tribune* correspondent was surprised to see Sprague, after "sitting silent these seven years," now speak with "vehement aggressiveness, which was as strange in manner as it was inexplicable in motive." At the same time, the reporter was at least somewhat impressed. "So incongruous, so queer," he wrote, "and yet so suggestive a speech I have never heard delivered in the Senate." The *New York Times* likened Sprague to an enraged prophet: a "voice in the wilderness" warning that the people would soon rise up and remove the other senators from their places. "His delivery is very poor, and it is absolutely painful to listen to him. His ideas seem to have no connection whatever, and his speeches lack all method. He . . . appears as regardless of the rules of rhetoric as of the feelings of his brother senators."[19]

Sprague's fourth speech, on March 30, was similar. He said that he was now under attack by the same "pernicious influences" that had "made cowards of men, disgraced regiments of men, disgraced a state, disgraced an army, disgraced a country." He claimed that financiers controlled the Congress and the country; indeed, "no people were ever so viciously controlled as the people of the United States now are." He insisted that he knew what he was talking about when he denounced American morals, adding: "Americans traveling abroad mingled with the dregs of European society and came back and inculcated upon society at home the immoralities and vices they had learned abroad." This was a clear attack on his wife, for everyone knew that Kate had spent many months in Europe in recent years.[20]

Kate was probably in the Senate galleries for this speech; the *Cleveland Plain Dealer* said that she was "always" present to hear Sprague and "watches him with great attention." Mary Viall, the Rhode Island woman with whom Sprague was still having an affair, was also in the galleries, for she described the scene in detail in the novel she published a few years later. According to Viall, Kate's beautiful face turned so red that it looked "like the face of any other angry red-faced woman" as she rushed up the narrow gallery steps and out of the Senate chamber. "For almost the first time in her life," Viall wrote, "the statesman's daughter dropped her mask."[21]

Within a few days after this speech, Kate and Nettie and Kate's son, Willie, left Washington, heading for a quiet resort in Aiken, South Carolina. A local paper reported that the two sisters intended to stay there until June. Chase wrote letter after letter to Kate, urging her to reconcile with her husband. "Let me entreat you to indulge no hard thoughts of him. You have both erred greatly; each ought to do all that is possible towards reconciliation." Kate should "humble your pride—yield even when you know you have the right on your side—remember the sacred obligation of your marriage vow—read it over and pray for strength and affection to keep it fully, in spirit as well as in act." Chase also tried, without much success, to talk with his son-in-law. He relayed to Kate her husband's claim that he was "sincerely anxious to have peace and goodwill restored," but the senator also insisted that he "could not be controlled by you."[22]

Sprague's speeches were one cause of the rift between him and his wife, but not the most serious cause. It seems that husband and wife each suspected the other of infidelity. For example, Chase wrote to Kate that Sprague had been looking for some papers in her room, especially the letters between her and one Colonel John Crosby. How Sprague knew that his wife was corresponding with Crosby and what her relations with him were, we do not know; nor do we know why he was searching her room. In another letter, Chase told Kate that he had received back in the post a letter that she had sent to a Mr. Ward; she had forgotten the stamp. "I am rather glad, for I don't want to have you write anything to anybody of the male variety of the human species."[23]

Meanwhile, in a letter to his son-in-law, who was in New York City for a few days, Chase noted that Sprague had hired as a house servant a "very fine-looking Englishwoman." Was it not, he asked, a "little risky to bring such a woman into the house while there are no other women here?" In 1880, when she filed a petition for divorce, Kate alleged that her husband committed adultery with this English servant, Harriet Brown, in 1869, as well as with Mary Viall and many other women, in this and other years. For his part, Sprague would later contend that the daughter Ethel, born to Kate in October 1869, was not his child.[24]

Although Chase believed that wives should generally defer to their husbands, he also believed that women should have stronger legal rights. In early 1869 Chase received a request from Elizabeth Smith Miller, daughter of Gerrit Smith and a prominent figure in the women's rights movement, for a letter on women's rights that she could read at a public meeting. Chase responded that he did not have time to "write anything which I should be willing to have read in public," but then he continued:

"You will not be mistaken if you believe me heartily desirous of all things which will really improve the condition of woman. Among such things, I count the increase of facilities for moral and intellectual culture; ample recognition and full protection to rights of property; and access to and perfect security in all employments for which she is qualified by strength, capacity, and integrity. I am, also, so far, at least, in favor of suffrage for women, that I should like to see the experiment tried in one or more of the states, and, if found to work well, extended to all. I am sufficiently confident of good results to be willing to vote for it in the state where I reside." In other words, although Chase was not in favor of a federal constitutional amendment granting women the right to vote, he would support women's suffrage in his home state if the issue was on the ballot.[25]

Chase left Washington in early May to hold circuit courts in the South, stopping first in Richmond. The key cases here involved the disqualification provision of the Fourteenth Amendment. The local district judge, John Underwood, had ruled that it took effect on the day the amendment was ratified and had thus invalidated some state court criminal convictions from the previous fall. Noting that Congress had passed legislation to establish a later effective date, Chase reversed Underwood, in a decision widely praised in Southern press.[26]

Chase's next stop was South Carolina, a state recently added to his circuit. Not long after arriving in Charleston, he was invited to an event to honor the Union dead in Magnolia Cemetery. Chase could not attend the event but applauded the purpose. "The nation cannot too tenderly cherish the memory of her dead heroes, or too watchfully guard the well-being of those who survive. And may we not indulge the hope that ere long we who adhered to the national cause will be prompt also to join in commemorating the heroism of our countrymen who fell on the other side, and that those who now specially mourn their loss, consenting to the arbitrament of arms, and resuming all their old love for their country and our country, one and indivisible, will join with us in like commemoration of the fallen brave of the army of the Union." Like Lincoln, who had called on the nation to learn from those who died at Gettysburg, Chase called on the nation to learn from those who died in the Civil War. "Why may not we all borrow from their sacred graves oblivion of past differences and henceforth unite in noble and generous endeavor to assure the honor and welfare of our whole country, of all her states and of all her citizens?"[27]

When Chase's letter was printed in the papers, he heard from an angry New York banker, who argued that the Union should honor only the Union soldiers. Chase replied that he had "no sympathy with the spirit which refuses to strew flowers upon the graves of the dead soldiers who fought against the side I took, and I am glad to know there was no such spirit among those who joined in decorating the graves of the soldiers of the Union who lie buried at Magnolia Cemetery." Responding to the suggestion that his letter was prompted by ambition, Chase wrote that the "chief justice is, I think, not ill employed when he inculcates goodwill among men." Chase was never as "ambitious as some unambitious people have represented me. At any rate, I am now unconscious of any other ambition than that of doing as much good and as little harm as possible." He would be "fully satisfied with my share of the general welfare, which it may be hoped wise and generous statesmanship, with God's blessing, will secure for our country."[28]

By mid-July, Chase was back in Washington to address the first phase of what would become a famous Supreme Court case, *Ex parte Yerger*. The dispute arose when the city authorities of Jackson, Mississippi, seized for unpaid back taxes the family piano of Edward Yerger, a former rebel officer and newspaper editor. Drunk and enraged, Yerger stabbed and killed on the streets of Jackson the Ohio lawyer serving as the town's temporary military mayor. Army officers immediately arrested Yerger and placed him on trial before a military commission. Yerger's lawyers, arguing that their client was entitled to a jury trial in the state courts, applied for a writ of habeas corpus to Justice Noah Swayne, whose circuit included Mississippi. Swayne declined to issue the writ but expressed (in Chase's words) "his perfect willingness that the application should be made to me and granted or denied according to my views of the law." Yerger's lawyers then applied to Chase, who believed that a military commission, four years after the end of the war, was not the right way to try a murder case. But he worried about whether he had authority outside his judicial circuit. Chase conferred by letter with two of his colleagues on the court, Samuel Nelson and Nathan Clifford. They advised that although each justice could hold circuit court only in his assigned circuit, issuing a writ of habeas corpus to free an unjustly imprisoned man was different; each justice had the right to issue such a writ with respect to any prisoner anywhere in the nation.[29]

For four hours, in a crowded conference room on a hot day in July, Chase heard arguments on these issues. He drafted but never issued an order to require the government to produce Yerger in Washington in October. Instead, with the chief justice's approval, and perhaps at his suggestion, counsel reached a compromise that would enable the case to proceed in a more typical way: Yerger's lawyers would apply to the district judge in Mississippi, seeking a writ from him, with the expectation that he would deny the writ, and thus allow the full Supreme Court to hear an appeal from that decision.[30]

Newspapers viewed both Chase's Southern tour and the *Yerger* case in political terms.

The *New York Herald* commented that "Chief Justice Chase, in his tour of the southern states, is gaining golden opinions from all the anti-radical Southern elements." A week later, the paper reported that Chase had "made a Southern political prospecting tour in view of the next Democratic presidential convention" and that he had "been hailed as the coming man by the Southern conservatives." The *Cincinnati Gazette*, covering the election in Virginia of a conservative Republican governor, claimed that "from first to last, Chief Justice Chase was consulted, and, for much of the time, he was upon the ground in person." The Virginia election could be "regarded as the first success of the Chase movement for the next presidential campaign." The *Baltimore American* agreed, seeing a strong conservative movement for Chase within the Republican Party. "The only real division," per the *American*, was between "earnest, active, and true Republicans, who support General Grant and his administration, and those who would destroy the Republican Party in the interest of Judge Chase."[31]

Some papers criticized Chase's handling of the *Yerger* case. Southern papers had hoped that he would not only release Yerger but also declare that military commissions were no longer constitutional. The *Louisville Courier-Journal* feared that Chase did not have "the courage to confront Congress squarely in the discharge of his functions. But if he means to be a candidate for the presidency, he had better have all sorts of courage." The *Chicago Tribune*, from the other side, believed that military commissions were still necessary in the South and feared that Chase wanted to use the *Yerger* case for political purposes. A decision that "Northern officials in Southern states have no rights which the chivalry are bound to respect, would raise a howl of demonic exultation from the whole rebel, Democratic, and Copperhead crew."[32]

Chase responded to these articles with letters to friends, denying that he had any political plans. To Daniel Butterfield, the former Union general, Chase explained that he was not touring the South for political purposes; he was simply attending the circuit courts to which he was assigned. Chase had not been anxious for the 1868 nomination, "whatever folks may say," and he was not looking for the 1872 nomination. "I hope, unfeignedly, that the nomination and election of General Grant will prove a real blessing to the country, and I shall be very glad if his administration proves so beneficial that the people will hear of nobody as his successor except himself." To William Rosecrans, another former Union general, Chase said that he had "very little interest in political movements except so far as general principles are involved or friends." He would leave political disputes to "younger men" and "look to nothing except the discharge of my judicial duties."[33]

Although Chase did a great deal of judicial work in the summer of 1869, there was also some personal time. Nettie and Kate left Aiken more or less when Chase arrived in Charleston. Nettie joined her father in Charleston and for the remainder of his Southern circuit, while Kate and her husband, having reconciled somewhat, went to their home in Narragansett, Rhode Island. Chase was able to visit them there for a few days in July, as well as for several weeks in late August and early September. In a letter to General Sherman, urging him to come to Narragansett with his daughters, Chase described the "big, old-fashioned house by the sea" and promised "plenty to eat from the farm, capital bathing, a delightful climate—all you want of tenpins and billiards." After returning to Washington, Chase wrote to Kate that he was pleased to learn she was expecting her second child and "delighted to see the restoration of the old affection between you and your husband. God grant that it may never be interrupted again."[34]

Chase was one of thousands who traveled to Hanover this summer to celebrate the hundredth anniversary of Dartmouth College. As president of the alumni association, Chase gave one of the principal speeches, stressing the college's role in the changes of the past hundred years: "Ninety-eight classes of young men have already gone forth from this institution; who can measure the religious, the moral, the intellectual, the political influence which they have exerted?" Dartmouth had some famous sons, such as Daniel Webster, but Chase was speaking mainly about the quiet contributions of lesser-known graduates. He closed by hoping that the "gladness and the gratitude with which we come together" would change as they departed into "earnest devotion to the best interests of our benignant mother in the future, so that the second centennial shall as much exceed the fulfillment of the present as the present one exceeds the feebleness and apparent insignificance of the days of small things which we commemorate." General Sherman was also among the Dartmouth guests, largely because Chase had urged him to come, writing playfully that as chief justice he might have to issue some orders, which Sherman, as head of the army, might have to enforce, to keep "the boys" in line.[35]

Chase decided this summer that he and Nettie would move out of the Washington house that they had long shared with Sprague and Kate. He wrote to Kate that "Nettie naturally feels that she wants a house of her own, or rather that her father should have a house and that she should be at the head of it." This may have been one reason to leave the shared house and move to rented quarters at 1827 I Street. Surely another was that (whatever he might write about the "restoration of the old affection") Chase knew that relations between Kate and her husband were strained. By moving out of the E Street house, he could get some distance from the difficulties between the two of them.[36]

At about this same time, Chase purchased a house with fifty wooded acres on high ground about two miles north of Capitol Hill. The structure was old and "bare and worn," Chase wrote Kate, but the "prospect of the Capitol and the Potomac beyond and the hills is splendid—nothing could be finer." To raise the purchase price, Chase had to sell some property in Cincinnati as well as borrow from Jay Cooke. Chase called this estate Edgewood, and the name persists as the name of the neighborhood in northeast Washington.[37]

The summer of 1869 was shorter for Chase and the other justices because they had agreed, before leaving on their circuits in April, that they would return to Washington and resume work in early October. The chief justice hoped that by holding court for two months in October and November, before the official term started in December, they could reduce the backlog of cases. Chase was no doubt annoyed when, on the agreed-upon date, Monday, October 5, only three of the other justices were present. He had to adjourn the court for a day, and then for another day, before there was a quorum.[38]

Despite the brief delay, this fall turned out to be productive for the court, which issued more than fifty opinions in the last three months of the year. Chase continued his practice of shouldering more than his share of the workload, drafting nine of these. There were only eight justices at this time, and one of them, Grier, was so aged and infirm that he could not contribute much. Congress had passed a law in April increasing the number of Supreme Court justices to nine and providing that any federal judge over the age of seventy, with at least ten years of service, could retire at full salary for the rest of his life. In a minor victory for Chase, this law used the formal title he preferred and that would ultimately become accepted—chief justice of the United States—rather than the more-common chief justice of the Supreme Court of the United States. The retirement section was drafted with Grier in mind, and a few days after it took effect in December, Chase and Nelson called at the seventy-five-year-old justice's house. According to a letter from Grier's daughter, Chase told him that the "politicians are determined to oust him" and that if he did not resign, Congress would "repeal the law giving the retiring salaries." Grier responded that "if they wished him to resign, he would do so." Two days later, Grier submitted his resignation to Grant, effective on the first of February 1870.[39]

Ulysses Grant thus had a chance given to few presidents: to make two appointments to the Supreme Court at the same time. His first choice was his attorney general, Ebenezer Hoar, but the conservative Massachusetts lawyer had alienated many senators, and it was soon clear that the Senate would not approve the nomination. Grant's second choice for associate justice, Edwin Stanton, was easily confirmed. But just four days later, on December 24, 1869, the fifty-five-year-old Stanton died of heart failure before he could take his seat on the court. Chase and Stanton had not been close in recent years, but Chase still mourned his death. "How sudden and how sad," he wrote to his friend James Pike. "Only yesterday, Sumner and Hooper were here, and we were talking of the prospect of perfect restoration, which we were all glad to think, his appointment to the Supreme Bench afforded to him. And already he is gone."[40]

The most controversial case on the court calendar this fall was that of Yerger, the Mississippi murderer. On October 15 the court heard a full day of argument on jurisdiction: whether the court had authority to review and decide the case. Only ten days later, Chase issued the court's detailed opinion, joined by all but one of the justices. He began by reviewing habeas corpus in both English and American law, noting that the "great writ of habeas corpus has been for centuries esteemed the best and only sufficient defense of personal freedom." The right to petition for habeas corpus was guaranteed by the Constitution, except in time of rebellion or invasion, and the first Congress, in the Judiciary Act of 1789, had confirmed that the Supreme Court, and individual justices, had the power to issue writs of habeas corpus. The purpose of the 1868 statute, Chase explained, was to prevent the court from deciding the *McCardle* case, not to take away the court's power to consider all habeas corpus petitions. Congress had repealed only one section of a single recent statute—not all the prior laws and principles authorizing the court to review by way of habeas corpus lower federal court decisions. The court therefore had jurisdiction.[41]

Chase's opinion did not address the merits of Yerger's claim, and, indeed, the court never decided whether his military trial was constitutional. On the day after the court issued this decision on jurisdiction, counsel informed the court that Yerger would not seek an immediate ruling on the merits; perhaps both sides feared an adverse decision from the court. A few months later, the federal military transferred Yerger to state authorities, who charged him with murder. Yerger was soon released on bail, however, and never tried by the state. Still, even limited to the question of jurisdiction, Chase's opinion in *Yerger* was one of his most important. After Chase's death, the court would use *Yerger* to protect black voting rights, and the court still cites *Yerger* in cases about federal judicial review. In 2006, for example, the Supreme Court relied on *Yerger* and other precedents to conclude that Congress had not precluded the court from reviewing the case of a prisoner being held in the Guantanamo Bay detention camp in Cuba.[42]

Another key case on the docket in late 1869 was *Hepburn v. Griswold*, the constitutional challenge to the legal tender law. The eight justices discussed this case for three hours at their conference on Saturday, November 29, and initially they were evenly divided, with Chase and three others against the law, and Grier and three others in favor. But then the justices discussed a related case, and it seemed that Grier believed it was not constitutional for Congress to force a creditor to accept notes in payment of a contract entered before the effective date of the legal tender law. So Chase, for a majority of five, including Grier, who may well have been confused, started drafting his opinion to declare the legal tender law unconstitutional with respect to prior agreements for specie payments.[43]

The chief justice was especially interested in a third major case, *Veazie Bank v. Fenno*, a constitutional challenge to a 10 percent tax imposed by Congress on notes issued by state banks. Chase's opinion for the court, issued in December, started with a brief financial history of the Civil War. He noted that at the outset of the war, the "circulating medium consisted almost entirely of banknotes issued by numerous independent corporations variously organized under state legislation, of various degrees of credit, and very unequal resources, administered often with great and not unfrequently with little skill, prudence, and integrity." To help finance the war, and to help create a single national currency, Congress passed and then revised the National Bank Act. For a while, Congress taxed the notes issued by state and national banks more or less equally, until 1866, when it imposed the 10 percent tax on state banknotes. Chase did not mention that he, as Treasury secretary, had argued for a steep tax to discourage state banks from issuing notes. The *New York World* complained that Chase should not have participated in the *Veazie* case, for he was the "father" of the national banks and the "instigator of the tax whose manifest design was to cripple and crush the rival state institutions."[44]

The first question in *Veazie* was whether the tax on state banknotes was a "direct tax" and therefore unconstitutional because it was not apportioned among the states by population. Conceding that the line between direct and indirect taxes was not easily drawn, Chase reviewed the history, especially the 1796 case of *Hylton v. United States*, decided when the justices were fresh from the process of drafting and ratifying the Constitution. Concluding that the banknote tax was not a direct tax, Chase turned to the second question: whether the tax was an impermissible interference with the sovereign rights of the states.[45]

Here he distinguished between state governments and private corporations created under state law, such as state-chartered banks. Congress could not impose taxes on state governments themselves, but it could impose taxes on corporations created under state laws or (as in this case) on contracts issued by such corporations. The bank insisted that the tax was "so excessive as to indicate a purpose on the part of Congress to destroy the franchise of the bank." Chase responded that the "power to tax may be exercised oppressively upon persons, but the responsibility of the legislature is not to the courts, but to the people by whom its members are elected. So if a particular tax bears heavily upon a corporation, or a class of corporations, it cannot, for that reason only, be pronounced contrary to the Constitution." In essence, Chase was saying that Congress was well within its powers when it used taxes to limit the operations of state banks and to encourage state banks to seek federal charters. Chief Justice John Roberts would note in his 2012 opinion on the Obamacare individual insurance mandate that "taxes that seek to influence conduct are nothing new."[46]

After the 1868 election, Chase called himself a Democrat, yet he remained close with many Republicans, including his friend Sumner. Early in January 1870 Chase called on Sumner, and they had a "long talk, principally about Cuba." Sumner was on the edge of a quarrel, which would turn into an all-out war, with Grant, primarily over the president's plan to annex the island nation of Santo Domingo, now the Dominican Republic. Chase may have had some sense of the incipient trouble, for he told Sumner that he was "satisfied generally with the administration and especially with the action of General Grant as to the colored citizens." Indeed, President Grant had shown himself a firm friend of African Americans, appointing the first black American ambassador and hundreds of blacks to less prominent positions, such as customs collectors, revenue officers, and postmasters. Only a few days before this, the papers noted that the new black ambassador from Haiti was "welcomed most cordially" at the White House by President Grant.[47]

Chase also agreed with Grant—and disagreed with most Democrats—about the Fifteenth Amendment. Democrats opposed the amendment because they believed that blacks did not deserve the right to vote and feared that if blacks secured suffrage, they would always vote for Republicans. But Chase, after his initial hesitation, not only supported the amendment but also lobbied for its ratification. In a long letter to George Hill, an Ohio legislator whose vote Chase had heard would be decisive on ratification in his home state, Chase said that he still favored "universal suffrage and universal amnesty." He regretted the delays in securing universal amnesty (many former rebels were still barred from holding office by the Fourteenth Amendment), but, in his view, the Fifteenth Amendment presented "an opportunity for universal suffrage." There was no reason to fear the section authorizing legislation, he wrote, because it would give "no power to Congress to interfere with suffrage in any state unless it is denied or abridged by the state, on account of race, color, or former slavery." If the Fifteenth Amendment was not ratified, and Ohio persisted in its practice of denying black men the right to vote, Chase predicted that the state would lose representatives in Congress under the Fourteenth Amendment. Chase sent similar letters to his friend Yeatman as the Ohio vote approached.[48]

On January 14 the Ohio Senate approved the constitutional amendment by a vote of nineteen to eighteen, with Chase's friend Yeatman the leader of those in favor. On January 20 the Ohio House approved the amendment, fifty-seven to fifty-five, with Chase's friend Hill in favor. Chase's pleasure was dimmed somewhat by seeing in the papers a version of one of his letters to Yeatman, which the *Chicago Tribune* characterized as just a "bid for the presidency."[49]

A few weeks later, after the Fifteenth Amendment had been ratified by enough states to become part of the Constitution, Chase wrote another letter, one that he fully intended to see published. A committee of Cincinnati blacks had invited him to speak at their celebration of the amendment. Chase had to decline because of work in Washington, but wrote that he was pleased to see the principles of equal voting rights, which he had advocated as long ago as his silver pitcher speech, now enshrined in the Constitution. "Every good man," Chase said, rejoiced "in the progress which the colored citizens of the United States have made in education, in religious culture, and in the general improvement of their condition. Every good man must earnestly desire their continued and accelerated progress in

the same direction." Nobody now advocated a return to slavery, and Chase
predicted that the day would soon arrive when nobody—not even those who
had opposed the new amendment—would oppose black voting rights.[50]

The key case on the court calendar in early 1870 was the legal tender
case, *Hepburn v. Griswold*. Chase took a long time to draft his opinion
before presenting it to his colleagues at their conference on January 29.
The three justices who planned to dissent, led by Miller, asked for more
time to prepare their opinion. Chase thus was not able, as he had hoped,
to deliver his *Hepburn* opinion on Grier's last day on the court, January
31. He read the decision on February 7 instead.[51]

The facts in *Hepburn* were simple enough. Susan Hepburn signed an
agreement in 1860 to pay $11,000 plus interest to Henry Griswold.
When she did not pay on the due date, Griswold filed suit, and Hepburn
finally offered to pay in Treasury notes, relying on the law making such
notes "legal tender in payment of all debts, public and private, within the
United States." Griswold refused to accept legal tender notes, insisting
on payment in gold or silver.[52]

In the first part of his opinion, Chase found that even though the
contract had not specified payment in specie, all contracts made before
1862 (the date of the first legal tender law) legally contemplated such
payment. He also found that he could not solve the problem by a narrow
interpretation of the law. The court would thus have to decide "whether
Congress has power to make notes issued under its authority a legal tender in payment of debts which, when contracted, were payable by law in
gold and silver coins."[53]

The federal government, Chase stressed, was a government of "limited
powers," and it was the role of the court to determine when Congress
had exceeded the limits imposed by the Constitution. Since there was no
explicit constitutional power to require people to accept federal notes as
legal tender, the question was whether this requirement was "necessary and
proper" for implementing some specific power. Here Chase quoted Chief
Justice John Marshall's opinion in the 1819 case, *McCulloch v. Maryland*:
"Let the end be legitimate, let it be within the scope of the constitution,
and all means which are appropriate, which are plainly adapted to that
end, which are not prohibited, but consist with the letter and spirit of
the constitution, are constitutional."[54]

But Chase looked quite closely and skeptically at whether it was really necessary for Congress to require people to accept the legal tender notes as payment for prior debts. He pointed out that the Treasury had issued notes both with and without the legal tender requirement during the Civil War; that those "not declared a legal tender at all constituted a very large proportion; and that they circulated freely and without discount." He argued that whatever benefit Congress gained by compelling people to accept legal tender notes for prior debts, was "far more than outweighed by the losses of property, the derangement of business, the fluctuations of currency and values, and the increase of prices to the people and the government, and the long train of evils which flow from the use of irre-deemable paper money." Chase therefore concluded that it was neither necessary nor proper for Congress to impose a legal tender requirement with respect to debts contracted before the date of the legal tender law.[55]

Chase also considered whether the legal tender requirement was con-sistent with the "spirit of the Constitution." Although he did not use the phrase, he relied on what we would call "substantive due process": the doctrine that some rights are so fundamental that they cannot be violated even if the government observes proper procedures. The legal tender law, Chase wrote, was like an act "compelling all citizens to accept, in satisfaction of all contracts for money, half or three-quarters or any other proportion less than the whole of the value actually due, according to their terms. It is difficult to conceive what act would take private property without process of law if such an act would not." In his private letters, Chase was even more scathing: "Honesty is always correct. Our constitution was made by honest men. No interpretation of it which makes it sanction dishonesty can be right. Our fathers did not believe in india-rubber yard sticks or in paper dollars."[56]

At the end of his *Hepburn* opinion, Chase alluded to his own change of course. Early 1862, when people were afraid that the Union might fail, was not a time "favorable to considerate reflection upon the constitutional limits of legislative or executive authority." Some (like Chase) were "strongly averse to making government notes a legal tender" but still "felt themselves constrained to acquiesce in the views of the advocates of the measure." Now, in a "calmer time," some (like Chase) had "reconsidered their conclu-sions."[57] Miller, joined by Davis and Swayne, dissented. Their fundamental disagreement with the chief justice was that they believed it *was* necessary and proper, under the Constitution, for Congress to impose the legal tender requirement. The dissenting justices criticized Chase for "second-guessing" the decision that Congress had made in the midst of the Civil War.[58]

Later in this same busy month, the Supreme Court, for the first time, invalidated a federal law because it exceeded the authority conveyed to Congress by the Commerce Clause: the authority to "regulate commerce with foreign nations, and among the several states, and with the Indian tribes." The law challenged in *United States v. Dewitt* prohibited anyone from selling certain types of oil; the prohibition applied even to making and selling such oil within the boundaries of a single state. In a short opinion for a unanimous court, Chase declared that the "power to regulate commerce among the states has always been understood as limited by its terms, and as a virtual denial of any power to interfere with the internal trade and business of the separate states, except, indeed, as a necessary and proper means for carrying into execution some other power expressly granted or vested." The government lawyers tried to defend this law as a necessary and proper means of enforcing federal tax laws, and pointed to federal rules for liquor distilleries, but Chase responded that the analogy failed because the "regulations referred to are restricted to the very articles which are the subject of taxation and are plainly adapted to secure the collection of the tax imposed; while, in the case before us, no tax is imposed on the oils the sale of which is prohibited." Chief Justice John Roberts would use a similar approach in 2012, when he ruled that the federal requirement to purchase health insurance could not be upheld as a regulation of commerce but was valid as a federal tax.[59]

The Senate was considering two controversial nominations to the Supreme Court in February 1870: those of Joseph Bradley, a railroad lawyer from New Jersey, and William Strong, a corporate lawyer and then state court judge from Pennsylvania. Grant made the nominations on the day of the *Hepburn* decision, and people expected that both Bradley and Strong would join with Miller and the other dissenters to reverse Chase's decision in that case. Some newspapers accused the president of packing the court for just this purpose. There is evidence pointing both ways on this issue, but it is interesting that Grant acknowledged later that he was keen to see the court sustain the constitutionality of the legal tender requirement and that he knew, when he named them, that Strong and Bradley were inclined to vote in favor of legal tender. Thus Grant, like most presidents, nominated justices whom he believed would agree with his position on important and controversial issues.[60]

At the first Saturday conference after both Bradley and Strong had joined the court, Miller urged that the court should consider two other legal tender cases and consider all the issues in these cases—including the constitutional issue just decided in *Hepburn*. Chase objected but was outvoted by Miller, Davis, Swayne, Bradley, and Strong. A few days later, there was a "very lively scene" in the courtroom, with Chase insisting and Miller denying that the court had informed counsel that they would not be allowed to raise the constitutional question, because it would be decided by *Hepburn*. The upshot was an order that the two cases would be heard in late April. On the appointed day, however, counsel for the appellants said that their clients wished to dismiss their appeals, so it seemed that Chase had prevailed over Miller. "We have had a desperate struggle in the secret conference of the court for three weeks over two cases involving the legal tender question," Miller complained to a relative. "The chief justice has resorted to all the stratagems of the lowest political trickery to prevent their being heard, and the fight has been bitter in the conference room." Miller managed to find another way to reach the legal tender question, however: the court would hear a different case. After another bitter discussion in conference, Chase had to announce on April 30, the last day of the term, that the court would hear in the fall another legal tender case, *Knox v. Lee*. Unless something changed, it looked like Miller and his four colleagues would use *Knox* to reverse *Hepburn*.[61]

When Chase arrived in Richmond in early May 1870 for a week of circuit court, he found the city in mourning. A few days before this, while the state supreme court was in session in its third-floor courtroom, above the high-ceilinged assembly chamber, the floor collapsed, sending many to their death. The governor appointed May 4 as a day of prayer, and Chase, before adjourning court on that day, gave a short speech. "Human emotions are poorly expressed by words," he began. "When the first vague rumors of the terrible event in this city, which has been so fitly named 'the Great Calamity,' went through the land a few days ago, all hearts felt a shock like that of a sudden and awful personal bereavement." Chase himself grieved to think of some Richmond residents whom he had known who were killed. "How terribly does such a calamity as this rebuke our vain expectations! How impressively does it admonish every one of us to look beyond the shadows of time to the realities of eternity!" Chase urged the people of Richmond, when they went to church that day, to take with them not only their sorrow but also the "consolations of faith" and to remember that "all is of God."[62]

Chase's own health was not particularly strong at this time. In fact, the sixty-two-year-old was so weak that some papers speculated that he would soon retire. Taking advantage of a new law, allowing the justices to visit each district only every other year, Chase did not travel to the other states in his circuit in the summer of 1870. When he visited New York City in June, he conferred with a famous physician, Alonzo Clark. Chase had been worried about his heart, but Dr. Clark did not think there was any serious cardiac issue; his primary concern was diabetes. It was probably at least in part at the doctor's recommendation that Chase spent this summer relaxing rather than working.[63]

Chase and Nettie left Washington in late June for the West. They spent time with family and friends in Ohio, Illinois, and Minnesota, staying both in cities (Chicago and Saint Paul) and remote villages (such as Ludlow, Illinois, where they visited some of the Ludlow family). On their way back east, they stopped in Niagara Falls, then boarded a train for New York City on August 16. It was on this train trip that Chase suffered a severe stroke, paralyzing the right side of his body "from the toe to the scalp," so that by the time he reached the city, he could "scarcely speak intelligibly." Nettie managed to get her father to their hotel and summoned doctors. After a week in New York, Kate and Nettie transferred their father to Narragansett, where he would rest and recover for the next several months.[64]

There were no press reports about the chief justice's stroke in August, and the first accounts in September were contradictory. The New York World reported that Chase had suffered a "paralytic stroke" in Rhode Island. "He is unable to walk, and his mind seems shattered and impaired." The Boston Journal disagreed, saying that Chase was "rapidly recovering from the illness brought on by his trip to Lake Superior, and yesterday was able to take his daily walk without any assistance." The New York Standard claimed that the "great statesman will resume his labors in the fall, sound in mind and body, and capable of doing the prodigious amount of work which has characterized every day of his public life." The patient himself told a friend that the newspapers exaggerated as usual. "I have neither been so ill nor am I quite so well now as they represent me," wrote Chase. "I can walk and ride very nearly as usual, but I am unable to write or to think with readiness or accuracy."[65]

This was one of dozens of letters that Chase dictated during his long, slow recovery, usually using a clerk, or sometimes one of his daughters, to write for him. He commented on legal and political developments, including the resignation of Interior Secretary Jacob Cox, who had disagreed with Grant about civil service reform. He wrote letters almost daily to his physician in New York City about his health. He wrote often to his friend Richard Parsons, who was serving as the marshal of the Supreme Court and, more generally, as Chase's personal agent in Washington, dealing, for example, with improvements at Edgewood. Chase drafted and submitted through Parsons a bill to revise aspects of the judicial system, including giving the power to appoint bankruptcy registers to the circuit justices rather than the chief justice.[66]

Interestingly, with the exception of one letter to Justice Nelson, it seems that Chase did not write to his colleagues on the court, nor did they write to him. Justice Miller wrote to a friend that it seemed that Chase would not resign "unless he is provided with something else" and that Grant would not give Chase the European appointment that would be "the only alternative to his remaining a figurehead to the court." Justice Davis groused to a relative that Chase's daughters were "contriving to keep his exact condition concealed from the public" because they feared that "his true condition, if known, might hurt his political prospects, and his family live in hopes he will ultimately get well, and certainly in season to be the Democratic candidate."[67]

It seems that Chase never considered retiring from the court. He was not eligible for the retirement provision devised for Grier, because he had not yet served ten years and was not yet seventy. There was no other retirement provision for federal judges, so there was a serious financial incentive for Chase to remain. He was also keen to take part in important cases, such as the legal tender dispute. And his daughters may well have encouraged him to stay; Miller wrote that Kate would "never consent to his retiring to private life."[68]

Chase hoped and expected to return to Washington and to his work in late November or early December—but this proved impossible. Instead, he made arrangements to rent rooms on Fifth Avenue in New York City, where he would be closer to his doctor, and Nettie closer to her future husband, Will Hoyt. After spending Christmas with Kate and her children in Narragansett, Chase and Nettie moved to Manhattan in the first few days of the new year.[69]

CHAPTER 26

"Quite Content"

1871–73

Chase's income never quite covered his expenses, and he wrote to Henry Cooke in early 1871 to say that he planned to overdraw his account at the Cooke bank by about $15,000 to cover the cost of work at Edgewood. Chase thus had a personal as well as professional interest in legislation under consideration at this time to increase the salaries of all federal judges. The House passed a bill to increase the salary of the chief justice from $6,500 to $8,500 and to increase other judges' wages proportionally. The Senate committee proposed that judicial salaries should be increased even further: in the case of the chief justice, to $10,500. After speaking with Sprague, Chase reported to Parsons in Washington that his son-in-law the senator would support these figures. On February 15, however, the full Senate amended the committee bill to reduce the salaries, down to $8,500 for the chief justice. The vote on this amendment was extremely close: twenty-nine in favor and twenty-eight against. Parsons was shocked that Sprague was one of the senators who voted for lower salaries. "Why would he not help us in this emergency?" he asked Chase, who could not explain Sprague's vote.[1]

Another issue of concern to Chase was the memory of his predecessor, Chief Justice Roger Taney. A movement was under way in early 1871 to honor Taney by raising funds to support his impoverished daughters. Although some Republicans saw no reason to honor a justice who had supported slavery, Chase disagreed, writing Parsons that "few better judges or purer men have sat upon the bench than Judge Taney." In the chief's view, Taney "made one great mistake"—the *Dred Scott* decision denying blacks citizenship—"but that does not affect my overall estimate of his character." Chase also believed that there should be a bust of Taney, along with those of the other former chief justices, in the courtroom of the Supreme Court. The main reason that there was no such bust was Charles Sumner, who had blocked the bill not long after Taney's death, declaring that the "name of Taney is to be hooted down the page of history." Chase hoped Congress would change its mind and pass a bill to pay for a sculptor, but this did not happen until after Chase's death.[2]

Chase returned to Washington in early March 1871 but did not return at once to his seat on the court. It seems that he was prepared to allow his colleagues to handle the routine cases on the calendar, but wanted to be on the bench when the legal tender issue was argued. Since construction was starting at Edgewood, Chase stayed with Kate, William, and their two children on E Street.[3]

The Chase-Sprague house was the scene of one of the main social events of the season: the reception after the March marriage of Nettie Chase and William Sprague Hoyt. The couple had known one another for several years, because Will Hoyt was a cousin of William Sprague. Like his cousin, twenty-four-year-old Will did not have a college education, for he had started working in his father's New York mercantile firm, Hoyt, Sprague & Co., at a young age. But in almost every other respect, Will Hoyt was at this point unlike William Sprague: sober, serious, faithful, and not quite rich.[4]

The church service was at St. John's Episcopal at one in the afternoon. The papers reported that Kate "wore a dress of rib-green silk, with a court-train," and that she entered the church on the arm of the groom. Then the twenty-three-year-old bride, dressed in "white illusion" with an "exquisite wreath of orange flowers," entered on the arm of her father, who "seemed to have thrown aside a score of years" and whose "tall form was proudly erect as he stepped forward to give away the bride." Because the rector of the church objected to weddings during the somber season of Lent, the couple was married by Chase's friend Bishop Charles McIlvaine, who did not have such scruples. The rector objected even more to the way in which the Chases changed the decorations of the church, from purple to white, complaining that the family "abused my hospitality in the most inexcusable way."[5]

The guests at the afternoon reception included President Grant, most members of the Cabinet, the justices of the Supreme Court, and many senators and representatives. From three until six, according to the *New York Times,* "the streets around the house were nearly impassable, from the throng of carriages, and at least five or six hundred persons were received." That night, the couple traveled by train to New York, from which they soon departed for several months in Europe. Will and Nettie were adventurous: in an illustrated letter from Wales, she described and sketched how they climbed the country's highest mountain, Snowdon, through rain and sleet. She closed with a word of advice for those considering the climb: "don't."[6]

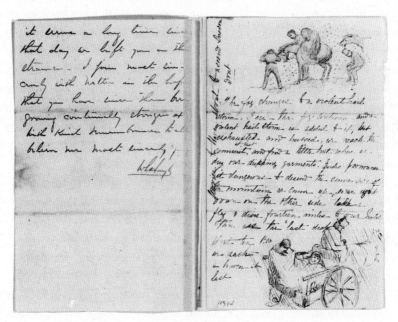

Part of Nettie's letter describing their ascent of Snowdon in Wales;
she sketched herself on horseback in the "violent hail" near the summit.

A few weeks later, on April 18, Chase and all the other justices were in their places in the courtroom to hear argument in two legal tender cases. Congressman Clarkson Potter, arguing against the legal tender requirement, urged the Supreme Court not to reverse itself so soon on such an important issue. To review "an abstract constitutional question so solemnly decided, not because of changes or doubts on the part of those who shared in the decision, but through a change in the composition of the court" would "divert the regard of the people from the court itself to the personnel of those who compose it." Attorney General Amos Akerman, defending the constitutionality of the legal tender requirement, insisted that the Supreme Court should defer to Congress. "The court may decide the question of congressional power," he stated, "but not the question of congressional wisdom."[7]

At their next Saturday conference, the justices divided as Chase had feared: Miller and four others voted to uphold the legal tender requirement. The chief justice was dismayed but commented in a letter to a friend that if five justices could reverse the decision that five others (counting Grier) had just made, then "under a new president, the later decision may be, itself, reversed." Chase was not as discouraged as his friend about the overall political situation: "My faith is that Providence always provides suitable men for the work of each generation. Clay, Webster, and Calhoun would hardly have suited the work of the war. Lincoln and his coworkers might not have suited the work of Reconstruction. They who have carried that work so near completion, will not, probably, be found competent to the work which the New Era will find for men to do. Men and their purposes change; God and his purposes change not."[8]

On the last day of the term, May 1, Justice Clifford announced that the court would uphold the legal tender requirement and that Chase and three others would dissent. The court did not read or release opinions at this time, however; those would not come until after the election.[9]

As much as he insisted that he was no longer interested in politics, Chase could never quite leave politics alone. In late May he wrote to Clement Vallandigham, who had returned to Ohio and to Democratic politics, a short letter praising him for a platform he had drafted for a state convention. Like other so-called New Departure Democrats, Vallandigham accepted the recent constitutional amendments, including black voting rights, but opposed further "centralization and consolidation," and decried Republican corruption. Chase wrote that Vallandigham had "rendered a great service to your country and to the party" and that he hoped to see the Democratic Party restored "to its ancient platform of progress and reform." The letter would probably have remained private if Vallandigham had not died a few weeks later, the victim of an accidental self-inflicted gunshot wound.[10]

Leaving Washington in June, Chase headed for a mineral spring in Michigan. On his way, he spoke in Cincinnati with a correspondent from the *New York Herald*. Asked whether Vallandigham's death would impede the New Departure movement, Chase said he thought not, for he believed Vallandigham had developed "a platform upon which the honest, patriotic men of both parties could come together." Asked about the Republicans, Chase said that there were divisions within the party and that "some of its leaders seem bent upon perpetuating the memories of the war and thus keeping alive the feeling of hatred and sectionalism which engendered it." Asked about Jefferson Davis, who was giving speeches saying that he did *not* accept the constitutional changes, Chase answered that Davis had been "acting very foolishly" and represented only a "small class of the Southern people."[11]

The *Herald* writer noted that Chase was "still tall, erect, and commanding" but had "grown so thin that his clothes seem to hang loosely upon him." The reporter also noticed that Chase paused several times in the conversation, at one point "staring at vacuity for a few minutes" before rousing himself. The chief justice spent a few weeks in July at the springs at St. Louis, Michigan, but found the climate unpleasant, so he went to a similar springs in Waukesha, Wisconsin, not far west of Milwaukee. He wrote to a friend that he was gradually getting stronger, in part from the waters, in part from "fresh air, simple diet, and exercise." While in Waukesha, Chase would go each Saturday morning to the local express office and stand on the scale; a small crowd would gather and cheer the news that he was slowly gaining weight. Since he weighed only 145 pounds when he left Washington and was still more than six feet tall, it is easy to understand why people thought Chase looked gaunt.[12]

The editors of the *Herald* argued in an August editorial that nominating Chase, on a New Departure platform, would give the Democrats their best chance of defeating Grant. The paper conceded that many Southerners would oppose this course because they viewed the constitutional amendments as "outrageous, scandalous, infamous, fraudulent, and void." If the Northern Democrats nominated Chase, however, on a progressive platform, and the Southern Democrats seceded from the party, the loss of Southern white votes would be offset by the "sure gain of a large portion of the black vote in every Southern state." Kate sent this article to her father in Waukesha, saying that if he met the "mutual friend" mentioned in the article—in other words, himself—Chase should "advise him not to make too many speeches or attend too many celebrations of one sort or another, but to devote all his energies for a while to getting quite well, that he may yet live a long while to gladden the hearts of his children and, if need be, serve his country."[13]

Chase followed her advice and did not give speeches, but in September he did consent to an interview with the *Cincinnati Enquirer.* Although he generally liked the ideas of the New Departure Democrats, Chase objected to the term. "I think the Democratic Party have taken no new departure. The change is simply a return to the original principles of Democracy as advocated by the great founders of the party." Wisconsin was in the midst of an election in which Republicans supported the Grant administration—especially its efforts to protect blacks against Klan violence in the South—while the Democratic platform denounced the president for "breaking down the distinction between the powers of the state government and those of the general government." Chase declared to the reporter that he "fully approved of the platform of the Wisconsin Democracy" and that he hoped the Democratic candidate for governor would be elected. Chase's old friend Horace Greeley called upon him in Waukesha at about this time, and papers reported they had a pleasant talk, supposedly "eschewing politics."[14]

Leaving Wisconsin in the middle of September, Chase made his way to the East, stopping to see Gerrit Smith in upstate New York and then spending a few days with Kate in Narragansett. When he reached Washington in October, work was nearly done on Edgewood. He wrote to Nettie that the house was "solid and substantial and large without show or pretension." The library and bedroom were both "really handsome rooms and look as if one might take genuine comfort in both, in one for the mind and in the other for the body." Chase returned at this time to his seat on the Supreme Court, hearing cases every weekday and leading the conferences every Saturday. Although he drafted seven opinions for the court in the last three months of 1871, out of the fifty-seven opinions issued in this quarter, almost all of Chase's opinions were short—some of them consisting of only two or three sentences. Clearly the chief justice was not quite the same after his stroke.[15]

As the new year started, Chase spent a few hours each day working on a much longer opinion: his dissent on the legal tender issue. The justices finally presented their opinions in the *Legal Tender Cases* on a cold day in the middle of January 1872. There were still five justices in favor of legal tender and four, headed by Chase, who believed the legal tender requirement was not constitutional. In his dissent, Chase elaborated on the arguments he had offered for the majority in the *Hepburn* case. On the due process point, he said that the legal tender requirement violated the "fundamental principle of all just legislation: that the legislature shall not take the property of A and give it to B." Forcing a person who had agreed to sell a farm to accept, instead of the promised purchase price, legal tender notes—"which may bear some proportion to the price or be even worthless"—seemed to Chase and his like-minded colleagues "a manifest violation of this clause of the Constitution." (The legal tender notes were worth somewhat less than gold dollars, but they were never worthless.) Although Chase complained that the court was reversing itself without good reason, he did not discuss the doctrine of stare decisis: the principle that the court should generally follow its prior precedents. Nineteenth-century justices, perhaps because they adhered to stare decisis more carefully, did not write elaborate discussions of the doctrine.[16]

Writing in his diary the evening the legal tender opinions were read in court, Chase called it a "sad day for the country and for the cause of constitutional government." He regretted that he had expressed even a "qualified opinion" that the legislation should include a legal tender requirement. Chase's opinion in early 1862 had hardly been "qualified"; he had told Congress that he supported the legal tender section "earnestly" and "decidedly." Now, however, he viewed this as a "sad mistake into which I was drawn by my anxiety for the passage of the bill then pending" and indeed the one great mistake of his financial administration.[17]

Chase hoped that someday the Supreme Court would reverse the legal tender decision, but it never happened. Indeed, federal law makes the banknotes we carry in our pockets, issued by the United States Federal Reserve, legal tender for all debts. But the *Legal Tender Cases* proved less important than Chase feared, for the United States returned to the gold standard (as he had hoped) not long after his death, and none of the opinions in the *Legal Tender Cases* are cited often these days. Another Chase decision, issued later in this same month, is cited and debated far more often: *United States v. Klein*.[18]

The *Klein* case started in the summer of 1863 in Vicksburg, Mississippi, when Union troops seized and the Treasury sold more than six hundred bales of cotton that belonged to a local merchant, Victor Wilson. At the end of the year, in the proclamation that Chase helped him draft, President Lincoln promised pardon, with restoration of all property rights, other than rights to slaves, to Southerners who would take and abide by an oath of loyalty to the Union. Wilson took the required oath in Vicksburg in 1864. After he died in 1865, his friend and executor, John Klein, filed suit in federal court, arguing that Wilson had never aided the rebellion, so therefore his estate was entitled to the proceeds from the sale of the cotton. The lower court ruled in Klein's favor, relying in part on a recent Chase decision in a similar case, *United States v. Padelford*, that a presidential pardon was a "complete substitute for proof that he gave no aid or comfort to the rebellion." Republicans in Congress disagreed with *Padelford,* and, in 1870, while the government's appeal in the *Klein* case was pending before the court, Congress enacted a law providing that federal courts should generally treat as disloyal any person who sought a pardon and should dismiss his or her claim. In oral arguments before the court, the government lawyers relied upon this new law to make the case that the court should dismiss Klein's claim on behalf of Wilson's estate.[19]

Chase viewed Lincoln's pardon proclamation, and Wilson's oath under the proclamation, as having established an agreement between the government and Victor Wilson. "The restoration of the proceeds became the absolute right of the persons pardoned," Chase wrote. If the government were now to retain the proceeds of the cotton sale, it "would be a breach of faith not less 'cruel and astounding' than to abandon the freed people whom the executive had promised to maintain in their freedom." The chief justice explained that the 1870 law was unconstitutional because it did not simply limit the authority of federal courts to hear a class of cases; it prescribed an "arbitrary rule of decision" for cases that were already pending in the federal courts. "We must think that Congress has inadvertently passed the limit which separates the legislative from the judicial power," Chase wrote. "It is of vital importance that these powers be kept distinct." Under the Constitution only the federal courts, and not Congress, could exercise judicial power. True, Congress had the right, as the court had noted in *McCardle*, to define in general terms the cases in which the Supreme Court could hear appeals from state and federal courts, but *Klein* underscored that Congress could not act as a court itself—it could not decide particular cases. Moreover, and perhaps more important, Chase held in *Klein* that the 1870 statute had the "effect of impairing the effect of a pardon, and thus infringing the constitutional power of the executive." In the twenty-first century, Chief Justice John Roberts has cited *Klein* more than once, writing in one case that "Congress violates [the Constitution] when it arrogates judicial power to itself and decides a particular case."[20]

In another important case this spring, Chase found himself alone in dissent. Although Edward Tarble was not of age and did not have the consent of his parents, he enlisted in the federal army in 1868. His father filed a petition for habeas corpus in the Wisconsin state courts, arguing that because his son (as a minor) could not enter into a binding agreement, there was no legal basis for the government to keep his son in the service. The state supreme court agreed and ordered the army to discharge Tarble, but the United States Supreme Court reversed. Relying heavily on an opinion by Taney, in a fugitive slave case, Field ruled that no state court could issue an order directing a federal officer to release a person detained by the federal government. Chase recalled all too well how blacks were often arrested or even kidnapped before the war on the flimsiest of "federal grounds," and how Chase and other lawyers used state writs of habeas corpus to secure their release—or at least to gain a fair hearing for their cases.[21]

"I have no doubt of the right of a state court to inquire into the jurisdiction of a federal court upon habeas corpus," Chase declared in his dissent. "I have still less doubt, if possible, that a writ of habeas corpus may issue from a state court to inquire into the validity of imprisonment or detention, without the sentence of any court whatever, by an officer of the United States." Field's approach would "deny the right to protect the citizen by habeas corpus against arbitrary imprisonment in a large class of cases" and was "never within the contemplation of the Convention which framed, or the people who adopted, the Constitution." Although brief, the dissent in *Tarble's Case* was a fine expression of Chase's concern for individual rights and freedom.[22]

The first months of 1872 were a pleasant period for Chase personally. He was living at Edgewood, with the company of a distant cousin, Caroline Moulton, and a few servants, including his longtime black valet William

Joice, whose help he now needed to shave and dress. Although William was a servant, he was also to some extent a member of the family, joining Chase and others for morning prayers, and receiving Chase's sympathy when his wife was sick and his child died. ("Your sincere friend," was how Chase signed one letter to him.) On January 10, Chase celebrated his birthday with Kate and her two children; there were sixty-four lighted candles on the cake, "much to the delight of William and Ethel." A few days later, he received a welcome telegram from Will Hoyt reporting that Nettie had just given birth to their first child, a daughter named Janet.[23]

From time to time, after the stroke, papers reported that Chase's health was failing or that he would soon retire from the court. He especially resented reports by the Washington correspondent of the *Cincinnati Commercial*, one of which said that "unless he ceases entirely from mental labor, his decease may be almost momentarily looked for." Chase wrote to his friend Murat Halstead, editor of the *Commercial*, to complain. The Supreme Court was hard at work, the chief justice wrote, and he was doing his full share, having missed only one day of the current term in order to attend a wedding. "My health is indeed not fully restored—perhaps will never be—but I am thankful that I can say that it is better than it was last winter, and my friends and brother judges congratulate me on my improvement."[24]

"The Japanese are all the rage just now," Chase wrote to Nettie in March, and indeed Washington was extremely excited by the arrival of a group of Japanese diplomats and students—including five young women whose "mission is to be educated here." The Iwakura Mission, named after its senior member, was part of Japan's effort to learn about Western ways and negotiate treaties with the Western powers. Chase attended several events with the Japanese, including a grand reception not long after their arrival and the Christian baptism of one young member of the delegation. He also hosted several senior members of the Japanese delegation for a dinner at Edgewood, noting in his diary that the other guests included "President and Mrs. Grant and Admiral and Mrs. Goldsborough"—his old friend Elizabeth Wirt Goldsborough.[25]

In April a reporter for the *New York Evening Post* visited Chase at Edgewood, calling the view from the piazza "one of the finest views of the city of Washington," with the "Capitol directly in front and seemingly but the distance of a rifle shot away." The correspondent was especially impressed by the chief justice's library and his learning, saying that he "reads French as readily as English" and could "translate Faust into his own strong and vigorous tongue." In English verse, Chase had a "high appreciation of Chaucer, Shakespeare, Milton, Dante, Goethe, and others." Chase's health was good, he was doing his work on the court, and he was enjoying life as well. "His old smile, his hearty laugh, and his buoyant cheerfulness have come back to him," the writer observed.[26]

Chase was invited this spring to attend an international conference in London on comparative criminal law. He was interested in the subject; indeed, he was working at this time on a short introduction for a revised edition of the works on criminal law by the early American legal reformer Edward Livingston. For a while, Chase considered crossing the Atlantic in order to attend the London conference, writing to Will and Nettie that he was "quite in earnest about going to Europe," and seeking their advice as to steamships and staterooms. In the end, however, he decided that his health was not strong enough for the voyage.[27]

Chase spent much of July in Narragansett with Kate and her children. In August he was in Northwood, New Hampshire, as the guest of his niece, Hannah Ralston Tucker, and her family. He enjoyed walks in the woods and services at the local Congregational church. He was back in Rhode Island in September, both in the quiet of Narragansett and the bustle of Newport. On his way back to Washington in October, he stopped for a few days in Philadelphia, where he visited the sights, including the Historical Society of Pennsylvania—later the home of many of Chase's papers.[28]

The presidential election of 1872, like many in Chase's long political life, involved three principal parties. In addition to the Democrats and the Republicans, there was a new party, the Liberal Republicans, opposed to Grant and in favor of civil service reform, lower tariffs, a return to the gold standard, and reconciliation between the North and South. Many of Chase's political friends were members of this movement, including Carl Schurz, Horace Greeley, Whitelaw Reid, and, to some extent, Charles Sumner. The Liberal Republicans planned their convention for early May, in Cincinnati, in the hope that they could persuade the Democrats, who would convene in July, to name the same candidates, and then work together to defeat the incumbent Grant.[29]

As the Cincinnati convention approached, there was some talk about whether the Liberal Republicans should nominate Chase for president. The

Cincinnati Enquirer reported that the delegates would probably nominate either Charles Francis Adams (wartime ambassador to Great Britain), longtime Republican senator Lyman Trumbull, or Salmon Chase. The *Springfield Republican,* a leading Massachusetts newspaper, disagreed, saying that the nominee would be Adams, Trumbull, or Horace Greeley. Many favored Justice David Davis, feeling that with his Democratic background, he could attract Democratic voters, but there was not much enthusiasm for him among former Republicans.[30]

Chase himself, this time around, was not really interested in the nomination. In a letter to his most ardent supporter, M. C. C. Church of Parkersburg, West Virginia, Chase complained that a public letter by Church seemed to "place me in the position of a man desiring the nomination for the presidency: I do not desire it." Chase also did not want to rival Davis. "He is my friend, and I hold him in the highest esteem as a man of honor and ability." Still, Chase did not quite close the door. "If those who agree with me in principle think that my nomination will promote the interests of the country, I shall not refuse the use of my name." When the ever-enthusiastic Alexander Long asked about his health, Chase replied that he often walked from Edgewood to the Capitol, "two and a half miles, with less fatigue than most men after fifty." Long urged Chase to write friends to press them to attend the convention, but Chase wrote no such letters. On the eve of the convention, he wrote to Church that it seemed from the papers that his name would "not be much considered" at the convention. "I am quite content that it should be so."[31]

Indeed, Chase's name was not discussed much at the Liberal Republican convention. The *New York Herald* reported the night before it opened that Long was telling people that Chase's health was so strong that he would serve the nation for another twenty-five years. But Long was essentially the only Chase man in Cincinnati; everyone else seemed to back other candidates. On the first ballot, more than six hundred votes were scattered among seven candidates, with Chase getting a paltry two and a half votes. On the sixth ballot, there were thirty-two votes for Chase, suggesting that some saw him as an alternative, but then there was a landslide for Greeley.[32]

Horace Greeley was a curious choice for president. With the exception of three months in Congress in the late 1840s, when he was appointed to fill the end of a term, Greeley had never served in government; his political experience was writing about politics in newspapers. Born in rural poverty, he worked as a printer and editor of various papers before starting the *New-York Tribune* in the early 1840s. Greeley was erratic and eccentric, in favor of vegetarianism, temperance, and women's rights but *not* women's suffrage. Particularly troubling for the Liberals, who favored lower tariffs, Greeley was a longtime advocate of higher protective tariffs. One of the leading Liberals, shortly after the nomination, wrote to Schurz that electing Greeley would be a "calamity of the first magnitude" because he was a "conceited, ignorant, half-cracked, obstinate old creature." Schurz agreed and tried without success to persuade Greeley to decline the nomination. Some Liberals decided to support President Grant. "That Grant is an ass, no man can deny," one Liberal wrote, "but better an ass than a mischievous idiot."[33]

Horace Greeley, editor of the New-York Tribune, *presidential candidate in 1872. When he died in New York in November 1872, both Grant and Chase attended his funeral.*

Chase had no concerns or qualms about Greeley. In a letter to Church, pressing him and others to support Greeley, Chase wrote that he and Greeley agreed "on the questions of finance and amnesty—more important, as I verily believe, than any now before the country." The question of "amnesty" at this time was whether Congress should exercise the authority granted to it by the Fourteenth Amendment to remove the prohibition against former rebels holding state or federal offices. Such legislation finally passed not long after the Liberal Republican convention, as Grant Republicans sought to reduce the Liberal threat to Grant.[34]

Neither in this letter to Church, nor in any of his other letters during the 1872 campaign, did Chase mention the issue of greatest concern to African Americans: federal protection for black rights and black lives in the South. Although Greeley had opposed slavery before the war and pressed Lincoln to issue an emancipation proclamation, his views changed after the war. In a letter to a friend in 1870, Greeley wrote that blacks were "an easy, worthless race, taking no thought for the morrow and liking to lean on those who befriend them." In an early 1872 editorial, he described the Southern state governments as being composed of ignorant local blacks and scheming Northern carpetbaggers, "and the result is a reign of corruption and oppression entirely without parallel in the history of the United States." In his letter accepting the Cincinnati nomination, Greeley declared that the American people were eager to forget the recent past and to "clasp hands across the bloody chasm." The hands that Greeley wanted to clasp were white hands.[35]

It is not surprising, then, that black leaders, almost without exception, favored Grant and opposed Greeley. Frederick Douglass campaigned for the president, saying that if blacks were sometimes "slighted" by the Republican Party, "we are as a class murdered by the Democratic Party." Most white abolition leaders agreed. William Lloyd Garrison wrote that "home rule," the slogan used by Greeley, was simply a way to weaken "protection of the Southern freedmen and loyalists against robbery, assassinations, and lynch-law barbarities." Gerrit Smith attended the regular Republican convention and endorsed Grant heartily as the true friend of black Americans. A leading scholar has estimated that three-quarters of all abolitionists supported Grant rather than Greeley.[36]

Not Chase. Before the war, he had overlooked the racism of many Democrats in his eagerness to ally with Northern Democrats; now he overlooked the racism of some of Greeley's supporters—and perhaps of Greeley himself—in his eagerness to see his friend elected. In July, when the Democratic convention in Philadelphia nominated Greeley, Chase wrote friends to say how pleased he was that Greeley would have the combined support of Democrats and Liberals. In August Chase wrote Sumner that he opposed Grant because of "delayed amnesty and interference with the Supreme Court in the matter of legal tender." This suggests that Chase agreed, at least in part, with the argument that Grant had packed the Supreme Court in order to reverse the legal tender decision. In September, as early election returns suggested that Grant would win a second term, Chase wrote that it was perhaps not surprising that the "bold experiment" of Democrats nominating a Republican was facing difficulties. Chase would vote for Greeley "with pleasure" because a Greeley administration would in no way "fundamentally clash with my views, while, in the important matters of currency, amnesty, and reform, it will thoroughly harmonize with them." In the end, Chase did not travel to Cincinnati in order to vote in November; he "paired off" informally with one of the other justices, who supported Grant, so neither of them had to vote. Perhaps another reason that Chase did not travel was that by November it was clear that the president would win—as he did, sweeping all but six of the thirty-seven states.[37]

After the election, during a brief recess in the work of the court in late November, Chase went to New York City to see his daughter Nettie. Thus, he was in the city when Greeley, doubly devastated by the death of his wife five days before the election as well as his landslide defeat, died there on the evening of November 29. Chase was shocked and grieved by his friend's passing and served as one of the pallbearers at the funeral on December 4. Fifteen hundred people, including Grant and other political and editorial leaders, packed the Universalist church of which Greeley was a member. Greeley's pastor, in his eulogy, declared that Greeley's goodness was more important than his greatness: "It may seem to us that because we cannot do great things, we can do nothing that is of worth, and that it matters little what we do. But goodness is richer than greatness. It lifts us nearer to God than any intellectual elevation, and, moreover, it is accessible for the humblest life." From the church, the funeral procession passed slowly through silent streets, filled with mourners, on its way south to the ferry to Brooklyn; Chase estimated the crowd at about three hundred thousand. The chief justice was one of those who continued with the coffin to the graveside in Green-Wood Cemetery, where, with a simple prayer at dusk, Greeley's body was committed to the grave.[38]

Like Greeley, Chase was known as a friend of reform of various sorts, and often received letters from reformers. Responding to a letter from a French leader about the effort to abolish the death penalty, he wrote that although he had not taken any personal part in the movement, his "sympathies are on the side of abolition, and my convictions are in favor of limiting it to the case of willful murder." Chase claimed that most Americans agreed with him on this issue and noted that a few states had already abolished the death penalty altogether.[39]

Answering a letter about women's rights, Chase said that when he started to hire women to work in the Treasury, there was no law that specifically allowed employment of women, "but the law sanctioned the employment of persons to do the work . . . and did not exclude females." He originally employed women "from motives of humanity"—to provide help for those who had been "deprived of the means of livelihood by the war"—but Chase added that he had "always favored the enlargement of the sphere of woman's work and the payment of just compensation for it." In another letter about women, to his old friend Gerrit Smith, Chase wrote that "my opinions and feelings are in favor of woman suffrage, but I would make haste slowly. It does well in Wyoming," where women already had the right to vote, "and would probably work equally well in Ohio or Massachusetts and might be adopted in other states progressively. I am afraid that our friend Miss [Susan B.] Anthony is a little too fast."[40]

Chase spent a fair amount of time in early 1873 thinking about biography, both his own and those of others. His friend and rival William H. Seward had died in late 1872 and was praised by Charles Francis Adams in a long address that many thought denigrated Lincoln. Responding to a letter from Montgomery Blair, who was planning a public response to Adams, Chase said that he saw no reason to fear "any damage to Lincoln's memory from the exaggeration of Mr. Seward's merits." In another letter, Chase wrote that he believed he had made two key contributions to history: first, in furthering the "emancipation of four millions of my countrymen," and second, in "securing to my country a uniform currency." In January Chase agreed to work with Robert Warden, a former Ohio judge, on a Chase biography and started to provide Warden with material, including his diaries and hundreds of letters. Some of this material was intensely personal, such as the diary describing the death of Chase's first wife. When Warden asked his subject whether he should quote the diaries, Chase replied that "where there was a doubt, perhaps the proper way would be to resolve that doubt against suppression." The diaries were "at least true," Chase said, "and the truth was very seldom really injurious to any interest."[41]

Chase and Warden talked several times about Grant. Chase told Warden that he had been mistaken about the general; in 1868 he had feared that Grant was not committed to protecting the former slaves, and, indeed, that Grant might be even less protective of their rights than Johnson. President Grant had proved himself, Chase said, the firm friend of black Americans. There were things that Grant had done of which Chase disapproved, but on the whole, Chase believed Grant "a man of good intentions" with a "really exalted love of country." Chase said similar things to Parsons, calling Grant an "absolutely honest, incorruptible, and patriotic man . . . earnestly striving to do his best to govern the country faithfully and well."[42]

Chase was thus pleased to take his part in Grant's second inauguration. As was usual in those days, events started in the Senate chamber, which Chase entered a little before eleven, leading the eight other justices down the aisle to their chairs. The *National Republican* reported that Chase, "having recovered much of his physical vigor, and showing a snow-white beard of several months' growth, was scarcely recognizable." After the new vice president, Henry Wilson, took his oath, and the new senators took their oaths, all the officials walked in a procession from the warmth of the chamber to the bitter cold outside, taking their places on a temporary platform. Grant's brief inaugural address was inaudible to all but a few because of the strong, cold wind. But the chief justice, at Grant's side, would have heard and approved of Grant's comment that although the former slaves were now citizens, they were "not possessed of the civil rights which citizenship should carry with it. This is wrong and should be corrected." At the end of the address, Grant approached Chase to take the oath of office. "As Chief Justice Chase held the holy book in his hand," the *Evening Star* reported, "and repeated the text of the oath, every head was uncovered, and deep silence pervaded the multitude."[43]

Warden moved in with Chase at Edgewood in March and started to work as the chief justice's private secretary. Relations were not always easy. Warden drafted (but perhaps did not send) a letter saying that he would quit if Chase continued to "treat me, your biographer, a person who has held high judicial position, a member of an honorable profession, and an educated gentleman, as though my perhaps over-proud poverty had reduced me to the condition of a sort of *valet*." Relations between Warden and Kate were also tense. She did not want a balanced biography of her father; she wanted a book to praise him. Without her father's knowledge, Kate started talking with Jacob Schuckers about writing a more flattering biography.[44]

Chase spent a few days in Richmond in early April, partly to attend circuit court, but mainly to help his friend Bradley Johnson, a Richmond lawyer who was working on a volume of Chase's circuit court opinions. Writing to Nettie upon his return to Washington, Chase said that the people of Richmond had welcomed him warmly and that the weather was delightful. "Peach trees and pear trees were in full bloom, and the trees generally had begun to put forth their foliage." Chase congratulated Nettie on the birth of her second child, Edwin, and said that he was anxious to meet his new grandchild.[45]

Chief Justice Chase near the end of his life.

When a reporter from the *Cincinnati Commercial* visited Chase in April at Edgewood, he gave her a tour of the house. "In the place of honor," she noted a fine portrait of Lincoln, "in which the ruggedness of the features is softened and the sad, patient eyes shadow forth the greatness of the soul." Under the portrait, in a frame, Chase displayed the letter in Lincoln's hand nominating him for chief justice. Chase said that Lincoln "has a martyr's crown, and he had all the traits of a martyr. He was truth and simplicity personified, and unselfish to a fault." Commenting on Lincoln in words that might apply to himself, Chase added: "I do not suppose that he was without ambition, but he never let it stand in the way of an obligation or a sense of right."[46]

On Monday, April 14, 1873, the justices read their opinions in one of the most important cases of the late nineteenth century: the *Slaughterhouse Cases*. The case arose out of an 1869 Louisiana law to require all butchers in New Orleans to use a single, large, central slaughterhouse, located south of the city and across the river, rather than slaughtering animals and polluting waters at more than one hundred places in and around the city. This slaughterhouse would be operated by a private company, but butchers who were not members of the company could use the facility by paying reasonable fees. An association of butchers challenged the law in the Supreme Court, claiming that it created an illegal monopoly and violated their rights under the Thirteenth Amendment (by creating a form of involuntary servitude) and the Fourteenth Amendment (by taking away their right to ply their trade).[47]

To understand the *Slaughterhouse Cases,* one must understand the racial and political context. Republicans, many of them black, some of them carpetbaggers who moved from the North to the South after the Civil War, dominated the Louisiana legislature that passed the slaughterhouse law. Democrats viewed every bill passed by this legislature as illegitimate. The *New Orleans Picayune* complained that whites had been "subjected to the terrible humiliation of seeing their former slaves, ignorant, brutal, and savage, placed above them in the political scale, and united with hordes of carpetbag adventurers and robbers, coming down from the North, now clothed with the lawmaking power." Democrats denounced the Republican legislature as corrupt, and, indeed, there was some corruption. The lead lawyer opposing the slaughterhouse law was John Archibald

Campbell, a former justice of the Supreme Court who had resigned his seat in early 1861, returned to the South, and served as an assistant secretary of war in the Confederacy. Starting in 1868, with lawsuit after lawsuit, Campbell attacked and impeded the Republican government of Louisiana; his challenges to the tax laws were so successful that the state had difficulty paying its bills for a while. The *Slaughterhouse Cases* were thus part of a much broader effort by Campbell and others against the Republican government—an attack in which he hoped to use the new constitutional amendments to undermine reconstruction.[48]

Justice Miller, for a majority of five justices, including the newest justice, Ward Hunt, ruled against the butchers and in favor of the slaughterhouse law. Miller stressed that the purpose of the Thirteenth and Fourteenth Amendments was to free the black slaves and to protect their rights; since the butchers were generally white, he viewed their claims skeptically. When Congress and the states amended the Constitution to provide that "no state shall make or enforce any law which shall abridge the privileges or immunities of citizens of the United States," what they had in mind, according to Miller, was a limited set of federal rights, such as the right to federal protection on the high seas, not the vast array of other rights, such as the right to free speech or the right to pursue a trade. For the protection of these rights, citizens had to look to their own state governments; they could not rely upon the federal courts. Moreover, Miller would not "look behind" the rationale of the Louisiana legislature for the slaughterhouse law. Any other approach, he wrote, would "fetter and degrade the state governments by subjecting them to the control of Congress, in the exercise of powers heretofore universally conceded to them of the most ordinary and fundamental character" and would "radically [change] the whole theory of the relations of the state and federal governments."[49]

The four dissenting justices argued that Miller was utterly wrong about the Privileges or Immunities Clause of the Fourteenth Amendment. In the principal dissent, Field accused Miller of reducing the clause to a "vain and idle enactment." Quoting from a case that was often cited in Congress during the debate on the amendment, Field insisted that the clause was intended to protect citizens in the "enjoyment of life and liberty, with the right to acquire and possess property of every kind, and to pursue and obtain happiness and safety." Bradley noted in his dissent that, before the Fourteenth Amendment, the "states were not prohibited from infringing any of the fundamental privileges and immunities," and it was the "intention of the people of this country" through the Fourteenth Amendment "to provide national security against violation by the states of the fundamental rights of the citizen." In similar language, Swayne declared that Miller's opinion turned "what was meant for bread into a stone." The Constitution before the Civil War already provided ample protections against violation of fundamental rights by the federal government but essentially no protection against such violations by the states; "that want was intended to be supplied by this amendment."[50]

Chase did not write his own opinion, simply joining the opinion of Field, the best of the three dissenting opinions. Chase surely would have written an opinion of his own if his health had been stronger. Indeed, if Chase had been in his full vigor, perhaps he would have been able to persuade one of the justices in Miller's majority to join an opinion giving a broader reading to the Fourteenth Amendment.[51]

Miller may well have reached the right result in *Slaughterhouse*, since the Louisiana law was a reasonable attempt to protect the health of New Orleans residents. But almost all scholars now agree that the justice's reasoning was wrong. Miller's opinion essentially eliminated the Privileges or Immunities Clause from the Fourteenth Amendment, and as one leading law professor has noted, "virtually no modern scholar—left, right, and center—thinks that this is a plausible reading of the amendment." By writing the Privileges or Immunities Clause out of the Constitution and leaving only the Equal Protection Clause to defend black rights, Miller's *Slaughterhouse* opinion paved the way for even more infamous decisions, such as *Plessy v. Ferguson* (1896), in which the Supreme Court would rule that "separate but equal" New Orleans streetcars did not violate the Equal Protection Clause. Indeed, the *Plessy* majority would cite *Slaughterhouse* in support of its decision not to inquire into whether the Louisiana segregation law was irrational or arbitrary. History has largely vindicated Chase and the others who dissented in the *Slaughterhouse Cases*.[52]

At the time, however, almost all papers agreed that Miller's approach was correct. The *New York Times*, a Grant Republican paper, praised Miller's *Slaughterhouse* decision, hoping that it would deal a "fatal blow to that school of constitutional lawyers who have been engaged, ever since the adoption of the Fourteenth Amendment, in inventing impossible consequences for that addition to the Constitution." The *New York World*, a Democratic paper, said that the key question in the *Slaughterhouse Cases* was whether the three recent constitutional amendments had changed the relationship between the states and the federal government. The Supreme Court had decided, quite sensibly in the *World*'s view, that the amendments "merely relate to the civil and political status of the African race, guaranteeing negro equality but leaving the Constitution in other respects unchanged." The *Nation*, a thoughtful Liberal weekly, agreed, saying that Miller's opinion gave an "able and clear construction" to the Constitution and showed that the court was "recovering from the war fever and getting ready to abandon sentimental canons of construction." The *Cincinnati Enquirer* criticized the decision, but only because the editors believed the court should not approve the action of the "so-called legislature of Louisiana, elected by the bayonet and through the agency of the most degraded and ignorant portion of the population." In other words, the *Enquirer* agreed with Campbell about the ignorance and corruption of the Louisiana legislature.[53]

On April 15, the day after the *Slaughterhouse* decision, the Supreme Court decided another important case: *Bradwell v. Illinois*. The supreme court of Illinois had denied the application of Myra Bradwell, editor of the *Chicago Legal News*, to become a lawyer in Illinois. Although she had passed the bar exam and was otherwise qualified, and although the statute in question did not refer to *men* or *women*, the Illinois court denied Bradwell's application because she was a woman. In her appeal to the Supreme Court, Bradwell argued that Illinois, by denying her the right to pursue her chosen profession, had violated the Privileges or Immunities Clause of the Fourteenth Amendment. Senator Matthew Carpenter, representing Bradwell in the Supreme Court, argued that the amendment "opens to every citizen of the United States, without distinction of color or sex, married or single, the honorable professions as well as the servile employments of life." The state could limit those admitted to the bar on the basis of "intelligence, integrity, and honor," but not on the basis of gender; "any honorable pursuit or profitable avocation, and all the privileges and immunities which are enjoyable by the colored citizen, are the right of our mothers, our sisters, and our daughters."[54]

Justice Miller, for the same group of five justices that formed the majority in *Slaughterhouse,* wrote the majority opinion in *Bradwell*. This was an easy case for Miller: just as the butchers could not rely on the

Fourteenth Amendment to challenge a state restriction upon their right to work, neither could Bradwell rely on the amendment to challenge the decision to exclude her from the legal profession. Bradley, joined by Field and Swayne, concurred in the result but reached it by a different route. They disagreed with Miller's reading of the Fourteenth Amendment, but they concluded that the alleged right of women to practice law was not one of the "fundamental rights" protected by the amendment. Newspapers reported that Bradley, "in an elaborate opinion, which seemed to cause no little amusement upon the bench and among the bar, cited common law and civil law, the law of nature and divine law, to prove that it was never intended that woman should practice law, but that woman's sphere was her home, and she violated all law in endeavoring to force her way into professional and public life." The *Nation* said the case showed why women were not qualified to be lawyers: Bradwell should have realized that her case was hopeless in the Supreme Court.[55]

Only Chief Justice Chase dissented in the *Bradwell* case. He was too sick to explain his reasons in an opinion, but it is not hard to guess at them. Chase believed that the right to pursue a profession was protected by the Privileges or Immunities Clause and that Illinois had violated Bradwell's constitutional rights when it excluded her from the legal profession. Chase probably agreed with Carpenter that voting rights and career rights were quite different; the reference in Section 2 of the Fourteenth Amendment to male voting showed that Section 1 did not affect voting rights. This did not prevent one newspaper from commenting that "Chase alone of all the judges upon the Supreme Bench can find law enough to help the women's suffrage movement." And, in a sense, the paper was right: of the nine justices on the Supreme Court, Chase was the most sympathetic to women's rights.[56]

After hearing and deciding a few more cases, including three in which Chase was the author of its opinions, the Supreme Court closed its term on May 1, 1873. Charles Sumner called the next day on his old friend Chase as the chief justice packed his bags to leave Washington for a few weeks. Sumner expressed doubt about Warden, asking Chase whether he could "grasp your life and character" and "put it on paper" properly. Chase said that perhaps Warden was not "up to your Massachusetts standards"—and that perhaps even *he* was not "quite up to them myself"—but, he added, Warden "knows the people of Ohio," which was where Chase expected Warden's book would be of most interest. Chase and Sumner also talked about recent events in Louisiana: there were two rival governments in the state, one Republican and one Democratic. Only two weeks earlier, political tension led to the Colfax Massacre, in which white Democrats killed about a hundred black Republicans who were sheltering in the county courthouse. Chase told Sumner that "such scenes as are being enacted in Louisiana were calculated, he thought, to destroy the faith of the people in a republican form of government."[57]

On Saturday, May 3, Chase boarded a train for New York City, intending to spend a few days there with his daughter Nettie and her family on West Thirty-Third Street. The family attended services on Sunday morning at the Presbyterian church, and Chase wrote a short letter to Warden that afternoon, asking whether he missed him. On Monday Chase took a carriage ride with Nettie in Central Park and walked a bit on Fifth Avenue with his friend Hiram Barney, "talking in a pleasant and familiar way of the topics of the hour." In a letter to his friend Parsons on this day, Chase wrote that "it seems odd to be so entirely out of the world in the midst of this great Babylon, but I am too much of an invalid to be more than a cipher. Sometimes I feel as if I were dead, though alive." Chase was on his "way to Boston, where I am to try a treatment from which great results are promised, but I expect little."[58]

As he wrote, however, Chase's energy returned, and he asked whether Parsons would join him on a trip to Colorado. "I think of going in late May or early June." Writing to his niece Alice Stebbins in Boston, Chase said that he would stay with her family there only if "you can receive me without the slightest inconvenience." He would stay in her spare room, for "all I want from you is love. I crave affection and its manifestation, but I do not want to have my ease consulted, while those who consult it change their arrangements for that purpose."[59]

On Tuesday morning, at about seven, Chase's black valet William Joice found him in his bed, unable to move or speak. Chase had suffered a second and more severe stroke. Doctors were summoned, but there was little they could do. Chase did not open his eyes or speak for the whole day. He died at the Hoyt home on Wednesday, May 7, 1873, at about ten in the morning, with his daughters and sons-in-law by his side. He was sixty-five years old.[60]

Conclusion

On the day after Chase's death, the *New-York Tribune*, now edited by Chase's friend Whitelaw Reid, observed that to Chase, "more than any other one man, belongs the credit of making the antislavery feeling what it had never been before: a power in politics. It had been the sentiment of philanthropists; he made it the inspiration of a great political party." Chase did this even though he was not good at people politics. "No man knew less of men as individuals, and none foresaw with such unerring instinct the course and current of men as masses. He was as incapable of the lesser arts of political intrigue as any hermit might have been, but he molded parties and organizations at his will." Without Chase's early work in the Liberty and Free Soil Parties, "it would have been scarcely possible to have constructed the great national party," the Republican Party, "which completed its organization in the campaign of 1856 and won its decisive victory four years later." As Treasury secretary, Chase managed to raise the "vast resources necessary to the support of an army of a million men," and, as chief justice, Chase showed "an easy mastery of legal principles."[1]

The *New York Sun*, edited by Chase's friend Charles Dana, largely agreed. Dana's obituary praised Chase's role in bringing together the Free Soil Party and organizing the Buffalo convention in 1848; Dana had heard Chase say in later years that the "blow struck at the Slave Power through Martin Van Buren in 1848 contributed most essentially to its final overthrow." Chase's four years as governor of Ohio were "marked by high intelligence, strict integrity, broad and comprehensive views of state

651

and national politics, and devotion to the cause of freedom." During the secession winter of 1860–61, although Dana and others pressed Chase to leave the Senate and lead the Treasury, he was reluctant. Chase told "some of his confidential friends" at the time that "questions of finance had never been among his favorite studies," and he "shrank from the responsibility of devising the ways and means of carrying on one of the most terrible and wasteful wars in history." Chase not only financed the war but also created a single American currency. "Now and for some time past, one currency has answered to carry the traveler from Maine to Louisiana, and to meet the demands of commerce from the Atlantic coast to the Pacific Ocean." Dana conceded that Chase was "intensely ambitious" but insisted that, although Chase was "sometimes accused of selfishness and even demagogism," he was never "suspected of dishonesty, [and] his hands were unquestionably free from the stain of corruption."[2]

Although the *New York Herald* had often criticized Chase as an antislavery agitator, the paper praised him after his death. The *Herald* particularly regretted that the Democrats had not nominated Chase in 1868, saying the party would have done far better with Chase's New Departure policies than with Seymour and his Southern allies. "Considered as statesman or politician, financier, or jurist, or in all these capacities together, the public life of Salmon P. Chase may be pronounced singularly consistent, sagacious, and successful. . . . It is the record of a conscientious, consistent, and patriotic philanthropist and reformer, who never lost sight of the boundaries of the Constitution." The *Herald* predicted that President Grant would have a hard time finding a suitable successor for Chase, and, indeed, it would take Grant a few tries before the Senate confirmed Morrison Waite as the next chief justice.[3]

The Washington weekly founded by Frederick Douglass in 1870, and now edited by his son Lewis Douglass, the *New National Era*, declared that "a great man has gone to an honored grave." In an obituary whose details suggest that it was penned by the senior Douglass, the paper quoted from several Chase speeches, including the 1845 address in which Chase said that all who claimed freedom for themselves, "as a birthright, precious beyond all price, and inalienable as life," knew instinctively that "no person can rightfully hold another as a slave." Douglass also noted that he had seen a recent statement by Chase, "fresh from his characteristic pen," in which Chase declared that he "demanded for himself no right, privilege, or opportunity which he was not willing to concede to every other man." Douglass closed by wishing that Chase's example "might hasten the day of relief from impurities, inequality, and injustice in the institutions of our republic."[4]

Murat Halstead, yet another editor whom Chase counted as a friend, shared some personal details in the *Cincinnati Commercial*. Halstead noted that Chase "even dallied with the Muses and wrote poetry, although from the examples handed down to us, it is fortunate that his ambition in that direction was quenched by a more mature judgment." Still, it was interesting that "at a time when he was pushing his way into the bar, compiling the statutes of Ohio, writing upon biographical, historical, and scientific subjects for newspapers and periodicals, he also found time to write verse and recreate himself in translations of the Latin poets into English." Chase's former student and law partner George Hoadly described Chase as the "most genial, companionable, and agreeable of friends," and his friend James Shepherd Pike wrote that Chase was "social and warmhearted," so that he was the "joy of his friends and the delight of his associates."[5]

Early on Saturday, May 10, Chase's coffin was moved from the Hoyt home to St. George's Episcopal Church on Stuyvesant Square in New York City. From eight in the morning until one in the afternoon, Chase's body lay in state in the church. Four thousand to five thousand people filed slowly past the open coffin, from "all classes of the community," including "bankers, merchants, professional men, mechanics, laborers." Many of the mourners were black, and there were "many remarkable instances of the deep veneration in which the chief justice was held by the colored people." In the afternoon, at the funeral service, the pallbearers included Gideon Welles, Gerrit Smith, William Evarts, William Cullen Bryant, Irvin McDowell, and William Tecumseh Sherman, with the two generals in their full military uniforms. In his funeral sermon, Reverend John Hall called upon those present to be "just and candid and generous" toward those who served in high offices: "Do not too soon whisper the word *ambition* regarding the men who render to us great public service, as if ambition were something wholly and absolutely and essentially wrong and wicked." Ambition was sometimes simply the recognition of God-given strength, "by which men are impelled to the work that they can do, and that none others are able to do."[6]

On Saturday evening, Chase's coffin was taken to Jersey City and placed on a train for Washington, accompanied by his family and a few others. When they arrived, early on Sunday morning, the coffin was taken to the Capitol, to lie in state there. The closed coffin was placed upon the same black catafalque that had served Abraham Lincoln and in the same spot where Henry Clay and John Calhoun had been placed, in what was then the Senate chamber, now the Supreme Court's chamber. The room was draped in black and adorned with flowers, including a large white floral cross in front of the chief justice's empty chair. The marshals opened the doors at ten, and a steady, silent stream of people entered the room and passed the coffin. One paper estimated that seven thousand people paid their respects, another reported the number of mourners as "fully ten thousand." Many were black.[7]

On Monday, with government offices closed in Washington, there was a second Chase funeral service, this time in the Senate chamber. Those present included President Grant, members of his Cabinet, senators, representatives, diplomats, justices, and judges. Again, in his eulogy, the minister addressed the ambition issue, quoting from a Chase letter in which he denied that he was a candidate for president. "An impression prevailed that Mr. Chase was a disappointed politician," but he did not act like one; "he was kind to all, a pure patriot, and an upright judge and Christian gentleman." After the services at the Capitol, as the bells of the city's churches tolled, the principal mourners went by carriage to Oak Hill Cemetery, in Georgetown, where there was another brief service, ending with a benediction. The next day, in a private ceremony, the body of Salmon P. Chase was buried in the Oak Hill plot of the Cooke family.[8]

Papers reported that Chase's will was "short and simple." He gave $10,000 to Dartmouth and another $10,000 to Wilberforce College—an immense amount for the small black college. Chase gave a lifetime annuity to his niece Jane Auld, and the remainder of his estate, estimated at $150,000, he divided equally between his daughters, Kate and Nettie.[9]

It was good in a way that Chase died when he did, for many later events would have pained him. Jay Cooke's firm failed in September 1873, prompting a nationwide financial panic and depression. The Hoyt family firm failed soon after that of Cooke, and Will Hoyt filed suit against William Sprague, claiming that the senator had cheated him, while he was a minor, out of his fair share of the Sprague family business. Because of the lawsuit and other disputes, Kate and Nettie almost never spoke with each other. Kate had a scandalous affair with Senator Roscoe Conkling in the latter part of the 1870s and then filed for divorce in 1880 from Sprague, claiming that he had committed adultery in every year since their marriage and abused her in other ways—including attempting to throw her out of an upstairs window. After the divorce was granted, Kate spent several years in Europe with her daughters, but by the 1890s, she was living in poverty at Edgewood, where she died in 1899. Nettie lived a somewhat happier life, finding success as an illustrator of children's books and sponsoring the summer art festival in Southampton, New York. In the 1890s, however, her husband Will "drank up most of the family fortunes" and abandoned the family to live in Puerto Rico. Nettie lived the last years of her life with a daughter in a small cottage in Thomasville, Georgia, where she died in 1925.[10]

Robert Warden and Jacob Schuckers were hard at work, in late 1873 and early 1874, on their competing biographies of Chase. Kate tried to prevent the publication of the Warden biography, demanding that he return her father's papers—even threatening litigation. When Warden's book appeared in early 1874, some of the early reviews were scathing. "Anything worse in the way of English composition has never been written," declared the *New York Herald*. Warden adopted a curious attitude toward Chase in the book, calling him "our hero" and yet criticizing Chase sharply at points, such as for accepting a loan from one of his principal subordinates, Hiram Barney. The Schuckers book, published in late 1874, was a more conventional nineteenth-century biography, full of praise for Chase.[11]

Warden and Schuckers were not the only men commenting on Chase's life in the months and years after his death. William Evarts, in a long address at Dartmouth in the summer of 1874, praised especially the fair and cautious way in which Chase, in the midst of partisan passions, presided over the Johnson impeachment trial. Chase's colleague on the Supreme Court, William Strong, writing to Evarts, agreed with this assessment but noted that it was unfortunate that Chase did not, after becoming chief justice, give up his ambition of becoming president. "Perhaps it was too much for human nature. It may be conceded he never allowed his political aspirations to warp his judicial conduct. But it was impossible to suppress the suspicion in some minds that his aspirations did in certain cases affect his legal judgments." Strong added that "had he not been chief justice, a more fit man for the head of the government could hardly be found." Justice Miller, in a private letter two years later, was far harsher. Miller described Chase as "religious by training and conviction and outward discipline, endowed by nature with a warm heart and a vigorous intellect, but all these warped, perverted, shriveled by selfishness generated by ambition. I doubt if for years before his death, his first thought in meeting any man of force was not invariably 'How can I utilize him for my presidential ambitions?'" But even Miller conceded that Chase was a "great man" and a "better man" than most men with long public careers.[12]

In September 1877 five men created what has proved Chase's most important monument: Chase National Bank. The leader in this effort was John Thompson, a New York banker and the publisher of *Thompson's Bank Note Reporter,* a guide to the thousands of different state banknotes. Thompson was one of the bankers with whom Chase corresponded during the Civil War, and, as an expert on state banknotes and the confusion, complexity, and counterfeits they created, Thompson strongly supported Chase's national bank scheme. Thompson founded one of the first banks under the new law in 1863, First National Bank of New York City, a predecessor of what is now Citibank. When Thompson and a few others formed Chase National Bank of New York City in 1877, they named it in honor of Chase, father of the national banking system. Chase Bank now has branches across the United States and provides credit cards, checking accounts, and other bank services to almost half of all American households.[13]

Kate Chase (no longer Kate Sprague after her divorce) arranged in 1886 for her father's remains to be transferred from Washington to Cincinnati for burial in Spring Grove Cemetery. There was a grand event at the music hall to celebrate Chase's return to Cincinnati, with an address by George Hoadly in which he described Chase as the "most unpopular man in Cincinnati" before the Civil War because he was an abolitionist in a "suburb of the South." And Chase was not a reclusive, philosophical abolitionist; Chase believed "in work and in methods; believed in parties, committees, machinery, organization, in newspapers, speeches, letters, persuasion; in short, in every species of agitation." There was another grand event in Cincinnati in 1923 to dedicate a monument to Chase at Spring Grove erected by the American Bar Association. Although the principal speaker, Chief Justice William Howard Taft, was the son of one of Chase's close Cincinnati friends, and was old enough that he must have known Chase at least slightly, he did not include much personal material in his address, focusing instead on how Chase guided the Supreme Court through a difficult period.[14]

Chase made his most important contribution to American history in the two decades before the Civil War, as an antislavery lawyer and leader. From the moment he joined the Liberty Party in 1841, Chase worked to turn it from a minor moral movement into a powerful political party. Chase realized that Americans would not join a party whose leaders denounced the Constitution as a compromise with slavery and who burned copies of the Constitution at public meetings. So Chase developed arguments that turned the Constitution into an antislavery charter—for example, that the Fugitive Slave Clause (since it was merely a compact among the states) did not authorize Congress to pass a fugitive slave law. Chase did not merely devise arguments, and press them in court cases, and publicize them through pamphlets. He also did the hard work of persuading people to join antislavery parties and to vote for antislavery candidates. Writing letters, giving speeches, courting editors, drafting platforms, melding factions into new parties—in all these ways, Chase paved the way for Lincoln's election in 1860.[15]

One could argue that Chase was a failure in his six years as senator. He opposed the Fugitive Slave Act of 1850 and the Kansas-Nebraska Act of 1854; they passed easily over his objections. Other bills that Chase favored, such as the homestead bill, or the legislation to fund a Pacific railroad, failed to pass while he was senator. Yet in another sense, Chase succeeded, for by the end of his Senate term, a new and more powerful antislavery party was emerging—the Republican Party—due to the work of Chase and colleagues. Similarly, one could argue that Chase was a failure during his four years as governor. The Ohio legislature largely ignored his suggestions about improving education and protecting black rights. Yet in 1860, the last year that Chase was governor, Lincoln carried Ohio in the presidential campaign and, indeed, all the states of the Northwest. Chase helped to ensure Lincoln's victory, first by forming and strengthening the Republican Party and then by speaking so widely for Lincoln in the 1860 campaign.

Chase hoped that slavery would end peacefully, as individual masters freed their slaves, as states changed their laws, and as antislavery leaders gained national power and changed national laws, limiting the spread of slavery into the territories and perhaps even prohibiting the interstate slave trade. Even as some of the slave states seceded, Chase did not believe that the federal government had the right to abolish slavery within the states; Chase and Lincoln still believed that each state had the right to make its own decisions about slavery. As the war continued, however, Chase and Lincoln came to see that the president, as commander in chief, had the power to free the slaves in the rebellious states. Chase supported Lincoln's emancipation proclamation, and pressed Lincoln to recognize black rights in other ways, such as through black voting rights.[16]

Chase's main role during the war was running the finances of the federal government. He made some mistakes as Treasury secretary, such as relying so heavily on bank loans in the fall of 1861, and demanding gold, thus contributing to the suspension by the banks of specie payments. Chase should have pressed Congress sooner for tax increases, although by the end of his tenure, he was pressing Congress as hard as possible on this front. Given the challenges, however, of taking federal spending from less than $80 million per year before the war, to $1.3 billion per year by the end of the war, it is not surprising that Chase made mistakes; what is amazing is that he managed to raise the funds. And he did so in novel ways, notably through the Cooke bond campaigns.

We are so accustomed to a single American currency, the dollar bills we carry in our wallets, that we forget that before the Civil War, the United States really did not have a single currency. The presence of so many different banknotes impeded commerce, encouraged counterfeiters, and injured consumers (when they accepted banknotes that proved worth less than they expected or indeed worthless). Chase's currency reform, creating a single currency printed and backed by the federal government, was a vital step in moving the American economy forward after the Civil War. Similarly, his national bank reform, enabling banks to operate on a national scale, helped pave the way for the new industrial economy. So Chase not only helped the United States survive the Civil War as a single nation, by raising the money to pay the military forces; he helped the United States emerge from the war stronger because of the new single currency and banking system.

By the end of the Civil War, Chase was no longer in the Treasury but rather in the Supreme Court, thanks to Lincoln's wise choice of Chase to succeed Roger Taney. When law professors list the great justices, they sometimes include Taney, but they do not include Chase. Yet the Chase Court decided a number of important cases, and Chase authored a number of important opinions, notably his opinion on secession and the states in *Texas v. White*. Chase would rank higher among the justices if he had served longer and if he had included more thorough legal analysis in his opinions. He would also rank higher if he could have written just a few more opinions; a strong dissent in the *Bradwell* case, for example, might have become an oft-quoted document in the fight for women's rights. As William Strong noted, Chase's reputation suffered during his lifetime, and has suffered since, because he did not abandon his presidential ambitions when he became chief justice. It is hard to find fault in Chase's cautious, evenhanded approach to the Johnson impeachment trial—until one reads his correspondence during the trial with Democratic political leaders, and wonders whether there was anything Chase would have done differently in the impeachment process had he not been seeking the Democratic nomination.[17]

Chase should not be evaluated, however, just on the basis of his years as chief justice, or his financial work during the Civil War, but on his whole life's work. On that basis, surely, Chase ranks as one of the great Americans of his generation. Perhaps the central message of Chase's life for our generation is that change is possible. When Chase predicted in the early 1840s that political pressure would end American slavery within a few years, it seemed absurd—almost laughable. The number of slaves, the extent of slave territory, the influence of the slave masters over state and federal policies—all of these were increasing when Chase made his prediction and would continue to increase. Slavery in the United States was not dying on the eve of the Civil War; it was booming. Yet Chase lived to see the end of American slavery, through the Civil War and the Thirteenth Amendment, and he lived to see black men vote not only in Ohio but even in South Carolina. Slavery ended in America not because of vast impersonal forces but because of the work of individual men and women, and Salmon P. Chase deserves his central place in this great American story.

Acknowledgments

It is a pleasure to thank some of those who helped to research and write this book.

My research assistants included Sean Andres, Robert Buchanan, Brittany Cathey, Mallory Fowler, Molly McCarthy, Alexandra Midler, Sophie Rizzieri and Jessica Ziparo.

Libraries and archives provide the raw material from which history books emerge. Many libraries and librarians helped with Chase, either in person or by email. I especially need to thank the staff members at University of California, Irvine; A. K. Smiley Public Library; Huntington Library; Library of Congress; Historical Society of Pennsylvania; and Cincinnati History Library and Archives. Many staff members were prepared to help even when their libraries were closed by the coronavirus pandemic.

Those who provided helpful comments on the draft included Frank Borchert, Stephen Dickey, Jane Flaherty, Jack Herney, Martin Johnson, Andy McCarthy, John McGinnis, Alexandra Midler, Robin Tiffney, and Jonathan White. None bears blame for the errors that remain.

My agent, Scott Waxman, helped frame my Chase idea into a proposal. Although Alice Mayhew at Simon & Schuster did not much like Chase as a person, she believed that he deserved a better biography, and she acquired this book. Sadly, Alice did not live to see the Chase manuscript. Megan Hogan then took over the book, and her comments and changes were most helpful. Copy editor Philip Bashe was thorough and thoughtful. Many others at Simon & Schuster have helped, including Jonathan Karp, Lisa Healy, Elise Ringo, and Christine Calella.

My wife, Masami, in the midst of her difficult teaching duties, supports me in my research and writing. I am more grateful than she knows.

This book is dedicated to my father, John Stahr, who died in October 2020, as I was writing the final paragraphs. He was, among other things, a great reader and collector of books. I am sorry that he did not live to add this one to his collection.

Notes

There are two main collections of Chase Papers: one at the Library of Congress and one at the Historical Society of Pennsylvania. The Library of Congress collection is available online, a huge help, especially in the pandemic. There are substantial collections of Chase letters in many other libraries around the country. John Niven and a team of Claremont students worked for years to gather Chase's diaries, and letters to and from Chase, and to publish selected items in two formats: a microfilm edition and five edited volumes. The edited Niven volumes are reliable and widespread, so that when an item is printed there, I have cited the relevant volume and page. Similarly, when letters are printed in other readily available sources, such as the Schuckers and Warden biographies, I have cited them, to save readers the tasks of going to manuscript collections and reading Chase's handwriting. Not many libraries have the Niven microfilm edition, however, so that instead of citing the film, I have cited the original letter or document. Most of the papers gathered by Niven and team are now at the A. K. Smiley Public Library, in Redlands, California, and in some cases, the Smiley library now has the only copy of a letter.

I have not changed words in quotes, but I have modernized spelling and punctuation. Perhaps I should say that I have not intentionally changed words, for Chase's handwriting was terrible, so I may well have misread some passages.

I have used the following abbreviations in the notes:

AKSPL: A. K. Smiley Public Library, Redlands, California.

ALPL: Abraham Lincoln Presidential Library.

Bourne: Edward Bourne, ed., "Diary and Correspondence of Salmon P. Chase," in the *Annual Report of the American Historical Association for the Year 1902,* vol. 2 (Washington, DC: Government Printing Office, 1903), 12–522.

CHLA: Cincinnati History Library and Archives.

CWL: The Collected Works of Abraham Lincoln, 8 vols., ed. Roy Basler (New Brunswick, NJ: Rutgers University Press, 1953–55).

HSP: Historical Society of Pennsylvania.

LC: Library of Congress.

NARG: National Archives Record Group.

NHHS: New Hampshire Historical Society.

NYHS: New-York Historical Society.

NYPL: New York Public Library.

OHC: Ohio History Center.

OR: *The War of the Rebellion: A Compilation of the Official Records of the Union and Confederate Armies,* 128 vols. (Washington, DC: Government Printing Office, 1880–1901). Series 1 unless indicated otherwise.

PAJ: The Papers of Andrew Johnson, 16 vols., ed. Leroy P. Graf and Ralph W. Haskins (Knoxville: University of Tennessee Press, 1967–2000).

Schuckers: Jacob Schuckers, *The Life and Public Services of Salmon Portland Chase, United States Senator and Governor of Ohio; Secretary of the Treasury and Chief-Justice of the United States* (New York: D. Appleton, 1874).

SPCP: The Salmon P. Chase Papers, 5 vols., ed. John Niven (Kent, OH: Kent State University Press, 1993–1998).

Spur: "Spur Up Your Pegasus": Family Letters of Salmon, Kate, and Nettie Chase, 1844–1873, ed. James P. McClure, Peg A. Lamphier, and Erika M. Kreger (Kent, OH: Kent State University Press, 2009).

Warden: Robert Warden, *An Account of the Private Life and Public Services of Salmon Portland Chase* (Cincinnati: Wilstach, Baldwin, 1874).

INTRODUCTION

1 "Public Meeting Today," *Charleston (SC) Courier*, May 12, 1865, 2; "Large Meeting at Zion Church," ibid., May 13, 1865, 2; "Our Charleston Correspondence," *New York Herald*, May 21, 1865, 1; Whitelaw Reid, *After the War: A Tour of the Southern States* (Cincinnati: Moore, Wilstach, and Baldwin, 1866), 79–83. General Rufus Saxton spoke first, followed by Major Robert Delany. Saxton started by saying that he expected Chase, but he was delayed.

2 "Large Meeting at Zion Church," *Charleston (SC) Courier*, May 13, 1865, 2; "Our Charleston Correspondence," *New York Herald*, May 21, 1865, 1; "Remarkable Story of a Negro," *Buffalo Weekly Express,* September 5, 1865, 3 ("old greenbacks"); Carl Schurz, *The Reminiscences of Carl Schurz* (New York: Doubleday, Page, 1909), 2:170.

3 "Large Meeting at Zion Church," *Charleston (SC) Courier*, May 13, 1865, 2; "Our Charleston Correspondence," *New York Herald*, May 21, 1865, 1. I have quoted the newspaper versions rather than Reid, whose version is "revised and expanded." See Reid, *After the War*, 581–86.

4 Chase to Hamilton Smith, March 31, 1828, *SPCP*, 2:25; see William Gienapp, *The Origins of the Republican Party, 1852–1856* (New York: Oxford University Press, 1987), 192 ("no individual made a more significant contribution to the formation of the Republican party than did Chase").

5 Chase, *The Address and Reply on the Presentation of a Testimonial to S. P. Chase, by the Colored People of Cincinnati* (Cincinnati: Henry W. Derby, 1845), 22. The case in which Lincoln represented the master was the *Matson* case. In another case, *Bailey v. Cromwell*, Lincoln argued that a black woman was not a slave, but Lincoln's client was a white man who was disputing whether he owed another white man on a promissory note. See Eric Foner, *The Fiery Trial: Abraham Lincoln and American Slavery* (New York: W. W. Norton, 2010), 45–50; David Reynolds, *Abe: Abraham Lincoln in His Times* (New York: Penguin Press, 2020), 264–67.

6 Chase to the Ohio State Teachers' Association, July 6, 1857, *SPCP*, 2:458; Lincoln-Douglas debate, September 18, 1858, *CWL*, 3:145–46.

7 Stephen Mihm, *A Nation of Counterfeiters: Capitalists, Con Men, and the Making of the United States* (Cambridge, MA: Harvard University Press, 2007), 3 ("more than ten thousand different kinds of paper"); Warren Weber, "Early State Banks in the United States: How Many Were There and Where Did They Exist?," *Quarterly Review of the Federal Reserve Bank of Minneapolis* 30 (2006): 33 (1,371 banks as of January 1, 1861).

8 Chase to Lincoln, April 11, 1865, *SPCP*, 5:15–16; Lincoln speech, April 11, 1865, *CWL*, 7:53–56; Chase to Lincoln, April 12, 1865, *SPCP*, 5:17–19; Frederick Douglass, *Autobiographies,* ed. Henry Louis Gates Jr. (New York: Library of America, 1994), 800; Louis P. Masur, *Lincoln's Last Speech: Wartime Reconstruction and the Crisis of the Union* (New York: Oxford University Press, 2015).

9 Chase to Hiram Barney, July 17, 1865, Barney Papers, Huntington.

CHAPTER 1: "He Called Me Yankee," 1808–26

1 Chase to Charles Cleveland, February 8, 1830, *SPCP,* 2:48; Chase to Hamilton Smith, May 29, 1832, Smith Papers, Indiana University; Chase to J. C. Rhodes, December 29, 1863, Chase Papers, HSP.

2 William Child, *History of the Town of Cornish New Hampshire,* 2 vols. (Concord, NH: Rumford Press, 1911), 1:17, 1:188–91; Chase to John Trowbridge, December 27, 1863, Warden, 25.

3 Simon Griffin, *The History of Keene, New Hampshire* (Bowie, MD: Heritage Books, 1980), 638; William and Nicholas Klingaman, *The Year Without a Summer: 1816 and the Volcano That Darkened the World and Changed History* (New York: St. Martin's Press, 2013). Some sources say there were ten Chase children, but Chase said there were eleven, one of whom died as an infant. Chase to Susan Walker, January 2, 1865, *SPCP,* 5:5.

4 Chase to John Trowbridge, December 29, 1863, Warden, 56.

5 Ibid., 61.

6 See George Knepper, *Ohio and Its People* (Kent, OH: Kent State University Press, 1989), 117–19.

7 "Lake Erie Steamboat," *Buffalo Journal,* May 15, 1821, 1 (advertised schedule); Daniel Walker Howe, *What Hath God Wrought: The Transformation of America, 1815–1848* (New York: Oxford University Press, 2007), 211–42; Henry Schoolcraft, *Narrative Journal of Travels Through the Northwestern Regions of the United States . . . in the Year 1820* (Albany, NY: E. E. Hosford, 1821), 47–48.

8 Chase to unknown, July 10, 1853, Chase Papers, LC; Chase to John Trowbridge, January 23, 1864, Warden, 69.

9 Virginia and Robert McCormick, *New Englanders on the Ohio Frontier: The Migration and Settlement of Worthington, Ohio* (Kent, OH: Kent State University Press, 1998). In the 1820 census, the population of Sharon Township, including the town of Worthington and rural areas, was 983 people. Ibid., 310n5.

10 Laura Smith, *The Life of Philander Chase* (New York: E. P. Dutton, 1903); Rima Schultz, "Philander Chase," in *American National Biography,* 24 vols., ed. John Garraty and Mark Carnes (New York: Oxford University Press, 1999), 4:736–37. For an excellent online exhibit about Philander Chase, see "The Papers of Philander Chase," Kenyon College, last modified February 21, 2002, https://www2.kenyon.edu/Khistory/chase/welcome2.htm.

11 Goodwin Berquist and Paul Bowers, *The New Eden: James Kilbourne and the Development of Ohio* (Lanham, MD: University Press of America, 1983), 182–83; McCormick and McCormick, *New Englanders on the Ohio Frontier,* 231–36.

12 Chase to Joseph Denison, November 15, 1831, Chase Papers, LC; Chase to John Trowbridge, January 25, 1864, Warden, 70–71.

13 Chase to unknown, July 10, 1853, Chase Papers, LC.

14 Philander Chase to Philander Chase Jr., July 4, 1822, Chase Papers, Kenyon (worried that boy's mother "may hear the school is broken up"); Chase to John

Trowbridge, January 26, 1864, Schuckers, 15; McCormick and McCormick, *New Englanders on the Ohio Frontier,* 148 (speech in Greek).

15 Philander Chase to Philander Chase Jr., July 8, 1822, Chase Papers, Kenyon; Philander Chase to Charles Wetmore, July 8, 1822, ibid.; Philander Chase to Philander Chase Jr., November 11, 1822, ibid.

16 Daniel Aaron, *Cincinnati, Queen City of the West* (Columbus: Ohio State University Press, 1992); Frances Trollope, *Domestic Manners of the Americans* (London: Whitaker, Treacher, 1832), 80.

17 Alexis de Tocqueville to father, December 20, 1831, in Olivier Zunz, ed., *Tocqueville and Gustave de Beaumont in America* (Charlottesville: University of Virginia Press, 2011), 191–92; Chase to Charles Cleveland, December 21, 1831, Chase Papers, HSP; Andrew DelBanco, *The War Before the War: Fugitive Slaves and the Struggle for America's Soul from the Revolution to the Civil War* (New York: Penguin Books, 2019), 107–30; Nikki Taylor, *Frontiers of Freedom: Cincinnati's Black Community, 1802–1868* (Athens: Ohio University Press, 2005), 37–58.

18 Philander Chase to Philander Chase Jr., December 1822, Chase Papers, Kenyon; Chase to John Trowbridge, January 1864, Schuckers, 15.

19 Philander Chase to Episcopal Bishops, July 29, 1823, in Philander Chase, *Bishop Chase's Reminiscences,* 2 vols. (Boston: J. B. Dow, 1848), 1:186 ("fainting"); Philander Chase to Intrepid Morse, July 23, August 1, 1823, Chase Papers, Kenyon; Chase to unknown, July 10, 1853, Chase Papers, LC.

20 Chase to Joseph Denison, October 26, 1823, *SPCP,* 2:3; Chase to Thomas Sparhawk, November 29, 1825, in Arthur Schlesinger, "Salmon Portland Chase, Undergraduate and Pedagogue," *Ohio State Archeological and Historical Quarterly* 28 (1919): 123; Chase to Sparhawk, February 6, 1826, in ibid., 127. The originals of the letters transcribed by Schlesinger are at the Ohio History Center.

21 Chase to Joseph Denison, March 20, 1824, Chase Papers, LC; Chase to Denison, July 17, 1824, Chase Papers, LC; Chase to Abigail Colby, August 31, 1824, Chase Papers, HSP.

22 Frederick Chase and John Lord, *A History of Dartmouth College and the Town of Hanover,* 2 vols. (Cambridge, MA: J. Wilson & Sons, 1891, 1913); Leon Richardson, *History of Dartmouth College* (Hanover, NH: Dartmouth College Publications, 1932); Jonathan Worcester, *A Memorial of the Class of 1827, Dartmouth College* (Hanover, NH: Centennial Anniversary of the College, 1869). Worcester was especially useful for the ages and backgrounds of Chase's college contemporaries; unfortunately, there is no similar book for the class of 1826.

23 *Dartmouth College v. Woodward,* 17 U.S. 518 (1819); Maurice Baxter, *Daniel Webster and the Supreme Court* (Amherst: University of Massachusetts Press, 1966), 84–85; Jean Edward Smith, *John Marshall: Definer of a Nation* (New York: Henry Holt, 1996), 433–38.

24 Chase to Joseph Denison, October 28, 1824, Chase Papers, LC; Chase to Charles Cleveland, February 8, 1830, *SPCP,* 2:48.

25 Chase to Joseph Denison, March 21, 1825, Chase Papers, Dartmouth; Chase to Hannah Chase Whipple, July 28, 1825, Chase Papers, HSP.

26 Chase to Thomas Sparhawk, February 6, 1826, in Schlesinger, "Chase, Undergraduate," 126; Chase to Sparhawk, February 20, 1826, ibid., 127; Chase to Adeline and Lauretta Hitchcock, December 19, 1826, *SPCP,* 2:10.

27 Chase to Thomas Sparhawk, March 16, 1826, in Schlesinger, "Chase, Undergraduate," 130; *Hopkinsian* 2 (1826): 119; George Punchard, *History of Congregationalism from A.D. 250 to the Present Time* (New York: Hurd & Houghton, 1865), 524–25.

28 Chase to Adeline Hitchcock, April 29, 1826, Chase Papers, HSP; Constantine Blodgett to Bezaleel Smith, May 1, 1826, Misc. mss. Dartmouth 826301; Arthur Livermore, class of 1829, quoted in Richardson, *History of Dartmouth,* 1:373.

29 Chase to Joseph Denison, June 20, 1826, *SPCP,* 2:8–9.

30 Alexander Chase to Chase, November 4, 1825, *SPCP,* 2:5; Moses Chase to Chase, November 15, 1826, Chase Papers, HSP; Chase to unknown, July 10, 1853, Chase Papers, LC; Chase to John Trowbridge, February 8, 1864, Warden, 118.

31 Moses Chase to Chase, November 15, 1826, Chase Papers, HSP; Chase to Adeline and Lauretta Hitchcock, December 19, 1826, *SPCP,* 2:10–14; Chase to unknown, July 10, 1853, Chase Papers, LC.

CHAPTER 2: "Metropolis of the Nation," 1826–30

1 Chase to Adeline and Lauretta Hitchcock, December 19, 1826, *SPCP,* 2:10–14.

2 Chase to Hamilton Smith, December 20, 1826, Smith Papers, Indiana University; *National Intelligencer* (Washington, DC), December 23, 1826; Chase to Thomas Sparhawk, January 13, 1827, *SPCP,* 2:16, and January 2, 1828, *SPCP,* 2:22. On the friendship between Henry Clay and Philander Chase, see Philander Chase, *Reminiscences of Bishop Chase* (1844), 1:250–55 (Clay provides Chase introductions in England).

3 Chase to John Trowbridge, February 10, 1864, Warden, 121–22. Warden interviewed Alexander Plumley, the schoolteacher who shared students with Chase, who corroborated Chase's recollection. Ibid., 122–23.

4 Chase to Hamilton Smith, May 31, 1827, *SPCP,* 2:17–19.

5 Chase diary, January 1, 1829, *SPCP,* 1:3 (Campbell), and July 12, 1829, *SPCP,* 1:16–17 (Johns), and February 21, 1830, *SPCP,* 1:39–41 (Methodists); Chase to John Trowbridge, February 10, 1864, Warden, 125 (Sunday School).

6 John Quincy Adams, *Diaries 1779–1821* (New York: Library of America Press, 2017), 39; Chase diary, December 31, 1829, *SPCP,* 1:34–35.

7 Chase to Joseph Denison, November 10, 1827, Chase Papers, LC; Chase to Thomas Sparhawk, January 2, 1828, *SPCP,* 2:21; Eugene Didier, "Salmon P. Chase," *The Chautauquan* 11 (1890), 184 (Chase never told a joke); Donald Cole, *Vindicating Andrew Jackson: The 1828 Election and the Rise of the Two-Party System* (Lawrence: University Press of Kansas, 2009), 150 (the Adams toast was "a gift from the gods" for the Jacksonians); Lynn Parsons, *The Birth of Modern Politics: Andrew Jackson, John Quincy Adams, and the Election of 1828* (New York: Oxford University Press, 2009), 167 ("Adams played into the enemy's hands").

8 Chase to Joseph Denison, November 10, 1827, Chase Papers, LC. On Wirt, see Gregory Glassner, *Adopted Son: The Life, Wit & Wisdom of William Wirt, 1772–1834* (Madison County, VA: Kurt, Ketner, 1997); Anya Jabour, *Marriage in the Early Republic: Elizabeth and William Wirt and the Compassionate Ideal* (Baltimore: Johns Hopkins University Press, 2012); John Kennedy, *Memoirs of the Life of William Wirt* (Philadelphia: Lee & Blanchard, 1850).

9 Chase to Thomas Sparhawk, January 2, 1828, *SPCP*, 2:21; Chase to Hamilton Smith, March 31, 1828, *SPCP*, 2:27; Chase to Sparhawk, February 29, 1829, Chase Papers, Dartmouth (annoyed at publication of the poem); William Coggeshall, ed., *The Poets and Poetry of the West* (Columbus, OH: Follett, Foster, 1860), 170 ("The Sisters," by Chase, "inscribed to E.G.W. and C.G.W.").

10 Chase to Thomas Sparhawk, May 15, 1828, in Schlesinger, "Chase, Undergraduate," 146; Liz Wirt to William Wirt, May 28, 1828, Wirt Papers, Maryland Historical Society; Chase to Charles Cleveland, June 3, 1828, Chase Papers, LC; Chase to Hamilton Smith, November 10, 1828, Smith Papers, Indiana University; Jabour, *Marriage in the Early Republic*, 302–3 (Edward Hazzard); James Dilts, *The Great Road: The Building of the Baltimore & Ohio Railroad, 1828–1853* (Stanford, CA: Stanford University Press, 1993), 63 (Hazzard one of the engineers).

11 Chase to Charles Cleveland, July 30, 1828, *SPCP*, 2:31; Chase to Thomas Sparhawk, September 3, 1828, in Schlesinger, "Chase, Undergraduate," 148–49; Chase to Sparhawk, February 23, 1829, Chase Papers, Dartmouth.

12 Elizabeth Wirt to William Wirt, September 22, 1828, Wirt Papers, Maryland Historical Society; Elizabeth Wirt to Laura Randall, November 1, 1828, ibid.; William Wirt to Chase, November 1, 1828, Chase Papers, HSP; Chase to Hamilton Smith, November 4, 1828, Smith Papers, Indiana University (sent Wirt "an immediate, very long, and elaborate answer").

13 William Wirt, *A Discourse on the Lives and Characters of Thomas Jefferson and John Adams* (Washington, DC: Gales & Seaton, 1826), 9; William Wirt to Teackle Wallis, August 25, 1833, in Kennedy, *Memoirs, William Wirt,* 2:412. On Wirt and Jefferson, see Glassner, *Adopted Son,* 105–9. On Wirt and Chase, see Peter Walker, *Moral Choices: Memory, Desire, and Imagination in Nineteenth-Century American Abolition* (Baton Rouge: Louisiana University Press, 1978), 318–26.

14 Chase to Thomas Sparhawk, January 2, 1828, *SPCP*, 2:22 (congressional debate); *Susquehanna Democrat*, May 30, 1828; *Charleston (SC) Courier*, July 23, 1828; *Charleston (SC) Mercury*, August 4, 1828; Howe, *What Hath God Wrought*, 270–75; William Freehling, *The Road to Disunion*, vol. 1: *Secessionists at Bay, 1776–1854* (New York: Oxford University Press, 1990), 253–70.

15 Chase to Thomas Sparhawk, November 10, 1828, in Schlesinger, "Chase, Undergraduate," 150–51.

16 Chase to Hamilton Smith, March 31, 1828, *SPCP*, 2:25, and July 30, 1828, *SPCP*, 2:31; *Abstract of the Returns of the Fifth Census* (Washington, DC: Government Printing Office, 1832), 45.

17 Petition, House Doc. No. 140, 23d Congress, 2d Sess. (1828); Chase to unknown, July 10, 1853, Chase Papers, LC; Don Fehrenbacher, *The Slaveholding Republic:*

An Account of the United States Government's Relations to Slavery (New York: Oxford University Press, 2001), 69; Albert Hart, *Salmon P. Chase* (Boston: Houghton, Mifflin, 1889), 46–47.

18 Chase to Charles Cleveland, June 3, 1828, Chase Papers, LC; Chase to Hamilton Smith, July 30, 1828, *SPCP,* 2:30; see Cole, *Vindicating Andrew Jackson*; Parsons, *Birth of Modern Politics.*

19 Chase to Thomas Sparhawk, November 10, 1828, in Schlesinger, "Chase, Undergraduate," 150–51; Cole, *Vindicating Andrew Jackson*, 179–95.

20 Chase to Joseph Denison, November 14, 1828, Chase Papers, LC.

21 Chase diary, January 1, 1829, *SPCP,* 1:3; Liz Wirt to William Wirt, January 2, 1829, Wirt Papers, Maryland Historical Society (misdated 1828).

22 Chase diary, January 13, 1829, *SPCP,* 1:6.

23 Ibid., February 14, 1829, *SPCP,* 1:10; *Wilkinson v. Leland*, 27 U.S. 627, 657 (1829); Legal Tender Cases, 79 U.S. 457, 671 (1870); Charles Fairman, *Reconstruction and Reunion 1864–88: Part 1* (New York: Macmillan, 1971), 27–28.

24 Chase diary, March 4, 1829, *SPCP,* 1:11; April 8, 1829, *SPCP,* 1:13; April 14, 1829, *SPCP,* 1:14; Chase to Thomas Sparhawk, April 20, 1829, in Schlesinger, "Chase, Undergraduate," 152–54; Parsons, *Birth of Modern Politics*, xi–xiv.

25 Chase to Thomas Sparhawk, April 20, 1829, in Schlesinger, "Chase, Undergraduate," 152–54.

26 Chase to Charles Cleveland, May 28 and July 11, 1829, Chase Papers, LC.

27 Chase diary, July 4, 1829, *SPCP,* 1:16 (notes "heavy rain"); *Washington (DC) Chronicle*, July 11, 1829; Chase to Charles Cleveland, July 11, 1829, Chase Papers, LC (asks his opinion on the printed speech).

28 *Washington (DC) Chronicle*, July 11, 1829; see Donald Cole, *Martin Van Buren and the American Political System* (Princeton, NJ: Princeton University Press, 1984).

29 *Washington (DC) Chronicle*, July 11, 1829.

30 Ibid.

31 Nathan Lord to Chase, June 6, 1829, Chase Papers, LC; Chase to Hamilton Smith, July 14, 1829, Smith Papers, Indiana University; Chase diary, August 1829, *SPCP,* 1:18–19; "Washington Monument at Baltimore," *Pittsfield (MA) Sun,* December 3, 1829, 2; Chase and Lord, *History of Dartmouth College*, 580.

32 Chase diary, August 1829, *SPCP,* 1:20–21; Chase to Thomas Sparhawk, September 30, 1829, in Schlesinger, "Chase, Undergraduate," 154–55.

33 Chase to Thomas Sparhawk, April 20, 1829, in Schlesinger, "Chase, Undergraduate," 152–54 (Maryland; law reform); Chase to William Wirt, June 16, 1829, Wirt Papers, Maryland Historical Society ("New York or Ohio or Alabama"); Chase to Charles Cleveland, March 18, 1830, Chase Papers, LC (Louisiana); Chase to Hamilton Smith, May 26, 1830, Smith Papers, Indiana University (Louisiana).

34 Chase to unknown, July 10, 1853, Chase Papers, LC; Schuckers, 30. Schuckers is quoting from some similar autobiographical letter, perhaps in HSP.

35 Chase diary, December 27, 1829, *SPCP,* 1:32–33; Howe, *What Hath God Wrought*, 562–63.

36 Chase diary, February 4, 1828, *SPCP*, 1:9 (Clay); December 29, 1828, 33 (Van Buren); January 1, 1829, 35–36; January 7, 1829, 36 (Jackson).

37 Liz Wirt to Chase, January 25, 1830, Chase Papers, HSP.

38 Chase to Liz Wirt, January 28, 1830, ibid. (draft).

39 Liz Wirt to Chase, January 30, 1830, ibid.

40 Chase to Charles Cleveland, February 8, 1830, *SPCP*, 2:48.

41 Chase diary, January 7, 1830, *SPCP*, 1:37; February 22, 1830, ibid. 1:42–43.

42 Ibid., February 1830, *SPCP*, 1:38–39.

43 Chase to Liz Wirt, January 28, 1830, Chase Papers, HSP; Chase to Charles Cleveland, February 8, 1830, *SPCP*, 2:47; Merrill Peterson, *The Great Triumvirate: Webster, Clay, and Calhoun* (New York: Oxford University Press, 1987), 170–79.

44 Chase diary, February 29, 1830, *SPCP*, 1:37; Chase to Charles Cleveland, December 21, 1831, Chase Papers, HSP. There was no February 29 in 1830; Chase probably means Sunday, February 28, 1830.

CHAPTER 3: *"First* in Cincinnati," 1830–35.

1 Chase diary, March 1830, *SPCP*, 1:45–47; Chase to Charles Cleveland, March 18, 1830, Chase Papers, LC. Chase notes that he arrived on a Saturday morning; this was probably Saturday, March 13, 1830.

2 *Cincinnati American*, August 23, 1830 (population); "Our City," ibid., January 3, 1831, reprinted in Warden, 185–87; Chase to Charles Cleveland, January 4, 1831, Chase Papers, HSP; see Aaron, *Cincinnati, Queen City.*

3 Chase to Charles Cleveland, March 18, 1830, Chase Papers, LC ("impossible for me to be admitted until the session of the Supreme Court which will sit here in June"); Chase to Hamilton Smith, June 30, 1830, Smith Papers, Indiana University (thanks for loan; has not yet opened office); Chase to Edward Chase, September 17, 1830, in Schuckers, 32–33; *Cincinnati Gazette*, September 27, 1830 (advertisement for office); Chase to Hamilton Smith, January 26, 1831, *SPCP*, 2:50, and May 9, 1831, Smith Papers, Indiana University.

4 Chase to Charles Cleveland, March 18, 1830, Chase Papers, HSP (seeks information about lyceums); *Cincinnati American*, October 1830 (benefits of a lyceum); "Lyceum Notice," ibid., November 1, 1830 (Chase on the committee to draft the constitution of the lyceum); ibid., November 29, 1830 (first lecture at the lyceum); ibid., December 27, 1830 (Chase to give lyceum lecture on Brougham); Chase to Charles Cleveland, January 4, 1831, Chase Papers, HSP (progress of the lyceum); Chase to Hamilton Smith, March 16, 1831, Smith Papers, Indiana University (gave lyceum lecture last night "to a very large and assuredly respectable audience"). The article about the benefits of a lyceum appears both in Chase's LC scrapbook and in Warden, 198–99.

5 Chase, "The Life and Character of Henry Brougham," *North American Review* 33 (July 1831): 227–29.

6 Ibid., 255–57.

7 Chase to Hamilton Smith, August 31, 1831, Smith Papers, Indiana University; Chase, "The Effects of Machinery," *North American Review* 34 (January 1832): 220–46.

8 Chase to Hamilton Smith, January 26, 1831, *SPCP,* 2:50; *Cincinnati American*, June 4, 1831. Warden, 185, describes Chase as editor pro tempore of the *Cincinnati American* at the time of the January 1831 article describing Cincinnati. I think Warden errs on the date, because of the references in the paper in the summer of 1831 to a temporary editor, and because of the density of articles from that period in the LC scrapbook.

9 *New York Daily Advertiser*, January 13, 1831; *Congressional Debates*, January 29, 1831, 541 (House vote on repeal of sec. 25 of the Judiciary Act); "The Supreme Court," *Cincinnati American*, June 1831, in Scrapbook, Chase Papers, LC, and partly in Warden, 783–84; see Charles Warren, *The Supreme Court in United States History* (Boston: Little, Brown, 1923), 2:196–200; Michael Kammen, *A Machine That Would Go of Itself: The Constitution in American Culture* (New York: Alfred A. Knopf, 1986), 49 ("between 1815 and 1835, attacks on the Supreme Court erupted frequently").

10 "Bank of the United States—The Currency," *Cincinnati American*, June 11, 1831. This article, and some of the others in this series, are in Chase Papers, LC, Scrapbook.

11 *Cincinnati American*, June 18, 25, 1831. On Jackson and the Bank, see Donald Cole, *The Presidency of Andrew Jackson* (Lawrence: University Press of Kansas, 1993), 95–106; Andrew Hill, "The Second Bank of the United States," December 5, 2015, https://www.federalreservehistory.org/essays/second-bank-of-the-us; Howe, *What Hath God Wrought*, 373–83.

12 Chase to Charles Cleveland, June 2, 1830, Chase Papers, LC (Indians); Chase to Hamilton Smith, June 15, 1830, Smith Papers, Indiana University (Maysville road); *Cincinnati American*, June 24, 1830 ("political humbug").

13 "The Virginia Springs," *National Gazette* (Philadelphia), September 26, 1831, 1; Thomas Chambers, *Drinking the Waters: Creating an American Leisure Class at Nineteenth-Century Mineral Springs* (Washington, DC: Smithsonian Institution Press, 2002); Alexander MacCorkle, *The White Sulphur Springs: The Traditions, History, and Social Life of the Greenbriar White Sulphur Springs* (Charleston, WV: W. A. MacCorkle, 1916).

14 William Wirt to Daniel Webster, August 17, 1831, in *Papers of Daniel Webster: Correspondence,* ed. Charles Wiltse (Hanover, NH: University Press of New England, 1977), 3:117 (introduces Chase); Chase to Hamilton Smith, October 10, 1831, Smith Papers, Indiana University (from Baltimore; has been in Washington); John Young to Chase, October 15, 1831, Chase Papers, LC (answers letter from New York of September 19); Chase to Hamilton Smith, November 10, 1831, Smith Papers, Indiana University (back in Cincinnati); Abigail Chase to Chase, April 10, 1832, Chase Papers, LC (mother has died; hoped to go to Cincinnati with her); Chase to unknown, July 10, 1853, Chase Papers, LC (went by way of White Sulphur Springs to Boston).

15 On the anti-Masons, see Howe, *What Hath God Wrought*, 266–70; Walter Stahr, *Seward: Lincoln's Indispensable Man* (New York: Simon & Schuster, 2012), 24–28; Sean Wilentz, *The Rise of American Democracy: Jefferson to Lincoln* (New York: W. W. Norton), 272–79.

16 Chase to Reverend Blanchard, November 18, 1868, Warden, 232 (father a Mason); see Stahr, *Seward*, 28–31.

17 William Wirt to Chase, November 11, 1831, in Kennedy, *Memoirs, William Wirt*, 2:314.

18 Chase to Charles Cleveland, December 21, 1831, Chase Papers, HSP.

19 Leo Damrosch, *Tocqueville's Discovery of America* (New York: Farrar, Straus & Giroux, 2010); Zunz, ed., *Alexis de Tocqueville and Gustave de Beaumont in America*, 167–68 (notes of Chase interview).

20 Gustave de Beaumont to his brother, December 4, 1831, in Zunz, ed., *Alexis de Tocqueville and Gustave de Beaumont in America*, 180–81; Alexis de Tocqueville to his mother, December 6, 1831, in ibid.,184; Chase to Charles Cleveland, December 21, 1831, Chase Papers, HSP.

21 Chase diary, April 10, 1832, *SPCP*, 1:64; Chase to Hamilton Smith, April 16, 1832, Smith Papers, Indiana University; Thomas Swann to Chase, April 23, 1832, Chase Papers, HSP; Alexander Everett to Chase, May 9, 1832, Chase Papers, HSP; Chase to Daniel Webster, May 10, 1832, *SPCP*, 2:51–52; "A Western Quarterly Review," *National Gazette* (Philadelphia), May 11, 1832, 2; William Wirt to Chase, May 16, 1832, Chase Papers, HSP; Chase to Hamilton Smith, May 29, 1832, Smith Papers, Indiana University (Walker both friend and rival); Isaac Jewett to Joseph Willard, August 26, 1832, in James Dunn, ed., "'Cincinnati Is a Delightful Place': Letters of a Law Clerk, 1831–34," *Bulletin of the Historical and Philosophical Society of Ohio* 10 (October 1852): 268.

22 Abigail Colby to Chase, May 28, 1832, Chase Papers, LC (on way to Cincinnati); Chase to Hamilton Smith, November 14, 1832, *SPCP*, 2:54; Chase diary, April 28, 1833, *SPCP*, 1:70; Harriet Beecher Stowe, *Men of Our Times: Leading Patriots of the Day* (Hartford: Hartford, 1868), 294. Some suggest that Chase was a member, along with Harriet Beecher, in a literary group, the Semi-Colons. Joan Hedrick, *Harriet Beecher Stowe: A Life* (New York: Oxford University Press, 1994), 82; Milton Rugoff, *The Beechers: An American Family in the Nineteenth Century* (New York: Harper & Row, 1981), 171. I do not see this in the early accounts of this group, however, by authors who would probably have mentioned someone as prominent as Chase. See Edward Mansfield, *Memoirs of the Life and Services of Daniel Drake, M.D.* (Cincinnati: Applegate, 1855), 223–27; John Foote, *Memoirs of the Life of Samuel E. Foote* (Cincinnati: R. Clarke, 1860), 177–78.

23 Chase, "The State of the South," *Illinois Monthly Journal*, July 1832, in *National Republican* (Washington, DC), December 27, 1860, 4; Jackson Nullification Proclamation, December 10, 1832, Miller Center UVA website (https://miller center.org/the-presidency/presidential-speeches/december-10-1832-nullification -proclamation). Although the *National Republican* claimed in 1860 that Chase's

article was widely copied in 1832, I do not see it in any 1832 papers, so there is some possibility that this is an 1860 forgery.

24 Chase to Charles Cleveland, August 13, 1832, Chase Papers, HSP.

25 Chase to Hamilton Smith, November 14, 1832, *SPCP*, 2:54.

26 Isaac Jewett to Joseph Willard, October 25, 1832, in Dunn, "Cincinnati Is a Delightful Place," 270; Chase to Hamilton Smith, November 14, 1832, *SPCP*, 2:53; Chase diary, January 1833, *SPCP*, 1:67–68.

27 Chase to Hamilton Smith, August 7, 1833, *SPCP*, 2:55; Chase, *The Statutes of Ohio and of the Northwestern Territory Adopted or Enacted from 1788 to 1833 Inclusive, Including a Preliminary Sketch of the History of Ohio* (Cincinnati: Corey & Fairbank, 1833–35).

28 Chase, *Statutes of Ohio*, 1:21–24, 32–34. See Frederick Blue, "Salmon P. Chase: First Historian of the Old Northwest," *Ohio History* 98 (1989): 52–69.

29 Chase, *Statutes of Ohio*, 1:47–48 (education), 1:393–94 (1804 statute), 1:555–56 (1807 statute). See Diane Barnes, "Only a Moral Power: African Americans, Reformers, and the Repeal of Ohio's Black Laws," *Ohio History* 124 (2017): 7–21; Stephen Middleton, *The Black Laws: Race and the Legal Process in Early Ohio* (Athens: Ohio University Press, 2005); Paul Finkelman, "The Strange Career of Race Discrimination in Antebellum Ohio," *Case Western Law Review* 55 (2004): 373–408. Finkelman is especially useful on the effects of the prohibition of black testimony.

30 Chase to James Kent, November 25, 1833, Chase Papers, HSP; Kent to Chase, December 20, 1833, ibid.; Joseph Story to Chase, March 1, 1834, in Schuckers, 36–37; "Fire," *Pittsburgh Gazette*, November 11, 1834, 2 (copies of Chase's book destroyed); Hart, *Chase*, 19 ($1,000 for "immense labor").

31 Chase to Daniel Caswell, November 1, 1832, Chase Papers, LC; Chase to Hamilton Smith, November 14, 1832, *SPCP*, 2:54 ("ablest lawyers"); Chase to Richard Peters, May 1, 1833, Chase Papers, HSP; Chase to Caswell, January 25, 1834, Chase Papers, LC; Chase diary, February 11, 1834, *SPCP*, 1:80.

32 Chase to Herman Cope, February 1834, April 12, 1834, February 6, 1835, Kirby Papers, CHLA.

33 Chase diary, February 8, 10, 1836, *SPCP*, 1:112–13; Josiah Lawrence to Chase, December 30, 1836, Chase Papers, LC.

34 Chase, Lecture for the Hamilton County Agricultural Society, December 1833, Chase Papers, HSP; Edward Mansfield to Chase, November 26, 1834, Chase Papers, HSP (colonization); "Temperance Meeting," *Western Monthly* 3 (1835): 182–83; Chase diary, February 21, 1836, *SPCP*, 1:117 (Sunday School Union); American Bible Society, *Annual Report of the American Bible Society* (New York: American Bible Society, 1838), 39; Chase to Charles Lanman, September 1, 1858, copy at AKSPL.

35 Chase to David Este, December 18, 1834, Virginia Historical Society (McLean will be nominated by state legislators); "Democratic Republican Recommendation," *Huron Reflector* (Norwalk, OH), January 13, 1835, 2 (public letter supporting McLean); Chase to Samuel Vinton, February 8, 1835, *SPCP*, 2:57–59; Chase to John McLean, February 16, 1835, Warden, 249–50; McLean to Chase,

February 25, 1835, *SPCP*, 2:59–60; Circular letter, August 10, 1835, Chase Papers, LC (supporting McLean); James Stegemoeller, "That Contemptible Bauble: The Birth of the Cincinnati Whig Party, 1834–1836," *Cincinnati Historical Society Bulletin* 39 (1981): 209–23; Francis Weisenberger, *The Life of John McLean: A Politician on the United States Supreme Court* (Columbus: Ohio State University Press, 1937), 82–92.

36 Chase diary, March 1, 1831, *SPCP*, 1:57; April 30, 1833, *SPCP*, 1:72; May 3, 1833, *SPCP*, 1:73; November 1835, *SPCP*, 1:81–83.

37 Warden, 241–42 (quoting from unnamed newspaper); "The First Love of Chief Justice Chase," *Atlanta Constitution*, February 15, 1874, 5 (longer quote suggesting neither partner was happy in this marriage). I am inclined to believe Chase, whose contemporary diary and letters show that he loved his wife, rather than an anonymous article forty years after the events.

38 Chase to Charles Cleveland, June 29, 1835, Chase Papers, HSP.

39 Chase diary, November 20, 1835, *SPCP*, 1:87; December 1, 1835, *SPCP*, 1:93–94.

40 Chase diary, December 25, 1835, *SPCP*, 1:94; December 26, 1835, *SPCP*, 1:96; December 29, 1835, *SPCP*, 1:100; December 31, 1835, *SPCP*, 1:102; Chase to Charles Cleveland, December 27, 1835, Chase Papers, HSP.

CHAPTER 4: "Some Great Scheme," 1836–41

1 On Garrison, see Henry Mayer, *All on Fire: William Lloyd Garrison and the Abolition of Slavery* (New York: St. Martin's Press, 1998). "Covenant with death" is at ibid., 313. On abolitionism generally, see Manisha Sinha, *The Slave's Cause: A History of Abolitionism* (New Haven, CT: Yale University Press, 2016). On the ways in which antislavery and abolitionism were linked, see Caleb McDaniel, "The Bonds and Boundaries of Antislavery," *Journal of the Civil War Era* 4 (2014): 84–105, and Randy Barnett, "Whence Comes Section One? The Abolitionist Origins of the Fourteenth Amendment," *Journal of Legal Analysis* 3 (2011): 165–264, especially note 6.

2 Chase diary, January 22, 1836, *SPCP*, 1:108–9. For more on the murder case, see Chase diary, December 25, 1836, *SPCP*, 1:95–96; "A Man by the Name of Gedney," *Boston Post*, January 5, 1836, 2; "Melancholy Homicide," *Sunbury (PA) Gazette*, January 23, 1836, 3; "Charles F. Gedney," *Richmond (IN) Weekly Palladium*, January 30, 1836, 2.

3 Chase to Charles Cleveland, April 6, 1836, *SPCP*, 2:60–62.

4 "Abolitionism in Cincinnati!," *Richmond Enquirer*, August 5, 1836, 3; "Abolitionism," *Pittsburgh Gazette*, August 6, 1836, 2; Betty Fladeland, *James Gillespie Birney: Slaveholder to Abolitionist* (Ithaca, NY: Cornell University Press, 1955), 125–43; David Grimsted, *American Mobbing, 1828–1861: Towards Civil War* (New York: Oxford University Press, 1998), 59–61; Leonard Richards, *"Gentlemen of Property and Standing": Anti-Abolition Mobs in Jacksonian America* (New York: Oxford University Press, 1970), 95–98; Richard Sewell, *Ballots for Freedom: Antislavery Politics in the United States, 1837–1860* (New York: Norton, 1976),

72 (Birney was "courageous and firm in his abolitionism, deeply religious, and skilled in the arts of propaganda").

5 *Cincinnati Daily Gazette*, August 1–2, 1836; *Cincinnati Whig*, August 1, 1836; *Daily Cincinnati Republican*, August 1, 1836; Chase to unknown, July 10, 1853, Chase Papers, LC.

6 *Cincinnati Daily Gazette*, August 2, 1836 (call for meeting); ibid., August 3, 1836 (report of meeting); ibid., August 4, 1836 (Chase letter) (also in *SPCP*, 2:62–63).

7 Chase to Charles Cleveland, February 17, 1837, Chase Papers, HSP; *Philanthropist* (Cincinnati), February 27, 1838, and April 30, 1839.

8 Chase, *Speech of Salmon P. Chase, in the Case of the Colored Woman, Matilda* (Cincinnati: Pugh & Dodd, 1837) 3–4; Chase to John Trowbridge, March 16, 1864, Warden, 282–83; Fladeland, *James Gillespie Birney*, 149–51; Charles Hickok, *The Negro in Ohio* (Cleveland: Williams, 1896), 141–42 ("nearly white, of striking beauty and engaging manners"); James Oakes, *Freedom National: The Destruction of Slavery in the United States, 1861–1865* (New York: W. W. Norton, 2012), 15–16.

9 Chase, *Matilda Speech*, 3–4; Chase to John Trowbridge, March 16, 1864, Warden, 282–83.

10 Chase, *Matilda Speech*, 5 (list of counsel); Fladeland, *James Gillespie Birney*, 152; Richards, *"Gentlemen of Property and Standing,"* 173 (list of anti-abolition rioters and supporters).

11 Chase, *Matilda Speech*, 5.

12 Ibid., 8. "Just exactly what *Somerset* decided is still being debated, over two hundred years after Lord Mansfield's opinion." Paul Finkelman, *An Imperfect Union: Slavery, Federalism, and Comity* (Chapel Hill: University Press of North Carolina, 1981), 38; see William Wiecek, *The Sources of Antislavery Constitutionalism* (Ithaca, NY: Cornell University Press, 1977), 40–61.

13 Chase, *Matilda Speech*, 10–11.

14 Ibid., 12–17.

15 Ibid., 17.

16 Ibid., 19–22. For more on the compact argument, see Richard Aynes, "Constricting the Law of Freedom: Justice Miller, the Fourteenth Amendment, and the *Slaughter-House Cases*," *Chicago-Kent Law Review* 70 (1994), 631n22; Randy Barnett, "From Antislavery Lawyer to Chief Justice: The Remarkable but Forgotten Career of Salmon P. Chase," *Case Western Law Review* 63 (2013): 659–63; Fehrenbacher, *Slaveholding Republic*, 208–12.

17 Chase, *Matilda Speech*, 23–26.

18 Ibid., 27–29.

19 For more on the *Matilda* case, see Finkelman, *Imperfect Union*, 160–64, and Steven Lubet, *Fugitive Justice: Runaways, Rescuers, and Slavery on Trial* (Cambridge, MA: Belknap Press of Harvard University Press, 2010), 25–27.

20 *Birney v. Ohio*, 8 Ohio 230 (1837).

21 Ibid.

22 *Cincinnati Gazette*, February 1838, in Scrapbook, Chase Papers, LC. I have not been able to find this in the paper, but there are gaps in the microfilm.

23 Elihu Wolcott to Chase, April 17, 1838, Chase Papers, HSP (from Jacksonville, Illinois, seeking advice in fugitive slave case); John Martin to Chase, March 1, 1840, Chase Papers, LC (from Macon, Georgia, seeking homes for emancipated slaves); Michael Benedict, "Salmon P. Chase and Constitutional Politics," *Law & Social Inquiry* 22 (1997): 463; Frederick Blue, *Salmon Chase: A Life in Politics* (Kent, OH: Kent State University Press, 1987), 40; Harold Hyman and William Wiecek, *Equal Justice Under Law: Constitutional Development 1835–1875* (New York: Harper & Row, 1982), 106 ("first major"); Schuckers, 72 ("attorney general for fugitive slaves").

24 "Suspension of Specie Payment," *New York Herald*, May 11, 1837, 2; *Cincinnati Gazette*, May 18, 1837; "Resumption by the Ohio Banks," *Huron Reflector* (Norwalk, OH), August 14, 1838, 2; "The Banks in the Several States," *New York Evening Post*, August 15, 1838, 2 (banks in Cincinnati resumed on August 7); Jessica Lepler, *The Many Panics of 1837: People, Politics and the Creation of a Transatlantic Financial Crisis* (Cambridge: Cambridge University Press, 2013); Katherine Liang, "Banking Crises at the Micro-Level: The Panic of 1837" (honors thesis, Wellesley College, 2017); Alasdair Roberts, *America's First Great Depression: Economic Crisis and Political Disorder After the Panic of 1837* (Ithaca, NY: Cornell University Press, 2012); Peter Rousseau, "Jacksonian Monetary Policy, Specie Flows, and the Panic of 1837," *Journal of Economic History* 62 (2002): 457–88.

25 James Birney to Lewis Tappan, August 23, 1837, in Dwight Dumond, ed., *Letters of James Gillespie Birney, 1831–1857* (New York: D. Appleton-Century, 1938), 419 (introduces Chase); Chase to Elizabeth Wirt, September 28, 1837, Wirt Papers, Maryland Historical Society; Lewis Tappan to Chase, October 7, 1837, Chase Papers, LC; Truman Thorpe to Chase, December 18, 1837, Chase Papers, LC (Chase in Columbus).

26 Act of February 25, 1839, sec. 2, in J. R. Swan, ed., *Statutes of the State of Ohio of a General Nature* (Columbus, OH: Samuel Medary, 1841), 126; see Charles Huntington, *A History of Banking and Currency in Ohio Before the Civil War* (Columbus, Ohio State Archeological and Historical Society, 1915), 162–64; Francis Weisenburger, *The Passing of the Frontier, 1825–1850* (Columbus: Ohio State Archeological and Historical Society, 1941), 346–52.

27 "Glories of Bank Reform," *Huron Reflector* (Norwalk, OH), February 19, 1839, 2; "The Bank Injunction," *Democrat & Herald* (Wilmington, OH), May 24, 1839, 3 (from *Cincinnati Advertiser*).

28 "Bank Injunction," *Ohio State Journal* (Columbus), May 29, 1839, 2 (from *Cincinnati Gazette*); "Bank Affairs," *Huron Reflector* (Norwalk, OH), June 25, 1839, 2.

29 *Philanthropist* (Cincinnati), January 23, 1838 (obituary); Chase diary, February 1838, *SPCP*, 1:119; Sauver Bonfils to Chase, December 8, 1838, Chase Papers, LC (asks to pay bill for Misses Chase and Skinner); Eliza Chase to Chase, June 22, 1844, *Spur*, 88–89 (only letter from Eliza); Helen Walbridge to Chase, February 6, 1864, Chase Papers, LC; Eliza Whipple to Jacob Schuckers, June 29, 1873,

in Schuckers, 630 ("His family then consisted of himself, his sister Helen, his little motherless child, Kitty, Jenny Skinner (another niece) and myself").

30 John Garniss to Chase, September 5, 1839, Chase Papers, HSP; Chase to Charles Cleveland, February 7, 1840, *SPCP,* 2:68 ("ardently attached"); "The Family Extended," *Spur,* 448.

31 Chase to Charles Cleveland, February 7, 1840, *SPCP,* 2:67–69.

32 Ibid., August 29, 1840, *SPCP,* 2:69–71; Chase diary, May 30, 1840, *SPCP,* 1:125; July 26, 1840, *SPCP,* 1:139; August 30, 1840, *SPCP,* 1:143.

33 Chase diary, June 26, July 1, 1840, March 15, 1841, *SPCP,* 1:127, 133, 156; Chase to Timothy Kirby, February 10, 1841, Kirby Papers, CHLA; Chase to Bank of the United States, March 31, 1841, Chase Papers, LC.

34 *Cincinnati Gazette,* April 6, 8, 1840; Chase diary, May 13, 1840 (worked "to defeat license to a tavern which I was persuaded ought not to have one and succeeded"); *Cincinnati Daily Republican,* March 12, 1841 (eight licenses, each with fee of $50, approved; Chase votes against all of them).

35 Cincinnati paper, October 16, 1838, in Scrapbook, Chase Papers, LC (reporting meeting of YMBSC); Chase diary, May 20–21, 1840, *SPCP,* 1:122–23; May 30, 1840, *SPCP,* 1:125; July 1, 1840, *SPCP,* 1:134; *Philanthropist* (Cincinnati), September 15, 1840, 2.

36 *Philanthropist* (Cincinnati), September 15, 1840, 2; Michael Holt, *The Rise and Fall of the American Whig Party: Jacksonian Politics and the Onset of the Civil War* (New York: Oxford University Press,1999), 89–121; Howe, *What Hath God Wrought,* 57–88; Wilentz, *Rise of American Democracy,* 482–518 (log cabin/hard cider quote on 498).

37 Chase to Charles Cleveland, August 29, 1840, *SPCP,* 2:69–71.

38 For the vote by county in Ohio, see "Ohio Presidential Election," *Huron Reflector* (Norwalk, OH), November 24, 1840, 2.

39 Chase diary, December 25, 1840, *SPCP,* 1:144; January 30, 1841, *SPCP,* 1:149; February 20, 1841, *SPCP,* 1:153.

40 Chase diary, January 3, 1841, *SPCP,* 1:147; William Ellery Channing, *Emancipation* (Boston: E.P. Peabody, 1840).

41 Chase diary, January 5, 1841, *SPCP,* 1:147; William Jay, *A View of the Action of the Federal Government, in Behalf of Slavery* (1839).

42 Chase diary, January 4, 1841, *SPCP,* 1:147; Theodore Dwight Weld, *The Power of Congress over the District of Columbia* (New York: American Anti-Slavery Society, 1838).

43 *Cincinnati Daily Gazette,* January 5, 7, 1841; *Daily Cincinnati Republican,* January 7, 1841; Howe, *What Hath God Wrought,* 512–15, 609–12.

44 Chase to the *Cincinnati Republican,* January 1841, Chase Papers, HSP (filed among undated letters). As best I can tell, the *Cincinnati Republican* did not print Chase's letter, but the film is not complete for this period. The Supreme Court case was *Barron v. Baltimore,* 32 U.S. 243 (1833).

45 Chase to William Henry Harrison, February 13, 1841, *SPCP,* 2:72–74; Chase to Daniel Webster, February 20, 1841, noted in Wiltse, *Webster Correspondence,* 5:355; Chase to Jacob Burnet, February 21, 1841, in Burnet Papers, OHC.

46 Chase diary, March 2–5, 1841, *SPCP*, 1:153–55; Howe, *What Hath God Wrought*, 570; Harriet Martineau, *The Hour and the Man: A Romance* (London: E. Moxon, 1841).

47 Chase diary, March 13, 1841, *SPCP*, 1:155–56; March 28, 1841, *SPCP*, 1:157; May 23, 1841, *SPCP*, 1:161; "Secret Drinking," *Philanthropist* (Cincinnati), March 31, 1841, 2 ("never was a city more agitated on the subject of temperance than Cincinnati is now"); *Cincinnati Daily Gazette*, April 7, 1841; *Daily Cincinnati Republican*, April 7, 1841; Ralph Grindrod, *Bacchus: An Essay on the Nature, Causes, Effects, and Cure, of Intemperance* (London: J. Pasco, 1839).

48 Chase diary, April 8–9, 1841, *SPCP*, 1:159–60; *Daily Cincinnati Republican*, April 9, 10, 1841; *Cincinnati Daily Gazette*, April 9, 10, 1841; "Proceedings of the Council," *Cincinnati Enquirer*, April 12, 1841, 3.

49 *Cincinnati Daily Gazette*, April 5, 1841, 2 (temperance candidates); ibid., April 13, 1841 (election results); "Dram-Selling Victory," *Philanthropist* (Cincinnati), April 21, 1841, 3; Chase diary, April 9–13, 1841, *SPCP*, 1:160–61.

50 "Fugitives from Labor," *Cincinnati Enquirer*, May 17, 1841, 2; *Cincinnati Daily Gazette*, May 21, 1841; Chase to Alvan Stewart, May 22, 1841, Stewart Papers, NYHS (comments on Towns case).

51 Chase to Charles Cleveland, May 18, 1841, *SPCP*, 2:74–76.

52 *Cincinnati Daily Gazette*, July 8–9, 1841; "The Remains of Gen. Harrison," *Cincinnati Enquirer*, July 8, 1841, 2; ibid., July 31, 1841, 2 (Chase defends Cornelius Burnett); Sylvester Holmes to Chase, August 20, 1841, Chase Papers, LC (hopes to see Chase in Boston soon); Flamen Ball to Chase, August 30, 1841, Chase Papers, HSP (Chase in New York); Chase to Joshua Giddings, December 30, 1841, *SPCP*, 2:81 ("at the funeral solemnities on the occasion of the removal of the body of General Harrison, I had the pleasure of being introduced to you").

53 *Cincinnati Daily Gazette*, August 20, 23, 1841; *Philanthropist* (Cincinnati), September 1, 1841; George Hoadly, *Address at Music Hall, Cincinnati, Ohio, on the Occasion of the Removal of the Remains of Salmon P. Chase to Spring Grove Cemetery* (Cincinnati: R. Clarke, 1887), 13.

54 Flamen Ball to Chase, August 30, 1841, Chase Papers, HSP; ibid., September 4, 1841, *SPCP*, 2:77–78; Stahr, *Seward*, 59–85; James Stewart, *Joshua R. Giddings and the Tactics of Radical Politics* (Cleveland: Press of Case Western University, 1970).

55 John Tyler, Veto Message Regarding the Bank of the United States, August 16, 1841, Miller Center UVA website (https://millercenter.org/the-presidency/presidential-speeches/august-16-1841-veto-message-regarding-bank-united-states); Tyler, Veto Message on the Creation of a Fiscal Corporation, September 9, 1941, Miller Center UVA website (https://millercenter.org/the-presidency/presidential-speeches/september-9-1841-veto-message-creation-fiscal-corporation).

56 Chase to Charles Cleveland, October 22, 1841, *SPCP*, 2:79–81.

57 See Chase to unknown, July 20, 1853, Chase Papers, LC (Colby and others were "pure, upright, and worthy citizens").

58 *Philanthropist* (Cincinnati), December 22, 1841; Chase to Flamen Ball, December 27, 1841, Chase Papers, HSP (plans for convention); "Proceedings of the Liberty Convention," *Philanthropist* (Cincinnati), January 5, 1842, 3.

59 "Proceedings of the Liberty Convention," *Philanthropist* (Cincinnati), January 5, 1842, 3. On the publication of Madison's notes, see Kammen, *Machine That Would Go of Itself*, 87–88, 100; Sean Wilentz, *No Property in Man: Slavery and Antislavery at the Nation's Founding* (Cambridge, MA: Harvard University Press, 2018), 223–24.

60 "Proceedings of the Liberty Convention," *Philanthropist* (Cincinnati), January 5, 1842, 3. See Chase to Gerrit Smith, May 14, 1852, *SPCP*, 2:97 ("the allegation against us of an intention to interfere with slavery in the states . . . prejudices against us many worthy and sensible people").

61 Chase, "Henry Brougham," 228; "Proceedings of the Liberty Convention," *Philanthropist* (Cincinnati), January 5, 1842, 3; Eric Foner, *Free Soil, Free Labor, Free Men: The Ideology of the Republican Party Before the Civil War* (New York: Oxford University Press, 1970).

CHAPTER 5: "To Limit and Localize . . . Slavery," 1841–48

1 "Presidential Nomination," *Baltimore Sun*, May 21, 1841, 2 ("abolitionists have again nominated James G. Birney"). For accounts of Chase's role in the Liberty Party, see Corey Brooks, *Liberty Power: Antislavery Third Parties and the Transformation of American Politics* (Chicago: University of Chicago Press, 2016), 83–93; Reinhard Johnson, *The Liberty Party: Antislavery Third Party Politics in the United States* (Baton Rouge: Louisiana State University Press, 2009), 31–36, 50–54, and Sewell, *Ballots for Freedom,* 90–92, 121–25.

2 Joshua Leavitt to Chase, December 6, 1841, Chase Papers, HSP.

3 Chase to Joshua Giddings, December 30, 1841, *SPCP,* 2:81–83; Giddings to Chase, January 4, 1842, Chase Papers, HSP; Chase to Giddings, January 21, 1842, *SPCP,* 2:85–87.

4 Chase to Giddings, January 21, 1842, *SPCP,* 2:85–87. On Adams and the gag rule, see Robert Remini, *John Quincy Adams: Militant Spirit* (New York: Times Books, 2002), 137–45. On Seward and Virginia, see Stahr, *Seward*, 65, 71, 81–82.

5 Chase to James Birney, January 21, 1842, *SPCP,* 2:84–85; Birney to Chase, February 2, 1842, Dumond, *Birney Letters*, 670–72; Joshua Leavitt to James Birney, February 14, 1842, ibid., 673.

6 Lewis Tappan to Chase, March 18, 1842, *SPCP,* 2:92–93; Chase to Tappan, May 26, 1842, Chase Papers, LC; Tappan to Chase, June 7, 1842, Chase Papers, HSP; Chase to Tappan, September 15, 1842, Chase Papers, LC. On Tappan, see Bertram Wyatt-Brown, *Lewis Tappan and the Evangelical War Against Slavery* (Cleveland, OH: Press of Case Western University, 1969).

7 Chase to Joshua Giddings, February 15, 1842, *SPCP,* 2:87–89; Chase to John Quincy Adams, February 15, 1842, Adams Papers, Massachusetts Historical Society; Chase to Lewis Tappan, September 24, 1842, *SPCP,* 2:99–101; Chase to John Quincy Adams, September 24, 1842, Chase Papers, HSP (draft).

8 Cassius Clay to Chase, March 1842, *SPCP*, 2:90–91; Clay to Chase, March 7, 1845, Chase Papers, HSP; David Smiley, *Lion of White Hall: The Life of Cassius Clay* (Madison: University of Wisconsin Press, 1962).

9 Chase to Thaddeus Stevens, April 8, 1842, Stevens Papers, LC; Chase to Gerrit Smith, May 14, 1842, *SPCP*, 2:96–98; Charles Sumner to Chase, December 11, 1845, Chase Papers, HSP; see David Donald, *Charles Sumner and the Coming of the Civil War* (New York: Alfred A. Knopf, 1967); Ralph Harlow, *Gerrit Smith, Philanthropist and Reformer* (New York: H. Holt, 1939), and Hans Trefousse, *Thaddeus Stevens: Nineteenth-Century Egalitarian* (Chapel Hill: University Press of North Carolina, 1997).

10 Liberty Roll of Hamilton County, May 13, 1842, Chase Papers, HSP; *Philanthropist* (Cincinnati), May 25, 1842; James Shedd to Chase, September 9, 1842, Chase Papers, LC; "The Result—Finally," *Carroll Free Press* (Carrollton, OH), October 28, 1842, 2.

11 Noah Worcester to Chase, September 5, 1842, *Spur*, 66; see Thomas Dormandy, *The White Death: A History of Tuberculosis* (London: Hambledon & London, 1999); Sheila Rothman, *Living in the Shadow of Death: Tuberculosis and the Social Experience of Illness in American History* (Baltimore: Johns Hopkins University Press, 1994), 13–15, 131–32; Nicole Smith, *The Problem of Excess Female Mortality: Tuberculosis in Western Massachusetts, 1850–1910* (MA thesis, University of Massachusetts, 2008). In his genealogical notes, Chase calculated the age at death of each of his wife's siblings. Chase Papers, LC.

12 Chase to Lafayette Bank, April 11, 1842, Chase Papers, LC (advice on mortgage); Statement of Condition of Lafayette Bank, January 6, 1845, in *Messages, Reports, and Other Communications, Made to the Forty-Third General Assembly of the State of Ohio* (Columbus: Samuel Medary, 1845), 6 (list of directors; Chase not listed); "Mahard's Assignee v. Lafayette Bank," *Cincinnati Enquirer*, September 24, 1846, 2; Mahard's Assignee v. Lafayette Bank, 1846, in John McLean, ed., *Reports of Cases Argued and Decided in the Circuit Court for the Seventh Circuit* (Columbus, OH: Derby, Bradley, 1847), 589 (Chase counsel for bank); Chase diary, November 22, 1848, *SPCP*, 1:197 (argued case for Lafayette Bank); Chase to unknown, July 10, 1853, Chase Papers, LC (autobiography).

13 Gamaliel Bailey to James Birney, March 31, 1843, Dumond, *Birney Letters*, 727; Chase to Lewis Tappan, May 15, 1843, *SPCP*, 2:102; William Jay to Chase, June 5, 1853, Chase Papers, HSP.

14 Chase to Lewis Tappan, September 12, 1843, *SPCP*, 2:103–5.

15 *Philanthropist* (Cincinnati), July 19, 1843; "Mr. Van Zant and his Persecutors," *Vermont Union Whig* (Rutland), August 17, 1843, 1; *Western Law Journal* 1 (October 1843): 2-14; ibid., November 1843: 56-69; transcript of circuit court hearing, *Jones v. Van Zandt*, November 29, 1843, NARG 267; Jones v. Van Zandt, 46 U.S. 215 (1847); see Lubet, *Fugitive Justice*, 27–30.

16 *Philanthropist* (Cincinnati), July 19, 1843.

17 Prigg v. Pennsylvania, 41 U.S. 539, 542 (1842); Chase to Charles Cleveland, February 3, 1845, Chase Papers, HSP; Paul Finkelman, "*Prigg v. Pennsylvania*

and Northern State Courts: Antislavery Use of a Proslavery Decision," *Civil War History* 25, no. 1 (March 1979): 5–35.

18 *Philanthropist* (Cincinnati), July 19, 1843; *Jones v. Van Zandt*, 46 U.S. at 224.

19 William Henry Seward to Chase, October 2, 1843, Chase Papers, HSP (willing to help; willing to collaborate with Stevens); Seward to Chase, October 22, 1843, ibid.; Chase to John McLean, December 7, 1844, Norcross Papers, Massachusetts Historical Society; McLean to Chase, January 10, 1845, Chase Papers, HSP.

20 William Birney to James Birney, March 28, 1844, Dumond, *Birney Letters*, 803–4; Chase and others to James Birney, March 30, 1844, ibid., 804–05; Chase to Lewis Tappan, April 3, 1844, Chase Papers, LC; "The Anti-Texas Meeting," *Cincinnati Weekly Herald & Philanthropist*, April 3, 1844, 1; "The Texas Meeting—Slavery Propagandists," ibid., April 10, 1844, 1. On American attitudes toward Mexico, see Amy Greenberg, *A Wicked War: Polk, Clay, Lincoln, and the 1846 U.S. Invasion of Mexico* (New York: Alfred A. Knopf, 2012), and Robert Johannsen, *To the Halls of the Montezumas: The Mexican War in the American Imagination* (New York: Oxford University Press, 1988).

21 James Birney to William Austin et al., February 23, 1844, Dumond, *Birney Letters*, 791; Chase to James Birney, April 2, 1844, ibid., 805–6; "Troy Convention," *Cincinnati Weekly Herald & Philanthropist*, May 22, 1844, 1 (Chase, in speech, argues that "slavery in the District of Columbia, in Florida, in the states created out of the territory of Louisiana, and in American vessels on the high seas was contrary to the plain letter and spirit of the Constitution"); "Liberty Man's Creed," ibid., September 11, 1844, 2.

22 "Still Later from Baltimore," *Cincinnati Weekly Herald & Philanthropist*, June 5, 1844, 2; Adam Jewett to Chase, June 7, 1844, Chase Papers, LC. On 1844 see Holt, *Whig Party*, 162–208, and Wilentz, *Rise of American Democracy*, 566–75.

23 Eliza Smith Chase to Chase, June 22, 1844, *Spur*, 68–69; Chase to Ebenezer Lane, June 27, 1844, Chase Papers, HSP; Chase to Flamen Ball, July 2, 1844, Chase Papers, LC (from Cumberland); Chase to William Mellen, July 2, 1844, Mellen Papers, Maine (from New York City); Chronology, *Spur*, 64 (death of daughter).

24 "To the Editor of the *Morning Herald*," *Cincinnati Weekly Herald & Philanthropist*, August 9, 1844, 3 (Chase letter declining nomination); "Meetings in Crosby etc." ibid., August 16, 1844, 2; "To the Liberty Men," ibid., August 23, 1844, 3; "Liberty Man's Creed," ibid., September 11, 1844, 2.

25 "Liberty Man's Creed," *Cincinnati Weekly Herald & Philanthropist*, September 11, 1844, 2.

26 Ibid.; see William Freehling, *The Road to Disunion*, vol. 2: *Secessionists Triumphant, 1854–1861* (New York: Oxford University Press, 2007), 367–72.

27 "Liberty Man's Creed," *Cincinnati Weekly Herald & Philanthropist*, September 11, 1844, 2; see Steven Deyle, *Carry Me Back: The Domestic Slave Trade in American Life* (New York: Oxford University Press, 2006), 173. ("Both the interregional trade and the local trade were essential for American slavery, and it's impossible to imagine the system surviving without the ability to transfer human property

from one owner to another or to transport it to another region, where it was more in demand. It was for this reason that the domestic slave trade, in all its components, was the lifeblood of the Southern slave system, and without it, the institution would have ceased to exist.")

28 "Liberty Man's Creed," *Cincinnati Weekly Herald & Philanthropist*, September 11, 1844, 2.

29 Seward to Chase, November 27, 1844, *SPCP*, 2:107–8; "Our Cause Ruined," *Cincinnati Weekly Herald & Philanthropist*, December 25, 1844, 1; Howe, *What Hath God Wrought*, 688–90 (Birney cost Clay enough votes to deny him New York); Johnson, *Liberty Party*, 44–47.

30 Chase to Charles Cleveland, February 3, 1845, Chase Papers, HSP.

31 "Important Case," *Cincinnati Weekly Herald & Philanthropist*, February 12, 1845, 2; Chase, *Address and Reply*, 4–5.

32 "Important Case," *Cincinnati Weekly Herald & Philanthropist*, February 12, 1845, 2; "The Duties of the Magistrate," ibid; Chase, *Address and Reply*, 5-8.

33 "Salmon P. Chase," *New-York Tribune*, August 1, 1855, 6. "The Case Decided," *Cincinnati Weekly Herald & Philanthropist*, February 19, 1845, 1, reported that after Chase's speech, there was "an involuntary and general burst of applause."

34 "Samuel Watson—The Citizens," *Cincinnati Weekly Herald & Philanthropist*, February 19, 1845, 1; "Salmon P. Chase," *New-York Tribune*, August 1, 1855, 6.

35 Chase, *Address and Reply*, 7–10.

36 Ibid., 11–18. On Andrew Gordon, see William and Aimee Cheek, *John Mercer Langston and the Fight for Black Freedom, 1829–1865* (Urbana: University of Illinois Press, 1989), 57 and 83, and Henry Louis Taylor Jr., *Race and the City: Work, Community, and Protest in Cincinnati: 1820–1970* (Champaign: University of Illinois Press, 1993), 39.

37 Chase, *Address and Reply*, 20-21.

38 Ibid., 22–26. On nativism, see Tyler Anbinder, *Nativism and Slavery: Northern Know Nothings and the Politics of the 1850s* (New York: Oxford University Press, 1992), and Ray Billington, *The Protestant Crusade, 1800–1860: A Study of the Origins of American Nativism* (New York: Macmillan, 1938).

39 Chase, *Address and Reply*, 27–32.

40 Ibid., 33–35.

41 Ibid.; Chase to Gerrit Smith, July 31, 1845, *SPCP*, 2:112; "Chase and His Antecedents," *Eaton (OH) Democrat*, September 20, 1855, 2; "Chase on Negro Suffrage," *Ashland (OH) Union*, September 26, 1855, 2; "The Political Sentiments of the Black Republicans," *M'Arthur (OH) Democrat*, October 4, 1855; Lincoln to Henry Raymond, December 18, 1860, *CWL*, 4:156. David Reynolds, in *Abe*, 407–12, emphasizes that Lincoln lived near and knew many blacks in Springfield.

42 "Southern and Western Liberty Convention," *Cincinnati Weekly Herald & Philanthropist*, April 23, 1845, 2; William Seward to Chase, May 28, 1845, Chase Papers, LC; "Southern and Western Liberty Convention," *Cincinnati Weekly Herald & Philanthropist*, June 18, 1845, 2.

43   Chase, *The Address of the Southern and Western Liberty Convention, Held at Cincinnati June 11 & 12, 1845, to the People of the United States* (Cincinnati: Printed at the Gazette Office, 1845).

44   Quintus Atkins to Chase, June 28, 1845, Chase Papers, LC; Chase to Atkins, July 2, 1845, *SPCP*, 2:109–11; William Henry Seward to Chase, August 4, 1845, *SPCP*, 2:113–15; William Jay to Chase, August 22, 1845, Chase Papers, HSP; see Barnett, "Whence Comes," 213–15.

45   Chase to Charles Cleveland, February 3, 1845, Chase Papers, HSP; Chase to Flamen Ball, July 24, 1845, Chase Papers, LC (from Columbus); Ball to Chase, July 28, 1845, Chase Papers, HSP (mentions Eliza, Helen, and Alice); Chase to Gerrit Smith, July 31, 1845, *SPCP*, 2:111–12; William Henry Seward to Chase, August 4, 1845, *SPCP*, 2:113; Ball to Chase, August 11, 1845, Chase Papers, HSP (Chase still not back in Cincinnati).

46   Chase to Charles Cleveland, October 1, 1845, *SPCP*, 2:121–22; Chase to Cleveland, October 20, 1845, Chase Papers, HSP; Chase to Edward Chase, November 3, 1845, in Julia Corbitt, *Echoes from Niagara: Historical, Political, Personal* (Buffalo: C. W. Moulton, 1890), 97.

47   "Liberty State Convention," *Cincinnati Weekly Herald & Philanthropist*, January 7, 1846, 2. On Hale, see Richard Sewell, *John P. Hale and the Politics of Abolition* (Cambridge, MA: Harvard University Press, 1965).

48   Chase to John Hale, January 30, 1846, *SPCP*, 2:122–23; Hale to Chase, April 3, 1846, Chase Papers, HSP.

49   James K. Polk, War Message to Congress, May 11, 1846, Miller Center UVA website (https://millercenter.org/the-presidency/presidential-speeches/may-11-1846-war-message-congress); "Our Country, Right or Wrong," *New-York Tribune*, May 12, 1846, 2; Richard L'Hommedieu to Chase, May 20, 1846, Chase Papers, LC ("full of the Mexican war fever here"); Greenberg, *Wicked War*, 101–10.

50   Cassius Clay to Chase, June 30, 1846, Chase Papers, HSP; Chase to Gerrit Smith, September 1, 1846, *SPCP*, 2:128–30; Smith to Clay, September 8, 1846, Chase Papers, HSP; Greenberg, *Wicked War*, 116 (abolitionists "loudly condemned the war with Mexico as unjust and part of a plot to strengthen slavery").

51   "New Hampshire U.S. Senator," *New-York Tribune*, June 11, 1846, 2 (election of Hale); "Meeting in Colerain Township—Disturbance," *Cincinnati Weekly Herald & Philanthropist*, June 17, 1846, 1 (rotten eggs); *Emancipator* (Boston), July 8, 1846 (same incident); Sewell, *Ballots for Freedom*, 125–30 (election of Hale).

52   *Congressional Globe*, August 8, 1846, 1217; "The Triumph," *Cincinnati Weekly Herald & Philanthropist*, August 19, 1846, 2; Chase to Gerrit Smith, September 1, 1846, *SPCP*, 2:130; see Jonathan Earle, *Jacksonian Antislavery and the Politics of Free Soil, 1824–1854* (Chapel Hill: University of North Carolina Press, 2004), 1–3, 66–68; David Potter, *The Impending Crisis: 1848–1861* (New York: Harper & Row, 1976), 20–25; Rachel Shelden, *Washington Brotherhood: Politics, Social Life, and the Coming of the Civil War* (Chapel Hill: University of North Carolina Press, 2013), 14–26.

53   Chase to Joshua Giddings, August 15, 1846, *SPCP*, 2:126; Giddings to Chase, August 31, 1846, *SPCP*, 2:127–28; Chase to Giddings, September 4, 1846,

Chase Papers, LC; Chase to Giddings, September 23, 1846, *SPCP,* 2:131; Chase
to Giddings, October 20, 1846, *SPCP,* 2:133.

54 Chase to Joshua Giddings, September 4, 1846, Chase Papers, LC; "The Convention at Mt. Pleasant," *Cincinnati Weekly Herald & Philanthropist,* September
9, 1846, 3; *Cleveland American,* October 7, 14, 1846; Chase to Joshua Giddings,
October 20, 1846, *SPCP,* 2:132; Vernon Volpe, *Forlorn Hope of Freedom: The Liberty
Party in the Old Northwest, 1838–1848* (Kent, OH: Kent State University Press,
1990), 117.

55 "From Washington," *Cincinnati Weekly Herald & Philanthropist,* August 5, 1846, 2;
"Capt. Mum vs. Capt. Do-Nothing," *Portage Sentinel* (Ravenna, OH), September
30, 1846, 2; "Repeal of the Black Laws," *Spirit of Democracy* (Woodsfield, OH),
October 3, 1846, 1; Stephen Maizlish, *Triumph of Sectionalism: The Transformation
of Ohio Politics, 1844–1856* (Kent, OH: Kent State University Press, 1983), 48.

56 "Governor's Election, 1846," *Spirit of Democracy* (Woodsfield, OH), October 31,
1846, 3 (election results by county).

57 Chase diary, March 2, 1846, *SPCP,* 1:179; Kate Chase to Chase, November 18,
1846, *Spur,* 70–71; Edwin Stanton to Chase, November 30, 1846, *SPCP* 2:135
(congratulates on marriage).

58 John McLean to Chase, December 19, 1846, *SPCP,* 2:137–38; William Seward
to Chase, December 26, 1846, January 2, 20, 22, 1847, Chase Papers, LC;
Washington Hunt to Chase, January 16, 26, 1847, Chase Papers, HSP; Seward
to Chase, February 18, 1847, *SPCP,* 2:141–42; Chase, *Reclamation of Fugitives from
Service: An Argument for the Defendant, Submitted to the Supreme Court of the United
States, at the December Term, 1846, In the Case of Wharton Jones vs. John Vanzandt*
(Cincinnati: R. P. Donogh, 1847).

59 Chase, *Reclamation of Fugitives,* 28–37, 46–52.

60 Ibid., 83–84, 88–92. For the connection between the Chase Van Zandt brief
and the Fourteenth Amendment, see Barnett, "Whence Comes Section One?,"
210–17.

61 Chase, *Reclamation of Fugitives,* 107–8.

62 *Jones v. Van Zandt,* 46 U.S. at 230.

63 Chase to Lewis Tappan, March 18, 1847, Chase Papers, LC.

64 Chase to John Hale, May 12, 1847, *SPCP,* 2:151.

65 Chase to Charles Sumner, April 24, 1847, *SPCP,* 2:149; Chase to Sydney Howard
Gay, April 28, June 20, 1847, Gay Papers, Columbia. Chase's second letter to Gay
seems intended for publication, but I do not see it in the *National Anti-Slavery
Standard.*

66 Chase diary, March 23–April 23, 1847, *SPCP,* 1:186–93; Schuckers, *Chase,* 3
(Nettie born September 19, 1847).

67 Chase to John Hale, May 12, 1847, *SPCP,* 2:152–53; Lewis Tappan to Chase,
June 23, 1847, Chase Papers, HSP (responding to a Chase letter not in the files);
Chase to Preston King, July 15, 1847, Bourne, 120.

68 Chase to John Hale, May 12, 1847, *SPCP,* 2:153 ("merest delusion"); "No
More Territory," *Huron Reflector* (Norwalk, OH), September 7, 1847, 2; "No

More Territory," *Washington Union*, September 13, 1847, 2; Chase to John Hale, September 23, 1847, Hale Papers, NHHS ("humbug"); "No More Territory," *Vermont Journal* (Windsor), September 24, 1847, 2; John Eisenhower, *So Far from God: The U.S. War with Mexico 1846–1848* (New York: Random House, 1989), 302–42.

69 *Cleveland True Democrat*, August 31, 1847 (Corwin for president); "For President in 1848," *Elyria (OH) Courier*, September 21, 1847, 2 (same); Chase to Charles Sumner, September 22, 1847, Bourne, 123; "Mr. Corwin—The Presidency," *National Era* (Washington, DC), September 30, 1847, 2 (speech quotes).

70 *Congressional Globe*, December 22, 1847, 64–65 (Lincoln); see Louis Fisher, "The Mexican War and Lincoln's 'Spot Resolutions,'" August 18, 2009, online on Library of Congress website, https://www.loc.gov/law/help/usconlaw/pdf/Mexican.war.pdf; Greenberg, *A Wicked War*.

71 Chase to Lewis Tappan, September 10, 1847, Barney Papers, Huntington ("I am still clearly of the opinion that we ought not to nominate this fall"); "Presidential Matters—National Liberty Convention," *National Era* (Washington, DC), September 16, 1847, 3 (letter signed Hampden); ibid., September 23, 1847 (resolutions of Hamilton county convention favor delay); Chase to John Hale, September 23, 1847, Hale Papers, NHHS (Hampden letter "expresses my views"); Joshua Leavitt to Chase, September 27, 1847, Chase Papers, HSP ("convinced that it is necessary for the Liberty Party to make nominations this fall").

72 Chase to John Thomas, June 24, 1847, Bourne, 119 ("comparatively young"); Gamaliel Bailey to Chase, September 14, 1847, *SPCP*, 2:156–58; Chase to John Hale, September 23, 1847, Hale Papers, NHHS (hopes that he will not be nominated); Joshua Leavitt to Chase, September 27, 1847, Chase Papers, HSP (hopes Chase will accept if he is nominated).

73 "National Liberty Convention," *Buffalo Courier*, October 23, 1847, 3 ("cheerfully"); *Emancipator* (Boston), October 27, 1847; "General Liberty Convention at Buffalo," *National Era* (Washington, DC), October 28, 1847, 3; Gerrit Smith to Chase, November 1, 1847, Chase Papers, OHC (printed public letter; addressed to Chase as principal opponent of Smith's resolution).

74 Chase to Charles Sumner, December 2, 1847, *SPCP*, 2:160–62; Earle, *Jacksonian Antislavery*, 68–73.

75 Chase to Belle Chase, November 9, 18, 19, 1847, Chase Papers, LC (in Columbus for Parish case); *Driskell v. Parish, Western Law Journal* 5 (1848): 206–8.

76 *Driskell v. Parish, Western Law Journal* 5 (1848): 206–8.

77 In re: Jane, a Woman of Color, *Western Law Journal* 5 (1848): 202–6; David Herbert Donald, *Lincoln* (New York: Simon & Schuster, 1995), 104 ("business was law"); Foner, *Fiery Trial*, 50; Charles McKirdy, *Lincoln Apostate: The Matson Slave Case* (Jackson: University Press of Mississippi, 2011); Reynolds, *Abe*, 265–67.

78 Edwin Stanton to Chase, December 2, 1847, Chase Papers, HSP; "Cincinnati Correspondence," *National Era* (Washington, DC), December 23, 1847, 3.

79 Edward Hamlin to Chase, December 3, 1847, Chase Papers, HSP; Chase to Belle Chase, January 7, 1848, Chase Papers, LC (in Columbus); Chase to Edwin Stanton, January 9, 1848, *SPCP*, 2:163–64; "Democratic State Convention," *Spirit of Democracy* (Woodsfield, OH), January 15, 1848, 2; Chase to Charles Sumner, January 16, 1848, Bourne, 127; Chase to Joshua Giddings, February 29, 1848, Chase Papers, HSP; *Cleveland True Democrat*, March 1, 1848; Chase to Joshua Giddings, March 10, 1848, *SPCP*, 2:167–68; Jacob Brinkerhoff to Chase, March 28, 1848, *SPCP*, 168; Chase to Benjamin Tappan, March 30, 1848, Tappan Papers, LC.

80 Jacob Brinkerhoff to Chase, March 28, 1848, *SPCP*, 2:168; "People's Convention," *Zanesville (OH) Courier*, May 19, 1848, 2; "Important Political Movement," *Buffalo Commercial*, May 20, 1848, 2 (2,500 signatories); Lewis Tappan to Chase, June 14, 1848, *SPCP*, 2:169.

81 "Loco-Foco National Convention," *New-York Tribune*, May 25, 1848, 1; Holt, *Whig Party*, 319–20; Earle, *Jacksonian Antislavery*, 74–77.

82 "All Whigs Not Blind," *Wyandot Pioneer* (Upper Sandusky, OH), June 30, 1848, 2 (from *Ashtabula (OH) Sentinel*); Holt, *Whig Party*, 320–34.

83 *Addresses and Proceedings of the State Independent Free Territory Convention of the People of Ohio, Held at Columbus, June 20 and 21, 1848* (Cincinnati: printed at the Herald Office, 1848); *Cleveland True Democrat*, June 26, 27, 1848; "Free Territory Club," *Ohio State Journal* (Columbus), July 25, 1848, 2.

84 Chase diary, December 29, 1833, *SPCP*, 1:33 ("cold, selfish"); Chase to John Hale, June 25, 1848, *SPCP*, 2:173–75.

85 Chase to John Hale, June 25, 1848, *SPCP*, 2:173–75; Henry Stanton to Chase, July 28, 1848, John McLean Papers, LC; Samuel Tilden to Chase, July 29, 1848, *SPCP*, 2:179–81 (New York delegates will insist on Van Buren).

86 Frederick Douglass, *Autobiographies*, 800; Holt, *Whig Party*, 338–39; John Mayfield, *Rehearsal for Republicanism: Free Soil and the Politics of Anti-Slavery* (Port Washington, NY: Kennikat Press, 1980), 111–19; Cynthia Nicoletti, *Secession on Trial: The Treason Prosecution of Jefferson Davis* (New York: Cambridge University Press, 2017), 225–30 (Dana); Joseph Rayback, *Free Soil: The Election of 1848* (Lexington: University Press of Kentucky, 1970), 223–30; Wilentz, *Rise of American Democracy*, 623–27.

87 "Free Soil Convention," *Buffalo Daily Commercial*, August 10, 1848, 1-2; see Earle, *Jacksonian Antislavery*, 161–62, on the Democratic antecedents of the platform.

88 "Free Soil Convention," *Buffalo Daily Commercial*, August 10, 1848, 1-2; Chase to Thomas Bolton, December 1, 1848, *SPCP*, 2:199.

89 "Free Soil Convention," *Buffalo Daily Commercial*, August 11, 1848, 2; Chase to James Taylor, August 15, 1848, *SPCP*, 2:183–85; George Julian, *Political Recollections, 1840–1872* (Chicago: Jansen, McClurg, 1884), 60–61.

90 "Proceedings of the National Free Soil Convention," *Buffalo Daily Republic*, August 12, 1848, 2.

91 *National Era* (Washington, DC), August 24, 1848.

CHAPTER 6: "Ambitious as Julius Caesar," 1848–49

1 Chase to Benjamin Butler, August 12, 1848, *SPCP,* 2:181 (from Lockport); Chase
   to James Taylor, August 15, 1848, *SPCP,* 2:183 (from Lockport); *Cleveland True
   Democrat,* August 16, 18, 1848 (speaking schedule). The population figures are
   from the 1850 census, adjusted downward because the population was growing
   so rapidly.

2 Chase to Belle Chase, August 19, 1848, Chase Papers, LC; Chase to Martin Van
   Buren, August 21, 1848, *SPCP,* 2:186; Van Buren to Chase et al., August 22,
   1848, in "Mr. Van Buren's Letter of Acceptance," *National Era* (Washington,
   DC), August 31, 1848, 2; "Mr. Van Buren's Letter," *Liberator* (Boston), September
   8, 1848, 3 (criticizes Van Buren's evasions).

3 Chase to Belle Chase, August 24, 1848, *SPCP,* 2:188; ibid., August 25, 1848,
   Chase Papers, LC; *Cleveland True Democrat,* August 26, 1848 ("listening").

4 Chase to Belle Chase, August 27, 1848, Chase Papers, LC; *Cleveland True Democrat,* August 28, 1848 ("former").

5 "The Amalgamated Party," *Buffalo Commercial,* September 2, 1848, 2 ("aspirant")
   (from *Cleveland Herald*); *New York Evening Post,* September 11, 1848 (letter from
   Cincinnati says Chase will be home soon); Chase to James Briggs, September
   12, 1848, Chase Papers, LC (regrets not seeing him in Columbus on way back
   from Lockport); *Cleveland Herald,* September 16, 1848 ("every member").

6 *Cleveland Herald,* September 11, 1848 (Townshend nominated as third-party
   candidate for legislature); "For President," *Elyria (OH) Courier,* September 12,
   1848, 2 (endorses Van Buren for president; Ford, the Whig, for governor).

7 *Ohio Standard* (Columbus), September 1848 (clipping in Chase Papers, LC scrapbook); "Ford and the Free Soilers," *Portage Sentinel* (Ravenna, OH), September
   27, 1848, 2 (Chase nominated); Chase to James Briggs, September 27, 1848,
   Chase Papers, LC (declines nomination); Chase to John Van Buren, September
   30, 1848, *SPCP,* 2:191.

8 "The Election," *Ohio State Journal* (Columbus), October 13, 1848, 2; "Ohio
   Election—The Result," ibid., October 14, 1848, 2; *Cleveland True Democrat,*
   October 17, 1848; "Ohio Election," *Ohio State Journal* (Columbus), October 27,
   1848, 2; Holt, *Whig Party,* 121–46.

9 Chase to Belle Chase, December 30, 1848, *SPCP,* 2:211.

10 Edward Hamlin to Chase, October 22, 1848, *SPCP,* 2:191; "The Successor of
    Senator Allen," *National Era* (Washington, DC), October 26, 1848, 2.

11 "Listen to Horace Greeley," *Huron Reflector* (Norwalk, OH), October 31, 1848, 2
    (Greeley letter); Daniel Crofts, *Lincoln & the Politics of Slavery: The Other Thirteenth
    Amendment and the Struggle to Save the Union* (Chapel Hill: University of North
    Carolina Press, 2016), 42; Donald, *Lincoln,* 129–33; Holt, *Whig Party,* 339–45;
    Stahr, *Seward,* 110–12.

12 "Election—The Returns," *Ohio State Journal* (Columbus), November 9, 1848,
    2; *Cleveland True Democrat,* November 10, 1848; Chase to Charles Sumner,

November 27, 1848, *SPCP,* 2:195 ("here in Ohio"); "The Western Reserve," *Huron Reflector* (Norwalk, OH), December 5, 1848, 2; see Joel Silbey, *Party over Section: The Rough and Ready Presidential Election of 1848* (Lawrence: University Press of Kansas, 2009).

13 Chase to Thomas Bolton, December 1, 1848, *SPCP,* 2:199.

14 "The First Monday in December 1848," *Ohio State Journal* (Columbus), December 4, 1848, 2; "Afternoon Session," ibid., December 5, 1848, 2; *Ohio Daily Standard* (Columbus), December 8, 9, 1848; "The Red Republic and Its Armed Legislators," *Ohio State Journal* (Columbus), December 19, 1848, 2 ("men go"); see Joanne Freeman, *The Field of Blood: Violence in Congress and the Road to Civil War* (New York: Farrar, Straus & Giroux, 2018).

15 Chase to Belle Chase, December 20, 1848, *SPCP,* 2:204.

16 Townshend, "Salmon Portland Chase," 117 ("there is a man"). Townshend needs a biography; in the meantime, see "Honest Independence": The Life of Norton Strange Townshend, on the website of the William Clements Library at the University of Michigan: https://clements.umich.edu/exhibit/townshend/.

17 Chase to Belle Chase, December 20, 1848, *SPCP,* 2:204; Chase to John Vaughan, December 21, 1848, *SPCP,* 2:207; "House of Representatives," *Ohio State Journal* (Columbus), December 21, 1848, 2; *Ohio Daily Standard* (Columbus), December 22, 1848.

18 Chase to Stanley Matthews, December 23, 1848, *SPCP,* 2:211; "The End," *Ohio State Journal* (Columbus), December 23, 1848, 2; Chase to Belle Chase, December 24, 1848, Chase Papers, LC (quotes); *Ohio Daily Standard* (Columbus), December 25, 1848; Chase to Belle Chase, December 25, 1848, Chase Papers, LC.

19 Chase to Belle Chase, December 30, 1848, *SPCP,* 2:211; "Free Soil Convention," *Ohio State Journal* (Columbus), January 2, 1849, 2 (resolutions); *Cleveland True Democrat,* January 3, 4, 1849 (convention reports).

20 Chase diary, January 1, 1849, *SPCP,* 1:201; *Kemper v. Trustees of Lane Seminary,* 17 Ohio 293 (1849); Fairman, *Reconstruction and Reunion,* 28 (count of cases; comments on *Kemper*).

21 Chase diary, January 5, 1849, *SPCP,* 1:201.

22 Ibid., January 5, 7, 10, 1849, *SPCP,* 1:201–3; *Ohio Daily Standard* (Columbus), February 10, 1849 (final text of bill).

23 Chase to Edward Hamlin, January 16, 1849, Bourne, 145; Chase to Edward Hamlin, January 17, 1849, ibid., 148; Chase to Stanley Matthews, January 18, 1849, Chase Papers, Wisconsin Historical Society; Chase to John Morse, January 19, 1849, *SPCP,* 2:216.

24 Albert Riddle to Joshua Giddings, January 15, 1849, Giddings Papers, OHC ("noble man"); Chase to Edward Hamlin, January 20, 1849, Bourne, 153; Riddle to Chase, January 21, 1849, Chase Papers, HSP; Chase to Riddle, January 23, 1849, Riddle Papers, Western Reserve Historical Society; *Cleveland True Democrat,* January 24, 1849 ("young man").

25 Chase to Norton Townshend, January 23, 1849, Townshend Papers, Clements; Chase to Edward Hamlin, January 27, 1849, Bourne, 160.

26 Chase to Stanley Matthews, January 27, 1849, *SPCP*, 2:220–21.

27 Chase to Frederick Douglass, May 4, 1850, Chase Papers, HSP (draft); Douglass to Chase, May 30, 1850, *SPCP*, 2:296–97; John Mercer Langston and Charles Langston to Chase, September 12, 1850, Chase Papers, LC; Chase to Langston and Langston, November 11, 1850, ibid; see David Blight, *Frederick Douglass: Prophet of Freedom* (New York: Simon & Schuster, 2018), 214–15, 457–58; William and Aimee Cheek, *John Mercer Langston*, 170–74; Sinha, *Slave's Cause*, 324–25; Stahr, *Seward*, 99–105; Nikki Taylor, *Frontiers of Freedom*, 114–15.

28 Edward Hamlin to Chase, January 27, 1849, Chase Papers, HSP; "House of Representatives," *Ohio State Journal* (Columbus), January 30, 1849, 2; Hamlin to Chase, January 30, 1849, Chase Papers, HSP ("will pass the Senate"); *Ohio Daily Standard* (Columbus), January 31, 1849.

29 Chase to Belle Chase, February 3, 1849, Chase Papers, LC; *Ohio Daily Standard* (Columbus), February 5, 7, 1849; "The Legislature," *Ohio State Journal* (Columbus), February 5, 1849, 2; "Correction," ibid., February 6, 1849, 2; Chase to Belle Chase, February 7, 1849, Chase Papers, LC ("quite Whiggish"); "Triumph of Right," *Huron Reflector* (Norwalk, OH), February 13, 1849, 2; "The Black Laws," *Ohio State Journal* (Columbus), February 21, 1849, 2.

30 Chase to Belle Chase, February 7, 1849, Chase Papers, LC; "Affairs at Columbus," *Zanesville (OH) Courier*, February 10, 1849, 2; Chase to Belle Chase, February 11, 1849, Chase Papers, LC. On the origin of the term Loco Foco, see Wilentz, *Rise of American Democracy*, 421.

31 Chase to Belle Chase, February 13, 1849, Chase Papers, LC; "Election of Senator, etc.," *Ohio State Journal* (Columbus), February 15, 1849, 2.

32 Chase to Belle Chase, February 15, 1849, Chase Papers, LC; Chase to Belle Chase, February 19, 1849, Chase Papers, LC ("more delay"); Chase to Belle Chase, February 20, 1849, Chase Papers, LC ("generally supposed"); "Coalition—Bargain Consummated," *Ohio State Journal* (Columbus), February 21, 1849, 2.

33 "Legislative Elections" and "The Bargain Consummated," *Ohio State Journal* (Columbus), February 22, 1849, 2; "Loco Foco Supper," ibid., February 23, 1849, 2; *Cleveland True Democrat*, February 23, 1849; *Ohio Daily Standard* (Columbus), February 23, 1849.

34 "Ohio," *Pittsburgh Gazette*, February 28, 1849, 2; "Ohio—The Consummation," *New-York Tribune*, February 26, 1849, 2.

35 "Senatorial and Other Elections," *Cincinnati Enquirer*, February 23, 1849, 2; "The New Senator," ibid., February 28, 1849, 2 (from *Cleveland Plain Dealer*).

36 "The New Senator from Ohio," *National Era* (Washington, DC), March 1, 1849, 2; "S.P. Chase, Ohio Senator," *Natchez (MS) Daily Courier*, March 13, 1849, 2.

37 Joshua Giddings to Sumner, February 1849, in George Julian, *The Life of Joshua R. Giddings* (Chicago: A. C. McClurg, 1892), 268; Doris Kearns Goodwin, *Team of Rivals: The Political Genius of Abraham Lincoln* (New York: Simon & Schuster, 2005), 136; John Niven, *Salmon P. Chase: A Biography* (New York: Oxford University Press, 1995), 74, 190.

CHAPTER 7: "Freedom Is National," 1849–50

1 Chase diary, March 6, 1849, *SPCP,* 1:208; Lincoln to John Clayton, March 10, 1849, *CWL,* 2:36–37; Sidney Blumenthal, *A Self-Made Man: The Political Life of Abraham Lincoln, 1809–1849* (New York: Simon & Schuster, 2016), 435–41; Donald, *Lincoln,* 137–41. For Lincoln's day-by-day activities, see the Lincoln Log: A Daily Chronology of the Life of Abraham Lincoln, accessed April 12, 2021: http://www.thelincolnlog.org/Home.aspx.

2 Chase to Joshua Giddings, February 27, 1849, March 6, 1849, Giddings Papers, OHC; see Reynolds, *Abe,* 297–99 (boardinghouse).

3 *Congressional Globe,* April 25, 1848, 670; see Reynolds, *Abe,* 302 (Lincoln "mentioned slavery only in passing in his congressional speeches").

4 Lincoln to Williamson Durley, October 3, 1845, *CWL,* 1:347–48; Lincoln Speech, September 12, 1848, *CWL,* 2:1–3; Lincoln Speech, November 1, 1848, *CWL,* 2:14.

5 Lincoln, Remarks and Resolution Introduced in the United States House of Representatives Concerning the Abolition of Slavery in the District of Columbia, January 10, 1849, *CWL,* 2:20–22.

6 Chase diary, March 6, 1849, *SPCP,* 1:208–9; Chase to Belle Chase, March 6, 1849, *SPCP,* 2:232–33.

7 Chase to Belle Chase, March 8, 1849, Chase Papers, LC; Elizabeth Goldsborough to Chase, March 26, 1849, ibid.; Louis Goldsborough, *A Reply to an Attack upon the Navy of the United States by Samuel E. Coues, President of the Peace Society* (Portsmouth, NH: C.W. Brewer, 1845).

8 *Senate Executive Journal,* March 7, 1849, 69; *Congressional Directory for the First Session of the Thirty-First Congress* (Washington, DC: Gideon, 1850), 34–35 (no committee assignments for Chase); *Congressional Directory for the First Session of the Thirty-Second Congress* (Washington, DC: Gideon, 1852), 35 (committee on Revolutionary claims); *Congressional Directory for the Second Session of the Thirty-Second Congress* (Washington, DC: G. S. Gideon 1853), 33–34 (no committee assignments for Chase); *Congressional Directory for the First Session of the Thirty-Third Congress* (Washington, DC: G. S. Gideon, 1854), 26 (Committees on Claims and on Patents); *Congressional Directory for the Second Session of the Thirty-Third Congress* (Washington, DC: G. S. Gideon, 1855), 25–26 (same).

9 *Senate Executive Journal,* March 13, 1849, 74–76; ibid., March 15, 1849, 81–83; ibid., March 19, 1849, 89–90; Chase to Belle Chase, March 17, 1849, Chase Papers, LC; "Called Session of the United States Senate," *New York Herald,* March 22, 1849, 4.

10 Chase diary, April 22, May 12–15, 1849, *SPCP,* 1:210–14; Chase to Charles Sumner, May 14, 1849, Chase Papers, OHC; see Donald Hutslar, "God's Scourge: The Cholera Years in Ohio," *Ohio History Journal* 105 (1996): 174–91; Matthew Smith, "Pandemic Redux: Revisiting Cincinnati's 1849 Cholera in the Age of Covid-19," *Origins: Current Events in Historical Perspective,* June 2020, online on

Ohio State University website, accessed April 12, 2021 (https://origins.osu.edu /connecting-history/cincinnati-cholera-covid-19-revisited.)

11 "People's Telegraph Line to New Orleans," *Louisville (KY) Courier*, September 19, 1848, 2; "The Foreign News," *New Orleans Crescent*, April 10, 1849, 2; Henry O'Reilly to Chase, May 15, 1849, Chase Papers, LC (first of many letters); Richard John, *Network Nation: Inventing American Telecommunication* (Cambridge, MA: The Belknap Press, 2010), 82–86; Kenneth Silverman, *Lightning Man: The Accursed Life of Samuel F. B. Morse* (New York: Alfred A. Knopf, 2003), 264–65, 280–83, 292–93. O'Reilly often spelled his name O'Rielly, but I have opted for the more standard spelling.

12 Chase to Belle Chase, May 30, 1849, Chase Papers, LC.

13 Ibid.; ibid., June 12, 1849, Chase Papers, LC; "The Decision in the Telegraph Case," *New York Evening Post*, June 18, 1849, 1; "Senator Chase of Ohio," *Louisville (KY) Courier*, June 19, 1849, 2; "Louisville and New Orleans Telegraph," *New Orleans Picayune*, June 29, 1849, 2.

14 Chase to Henry O'Reilly, June 18 and June 20, 1849, O'Reilly Papers, NYHS ("may come down tomorrow"); O'Reilly to Chase, June 19 and June 22, 1849, Chase Papers, LC ("come by first boat"); Chase to Belle Chase, June 27, 1849, Chase Papers, LC (from Louisville); Chase diary, June 30–July 1, 1849, *SPCP*, 1:214–15.

15 Chase to George Bradburn, July 4, 1849, in Frances Bradburn, *A Memorial of George Bradburn* (Boston: Cupples, Upham, 1883), 174; Chase to Kate Ludlow, July 6, 1849, Clarkson Family Papers, State Historical Society of Missouri.

16 Chase to George Bradburn, July 4, 1849, in Bradburn, *Memorial of George Bradburn*, 173–74; Chase to Belle Chase, July 13, 1849, Chase Papers, LC; *Cleveland True Democrat*, July 14, 15, 1849; Chase to Belle Chase, July 19, 1849, *SPCP*, 2:245–46 (from Cleveland); "Extract from a Letter," *Buffalo Weekly Republic*, July 24, 1849, 3; Chase to John Breslin, July 30, 1849, in Schuckers, 101–3.

17 Chase to Belle Chase, August 19, 1849, *Spur*, 71–73 (from Albany, NY); ibid., August 26, 1849, Chase Papers, LC (from Concord); Chase to John Hale, August 26, 1849, Hale Papers, NHHS; Chase to Charles Sumner, September 2, 1849, Bourne, 182–83 (heading to Boston to take Henry deposition); ibid., September 4, 1849, Sumner Papers, Harvard (from Boston); Chase to Belle Chase, September 11, 1849, Chase Papers, LC (from Portland); Chase to Henry O'Reilly, September 15, 1849, O'Reilly Papers, NYHS (from New Haven, CT); ibid., September 18, 1849, O'Reilly Papers, NYHS (heading to Philadelphia and Washington); Chase to Belle Chase, September 25, 1849, Chase Papers, LC (from Washington); "Free Soil Meeting," *Pittsburgh Daily Post*, October 2, 1849, 2. The evidence Chase gathered in these weeks is in the printed Supreme Court record in *O'Reilly v. Morse*.

18 John Dix to Chase, November 30, 1849, *SPCP*, 2:264; Potter, *Impending Crisis*, 90–97; Stahr, *Seward*, 120–22.

19 *Congressional Globe*, December 13, 1849, 27–28; Chase to Charles Sumner, December 14, 1849, *SPCP*, 2:265; Chase to Edward Hamlin, December 15, 1849, *SPCP*, 2:266–68.

20 Chase to Edward Hamlin, December 21, 1849, Chase Papers, LC, and December 30, 1849, *SPCP,* 2:271.

21 Ibid., *SPCP,* 2:271; "The Parkeville Hydropathic Institute," *National Era* (Washington, DC), May 16, 1850, 4 (Dexter advertisement); Chase to Kate Chase, September 10, 1851, *Spur,* 98 ("glad to have a homeopathic physician"), and January 1862, *Spur,* 192 ("never forget how futile was allopathic practice"); Susan Cayleff, *Wash and Be Healed: The Water-Cure Movement and Women's Health* (Philadelphia: Temple University Press, 1987), 143–44, 148–51; Jane Donegan, *"Hydropathic Highway to Health": Women and Water-Cure in Antebellum America* (New York: Greenwood Press, 1987); Harry Weiss and Howard Kemble, *The Great American Water-Cure Craze: A History of Hydrotherapy in the United States* (Trenton, NJ: Past Times Press, 1967). Some have suggested that Kate started with Mrs. Haines in late 1849, but the first mention I find of her there is from January 1850. John Garniss to Chase, January 7, 1850, Chase Papers, LC.

22 Chase to Edward Hamlin, January 2, 1850, *SPCP,* 2:273; George Dexter to Chase, January 2, 1850, Chase Papers, LC (first of many); Chase to Belle Chase, January 7, 1850, *SPCP,* 2:276.

23 Chase to Cleveland, January 18, 1850, Chase Papers, HSP (snow); Cheney & Co. to Chase, January 28, 1850, Chase Papers, LC (telegram); Chase to Sumner, January 30, 1850, *SPCP,* 2:278.

24 *Congressional Globe,* January 10, 1850, 133.

25 Ibid., 134–36.

26 Ibid., January 24, 1850, app., 80–81.

27 Ibid., 83.

28 Ibid., January 29, 1850, 244–47; Chase to Hamlin, February 2, 1850, Chase Papers, LC; *Congressional Globe,* February 5–6, 1850, app., 115–26; Chase to Belle Chase, February 5, 6, 1850, Chase Papers, LC; Fergus Bordewich, *America's Great Debate: Henry Clay, Stephen A. Douglas, and the Compromise That Preserved the Union* (New York: Simon & Schuster, 2012), 5–7, 134–44; Potter, *Impending Crisis,* 97–100.

29 Chase to Lewis Tappan, February 3, 8, 12, 17, 27, March 15, 1850, Barney Papers, Huntington. The letter with the draft petitions is February 3; the letter quoted is March 15, 1850.

30 *Congressional Globe,* March 4, 1850, 451–53; Chase to unknown, March 5, 1850, George Milton Papers, LC; Bordewich, *America's Great Debate,* 156–58.

31 *Congressional Globe,* March 7, 1850, 476–83; Chase to Charles Sumner, March 7, 1850, *SPCP,* 2:284; Sumner to Chase, March 9, 1850, *SPCP,* 2:284–85.

32 *Congressional Globe,* March 11, 1850, app., 260–65; "From an Occasional Correspondent," *New York Evening Post,* March 14, 1850, 2; "Mr. Seward's Speech," *Brattleboro (VT) Eagle,* March 18, 1850, 2; Stahr, *Seward,* 123–27.

33 Chase to Charles Sumner, March 15, 1850, Bourne, 203–4; Chase to Belle Chase, March 20, 1850, Chase Papers, LC (to speak Tuesday); Sumner to Chase, March 22, 23, 1850, ibid.

34 *Congressional Globe,* March 26, 1850, 602–4. Freeman, *Field of Blood,* 148–56, has a great discussion of the Benton-Foote fight.

35 *Congressional Globe*, March 26, 1850, app., 468–74.

36 Ibid. ("freedom is national" on 474). See Charles Sumner, *Freedom National, Slavery Sectional* (Washington, DC: Buell & Blanchard, 1852) (speech of August 26, 1852); James Oakes, *Freedom National: The Destruction of Slavery in the United States, 1861–1865* (2012).

37 *Congressional Globe*, March 26, 1850, app., 474; see Lisa Jardine, *On a Grander Scale: The Outstanding Career of Sir Christopher Wren* (New York: HarperCollins, 2003), 483.

38 *Congressional Globe*, March 27, 1850, 609–11.

39 Ibid., app. 474–77.

40 Ibid., 477–80. For the pamphlet version, see Chase, *Union and Freedom, Without Compromise: Speech of Mr. Chase, of Ohio, on Mr. Clay's Compromise Resolutions* (Washington, DC: Buell & Blanchard, 1850).

41 Chase to Belle Chase, March 27, 1850, *SPCP,* 2:286; ibid., March 31, 1850, Chase Papers, LC; "Thirty-First Congress," *New York Herald*, March 28, 1850, 2; "XXXIst Congress," *New-York Tribune*, March 28, 1850, 3; "Orders of the Day," *Washington (DC) Union*, March 28, 1850, 3 (speech will be printed "at an early day"); *National Intelligencer* (Washington, DC), April 4, 1850; "Speech of Mr. Chase of Ohio," *National Era* (Washington, DC), April 11, 1850, 1.

42 Chase to Charles Sumner, April 13, 1850, *SPCP,* 2:287; Chase to Edward Hamlin, April 16, 1850, Bourne, 210.

43 "The Compromise Committee," *National Era* (Washington, DC), May 2, 1850, 2 ("omnibus bill"); Chase to Frederick Douglass, May 4, 1850, Chase Papers, HSP (draft); Douglass to Chase, May 30, 1850, *SPCP,* 2:296–97.

44 John Mercer Langston and Charles Langston to Chase, September 12, 1850, Chase Papers, LC; Chase to Langston and Langston, November 11, 1850, ibid; see William and Aimee Cheek, *John Mercer Langston.*

45 Chase to unknown, May 8, 1850, *SPCP,* 2:294–95; Chase to Tappan, May 10, 1850, *SPCP,* 2:295–96.

46 Chase diary, May 18–20, 1850, *SPCP,* 1:223–24; Chase to Belle Chase, May 20, 1850, Chase Papers, LC (from Baltimore on return); Chase to Sumner, May 25, 1850, Bourne, 211 (wife in Round Hill, Massachusetts).

47 Chase to Cleveland, May 31, 1850, Chase Papers, HSP; Chase to Belle Chase, June 1, 1850, Chase Papers, LC; Chase to Sumner, June 22, 1850, Bourne, 213.

48 Samuel Fitch, *Six Lectures on the Uses of the Lungs; and Causes, Prevention, and Cure of Pulmonary Consumption, Asthma, and Diseases of the Heart* (New York: H. Carlisle, 1847); Chase to Belle Chase, June 30, 1850, Chase Papers, LC; Chase to Ralston Skinner, July 8, 1850, ibid. (in NYC seeing Fitch); Chase to Belle Chase, July 10, 1850, ibid. (back in DC).

49 Chase to Belle Chase, July 12, 13, 1850, Chase Papers, LC.

50 Ibid., July 28, 1850, *Spur,* 80–81; see also ibid., July 29, 1850, ibid., 81–82.

51 *Congressional Globe*, August 1, 1850, 1503; *New York Express*, August 2, 1850; *Washington (DC) Union*, August 6, 1850 (Chase speaking August 2); Bordewich, *America's Great Debate*, 298–302; David Heidler and Jeanne Heidler, *Henry Clay: The Essential American* (New York: Random House, 2010), 474–77.

52 Chase to Belle Chase, February 28, 1850, *SPCP,* 2:76; *New York Evening Post,* August 9, 1850 (train to White House with onward carriage to Schooley's Mountain); Chase to Kate, August 13, 1850, *Spur,* 82–84.

53 Chase to Belle Chase, August 9, 1850, Chase Papers, LC; *Congressional Globe,* August 9, 1850, 1554; Chase to Townshend, August 10, 1850, Townshend Papers, Clements Library; Chase to Hamlin, August 14, 1850, *SPCP,* 2:302–4 (quote).

54 Chase to Sumner, August 13, 1850, Bourne, 214–15.

55 *Congressional Globe,* August 19, 1850, app. 1582; Bordewich, *America's Great Debate,* 320–21.

56 Ibid., app., 1584–87; ibid., 324–25.

57 *Congressional Globe,* August 23, 1850, app., 1619–21.

58 Ibid., app., 1621–23, 1647. Technically this was the vote on the third reading, not final passage, but there was no recorded vote on final passage. Ibid., app., 1659–60.

59 Chase to Charles Sumner, September 8, 1850, *SPCP,* 2:304–5; "Washington After the Settlement," *New-York Tribune,* September 10, 1850, 6 (quote); *New York Evening Post,* September 10, 1850 (similar).

60 *Congressional Globe,* September 18, 1850, 1858–59; see Hyman and Wiecek, *Equal Justice Under Law,* 146.

61 *Congressional Globe,* September 23, 1850, 1945; Chase to unknown, September 28, 1850, Chase Papers, OHC.

62 Only the second session of the fortieth Congress, from December 2, 1867, to November 10, 1868, was longer than the first session of the thirty-first Congress. The first uses I can find of the capitalized term "Compromise of 1850" are in 1851. *Buffalo Daily Republic,* May 24, 1851; *Natchez (MS) Daily Courier,* June 24, 1851.

CHAPTER 8: "The Question Is Not Settled," 1850–53

1 Chase to Joshua Giddings, October 22, 1850, *SPCP,* 2:307–09; Chase to John Morse, October 30, 1850, *SPCP,* 2:310–11.

2 Chase to Kate Chase, October 26, 1850, *SPCP,* 2:309; Chase to Belle Chase, November 8, 9, 21, 1850, Chase Papers, LC; Belle Chase to Chase, December 1850, Chase Papers, HSP; Belle Chase to Kate Chase, December 11, 1850, *Spur,* 88–89; Nettie Chase to Kate Chase, January 9, 1851, *Spur,* 89–90.

3 Chase to Belle Chase, December 7 and 25, 1850, Chase Papers, LC; Chase to Kate Chase, January 22, 1851, *Spur,* 91; Chase to Kate Chase, February 14, 1851, ibid., 92; Chase to Kate Chase, March 4, 1852, ibid., 115.

4 Chase to Kate Chase, January 15, 1851, *Spur,* 90–91; Kinsley Bingham to Anne Bingham, January 20, 26, February 10, 1851, Bingham Papers, Bentley Historical Library, Michigan; George Julian to Anne Julian, January 22, February 20, 1851, in Grace Clarke, ed., "Home Letters of George W. Julian, 1850–1851," *Indiana Magazine of History* 29 (1933): 157, 160; Chase to Belle Chase, February 26, 1851, Chase Papers, LC; Stanley Harrold, *Gamaliel Bailey and Antislavery*

Union (Kent, OH: Kent State University Press, 1986), 133–34; Shelden, *Washington Brotherhood*, 85; Bela Vassady, "The 'Tochman Affair': An Incident in Mid-Nineteenth Century Hungarian Emigration to America," *Polish Review* 25 (1980): 12–27 (on Jagiello).

5 *Buffalo Commercial*, February 21, 1851 (quoting Clay); Chase to Edward Hamlin, February 24, 1851, *SPCP*, 2:313; Lewis Campbell, *The Slave Catchers: Enforcement of the Fugitive Slave Law, 1850–1860* (Chapel Hill: University Press of North Carolina, 1970), 148–51.

6 *Washington (DC) Union*, February 26, 1851.

7 Chase to Charles Sumner, February 26, 1851, Sumner Papers, Harvard (hoping for his election); Chase to Joshua Giddings, March 24, 1851, Giddings Papers, OHC (disappointed by election of Wade); Chase to Edward Stansbury, April 1, 1851, *SPCP*, 2:315–16 (distrusts Wade as Whig); Chase to Charles Sumner, April 28, 1851, Bourne, 235–36.

8 Belle Chase to Kate Chase, December 1850, *Spur*, 89 (expects to leave in late April or early May); Chase to Belle Chase, April 15, 1851, Chase Papers, LC; Chase to Kate Chase, April 19, 1851, *Spur*, 94–95. It is hard to date Belle's return, but it seems she was in Ohio by June 1. See Chase to Belle Chase, June 1, 1851, Chase Papers, LC.

9 "Senator Chase's Speech," *National Era* (Washington, DC), June 19, 1851, 1. For the pamphlet version, see Chase, *Speech of Senator Chase, Delivered May 30, 1851, Before a Mass Convention of the Democracy of Northwestern Ohio* (Cincinnati: Ben Franklin Book & Job Office, 1851).

10 "Senator Chase's Speech," *National Era* (Washington, DC), June 19, 1851, 1.

11 Ibid.

12 Chase to Belle Chase, June 1, 1851, Chase Papers, LC.

13 Chase to Charles Sumner, June 28, 1851, Bourne, 237; "Freedom Convention at Ravenna," *Summit County Beacon* (Akron, OH), July 2, 1851, 2; Chase to W. T. Tillinghast, July 7, 1851, in *Southern Press*, August 21, 1851; *Green Mountain Freeman* (Montpelier, VT), July 10, 1851 (Ravenna); Chase to unknown, July 29, 1851, Buffalo Historical Society.

14 "Democratic State Convention," *Portage Sentinel* (Ravenna, OH), August 11, 1851, 2; "Proceedings of the Democratic State Convention," ibid., August 18, 1851, 1-2; "Ohio Democracy," *Oshkosh (WI) Democrat*, August 22, 1851, 2 (Fulton County); Chase to Charles Miller, August 25, 1851, *SPCP*, 2:325–26 (other counties).

15 Chase to Joshua Giddings, August 9, 1851, *SPCP*, 2:321–23; Chase to Charles Miller, August 25, 1851, *SPCP*, 2:323–32.

16 *Cleveland True Democrat*, September 8, 11, 1851; "The Disguise Off At Last," *Summit County Beacon* (Akron, OH), September 10, 1851, 3; "Ohio Politics," *National Era* (Washington, DC), September 11, 1851, 2; "Mr. Chase and the Free Soilers of Ohio," ibid., October 2, 1851, 2; "Senator Chase," *Gallipolis (OH) Journal*, October 9, 1851, 1. (Chase's letter "has elicited universal surprise among his Free Soil friends and meets with universal condemnation.")

17 "National Convention of the Friends of Freedom," *National Era* (Washington, DC), October 2, 1851, 3; *Cleveland True Democrat*, October 24, 1851.

18 Chase to Belle Chase, December 2, 1851, Chase Papers, LC; ibid., December 7, 1851, *Spur,* 101–2.

19 Ibid., December 10, 1851, Chase Papers, LC; Chase diary, January 2, 1853, *SPCP,* 1:233; Jane Swisshelm, *Half a Century* (Chicago: J. G. Swisshelm, 1880), 125–27; Wilentz, *Rise of American Democracy*, 655–57.

20 Chase to Belle Chase, December 11, 13, 1851, Chase Papers, LC; Joseph Potter to Chase, December 10, 19, 1851, ibid.; Chase to Belle Chase, December 14, 1851, *Spur,* 103–4; Caroline Clopper to Mary Ann Clopper, December [19?], 1851, in Edward Clopper, *An American Family: Its Ups and Downs Through Eight Generations* (Cincinnati: 1950), 422; Chase to Sumner, December 20, 1851, Sumner Papers, Harvard (from Cincinnati). It seems Chase had not received Potter's letter of December 10 when he wrote to Belle on December 14 and that he changed plans to come home earlier.

21 Chase to Edward Hamlin, January 1 and 9, 1852, Chase Papers, LC; Chase to unknown, January 3, 1852, Chase Papers, HSP (filed in 1851) ("feel like a criminal"); *Cincinnati Daily Gazette*, January 15, 1852 (death and funeral arrangements).

22 "The Death of Mrs. Chase," *Washington (DC) Union*, January 16, 1852, 3; *Albany (NY) Evening Journal*, January 19, 1852; *Cleveland True Democrat*, January 20, 1852; "Death of Mrs. Chase," *Buffalo Daily Republic*, January 22, 1852, 2.

23 Chase to Kate Chase, February 12, 1852, *Spur,* 111; Chase to Edward Hamlin, February 25, 1842, Chase Papers, LC, and March 10, 1852, Bourne, 240–41.

24 Chase to unknown, June 3, 1852, William Smith Mason Papers, Yale ("confusion"); "The Baltimore Platform," *Burlington (VT) Free Press*, June 9, 1852, 2; Charles Sumner to Charles Francis Adams, June 13, 1852, in *The Selected Letters of Charles Sumner,* ed. Beverly Palmer (Boston: Northeastern University Press, 1990), 1:362; Chase to E. L. Keyes, July 2, 1852, in "Letter of Mr. Chase to the Worcester Convention," *National Era* (Washington, DC), July 15, 1852, 3; Chase, *Speech at the Republican Mass Meeting in Cincinnati* (Columbus: Ohio State Journal, 1855) ("deeply interested spectator"); Allan Nevins, *Ordeal of the Union: A House Dividing, 1852–1857* (New York: Charles Scribner's Sons, 1947), 2:3–23 (Democratic nomination).

25 Chase to Kate Chase, July 25, 1852, Chase Papers, HSP; Chase to Edward Hamlin, August 3, 1852, Chase Papers, LC.

26 Chase to Edward Hamlin, July 19, 1852, Bourne, 243–44; Chase to John Hale, August 5, 7, Hale Papers, NHHS; "Independent Democratic Nominations," *National Era* (Washington, DC), August 19, 1852, 2 (Townshend letter); Schuyler Marshall, "The Free Democratic Convention of 1852," *Pennsylvania History* 22 (1955): 146–67; Sewell, *John P. Hale,* 145–48.

27 Chase to Kate Chase, August 27, 1852, *Spur,* 122–23; Shelden, *Washington Brotherhood,* 18–26.

28 Chase to Charles Sumner, September 9, 1852, Bourne, 247–48; *Cleveland True Democrat*, September 21, 30, October 5, 1852; "Senators Hale and Chase," *Oberlin*

(OH) Evangelist, October 13, 1852, 166; "Presidential Preferences of the Free Democracy," *National Era* (Washington, DC), October 14, 1852, 2; Brent Morris, *Oberlin, Hotbed of Abolitionism: College, Community, and the Fight for Freedom and Equality in Antebellum America* (Chapel Hill: University of North Carolina Press, 2014), 170; Gary Kornblith and Carol Lasser. *Elusive Utopia: The Struggle for Racial Equality in Oberlin, Ohio* (Baton Rouge: Louisiana State University Press, 2018), 89–90.

29 Charles Sumner to W. H. Seward, November 6, 1852, Seward Papers, Rochester. On 1852 more generally, see Holt, *Whig Party*, 753–64; Sewell, *Ballots for Freedom*, 242–51; Wilentz, *Rise of American Democracy*, 658–67.

30 Chase to Wendell Phillips, December 26, 1852, *SPCP*, 2:352.

31 "Supreme Court of the United States," *Baltimore Sun*, December 30, 1852, 4; Chase, *The Electric Telegraph: Substance of the Argument of S. P. Chase . . . in the case of H. O'Reilly and Others vs. S.F.B. Morse and Others* (New York: Baker, Godwin, 1853); O'Reilly v. Morse, 56 U.S. 62 (1853); *Cleveland True Democrat*, February 25, 1853; Adam Mossoff, "*O'Reilly v. Morse*" (research paper 14–22, George Mason Law & Economics, August 18, 2014), at SSRN, https://dx.doi.org/10.2139/ssrn.2448363.

32 Chase to John Bigelow, March 15, 28, 30, 1853, Bigelow Papers, Union College; see Lorman Ratner and Dwight Teeter, *Fanatics and Fire-Eaters: Newspapers and the Coming of the Civil War* (Urbana: University of Illinois Press, 2003), 4–25.

33 Franklin Pierce, Inaugural Address, March 4, 1853, Miller Center UVA website: https://millercenter.org/the-presidency/presidential-speeches/march-4-1853-inaugural-address.

34 *Congressional Globe*, April 9, 1853, 323–30; "United States Senate Extra Session," *New York Herald*, April 10, 1853, 2; "Patronage to Newspapers," *National Era* (Washington, DC), April 14, 1853, 2; "Patronage and the Press," ibid. April 21, 1853, 2; Holt, *Whig Party*, 401; Wilentz, *Rise of American Democracy*, 316.

35 Chase diary, May 26, 1843, *SPCP*, 1:163; *Congressional Globe*, April 9, 1853, 327; "United States Senate Extra Session," *New York Herald*, April 10, 1853, 2. I have relied both on the *Globe* and the *Herald* in this case because the *Herald* is probably closer to what Chase and Weller said. See Shelden, *Washington Brotherhood*, 29–32.

36 *Congressional Globe*, April 9, 1853, 327–30; "United States Senate Extra Session," *New York Herald*, April 10, 1853, 2.

37 "The News," *New York Herald*, April 10, 1853, 2; "Ohio Politics—Chase and Weller," *National Era* (Washington, DC), April 21, 1853, 2; "The Free Democratic Senators," *Ohio Star* (Ravenna), May 18, 1853, 2 (from *Baltimore Sun*).

38 Chase diary, April 13–20, 1853, *SPCP*, 1:257; *Sandusky (OH) Register*, April 24, 1853; "Political Integrity," *Ohio State Journal* (Columbus), May 27, 1853, 2; "Opening of the Campaign," *Portage Sentinel* (Ravenna, OH), June 1, 1853, 2.

39 Montgomery Blair to Chase, April 21, 1851, Chase Papers, LC; Frank Blair to Chase, June 1, 1853, Chase Papers, HSP; Chase to Charles Sumner, June 13, 1853, Bourne, 251; Chase to Kate Chase, July 4, 1853, Chase Papers, HSP;

William Smith, *The Francis Preston Blair Family in Politics* (New York: Macmillan, 1933).

40 Chase to John Bigelow, June 15, 1853, Bigelow Papers, Union College; *New York Evening Post*, June 29, 1853; "Senator Chase in Missouri," *National Era* (Washington, DC), June 30, 1853, 3 (prints correspondence between Chase and Saint Louis leaders).

41 Chase to Edward Hamlin, July 21, 1853, Chase Papers, LC (from Philadelphia); Chase to Kate Chase, August 4, 1853, *SPCP*, 2:357–58 (visited Ellicott family "on my way to Washington").

42 "Opening of the Campaign," *Portage Sentinel* (Ravenna, OH), June 1, 1853, 2; "The National Era," *Ohio Star* (Ravenna), September 28, 1853, 2; "State Ticket," *Cincinnati Enquirer*, October 11, 1853, 2 (no Senate candidate).

43 Chase diary, June 20, 1853, *SPCP*, 1:239 ("very hot"); *Ohio Columbian* (Columbus), June 30, 1853; Chase to Sumner, September 3, 1853, Bourne, 252 (twenty counties); *Freeman's Manual* (Columbus, OH), September 1, 1853 (Ironton); ibid., September 10, 1853 (Syracuse); ibid., September 28, 1853 (clear thought); "Senator Chase's Speech," *Wilmington (OH) Herald of Freedom*, October 7, 1853, 1 (Syracuse). Forty speeches is my estimate based on Chase's incomplete diary and the newspapers, also far from complete. See Chase diary, May 9–August 17, 1853, *SPCP*, 1:238–42; *Ohio Columbian* (Columbus), June 2, 23, 1853; Chase to Norton Townshend, September 12, 1853, *SPCP*, 2:359–60; *Ohio Columbian* (Columbus), September 28, 1853.

44 Chase to Hamlin, June 6, 1853, *SPCP*, 2:353–57; *Cleveland True Democrat*, July 21, August 2, 1853; *National Era* (Washington, DC), August 11, 25, September 8, 1853; *Freeman's Manual* (Columbus, OH), August 15, 1853 (available Google books).

45 Chase to unknown, July 10, 1853, Chase Papers, LC. See Chase to Charles Sumner, July 4, 1853, Sumner Papers, Harvard (possible printed version of Chase's speeches).

46 Chase to Alfred Edgerton, November 14, 1853, *SPCP*, 2:361–77 (quote 370).

47 Chase to Gerrit Smith, August 1, 1851, *SPCP*, 2:318–21; Chase to Edward Hamlin, July 21, 1853, Chase Papers, LC; *Freeman's Manual* (Columbus, OH), August 1, 15, 1853; *Cleveland True Democrat*, October 11, 1853. For an excellent general account, see Gienapp, *Republican Party*, 56–60.

48 Chase to Joshua Giddings, July 4, 1853, Chase Papers, LC; Chase to Charles Sumner, September 3, 1853, Bourne, 252; Chase to Edward Hamlin, October 17, 1853, Chase Papers, LC; Chase to Norton Townshend, October 31, 1853, *SPCP*, 2:360.

49 Franklin Pierce, First Annual Message, December 5, 1853, Miller Center UVA website (https://millercenter.org/the-presidency/presidential-speeches/december-5-1853-first-annual-message); Charles Sumner to Samuel Howe, December 8, 1853, in *Memoir and Letters of Charles Sumner*, ed. Edward Pierce (Boston: Roberts Brothers, 1893), 3:361; see Chase to Edward Hamlin, December 31, 1853, *SPCP*, 2:381 (predicting that the Pierce administration would "worry along, without any marked defeats").

CHAPTER 9: "The Nebraska Iniquity," 1854

1 "Senate," *Washington (DC) Union*, January 5, 1854, 1; "Senate," ibid., January 6, 1-2; Alice Malavasic, *The F Street Mess: How Southern Senators Rewrote the Kansas-Nebraska Act* (Chapel Hill: University of North Carolina Press, 2017), 88–89; Potter, *Impending Crisis*, 145–58.

2 Chase to John Wilson, January 11, 15, 1854, Chase Papers, LC; Wilson to Chase, January 13, 18, 1854, Chase Papers, LC; "The Nebraska Bill—Agitation in Prospect," *National Era* (Washington, DC), January 12, 1854, 2; "From Washington," *New York Times*, January 19, 1854, 1; *New-York Tribune*, January 6, 14, 1854; *Washington (DC) Union*, January 5, 6, 1854.

3 *Congressional Globe*, January 23, 24, 1854, 221–22, 239–40; *New-York Tribune*, January 24, 1854; *Washington (DC) Union*, January 24, 25, 1854; Chase to Edward Pierce, August 5, 1854, Pierce Papers, Harvard; Gienapp, *Republican Party*, 72; Malavasic, *F Street Mess*, 98–101.

4 *National Era* (Washington, DC), January 24, 1854; "Slavery Extension," *New York Times*, January 24, 1854, 2; *Appeal of the Independent Democrats in Congress to the People of the United States* (Washington, DC: Tower's Printers, 1854) (pamphlet version); see Hyman and Wiecek, *Equal Justice Under Law*, 168–69; Potter, *Impending Crisis*, 163–64.

5 Chase to John Jay, January 23, 1854, Chase Papers, HSP; Chase to Edward Hamlin, January 24, 1854, *SPCP*, 2:381–82. For more on Atchison, see Freehling, *Secessionists Triumphant,* 61–73, and Malavasic, *F Street Mess*, 41–46. For more on the Chase-Jay connection, see Jay to Chase, February 8, 1854, Chase Papers, LC (misfiled under 1853); Chase to Kate Chase, April [6?], 1854, *Spur,* 137–38 ("Jays are on a visit to Washington"); "List of Arrivals at the Hotels," *Washington (DC) Evening Star*, April 6, 1854, 4 (Jay family at Willard's Hotel); Chase to Jay, June 14, 1854, Jay Family Papers, Columbia (left portrait at Katonah train station); Chase to Jay, June 24, 1854, ibid. (pleased he has recovered portrait); Chase to Jay, June 28, 1854, ibid. (arrangements for Kate to visit Katonah); Chase to Kate Chase, July 5, 1854, *Spur,* 138 (she is with the Jays); Chase to Jay, July 7, 1854, Jay Family Papers, Columbia (sends money for Kate); Chase to Jay, July 16, 1854, ibid. (sends article for possible publication); and Chase to Jay, August 8, 1854, ibid. (travel plans).

6 "Senator Douglas' Nebraska Bill," *Chicago Tribune*, January 25, 1854, 2; *New York Evening Post*, January 25, 31, 1854; *New-York Tribune*, January 31, February 2, 1854.

7 *Congressional Globe*, January 30, 1854, 275–81; "Congressional," *New York Times*, February 1, 1854, 4; *New-York Tribune*, January 31, February 1, 1854.

8 "Senate," *New-York Tribune*, February 4, 1854, 5. There are slight differences between the *Tribune* report and the *Globe*; I have opted in this case for the newspaper. On the crowd, see "From Washington," *New York Times*, February 6, 1854, 1.

9 "Senate," *New-York Tribune*, February 4, 1854.

10 Ibid.; "From Washington," *New York Times*, February 6, 1854, 1.

11 Chase to Norton Townshend, February 10, 1854, Chase Papers, HSP; Chase to Townshend, February 10, 1854, Townshend Papers, Clements Library; see Chase to Edward Hamlin, February 10, 1854, Bourne, 257–58 (pleased by the "profound attention of the immense audience").

12 James Pike to William Fessenden, February 10, 1854, Pike Papers, LC; George Sumner to Chase, February 14, 1854, Chase Papers, HSP ("every day's delay in the Senate is a real gain"); *Congressional Globe*, February 15, 1854, 421 (Chase amendment); Nevins, *Ordeal of the Union*, 2:141 ("at every juncture Douglas labored for haste").

13 *Congressional Globe*, March 2, 1854, app., 281–82.

14 Ibid., March 3–4, 1854, 531–32, app., 332–36; Robert Johannsen, *Stephen A. Douglas* (New York: Oxford University Press, 1973), 430–32; Malavasic, *F Street Mess*, 135–42; Nevins, *Ordeal of the Union,* 2:143–45.

15 *Congressional Globe*, March 3–4, 1854, app., 335–36; Chase to Sankey Latty, March 6, 1854, copy at AKSPL; *New-York Tribune*, March 7, 1854. The *Tribune* printed two letters from Washington on March 7, the one quoted, and another, which Pike later claimed as his own. See James Pike, *First Blows of the Civil War: The Ten Years of Preliminary Conflict* (New York: American News, 1879), 216–20.

16 Chase to Edward Pierce, March 12, 1854, Bourne, 259; Chase to Sydney Howard Gay, March 14, 1854, Gay Papers, Columbia; *Washington (DC) Sentinel*, March 15, 1854; "Democratic Anti-Nebraska Meeting in Cincinnati," *Pittsburgh Gazette,* March 28, 1854, 2; "The Great Anti-Nebraska Convention," *Belmont Chronicle* (St. Clairsville, OH), March 31, 1854, 2; Nevins, *Ordeal of the Union*, 2:125–32.

17 Chase to Townshend, March 9, 1854, Chase Papers, HSP; *Middlebury (VT) Register*, March 29, 1854; Chase to William Allen, April 8, 1854, Allen Papers, LC; see Andrew Crandall, *The Early History of the Republican Party, 1854–1856* (Boston: R. G. Badger, 1930), 20–21; Wilentz, *Rise of American Democracy*, 674–79.

18 Chase to Norton Townshend, March 9, 1854, Chase Papers, HSP (probably will not attend), and March 18, 1854, Townshend Papers, Clements Library (decided to attend); "The Great Anti-Nebraska Convention," *Ohio State Journal* (Columbus), March 23, 1854, 2; "The Meeting on Wednesday Evening," ibid., March 24, 1854, 2; *Ohio Columbian* (Columbus), March 29, 1854.

19 Chase to Theodore Parker, April 5, 1854, Chase Papers, HSP; Chase to Ichabod Codding, April 22, 1854, *SPCP,* 2:385; Chase to Edward Pierce, May 16, 1854, Bourne, 260–61; Gienapp, *Republican Party*, 77 ("throughout March and April, the president and his advisers applied pressure to recalcitrant Democrats"); Michael Landis, *Northern Men with Southern Loyalties: The Democratic Party and the Sectional Crisis* (Ithaca: Cornell University Press, 2014), 115 ("Pierce did everything he could to aid the bill"); Roy Nichols, *Blueprints for Leviathan: American Style* (New York: Atheneum, 1963), 107–9.

20 "Passage of the Nebraska Bill," *New York Times*, May 23, 1854, 1; James Cutts, *A Brief Treatise upon Constitutional and Party Questions* (New York: D. Appleton, 1866), 122–23 (Douglas quote); Richard Johnston and William Browne, *Life*

of Alexander H. Stephens (Philadelphia: J.B. Lippincott, 1878), 277 (Stephens quote); Nevins, *Ordeal of the Union*, 2:154–57.

21 *Congressional Globe,* May 25, 1854, app. 780–82.

22 Ibid., app. 787–88 (Douglas). Most secondary accounts place Chase's comment about the cannon fire in March, when the bill passed the Senate for the first time. See Goodwin, *Team of Rivals*, 163; Nevins, *Ordeal of the Union*, 2:145; Schuckers, *Chase*, 156. But Chase said that the cannon fire was at the time of final passage. See Chase, *Speech of Hon. Salmon P. Chase, Delivered at the Republican Mass Meeting in Cincinnati, August 21, 1855* (Columbus: Ohio State Journal, 1855), 10–11. And the newspapers did not mention cannon fire in March, only in May. See *Washington (DC) Sentinel*, May 27, 1854; "The Hour and the Hour to Come," *National Era* (Washington, DC), June 1, 1854, 2 ("At half past one, we were awakened by the booming of cannon from Capitol Hill, announcing the passage of the bill").

23 *Congressional Globe*, July 12, 1854, 1702–3; see Chase to Norton Townshend, July 22, 1854, Chase Papers, HSP (could not attend convention because of homestead bill).

24 "The Know Nothings," *New York Herald*, June 4, 1854, 2; Anbinder, *Nativism and Slavery*, 3–15; Gienapp, *Republican Party*, 92–102; Maldwyn Jones, *American Immigration* (Chicago: University Press of Chicago, 1992); Wilentz, *American Democracy*, 679–86.

25 For homestead legislation in 1854, see George Stephenson, *The Political History of the Public Lands, from 1840 to 1862* (Boston: R. G. Badger, 1917), 168–89.

26 Chase to Kate Chase, July 5, 1854, *Spur,* 138–39. For more on Chase in August, see Chase to Edward Pierce, August 8, 1854, Bourne, 263; Chase to John Jay, August 8, 1854, Jay Family Papers, Columbia; Chase to John Hale, August 11, 1854, Hale Papers, NHHS (from Concord; invites to White Mountains); Chase to Norton Townshend, August 14, 1854, Townshend Papers, Clements Library (from Concord; "taking a little rest and visiting some relatives"); Chase to Edward Pierce, September 1, 1854, Pierce Papers, Harvard (in Concord; leaving for Ohio).

27 *New Hampshire Statesman* (Concord), September 2, 1854; "Speech of Hon. S.P. Chase," *Green Mountain Freeman* (Montpelier, VT), September 7, 1854, 2.

28 Chase to Kate Chase, September 15, 23, 1854, *SPCP,* 2:150–51; *Spur,* 452–53 (Catharine Collins).

29 "The Canvass for Congressmen," *Ohio State Journal* (Columbus), September 6, 1854, 2; Chase to Sankey Latty, September 9, 1854, copy at AKSPL; "Senator Chase in Perrysburg," *Perrysburg (OH) Journal*, September 30, 2; "Meeting at Findlay," ibid., October 7, 1854, 2; "Political News," *Plymouth (OH) Advertiser*, September 30, 1854, 2 ("Chase is stumping the western counties of the state for the Republican ticket"); Holt, *Whig Party*, 862–63.

30 *Ohio Columbian* (Columbus), October 18, 1854; *Ashtabula (OH) Sentinel*, October 19, 1854; Gerard Magliocca, *American Founding Son: John Bingham and the Invention of the Fourteenth Amendment* (New York: New York University Press,

2013); Gienapp, *Republican Party*, 119 ("Every Democratic district had been lost, and, although the state's delegation was a conglomeration of Know-Nothings, anti-Nebraska Democrats, and antislavery fusionists, its members were united in their opposition to Pierce and the Kansas-Nebraska Act").

31 "Chase and Giddings," *Summit County Beacon* (Akron, OH), October 25, 1854, 1 (from *Chicago Tribune*); "The Movement in Illinois," *National Era* (Washington, DC), October 26, 1854, 3.

32 "Hon. S. P. Chase," *Chicago Tribune*, September 30, 1854, 2 (schedule); *Belvidere (IL) Standard*, October 17, 1854; *Free West* (Chicago), October 26, 1864; *Wisconsin Free Democrat* (Milwaukee), October 27, 1854, (from *Galena (IL) Jeffersonian*); Chase to Norton Townshend, October 31, 1854, Townshend Papers, Clements Library; Chase to James Grimes, October 31, 1854, Chase Papers, HSP.

33 *Illinois State Register* (Springfield), October 19, 1854; *Illinois State Journal* (Springfield), October 20, 1854. For the *State Journal*, see Harold Holzer, *Lincoln and the Power of the Press* (New York: Simon & Schuster, 2014), 151–52, 162–63. For Lincoln as a Whig in 1854, see Donald, *Lincoln*, 170–71.

34 Chase to Norton Townshend, October 31, 1854, Townshend Papers, Clements Library; Chase to Edward Hamlin, November 11, 1854, Bourne, 365.

35 David Atchison to Jefferson Davis, September 24, 1854, in *The Papers of Jefferson Davis, 1853–1855,* ed. Lynda Crist (Baton Rouge: Louisiana State University Press, 1985), 83–84; Anbinder, *Nativism and Slavery,* 75–102; Freehling, *Secessionists Triumphant,* 71–73; Gienapp, *Republican Party*, 133–39, 147–60; Wilentz, *American Democracy*, 685–86.

36 Chase to Charles Sumner, October 30, 1854, Sumner Papers, Harvard; Chase to Edward Hamlin, November 21, 1854, *SPCP*, 2:388–89; Chase to John Paul, December 27, 1854, *SPCP*, 2:391–93.

37 Chase to Edward Pierce, November 28, 1854, Pierce Papers, Harvard; *Boston Evening Transcript*, December 7, 1854; "Senator Chase," *National Era* (Washington, DC), January 25, 1855, 3 (from *Boston Traveller*).

38 Chase speech, December 7, 1854, Chase Papers, HSP; *Boston Daily Atlas*, December 8, 1854; *Boston Evening Transcript*, December 8, 1854. The quotes are from the manuscript at HSP rather than the brief news reports.

39 Chase speech, December 7, 1854, Chase Papers, HSP; see Don Fehrenbacher, *The Dred Scott Case: Its Significance in American Law and Politics* (New York: Oxford University Press, 1978). I have translated a bit of legal Latin in the quote about Wythe.

40 Chase speech, December 7, 1854, Chase Papers, HSP; *Dred Scott v. Sandford*, 60 U.S. 393 (1857).

41 "Slavery Eternal," *Green Mountain Freeman* (Montpelier, VT), October 26, 1854, 2 (from *Richmond Examiner*); Chase speech, December 7, 1854, Chase Papers, HSP. Chase's critique is similar to the conservative critique of the progressives, that they discard the Jeffersonian view of rights. See George Will, *The Conservative Sensibility* (New York: Hachette Books, 2019), 32–50.

42 Chase speech, December 7, 1854, Chase Papers, HSP. "Mr. Chase concluded his eloquent lecture, of which the above is but a brief sketch, with an eloquent

appeal to the friends of human liberty to be true to each other, to humanity, and to God, and to labor for the restoration of the theories of 1784, in regard to slavery." *Boston Atlas*, December 8, 1854.

CHAPTER 10: "Our Victory Is Glorious," 1855

1 *Congressional Globe*, January 9, 1855, 216–17; *New York Evening Post*, January 12, 1855 (supports Chase's amendment). On circuit riding, see Joshua Glick, "The Supreme Court and Circuit Riding," *Cardozo Law Review* 24 (2003), 1753 (online at Supreme Court Historical Society).

2 *Congressional Globe*, January 16, 17, February 19, February 28, 1855, 272–75; 810–11, app., 303.

3 Ibid., February 16, 1855, 771–72.

4 Ibid., February 23, 1855, app., 211 (Chase), 244 (Sumner), and 247 (vote).

5 "Senator Chase," *New York Evening Post*, March 9, 1855, 2.

6 "Hon. S.P. Chase of Ohio," *Frederick Douglass' Paper* (Rochester, NY), March 16, 1855, 2. On the relationship between Douglass and Julia Griffiths, see Blight, *Frederick Douglass,* 202–8, 265–67.

7 Chase diary, March 24–25, 1855, *SPCP,* 1:245–46; "Rosetta Again Arrested" and "Rosetta's Case," *Anti-Slavery Bugle* (New Lisbon, OH), March 31, 1855, 2; *Ex parte Robinson*, 20 Fed. Cases 296 (1855); Chase to John Trowbridge, March 19, 1864, Warden, 344–45; Finkelman, *Imperfect Union*, 174–77; R. J. M. Blackett, *The Captive's Quest for Freedom: Fugitive Slaves, the 1850 Fugitive Slave Law, and the Politics of Slavery* (New York: Cambridge University Press, 2018), 247–48.

8 Chase to Oran Follett, January 1, 1855, Follett Papers, in Belle Hamlin, ed., "Selections from the Follett Papers," *Quarterly Publication of the Historical and Philosophical Society of Ohio* 13 (1918): 61.

9 Chase to Edward Hamlin, February 9, 1855, *SPCP,* 2:401–2; "Politics of Our State—Division Among the Opposition," *Cadiz (OH) Democratic Sentinel*, February 14, 1855, 1 (predicting split between Free-Soil and Know-Nothing factions would lead to Democratic victory).

10 Chase to Norton Townshend, February 14, 1855, Townshend Papers, Clements Library. The line from Burns should read "come counsel, dear Tittie, don't tarry" where "tittie" is Scottish for sister. Donald Low, ed., *The Songs of Robert Burns* (London: Routledge, 1993), 309.

11 Chase to James Shepherd Pike, March 22, 1855, in Pike, *First Blows*, 294.

12 "Kansas—The Giant Fraud," *New-York Tribune*, April 2, 1855 4; *Cincinnati Enquirer*, April 3, 1855; *Toledo (OH) Blade*, April 11, 1855; *National Era* (Washington, DC), April 19, 1855; William Baughin, "Bullets and Ballots: The Election Day Riots of 1855," *Bulletin of the Historical and Philosophical Society of Ohio* 21 (1963): 267–73; Gienapp, *Republican Party*, 168–72, 196–97; Maizlish, *Triumph of Sectionalism*, 110–11.

13 Chase to John Bigelow, March 21, 1855, Bigelow Papers, Union College; "Who Shall Be Governor?," *New York Times*, May 16, 1855, 4; *New York Evening Post*,

May 17, 1855; *New-York Tribune*, May 18, 1855; *National Era* (Washington, DC), May 24, 1855; Chase to Kate Chase, May 27, 1855, *SPCP*, 2:163; Chase to James Pike, June 20, 1855, in Pike, *First Blows*, 296 ("in our conversations at New York").

14 Chase to Edward Pierce, May 14, 1855, Pierce Papers, Harvard; "The Freesoilers Cracking the Whip at the Know Nothings," *Cadiz (OH) Sentinel,* May 23, 1855, 1 (quoting *Ohio Columbian* (Columbus)); James Coulter to Chase, May 27, 1855, Chase Papers, LC.

15 Lewis Campbell to Isaac Strohm, May 24, 1855, OHC; Chase to Lewis Campbell, May 25, 1855, Chase Papers, LC; Campbell to Chase, May 28, 1855, ibid.; Chase to Campbell, May 29, 1855, *SPCP*, 2:409–11; Campbell to Chase, May 31, 1855, *SPCP*, 2:411–13; Chase to Campbell, June 2, 1855, *SPCP*, 2:414–16.

16 *Ohio Columbian* (Columbus), June 13, 1855; *New-York Tribune*, June 13, 14, 15, 16, 1855 (Philadelphia); James Ashley to Chase, June 16, 1855, *SPCP*, 2:417; *Louisville (KY) Daily Courier*, June 18, 1855 (Cleveland); Anbinder, *Nativism and Slavery*, 167–72; Gienapp, *Republican Party*, 182–87.

17 Chase to Lyman Hall, June 15, 1855, in "Letter from Mr. Chase," *National Era* (Washington, DC), June 28, 1855, 3; Chase to James Pike, June 20, 1855, in Pike, *First Blows*, 296; Chase to Edward Pierce, June 20, 1855, Pierce Papers, Harvard; Chase to Kate Chase, June 21, 1855, *Spur,* 163–64; *Herald of Freedom* (Wakarusa, Kansas Territory), July 28, 1855.

18 *Ohio State Journal* (Columbus), July 11, 1855, 2 (from *Cincinnati Gazette*); *Ohio Columbian* (Columbus), July 11, 1855; *Cincinnati Enquirer,* July 12, 1855 (from *Ohio Statesman* (Columbus)).

19 "Ohio Republican Convention," *Ohio State Journal* (Columbus), July 13, 1855, 2; "Ohio Republican Convention," ibid., July 14, 1855, 2; *Toledo (OH) Blade*, July 16, 1855; "Ohio Republican State Convention," *New-York Tribune*, July 16, 1855, 5. Secondary sources include Anbinder, *Nativism and Slavery*, 177–78; William Gienapp, "Salmon P. Chase, Nativism, and the Formation of the Republican Party in Ohio," *Ohio History* 93 (1984): 24–39; Maizlish, *Triumph of Sectionalism*, 211–17.

20 "Ohio Republican Convention," *Ohio State Journal* (Columbus), July 14, 1855, 2. For a slightly different version, see "Ohio Republican State Convention," *New-York Tribune*, July 16, 1855, 5.

21 "Republican Mass Meetings," *Ohio State Journal* (Columbus), September 3, 1855, 2; *Toledo (OH) Blade*, September 10, October 3, 1855; Chase to Kate Chase, September 30, 1855, *SPCP,* 2:422–25; Chase to Charles Sumner, October 15, 1855, Sumner Papers, Harvard; Chase to James Pike, October 18, 1855, *SPCP,* 2:426.

22 "Great Republican Mass Meeting at Circleville," *Belmont Chronicle* (St. Clairsville, OH), August 30, 1855, 1. It appears from his speaking schedule that Chase gave this speech on August 4. See *Ohio State Journal* (Columbus) August 1, 1855.

23 Chase, *Speech of August 21, 1855*, 3–8.

24 Ibid., 8–9. On Washington and Jefferson, see Mary Thompson, *"The Only Unavoidable Subject of Regret": George Washington, Slavery, and the Enslaved Community at Mount Vernon* (Charlottesville: University of Virginia Press, 2019);

Henry Wiencek, *Master of the Mountain: Thomas Jefferson and His Slaves* (New York: Farrar, Straus & Giroux, 2012).

25 Chase, *Speech of August 21, 1855*, 11–12.

26 Ibid., 12. Although the details do not quite square, it seems that Chase was referring to William Phillips. See Freehling, *Secessionists Triumphant*, 76.

27 Chase, *Speech of August 21, 1855*, 12–13.

28 *Sandusky (OH) Commercial Register*, September 5, 1855.

29 "The Movement in Illinois," *National Era* (Washington, DC), October 25, 1854, 3; *Ohio Columbian* (Columbus), September 26, 1855 ("clear, frank"); *New York Evening Post*, June 5, 1856; *Brooklyn Times Union*, September 27, 1871; Blue, *Chase*, 102 ("oratorical skills were limited"); Niven, *Chase*, 138 ("emotional content was nil"); Goodwin, *Team of Rivals*, 147 ("nor did Chase possess Seward's compelling speaking style"); Alonzo Rothschild, *Lincoln, Master of Men* (Boston: Houghton, Mifflin, 1906), 163 (Chase lacked the "wit, play of fancy, sympathetic fervor" of Lincoln); Schuckers, 167–68 (quotes *Times Union*).

30 Chase to Kate Chase, August 10, 1855, Chase Papers, HSP; *Buffalo Daily Republic*, August 10, 1855; *Ohio Columbian* (Columbus), August 15, 1855; Samuel Galloway to Chase, August 16, 1855, Chase Papers, HSP; *Gallipolis (OH) Journal*, October 4, 1855; John Weaver, *Nativism and the Birth of the Republican Party in Ohio, 1854–56* (PhD diss., Ohio State University, 1982), 57 ("soon the sons").

31 "Chase Praising the Know Nothings," *Portage Sentinel* (Ravenna, OH), September 15, 1855, 2; *Cadiz (OH) Sentinel*, September 19, 1855; "Chase and His Antecedents," *Eaton (OH) Democrat*, September 20, 1855, 2; "Chase on Negro Suffrage," *Ashland (OH) States & Union*, September 26, 1855, 2; *Cincinnati Enquirer*, October 2, 1855; *Gallipolis (OH) Journal*, October 4, 1855; "The Political Sentiments of the Black Republicans," *M'Arthur (OH) Democrat*, October 4, 1855.

32 *Cleveland Leader*, September 20, October 3, 1855; *Fremont (OH) Weekly Journal*, September 28, 1855 (quote); *Pomeroy (OH) Weekly Telegraph*, October 2, 1855.

33 Chase to Kate Chase, September 15, 1854, *Spur*, 149; ibid, September 30, 1855, *SPCP*, 2:422.

34 Ibid., September 30, 1855, *SPCP*, 2:422–24.

35 Ibid., 2:425; *Toledo (OH) Blade*, October 3, 5, 1855; *Cleveland Leader*, October 9, 1855; "They Can't Do It," *Ohio State Journal* (Columbus), October 9, 1855, 2; "The Election—The Result," ibid., October 10, 1855, 2; "Chase Elected Governor!," ibid., October 11, 1855, 2; *Toledo (OH) Blade*), October 12, 1855 ("glorious Democratic gains"); *Western Reserve Chronicle* (Warren, OH), October 17, 1855 (accuses Democrats of "crowing too soon"); Gienapp, *Republican Party*, 200–203; Weaver, *Nativism and the Birth*, 97–100.

36 Chase to Charles Sumner, October 15, 1855, Sumner Papers, Harvard; Chase to James Grimes, October 17, 1855, Chase Papers, HSP; *Ohio Columbian* (Columbus), October 31, 1855.

37 Chase to Kinsley Bingham, October 19, 1855, *SPCP*, 2:428–29; John Paul to Chase, October 24, 1855, Chase Papers, HSP; T. M. Tweed to Chase, October 25, 1855, Chase Papers, LC ("I cannot see how you are to avoid being a candidate

for the presidency"); Kinsley Bingham to Chase, November 14, 1855, Chase
Papers, LC.

38 *Albany (NY) Argus*, October 20, 1855; Theodore Parker to William Herndon,
November 30, 1855, Parker Papers, Massachusetts Historical Society; Gienapp,
Republican Party, 239–60.

39 Chase to John Hale, December 10, 1855, Hale Papers, NHHS; Alfred Stone to
Cassius Clay, December 14, 1855, in *New-York Tribune*, December 25, 1855;
Clay to Stone, December 15, 1855, in ibid.

40 Gamaliel Bailey to Chase, November 27, 1855, Chase Papers, HSP.

41 William Seward to Francis Blair, December 29, 1855, Blair-Lee Papers, Princeton;
William Seward to Thurlow Weed, December 31, 1855, in Frederick Seward,
Seward at Washington, as Senator and Secretary of State, 1846–1861 (New York:
Derby & Miller, 1891), 264. On the dinner, see John Bicknell, *Lincoln's Pathfinder:
John C. Frémont and the Violent Election of 1856* (Chicago: Chicago Review Press,
2017), 19–21, 27–29; Gienapp, *Republican Party*, 250–51; Harrold, *Gamaliel
Bailey*, 174; Niven, *Chase*, 178–79.

42 William Seward to Thurlow Weed, December 31, 1855, in Seward, *Seward
at Washington*, 264; Preston King to Gideon Welles, January 3, 1856, Welles
Papers, LC.

CHAPTER 11: "Avowed and Determined," 1856–57

1 "Supreme Court," *Washington (DC) Evening Star*, January 5, 1856, 3; *Ohio State
Journal* (Columbus), January 11, 1856; Jones v. Johnston, 59 U.S. 150 (1855)
(Chase counsel); *Ohio State Journal*, January 15, 1856; "For the Beacon," *Summit
County Beacon* (Akron, OH), January 23, 1856, 1; Bob Hunter and Lucy Wolfe,
*A Historical Guidebook to Old Columbus: Finding the Past in the Present in Ohio's
Capital City* (Athens: Ohio University Press, 2012), 35–36.

2 Chase, *Inaugural Address of Salmon P. Chase, Governor of the State of Ohio* (Columbus,
OH: Statesman Steam Press, 1856), 3-4.

3 Ibid., 13–15.

4 *Ohio State Journal*, January 15, 1856; *New-York Tribune*, January 16, 1856; *M'Arthur (OH) Democrat*, January 24, 1856; *National Era* (Washington, DC), January
24, 1856.

5 Chase to Adeline Hitchcock, April 29, 1826, Chase Papers, HSP ("poisonous);
Chase diary, May 16, 20, October 18–19, 1857, *SPCP*, 1:277–79 and 306–7;
Spur, 146–47; Janet Chase Hoyt, "A Woman's Memories," *New-York Tribune*,
February 15, 1891, 16. We have to "extrapolate" from 1857, for which there
is a detailed diary, because there is no diary for 1856 and only a few pages for
1858 and 1859.

6 Chase to Kate Chase, July 25, 1856, *Spur*, 164 (corrected "with" to "without");
Chase diary, January 27, February 5–6, 1857, *SPCP*, 1:260–64.

7 William Dean Howells, *Years of My Youth* (New York: Harper & Brothers,
1916), 154–55; Schurz, *Reminiscences* (1907–09), 2:169–70; Isabella Trotter,

First Impressions of the New World on Two Travelers from the Old (London: Longman, Brown, 1859), 189–91; John Oller, *American Queen: The Rise and Fall of Kate Chase Sprague, Civil War "Belle of the North" and Gilded Age Woman of Scandal* (Boston: Da Capo Press, 2014), 31–36.

8 Chase to Kate Chase, December 4, 5, 1857, *Spur,* 166–67; ibid., December 6, 1857, Chase Papers, HSP; Trotter, *First Impressions,* 190–93.

9 Chase to Kate Chase, September 15, 1854, *Spur,* 150; Chase diary, February 18, 1858, *SPCP,* 1:267; Nettie Chase to Kate Chase, September 26, 1858, *Spur,* 168. The notes in *Spur* provide the best biography of Nettie, at least up to the time of her father's death.

10 Elizabeth Pike to Chase, January 27, 1856, Chase Papers, HSP; Pike to Chase, February 27, 1858, Chase Papers, HSP; Pike to Chase, July 7, 1859, Chase Papers, LC; Chase to Pike, July 13, 1859, Pike Papers, Maine.

11 Elizabeth Goldsborough to Chase, January 25, 1856, Chase Papers, LC; "Gov. Chase," *Baltimore Sun,* August 25, 1856, 1 (Chase visited Annapolis); Goldsborough to Chase, September 29, 1856, Chase Papers, LC; Chase to Goldsborough, July 16, 1857, Goldsborough Papers, Duke (impending visit); Chase to Goldsborough, July 17, 1857, Goldsborough Papers, NYPL (same); Goldsborough to Chase, August 5, 1857, Chase Papers, LC.

12 Chase diary, December 16, 1852, *SPCP,* 1:232; Margaret Bailey to Chase, January 11, 1857, Chase Papers, LC; Chase diary, January 27, 29, March 5, May 1, 19, July 4, 1857, *SPCP,* 1:259–60, 273, 277, 279, 289–90.

13 "Wisconsin Affairs," *New York Herald,* February 7, 1856, 1 (death of Ben Eastman); Chase diary, March 6, 1857, *SPCP,* 1:273 (letter from Eastman); Chase to Kate Chase, April 30, 1859, *Spur,* 170 (possible visit from Eastman); ibid., [1861?], ibid., 183 (he called on Eastman); Chase to Jacob Schuckers, September 24, 1866, *SPCP,* 5:125 ("sweet and lovely").

14 *Louisville (KY) Courier,* January 30, 1856; Mark Reinhardt, *Who Speaks for Margaret Garner?* (Minneapolis: University of Minnesota Press, 2010). Reinhardt's book compiles and comments on primary documents.

15 Chase to John Trowbridge, March 13, 1864, *SPCP,* 4:324.

16 *SPCP,* 326 ("great interest"); *New-York Tribune,* February 8, 1856; *Cincinnati Gazette,* February 29, 1856.

17 Joseph Cox to Chase, February 29, 1856, Chase Papers, LC; Chase to Charles Morehead, March 4, 1856, in Reinhardt, *Who Speaks,* 127–30; Morehead to Chase, March 7, 1856, in ibid., 130–33; *Louisville (KY) Courier,* March 10, 1856; *Cincinnati Enquirer,* March 11, 1856; Edward Hamlin to Chase, March 11, 1856, Chase Papers, LC; Joseph Cooper to Chase, March 11, 1856, ibid.; *National Era* (Washington, DC), March 20, 1856 (defends Chase); Chase to George Denison, December 31, 1863, *SPCP,* 4:237–39 (defends his conduct in the Garner case); Chase to John Trowbridge, March 13, 1864, in Reinhardt, *Who Speaks,* 141–42 (similar).

18 Chase to Joseph Cox, May 13, 1856, Chase Papers, OHC (pardon); Chase to George Hoadly, May 20, 1856, ibid. (appointment); *Cincinnati Enquirer,* April

21, 1857 (Mansfield); *Pomeroy (OH) Weekly Telegraph*, April 28, 1857 (Mansfield); Hoadly, *Address at Music Hall*, 16; John Fairlie, "The Veto Power of the State Governor," *American Political Science Review* 11 (1917): 473–93.

19 Benjamin Wade to Chase, March 7, 1856, Chase Papers, HSP; Chase to Harvey Pollock, May 8, 1856, Chase Papers, OHC (extradition).

20 James Ashley to Chase, January 16, 1856, Chase Papers, LC; *National Era* (Washington, DC), January 17, 1856; *New-York Tribune*, January 17, 1856; Gienapp, *Republican Party*, 251–53.

21 *Steubenville (OH) True American*, November 28, 1855; Thomas Spooner to Chase, February 5, 1856, Chase Papers, LC; Chase to Charles Cleveland, February 11, 1856, Chase Papers, HSP; Gienapp, *Republican Party*, 253–54.

22 "The Republicans at Pittsburg," *New York Times*, February 22, 1856, 1, 4; "The Republican Convention," *New-York Tribune*, February 23, 1856, 4; Russell Errett, "Formation of the Republican Party in 1856," *Magazine of Western History* 7 (December 1887): 182–83; Gienapp, *Republican Party*, 254–56.

23 "National Republican Convention," *New York Times*, February 25, 1856, 1; "Republican National Convention," *New-York Tribune*, February 25, 1856, 4; "Second Day's Proceedings," *Pittsburgh Gazette*, February 25, 1856, 1; Gienapp, *Republican Party*, 256–59.

24 "National Republican Convention," *New York Times*, February 25, 1856, 1; "Republican National Convention," *New-York Tribune*, February 25, 1856, 4; "Second Day's Proceedings," *Pittsburgh Gazette*, February 25, 1856, 1; Bicknell, *Lincoln's Pathfinder*, 92–97; Gienapp, *Republican Party*, 256–59.

25 Chase to Hiram Barney, February 25, 1856, Barney Papers, Huntington ("a good convention" and "my name was greatly preferred for a certain place"); Thomas Bolton to Chase, February 25, 1856, Chase Papers, HSP; James Ashley to Chase, February 26, 1856, Chase Papers, OHC; John Bigelow to Chase, February 26, 1856, Chase Papers, LC. On Bigelow and Frémont, see Bicknell, *Lincoln's Pathfinder*, 33; Margaret Clapp, *Forgotten First Citizen: John Bigelow* (Boston: Little, Brown, 1947, 99–103.

26 Horace Greeley to Schuyler Colfax, May 6, 1856, Greeley-Colfax Papers, NYPL; Bicknell, *Lincoln's Pathfinder*, 34–35, 89–91; Gienapp, *Republican Party*, 307–29; Stahr, *Seward*, 159–64.

27 *Washington (DC) Union*, September 11, 1850; *Congressional Globe*, September 24, 1850, app., 1363–65; *New York Evening Post*, September 28, 1850; *Louisville (KY) Courier*, October 4, 1850; Tom Chaffin, *Pathfinder: John Charles Frémont and the Course of American Empire* (Norman: University of Oklahoma Press, 2014).

28 Bicknell, *Lincoln's Pathfinder*, 26–38; Chaffin, *Pathfinder*, 435–37; Gienapp, *Republican Party*, 321–23.

29 *Ashland (OH) Ohio States & Union*, March 26, 1856 (Benton letter); Chase to John Bigelow, March 28, 1856, Chase Papers, NYPL; *New York Times*, March 29, 1856; Chase to Hiram Barney, April 3, 1856, Barney Papers, Huntington; Chase to Hiram Barney, May 13, 1856, ibid. ("Politicians are always short-sighted. They now want to prepare our party for a race by cutting off its feet").

30 Gamaliel Bailey to Chase, April 18, 1856, *SPCP*, 2:434–35; Chase to Seward, April 21, 1856, Seward Papers, Rochester.

31 *New-York Tribune*, April 1, 1856; *National Era* (Washington, DC), April 10, 1856; Nevins, *Ordeal of the Union*, 426–34.

32 *Congressional Globe*, May 19–20, 1856, app. 529–47; Donald, *Sumner and the Coming of the Civil War*, 290–307; Freehling, *Secessionists Triumphant*, 79–84; Freeman, *Field of Blood*, 219–21; Stahr, *Seward*, 160–61.

33 Chase to Charles Sumner, May 23, 1856, Sumner Papers, Harvard.

34 *Cincinnati Gazette*, May 24, 1856; *New-York Tribune*, May 24, 1856; *Ohio State Journal* (Columbus), May 29, 1856; Nicole Etcheson, *Bleeding Kansas: Contested Liberty in the Civil War Era* (Lawrence: University Press of Kansas, 2004), 100–12.

35 *New York Evening Post*, May 18, 1856; "The Selection of a Presidential Candidate," *New-York Tribune*, June 6, 1856, 6; Bicknell, *Lincoln's Pathfinder*, 188 (Bigelow's biography).

36 Chase to Hiram Barney, June 6, 1856, *SPCP*, 2:438–39; Chase to Edward Hamlin, June 12, 1856, *SPCP*, 2:440–41; Chase to George Hoadly, June 12, 1856, ibid., 441–42 (authorizing withdrawal of Chase's name); Chase to T. G. Mitchell, June 13, 1856, in "Mr. Chase Is Withdrawn," *New York Times*, June 19, 1856, 1 (similar); "The Republican Convention," *New-York Tribune*, June 17, 1856, 5 ("inevitable"); Gienapp, *Republican Party*, 334–46.

37 Hiram Barney to Chase, June 21, 1856, *SPCP*, 2:443–44; Chase to John Frémont, June 27, 1856, Chase Paper LC (congratulates); Chase to George Julian, July 17, 1856, Giddings-Julian Papers, LC (praises platform); Chase to "my dear cousin," July 22, 1856, Chase Papers, OHC; Elizabeth Pike to Chase, September 14, 1856, Chase Papers, HSP.

38 *Washington (DC) Sentinel*, June 10, 1856; *Louisville (KY) Courier Journal*, July 2, 1856; see Robert Rayback, *Millard Fillmore: Biography of a President* (Buffalo: Buffalo Historical Society, 1959), 327–29.

39 *North American & United States Gazette* (Philadelphia), August 4, 1856 (Chase in Springfield); *Pomeroy (OH) Weekly Telegraph*, August 5, 1856 (Athens); *Western Reserve Chronicle* (Warren, OH), August 6, 1856 (Yellow Springs); Charles Dana to James Pike, August 9, 1856, Pike Papers, Maine; *Ohio State Journal* (Columbus), August 14, 1856 (Zanesville); *Pittsburgh Gazette*, August 20, 1856 (same); *Ohio State Journal* (Columbus), September 2, 1856 (Chase speaking schedule for September); *Cleveland Leader*, September 11, 1856 (Sandusky); Chase to Hannibal Hamlin, September 12, 1856, Charles Aldrich Papers, State Historical Society of Iowa (reaction in Ohio to Maine election); *Cadiz (OH) Sentinel*, September 24, 1856 (Cadiz); *Toledo (OH) Blade*, October 6, 1856 (Napoleon).

40 Chase to "my dear cousin," July 22, 1856, Chase Papers, OHC; *North American & United States Gazette* (Philadelphia), August 4, 1856 (Chase predicts a hundred thousand majority); Gienapp, *Republican Party*, 401 ("all but extinguished").

41 For a detailed analysis, see Gienapp, *Republican Party*, 413–15 (including county-by-county maps).

42 Chase to Charles Sumner, November 8, 1856, Sumner Papers, Harvard; Bicknell, *Lincoln's Pathfinder*, 275–80; Michael Holt, *The Election of 1860: "A Campaign Fraught With Consequences"* (Lawrence: University Press of Kansas, 2017), 11–12. Republicans had majorities in the six New England states, Michigan, and Wisconsin.

43 Chase diary, January 2–3, 1857, *SPCP*, 1:247–48; Chase, *Message of the Governor of Ohio to the Fifty-Second General Assembly, at the Adjourned Session, Commencing January 5, 1857* (Columbus, OH: Statesman Steam Press, 1857), 6–7, 25–26, 29–30; *Cincinnati Enquirer*, January 7, 1857; *New York Evening Post*, January 8, 1857.

44 *Ohio State Journal* (Columbus), January 7, 1857 (quotes); *Columbus (OH) Gazette*, January 9, 1857; *Scioto Gazette* (Chillicothe, OH), January 9, 1857.

45 *Cleveland Herald*, February 20, 1857; Chase, "Galileo," Chase Papers, LC.

46 Chase to the Ohio State Teachers' Association, July 6, 1857, *SPCP*, 2:457–48.

47 *Ohio State Journal* (Columbus), June 4, 1857; *National Era* (Washington, DC), June 18, 1857; "Speech of Gov. Chase, of Ohio," *Baltimore Sun*, July 20, 1857, 1 (quotes); *Columbus (OH) Gazette*, July 31, 1857.

48 "The Dred Scott Case," *New York Times*, March 9, 1857, 2; *New-York Tribune*, March 9, 1857. The Supreme Court did not issue its final opinions until late May, with considerable changes, so I have cited the newspaper summaries Chase would have seen in March. See Fehrenbacher, *Dred Scott Case*, 314–21.

49 *Anti-Slavery Bugle* (New Lisbon, OH), April 11, 1857 (committee report); Act of April 16, 1857, 54 *Ohio Laws* 170 (against use of jails); Act of April 17, 1857, 54 *Ohio Laws* 186 (against bringing slaves into state); Act of April 17, 1857, 54 *Ohio Laws* 220 (against kidnapping); Chase diary, April 17, 1857, *SPCP*, 1:275–76; Chase to Edward Pierce, April 27, 1857, Pierce Papers, Harvard; *Summit County Beacon* (Akron, OH), June 17, 1857 (reprints kidnapping law). See Paul Finkelman, "Race Discrimination in Antebellum Ohio," 401–3.

50 Chase to Frederick Haussarek, April 7, 1857, Haussarek Papers, OHC; Draft resolutions, April 7, 1857, Chase Papers, HSP; Haussarek to Chase, April 11, 1857, ibid.; see Anbinder, *Nativism and Slavery*, 257–60; Eugene Roseboom, *The Civil War Era, 1850–1873* (Columbus: Ohio State Archeological & Historical Society, 1944), 226 (*History of the State of Ohio*, vol. 4).

51 James Ashley to Chase, November 27, 1856, Chase Papers, LC; Chase to Edward Pierce, April 27, 1857, Pierce Papers, Harvard; Chase to John Hale, May 5, 1857, Hale Papers, NHHS; *Ohio State Journal* (Columbus), May 13, 1857; *Summit County Beacon* (Akron, OH), May 13, 1857, 2 (Chase "will consent to be a candidate"); *Tiffin (OH) Tribune*, May 15, 1857 (Chase is "the gubernatorial candidate of the people"); *Highland Weekly News* (Hillsboro, OH), May 28, 1857; Rufus Spalding to Chase, June 23, 1857, Chase Papers, HSP. Blue argues that the Gibson-Breslin scandal was a "major factor in Chase's decision to seek reelection." Blue, *Chase*, 115. Because of the May newspaper articles, I disagree.

52 "The Fugitive Slave Law," *Summit County Beacon* (Akron, OH), June 3, 1857, 2; *Holmes County Republican* (Millersburg, OH), June 4, 1857; "The Progress of the Treason," *Cincinnati Enquirer*, June 10, 1857; *Ohio State Journal* (Columbus),

June 11, 1857 (responds to *Enquirer*); see Benjamin Prince, "The Rescue Case of 1857," *Ohio Archeological & Historical Society Publications* 16 (1907): 292–309.

53   Chase diary, June 12, 1857, *SPCP*, 1:286; *Ohio State Journal* (Columbus), June 16, 1857; Chase to Henry Reed, June 25, 1857, *SPCP*, 2:456–57; Chase notes, "Wright's Statement of Interview with Gibson," June 1857, Chase Papers, HSP.

54   Chase diary, June 13, 1857, *SPCP*, 1:286; "Large Defalcation," *Ohio State Journal* (Columbus), June 13, 1857, 2; Chase to Henry Reed, June 25, 1857, *SPCP*, 2:456–57; Chase to John Trowbridge, March 21, 1864, *SPCP*, 4:340–41.

55   *Cincinnati Enquirer*, June 14, 16, 1857; *Ohio State Journal* (Columbus), June 17, 20, 1857; "The Great Ohio Defalcation," *Chicago Tribune*, June 26, 1857, 2; "The Defalcation—Chase and Medill," ibid., June 29, 1857, 2. See Mark Summers, *The Plundering Generation: Corruption and the Crisis of the Union, 1849–1861* (New York: Oxford University Press, 1988), 74–78.

56   Francis Wright to Chase, June 18, 1857, Chase Papers, OHC; Chase to John Andrews, June 18, 1857, ibid.; Chase to Wright, June 22, 23, 1857, *SPCP*, 2:452–55; Wright to Chase, June 24, 1857, Chase Papers, HSP (telegram); Andrews to Chase, June 27, 1857, Chase Papers, OHC; Chase diary, June 27, 1857, *SPCP*, 1:259 ("relieved"); "Erie Bonds," *New York Times*, June 29, 1857, 8 (notice from Wright).

57   Chase to Thomas Sparrow, June 22, 1857, Chase Papers, OHC; William Dennison to Chase, June 23, 1857, ibid.; *Holmes County Republican* (Millersburg, OH), July 2, 1857; *Ohio State Journal* (Columbus), July 17, 1857; "The Defaulters Indicted," *Summit County Beacon* (Akron, OH), July 22, 1857, 2; *Ohio State Journal* (Columbus), August 17, 1857 (Breslin quoted in Sparrow report); "Ohio Politics," *New York Times*, August 29, 1857, 3 (Chase speech); *Delaware (OH) Gazette*, March 12, 1858; Summers, *Plundering Generation*, 75–80; *Report of the Investigating Commission Appointed to Enquire into the Causes of the Defalcation in the State Treasury* (1859).

58   *Cincinnati Enquirer*, July 10, 1857; *Anti-Slavery Bugle* (New Lisbon, OH), July 11, 1857; Prince, "The Rescue Case of 1857," 292–309.

59   Henry Carrington to L. L. Rice, July 24, 1857, Chase Papers, OHC; Chase to Lewis Cass, July 27, 1857, ibid.; Cass to Chase, August 4, 1857, ibid.; Chase to Cass, August 15, 1857, ibid.; Cass to Chase, August 27, 1857, ibid.; *Columbus (OH) Gazette*, December 23, 1859 (Gibson found guilty); *Fremont (OH) Weekly Journal*, February 3, 1860 (Gibson free on bail until new trial); *Lancaster (OH) Gazette*, January 5, 1865 (Breslin obtains *nolle prosequi*); *Delaware (OH) Gazette*, January 25, 1867 (case against Gibson dropped). There is no question that Buchanan and Chase met in Washington in July 1857, for Chase thanked Cass for setting up the meeting with Buchanan, saying that he hoped it would have "beneficial effects." Chase to Cass, July 27, 1857, Chase Papers, OHC. Whether Buchanan and Chase agreed upon a cease fire, however, is open to question. The source for this is Schuckers, whose source was clearly Carrington. Schuckers summarized the Chase proposal and then said that "the result" of the meeting between Chase and Buchanan was "that the prosecutions were soon

after dropped without embarrassment to either jurisdiction." Schuckers, *Chase*, 181–82. If a cease fire was agreed in July, however, would Chase have continued to attack the federal government in August for arresting state officers? See *Ohio State Journal* (Columbus), August 13, 1857; "Ohio Politics," *New York Times*, August 29, 1857, 3. And if he really reached an agreement with Buchanan, why didn't Chase mention this in 1864, when he summarized the rescue case for Trowbridge? See Chase to John Trowbridge, March 19, 1864, Warden, *Chase*, 350–51.

60 *Ohio State Journal* (Columbus), August 13, 1857.

61 Ibid.

62 *Cadiz (OH) Sentinel*, September 3, 10, 1857; *Coshocton (OH) Progressive Age*, October 7, 1857; *Eaton (OH) Democrat*, September 10, 17, 1857; *M'Arthur (OH) Democrat*, September 3, 10, 17, 1857; *Steubenville (OH) True American*, October 7, 1857; *Cincinnati Enquirer*, August 27, October 7, 1857 (quote in October 7); "Negro Suffrage," *Summit County Beacon* (Akron, OH), October 7, 1857, 2.

63 Chase to Alphonso Taft, May 3, 1857, Taft Papers, LC; "Grand Republican Demonstration," *Ohio State Journal* (Columbus), August 21, 1857, 2; "Ohio Politics," *New York Times*, August 29, 1857, 3; Chase to Alphonso Taft, March 5, 1858, Taft Papers, LC.

64 "Grand Republican Demonstration," *Ohio State Journal* (Columbus), August 21, 1857, 2; "Ohio Politics," *New York Times*, August 29, 1857, 3; Michael Woods, "'Tell Us Something About State Rights': Northern Republicans, State Rights, and the Coming of the Civil War," *Journal of the Civil War Era* 7 (2017): 242–68.

65 Chase diary, August 1857, *SPCP*, 1:297–99; *Ohio State Journal* (Columbus), September 14, 1857; Chase diary, September 14–October 13, 1857, *SPCP*, 1:299–305; *Ohio State Journal* (Columbus), October 27, 1857 (Chase traveled 3,700 miles); Chase to Charles Sumner, November 23, 1857, *SPCP*, 2:466.

66 Chase to Nettie Chase, September 13, 1857, *SPCP*, 2:459–61.

67 Chase diary, October 13–17, 1857, *SPCP*, 1:304–6; Chase to Edward Pierce, October 15, 1857, Pierce Papers, Harvard; "Republicans!," *Ohio State Journal* (Columbus), October 13, 1857, 2; "The Election," ibid., October 14, 1857, 2; "The State Ticket Still in Doubt," ibid., October 15, 1857, 2; "The Election Still in Doubt," ibid., October 16, 1857, 2; *Ohio Statesman* (Columbus), October 13, 14, 15, 16, 17, 1857.

68 "The Election—Chase Ahead," *Ohio State Journal* (Columbus), October 17, 1857, 2; *New-York Tribune*, October 19, 1857; *New York Evening Post*, October 20, 1857; *Ohio Statesman* (Columbus), October 20, 21, 1857; *Cincinnati Enquirer*, October 24, 1857. On black voting, see Finkelman, "Race Discrimination in Antebellum Ohio," 377n18 ("adult males of mixed ancestry who were more than half white could vote"); Kennet Kusmer, *A Ghetto Takes Shape: Black Cleveland, 1870–1930* (Urbana: University of Illinois Press, 1976), 14–17; Kornblith and Lasser, *Elusive Utopia*, 70–72.

69 Chase to Charles Cleveland, November 3, 1857, *SPCP*, 2:462–63; Chase to Edward Pierce, November 7, 1857, Pierce Papers, Harvard; Kenneth Stampp,

America in 1857: A Nation on the Brink (New York: Oxford University Press, 1990), 242–50.

70 Potter, *Impending Crisis*, 297–321; Stampp, *America in 1857*, 281–303.

71 *New-York Tribune*, December 21, 1857; Lincoln to Lyman Trumbull, December 27, 1857, *CWL*, 2:430; Charles Sumner to Chase, January 10, 1858, in Palmer, *Sumner Letters*, 1:488; Chase to Sumner, January 18, 1858, in Bourne, 275–77; see Allen Guelzo, *Lincoln and Douglas: The Debates that Defined America* (New York: Simon & Schuster, 2008), 47–53.

CHAPTER 12: "Your Noble Lincoln," 1858–59

1 Chase, *Message of the Governor of Ohio to the Fifty-Third General Assembly at the Regular Session Commencing January 4, 1858* (Columbus, OH: Statesman Steam Press, 1858), 9–13. On the Panic of 1857, see Charles Calomiris and Larry Schweikart, "The Panic of 1857: Origins, Transmission, and Containment," *Journal of Economic History* 51 (1991): 807–34; James Huston, *The Panic of 1857 and the Coming of the Civil War* (Baton Rouge: Louisiana State University Press, 1987); Timothy Riddiough and Howard Thompson, "When Prosperity Merges into Crisis: The Decline and Fall of Ohio Life, Political Economy of Bank Suspension, and the Panic of 1857" (paper, December 21, 2016), available at SSRN, http://dx.doi .org/10.2139//ssrn.2888689.

2 Chase, *1858 Message*, 15–24. The legislature, over Chase's objection, appointed a commission to investigate the Breslin-Gibson defalcation.

3 Ibid., 36–38.

4 "Message of Governor Chase," *Chicago Tribune*, January 7, 1858, 3; *New-York Tribune*, January 8, 1858; *New York Evening Post*, January 8, 1858; *Ohio State Journal* (Columbus), January 13, 1858; Lincoln, Gettysburg Address, November 19, 1863, *CWL*, 7:23.

5 *Columbus (OH) Gazette*, January 15, 1858; *Perrysburg (OH) Journal*, January 21, 1858.

6 Joshua Giddings to Chase, February 1, 1858, Chase Papers, HSP; James Ashley to Chase, February 17, 1858, Chase Papers, LC; William Schouler to Chase, March 23, 1858, Chase Papers, HSP; Theodore Parker to Chase, March 29, 1858, *SPCP*, 3:6–7; Calvin Stowe to Chase, March 30, 1858, Chase Papers, LC; John Bingham to Chase, May 11, 1858, Chase Papers, LC.

7 Joshua Giddings to Chase, February 1, 1858, Chase Papers, HSP (Banks a weak candidate); *Congressional Globe*, February 2, 1858, 521 (Seward remarks); John Jay to Chase, February 22, 1858, Jay Family Papers, Columbia (Seward "seriously damaged"); Hiram Barney to Chase, February 23, 1858, Chase Papers, HSP (Seward "effectually disposed of"); Chase to John Bigelow, February 23, 1858, Bigelow Papers, Union College; William Schouler to Chase, March 23, 1858, Chase Papers, HSP; John Bingham to Chase, May 11, 1858, Chase Papers, LC; Stahr, *Seward*, 169–71.

8 Chase to John Jay, January 12, 1858, Jay Family Papers, Columbia; Chase to Edward Stansbury, February 27, 1858, Chase Papers, Huntington; Chase to Hiram Barney, February 28, 1858, Chase Papers, HSP.

9 Chase to Edward Pierce, January 30, 1858, Pierce Papers, Harvard (Richmond); Chase to W. F. Ritchie, February 19, 1858, in *Richmond Enquirer*, March 4, 1858.

10 Chase to Edward Pierce, June 28, 1858, Pierce Papers, Harvard (Ohio University and Marietta College); "The Annual Commencement at Hudson," *Summit County Beacon* (Akron, OH), July 14, 1858, 2 (Western Reserve College); *Ohio State Journal* (Columbus), July 14, 1858 (same); "Oberlin College Commencement," *Cleveland Daily Leader*, August 26, 1858, 2; *Pittsburgh Daily Post*, August 30, 1858; *Oberlin (OH) Evangelist*, September 1, 1858.

11 *Anti-Slavery Bugle* (New Lisbon, OH), February 21, 1857; Chase diary, February 24–25, 1857, *SPCP*, 1:269–70 (Chase attends trustee meeting at Wilberforce); *Holmes County Republican* (Millersburg, OH), March 5, 1857; Chase to Granville Waldegrave, November 1, 1863, *SPCP*, 4:169; Chase to Daniel Payne, September 29, 1868, Chase Papers, LC; "Late Chief Justice Chase," *Chicago Tribune*, May 22, 1873, 4 (Chase's will); see Charles Butcher, *Wilberforce University* (Wilberforce, OH: Wilberforce University, 1910); Nelson Strobert, *Daniel Alexander Payne: The Venerable Preceptor of the African Methodist Episcopal Church* (Lanham, MD: University Press of America, 2012), 74–81.

12 *Richmond Enquirer*, March 5, 1858 (Chase letter); Chase to George Brown, March 12, 1858, in *Herald of Freedom* (Wakarusa, Kansas Territory), March 28, 1858; Chase to Edward Pierce, April 29, 1858, Pierce Papers, Harvard; Chase to James Briggs, May 14, 1858, Chase Papers, HSP; Chase to Alexander Ramsay to Chase, May 27, 1858, Ramsay Papers, Minnesota; Abraham Lincoln, House Divided Speech, June 16, 1858, *CWL*, 2:461–62; Chase to Lincoln, June 13, 1859, *SPCP*, 3:14; see Guelzo, *Lincoln and Douglas*, 53–63; Holt, *Election of 1860*, 20 ("highly unusual" to nominate candidate for Senate).

13 Nathaniel Banks to Chase, July 20, 1858, Chase Papers, HSP (filed under 1859); "Commencement at Harvard College," *New York Herald*, July 23, 1858, 3; *Baltimore Exchange*, July 24, 1858; Theodore Parker to Chase, July 25, 1858, in John Weiss, ed., *Life and Correspondence of Theodore Parker* (New York: D. Appleton, 1864), 2:232; Chase to Parker, August 16, 1858, in ibid., 520–21; Parker to Chase, August 30, 1858, in ibid., 230–31; *New York Evening Post*, October 7, 1858 (thirty hours from NYC to Cincinnati). On Chase and Banks, see note 7 supra and Chase to Banks, November 11, 1855, Banks Papers, LC (introduction); Chase to Banks, February 4, 1856, ibid. (congratulates on election as speaker); Chase to Edward Pierce, November 7, 1857, Chase Papers, HSP (glad that Banks elected as governor); Banks to Chase, December 10, 1857, ibid. (glad Chase reelected).

14 Chase to Edward Pierce, August 3, 1858, Pierce Papers, Harvard; "Gov. Chase at Dartmouth College," *Cleveland Daily Leader*, August 3, 1858, 2; *Vermont Chronicle* (Bellows Falls), August 3, 1858; Amos Tuck to Chase, October 21, 1858, Chase Papers, LC.

15 *Newburyport (MA) Herald*, August 9, 1858; "Dinner to Governor Chase of Ohio," *New York Herald*, August 11, 1858, 4; "Dinner to Gov. Chase," *New York Times*, August 11, 1858, 5; *New-York Tribune*, August 11, 1858; *Cleveland Herald*, August 12, 1858 (from *Boston Courier*).

16 *Cleveland Herald*, August 12, 1858; *Perrysburg (OH) Journal*, August 19, 1858; *Holmes County Republican* (Millersburg, OH), August 26, 1858; Reynolds, *Abe*, 424–25 (connection between antislavery and Puritans).

17 Chase to Elizabeth Pike, August 12, 1858, Pike Papers, Maine.

18 Chase to Parker, August 16, 1858, in Weiss, *Theodore Parker*, 2:520 (from Newport); "Our Summer Retreats: Newport," *New York Herald*, August 20, 1858, 3 (Chase in Newport); *New-York Tribune*, August 21, 1858 (Chase at Field's reception); "Gov. Chase in New York," *Cleveland Daily Leader*, August 30, 1858, 2; see John Steele Gordon, *A Thread Across the Ocean: The Heroic Story of the Transatlantic Cable* (New York: Walker, 2003).

19 Chase to Charles Sumner, July 16, 1858, Bourne, 279.

20 *M'Arthur (OH) Democrat*, August 19, 1858; *Newark (OH) Advocate*, August 25, 1858; *National Era* (Washington, DC), August 26, 1858; *Ohio State Journal* (Columbus), September 1, 1858; Chase to John Bigelow, September 1, 1858, Bigelow Papers, Union College; "Gov. Corwin and Gov. Chase," *Cleveland Daily Leader*, September 3, 1858, 2; *New York Evening Post*, September 6, 1858. For more on Corwin, see Crofts, *Lincoln & the Politics of Slavery*, 125–30.

21 *Ohio State Journal* (Columbus), September 11, 1858; Chase to Kate Chase, September 15, 1858, Chase Papers, HSP. Several words in Chase's letter are illegible.

22 Chase to Kate Chase, September 15, 1858, Chase Papers, HSP; *Cincinnati Commercial*, October 1, 1858; *Ohio State Journal* (Columbus), October 1, 2, 1858.

23 *Ohio State Journal* (Columbus), October 2, 1858; "Great Doings in Hamilton County," *Chicago Tribune*, October 5, 1858, 2; "Gov. Chase's Speech," *Cleveland Daily Leader*, October 5, 1858, 2; *Weekly Hawk-Eye* (Burlington, IA), October 12, 1858.

24 *Ohio State Journal* (Columbus), August 31, 1858; "The State Elections," *New York Herald*, October 13, 1858, 4; *Illinois State Journal* (Springfield), October 14, 1858; "The Douglas Contest," *New York Times*, October 25, 1858, 4; Chase scrapbook, Chase Papers, HSP.

25 Chase to James Pike, May 12, 1858, in Pike, *First Blows*, 418–20 (opposes Douglas); Lincoln-Douglas debate, September 18, 1858, *CWL*, 3:145–46; Chase to Kate Chase, October 28, 1858, *Spur*, 169–70; Chase to Anson Miller, December 11, 1858, Miller Papers, Illinois Historical Society; Foner, *Fiery Trial*, 107–8.

26 "Gov. Chase of Ohio Coming," *Chicago Tribune*, October 19, 1858, 1; "Gov. Chase Coming," ibid., October 20, 1858, 1; *New York Times*, October 25, 1858. As late as October 18, Illinois Republicans were unsure whether Chase would come to speak. See Joseph Medill to Elihu Washburne, October 18, 1858, Washburne Papers, LC.

27 "The Ball Rolling On," *Chicago Tribune*, October 27, 1858, 1; Chase to Kate Chase, October 28, 1858, *Spur*, 169–70; "Senator Chase and Owen Lovejoy,"

Daily Morning News (Davenport, IA), November 2, 1858, 1; *Rock Island (IL) Daily Commercial*, November 2, 1858; *Mendota (IL) Press*, November 4, 1858; *Bureau County Republican (Princeton, IL)*, November 4, 1858; Chase to Edward Pierce, November 10, 1858, Pierce Papers, Harvard.

28 "Chase and Payne Off for Illinois," *Eaton (OH) Democrat*, October 28, 1858, 2 (from *Cleveland Plain Dealer*); *Cincinnati Gazette*, November 1, 1858.

29 *Chicago Times*, October 7, 1858 (Illinois should not disgrace itself by electing Lincoln, an "advocate of negro equality and negro citizenship"); *Illinois State Journal* (Springfield), October 21, 1858 (insisting that Lincoln was *not* in favor of "nigger equality"); "The Ball Rolling On," *Chicago Tribune*, October 27, 1858, 1 (too late for printed speeches); *Rock Island (IL) Argus*, November 1, 1858 (Chase and Lovejoy "nigger equality champions").

30 *Rock Island (IL) Commercial*, November 3, 1858 ("Lincoln Will Be Our Next Senator!"); *Mendota Press*, November 4, 1858; *Ottawa Republican*, November 6, 1858; Chase to Anson Miller, December 11, 1858, Miller Papers, Illinois Historical Society; Lincoln to Chase, April 30, 1859, *CWL*, 3:378; see Guelzo, *Lincoln and Douglas*, 281–93.

31 *Ohio State Journal* (Columbus), November 8, 1858; Howells, *Years of My Youth*, 154–55.

32 Chase, *Message of the Governor of Ohio to the Fifty-Third General Assembly at the Adjourned Session Commencing January 3, 1859* (Columbus, OH: Statesman Steam Press, 1859); *Highland Weekly News*, January 13, 1859; see Forrest Nabors, *From Oligarchy to Republicanism: The Great Task of Reconstruction* (Columbia: University of Missouri Press, 2017), 46–51 (contrasting Northern and Southern education).

33 Gamaliel Bailey to Chase, January 16, 1859, Chase Papers, HSP.

34 Chase to Gamaliel Bailey, January 24, 1859, Chase Papers, HSP.

35 *New-York Tribune*, January 17, 1859; *Albany (NY) Evening Journal*, January 18, 1859.

36 Chase to John Jay, March 3, 1859, Jay Family Papers, Columbia; Donn Piatt to Chase, March 4, 1859, Chase Papers, HSP; Chase to my dear friend, March 23, 1859, ibid.; Gamaliel Bailey to Chase, March 23, 1859, ibid.; *Ohio Statesman* (Columbus), March 31, 1859; *National Era* (Washington, DC), April 7, 1859; *Columbus (OH) Gazette*, April 22, 1859.

37 James Briggs to Chase, April 16, 1859, Chase Papers, LC; *New-York Tribune*, April 16, 1859; Chase to James Briggs, April 19, 1859, Chase Papers, LC; *New-York Tribune*, April 26, 1859; Chase to T. R. Stanley, October 25, 1859, Bourne, 281–82; *Fremont (OH) Weekly Journal*, December 16, 1859.

38 Chase diary, February 17, 1859, *SPCP*, 1:310–11; *Ohio State Journal* (Columbus), February 18, 1859 (obituary); Chase to Charles Sumner, February 19, 1859, Sumner Papers, Harvard; Chase to Edward Pierce, February 28, 1859, Pierce Papers, Harvard; Chase to John Jay, March 3, 1859, Jay Family Papers, Columbia.

39 For good accounts of the Oberlin-Wellington Rescue; see Lubet, *Fugitive Justice*, 229–314; Kornblith and Lasser, *Elusive Utopia*, 94–104; Brent Morris, *Oberlin*, 208–22.

40 "Siege of Oberlin," *Anti-Slavery Bugle* (New Lisbon, OH), December 18, 1858, 3; Lubet, *Fugitive Justice*, 248–51.

41 Lubet, *Fugitive Justice*, 250–77.

42 "Langston Sentenced," *Cleveland Daily Leader*, May 13, 1859, 1; *Ashtabula (OH) Weekly Telegraph*, May 28, 1859; *St. Cloud (MN) Democrat*, June 16, 1859; *Vermont Journal* (Windsor), June 18, 1859; Lubet, *Fugitive Justice*, 278–98.

43 *Ohio State Journal* (Columbus), May 19, 1859; "Mass Convention on Tuesday," *Cleveland Daily Leader*, May 23, 1859, 2; Jacob Shipherd, ed., *History of the Oberlin-Wellington Rescue* (Boston: J. P. Jewett & Co., 1859), 196–225 (Wolcott's argument).

44 "Afternoon Meeting," *Cleveland Daily Leader*, May 25, 1859, 1; Chase to John Sherman, March 3, 1866, *SPCP*, 5:79.

45 "Afternoon Meeting," *Cleveland Daily Leader*, May 25, 1859, 1; Lubet, *Fugitive Justice*, 304 ("now there was no mistaking Salmon Chase's direct challenge to President Buchanan").

46 Chase diary, August 9, 1851, and January 17, 1857, *SPCP*, 1:224 and 255; *Cincinnati Daily Press*, May 26–27, 1859; "Habeas Corpus Before the Supreme Court," *Ohio State Journal* (Columbus), May 26, 1859, 2; "The Habeas Corpus Cases," ibid., May 28, 1859, 2; "The Decision," ibid., May 30, 1859, 2; "The Habeas Corpus Cases," ibid., May 31, 1859, 2; "Opinion of Justice Swan," ibid., June 1, 1859, 2; "The Habeas Corpus Case," *Cleveland Daily Leader*, May 31, 1859, 2; Lubet, *Fugitive Justice*, 307–11.

47 Chase draft platform, June 2, 1859, Chase Papers, LC; Chase to Edward Pierce, June 2, 1859, Pierce Papers, Harvard; "Republican State Convention," *Ohio State Journal* (Columbus), June 3, 1859, 2; "Republican State Convention," *Cleveland Daily Leader*, June 4, 1859, 2; see Anbinder, *Nativism and Slavery*, 250–53; Sinha, *Slave's Cause*, 365–69.

48 Lincoln to Chase, June 9, 1859, *CWL*, 3:384.

49 Chase to Lincoln, June 13, 1859, *SPCP*, 3:14–15.

50 Lincoln to Chase, June 20, 1859, *CWL*, 3:386. I have translated a bit of Latin into English.

51 *Burlington (VT) Daily Times*, May 31, 1859; *Wisconsin State Journal* (Madison), June 1, 1859; Chase to Charles Sumner, June 20, 1859, Bourne, 281; *Buffalo Commercial*, June 24, 1859; "The Late Dr. Bailey," *Chicago Tribune*, June 24, 1859, 2; *National Era* (Washington, DC), June 30, 1859; Elizabeth Pike to Chase, July 7, 1859, Chase Paper LC; Chase to Pike, July 13, 1859, Pike Papers, Maine.

52 Chase to Robert Hosea, July 25, 1859, Hosea Papers, Harvard (leaving Columbus that day for New England); *Hartford Courant*, July 29, 1859; "Governor Chase at Yale," *Cleveland Daily Leader*, July 30, 1859, 2; "The Plymouth Monument Celebration," *Cleveland Daily Leader*, August 6, 1859, 2. On the settlement of Ohio, see David McCullough, *The Pioneers: The Heroic Story of the Settlers Who Brought the American Ideal West* (New York: Simon & Schuster, 2019).

53 Chase to Simon Cameron, August 6, 1859, Cameron Papers, LC; "Interesting from Washington," *New York Herald*, August 29, 1859, 4; Paul Kahan, *Amiable Scoundrel: Simon Cameron, Lincoln's Scandalous Secretary of War* (Hastings, NE: Potomac Press 2016), 137.

54 Joseph Medill to Chase, April 26, 1859, *SPCP*, 3:10–11; ibid., May 11, 1859, Chase Papers, HSP; ibid., June 8, 1859, *SPCP*, 3:13–14; ibid., July 27, 1859, Chase Papers, HSP; James Ashley to Chase, July 29, 1859, Chase Papers, LS (re: Medill); Joseph Medill to Chase, August 30, 1859, Chase Papers, HSP.

55 William Brisbane to Chase, March 14, 1859, Chase Papers, OHC; Carl Schurz to Chase, July 30, 1859, September 3, 1859, Chase Papers, HSP.

56 *Ohio State Journal* (Columbus), August 9, 1859 (speaking schedule); *Highland Weekly News*, August 11, 1859 (fabrication); *Ravenna Ohio Democrat*, August 24, 1859; Chase to Edward Pierce, August 28, 1859, *SPCP*, 3:16–17; "Republican Meeting in Lake," *Cleveland Daily Leader*, September 2, 1859, 2; Chase to Kate Chase, September 2, 1859, *Spur,* 172–73; *Ohio State Journal* (Columbus), September 12, 1859 (speaking schedule); Chase to Lincoln, September 29, 1859, Lincoln Papers, LC (from Toledo); Chase to Kate Chase, October 1, 1859, Chase Papers, HSP (not home for several more days); Chase diary, September 29–30, 1859, *SPCP*, 1:312; Chase to Edward Pierce, October 7, 1859, Chase Papers, HSP (on way to make last speech of campaign).

57 *Ohio State Journal* (Columbus), August 29, 1859; "Speech of Gov. Chase," *Chicago Tribune*, August 29, 1859, 3; "Speech of Governor Chase at Sandusky," *Cleveland Daily Leader*, August 30, 1859, 1; ibid. August 31, 1859, 1; ibid., September 1, 1859, 1; *New York Times*, September 3, 1859.

58 *Ohio Statesman* (Columbus), October 16, 1859; Lincoln speech, October 16, 1859, *CWL*, 3:401–2; *Ohio State Journal* (Columbus), September 17, 1859; "Douglas—Ranney—Pugh & Co.," *Cleveland Daily Leader*, September 20, 1859, 2; Lincoln to Chase, September 21, 1859, *CWL,* 3:470–71; Chase to Lincoln, September 29, 1859, Lincoln Papers, LC; see Gary Ecelbarger, *The Great Comeback: How Abraham Lincoln Beat the Odds to Win the 1860 Republican Nomination* (New York: Thomas Dunne Books, 2008), 54–76.

59 *New-York Tribune*, October 13, 1859; *Ohio State Journal* (Columbus), November 4, 1859.

60 "Insurrection and Bloodshed at Harper's Ferry," *Cleveland Daily Leader*, October 19, 1859, 2; *Cincinnati Enquirer*, October 19, 1859; *Illinois State Register* (Springfield), October 20, 1859; Chase to Joseph Barrett, October 29, 1859, *SPCP,* 3:22–23. On Brown, see Tony Horwitz, *Midnight Rising: John Brown and the Raid That Sparked the Civil War* (New York: Henry Holt, 2013). On the press coverage of Brown, see Ratner and Teeter, *Fanatics and Fire-Eaters,* 71–84.

61 Chase endorsement, December 20, 1856, in Franklin Sanborn, *The Life and Letters of John Brown* (Boston: Roberts Brothers, 1885), 363–64; Chase to Nelson Hawkins, June 6, 1857, in ibid., 363–64.

62 *Ohio State Journal* (Columbus), October 24, 1859.

63 Joseph Medill to Lincoln, September 10, 1859, Lincoln Papers, LC; Chase to James Briggs, October 24, 1859, Chase Papers, LC (hopes New York papers publish speech); Chase to James Briggs, October 24, 1859, Chase Papers, HSP (hopes Cleveland papers publish speech); Joseph Medill to Chase, October 30, 1859, Chase Papers, HSP.

64 Henry Wise to Chase, November 25, 1859, and Chase to Wise, December 1, 1859, both in "Correspondence Between Governor Wise of Virginia, President Buchanan and Governor Chase of Ohio," *Detroit Free Press*, December 11, 1859, 1. On Brown's role, see Allen Guelzo, *Fateful Lightning: A New History of the Civil War and Reconstruction* (New York: Oxford University Press, 2012), 118–20; Potter, *Impending Crisis*, 372–84.

65 Chase to Thomas Spooner, December 18, 1859, *SPCP*, 3:23–24; "Meeting of the Republican National Committee," *New York Herald*, December 22, 1859, 4; *New-York Tribune*, December 23, 1859; Ecelbarger, *Great Comeback*, 113. For Welles and Chase, see Chase to Welles, August 22, 1855, Welles Papers, LC; George Bunce to Chase, October 22, 1855, ibid.; Chase to Welles, October 26, 1855, ibid.; Preston King to John Bigelow, May 10, 1860, in John Bigelow, *Retrospections of an Active Life* (New York: Baker & Taylor, 1909–13), 1:289 (Welles supports Chase).

CHAPTER 13: "The Interests of the Cause," 1860

1 Chase, *Message of the Governor of Ohio to the Fifty-Fourth General Assembly at the Session Commencing January 2, 1860* (Columbus, OH: Statesman Steam Press, 1860), 3, 28; "Inaugural Address of William Dennison," *Cleveland Daily Leader*, January 10, 1860, 2.

2 Chase, *1860 Message*, 30–31.

3 "Message of Governor Chase," *Cleveland Daily Leader*, January 4, 1860, 2; *Cincinnati Enquirer*, January 4, 1860; "Ohio's Response," *Chicago Tribune*, January 5, 1860, 2; "Message of Governor Chase," *New York Times*, January 6, 1860, 1; *New York Evening Post*, January 9, 1860; "Commercial Matters," *New York Tribune*, January 7, 1860, 7; Chase, *1860 Message*, 30 ("earnestly condemn"); see Matthew Clavin, *Toussaint Louverture and the American Civil War: The Promise and Peril of a Second Haitian Revolution* (Philadelphia: University of Pennsylvania Press, 2011).

4 "Visits of the Governors and Legislatures of Kentucky and Tennessee in Ohio," *Ohio State Journal* (Columbus), January 27, 1860, 2; *Louisville (KY) Courier*, January 28, 1860; "Speech of Ex-Gov. Chase at Columbus," *New York Times*, January 31, 1860, 3; *Ravenna (OH) Republican Democrat*, February 1, 1860; *New-York Tribune*, February 4, 1860.

5 Chase to James Briggs, November 21, 1859, Chase Papers, HSP (Hayes); James Ashley to Chase, December 19, 1859, Chase Papers, LC; *Columbus (OH) Gazette*, January 13, 1860; Ashley to Chase, January 14, 1860, Chase Papers, LC; "Democratic Convention—U.S. Senator," *Pomeroy (OH) Weekly Telegraph*, January 17, 1860, 1; "Republican Caucus—United States Senator," ibid.,

January 24, 1860, 2; "The Senatorial Question," *Ohio State Journal* (Columbus), February 1, 1860, 2; "Editorial Correspondence," *Pomeroy (OH) Weekly Telegraph,* February 7, 1860. The best account of the struggle to make Chase senator is in the *Pomeroy (OH) Weekly Telegraph*, whose editor, Tobias Plant, was also a Republican member of the Ohio House.

6 "Senatorial Nomination," *Ohio State Journal* (Columbus), February 2, 1860, 2; "Gov. Chase Nominated," *Cleveland Daily Leader*, February 2, 1860, 2; *Columbus (OH) Gazette*, February 3, 1860; "Editorial Correspondence," *Pomeroy (OH) Weekly Telegraph*, February 14, 1860, 2 ("we shall see").

7 *Ohio State Journal* (Columbus), February 3, 1860; "The Reception," ibid., February 4, 1860, 2; "Election of United States Senator," *Cleveland Daily Leader*, February 4, 1860, 2; *Pomeroy (OH) Weekly Telegraph*, February 14, 1860.

8 *Ohio State Journal* (Columbus), February 3, 1860; "S. P. Chase Elected Senator," *Cleveland Daily Leader*, February 3, 1860, 2; "Election of United States Senator," *Cleveland Daily Leader*, February 4, 1860, 2; "Salute Fired in Honor of the Election of Gov. Chase," *Quad-City Times* (Davenport, IA), February 4, 1860, 1.

9 "Republican State Conventions," *Cleveland Daily Leader*, January 23, 1860, 2 (district conventions should be held on or about February 24); "Republican District Convention," *Cleveland Daily Leader*, February 24, 1860, 2; *Columbus (OH) Gazette*, February 24, 1860; "District Convention," *Jeffersonian Democrat* (Chardon, OH), February 24, 1860, 2; *Ravenna (OH) Republican Democrat*, February 29, 1860 ("said that all the congressional delegates north of the National Road are favorable to Chase"); Chase to David Cartter, April 1, 1860, Cartter Papers, LC ("I desire nobody to prefer me to the cause"); Chase to Benjamin Cowan, May 11, 1860, Chase Papers, CHLA ("love the cause better than myself").

10 "The Presidency—Abraham Lincoln," *Chicago Tribune*, February 16, 1860, 2; *New-York Tribune*, February 20, 1860.

11 Republican Central Committee to Chase, October 29, 1859, Chase Papers, LC (invitation for November 3 celebration); "Republican Ratification Meeting," *New York Times*, November 4, 1859, 1 (report on Cooper Union celebration; includes Chase declination); Lincoln, Cooper Union speech, February 27, 1860, *CWL*, 3:522–50; Harold Holzer, *Lincoln at Cooper Union: The Speech That Made Lincoln President* (New York: Simon & Schuster, 2005); Goodwin, *Team of Rivals*, 219 (Chase "turned down an invitation to speak at Cooper Union"). Goodwin fails to note that the invitation to Chase was in late 1859, for a postelection celebration, not the right occasion for a speech like Lincoln made in early 1860. Republican Central Committee to Chase, October 29, 1859, Chase Papers, LC (invitation for November 3 celebration); "Republican Ratification Meeting," *New York Times*, November 4, 1859, 1 (includes Chase letter declining invitation).

12 "The Irrepressible Conflict," *New York Times*, March 1, 1860, supp. 1–2 (Seward speech); *New York Evening Post*, March 2, 1860; Chase to Benjamin Wade, March 4, 1860, Wade Papers, LC; Chase to Charles Sumner, April 6, 1860, Sumner Papers, Harvard; Stahr, *Seward*, 182–84.

13 *Albany (NY) Argus*, February 23, 1860 (advertises speech); Chase speech, February 23, 1860, Chase Papers, HSP; *Albany (NY) Evening Journal*, February 24, 1860 (reports speech).

14 *Ohio State Journal* (Columbus), March 2, 1860; Chase to Benjamin Wade, March 4, 1860, Wade Papers, LC; *New-York Tribune*, March 5, 1860; Chase to James Briggs, March 8, 1860. There is a letter from Wade to Chase, of March 5, 1860, among the Chase Papers at HSP, but this is not a response to Chase's letter of March 4, but instead a response to a request for a copy of a recent Wade speech. See Blue, *Chase*, 124 ("Wade's response was polite but noncommittal").

15 Charles Cleveland to Chase, March 3, 1860, Chase Papers, HSP; Erastus Hopkins to Chase, March 10, 1860, Chase Papers, LC; Edward Pierce to Chase, March 12, 1860, Chase Papers, HSP; Amos Tuck to Chase, March 14, 1860, Chase Papers, LC; Chase to Robert Hosea, March 18, 1860, Hosea Papers, Harvard; Chase to Pierce, March 19, 1860, Pierce Papers, Harvard; *Cincinnati Enquirer*, March 19, 1860 (Schurz lecture).

16 Chase to James Pike, March 19, 1860, in Pike, *First Blows*, 502; Joshua Giddings to Chase, March 26, 1860, Chase Papers, HSP ("Seward has the inside track"); Pike to Chase, April 7, 1860, Chase Papers, HSP ("Bates I have always regarded as an impossible candidate"); Chase to Richard Parsons, April 10, 1860, Chase Papers, HSP; Chase to Edward Pierce, May 10, 1860, Pierce Papers, Harvard; Chase notes re: Chicago delegates, May 1860, Chase Papers, HSP.

17 Chase to James Pike, March 19, 1860, in Pike, *First Blows*, 503; Chase to Charles Sumner, April 6, 1860, Sumner Papers, Harvard; Chase to Richard Parsons, April 10, 1860, Chase Papers, HSP; Chase to James Briggs, April 23, 1860, Chase Papers, LC; Chase to Richard Parsons, April 25, 1860, Chase Papers, HSP (from Washington); Chase to James Briggs, April 27, 1860, ibid.; "News from Washington," *New York Herald*, April 28, 1860, 6; Chase to James Briggs, April 29, 1860, Chase Papers, HSP; Holt, *Election of 1860*, 50–66 (Charleston).

18 Chase to Henry Cooke, May 5, 1860, Cooke Papers, Huntington.

19 "Baltimore Union Convention," *New York Times*, May 11, 1860, 1; Holt, *Election of 1860*, 67–82.

20 "The Presidential Contest," *New York Times*, May 11, 1860, 4; "Will the Game Win?," *Chicago Tribune*, May 12, 1860, 3; Holt, *Election of 1860*, 83–87.

21 See Stahr, *Seward*, 33, 185–86. Goodwin faults Chase for failing "to appoint a campaign manager" to "bargain and maneuver for him." Goodwin, *Team of Rivals*, 219.

22 Edward Pierce to Chase, May 13, 1860, *SPCP*, 3:27–28; "Our Special Chicago Despatch," *New York Herald*, May 16, 1860, 3. For the Chicago convention, see Ecelbarger, *Great Comeback*, 189–231; Holt, *Election of 1860*, 88–114.

23 *Proceedings of the National Republican Convention, Held at Chicago May 16th, 17th & 18th, 1860* (Chicago: Press & Tribune Office, 1860), 30; Stahr, *Seward*, 188–90.

24 *Proceedings of the National Republican Convention, 1860*, 30; "How Ohio Voted at Chicago," *Cleveland Daily Leader*, June 9, 1860, 2 (ballot-by-ballot vote of the Ohio delegation).

25 *Proceedings of the National Republican Convention, 1860,* 31–32; Ecelbarger, *Great Comeback,* 223–31; Holt, *Election of 1860,* 109–11; Stahr, *Seward,* 188–91.

26 *Ohio State Journal* (Columbus), May 19, 1860; *Daily Ohio Statesman* (Columbus), May 19, 1860.

27 Chase to Lincoln, May 19, 1860, *SPCP,* 3:28–29 (misdated by Chase as May 17); *Ohio State Journal* (Columbus), May 23, 1860; Chase to Samuel Wood, May 24, 1860, Kansas Historical Society; Chase to Richard Parsons, May 30, 1860, Chase Papers, HSP.

28 Chase to Hiram Barney, June 22, 1860, Barney Papers, Huntington; Elizabeth Pike to Chase, August 8, 1860, Chase Papers, HSP; Chase to Lyman Trumbull, October 14, 1860, Trumbull Papers, LC.

29 *Ohio State Journal* (Columbus), May 23, 1860.

30 Chase to James Underhill, June 11, 1860, Chase Papers, HSP; *Cincinnati Enquirer,* June 17, 1860; Caleb Smith to Chase, August 9, 1860, Chase Papers, LC; Chase to Smith, August 11, 1860, Chase Papers, Dartmouth.

31 "Gov. Chase in Michigan," *Cleveland Daily Leader,* August 2, 1860, 2; *Cass County Republican* (Dowagiac, MI), August 9, 16, 1860; *New-York Tribune,* August 18, 1860.

32 *Richmond (IN) Weekly Palladium,* August 30, 1860.

33 Ibid.

34 Elizabeth Pike to Chase, August 8, 1860, Chase Papers, HSP; Chase to Edward Pierce, August 31, 1860, Pierce Papers, Harvard; *New Hampshire Statesman* (Concord), September 8, 1860; "The Mass Meeting," *Exeter (NH) News-Letter,* September 10, 1860, 2.

35 Chase to William Child, September 10, 1860, Chase Papers, Dartmouth; *Burlington (VT) Times,* September 5, 12, 1860; *Vermont Watchman & State Journal* (Montpelier), September 14, 1860.

36 "Gov. Chase Returned," *Ohio State Journal* (Columbus), September 12, 1860, 2; "Republican Mass Meetings," ibid., September 17, 1860, 2; "Great Demonstration at Urbana," ibid., September 22, 1860, 1; Chase to Hiram Barney, September 22, 1860, Barney Papers, Huntington; Chase to John Stevens, September 23, 1860, Stevens Papers, NYHS; Chase to Hiram Barney, October 1, 1860, Barney Papers, Huntington (cannot come to New York before Ohio election day "without breach of positive engagements in our doubtful congressional districts"); "Governor Chase in Licking," *Ohio State Journal* (Columbus), October 5, 1860, 2.

37 Chase to William Mellen, September 24, 1860, Mellen Papers, Bowdoin. We do not have Mellen's letter but can infer much from Chase's response: "I am very much struck by your account of the state of sentiment in Kentucky and the South generally. It is I doubt not in the main correct, and yet I cannot but think there is more free soil sentiment in Kentucky willing to avow itself than you seem to think." On the Lower South's fears about the border states, see Freehling, *Secessionists Triumphant,* 22–24, 438–39.

38 "The Great Triumph in Ohio," *Ohio State Journal* (Columbus), October 13, 1860, 2; *Cleveland Herald,* October 15, 1860. On the fusion ticket, see Stahr, *Seward,* 207–8.

39 "Gov. Chase at Fort Plains," *New-York Tribune*, October 20, 1860, 6.

40 "Gov. Chase in Troy," *New-York Tribune*, October 20, 1860, 6.

41 Ibid.

42 "Gov. Chase at Fort Plains" and "Gov. Chase in Troy," *New-York Tribune*, October 20, 1860, 6.

43 "Speech of Gov. Chase of Ohio," *New York Times,* October 22, 1860, 1; "Third Congressional District," *New-York Tribune*, October 22, 1860, 1; "Hon. Salmon P. Chase," ibid., October 23, 1860, 1; "Gov. Chase in Brooklyn," ibid., October 24, 1860, 5; "Ex-Gov. Chase," ibid., October 26, 1860, 5 ("speaking daily"); *Brooklyn Evening Star*, October 24, 1860; *Cleveland Morning Leader*, October 25, 1860; *Poughkeepsie (NY) Eagle*, October 27, 1860.

44 Chase to William Cullen Bryant, November 2, 1860, Bigelow Papers, Union College; Chase to John Greenleaf Whittier, November 4, 1860, Whittier Papers, University of Virginia; Chase to Hiram Barney, November 5, 1860, Barney Papers, Huntington.

45 *Cleveland Morning Leader*, November 3, 1860; "Governor Chase in Kentucky," *New-York Tribune*, November 7, 1860, 6. For the context of Jackson's toast, see Howe, *What Hath God Wrought*, 372–73.

46 *New-York Tribune*, November 7, 1860. On secession, see Cynthia Nicoletti, *Secession on Trial*, 14–19.

47 Holt, *Election of 1860*, xi ("most consequential").

48 Chase to John Jay, November 6, 1860, Jay Family Papers, Columbia; Chase to Lincoln, November 7, 1860, Lincoln Papers, LC.

CHAPTER 14: "Inauguration First, Adjustment Afterwards," 1860–61

1 Charles Dana to Chase, November 7, 1860, Chase Papers, HSP; George Fogg to Chase, November 7, 1860, Chase Papers, LC; James Pike to Chase, January 4, 1861, Chase Papers, HSP.

2 Chase to Charles Dana, November 10, 1860, *SPCP,* 3:32; Chase to Hiram Barney, November 13, 1860, Barney Papers, Huntington; Barney to Chase, November 26, 1860, Chase Papers, HSP; Chase to Benjamin Cowen, November 26, 1860, Chase Papers, CHLA; Chase to Barney, November 29, 1860, Barney Papers, Huntington.

3 Chase to Lyman Trumbull, November 12, 1861, *SPCP,* 3:34. On the initial Republican response, see Crofts, *Lincoln & the Politics of Slavery,* 88–92; Russell McClintock, *Lincoln and the Decision for War: The Northern Response to Secession* (Chapel Hill: University of North Carolina Press, 2008), 46–57; David Potter, *Lincoln and His Party in the Secession Crisis* (New Haven, CT: Yale University Press, 1942), 1–17. For a brilliant account of how the minority in the Lower South in favor of immediate secession defeated the majority in favor of delay, see Freehling, *Secessionists Triumphant*, 345–498.

4 Ruhamah Hunt to Chase, November 23, 1860, Chase Papers, LC; Chase to Ruhamah Hunt, November 30, 1860, *SPCP,* 3:37–39. Ruhamah Hunt to Chase,

May 30, 1861, Chase Papers, LC. Chase considered and decided against publishing the letter to Hunt. Chase made a similar compensation proposal in Chase to John Greenleaf Whittier, November 23, 1860, *SPCP,* 3:35–37.

5 Buchanan message, December 3, 1860, in *Ohio State Journal* (Columbus), December 6, 1860; Chase to Elizabeth Goldsborough, December 30, 1860, Chase Papers, OHC.

6 Villard dispatches, November 29, 30, 1860, in Michael Burlingame, ed., *Sixteenth President-in-Waiting: Abraham Lincoln and the Springfield Dispatches of Henry Villard* (Carbondale: Southern Illinois University Press, 2018), 61–62 (Fogg in Springfield); George Fogg to Chase, December 12, 1860, Chase Papers, LC; Fogg to Lincoln, December 13, 1860, Lincoln Papers, LC.

7 *Albany (NY) Evening Journal,* November 24, 30, December 17, 1860; *New-York Tribune,* December 19, 1860 (Crittenden) and December 25, 1860 (Seward); see Crofts, *Lincoln & the Politics of Slavery,* 106–19; McClintock, *Lincoln and the Decision,* 95–104.

8 Chase draft article, December? 1860, Chase Papers, LC; Chase to George Fogg, December 15, 1860, *SPCP,* 3:41; Chase to William Seward, December 27, 1860, Seward Papers, Rochester. On the Niven microfilm, the draft article starts at 41:1166.

9 "Resignation of Gen. Cass," *Cleveland Daily Leader,* December 17, 1860, 2; "The News," *New York Herald,* December 17, 1860, 4 (Scott has resigned); "Who Is Responsible?," *Ohio State Journal* (Columbus), December 20, 1860, 2; "Washington Intelligence," *Chicago Tribune,* December 21, 1860, 2; "The Revolution in South Carolina," *New York Herald,* December 28, 1860, 4; "The War Commenced," ibid., December 29, 1860, 6; "The Ultimatum" and "Summary of Washington Gossip," *Ohio State Journal* (Columbus), December 29, 1860, 2; Freehling, *Secessionists Triumphant,* 476–79; Adam Goodheart, *1861: The Civil War Awakening* (New York: Alfred A. Knopf, 2001), 4–20; Stephen Sears, *Lincoln's Lieutenants: The High Command of the Army of the Potomac* (Boston: Mariner Books, 2017), 10–11; Walter Stahr, *Stanton: Lincoln's War Secretary* (New York: Simon & Schuster, 2017), 110–17.

10 Chase to Winfield Scott, December 29, 1860, *SPCP,* 3:43–44; Freehling, *Secessionists Triumphant,* 486–88; Stahr, *Stanton,* 114–17, 124–25.

11 Lincoln to Chase, December 31, 1860, *CWL,* 4:168; Chase to Lincoln, January 2, 1861, Lincoln Papers, LC; Chase to George Fogg, January 3, 1861, Fogg Papers, NHHS ("I go to Springfield today"); Villard dispatch, January 4, 1861, in Burlingame, *Sixteenth President-in-Waiting,* 159 (Chase arrived in Springfield); *Illinois State Journal* (Springfield), January 4, 1861; "The Revolutionary News of Yesterday," *New York Herald,* January 4, 1861, 4; "Progress of the Revolution in the South," ibid., January 5, 1861, 6; "The National Troubles," *New York Times,* January 4, 5, 1861, 1; see Freehling, *Secessionists Triumphant,* 476–96.

12 Villard dispatches, January 6, 1861, in Burlingame, *Sixteenth President-in-Waiting,* 160–63; Chase to Nathaniel Banks, January 6, 1861, Chase Papers, Yale; William Wallace to Ann Wallace, January 6, 1861, Wallace-Dickey Family

Papers, ALPL (sermon); Lincoln to Lyman Trumbull, January 7, 1861, *CWL,*
4:171; Chase to George Opdyke, January 9, 1861, *SPCP,* 3:44–45; Chase to
James Worthington, January 14, 1861, Chase Papers, Brown.

13 Villard dispatches, January 6, 1861, in Burlingame, *Sixteenth President-in-Waiting,*
160–61.

14 Lincoln to William Seward, December 8, 1860, *CWL,* 4:148–49 (offer); Seward to
Lincoln, December 26, 1860, Lincoln Papers, LC (acceptance); Lincoln to Simon
Cameron, December 31, 1860, *CWL,* 4:168; Lyman Trumbull to Lincoln, Janu-
ary 31, 1860, Lincoln Papers, LC; Lincoln to Simon Cameron, January 3, 1861,
CWL, 4:169–70; Villard dispatch, January 6, 1861, in Burlingame, *Sixteenth
President-in-Waiting,* 160–61; Lincoln to Lyman Trumbull, January 7, 1861, *CWL,*
4:171; Charles Ray to Elihu Washburne, January 7, 1861, Washburne Papers, LC;
Chase to George Opdyke, January 9, 1861, *SPCP,* 3:44–45; Chase to James Pike,
January 10, 1861, ibid., 46–47; Chase to Lincoln, January 11, 1861, ibid., 48;
John Killinger to Lincoln, January 15, 1861, Lincoln Papers, LC ("protest against
the selection of a gentleman with so offensive a tariff record as Mr. Chase for the
Treasury"); see Harold Holzer, *Lincoln President-Elect: Abraham Lincoln and the Great
Secession Winter 1860–1861* (New York: Simon & Schuster, 2008), 200–209.

15 Chase to George Opdyke, January 9, 1861, *SPCP,* 3:44–45; Chase to Elihu
Washburne, January 14, 1861, Washburne Papers, LC.

16 Chase to Hiram Barney, January 8, 1861, Chase Papers, LC; Chase to George
Opdyke, January 9, 1861, *SPCP,* 3:45–46; Chase to John Jay, January 16, 1861,
Jay Family Papers, Columbia; Elizabeth Lee to Phillip Lee, January 17, 1861,
in Virginia Laas, ed., *Wartime Washington: The Civil War Letters of Elizabeth Blair
Lee* (Urbana: University of Illinois Press, 1991), 25.

17 Chase to William Seward, January 10, 1861, Seward Papers, Rochester; *Ohio
State Journal* (Columbus), January 16, 1861 (Seward speech); Chase to Stephen
Harding, January 27, 1861, Harding Papers, Indiana; Chase to John Greenleaf
Whittier, February 1, 1861, Whittier Papers, Essex Institute (quote); Stahr,
Seward, 222–25.

18 Villard dispatches, January 4, 10, 1861, in Burlingame, *Sixteenth President-in-Waiting,* 160 and 174; Chase to Lincoln, January 11, 1861, *SPCP,* 3:48–49.

19 Chase to Norman Judd, January 20, 1861, *SPCP,* 3:50–51.

20 Chase to Charles Sumner, January 26, 1861, Sumner Papers, Harvard; Chase to
Stephen Harding, January 27, 1861, Harding Papers, Indiana; Chase to Lincoln,
January 28, 1861, *SPCP,* 3:52–53; *Ohio State Journal* (Columbus), February 1,
1861; *Cincinnati Commercial,* February 2, 1861; *Fremont (OH) Journal,* February 8,
1861; *Leavenworth (KS) Times,* February 13, 1861; *Evansville (IL) Daily Journal,*
February 14, 1861; "Mottoes for the Day," *Chicago Tribune,* February 16, 1861,
2; "Mottoes for Our Flag," *Cleveland Daily Leader,* February 22, 1861, 2; *New-
York Tribune,* February 28, 1861.

21 Chase to Andrew Johnson, January 11, 1861, *PAJ,* 4:152; "Passage of the Kansas Bill," *New York Times,* January 22, 1861, 1; *Ohio State Journal* (Columbus),
January 29, 1861.

22 *Philadelphia Inquirer*, January 19, 1861 (Virginia resolution); *Ohio State Journal* (Columbus), January 29, 30, 31, 1861; Chase to Joshua Giddings, January 31, February 1, 1861, Giddings Papers, OHC; Chase to Robert Hosea, February 1, 1861, Hosea Papers, Harvard; "Columbus Correspondence," *Cleveland Daily Leader*, February 1, 1861, 2; Chase to Norton Townshend, February 1, 1861, Townshend Papers, Clements Library (leaves for Washington tomorrow); Chase to Henry Carrington, February 3, 1861, Carrington Papers, Yale (from Washington); "The Peace Convention," *Washington (DC) Evening Star*, February 4, 1861, 3 (Chase in convention); Robert Gunderson, *Old Gentlemen's Convention: The Washington Peace Conference of 1861* (Madison: University of Wisconsin Press, 1961), 36–37.

23 "The Peace Convention," *Washington (DC) Evening Star*, February 4, 1861, 3; "Personal," ibid., February 14, 1861, 2 ("probably there"); Lucius Chittenden, *A Report of the Debates and Proceedings in the Secret Sessions of the Conference Convention for Proposing Amendments to the Constitution of the United States, Held at Washington, D.C., in February A.D. 1861* (New York: D. Appleton, 1864), 11; Crofts, *Lincoln & the Politics of Slavery*, 189–91; Goodheart, *1861*, 87–88; Gunderson, *Old Gentlemen's Convention*, 10–13, 43, 105–6.

24 George Fogg to Lincoln, February 5, 1861, Lincoln Papers, LC; Stahr, *Seward*, 233–34, 241–42.

25 Chittenden, *Report of the Debates*, 34–35; Gunderson, *Old Gentlemen's Convention*, 46–50. Examples of news reports include *New York Evening Post*, February 15, 1861; "The National Crisis," *New York Herald*, February 15, 1861, 1; "Mr. Guthrie's Propositions," *Detroit Free Press*, February 16, 1861, 2; "Important from Washington," *New York Herald*, February 27, 1861, 1. One of the Ohio delegates advised his brother that "you can rely upon nothing you see in the papers" and that "I have not yet seen a true report of anything done in convention." Reuben Hitchcock to Peter Hitchcock, February 16, 1861, in Robert Gunderson, "Letters from the Washington Peace Conference of 1861," *Journal of Southern History* 22 (1951): 388.

26 Chase et al to Austin Blair, February 15, 1861, in "Another Effort to Appoint Commissioners," *Detroit Free Press*, February 17, 1861, 1; *New York Evening Post*, February 18, 1861 (Republican states should send delegates); Gunderson, *Old Gentlemen's Convention*, 72–80.

27 Chittenden, *Report of the Debates*, 43–45.

28 "Mr. Lincoln in Washington," *New York Times*, February 25, 1861, 1; "At Willard's," *Washington (DC) Evening Star*, February 25, 1861, 3; "The Irrepressible Conflict Among Republicans," *New York Herald*, February 26, 1861, 4; Lucius Chittenden, *Recollections of President Lincoln and His Administration* (New York: Harper & Brothers, 1891), 70–72; Gunderson, *Old Gentlemen's Convention*, 62–71, 84–85; Brad Meltzer and Josh Mensch, *The Lincoln Conspiracy* (New York: Flatiron Books, 2020), 307–18; Stahr, *Seward*, 237–39.

29 Chittenden, *Report of the Debates*, 426–33; see Freehling, *Secessionists Triumphant*, 436 ("no more territory").

30 "Glorious Result," *Washington (DC) Evening Star*, February 27, 1861, 2; "The Peace Conference," *New York Herald*, February 28, 1861, 1; Michael Burlingame, *Abraham Lincoln: A Life* (Baltimore: Johns Hopkins University Press, 2008), 2:43–44; Chittenden, *Report of the Debates,* 433–34, 437–39, 440–46, 452; Gunderson, *Old Gentlemen's Convention,* 86–92. Chase is not recorded as opposing the second article, but I think this is probably an oversight by the reporter. See Chittenden, *Report of the Debates,* 443.

31 "The Compromisers' Action," *New-York Tribune*, March 2, 1861, 4; Crofts, *Lincoln & the Politics of Slavery,* 213–21.

32 *New York Times*, February 25, 1861; "Mr. Lincoln's Cabinet," *New York Herald*, February 28, 1861, 1; "The Struggle for Cabinet Portfolios," *Washington (DC) Evening Star*, March 1, 1861, 2; Lincoln list, March 1, 1861, Lincoln Papers, LC; "The New Cabinet Officers," *New York Herald*, March 2, 1861, 3 (Pennsylvania men oppose Chase "on account of his free trade notions"); "From Washington," *New-York Tribune*, March 7, 1861, 5 (Weed "denouncing Chase"); "Our Washington Letter," *Chicago Tribune*, March 11, 1861, 2 ("Chase would be dropped"); Burlingame, *Lincoln*, 2:52–58; Holzer, *Lincoln President-Elect*, 430–34; Stahr, *Seward*, 241–45.

33 "The Levee of the President Elect," *New York Herald*, March 1, 1861, 1; Charles Francis Adams diary, March 1, 1861, Massachusetts Historical Society.

34 Chase to Charles Dana, March 1, 1861, Chase Papers, ALPL; *New-York Tribune*, March 6, 1861.

35 *Congressional Globe*, March 4, 1861, 1433; "Inauguration of Abraham Lincoln," *Washington (DC) Evening Star*, March 4, 1861, 3; Burlingame, *Lincoln*, 2:60; Crofts, *Lincoln & the Politics of Slavery,* 226–33; Stahr, *Seward*, 245–47.

36 Lincoln inaugural address, March 4, 1861, *CWL,* 4:266–71; "Inauguration of Abraham Lincoln," *Washington (DC) Evening Star*, March 4, 1861, 3; Burlingame, *Lincoln*, 2:61–62.

37 "Rumors About the Cabinet," *New York Herald*, March 5, 1861, 8; "Inauguration Day," *New York Times*, March 6, 1861, 1; Chase to William Fessenden, March 13, 1861, Chase Papers, NYHS (from Rugby House); Simon Cameron to Chase, May 11, 1861, Chase Papers, HSP (will come to Rugby House); "A Woman's Memories," *New-York Tribune*, March 8, 1891, 16 (Nettie's recollections); Goodwin, *Team of Rivals*, 329 (inaugural ball); Peg Lamphier, *Kate Chase and William Sprague: Politics and Gender in a Civil War Marriage* (Lincoln: University of Nebraska Press, 2003), 54 (same).

38 *Congressional Globe*, March 5, 1861, 1435; "The New Cabinet," *Washington (DC) Evening Star*, March 5, 1861, 2; *New-York Tribune*, March 5, 1861; "Our Washington Letter," *Chicago Tribune*, March 11, 1861, 2 (five minutes); Chase to John Trowbridge, March 21, 1864, *SPCP,* 4:344.

39 Chase to Lincoln, March 6, 1861, Lincoln Papers, LC; Chase to William Dennison, March 6, 1861, Chase Papers, HSP; *National Republican* (Washington, DC), March 7, 1861 (all the heads of department "have accepted the positions tendered to them"); *New-York Tribune*, March 7, 1861 (Chase called on Dix);

"The New Administration," *New York Herald*, March 8, 1861, 1 (Cabinet officers took charge of their departments on Thursday morning).

CHAPTER 15: "We Have the War upon Us," 1861

1 "Lincoln Playing a New Role," *Nashville Union*, March 13, 1861, 2 (Cabinet composed of "men of the most ultra and dangerous character"); "The Commissioners of the Southern Confederacy," *New York Herald,* March 14, 1861, 4 ("abolitionist ultraism" in the Cabinet); Bray Hammond, *Sovereignty and an Empty Purse: Banks and Politics in the Civil War Era* (Princeton, NJ: Princeton University Press, 1970), 39; Mihm, *Nation of Counterfeiters*, 309; Heather Cox Richardson, *The Greatest Nation of the Earth: Republican Economic Policies During the Civil War* (Cambridge, MA: Harvard University Press, 1997), 31 ("more ambitious and self-confident than knowledgeable about finances").

2 *New-York Tribune*, October 20, 1860; *New York Times*, January 25, 1861; *Hartford Courant*, February 14, 1861; Lucius Chittenden, *Personal Reminiscences, 1840–1890* (New York: Richmond, Croscup, 1893), 90; Jane Flaherty, "'The Exhausted Condition of the Treasury' on the Eve of the Civil War," *Civil War History* 55: (1999), 244-77.

3 "News of the Day," *New York Times*, March 23, 1861, 4; *Baltimore Exchange*, March 25, 1861; Chase to Lincoln, April 2, 1861, Lincoln Papers, LC (claiming that bids show "decided improvement in finances"); "The New Treasury Loan," *Chicago Tribune*, April 3, 1861, 1; "Financial and Commercial," *New York Herald*, April 4, April 8, 1861, 5; Chase to John Jay, April 6, 1861, Jay Family Papers, Columbia.

4 Lincoln inaugural address, March 4, 1861, *CWL*, 4:266; see William Cooper, *We Have the War upon Us: The Onset of the Civil War, November 1860–April 1861* (New York: Alfred A. Knopf, 2012), 204–40; McClintock, *Lincoln and the Decision*, 187–225.

5 "Formidable Preparations at Charleston," *Chicago Tribune*, February 28, 1861, 2; "Condition of Affairs in Charleston Harbor," *Cleveland Daily Leader*, March 4, 1861, 2; Joseph Holt and Winfield Scott to Lincoln, March 5, 1861, Lincoln Papers, LC; see McClintock, *Lincoln and the Decision*, 199–216; Stahr, *Seward*, 259–61.

6 Lincoln to Cabinet members, March 15, 1861, *CWL*, 4:284–85; Chase to Lincoln, March 16, 1861, Lincoln Papers, LC.

7 Lincoln to Chase, March 18, 1861, *CWL*, 4:292.

8 Chase to Lincoln, March 1861, Lincoln Papers, LC; see "Threatened Trouble in the Cabinet," *New York Herald*, April 8, 1861, 1 ("the frantic efforts to blockade Southern ports that are being made, will not prevent goods from being distributed, via New Orleans, Charleston, and Savannah, throughout the North and Northwest").

9 Dr. Elkanah Williams to Chase, June 17, 1859, Chase Papers, LC; John Nicolay, seating chart, March 28, 1861, Nicolay Papers, LC; William Howard Russell, *My Diary North and South* (Boston: T. O. H. P. Burnham, 1863), 62.

10 Winfield Scott to Simon Cameron, March 28, 1861, *OR*, vol. 1, 200–201; Chase to Lincoln, March 29, 1861, Lincoln Papers, LC; McClintock, *Lincoln and the Decision*, 230–33; Sears, *Lincoln's Lieutenants*, 21–23; Stahr, *Seward*, 266–68.

11 Lincoln to Robert Chew, April 6, 1861, *CWL*, 4:323–24; "No News Today from Charleston," *Washington (DC) Evening Star*, April 12, 1861, 2; Edwin Stanton to James Buchanan, April 12, 1861, in George Curtis, *Life of James Buchanan* (New York: Harper & Brothers, 1883), 2:541–42; "The War Commenced," *Washington (DC) Evening Star*, April 13, 1861, 3; "The Surrender of Fort Sumter," ibid., April 15, 1861, 3.

12 Lincoln proclamation, April 15, 1861, *CWL*, 4:331–32; Lincoln proclamation, April 19, 1861, ibid., 338–39; Chase to George Bancroft, February 6, 1866, *SPCP*, 5:76–77; Guelzo, *Fateful Lightning*, 280–84; Sears, *Lincoln's Lieutenants*, 30–32; Stahr, *Seward*, 280–83.

13 "Mayor Brown's Speech," *Baltimore Sun*, April 20, 1861, 1; Michael Kline, *The Baltimore Plot: The First Conspiracy to Assassinate President Lincoln* (Yardley, PA: Westholme, 2008), 348–50.

14 Chase to Alphonso Taft, April 28, 1861, *SPCP*, 3:63–64.

15 Chase to Lincoln, April 25, 1861, *SPCP*, 3:61–62; Lincoln to Scott, April 25, 1861, *CWL*, 4:344; Stahr, *Seward*, 283–84.

16 "Arrival and Departure of the Troops," *New York Herald*, April 19, 1861, 3; "The News," ibid., April 20, 1861; 4; *National Republican* (Washington, DC), April 24, 30, 1861; "The Rhode Island Regiment," *Washington (DC) Evening Star*, April 29, 1861, 2; Goodheart, *1861*, 176–96; Goodwin, *Team of Rivals*, 352–54; McPherson, *Battle Cry of Freedom: The Civil War Era* (New York: Oxford University Press, 1988), 274–75, 284–87.

17 *New York Evening Post*, March 29, April 4, 1860; "The Rhode Island Election," *Wisconsin State Journal* (Madison), April 5, 1860, 1; "Rhode Island Election," *Hillsdale (MI) Standard*, April 17, 1860, 2 ($50 per voter); Hay diary, April 26, 1861, in Michael Burlingame and John Ettlinger, eds., *Inside Lincoln's White House: The Complete Civil War Diary of John Hay* (Carbondale: Southern Illinois University Press, 1997), 12; John Oller, *American Queen*, 45–59.

18 *Cadiz (OH) Sentinel*, May 29, 1861; *Rock Island (IL) Argus*, May 29, 1861; "Gov. Sprague," *Baltimore Sun*, May 30, 1861, 1.

19 Harry Carman and Reinhard Luthin, *Lincoln and the Patronage* (New York: Columbia University Press, 1943); Stahr, *Seward*, 252–59.

20 Chase to W. H. Seward, March 20, 1861, *SPCP*, 3:54–55; Lincoln to Chase, May 8, 1861, *CWL*, 4:361–62.

21 Chase to W. H. Seward, March 20, 1861, Seward Papers, Rochester; Seward to Chase, March 27, 1861, Huntington; Seward to Chase, March 27, 1861, Chase Papers, HSP; Seward to Lincoln, March 28, 1861, Lincoln Papers, LC; Chase to John Sherman, March 28, 1861, John Sherman Papers, LC; *Buffalo Commercial*, October 14, 1862 (death of Edward); "Chief Justice Chase," *New York Herald*, May 8, 1873, 3 (parallels between brothers); Carman and Luthin, *Patronage*, 167–68; Stahr, *Seward*, 256.

22 Chase to Hiram Barney, March 23, 1861, Chase Papers, LC; Barney to Chase, March 25, 1861, Chase Papers, HSP; "The Rush for Office," *New York Herald*, March 25, 1861, 1; Chase to William Allen Butler, June 17, 1861, Chase Papers, LC; Butler to Chase, June 25, July 1, 1861, ibid.; Niven, *Chase*, 239–40; Stahr, *Seward*, 257–58.

23 Chase to Lincoln, April 18, 1861, Lincoln Papers, LC; Chase to John Cisco, May 24, 25, 1861, Cisco Papers, LC; Cisco to Chase, May 29, 1861, NARG 56.

24 William Mellen to Chase, February 20, 1861, Chase Papers, HSP; Chase to Mellen, March 22, 1861, NARG 366; Mellen to Chase, March 25, 1861, Chase Papers, HSP; Chase to Mellen, April 6, 1861, NARG 366; Chase to Mellen, April 7, 1861, Mellen Papers, Bowdoin; Mellen to Chase, April 10, 1861, Chase Papers, HSP.

25 James Gallatin to Chase, March 27, 1861, in Albert Bolles, *The Financial History of the United States from 1861 to 1885* (New York: D. Appleton & Co., 1886), 7–8; George Coe to John Stevens, May 10, 1861, Stevens Papers, NYHS; "Dispatch to the Associated Press," *New York Times*, May 12, 1861, 1; Chase to John Cisco, May 17, 1861, *SPCP*, 3:64–65; Chase to John Stevens, May 22, 1861, Stevens Papers, NYHS; Chase to William Gray, May 25, 1861, NARG 53; "Financial and Commercial," *New York Herald*, May 27, 1861, 2.

26 Chase to Thornton Lathrop, January 2, 1869, *SPCP*, 5:289–91.

27 Jay Cooke to Henry Cooke, March 25, 1861, Cooke Papers, HSP; Henry Cooke to Jay Cooke, April 9, 1861, ibid.; Chase to Jay Cooke, April 20, 1861, in Ellis Oberholtzer, *Jay Cooke: Financier of the Civil War* (Philadelphia: G. W. Jacobs, 1907), 1:136–37; Jay Cooke to Chase, May 15, 1861, ibid., 137–38; Jay Cooke to Henry Cooke, May 15, 1861, ibid., 138–39; Henry Cooke to Jay Cooke, May 17, 1861, Cooke Papers, HSP. Cooke needs a new biography: the most recent one is Henrietta Larson, *Jay Cooke, Private Banker* (Cambridge, MA: Harvard University Press, 1936).

28 Lincoln proclamation, May 3, 1861, *CWL*, 4:353–54; General Orders Nos. 15 & 16, May 4, 1861, *OR*, ser. 3, vol. 1, 151–57; Chase to John Trowbridge, March 20, 1864, *SPCP*, 4:345 (Chase worked with McDowell and Franklin on orders); Emory Upton, *The Military Policy of the United States* (Washington, DC: Government Printing Office, 1904) (quoting Franklin on Chase's role). The draft proclamation appears to have some editing by Chase. Draft proclamation, May 3, 1861, Lincoln Papers, LC.

29 Irvin McDowell to Chase, May 16, 1861, Chase Papers, HSP; "Important Letter from Mr. Seward," *New York Herald*, May 18, 1861, 1 (McDowell promoted to brigadier general); General Orders No. 26, May 27, 1861, *OR*, vol. 2, 653 (forming department; placing McDowell in charge); McDowell testimony, December 26, 1861, in *Report of the Joint Committee on the Conduct of the War* (Washington, DC: Government Printing Office, 1863), 2:35–38; *Alexandria (VA) Gazette*, July 16, 1862 (McDowell a Chase protégé); Chase to Enoch Carson, September 8, 1862, Stern Papers, LC (meeting McDowell); Chase to William Bryant, September 4, 1862, *SPCP*, 3:259 ("I recommended General McDowell as I did

General McClellan"); "A Woman's Memories," *New York Tribune*, June 7, 1891, 16 (Nettie); Donald, *Lincoln*, 305–7; Sears, *Lincoln's Lieutenants*, 37–40.

30 Benjamin Butler to Winfield Scott, May 24, 27, 1861, *OR,* vol. 2, 52, 648; Simon Cameron to Chase, May 25, 1861, Chase Papers, HSP; "Important from Fort Monroe," *New York Times*, May 27, 1861, 1; see Goodheart, *1861*, 312–15.

31 Simon Cameron to Benjamin Butler, May 30, 1861, *OR,* ser. 3, vol. 1, 243; Chase to John Trowbridge, March 21, 1864, *SPCP,* 4:346 ("The secretary of war conferred with me, and I submitted my suggestions to him in the form of a letter, which he adopted with some slight modification"); see Goodheart, *1861*, 327–47; Louis Masur, *Lincoln's Hundred Days: The Emancipation Proclamation and the War for the Union* (Cambridge, MA: Belknap Press, 2012), 15–18.

32 *Philadelphia Inquirer*, April 10, 1861 (copperhead); *New York Times*, April 17, 1861; *Louisville (KY) Daily Courier*, June 21, 1861; Lovell Rousseau to Chase, June 22, 1861, Chase Papers, HSP; *The Tennessean*, July 3, 1861; Chase to George McClellan, July 7, 1861, *SPCP,* 3:74; Chase to Rousseau, July 11, 1861, NARG 56; Chase to John Trowbridge, March 21, 1864, *SPCP,* 4:345–46; Chase to Murat Halstead, August 31, 1868, Chase Papers, OHC ("sort of Assistant Secretary of War for Kentucky & Tennessee"); William Harris, *Lincoln and the Border States: Preserving the Union* (Lawrence: University Press of Kansas, 2014), 80–118.

33 Chase to George McClellan, July 7, 1861, *SPCP,* 3:74; William Nelson to Andrew Johnson, July 11, 1861, *PAJ,* 4:558; Nelson to Chase, July 16, 1861, Johnson Papers, LC; Nelson to Chase, July 23, 1861, *SPCP,* 3:80–82; Nelson to Chase, September 26, 1861, Anderson Papers, LC (denies that he has been drinking); Donald Clark, *The Notorious "Bull" Nelson: Murdered Civil War General* (Urbana: Southern Illinois University Press, 2011).

34 Chase to Henry Carrington, May 5, 1861, Carrington Papers, Yale (claims credit for McClellan's appointment); George McClellan to Chase, June 26, 1861, in Stephen Sears, ed., *The Civil War Papers of George B. McClellan* (New York: Ticknor & Fields, 1989), 36–37 (responds to letters of 19 and 20 June); Chase to McClellan, July 7, 1861, *SPCP,* 3:74–75; McClellan to Chase, July 10, 1861, in Sears, *Papers of McClellan*, 50; Stephen Sears, *George B. McClellan: The Young Napoleon* (New York: Ticknor & Fields, 1988).

35 *Ohio Statesman* (Columbus), June 16, 1861 (from *Cincinnati Commercial*); Chase to Simon Cameron, June 28, 1861, NARG 56; Chase to Martin Potter, July 8, 1861, Cameron Papers, LC; Chase to Potter, July 22, 1861, Chase Papers, HSP; Chase to William Gray, September 18, 1861, Schuckers, 431; Paul Kahan, *Amiable Scoundrel: Simon Cameron, Lincoln's Secretary of War* (2016).

36 John Motley to Mary Motley, June 23, 1861, in George William Curtis, ed., *The Correspondence of John Lothrop Motley* (New York: Harper & Brothers, 1889), 1:387; William Sommers, "John Lothrop Motley: The Witty US Minister to Vienna," *American Diplomacy* (September 2017) (quoting Motley to Sumner).

37 John Motley to Mary Motley, June 23, 1861, in Curtis, *John Motley,* 389.

38 Ibid., 1:389–90.

39 Ibid., 1:390–91.

40 There is a debate among historians about whether Lincoln and Chase, as early as 1860 or 1861, planned to emancipate the Southern slaves. James Oakes, in *Freedom National*, 49–54, claims they did. Daniel Crofts responds that this is "history written as we might like it to have been" and that the Oakes interpretation "cannot stand scrutiny." Crofts, *Lincoln and the Politics of Slavery*, 277; see Gary Gallagher, *The Union War* (Cambridge, MA: Harvard University Press, 2011). I agree with Crofts and Gallagher.

41 "The Review" and "The Flag Raising," *Washington (DC) Evening Star*, July 5, 1861, 3.

42 Lincoln, Message, July 4, 1861, *CWL*, 4:436–41.

43 Chase, *Report of the Secretary of the Treasury on the Finances* (July 1861), 5–7. Much of the report was printed in the papers. See "Report of Secretary Chase," *New York Times*, July 6, 1861, 5.

44 Chase, *Report of July 1861*, 12–13.

45 Ibid., 9–11.

46 "The Treasury Report," *New York Times*, July 8, 1861, 4; *New-York Tribune*, July 8, 1861.

47 Chase to William Fessenden, June 18, 1861, Fessenden Papers, Bowdoin; William Fessenden to Andrew Johnson, June 24, 1861, *PAJ*, 4:152; Chase to Thaddeus Stevens, July 15, 1861, NARG 56; Elihu Washburne to Chase, July 15, 1861, NARG 56.

48 Act of July 17, 1861, *Statutes at Large*, 12:259–60; Max Edling, *A Hercules in the Cradle: War, Money, and the American State, 1783–1867* (Chicago: University of Chicago Press, 2014), 187; Oberholtzer, *Cooke*, 145.

49 *National Republican* (Washington, DC), July 18–20, 1861; Simon Cameron to Chase, July 21, 1861, Chase Papers, HSP; Goodwin, *Team of Rivals*, 370–76; McPherson, *Battle Cry of Freedom*, 339–47; Stahr, *Seward*, 299–300.

50 "A Woman's Memories," *New-York Tribune*, June 7, 1891, 16.

51 Chase to John Cisco, July 22, 1861, NARG 53; Chase to William Mellen, July 23, 1861, *SPCP*, 3:79–80 ("prestige of victory"); Sears, *Lincoln's Lieutenants*, 76–78.

52 Trade Act of 1861, July 13, 1861, *Statutes at Large*, 12:255–58; Chase to William Fessenden, July 22, 1861, NARG 56; Chase to Thaddeus Stevens, July 23, 1861, NARG 56; Revenue Act of 1861, August 5, 1861, *Statutes at Large*, 12:292–313; Lincoln proclamation, August 16, 1861, *CWL*, 4:487–88; Richardson, *Greatest Nation*, 110–15.

53 Chase to William Fessenden, July 26, 1861, NARG 107; Act of August 5, 1861, *Statutes at Large*, 12:313 ("deposit any"); First Confiscation Act, August 6, 1861, ibid., 12:319; Richardson, *Greatest Nation*, 213–17.

54 "Gen. Fremont at St. Louis," *Chicago Tribune*, July 26, 1861, 2; Chase to John Frémont, August 4, 1861, *SPCP*, 4:85–86; Chase to Joseph Cable, October 23, 1861, Chase Papers, HSP ("I did not favor General Frémont's appointment"); Chaffin, *Pathfinder*, 456–59.

55 Chase to Lincoln, August 9, 1861, Lincoln Papers, LC ("obliged to go to New York today"); "Financial and Commercial," *New York Herald*, August 12, 1861, 3;

ibid., August 13, 1861, 3; ibid., August 14, 1861, 3; ibid., August 15, 1861, 5; ibid., August 17, 1861, 2 (includes copy of the plan as adopted); *New-York Tribune*, August 12–17, 1861; George Coe notes, August 1861, in Theodore Patterson, *History of the Banks in 1861* (1927) (typescript in the Patterson Papers, LC); Chase to John Stevens, August 16, 1861, Stevens Papers, NYHS; Chase to John Stevens, August 19, 1861, NARG 53.

56 "Inspection Reviews," *Washington (DC) Evening Star*, August 21, 1861, 2; *Philadelphia Inquirer*, August 22, 1861; Oberholtzer, *Cooke*, 155–57 (quoting Cooke memoir).

57 *Philadelphia Inquirer*, September 2, 1861; "The National Loan," *Chicago Tribune*, September 5, 1861, 2; *Burlington (VT) Daily Times*, September 7, 1861; "The Great National Loan," *New York Herald*, September 10, 1861, 8.

58 Frémont proclamation, August 30, 1861, *OR*, vol. 3, 466–67; Joshua Speed to Chase, September 2, 1861, *SPCP*, 3:92–94; Garrett Davis to Chase, September 3, 1861, *SPCP*, 3:94–95; Green Adams to Chase, September 4, 1861, Chase Papers, HSP; Chase to Adams, September 5, 1861, *SPCP*, 3:95–97; William Nelson to Chase, September 8, 1861, Chase Papers, HSP (Frémont proclamation a "Godsend" to the opposition in Kentucky).

59 Lincoln to John Frémont, September 2, 1861, *CWL*, 4:506–7; Frémont to Lincoln, September 8, 1861, Lincoln Papers, LC; Lincoln to Frémont, September 11, 1861, *CWL*, 4:517–18; Joseph Medill to Chase, September 15, 1861, *SPCP*, 3:97–98; Benjamin Plumly to Chase, September 15, 1861, Chase Papers, LC (supports Frémont); "Lincoln's Instructions to Fremont," *Chicago Tribune*, September 16, 1861, 1; Benjamin Farrar to Chase, September 16, 1861, Chase Papers, LC.

60 Chase to August Belmont, July 1, 1861, in August Belmont, *Letters Speeches and Addresses of August Belmont* (printed privately, 1892), 109; Jay Cooke to Chase, September 7, 1861, in Oberholtzer, *Cooke*, 159; James Gordon Bennett to Chase, September 9, 1861, Chase Papers, LC; *Philadelphia Inquirer*, September 13, 1861; Chase to August Belmont, September 13, 1861, in Belmont, *Letters Speeches*, 110–11; *Daily Green Mountain Freeman* (Montpelier, VT), September 16, 1861; *New York Herald*, September 17, 1861. Hammond, who viewed the 1861 national loan as pointless, ignored these reports. See Bray Hammond, *Sovereignty and an Empty Purse: Banks and Politics in the Civil War* (1970), 109–10. Richardson, in *Greatest Nation*, 41–45, has a good discussion of the 1861 national loan.

61 "The Preparation of Treasury Notes," *New York Herald*, September 15, 1861, 1; Chase to John Hamilton, October 1, 1861, Schuckers, 278.

62 *Reading (PA) Times*, September 18, 1861; *Philadelphia Ledger*, September 19, 1861; Chase to Augustus Boyle, December 11, 1872, *SPCP*, 5:363–64 ("motives of humanity"); see "General Spinner and the Women Clerks," *Women's Journal*, January 10, 1891, 16–17; Jessica Ziparo, *This Grand Experiment: When Women Entered the Federal Workforce in Civil War-Era Washington, D.C.* (Chapel Hill: University of North Carolina Press, 2017), 20–23.

63 Chase to Henry Vail, September 10, 1861, NARG 53; Chase to John Sherman, October 1, 1861, Sherman Papers, LC; Chase to Larz Anderson, October 2, 1861, Schuckers, 430–31.

64 Chase to Simeon Nash, September 26, 1861, Schuckers, 277–78; Minutes of meeting with Chase, September 28, 1861, Stevens Papers, NYHS; "Financial and Commercial," *New York Herald*, September 30, 1861, 8; Chase to John Williams, October 1, 1861, NARG 53 ("however harmless"); Chase to William Aspinwall, October 1, 1861, NARG 53; "Financial and Commercial," *New York Herald*, October 1, 1861, 5; ibid., October 2, 1851, 8. Hammond's criticism of Chase fails, in my view, to consider the practical and political problems he faced in accepting banknotes. See Hammond, *Sovereignty and an Empty Purse*, 110–30.

65 *Cincinnati Daily Press*, October 7, 1861 (Blair's charges); Chase to Simon Cameron, October 7, 1861, *SPCP*, 3:100; Howard Beale, ed., *The Diary of Edward Bates, 1859–1866*, October 22, 1861 (Washington, DC: Government Printing Office, 1933), 198–99; Chaffin, *Pathfinder*, 459–71; John Marszalek, *Commander of All Lincoln's Armies: A Life of Henry W. Halleck* (Cambridge, MA: Harvard University Press, 2004); Michael Smith, *The Enemy Within: Fears of Corruption in the Civil War North* (Charlottesville: University of Virginia Press, 2011), 67–94. For a few days, David Hunter commanded the Department of the West; then Lincoln divided the department and placed Henry Halleck in charge of the Department of the Missouri.

66 Chase to Joseph Cable, October 23, 1861, Schuckers, 423; Chase to Jesse Stubbs, November 1, 1861, *SPCP*, 3:105–6.

67 "Speech of Hon. Chas. Sumner," *Fall River (MA) Evening News*, October 12, 1861, 1.

68 Chase to Kate Chase, September 2, 1861, *Spur*, 183–84; ibid., September [1861?], Chase Papers, HSP; Nettie Chase to Kate, September 19, 1861, *Spur*, 184–85; William Sprague to Chase, September 23, 1861, Chase Papers, HSP. The undated letter seems to fit in with the September 2 letter, which says that Kate had been in Newport. Curiously, Sprague does not mention Kate in his letters to Chase from this period.

69 Rutherford Hayes to Chase, June 29, 1861, Chase Papers, LC; Chase to William Nelson, September 18, 1861, Schuckers, 429–30; Chase to John Sherman, October 1, 1861, Sherman Papers, LC; Chase to Larz Anderson, October 2, 1861, Schuckers, 430–31; Chase to W. T. Sherman, October 13, 1861, *SPCP*, 3:101–2; Chase to John Sherman, November [18?], 1861, Sherman Papers, LC; *Chicago Tribune*, November 18, 1861 (Sherman assigned to Halleck).

70 Chase to Lincoln, November 1, 1861, Lincoln Papers, LC (draft paragraph re: Scott); Chase to Thomas Key, November 1, 1861, McClellan Papers, LC; Lincoln remarks, November 1, 1861, *CWL*, 5:10–11; Burlingame and Ettlinger, *Diary of John Hay*, November 1, 1861, 30; Sears, *McClellan*, 122–25; Stahr, *Stanton*, 146–47.

71 "Highly Important News," *New York Herald*, November 17, 1861, 1; "Slidell and Mason," ibid., November 18, 1861, 1; "Great Financial Success," ibid.,

November 19, 1861, 6; Stahr, *Seward*, 307–10: Gordon Warren, *Fountain of Discontent: The Trent Affair and Freedom of the Seas* (Boston: Northeastern University Press, 1981).

72 Chase to James Pollack, November 20, 1861, NARG 104; ibid., December 9, 1863, NARG 53 ("in God we trust"); ibid., May 10, 1864, NARG 53; Chase to Charles McIlvaine, April 14, 1865, Warden, 637; U.S. Treasury, "History of 'In God We Trust,'" Treasury Department website, https://www.treasury.gov/about/education/pages/in-god-we-trust.aspx.

73 Edwin Stanton to H. L. M. Barlow, November 23, 1861, in Stahr, *Stanton*, 148; *New-York Tribune*, November 25, 1861; Chase to Simon Cameron, November 26, 1861, NARG 53, and November 27, 1861, Schuckers, 279–81; Edward Pierce, "The Contrabands at Fortress Monroe," *Atlantic Monthly* (November 1861), 626–40; Chase to John Trowbridge, March 21, 1864, *SPCP*, 4:346 (Chase and Cameron "agreed very early that the necessity of arming them was inevitable," but they were "alone in that opinion.").

74 Lincoln message, December 3, 1861, *CWL*, 5:35–53; Worthington Snethen to Chase, December 10, 1861, Chase Papers, LC; Donald, *Lincoln*, 320; Masur, *Lincoln's Hundred Days*, 30–33.

75 Lincoln message, December 3, 1861, *CWL*, 5:35–53; "Report of the Secretary of War," *Baltimore Sun*, December 4, 1861, 1; *Chicago Tribune*, December 5, 1861 (praises Cameron's report); ibid., December 7, 1861 (condemns "emasculation"); Worthington Snethen to Chase, December 10, 1861, Chase Papers, LC; Donald, *Lincoln*, 320; Goodwin, *Team of Rivals*, 404–5; Stahr, *Stanton*, 148–49. I do not accept Goodwin's view that Cameron blindsided Lincoln. Welles recalled that the Cabinet heads "presented to the president an abstract of the essential parts of their respective reports." If this is right, Lincoln's failure was not only that he did not ask to see Cameron's report in draft form, but also he did not bother to *read* the summary that Cameron provided him. Howard Meneely, ed., "Three Manuscripts of Gideon Welles," *American Historical Review* 31 (1926): 485.

76 Chase, *Report of the Secretary of the Treasury on the State of the Finances for the Year Ending June 30, 1861* (Washington, DC: Government Printing Office, December 1861).

77 Ibid., 17–20.

78 "Financial and Commercial," *New York Herald*, December 12, 1861, 2; *Boston Daily Advertiser*, December 13, 1861; *Chicago Tribune*, December 13, 1861; *Cleveland Morning Leader*, December 13, 1861; "Financial and Commercial," *New York Herald*, December 13, 1861, 8.

79 Chase, draft message, December 1861, *SPCP*, 1:329–31; Chase, draft message, February 1862, Lincoln Papers, LC; Lincoln, message, March 6, 1864, *CWL*, 5:144–46. There are differences between the two Chase versions, perhaps because Chase did not retain a copy of what he first provided Lincoln.

80 Chase diary, December 9, 1861, *SPCP*, 1:312–13.

81 Ibid., December 10–12, 1861, 1:313–17.

82 William Sprague to Chase, December 1, 1861, NARG 366; William Reynolds to Chase, December 11, 1861, ibid. (about to depart from New York); Chase to

Edward Pierce, December 20, 1861, Chase Papers, LC (come to Washington); William Reynolds to Chase, December 23, 1861, NARG 366 (just arrived South Carolina); Chase to Hiram Barney, December 31, 1861, NARG 56; William Reynolds to Chase, January 1, 1862, *SPCP,* 3:116–18; Chase to Edward Pierce, January 4, 1862, *SPCP,* 118–19 ("sympathize with"); *Chicago Tribune,* January 8, 1862; *Liberator* (Boston), January 10, 1862. Many of the primary sources are in Ira Berlin et al., eds., *The Wartime Genesis of Free Labor: The Lower South* (Cambridge: Cambridge University Press, 1990). For secondary accounts, see Willie Lee Rose, *Rehearsal for Reconstruction: The Port Rose Experiment* (Indianapolis: Bobbs-Merrill 1964), 3–26, and Chandra Manning, *Troubled Refuge: Struggling for Freedom in the Civil War* (New York: Alfred A. Knopf, 2016), 78–95.

83 "Startling News from England—Imminent Prospect of War," *New York Times,* December 16, 1861, 4; John Cisco to Chase, December 16, 1861, *SPCP,* 3:112–13.

84 John Cisco to Chase, December 17, 1861, NARG 56; Chase diary, December 18, 1861, *SPCP,* 1:317; "Financial and Commercial," *New York Herald,* December 18, 1861, 2; *New-York Tribune,* December 18, 1861; "Financial and Commercial—Mr. Chase Arrived," *New York Herald,* December 19, 1861, 5; "Financial and Commercial—The Bank Presidents," ibid., December 20, 1861, 2; Chase to Jay Cooke, December 23, 1861, Oberholtzer, *Cooke,* 186–87; "Financial and Commercial," *New York Herald,* December 24, 1861, 5 (weekly specie report and "the gold having gone into private safes in the city and into the vaults of the country banks").

85 Chase diary, December 25, 1861, *SPCP,* 1:318–20; "The *Trent* Affair," *New York Times,* December 29, 1861, 1 (prints *Trent* correspondence); Stahr, *Seward,* 312–23.

86 Chase to John Cisco, December 29, 1861, *SPCP,* 3:113–14; "Financial and Commercial," *New York Herald,* December 30, 1861, 3; *New-York Tribune,* December 30–31, 1861.

CHAPTER 16: "Slavery Must Go," Early 1862

1 Chase diary, January 1–2, 1862, *SPCP,* 1:320–21; Beale, *Diary of Edward Bates,* January 1, 1862, 221; Goodwin, *Team of Rivals,* 409–10; Stahr, *Seward,* 324.

2 Chase diary, January 6, 1862, *SPCP,* 1:321–22; see Bruce Tap, *Over Lincoln's Shoulder: The Committee on the Conduct of the War* (Lawrence: University Press of Kansas, 1998).

3 Chase diary, January 9, 1862, *SPCP,* 1:324; Henry Cooke to Chase, January 10, 1862, Chase Papers, HSP; Chase to Kate Chase, January 10, 12, 1862, *SPCP,* 3:102–3; Chase to John Stevens, January 17, 1862, *SPCP,* 120; Nettie Chase to Kate Chase, January 26, 28, 1862, *Spur,* 195–96; Jay Cooke to Chase, January 31, 1862, Cooke Papers, HSP (Nettie not quite well enough to travel).

4 *New-York Tribune,* January 1, 1862; Lincoln to Chase, January 2, 1862, *CWL,* 5:88; "News from Washington," *New York Herald,* January 11, 1862, 5; Chase diary, January 11, 1862, *SPCP,* 1:324; Ethan Rafuse, "Typhoid and Tumult:

Lincoln's Response to General McClellan's Bout with Typhoid Fever in the Winter of 1861–62," *Journal of the Abraham Lincoln Association* 18 (1997): 5–10; Sears, *McClellan*, 136–37; Stahr, *Stanton*, 152.

5 Lincoln to Simon Cameron, January 11, 1862, *CWL*, 5:96; Chase to Kate Chase, January 12, 1862, Chase Papers, HSP; Chase diary, January 12, 1862, *SPCP*, 1:324–26; Stahr, *Stanton*, 153.

6 Lincoln to Simon Cameron, January 11, 1862, *CWL*, 5:96–97 (issued January 13 but backdated); Chase memo, September 1862, in Schuckers, 446; George McClellan, *McClellan's Own Story* (New York: C. L. Webster, 1887), 155–59; Montgomery Meigs, "General M. C. Meigs on the Conduct of the War," *American Historical Review* 26 (1921): 292–93; Sears, *McClellan*, 140–41; Sears, *Lincoln's Lieutenants*, 137–40; Stahr, *Stanton*, 153. Sears rightly notes that McClellan's rudeness was "inexplicable." Sears, *Lincoln's Lieutenants*, 139.

7 Chase diary, January 14, 1862, *SPCP*, 1:326; Chase to William Fessenden, January 15, 1862, Fessenden Papers, Bowdoin (Fessenden note on the reverse side); *Chicago Tribune*, January 15, 1862; Chase to John Stevens Jr., January 17, 1862, *SPCP*, 3:120; Chase to Simon Cameron, January 18, 1862, Cameron Papers, LC; Fessenden to Elizabeth Warriner, January 19, 1862, Fessenden Papers, Bowdoin; Fessenden to Samuel Fessenden, January 19, 1862, ibid.; Stahr, *Stanton*, 154–57.

8 Chase to Martin Potter, February 17, 1862, *SPCP*, 2:135–36; Chase to Charles McIlvaine, February 17, 1862, Warden, 416; Edwin Stanton to Frederick Lander, February 17, 1862, in *New York Herald*, February 20, 1862. It is not clear when and how Chase met Lander, but they were friends by early 1862. See Chase to Lander, February 8, 1862, Chase Papers, HSP; Lander to Chase, February 8, 1862, Chase Papers, LC; Gary Ecelbarger, *Frederick W. Lander: The Great Natural American Soldier* (Baton Rouge: Louisiana State University Press, 2000), 208–12.

9 *New York Herald*, February 24, 1862; Goodwin, *Team of Rivals*, 418–21.

10 *Chicago Tribune*, March 6, 1862; *National Republican* (Washington, DC), March 6, 1862; "The Funeral of Gen. Lander," *New York Herald*, March 7, 1862, 1; *Philadelphia Inquirer*, March 7, 1862; Ecelbarger, *Frederick W. Lander*, 278–85.

11 Chase to Lincoln, March 8, 1862, Lincoln Papers, LC; George Meade to Margaretta Meade, March 9, 1862, Meade Papers, HSP; Lincoln to George McClellan, April 9, 1862, *CWL*, 5:185; Stephen Sears, *To the Gates of Richmond: The Peninsula Campaign* (New York: Ticknor & Fields, 1989), 9–11; Sears, *Lincoln's Lieutenants*, 155–56.

12 Stahr, *Stanton*, 181–83; Craig Symonds, *Lincoln and His Admirals* (New York: Oxford University Press, 2008), 136–41. I use the spelling used by Chase and his contemporaries, *Merrimac*.

13 George McClellan to Lincoln and Edwin Stanton, March 9, 1862, in Stephen Sears, *The Civil War Papers of George B. McClellan* (1989), 200; Chase diary, March 10, 1862, *SPCP*, 1:331; *New-York Tribune*, March 13, 1862; Sears, *Gates of Richmond*, 13–14; Sears, *Lincoln's Lieutenants*, 163–64; Stahr, *Stanton*, 182–83.

14 Lincoln order, March 11, 1862, *CWL*, 5:155; George McClellan to Randolph Marcy, March 11, 1862, in Sears, *Papers of McClellan*, 201–2; McClellan to the

Army of the Potomac, March 14, 1862, ibid., 211; Sears, *Gates of Richmond*, 21–22.

15 George McClellan to Lincoln, April 5, 1862, in Sears, *Papers of McClellan,* 228; Thomas Key to Chase, April 10, 1862, Chase Papers, HSP; Chase to Key, April 18, 1862, *SPCP,* 3:176–77.

16 John Dahlgren diary, April 19, 1862, in Madeline Dahlgren, *Memoir of John A. Dahlgren, Rear-Admiral United States Navy, by his Widow, Madeline Vinton Dahlgren* (Boston: J. R. Osgood, 1882), 364. There were short reports about this trip in the newspapers: see "General M'Dowell and the President," *New York Times,* April 22, 1862, 1; *New-York Tribune,* April 22, 1862; *Ohio Statesman* (Columbus), April 22, 1862. For some reason, this trip to see McDowell has not received much attention.

17 John Dahlgren diary, April 19, 1862, in Dahlgren, *Memoir,* 364–65; "Advance of Gen. McDowell," *New York Herald,* April 20, 1862, 1.

18 John Dahlgren diary, April 19, 1862, in Dahlgren, *Memoir,* 365. Dahlgren is not quite clear where he and Chase met "in the evening" of April 20.

19 Here is a sample of Chase letters to or from Union generals: Chase to Robert Anderson, August 31, 1861, Anderson Papers, LC; Chase to Nathaniel Banks, May 19, 1863, *SPCP,* 4:33–35; William Birney to Chase, July 21, 1863, *SPCP,* 4:90–91; Chase to James Blunt, May 4, 1864, Warden, 582–83; Napoleon Buford to Chase, March 1, 1864, *SPCP,* 4:312–13; Chase to Don Carlos Buell, July 29, 1862, Chase Papers, HSP; Chase to Ambrose Burnside, May 11, 1862, Chase Papers, ALPL; Chase to Benjamin Butler, June 24, 1862, *SPCP,* 3:218–19; Daniel Butterfield to Chase, December 20, 1862, Chase Papers, HSP; Henry Carrington to Chase, May 26, 1863, *SPCP,* 4:42–45; Chase to John Cochrane, October 18, 1862, Schuckers, 457–58; Chase to Jacob Cox, June 13, 1861, *SPCP,* 3:67; John Dix to Chase, November 21, 1861, *OR,* vol. 5, 662; Chase to John Frémont, August 4, 1861, *SPCP,* 3:85–86; James Garfield to Chase, May 5, 1863, *SPCP,* 4:22–23; Chase to Quincy Adams Gillmore, December 29, 1863, *SPCP,* 4:232–34; Chase to Ulysses Grant, July 4, 1863, *SPCP,* 4:75–76; Chase to Henry Halleck, March 9, 1862, Warden, 418–19; Rutherford Hayes to Chase, June 29, 1861, Chase Papers, LC; Chase to Joseph Hooker to Chase, May 25, 1863, *OR,* vol. 25, pt. 2, 524; Chase to David Hunter, February 14, 1863, *SPCP,* 3:381–82; Chase to Thomas Kane, September 2, 1863, Chase Papers, HSP; Erasmus Keyes to Chase, June 17, 1862, *SPCP,* 3:211–13; Frederick Lander to Chase, February 8, 1862, Chase Papers, HSP; Chase to Benjamin Ludlow, May 12, 1863, *SPCP,* 4:28–29; George McClellan to Chase, July 10, 1861, Sears, *Papers of McClellan,* 50–51; Irvin McDowell to Chase, October 17, 1861, Lincoln Papers, LC; Montgomery Meigs to Chase, November 17, 1864, Chase Papers, LC; Chase to Ormsby Mitchel, October 4, 1862, *SPCP,* 3:289–90; William Nelson to Chase, February 28, 1862, Chase Papers, HSP; Chase to John Pope, August 1, 1862, Chase Papers, HSP (sends photographs); William Rosecrans to Chase, August 3, 1862, *SPCP,* 3:239–40; Chase to Lovell Rousseau, October 25, 1862, Schuckers, 457–58; Rufus Saxton to Chase, January 22, 1864, *SPCP,* 4:259–60;

Chase to John Schofield, May 7, 1865, *OR,* vol. 47, pt. 3, 427; Chase to William Sherman, January 2, 1865, *SPCP,* 5:3–4; Chase to Lincoln, May 25, 1862, *OR,* vol. 12, pt. 3, 230 (coming to Washington with James Shields); Chase to Franz Sigel, September 18, 1863, Chase Papers, NYHS; Chase to George Thomas, December 23, 1864, Chase Papers, Indiana Historical Society; Egbert Viele to Chase, September 25, 1862, Chase Papers, LC; James Wadsworth to Chase, March 26, 1864, NARG 56.

20 William Nelson to Chase, April 10, 1862, *SPCP,* 3:167–70; Lovell Rousseau to Chase, April 15, 1862, *SPCP,* 3:171–76; Ron Chernow, *Grant* (New York: Penguin Press, 2017), 199–209; McPherson, *Battle Cry of Freedom,* 405–14; Williamson Murray and Wayne Hsieh, *A Savage War: A Military History of the Civil War* (Princeton, NJ: Princeton University Press, 2016), 147–59.

21 *National Republican* (Washington, DC), January 13, 1862; Chase to Kate Chase, January 14, 1862, Chase Papers, HSP ("bankers had gathered at our house"); Chase diary, January 15, 1862, *SPCP,* 1:326–27; *National Republican* (Washington, DC), January 16, 1862 (Chase points); Chase to John Stevens, January 21, 1862, Chase Papers, HSP; see Hammond, *Sovereignty and an Empty Purse,* 196–200.

22 Chase to Elbridge Spaulding, January 22, 1862, NARG 56; "The Finances of the Government," *New York Times,* January 22, 1862, 1 (Chase would "accept and cordially support" legal tender); "Financial and Commercial," *New York Herald,* January 23, 1862, 3.

23 Chase to Thaddeus Stevens, January 29, 1862, *SPCP,* 3:126–27.

24 Chase to Elbridge Spaulding, February 3, 1862, in Schuckers, 245–46; *Congressional Globe,* February 3, 1862, 617–18 (Spaulding); ibid., February 4, 1862, 630 (Morrill); ibid., 633 (Conkling); see Hammond, *Sovereignty and an Empty Purse,* 185–96.

25 Chase to John Bingham, February 6, 1862, NARG 56; Chase to William Fessenden, February 7, 1862, in *Congressional Globe,* February 7, 1862, 704; *Hartford Courant,* February 11, 1862; "Passage of the Treasury Note Bill," *New York Herald,* February 14, 1862, 1; see Ajit Pai, "Congress and the Constitution: The Legal Tender Act of 1862," *Oregon Law Review* 77 (1998): 535–99.

26 Chase to William Fessenden, February 10, 1862, *SPCP,* 3:132–33; Legal Tender Act, February 25, 1862, *Statutes at Large,* 12:345–48; Richardson, *Greatest Nation,* 47–48.

27 Chase to Thaddeus Stevens, February 25, 1862, *SPCP,* 3:141–42; Act of March 1, 1862, *Statutes at Large,* 12:352–53.

28 Fessenden remarks, *Congressional Globe,* February 12, 1862, 766; "House of Representatives," *New York Herald,* March 15, 1862, 1; *Chicago Tribune,* March 18, 1862 (Chase tax bill); *New-York Tribune,* April 9, 1862; "Passage of the Tax Bill," *New York Herald,* June 7, 1862, 5 (Senate tax bill "unrecognizable" to House); Revenue Act, July 1, 1862, *Statutes at Large,* 12:432–89. The license fee for jugglers is on page 457.

29 John Martin to Thomas Ewing, January 22, 1862, Ewing Papers, LC; Rush Sloane to Chase, January 22, 1862, Chase Papers, LC; *Holmes County Republican*

(Millersburg, OH), February 6, 1862 (Chase reportedly not interested); "The Ohio Senatorship," *Cleveland Daily Leader*, February 8, 1862, 2 (favors Wade); Chase to Martin Potter, February 17, 1862, *SPCP*, 3:135; Chase to James Monroe, March 3, 1862, *SPCP*, 3:143 (favors Spalding); Chase to Jay Cooke, May 31, 1862, Cooke Papers, HSP. David Von Drehle, *Rise to Greatness: Abraham Lincoln's Most Perilous Year* (New York: Henry Holt, 2012), 39, errs in calling Martin a "confidant" of Chase. There was no correspondence between them; Martin was a friend and adviser of Ewing. See Charles Wiseman, *Centennial History of Lancaster Ohio* (Lancaster, OH: C. M. L. Wiseman, 1898), 229–31.

30 Chase to Robert Warden, November 6, 1861, Warden, 389 ("patience of God"); Chase to William Reynolds, January 6, 1862, Amistad Center (introducing French); Chase to Hamilton Pierson, February 1, 1862, Warden, 397; Rose, *Rehearsal*, 26–28.

31 Edward Pierce to Chase, January 19, 1862, *SPCP*, 3:120–24.

32 Pierce report, February 3, 1862, in *New-York Tribune*, February 19, 1862. The "official" copy of Pierce's report is the version printed in the *Tribune* with some handwritten corrections. See Berlin, *Lower South*, 151.

33 Mansfield French to Chase, February 16, 1862, *SPCP*, 3:133–34; Chase to Edward Pierce, February 18, 1862, Chase Papers, LC; Chase to Pierce, February 19, 1862, *SPCP*, 3:136–37; Pierce to Chase, February 21, 1862, *SPCP*, 3:138–39; *New-York Tribune*, February 21, 1862 (Cooper Union).

34 Edward Pierce to Chase, February 21, 1862, *SPCP*, 3: 138–39; Chase to Pierce, February 24, 1862, Chase Papers, LC (two letters same date); Chase to Hiram Barney, February 24, 1862, *SPCP*, 3:139–40; George William Curtis to Chase, February 24, 1862, *SPCP*, 3:140–41; William Sprague to Chase, February 26, 1862, Chase Papers, LC; Chase to Pierce, February 27, 28, 1862, Chase Papers, LC; Chase to Barney, February 28, 1862, NARG 56.

35 Edward Pierce to Chase, March 2, 1862, in Berlin, *Lower South*, 155–62; Chase to Pierce, March 2, 1862, Chase Papers, CHLA; Chase to Hiram Barney, March 3, 1862, NARG 56; "A Peaceful Expedition to Port Royal," *New York Herald*, March 4, 1862, 8 (departure of the *Atlantic*).

36 Chase diary, March 13, 1862, *SPCP*, 1:331; Edward Pierce to Chase, March 14, 1862, *SPCP*, 3:150–51.

37 Edward Pierce to Chase, March 14, 1862, *SPCP*, 3:148–51; Mansfield French to Chase, March 1862, *SPCP*, 3:146–48; "Port Royal Correspondence," *New York Times*, March 20, 1862, 1; Chase to William Reynolds, March 20, 1862, Chase Papers, CHLA; Pierce to Chase, March 30, 1862, *SPCP*, 3:154–56; Reynolds to Chase, April 1, 1862, *SPCP*, 3:157–58; Chase to Pierce, April 11, 1862, Chase Papers, LC.

38 "The Bill for the Abolition of Slavery in the District of Columbia," *New York Times*, April 4, 1862, 1; Compensated Emancipation Act, April 16, 1862, *Statutes at Large*, 12:376–78; see Wilentz, *No Property in Man*, 110–14.

39 Chase diary, April 11, 1862, *SPCP*, 1:333 (House passed Senate bill after "long and exciting session"); "Passage of the Bill," *New York Herald*, April 12, 1862, 7; "The Bill Abolishing Slavery in the District of Columbia Passed in the House,"

New York Times, April 12, 13, 1862, 5; "Emancipation!," *New-York Tribune*, April 12, 1862, 4; "The District Emancipation Bill Not Yet Signed by the President," *New York Times*, April 13, 1862, 5; "Effect of the Passage," *New York Herald*, April 13, 1862, 4; Chase diary, April 16, 1862, *SPCP*, 1:333 (Lincoln signed bill this morning); Chase to Thomas Key, April 18, 1862, *SPCP*, 3:177; Alexander and James Hays to Chase, April 19, 1862, *SPCP*, 3:177–78. I cannot find news accounts of the serenade, but since the leaders described it as "private," that is perhaps to be expected.

40 Homestead Act, May 20, 1862, *Statutes at Large*, 12:392–93; Pacific Railway Act, July 1, 1862, ibid., 489–98; Morrill Act, July 2, 1862, ibid., 503–5; Henry Carey to Chase, July 9, 1862, Edward Carey Gardiner Papers, HSP (every immigrant "a machine that represents a capital of at least $1,000"); Chase, *Report of the Secretary of the Treasury on the State of the Finances for the Year Ending June 30, 1862* (Washington, DC: Government Printing Office, 1863), 23 ("working millions"); Chase to Kate Chase, August 18, 1863, *Spur*, 220–21 ("great work"); Chase to John Dix, November 25, 1863, *SPCP*, 4:199–201 (Pacific Railroad); Chase to Francis Gillette and John Hooker, July 9, 1864, Chase Papers, HSP (immigrants would increase the "moral, intellectual & physical power" of the United States); see Richardson, *Greatest Nation*, 144–49, 155–62, 176–87.

41 Chase diary, May 1, 1862, *SPCP*, 1:335; George McClellan to Edwin Stanton, May 4, 1862, Sears, *Papers of McClellan*, 253; McClellan to Winfield Scott, May 4, 1862, ibid., 253; Chase to Nettie Chase, May 7, 1862, *SPCP*, 1:336; Egbert Viele, "A Trip with Lincoln, Chase, and Stanton," *Scribner's Monthly* 16 (1878), 813; Stahr, *Stanton*, 196–97; Symonds, *Lincoln and His Admirals*, 145–46.

42 Chase to Nettie Chase, May 7, 1862, *SPCP*, 1:336–37. There are two versions of each of Chase's three letters to Nettie, with slight differences. See Chase to Nettie, May 7, 1862, *SPCP*, 3:186–87.

43 Chase to Nettie Chase, May 7, 1862, *SPCP*, 1:337–38; Anne Holloway & Jonathan White, *"Our Little Monitor": The Greatest Invention of the Civil War* (Kent, OH: Kent State University Press, 2018); Sears, *Lincoln's Lieutenants*, 210 ("McClellan's contempt for Lincoln, and for Stanton and Chase too, led him to deliberately refuse to share confidences"); Stahr, *Stanton*, 197 ("other generals would have viewed this as an order").

44 Chase to Nettie Chase, May 7, 1862, *SPCP*, 1:337–38; Chase to Nettie, May 8, 1862, *SPCP*, 1:338–39.

45 Ibid., May 8, 1862, *SPCP*, 3:189–90; see Manning, *Troubled Refuge*, 53.

46 Chase to Nettie Chase, May 11, 1862, *SPCP*, 1:340–42.

47 Ibid. 342; "Our Special Army Correspondence," *New York Herald*, May 13, 1862, 3; "From Fortress Monroe," *New York Times*, May 13, 1862, 1; Viele narrative, May 18, 1862, Chase Papers, HSP, box 13.

48 Chase to Nettie Chase, May 11, 1862, *SPCP*, 1:342; "Our Special Army Correspondence," *New York Herald*, May 13, 1862, 3; "From Fortress Monroe," *New York Times*, May 13, 1862, 1 (including Wool's order). The quotes are from Chase's letter, but the newspapers provide key details.

49 Chase to Nettie Chase, May 11, 1862, *SPCP,* 1:342; "Our Special Army Correspondence," *New York Herald*, May 13, 1862, 3; *New York Times*, May 13, 1862.
Wool's order was printed in the papers.

50 Chase to Nettie Chase, May 11, 1862, *SPCP,* 1:342; Chase to Ambrose Burnside,
May 11, 1862, Chase Papers, ALPL; Chase to George Carlisle, May 12, 1862,
Chase Papers, CHLA; "Our Special Army Correspondence," *New York Herald,*
May 13, 1862, 3; see Symonds, *Lincoln and His Admirals*, 155.

51 Chase to Nettie Chase, May 11, 1862, *SPCP,* 1:344; Chase to Irvin McDowell,
May 14, 1862, Chase Papers, HSP.

52 Edward Pierce to Chase, May 7, 1862, *SPCP,* 3:188–89; Pierce to Chase, May 7,
1862, NARG 366 (second letter same day); Pierce to Chase, May 8, 1862, *SPCP,*
3:191; Chase to Rufus Saxton, May 16, 1862, NARG 56; Chase to Pierce, May
17, 1862, *SPCP,* 3:200–201; Chase to Edwin Stanton, May 17, 1862, NARG
56.

53 "Important Order by General Hunter," May 9, 1862, in *New York Times*, May
16, 1862, 7; Chase to Lincoln, May 16, 1862, Lincoln Papers, LC.

54 Lincoln to Chase, May 17, 1862, *CWL,* 5:219; Lincoln proclamation, May 19,
1862, *CWL,* 5:222–23; "A Proclamation," *Washington (DC) Evening Star*, May
19, 1862, 2; Chase to Horace Greeley, May 21, 1862, *SPCP,* 3:203 (saw the
proclamation Monday evening in the *Star*).

55 Chase to David Hunter, May 20, 1862, *SPCP,* 3:202; Chase to Hiram Barney,
May 21, 1862, NARG 56; Chase to Horace Greeley, May 21, 1862, *SPCP,*
3:202–3.

56 Edward Pierce to Chase, May 12, 1862, *OR,* ser. 3, vol. 2, 52–53; Pierce to Chase,
May 13, 1862, *SPCP,* 3:198–99; Chase to Edwin Stanton, May 21, 1862, *OR,*
ser. 3, vol. 2, 50–60; see Manning, *Troubled Refuge*, 92–93.

57 Lincoln to Irvin McDowell, May 24, 1862, *OR,* vol. 12, pt. 3, 219; Edwin
Stanton to McDowell, May 24, 1862, *OR,* 220 (Chase arriving at Aquia at about
midnight); McDowell to Lincoln, May 24, 1862, *OR,* 220–21 (hope to see Chase
tonight); Chase diary, June 26, 1862, *SPCP,* 1:345; see Stahr, *Stanton*, 205–7.

58 Chase to Edwin Stanton, May 25, 1862, *OR,* vol. 12, pt. 3, 229–30 (four messages); Lincoln to Chase, May 25, 1862, *CWL,* 5:234–35; Chase to Lincoln, May
25, 1862, *OR,* vol. 12, pt. 3, 230; Chase diary, June 26, 1862, *SPCP,* 1:345–46.

59 Chase diary, June 26, 1862, *SPCP,* 1:345–46; Chase to Simon Cameron, May
26, 1862, Cameron Papers, LC; William Nelson to Chase, May 30, 1862, Chase
Papers, HSP; Chase to Irvin McDowell, June 3, 1862, Chicago Historical Society.

60 McPherson, *Battle Cry of Freedom*, 464–71; Sears, *Gates of Richmond*, 181–336;
Stahr, *Stanton*, 213–16; Williamson and Hsieh, *Savage War*, 181–89.

61 Ormsby Mitchel to Chase, April 20, 1862, *SPCP,* 3:178–81; Chase to Mitchel,
May 2, 1862, NARG 56; Mitchel to Chase, May 19, 1862, NARG 56; Mitchel
to Chase, June 2, 1862, Chase Papers, HSP; Chase to Mitchel, June 5, 1862,
ibid.

62 "Departure of Gov. Johnson and Suite for Tennessee," *New York Herald*, March 8,
1862, 3; Chase to Andrew Johnson, April 3, 1862, Johnson Papers, LC; Chase

to Johnson, April 4, 1862, *PAJ,* 5:267; Johnson to Chase, April 29, 1862, *PAJ,* 5:350; "Letter from the Hon. Ed. Stanly," *New York Times,* May 15, 1862, 3; Chase to Johnson, September 12, 1863, *PAJ,* 6:364–65; Chase to Johnson, October 19, 1863, *PAJ,* 6:426; Chase to Hobart Berrien, Feb. 5, 1866, Chase Papers, HSP; see Hans Trefousse, *Andrew Johnson: A Biography* (New York: W. W. Norton, 1989), 152–53.

63 *Chicago Tribune,* June 3, 1862; "Governor Stanly's Closing," *New York Herald,* June 3, 1862, 78; "The Last Assault," ibid., June 6, 1862, 4; "The Jacobin Clubs," ibid., June 7, 1862, 4.

64 George Denison to Chase, May 15, 1862, Bourne, 298–300; Chase to Denison, May 16, 1862, NARG 36; Chase to M. F. Bonzano, May 16, 1862, ibid.; see Terry Jones, "The Beast in the Big Easy," *New York Times,* May 18, 2012; Chester Hearn, *When the Devil Came Down to Dixie: Ben Butler in New Orleans* (Baton Rouge: Louisiana State University Press, 2000), 76–89.

65 Charles Sumner to John Andrew, May 28, 1862, in Palmer, *Sumner Letters,* 2:115; Chase to Benjamin Butler, June 24, 1862, *SPCP,* 3:218–19. For more routine correspondence, see Benjamin Butler to Chase, June 17, 19, 23, 1862, Butler Papers, LC.

CHAPTER 17: "A New Era," Late 1862

1 Chase to Jay Cooke, July 4, 1862, Oberholtzer, *Cooke,* 1:198; "The Fourth," *Washington (DC) Evening Star,* July 5, 1862, 3; Chase to Kate Chase, July 6, 1862, *Spur,* 206–7; Harris Fahnestock to Jay Cooke, July 7, 1862, Oberholtzer, *Cooke,* 197–98; see Goodwin, *Team of Rivals,* 445.

2 George McClellan to Lincoln, July 7, 1862, in Sears, *Papers of McClellan,* 344–45; see Goodwin, *Team of Rivals,* 450–52; Sears, *Gates of Richmond,* 350–51.

3 George McClellan to Chase, July 11, 1862, Dickson Papers, Clements Library, Michigan; James Randall, ed., *The Diary of Orville Hickman Browning,* 2 vols., July 11, 1862 (Springfield: Illinois State Historical Library, 1925, 1933), 1:557; Henry Cooke to Jay Cooke, July 12, 1862, in Cooke Papers, HSP.

4 Edwin Stanton to Henry Halleck, July 11, 1862, NARG 107; Lincoln to Halleck, July 11, 1862, *CWL,* 5:312–13; Chase to Kate Chase, July 13, 1862, *SPCP,* 3:226–27; Chase to Richard Parsons, July 20, 1862, *SPCP,* 3:230–31; "General Halleck Assigned to General Command," *Washington (DC) Evening Star,* July 23, 1862, 3 (prints Lincoln's July 11 order promoting Halleck).

5 Pope proclamation, July 14, 1862, in "Address of Major General Pope," *Baltimore Sun,* July 15, 1862, 2; Chase diary, July 21, 1862, *SPCP,* 1:349–50; Chase, Notes on the Army of the Potomac and Army of Virginia, September 2, 1862, in Schuckers, *Chase,* 448.

6 Chase to William Fessenden, June 2, 1862, NARG 46; Chase to Fessenden, June 30, 1862, *SPCP,* 3:225 (comments on revised legal tender bill); Pacific Railway Act, July 1, 1862, *Statutes at Large,* 12:489–98; Second Legal Tender Act, July 11, 1862, ibid., 532–33.

7 "The Confiscation Bill," *New York Times*, July 12, 1862, 4 (confiscation bill); *New-York Tribune*, July 14, 1862 (confiscation bill); Lincoln message, July 17, 1862, *CWL*, 5:328–31; Second Confiscation Act, July 17, 1862, *Statutes at Large*, 12:589–92; *Buffalo Evening Courier*, July 18, 1862 (attacks "unreason, fanaticism, and passion" of confiscation law).

8 Randall, *Diary of Orville Hickman Browning*, July 14, 1862, 1:558; Henry Cooke to Jay Cooke, July 16, 1862, Oberholtzer, *Cooke*, 1:199.

9 "Both Houses of Congress," *New York Times*, July 17, 1862, 4; *Chicago Tribune*, July 17, 1862; Second Confiscation Act, July 17, 1862, *Statutes at Large*, 12:589–92; Burlingame, *Abraham Lincoln*, 2:357–60.

10 Chase to Richard Parsons, July 20, 1862, *SPCP*, 3:231; Chase diary, July 21, 1862, *SPCP*, 1:348; Stanton order, July 22, 1862, in "Important Executive Order," *Washington (DC) Evening Star*, July 23, 1862, 2. Although dated July 20, the letter to Parsons describes the discussion of the several orders on July 21. The quotes are from the order as finally issued, which combined the three orders into one document.

11 Chase diary, July 22, 1862, *SPCP*, 1:350–51; see Chase to Edward Haight, July 24, 1862, *SPCP*, 3:232 ("such generals as McClellan cost too much money—to say nothing of the lives of our young men").

12 Chase diary, July 22, 1862, *SPCP*, 1:351; see Stahr, *Seward*, 341–44; Stahr, *Stanton*, 225–27 (discussing other sources).

13 Lincoln draft emancipation proclamation, July 22, 1862, *CWL*, 5:336–37; Chase diary, July 22, 1862, *SPCP*, 1:351.

14 Ibid.

15 Chase diary, July 22, 1862, *SPCP*, 1:351; Stanton notes, July 22, 1862, Stanton Papers, LC.

16 Ibid.; Christopher Wolcott to Pamphila Wolcott, July 27, 1862, in Stahr, *Stanton*, 226.

17 Chase to Kate Chase, July 14, 1862, *SPCP*, 3:227; Chase to Lincoln, July 29, 1862, Lincoln Papers, LC; "The President and Cabinet," *Baltimore Sun*, July 30, 1862, 2 ("industrious clerks"); John Sherman to Chase, August 3, 1863, *SPCP*, 3:241; Helen McDowell to Chase, August 1862, in Mary Phelps, *Kate Chase: Dominant Daughter* (New York: Thomas Crowell, 1935), 121 (Nettie and Kate).

18 Chase to Lincoln, August 4, 1862, Lincoln Papers (two letters); Chase diary, August 7, 1862, *SPCP*, 1:361 ("engaged nearly all day on selections of recommendations for collectors and assessors"); Chase to Lincoln, August 12, 13, 14, 1862 (five letters); Chase diary, August 15, 1862, *SPCP*, 1:363 (meeting with Lincoln and Welles about Connecticut appointments); Chase to Lincoln, August 19, 20, 21, 1862 (five letters); Chase to Lincoln, August 23, 24, 25, 26 (six letters), Lincoln Papers, LC; Chase to Henry Anthony, August 22, 1862, in Jessy Emilie Young, *Some Unpublished Letters of Chase* (master's dissertation, Columbia University, 1922). Young transcribed and edited two volumes of letters that are still in family hands. In his memoir, Boutwell claimed that Chase was not much involved with these appointments, but the Lincoln Papers and Chase

Papers show that Chase was deeply involved. See George Boutwell, *Reminiscences of Sixty Years in Public Life* (New York: McClure, Phillips, 1902), 1:307.

19 Chase diary, August 3, 1862, *SPCP,* 1:357–58.

20 Chase to William Cullen Bryant, August 4, 1862, *SPCP,* 3:244–45; *New York Evening Post,* August 7, 8, 1862.

21 Chase diary, August 6, 1862, *SPCP,* 1:360; *National Republican* (Washington, DC), August 7, 1862; "Great War Meeting Held at the Capitol," *New York Times,* August 7, 1862, 1; Chase diary, August 7, 1862, *SPCP,* 1:360; Benjamin Brown French, diary entry, August 10, 1862, in *Witness to the Young Republic: A Yankee's Journal: The Diary of Benjamin Brown French, 1828–1870,* ed. Donald Cole and John McDonough (Hanover, NH: University Press of New England, 1989), 405.

22 Chase diary, August 7, 1862, *SPCP,* 1:360; "Great War Meeting Held at the Capitol," *New York Times,* August 7, 1862, 1.

23 Lincoln remarks, August 14, 1862, *CWL,* 5:370–71; Chase diary, August 15, 1862, *SPCP,* 1:362; Foner, *Fiery Trial,* 17–25, 123–33, 185–86, 222–25.

24 Henry Halleck to George McClellan, August 3, 1862, *OR,* vol. 11, pt. 1, 80–81; Chase diary, August 19, 1862, *SPCP,* 1:366; Chase to Henry Anthony, August 22, 1862, in Young, *Some Unpublished Letters;* Chase to Seward, August 27, 1862, Seward Papers, Rochester; see John Hennessy, *Return to Bull Run: The Campaign and Battle of Second Manassas* (New York: Simon & Schuster, 1993), 114–20; Stahr, *Stanton,* 234–36.

25 Irvin McDowell to Chase, August 30, 1862, in "The Second Battle of Bull Run," *New York Herald,* September 1, 1862, 8; John Pope to Henry Halleck, August 30, 1862, in "Thrilling News from the Battlefield," *Washington (DC) Evening Star,* August 30, 1862, 3; see Hennessy, *Return to Bull Run,* 464–65.

26 Chase diary, August 31, 1862, *SPCP,* 1:367; Chase to Thaddeus Stevens, August 31, 1862, Warden, 457; see Hennessy, *Return to Bull Run,* 464–65.

27 William and Erica Gienapp, eds., *The Civil War Diary of Gideon Welles, Lincoln's Secretary of the Navy,* August 31, 1862 (Urbana: University of Illinois Press, 2014), 17–18; Stahr, *Stanton,* 236–37.

28 Chase diary, September 1, 1862, *SPCP,* 1:367–68; Gienapp and Gienapp, *Diary of Gideon Welles,* September 1, 1862, 24–26; Stahr, *Stanton,* 238.

29 Chase diary, September 2, 1862, *SPCP,* 1:367–68.

30 Chase draft proclamation, September 2, 1862, Chase Papers, Brown University; Chase draft proclamation, September 1862, Lincoln Papers. The version at Brown is in Chase's handwriting; the version in the Lincoln papers the handwriting of a clerk.

31 "Latest from the Front," *Washington (DC) Evening Star,* September 3, 1862, 2nd ed., 3; McClellan to Halleck, September 10, 1862, in Sears, *Papers of McClellan,* 444–45; *National Republican* (Washington, DC), September 12, 1862; see Stephen Sears, *Landscape Turned Red: The Battle of Antietam* (New York: Ticknor & Fields, 1983), 72–73, 85–93.

32 Chase diary, September 12, 14, 1862, *SPCP,* 1:381–82 and 386; McClellan to Lincoln, September 13, 1862, in Sears, *Papers of McClellan,* 453; McClellan to

Halleck, September 13, 1862, in ibid., 456; see Murray and Hsieh, *Savage War*, 225–26; Sears, *Landscape Turned Red*, 112–13.

33 Chase diary, September 17, 1862, *SPCP*, 1:391; Chase to Alexander Latty, September 17, 1862, *SPCP*, 3:273–74.

34 *National Republican* (Washington, DC), September 18, 1862; McClellan to Halleck, September 18, 1862, in Sears, *Papers of McClellan*, 468.

35 *New-York Tribune*, September 29, 1862 ("fatal Thursday"); Sears, *Landscape Turned Red*, 298–309.

36 McClellan to Halleck, September 19, 1862, in ibid., 470 (three messages); Sears, *Landscape Turned Red*, 298–309.

37 Chase to John Sherman, September 20, 1862, *SPCP*, 3:277–78; Chase to Chandler, September 20, 1862, *SPCP*, 3:276–77. For similar comments, see Chase to Sherman, September 10, 1862, John Sherman Papers, LC; James Garfield to Burke Hinsdale, October 30, 1862, in Frederick Williams, ed., *The Wild Life of the Army: Civil War Letters of James A. Garfield* (Kalamazoo: Michigan State University Press, 1964), 170 ("misnomer to call it a Cabinet").

38 Robert Dale Owen to Lincoln, September 17, 1862. Lincoln Papers; Chase to Robert Dale Owen, September 20, 1862, *SPCP*, 3:277.

39 Chase to Hiram Barney, October 26, 1862, *SPCP*, 3:305–07; Chase diary, September 22, 1862, *SPCP*, 1:393; see Gienapp and Gienapp, *Diary of Gideon Welles*, September 22, 1862, 52–55; Masur, *Lincoln's Hundred Days*, 1–7.

40 Chase diary, September 22, 1862, *SPCP*, 1:393–94. Chase noted that Lincoln hesitated before mentioning his "Maker."

41 *SPCP*, 1:394.

42 Lincoln, Preliminary Emancipation Proclamation, September 22, 1862, *CWL*, 5:433–36.

43 Chase diary, September 22, 1862, *SPCP*, 1:394–95.

44 "Proclamation by the President," *Chicago Tribune*, September 23, 1862, 1; *New York Times*, September 23, 1862; *Luzerne (PA) Union*, September 24, 1862; see Masur, *Lincoln's Hundred Days*, 102–16.

45 *National Republican* (Washington, DC), September 25, 1862; "Serenade to the President," *New York Herald*, September 25, 1862, 1; "Serenade to the President," *Washington (DC) Evening Star*, September 25, 1862, 3; *Chicago Tribune*, September 26, 1862. There are slight differences among these.

46 Garfield to Lucretia Garfield, September 20, 1862, in Williams, *Wild Life of the Army*, 137; Chase diary, September 23, 25, 1862, *SPCP*, 396–97, 400–401; Garfield to Harrison Rhodes, September 26, 1862, in Williams, *Wild Life of the Army*, 141–42; Garfield to Lucretia Garfield, September 27, 1862, in ibid., 145; see Ira Rutkow, *James A. Garfield* (New York: Times Books, 2006).

47 Garfield to Harrison Rhodes, October 5, 1862, in Williams, *Wild Life of the Army*, 148–54.

48 Lucretia Garfield to Garfield, October 8, 1862, in ibid., 159; Garfield to Lucretia Garfield, October 12, 1862, in ibid., 157–59.

49 DuPont to Sophia DuPont, October 17, 21, 1862, in John Hayes, ed., *Samuel Francis DuPont: A Selection from His Civil War Letters* (Ithaca: Cornell University Press, 1969), 2:248 and 2:255–56; Harriet Beecher Stowe to James Fields, November 27, 1862, Huntington. For some reason Kate was not close with Sprague this fall. See Lamphier, *Kate Chase & William Sprague*, 47; Oller, *American Queen*, 71–73.

50 John Sherman to Chase, September 28, 1862, *SPCP,* 3:286–87; Hezekiah Bundy to Chase, October 3, 1862, Chase Papers, LC; *Western Reserve Chronicle*, October 8, 1862 (Garfield); *Gallipolis (OH) Journal*, October 9, 1862 (Bundy); Chase to Robert Hosea, October 17, 1862, Hosea Papers, Harvard; *National Republican* (Washington, DC), October 17, 1862; *New-York Tribune*, October 20, 1862.

51 "The Real Meaning of the Late Elections," *New York Herald*, October 23, 1862, 4.

52 *New York World*, October 23, 1862; *New-York Tribune*, October 24, 1862; "Wadsworth and Seymour," *New York Herald*, October 24, 1862, 4; *New York Evening Post*, November 1, 1862; *New-York Tribune*, November 1, 1862.

53 "The President and the Radical Abolitionists," *New York Herald*, November 3, 1862, 4.

54 Chase to Barney, October 22, 1862, Chase Papers, HSP; Chase to Barney, October 26, 1862, *SPCP,* 3:305–06; Chase to John Young, October 27, 1862, Schuckers, 458–59; Chase to Barney, October 28, 1862, Barney Papers, Huntington; Chase to Richard Parsons, October 31, 1862, *SPCP,* 3:311 ("handsomely"); Sears, *Lincoln's Lieutenants*, 432–33.

55 Chase to Sumner, November 9, 1862, *SPCP,* 3:314–15; Chase diary, November 9, 1862, *SPCP,* 1:423; Chase to Joseph Geiger, November 12, 1862, *SPCP,* 3:316; Chase to Hiram Barney, December 5, 1862, Barney Papers, Huntington.

56 Chase to Butler, November 14, 1862, *SPCP,* 3:318–19; Chase to Butler, December 14, 1862, *SPCP,* 3:336–37; *Hartford Courant*, December 29, 1862 (arrival of Banks and departure of Butler); *Chicago Tribune*, December 29, 1862 (Butler on way to Washington).

57 "Financial and Commercial," *New York Herald*, September 8, 1862, 2 (Hamilton); Chase to Joseph Hoxie et al., September 8, 1862, in Young, *Some Unpublished Letters* (Bonner); *Pittsburgh Gazette*, September 11, 1862 (*Herald*); Carey to Chase, September 14, 1862, Chase Papers, HSP; Chase to Cisco, September 15, 1862, *SPCP,* 3:265–67 (Cooke); Chase to Cisco, October 7, 1862, Chase Papers, HSP; Chase to Bonner, October 8, 1862, ibid.; James Garfield to Harrison Rhodes, in Williams, *Wild Life*, 190–91. (Chase and Garfield discussed currency with Carey.)

58 Chase to Butler, September 23, 1862, *SPCP,* 3:283–84; Chase, *Report of the Secretary of the Treasury for the Year Ending June 30, 1862,* 12 (inflation) and 43 (third quarter).

59 Chase to Jay Cooke, October 23, 1862, *SPCP,* 3:299–300; Richardson, *Greatest Nation*, 50–51.

60 *Reading (PA) Times*, November 5, 1862; *Altoona (PA) Tribune*, November 6, 1862; Chase to Jay Cooke, November 8, 13, 1862, in Oberholtzer, *Cooke*, 221–22; Edling, *Hercules in the Cradle*, 195–200.

61 Lincoln message, December 1, 1862, *CWL,* 5:522–23 and 537.

62 Chase, *Report of the Secretary of the Treasury for Year Ending June 30, 1862,* 14–16; Henry Cooke to Jay Cooke, November 29, 1862, in Oberholtzer, *Cooke,* 329–30.

63 Chase, *Report of the Secretary of the Treasury for the Year Ending June 30, 1862,* 17–20.

64 Ibid., 22–23.

65 *New York Evening Post,* December 10, 1862; *Chicago Tribune,* December 10, 1862; Chase to John Cisco, December 10, 1862, *SPCP,* 3:327; James Hamilton to Chase, December 11, 1862, *SPCP,* 3:333–34; Chase to Joseph Medill, December 13, 1862, *SPCP,* 3:334–36; *Sunbury (PA) Gazette,* December 13, 1862 (Stevens bill); William Cullen Bryant to Chase, December 18, 1862, Chase Papers, HSP (apologizes for *Post*'s opposition); Richardson, *Greatest Nation,* 84–85.

66 "Seward's Policy," *Brownson's Quarterly Review* (October 1862): 487–521; "Who Is Responsible?," *New York Herald,* October 6, 1862, 4 (quoting Brownson); "Just As Mephistopheles," *New York Herald,* November 9, 1862, 4 (Brownson and Chase); "Remove Him!," *Boston Commonwealth,* December 6, 1862 (remove Seward); see Stahr, *Seward,* 353–56.

67 Chase to Kate Chase, January 12, 1862, Chase Papers, HSP; Chase diary, September 10, 1862, *SPCP,* 1:377 ("however vigorous"); Chase to John Sherman, September 20, 1862, *SPCP,* 3:277–78; Chase to Zachariah Chandler, September 20, 1862, *SPCP,* 3:276–77; Chase diary, October 1–2, 1862, *SPCP,* 1:409–11 (joint letter); "Great Honors to a Negro," *Cincinnati Enquirer,* March 21, 1863, 2.

68 Randall, *Diary of Orville Hickman Browning,* December 16, 1862, 1:596–97; Francis Fessenden, *The Life and Public Services of William Pitt Fessenden* (Boston: Houghton, Mifflin, 1907), 1:233–36; see Amanda Foreman, *A World on Fire: An Epic History of Two Nations Divided* (New York: Random House, 2010), 343–44 ("so close"); Goodwin, *Team of Rivals,* 486–88; Murray and Hsieh, *Savage War,* 242–46; Stahr, *Seward,* 356–57.

69 Randall, *Diary of Orville Hickman Browning,* December 17, 1862, 1:598–99; Fessenden, *Fessenden,* 1:237–38.

70 Fessenden, *Fessenden,* 1:240–43; Beale, *Diary of Edward Bates,* December 19, 1862, 469; Gienapp and Gienapp, *Diary of Gideon Welles,* December 19, 1862, 98–100; "The Cabinet Crisis," *New York Times,* December 22, 1862, 1 ("military success").

71 Fessenden, *Fessenden,* 1:243–48.

72 Gienapp and Gienapp, *Diary of Gideon Welles,* December 20, 1862, 104–5.

73 Chase to Lincoln, December 20, 1862, *SPCP,* 3:340–41.

74 Fessenden, *Fessenden,* 1:249; see Henry Cooke to Jay Cooke, December 20, 1862, in Oberholtzer, *Cooke,* 1:225–26 (similar).

75 Fessenden, *Fessenden,* 1:249.

76 Lincoln to Chase and Seward, December 20, 1862, *CWL,* 6:12; Chase to Seward, December 21, 1862, *SPCP,* 3:342; Seward to Lincoln, December 21, 1862, Lincoln Papers; Chase to Lincoln, December 22, 1862, *SPCP,* 3:342–43; Goodwin, *Team of Rivals,* 494–95; Stahr, *Seward,* 359–60.

77 Lincoln to Seward et al., December 23, 1862, *CWL,* 6:17; Chase to Lincoln, December 29, 1862, *SPCP,* 3:347–49.

78 Chase to Lincoln, December 29, 1862, *SPCP,* 3:350–51.

CHAPTER 18: "My Fixed Faith," Early 1863

1 Chase diary, January 1, 1863, *SPCP,* 1:424–25; Fanny Seward diary, January 1, 1863, Seward Papers, Rochester; Chase to Susan Walker, January 2, 1865, *SPCP,* 5:4 ("paralysis"); Goodwin, *Team of Rivals,* 497–99; Trudy Krisher, *Fanny Seward: A Life* (Syracuse, NY: Syracuse University Press, 2015), 78–81; Stahr, *Seward,* 361.

2 Chase diary, January 1, 1863, *SPCP,* 1:424–25; *Sacramento (CA) Daily Union,* January 29, 1863; Stahr, *Seward,* 361–62.

3 Lincoln, Emancipation Proclamation, January 1, 1863, *CWL,* 6:28–30; "The Proclamation," *Washington (DC) Evening Star,* Jan. 1, 1863, 2 (second edition).

4 Mansfield French to Chase, January 2, 1863, *SPCP,* 3:352; Masur, *Lincoln's Hundred Days,* 206–10.

5 Mansfield French to Chase, January 2, 1863, *SPCP,* 3:352–53; John Andrew to Chase, January 3, 1863, *SPCP,* 3:355–56; Chase to Hannibal Hamlin, January 25, 1863, in Senate Executive Document No. 26, 37th Congressional, 3d Sess.

6 Act of February 6, 1863, *Statutes at Large,* 12:640–41; Lincoln to David Hunter et al., February 10, 1863, *CWL,* 6:98; Rose, *Rehearsal for Reconstruction,* 212–13. Although there is no draft of the order in Chase's hand, the inclusion of the tax commissioners and the requirement that the commissioners report to Chase indicate that it was a Treasury document.

7 David Hunter to Chase, February 8, 1863, *SPCP,* 3:382 note; Chase to Hunter, February 14, 1863, *SPCP,* 3:381–82; Hunter order, March 6, 1863, *OR,* vol. 14, 1020–21; Edward Pierce to Chase, April 2, 1863, *SPCP,* 4:3–5.

8 Lincoln to Andrew Johnson, March 26, 1863, *CWL,* 6:149–50; Chase to George Opdyke et al., April 8, 1863, *SPCP,* 4:7–9. For the Chase letter in the papers, see *National Republican* (Washington, DC), April 13, 1863; "Letter from Secretary Chase," *Chicago Tribune,* April 15, 1863, 2; "Letter from Mr. Chase," *Philadelphia Inquirer,* April 24, 1863, 1; *Cleveland Daily Leader,* April 24, 1863.

9 George Denison to Chase, March 29, 1863, *SPCP,* 3:405 ("slavery has been reestablished"); Denison to Chase, March 31, 1863, *SPCP,* 3:417 ("four full regiments"); Chase to William Aspinwall and John Forbes, May 14, 1863, *SPCP,* 4:32; Chase to Robert Walker, June 8, 1863, *SPCP,* 4:57–58 ("most remarkable"); Dudley Cornish, *The Sable Arm: Black Troops in the Union Army, 1861–1865* (New York: Longman, Greens, 1957), 142–43; William Harris, *With Charity for All: Lincoln and the Restoration of the Union* (Lexington: University Press of Kentucky, 1997), 114–15; Noah Trudeau, *Like Men of War: Black Troops in the Civil War, 1862–1865* (Boston: Little, Brown,1998), 34–46; Stahr, *Stanton,* 282–84.

10 Chase to Benjamin Flanders, May 24, 1863, *SPCP,* 4:40 ("universal suffrage"); Chase to Edwin Stanton, June 12, 1863, *SPCP,* 4:63–65.

11 Chase to Galusha Grow, January 10, 1863, *SPCP,* 3:363–65; "The Finances of the Government," *New York Times,* January 10, 1863, 1; Chase to William Fessenden, January 11, 1863, *SPCP,* 3:366–68; Joint Resolution, January 17, 1863, *Statutes at Large,* 12:822; Chase draft message, January 17, 1863, Chase Paper LC; Lincoln message, January 17, 1863, *CWL,* 5:60–61; "From Washington," *Chicago Tribune,* January 20, 1863, 1.

12 Chase to William Fessenden, January 11, 1863, *SPCP,* 3:366 (concerns about House finance bill); *Congressional Globe,* January 15, 1863, 342 (Gurley comments on banking bill); Chase to Elbridge Spaulding, January 21, 1863, *SPCP,* 3:371 (comments on finance bill); "Congress," *New York Herald,* January 27, 1863, 4 (House passes finance bill); Chase to William Mellen, January 27, 1863, *SPCP,* 3:374–75 (comments on finance bill); see Hammond, *Sovereignty and an Empty Purse,* 296–317.

13 Chase to Horace Greeley, January 28, 1863, *SPCP,* 3:375–77; see David Gische, "The New York City Banks and the Development of the National Banking System, 1860–1870," *American Journal of Legal History* 23 (1979): 36–38.

14 Chase diary, January 23, 1863, *SPCP,* 1:425–26; Horace Greeley to Chase, January 31, 1863, *SPCP,* 3:377–78; Randall, *Diary of Orville Hickman Browning,* January 31, 1863, 1:622; "The National Banking Scheme," *New York Times,* January 31, 1863, 4; "The Bank Scheme of Secretary Chase," *New-York Tribune,* February 2, 1863, 5; "National Banking," *New-York Tribune,* February 3, 1863, 4; "Mr. Chase's Plan," *Chicago Tribune,* February 7, 1863, 2. We do not have Chase's diary for February through June 1863; if we did, it would surely show other face-to-face meetings with legislators. See Chase diary, July 1, 1863, *SPCP,* 1:426.

15 *Congressional Globe,* February 10, 1863, 843–44 (Sherman); see Chase to Sherman, January 30, February 5, 1863, Sherman Papers, LC; Sherman to Chase, February 7, 1863, *SPCP,* 3:379; Chase to Sherman, February 9, 10, 1863, Sherman Papers, LC (four letters).

16 *Congressional Globe,* February 12, 1863, 896–97; "Financial and Commercial," *New York Herald,* February 14, 1863, 2; "How Chase's Bank Bill Was Hurried Through the Senate," *Cincinnati Enquirer,* February 21, 1863, 1 (from *Chicago Times*); Richardson, *Greatest Nation,* 89–90.

17 Chase to Lincoln, February 19, 1863, Lincoln Papers, LC; "The Bank Bill in the House," *New-York Tribune,* February 20, 1863, 1 ("Chase was at the House"); Chase to Lincoln, February 20, 1863, Lincoln Papers, LC; "The Bank Bill," *Philadelphia Inquirer,* February 21, 1863, 1 (Chase and Usher in the Speaker's room); "From Washington," *Chicago Tribune,* February 21, 1863, 1; National Banking Act, February 25, 1863, *Statutes at Large,* 12:665–82.

18 National Banking Act, February 25, 1863, *Statutes at Large,* 12:665–82; Gische, "New York City Banks," 38–40; Richardson, *Greatest Nation,* 90–91.

19 "From Washington," *Chicago Tribune,* February 21, 1863, 1; "The Conference Committee's Report Adopted," ibid., February 27, 1863, 1; George Opdyke to Chase, February 27, 1863, *SPCP,* 3:392–93; Finance Act, March 3, 1863, *Statutes at Large,* 12:709–13.

20 Edling, *Hercules in the Cradle*, 189 (banking bill's "contribution to the financing of the Civil War was marginal"); Hammond, *Sovereignty and an Empty Purse*, 339–40 ("passage of the bill was no help to the financing of the war"); "Rahm Emanuel on the Opportunities of Crisis," YouTube, 2:47, *Wall Street Journal* interview, November 19, 2008), https://www.youtube.com/watch?v=_mzcbXi1Tkk&ab_channel=WallStreetJournal.

21 *York (PA) Gazette*, February 3, 1863; *Reading (PA) Times*, February 19, 1863; Henry Cooke to Jay Cooke, March 24, 25, 1863, Oberholtzer, *Cooke*, 229–30.

22 "The New Five-Twenties," *Philadelphia Inquirer*, March 27, 1863, 2; "Monetary Affairs," *New York Times*, March 29, 1863, 3; *Lancaster (PA) Inquirer Gazette*, April 7, 1863; *Pittston (PA) Gazette*, April 16, 1863.

23 *Philadelphia Ledger*, March 28, 1863; "A Day at the Agency of the Five Twenties," *Lancaster (PA) Evening Express,* April 10, 1863, 1.

24 Finance Act, March 3, 1863, *Statutes at Large,* 12:711 (last sentence of sec. 3); "The New Five-Twenties," *Philadelphia Inquirer*, March 27, 1863, 2; *Lancaster (PA) Intelligencer*, April 7, 1863; Chase to John Cisco, June 26, 1863, *SPCP,* 4:70–71.

25 "A Day at the Agency for the Five-Twenties," *Philadelphia Inquirer*, April 9, 1863, 4; Chase to William Aspinwall and John Forbes, May 14, 1863, *SPCP,* 4:29–31; *Leavenworth (KS) Times*, May 20, 1863; Edling, *Hercules in the Cradle*, 195–97; Larson, *Cooke*, 126–32; Richardson, *Greatest Nation*, 50–55.

26 Chase to Jay Cooke, June 1, 1863, *SPCP,* 4:50–51, and June 2, 1863, *SPCP,* 4:52–53.

27 *Senate Journal,* March 5, 1863, 449 (Sprague sworn in as senator); William Sprague to Hiram Barney, May 18, 1863, Chase Papers, HSP; Gienapp and Gienapp, *Diary of Gideon Welles,* May 19, 1863, 191.

28 William Sprague to Chase, May 31, 1863, *SPCP,* 4:49–50; Chase to Sprague, June 4, 1863, *SPCP,* 4:55–56; Sprague to Chase, June 8, 1863, *SPCP,* 4:59.

29 William Sprague to Chase, June 12, 1863, Chase Papers, LC.

30 Ibid. This was not the only time that Sprague sought help with cotton permits. See Sprague to Chase, October 14, 1862, *SPCP,* 3:297. Lamphier speculates that Kate's anger about Sprague's questionable cotton trading was the reason for the suspension of their engagement. Lamphier, *Kate Chase and William Sprague*, 47–49. Oller disagrees. Oller, *American Queen*, 60–62.

31 Chase to Kate Chase, June 29, 1863, *SPCP,* 4:72–73; Chase to David Dudley Field, June 30, 1863, *SPCP,* 1862, 4:73–74.

32 Murat Halstead to Chase, April 1, 1863, Lincoln Papers, LC; Chase to Lincoln, April 4, 1863, ibid. On Grant's drinking, see Chernow, *Grant*, 250–53.

33 Chase to Lincoln, April 22, 1863, *SPCP,* 4:15–16; James Garfield to Chase, May 5, 1863, ibid., 22 ("true objective point"); Lincoln to Chase, May 13, 1863, *CWL,* 6:213 ("I return the letters of General Garfield"); Lincoln to Joseph Hooker, June 10, 1863, *CWL,* 6:257 ("true objective point"). On "true objective point," see McPherson, *Battle Cry of Freedom*, 651; Stephen Sears, *Gettysburg* (New York: Houghton, Mifflin, 2004), 84.

34 Chase to Charles McIlvaine, January 25, 1863, *SPCP,* 3:372–73.

35 Gienapp and Gienapp, *Diary of Gideon Welles,* February 10, 18, 1863, 136, 140; Chase to Lincoln, February 27, 1863, *SPCP,* 3:391–92; "Nominations and Rejections," *New-York Tribune,* March 2, 1863, 4.

36 Chase to James Dixon, February 28, 1863, Chase Papers, HSP; Lincoln to Chase, March 2, 1863, *CWL,* 6:122–23; Chase to Lincoln, March 2, 1863, Lincoln Papers, LC; Dixon to Lincoln, March 5, 1863, Lincoln Papers, LC; Gienapp and Gienapp, *Diary of Gideon Welles,* March 9, 1863, 145–46 (conversation with Dixon); *Hartford Courant,* March 11, 1863 (appointment of Bolles).

37 Chase to Gideon Welles, February 23, 1863, Flagg Papers, Yale (introducing Smith); Lincoln to Chase, March 21, 1863, *CWL,* 6:144; Chase to George Harrington, March 23, 1863, Harrington Papers, Missouri Historical Society; Anson Henry to Chase, April 13, 1863, Lincoln Papers, LC; Henry to Lincoln, April 23, 1863, ibid. (asking whether Smith has been removed); see Daryl McClary, "Victor Smith Forcibly Moves the U.S. Customs Port of Entry from Port Townsend to Port Angeles on August 1, 1862," HistoryLink.org, last modified September 21, 2005, https://www.historylink.org/File/7474.

38 Lincoln to Chase, May 8, 1863, *CWL,* 6:202 (two letters); Chase to Lincoln, May 11, 1863, *SPCP,* 4:26; Lincoln to Anson Henry, May 13, 1863, *CWL,* 6:215 ("Chase's feelings were hurt by my action in his absence").

39 Chase to Lincoln, May 11, 1863, *SPCP,* 4:26–27; Lincoln to Chase, May 13, 1863, *CWL,* 6:213 (requests commission for Gunn "as you request"); *Buffalo Morning Express,* May 20, 1863 (Gunn appointed in place of Smith). After both Chase and Lincoln were dead, Field claimed that Lincoln went to Chase's house, placed his arm around Chase's neck, and persuaded Chase not to resign. "It was difficult to bring him to terms," Lincoln supposedly said. "I had to plead with him a long time, but I finally succeeded and heard no more of that resignation." Maunsell Field, *Memories of Many Men and Some Women* (New York: Harper, 1874), 302–3. The whole passage seems an invention by Field rather than an accurate account. See Don and Virginia Fehrenbacher, *Recollected Words of Abraham Lincoln* (Stanford, CA: Stanford University Press, 1996), 159–60 (noting that Lincoln would be unlikely to confide in a Chase confidante).

40 Burnside order no. 38, April 13, 1863, *OR,* ser. 2, vol. 5, 480; *Brooklyn Daily Eagle,* April 14, 1863 (Vallandigham for president); "Vallandigham," *New-York Tribune,* May 15, 1863, 4; *New York Evening Post,* May 19, 1863; "Vallandigham and Burnside," *New York Herald,* May 20, 1863, 6; see Michael Curtis, "Lincoln, Vallandigham, and Anti-War Speech in the Civil War," *William & Mary Bill of Rights Journal* 7 (1998): 105–92; Stahr, *Stanton,* 276–77.

41 Chase to Richard Parsons, June 15, 1863, *SPCP,* 4:66–67; Chase to Hiram Barney, June 17, 1863, Chase Papers, HSP; see Ex parte Milligan, 71 U.S. 2 (1866).

42 Chase to Richard Parsons, February 16, 1863, *SPCP,* 3:384–85; see Chase to Benjamin Butler, December 14, 1862, *SPCP,* 3:337.

43 *New York Herald,* May 23, 1863; *Buffalo Courier,* May 29, 1863; "The Loyal Leagues," *New-York Tribune,* May 29, 1863, 4; "The Greatest Joke of the Day,"

New York Herald, June 3, 1863, 4; Paul Taylor, *The Most Complete Political Machine Ever Known: The North's Union Leagues in the American Civil War* (Kent, OH: Kent State University Press, 2018).

44 "Presidential Movements—Secretary Chase in the Field," *New York Herald*, June 20, 1863, 6; Chase to David Dudley Field, June 30, 1863, *SPCP*, 4:74.

45 "From the Army of the Potomac," *New York Times*, May 3, 1863, 1; "Secretary Chase in Boston," *National Republican* (Washington, DC), May 5, 1863, 1 (from *Boston Traveller*); Stahr, *Stanton*, 290–91.

46 Benjamin Ludlow to Chase, May 8, 1863, Chase Papers, LC; Chase to Ludlow, May 12, 1863, *SPCP*, 4:28–29; Chase to William Aspinwall and John Forbes, May 14, 1863, *SPCP*, 4:32; Chase to Joseph Hooker, May 14, 1863, Schuckers, 461; Chase to James Garfield, May 14, 1863, ibid., 467; see Murray and Hsieh, *Savage War*, 265; Sears, *Lincoln's Lieutenants*, 510–11.

47 Chase to Lincoln, May 21, 1863, Lincoln Papers, LC (from Hooker's headquarters); *Janesville (WI) Gazette*, May 21, 1863 (Chase and Sprague have gone to visit army); Chase to Hooker, May 23, 1863, *SPCP*, 4:35–36; Chase to Hooker, May 25, 1863, *OR*, vol. 25, pt. 2, 523; Hooker to Chase, May 25, 1863, *OR*, 524; Daniel Butterfield to Chase, June 5, 1863, Chase Papers, HSP; Butterfield to Chase, June 11, 1863, *SPCP*, 4:61–63; Butterfield to Chase, June 17, 1863, Chase Papers, HSP; Chase to Butterfield, June 20, 1863, ibid.; Chase to Kate Chase, June 25, 1863, *SPCP*, 4:69–70; Chase to Butterfield, June 25, 1863, Chase Papers, HSP; Hooker to Halleck, June 26, 1863, *OR*, vol. 27, pt. 1, 58; Halleck to Hooker, June 27, 1863, *OR*, 59; Hooker to Halleck, June 27, 1863, *OR*, 60; Halleck to George Meade, June 27, 1863, *OR*, 61; Sears, *Lincoln's Lieutenants*, 528–40; Stahr, *Stanton*, 292–93.

48 Gienapp and Gienapp, *Diary of Gideon Welles*, June 28, 1863, 228–30.

CHAPTER 19: "Bringing to a Second Birth This Same Mighty Nation," Late 1863

1 Chase diary, July 1, 1863, *SPCP*, 1:426; Chase notes, July 3, 1863, Chase Papers, HSP; Edwin Stanton to John Dix, July 4, 1863, *OR*, vol. 27, pt. 3, 529; Stahr, *Stanton*, 296–97.

2 Chase to Ulysses Grant, July 4, 1864, Schuckers, 461. The clerk's copy of this letter does not have the complimentary language quoted in Schuckers; the clerk indicated its omission with "&c &c &c." Chase to Ulysses Grant, July 4, 1864, *SPCP*, 4:75.

3 Chase to Thomas Kane, July 9, 1863, Schuckers, 471; Chase to John Bigelow, July 10, 1863, Chase Papers, NYHS; Chase to William Sprague, July 15, 1863, *SPCP*, 4:82; Goodwin, *Team of Rivals*, 535–36; Stahr, *Stanton*, 298–300.

4 John Cisco to Chase, July 13, 1863, NARG 56 (two messages); Chase to Hiram Barney, July 13, 1863, NARG 56; Chase to Cisco, July 14, 1863, NARG 56 (asks status); Cisco to Chase, July 14, 1863, NARG 56; *National Republican* (Washington, DC), July 14, 1863; Chase to Cisco, July 15, 1863, NARG 56 ("am assured that adequate force is on its way"); Barney to Chase, July 15, 1863, *SPCP*, 4:84–85;

Cisco to Chase, July 15, 1863, NARG 56 (two messages); David Dudley Field to Chase, July 15, 1863, Chase Papers, HSP; Chase to Field, July 16, 1863, ibid.; Barney to Chase, July 16, 1863, Chase Papers, Huntington; Cisco to Chase, July 23, 1863, *SPCP,* 4:93–95; Edwin Burrows and Mike Wallace, *Gotham: A History of New York City to 1898* (New York: Oxford University Press, 1999), 887–95.

5　Nathaniel Banks to Henry Halleck, July 8, 1863, in "Fall of Port Hudson," *Washington (DC) Evening Star,* July 16, 1863, 2; Chase to Banks, July 16, 1863, Chase Papers, HSP; George Denison to Chase, August 12, 1863, *SPCP,* 4:101; *Daily True Delta* (New Orleans), August 12, 1863.

6　*Daily True Delta* (New Orleans), August 14, 1863; Chase to George Denison, August 26, 1863, *SPCP,* 4:117; Chase to S. M. Breckinridge et al., September 3, 1863, *SPCP,* 4:130–32.

7　Chase to James Garfield, August 17, 1863, *SPCP,* 4:103; Chase to John Weiss, August 21, 1863, Schuckers, 392; Shelby Foote, *The Civil War: A Narrative,* 3 vols. (New York: Random House, 1948–74), 2:620–21; Murray and Hsieh, *Savage War,* 330–32; Sears, *Lincoln's Lieutenants,* 593–95; Stephen Wise, *Gate of Hell: Campaign for Charleston Harbor, 1863* (Columbia: University of South Carolina Press, 1994), 154–87.

8　Charles Dana to Edwin Stanton, September 20, 1863, *OR,* vol. 30, pt. 1, 192–93; Chase diary, September 20, 1863, *SPCP,* 1:448; Stahr, *Stanton,* 309–12.

9　Chase diary, September 23, 1863, *SPCP,* 1:450 ("silent & stern"); James Garfield to Chase, *OR,* vol. 30, pt. 3, 792; Charles Dana to Edwin Stanton, *OR,* pt. 1, 197; William Rosecrans to Lincoln, *OR,* pt. 1, 168.

10　Chase diary, September 23, 1863, *SPCP,* 1:450–52. For the cast of characters, see Stahr, *Stanton,* 312.

11　Chase diary, September 23, 1863, *SPCP,* 1:452–53. There is a second version of this meeting in Chase's diary, shorter but similar. For a longer account, see Stahr, *Stanton,* 313–15.

12　Chase to Kate Chase, September 30, 1863, *Spur,* 230; Chase to Joseph Hooker, December 21, 1863, *SPCP,* 4:222–23; Foote, *Civil War,* 2:846–49; Stahr, *Stanton,* 313–23.

13　William Birney to Chase, July 21, 1863, *SPCP,* 4:90–91; Chase to Edwin Stanton, July 23, 1863, *SPCP,* 4:92–93; Chase to Stanton, September 4, 1863, in Ira Berlin et al., eds., *The Black Military Experience* (Cambridge: Cambridge University Press, 1982), 359; Chase diary, September 26–27, 1863, *SPCP,* 1:454–56; "Personal," *Baltimore Sun,* September 28, 1863, 1; Berlin, *Black Military Experience,* 184–86 (Birney recruiting in Maryland).

14　Chase to Jay Cooke, May 31, 1861, Oberholtzer, *Cooke,* 188; Chase to Jay Cooke, September 1, 1863, *SPCP,* 4:129; Ernest Furgurson, *Freedom Rising: Washington in the Civil War* (New York: Alfred A. Knopf, 2004), 332–33; Kate Masur, *An Example for All the Land: Emancipation and the Struggle over Equality in Washington, D.C.* (Chapel Hill: University of North Carolina Press, 2010), 99–111.

15　Burlingame and Ettlinger, *Diary of John Hay,* July–August 1863, 77; "The Administration and the Union Question," *New York Herald,* August 10, 1863,

4; "Presidential Movements," *New York Herald*, August 13, 1863, 4; *New-York Tribune*, September 19, 1863; "The Chase and Seward Factions in the Cabinet," *New York Herald*, September 22, 1863, 6; "From St. Louis," *Chicago Tribune*, October 1, 1863, 2 (Blair's speech "a blast against Sec. Chase"); Elizabeth Blair Lee to Phillip Lee, October 7, 1863, Laas, *Wartime Washington*, 311 ("Wade is against Chase because he is for himself"); *St. Joseph (MO) Weekly Herald*, October 8, 1863; *Wheeling Daily Register*, October 10, 1863; "The Presidential Question in the Cabinet," *New York Herald*, October 20, 1863, 6.

16 "Speech of Hon. Montgomery Blair," *New York Herald*, October 6, 1863, 4; Thaddeus Stevens to Chase, October 8, 1863, Chase Papers, HSP; "The Presidential Question in the Cabinet," *New York Herald*, October 20, 1863, 6; Beale, *Diary of Edward Bates*, October 20, 1863, 311; *Sioux City (IA) Register*, October 24, 1863; "President Lincoln and His Peace Negotiations," *New York Herald*, October 28, 1863, 6.

17 Charlotte Eastman to Chase, July 19, 1863, Chase Papers, HSP; Horace Greeley to Chase, September 29, 1863, *SPCP*, 4:145–46; Joshua Leavitt to Chase, September 30, 1863, Chase Papers, LC.

18 Chase to Charlotte Eastman, August 22, 1863, *SPCP*, 4:112–13; Chase to Joshua Leavitt, October 7, 1863, *SPCP*, 4:148–49; Chase to Horace Greeley, October 9, 1863, *SPCP*, 4:150–51.

19 Chase to John Brough, June 30, 1863, Chase Papers, LC; "The Campaign in Ohio," *Cincinnati Enquirer*, August 21, 1863, 1; Murat Halstead to Chase, August 24, 1863, Chase Papers, LC; Chase to Franz Sigel, September 18, 1863, Chase Papers, NYHS; "The Political Campaign in Ohio," *New-York Tribune*, October 3, 1863, 6; Gienapp and Gienapp, *Diary of Gideon Welles*, October 14, 1863, 309; *London Times*, October 20, 1863; George Porter, *Ohio Politics During the Civil War Period* (New York: Columbia University Press, 1911), 178–84; Jennifer Weber, *Copperheads: The Rise and Fall of Lincoln's Opposition in the North* (New York: Oxford University Press, 2006), 118–23.

20 *Cleveland Daily Leader*, October 14, 1863; *Indianapolis Star*, October 15, 1863.

21 "Mr. Chase on the War," *New York Herald*, October 17, 1863, 8; "Secretary Chase on the Presidential Stump," ibid., 6.

22 Chase to Lincoln, October 13, 14, 1863, Lincoln Papers, LC; Chase, *"Going Home to Vote": Authentic Speeches of S.P. Chase . . . October 1863* (Washington, DC: W. H. Moore, 1866) 19–20.

23 *Indianapolis Star*, October 15, 1863; "Secretary Chase on His Travels," *Philadelphia Inquirer*, October 20, 1863, 2.

24 Ibid.; Chase, *"Going Home to Vote,"* 22–31.

25 Chase to Edward Mansfield, October 18, 1863, *SPCP*, 4:155–56; Chase to Nettie Chase, October 23, 1863, *Spur*, 234.

26 Beale, *Diary of Edward Bates*, October 17, 1863, 310. The letters from Judge Turner, in Carson City, to Chase, in Washington, suggest that he was a friend of Chase. See George Turner to Chase, January 21, 1862, May 28, July 20, October 30, 1863, Chase Papers, LC. After accusations that he was taking bribes, Turner

was forced to resign. See Patricia Cafferata, "Nevada's Crooked Territorial Justices," *Nevada Lawyer* (October 2014), 6-11.

27 Burlingame and Ettlinger, *Diary of John Hay,* June 1863 and October 18, 1863, 78, 93; Fehrenbacher and Fehrenbacher, *Recollected Words*, 216.

28 Burlingame and Ettlinger, *Diary of John Hay,* October 29, 1863, 103; *New York World*, November 3, 1863; Homer Plantz to Chase, November 12, 1863, *SPCP,* 4:182 (in New York on way to Florida).

29 "Great Union Meeting at Baltimore," *Philadelphia Inquirer*, October 29, 1863, 1; "Unconditional Union Mass Meeting in Baltimore," *Washington (DC) Evening Star*, October 29, 1863, 2; James Garfield to Lucretia Garfield, October 30, 1863, in Williams, *Wild Life of the Army*, 299; Chase to William Sprague, October 31, 1863, *SPCP,* 4:165 ("immense concourse" in Baltimore); Chase to Charles Sumner, October 31, 1863, *SPCP,* 4:166 ("was not the Baltimore reception still more remarkable?"); Harris, *Lincoln and the Border States*, 277–83; Stahr, *Stanton*, 325–26.

30 Chase to Kate Chase, August 12, 1863, *Spur,* 216 ("be careful to do nothing which will in the slightest degree diminish his respect for you"); William Sprague to Kate, September 19, 1863, in Oller, *American Queen*, 76 ("great discomfort"); Sprague to Kate, October 19, 1863, ibid. ("indulge in"); Sprague to Chase, November 4, 1863, *SPCP,* 4:176–77; Sprague to Kate, November 4, 1863, Oller 75–76 ("tobacco smoke"); see Lamphier, *Kate Chase and William Sprague*, 108–12.

31 "Marriage of Miss Kate Chase," *Washington (DC) Evening Star*, November 13, 1863, 2; "Marriage in Official Circles," *Brooklyn Daily Eagle,* November 14, 1863, 2; "The Nuptials of Miss Kate Chase," *New York Times*, November 15, 1863, 8 (from *Washington Chronicle*); Oller, *American Queen*, 80–84; *Spur,* 239.

32 Chase to David Wills, November 16, 1863, in "The National Necropolis," *New York Herald*, November 20, 1863, 10 ("impossible for me to be present at the consecration of the grounds"); Lincoln to Chase, November 17, 1863, *Warden*, 555; Chase to Kate Sprague, November 18, 1863, *Spur,* 243–44; Chase to William Sprague, November 18, 1863, ibid., 245.

33 Chase to Lincoln, November 25, 1863, *SPCP,* 4:202–3; Lincoln proclamation, December 8, 1863, *CWL,* 7:53–56; Harris, *With Charity for All,* 133.

34 Lincoln to Chase, September 2, 1863, *CWL,* 6:428–29; Chase to Lincoln, November 25, 1863, *SPCP,* 4:202–3; Lincoln proclamation, December 8, 1863, *CWL* 7:53–56; Chase to Henry Ward Beecher, December 26, 1863, *SPCP,* 4:225.

35 Chase to Thomas Swann, December 18, 1863, *SPCP,* 4:222.

36 Lincoln message, December 8, 1863, *CWL,* 7:41.

37 Chase, *Report of the Secretary of the Treasury on the State of the Finances for the Year Ending June 30, 1863* (Washington, DC: Government Printing Office, 1863), 14, 15, 20, 21.

38 Ibid., 9–10, 21–22, 32–33.

39 Charles Schmidt to Chase, November 3, 1863, *SPCP,* 4:174 ("one-term principle"); Chase to William Sprague, November 26, 1863, *SPCP,* 4:204–5.

40 Chase to Hiram Barney, November 7, 1863, *SPCP*, 4:178.

41 Chase to John Trowbridge, December 27, 1863, Chase Papers, HSP; John Trowbridge, *My Own Story: With Recollections of Noted Persons* (New York: Houghton, Mifflin, 1903), 370–72.

42 Trowbridge, *My Own Story*, 377–78; Ralph Waldo Emerson to Chase, January 10, 1863, online at Whitman Archive; Whitman notes, December 11, 1863, in Thomas Donaldson, *Walt Whitman the Man* (New York: Francis P. Harper, 1896), 156; Trowbridge to Chase, February 5, 1864, *SPCP*, 4:278 (reminds Chase about Whitman); see Rufus Coleman, "Trowbridge and Whitman," *Publications of the Modern Language Association of America* 63 (1948): 262–73; Garret Peck, *Walt Whitman in Washington, D.C.* (Charleston, SC: History Press, 2015), 90–92.

43 Chase to John Trowbridge, December 27, 1863, Chase Papers, HSP; Chase to Helen Walbridge, January 2, 1864, Warden, 561 ("boys and girls"); Chase to Flamen Ball, February 2, 1864, *SPCP*, 4:274–75. For examples of the letters, see Chase to Trowbridge, January 24, February 10, March 20, March 21, 1864, *SPCP*, 4:263–66, 280–84, 332–34, 335–50.

44 Chase to Susan Walker, December 23, 1863, *SPCP*, 4:224.

45 "Wendell Phillips on the Amnesty Proclamation," *New-York Tribune*, December 23, 1863, 1; "Wendell Phillips at Cooper Union," *New York Times*, December 23, 1863, 10; "Wendell Phillips—Gov. Chase," *New-York Tribune*, December 24, 1863, 4; "Wendell Phillips at Cooper Institute," *Chicago Tribune*, December 28, 1863, 1.

46 Chase to Henry Ward Beecher, December 26, 1863, *SPCP*, 4:225–26; Henry Ward Beecher to Chase, December 28, 1863, *SPCP*, 4:231–32; Chase to William Dennison, December 31, 1863, *SPCP*, 4:237–39; Chase to Edward Pierce, January 14, 1864, Pierce Papers, Harvard; Chase to John Bailey, January 22, 1864, Warden, 559–60; Chase to John Trowbridge, March 13, 1864, *SPCP*, 4:323–29.

47 Lyman Stickney to Lincoln, December 2, 1863, Lincoln Papers, LC; Benjamin Flanders to Chase, December 12, 1863, *SPCP*, 4:211–12 (Louisiana); Stickney to Chase, December 21, 1863, Chase Papers, LC; Chase to Thomas Durant, December 28, 1863, *SPCP*, 4:229–30; Chase to Quincy Adams Gillmore, December 29, 1863, *SPCP*, 4:232–33; Chase to Horace Greeley, December 29, 1863, *SPCP*, 4:234–35; "The Department of the South," *New-York Tribune*, December 29, 1863, 1 (Florida meeting); Chase to Lyman Stickney, December 29, 1863, Chase Papers, HSP; see Ovid Futch, "Salmon P. Chase and Civil War Politics in Florida," *Florida Historical Quarterly* 32 (1954): 163–73.

CHAPTER 20: "The Salmon Is a Queer Fish," Early 1864

1 *Hartford Courant*, January 7, 1864 (New Hampshire); Chase to William Dickson, January 14, 1864, Chase Papers, HSP; Chase to James Hall, January 18, 1864, Warden, 560; Chase to Thomas Heaton, January 28, 1864, ibid., 565–66; "Popular Manifestations for Mr. Lincoln," *New York Times*, February 29, 1864,

4; see Blue, *Chase*, 221–22; Charles Flood, *1864: Lincoln at the Gates of History* (New York: Simon & Schuster, 2009), 33–37; Charles Wilson, "The Original Chase Organization Meeting and The Next Presidential Election," *Mississippi Valley Historical Review* 23 (1936): 61 –79.

2 James Hall to Chase, January 14, 1864, Chase Papers, LC; Chase to William Lindsley, February 1, 1864, Warden, 568; Richard Parsons to Chase, February 4, 1864, Chase Papers, LC; Alfred Stone to Chase, February 5, 1864, ibid.; S. S. Osborn to Benjamin Wade, February 8, 1864, Wade Papers, LC; Lewis Gunckel to Chase, February 12, 1864, *SPCP*, 4:291–92.

3 *Washington (DC) Union*, February 20, 1864; *National Republican* (Washington, DC), February 22, 1864; "The First Manifesto of the Chase Men," *New York Herald*, February 22, 1864, 6.

4 "The Circular in Favor of Mr. Chase," *New York Times*, February 24, 1864, 4.

5 Chase to Lincoln, February 22, 1864, *SPCP*, 4:303–4; ibid., February 23, 1864, Lincoln Papers, LC.

6 "From Columbus," *Chicago Tribune*, February 29, 1864, 1; *Cincinnati Commercial*, February 29, 1864; *Cleveland Morning Leader*, February 29, 1864; W. H. West to Lincoln, February 29, 1864, Lincoln Papers, LC; Richard Parsons to Chase, March 2, 1864, *SPCP*, 4:315–16; James Hall to Chase, March 2, 1864, Chase Papers, LC; Elizabeth Yager, "The Presidential Campaign of 1864 in Ohio," *Ohio State Archeological & Historical Quarterly* 34 (1925): 553 –55; William Zornow, "Lincoln, Chase, and the Ohio Radicals in 1864," *Bulletin of the Historical & Philosophical Society of Ohio* 9 (1951): 24–28.

7 Blair speech, *Congressional Globe*, February 27, 1864, app., 50; Chase to Horace Greeley, February 29, 1864, *SPCP*, 4:309–10.

8 Lincoln to Chase, February 29, 1864, *CWL*, 7:212–13.

9 James Garfield to Chase, February 25, 1864, in John Waugh, *Re-Electing Lincoln: The Battle for the 1864 Presidency* (New York: Crown, 1997), 120; Horace Greeley to Chase, March 2, 1864, *SPCP*, 4:314.

10 Chase to William Orton, March 4, 1864, Chase Papers, HSP; Chase to James Hall, March 5, 1864, in "The Presidency," *New York Times*, March 11, 1864, 4; Chase to James Hall, March 6, 1864, Chase Papers, HSP.

11 *New York Evening Post*, March 10, 1864; "Mr. Chase's Declination," *Chicago Tribune*, March 11, 1864, 2; "The Declination of Mr. Chase," *New York Times*, March 12, 1864, 6.

12 "Withdrawal of Gov. Chase," *New-York Tribune*, March 11, 1864, 4.

13 "Secretary Chase and the Presidency," *New York Herald*, March 12, 1864, 4.

14 "The Declination of Mr. Chase," *New York Times*, March 12, 1864, 6; see Chase to Lincoln, November 25, 1863, *SPCP*, 4:202–3.

15 Thomas Durant to Lincoln, February 10, 1864, Lincoln Papers, LC; "From Washington," *Cleveland Daily Leader*, March 5, 1864, 1; "The Petition of the New Orleans Creoles to the President," *Chicago Tribune*, March 10, 1864, 1; Lincoln to Michael Hahn, March 13, 1864, *CWL*, 7:242; Harris, *With Charity for All*, 182–83; Benjamin Quarles, *Lincoln and the Negro* (New York: Oxford University

Press, 1962), 226–29. Harris says that Hahn shared Lincoln's private letter in 1864, but his only support for this is a letter that Hahn wrote *after Lincoln's death*. See Hahn to William Kelley, June 21, 1865, in "The Late President Lincoln on Negro Suffrage," *New York Times*, June 23, 1865, 8.

16 Chase to Horace Greeley, March 4, 1864, *SPCP*, 4:317; Chase to Benjamin Flanders, March 7, 1864, *SPCP*, 4:320–21; Chase to Cyrus Field, April 6, 1864, *SPCP*, 4:364–65; Chase to Nathaniel Banks, April 13, 1864, *SPCP*, 4:374.

17 For a summary of the political situation in early 1864, see Flood, *1864*, 33–52. For questions about whether Lincoln was too deferential to public opinion, see Elizabeth Pryor, *Six Encounters with Lincoln: A President Confronts Democracy and Its Demons* (New York: Viking, 2016), 137–45.

18 Chase to James Wadsworth, June 3, 1864, in "Letter from Hon. S. P. Chase," *New York Herald*, June 5, 1864, 8; "The Grant Testimonial," *Chicago Tribune*, June 8, 1864, 2; "Shall the Black Soldier Have Political Rights?," *Burlington (VT) Daily Times*, June 13, 1864, 1 ("brave words"); Chase to Simeon Nash, June 15, 1864, *SPCP*, 4:397; *Louisville (KY) Daily Journal*, June 16, 1864; "Salmon P. Chase," *Cleveland Daily Leader*, July 7, 1864, 2; *Daily True Delta* (New Orleans), August 28, 1864 (legislature "shall have the power to pass laws extending suffrage to such other persons, citizens of the United States, as by military service, by taxation to support the government, or by intellectual fitness, may be deemed entitled thereto"); Harris, *With Charity for All*, 182–85.

19 Chase to Nettie Chase, September 30, 1863, *SPCP*, 4:148; see Chase to Nettie, November 23, 1863, *Spur*, 247; William Sprague to Chase, December 2, 1863, ibid., 249; Nettie to Chase, February 20, 1864, ibid., 251.

20 Chase diary, August 15, 1862, *SPCP*, 1:362 (reading Victor Hugo in French); Chase to Charlotte Eastman, June 8, 1863, Chase Papers, HSP; Chase to Eastman, February 1, 1864, ibid.; Chase to Nettie Chase, February 26, 1864, *SPCP*, 4:308–9; Chase to Adolphus Mot, October 1866, Chase Papers, HSP.

21 "Grand Vocal and Instrumental Concert," *Philadelphia Inquirer*, April 29, 1864, 8; *Delaware State Journal* (Wilmington), May 3, 1864; *National Republican* (Washington, DC), May 18, 1864; Burlingame and Ettlinger, *Diary of John Hay*, May 20, 1864, 197; Gienapp and Gienapp, *Diary of Gideon Welles*, May 21, 1864, 414; "Concert at the Residence of Secretary Chase," *New York Herald*, May 23, 1864, 1.

22 Chase to Nettie Chase, May 5, 1864, *Spur*, 256.

23 "Proceedings of Congress," *Chicago Tribune*, January 6, 1864, 1 (House questions about Cooke); Jay Cooke to Chase, January 16, 1864, Oberholtzer, *Cooke*, 1:300–308 (reviewing five-twenty sales process); Chase to Cyrus Field, February 17, 1864, *SPCP*, 4:294–95; Chase to Jay Cooke, March 19, 1864, Chase Papers, HSP (personal finances); Chase to Schuyler Colfax, April 1, 1864, in "Secretary Chase and the Firm of Jay Cooke & Co.," *Philadelphia Inquirer*, April 8, 1864, 4 (responds to House questions about Cooke); *New York World*, May 5, 1864 (more questions about Chase-Cooke relations); Edling, *Hercules in the Cradle*, 198–99; Larson, *Jay Cooke*, 145–46, 160–62.

24 Chase to Cyrus Field, April 6, 1864, *SPCP,* 4:365; Chase to Horace Greeley, April 6, 1864, *SPCP,* 4:366–67; Chase to Richard Smith, May 27, 1864, *SPCP,* 4:393; see Gische, "New York City Banks," 24–31, 40–45.

25 "Monetary Affairs," *New York Times,* February 8, 1864, 2 ("undoubtedly"); ibid., February 24, 1864, 2 (additional capital for Fourth Bank); Chase to Thaddeus Stevens, April 11, 1864, *SPCP,* 4:370–72 (forwards bill to tax state bank notes); Chase to Richard Smith, May 27, 1864, *SPCP,* 4:393; Gische, "New York City Banks," 48–49.

26 Chase to Richard Smith, May 27, 1864, *SPCP,* 4:393.

27 National Banking Act, February 25, 1863, *Statutes at Large,* 12:668 (sec, 12; shareholder liability); *Congressional Globe,* March 23, 1864, 1256–57 (Hooper); National Banking Act, June 3, 1864, *Statutes at Large,* 13:103 (sec. 12; shareholder liability); Gische, "New York City Banks," 46–52.

28 National Banking Act, June 3, 1864, *Statutes at Large,* 13:99–118; "Financial and Commercial," *New York Herald,* November 23, 1864, 2 (Bank of Commerce about to become national bank); William Fessenden, *Report of the Secretary of the Treasury on the State of the Finances for the Year 1864* (Washington, DC: Government Printing Office, December 1864), 24; Gische, "New York City Banks," 57–61.

29 Chase to Jay Cooke, April 4, 1864, Oberholtzer, *Cooke,* 1:362; Chase to Lyman Stickney, May 25, 1864, Warden, 695; Chase to Seward, May 30, 1864, Warden, 597–98.

30 "The Widening Rupture in the Republican Party," *New York Herald,* April 27, 1864, 4; Chase to John Brough, May 19, 1864, *SPCP,* 4:384.

31 Chase to John Trowbridge, March 13, 20, 21, 1864, *SPCP,* 4:323–28, 332–34, and 335–50; William Wise to Jay Cooke, April 25, 1864, Oberholtzer, *Cooke,* 1:364; Chase to Trowbridge, May 11, 1864, Warden, 589; John Trowbridge, *The Ferry Boy and the Financier* (Boston: Walker, Wise, 1864), 72, 311–32.

32 Gideon Welles to Chase, May 20, 1864, *SPCP,* 4:386; Chase to Welles, May 24, 1864, *SPCP,* 4:386, note 1; Gienapp and Gienapp, *Diary of Gideon Welles,* June 25, 1864, 431–32.

33 *Congressional Globe,* April 23, 1864, 1829–31 (Blair); "Frank Blair's Attack on Secretary Chase," *New York Herald,* April 24, 1864, 4; "The Sanitary Fair," *Baltimore Sun,* April 25, 1864, 1; *Congressional Globe,* April 29, 1864, 1868 (Brooks); "The Charges Against the Treasury Department," *Cincinnati Enquirer,* May 2, 1864, 3. For an insightful discussion, see Smith, *Enemy Within,* 97–126.

34 Lincoln to Stanton, April 21, 1864, *CWL,* 7:307; "The Sanitary Fair," *Baltimore Sun,* April 25, 1864, 1; "Secretary Chase at the Sanitary Fair," *Philadelphia Inquirer,* April 25, 1864, 4; "Blair on Chase," *New York Herald,* April 25, 1864, supplement 1; Gienapp and Gienapp, *Diary of Gideon Welles,* April 28, 1864, 398; "Frank Blair's Re-Appointment," *New-York Tribune,* April 29, 1864, 4; Lincoln to House, May 2, 1864, *CWL,* 7:326–27 (listing Blair correspondence); Chase to Jay Cooke, May 5, 1864, *SPCP,* 4:379–80; Chase to Nettie Chase, May 5, 1864, *Spur,* 256–57; Chase to Richard Parsons, May

7, 1864, Warden, 586–87. Albert Riddle later described Chase losing his temper on the train to Baltimore about Blair. Albert Riddle, *Recollections of War Times* (New York: G. P. Putnam's Sons, 1895), 266–68; see Blue, *Chase*, 229–30. I question Riddle's account because the newspapers do not mention Riddle being in Baltimore. See "The Sanitary Fair," *Baltimore Sun*, April 25, 1864, 1; "Secretary Chase at the Sanitary Fair," *Philadelphia Inquirer*, April 25, 1864, 4.

35 "Mr. Chase on Arbitrary Arrests," *New-York Tribune*, May 25, 1864, 4; *New York World*, May 26, 1864.

36 Chase to Cyrus Field, February 17, 1864, *SPCP*, 4:294 (favors constitutional amendment); "National Radical Democratic Convention," *Chicago Tribune*, June 3, 1864, 2 (Cleveland convention); "The Platform," *New York Times*, June 9, 1864, 1 (Baltimore convention); Lincoln to Committee, June 9, 1864, *CWL*, 7:380; "House of Representatives," *New York Times*, June 16, 1864, 4 (constitutional amendment rejected in House); see Burlingame, *Abraham Lincoln*, 2:641–45; Flood, *1864*, 107–11, 118–34; Foner, *Fiery Trial*, 291–300; Goodwin, *Team of Rivals*, 686–90; Stahr, *Seward*, 417–21.

37 Chase to Simeon Nash, June 15, 1864, *SPCP*, 4:397. On the chief justice question, see Charles Sumner to Chase, October 14, 1864, Schuckers, 512; William Fessenden to Chase, October 20, 1864, Schuckers, 512.

38 "Secretary Chase Serenaded," *National Republican* (Washington, DC), June 14, 1864, 2; McPherson, *Battle Cry of Freedom*, 718–43.

39 "Secretary Chase Serenaded," *National Republican* (Washington, DC), June 14, 1864, 2. I have not been able to identify the relative to whom Chase referred in this speech.

40 Ibid. I have quoted the first version rather than the corrected version in the second edition of the paper. See "Secretary Chase's Speech," ibid. (2nd ed.).

41 Chase diary, June 24, 1864, *SPCP*, 1:461–62.

42 Chase to John Forbes, June 25, 1864, *SPCP*, 4:404; Chase to Thaddeus Stevens, June 25, 1864, NARG 233; Chase to Reuben Fenton, June 25, 1864, Warden, 608; Abandoned Property Act of 1864, July 2, 1864, *Statutes at Large*, 13:276; Chase diary, July 2, 1864, *SPCP*, 1:474 ("how much good I expected to accomplish under this bill!"); Chase to Cyrus Grosvenor, July 11, 1864, Chase Papers, HSP; Fessenden, *Report of the Secretary of the Treasury . . . for the Year 1864*, 26–27 (explaining why he allowed "the freedmen to remain as they had been, under military protection").

43 Chase to John Cisco, May 24, 1864, *SPCP*, 4:387–88; Chase to Deming Duer, June 20, 1864, Warden, 605; Chase to John Cisco, June 20, 1864, *SPCP*, 4:399; Chase to John Stewart, June 25, 1864, Warden, 608; Chase to William Noyes, July 11, 1864, *SPCP*, 4:418–19.

44 *New York Evening Post*, June 24, 1864 (letter to the editor from "a loyal private banker"); Chase diary, June 26, 1864, *SPCP*, 1:463; Chase to John Cisco, June 26, 1864, Warden, 610–11; Chase to William Cullen Bryant, June 26, 1864, ibid., 611; Chase to Jay Cooke, June 26, 1864, *SPCP*, 4:405.

45 Chase diary, June 27, 1864, *SPCP*, 1:463–65; Chase to Lincoln, June 27, 1864, Lincoln Papers, LC; Chase to John Cisco, July 2, 1864, *SPCP*, 4:413–14; Chase to Horace Greeley, July 4, 1864, *SPCP*, 4:416–17.

46 Chase diary, June 28, 1864, *CWL*, 1:465–66; Lincoln to Chase, June 28, 1864, *CWL*, 7:412–13; Chase to Lincoln, June 28, 1864, Lincoln Papers, LC (requests conversation); Chase to Lincoln, June 28, 1864, *SPCP*, 4:406–7 (two letters); Chase to John Cisco, June 28, 1864, Warden, 611; Chase to John Cisco, July 2, 1864, *SPCP*, 4:413–14.

47 Chase diary, June 28, 1864, *CWL*, 1:465–68; Chase to Justin Morrill, June 28, 1864, NARG 56 (two letters); John Cisco to Chase, June 28, 1864, Lincoln Papers, LC.

48 Lincoln to Chase, June 28, 1864, *CWL*, 7:413–14; Chase diary, June 29, 1864, *SPCP*, 1:468 (received Lincoln's reply "this morning").

49 Chase to Lincoln, June 29, 1864, *SPCP*, 4:409–10.

50 Chase to Thaddeus Stevens, June 29, 1864, Lincoln Papers, LC.

51 Chase to Lincoln, June 30, 1864, Lincoln Papers, LC; Chase diary, June 30, 1864, *SPCP*, 1:469–70.

52 Lincoln to Chase, June 30, 1864, *CWL*, 7:419; Burlingame and Ettlinger, *Diary of John Hay*, June 30, 1864, 213; Goodwin, *Team of Rivals*, 632–33.

53 Chase diary, June 30, 1864, *SPCP*, 1:471; Jay Cooke to Chase, June 30, 1864, Chase Papers, HSP; Chase to Edwin Stanton, June 30, 1864, Warden, 618; Chase to William Cullen Bryant, June 30, 1864, *SPCP*, 4:411–12; Chase to John Cisco, July 2, 1864, *SPCP*, 4:412–15.

54 Chase diary, June 30, 1864, *SPCP*, 1:471–72.

CHAPTER 21: "So Help Me God," Late 1864

1 Chase to Abraham Lincoln, December 20, 1862, Lincoln Papers, LC; Chase to John Cisco, July 1, 1864, *SPCP*, 4:412–15; Chase to Horace Greeley, July 4, 1864, *SPCP*, 4:416–17; Chase to William Curtis Noyes, July 11, 1864, *SPCP*, 4:418–20.

2 "Senator Fessenden Secretary of the Treasury!," *Washington (DC) Evening Star*, July 1, 1864, 2; *Brooklyn Daily Eagle*, July 2, 1864 ("jolly story-teller"); "Our New Financier," *New-York Tribune*, July 2, 1864, 4; "The Resignation of Chase," *Ohio Statesman* (Columbus), July 4, 1864, 2 (from *New York World*) ("jolly fellow").

3 Chase diary, July 1, 1864, *SPCP*, 1:473–74; Stahr, *Stanton*, 354.

4 Chase diary, July 4, 1865, *SPCP*, 1:474–76. For more on the Wade-Davis bill, see Flood, *1864*, 180–85; Harris, *With Charity for All*, 186–90; Stahr, *Stanton*, 360–62. Louis Masur, in *Lincoln's Last Speech*, 111, comments on Chase's diary entry that "Chase and other radicals held on to the idea that Lincoln was not fully committed to abolition and used it as fuel to energize their opposition."

5 "Secretary Fessenden Sworn In," *Washington (DC) Evening Star*, July 5, 1864 (3rd ed.), 2; Chase diary, July 4–6, 1865, *SPCP*, 1:476–79; Chase to Nettie Chase, July 5, 1865, *Spur*, 258.

6 Chase to Kate Sprague, July 11, 1864, *Spur,* 259–60; Chase to William Curtis Noyes, July 11, 1864, Chase Papers, HSP; Benjamin Cooling, *Jubal Early's Raid on Washington 1864* (Baltimore: Nautical & Aviation, 1989), 83–156.

7 Chase diary, July 13–17, 1865, *SPCP,* 1:479–82; "The Railroad Clear Again," *Washington (DC) Evening Star,* July 13, 1864, 2 (checking the rail line).

8 Chase diary, July 17–August 2, 1864, *SPCP,* 1:482–85; "Serenade to Secretary Chase," *Washington (DC) Evening Star,* September 21, 1864, 1 (few weeks of vacation "after unremitted labor for eight or nine years").

9 Chase diary, August 3–4, 1864, *SPCP,* 1:485; Chase to William Mellen, August 5, 1864, *SPCP,* 4:422; *Cincinnati Daily Commercial,* August 6, 8, 1864; "The Lincoln Convention Yesterday," *Cincinnati Enquirer,* August 8, 1864, 3; "Ben. Eggleston," *Ohio Statesman* (Columbus), August 8, 1864, 2; "The Cincinnati Commercial on Eggleston's Nomination," *Ohio Statesman* (Columbus), August 9, 1864, 2; Mellen to Chase, August 10, 1864, *SPCP,* 4:420–21; Chase to Mellen, August 17, 1864, Mellen Papers, Bowdoin; Chase to Charles May, August 31, 1864, Warden, 628–29.

10 "President Lincoln Denounced by His Party," *New York Herald,* August 6, 1864, 4; Thurlow Weed to W. H. Seward, August 22, 1864, Lincoln Papers, LC; Henry Raymond to Lincoln, August 22, 1864, ibid.; Lincoln, memorandum, August 23, 1864, *CWL,* 7:514; Lincoln, draft commission for Raymond, August 24, 1864, Lincoln Papers, LC; Goodwin, *Team of Rivals,* 647–53; Reynolds, *Abe,* 814–17; Stahr, *Seward,* 404–7.

11 Chase to William Noyes, July 11, 1864, *SPCP,* 4:419 ("great and almost universal dissatisfaction with Mr. Lincoln"); Chase to William Mellen, August 5, 1864, *SPCP,* 4:422; Chase to Charles Schmidt, August 12, 1864, Chase Papers, CHLA; Chase diary, August 25, 1864, *SPCP,* 1:494; Chase to Charles May, August 31, 1864, Warden, 628–29; "Mr. Chase," *Fall River (MA) Evening News,* September 1, 1864, 2 (Chase's letter to Schmidt).

12 Chase diary, August, September 2–10, 1864, *SPCP,* 1:498–501; *New Orleans Times Picayune,* September 21, 1864 (speech); Chase to Kate Sprague, June 24, 1865, *Spur,* 284 ("one to whom your first duties belong"); Chase to Nettie Chase, January 24, 1867, *Spur,* 341 ("no woman could have a kinder more indulgent husband").

13 "The Democratic National Convention," *New York Herald,* August 31, 1864, 1; "The Rival Platforms," *New-York Tribune,* September 1, 1864, 4; "Fall of Atlanta," *New York Herald,* September 3, 1864, 1; Stahr, *Seward,* 407–9; Waugh, *Re-Electing Lincoln,* 276–94; Weber, *Copperheads,* 166–76.

14 Samuel Hooper to Chase, September 13, 1864, Chase Papers, HSP. We do not have Chase's letter to Hooper, but Hooper more or less quoted it back to Chase.

15 Chase diary, September 12–19, 1864, *SPCP,* 1:501–4; Chase to John Milliken, September 14, 1864, private collection, on Heritage Auctions website, accessed January 2020; Chase to Samuel Hooper, September 16, 1864, *SPCP,* 4:430; Chase to Kate Sprague, September 17, 1864, *SPCP,* 4:431–33; J. K. Herbert to Benjamin Butler, September 26, 1864, Jesse Marshall, ed., *Private and Official*

Correspondence of General Benjamin F. Butler During the Period of the Civil War (printed privately, 1917), 5:167–68 (Chase had long interview with Lincoln; perhaps promised chief justice position).

16 "Another Campaign Flag Flung to the Breeze," *Washington (DC) Evening Star*, September 20, 1864, 1; "Serenade to Secretary Chase," *Washington (DC) Evening Star*, September 21, 1864, 1; *Pittsburgh Daily Commercial*, September 21, 1864; "Speech by Secretary Chase," *Chicago Tribune*, September 22, 1864, 3; *Buffalo Courier*, September 23, 1864; *Xenia (OH) Sentinel*, September 27, 1864; "Speech of Hon. S.P. Chase," *Liberator* (Boston), October 7, 1864, 1.

17 Chase diary, September 20–24, 1864, *SPCP*, 1:506–7; *Cleveland Daily Herald*, September 21, 1864; Chase to Kate Sprague, September 23, 1864, Chase Papers, HSP.

18 "Grand Demonstration in Cincinnati," *Chicago Tribune*, September 28, 1864, 2; "Great Speech of Hon. S. P. Chase," *Chicago Tribune*, September 30, 1864, 3.

19 "Great Speech of Hon. S. P. Chase," *Chicago Tribune*, September 30, 1864, 3. Although the Northern papers praised Farragut's bravery in 1864, they did not quote him as saying "damn the torpedoes." That famous phrase did not appear in print until 1870. See "Farragut," *New York Herald*, August 27, 1864, 1; "The Birthday Ball," *Washington (DC) Evening Star*, February 23, 1870, 1; *Atlanta Constitution*, August 18, 1870; *Brooklyn Daily Eagle*, September 30, 1870.

20 Chase diary, September 28–October 11, 1864, *SPCP*, 1:507–8; Chase to John Sherman, October 2, 1864, Sherman Papers, LC (from Louisville); Chase to John Stevens Jr., October 3, 1864, Stevens Papers, NYHS; *Louisville (KY) Daily Journal*, October 3, 1864; "Union Men of Ohio Attention," *Cleveland Daily Leader*, October 6, 1864, 2; Chase to Lincoln, October 11, 1864, Lincoln Papers, LC; "The News," *Chicago Tribune*, October 12, 1864, 1; "The October Elections," *New-York Tribune*, October 12, 1864, 1; "From Kentucky," *New York Times*, October 16, 1864, 6 (Louisville speech); Chase to George Harrington, October 16, 1864, Harrington Papers, Missouri Historical Society ("we must take nothing for granted"); Chase to Hiram Barney, October 18, 1864, Chase Papers, LC ("we must not be found napping").

21 Edwin Stanton to Chase, October 13, 1864, Chase Papers, HSP; Chase to Stanton, October 13, 1864, *SPCP*, 4:434–35. On the choice of chief justice, see Burlingame, *Abraham Lincoln*, 2:731–36; Fairman, *Reconstruction and Reunion*, 5–31; David Silver, *Lincoln's Supreme Court* (Urbana: University of Illinois Press, 1956), 185–209.

22 Charles Sumner to Chase, October 14, 1864, Schuckers, 512; Horace Greeley to Chase, October 19, 1864, *SPCP*, 4:435–36; Samuel Hooper to Chase, October 21, 1864, Chase Papers, HSP; Charles Cleveland to Chase, October 23, 1864, Chase Papers, HSP; Edwin Stanton to Chase, November 19, 1864, Schuckers, 512–13.

23 "For Chief Justice—Salmon P. Chase," *Chicago Tribune*, October 15, 1864, 2.

24 "The New Chief Justice," *New York Herald*, October 16, 1864, 4; "Who Shall Be the Next Chief Justice?," *New York Herald*, October 18, 1864, 4; *New York World*, October 20, 1864 ("we consider Chase out of the question"); Chase to Horace

Greeley, October 21, 1864, Greeley Papers, NYPL (Davis favors Swayne and "his desires would have more weight"); "News from Washington," *Ohio Statesman* (Columbus), October 22, 1864, 2 ("Lincoln will not nominate Chase"); David Davis to Lincoln, October 22, 1864, Lincoln Papers, LC (urging Swayne).

25 Chase to Charles Sumner, October 19, 1864, Chase Papers, LC; William Fessenden to Chase, October 20, 1864, Schuckers, 512; Sumner to Lincoln, October 24, 1864, Lincoln Papers, LC.

26 Chase diary, October 13–22, 1864, *SPCP*, 1:508; "Ex-Secretary Chase," *New-York Tribune*, October 19, 1864, 4 (Covington speech); Chase to Edwin Stanton, October 24, 1864, Stanton Papers, LC; Henry S. Graham and E. Hergesheimer, *Map Showing the Distribution of the Slave Population of the Southern States of the United States, Compiled from the Census of 1860* (Washington, DC: Henry S. Graham, 1861), available at Library of Congress online, accessed April 12, 2021, https://www.loc.gov/item/99447026/; Anne Marshall, *Creating a Confederate Kentucky: The Lost Cause and Civil War Memory in a Border State* (Chapel Hill: University of North Carolina Press, 2010), 26–31.

27 Johnson speech, October 24, 1864, *PAJ*, 7:252–53; Chase to Robert Corwin, April 24, 1866, *SPCP*, 5:84 ("heroic utterance").

28 "Hon. S. P. Chase in Philadelphia," *Philadelphia Inquirer*, October 28, 1864, 8.

29 Chase diary, October 28–31, 1864, *SPCP*, 1:509; "Hon. S. P. Chase to Speak," *Cleveland Daily Leader*, October 31, 1864, 3; "Great Speech of Hon. S. P. Chase," ibid., November 1, 1864, 4.

30 Chase diary, November 1–8, 1864, *SPCP*, 1:509–10; "The Campaign in Michigan," *Chicago Tribune*, November 4, 1864, 1; "Hon. S. P. Chase," ibid., November 5, 1864, 4; Chase to George Harrington, November 8, 1864, Harrington Papers, Missouri Historical Society.

31 Whitelaw Reid to Chase, October 19, 27, 1864, Chase Papers, HSP; "A Victory of Gigantic Proportions," *Chicago Tribune*, November 9, 1864, 1; "The Election," *Cleveland Daily Leader*, November 9, 1864, 1; Chase to George Denison, November 11, 1864, *SPCP*, 4:437.

32 Chase to Hugh McCulloch, November 10, 1864, McCulloch Papers, LC; Chase to George Denison, November 11, 1864, *SPCP*, 4:437–38; Chase to Jacob Schuckers, November 19, 1864, Chase Papers, LC; Chase to Charles Sumner, December 2, 1864, Chase Papers, LC ("I should have been there earlier").

33 Chase to Charles Sumner, November 12, 1864, *SPCP*, 4:438–40.

34 "The Chief Justiceship," *Ohio Statesman* (Columbus), November 15, 1864, 2 (from *New York Times*); "From Washington," *New-York Tribune*, November 17, 1864, 5; Edwin Stanton to Chase, November 19, 1864, Schuckers, 512–13; "Mr. Chase to be Chief Justice," *Cincinnati Enquirer*, November 25, 1864, 3; *Buffalo Courier*, November 26, 1864.

35 Randall, *Diary of Orville Hickman Browning*, October 13, 1864, 1:686–87; Horace Greeley to Chase, November 13, 1864, Chase Papers, HSP; William Fessenden to Chase, November 18, 1864, Chase Papers, HSP; Charles Sumner to Chase, November 20, 1864, Chase Papers, HSP.

36 Chase to John Sherman, November 12, 1864, Sherman Papers, LC; Chase to Richard Parsons, November 22, 27, 1864, Chase Papers, HSP; Chase to Robert Carter, November 23, 1864, Marble Papers, LC.

37 Chase to Dwight Bannister, November 29, 1864, Chase Papers, LC (passing through Columbus tomorrow; intends to spend Sunday in Cleveland); Chase to Charles Sumner, December 2, 3, 1864, ibid. (two letters from Cleveland); "Hon. S. P. Chase in Town," *Cleveland Daily Leader*, December 3, 1864, 4; Chase to Warner Bateman, December 6, 1864, Bateman Papers, Western Reserve Historical Society (from Philadelphia); Charles Cleveland to Chase, December 7, 1864, Chase Papers, LC (sorry to miss him in Philadelphia).

38 "Meeting of the Supreme Court," *New York Herald*, December 6, 1864, 4; *New York World*, December 6, 1864; *National Republican* (Washington, DC), December 6, 1864 (second edition reports nomination and confirmation); Chase to Lincoln, December 6, 1864, Lincoln Papers, LC. There is a copy of the letter, also in Chase's hand, with slightly different wording, in the Chase Papers, NYHS.

39 Warden, 630. See Blue, *Chase*, 245; Oller, *American Queen*, 94. Oller questions the tale.

40 "The Chief Justiceship," *New-York Tribune*, December 7, 1864, 4; *New York World*, December 7, 1864; "The New Appointment," *New York Times*, December 8, 1864, 4; "The New Chief Justice," *Philadelphia Inquirer*, December 8, 1864, 1; Charles Dana to James Pike, December 12, 1864, Pike Papers, Maine.

41 Charles Cleveland to Chase, December 7, 1864, Chase Papers, LC; John Jay to Chase, December 7, 1864, ibid.; William Schouler to Chase, December 7, 1864, ibid.; Alphonso Taft to Chase, December 7, 1864, ibid.; John Wright to Chase, December 7, 1864, ibid.

42 "The Nomination of Hon. S. P. Chase as Chief Justice," *Cincinnati Enquirer*, December 7, 1864, 2; Gienapp and Gienapp, *Diary of Gideon Welles*, December 15, 1864, 546.

43 Foster interview with Nicolay, October 23, 1878, Fehrenbacher and Fehrenbacher, *Recollected Words*, 162. For other examples, see ibid., 38 (George Boutwell, 1895); ibid., 55 (Noah Brooks, 1895). On the general problem of recalling Lincoln's words, see the Fehrenbachers' introduction.

44 *Baltimore American*, December 8, 1864; "The Visit of the Maryland Electors," *Chicago Tribune*, December 25, 1864, 1; Fehrenbacher and Fehrenbacher, *Recollected Words*, 15 (reprints *Baltimore American*).

45 "Correspondence of the *Baltimore Sun*," *Baltimore Sun*, December 6, 1864, 4 (Supreme Court had no quorum yet); ibid., December 7, 1864, 4 (Supreme Court honors Taney); *Lancaster (PA) Daily Evening Express*, December 12, 1864 (crowd hoped to see Chase); "Chief Justice Chase," *Philadelphia Inquirer*, December 13, 1864, 1.

46 Act to Prescribe an Oath of Office, July 2, 1862, *Statutes at Large*, 12:502; "The News," *Chicago Tribune*, December 16, 1864, 1; *Cincinnati Gazette*, December 16, 1864; "The Supreme Court," *Detroit Free Press*, December 16, 1864, 4; "Inauguration of Chief Justice Chase," *New York Herald*, December 16, 1864, 4; "Chief

Justice Chase on the Bench," *Philadelphia Inquirer*, December 16, 1864, 1; *Pittsburgh Daily Commercial*, December 16, 1864; "Chief Justice Chase," *Washington (DC) Evening Star*, December 15, 1864, 1; *Washington (DC) Morning Chronicle*, December 16, 1864; Noah Brooks, *Washington, D.C., in Lincoln's Time* (Athens: University of Georgia Press, 1989), ed. Herbert Mitgang, 175 ("gorgeously dressed").

CHAPTER 22: "Universal Suffrage," 1864–65

1 Fairman, *Reconstruction and Reunion*, 32–35, 62–69.
2 Chase to Margaret Bailey, January 6, 1865, in Young, *Some Unpublished Letters*, 91–92; Chase to Susan Walker, March 17, 1865, *SPCP*, 5:13–14; Chase to Susan Trimble, April 14, 1865, Warden, 637–38 ("caring nothing"); Tobey v. Leonards, 69 U.S. 423 (1865); Fairman, *Reconstruction and Reunion*, 34–35.
3 See Gordon v. United States, 69 U.S. 561 (1865); Ex parte Garland, 71 U.S. 633 (1866); Reichart v. Felps, 73 U.S. 160 (1868); The Alicia, 74 U.S. 571 (1869); Hepburn v. Griswold, 75 U.S. 603 (1870); United States v. Dewitt, 76 U.S. 41 (1870); The Justices v. Murray, 76 U.S. 274 (1870); Collector v. Day, 78 U.S. 113 (1871); United States v. Klein, 80 U.S. 128 (1872); United States v. Railroad Company, 84 U.S. 322 (1873). As Stanley Kutler notes, in *Judicial Power and Reconstruction Politics* (Chicago: University of Chicago Press, 1968), 114, there is some disagreement about whether some of these cases should be included on this list.
4 The nineteenth-century justices who ran for president were Salmon Chase, David Davis, Stephen Field, and John McLean. On consensus in the court, see Stacia Haynie, "Leadership and Consensus on the U.S. Supreme Court," *Journal of Politics* 54 (1992): 1158–69; Thomas Walker, Lee Epstein, and William Dixon, "On the Mysterious Demise of Consensual Norms in the United States Supreme Court," *Journal of Politics* 50 (1988): 361–89.
5 Fairman, *Reconstruction and Reunion*, 62–63; W. H. Smith, "Supreme Court and Its Justices in Days Following the Civil War," *Washington (DC) Evening Star*, April 22, 1923, 77; Edward White, "Salmon Portland Chase and the Judicial Culture of the Supreme Court in the Civil War Era," in *The Supreme Court and the Civil War*, ed. Jennifer Lowe (Washington, DC: Supreme Court Historical Society, 1996), 39.
6 Fairman, *Reconstruction and Reunion*, 69–80; White, "Salmon Portland Chase," 40–41. The description of the role of the chief in conference is from an 1875 obituary, by John Archibald Campbell, of his colleague Benjamin Curtis. See John William Wallace, *Cases Argued and Adjudged in the Supreme Court of the United States* (Washington, DC: William H. Morrison, 1875), vol. 20, x (Campbell's remarks).
7 See David Hughes, "Salmon P. Chase as Chief Justice," *Vanderbilt Law Review* 18 (1965): 599–614 (Chase's relations with other justices); Jonathan Lurie, *The Chase Court: Justices, Rulings, and Legacy* (Santa Barbara, CA: ABC-Clio, 2004),

15 (Chase "had to deal with self-confident if not egotistical colleagues while he sought a harmonious judicial environment").

8 Chase diary, January 14, 1865, *SPCP*, 1:517 (walking with Wayne); Chase to Kate Sprague, March 28, 1865, *Spur*, 263; Lurie, *Chase Court*, 27–30; Silver, *Lincoln's Supreme Court*, 16–18.

9 Fairman, *Reconstruction and Reunion*, 3 (Catron "absent throughout the term"); Lurie, *Chase Court*, 30–32.

10 Lurie, *Chase Court*, 32–35; Silver, *Lincoln's Supreme Court*, 22; Chase to Samuel Nelson, October 6, 1866, Chase Papers, HSP; Chase to Samuel Nelson, May 28, 1867, October 17, 1870, Chase Papers, LC.

11 Fairman, *Reconstruction and Reunion*, 82–84, 560, 719 (Grier "was not up to the work at hand"); Lurie, *Chase Court*, 35–36; Silver, *Lincoln's Supreme Court*, 22; Chase to Samuel Miller, July 3, 1866, *SPCP*, 5:120 (Grier's health).

12 Phillip Clifford, *Nathan Clifford: Democrat* (New York: G. P. Putnam's Sons, 1922), 1–25; Lurie, *Chase Court*, 37–39; Silver, *Lincoln's Supreme Court*, 22–23; W.H. Smith, "Supreme Court," *Washington (DC) Evening Star*, April 22, 1923, 77.

13 Chase diary, January 1, March 9, 1857, *SPCP*, 1:247 and 275 (meetings with Swayne); Noah Swayne to Chase, April 4, 1861, Chase Papers, LC; Chase to Horace Greeley, October 21, 1864, Greeley Papers, NYPL (describing Swayne as a "friend and neighbor in Columbus"); Lurie, *Chase Court*, 39–41; Silver, *Lincoln's Supreme Court*, 57–63.

14 John Sherman to Lincoln, October 22, 1864, Lincoln Papers, LC; Schuyler Colfax to Lincoln, November 3, 1864, ibid.; Chase to Charles Sumner, November 12, 1864, *SPCP*, 4:439; Lurie, *Chase Court*, 41–43; Michael Ross, *Justice of Shattered Dreams: Samuel Freeman Miller and the Supreme Court During the Civil War Era* (Baton Rouge: Louisiana State University Press, 2003), 1–81.

15 David Davis to Lincoln, October 22, 1864, Lincoln Papers, LC; Davis to Julius Rockwell, December 12, 1864, Davis Papers, ALPL; Chase to Davis, June 24, 1867, *SPCP*, 5:157; Davis to Chase, August 12, 1867, Chase Papers, LC; Goodwin, *Team of Rivals*, 150–51; Willard King, *Lincoln's Manager: David Davis* (Cambridge, MA: Harvard University Press, 1960).

16 Chase to Charles Sumner, November 12, 1864, *SPCP*, 4:439 (Field supports Chase); Chase diary, January 6, 1866, *SPCP*, 1:607; Chase to Stephen Field, April 30, 1866, *SPCP*, 5:88; Paul Kens, *Justice Stephen Field: Shaping Liberty from the Gold Rush to the Gilded Age* (Lawrence: University Press of Kansas, 1997), 1–97; Silver, *Lincoln's Supreme Court*, 88–93.

17 Chase diary, January 16, 1865, *SPCP*, 1:517; Chase to Susan Walker, March 17, 1865, *SPCP*, 5:14; Richard Aynes, "Kate Chase, the 'Sphere of Women's Work,' and Her Influence upon Her Father's Dissent in *Bradwell v. Illinois*," *Ohio History* 117 (2010), 36–37 (dissent count); Benedict, "Salmon P. Chase," 480 (seven of eighteen important Reconstruction opinions); Hughes, "Salmon P. Chase," 602–3 ("wrote more opinions than any other member in every term except those when he was presiding in the impeachment trial and after his stroke").

18　Chase to Lincoln, January 2, 1865, Lincoln Papers, LC; Lincoln to Chase, January 2, 1865, *CWL*, 8:195; Chase to Susan Walker, January 2, 1865, *SPCP*, 5:4–5.

19　Charles Sumner to Chase, December 21, 1864, in Palmer, *Sumner Letters*, 2:259–60; Sumner to Chase, January 5, 1865, ibid., 260n3 (Chase replied "not forgotten"); Chase diary, January 21, 1865, *SPCP*, 1:519; Chase to Sumner, January 23, 1865, Sumner Papers, Harvard; Chase diary, February 1, 1865, *SPCP*, 1:521; Sumner notes re: John Rock, February 1, 1865, John Hay Papers, LC; David Davis to Julius Rockwell, February 19, 1865, Davis Papers, ALPL; Fairman, *Reconstruction and Reunion*, 59–60.

20　The Circassian, 69 U.S. 135 (1865); Mrs. Alexander's Cotton, 69 U.S. 404 (1865); The Slavers (Kate), 69 U.S. 350 (1865); Fairman, *Reconstruction and Reunion*, 39 ("it was a matter with which he was thoroughly conversant").

21　"The Rev. Henry Ward Beecher," *Baltimore Sun*, February 1, 1865, 1; *National Republican* (Washington, DC), February 1, 1865; Eric Foner, *The Second Founding: How the Civil War and Reconstruction Remade the Constitution* (New York: W. W. Norton, 2019), 35–37; Goodwin, *Team of Rivals*, 686–90.

22　Chase to W. T. Sherman, January 2, 1865, *SPCP*, 5:3–4; Sherman to Chase, January 11, 1865, *SPCP*, 5:6–7; Chase to George Denison, January 22, 1865, Warden, 633; Chase to William Kelley, January 22, 1865, ibid.; Chase to Wendell Phillips, February 7, 1865, *SPCP*, 5:10–11; Chase to Francis Lieber, February 14, 1865, *SPCP*, 5:11–12.

23　"The Inauguration," *Washington (DC) Evening Star*, March 4, 1865, 2; Chase to Susan Walker, March 1865, *SPCP*, 5:14; Donald, *Lincoln*, 575; David Donald, *Charles Sumner and the Rights of Man* (New York: Alfred A. Knopf, 1970), 218–19; William Harris, *Lincoln's Last Months* (Cambridge, MA: Belknap Press, 2004), 87–90; Reynolds, *Abe*, 866–69; Stahr, *Stanton*, 401–2; Trefousse, *Johnson*, 189–90.

24　"The Inauguration," *Washington (DC) Evening Star*, March 4, 1865, 2; see Kenneth Winkle, *Lincoln's Citadel: The Civil War in Washington, D.C.* (New York: W. W. Norton, 2013), 404 (contrasting 1861 and 1865).

25　Lincoln, Second Inaugural Address, March 4, 1865, *CWL*, 8:332–33.

26　"The Inauguration," *Washington (DC) Evening Star*, March 4, 1865, 2; Chase to Mary Todd Lincoln, March 4, 1865, Lincoln Papers, LC.

27　Chase to Lincoln, March 6, 1865, Lincoln Papers, LC; Gienapp and Gienapp, *Diary of Gideon Welles*, March 7, 1865, 599.

28　Chase to Susan Walker, March 1865, *SPCP*, 5:14–15; White, "Salmon Portland Chase," 39–40. The changing boundaries of the circuits are shown on the website of the Federal Judicial Center, accessed April 12, 2021. https://www.fjc.gov/history/exhibits/graphs-and-maps/federal-judicial-circuits.

29　"Grant in Motion," *Washington (DC) Evening Star*, March 30, 1865, 2; "From Grant's Army," *Chicago Tribune*, April 1, 1865, 1; Chase diary, April 1–2, 1865, *SPCP*, 1:522–23; Chernow, *Grant*, 487–92.

30　Chase diary, April 3, 1865, *SPCP*, 1:523–24; "United States Circuit Court," *Baltimore Sun*, April 4, 1865, 1.

31 Chase diary, April 4, 1865, *SPCP*, 1:524; *National Republican* (Washington, DC), April 5, 1865.

32 Chase diary, April 7, 1865, *SPCP*, 1:525–26; "United States Circuit Court," *Baltimore Sun*, April 8, 1865, 1.

33 Chase diary, April 8–9, 1865, *SPCP*, 1:526; Charles Sumner to Chase, April 10, 1865, in Palmer, *Sumner Letters*, 2:282–83; *National Republican* (Washington, DC), April 10, 1865 (Lincoln's return; news of Lee's surrender); Goodwin, *Team of Rivals*, 723–26; Stahr, *Seward*, 432–33.

34 Chase diary, April 10–11, 1865, *SPCP*, 1:526–27; Chase to Lincoln, April 11, 1865, *SPCP*, 5:15–16. The Lincoln letter is the last item in Chase's diary entry for April 11, suggesting that he wrote it at day's end. For Lincoln in Richmond, see Harris, *Lincoln's Last Months*, 204–7, and Stahr, *Stanton*, 409.

35 Chase to Lincoln, April 11, 1865, *SPCP*, 5:15–16.

36 Lincoln speech, April 11, 1865, *CWL*, 8:399–405; Masur, *Lincoln's Last Speech*, 162–68.

37 Chase to Lincoln, April 12, 1865, *SPCP*, 5:17–19.

38 Chase diary, April 13–14, 1865, *SPCP*, 1:528–29; Chase to William Sprague, April 14, 1865, *SPCP*, 5:22–23.

39 Chase diary, April 14, 1865, *SPCP*, 1:528–29; Chase to Charlotte Eastman, April 24, 1865, *SPCP*, 5:29–31.

40 Chase diary, April 15, 1865, *SPCP*, 1:529–30; Chase to Charlotte Eastman, April 24, 1865, *SPCP*, 5:29–31; Stahr, *Seward*, 1–3, 435–37.

41 Chase diary, April 15, 1965, *SPCP*, 1:529–30; Chase to Charlotte Eastman, April 24, 1865, *SPCP*, 5:29–31.

42 Chase diary, April 15, 1865, *SPCP*, 1:530–31; Chase notes, April 15, 1865, Warden, 630–31; Elizabeth Blair Lee to Phillip Lee, April 15, 1865, Laas, *Wartime Washington*, 495; "Inauguration of Andrew Johnson," *Washington (DC) Evening Star*, April 15, 1865, 2 (second edition); Chase to Andrew Johnson, April 16, 1865, *PAJ*, 7:564; Chase to Charlotte Eastman, April 24, 1865, *SPCP*, 5:30–31; Trefousse, *Johnson*, 194–95.

43 Chase diary, April 15, 1865, *SPCP*, 1:530–31; Chase to John Van Buren, April 17, 1865, Chase Papers, HSP; Henry Buttz, ed., *The New Life Dawning, and Other Discourses, of Bernard H. Nadal* (New York: Nelson & Phillips, 1873), 63–68; Martha Hodes, *Mourning Lincoln* (New Haven, CT: Yale University Press, 2015), 97–114. Although the editor did not give a date for Nadal's sermon, the text makes clear that it must have been preached on Easter.

44 James Woodburn, ed., "George W. Julian's Journal—The Assassination of Lincoln," *Indiana Magazine of History* 11 (1915): 335; "The Principles and Policy of President Johnson," *New York Herald*, April 24, 1865, 4; Trefousse, *Johnson*, 197–98.

45 Chase to Jacob Schuckers, April 4, 1865, Chase Papers, HSP; Chase diary, April 18, 20, 1865, *SPCP*, 1:531; Chase to Johnson, April 18, 1865, *PAJ*, 7:258; Chase to Charlotte Eastman, April 24, 1865, *SPCP*, 5:31; Charles Sumner to the Duchess of Argyll, April 24, 1865, Palmer, *Sumner Letters*, 2:295; Sumner to John Bright, April 24, 1865, ibid., 297; Johnson order, April 29, 1865, Warden,

642; Stanton order, April 29, 1865, ibid.; Chase to Theodore Tilton, May 1, 1865, Chase Papers, NYHS; Sumner to John Bright, May 1, 1865, in Pierce, ed., *Memoir and Letters of Charles Sumner*, 4:242–43; Sumner to Wendell Phillips, May 1, 1865, Palmer, *Sumner Letters*, 2:298–99; Sumner to Francis Lieber, May 2, 1865, ibid., 299–300.

46 Chase to Thomas Key, April 28, 1865, Chase Papers, HSP (reorganization by "whole loyal people without distinction of color"); Chase diary, April 29, 1865, *SPCP*, 1:533; Chase, Draft Address, April 29, 1865, Johnson Papers, LC.

47 Chase, Draft Address, April 29, 1865, Johnson Papers, LC.

48 Chase diary, April 29, 1865, *SPCP*, 1:534; Chase, Draft Address, April 29, 1865, Johnson Papers, LC; Chase to William Sprague, April 30, 1865, Chase Papers, HSP ("I fear his diffidence will prevent him from doing it; though his heart inclines to it.") Niven was unsure about a few words in Chase's diary entry, so I have also consulted David Donald, ed., *Inside Lincoln's Cabinet: The Civil War Diaries of Salmon P. Chase* (New York: Longman, Greens, 1954), 271–72.

49 Chase diary, May 1–9, 1865, *SPCP*, 1:536–43; Chase to Kate Sprague, May 2, 1865, *Spur*, 270–72; Chase to Benjamin Butler, May 2, 1865, in Marshall, *Private and Official Correspondence of General Benjamin F. Butler*, 5:610–11; Chase to Edwin Stanton, May 5, 1865, *SPCP*, 5:40; Chase to Kate Sprague, May 5, 1865, *Spur*, 272–73; Chase to Kate Sprague, May 5, 1865, *SPCP*, 5:38 (second letter same day); W. T. Sherman to Chase, May 6, 1865, *SPCP*, 41; Chase to Sherman, May 6, 1865, *SPCP*, 44–45; Reid, *After the War*, 12–13.

50 "President Johnson and His Policy," *New York Herald*, May 3, 1865, 4; "The Negro Question," ibid., May 6, 1865, 4; Chase diary, May 11, 1865, *SPCP*, 1:545 (saw *Herald* for May 2–8); Chase to Andrew Johnson, May 12, 1865, Johnson Papers, LC. For transcripts and comments on Chase's letters to Johnson from the South, see James Sefton, "Chief Justice Chase as an Advisor on Presidential Reconstruction," *Civil War History* 13 (1967): 242–64.

51 Chase diary, May 12, 1865, *SPCP*, 1:547; *Charleston (SC) Courier*, May 13, 1865; Chase to Johnson, May 17, 1865, *SPCP*, 5:47; "Mr. Chase's Speech," *New York Herald*, May 21, 1865, 1.

52 Chase diary, May 12, 1865, *SPCP*, 1:547; *Charleston (SC) Courier*, May 12–13, 1865; Chase to Johnson, May 17, 1865, *SPCP*, 5:47–48. The *Courier*, on the morning of the twelfth, reported that Chase would leave that afternoon and that Saxton would address the Zion meeting. Chase, in his letter to Johnson, said Saxton asked him to attend the Zion meeting.

53 "Large Meeting at Zion Church," *Charleston (SC) Courier*, May 13, 1865, 2; "Mr. Chase's Speech," *New York Herald*, May 21, 1865, 1. Chase forwarded the *Courier* version of the speech to Johnson. Chase to Johnson, May 17, 1865, *SPCP*, 5:47. These contemporary versions seem more reliable than the one usually quoted, Reid's version, printed a year later. See Niven, *Chase*, 388; Reid, *After the War*, 581–86.

54 "Large Meeting at Zion Church," *Charleston (SC) Courier*, May 13, 1865, 2; "Mr. Chase's Speech," *New York Herald*, May 21, 1865, 1.

55 Ibid.

56 Ibid.

57 Chase diary, May 13–16, *SPCP*, 1:548–51; Chase to Johnson, May 17, 1865, *SPCP*, 5:47–48.

58 Chase to Johnson, May 12, 1865, Johnson Papers, LC; Chase to Johnson, May 17, 1865, *SPCP*, 5:47–51; Chase to Edwin Stanton, May 20, 1865, *SPCP*, 5:52–53 (urges him to read letters to Johnson; "universal suffrage essential").

59 Chase diary, May 17–24, *SPCP*, 1:551–55; Chase to Kate Sprague, May 22, 1865, *Spur*, 277–79; Chase to Charles Sumner, May 22, 1865, *SPCP*, 5:53–55.

60 Chase diary, May 25–28, *SPCP*, 1:555–60; Chase to Kate Sprague, May 28, 1865, *Spur*, 280–83.

61 "Chief Justice Chase and His Presidential Program," *New York Herald*, May 22, 1865, 4; *New York World*, May 22, 1865; "Chief Justice Chase the Great Negro Worshipper," *New York Herald*, May 24, 1865, 4; Johnson amnesty proclamation, May 29, 1865, *PAJ*, 8:128–30; Johnson North Carolina proclamation, May 29, 1865, *PAJ*, 8:136–38; Chase diary, June 2–5, 1865, *SPCP*, 1:563–65; *New Orleans Picayune*, June 3, 1865 (summary of proclamations); Charles Sumner to Carl Schurz, October 20, 1865, Palmer, *Sumner Letters*, 2:339 (Chase learned of proclamations in Mobile).

62 Chase diary, June 5–11, 1865, *SPCP*, 1:564–69; Chase to J. B. Roudanez et al, June 6, 1865, in *National Republican* (Washington, DC), June 20, 1865; *New Orleans Picayune*, June 7, 1865; *Cleveland Daily Leader*, June 22, 1865.

63 Chase diary, June 15–22, 1865, *SPCP*, 1:572–78; Chase to Kate Sprague, June 19, 1865, *Spur*, 283–84, June 24, 1865, 284–87; Chase to James Pike, July 8, 1865, *SPCP*, 5:57–59.

64 Chase to Charles Sumner, June 25, 1865, *SPCP*, 5:55–56; Chase to W. H. Seward, June 25, 1865, Chase Papers, HSP; Chase to Henry Carrington, June 30, 1865, Carrington Papers, Yale.

65 Chase to Jacob Schuckers, July 7, 1865, *SPCP*, 5:61–62.

66 Ibid., *SPCP*, 5:61; Chase to James Pike, July 8, 1865, *SPCP*, 5:59; Chase to Hiram Barney, July 17, 1865, Barney Papers, Huntington; Chase to Hiram Barney, August 1, 1865, ibid.

67 "Chief Justice Chase at Dartmouth College Commencement," *Cincinnati Enquirer*, July 14, 1865, 3; *New York World*, July 24, 1865; "Speech of Chief Justice Chase at Dartmouth College," *Cleveland Daily Leader*, July 26, 1865, 2; *Rock Island (IL) Argus*, August 1, 1865; *Holmes County Farmer* (Millersburg, OH), August 3, 1865.

68 "Speech by Secretary Chase," *Chicago Tribune*, September 22, 1864, 3 ("wherever rebellion and treason are found"); Chase draft address, April 29, 1865 (secession was "treason and rebellion"); "Supporters of Jeff. Davis," *New York Times*, August 5, 1865, 1; Johnson to Chase, August 10, 1865, *PAJ*, 8:554; Chase to Johnson, August 12, 1865, Johnson Papers, LC; "The Trial of Jeff. Davis," *Philadelphia Inquirer*, August 21, 1865, 1; *Columbia (SC) Daily Phoenix*, August 25, 1865; Francis Blair to Johnson, September 6, 1865, *PAJ*, 9:32–33; see Nicoletti, *Secession on Trial*, 24–79.

69 Chase to Charles Sumner, August 24, 1865, *SPCP,* 5:64–65; Chase to William Sprague, September 5, 1865, *SPCP,* 5:66–68. On suffrage for women, see Mark Summers, *The Ordeal of the Reunion: A New History of Reconstruction* (Chapel Hill: University of North Carolina Press, 2014), 243–46.

70 Chase to William Sprague, September 5, 1865, *SPCP,* 5:67–68.

71 "The Religious Convention," *Cleveland Daily Leader,* September 29, 1865, 4; *Western Reserve Chronicle* (Warren, OH), October 11, 1865; James Pollard, ed., *The Journal of Jay Cooke; or, The Gibraltar Records, 1865–1905* (Columbus: Ohio State University Press, 1935), 47–52, 117–25.

72 Johnson to Chase, October 2, 1865, *PAJ,* 9:161; Chase to Johnson, October 12, 1865, *SPCP,* 5:70–71 (received letter only two days earlier).

73 Eric Foner, *Reconstruction: America's Unfinished Revolution, 1863–1877* (New York: Harper & Row, 1968), 239–53; Foner, *Second Founding,* 57–59; Stahr, *Stanton,* 463–64; Summers, *Ordeal of the Reunion,* 72–86.

74 *New-York Tribune,* December 5, 1865 (first session of the court); "Argument in the Supreme Court," *Cleveland Daily Leader,* December 16, 1865, 1; *Wheeling Daily Intelligencer,* December 18, 1865 (Garland argument).

75 *Wilmington (NC) Daily Dispatch,* November 25, 1865; *Raleigh (NC) Daily Standard,* November 27, 1865; "The Constitutional Amendment," *Cleveland Daily Leader,* December 11, 1865, 1; Chase diary, December 18, 1865, *SPCP,* 1:599–600; Act to Establish and Regulate the Domestic Relations of Persons of Color, December 21, 1865, on College of Charleston website, accessed April 12, 2021 (http://ldhi.library.cofc.edu/exhibits/show/after_slavery_educator/ unit _three_documents/document_eight); "Thad. Stevens' Speech," *Ohio Statesman* (Columbus), December 22, 1865, 1; Foner, *Second Founding,* 38–40; Summers, *Ordeal of the Reunion,* 72–77.

CHAPTER 23: "The Most Dangerous Man," 1866–67

1 Johnson veto message, February 19, 1866, in "Washington News," *New York Times,* February 20, 1866, 1; Johnson speech, February 22, 1866, in "Washington News," *New York Times,* February 23, 1866, 4; William Hilton to Andrew Johnson, February 26, 1866, *PAJ,* 10:177; Trefousse, *Andrew Johnson,* 244 (Johnson's speech a "tactless harangue").

2 Cummings v. Missouri, 71 U.S. 277 (1867); David Currie, *The Constitution in the Supreme Court: The First Hundred Years 1789–1888* (Chicago: University of Chicago Press, 1985), 292–96; William Johnson, "Missouri Test Oath," in *The Catholic Encyclopedia,* ed. Charles Herbermann et al. (New York: Universal Knowledge Foundation, 1912), 14:538–39.

3 Ex parte Milligan, 71 U.S. 2 (1866); Anne Ashmore, *Dates of Supreme Court Decisions and Arguments* (2006) (typescript on Supreme Court website); Michael Benedict, "Ex Parte Milligan in Context and History: David Davis and the Constitutional Politics and Law of Civil Liberty," in Stewart Winger and Jonathan White, eds., *Ex Parte Milligan Reconsidered: Race and Civil Liberties from the Lincoln*

Administration to the War on Terror (Lawrence: University of Kansas Press, 2020), 195–221; Currie, *Constitution in the Supreme Court*, 288–92; Fairman, *Reconstruction and Reunion*, 143–44, 192–214.

4 Randall, *Diary of Orville Hickman Browning,* April 3, 1866, 2:69 (test oath); "From Washington," *Chicago Tribune*, April 4, 1866, 1 (Milligan order); "Important Decision of the Supreme Court," *Philadelphia Inquirer*, April 4, 1866, 1; Chase to Charles Drake, April 24, 1866, *SPCP,* 5:86 ("too important").

5 Randall, *Diary of Orville Hickman Browning,* March 25, 1866, 2:67 (test oath); Samuel Miller to Chase, June 5, 1866, *SPCP,* 5:108–09; Chase to Miller, June 9, 1866, *SPCP,* 5:110–12; Miller to Chase, June 27, 1866, *SPCP,* 5:114–15; Fairman, *Reconstruction and Reunion*, 151–60.

6 Chase to Nettie Chase, April 16, 1866, *Spur,* 300; Chase to Nettie, May 14, 1866, ibid., 306 ("deadlock"); Chase to Kate Sprague, June 15, 1866, ibid., 308–9 ("you and Nettie"); Chase to Nettie, June 18, 1866, ibid., 311 ("Spur up"); Chase to Nettie, July 2, 1866, ibid., 315 ("two or three words were defective").

7 William Sprague to Kate Sprague, April 14, May 18, 1866, quoted in Oller, *American Queen*, 101–3; *Buffalo Commercial*, June 20, 1866 (shirt collar).

8 "The President's Veto," *New York Times*, March 28, 1866, 1; "The Veto in the House," *Washington (DC) Evening Star*, April 9, 1866, 2; "Speech of Chief Justice Chase," *Cleveland Daily Leader*, April 14, 1866, 2; Stahr, *Stanton*, 469–70; Trefousse, *Andrew Johnson*, 245–47.

9 Chase draft amendment, early 1866, Chase Papers, HSP; Chase draft resolution, early 1866, Chase Papers, LC; Chase to Stephen Field, April 30, 1866, *SPCP,* 5:88–89 (shares draft amendment and draft resolution); Chase to John Bingham, June 9, 1866, Chase Papers, HSP; Foner, *Second Founding*, 80–81 (Stanton).

10 "Report from the Reconstruction Committee," *New York Herald*, April 29, 1866, 1; Chase to John Bingham, June 9, 1866, Chase Papers, HSP; Magliocca, *American Founding Son*, 108–27 (Bingham's role). Chase's letter to Bingham was reacting to the Senate version of the Amendment, which included the Citizenship Clause. The Supreme Court, at least initially, did not agree with Chase's view on Indian citizenship. See Elk v. Wilkins, 112 U.S. 94 (1884).

11 "Report from the Reconstruction Committee," *New York Herald*, April 29, 1866, 1; Magliocca, *American Founding Son*, 108–27 (Bingham's role).

12 Chase to Stephen Field, April 30, 1866, *SPCP,* 5:88–89; Chase to Wendell Phillips, May 1, 1866, *SPCP,* 5:91; Chase to Jacob Schuckers, May 15, 1866, *SPCP,* 5:96 ("the amendment to the Constitution proposed by the House is on the whole fair and just"); Chase to Nettie Chase, June 5, 1866, *SPCP,* 5:104 ("my opinion is that it covers too much ground").

13 Chase to William Brownlow, July 2, 1866, *SPCP,* 5:117–18; Chase to Nettie Chase, July 2, 1866, *Spur,* 316; Chase to Robert Hill, July 11, 1866, Chase Papers, HSP (urges South to accept amendment); Trefousse, *Andrew Johnson*, 252–54.

14 Chase draft bill, April 1866, Chase Papers, HSP; Chase to Samuel Miller, June 15, 1866, *SPCP,* 5:113; Chase to Samuel Miller, July 3, 1866, *SPCP,* 5:119–20;

Chase to William Sprague, July 25, 1866, *SPCP,* 5:121–22; Fairman, *Reconstruction and Reunion,* 160–69 (includes Chase draft).

15 Act of July 23, 1866, *Statutes at Large,* 14:209; Chase to Noah Swayne, September 29, 1866, *SPCP,* 5:129–30; Chase to David Davis, October 4, 1866, *SPCP,* 5:133–35; Fairman, *Reconstruction and Reunion,* 172–75.

16 Chase to Andrew Hamilton, June 7, 1866, Chase Papers, HSP ("throw off the robes"); Chase to Thomas Heaton, June 27, 1866, ibid.; Chase to Nettie Chase, July 2, 1866, *Spur,* 318; Chase to Jay Cooke, August 24, 1866, Cooke Papers, HSP; Albert Castel, *The Presidency of Andrew Johnson* (Lawrence: University Press of Kansas, 1979), 77–84; Stahr, *Stanton,* 474–75; Summers, *Ordeal of the Reunion,* 93–95; Trefousse, *Andrew Johnson,* 255–62.

17 Philip Sheridan to Ulysses Grant, August 2, 1866, John Simon, ed., *The Papers of Ulysses Grant* (Urbana: Southern Illinois University Press, 1967–2009), 16:289; Foner, *Reconstruction,* 262–64; Summers, *Ordeal of the Reunion,* 95–97.

18 "National Union Convention," *New York Times,* August 15, 1866, 5; Castel, *Presidency of Andrew Johnson,* 85; Foner, *Reconstruction,* 264; Stahr, *Seward,* 470–71; Summers, *Ordeal of the Reunion,* 94–95.

19 Chase diary, August 14–15, 1866, *SPCP,* 1:624–25.

20 Chase to Jacob Schuckers, September 24, 1866, *SPCP,* 5:125; Chase to Nettie Chase, March 27, 1867, Chase Papers, LC.

21 Chase to Kate Chase, August 17, 1865, Chase Papers, HSP (Walker); Chase to Elizabeth Pike, December 23, 1865, Chase Papers, HSP; Pike to Chase, February 28, 1866, Chase Papers, HSP; Chase to Pike, March 20, 1866, *SPCP,* 5:82–83; Chase diary, September 16–17, 1866, *SPCP,* 1:636; Chase to Nettie Chase, October 29, 1866, Chase Papers, LC; James Durden, "James S. Pike: President Lincoln's Minister to the Netherlands," *New England Quarterly* 29 (1956): 341–64; Carol Faulkner, *Women's Radical Reconstruction: The Freedmen's Aid Movement* (Philadelphia: University of Pennsylvania Press, 2007), 136–38 (Walker).

22 Johnson speech, September 3, 1866, *PAJ,* 11:175–76; "The President's Mistake," *New York Times,* September 7, 1866, 4; Stahr, *Seward,* 471–73; Trefousse, *Andrew Johnson,* 262–66.

23 Chase to Jacob Schuckers, September 24, 1866, *SPCP,* 5:125–28; "Why Mr. Davis Has Not Been Tried," *New-York Tribune,* September 26, 1866, 4; *New Orleans Crescent,* October 8, 1866; "Who Holds Jeff Davis," *Chicago Tribune,* October 15, 1866, 2; "Why Jeff Davis Is Not Tried or Released," *New York Herald,* October 15, 1866, 4.

24 Chase diary, September 3–6, 1866, *SPCP,* 1:631–32; "The Southern Loyalists' Convention," *New-York Tribune,* September 4, 1866, 1; "The Southern Loyalists' Convention, Second Day," ibid., September 5, 1866, 1; Chase to Jacob Schuckers, September 8, 1866, Chase Papers, LC (describing one of the Philadelphia meetings).

25 Chase to Flamen Ball, April 10, 1866, Chase Papers, CHLA ("some people seem"); Hugh Bond to Chase, October 10, 1866, Chase Papers, LC; Chase to

Hugh Bond, October 10, 1866, Chase Papers, Cornell University; Chase to Kate Sprague, October 12, 1866, *Spur,* 324; "Improvement of the Colored People," *Baltimore Sun*, October 12, 1866, 1; "Meeting of the American Union Commission," *Philadelphia Inquirer*, October 12, 1866, 1; "Speech of Chief Justice Chase," *New York Times*, November 25, 1866, 3.

26 "The Elections," *New-York Tribune*, October 10, 1866, 1; ibid., October 11, 1866, 1; Chase to Nettie Chase, October 15, 1866, *Spur,* 328.

27 *New Orleans Crescent*, October 4, 1866; Chase to Horace Greeley, November 27, 1866, *SPCP,* 5:138–39; Castel, *Presidency of Andrew Johnson*, 99–103.

28 "The Elections," *New-York Tribune*, November 7, 1866, 4; Chase to Benjamin Cowan, November 8, 1866, *SPCP,* 5:136–37; Howells, *Years of My Youth*, 156.

29 *New York World*, November 13, 1866; "Interviews with the President," *Chicago Tribune*, November 19, 1866, 1; "Chief Justice Chase and the President," *New-York Tribune*, November 19, 1866, 1; Chase to Horace Greeley, November 27, 1866, *SPCP,* 5:138–39.

30 Chase to Kate, September 18, 1866, Chase Papers, LC; "Scandal," *New-York Tribune*, October 31, 1866, 4; *Burlington (VT) Free Press*, November 26, 1866; Chase to Nettie Chase, November 27, 1866, *Spur,* 335–36; Chase to Nettie, December 12, 1866, ibid., 342–43; Oller, *American Queen*, 106–7.

31 *National Republican* (Washington, DC), December 18, 1866; *Ex parte Milligan*, 71 U.S. at 2.

32 *Richmond Times*, December 20, 1866; *Raleigh (NC) Daily Standard*, December 25, 1866; *Wisconsin State Journal* (Madison), December 26, 1866; *Jackson (MS) Daily Clarion*, December 28, 1866; Fairman, *Reconstruction and Reunion*, 214–15; Michael Haggerty, "To Leave Behind the Law of Force: Salmon Chase and the Civil War Era," in Winger and White, *Ex Parte Milligan Reconsidered*, 222–42.

33 *National Republican* (Washington, DC), January 15, 1867; *Cummings v. Missouri*, 71 U.S. at 277; *Ex parte Garland,* 71 U.S. at 333; Kens, *Justice Stephen Field*, 116–17.

34 *Cummings v. Missouri*, 71 U.S. at 332 (noting dissent); *Ex parte Garland*, 71 U.S. at 382–99 (dissenting opinion); Currie, *Constitution in the Supreme Court*, 292–96; Ross, *Justice of Shattered Dreams*, 142–44.

35 Lincoln first inaugural, March 4, 1861, *CWL,* 4:268; "Congress and the Supreme Court," *Chicago Tribune*, January 17, 1867, 2; Fairman, *Reconstruction and Reunion*, 244–46.

36 Military Reconstruction Act, March 2, 1867, *Statutes at Large,* 14:428–29; Castel, *Presidency of Andrew Johnson*, 106–10; Summers, *Ordeal of the Reunion*, 102–6.

37 Judiciary Act, March 2, 1867, *Statutes at Large,* 14:433; Bankruptcy Act, March 2, 1867, ibid., 517–19; Tenure of Office Act, March 2, 1867, ibid., 430–31; Stahr, *Stanton*, 485–89.

38 Chase to Nettie Chase, February 15, 1867, *Spur,* 355; "The New Congress," *New-York Tribune*, March 5, 1867, 4; Draft bill, March 1867, Chase Papers, HSP; Act of March 23, 1867, *Statutes at Large,* 15:2–4; Fairman, *Reconstruction and Reunion*, 324–27.

39 *Louisville (KY) Courier*, April 10, 1867 (quotes petition); Mississippi v. Johnson, 71 U.S. 475, 498–99 (1867); Marbury v. Madison, 5 U.S. 137, 170 (1803).

40 "Governor Sharkey's Mississippi Case," *Philadelphia Inquirer*, April 27, 1867, 1; "Dismissal of Mississippi and Georgia Injunction," ibid., May 14, 1867, 4; *The Nation*, May 27, 1867; Georgia v. Stanton, 73 U.S. 50 (1868).

41 "Distinguished Arrival," *Richmond Dispatch*, June 5, 1867, 1; Chase to Nettie Chase, June 7, 1867, *SPCP*, 5:153–54.

42 Chase to Nettie Chase, June 7, 1867, *SPCP*, 5:153–54; *Raleigh (NC) Daily Standard*, June 8, 1867.

43 *Raleigh (NC) Daily Standard*, June 8, 11, 18, 1867; Chase to David Davis, June 24, 1867, *SPCP*, 5:157–58; Chase to Gerrit Smith, June 25, 1867, *SPCP*, 5:161–62.

44 *Raleigh (NC) Daily Standard*, June 20, 1867 (reporting *Shortridge v. Macon*); "The Law of Treason," *New York Times*, June 22, 1867, 8; Nicoletti, *Secession on Trial*, 217–24. I prefer to rely upon contemporary papers for Chase's circuit court opinions rather than the "official" report, prepared years later, which Chase edited. See Bradley Johnson, *Reports of Cases Decided by Chief Justice Chase in the Circuit Court of the United States Fourth Circuit During the Years 1865–1869* (New York: Diossy, 1876), iii–v.

45 *Nashville Union*, June 7, 1866 (Smith's letter to Chase); "The Law of Treason," *New York Times*, June 22, 1867, 8.

46 "Chase on Rebellion," *New-York Tribune*, June 24, 1867, 4; Chase to Horace Greeley, June 25, 1867, *SPCP*, 5:159–60; Chase to Gerrit Smith, June 25, 1867, *SPCP*, 5:161–62.

47 Chase to Nettie Chase, March 23, 1867, *Spur*, 357 (Kate hopes to meet Nettie in Paris); "Passengers Sailed," *New York Times*, April 7, 1867, 8 (Kate's departure); Chase to Nettie, July 11, 1867, *SPCP*, 5:169 (presidential); ibid., September 12, 1867, *Spur*, 358 (she is on way to Paris).

48 Chase to John Russell Young, June 26, 1867, *SPCP*, 5:164; Chase to Theodore Tilton, July 9, 1867, *SPCP*, 5:167; Trefousse, *Andrew Johnson*, 280, 299, 334.

49 Henry Stanbery to Andrew Johnson, June 12, 1867, in *Official Opinions of the Attorneys-General* (Washington, DC: Government Printing Office, 1870), 12:141–68; "Mr. Stanbery's Opinion," *New-York Tribune*, June 17, 1867, 4 ("Mr. Stanbery cuts the heart out of the military bill"); Philip Sheridan to Ulysses Grant, June 22, 1867, in John Simon, ed., *The Papers of Ulysses Grant* (1991), 17:198; "Sheridan's 'Insubordination,'" *Philadelphia Evening Telegraph*, June 25, 1867, 4; Chase to John Russell Young, June 26, 1867, *SPCP*, 5:164; Chase to Theodore Tilton, *SPCP*, 5:167–68; Stahr, *Stanton*, 491–92.

50 Chase to Horace Greeley, August 5, 1867, *SPCP*, 5:170–71; Chase to James Garfield, August 7, 1867, Garfield Papers, LC; Chase to Joseph Snodgrass, March 16, 1868, *SPCP*, 5:192–93 (Chase warned Johnson against removing Stanton and Seward).

51 Andrew Johnson to Edwin Stanton, August 5, 1867, *PAJ*, 12:461 (demanding resignation); Stanton to Johnson, *PAJ*, 12:461 (refusing to resign); "The Cabinet Difficulty," *Washington (DC) Evening Star*, August 8, 1867, 1 (from *Philadelphia*

Evening Telegraph); "Secretary Stanton," *Philadelphia Evening Telegraph*, August 6, 1867, 4; Stahr, *Stanton*, 494–96.

52 "Negro Suffrage in Ohio," *New York Herald*, September 20, 1867, 4; "Chief Justice Chase in Ohio," *Ohio Statesman* (Columbus), September 24, 1867, 2; *Columbus (OH) Morning Journal*, September 25, 1867; Michael Benedict, "The Rout of Radicalism: Republicans and the Election of 1867," *Civil War History* 18 (1972): 334–44.

53 *New York Evening Post*, September 27, 1867; "Female Suffrage," *Baltimore Sun*, October 2, 1867, 2; *Nashville Union*, October 2, 1867; "Chief Justice Chase Committed to Female Suffrage," *Ohio Statesman* (Columbus), October 4, 1867, 2; *Yorkville (SC) Enquirer*, October 10, 1867. There is no letter along these lines from Chase to Stone in the archives, but there is no reason to think that Stone misrepresented what Chase told her in conversation. Chase's words would continue to be quoted into the early twentieth century. See *Vermont Standard* (Woodstock), May 5, 1904.

54 "Speech of Hon. S.P. Chase," *Baltimore Sun*, October 7, 1867, 1; *Ohio State Journal* (Columbus), October 7, 1867; Chase to Henry Walbridge, January 2, 1868, *SPCP*, 5:185 (visited Jane Auld and her children); Pollard, *Journal of Jay Cooke, or Gibraltar Records*, 172 (visited Jay Cooke).

55 "The End of S. P. Chase," *Cincinnati Enquirer*, October 10, 1867, 2; "Radical Abolition View of the Late Elections," *New York Herald*, October 11, 1867, 4; *Cincinnati Enquirer*, October 12, 1867; *Nashville Union*, October 12, 1867. For more on the 1867 election, see Benedict, "Rout of Radicalism," and Edward Gambill, *Conservative Ordeal: Northern Democrats and Reconstruction, 1865–1868* (Ames: Iowa State University Press, 1981), 100–104.

56 "A Chase Organ Against the Grant Movement," *Ohio Statesman* (Columbus), October 18, 1867, 1 (from *Cincinnati Commercial*).

57 "Important Manifesto of Mr. Chase," *New York Herald*, October 22, 1867, 6; *New York World*, October 22, 1867; *Buffalo Commercial*, October 23, 1867.

58 Chase to Napoleon Buford, October 17, 1867, Chase Papers, LC.

59 The apprenticeship agreement recited that Turner was born on October 18, 1856. "Before Chief Justice Chase," *Baltimore Sun*, October 16, 1867, 1; "Important Decision by Chief Justice Chase," *Philadelphia Inquirer*, October 17, 1867, 1; see Harold Hyman, *The Reconstruction Justice of Salmon P. Chase: In re Turner & Texas v. White* (Lawrence: University Press of Kansas, 1997), 123–28.

60 "Before Chief Justice Chase," *Baltimore Sun*, October 16, 1867, 1; "Important Decision by Chief Justice Chase," *Philadelphia Inquirer*, October 17, 1867, 1.

61 Ibid.

62 "Before Chief Justice Chase," *Baltimore Sun*, October 17, 1867, 1; "Important Decision," *Chicago Tribune*, October 17, 1867, 1; "Chief Justice Chase," *New-York Tribune*, October 17, 1867, 4; "Important Decision by Chief Justice Chase," *Philadelphia Inquirer*, October 17, 1867, 1.

63 *Buffalo Commercial*, October 17, 1867; "Baltimore," *Detroit Free Press*, October 17, 1867, 1; *New York World*, October 18, 1867; "The Just Judge," *Philadelphia Evening Telegraph*, October 25, 1867, 2 (from *New York Independent*).

64 Andrew Johnson, Third Annual Message to Congress, December 3, 1867, Miller Center UVA website (https://millercenter.org/the-presidency/presidential-speeches/december-3-1867-third-annual-message-congress); David Stewart, *Impeached: The Trial of President Andrew Johnson and the Fight for Lincoln's Legacy* (New York: Simon & Schuster, 2009), 108 ("not exactly oil on troubled waters").

65 Chase to James Garfield, August 7, 1867, Chase Papers, LC; Stewart, *Impeached*, 108–13.

CHAPTER 24: "Mad with the Presidential Fever," 1868

1 Chase to Thomas Conway, January 1, 1868, *SPCP,* 5:182–83.

2 Chase to Henry Walbridge, January 2, 1868, *SPCP,* 5:184–85.

3 *New York Independent*, January 16, 1868; *New-York Tribune*, January 18, 1868.

4 Chase to Greeley, January 17, 1868, *SPCP,* 5:186–88; "The Presidency Ahead," *New-York Tribune*, January 17, 1868, 2; Stahr, *Stanton*, 504–7.

5 Chase to Dwight Bannister, January 15, 1868, Chase Papers, LC; "Grant," *Chicago Tribune*, January 30, 1868, 2; "A Straw," *Richmond Dispatch*, February 8, 1868, 2; Chase to George Senter, February 17, 1868, Chase Papers, LC; "Ohio," *Chicago Tribune*, March 5, 1868, 1 (Columbus convention).

6 Fairman, *Reconstruction and Reunion*, 411–21, 437–40, 449–50 (quote on 416).

7 "Passage of the Bill for the Regulation of the Supreme Court," *Detroit Free Press*, January 14, 1868, 4; "Passage of the Supreme Court Quorum Bill in the House," *New York Herald*, January 14, 1868, 4.

8 "Military Tribunals Before the Supreme Court," *Richmond Dispatch*, January 20, 1868, 3; *Wisconsin State Journal* (Madison), January 22, 1868; *Vicksburg (MS) Herald*, January 24, 1868; *New Orleans Picayune*, January 31, 1868; Fairman, *Reconstruction and Reunion*, 449–50; Ross, *Justice of Shattered Dreams*, 152–57.

9 "Washington," *New-York Tribune*, February 22, 1868, 1; Stewart, *Impeached*, 127–48; Stahr, *Stanton*, 503–13.

10 *National Republican* (Washington, DC), February 25–26, 1868; Stewart, *Impeached*, 148–53; Stahr, *Stanton*, 513.

11 Chase diary, February 26, 1868, *SPCP,* 1:641–42; Chase to Jacob Howard, February 27, 1868, *SPCP,* 1:642; *Cincinnati Enquirer*, March 3, 4, 5, 1868; "Senatorial Debate on Rules Governing the Trial," *New York Herald*, March 3, 1868, 3; Stahr, *Stanton*, 513.

12 Chase to the Senate, March 4, 1868, *SPCP,* 5:189–91; *National Republican* (Washington, DC), March 5, 1868; Stewart, *Impeached*, 162–63.

13 "Views of Chief Justice Chase on the Rules of the Court," *New York Herald*, March 5, 1868, 1; see "The Sensation of Yesterday," *Cincinnati Enquirer*, March 5, 1868, 2; *National Republican* (Washington, DC), March 5, 1868.

14 *National Republican* (Washington, DC), March 6, 1868; "The Trial of President Johnson," *New York Herald*, March 6, 1868, 5; Chase to Elizabeth Wirt Goldsborough, 1868, Goldsborough Papers, NYPL (two letters re: tickets).

15 "Progress of Impeachment," *Cincinnati Enquirer*, March 6, 1868, 3; *National Republican* (Washington, DC), March 6, 1868; "The Trial of President Johnson," *New York Herald*, March 6, 7, 1868, 5.

16 R. C. Root to Samuel Tilden, February 10, 1868, Tilden Papers, NYPL; see Erik Alexander, "The Fate of Northern Democracy After the War: Another Look at the Election of 1868," in *A Political Nation: New Directions in Mid-Nineteenth-Century American History,* ed. Gary Gallagher and Rachel Shelden (Charlottesville: University of Virginia Press, 2012), 188–95.

17 Chase to William Thomas, March 10, 1868, Warden, 680–81.

18 "Wendell Phillips's Organ," *Brooklyn Daily Eagle*, March 13, 1868, 2; "Chief Justice Chase and the President," *New York Herald*, March 13, 1868, 5; *National Anti-Slavery Standard*, March 14, 1868. Although the issue of the *Standard* was dated March 14, the quotes in other papers show that the report appeared on March 12.

19 Chase to Joseph Snodgrass, March 16, 1868, *SPCP*, 5:192–93.

20 *Hartford Courant,* March 17, 1868, 2 (from *New York Atlas*); "Judge Chase as the Democratic Nominee," *Buffalo Commercial,* March 18, 1868, 2 (from *New York Sun*); *Tiffin (OH) Weekly Tribune,* March 19, 1868; *New York Herald*, March 22, 1868; *New York Evening Post*, March 23, 1868; *Leavenworth (KS) Daily Commercial*, March 24, 1868, 1 (from *New York Sun*). On Dana and the *Sun*, see Frank O'Brien, *The Story of the Sun: New York, 1833–1918* (New York: George H. Doran, 1918), 198–201, 237–42.

21 *New York Herald*, March 25, 1868 (from *Cincinnati Gazette*).

22 Chase to Murat Halstead, March 26, 1868, ibid., 195–97; *New York Herald*, June 8, 1871.

23 "Read Out," *Washington (DC) Evening Star*, April 15, 1868, 2 (from *Independent*); "Mr. Chase and the Republican Party," *New York Times*, April 15, 1868, 4 (from *Independent*); *Independent* (New York), April 16, 1868; Chase to Theodore Tilton, April 19, 1868. Although the *Independent* was dated April 16, the quotes in other papers show the article appeared earlier.

24 Chase to Theodore Tilton, April 19, 1868, *SPCP*, 5:210–11; see Chase to Gerrit Smith, April 19, 1868, *SPCP*, 5:209 (Tilton's article was "an abuse of hospitality").

25 Thomas Jefferson to Elbridge Gerry, January 26, 1799, Founders Online website (https://founders.archives.gov/?q=Jefferson%20to%20elbridge%20gerry%20 1799%20Author%3A%22Jefferson%2C%20Thomas%22&s=1111311111&r= 4&sr=); Chase to John Bigelow, February 23, 1858, Bigelow Papers, Union College (West Point).

26 Chase to John Van Buren, March 25, 1868, *SPCP*, 5:194–95; Charles Halpine to Chase, April 1, 1868, *SPCP*, 5:197 (thanks Chase for recent letter; favors Chase for president); Chase to Van Buren, April 5, 1868, *SPCP*, 5:200–201; Chase to Alexander Long, April 8, 1868, *SPCP*, 5:201–2; Long to Chase, April 11, 1868, Long Papers, CHLA; Chase to Long, April 19, 1868, *SPCP*, 5:205–7; ibid., April 20, 1868, Long Papers, CHLA (asking him to keep his letters confidential).

27 *New York Herald*, March 13, 1868; *Congressional Globe*, March 14, 1868 (remarks of Schenk); Fairman, *Reconstruction and Reunion*, 464–65.

28 Welles diary, March 23, 1868, Welles Papers, LC; Chase to John Van Buren, April 5, 1868, *SPCP*, 5:200; Randall, *Diary of Orville Hickman Browning*, April 9, 1868, 2:191; David Davis to Julius Rockwell, April 22, 1868, Davis Papers, ALPL; Ashmore, *Dates of Supreme Court Decisions*, 89–92; Fairman, *Reconstruction and Reunion*, 467–69, 478–87.

29 Johnson veto message, March 25, 1868, in National Republican (Washington, DC), March 26, 1868; Act of March 27, 1868, *Statutes at Large*, 14:44; *Louisville (KY) Daily Courier*, April 1, 1868; *New Orleans Picayune*, April 1, 1868; Fairman, *Reconstruction and Reunion*, 478–79 (*Enquirer* quoted page 479).

30 *New York World*, April 1, 2, 1868; *New York Herald*, May 5, 6, 1868 (re: charge to the jury); Stewart, *Impeached*, 177–79.

31 Chase diary, April 17, 1857, *SPCP*, 1:276 (Bingham supports Chase for second term); Chase to Benjamin Butler, June 24, 1862, *SPCP*, 3:218–29 (one of more than a dozen wartime letters); Chase diary, July 23, 1866, *SPCP*, 1:617–18 (visit with Evarts); Chase to John Russell Young, June 26, 1867, *SPCP*, 5:164 (Chase has known Stanbery a long time); Chase to Kate, July 26, 1869, Chase Papers, HSP (visit with Evarts); Magliocca, *American Founding Son*, 27 ("Chase and Bingham were not close friends, but Chase loomed over Bingham's career").

32 *New York Herald*, April 1, 1868; Stewart, *Impeached*, 197–98; Frank Bowman, "The Role of the Chief Justice in an Impeachment Trial," *Scotusblog*, January 10, 2020; Siobahn Hughes, "Chief Justice Roberts Says He Wouldn't Break a Tie in Impeachment Trial," *Wall Street Journal*, January 20, 2020.

33 *New York Herald*, April 18, 19, 1868; Chase to Alexander Long, April 19, 1868, *SPCP*, 5:206; Chase to Gerrit Smith, April 19, 1868, *SPCP*, 5:209; John Pruyn diary, April 20, 1868, in Jerome Mushkat, ed., "The Impeachment of Andrew Johnson: A Contemporary View," *New York History* 48 (1967): 280; Stewart, *Impeached*, 216–17 (Republicans erred in "muzzling" Cabinet members).

34 *New York Herald*, April 20, 1868; James Garfield to James Rhodes, April 28, 1868, in *The Life and Letters of James Abram Garfield*, ed. Theodore Smith, (New Haven, CT: Yale University Press, 1925), 1:424; Chase to James Shepherd Pike, April 28, 1868, Pike Papers, Maine; Stewart, *Impeached*, 229–39.

35 *New York Herald*, May 5, 6, 1868; Chase to John Van Buren, May 6, 1868, Chase Papers, LC; Gambill, *Conservative Ordeal*, 120 ("Democrats looked to Chase to instruct the Senate before the final verdict and possibly influence the outcome of the trial").

36 "Chief Justice Chase and the Presidency," *New York Herald*, May 7, 1868, 6; "New Phase in the Impeachment," *New York Herald*, May 8, 1868, 6; "Counsel in Extremity," *New-York Tribune*, May 9, 1868, 4.

37 "Impeachment," *New York Herald*, May 12, 1868, 3; *Washington (DC) Morning Chronicle*, May 15, 1868.

38 "Impeachment," *Washington (DC) Evening Star*, May 16, 1868, extra ed., 1; "Impeachment," *New York Herald*, May 17, 1868, 3; *National Republican*

(Washington, DC), May 18, 1868; "News from Washington," *Philadelphia Inquirer*, May 18, 1868, 1; Stewart, *Impeached*, 275–77.

39 "Impeachment," *Washington (DC) Evening Star*, May 16, 1868, 1; "Impeachment," *New York Herald*, May 17, 1868, 3; *National Republican* (Washington, DC), May 18, 1868; "News from Washington," *Philadelphia Inquirer*, May 18, 1868, 1 ("nervously busy with tearing a white paper"); Stewart, *Impeached*, 277–78.

40 Chase to Clark Williams, May 16, 1868, *SPCP*, 5:215–16. Chase was referring to Senator Fessenden's comment that there would be no difficulty convicting and removing Johnson if it could be done "for general cussedness." Stewart, *Impeached*, 151.

41 "The Verdict," *New-York Tribune*, May 17, 1868, 4; *Washington (DC) Morning Chronicle*, May 18, 1868.

42 Chase to Horace Greeley, May 19, 1868, *SPCP*, 5:216–17; Chase to *Washington Chronicle*, draft, May 18, 1868, Chase Papers, LC (filed under "Speeches and Writings").

43 Chase to James Gordon Bennett, May 22, 1868, *SPCP*, 5:218–20; see "President Johnson and His Policy," *New York Herald*, May 3, 1865, 4; "The Negro Question," ibid., May 6, 1865, 4.

44 Chase to James Gordon Bennett, May 22, 1868, *SPCP*, 5:220.

45 "Impeachment," *New York Herald*, May 27, 1868, 3; "News from Washington," *Philadelphia Inquirer*, May 27, 1868, 1; Stewart, *Impeached*, 280–81.

46 "Chief Justice Chase and the Presidency," *Washington (DC) Evening Star*, May 19, 1868, 2; "The Presidential Contest," *New York Herald*, June 2, 1868, 6; "Let Us Hear from Mr. Vallandigham," *New York Herald*, June 3, 1868, 6; *Nashville Tennessean*, June 7, 1868; "Political Summary," *Charleston (SC) Daily News*, June 9, 1868, 1 (from *Boston Post*); Arphaxed Loomis to Samuel Tilden, June 8, 1868, in John Bigelow, ed., *Letters and Literary Memorials of Samuel J. Tilden* (New York: Harper, 1908), 1:230 ("greatest calamity"); Sanford Church to Tilden, June 10, 1868, ibid., 1:229 ("out of the question"); Foner, *Reconstruction*, 338–40; Gambill, *Conservative Ordeal*, 123–34; Summers, *Ordeal of the Reunion*, 141–42.

47 Chase to August Belmont, May 30, 1868, *SPCP*, 5:221–24; Chase to "dear sir," May 30, 1868, Marble Papers, LC; "Chief Justice Chase on the Situation," *New York Herald*, June 3, 1868, 3; Chase to John Van Buren, June 17, 1868, *SPCP*, 5:233–35. The letter in the Marble papers appears to be a copy of the Belmont letter. For more about Chase and the Democrats, see Alexander "The Fate of Northern Democracy," 188–99.

48 Chase to Milton Sutliff, June 3, 1868, *SPCP*, 5:226–27.

49 "Mr. Chase and the Presidency," *Richmond Dispatch*, June 9, 1868, 3 (from *Syracuse {NY} Journal*); Chase to Jacob Schuckers, June 9, 1868, Chase Papers, LC.

50 Chase to Jacob Schuckers, June 3, 1868, *SPCP*, 5:224–25; Chase to Milton Sutliff, June 3, 1868, *SPCP*, 5:227; "Trial of Jeff. Davis," *Richmond Dispatch*, June 4, 1868, 1; George Lathrop, "The Bailing of Jefferson Davis," *Century* 33 (1887): 639; Nicoletti, *Secession on Trial*, 293–96. As Nicoletti notes in *Secession on Trial*, 295n16, it is not clear that Chase's actions were improper under nineteenth-century standards of judicial ethics.

51 Chase to Jacob Schuckers, June 3, 1868, *SPCP,* 5:225; Chase to Milton Sutliff, June 3, 1868, *SPCP,* 5:227; Chase to Gerrit Smith, June 17, 1868, *SPCP,* 5:232.

52 John Van Buren to Chase, June 9, 1868, Chase Papers, HSP; Daniel Goodloe to Chase, June 10, 1868, Chase Papers, LC (from Raleigh); George Gordon to Chase, June 10, 1868, ibid. (from Philadelphia); William Cullen Bryant to Chase, June 13, 1868, *SPCP,* 5:228–30; Josiah Tucker to Chase, June 15, 1868, Chase Papers, LC (from Boston); Chase to John Van Buren, June 17, 1868, *SPCP,* 5:233–35; Chase to William Cullen Bryant, June 19, 1868, *SPCP,* 5:237–39.

53 Chase to John Bailey, June 17, 1868, Chase Papers, LC; "Chase's Platform," *Ohio Statesman* (Columbus), June 19, 1868, 3; *Wheeling Intelligencer,* June 19, 1868; "Chief Justice Chase and the Democrats," *New York Times,* June 20, 1868, 5; "The Chase Platform," *Pittsburgh Gazette,* June 20, 1868, 4. Why Chase wrote on June 17 about a platform that first appeared (it seems) on June 18 is puzzling; perhaps he misdated his letter.

54 Chase to Hamilton Smith, June 20, 1868, Chase Papers, LC; Chase to Sankey Latty, June 20, 1868, ibid.; Chase to John Martin, June 22, 1868, ibid; *New York World,* June 15, 1868; "The Platform and the Candidate for the Times," *New York Herald,* June 22, 1868, 4; Chase to John Cisco, June 25, 1868, *SPCP,* 5:240–41; "Negro Suffrage in the South," *New York Herald,* June 25, 1868, 6; Samuel Ward to Chase, June 26, 1868, *SPCP,* 5:245 (Tilden and Van Buren). For more on the "Chase movement," see Charles Coleman, *The Election of 1868: The Democratic Effort to Regain Control* (New York: Columbia University Press, 1933), 102–40.

55 Frederick Aiken to Chase, June 26, 1868, Chase Papers, LC; Kate to Chase, July 2, 1868, *SPCP,* 5:246–47.

56 *Raleigh (NC) Daily Standard,* May 16, 1868; "National Democratic Convention," *New York Herald,* June 17, 1868, 4; "The Chase Movement in the South," *New York Herald,* June 21, 1868, 5; *Carlisle (PA) Weekly Herald,* July 10, 1868; *Evansville (IL) Daily Journal,* August 4, 1868. For the full list of delegates, see *Official Proceedings of the National Democratic Convention, Held at New York, July 4–9, 1868* (Boston: Rockwell & Rollins, 1868), 31–40.

57 *Hartford Courant,* July 3, 1868 (Blair to Broadhead letter); Alexander Long to Chase, July 3, 1868, *SPCP,* 5:250; Chase to Frederick Aiken, July 4, 1868, *SPCP,* 5:251; Chase to John Van Buren, July 4, 1868, *SPCP,* 5:253–54; Summers, *Ordeal of the Reunion,* 141–42 (Blair letter).

58 *Official Proceedings,* 3–20; Hamilton Smith to Chase, July 5, 1868, *SPCP,* 5:254–55; Kate to Chase, July 5, 1868, *SPCP,* 5:256; Stewart Mitchell, *Horatio Seymour of New York* (Cambridge, MA: Harvard University Press, 1938), 411–12.

59 *Official Proceedings,* 20–54, 58–60; Chase to Prentice Tucker, July 7, 1868, Warden, 706; Chase to Kate Sprague, July 7, 1868, *SPCP,* 5:258; "National Democratic Convention," *Washington (DC) Evening Star,* July 7, 1868, 1; "Democratic Convention," *Philadelphia Inquirer,* July 8, 1868, extra ed., 1.

60 *Official Proceedings* 55–103; "Democratic Convention," *Philadelphia Inquirer,* July 8, 1868, 1.

61 *Official Proceedings* 104–39; "Democrats in Council," *Philadelphia Inquirer*, July 9, 1868, 1.

62 *Official Proceedings* 140–73; Gambill, *Conservative Ordeal,* 142 ("Seymour was suddenly and forcibly removed"); Mitchell, *Horatio Seymour*, 431 ("the unwilling candidate was pushed out of the hall"); Summers, *Ordeal of the Reunion*, 142 ("hustled from the hall").

63 Kate to Chase, July 10, 1868, *SPCP,* 5:263–64; *Cincinnati Enquirer*, July 10, 1868; Chase to Jay Cooke, July 11, 1868, *SPCP,* 5:265; Chase to Gerrit Smith, July 26, 1868, *SPCP,* 5:269–70; Coleman, *Election of 1868*, 225–33; Gambill, *Conservative Ordeal*, 141–42.

64 *Brooklyn Daily Eagle*, July 11, 1868; *Chicago Tribune*, July 21, 1868.

65 Chase to Gerrit Smith, July 26, 1868, *SPCP,* 5:269–70.

66 "The Mask Lifted," *Brownlow's Knoxville (TN) Whig*, September 16, 1868, 3 (Forrest); *Chicago Tribune*, September 23, 1868; *Buffalo Commercial*, September 25, 1868; *Chicago Tribune*, November 30, 1868; William Darrow, "The Killing of Congressman James Hinds," *Arkansas Historical Quarterly* 74 (2015): 18–55; Lee Formwalt, "The Camilla Massacre of 1868: Racial Violence as Political Propaganda," *Georgia Historical Quarterly* 71 (1987): 399–426; Foner, *Reconstruction*, 342–43; Summers, *Ordeal of the Reunion*, 146–50.

67 Chase to Hiram Barney, August 9, 1868, *SPCP,* 5:273; Chase to Murat Halstead, August 31, 1868, Halstead Papers, Ohio History Center; Chase to Gerrit Smith, September 30, 1868, *SPCP,* 5:278–79; Chase to Joseph Snodgrass, October 1, 1868, Chase Papers, LC; Chase to James Shepherd Pike, October 5, 1868, Pike Papers, Maine.

68 Alexander Long to Chase, October 3, 1868, Long Papers, NYHS; *New York World*, October 15, 1868; Alexander Long to Chase, October 15, 1868, Long Papers, NYHS; *New York Sun*, October 16, 1868; *Cincinnati Enquirer*, October 17, 1868; "The Prospects in November," *Ohio Statesman* (Columbus), October 17, 1868, 2; Fairman, *Reconstruction and Reunion*, 550–51; Gambill, *Conservative Ordeal*, 150–52.

69 Chase to John Van Buren, October 17, 1868, Chase Papers, LC; Chase to Thomas Hendricks, October 24, 1868, *SPCP,* 5:283.

70 Chase to Whitelaw Reid, October 31, 1868, Reid Papers, LC (from Washington); Chase to Robert Warden, November 3, 1866, Warden, 716 (from Washington); Chase to Gerrit Smith, November 6, 1866, Chase Papers, HSP (from Washington); Foner, *Reconstruction*, 342–45; Summers, *Ordeal of the Reunion*, 151–52.

71 *Keppel v. Petersburg Railroad Co.*, 14 *Federal Cases* 24 (1868); *Charleston (SC) Daily Courier*, November 26, 1868; "Test Oath Decision of Chief Justice Chase," *Baltimore Sun*, November 26, 1868, 1; "Interesting Case," *Richmond Dispatch*, December 2, 1868, 1; *New Orleans Picayune*, December 11, 1868.

72 "Interesting Case," *Richmond Dispatch*, December 2, 1868, 1; *New Orleans Picayune*, December 11, 1868.

73 "The Case of Jefferson Davis," *Richmond Dispatch*, December 3, 1868, 1; ibid., December 4, 1868, 2; "Quashing the Davis Indictment," *Baltimore Sun*, December

5, 1868, 1; "The Case of Jeff. Davis," *Richmond Dispatch*, December 5, 7, 1868, 2; Nicoletti, *Secession on Trial*, 297–300. Again, I have relied more on contemporary papers than on Johnson's report.

74 "General Amnesty," *New-York Tribune*, December 25, 1868, 3; *Burlington (VT) Free Press*, December 26, 1868; *Harrisburg (PA) Daily Telegraph*, December 28, 1868; *Montgomery (AL) Weekly Advertiser*, December 29, 1868; *Janesville (WI) Daily Gazette*, December 29, 1868. Although Johnson's order was dated December 25, it could not have been printed in the papers on that day unless it was issued the prior day.

CHAPTER 25: "Indestructible Union . . . Indestructible States," 1869–70

1 *Hartford Courant*, January 16, 1869; "The Constitutional Amendment Passed," *New York Herald*, February 27, 1869, 6; "The Final Step," *New-York Tribune*, February 27, 1869, 4; Foner, *Reconstruction*, 445–49; Foner, *Second Founding*, 98–106; Summers, *Ordeal of the Reunion*, 153–54.

2 Chase, *Address and Reply*, 22 ("true democracy"); Chase to William Byrd, April 3, 1869, *SPCP*, 5:294.

3 Chase to Thomas Yeatman, October 19, 1869, *SPCP*, 5:318; see Chase to John Van Buren, November 20, 1869, *SPCP*, 5:321; Chase to George Hill, January 7, 1870, *SPCP*, 5:323–25.

4 Lane County v. Oregon, 74 U.S. 71; Bronson v. Rodes, 74 U.S. 229 (1868); Butler v. Horwitz, 74 U.S. 258 (1868); Fairman, *Reconstruction and Reunion*, 704–8; Henry Friendly, "Federalism: A Forward," *Yale Law Journal* 86 (1977): 1019 (quoting *Lane County*).

5 "President Grant," *New York Herald*, March 5, 1869, 3; Chase to Julia Grant, March 5, 1869, Warden, 717; Chernow, *Grant*, 629–33; Stahr, *Seward*, 528–29; Ronald White, *American Ulysses: A Life of Ulysses S. Grant* (New York: Random House, 2016), 471–73.

6 Chase to John Nicolay, March 8, 1869, Chase Papers, LC; Chase to Nettie Chase, April 12, 1869, *SPCP*, 5:296; Chase diary, January 5, 1870, *SPCP*, 1:645–46 (Chase approved Grant's administration, especially "as to colored citizens"); Chernow, *Grant*, 626–29; Summers, *Ordeal of the Reunion*, 154–59.

7 Ex parte McCardle, 74 U.S. 506 (1869); Chase to Nettie Chase, April 12, 1869, *SPCP*, 5:296; see John Beerbower, "*Ex Parte McCardle* and the Attorney General's Duty to Defend Acts of Congress," *University of San Francisco Law Review* 47 (2013): 679 (*McCardle* case is a "staple of federal courts classes"); Currie, *Constitution in the Supreme Court*, 304–6; William Van Alstyne, "A Critical Guide to *Ex Parte McCardle*," *Arizona Law Review* 15 (1973): 229–69.

8 Texas v. White, 74 U.S. 700 (1869).

9 Ibid., 722–24.

10 Ibid., 724–25.

11 Ibid., 725.

12 Ibid., 726–27.

13 Ibid., 728–31.

14 Ibid., 728–29.

15 Ibid., 732–34.

16 Ibid., 737–41 (dissents); Chase to Nettie Chase, April 12, 1869, *SPCP,* 5:296. See Currie, *Constitution in the Supreme Court,* 311–16 (quote 312); Nicoletti, *Secession on Trial,* 313–26; National League of Cities v. Usery, 426 U.S. 833, 844 (1976); Gregory v. Ashcroft, 501 U.S. 452, 457 (1991); New York v. United States, 505 U.S. 144, 162 (1992); Printz v. United States, 521 U.S. 898, 919 (1997); Wyeth v. Levine, 129 S. Ct. 1187, 1206 (2009) (Thomas); Upper Skagit Indian Tribe v. Lundgren, 138 S. Ct. 1649, 1662 (2018) (Thomas).

17 *Congressional Globe,* March 15, 1869, 64–66; "Senate," *New York Herald,* March 16, 1869, 3; *Congressional Globe,* March 19, 1869, 157–59; "Startling Speech of Senator Sprague," *New York Herald,* March 20, 1869, 3.

18 *Congressional Globe,* March 24, 1869, 245–46; *Chicago Tribune,* March 25, 1869; "Senate," *New York Herald,* March 25, 1869, 3; "Congressional," *Philadelphia Inquirer,* March 25, 1869, 8. I have quoted from the papers, which seem closer to Sprague's words.

19 "The Debate on the Tenure of Office Act," *Chicago Tribune,* March 26, 1869, 2; "Senator Sprague in the Arena," *New York Times,* March 31, 1869, 3.

20 *Congressional Globe,* March 30, 1869, 358–61; "Senate," *New York Herald,* March 31, 1869, 5; "Senator Sprague in the Arena," *New York Times,* March 31, 1869, 3.

21 *Cleveland Daily Leader,* April 9, 1869; Mary Viall Anderson, *The Merchant's Wife* (1876), 41–42; Belden and Belden, *So Fell the Angels,* 228–29; Oller, *American Queen,* 136–37.

22 Chase to Kate, April 8, 1869, Chase Papers, HSP; ibid., April 17, 1869, *Spur,* 385–87, and May 4, 1869, ibid., 390–91.

23 Ibid.

24 Chase to William Sprague, May 2, 1869, Chase Papers, LC; "Mrs. Sprague Sues for Divorce," *New York Times,* December 20, 1880, 2; Oller, *American Queen,* 136–41.

25 Chase to Elizabeth Smith Miller, May 2, 1869, *SPCP,* 5:302–3; "The Woman's Suffrage Association," *New York Times,* May 18, 1869, 5; Summers, *Ordeal of the Reunion,* 245–46. The timing suggests that Miller may have wanted Chase's letter for the initial meeting of the Woman's Suffrage Association.

26 "Chief Justice Chase's Opinion in the Caesar Griffin Case," *Richmond Dispatch,* May 11, 1869, 2; "Judge Chase's Reversal of Underwood," *Baltimore Sun,* May 12, 1869, 2.

27 Chase to Nettie Chase, May 4, 1869, *Spur,* 392 (she is still in Aiken); Chase to Kate, May 15, 1869, Chase Papers, HSP (arrangements for her travel from Aiken); *Charleston (SC) Daily News,* May 21, 1869 (Chase and daughter in Charleston); Chase to B. H. Manning, May 29, 1869, Schuckers, 529; Chase to W. T. Sherman, June 24, 1869, Sherman Papers, LC (Chase and daughter going to White Sulphur Springs). For reprints of Chase's letter, see "Decorating Soldiers' Graves," *Richmond Dispatch,* June 2, 1869, 3; "A Letter from Chief Justice Chase," *New-York*

Tribune, June 4, 1869, 5; *Norfolk (VA) Virginian,* June 7, 1869; *Wilmington (NC) Journal,* June 11, 1869; and *Semi-Weekly Wisconsin* (Milwaukee), June 12, 1869.

28 John Williams to Chase, June 4, 1869, *SPCP,* 5:306–7; Chase to Williams, June 10, 1869, *SPCP,* 5:307–8.

29 *Charleston (SC) Daily News,* May 22, June 7, 1869; Chase to Richard Parsons, June 8, 1869, Chase Papers, HSP; *Wilmington (NC) Journal,* June 18, 1869; Chase to Nathan Clifford, June 22, 1869, *SPCP,* 5:309 (from Richmond); "Chief Justice Chase," *New York Times,* July 12, 1869, 1 (Chase back in Washington); Chase to Kate, August 1, 1869, *SPCP* 5:312 (from Parkersburg).

30 *Memphis Public Ledger,* June 9, 1869; *Chicago Evening Post,* June 14, 1869; Chase to Nathan Clifford, June 22, 1869, *SPCP,* 5:309–10; Samuel Nelson to Chase, June 28, 1869, Chase Papers, HSP; Clifford to Chase, July 6, 1869, ibid.; "The Argument on the Yerger Habeas Corpus Case," *Baltimore Sun,* July 15, 1869, 1; *New York Herald,* July 15, 1869, 11; "US Supreme Court—The Yerger Case," *Philadelphia Inquirer,* July 15, 1869, 1; Fairman, *Reconstruction and Reunion,* 564–78. Fairman prints many key documents, including Chase's draft order.

31 "The Confusion in Our Political Parties," *New York Herald,* June 22, 1869, 6; *New York Herald,* June 30, 1869, 4; *Fort Wayne (IN) Gazette,* July 28, 1869; "The Chase Presidential Movement," *Richmond Dispatch,* July 31, 1869, 3 (from the *Baltimore American*); Summers, *Ordeal of the Reunion,* 167 (VA election).

32 *Louisville (KY) Courier-Journal,* July 19, 1869; *Galveston (TX) Daily News,* August 14, 1869; *Chicago Tribune,* August 23, 1869; Fairman, *Reconstruction and Reunion,* 578–79.

33 Chase to Daniel Butterfield, July 2, 1869, *SPCP,* 5:311–12; Chase to William Rosecrans, August 16, 1869, *SPCP,* 5:314–15; see Chase to Hamilton Fish, May 26, 1869, *SPCP,* 5:304–5 ("earnestly desire the success of the administration").

34 Chase to Kate, May 14, 1869, Chase Papers, HSP; *Charleston (SC) Daily News,* May 21, 1869; Chase to W. T. Sherman, July 7, 1869, Sherman Papers, LC; Chase to Kate, September 15, 1869, *SPCP,* 5:317.

35 Chase to W. T. Sherman, June 24, July 7, 1869, Sherman Papers, LC; *New York Herald,* July 21, 1869, 5; "Address of Chief Justice Chase," *New York Herald,* July 22, 1869, 10; "Dartmouth College," *New York Herald,* July 23, 1869, 8.

36 Chase to Kate, September 15, 1869, *Spur,* 394–95; Chase to Anna Hoover, September 26, 1869, Chase Papers, LC; Chase to Kate, October 1, 1869, *Spur,* 396–97; Oller, *American Queen,* 139.

37 Chase to Flamen Ball, October 4, 1869, Chase Papers, CHLA; Chase to Kate, November 7, 1869, *SPCP,* 5:319–20.

38 *National Republican* (Washington, DC), October 5, 6, 7, 1869; G. Edward White, "Salmon P. Chase and the Judicial Culture of the Supreme Court in the Civil War Era," in *The Supreme Court in the Civil War Era,* ed. Jennifer Lowe, (Washington, DC: Supreme Court Historical Society, 1996), 39 (on Chase's effort to lengthen terms).

39 Judiciary Act, April 10, 1869, *Statutes at Large,* 16:44; Sarah Grier Beck to George Harding, December 9, 1869, in Fairman, *Reconstruction and Reunion,* 730;

Ulysses Grant to Robert Grier, December 15, 1869, John Simon, ed., *Papers of Ulysses Grant* (1994), 20:52 (accepting resignation letter of December 11); Ashmore, *Dates of Supreme Court Decisions*, 94–96; Fairman, *Reconstruction and Reunion*, 82–84, 166, 725–30.

40 Chase to James Pike, December 24, 1869, *SPCP*, 5:322–23; Chernow, *Grant*, 687–89; Stahr, *Stanton*, 530–32; Warren, *Supreme Court*, 3:223–29.

41 Ex parte Yerger, 75 U.S. 85 (1869).

42 For the subsequent history of *Yerger*, see Fairman, *Reconstruction and Reunion*, 584–91. Cases citing *Yerger* include: Ex parte Virginia, 100 U.S. 339 (1880); Hamdan v. Rumsfeld, 547 U.S. 557 (2006); Boumediene v. Bush, 128 S. Ct. 2229 (2008); Ortiz v. United States, 138 S. Ct. 2165 (2018); Department of Homeland Security v. Thuraissagam, 140 S. Ct. 1959 (2020).

43 Fairman, *Reconstruction and Reunion*, 716–17.

44 Veazie Bank v. Fenno, 75 U.S. 533 (1869); *New York World*, December 16, 1869.

45 *Veazie Bank v. Fenno*, 75 U.S., at 540–47.

46 Ibid., at 548–49; NFIB v. Sebelius, 567 U.S. 519, 567 (2012). Roberts quoted from a 1937 case holding that "every tax is in some measure regulatory. To some extent, it interposes an economic impediment to the activity taxed as compared with others not taxed." Sonzinsky v. United States, 300 U.S. 506, 513 (1937). This section of *Sonzinsky* cited *Veazie*, adding that "it has long been established that an Act of Congress, which, on its face, purports to be an exercise of the taxing power is not any the less so because the tax is burdensome or tends to restrict or suppress the thing taxed." *Sonzinsky* at 513. So Roberts, in one of his most famous opinions, relied indirectly upon Chase.

47 "Letter from Washington," *Baltimore Sun*, January 3, 1870, 4; Chase diary, January 5, 1870, *SPCP*, 1:645–46; Chernow, *Grant*, 641–42, 681–82, 690–94; Donald, *Sumner*, 433–53.

48 Chase to Thomas Yeatman, January 3, 1870, Chase Papers, CHLA; Chase to George Hill, January 7, 1870, *SPCP*, 5:323–25; Chase diary, January 8, 1870, *SPCP*, 1:646; Chase to Yeatman, January 12, 1870, Chase Papers, CHLA.

49 *Ohio State Journal* (Columbus), January 14, 15, 20, 21, 1870; *Pittsburgh Weekly Gazette*, January 22, 1870; Chase to Thomas Yeatman, January 23, 1870, Chase Papers, CHLA; *Chicago Tribune*, January 24, 1870.

50 Chase to Cincinnati Committee, March 30, 1870, in "Chief Justice Chase on the Fifteenth Amendment," *Baltimore Sun*, April 15, 1870, 1; for reprints, see *Pittsburgh Weekly Gazette*, April 14, 1870; *Memphis Daily Appeal*, April 15, 1870; *Selma (AL) Morning Times*, April 19, 1870; and *Wilmington (NC) Journal*, April 22, 1870. Niven printed the letter as edited by Chase; I have used the version in the papers. See *SPCP*, 5:330–31.

51 Hepburn v. Griswold, 75 U.S. at 626; "The Legal Tender Cases," *Washington (DC) Evening Star*, February 7, 1870, 1.

52 Hepburn v. Griswold, 75 U.S. at 604–5.

53 Ibid., at 606–10.

54 Ibid., at 611–15; see McCulloch v. Maryland, 17 U.S. 316, 421 (1819).

55 *Hepburn v. Griswold*, 75 U.S. at 615–21.

56 Ibid., at 622–25; Chase to James Ward, May 15, 1870, *SPCP*, 5:334.

57 *Hepburn v. Griswold*, 75 U.S. at 625.

58 Ibid., at 626–39.

59 United States v. Dewitt, 76 U.S. 41, 44 (1869); *NFIB v. Sebelius*, 567 U.S. at 567; see Barnett, "Remarkable but Forgotten," 685–87.

60 "Nominations," *Washington (DC) Evening Star*, February 7, 1870, 1; "Nominations by the President," *New-York Tribune*, February 8, 1870, 1; *Memphis Daily Appeal*, April 29, 1870, 1 (from *New York World*) ("Grant had packed the bench to humiliate Chief Justice Chase and the majority who concurred with him"); Hamilton Fish diary, October 28, 1876, in John Simon, ed., *Papers of Ulysses Grant* (1994), 27:448–49; Fairman, *Reconstruction and Reunion*, 719–32; Sidney Ratner, "Was the Supreme Court Packed by President Grant?" *Political Science Quarterly* 50 (1935): 343–58; Leon Sachs, "*Stare Decisis* and the Legal Tender Cases," *Virginia Law Review* 20 (1934): 856–85.

61 Chase diary, March 26–31, 1870, *SPCP*, 1:650–52; "Probable Re-Opening of the Legal Tender Question in the Supreme Court," *New-York Tribune*, April 1, 1870, 1; *Chicago Tribune*, April 12, 1870; *Wheeling Daily Intelligencer*, April 13, 1870 ("very lively scene"); *Pittsburgh Daily Commercial*, April 21, 1870; Samuel Miller to William Ballinger, April 21, 1870, Miller Papers, LC; Chase to John Tucker, May 1, 1871, *SPCP*, 5:547–48; Fairman, *Reconstruction and Reunion*, 738–52.

62 "Frightful Calamity," *New York Herald*, April 28, 1870, 7; "Circuit Court of the United States," *Richmond Dispatch*, May 3, 1870, 1; "Chief Justice Chase on the Calamity," ibid., May 6, 1870, 2; Chase to Ulysses Grant, May 24, 1870, Warden, 720.

63 Chase diary, June 10, 13, 1870, *SPCP*, 1:653; *St. Joseph (MO) Herald*, June 18, 1870 (retirement).

64 Chase diary, June 23–July 21, 1870, *SPCP*, 1:653–60; "Chief Justice Chase," *Philadelphia Evening Telegraph*, July 8, 1870, 1; *Minneapolis Star Tribune*, July 15, 23, 26, 1870; *Chicago Tribune*, August 11, 1870; "Prominent Arrivals," *New York Herald*, August 18, 1870, 6 (Chase at New York hotel); Chase to Richard Parsons, September 26, 1870, *SPCP*, 5:338–39.

65 "Sad Condition of Chief Justice Chase," *Memphis Daily Appeal*, September 4, 1870, 1 (from *New York World*); *Charleston (SC) Daily Courier*, September 9, 1870 (from *Boston Journal*); "Chief Justice Chase," *Richmond Dispatch*, September 16, 1870, 2 (from *New York Standard*); Chase to Alfred Mullett, September 26, 1870, Chase Papers, LC.

66 Chase to Joshua Leavitt, October 27, 1870, in "Dr. Leavitt's Golden Wedding," *New-York Tribune*, November 3, 1870, 8; Chase to John Perry, November 14, 1870, Chase Papers, LC (one of twenty letters to his doctor); Chase to Richard Parsons, December 12, 1870, ibid.; Chase to Albert Riddle, December 15, 1870, ibid.

67 Chase to Samuel Nelson, October 17, 1870, Chase Papers, LC; Samuel Miller to William Ballinger, November 6, 1870, Miller Papers, LC; David Davis to

Julius Rockwell, November 30, 1870, Davis Papers, ALPL; Chase to Richard Parsons, December 26, 1870, *SPCP*, 5:340–41 (sending regards to justices).

68 Judiciary Act, April 10, 1869, *Statutes at Large*, 16:44; Samuel Miller to William Ballinger, November 6, 1870, Miller Papers, LC.

69 Chase to Bradley Johnson, September 28, 1870, Chase Papers, LC (estimates another six weeks); Chase to Samuel Nelson, October 17, 1870, ibid. (probably not there until December); Chase to Hiram Barney, December 12, 1870, ibid.; Chase to Richard Parsons, December 26, 1870, ibid. (from Narragansett); Chase to Jay Cooke, January 3, 1871, Cooke Papers, HSP (from New York).

CHAPTER 26: "Quite Content" 1871–73

1 Chase to Richard Parsons, February 8, 1871, Chase Papers, LC; Chase to William Sprague, February 10, 1871, ibid.; *Congressional Globe*, February 15, 1871, 1256–62; Parsons to Chase, February 16, 1871, *SPCP*, 5:342; Chase to Parsons, February 17, 1871, Chase Papers, LC.

2 *Congressional Globe*, February 23, 1865, 1012 (Sumner); "The Late Chief Justice Taney," *Baltimore Sun*, February 4, 1871, 1; *Buffalo Morning Express*, February 13, 1871; Chase to Richard Parsons, February 13, 1871, Chase Papers, LC; "The Proceedings of Congress Yesterday," *Baltimore Sun*, January 27, 1874, 1 (busts of Chase and Taney).

3 "Chief Justice Chase and Daughter," *New York Times*, March 7, 1871, 1; "Letter from Washington," *Baltimore Sun*, March 9, 1871, 4.

4 For this sketch of Will Hoyt, I have relied on *Spur*, with its excellent notes, and an unpublished Hoyt family history shared by family members.

5 *Chicago Tribune*, March 17 and 24, 1871; "Marriage of Miss Chase," *New York Times*, March 19, 1871, 1; "Marriage of the Daughter of Chief Justice Chase," *Baltimore Sun*, March 24, 1871, 4; "Wedding in High Life," *New York Herald*, March 24, 1871, 10; "A Distinguished Wedding," *New York Times*, March 24, 1871, 5; "A Fashionable Wedding," *Philadelphia Inquirer*, March 24, 1871, 1; John Lewis to William Whittington, March 25, 1871, in Richard Grimmet, *St. John's Church, Lafayette Square: The History and Heritage of the Church of the Presidents, Washington, DC* (Minneapolis: Mill City Press, 2009), 67.

6 "Marriage of the Daughter of Chief Justice Chase," *Baltimore Sun*, March 24, 1871, 4; "Wedding in High Life," *New York Herald*, March 24, 1871, 10; "A Distinguished Wedding," *New York Times*, March 24, 1871, 5; Nettie Hoyt to Chase, April 30, 1871, *Spur*, 408–11.

7 "Legal Tender Cases in the Supreme Court," *Baltimore Sun*, April 19, 1871, 1; *Legal Tender Cases*, 79 U.S. at 517 (Potter) and 525 (Akerman).

8 Chase to Edward Mansfield, April 24, 1871, *SPCP*, 5:343–44; *Wisconsin State Journal* (Madison), April 25, 1871; *Hartford Courant*, April 26, 1871.

9 Chase to John Tucker, May 1, 1871, *SPCP*, 5:344–45; "United States Supreme Court," *New York Times*, May 2, 1871, 1; *Fall River (MA) Daily Evening News*, May 2, 1871 ("father of our currency").

10 Chase to Clement Vallandigham, May 20, 1871, *SPCP*, 5:349; "Vallandigham," *New York Herald*, June 18, 1871, 7. For more on the New Departure Democrats, see Foner, *Reconstruction* 412–21, and Summers, *Ordeal of the Reunion*, 301–5.

11 Chase to Nettie Hoyt, June 5, 1871, *Spur*, 415; Chase to Murat Halstead, June 13, 1871, Chase Papers, CHLA; "Chief Justice Chase," *New York Herald*, June 26, 1871, 6.

12 "Chief Justice Chase," *New York Herald*, June 26, 1871, 6; Chase to William Dickson, August 4, 1871, Warden, 724–25; Chase to Richard Parsons, August 9, 1871, Chase Papers, LC; Chase to Alexander Plumley, August 19, 1871, Warden, 726; *Buffalo Commercial*, September 26, 1871; "Salmon P. Chase," *New-York Tribune*, May 8, 1873, 1 ("always ascribed the benefit derived to diet, air, and exercise, rather than to any curative properties in the waters").

13 "Chief Justice Chase as the Democratic Candidate," *New York Herald*, August 24, 1871, 4; Kate to Chase, August 29, 1871, *Spur*, 418.

14 *Janesville (WI) Gazette*, August 25, 1871; *Chicago Tribune*, September 7, 1871; *Wisconsin State Register* (Madison), September 9, 1871; *Cincinnati Enquirer*, September 16, 1871; *Pittsburgh Commercial*, September 16, 1871; *Racine (WI) Journal*, September 20, 1871.

15 *Burlington (VT) Free Press*, September 25, 1871; "Telegraphic Summary," *Baltimore Sun*, September 26, 1871, 4 (Chase with Smith); Chase to Jacob Schuckers, October 3, 1871, Chase Papers, LC (from Narragansett); Chase to Nettie Hoyt, October 14, 1871, *Spur*, 420–21; "The Supreme Court," *Baltimore Sun*, October 16, 1871, 1; Ashmore, *Dates of Supreme Court Decisions*, 102–5; United States v. Crusell, 79 U.S. 175 (1871); Hennessy v. Shelden, 79 U.S. 440 (1871); The Patapsco, 79 U.S. 451 (1871); Hall v. Allen, 79 U.S. 452 (1871).

16 Chase diary, January 2, 6, 1872, *SPCP*, 1:664, 667; *Legal Tender Cases*, 79 U.S. at 570–87; see Payne v. Tennessee, 501 U.S. 808, 827 (1986); Planned Parenthood of Southeastern Pennsylvania v. Casey, 505 U.S. 833, 854–55 (1992); Ramos v. Louisiana, 140 S. Ct. 1390 (2020).

17 Chase to Elbridge Spaulding, February 3, 1862, Schuckers, 245–46; Chase diary, January 15, 1872, *SPCP*, 1:668–69.

18 Gordon Young, "*United States v. Klein*, Then and Now," *Loyola University of Chicago Law Journal* 44 (2012): 268 (*Klein* cited in thirty-three Supreme Court cases).

19 United States v. Padelford, 76 U.S. 531, 542–43 (1870); Act of July 25, 1870, *Statutes at Large*, 16:235; United States v. Klein, 80 U.S. 128 (1872); Fairman, *Reconstruction and Reunion*, 840–46; Gordon Young, "Congressional Regulation of Federal Courts' Jurisdiction and Processes: *United States v. Klein* Revisited," *Wisconsin Law Review* (1981): 1197–210.

20 *United States v. Klein*, 80 U.S. at 142–48; see Patchak v. Zinke, 138 S.Ct. 897, 915–16 (2018) (Roberts dissenting); Bank Markazi v. Peterson, 136 S. Ct. 1310, 1333–35 (2016) (Roberts dissenting).

21 *Tarble's Case*, 80 U.S. 397 (1871). Field relied heavily upon Ableman v. Booth, 62 U.S. 506 (1859).

22 *Tarble's Case*, 80 U.S. at 412–13 (Chase dissent).

23 Chase diary, January 1, 1872, *SPCP,* 1:663–64; Chase to Ludlow Jones, January 10, 1872, Ludlow Papers, CHLA; Chase diary, January 14, 1872, *SPCP,* 1:668 (includes telegram); Chase to Nettie Hoyt, February 4, 1872, *Spur,* 422–23; Chase to Gerrit Smith, March 1, 1872, Chase Papers, LC; Chase to William Joice, July 22, 1872, Chase Papers, HSP.

24 Chase to Hiram Barney, March 29, 1872, Barney Papers, Huntington; *Cincinnati Commercial,* May 17, 1872; Chase to Murat Halstead, May 20, 1872, *SPCP,* 5:358–59; *Reading (PA) Times,* October 28, 1872; *Cincinnati Commercial,* November 5, 1872; *Chicago Tribune,* November 5, 1872; Chase to Murat Halstead, November 7, 1872, Whelpley Papers, CHLA (copy in Warden, 735–36); *Boston Globe,* November 18, 1872 (Chase "emphatically denies").

25 "Our Japanese Visitors," *Washington (DC) Evening Star,* February 29, 1872, 1; "Our Oriental Visitors," ibid., March 2, 1872, 1; "Congress Yesterday," *New York Herald,* March 6, 1872, 5; Chase to Nettie Hoyt, March 8, 1872, *Spur,* 425; Chase diary, April 28, 1872, *SPCP,* 1:677; *Pittsburgh Daily Commercial,* April 29, 1872; Chase diary, May 25, 1872, *SPCP,* 1:683–84; W. G. Beasley, *Japan Encounters the Barbarian: Japanese Travelers in America and Europe* (New Haven, CT: Yale University Press, 1995), 162–65.

26 *New York Evening Post,* April 7, 1872.

27 Chase diary, May 15, 18, 1872, *SPCP,* 1:681–82; Chase to Nettie Hoyt, May 20, 1872, *Spur,* 426; Chase diary, June 12, 14, 16, 1872, *SPCP,* 1:689; Edward Livingston, *The Complete Works of Edward Livingston on Criminal Jurisprudence* (New York : National Prison Association of the United States of America, 1873), v–viii (introduction by Chase).

28 Chase to Hiram Barney, July 12, 1872, Chase Papers, HSP (from Narragansett); Chase diary, August 18–30, September 13, 1872, *SPCP,* 1:696–99; Chase to David Lloyd, September 15, 1872, *SPCP,* 5:359 (from Narragansett); Chase diary, October 4, 1872, *SPCP,* 1:702 (visits HSP).

29 On the Liberal Republicans, see Chernow, *Grant,* 739–43; Donald, *Sumner,* 516–20, 539–44; Foner, *Reconstruction,* 497–503; Andrew Slap, *The Doom of Reconstruction: The Liberal Republicans in the Civil War Era* (New York: Fordham University Press, 2007), 126–50; Summers, *Ordeal of the Reunion,* 303–9.

30 Charles Grady to Chase, March 29, 1872, *SPCP,* 5:354–55 (seeking comment on Liberal Republican platform); "Chief Justice Chase for the Presidency," *Philadelphia Inquirer,* April 19, 1872, 4; *Cincinnati Enquirer,* April 24, 1872; "The Cincinnati Convention," *New York Herald,* April 25, 1872, 3; *Springfield (MA) Daily Republican,* April 26, 1872; Earle Ross, *The Liberal Republican Movement* (New York: H. Holt, 1919), 76–78; Slap, *Doom of Reconstruction,* 134–38, 146–50.

31 Chase to M. C. C. Church, March 20, 1872, *SPCP,* 5:352–53; Chase to Flamen Ball, April 8, 1872, Warden, 729; Chase to Alexander Long, April 15, 1872, Long Papers, CHLA; Long to Chase, April 22, 1872, *SPCP,* 5:355–56; Chase to Church, April 29, 1872, in "Letter from Chief Justice Chase," *Baltimore Sun,* May 3, 1872, 1.

32 "Cincinnati," *New York Herald,* April 29, 1872, 3; *Proceedings of the Liberal Republican Convention, in Cincinnati, May 1st, 2d and 3d, 1872* (1872), 21–29; Matthew

Downey, "Horace Greeley and the Politicians: The Liberal Republican Convention in 1872," *Journal of American History* 53 (1967): 727–50.

33 E. L. Godkin to Carl Schurz, May 19, 1872, in Frederic Bancroft, ed., *Speeches, Correspondence and Political Papers of Carl Schurz* (New York: G. P. Putnam's Sons, 1913), 2:276; Lester Taylor to Edward Atkinson, July 27, 1872, Atkinson Papers, Massachusetts Historical Society; Robert Williams, *Horace Greeley: Champion of American Freedom* (New York: New York University Press, 2007), 113–17, 274–78, 299–302.

34 Chase diary, May 4, 1872, *SPCP*, 1:679; Chase to M. C. C. Church, May 10, 1872, *SPCP*, 5:357–58; Amnesty Act, May 22, 1872, *Statutes at Large*, 17:142; Foner, *Reconstruction*, 504.

35 Horace Greeley to J. S. Griffing, September 7, 1870, in *New National Era* (Washington, DC), October 31, 1872; "Civilization at the South," *New-York Tribune*, March 23, 1872, 4; *Memphis Public Ledger*, May 22, 1872 ("clasp hands across the bloody chasm"); Foner, *Reconstruction*, 504–7; Summers, *Ordeal of the Reunion*, 310–12.

36 *Belmont Chronicle* (St. Clairsville, OH), April 11, 1872 (Garrison); Blight, *Frederick Douglass*, 531–36; Chernow, *Grant*, 745–46 (Douglass); James McPherson, "Grant or Greeley: The Abolitionist Dilemma in the Election of 1872," *American Historical Review* 71 (1965): 43–61.

37 Chase to Hiram Barney, July 12, November 9, 1872, Chase Papers, HSP; Chase to Richard Parsons, July 12, 1872, ibid.; Chase to Charles Sumner, August 2, 1872, Sumner Papers, Harvard; Chase to David Lloyd, August 14, 1872, Schuckers, 593; Chase to Lloyd, September 15, 1872, *SPCP*, 5:359–60; Chase to Flamen Ball, November 4, 1872, Chase Papers, CHLA; Chase to Hiram Barney, November 9, 1872, Chase Papers, HSP.

38 Chase diary, November 29–December 4, 1872, *SPCP*, 1:706–9; "Horace Greeley," *New-York Tribune*, November 30, 1872, 1; "Horace Greeley, the Closing Ceremonies," *New-York Tribune*, December 5, 1872, 1.

39 Chase to Charles Lucas, November 19, 1872, *SPCP*, 5:361.

40 Chase to Augustus Boyle, December 11, 1872, *SPCP*, 5:363–64; Chase to Gerrit Smith, February 15, 1873, *SPCP*, 5:367.

41 Warden, 772 ("where there"), 791 ("no secrets"); Chase to Charles Lucas, November 19, 1872, *SPCP*, 5:361 ("four millions"); Chase to Montgomery Blair, April 28, 1873, Warden, 779; Frederick Blue, "Kate's Paper Chase: The Race to Publish the First Biography of Salmon P. Chase," *Old Northwest* 8 (1982–83): 353–58.

42 "Mr. Chase and the Administration," *New-York Tribune*, May 21, 1873, 6 (Parsons); Charles Sumner to Hiram Barney, May 24, 1873, in Palmer, *Sumner Letters*, 2:620–21; Warden, 776–78.

43 Chase to Gerrit Smith, February 14, 1873, *SPCP*, 5:367 (inviting to come for inauguration); "Taking the Oath," *Washington (DC) Evening Star*, March 4, 1873, 4; *National Republican* (Washington, DC), March 5, 1873; "Inauguration Day," *New York Herald*, March 5, 1873, 3; "Inauguration Scenes," *Richmond Dispatch*, March 6, 1873, 3; Chernow, *Grant*, 754–56; Charles Lane, *The Day Freedom Died: The Colfax Massacre, the Supreme Court, and the Betrayal of Reconstruction* (New York: Henry Holt, 2008), 1–2, 6–8.

44 Robert Warden to Chase, April 5, 1873, Chase Papers, CHLA; Blue, "Kate's Paper Chase," 353–61. Warden's letter to Chase is signed and is among Chase's papers, but it is heavily edited, suggesting this is a draft placed in Chase's papers after his death.

45 "Chief Justice Chase in Richmond," *New York Herald*, April 6, 1873, 11; *Alexandria (VA) Gazette*, April 7, 1873; "Deputation to Chief Justice Chase," *Richmond Dispatch*, April 11, 1873, 2; Chase to Nettie Hoyt, April 12, 1873, *Spur*, 432–33.

46 "Chief Justice Chase at Home," *Richmond Dispatch*, April 8, 1873, 3 (from *Cincinnati Commercial*).

47 *The Slaughterhouse Cases*, 83 U.S. 36 (1873). Useful secondary sources include: Richard Aynes, "Constricting the Law of Freedom: Justice Miller, the Fourteenth Amendment, and the *Slaughterhouse Cases*," *Chicago-Kent Law Review* 70 (1994): 627–88; Randy Barnett, "The Three Narratives of the *Slaughter-House Cases*," *Journal of Supreme Court History* 41 (2016): 295–309; Lackland Bloom Jr., *Do Great Cases Make Bad Law?* (New York: Oxford University Press, 2014), 115–35; Michael Curtis, "Resurrecting the Privileges or Immunities Clause and Revising the *Slaughter-house Cases* Without Exhuming *Lochner*: Individual Rights and the Fourteenth Amendment," *Boston College Law Review* 38 (1997): 1–106; Michael Ross, "Justice Miller's Reconstruction: The *Slaughter-House Cases*, Health Codes and Civil Rights in New Orleans," *Journal of Southern History* 64 (1998): 649–76; Michael Ross, "Obstructing Reconstruction: John Archibald Campbell and the Legal Campaign Against Louisiana's Republican Government, 1868–1873," *Civil War History* 49 (2003): 235–53.

48 *New Orleans Daily Picayune*, April 20, 1870; Barnett, "Three Narratives," 299–302; Ross, "Obstructing Reconstruction," 240–51; Robert Saunders, *John Archibald Campbell: Southern Moderate, 1811–1889* (Tuscaloosa: University of Alabama Press, 1997), 150–57, 186–97.

49 *Slaughterhouse Cases*, 83 U.S. at 77.

50 Ibid., at 96–97 (Field), 121–22 (Bradley), and 129 (Swayne).

51 Ibid., at 111 (Chase joins Field); Barnett, "Three Narratives," 307; Robert Kaczorowski, "The Chase Court and Fundamental Rights: A Watershed in American Constitutionalism," *Northern Kentucky Law Review* 21 (1993): 189–91.

52 Akhil Reed Amar, "Substance and Method in the Year 2000," *Pepperdine Law Review* 28 (2001): 631 ("virtually no"); Barnett, "Three Narratives," 307–8; Brief of Constitutional Law Professors as *Amici Curiae* in Support of Petitioners, *McDonald v. Chicago*, 561 U.S. 742 (2010), 33–34.

53 "Highly Important Decision of the Supreme Court," *New York Herald*, April 15, 1873, 12; *Boston Daily Advertiser*, April 16, 1873; *Cincinnati Enquirer*, April 16, 1873; "The Scope of the Thirteenth and Fourteenth Amendments," *New York Times*, April 16, 1873, 6; "Women's Rights and State Rights," *New-York Tribune*, April 16, 1873, 4; *Rochester (NY) Democrat*, April 17, 1873; "The New Orleans Abattoir Decision," *Chicago Tribune*, April 19, 1873, 4 (useful check upon national government infringing "constitutional prerogatives of the states"); *Nation*, April 24, 1873.

54 "Woman's Rights," *Philadelphia Inquirer*, January 20, 1872, 3 (Bradwell argument); Bradwell v. Illinois, 83 U.S. 130 (1873); Richard Aynes, *"Bradwell v. Illinois*: Chief Justice Chase's Dissent in and the 'Sphere of Women's Work,'" *Louisiana Law Review* 59 (1999): 521–41; Nancy Gilliam, "A Professional Pioneer: Myra Bradwell's Fight to Practice Law," *Law and History Review* 5 (1987): 105–33.

55 *Bradwell v. Illinois*, 83 U.S. at 137–39 (Miller) and 139–42 (Bradley); *Topeka (KS) Daily Commonwealth*, April 20, 1873; "Chief Justice Chase," *Summit County Beacon* (Akron, OH), April 23, 1873, 1; *Nation*, April 24, 1873.

56 *Bradwell v. Illinois*, 83 U.S. at 139 (Chase "dissented from the judgment of the court and from all the opinions"); "Chief Justice Chase," *Summit County Beacon* (Akron, OH), April 23, 1873, 1; see Aynes, *"Bradwell v. Illinois,"* 537–38 (sketch of Chase's opinion).

57 *New Orleans Republican*, April 17, 1873; "The Louisiana Troubles," *New York Times*, April 21, 1873, 4; Ripley v. Railway Passengers' Assurance Co., 83 U.S. 336 (1873); Osborne v. Mobile, 83 U.S. 479 (1873); Rodd v. Heartt, 84 U.S. 354 (1873); "Adjournment of the United States Supreme Court Until October 1," *Detroit Free Press*, May 2, 1873, 1; Warden, *Chase*, 802–3 (meeting with Sumner); "Chief Justice Chase," *New York Herald*, May 8, 1873, 3; Charles Lane, *Day Freedom Died*, 9–22.

58 Chase to Robert Warden, May 4, 1873, Warden, 805; Chase to Richard Parsons, May 5, 1873, *SPCP*, 5:370; "Salmon P. Chase," *New-York Tribune*, May 8, 1873, 1 ("pleasant and familiar way").

59 Chase to Richard Parsons, May 5, 1873, *SPCP*, 5:370; Chase to Alice Stebbins, May 5, 1873, Schuckers, 624; "Chief Justice Chase," *New York Herald*, May 8, 1873, 3 (Chase planned to go to Colorado with former governor Gilpin).

60 "Chief Justice Chase," *New York Herald*, May 8, 1873, 3; "Salmon P. Chase," *New-York Tribune*, May 8, 1873, 1.

CONCLUSION

1 "A Great Life," *New-York Tribune*, May 8, 1873, 4.

2 *New York Sun*, May 8, 1873.

3 "The Death of Chief Justice Chase," *New York Herald*, May 8, 1873, 6. On Grant's circuitous path to Waite, see Chernow, *Grant*, 764–67.

4 *New National Era* (Washington, DC), May 15, 1873. I believe that Douglass wrote this article because the author stated that he recognized Chase's handwriting, and I doubt that Douglass's sons, who now edited the paper, would have known Chase's hand. See Blight, *Douglass*, 524–29.

5 "About Mr. Chase," *Washington (DC) Evening Star*, May 10, 1873, 1 (from *Cincinnati Commercial*); Warden, 796: James Pike, *Chief Justice Chase* (1873), 16.

6 "Chief Justice Chase," *New York Herald*, May 11, 1873, 5; "The Nation's Loss," *New-York Tribune*, May 12, 1873, 1.

7 *National Republican* (Washington, DC), May 12, 1873 ("fully ten thousand people"); "The Dead Jurist," *Philadelphia Inquirer*, May 12, 1873, 1; "The Chase Obsequies," *Washington (DC) Evening Star*, May 12, 1873, 1 ("over seven thousand").

8 "The Chase Obsequies," *Washington (DC) Evening Star*, May 12, 1873, 1; *National Republican* (Washington, DC), May 13, 1873; "The Nation's Loss," *New-York Tribune*, May 13, 1873, 1.

9 *Alexandria (VA) Daily State Journal*, May 19, 1873; *Rutland (VT) Daily Globe*, May 22, 1873; *Clinton (IL) Register*, May 30, 1873.

10 *Chicago Tribune*, December 19, 1880 (divorce); ibid., August 1, 1899 (Kate obituary); "Mrs. J. R. C. Hoyt Dead," *Washington (DC) Evening Star*, November 20, 1925, 7; Oller, *American Queen*, 156–71, 252–64 ("drank up" on 257).

11 "Salmon P. Chase," *New York Herald*, March 16, 1874, 4; *Boston Post*, May 27, 1874; *Boston Globe*, May 28, 1874; *Christian Journal*, September 12, 1874; Blue, "Kate's Paper Chase," 353–61.

12 William Evarts, "Eulogy on Mr. Chase," in Schuckers, 654–56; William Strong to William Evarts, September 10, 1874, Strong Papers, LC; Samuel Miller to William Ballinger, October 15, 1876, Miller Papers, LC.

13 John Thompson to Chase, May 1, 1862, Chase Papers, LC; Thompson to Chase, June 2, 1862, ibid.; Chase to Thompson, April 11, 1864, Chase Papers, HSP; Chase National Bank, *Chase National Bank of the City of New York*, 1877–1922 (New York: Chase National Bank, 1922), 3–10; Chase Bank website ("We're proud to serve nearly half of America's households with a broad range of financial services, including personal banking, credit cards, mortgages, auto financing, investment advice, small business loans and payment processing") (https://www .chase.com/digital/resources/about-chase).

14 *Springville (NY) Journal*, October 12, 1886; *Akron (OH) Beacon Journal*, October 15, 1886; *Cincinnati Enquirer*, May 31, 1923; Hoadly, *Address at Music Hall*, 5–6; Oller, *American Queen*, 244–48.

15 See Foner, *Free Soil, Free Labor*, 73 ("Chase's interpretation of the Constitution formed the legal basis for the political program which was created by the Liberty Party and inherited in large part by the Free-Soilers and Republicans").

16 See Chase to Lincoln, draft message, December 1861, *SPCP*, 1:329 (Republicans regarded slavery in the slave states as beyond federal power); Chase to Lincoln, December 29, 1862, *SPCP*, 3:350–51 (urging him to expand emancipation proclamation); Chase to Lincoln, April 12, 1864, *SPCP*, 5:17–19 (urging him to extend voting rights to all Southern blacks).

17 See Barnett "From Antislavery Lawyer to Chief Justice," 697–702 (speculating on why Chase has been "forgotten"); Albert Blaustein and Roy Mersky, "Rating Supreme Court Justices," *American Bar Association Journal* 58 (1972): 1183–89; Currie, *Constitution in the Supreme Court*, 357 ("not one of these four [Chase] opinions is satisfying from the standpoint of legal analysis"); Bernard Schwartz, "Supreme Court Superstars: The Ten Greatest Justices," *Tulsa Law Review* 31 (1995): 931–59; William Strong to William Evarts, September 10, 1874, Strong Papers, LC. None of the justices on Schwartz's list served less than fifteen years, and several of them served more than thirty years.

Illustration Credits

All images are from the Prints & Photographs collection at the Library of Congress, except the following:

Page

212 Library Company of Philadelphia

233 William Alexander Taylor, *Centennial History of Columbus and Franklin County, Ohio* (Columbus, OH: S. J. Clarke, 1909): 335

265 New York Public Library

271 Library Company of Philadelphia

326 Cincinnati Museum Center

359 Library Company of Philadelphia

437 Ellis Oberholtzer, *Jay Cooke: Financier of the Civil War,* vol. 1 (Philadelphia: George W. Jacobs, 1907)

438 Library Company of Philadelphia

462 National Archives

533 National Archives

577 United States Senate

Index

Page numbers in *italics* refer to illustrations.

About the Author

Walter Stahr is the *New York Times* bestselling author of *Seward: Lincoln's Indispensable Man*, as well as *Stanton: Lincoln's War Secretary*, and *John Jay: Founding Father*. A two-time winner of the Seward Award for Excellence in Civil War Biography, Stahr practiced law in Washington and Asia for more than two decades, before turning to writing history. He lives with his wife, Dr. Masami Miyauchi Stahr, in Newport Beach, California. Visit him at walterstahr.com.